THE OXFORD HANDB

POSTWAR EUROPEAN HISTORY

The postwar period is no longer current affairs but is becoming the recent past. As such, it is increasingly attracting the attentions of historians. Whilst the Cold War has long been a mainstay of political science and contemporary history, recent research approaches postwar Europe in many different ways, all of which are represented in the thirty-five chapters of this book. As well as diplomatic, political, institutional, economic, and social history, *The Oxford Handbook of Postwar European History* contains chapters which approach the past through the lenses of gender, espionage, art and architecture, technology, agriculture, heritage, postcolonialism, memory, and generational change, and shows how the history of postwar Europe can be enriched by looking to disciplines such as anthropology and philosophy.

The *Handbook* covers all of Europe, with a notable focus on Eastern Europe. Including subjects as diverse as the meaning of 'Europe' and European identity, southern Europe after dictatorship, the cultural meanings of the bomb, the 1968 student uprisings, immigration, Americanization, welfare, leisure, decolonization, the Wars of Yugoslav Succession, and coming to terms with the Nazi past, the essays in this Handbook offer an unparalleled coverage of postwar European history that offers far more than the standard Cold War framework. Readers will find self-contained, state-of-the-art analyses of major subjects, each written by an acknowledged expert, as well as stimulating and novel approaches to newer topics. Combining empirical rigour and adventurous conceptual analysis, this *Handbook* offers in one substantial volume a guide to the numerous ways in which historians are now rewriting the history of postwar Europe.

Dan Stone is Professor of Modern History at Royal Holloway, University of London. His recent publications include *Histories of the Holocaust* (2010) and (as editor) *The Historiography of Genocide* (2008).

Praise for *The Oxford Handbook of Postwar European History*

'a fascinating and well-informed read ... a useful resource for years to come'

Martijn Lak, *European History Quarterly*

'essential reading for specialists and their students'

Mark Smith, *Reviews in History*

'an important and worthwhile volume'

Jeremy Black, *Journal of European Studies*

THE OXFORD HANDBOOK OF

....

POSTWAR
EUROPEAN
HISTORY

....

Edited by

DAN STONE

OXFORD
UNIVERSITY PRESS

OXFORD
UNIVERSITY PRESS

Great Clarendon Street, Oxford, OX2 6DP,
United Kingdom

Oxford University Press is a department of the University of Oxford.
It furthers the University's objective of excellence in research, scholarship,
and education by publishing worldwide. Oxford is a registered trade mark of
Oxford University Press in the UK and in certain other countries

First published 2012
First published in paperback 2014
Impression: 1

Published in the United States of America by Oxford University Press
198 Madison Avenue, New York, NY 10016, United States of America

British Library Cataloguing in Publication Data
Data available

ISBN 978-0-19-956098-1 (Hbk.)
ISBN 978-0-19-872917-4 (Pbk.)

Contents

PART III: BLOCS, PARTIES, POLITICAL POWER

PART IV: RE-CONSTRUCTION: STARTING AFRESH OR REBUILDING THE OLD

PART V: FEAR

PART VI: CULTURE AND HISTORY

PART VII: COMING TO TERMS WITH THE WAR

List of Illustrations

Figures

Tables

LIST OF ABBREVIATIONS

AEC	Aero Engine Controls
AGA	Spanish State Archives
AK	Armia Kraiova (Home Army) (Poland)
AML	Amis du Manifeste de la Liberté (Algeria)
AOC	Appellation d'origine contrôlée
ARD	Arbeitsgemeinschaft der öffentlich-rechtlichen Rundfunkanstalten der Bundesrepublik Deutschland (Consortium of Public-law Broadcasting Institutions of the Federal Republic of Germany)
ARP	Air Raid Precautions
ATM	Automated teller machine
BBC	British Broadcasting Corporation
BCP	Bulgarian Communist Party
BR	Brigate rosse (Red Brigades) (Italy)
BSE	Bovine spongiform encephalitis (mad cow disease)
CAP	Common Agricultural Policy
CCF	Congress for Cultural Freedom
CCP	Chinese Communist Party
CDU	Christlich-Demokratische Union (Christian Democratic Union) (Germany)
CEA	Atomic Energy Commission
CER	European Organization for Atomic Research
CGT	Confédération Générale du Travail (France)
CIA	Central Intelligence Agency (US)
CIS	Commonwealth of Independent States
CLN	Committee of National Liberation (Italy)
CMEA	Council for Mutual Economic Assistance (Comecon)
CNC	Centre National de la Cinématographie (France)
CND	Campaign for Nuclear Disarmament (UK)
CNN	Cable News Network
CNR	Conseil national de la résistance (National Resistance Council) (France)
COMECON	see CMEA
CP	Communist Party
CPSU	Communist Party of the Soviet Union
CSCE	Conference on Security and Cooperation in Europe

CSSR	Czechoslovak Soviet Socialist Republic
DC	Democrazia Cristiana (Christian Democrats) (Italy)
DDR	Deutsche Demokratische Republik, see GDR
DDT	Dichlorodiphenyltrichloroethane (insecticide)
DGS	Direcção Geral de Segurança (General Security Directorate) (Portugal)
DPs	Displaced persons
DR2	Danmarks Radio 2 (Denmark)
EAM	National Liberation Front (Greece)
EBU	European Broadcasting Union
EC	European Community
ECHR	European Court of Human Rights
ECR	European Conservatives and Reformists Group
ECSC	European Coal and Steel Community
EDC	European Defence Corps
EEC	European Economic Community
EFTA	European Free Trade Association
ELAS	Ellinikós Laïkós Apeleftherotikós Stratós (Greek People's Liberation Army)
EMU	European Monetary Union
EPU	European Payments Union
ERP	European Recovery Program (Marshall Plan)
ERW	Enhanced-Radiation Weapon (neutron bomb)
ETA	Basque Homeland and Freedom
EU	European Union
EURODAC	European Dactyloscopy
EXCOMM	Executive Committee of the National Security Council (US)
FIDESZ-MPP	Alliance of Young Democrats-Hungarian Civic Party
FLN	Front pour la Libération National (National Liberation Front) (Algeria)
FND	National Democratic Front (Romania)
FRG	Federal Republic of Germany
FRY	Federal Republic of Yugoslavia
GATT	General Agreement on Tariffs and Trade
GDP	Gross domestic product
GDR	German Democratic Republic
GERB	Citizens for European Development of Bulgaria
GNP	Gross national product
HDZ	Croat Democratic Union
HSP	Croatian Party of Rights
HVO	Hravatsko vijeće obrane (Croatian Defence Council)
ICOM	International Council of Museums

ICOMOS	International Council on Monuments and Sites
ICT	Information and Communication Technology
ICTY	International Criminal Tribunal for the Former Yugoslavia
IDP	Internally Displaced Person
IEPC	Agreement for Intra-European Payments and Compensations
IISS	International Institute for Strategic Studies
IMF	International Monetary Fund
INF	Intermediate-Range Nuclear Forces Treaty
INSEAD	Institut Européen d'Administration des Affaires (European Institute of Business Administration)
IRA	Irish Republican Army
ISUY	International Union of Socialist Youth
ITV	Independent Television (UK)
IUCN	International Union for Conservation of Nature
JNA	Yugoslavian National Army
Jobbik	Movement for a Better Hungary Party
KGB	Komitet gosudarstvennoy bezopastnosti (Committee for State Security) (USSR)
KKE	Greek Communist Party
KLA	Kosovo Liberation Army
KPD	Kommunistische Partei Deutschlands (German Communist Party)
KPRF	Communist Party of the Russian Federation
KSČ	Czechoslovak Communist Party
LCY	League of Communists of Yugoslavia
LNNK	Latvian Fatherland and Freedom Party
LPR	League of Polish Families
LSE	London School of Economics and Political Science
MAD	Mutual Assured Destruction
MFA	Movimento das Forças Armadas (Armed Forces Movement) (Portugal)
MIÉP	Justice and Life Party (Hungary)
MKP	Hungarian Communist Party
MLF	Multilateral Nuclear Force (NATO)
MPs	Members of Parliament
MRP	Mouvement Républicain Populaire (People's Republican Movement) (France)
MTV	Music Television
NATO	North Atlantic Treaty Organization
ND	New Democracy (Greece)
NDH	Independent State of Croatia
NDR3	Norddeutscher Rundfunk 3 (FRG)
NGO	Non-Governmental Organization
NKVD	Narodnyy komissariat vnutrennikh del (People's Commissariat for Internal Affairs) (Soviet Security Service)

NYT	New York Times
OAS	Organisation de l'Armée Secrète (Secret Army Organization) (France)
OECD	Organization for Economic Cooperation and Development
OEEC	Organization for European Economic Cooperation
OPEC	Organization of Petroleum Exporting Countries
ORTF	Office de Radiodiffusion-Télévision Française (French Radio and Television Broadcasting)
OWI	Office of War Information (US)
PASOK	Panel'linio Sosialistiko Cinima (Panhellenic Socialist Movement) (Greece)
PCF	Partie Communiste Française (French Communist Party)
PCI	Partito Comunista Italiano (Italian Communist Party)
PCP	Portuguese Communist Party
PDA	Personal Digital Assistant
PDL	Partidul Liberal Democrat (Liberal-Democratic Party) (Romania)
PIDE	Policia Internacional e de Defesa do Estado (International and State Police) (Portugal)
'PIIGS'	Portugal, Italy, Ireland, Greece and Spain
PiS	Prawo i Sprawiedliwość (Law and Justice Party) (Poland)
PLA	Party of Labour in Albania
POW	Prisoner of war
PRC	People's Republic of China
PS/SFIO	Partie Socialiste/Section Française de l'Internationale Ouvrière (French Socialist Party)
PSDI	Partito Socialista Democratico Italiano (Italian Democratic Socialist Party)
PSI	Partito Socialista Italiano (Italian Socialist Party)
PSL	Polskie Stronnictwo Ludowe (Polish Peasants' Party)
PSOE	Partido Socialista Obrero Español (Spanish Socialist Party)
PZPR	Polska Zjednoczona Partia Robotnicza (Polish United Workers' Party)
RAF	Red Army Faction (West Germany)
R&D	research and development
RCP	Romanian Communist Party
RSFSR	Russian Federation
RTP	Rádio e Televisão de Portugal (Portuguese Radio and Television)
SALT	Strategic Arms Limitation Treaty
SAP	Sveriges socialdemokratiska arbetareparti (Swedish Social Democratic Party)
SDS	Sozialistische deutsche Studentenbund (German Socialist Student League)
SDS	Srpska demokratska stranka (Serbian Democratic Party)
SED	Sozialistische Einheitspartei Deutschlands (German Socialist Unity Party)
SMER	Sociálna demokracia (Direction – Social Democracy) (Slovakia)
SNP	Scottish National Party
SNS	Slovenská národná strana (Slovak National Party)

SPD	Sozialdemokratische Partei Deutschlands (German Social Democratic Party)
SPÖ	Sozialdemokratische Partei Österreichs (Austrian Social Democratic Party)
SS	Schutzstaffel
STS	Science, Technology and Society
TFP	Total Factor Productivity
TGV	Train à Grande Vitesse
TV	Television
TVE	Televisión Española (Spanish Television)
TVN	TV Nowa (Poland)
TVP1, 2, 3	Telewizja Polska (Polish Television)
UN	United Nations
UNESCO	United Nations Educational, Scientific and Cultural Organization
UNHCR	United Nations High Commission for Refugees
UNMIK	United Nations Interim Administration Mission in Kosovo
UNRRA	United Nations Relief and Rehabilitation Administration
UNURI	Unione nazionale universitaria rappresentativa italiana (Central student organization) (Italy)
USHMM	United States Holocaust Memorial Museum
US/USA	United States/United States of America
USSR	Union of Soviet Socialist Republics (Soviet Union)
VE	Victory in Europe
VJ	Yugoslav Army
VRS	Bosnian Serb Army
WEU	Western European Union
WP	Warsaw Pact
WTO	World Trade Organization
yBa	young British artists
YLE	Yleisradio (Finnish Broadcasting Company)
ZboWiD	Związek Bojowników o Wolność i Demokrację (Union of Fighters for Freedom and Democracy) (Poland)
ZDF	Zweites Deutsches Fernsehen (Second German TV Channel)

LIST OF CONTRIBUTORS

G.J. Ashworth was educated at the Universities of Cambridge, Reading, and London (PhD. 1974). He taught at the Universities of Wales and Portsmouth, and since 1979 Groningen. Since 1994, he has been professor of heritage management and urban tourism in the Department of Planning, Faculty of Spatial Sciences, University of Groningen (Netherlands). He is also Visiting Professor, Institute of Conservation, University of Gothenburg, Sweden. He received an honorary doctorate from the University of Brighton in 2009. Main research interests include heritage management, urban tourism and place marketing.

Ivan T. Berend is a Distinguished Professor at the Department of History, University of California, Los Angeles. Previously, he was professor of economic history at the Budapest University of Economics (1953–1985); President of the Hungarian Academy of Sciences (1985–90); and President of the International Committee of Historical Sciences (1995–2000). He is a Member of the British Academy and five other European academies of sciences. His most recent book is *Europe since 1980* (2010). Among his earlier works, he published a tetralogy on nineteenth- and twentieth-century Central and Eastern Europe, *The European Periphery and Industrialization, 1780–1914* (1984), and *An Economic History of 20th Century Europe* (2006). He is currently working on an economic history of nineteenth-century Europe.

Luiza Bialasiewicz is Associate Professor in the Department of European Studies at the University of Amsterdam. Her main interests lie with the historical and political geographies of European integration and European geopolitics. She is the co-author of *Spazio e Politica: Riflessioni di geografia critica* (2004) and the editor of *Europe in the World: EU Geopolitics and the Making of European Space* (2011). She is currently completing a research monograph on the transnational geographies of the idea of Europe entitled *Traces of Europe*.

Robert Bideleux was born in Argentina and educated in Brazil and the UK, and is a Reader in Political and Cultural Studies at Swansea University, where he teaches on political economy, genocide and global politics and runs a PPE programme. He has written extensively on political and economic change in modern Europe (especially its eastern half). He is currently working on the impact of the Great Recession of 2008–09 on the post-Communist states, writing books entitled *Genocidal Europe* and *Rethinking Europe's East-West Divides*, and co-writing (with Ian Jeffries) *East Central Europe After Communism* and *The Caucasus States After Communism*.

Ib Bondebjerg is Professor at the Department of Media, Cognition and Communication, University of Copenhagen (www.mef.ku.dk) and Director of the Centre for Modern European Studies (www.cemes.ku.dk), University of Copenhagen, Denmark. He was the founder and editor-in-chief of the international journal *Northern Lights. Film and Media Studies Yearbook* (2000–2009) and is a member of the editorial board of the international journal *Studies in Documentary Film*. He has published more than 100 articles in national and international journals and books. His most important single-authored books are: *Electronic Fictions. Television as a Narrative Medium* (1993, in Danish), *Film and Modernity. Film Genres and Film Culture in Denmark 1940–1972* (2005, in Danish), *Narratives of Reality. History of the Danish TV-Documentary* (2008, in Danish), *Images of Reality. The Modern Danish Film Documentary,* 2011, in Danish) and *Engaging with Reality: Documentary and Politics* (2011). Among his edited and co-edited books are: *Moving Images, Culture and the Mind* (2000), *The Danish Director: Dialogue on a National Cinema* (2001, with Mette Hjort), *European Culture and the Media* (2004, with Peter Golding) and *Media, Democracy and European Culture* (2008, with Peter Madsen).

Cathie Carmichael is Reader in Eastern European History at the University of East Anglia, Norwich. She studied at the London School of Economics and the Universities of Ljubljana and Bradford. She is the author of *Ethnic Cleansing in the Balkans: Nationalism and the Destruction of Tradition* (2002) and *Genocide before the Holocaust* (2009), co-editor (with Stephen Barbour) of *Language and Nationalism in Europe* (2000), and co-author (with James Gow) of *Slovenia and the Slovenes* (2000). She is on the International Advisory Board *of Europe-Asia Studies,* a member of the Executive Board of the British Association of Slavonic and East European Studies and an editor of the *Journal of Genocide Research.*

Stephen Castles is Research Professor of Sociology at the University of Sydney and Associate Director of the International Migration Institute (IMI), University of Oxford. He works on international migration dynamics, global governance and migration and development. His recent books include: *The Age of Migration: International Population Movements in the Modern World* (4th edn, with Mark Miller, 2009); and *Migration and Development: Perspectives from the South* (edited with Rúal Delgado Wise, 2008).

Hugh D. Clout is Professor Emeritus of Geography and former dean of social and historical sciences at University College London. His most recent books are *Patronage and the Production of Geographical Knowledge in France* (2009) and *Contemporary Rural Geographies* (ed., 2007). Previous books include: *Times History of London* (ed., 2007); *After the Ruins: Restoring the Countryside of Northern France after the Great War* (2007); and *Agriculture in France on the Eve of the Railway Age* (1980). He is currently working on the reconstruction of towns and villages in France after World War II, and on the historiography of academic geography in France. He serves on the editorial board of several French geographical periodicals. He is a Fellow of the British Academy, of the Academia Europaea, and of University College London.

Nicholas Crafts has been Professor of Economic History at the University of Warwick since 2006. He is also Director of the ESRC Research Centre on Competitive Advantage in the Global Economy (CAGE), at Warwick. Previous academic appointments have included full-time positions at London School of Economics and Oxford University, and visiting positions at UC Berkeley and Stanford. He is a Fellow of the British Academy and is a past President of the Economic History Society. His main fields of interest are long-run economic growth, British economic performance and policy in the twentieth century, the Industrial Revolution, and the historical geography of industrial location.

Geoff Eley is the Karl Pohrt Distinguished University Professor of Contemporary History at the University of Michigan, where he has taught since 1979; he is currently chairing the History Department. His most recent books include *Forging Democracy: The History of the Left in Europe, 1850–2000* (2002); *A Crooked Line: From Cultural History to the History of Society* (2005); *The Future of Class in History: What's Left of the Social?* (with Keith Nield, 2007); and *After the Nazi Racial State: Difference and Democracy in Germany and Europe*, coauthored with Rita Chin, Heide Fehrenbach, and Atina Grossmann (2009). He is co-editor of a volume of essays on German colonialism with Bradley Naranch. He is currently finishing a book on fascism and the German Right called *Genealogies of Nazism: Conservatives, Radical Nationalists, Fascists in Germany, 1860–1930*.

Martin Evans is Professor of Contemporary History at the University of Portsmouth. He is the author of *Memory of Resistance: French Opposition to the Algerian War* (1997) and *Algeria: France's Undeclared War* (2011), and the co-author (with John Phillips) of *Algeria: Anger of the Dispossessed* (2007). He is on the editorial board *of History Today*. In 2007–08 he was a Leverhulme Senior Research Fellow at the British Academy.

Philipp Gassert is Professor of Transatlantic Cultural History at the University of Augsburg. His books include a history of anti-Americanism in Nazi Germany, *Amerika im Dritten Reich: Ideologie, Volksmeinung und Propaganda* (1997) and many other publications dealing with postwar European history, including *1968: The World Transformed* (co-edited with Carole Fink and Detlef Junker, 1998); *Coping with the Nazi Past: West German Debates on Nazism and Generational Conflict, 1955–1975* (co-edited with Alan E. Steinweis, 2006). He has taught at the University of Heidelberg and the University of Pennsylvania in Philadelphia. He was also deputy director of the German Historical Institute in Washington, D.C. in 2008–09.

Brian Graham is Emeritus Professor of Human Geography at the University of Ulster, Northern Ireland. His most recent books are *Pluralising Pasts: Heritage, Identity and Place in Multicultural Societies* (2007), co-authored with G.J. Ashworth and J.E. Tunbridge; and *The Ashgate Research Companion to Heritage and Identity* (2008), co-edited with Peter Howard. He is currently writing a study of the role of commemoration of conflict in peace processes with Sara McDowell and completing a cultural geography of the Irish borderlands with Catherine Nash. His previous books include *A Geography of Heritage: Power, Culture, Economy* (2000), also co-authored with G.J. Ashworth and J.E. Tunbridge and several edited volumes such as *Modern Historical Geographies* (with Catherine Nash, 2000), *Modern Europe: Place, Culture, Identity* (1998), and *In Search of Ireland* (1997). He has also published numerous articles and book chapters on issues concerned with heritage, identity and memory in Ireland and Europe. He lives in Northern Ireland.

Helen Graham teaches modern European history at Royal Holloway, University of London. Her books include *The Spanish Republic at War* (2003), *The Spanish Civil War: A Very Short Introduction* (2005), which has been translated into German, Spanish, Portuguese, and Greek, and *The War and its Shadow: Spain's Civil War in Europe's Long Twentieth Century* (2012). She is currently researching a book about Franco's prisons and writing another, *Lives at the Limit*, which explores the reverberations of Republican defeat internationally through a series of interlocking biographical essays. Her research interests include the social history of Spanish communism; comparative civil wars and comparative cultural and gender history. In 1995 she edited (with Jo Labanyi) the Oxford University Press volume *Spanish Cultural Studies*.

Ido de Haan is Professor of Political History at Utrecht University (the Netherlands). His fields of interest are the history of modern democracy, citizenship, and the state, the history and memory of large-scale violence, the comparative study of political transitions, the history of political thought, and contemporary Jewish history. He has published on the memory of war, occupation, and the Holocaust in the Netherlands, on the political history of the Netherlands in the nineteenth century, and on the history of the Dutch welfare state. He has also edited volumes on the social question, the history of 'maakbaarheid' (the untranslatable Dutch concept for 'constructing society'), and a volume on 'borders and boundaries' in Jewish history. He is currently leading a research project on the history of functional, corporatist and associational forms of democracy since the end of the nineteenth century until the present. He regularly contributes to the public debate in the Netherlands. Ido de Haan lives in Amsterdam.

Jussi M. Hanhimäki is Professor of International History and Politics at the Graduate Institute of International and Development Studies in Geneva, Switzerland and Finland Distinguished Professor (Academy of Finland). His most recent publications include *The United Nations: A Very Short Introduction* (2008) and *The Flawed Architect: Henry Kissinger and American Foreign Policy* (2004). Professor Hanhimäki is one of the founding editors of the journal *Cold War History* and a member of the editorial boards of *Relations Internationales, Refugee Survey Quarterly,* and *Ulkopolitiikka*.

Andrew Jamison has an undergraduate degree in history and science from Harvard University (1970) and a PhD from University of Gothenburg in theory of science (1983). He was director of the graduate programme in science and technology policy at the University of Lund from 1986 to 1995, and since 1996, has been professor of technology and society at the Department of Development and Planning at Aalborg University. He was coordinator of the EU-funded project, Public Participation and Environmental Science and Technology Policy Options (PESTO), from 1996 to 1999, and is currently coordinating a Programme of Research on Opportunities and Challenges in Engineering Education in Denmark (PROCEED), from 2010 to 2013, funded by the Danish Strategic Research Council. He has published widely in the areas of environmental politics, social movements, and cultural history, most recently *The Making of Green Knowledge: Environmental Politics and Cultural Transformation* (2001) and, with Mikael Hård, *Hubris and Hybrids: A Cultural History of Technology and Science* (2005).

Martin Klimke is an Assistant Professor of History at New York University, Abu Dhabi. From 2006 to 2010, he was the coordinator of the EU-funded conference and training series 'European Protest Movements since 1945'. His many publications include: *The Other Alliance: Student Protest in West Germany and the United States in the Global Sixties* (2010); *A Breath of Freedom: The Civil Rights Struggle, African American GIs, and Germany* (with Maria Höhn, 2010); *Changing the World, Changing the Self: Political Protest and Collective Identities in the 1960s and 1970s* (co-edited with Belinda Davis, Carla MacDougall and Wilfried Mausbach, 2010); *1968: Memories and Legacies of a Global Revolt* (co-edited with Philipp Gassert, 2009); and *1968 in Europe: A History of Protest and Activism, 1956–77* (co-edited with Joachim Scharloth, 2008).

Catherine Lee is Head of the Research and Postgraduate Office at London Metropolitan University. Her research is trans-disciplinary with a focus on political sociology. She has a long-standing interest in theories of practice and governmentality. Her work has investigated conceptions and understandings of Europe as well as practices of the knowledge economy.

Uli Linke is Professor of Anthropology at Rochester Institute of Technology (http://www.rit.edu/cla/sociology/faculty/linke.html). Her research is focused on the cultural politics of nationhood in Europe, with particular attention to regimes of exclusion, gender, genocide, trauma and memory, and the semiotics of the body. Her books include *Cultures of Fear: A Critical Reader* (co-edited with Danielle Taana Smith, 2009), *German Bodies: Race and Representation after Hitler* (1999), and *Blood and Nation: The European Aesthetics of Race* (1999). She has taught at the University of Toronto, the Central European University in Budapest, Rutgers University, and the University of Tübingen, where she was a faculty member at the Ludwig Uhland Institute. Her essays have appeared in *Comparative Studies of Society and History, New German Critique, History and Anthropology* and *Anthropological Theory* among other journals.

Roger Markwick is Associate Professor of Modern European History and Head of the School of Humanities and Social Science, University of Newcastle, Australia (http://www.newcastle.edu.au/staff/research-profile/Roger_Markwick). His *Rewriting History in Soviet Russia: The Politics of Revisionist Historiography in the Soviet Union, 1956–1974* won the Alexander Nove Prize in Russian, Soviet, and Post-Soviet Studies for 2001.

Among his other writings is 'Communism: Fascism's "Other"?', in *The Oxford Handbook of Fascism* (2009). He is co-author (with Euridice Charon Cardona) of *Soviet Women on the Frontline in the Second World War* (2012). His latest research is on Soviet women on the home front during the Second World War.

Samuel Moyn is Professor Law and History at Harvard University. He has published three books, including *Origins of the Other: Emmanuel Levinas between Revelation and Ethics* (2005) and *The Last Utopia: Human Rights in History* (2010). He reviews frequently for *The Nation*, and lives in New York City.

Stefan Muthesius is an art historian, specialising in the history of architecture and design of the last 200 years in Europe and North America. He taught at the School of World Art Studies at the University of East Anglia in Norwich. His last book is *The Poetic Home: Designing the 19th Century Domestic Interior* (2009); earlier books include *The Postwar University: Utopianist College and Campus* (2000), *An Introduction to Art, Architecture and Design in Poland* (1994) and *The English Terraced House* (1984).

Leopoldo Nuti is Professor of History of International Relations at the University of Roma Tre and Director of CIMA, an Italian Inter-university Center for Cold War Studies. Prof. Nuti has been a Fulbright student at George Washington University (MA, class of '86), NATO Research Fellow, Jean Monnet Fellow at the European University Institute, Research Fellow at the CSIA, Harvard University, Research Fellow for the Nuclear History Program, Senior Research Fellow at the Norwegian Nobel Institute, and Visiting Professor at the Institut d'Etudes Politiques in Paris. He has published extensively in Italian, English and French on US-Italian relations and Italian foreign and security policy. His latest books are a history of nuclear weapons in Italy during the Cold War, *La sfida nucleare. La politico estera italiana e le armi nucleari, 1945–1991* (2007) and, as an editor, *The Crisis of Detente in Europe: From Helsinki to Gorbachev, 1975–1985* (2008).

Richard Overy is Professor of History at the University of Exeter after teaching for 24 years at King's College, London. He has written more than 25 books on the Second World War, the history of airpower, and of the Soviet and German dictatorships. His most recent books have been *The Dictators: Hitler's Germany and Stalin's Russia* (2004) (which won the Wolfson and the Hessell Tiltman Prizes for History), *The Morbid Age: Britain and the Crisis of Civilisation 1919–1939* (2009), and *The Third Reich: A Chronicle* (2010). He is a Fellow of the British Academy and a Fellow of the Royal Historical Society. In 2001 he was awarded the Samuel Eliot Morison Prize for his contributions to military history, and in 2010 the James Doolittle Award for his writings on air power.

Luisa Passerini is a retired Professor of Cultural History at the University of Turin, Italy (www.personalweb.unito.it/luisa.passerini/). Her most recent book is *Love and the Idea of Europe* (2009) and she has started a study on the connections between memory, visuality, and new forms of European identity. Among her previous books are *Europe in Love, Love in Europe: Imagination and Politics between the Wars* (1999) and *Memory and Utopia: The Primacy of Inter subjectivity* (2007). She is an External Professor at the European University Institute, Florence, and a Visiting Professor at Columbia University.

Mark Pittaway was Senior Lecturer in European Studies in the History Department at the Open University. His publications included *Eastern Europe, 1939–2000* (2004). He passed away in 2010, during the preparation of this volume.

Alejandro Quiroga is a Reader in Spanish History at the School of Historical Studies, Newcastle University. His most recent book is *Right-Wing Spain in the Civil War Era. Soldiers of God and Apostles of the Fatherland, 1914–45* (co-edited with Miguel Ángel del Arco, 2012). He is the author of *The Reinvention of Spain: Nation and Identity since Democracy* (with Sebastian Balfour, 2007), *Making Spaniards: Primo de Rivera and the Nationalization of the Masses, 1923–1930* (2007), and *Los orígenes del Nacionalcatolicismo. José Pemartín y la Dictadura de Primo de Rivera* (2006). He is currently writing a monograph on football and national identities in contemporary Spain.

Douglas Selvage is staff researcher at the Office of the Federal Commissioner for Stasi Records in Berlin for the project, 'The Ministry for State Security and the CSCE Process'. Previously, at the Historian's Office of the U.S. Department of State, he edited *Foreign Relations of the United States: European Security, 1969–1976*, along with other co-edited volumes. He also won the Link-Kuehl Prize for Documentary Editing of the Society for Historians of American Foreign Relations for *Soviet-American Relations: The Detente Years, 1969–1972* (co-edited with David Geyer, 2007). He is a frequent contributor to the publications of the Cold War International History Project and the Parallel History Project. He also served as principal investigator for the National Endowment for the Humanities grant project, 'The Cold War and Human Security: Translations for the Parallel History Project'.

Michael Shafir is Professor of International Relations at Babes-Bolyai University, Cluj-Napoca, Romania. He is the author *of Romania: Politics, Economics and Society. Political Stagnation and Simulated Change* (1985); *Between Negation and Comparative Trivialization: Holocaust Denial in Post-Communist East-Central Europe* (2002); and *X-Rays and other Phobias* (2010). He has published over 300 articles on communist and post-communist affairs in American, Austrian, British, Czech, Dutch, French, German, Hungarian, Israeli, Romanian, and Slovak journals, and has contributed chapters to books published in Austria, the Czech Republic, Great Britain, Romania, Slovakia, and the USA. Professor Shafir is the head of the Romanian delegation to the Task Force for International Cooperation on Holocaust Education, Remembrance, and Research (ITF).

P.D. Smith is an independent researcher and writer (www.peterdsmith.com). His most recent book is *City: A Guidebook for the Urban Age* (Bloomsbury, 2012). His previous books are *Doomsday Men: The Real Dr Strangelove and the Dream of the Superweapon* (2007); *Metaphor and Materiality: German Literature and the World-View of Science 1780–1955* (2000); and a succinct biography of Einstein (2003). He has taught at University College London where he is an Honorary Research Associate in the Department of Science and Technology Studies. He regularly reviews books for the *Guardian* and the *Times Literary Supplement,* and has written for the *Independent* and the *Financial Times* among other journals. He lives in Hampshire.

Dan Stone is Professor of Modern History at Royal Holloway, University of London. He works on historiographical and philosophical interpretations of the Holocaust, comparative genocide, modern European history of ideas, and the cultural history of the British Right. His publications include: *Breeding Superman: Nietzsche, Race and Eugenics in Edwardian and Interwar Britain* (2002); *Constructing the Holocaust: A Study in Historiography* (2003); *Responses to Nazism in Britain 1933–1939: Before War and Holocaust* (2003); *The Historiography of the Holocaust* (ed., 2004); *History, Memory and Mass Atrocity: Essays on the Holocaust and Genocide* (2006), *Hannah Arendt and the Uses of History: Imperialism, Nation, Race and Genocide* (ed. with Richard H. King, 2007); *The Historiography of Genocide* (ed., 2008); *Histories of the Holocaust* (2010); *The Holocaust and Historical Methodology* (ed., 2012) and *Goodbye To All That? The Story of Europe since 1945* (2014).

Philipp Ther is Professor of Central European History at the University of Vienna. He has published several books about nationalism, violence, and ethnic cleansing. Among them are *Deutsche und polnische Vertriebene. Gesellschaft und Vertriebenenpolitik in der SBZ/DDR und in Polen 1945–1956* (1998), *Redrawing Nations: Ethnic Cleansing in East-Central Europe 1944–1948* (ed. with Ana Siljak, 2001), *Nationalitätenkonflikte im 20. Jahrhundert: Ursachen von inter-ethnischer Gewalt im Vergleich* (ed. with Holm Sundhaussen, 2001), and *Die dunkle Seite der Nationalstaaten: Ethnische Säuberungen im modernen Europa* (2011). His other, more pleasant field of interest, is cultural history, especially the history of music and society.

Vladimir Tismaneanu is Professor of Politics at University of Maryland (College Park) and President of the Scientific Council of the Institute for the Investigation of Communism Crimes and the Memory of the Romanian Exile (Romania). Most recently, he edited the volume *Promises of 1968: Crisis, Illusion, and Utopia* (2010). Among his books are *Reinventing Politics: Eastern Europe from Stalin to Havel* (1992, paperback with a new epilogue, 1993); *Fantasies of Salvation: Nationalism, Democracy, and Myth in Post-Communist Europe* (1998); *Stalinism for All Seasons: a Political History of Romanian Communism* (2003). His next book, *The Devil in History: Lessons of the 20th Century,* is forthcoming with University of California Press.

Gianni Toniolo is Research Professor of Economics and History at Duke University (North Carolina), Visiting Professor at Libera Università Internazionale degli Studi Sociali (Rome), Research Fellow at the Centre for Economic Policy Research (London), and a member of the European Academy. His research interests focus on European economic growth since 1800 and on financial history. Among his books are: *The World Economy between the Wars* (with C.H. Feinstein and P. Temin, 2008); *The Global Economy in the 1990s. A Long-run Perspective* (with P. Rhode 2006); *Central Bank Cooperation at the BIS* (2005); and *Economic Growth in Europe since 1945* (with N. Crafts, 1996).

Rosemary Wakeman is Professor of History and Director of the Urban Studies Program at Fordham University in New York. She is the author of *The Heroic City: Paris 1945–1958* (2009) and *Modernizing the Provincial City: Toulouse, 1945–1975* (1997). She has also edited *Themes in Modern European History since 1945* (2003). She has published numerous articles on urban history and on cities, and writes regularly for the *Revue Urbanisme*. Her current book project is an intellectual history of the New Town Movement in Europe and the United States.

Robert J.C. Young is Julius Silver Professor of English and Comparative Literature at New York University. He was formerly Professor of English and Critical Theory at Oxford University and a fellow of Wadham College. He has published *White Mythologies: Writing History and the West* (1990, new edition 2004), *Colonial Desire: Hybridity in Culture, Theory and Race* (1995), *Postcolonialism: An Historical Introduction* (2001), *Postcolonialism: A Very Short Introduction* (2003), and *The Idea of English Ethnicity* (2008). Editor of *Interventions: International Journal of Postcolonial Studies,* he was also a founding editor of the *Oxford Literary Review* which he edited from 1977 to 1994. His work has been translated into 20 languages.

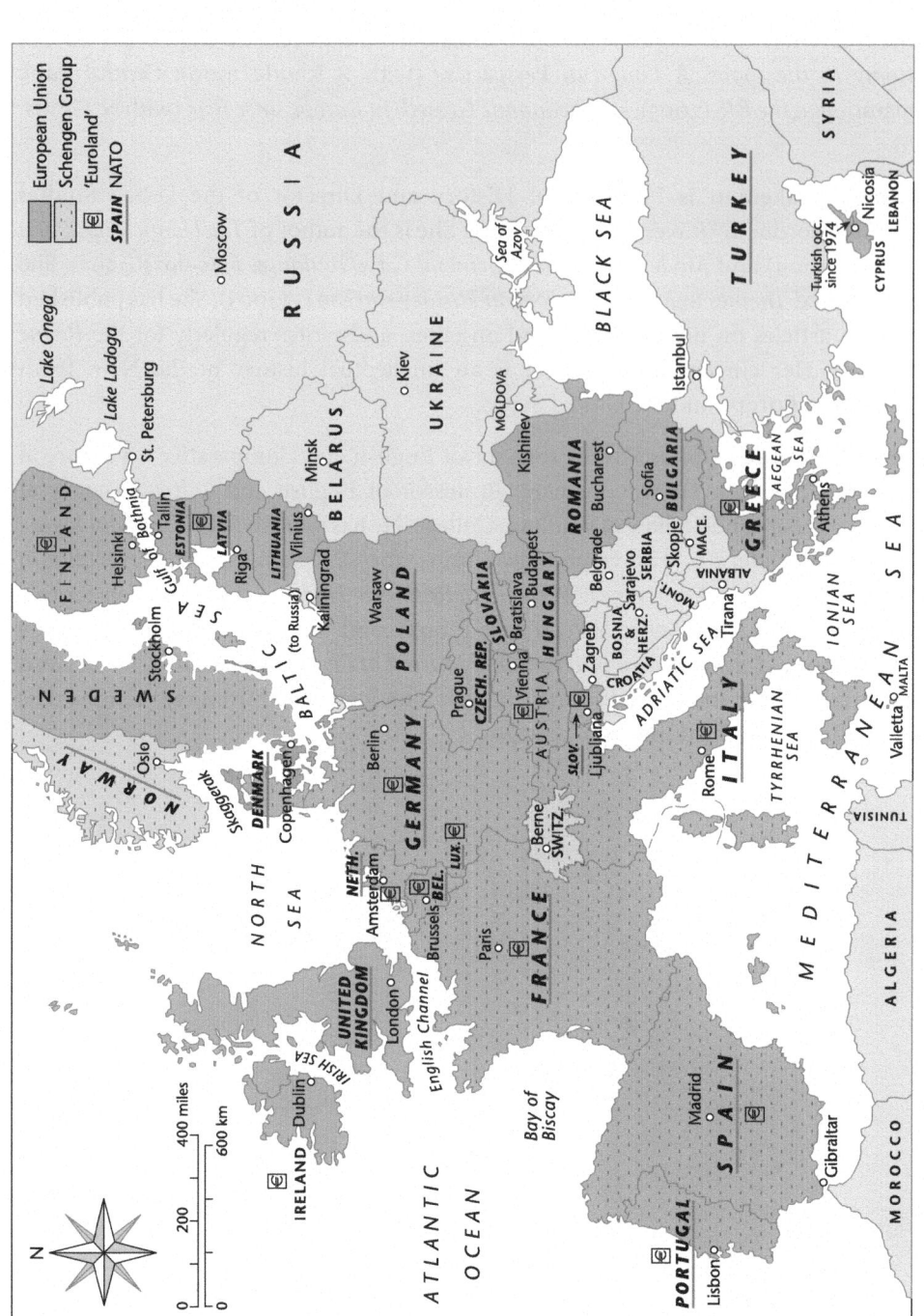

FIGURE 1: Europe 2012

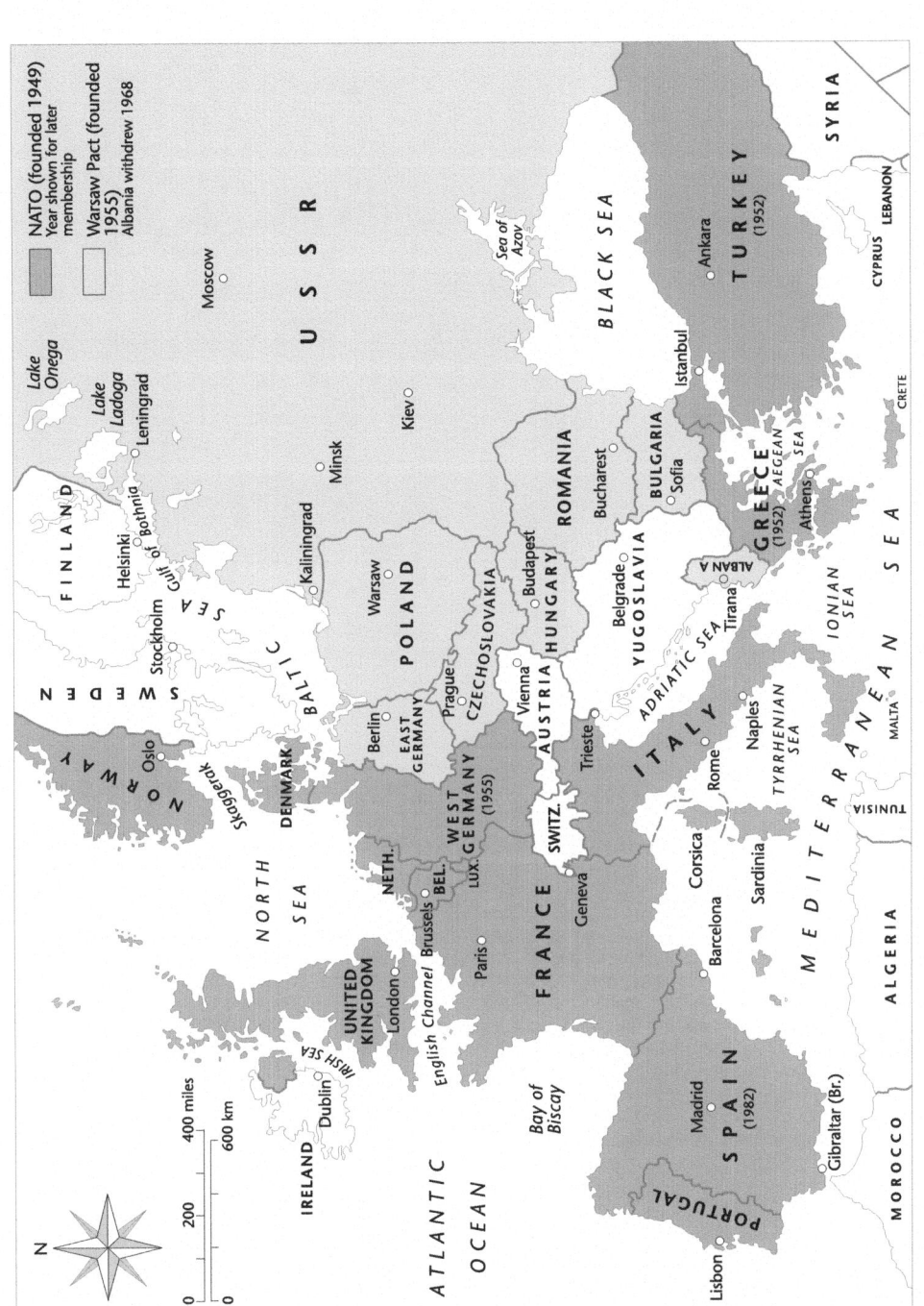

FIGURE 2: Cold War Europe 1945–89

EDITOR'S INTRODUCTION

Postwar Europe as History

DAN STONE

'Who would dare to impute to those masses who have risen in Europe against Nazi rule that they are fighting for the revival of a past whose profound weaknesses and irrevocable collapse they have experienced? Their goal is a new world!'

Le Franc-tireur, 1 March 1944

'We live on the cusp of two worlds. If we find an ethic that will have as its goal the welfare of man and not economic profit or the selfish interests of some race, nation, or social class, then, perhaps, we will be able to clear the rubble from our continent and provide education and comfort to people who crave housing, work, and books more than uniforms, guns, and tanks.'

Anatol Girs

'You are likely to lose faith in yourself and in mankind when you see the survivors of the cataclysm trying to build up a new world by building into it all the same structures that led to the decomposition of the old.'

Gregor von Rezzori[1]

PRIMO Levi is famous as the author of one of the great testimonies of Europe's catastrophe. Indeed, the rise to prominence of the genre of testimony in the late twentieth

---

[1] *Le Franc-tireur, Organe du Mouvement de Libération Nationale*, Édition Sud, 1 March 1944, cited in Walter Lipgens, 'European Federation in the Political Thought of Resistance Movements during World War II', *Central European History* 1:1 (1968), 9; Anatol Girs, 'From the Publisher', in Janusz Nel Siedlecki, Krystyn Olszewski and Tadeusz Borowski, *We Were in Auschwitz* (New York: Welcome Rain, 2000 [1946]), 2; Gregor Von Rezzori, *Memoirs of an Anti-Semite: A Novel in Five Stories* (London: Pan Books, 1983), 251. My thanks to Roger Markwick for comments on an earlier version of this introduction.

century is unthinkable without him. But Levi was also the author of numerous short stories, which he published in Italian journals in the 1960s and 1970s. Where *If This Is a Man* and *The Truce* eventually came to define the Holocaust and to establish Auschwitz as postwar Europe's epitome of evil, 'Gladiators', first published in *L'Automobile* in 1976, seems to sum up many of the postwar period's characteristics: technology, wealth, leisure, sport, and changing gender relations; but also mass consumption, alienation, 'massifica-tion', and violence. All are exemplified in Levi's story, in which the eponymous fighters—mostly convicts—are thrown into an arena where, armed only with a hammer, they must face being mown down by cars.[2] The spectators applaud when a gladiator performs an acrobatic manoeuvre that facilitates his escape, but the wildest applause is reserved for the gladiator who smashes in the head of a driver with his hammer. The violence in this story is shocking, all the more so for being juxtaposed with leisure, relaxation, and that epitome of postwar mass culture, the automobile. But coming from the pen of Levi, with the ominous threat of Auschwitz always in the background, 'Gladiators' also suggests that the apparent stability of postwar European consumer society belies the fact that Europe's darker history is still present, just below the surface. In contrast to a novel like Georges Perec's *W or The Memory of Childhood* (1975), in which an entire society is based on the rigid lines of sport—an allegory of the attempt to turn interwar and wartime society into a grand barracks—Levi's vision is of a society not permanently mobilized, as under fascism, but nevertheless ready and willing to employ and enjoy violence.

Italy in the 1970s, when Levi wrote 'Gladiators', was a society scarred by the memory of fascism. In its most violent manifestation, the extreme-left Red Brigades (*Brigate Rosse*) sought to expose the 'objective' fascism of the modern state by provoking it into a clampdown, forcing a rightward shift. As with the Red Army Faction in West Germany at the same time, the Red Brigades were, unwittingly, doing the work of the fascists for them; indeed, their immature psychological proclivities towards violence made them, despite their stated ideologies, heirs to European fascism in a complex way. In a time defined by both Eurocommunism and Eurosclerosis, the everyday chaos of postwar Italian politics meant that violence, corruption (including the machinations of the P2 masonic lodge), instability, and terrorism coexisted with historically unprecedented economic prosperity in the new, peaceful context of the EEC.

It is tempting to tell the story of Europe in the twentieth century in two halves: the first, a sorry, bleak tale of poverty, war, and genocide; and the second, a happy narrative of stability and the triumph of boring normality over dangerous activism and exuberant politics. This is not entirely unwarranted, especially if we stick to Eric Hobsbawm's 'short twentieth century' of 1914–1989.[3] However, as the Italian example shows, while the extremes of the 'second thirty years war' did not return to Europe between 1945 and 1989, it behoves us to dig a little deeper and uncover some of the subplots of the redemp-tive narrative which is so appealing. Quite apart from the fact that Europe in 1944–45

---

[2] Primo Levi, 'Gladiators', in *A Tranquil Star: Unpublished Stories* (London: Penguin, 2008), 83–9.

[3] Eric Hobsbawm, *The Age of Extremes: A History of the World, 1914–1991* (London: Michael Joseph, 1994).

could not feed itself—and therefore that the view from the early twenty-first century should avoid whiggish triumphalism—there were numerous fault lines along which European politics, culture, and society split, sometimes very dangerously. Most obvious of these is of course the Cold War, which divided the continent in a way that defined it for forty years and whose after-effects are still evident. I will say more about the Cold War shortly, but it should not be taken as synonymous with the postwar period *tout court*, for this would lead one to overlook many other significant pressure points.

The impact of World War II, the largest and bloodiest conflict in world history, leaving so many dead that 'the very earth seemed to breathe', did not end in 1945.[4] Without understanding the nature of World War II, one cannot get to grips with what followed. It was not just a classic territorial struggle best understood in terms of military strategy, but an ideological clash, in which a racialized vision of a Europe united under German domination fought, after 1941, against an uneasy alliance of liberals and communists. This war of ideologies, inspired primarily by Nazi chiliasm, gave the war its millenarian character, and accounts for the fact that in every state there was a mini-war going on, with large sections of the European population believing—with a peak in about 1941–42—that a Nazified Europe was an unstoppable reality. Military and ideological collaboration with Nazism meant that the viciousness of the fighting was akin to a civil war.[5] As the Italian fascist novelist Curzio Malaparte wrote:

> all over Europe, a frightful civil war was festering like a tumour beneath the surface of the war which the Allies were fighting against Hitler's Germany. In their efforts to liberate Europe from the German yoke Poles were killing Poles, Greeks were killing Greeks, Frenchmen were killing Frenchmen, Rumanians were killing Rumanians, and Jugoslavs were killing Jugoslavs... While the Allies were allowing themselves to be killed in the attempt to liberate Italy from the Germans, we Italians were killing one another.[6]

In the Yugoslav context, renegade communist Milovan Djilas put it even more succinctly: 'A people was at grips with the invader, while brothers slaughtered one another in even more bitter warfare'.[7] The Liberation itself was a bloody and frightening process for millions of Europeans, from the citizens of Normandy whose towns were bombed by the Allies on and after D-Day, to the inhabitants of Nazi camps who were too dazed and weak to comprehend what was happening, and who continued to die in droves after being 'liberated'.[8] In the immediate postwar years, many millions of people—especially Germans—were displaced as borders were shifted and populations expelled or forcibly 'transferred', in the largest internal population migration in recorded European

---

[4] Milovan Djilas, *Wartime* (London: Secker &Warburg, 1980), 447.

[5] See Dan Stone, *Histories of the Holocaust* (Oxford: Oxford University Press, 2010), ch. 1 for more detail.

[6] Curzio Malaparte, *The Skin* (London: Ace Books, 1959), 228–9.

[7] Milovan Djilas, *Conversations with Stalin* (Harmondsworth: Penguin, 1969), 19.

[8] William I. Hitchcock, *Liberation: The Bitter Road to Freedom, Europe 1944–1945* (London: Faber and Faber, 2009).

history.[9] By the end of the war, the Allies were in effect promoting what the Nazis had advocated in the 1930s: 'ethnic homogeneity as a desirable feature of national self-determination and international stability'.[10] Purges of collaborators—often carried out by people who themselves had dubious pasts—resulted in tens of thousands of deaths before the return of governments-in-exile. Even so, it is remarkable that, after the violence of the war, retribution was not more terrible.[11]

Displaced Persons (DP) camps, especially housing Jewish survivors of the Nazi camps and of postwar antisemitic violence in Eastern Europe, were a blot on the Central European landscape until more than ten years after the war, when the establishment of the state of Israel permitted the last remaining DPs to go where they wanted. Violence and civil war continued in many parts of Europe. Communist authorities did not put down the last pockets of nationalist resistance in Poland until the early 1950s; civil war in Greece precipitated British withdrawal from Great Power status and permanent American intervention in Europe, in the shape of the Truman Doctrine and the Marshall Plan (the European Recovery Programme). In the midst of the bloodiest war of European decolonization, in Algeria, France nearly succumbed to civil war in 1958, following a right-wing military plot. Decolonization in general was a great shock to European notions of superiority and power, which had long been casually assumed. The leaders of the decolonization movements simply continued the struggles they had fought against the Japanese or in service in Europe during World War II against the colonial powers that sought to reassert their control after liberation. Even in the continuing arrangements of neocolonialism and clientelism, which benefited the former colonial powers, decolonization brought new challenges: mass, non-white immigration into Europe, Third Worldism, and other political positions broadly associated with the 'New Left' that did not fit comfortably into paradigms that the establishment could understand. Dictatorships continued to exist in Spain and Portugal until the 1970s, as the Franco and Salazar regimes played on their supposed wartime neutrality and their anti-communist credentials to persuade the US and its allies that in the context of the Cold War they ought to be tolerated. Twenty years after the end of its civil war, Greece in 1967 fell prey

---

[9] Mark Mazower, *Dark Continent: Europe's Twentieth Century* (London: Allen Lane The Penguin Press, 1998), 217–24. As Mazower notes (224), close to ninety million people were either killed or displaced in Europe between 1939 and 1948. Thus: 'We cannot hope to understand the subsequent course of European history without attending to this enormous upheaval and trying to ascertain its social and political consequences.' See also Philipp Ther and Ana Siljak (eds), *Redrawing Nations: Ethnic Cleansing in East-Central Europe, 1944–1948* (Lanham, MD: Rowman and Littlefield, 2001); Alfred-maurice De Zayas, *A Terrible Revenge: The Ethnic Cleansing of the East European Germans*, 2nd edn (Basingstoke: Palgrave Macmillan, 2006); Pertti Ahonen, Gustavo Corni, Jerzy Kochanowski, Rainer Schulze, Tamás Stark, and Barbara Stelzl-Marx, *People on the Move: Forced Population Movements in Europe in the Second World War and its Aftermath* (Oxford: Berg, 2008).

[10] Mark Mazower, *No Enchanted Palace: The End of Empire and the Ideological Origins of the United Nations* (Princeton, NJ: Princeton University Press, 2009), 143.

[11] István Deák, Jan T. Gross and Tony Judt (eds), *The Politics of Retribution in Europe: World War II and Its Aftermath* (Princeton, NJ: Princeton University Press, 2000); Roderick Kedward and Nancy Wood (eds), *The Liberation of France: Image and Event* (Oxford: Berg, 1995).

to military dictatorship, a brutal junta that rose and fell over the question of Cyprus, itself one of the longest running sores of postwar politics.

The Cold War itself—in the broader context of US–Soviet rivalry—obviously threatened the stability not just of Europe but of the world as a whole. The Cuban Missile Crisis of 1962 brought the world shockingly close to nuclear annihilation—it is impossible to read the transcripts of President Kennedy's discussions with EXCOMM (Executive Committee of the National Security Council) and the Joint Chiefs of Staff without one's palms sweating[12] —and the revival of the nuclear arms race in the 1980s not only reawoke fears of Mutual Assured Destruction (as in films such as *The Day After*) but understandably contributed to preventing the vast majority of Kremlin watchers from predicting the demise of communist Europe just a few years later. From the communist takeover of Eastern Europe in the immediate postwar years to the various Berlin crises, the establishment of NATO and the Warsaw Pact, the violent suppression of the workers' uprisings of 1953, the Hungarian revolution of 1956, and the 'Prague Spring' of 1968, the Korean war, the Vietnam war and many other episodes, the global Cold War both influenced and was influenced by events in Europe.[13]

Moving away from high politics, many other spheres of life changed dramatically in the postwar period, so that simplistic notions of stability and normality cannot do justice to the complex realities. In the field of gender relations and sexuality, the period was the first in human history in which women could take control of the reproductive process. Even if feminism and the 'sexual revolution' look somewhat jaded from the perspective of the twenty-first century, when the gender stereotypes against which feminism fought are being staunchly reinforced, the phenomenon of women's rights (to equal pay for equal work, to divorce, to protection from rape, especially in marriage, to contraception, and to abortion) backed by legislation was still unprecedented. Homosexuality was a subject that was not only unthinkable for most Europeans, but certainly unmentionable in 'respectable' society in the 1940s; from the late 1960s onwards, gay rights, though achieved steadily and unevenly, and sometimes in the face of violent opposition, made their appearance in Western European law. The expansion of higher education, the rise of mass consumerism and tourism, the obsession with 'things', ownership and wealth, the availability of cheap credit; all were phenomena of the postwar world. As Max-Stephan Schulze notes, 'the increase in material prosperity was probably *the* major characteristic of economic and social development in Western Europe since 1945'.[14] The same is true for Eastern Europe; even though from the 1960s onwards, standards of living fell sharply below those in the West, for many, conditions were better than before the war and, importantly, the perception that improvements were possible became widespread.

---

[12] See http://www.hpol.org/jfk/cuban/ for audio transcripts, accessed March 2010.

[13] Odd Arne Westad, *The Global Cold War: Third World Interventions and the Making of Our Times* (Cambridge: Cambridge University Press, 2005). See also Jeremi Suri, 'The Cold War, Decolonization, and Global Social Awakenings: Historical Intersections', *Cold War History* 6:3 (2006), 353–63.

[14] Max-Stephan Schulze, 'Introduction', in Schulze (ed.), *Western Europe: Economic and Social Change since 1945* (London: Longman, 1999), 1.

However, postwar phenomena also included, in Western Europe, racialized under-standings of immigration and decolonization, often resulting in riots and the rise of new far-right parties, sometimes with direct linkages to interwar fascism; terrorism of the radical left and right, as well as nationalist movements such as the IRA or ETA; the sup-pression of critical thought in the postwar period as old elites pushed with all their might for their rehabilitation at the expense of those with new ideas for anti-fascist grassroots politics. In Eastern Europe, the period saw the creation of police states backed up by powerful and all-pervasive secret police forces that were far more extensive than the Gestapo; the homogenization of living and working conditions; and the dominance of ideology over the private sphere, with sometimes tragicomic, sometimes lunatic results.[15] Indeed, if one compares Western or Eastern Europe in 1945 with Europe in 2000, in every sphere—political, economic, cultural, social, educational, and sexual—the difference between the start and the end of the period is so vast that probably no other comparably short period of European history has ever witnessed such remarkable change.

Recognizing that fact and explaining it is the historian's task, and thus we can see that postwar Europe is fast becoming history. This process of historicization is being set in train in many ways, but clearly, comfortable notions of stability and progress are insuffi-cient for the job. In his 1895 inaugural lecture at Cambridge, Lord Acton noted that 'there is far more fear of drowning than of drought' when encountering the sources for writing modern history—and that in an age when history was restricted to diplomatic history. Some clear-cut conceptual parameters are therefore required in order to make sense of this mass of material, encompassing every conceivable sphere of human activity.

Conceptual Parameters

Since the end of the Cold War, Europe's postwar years have increasingly been histori-cized. Where earlier postwar Europe was—understandably—confined to the sphere of current affairs, and was written about by journalists, politicians, political scientists, and sociologists, now historians have made their mark, with a stream of research on all aspects of the period, from diplomacy to consumerism. Yet, despite the appearance of several superb synthetic works, there is as yet no real sense of a coherent historical field or any consensus about what 'postwar Europe' means. How did a continent in ruins in 1945 become one of the most prosperous and privileged corners of the world? What changes had to be made to 'late European modernity' to maintain economic and social stability at the end of the century? The objective of this *Handbook* is to attempt to main-tain a productive tension between, on the one hand, bringing some coherence to the field and, on the other hand, giving readers a sense of the multifaceted nature of the existing and forthcoming research.

---

[15] For example, Norman Manea, *On Clowns: The Dictator and the Artist* (London: Faber and Faber, 1994).

The *Handbook* is distinct from existing syntheses in two main ways: first, it is structured thematically rather than chronologically; second, it modifies (though of course does not altogether remove) the emphasis usually placed on the Cold War as the main historical framework for understanding the period. Thanks to its size, the *Handbook* differs from the few existing thematic collections in that it has unusually wide coverage, with a considerable stress on cultural history. This structure allows a number of interesting chronological questions to be raised, rather than taken as given. It also means that among the authors there are not only historians but historical geographers, political scientists, anthropologists, and literary scholars. The result is a collection of essays that indicate how what remains for many people a living part of the present is being historicized in inventive and innovative ways.

The following guidelines have structured this *Handbook* from its initial conception:

1. Without unthinkingly overturning the standard periodization that divides the twentieth century into two discrete halves, the *Handbook* questions the extent to which 1945 was really a 'zero hour'. Instead, lines of continuity as well as discontinuity are traced from the late nineteenth and early twentieth centuries through to the beginning of the twenty-first century.[16] For example by contrast with obvious breaks in the sphere of politics, in social life continuities and more gradual changes are easier to trace from the pre-war period to the postwar years. The following questions have been borne in mind: is 'postwar' a period or a concept? Did the postwar period begin in 1945 or has the extent of the break been exaggerated, perhaps being itself part of postwar Europeans' self-understanding? Maybe the 'real' postwar period began only in 1989, after the 'Cold War parenthesis'? The Cold War can itself now be historicized, instead of being seen as the framework which explains everything else, and set into contexts of longer-term narratives and 'larger geopolitical frameworks, particularly the collapse of empires and the proliferation of states'.[17]

2. This questioning of chronology in turn permits the thematic investigation of various facets of postwar life—from high politics to economics to tourism and consumerism—in a far-reaching way, around the axes of time and place.

3. 'Europe' in this *Handbook* is understood to mean all of Europe, including a notable emphasis on Eastern Europe as well as on the creation of 'neo-Europes' overseas

---

[16] An example is Charles S. Maier's notion of 'territoriality', a process, described in a structural rather than chronological narrative, which lasted from about 1860 for a century or so, and has since then unravelled. See 'Consigning the Twentieth Century to History: Alternative Narratives for the Modern Era', *American Historical Review* 105:3 (2000), 807–31. Cf. Giovanni Arrighi, *The Long Twentieth Century: Money, Power, and the Origins of Our Times* (London: Verso, 1994) for a narrative framed by cycles of capitalist domination, and Eric D. Weitz, 'From the Vienna to the Paris System: International Politics and the Entangled Histories of Human Rights, Forced Deportations, and Civilizing Missions', *American Historical Review* 113:5 (2008), 1313–43 for a focus less on territory and more on population management in the context of changing conceptions of diplomacy and international relations.

[17] David Reynolds, 'World War II and Modern Meanings', *Diplomatic History* 25:3 (2001), 466. See also Reynolds, '1940: Fulcrum of the Twentieth Century?', *International Affairs* 66:2 (1990), 325–50.

and 'reverse colonialism' in Europe itself.[18] For, as Catherine Lee and Robert Bideleux note, to give one example among many, Europe's 'peripheries and perimeters are no less important than the core', and 'Europe' should be understood neither as a geographical nor as a political entity, but rather as a narrative or an idea.[19]

4. 'History' is understood to mean as many ways of approaching the past as possible, with considerable emphasis on the achievements of cultural history, the emergence of which is itself a notable postwar phenomenon. Many of the ways in which the past is discussed in this *Handbook* have been developed within the contexts of the changes that have taken place in the historical profession since 1945. Where before the war, the field was dominated by diplomatic history, high politics, and the historical development of nations, with other approaches, such as social and intellectual history, regarded as distinctly inferior, since 1945 the postwar profession has been vastly expanded in terms of the numbers of historians researching and teaching at higher education institutions and the variety of approaches that are considered acceptable. Political history remains important, for good reason, and diplomatic history, especially in the context of human rights and international relations, is undergoing something of a renaissance, but social, cultural, economic, and intellectual history are all now enormously productive areas of historical research. Within these major divisions, new fields such as gender, the history of the body or of the emotions, the history of the book, memory studies, environmental history, media history, or the history of science and medicine are all major developments. Some existed in a nascent state before 1945, but only with the expansion of the profession since then have they come into their own. In other words, the descriptions of the past that the chapters of this *Handbook* provide have themselves only become possible because of—and are thus products of—changes in the postwar world. Even a book of thirty-six chapters cannot cover everything, but my aim as editor has been to represent as wide a variety of historical approaches as possible, for this variety in itself tells us something about the period the book is describing and narrating.

---

[18] The term 'neo-Europes' comes from Alfred W. Crosby, *Ecological Imperialism: The Biological Expansion of Europe, 900–1900*, 2nd edn (Cambridge: Cambridge University Press, 2004). Cf. James Belich, *Replenishing the Earth: The Settler Revolution and the Rise of the Anglo-World, 1783–1939* (Oxford: Oxford University Press, 2009).

[19] Catherine Lee and Robert Bideleux, ' "Europe": What Kind of Idea?', *The European Legacy* 14:2 (2009), 163–76; see also Ksenija Vidmar-Horvat and Gerard Delanty, '*Mitteleuropa* and the European Heritage', *European Journal of Social Theory* 11:2 (2008), 203–18; Anthony Pagden (ed.), *The Idea of Europe: From Antiquity to the European Union* (Washington, DC: Woodrow Wilson Center Press/ Cambridge: Cambridge University Press, 2002); Michael Wintle (ed.), *Imagining Europe: Europe and European Civilisation as Seen from its Margins and by the Rest of the World, in the Nineteenth and Twentieth Centuries* (Brussels: Peter Lang, 2008); Tony Judt, *Postwar: A History of Europe since 1945* (London: William Heinemann, 2005), ch. 23.

5. The contributions stress the interplay between the local, national, and international, and between the political and the intimate, especially in the Cold War context. As well as highlighting the variety of historical approaches, the *Handbook* also seeks to break down disciplinary boundaries where appropriate (i.e. not just for the sake of it); between for example economic history and history of ideas. Doing so provides two things: first, a rich picture of the complexity of postwar life; second, a sense of the extraordinary expansion of historiographical approaches as both product and producer of postwar European culture.

6. Throughout the *Handbook*, strict chronological divisions have been avoided, in order to stress that long-term historical factors were at work after 1945 as much as, if not more than short-term self-contained matters, as well as to suggest the interconnectedness of political, social, economic, cultural, and other factors.

No book on postwar Europe can exclude the Soviet–American rivalry and the way in which it played out in and was in turn affected by developments in Europe. But the Cold War does not provide the only focus or conceptual framework for the *Handbook*. Silvio Pons and Federico Romero write that

> The pervasiveness of the Cold War has often been used as an argument for studying it on its own terms: the bipolar system and its dynamics dominated all the nooks and crannies of the societies involved. But its very pervasiveness means that it was also porous, permeable and subject to myriad influences and transformative trends.[20]

In other words, one can show how the ubiquitous Cold War context shaped and informed all areas of life, not just politics in the narrow sense of international relations or military strategy. The Cold War, as Joel Isaac reminds us, 'was more than a high-political drama'.[21] Film, television, sport, gender relations, industrial relations, and the development of the social sciences, to name just a few areas, were all affected by the basic fact of the division of Europe into two ideologically-opposed camps. They were affected not only at an institutional level, in terms of funding or status, but also at the level of the imagination, as Cold War fears and insecurities crept, for example, into popular culture or family life. The reverse is also true: the way in which the Cold War was played out in international politics was also affected by gendered tropes, with Khrushchev's macho posturing and the phallic imagery of the space race being among the obvious ways in which cultural and social mores bled into the big political issues of the day.[22] Theodor

---

[20] Silvio Pons and Federico Romero, 'Introduction', in Pons and Romero (eds), *Reinterpreting the End of the Cold War: Issues, Interpretations, Periodizations* (London: Frank Cass, 2005), 9.

[21] Joel Isaac, 'The Human Sciences in Cold War America', *Historical Journal* 50:3 (2007), 731.

[22] Frank Costigliola, 'The Nuclear Family: Tropes of Gender and Pathology in the Western Alliance', *Diplomatic History* 21:2 (1997), 163–83; Robert D. Dean, 'Masculinity as Ideology', *Diplomatic History* 22:1 (1998), 29–62; Peter Carlson, *K Blows Top* (London: Old Street, 2009); Ruth Oldenziel and Karin Zachmann (eds), *Cold War Kitchen: Americanization, Technology, and European Users* (Cambridge, MA: MIT Press, 2009).

Adorno wrote of Hitler's 'robot bombs' that they manifested 'world spirit' and, at the same stroke, refuted Hegel's philosophy of history.[23] It was perhaps even harder to be a Hegelian during the Cold War, in the face of nuclear annihilation.[24]

But if one can show that the Cold War as a phenomenon was porous, one should also note that it did not determine every area of postwar Europeans' life. Certainly the focus on explaining the origins and course of the Cold War has tended to obscure the significance of the first two or three postwar years, in which the future was open and the formal division of the continent was by no means inevitable. But rock 'n' roll, the pill, and foreign holidays were all part of postwar Europe. Indeed, for many people, they were more so than the thought of nuclear destruction, which many preferred to box off in order to remain sane—and can equally validly be the subjects of historical analysis. The many studies that have recently appeared on tourism, consumerism, family life, religion, industry, fashion and design, science and technology, art, architecture, music, film, the press and photography all intersect with conventional narratives of the postwar period that take it as synonymous with the Cold War; but they also offer ways of understanding postwar society, culture, and economics that do not see those spheres of life as overdetermined by the capitalism–communism rivalry.[25] All of these topics both slot into and cut across a standard chronological account of postwar Europe. The following chapters assume a working knowledge of the series of events of the period, and so I will use the rest of this introduction to provide a basic high political and institutional chronological framework that can help orient the reader.

CHRONOLOGY

It is helpful to break up the postwar period into distinct phases, following Tony Judt and Charles Tilly. Tilly's periodization is based largely on economic indicators: up to 1950, when all of Europe was engaged in recovering from the war; 1950–65, when robust

[23] Theodor Adorno, *Minima Moralia: Reflections from Damaged Life* (London: Verso, 1989 [1951]), 55. For classic studies of the bomb, see John Hersey, *Hiroshima* (Harmondsworth: Penguin, 1946); Robert Jungk, *Brighter Than a Thousand Suns: A Personal History of the Atomic Scientists* (Harmondsworth: Penguin, 1960 [1956]); Karl Jaspers, *The Future of Mankind* (Chicago, IL: University of Chicago Press, 1961).

[24] As two famous works that book-end the period attest: Karl Popper's *The Open Society and Its Enemies* (2 vols, 1944), with its famous condemnation of Hegelianism as the precursor to terror, and Francis Fukuyama's *The End of History and the Last Man* (1992), which marked the return of Hegelianism, albeit with short-lived enthusiasm.

[25] On culture, see the useful essays by Patrick Major and Rana Mitter: 'Culture', in Saki R. Dockrill and Geraint Hughes (eds), *Palgrave Advances in Cold War History* (Basingstoke: Palgrave Macmillan, 2006), 240–62; 'East is East and West is West? Towards a Comparative Socio-Cultural History of the Cold War', *Cold War History* 4:1 (2003), 1–22. As they note ('Culture', 255), 'what seems undeniable is that popular culture exploited the cold war as much as cold warriors used the culture industry'.

growth characterized most of the continent; 1965–90, when growth slowed again.[26] This is a useful division, but does little to explain the variation in living standards between east and west, and the reasons why the West outstripped the East despite the end of the postwar boom from 1973 onwards. Here Judt is more helpful, dividing the period into four: 1945–53 ('postwar'); 1953–71 ('prosperity and its discontents'); 1971–89 ('recessional'); 1989–2005 ('after the fall'). This chronology broadly makes sense, and although the sections of this *Handbook* are not structured around it, they nevertheless confirm its appositeness.

The first ('postwar') phase has been investigated in great detail by historians, mainly with the aim of explicating the origins of the Cold War. But by seeing these immediate postwar years as no more than precursors to the definitive postwar settlement, the radical contestation and openness that characterized them can easily be overlooked. As Geoff Eley writes, the 'lasting framework of policy, reforms and dominant thinking that eventually solidified out of the intensely contested politics of 1945–46' has 'retroactively acquired a much stronger logic of inevitability', with the arrangements of 1947–48 being 'projected backwards onto the preceding moment of Liberation'. For Eley, this retroactive determinism means that historians miss the possibility that existed in 1945 of a 'Third Way', a social vision 'situated somewhere between or beyond the starkly polarized options of Stalinism and the anti-Communist consensus of "the West"'.[27] This is a viewpoint shared by Mazower, who notes that 'many former partisans and members of the underground were left with the feeling that they and their cause had been betrayed'.[28]

These claims can be tested by taking as an example the communist takeover of Europe, and the way in which that process has been interpreted by historians. One of the longest running debates in Cold War historiography has been the question of Stalin's role: did he set the pace with his threats of expansionism or merely react to western, especially American aggression? John Lewis Gaddis argues that 'as long as Stalin was running the Soviet Union a cold war was unavoidable', a claim that has been the basis of traditionalist Cold War historiography since the beginning of the Cold War itself.[29] Since the partial opening of the Soviet era archives, one can now defend the claim that 'Stalin had the intention, the means, and the ability to control the overall design, as well as the thrusts and parries of Soviet foreign policy'. But it is also clear that the Soviets did not intend to divide the continent in 1944–45, and that, for the first years after the war, the countries of

[26] Charles Tilly, 'Europe Transformed, 1945–2000', in Chris Rumford (ed.), *The Sage Handbook of European Studies* (London: Sage, 2009), 20–1.

[27] Geoff Eley, 'Europe after 1945', *History Workshop Journal* 65 (2008), 208. See also Eley, 'When Europe Was New: Liberation and the Making of the Post-War Era', in Monica Riera and Gavin Schaffer (eds), *The Lasting War: Society and Identity in Britain, France and Germany after 1945* (Basingstoke: Palgrave Macmillan, 2008), 17–43.

[28] Mazower, *Dark Continent*, 211; cf. James D. Wilkinson, *The Intellectual Resistance in Europe* (Cambridge, MA: Harvard University Press, 1981); Örjan Appelqvist, 'International Socialist Attempts at Bridge-Building in the Early Postwar Period', in Konrad H. Jarausch and Thomas Lindenberger (eds), *Conflicted Memories: Europeanizing Contemporary Histories* (New York: Berghahn, 2007), 221–36.

[29] John Lewis Gaddis, *We Now Know: Rethinking Cold War History* (Oxford: Clarendon Press, 1997), 292.

what became 'eastern Europe' had 'very different political constellations that, at least from the perspective of the time, might well have indicated diverse futures'.[30]

Some historians have pointed to Stalin's policy of building 'National Fronts' (i.e. creating communist-dominated coalitions that would gradually dispense with the non-communists) as proof of his intentions to take over the whole of the European area occupied by the Red Army in 1945. Eduard Mark, for example, cites Stalin's advice to the East Germans in 1948—'you should advance towards socialism not by taking a straight road but move in zigzags'—as evidence that Stalin's apparent willingness to accommodate the wartime allies' and local democratic politicians' points of view was a sham, and argues that the National Front strategy was a way of taking power for the communists without threatening the wartime Grand Alliance through appearing bellicose.[31]

Stalin undoubtedly acted to secure the Soviet Union's new westward-shifted borders by installing friendly regimes in Poland and Romania. Yet it remains the case that elsewhere, notably Hungary and Czechoslovakia, Stalin was far more relaxed about the progress of communism. Finland was exempted altogether and, as one historian notes, had Stalin been willing to permit the 'Finlandization' of the rest of Eastern Europe, 'then the West would have been much less alarmed'.[32] Only in 1947, with the failure of the Conference of Foreign Ministers to agree terms of a German peace treaty, the declaration of the Truman Doctrine in 1947, the announcement of the ERP—which was also offered to the Eastern European countries—and the exclusion of communists from government in France and Italy, was Stalin motivated into initiating the coup in Czechoslovakia in February 1948 which brought the communists to power there and to creating the Cominform in September 1947, in an attempt to imitate the Marshall Plan.[33] Stalin, it seems, aimed neither to divide the continent at the end of the war, nor to force all countries in the region into the same straitjacket at the same pace.

Thus, although one can trace its origins back to the Bolshevik Revolution, and tensions between the Allies began shortly after the German invasion of the USSR in June 1941, the Cold War did not begin in earnest until 1948. Following the Prague coup, the French-occupied zone of Germany was merged with the British–American 'Bizonia', the Soviets blockaded Berlin's western sectors, culminating in the Berlin airlift, and within

[30] Norman M. Naimark, 'Stalin and Europe in the Postwar Period, 1945–53: Issues and Problems', *Journal of Modern European History* 2:1 (2004), 29, 33. See also Melvyn P. Leffler, 'The Cold War: What Do "We Now Know"?', *American Historical Review* 104:2 (1999), 501–24; Alfred J. Rieber, 'The Origins of the Cold War in Eurasia: A Borderland Perspective', in Jarausch and Lindenberger (eds), *Conflicted Memories*, 117–29.

[31] Eduard Mark, 'Revolution by Degrees: Stalin's National-Front Strategy for Europe, 1941–1947', *Cold War International History Project Working Paper* 31 (Washington, DC: Woodrow Wilson Center, 2001), 17, 20–1. Also Mark, 'American Policy toward Eastern Europe and the Origins of the Cold War, 1941–1946: An Alternative Interpretation', *Journal of American History* 68:2 (1981), 313–36.

[32] William Taubman, 'How Much of the Cold War was Inevitable?', in Francesca Gori and Silvio Pons (eds), *The Soviet Union and Europe in the Cold War, 1943–53* (Basingstoke: Macmillan Press, 1996), 192.

[33] Anna Di Biagio, 'The Marshall Plan and the Founding of the Cominform, June–September 1947', in Gori and Pons (eds), *The Soviet Union and Europe in the Cold War*, 208–21.

a year the Federal Republic of Germany and the German Democratic Republic had been born, ironically normalizing German statehood and permitting Adenauer (though not the SED to the same extent) to act as the head of a sovereign nation. The Treaty of Brussels created a military alliance in Western Europe, aimed at defending the region from the Soviet Union rather than Germany, and within a few years the new Germanies, which lay at the heart of Cold War Europe in all senses, had been relieved of their very short period of denazification purdah and, now functioning as independent states, were willingly incorporated into NATO and the Warsaw Pact.[34]

The birth of the new German states and the reluctant French agreement to the rearming of West Germany in the context of NATO (after the National Assembly first demanded and then eventually rejected a European Defence Community) also help explain the emergence of another key postwar institution: the European Coal and Steel Community, the forerunner of today's European Union. Unfortunately, hagiographical narratives that explain the emergence of the Franco–German partnership out of the World War II resistance movements' plans and blueprints are some way from the truth. Resistors could dream about a world in which the 'maintenance of freedom and security on the entire continent should be solely in the hands of the European federation and its executive, legislative, and judiciary organs'.[35] Robert Schuman clarified what was really going on in his speech that initiated the ECSC:

> The solidarity in production thus established [by joining coal & steel production] will make it plain that any war between France and Germany becomes not merely unthinkable, but materially impossible...this proposal will build the first concrete foundation of a European federation which is indispensable to the preservation of peace.[36]

With protests from the Communist resistance and the USSR, that moves towards European federation would be tantamount to creating a 'bourgeois' anti-Soviet bloc, the USA and Britain backed down to Stalin's objections in Tehran (November 1943). Hence, when the great powers met in 1945 they, in Lipgens's words, 'did nothing more than arrange for the restoration of the system of national states'.[37] The move towards the pooling of resources and the creation of a common market in the Treaties of Rome (European Coal and Steel Community, 1951) and Paris (European Economic Community, Euratom, 1957) was based primarily on national interest. This was a realization that the haughty British came to later. In 1946, Churchill famously called, in a speech in Zurich, for a 'United States of Europe', but made it clear that it should be without Britain or its Commonwealth, which, with 'mighty America', would be 'the friends and sponsors of the new Europe'. But, after the failure of Britain's rival European Free Trade Area (EFTA), a

---

[34] Vojtech Mastny, 'The New History of Cold War Alliances', *Journal of Cold War Studies* 4:2 (2002), 55–84.

[35] Movimento Federalista Europeo, 28 August 1943, cited in Lipgens, 'European Federation in the Political Thought of Resistance Movements', 13.

[36] John Pinder, *The Building of the European Union*, 3rd edn (Oxford: Oxford University Press, 1998), 3.

[37] Lipgens, 'European Federation in the Political Thought of Resistance Movements', 16.

random assortment of states not in the EEC, the country finally applied for membership, only to be twice rebuffed by de Gaulle, until, in response to Willy Brandt's *Ostpolitik*, it suited French interests to let Britain join.

It would be strange to explain the readiness of states to enter into this sort of multilateral, international agreement if notions of federalism were wholly irrelevant.[38] Nevertheless, national interest has sustained the EEC/EU ever since, which (despite Schuman's talk of 'European federation', a phrase that has never appeared since the Treaty of Rome spoke of 'ever closer union') is an economic rather than a political union. The key moments of the union's development, from the creation and renegotiation of the Common Agricultural Policy to the Maastricht Treaty and the post-communist accessions, have been driven by national interests, especially French fear of Germany, far more than by federalism. The 'founding fathers', Monnet, Schuman, Spaak, de Gasperi, and so on, might be cheered by the fact that the union has contributed to keeping Europe in a state of peace since World War II (with the admittedly rather significant exception of Yugoslavia in the 1990s), but they would soon see that it is economic interdependence that holds Europe's nation states together in the EU. Political power in the EU, even in the twenty-first century, resides not in a supranational European 'state' but in the context of the Council of Ministers, which means a voluntarily entered into sharing of sovereignty. A 'state' that has a toothless parliament and a shared currency but that cannot raise taxes or make war is unlikely to replace the European nation states any time soon.[39]

In the context of the early Cold War, the rearming of West Germany, the establishment of NATO, and the creation of the EEC, what we see in Western Europe is a period in which the glimpse of the radical new political opportunities that briefly shone in the immediate aftermath of the war was gradually but surely snuffed out. The centre-right governments in power and the institutions that took shape in the 1940s and 1950s helped to give a conservative cast to Western European political culture. Stability through parliamentary democracy was certainly one result—though not in southern Europe— especially since it came nicely wrapped in shiny consumer goods. Christian Democrats succeeded where socialist parties did not in creating some cross-class participation.[40] There is nevertheless something remarkable about a situation in which vast numbers of former Nazis could still be working as teachers, judges, and policemen, not to mention become General Secretary of the United Nations, as did the Austrian Kurt Waldheim, or in which representatives of political parties that (in the most charitable reading) had

---

[38] Perry Anderson, *The New Old World* (London: Verso, 2009). Cf. Mazower's comments about the UN in *No Enchanted Palace*.

[39] But see Jean Leca, '"The Empire Strikes Back!" An Uncanny View of the European Union. Part I—Do We Need a Theory of the European Union?', *Government and Opposition* 44:3 (2009), 285–340, for a sophisticated analysis, which shows that the dichotomy between federalism and a Europe of nation states is no longer satisfactory for understanding the way the EU works.

[40] Martin Conway, 'Democracy in Postwar Western Europe: The Triumph of a Political Model', *European History Quarterly* 32:1 (2002), 59–84; Conway, 'The Rise and Fall of Western Europe's Democratic Age, 1945–1973', *Contemporary European History* 13:1 (2004), 67–88.

failed to prevent the slide into the apocalypse were once again at the helm, not ten years after the war. Adorno was being dramatic, but when he penned his extraordinary essay, 'The Meaning of Working through the Past' (1959), it was not entirely hyperbolic to write:

> I consider the survival of National Socialism *within* democracy to be potentially more menacing than the survival of fascist tendencies *against* democracy. Infiltration indicates something objective; ambiguous figures make their *comeback* and occupy positions of power for the sole reason that conditions favour them.[41]

Adorno's warning was startlingly echoed in the writings of anti-colonial thinkers such as Aimé Césaire, Frantz Fanon, and Albert Memmi. Although many of the overseas colonies, such as Singapore, Malaya, and the Dutch East Indies were occupied during the war, the European powers considered it their right to reassert their rule at the conclusion of the conflict. But the newly empowered colonial subjects disagreed and, in one of the more remarkable phenomena of postwar history, the decolonization process became an unstoppable force. Decolonization had taken place before World War II (Brazil in 1830, for example), but the year 1960 brought European colonial history—barring a few exceptions—to a close, at least in the formal sense (informal empire and exploitative relationships did not end). Here the European self-image was severely tried.

The British decolonization process was neither as peaceful nor ordained from above as the official (and popular) narrative would have us believe.[42] Still, the shameful abandonment of the Belgian Congo (Zaire) in 1960, and the wars in Indochina and, especially, Algeria, were of a different order. When the French army surrendered at Dien Bien Phu in 1954, and lost Indochina, Algeria was the only remaining colony of significance for the French. In fact, it was not formally a colony but part of metropolitan France, split into three departments and returning deputies to the National Assembly. Thus, it was all the more galling that the Algerians rejected the benefits of French civilization. The 'war' saw the use of torture—the army was condemned as 'your Gestapo in Algeria' as early as 1955 by Claude Bourdet in *France-Observateur*[43]—and precipitated a crisis in the Fourth Republic when the OAS (*Organisation de l'Armée Secrète*) came close to unleashing civil war in France. The generals' failure did not prevent the massive loss of life in Algeria, the notorious cover up of the killing in Paris during the pro-FLN demonstration of 17 October 1961, or the migration of over one million French settlers (*pieds noir*) back to mainland France in the wake of Algerian independence a year later. These events help set Fanon's violent anti-colonial tirades into a meaningful context. When he wrote that

---

[41] Theodor Adorno, 'The Meaning of Working through the Past', in *Critical Models: Interventions and Catchwords* (New York: Columbia University Press, 1998), 90. For a powerful depiction of the political culture of Bonn, West Germany's unlikely capital city, see Wolfgang Koeppen's 1953 Novel, *The Hothouse* (London: Granta Books, 2002).

[42] See the comments in Martin Shaw, 'Britain and Genocide: Historical and Contemporary Parameters of National Responsibility', *Review of International Studies* (forthcoming).

[43] Cited in Robert Gildea, *France since 1945* (Oxford: Oxford University Press, 1996), 24.

in the colonial context the settler only ends his work of breaking in the native when the latter admits loudly and intelligibly the supremacy of the white man's values. In the period of decolonization, the colonized masses mock at these very values, insult them and vomit them up

Fanon was merely echoing the reality of the decolonization struggle.[44] But if the decolonization process was traumatic and violent, it soon became apparent that it was economically beneficial for the Europeans to reap the benefits of trade and other links with former colonial countries without having the expense of maintaining a military or civil presence. The exception was Portugal; in a reversal of the experience of the other colonial powers' experiences, the military was responsible for forcing the hand of the authoritarian government in the colonial metropole, Lisbon. Their actions began the process that saw the end of dictatorship in Portugal as well as independence for the Portuguese colonies (although, for Angola especially, this would usher in several decades of vicious warfare). In 1960, President Dwight Eisenhower said of the Salazar regime that: 'Dictatorships of this type are sometimes necessary in countries whose political institutions are not so far advanced as ours.'[45] It was therefore all the more surprising that the army—not usually at the vanguard of progressive thought—was the institution that promoted a new thinking. As Colonel Vasco Gonçalves said in June 1975:

> The same forces that oppressed the peoples of the former territories under Portuguese administration also oppressed the Portuguese people. It is with great modesty and humility that we must say, without ambiguities, that the struggle of the colonial peoples against Portuguese fascism also aided our liberation from the same fascism.[46]

Thus, as well as contributing to European prosperity in general, both economically and morally, decolonization in Portugal also helped to bring about the passage from dictatorship to democracy in that country—though not in Lusophone Africa—at the same time as the dictatorship in Spain was also coming to its negotiated end.

While the western half of the continent was rebuilding in the context of American assistance and new collective settlements concerning defence (Western Union and NATO) and economics (Bretton Woods, ECSC, EEC, GATT, OECD), the eastern half, now firmly under communist rule, was attempting to do something similar. But it faced different problems altogether. First, in terms of defence, the communists were not only concerned to shore up their region against the perceived threat from the West by creating the Warsaw Pact, but had to face down considerable internal opposition too. In terms of economics, while Comecon was established to rival the Marshall Plan, and was not without achievements, it lacked the flexibility of the ERP system and failed to adapt.

---

[44] Frantz Fanon, *The Wretched of the Earth* (London: Penguin, 1990 [1961]), 33–4.

[45] Cited in Kenneth Maxwell, *The Making of Portuguese Democracy* (Cambridge: Cambridge University Press, 1995), 7.

[46] Maxwell, *The Making of Portuguese Democracy*, 96. For an interesting discussion, see Ellen W. Sapega, 'Remembering Empire/Forgetting the Colonies: Accretions of Memory and the Limits of Commemoration in a Lisbon Neighborhood', *History & Memory* 20:2 (2008), 18–38.

The economic and political stagnation of the Brezhnev years could not, however, be foreseen at first. Tilly notes that 'from the West it looked for a while as though the Warsaw Pact would bring off the combination of socialism, authoritarianism, and vigorous economic growth'.[47] 'For a time', as Gianni Toniolo reminds us, 'communist regimes commanded a sufficient degree of consensus, not so surprising in light of their early achievements and of eastern Europe's interwar history'.[48] This was not universally true—in Romania, for example, with its tiny Communist Party and interwar and wartime history dominated by ethno-nationalism and fascism, communism was installed by force[49]—but across the continent there was considerable admiration for the victory of anti-fascism and for the economic achievements of the people's republics in the early postwar years.[50]

But if communism managed to sustain a standard of living comparable with the West for the first decade and half after the war, no such comparison can be made in the sphere of politics. It quickly became clear, with the massive seizures of property and land, the purges of 'collaborators' that became excuses to do away with anyone 'bourgeois', and the suppression of alternative opinions, that the overthrow of the Nazi dictatorship had resulted in the ushering in of another one, albeit of a different sort. If, in Western Europe, the postwar atmosphere was fundamentally conservative, this was largely a reflection of popular will; in Eastern Europe, the suppression of national sovereignty, especially in the Baltic States, the Polish *kresy*, and other regions incorporated directly into the Soviet Union, and the elimination of opposition, at least in the public sphere, was centrally, and violently, imposed. 'There will be a Lithuania,' one apparatchik put it, 'but there will be no Lithuanians.'[51] Post-Cold War disagreements between eastern and western memories of World War II and its aftermath, as I discuss in my chapter below, are direct reflections of these different circumstances. As the Lithuanian poet Tomas Venclova laconically wrote: 'I do not envy the leaders of those days to whom history presented a choice among Hitler, Stalin, and death, each choice not necessarily excluding the other two.'[52]

Despite the efforts of destalinization, following Stalin's death in 1953, the arrest of Beria, and Khrushchev's denunciation in his 'secret speech' at the 20th Party Congress in 1956, these moves were not sufficient to meet the needs and demands of the people. Thus, in the wake of uprisings in Poland, Czechoslovakia, and East Germany in 1953, the Berlin

---

[47] Tilly, 'Europe Transformed', 20.

[48] Gianni Toniolo, 'Europe's Golden Age, 1950–1973: Speculations from a Long-Run Perspective', *Economic History Review* 51:2 (1998), 265. See also Toniolo and Crafts's chapter below.

[49] Kevin Adamson, 'Discourses of Violence and the Ideological Strategies of the Romanian Communist Party, 1944–1953', *East European Politics and Societies* 21:4 (2007), 559–87.

[50] For brilliant depictions of people adapting to the reality of the communist takeover in Poland, see Czesław Miłosz's Novel, *The Seizure of Power* (London: Abacus, 1985) and Jerzy Andrzejewski's, *Ashes and Diamonds* (Harmondsworth: Penguin, 1982), the latter famously filmed by Andrzej Wajda (1958). On Wajda, see David Caute, *The Dancer Defects: The Struggle for Cultural Supremacy during the Cold War* (Oxford: Oxford University Press, 2003), ch. 13.

[51] Czesław Miłosz, *The Captive Mind* (London: Penguin, 1985), 230.

[52] Cited in John Hiden and Patrick Salmon, *The Baltic Nations and Europe: Estonia, Latvia and Lithuania in the Twentieth Century*, rev. edn (London: Longman, 1994), 109.

Airlift of 1948, and the Hungarian Revolution of 1956, communism suffered a severe loss of the status it had acquired by virtue of defeating the Third Reich in Europe. When Imre Nagy spoke of the need to 'develop toward socialism by systematically decreasing the use of force [and] utilizing democratic forms and methods in the interest of close co-operation on the widest possible scale with the masses of working people', what he actually meant was that Hungary should withdraw from the Warsaw Pact and, as a neutral state, work towards a renewed system of democracy.[53] The year 1956 was the key moment, for it ended with the Warsaw Pact's invasion of Hungary. The sight of tanks on the streets of Budapest shocked western fellow travellers, whose image of the golden age being realized in the here and now was shattered,[54] and provided an echo of Brecht's comment on the 1953 uprising: that the leadership should elect a new people.

By contrast, the 'Prague Spring' of 1968 was never such a threat to the system. Although Dubček was an idealistic reformer *within* the party, whose concern for legality made him hard to deal with, he never sought to withdraw from the Warsaw Pact or to declare Czech neutrality. Once the tanks had cleared the streets there was no opportunity for further reform and the period of gerontocratic stagnation set in. The conditions of 1956—Tito's and Khrushchev's anti-Stalinist reformism—were not present in 1968. Thus although Prague 1968 marked the last chance for reform in the Soviet bloc, its real importance lay in its adumbration of Gorbachev. Mazower cites the remarkable prescience of François Fejtö: 'One may hope that the next Dubček will appear in the nerve centre of the system: Moscow.'[55]

The supreme symbol of communism's need to hold its people by force, and the greatest symbol of the Cold War, was of course the Berlin Wall, or, as the East Germans called it, the 'anti-fascist protective rampart'.[56] In the Brezhnev era, the old men in power—Honecker (GDR), Zhivkov (Bulgaria), Jaruzelski (Poland), and Kádár (Hungary)—did not return to the paranoia of Stalinism. But there were exceptions. Enver Hoxha's Albania was based on a variety of Maoism (following Albania's break with the USSR in 1961 and alignment with China), and Nicolae Ceaușescu had turned Romania into a personal fiefdom by the 1980s.[57] In retrospect, life in these regimes could have its funny side, as in the 2009 film *Tales from the Golden Age* (dir Cristian Mungiu) or György Dragomán's *The*

---

[53] Imre Nagy, 'On Communism' (1956), cited in Geoffrey Swain and Nigel Swain, *Eastern Europe since 1945* (Basingstoke: Macmillan, 1993), 85.

[54] Miłosz, *The Captive Mind*, 234: 'The Western Communist needs a vision of a golden age which is *already* being realized on earth. The Stalinist of the East does everything in his power to instil this vision in the minds of others, but he never forgets that it is merely a useful lie.'

[55] Mazower, *Dark Continent*, 289. See also Hannah Arendt's penetrating analysis, 'Totalitarian Imperialism: Reflections on the Hungarian Revolution', *Journal of Politics* 20:1 (1958), 5–43.

[56] On the GDR, see Patrick Major, *Behind the Berlin Wall: East Germany and the Frontiers of Power* (Oxford: Oxford University Press, 2010); Noel D. Cary, 'Farewell without Tears: Diplomats, Dissidents, and the Demise of East Germany', *Journal of Modern History* 73:3 (2001), 617–51.

[57] Miranda Vickers, *The Albanians: A Modern History* (London: I. B. Tauris, 1997), ch. 9; Vladimir Tismaneanu, *Stalinism for All Seasons: A Political History of Romanian Communism* (Berkeley: University of California Press, 2003), ch, 7; Dennis Deletant, *Ceaușescu and the Securitate: Coercion and Dissent in Romania, 1965–89* (London: C. Hurst &Co., 1996). See Tismaneanu's chapter in this volume.

White King (2008, in English), but the laughter is always tinged with a manic edge. In a country in which the Piteşti 're-education camp' could exist—where people were forced to torture and sexually abuse their family members—the worst excesses of Stalin were by no means over, even if (or rather, because) Romania took an independent line from Moscow and was feted by the West for doing so. In the USSR too, the camp system did not disappear with Stalin's death, as Avraham Shifrin's 1980 publication, *The First Guidebook to Prisons and Concentration Camps of the Soviet Union*, testifies.[58]

The year 1968 was not only a year of revolt in Eastern Europe. Discontent with prosperity in the West came from critics of consumerism, who believed that the 'culture industry' was being cynically employed by elites to 'buy off' the masses and keep them politically quiescent, and an anti-Americanism fuelled by the Vietnam war. Conservatives trod a delicate balance between anti-communism (as in the CIA-funded Congress for Cultural Freedom[59]) and anti-Americanization, with the latter usually losing out, but not without generating a substantial repertoire of distaste for supposed American vulgarity and brashness, as if a continent that had recently destroyed itself had a claim to greater civilization.[60] 'The idea that after this war life will continue "normally"', wrote Adorno, 'or even that culture might be "rebuilt"—as if the rebuilding of culture were not already its negation—is idiotic.'[61] The rise of the New Left, which rejected orthodox Marxism–Leninism as represented by the USSR and looked instead to third world leaders such as Che Guevara and Fidel Castro for inspiration, and drew its theoretical inspiration from Marcuse and McLuhan rather than from Lenin and Stalin, was predicated on this rejection of postwar culture, which it regarded as a continuation of fascism by other means. Hence student leader Rudi Dutschke could argue that:

> Our life is more than money. Our life is thinking and living. It's about us, and what we could do in this world...It is about how we could use technology and all the other things which at the moment are used against the human being...My question in life is always how we can destroy things that are against the human being, and how we can find a way of life in which the human being is independent of a world of trouble, a world of anxiety, a world of destruction.[62]

[58] Avraham Shifrin, *The First Guidebook to Prisons and Concentration Camps of the Soviet Union* (Toronto, ON: Bantam Books, 1982).

[59] Peter Coleman, *The Liberal Conspiracy: The Congress for Cultural Freedom and the Struggle for the Mind of Post-War Europe* (New York: Free Press, 1989); Giles Scott-Smith, 'The Congress for Cultural Freedom, the End of Ideology and the 1955 Milan Conference: "Defining the Parameters of Discourse"', *Journal of Contemporary History* 37:3 (2002), 437–55; Scott-Smith, *The Politics of Apolitical Culture: The Congress for Cultural Freedom, the CIA, and Post-War American Hegemony* (London: Routledge, 2002). For the broader context see Hans Krabbendam and Giles Scott-Smith (eds), *The Cultural Cold War in Europe, 1945–1960* (London: Routledge, 2004).

[60] Alexander Stephan (ed.), *The Americanization of Europe: Culture, Diplomacy, and Anti-Americanism after 1945* (New York: Berghahn, 2006); Jessica C. E. Gienow-Hecht (ed.), *Decentering America* (New York: Berghahn, 2007); Dan Diner, *America in the Eyes of the Germans: An Essay on Anti-Americanism* (Princeton, NJ: Markus Wiener, 1996).

[61] Adorno, *Minima Moralia*, 55.

[62] Cited in Ingo Cornils, '"The Struggle Continues": Rudi Dutschke's Long March', in Gerard DeGroot (ed.), *Student Protest: The Sixties and After* (London: Longman, 1998), 114.

Thus, student rebellions in France, West Germany, Italy, and even Britain in 1968 were not just protests about poor conditions in universities. They were the revolts of a generation that had never known war and its compromises, attempts to overthrow the mores of their parents' generation which, they believed, had failed or, worse, collaborated with fascism. The disjunction between the conservative cultural atmosphere of Western Europe in the 1950s and 1960s and the burgeoning consumer society, with its unheard-of excess wealth, was no longer sustainable.

Yet the student rebels' aspirations were inherently unattainable. As one scholar says,

> 'power to the imagination' remained a vital programme that fascinated and mobilized individuals but was unsuccessful in gaining power because power is based on entirely different organizational and decision-making premises than is the mobilization of the imagination. The internal tension and limited effectiveness of the New Left were due to the fact that it could not assume power without destroying itself.[63]

Hannah Arendt was harsher when she spoke of the 'theoretical sterility and analytical dullness' of the student movement, which for her was 'just as striking and depressing as its joy in action is welcome'.[64] But perhaps more important than problems internal to the student movements is the role of the establishment. In France, for example, the revolts certainly shook the Gaullist regime, but it ultimately came out strengthened. Apart from the fact that the radical actions of the extreme left split the left alliance—the Radicals could no longer cooperate with the Communists, and neither could the SFIO (Socialists)—de Gaulle's appeal to the people to choose between Gaullism and communism brought hundreds of thousands of pro-government demonstrators onto the streets of Paris. The subsequent cleverly timed general election in June provided an opportunity for the shocked middle-classes to register their distaste for street action. One political commentator wrote that 'each barricade, each burning car brought tens of thousands of votes to the Gaullist party; that's the truth'.[65] In the 1969 presidential election Pompidou scored more votes (57.6 per cent) than even de Gaulle had done in 1964 (54.5 per cent).

Paradoxically, the revolt against postwar 'fascism' (as the students saw it) was carried out by a middle-class generation which was wealthier, healthier, and more materially comfortable than any such cohort in history. And while a tiny minority of the rebels went on to careers as terrorists in the paranoid worlds of the RAF, the BR, or the extreme right,[66] most successfully negotiated the perils of the recessions and economic challenges that lay only a few years ahead. But if the students could never overthrow the postwar

---

[63] Ingrid Gilcher-Holtey, 'May 1968 in France: The Rise and Fall of a New Social Movement', in Carole Fink, Philipp Gassert, and Detlef Junker (eds), *1968: The World Transformed* (Cambridge: Cambridge University Press, 1998), 272. For a general survey, see Martin Klimke and Joachim Scharloth (eds), *1968 in Europe: A History of Protest and Activism, 1956–1977* (New York: Palgrave Macmillan, 2008) and Klimke's chapter in this volume.

[64] Hannah Arendt, *Crises of the Republic* (Harmondsworth: Penguin, 1973), 168.

[65] René Andrieu in *L'Humanité*, cited in Gilcher-Holtey, 'May 1968 in France', 269.

[66] Andrea Mammone, 'The Transnational Reaction to 1968: Neo-Fascist Fronts and Political Cultures in France and Italy', *Contemporary European History* 17:2 (2008), 213–36.

order, they certainly achieved forcing a rethink of its norms, and contributed to bringing about a liberalization of attitudes and laws.

Somewhat ironically, however, the greatest impact of this liberalizing process was to be felt in the sphere of economics in the years after 1973. The major theme of the period that Judt terms 'recessional' was how to deal with the unprecedented challenges that had brought about and sustained economic crisis. It ended only with the 'restructuring' of the economies of Europe with the rise of neoliberalism, and the latter's application to the whole of Europe following the collapse of communism, now in the very different circumstances of a global economy. The postwar economic boom—which was in fact a continuation of interwar economic trends—could not be sustained indefinitely, and not just because of the inevitable loss of market share brought about by the rise to prominence of new capitalist economies, especially in Japan, Taiwan, and South Korea. In fact, by the time the oil crisis—brought about by OPEC's raising the price of a barrel of oil from $2 in mid-1973 to $12 in 1975—took effect, the Western European economies were already suffering from low rates of productivity, outdated industrial plant, and lack of investment. From an average in OECD countries of 4.8 per cent per annum in the 1960s, the growth rate slowed to 3.4 per cent and then, between 1974 and 1976, almost to zero. OPEC's decision to punish countries it deemed to have supported Israel during the Yom Kippur war simply exacerbated a trend that was already in train. And apart from the economic blows, the unseemly scrabble for oil exemplified the problem of Eurosclerosis that afflicted the EEC in the 1970s, with individual states desperately trying to ensure their own continuity of supply rather than working towards a collective solution.

The response to the oil crisis and to the novel problem of stagflation—which combined the phenomena of high inflation and unemployment, thought to be mutually exclusive in orthodox Keynesianism—was, over a fairly short time frame and with dramatic social consequences, to shut down the industries on which postwar prosperity had been built and to turn the Western European economy into a high-tech service sector. The process was carried through most radically in Britain under Margaret Thatcher, with her monetarist advisors, but applied also to West Germany, France, Italy, and even the Scandinavian countries, where the long-dominant Social Democrats saw their grip on power weaken (and where, in a rare moment of excitement in Swedish politics, Prime Minister Olof Palme was assassinated in 1986).

As well as increasing unemployment, the restructuring also saw conservative retrenchment in the social and cultural sphere: liberalization of the economy but control measures elsewhere. This meant a new liberalism which de-emphasized the social contract that had been accepted in 1945 as a necessary component of reconstruction: guaranteeing health and education, and benefits to those unable to support themselves. This programme was first promoted by Christian Democrat or conservative parties, but was eventually accepted even by the 'centre-left', exemplified by Tony Blair, Lionel Jospin, and Gerhard Schröder. But it owed little to traditional conservative values of probity, social order, and economic caution. The extraordinary changes that took place in the European economy in the 1980s and 1990s, which largely did away with heavy industry (exceptions include the industrial belt of the Ruhr and car manufacturing in Germany and France) came at a very high price in terms of the values that provided the mood music to the postwar Western European consensus. The rise of individualism and the *enrichissez-vous* mentality reached its fitting conclusion in the early twenty-first century with celebrity culture, misery memoirs, and the stunning mediocrity of television 'talent' shows on the one hand, and widening wealth and health disparities, the 'return of religion', populism, and social division in the public sphere on the other.

Economics, however, is not in itself the main driving force of historical change. The decisions taken by OPEC reveal that clearly enough. And nowhere is this fact more evident than in the history of the collapse of communism. Although by the 1980s living standards behind the Iron Curtain had fallen way behind those of Western Europe, vanishingly few commentators believed that that meant the end of the communist regimes. Daniel Chirot elegantly notes:

> By the 1970s the USSR had the world's most advanced late nineteenth-century economy, the world's biggest and best, most inflexible rustbelt. It is as if Andrew Carnegie had taken over the entire United States, forced it into becoming a giant copy of US Steel, and the executives of the same US Steel had continued to run the country into the 1970s and 1980s.

Or, as Ken Jowitt succinctly put it, 'After 70 years of murderous effort, the Soviet Union had created a German industry of the 1880s in the 1980s'.[67] The Brezhnev Doctrine institutionalized ossification, 'as if', philosopher Karl Jaspers had written some years before, 'a principle were, so to speak, alive and as if everyone, including the dictator of the moment, had become mere functionaries of it'.[68] The 'hegemony of form' meant that even if people were only paying lip-service to the reigning ideology, they nevertheless expected the 'tyrannies of certitude' to continue to hold on to power.[69] So when Mikhail Gorbachev came to power in 1985, following the interim filled by the living dead Yuri Andropov and Konstantin Chernenko, few expected that empty shops and dreadful pollution would by themselves bring about change. And indeed, not economic factors in the narrow sense—appalling though all the indicators were—but political ones hold the key to the collapse.[70]

Much has been written, in the wake of the twentieth anniversary of the fall of communism, to try and explain a sequence of events that almost no one had been able to

[67] Daniel Chirot, 'What Happened in Eastern Europe in 1989?', in Vladimir Tismaneanu (ed.), *The Revolutions of 1989* (London: Routledge, 1999), 22; Ken Jowitt, 'The Leninist Extinction', in *New World Disorder*, 256.

[68] Karl Jaspers to Hannah Arendt, 23 November 1957, in Lotte Kohler and Hans Saner (eds), *Hannah Arendt/Karl Jaspers Correspondence 1926–1969* (San Diego, CA: Harcourt Brace, 1993), 334.

[69] Alexei Yurchak, *Everything Was Forever, Until It Was No More: The Last Soviet Generation* (Princeton, NJ: Princeton University Press, 2006), esp. ch. 2; 'tyrannies of certitude' is Daniel Chirot's phrase.

[70] For a useful analysis of the various factors that contributed to the demise of communism, see Georg Schöpflin, *Politics in Eastern Europe 1945–1992* (Oxford: Blackwell, 1993), ch. 9.

foresee. To a large extent, the collapse is overdetermined, and it is impossible to provide a definitive explanation of such large-scale, continent-wide events. From economic stagnation to the daring of Solidarity in Poland to the bravery of the crowds in taking to the streets in 1989 in Leipzig, Prague, Sofia, and Timişoara, there are many factors that contributed to communism's demise, not least the role played by political commemorations in mobilizing protest.[71] In the US, the end of the Cold War is popularly and erroneously ascribed to Ronald Reagan 'defeating' the 'evil empire', a narrative that won widespread support before the attacks of 11 September 2001 on the US put the brakes on American liberal triumphalism. All of these factors (Reagan included) did have some bearing on communism's collapse. But none of them would have mattered were it not for the decisions taken by the CPSU's new General Secretary, Mikhail Gorbachev, first to initiate reform in the USSR and, second, not to intervene militarily when the reform process took on a life of its own.[72]

As Gorbachev noted, with more prescience than he knew, shortly after initiating the programmes of *perestroika* and *glasnost* that were to spiral irretrievably out of his control,

> To threaten the socialist order, try to undermine it from outside, and tear one country or another from the socialist community means encroachment not only on the will of the people but also on the entire post-war order and, in the final analysis, on peace.[73]

This threat to communism had been recognized by Hannah Arendt, when she wrote years before Gorbachev's accession that 'a new model' of socialism meant 'to the Russians, not only a more humane handling of the economic or intellectual questions but also the threat of the decomposition of the Russian empire'.[74] Gorbachev's experiment was, therefore, a brave one from the point of view of Soviet orthodoxy. But the stagnation of the Warsaw Pact, its 'backwardness' in terms of economic indicators, meant that for the vast majority of the population the stability of guaranteed employment could no longer act as sufficient compensation for living in a system of 'order without life', as Václav Havel called it.

---

[71] Steven Pfaff and Guobin Yang, 'Double-edged Rituals and the Symbolic Resources of Collective Action: Political Commemorations and the Mobilization of Protest in 1989', *Theory and Society* 30:4 (2001), 539–89.

[72] But, for the importance of a bottom-up approach, see Padraic Kenney, *A Carnival of Revolution: Central Europe 1989* (Princeton, NJ: Princeton University Press, 2003), and Vojtech Mastny, 'Did Gorbachev Liberate Eastern Europe?', in Olav Njølstad (ed.), *The Last Decade of the Cold War: From Conflict Escalation to Conflict Transformation* (London: Frank Cass, 2004), 402–23.

[73] Mikhail Gorbachev, speech to the Warsaw Congress, 30 June 1986, cited in Vladimir Tismaneanu, *The Crisis of Marxist Ideology in Eastern Europe: The Poverty of Utopia* (London: Routledge, 1988), 203. See also Vladislav M. Zubok, 'Gorbachev and the End of the Cold War: Perspectives on History and Personality', *Cold War History* 2:2 (2002), 61–100; Archie Brown, 'Perestroika and the End of the Cold War', *Cold War History* 7:1 (2007), 1–17; Melvyn P. Leffler, 'The Beginning and the End: Time, Context and the Cold War', in Njølstad (ed.), *The Last Decade of the Cold War*, 29–59.

[74] Arendt, *Crises of the Republic*, 179.

The hard-line communists, typified by Nicolae Ceauşescu, the region's staunchest defender of 'national Stalinism', condemned Gorbachev as a 'right-wing deviationist':

> We must bear in mind that there are a number of theoretical and practical deviations, both on the right and on the left. Of course, both of them are equally danger-ous...However, it is my opinion that the main danger today comes from the rightist deviations, which can seriously harm socialist construction and the struggle for dis-armament, peace, and mankind's overall progress.[75]

Following the introduction of *perestroika*, Vasil Bilak, Gustav Husák's hard-line lieuten-ant in charge of ideological affairs in Czechoslovakia, sought to offer reassurance to those who needed it of the clear difference between Gorbachev's aims and those of the 'right-wing opportunists' of the 1968 Prague Spring:

> Nothing is identical. The CPSU leadership is striving to strengthen socialism and the unity of the socialist community, whereas our 'fighters for socialism with a human face' strove in 1968 to dismantle socialism and to break up the socialist community...Certain posthumous children of right wing opportun-ists, who are striving to 'rehabilitate' those who were politically shipwrecked...are pursuing the same goal as in 1968—to return Czechoslovakia to the lap of capitalism.[76]

It must be said that Ceauşescu had a point—he was never taken in by naive reformers who believed that communism could be made more acceptable, and would never have tolerated a loss of nerve or confidence among the leadership, which is why he had to be violently ejected from power. In the cases of revolution and reform (1956 and 1968) the aspirations of the reformers ended in the attainment of the exact opposite of what was intended: renewed Stalinism in post-1956 Hungary and post-1968 Czechoslovakia, and the demise of the communist system in the Soviet Union in 1991. Ironically, the drive to free countries from communist rule (1953, 1956, 1968) ended by tightening it, while the desire to reform and improve communist rule (Gorbachev's accession in 1985) ended in its collapse. In fact, one could go so far as to say that it was precisely because the signals emanating from Moscow were for limited and gradual reform rather than for a complete overhaul of the system that major change could take place. Only because the impetus for reform came from the heart of the system itself could the dreams of the 1956 and 1968 reformers finally be realized, even if that was the opposite of what Gorbachev set out to achieve.

On 8 December 1991, two years after the unplanned collapse of the Berlin Wall, fol-lowing the renunciation of a treaty preventing East German tourists holidaying in Hungary from crossing the border into Austria (and thence to West Germany), the lead-ers of Russia, Ukraine, and Belarus conspired against Gorbachev's wishes and signed the Belovezha Accord, which abolished the superpower and replaced it with the CIS. The Supreme Soviet was powerless to prevent the break-up of the Soviet Union, and

---

[75] Nicolae Ceauşescu in *Scînteia*, 4 May 1988, cited in Tismaneanu, *Stalinism for All Seasons*, 32.
[76] Cited in Tismaneanu, *The Crisis of Marxist Ideology*, 202.

recognized that fact by dissolving itself on 26 December.[77] Despite some feeble attempts to hold on to the Baltic States in 1991, the end was remarkably free of violence.[78] The role played by Russian President Boris Yeltsin, in preventing the August 1991 coup of hardline Soviet ministers from succeeding in toppling Gorbachev, was key both to the success of 'reform' and to undermining Gorbachev's authority. Who could have predicted that communism would die not with a bang but with a whimper?[79]

At this point, the postwar histories of Eastern and Western Europe converged in a way that had not been true for forty years. For that reason, the post-communist years ('after the fall') deserve separate treatment.

POST-1989

Twenty years is insufficient time for a meaningful historicization process to have occurred, if only because many of the sources that historians will need remain inaccessible.[80] Nevertheless, the post-1989 years are becoming history; for example the twentieth anniversary of the revolutions in 2009 saw a slew of academic and popular studies devoted to rethinking the meaning of '1989' or 'telling the unknown story' of what happened to bring about the collapse of communism.[81] Much of what has happened in Eastern Europe since then has been the preserve of political scientists (discussing issues

---

[77] Graeme Gill and Roger D. Markwick, *Russia's Stillborn Democracy? From Gorbachev to Yeltsin* (Oxford: Oxford University Press, 2000), 110; Katherine Verdery, 'What Was Socialism, and Why Did It Fall?', in Tismaneanu (ed.), *The Revolutions of 1989*, 75; Hans-Hermann Hertle, 'The Fall of the Wall: The Unintended Self-Dissolution of East Germany's Ruling Regime', *Cold War International History Project Bulletin* 12–13 (2001), 131–64; Jacques Lévesque, 'The Emancipation of Eastern Europe', in Richard K. Hermann and Richard Ned Lebow (eds), *Ending the Cold War: Interpretations, Causation, and the Study of International Relations* (New York: Palgrave Macmillan, 2004), 107–29.

[78] Stephen Kotkin, *Armageddon Averted: The Soviet Collapse 1970–2000* (Oxford: Oxford University Press, 2001).

[79] For a useful discussion, see David Rowley, 'Interpretations of the End of the Soviet Union: Three Paradigms', *Kritika: Explorations in Russian and Eurasian History* 2:2 (2001), 395–426.

[80] On the problem of dealing with the recent past, see Hayden White's thoughtful comments in 'The Metaphysics of (Western) Historiography', *Taiwan Journal of East Asian Studies* 1:1 (2004), 1–16. The recent past 'is becoming something that will have been', as White puts it (5).

[81] For example: Victor Sebestyen, *Revolution 1989: The Fall of the Soviet Empire* (London: Weidenfeld and Nicolson, 2009); Mary Elise Sarotte, *1989: The Struggle to Create Post-Cold War Europe* (Princeton, NJ: Princeton University Press, 2009); Michael Meyer, *The Year that Changed the World: The Untold Story Behind the Fall of the Berlin Wall* (London: Simon and Schuster, 2009); Constantine Pleshakov, *There Is No Freedom without Bread! 1989 and the Civil War that Brought down Communism* (New York: Farrar Straus Giroux, 2009); Stephen Kotkin, *Uncivil Society: 1989 and the Implosion of the Communist Establishment* (New York: Modern Library, 2009); Jeffrey A. Engel(ed.), *The Fall of the Berlin Wall: The Revolutionary Legacy of 1989* (New York: Oxford University Press, 2009); Padraic Kenney, *1989: Democratic Revolutions at the Cold War's End* (New York: Palgrave Macmillan, 2010). In 2009 the journals *Contemporary European History* and *East European Politics and Societies* both ran special issues devoted to thinking about the meaning of 1989.

of democratic legitimization, elections, party structures, transitional justice, and so on); economists (discussing the varieties of capitalism being developed in Eastern Europe); and 'transitologists' of all sorts, who are starting to learn that there is no preordained path towards western-style democratic, predictable stability. Rather, 'post-totalitarian blues', as Jacques Rupnik names it, is not just a theoretical possibility.[82] Indeed, since postwar stability has been threatened by the rise of populism in the western half of the continent, there should be no surprise that it exists—and is growing—in the eastern half.[83] But many properly historical questions, especially concerning what transpired in 1989 and why the course of events followed the shape it did, are being asked. What is abundantly clear is that the postwar consensus is, if not dead, semi-comatose. Both west and east failed to live up to the fundamental premises that underpinned them, as Susan Buck-Morss points out:

> Thus: the Communist Party, the self-proclaimed vanguard of history, attempted to sustain power within an economic system that by its own definition repeatedly fell behind industrial development in the West. Thus: the nation-state system attempted to maintain its hegemony within a capitalist global economy that increasingly threatened to escape the control of nation-state political units.[84]

Probably the most pressing concern from a Western European point of view following the end of the Cold War was German unification. This was a process driven by Chancellor Kohl, who promised the East Germans 'flourishing landscapes'; their enthusiasm for the project is encapsulated in the switch in their rally slogan from '*Wir sind das Volk*' ('we are the people') to '*Wir sind ein Volk*' ('we are one people'). The number of Germans who agreed with Günter Grass that the Germanies should be left as 'two states, one nation' was vanishingly small.[85] Like Grass, but for rather different reasons, western leaders were less sure that unifying the two Germanies and making Germany the most populous country and the largest economy in Europe was in their interest. Giulio Andreotti, Italy's 'experienced and enigmatic' Christian Democrat prime minister, had as early as 1984 let slip a remark about the coming '*pan-Germanismus*' and, after the fall of the Berlin Wall, reputedly remarked: 'We love the Germans so much that the more Germanies there are the better'.[86]

---

[82] Jacques Rupnik, 'The Post-Totalitarian Blues', in Tismaneanu (ed.), *The Revolutions of 1989*, 231–43. On post-1989 in general, see Sorin Antohi and Vladimir Tismaneanu (eds), *Between Past and Future: The Revolutions of 1989 and Their Aftermath* (Budapest: Central European University Press, 2000).

[83] Daniele Albertazzi and Duncan McDonnell (eds), *Twenty-First Century Populism: The Spectre of Western European Democracy* (Basingstoke: Palgrave Macmillan, 2008).

[84] Susan Buck-Morss, *Dreamworld and Catastrophe: The Passing of Mass Utopia in East and West* (Cambridge, MA: MIT Press, 2000), 39.

[85] Günter Grass, *Two States – One Nation? The Case against German Reunification* (London: Secker & Warburg, 1990).

[86] Leopoldo Nuti, 'Italy, German Unification and the End of the Cold War', in Frédéric Bozo, Marie-Pierre Rey, N. Piers Ludlow and Leopoldo Nuti (eds), *Europe and the End of the Cold War: A Reappraisal* (London: Routledge, 2008), 192; Andreotti cited in Pleshakov, *There Is No Freedom Without Bread!*, 208.

Mitterand and Thatcher were notoriously twitchy about the idea, and were dragged along by Kohl's influence over George Bush Sr, and the latter's desire for a US–German axis in foreign policy. So too was Gorbachev, though Russia was in no position really to influence the course of events. Following so-called 2+4 talks (the two German states and the four allied states—Berlin was still officially under allied control at this point), the 2+4 Treaty of 12 September 1990 formally ended the division of Germany and restored full German sovereignty, including ending the special status of Berlin. Although international authorization was formally required for this process, Bonn set the pace, backed by overwhelming popular support in both Germanies. After the CDU's Alliance for Germany won 48.1 per cent of the East German election of 18 March 1990—a victory for Kohl's promise of money—monetary union at 1:1 took place on 1 July, and unification officially followed on 3 October. The CDU victory on 2 December, the date of the first all-German election, was massive, saving Kohl's chancellorship after dwindling support in the FRG.[87]

The two countries were unified according to article 23 of the West German constitution, which did not require a new constitution to be written, unlike article 46—in other words, East Germany would essentially be 'colonized'. At the time, no one cared. The Cold War in Germany had always been about the national question—which is why 'the "German question" was always too important to leave to the Germans'[88]—and the end of the Cold War saw the national question reassert its primacy. Hence, the unification of Germany was one of those key moments in the history of the EU when further integration—in this case, the Maastricht Treaty on European Union—was precipitated by the 'German question'. Indeed, following the remarkable incorporation of the 'new *Länder*' (the former GDR) into West Germany, an economic feat that would have brought any other European economy to its knees, Germany lost none of its enthusiasm for the European project, at least not until it was called on to rescue the Greek and Irish economies in 2010.

In the former Soviet Bloc, the USSR was replaced by the CIS, headed by Yeltsin, which kept the Eurasian border states within Russia's orbit. With respect to international communist structures, it was only once Gorbachev had signalled his unwillingness to use force to hold on to the East European satellite states that the communist bloc discovered a sense of unity of purpose. As Mastny says with respect to the Warsaw Pact, it is ironic that

> the end of the cold war gave the alliance a new lease on life by making it serve for the first time a clear and constructive purpose—namely, the dismantling of the outsized conventional forces and armaments that remained the cold war's legacy.[89]

---

[87] For more details, see Charles S. Maier, *Dissolution: The Crisis of Communism and the End of East Germany* (Princeton, NJ: Princeton University Press, 1997); Sarotte, *1989*, on German influence; Frédéric Bozo, *Mitterand, the End of the Cold War, and German Unification* (Oxford: Berghahn, 2009); documents in Konrad H. Jarausch and Volker Gransow, *Uniting Germany: Documents and Debates, 1944–1993* (Providence, RI: Berghahn, 1994).

[88] Jost Dülffer, 'Cold War History in Germany', *Cold War History* 8:2 (2008), 135.

[89] Vojtech Mastny, 'The Warsaw Pact: An Alliance in Search of a Purpose', in Ann Heiss and S. Victor Papacosma (eds), *NATO and the Warsaw Pact: Intrabloc Conflicts* (Kent, OH: Kent State University Press, 2008), 155.

In former communist Eastern Europe, 'round-table talks' were generally the method used to smooth the passage of the 'velvet revolution', to prevent bloodshed, and to allow the communist apparatchiks to disappear into obscurity as parliamentary democracy gradually took control. More vigorous attacks on communism, including threats of legal action, only came in the first decade of the twenty-first century, when they became a useful instrument of social and moral control, as in Hungary, the Baltic States, or the Kaczyński brothers' Poland.

Certainly, there were many problems: economic liberalization was a terrible shock to people who had had their economically unviable jobs protected by the state (albeit at the cost of low productivity, waste, shortages, and environmental degradation) and who now faced a future of unemployment coupled with a loss of services such as free childcare. In the communist countries, such services were provided by the state less out of solidarity with the working class than as a stick with which to force people (especially women) into work. But still, exposure to the harsh realities of western capitalism, especially in its short-lived robber–capitalist variant, sent many running to the illusory warmth of *Ostalgie* (nostalgia for the east). And politically, the vacuum opened up by the collapse of the Party and its dominant narrative left plenty of room for populists with 'fantasies of salvation'.[90] In cases such as Romania, it was not even clear whether a genuine sweeping away of the old order had taken place at all; one scholar talks about 'quasi-democratic communism' lasting there until after the December 2004 elections.[91]

But if there has been a 'general deterioration of memory discourses after 2000', the remarkable nature of what happened in 1989 should not be forgotten.[92] Adam Michnik says that for him and his colleagues at *Gazeta Wyborcza*, 'manna did fall from

---

[90] Vladimir Tismaneanu, *Fantasies of Salvation: Democracy, Nationalism, and Myth in Post-Communist Europe* (Princeton, NJ: Princeton University Press, 1998). See my chapter below for a discussion of post-1989 European memory, and Michael Shafir's chapter for a discussion of Tismaneanu's claims.

[91] Padraic Kenney, *The Burdens of Freedom: Eastern Europe since 1989* (London: Zed Books, 2006), 117. See also Vladimir Tismaneanu, 'The Quasi-Revolution and its Discontents: Emerging Political Pluralism in Post-Ceauşescu Romania', *East European Politics and Societies* 7:2 (1993), 309–48; Peter Siani-Davies, 'Romanian Revolution or Coup d'état? A Theoretical View of the Events of December 1989', *Communist and Post-Communist Studies* 29:4 (1996), 453–65. But as Jowitt noted ('The Leninist Extinction', 259), with reference to Bulgaria and Romania in an essay of 1991, 'even regimes whose new political profiles contain elements recognizably derived from their Leninist predecessors will no longer be Leninist or part of an international regime world'. Mircea Munteanu, 'The Last Days of a Dictator', *Cold War International History Project Bulletin* 12–13 (2001), 217–25, includes the transcript of the key conversation on 4 December 1989 between Gorbachev and Ceauşescu.

[92] Eric Langenbacher, 'Ethical Cleansing? The Expulsion of Germans from Central and Eastern Europe', in Nicholas A. Robins and Adam Jones (eds), *Genocides by the Oppressed: Subaltern Genocide in Theory and Practice* (Bloomington, IN: Indiana University Press, 2009), 67; cf. Eva Hahn and Hans Henning Hahn, 'The Holocaustizing of the Transfer-Discourse: Historical Revisionism or Old Wine in New Bottles?', in Michal Kopeček (ed.), *Past in the Making: Historical Revisionism in Central Europe after 1989* (Budapest: Central European University Press, 2008), 39–58.

heaven... the democratic opposition won everything there was to gain at the bargaining table'.[93] Given the lack of democratic traditions in much of Eastern Europe—with the exception of Czechoslovakia between the wars—and given the underhand strategies that ordinary people had to develop to outwit the authorities in order to survive, especially in the most authoritarian cases of Albania and Romania, not to mention the impact of the credit crisis of the last few years, which has hit Hungary, Latvia, and Ukraine especially hard, we do not need to wonder at the existence of challenges to liberal democracy. And if in some instances—Russia, most obviously—we see democratic structures without democratic practice, it is still stability, albeit wobbly, rather than disintegration or rising radicalism that is the most striking characteristic of 1989's aftermath. The 'ethnic rivalries, unsavoury political bickering, rampant political and economic corruption, and the rise of illiberal parties and movements' are all deplorable, but should not lead one to diminish the revolutions' 'generous message and colossal impact' or to question the validity of change per se.[94]

The exception, of course, is the break-up of Yugoslavia and the series of wars that engulfed it. It is often forgotten that Slobodan Milošević emerged out of a communist context, gradually developing his ultra-nationalist message in the period of Yugoslavia's fragmentation following Tito's death in 1980. Yugoslavia is the prime example of 'memory' being mobilized in the name of violent ideologies, with Milošević's 1989 speech commemorating the 600th anniversary of the Battle of Kosovo Polje regularly cited as a key moment in the mobilization of nationalist fear and hatred. Recalling the vicious history of World War II, in which Serbs had been victims of Croatian-perpetrated genocide, Milošević and his allies set out to impose Serb domination on the Yugoslav republics that were seceding from the state.[95]

Yugoslavia was a remarkable creation, in both its monarchical and republican forms. During the 1960s and 1970s, with its independence from Moscow, relative openness to the West, and a standard of living higher than most of its communist counterparts, Yugoslavia appeared to have brought an impressive degree of harmony to the various South Slav nations that made up the federation, with increasing numbers identifying as 'Yugoslav' in preference to one of the constituent national groups. The extraordinary 'success' of Serb ultra-nationalism in the late 1980s and early 1990s was that it convinced

---

[93] Adam Michnik, 'Independence Reborn and the Demons of the Velvet Revolution', in Antohi and Tismaneanu (eds), *Between Past and Future*, 85.

[94] Vladimir Tismaneanu, 'The Revolutions of 1989: Causes, Meanings, Consequences', *Contemporary European History* 18:3 (2009), 272. See also, in the same issue (253–69), Charles S. Maier, 'What Have We Learned since 1989?' On the radical right in post-communist Eastern Europe, see the special issue of *Communist and Post-Communist Studies* 42:4 (2009), and on Western Europe, see Paul Hainsworth, *The Extreme Right in Western Europe* (London: Routledge, 2008).

[95] Gino Raymond and Svetlana Bajic-Raymond, 'Memory and History: The Discourse of Nation-Building in the Former Yugoslavia', *Patterns of Prejudice* 31:1 (1997), 21–30; Florian Bieber, 'Nationalist Mobilization and Stories of Serb Suffering: The Kosovo Myth from 600th Anniversary to the Present', *Rethinking History* 6:1 (2002), 95–110; Milica Bakić-Hayden, 'Nesting Orientalisms: The Case of Former Yugoslavia', *Slavic Review* 54:4 (1995), 917–31.

people that the past would always invade the present, and forced people to drop their multiple identities and to identify wholly as one thing or another.[96]

In terms of events, the facts are both complex and straightforward. They are complex because the disintegration of Yugoslavia took place over a decade and because in reality the 'war' was made up of several discrete but related conflicts. But it was straightforward too, because the driving force was the same throughout: a Serb ultra-nationalist drive to create a Greater Serbia. Certainly Croatian Serbs were being mistreated in Croatia, and there is no room either for trying to make Franjo Tudjman, the head of independent Croatia, look like a respectable politician (he was a Holocaust denying admirer of the Nazi-backed NDH). The mistreatment of Serbs and Romanies by ethnic Albanian Kosovars following the Serbian withdrawal from Kosovo in 1999 was a shabby reminder that victimhood does not make people nicer. Nor does the western demonization of Serbia—which many Serbs and their friends in the region (in Romania and Greece, for example) found inexplicable—necessitate the condemnation of an entire people, for this would be to think in the same ethnic pigeonholing terms as a Milošević, Karadzic, or Mladic.[97] But the evidence suggests that, under the guise of defending Yugoslav territorial integrity (a claim that bamboozled the US and the EU with their memories of German-sponsored Croatian fascism), Milošević set out not to reassert the legitimacy of Yugoslav federalism but to impose Serbian hegemony over the region.[98]

Following Tudjman's victory in Croatia's first post-communist election in April 1990 and Croatia's declaration of independence from Yugoslavia on 25 June 1991, the JNA (Yugoslav National Army), which was largely in Serbian hands, was used to step up the level of violence in Croatia. Air raids on Zagreb suggested that the Serbs were engaged in more than merely protecting ethnic Serbs in Croatia, but it was only once Vucovar, Eastern Slavonia, and the Krajina had been taken, and the UNESCO world heritage site of Dubrovnik was besieged, that the West realized that Serbia was overrunning Croatia. By the time of the deal brokered by Lord Carrington, Milošević was in control of more than a quarter of Croatian territory.

But it was Bosnia where the real conflict would take place, and where the term 'ethnic cleansing' took on a relevance that it had not had in Europe since World War II.

---

[96] Dan Stone, 'Genocide and Memory', in Donald Bloxham and A. Dirk Moses (eds), *The Oxford Handbook of Genocide Studies* (Oxford: Oxford University Press, 2010), 102–19; Anthony Oberschall, 'The Manipulation of Ethnicity: From Ethnic Cooperation to Violence and War in Yugoslavia', *Ethnic and Racial Studies* 23:6 (2000), 982–1001.

[97] Janine Natalya Clark, 'Collective Guilt, Collective Responsibility and the Serbs', *East European Politics and Societies* 22:3 (2008), 668–92.

[98] For good analyses of the violent collapse of Yugoslavia, see, among others: Jasminka Udovicki and James Ridgeway (eds), *Burn This House: The Making and Unmaking of Yugoslavia*, rev. edn (Durham, NC: Duke University Press, 2000); Nebojša Popov (ed.), *The Road to War in Serbia: Trauma and Catharsis* (Budapest: Central European University Press, 2000); Susan L. Woodward, *Balkan Tragedy: Chaos and Dissolution after the Cold War* (Washington, DC: The Brookings Institution, 1995); John R. Lampe, *Yugoslavia as History: Twice There Was a Country* (Cambridge: Cambridge University Press, 1996); Jasna Dragović-Soso, *Saviours of the Nation? Serbia's Intellectual Opposition and the Revival of Nationalism* (London: C. Hurst, 2002).

Following Muslim President Izetbegović's declaration of Bosnian independence on 3 March 1992, the Bosnian Serbs, under Radovan Karadzic, announced the establishment of the Serbian Republic of Bosnia-Herzegovina, later renamed the Republika Srpska, based in Banja Luka. Within weeks of fighting, the Bosnian Serbs controlled 70 per cent of Bosnian territory. Of Bosnia's 4.4 million inhabitants, almost all were dislocated: 3 million were internally displaced, and 1.3 million fled as refugees abroad. The massacre at Srebrenica in July 1995, after the UN had declared it a 'safe area', was the single worst massacre of the war, and has prompted many, including the ICTY, to talk of genocide in Bosnia.[99] The Muslim–Croat Federation's fight back in April 1995 therefore took the Serbs and the international community by surprise, and succeeded in pushing the Serbs out of most of the Krajina. The Dayton Agreement, it has been argued, froze events before they could take their natural course; it would have been preferable, so this version of events goes, to allow the Muslim–Croat Federation to defeat the Serbs completely. But no doubt Dayton also saved further large-scale bloodshed.[100]

The Serbs' last stab at victory was in Kosovo, in some ways the most significant of all the wars of Yugoslav succession, for Kosovo was part of Serbia (albeit autonomous until 1981) and the 'heartland' of Serb national identity. The movement of Bosnian Serb refugees into Kosovo was a deliberate strategy to counter the ethnic balance, which was heavily in the favour of the Albanians. But Kosovo, and unofficial President Ibrahim Rugova, were ignored by Dayton, and this gave Serbia its chance to impose its will on the territory. The ensuing massacres, particularly at Račak on 15 January 1999, gave rise to large-scale refugee movements into Macedonia and Montenegro, and feverish international talks aimed at solving the crisis at Rambouillet, near Paris. When the talks broke down, NATO bombed Serbia from 24 March for 78 days, until the country's infrastructure was ruined, and the state was turned into an international pariah. Although the bombing seemed at first to harden nationalist resolve, Milošević was deposed late in 2000. But if, a decade later, noises are being made that will gradually rehabilitate Serbia, and eventually permit it to join the EU, many across Europe think that NATO and the EU lost prestige by using their military might to smash a small country.

The wars in Yugoslavia revived the frightening World War II memories of Chetniks and Ustashe, and showed how rapidly alternatives could be eliminated if circumstances permitted. Europe still lives with the consequences of the wars, with stability in Kosovo and Bosnia now extremely fragile, and guaranteed only by large international peacekeeping forces.[101] They also confirm what Tony Judt says about memory. Reinforcing the

[99]   Robert M. Hayden, 'Mass Killings and Images of Genocide in Bosnia, 1941–5 and 1992–5', in Dan Stone (ed.), *The Historiography of Genocide* (Basingstoke: Palgrave Macmillan, 2008), 487–516; see Cathie Carmichael's chapter below.

[100]   Noel Malcolm, *Bosnia: A Short History*, rev. edn (London: Macmillan, 1996), 270–1.

[101]   Robert M. Hayden, ' "Democracy" without a Demos? The Bosnian Constitutional Experiment and the Intentional Construction of Nonfunctioning States', *East European Politics and Societies* 19 (2005), 226–59; Paul B. Miller, 'Contested Memories: The Bosnian Genocide in Serb and Muslim Minds', *Journal of Genocide Research* 8:3 (2006), 311–24.

claim that the initial postwar years hold the key to much of what subsequently occurred, Judt argues that the years 1945–48 'were the moment not only of the division of Europe and the first stage of its postwar reconstruction but also, and in an intimately related manner, the period during which Europe's postwar memory was molded'.[102] Even if, following the end of the Cold War, the politics of memory does not always follow predictable paths, Judt's point still holds.[103]

Indeed, the focus on memory reminds us that even if historians like to break time up into neatly packaged periods to ease the process of analysis and comprehension, reality is not so accommodating. It is of course still possible to provide overarching narratives for the postwar period, as has most commonly been done in a triumphalist mode by the likes of Francis Fukuyama, who saw the end of the Cold War in Hegelian terms as the victory for a certain philosophy of history—the unfolding of liberal reason in the shape of the parliamentary democratic state. In the years since 1989, Fukuyama's pleasing telos has been somewhat shaken, with war in Yugoslavia, the so-called 'war on terror', and the infantilization of politics that has taken over much of the current European scene, with sexual antics (Italy and France), MPs' expenses (Britain), 'reality' TV, nostalgia for pasts that never existed, and scaremongering over Islam (Switzerland, Austria, the Netherlands, and everywhere else) taking up more time in parliaments and the press than global warming, growing social divisions, and economic crisis.

Tony Judt recently argued that we should be far angrier than we are that the achievements of a century of social democracy have been so substantially dismantled in the last three decades. Europe may have become a rich and privileged corner of the world, but the manner of its survival of the 1970s recession and its transformation into a service-sector paradise has come at a high cost—of social cohesion, respect for the worth of individuals, and deepening socio-economic divisions, with all the attendant ills of poverty, crime, and violence that highly unequal societies suffer. Today's problem, according to Judt, is how to return to social democratic values in an age that still uses a social democratic vocabulary (of fairness, liberalism, tolerance) but which acts in ways that scorn those values.[104] Whatever one thinks of Judt's argument, the challenge that faces contemporary Europe is that in the post-Cold War, 'war on terror' age in which we now live, the legacies of World War II are acquiring meanings that fundamentally shake what are usually supposed to be 'European values'.

From their study of revolution, anti-communist intellectuals such as Adam Michnik learned that 'those who start by storming Bastille will end up building Bastille'.[105] Much

---

[102] Tony Judt, 'The Past is Another Country: Myth and Memory in Postwar Europe', in Deák, Gross and Judt (eds), *The Politics of Retribution*, 296.

[103] cf. Padraic Kenney, 'Martyrs and Neighbors: Sources of Reconciliation in Central Europe', *Common Knowledge* 13:1 (2007), 149–69.

[104] Tony Judt, 'What is Living and What is Dead in Social Democracy?' Lecture at New York University, 19 October 2009, online at: http://remarque.as.nyu.edu/object/io_1256242927496.html, accessed March 2010. See the fuller discussion in Judt, *Ill Fares the Land: A Treatise on Our Present Discontents* (London: Allen Lane, 2010).

[105] Michnik cited in Timothy Garton Ash, 'Conclusions', in Antohi and Tismaneanu (eds), *Between Past and Future*, 397.

of recent European history is about what shape the new Bastille in the guise of Fortress Europe will take. When one examines the 'return of memories' that could not be articulated in the public sphere during the Cold War—when the anti-fascist narrative was imposed on the East and prevailed in the West, albeit in a conservative, anti-communist form—one can see that the years since 1989 are intimately connected to World War II and its aftermath. In many ways, we are only now living through the postwar period.

PART I

WHAT IS POSTWAR EUROPE?

CHAPTER 1

CORPORATISM AND THE SOCIAL DEMOCRATIC MOMENT: THE POSTWAR SETTLEMENT, 1945–1973

GEOFF ELEY

CERTAIN facts about postwar Eursope seem self-evidently true. Undoubtedly the most salient was the division of Europe and the political, economic, social, and cultural antinomies that separated western capitalism from Soviet-style communism in the overarching context of the Cold War. That exorbitantly conventional binary framework authorized familiar narratives of the securing of freedom or its absence, whose dominance implied certain enduring stabilities remarkably encompassing in their reach. Yet, while their constraining and enabling power can hardly be underestimated, the Cold War's normativities are easily made to explain too much. They certainly obscure the messier contingencies that actually brought the postwar into being. Moreover, if the Cold War itself stretched across four decades, from the heightening of international tensions in 1947–48 to the collapse of the Soviet Union in 1989–91, the postwar settlement's reliable solidities had already been breaking apart in the 1970s, reeling from the shocks of 1968. Politics dramatically registered the societal transformations occurring in what Eric Hobsbawm rightly called the 'golden age', whose consequences for urban living, access to education, and patterns of consumption unfolded on either side of the boundary between east and west.[1] Then, with disconcerting rapidity, the global economic downturn of 1973–74 ended the postwar boom, shelving its promises of permanent growth and continuously unfolding prosperity. In those terms, the core of the postwar settlement lies in the years 1947–73.

---

[1] Eric Hobsbawm, *The Age of Extremes: A History of the World, 1914–1991* (New York: Pantheon, 1994), 225–400, especially 257–319.

There would be many ways of drawing out the coherence of that settlement. One would be the international history of the Cold War per se. Another would be the history of the ideas that sustained it. A third approach, using the now popular analytics of memory and memorializing, implies a vantage point situated unequivocally *inside* the later 'post' of the early twenty-first century present, as does the new aspirant master narrative of European integration or the related commitment to rewriting the history of Europe in avowedly 'transnational' ways. We might also pull together what we have learned about the social histories of the immediate post-1945 decades. One such perspective would address the re-gendering of social relations and political life, particularly with regard to the consequences for women and girls. Another would foreground questions of migration and migrancy, the organization of labour markets, and the changing bases of working-class formation. Yet another would emphasize the changing relations of Europe to the rest of the world, particularly its colonial theatres of influence and power.

In the interests of clarity, this essay will focus on the single most striking particularity of the post-1945 settlement, namely the centrality acquired by organized labour for the polities, social imaginaries, and public cultures of postwar European societies. Measured either by what came before or by the succeeding years of capitalist restructuring and deindustrialization, the 1950s and 1960s appear more and more as an exceptional moment in the several centuries' history of industrial capitalism. The public legitimacy of labour, grounded in the acknowledged terms of postwar reconstruction, and borne by an unprecedented growth of democratic capacities, acquired a generality of acceptance it had never enjoyed before and has never regained since.

DEMOCRACY AS A CULTURAL PROJECT, 1945–68

The settlements accompanying the successive world wars saw the twentieth century's two great waves of pan-European democratization, whose contrasting scale and resilience were vitally linked in each case to the unevenness and fragility of the achieved forms of societal cohesion and the stability of political arrangements at the level of the state.[2] To pose the question in these terms presupposes an avowedly dynamic definition of democracy, one that joins formal criteria to the societal circumstances under which democratic gains are most likely to occur. Whereas the formal definition might emphasize popular sovereignty and accountable government based on universal, secret, adult, and equal suffrage, secured by freedoms of speech, conscience, association, assembly, and the press, and backed by rights under the law, then democracy's dynamics require the contingencies of conjunctures and events. In other words, we need an argument about democracy's actual emergence in twentieth-century Europe—the conflicts sur-

[2] A third democratizing wave occurred in 1989–91, though confined to the continent's eastern half.

rounding its recorded eventuations and the complicated histories producing its actually accomplished forms.

Thus to grasp the full extent of the changes encompassed in 1918 and 1945 requires focusing not only on the obvious political arenas of parliaments, party conflicts, and citizenship rights guaranteed by law, but also on a much wider range of contexts. These would include:

1. expansive conceptions of social rights implied by the rise of the welfare state;
2. the enlargement of citizenship capacities in ways that might not always receive explicit ratification on the national stage of politics or become institutionalized quickly and easily into law. Here we should note the raising of new claims for recognition well in advance of the attainment of any juridical standing, as well as the persisting unevenness in the law's ability to resolve discrepancies and imperfections;
3. the mobile boundary of distinctions between the public and the private in fields of regulation and intervention concerning issues of personhood, intimate relations, and the social body, particularly those concerning family, sexualities, and moral order;
4. the variegated political space of an increasingly mass-mediated public sphere.

In the case of 1918, the longer term record was extremely mixed. On the one hand, the European-wide process of democratic constitution making during 1918–19 produced a dramatically transformed set of polities and international system. The new successor states of East-Central Europe in particular were all equipped with constitutions that were originally strongly democratic, linked to impressive projects of social reform, and further challenged and incited by the direct democracy of the soviets and workers' councils further to the left. Yet by the end of the 1920s across Europe as a whole very little of this settlement still remained. Few of the freshly generated democratic capacities proved capable of outlasting that initial postwar decade.

Why did this earlier settlement prove so impermanent? The instabilities of the new arrangements had many explanations, to be sure, but the fractured shallowness of popular identifications with democracy proved one of the most decisive. To make sense of this we might distinguish between the act of *constitution making* and processes of *culture building*. For as suggested above, the political breakdowns of the 1920s and 1930s reflected the relative thinness of the emergent societal consensus and the bitterly contested novelty of its democratic values. Understanding that brittleness of the new political arrangements—and conversely the possible ground from which more lasting democratic cultures might have been formed—then requires discussion of the public sphere. Moreover, if the toughening of civil society through the enhancement of the public sphere was a vital part of the democratic quality of the postwar political settlements in both 1918 and 1945, then that process encompassed far more than simply the making of public opinion via the press and other media of public communication. Rather, it brought into play all the ways in which society's self-organization acquired legitimacy and legally protected public space—through collective organization of all kinds, through the formation of political identities, through the expression of opinion, through the circulation of ideas, and so forth.[3]

The strengthening of the public sphere may well be approached constitutionally as a matter of legal innovation and institutional change, as the securing of the freedoms of ideas and exchange against censorship and coercive restraint. But any genuine and lasting enhancement of the public sphere would have to encompass *all* of the aspects of the new breakthrough to democracy—from the newly created republican sovereignties and associated discourse of citizenship, through the strengthening of parliamentary government, to protections for the press, expansion of workers' rights under the law, corporative recognition of trade unions, growth of civil liberties, social legislation, protection for vulnerable populations and disfranchised minorities, and so forth.

Without benefit of this expanded and legally protected public sphere, whose rules and opportunities could be enjoyed on a national or society-wide scale, social movements would remain confined to their own defensive and self-referential, largely ghettoized, subcultural space. For popular democratic purposes, such a strengthening of the public sphere was a *sine qua non*, and at all events a huge strategic gain. Under the most repressive forms of rule, after all, self-organization at a subcultural level is still possible in a defensive and inward-looking sense. But without secure or predictable access to any wider public domain, subcultures remain chronically weak. They become deprived of access to possible coalitions and therefore to the support of a broad enough societal consensus. They lack either the national–popular credibility of a plausible counter-hegemonic claim—the necessary moral–political capital for governing—or the resources for resisting anti-democratic or counter-revolutionary repression, if that came.

Thus the overall field of interaction between reforms under the law, institutional developments, and changing political culture was crucially important. Where a robust societal consensus could be constructed, enjoying simultaneous legitimacy at the level of the state and breadth in popular culture, the grounding and resilience of popular democracy could be very strong. Thus in contrast to the fragilities of the post-1918 settlements, in fact, a consensus of that kind *was* elaborated after 1945, drawing upon the democratic patriotisms of the war years, fusing the aspirations for a new beginning with the logics of economic reconstruction, and organizing itself within the anti-fascist integument of the postwar settlements. Between the late 1940s and the next breaking point of 1968, a democratically centred or inflected societal consensus was produced, providing a kind of template for the popular political imagination. That consensus was organized around a strongly liberal public sphere, with all the concomitant legal protections. It was fashioned from the popular democratic momentum of a wartime mobilization, which became linked to the social contract imagined for the peacetime about to come. The reformist strengths of that settlement made it possible for popular consciousness to identify with the state, which thereby acquired a new and lasting reservoir of moral capital.

---

[3] See Geoff Eley, 'Nations, Publics, and Political Cultures: Placing Habermas in the Nineteenth Century', in Craig Calhoun (ed.), *Habermas and the Public Sphere* (Cambridge, MA: MIT Press, 1992), 289–339, and 'Politics, Culture, and the Public Sphere', *positions* 10 (2002), 219–36.

This was the decisive difference separating the postwar settlement after 1945 from its predecessor in 1918–19. We can see this very clearly in the case of post-1945 Britain. The institutional features of the British version of the Keynesian welfare state synthesis are well known. They included social security 'from the cradle to the grave', the National Health Service, the Butler Education Act, progressive taxation, strong public-sector policies, corporative economic management, strong ideals of trade union recognition, and an integrative discourse of social citizenship.[4] But the persuasiveness and democratic breadth of this package also acquired vital foundations in popular culture.

In this context, patriotism—British national feeling—had acquired powerful inflections to the Left. Pride in being British implied not just identification with the Empire and the flag, but especially the egalitarianism of the Second World War, the achievement of the welfare state, and a complex of democratic traditions stressing decency, tolerance, and the importance of everyone pulling together, in a way that honoured the value and values of ordinary working people. In the legitimizing narratives of popular memory surrounding this patriotism, both the founding rigours of the postwar Labour Government and the normalizing complacencies of the succeeding Conservative administrations of the 1950s became important in their differing ways. But the lasting stability of this consensus, which endured into the 1970s, also depended on a larger cultural script binding the experiences of the 1930s and 1940s together. The postwar consensus also evoked images of the Depression, and by these means the patriotic comradeship of wartime became reworked into a social democratic narrative of suffering and social redress.

In that narrative, the poverty attributed to the 1930s became a sign for the difference and desirability of what was expected to become the new postwar present.[5] From the vantage-point of the 1950s, the 1930s signified a massive failure of the system—the 'low, dishonest decade', the 'devil's decade', the 'wasted years' of the familiar parlance of the day. The imagery of dismal hardship, mass unemployment, and hunger marches described an unacceptable history that could never be readmitted to the legitimate agenda, a past that could never be repeated, a societal misery demanding public responsibility and collective action. The Second World War was a 'good war', not just because of its anti-fascist character (the quality most commonly adduced in such discussions), but

---

[4] For more than two decades the character of the postwar settlement in Britain has been the subject of much continuing debate. For my own thoughts, see Geoff Eley, 'Legacies of Antifascism: Constructing Democracy in Postwar Europe', *New German Critique* 67 (1996), 73–100, and 'Finding the People's War: Film, British Collective Memory, and World War II', *American Historical Review* 105 (2001), 818–38.

[5] Since the later 1970s, the Depression's place in British collective memory has been radically reshaped. Under the impact of Thatcherism's retelling of the story, the new 'present' of the 1980s became itself fundamentally different from the older 'present' that previously prevailed. The reworking of popular memory became a central feature of public rhetoric, pedagogy, and popular culture during the 1980s. See Geoff Eley, '*Distant Voices, Still Lives*. The Family is a Dangerous Place: Memory, Gender, and the Image of the Working Class', in Robert Rosenstone (ed.), *Revisioning History: Film and the Construction of the Past* (Princeton, NJ: Princeton University Press, 1995), 17–43; and 'Finding the People's War'.

because the egalitarianism and social solidarities needed for victory also made an irrefutable case for equitable social policies in the world to come. The breadth of the resulting post-1945 consensus behind the welfare state rested rhetorically on this suturing of the Depression and the war together, of *patriotism* and *social need*, *national interest* and *common good*. In popular memory this rendition of the 1930s and 1940s became an especially effective and resonant narrative holding intact a coherent sense of Britishness after the war. Here, for instance, is the playwright Dennis Potter, in other respects the least sentimental of cultural critics:

> ...we were, at that time, both a brave and a steadfast people, and we shared an aim, a condition, a political aspiration if you like, which was shown immediately in the 1945 General Election, and then [in] one of the great governments of British history—those five, six years of creating what is now being so brutally and wantonly and callously dismantled was actually a period to be proud of, and I'm proud of it.[6]

The key here is far less any historical accuracy of Potter's description—the forms national history may actually have assumed during the 1940s or the actual record of the postwar Labour Government—than its plausible resonance for the affected postwar generations. *That* ground of cultural identification—less tangible than either the juridical weight of constitutions or the material benefits of welfare states—became crucial to the longlasting stabilities of the post-1945 settlements, supplying the necessary staying power that post-1918 democracies had patently lacked. Indeed, to grasp fully the resilience of the socio-political arrangements accompanying the defeat of fascism requires acknowledging precisely this cultural dimension. That means exploring the fields of popular identification the wartime experience brought into being, the complicated ways in which these became articulated to a postwar system of politics, the forms of legitimation they provided for the postwar state, and the support they delivered for one kind of politics as against another.

The forms of cohesion and stability in a society—and the conditions under which these may be effectively renewed—depend crucially on the forms of identification forged in popular memory and popular culture with that society's political institutions and the form of its state. For the twentieth century, the European transnational constitution-making conjunctures in the aftermaths of the two world wars were undoubtedly the key moments. In each case, the scale of societal mobilization, the radicalism of the institutional changes, and the turbulence of popular hopes all fractured the stability of existing allegiances and ripped the fabric of social conformity wide enough for big democratic changes to break through. But in the case of 1918, the forging of a new societal consensus around sufficiently strong popular loyalties to the democratic state proved uneven, fragile, and highly contested, as the political polarizations of the interwar years and the rise of fascism only too tragically confirmed. After 1945, in contrast,

[6] Dennis Potter, *Seeing the Blossom: Two Interviews and a Lecture* (London: Faber and Faber, 1994), 9.

the Western European consensus proved both broad and deep, engendering remarkably dense and resilient popular faith in the postwar social and political order.

This Western European postwar consensus lasted for two decades, subsisting on the doubled memories of war and Depression. Its boundaries were only reached generationally, as capitalist reconstruction, the long boom, and the consumer prosperity gradually changed the political landscape. By the 1960s, amid the resulting cultural tensions, the reflex of continuing to invoke the benefits of the postwar reforms seemed to a younger generation too much like complacency. Moreover, the new clash of generations became all the more painful when parents absolutized their own experience, wielding 'the blackmail of past hardships' in order to silence critiques of the present. As Alessandro Portelli remarks of the Italian version of this transition: 'Older generations, those that went through Fascism, war, Resistance, hard times in the factories, poverty, and the Depression, often think they have a monopoly on history and blackmail the younger generation with it'.[7] Thus for Gaetano Bordoni, a communist barber in San Lorenzo in Rome, his daughter's political complaining and dismissiveness towards hard-won material comforts only dishonoured his own generation's earlier anti-fascist sacrifices. As he put it:

> when I was ten years old, I carried a machine gun in the hills of Frosinone, along with my father, shooting it out…I mean, now at age ten you have a toy; I had a machine gun.

By leaving her steak uneaten on the dinner plate, Bordoni's daughter demeaned her father's life's meaning, Portelli argues, because material betterment was coupled in his mind with the winning of democracy. By dismissing material comforts as having nothing to do with 'freedom' and by 'calling for more radical forms of struggle, the younger generation questions both the achievements of the anti-Fascist struggle and the current politics of the working-class Left'.[8]

For the older generation, the Second World War had become *the* defining experience. In countries occupied by the Nazis (especially Italy and France), the anti-fascist legacies of the Resistance combined very powerfully with the reformist languages of reconstruction to make the prosperity of the 1960s feel like a final realizing of the promise of Liberation. In Italy, where workers had barely escaped from the extreme bleakness of the 1950s, the improving standards acquired extra emotional power. 'What was the image of socialism then [in the 1950s]? It was, Everybody eats. Food for all. At the time, that was the most urgent problem, rather than alienation, say, or man–machine relationships [the big issues of 1968].'[9] Britain was spared Nazi rule, and there the post-1945 welfare state and the wartime collectivism functioned in fully analogous ways.

---

[7] Alessandro Portelli, 'Luigi's Socks and Rita's Makeup: Youth Culture, the Politics of Private Life, and the Culture of the Working Classes,' in *The Battle of Valle Giulia: Oral History and the Art of Dialogue* (Madison, WI: University of Wisconsin Press, 1997), 241.

[8] Ibid., 243–4.

[9] Ibid., 240.

Postwar Social Democracy

What might be said more specifically about the form of the postwar settlement as it was actually realized after 1945? As already argued, any account has to begin from the massive constraints imposed by the Cold War on the European political imaginary between the late 1940s and our own time. Whether in the Soviet East or the capitalist West, the Cold War closed down any more radical possibilities glimpsed in 1945. By the summer of 1947, the sharpening of tensions between the USSR and the USA had defined a new period of conservative resurgence and capitalist consolidation for Western Europe, through which the hopes inspired by the resistance struggles during the moment of antifascist opportunity were now continuously scaled back. A complex dialectic was brought into play, through which the slow revival of indigenous conservatisms and international pressures continually reinforced one another, repeatedly breaching the autonomies of national arenas with the global determinations of the Cold War. The result was an unanticipated conservative normalizing whose consequences then defined the political landscape well into the 1960s. But in light of this resurgence, what had changed? What made the conservative Europe emerging from the 1940s *different* from the conservative Europe of the prewar? In what sense might the postwar settlement in Western Europe be called *social democratic*, even despite the return of conservatives to office?

In summarizing the coordinates of postwar reconstruction, I would make the following *five* points:

1. This was a key moment of pan-European constitution making, comparable to the earlier conjunctures of 1917–23, the 1860s, and the time of the great French Revolution. Western Europe saw a further strengthening of its liberal–democratic polities. Most notably, new constitutions were made in France (1946), Italy (1947), and West Germany (1949), each of which adopted republicanism, regionalism, nationalization and other forms of economic regulation, progressive taxation, and stronger protections for civil liberties. Of course, new constitutions were adopted in the People's Democracies of Eastern Europe too, building on the coalition governments formed with the Liberation between September 1944 and March 1945 (in Bulgaria, Romania, Hungary, Poland, and Czechoslovakia), but prospects for any democratic consolidation were quickly severed by the process of Stalinization.[10]

2. The postwar settlement included strong elements of nationalization and public ownership in the economy, organized around the legitimacy of a strong public sector, notions of the mixed economy, and the paramount necessity of planning.

3. The settlement reflected powerful commitments to social welfare and an active labour policy, decisively influenced by the memory of the Depression and shaped

---

[10] In Albania and Yugoslavia the Communist Parties had formed provisional governments much earlier, the former by creating the National Liberation Front in October 1944, the latter by proclaiming the provisional government as early as November 1943.

by the popular societal mobilizations of the war. *Collectivism*, as a complex amalgam of patriotism, national identification, public responsibilities, and public good, was the defining characteristic of this mood. It centred around the following policy areas, in varying configurations: (a) improved social security; (b) progressive taxation; (c) public health care; (d) housing programmes; (e) social and moral support for particular family forms; (f) trade union rights and recognition; and perhaps most important of all (g) full employment.

4. The settlement brought the integration of the Labour movement into the active life of the state, by means of trade union recognition, free collective bargaining, and the maintenance of civil liberties (always a key enabling condition for labour movements), including all the classic liberal freedoms that now properly entered the entailments of universal citizenship in western Europe for the first time. There was a major blot on this achievement after 1947, resulting from the exclusion and harassment of the Communist Parties, which at times extended to more generalized limits on civil freedoms. Here the Cold War licensed a severe compromising of democracy.

5. There were important moves towards transnational integration and European federation, via the initial impetus of Marshall Aid and the OEEC, reinforced by the division of Europe and the launching of NATO, and then through the Council of Europe (1949), and Franco–German economic cooperation leading to the Common Market in the Treaty of Rome (1957).[11]

Aside from re-securing constitutional democracy itself, the greatest single contrast with the aggregate circumstances of 1939 concerned the political legitimacy of labour. Not only had the labour *movements* moved to the centre of the political systems, but *labour itself* was now recognized as a social good. Here the postwar settlement registered a key transition from the classic liberal democratic principles of 1789—the sufficiency of political rights for freedom and liberty—towards the need for *social* democracy and the centrality of rights in the social and economic spheres. This brings us to the importance of the welfare state.

Here, the notion of *social citizenship* was a decisive breakthrough. An abstraction from the wartime collectivism and associated solidaristic models of society, this also drew on Christian socialist and Christian democratic ideals of social responsibility and

[11] The OEEC (Organisation for European Economic Cooperation) formed in April 1948 oversaw the disbursement of Marshall Aid through the ERP (European Recovery Program). Outlasting the Marshall Plan per se, it transmuted in 1960 into the OECD (Organisation for Economic Cooperation and Development), adding the USA and Canada to the original Western European members. Japan joined in 1964. The Council of Europe was created on 5 May 1949 by ten states (Belgium, Netherlands, Luxemburg, France, Britain, Ireland, Italy, Denmark, Norway, Sweden), joined by Greece and Turkey (1949), Iceland (1950), West Germany (1951), Austria (1956), Cyprus (1961), Switzerland (1963), and Malta (1965). It comprised a committee of ministers and a public consultative body, with permanent offices in Strasbourg. Though conceived more ambitiously for the promotion of European unity, its effectiveness was limited by British and Scandinavian reluctance.

the humanistic liberalism of many social policy and public health professionals reacting to the disasters of the Depression.[12] In Britain, where absence of Nazi occupation had permitted a relatively free public life, the practical egalitarianism of 'everyone pulling together' could become integral to the public rhetoric of the war itself, while for continental Europe such ideas were formed in the planning circles of resistance and exile. To exercise their democratic rights effectively, it was argued, people needed a minimum standard of living, because otherwise social inequalities would undermine citizenship in the vote. Political rights required complementing with a range of social rights too— the right to a job, to unemployment and sickness insurance, to old age pensions, to universally provided health care, to decent housing, to equal educational opportunity, to a minimum wage. All became established as entitlements during the process of postwar reform, remaining until the mid-1970s an accepted part of the political landscape. It was no accident that many of them were long-standing demands of European labour movements.

Women proved central to the welfare state legislation—as the objects of policy, as the subjects of the new socially inflected citizenship talk, and as addressees of political campaigns. Women were newly enfranchised in France, Italy, and Belgium, while elsewhere (West Germany, Austria) they regained the briefly held rights fascism had severed between the wars; only in Britain and Scandinavia did female suffrage have any longer continuity, dating from World War I. Women's economic mobilization also brought a sense of expectation, linking their wartime contribution to rhetoric of equality. As before, however, the resulting citizenship claims centred around maternity, and once again women's patriotic service made little difference to how policymaking became justified after the war. Pressure of returning soldiers for their old jobs, trade unions' longstanding maintenance of the gender bar, deep ideological assumptions regarding women's place, and the desire to rebuild society on the 'healthy' foundations of a reassembled familialism—all these factors re-masculinized the world of work and the public sphere, constructing for women a re-naturalized domestic future. Crude trends towards rising female employment prevented women from being straightforwardly returned to the home. But public languages certainly *imagined* them there. If women participated in the postwar romance of democracy, they did so on terms already familiar from the recharged gender regimes after 1918.

This proved one of the easiest fronts of normalization. In Catholic Europe, the resurgent right vigorously mobilized familial rhetoric of the most reactionary Christian kind. For the Italian DC the family was the battleground for reviving the nation after fascism and defending it against communism, a 'fortress' of established values. In West Germany the Christian Democrats made 'restoring' the family a central priority of postwar policy, reaffirming privacy, male prerogatives, female domesticity, and the sanctity of motherhood as the primary markers of de-nazification, the necessary bulwark against communism, and the bearer of the 'Christian occidental' tradition.

---

[12] See T. H. Marshall's classic work, *Citizenship and Social Class, and Other Essays* (Cambridge: Cambridge University Press, 1950).

Family policy became a key weapon in the Cold War, with 'totalitarian' control in the communist East an ever present figure of fear. In the West German constitution, legal equality (Article 3) was immediately negated by 'protection of the family' (Article 6), and despite the Constitutional Court's limited overriding of paternal authority in 1959 (qualifying the new Family Law of 1957), women became soldered into a narrow range of social opportunities, backed by the Law for the Protection of Mothers of 1952, which severely constrained married women's employment. Typically, the rival SPD rarely departed from these principles, as the nexus of 'a healthy economy, a self-supporting welfare state, large families, good mothers, and national vitality' was vital to the consensus of the 1950s.[13] The same applied in Britain, where the twin charters of welfare state innovation, the 1942 *Beveridge Report* and the 1944 *White Paper on Employment Policy*, shaped the 1946 legislation around the family as a male-headed economic unit with women located firmly inside the home. Even women's principal gain, family allowances paid directly to mothers, a main interwar feminist demand, reflected the maternalist assumptions.

Nonetheless, for Labour and SPD women (and activist women elsewhere) maternalist politics contested the male trade-unionist nostrum of the 'family wage' by addressing women's specific needs, and so was an emancipatory demand. As Moeller says, 'women's entry into the state should be measured less by their participation in electoral politics than by their direct involvement in advocating and promoting social welfare policies affecting families, maternity, and children's welfare', which certainly in its own way problematized the 'private/public divide and the separation of spheres'.[14]

This ambivalence of postwar reforms should be judged in a wider social field, recognizing both the limited but meaningful women's gains (whether constitutionally, or materially in the form of family allowances) and the underlying hegemony of the family form, into which women's futures were so potently subsumed. Women may have felt validated by the public recognition of mothering, in a vision of the 'equality of worth [which] acknowledges difference', as one SPD spokeswoman called it. But 'that vision was completely consistent with a legal order that fully legitimated a normative vision of the home as women's most important [domain]'.[15] Much rested on how exactly this balance was weighted, and the precise space allowed by the validation of maternal citizenship.

The language of rights and entitlements brought by social citizenship and the state's corrective agency made a climate conducive to other claims, and while later feminisms hardly descended directly from the postwar settlement, it contained important contradictions where they could work. The logics of feminist advocacy in the 1960s extended earlier arguments to the circumstances of women, for if effective citizenship required

---

[13] Robert G. Moeller, *Protecting Motherhood: Women and the Family in the Politics of Postwar West Germany* (Berkeley, CA: University of California Press, 1993), 214.

[14] Robert G. Moeller, 'The State of Women's Welfare in European Welfare States', *Social History* 19:3 (1994), 391.

[15] Moeller, *Protecting Motherhood*, 208–9. The SPD spokeswoman was Elisabeth Selbert.

legislative action for a series of social rights, then other affirmative action could easily follow—against *gender* as well as *class* inequalities, via equal pay, anti-discrimination laws, reproductive rights, and so forth. In a complex indirect manner, welfare state measures and citizenship reforms built up a language of rights and capacities that later radicalisms could also deploy.

Postwar reforms had a vital multivalent quality. Welfare state measures after 1945 were as much concerned with population policy and industrial modernization, with international competitiveness and national efficiency, as with social amelioration and democratic progress in any altruistic sense. Technocratic policies of economic and social reconstruction were also at issue—whether as social policies aimed at strengthening the family and securing social reproduction, maintaining a particular gender regime and the sexual division of labour, and promoting particular models of mass consumption, or as educational reforms servicing the needs of the changing economy for categories of skilled and unskilled labour. But it was precisely the ability to harmonize such functionalist arguments with the popular hopes of large social constituencies, and to combine capitalist prosperity with the reformist project of a Left political base, that gave the key to the stability of the new political arrangements in the Cold War realignment.

Patterns of Stability

If the Western European settlements shared a social democratic logic of collectivism, public goods, and social provision, that politics presented a striking paradox, as the new arrangements were often administered by solidly conservative governments. This implied convergence required a major reorientation, moving Conservatives and Christian Democrats away from an earlier die-hard intransigence onto a new ground of social reconstruction, corporatist pragmatics, and post-fascist democratic recognition. It was eased by a basic de-radicalizing of social democracy itself. After the immediate postwar moment, once the Cold War marked its boundary strictly against Communists and other radicals, socialist parties now shed their Marxist affiliations. Such ideas lived henceforth in the intellectual margins, some trade unions, and locally bounded subcultures. Social Democrats grew nervous about the class struggle and sceptical about transforming capitalism in any revolutionary or structural sense. The resulting social democratic presence revealed the following pattern:

1. unmediated dominance, as single governing social democratic parties won repeated elections on sustained programmes of structural reform, based on liberal democracy, the mixed economy, trade union corporatism, and a strong welfare state. This was the Scandinavian model of Sweden, Norway, and Denmark;
2. consensus government, where strong parties performed consistently highly in elections (20–45 per cent of the popular vote), and joined continuously in coalition governments, from complex institutionalized multi-party arrangements

(Switzerland, Finland, Iceland) to more pragmatic coalitions in the Benelux countries and a bilateral 'great coalition' in Austria. At a stretch, we might add France, where a weak socialist party joined 21 of 27 governments during 1944–58, but in centrist coalitions with minimal radical content. Similarly, the Labour Governments of 1945–51 reshaped the British political climate so effectively that its accomplishments outlasted Labour's ensuing period of continuous opposition in 1951–64;

3. permanent opposition, where strong parties found themselves blocked by the repeated election victories of a successful popular conservatism. The British Labour Party lost three consecutive elections on an enviably high vote, in 1951 (48.8 per cent), 1955 (46.4 per cent), and 1959 (43.8 per cent), while in contrast the West German SPD's support hovered at disappointingly low levels of 29.2 per cent (1949), 28.8 per cent (1953), and 31.8 per cent (1957). The much weaker Irish case may be added, where Labour was permanently marginalized by the nationalist political frame. In five elections during 1948–61 it attained a peak of only 12 per cent, in 1957;

4. decline and disarray, where socialists faced strong Communist Parties from a dwindling electoral base, vacillating between left-wing posturing to centrist accommodation. Examples were the PS/SFIO in France, whose popular vote dropped from 23.4 per cent of the total in 1945 to only 12.6 per cent in 1962; and the PSI in Italy, which between 1946 and 1958 declined from 20.7 per cent to 14.2 per cent;[16]

5. illegality in Spain, Portugal, and Greece, where functioning socialist parties only returned in the mid-1970s with the collapse of the dictatorships and the restoration of parliamentary democracy.

By successfully canalizing society's progressive aspirations, the strongest social democratic parties exercised hegemony over reform. For that to happen, several obstacles had to be absent. The rivalry of a mass Communist Party, the divisiveness of confessionalism or ethnolinguistic differences among the working class and its potential allies, and the persistence of a strong doctrinal tradition or revolutionary heritage could all impede the party's advance. Thus in Italy, France, Finland, and Iceland, communist strength severely capped the efficacy of the socialist parties concerned. Likewise, the Christian Democracies of Italy and Germany divided the national working class, if less persistently than such divisions in the Low Countries and Switzerland, where society's segmentation permanently constrained social democracy's popular appeal. Finally, during the 1950s the Marxist attachments of the SPD and some smaller parties like the Italian PSI compromised their ability to embrace the new self-limiting reformism.

Without such handicaps, the progress of social democracy then became much surer. Exercising sole or decisive predominance over the national Labour movement, with benefit of cultural homogeneity, and making a virtue of political eclecticism or doctrinal

---

[16] In 1958 the socialist vote could be augmented by the 4.5 per cent of the extremely right-wing PSDI (*Partito Socialista Democratico Italiano*).

flexibility, socialist parties laid convincing moral claim to the voice of 1945, rallying broader social coalitions around the Labour movement's central progressive project. This was pre-eminently true of the Labour Party in Britain, of the Social Democrats in Denmark, Norway, and Sweden, and of the Socialist Party in Austria. These were the only socialists consistently to break the 40 per cent electoral barrier in the years 1945–60.

The international situation was critical to this social democratic success. On the one hand, Marshall Aid decisively underpinned the reformist project in Britain; on the other hand, the strong electoral showing of Scandinavian Communists (10.3 per cent in Sweden in 1944, 12.5 per cent Denmark and 11.9 per cent in Norway in 1945) was abruptly wiped out by the Cold War. This double-edged action—the economics of Marshall Aid, the politics of anti-communism—decisively solidified the postwar settlement elsewhere. By 1945 liberal democratic constitutionalism was already shaping political expectations, pulling Communists no less than Social Democrats away from the participatory experiments so key to 1917–23, for which anti-fascist resistance again offered fertile ground. When the Cold War properly began, and Stalin hauled Communists back to a language of proletarian dictatorship and soviets, this sanctifying of parliamentarism once more marked the decisive schism in the Left. As Europe divided—inside individual societies, no less than geopolitically—collective defence of 'the West' became essential to social democracy's identifying vocabulary, changing the valency of internationalist appeals. Henceforth, both European integration and European assertiveness overseas became harnessed to the cohesion of the Western political community of the Cold War. Ernest Bevin notably committed the Labour Party to a very traditional policy of imperial defence. Via the viciously repressive late-colonial wars accompanying decolonization in Africa and Asia, the French Socialists too took a prominent role. In 1946 Guy Mollet led the SFIO in the name of 'that fundamental reality, the class struggle'; but as head of government during 1956–57 treated the Algerian and other liberation movements with draconian repression, not to speak of the disastrous Suez adventure.[17] This compromising of old socialist principles, all too predictable during the 1950s, was inscribed in the anti-communist option: the most fundamental cleavage was between those socialists aligning themselves with NATO, and those on the Left who did not.

The thinking behind the Marshall Plan had a partially explicated social dimension, attached to a modernizing package of high productivity, high wages, redistributive taxation, and mass consumption.[18] Where this strategy encountered a militant indigenous labour movement led by Communists, as in Italy and Greece, it clashed with the Truman Doctrine's simultaneous anti-communist priorities, and consequently gave

---

[17] Guy Mollet (1905–75), the schoolteacher son of a weaver, was Secretary-General of the PS (SFIO) from 1946–69, and led the party to its sordid demise. He served in five governments between 1946 and 1958, becoming Prime Minister from 1956–57, during one of the several low points of postwar French politics.

[18] This emerges strongly from Michael J. Hogan, *The Marshall Plan: America, Britain, and the Reconstruction of Western Europe, 1947–1952* (Cambridge: Cambridge University Press, 1987).

way. On the other hand, where the Communist Party (CP) was successfully marginal-ized, and the national labour movement securely social democratic and linked to broader middle-class progressivism, as in Britain, the Low Countries, and Scandinavia, Marshall's social purposes worked with the grain of an indigenous reformism, making the resulting settlement quite robust. If far less radical than the wartime anti-fascism, this new convergence of international and national developments still sustained a via-ble reformism in parts of Western Europe, notably theorized into social democracy's historic opportunity.

Keynesianism, a summary term for the range of counter-cyclical proposals for a polit-ically regulated capitalism that coalesced between the later 1930s and the end of the war, gave the key to this social democratic agenda.[19] On this basis, the implied social contract of 1945, rewarding popular patriotism with democracy and social justice, could be attained without attacking the fundamental legitimacy of capitalism as the source of future prosperity. The interests of capital would be guaranteed by national economic management, social peace, and rising productivity; the people would be served by full employment, rising incomes, expanding social services, and the government's commit-ment to social equality.

The guarantors of this Keynesian welfare state arrangement were the national trade-union leaders, who, epitomized by Ernest Bevin as British Minister of Labour (1940–5), had emerged to broker their members' productivity and discipline. Industrial relations were another key site of the settlement: a leading section of the working class—organ-ized, skilled or semi-skilled, usually male—won unprecedented economic security, based not only on full employment and rising real wages, but also on a new shop floor self-respect. Organized workers' political loyalty became embedded in new workplace relations, bringing trade-union recognition, legally established seniority and demarca-tion rules, job protections, fringe benefits, and the constraining of management's power in production, all secured by a national system of negotiations between employers and unions backed by the state. In return, management could invest in higher productivity, including new machinery, new plant, new divisions of labour, and new techniques of production, without union disruptions or challenges to its right of control. The produc-tion line became more common, with cars as the classic industry. This new factory regime—high wages, absence of strikes, guaranteed shop-floor discipline, high produc-tivity—would potentially feed a new era of consumer-oriented prosperity, freeing prof-its from the old bugbear of labour movement challenges to the nature of the system.

At the apex of this system was the state. Postwar labour relations depended on a cor-poratist political triangulation: through its national trade-union federation the organ-ized working class won tangible economic benefits and political influence; capital won the space to pursue a new accumulation strategy based on *Fordism*, meaning workplace-

---

[19] I am using the term in a loose and summary way to encompass the range of macroeconomic policy innovations aimed at producing both regularized economic growth and social stabilty on the basis of full employment, some of which (as in Sweden) originated independently of John Maynard Keynes himself.

focused deals combining high wages, productivity, and a modernized labour process, linked to the promise of consumer driven growth; and the state won a new role for itself as the overseer of this large-scale societal deal. At the level of the economy as a whole, this corporatism was held together partly by national systems of consultation and negotiation between all three partners (government, employers, unions), and partly by the Keynesian system of demand management that claimed to have eliminated mass unemployment as the unacceptable face of capitalism. In economic terms, it produced a system of 'reform or managed capitalism', which held a central place for the organized working class, but had little to do with socialism as such.

The axiomatic belief in an assured future of *economic growth* anchored this entire Keynesian welfare state package, making the rapprochement of labour and capital feasible in the first place:

> With growth it was possible to envisage a continuous increase in welfare spending and the incomes of working-class people without either having to raise income tax to punitive levels or to reduce the real living standards of the middle and property-owning class.[20]

This was indeed an unprecedented period of expansion, a long capitalist boom that drastically shifted most social and political thought. The period's economic orthodoxies reflected a self-conscious rejection of the interwar past. Reconstruction was linked for most non-socialist decision makers to capitalism's recovery of political legitimacy in this sense, to its capacity for restructuring in global and national ways. On the one hand, a renewed disintegration of the world economy into protectionist national units or empires had become unthinkable, so the trading and fiscal system was to be globalized through US-brokered arrangements like the World Bank and IMF descending from the 1944 Bretton Woods Agreements. On the other hand, public planning and the 'mixed economy' were essential domestically to allow free enterprise to do its work. High levels of government intervention could now be tolerated, assuring a healthy economic and political future through full employment and the continuous growth of disposable incomes—through a 'democratizing of the market', in Hobsbawm's phrase.[21] Capitalism was to be regulated, rationalized by a set of compelling political imperatives:

> ...if the economic memory of the 1930s was not enough to sharpen [the] appetite for reforming capitalism, the fatal political risks of not doing so were patent to all who had just fought Hitler's Germany, the child of the Great Slump, and were confronted with the prospect of Communism and Soviet power advancing westwards across the ruins of capitalist economies that did not work.[22]

---

[20] William E. Paterson and Alastair H. Thomas, 'Introduction', in Paterson and Thomas (eds), *The Future of Social Democracy. Problems and Prospects of Social Democratic Parties in Western Europe* (Oxford: Oxford University Press, 1986), 4.

[21] Hobsbawm, *Age of Extremes*, 269.

[22] Ibid., 271.

The encounter with this socially rationalized, politically regulated capitalist recovery incited Social Democrats into remarkable optimism, guided not (as in the past) by a conviction in the inevitable capitalist collapse, but by the humanized viability of a prosperous capitalist future. 'Traditionally socialist thought has been dominated by the economic problems posed by capitalism, poverty, mass unemployment, squalor, instability, and even the possibility of the collapse of the whole system', Anthony Crosland argued. But now these perspectives could be decisively revised:

> Capitalism had been reformed out of all recognition. Despite occasional minor recessions and balance of payments crises, full employment and at least a tolerable degree of stability are likely to be maintained. Automation can be expected steadily to solve any remaining problems of under-production. Looking ahead, our present rate of growth will give us a national output three times as high in fifty years.[23]

Moreover, beyond the impact of the postwar economy's sustained growth, the structural reforms of the immediate postwar years had also survived, for the conservative governments dominating non-Scandinavian north-western Europe during the 1950s made few efforts to roll back the fundamental features of the settlement. This situation encouraged non-Marxist socialists to overhaul their underlying analysis. The slow betterment of the standard of living, accelerating after 1960 into a full-blown consumer economy, had its counterpart in the structural growth of the service sector and the upward mobility of non-manual workers with secondary and higher educational qualifications, not least in expanding public employment. In short, the Keynesian formula—'economic growth in a capitalist economy based on the mass consumption of a fully employed and increasingly well-paid and well-protected labour force', backed by the postwar welfare state—produced a major de-radicalizing of the social democratic imagination.[24]

Of course, the arrival of prosperity was neither universal nor evenly spread, whether inside societies or in overall national performance. Unemployment dropped below four per cent in West Germany only in the late 1950s, and in Italy after 1960, whereas in Britain, Sweden, and the Netherlands it kept that level throughout 1945–60 and was usually much lower. But socialist strategists soon saw the revisionist logic, accepting the permanence of prosperity as an appealing substitute for the older goal of abolishing capitalism, for which in any case they had no plan. The Cold War and the political community of NATO were crucial to this choice, and the postwar social changes now heightened the pressure for a more consistent redesigning of the socialist appeal. The rhetoric of revolution, certainly as a model of insurrectionary politics or confrontational challenge to existing state power, had long receded, but the engagement with extra-parliamentary arenas and activism (whether through local government, workplace democracy, or direct action and the mass strike), however vestigial, now too disappeared. The languages of class, with their assumption of structural and irreconcilable conflicts of interest in the

---

[23] Anthony Crosland, *The Future of Socialism* (London: Cape, 1956), 517, cited in Hobsbawm, *Age of Extremes*, 268.

[24] Ibid., 282.

economy, grounded in the exploitative wage relation, were increasingly discarded. New strategists called for a fundamental shift of priorities—away from the primary interests and agency of the working class, and towards the continuing transformations of the class structure and a broader social coalition of support. Instead of the class struggle, revisionists focused wholly on elections and the ideal of a 'people's party' garnering all manner of social support.

The SPD's Godesberg Programme, adopted at its 1959 congress, became a benchmark for this 'modernizing' approach. All talk of the end of capitalism disappeared, as did the Marxist affiliations, and indeed the very mention of the word 'socialism' itself. Remaining was the desire to govern by winning an election. The promise of the mixed economy, with its architecture of welfare state, full employment, and strong public sector, reconciled Social Democrats to the essentials of private ownership and control. By the 1960s, this stance wholly dominated the British Labour Party, the socialist parties of the Low Countries and France, the SPD, and the social democracies of Scandinavia, where it was presaged in the demand management strategies and welfare initiatives of the 1930s. The push towards this programmatic embrace was completed by the conservative political logic of the Cold War, for outside Scandinavia, Western Europe was governed not by Social Democrats themselves, but by their conservative enemies. If Social Democrats shaped the Keynesian and welfare-statist underpinnings of the settlement, it was conservatives who reaped the political benefits. Parties like Labour and the SPD found themselves once again in opposition, sustaining the postwar consensus from without. Moreover, neither the thirteen years of Conservative rule in Britain (1951–64), nor the seventeen years of the 'CDU state' in West Germany (1949–66), could have worked without trade union cooperation. In light of so much consensus, traditional socialist analysis lost its traction. Labour and the SPD cleaved strongly to the centrist ground, stressing their commonalities with conservatives rather than older differences that kept them apart.

Yet the *strongest* case of the Keynesian welfare state synthesis, where things took explicitly social democratic form, with socialists in the driving seat, was Sweden. Structural particularities of Swedish capitalism and working-class formation conjoined with the crucial enabling conditions mentioned above (a united labour movement without communist competition, cultural homogeneity, doctrinal flexibility) to open the way. Postwar social democracy's three pillars—Keynesianism, welfare state, corporatism—made an integral unity, shaped by a certain quality of leadership into a vision of societal transformation lacking elsewhere. The basic corporatist trade-off—wage restraint in the interests of economic reconstruction, matched by welfare reforms and full employment—was actually delivered upon by the SAP, allowing Swedish workers to see the state as their own, with more than just rising real wages at stake. That moral–political loyalty became skillfully extended by the SAP in the late 1950s and 1960s towards the white-collar and professional middle classes. Apart from fellow Scandinavians, no other socialists attained quite the sustained national leadership, governmental competence, humane political values, and strategic understanding of the SAP during its long ascendancy between 1932 and 1976.

Social Democrats in most of Europe had abandoned thoughts of abolishing capitalism. Radical factions remained, but mostly among intellectuals or in some localities or sections of youth, with small chance of capturing their movements. Socialists placed their faith in economic growth, industrial prosperity, rising living standards, and a time when 'ideological questions' and the 'class struggle' no longer applied. Maintaining full employment, reducing inequality by progressive taxation and social reform, improving life chances via education and social services, making society generally more humane— such goals dispensed with critiques of the structural bases of capitalism or the existing parliamentary state. Social Democrats could still credit themselves with the settlement's reforming accomplishments. But outside Scandinavia they were now watching mainly from opposition. This was a far cry from the mood of only ten years before. At the birth of the British wartime coalition, in a speech before 2000 union leaders on 25 May 1940, Ernest Bevin (newly appointed Minister of Labour) affirmed the unity of socialism and patriotism in the promise of a corporative Labour-dominated future:

> I have to ask you virtually to place yourselves at the disposal of the state. We are Socialists and this is the test of our Socialism. It is the test whether we have meant the resolutions which we have so often passed…If our Movement and our class rise with all their energy now and save the people of this country from disaster, the country will always turn with confidence to the people who saved them…And the people are conscious at this moment that they are in danger.[25]

In realizing that promise, '1945' endowed an ethic of collectivism that resonated politically for another three decades. But the larger vision of exercising moral–political leadership of the nation to accomplish more basic anti-capitalist change had gone.

CONCLUSION

This discussion has focused on the postwar settlement in the West, giving little attention either to the dictatorships of the Mediterranean or to the Soviet-style societies of the East. But there are certainly ways in which eastern Europe might be included. Without the unforgiving juggernaut of Stalinization, anti-fascist optimism might easily have sustained a more coercively centralist version of the Keynesian–welfarist policies discussed above, however dangerously beholden to increasingly top-down communist rule. The People's Democracies also rested sociologically on the brute egalitarianism of a recognizable social contract. During 1948–53 in Czechoslovakia 'an estimated 200,000 to 400,000 workers were promoted from the shopfloor into state administration: in the economy, but more particularly in the army and the police'. Across Eastern Europe the promise of social mobility via education and jobs gave the socialist regimes a fund of

---

[25] Keith Middlemas, *Politics in Industrial Society: The Experience of the British System since 1911* (London: Deutsch, 1979), 275.

legitimacy among workers.[26] By the 1960s those economies were delivering jobs, heavily subsidized food, clothing, housing, and transportation, and access to health care and schools, even if inefficiencies notoriously undermined those relative goods. At far lower levels, and without the 1960's intoxicating take-off into consumption, communist rule relied on this operative social contract of the social minimum and the welfare state, linked to higher wages, cheap food, and social recognition.

Of course, what fundamentally distinguished the settlements in the two parts of the continent was Stalinism's violent and pervasive machinery of repression. This darkest side of the Cold War bleakly qualifies the general European story of improvement and reform. In addition to the stain of Stalinism, two other histories heavily relativize the optimism of that account: on the one hand, the disordering flux of displaced and migrating peoples strewn across Europe's geography by war's end; on the other hand, decolonization and the ending of Europe's direct rule over other parts of the world.

The final stages of war found some 23 million Europeans stranded and subject to the vicissitudes of territorial changes and repatriation. As Europe's bedraggled peoples began resuming their barely remembered or attainable lives, postwar social relations and public mores became vitally shaped by the challenge of integrating this literally un-homed population. It included the many categories of refugees, camp inmates, and DPs who ended up staying where they were marooned; migrant workers recruited from inside and outside Europe's borders; POWs and other returnees; repatriated populations of various kinds; German, Italian, Polish, and Ukrainian expellees; and the special case of orphaned and evacuated children.

This disordering of Europe's settled demography gave postwar circumstances an exceptional quality ('violent peacetime', in Peter Gatrell's arresting phrase) that left displaced civilians particularly vulnerable to coercion, whether from the reconstituted national governments and the inter-Allied occupying regimes, or the wider machinery of professional expertise and relief arrangements organized through charitable, semi-official, and voluntary organizations.[27] During 1945–50, 12.5 million German speakers were expelled from Poland, Czechoslovakia, and elsewhere in Eastern Europe in a torrent of dispossession and ethnic homogenization that left the beneficiary populations heavily beholden to the presiding postwar regimes, while making the expellees themselves a significant constituency in their newly acquired homeland.[28] For these large

---

[26] Jacques Rupnik, 'The Roots of Czech Stalinism', in Raphael Samuel and Gareth Stedman Jones (eds), *Culture, Ideology and Politics: Essays for Eric Hobsbawm* (London: Routledge, 1983), 312; also Padraic Kenney, *Rebuilding Poland: Workers and Communists, 1945–1950* (Ithaca, NY: Cornell University Press, 1997).

[27] See Peter Gattrell, 'Trajectories of Population Displacement in the Aftermath of Two World Wars', in Jessica Reinisch (ed.), *The Disentanglement of Populations: Migration, Expulsion and Displacement in Post-War Europe, 1944–1949* (London: Palgrave Macmillan, 2010), 3–26.

[28] See Pertti Ahonen, *After the Expulsion: West Germany and Eastern Europe 1945–1990* (Oxford: Oxford University Press, 2003), 20–1; Philipp Ther and Ana Siljak (eds), *Redrawing Nations: Ethnic Cleansing in East-Central Europe, 1944–1948* (Oxford: Rowman and Littlefield, 2001).

anomalous populations, claiming citizenship in the postwar settlement was a complex process.

The largest category of migrants excluded over the longer term from the settlement's social goods were not forcibly displaced refugees but workers drawn into Western Europe by its attractive labour market. The major post-colonial immigrations—from the West Indies and South Asia to Britain; from North Africa, the Caribbean, and West Africa to France; from Surinam to the Netherlands—occurred only from the 1960s. Until that time West Germany, the Low Countries, France, and Switzerland met their labour needs from southern Europe (Italy, Spain, and Portugal), expanding later towards Greece, Turkey, Yugoslavia, and North Africa. Typically, the flow became regularized via bilateral agreements—in the Dutch case with Italy (1960), Spain (1961), Portugal (1963), Turkey (1964), Greece (1966), Morocco (1969), Yugoslavia (1970), and Tunisia (1970); or in West Germany with Italy (1955), Spain (1960), Greece (1960), Turkey (1961), Morocco (1963), Portugal (1964), Tunisia (1965), and Yugoslavia (1968).[29] The social citizenship of the working-class majority in each of these countries—their job security, higher wages and greater benefits, access to health care and housing, expectation of pensions, protections under the law—always presupposed this mobile, insecure, low-waged, and unprotected Mediterranean reservoir of cheap and disposable labour power. It also presumed a variable history of colonialism in the larger than European world, which after 1945 had begun its long and violent descent into decolonization. This, too, was a profoundly damaging handicap on the social goods of the settlement.

Europe's relations with the non-western world cast those goods in a sobering light. For this Western European experience of relatively humanized capitalism was no less beholden to globalized systems of exploitation of natural resources, human materials, and grotesquely unequal terms of trade than the preceding era of imperialist expansion. Social democratic gains were embedded in the privileged prosperity of a metropolitan boom whose very possibility rested on historically specific repertoires of extraction and exploitation operating on a world scale. Moreover, while histories of capitalism are customarily presented as a progressive story of industrialization centred around a particular model of social development and working-class formation, it becomes increasingly clear that the presumed centrality of waged work in manufacturing and extractive industry has proven a transitory rather than a permanent feature. It was extremely particular to the roughly 150 years between the British and Belgian industrializations and the dismantling of manufacturing economies in the 1970s and 1980s. The socially valued forms of organized labour prevalent after 1945, still more the redistributive vision of a regulated capitalism celebrated by Crosland, stand revealed as a finite and exceptional project. At ever-accelerating pace, the social relations of work have been transformed since the 1980s into the new low-waged, semi-legal, and deregulated labour market of

---

[29] For a full survey of the Western European labour migrancy, see Geoff Eley, 'The Trouble with "Race": Migrancy, Cultural Difference, and the Remaking of Europe', in Rita Chin, Heide Fehrenbach, Geoff Eley, and Atina Grossmann, *After the Nazi Racial State: Difference and Democracy in Germany and Europe* (Ann Arbor, MI: University of Michigan Press, 2009), 155–60.

a mainly service-based and transnationalized economy. This de-skilling, de-unionizing, de-benefiting, and de-nationalizing of labour via the rampant processes of metropolitan deindustrialization and global capitalist restructuring has comprehensively undermined the model of corporatism around which so much of the postwar settlement was built.

This *reproletarianizing* of labour radically relativizes the post-1945 changes. To contemporaries, postwar reconstruction seemed the forecourt to an indefinitely unfolding future of economic growth, social prosperity, and social peace. Labour had won unprecedented legitimacy in the life of the state, both collectively organized and socially valued via unions, public policy, the wider common sense, and the acceptable ethics of a society's shared collective life. Yet from a vantage point in the early 2000s, that appears more as a passing interlude in the life of capitalist social formations whose ordering principles look very different over the fullest span of their history. From the mid-1970s, every element in the democratizing architecture of the post-1945 settlement—planning, full employment, social services for all, redistributive taxation, recognition of unions, public schooling, collectivist ideals of social improvement, a general ethic of public good—was brought under brutally effective political attack. By the 1990s, little remained of either the practices or the principles, let alone the material structures and institutional architecture, that organized the political common sense of the three decades after 1945.

The social contract binding the Keynesian–welfarist synthesis together was gone. Instead the post-communist era now brought compelling evidence of a radically stripped-down version of the labour contract. New forms of the exploitation of labour relentlessly accumulated around the expanding prevalence of minimum wage, unqualified and unskilled, disorganized and deregulated, semi-legal, and migrant labour markets, in which livelihoods are systematically stripped of precisely those forms of security and organized protection that the politics of anti-fascist reconstruction had sought centrally to instate. In those terms, the postwar settlement described a remarkably brief segment of European time.

FURTHER READING

Bessel, Richard and Dirk Schumann (eds), *Life after Death: Approaches to the Cultural and Social History of Europe during the 1940s and 1950s* (Cambridge: Cambridge University Press, 2003).

Chin, Rita, Heide Fehrenbach, Geoff Eley and Atina Grossmann, *After the Nazi Racial State: Difference and Democracy in Germany and Europe* (Ann Arbor, MI: University of Michigan Press, 2009).

Conway, Martin, Peter Romijn, et al., *The War on Legitimacy in Politics and Culture, 1936–1946* (Oxford: Berg, 2008).

Davis, Belinda, 'What's Left? Popular and Democratic Political Participation in Postwar Europe', *American Historical Review* 113:2 (2008), 363–90.

Eley, Geoff, *Forging Democracy: The History of the Left in Europe, 1850–2000* (New York: Oxford University Press, 2002).

Eley, Geoff, 'When Europe was New: Liberation and the Making of the Postwar', in Monica Riera and Gavin Schaffer (eds), *The Lasting War: Society and Identity in Britain, France and Germany after 1945* (Basingstoke: Palgrave Macmillan, 2008), 17–43.

Gillingham, John, *European Integration, 1950–2003: Superstate or New Market Economy?* (Cambridge: Cambridge University Press, 2003).

Hogan, Michael J., *The Marshall Plan: America, Britain, and the Reconstruction of Western Europe, 1947–1952* (Cambridge: Cambridge University Press, 1987).

Horn, Gerd-Rainer and Emmanuel Gerard (eds), *Left Catholicism 1943–1955: Catholics and Society in Western Europe at the Point of Liberation* (Leuven: Leuven University Press, 2001).

Judt, Tony, *Postwar: A History of Europe since 1945* (New York: Penguin Press, 2005).

Lebow, Richard Ned, Wulf Kansteiner and Claudio Fogu (eds), *The Politics of Memory in Postwar Europe* (Durham, NC: Duke University Press, 2006).

Pittaway, Mark, *Eastern Europe 1939–2000* (London: Bloomsbury, 2004).

Therborn, Göran, *European Modernity and Beyond: The Trajectory of European Societies 1945–2000* (London: Sage Publications, 1995).

CHAPTER 2

··

INTERWAR, WAR, POSTWAR: WAS THERE A ZERO HOUR IN 1945?

··

RICHARD OVERY

'Personal liberty, presumably, will be gone from Continental Europe for at least a generation; for obviously the existing chaos cannot be controlled except by an iron tyranny...'

Aldous Huxley, 7 May 1945[1]

WHEN the Second World War ended in Europe—there were still a little over three months of bitter fighting left in the war against Japan—there were many like Aldous Huxley who assumed that the sheer level of destruction, hatred, and fear unleashed by the conflict would produce a Europe even worse than the one they recalled from the 1930s. Only in Germany was the moment captured linguistically in the concept of *Stunde Null*, hour zero, for the German population almost certainly expected the worst from the catastrophic defeat of Hitler's Reich.[2] They knew there was no going back to the interwar years. Observers then and since were struck by the capacity of ordinary Germans to live in 1945 and its immediate aftermath as if in a permanent present, an obsession with what Richard Bessel has described as the 'day-to-day struggle for existence', the here and now.[3]

It is not difficult to understand the response in Germany to the reality of defeat in 1945. It clearly brought down a curtain on a particular period in Germany's history that

[1] Grover Smith (ed.), *Letters of Aldous Huxley* (London: Chatto & Windus, 1969), 520, letter from Huxley to Hermann Broch, 7 May 1945.

[2] The term *Stunde Null* is often rendered as 'zero hour' but this English form has another meaning and does not sufficiently convey the idea, implicit in the term 'hour zero', that this was a point caught precisely between two moments: a past that had disappeared and a future that was as yet unshaped.

[3] Richard Bessel, *Germany 1945: From War to Peace* (London: HarperCollins, 2009), 6.

could be dated back to the nationalist and imperial aspirations prior to 1914. As soon as the war ended, sometimes sooner, Germans who had been enthusiasts for the Third Reich tried to distance themselves from association with it or to escape altogether from its historical clutches. Not all of them were as unfortunate as the character in Günter Grass's *The Tin Drum*, who tried to swallow his Party badge and chokes to death, but the metaphor was an apt one.

In Germany in 1945 the past melted away almost overnight. In Berchtesgaden a young girl observed her mother remove a wax relief portrait of Hitler from the wall in early May 1945, place it in a pot over the stove and watch it dissolve, leaving no trace of the disgraced leader.[4] The victorious Allies also wanted to eradicate the memory and the physical presence of the Third Reich, but much of the German population practised a self-imposed censorship of their recent past. There was a widespread recognition that there was no going back to the old Germany. A captured German admiral, bugged by his captors, was overheard explaining this reality to his fellow-prisoners:

> I can't help thinking that once the enemy is on German soil the whole German tradition—the marching up and down, the rolling of drums—will be a thing of the past. No more parades, no more shouting—it's difficult to imagine a Germany like that. We were so used to the old Germany.[5]

This was also Hitler's anxiety shortly before his suicide, when he told his deputy, Martin Bormann, that he could not contemplate living through the 'transition period' following Germany's defeat.[6]

When the Allies arrived in Germany, they were uncertain about what might be the reaction of the population. Plans were prepared against a possible insurgency, and hundreds of thousands of Germans who had been in the National Socialist Party or one of its ancillary associations, including the League of German Girls and the Women's Association, were put in camps and prisons. In the Soviet zone of occupation, 122,671 passed through Special Camp No. 1 for fascist prisoners, of whom 42,889 died in captivity. In the American zone in south-central Germany the Counter-Intelligence Corps had arrested 117,500 people by the end of 1945; the British interned 100,000, the French 21,500.[7] It was the intention of the Allies, confirmed in the founding meeting of the United Nations in San Francisco in May 1945, to hold trials of those defined as major war criminals so that the wider international community (and those Germans still ignorant of them) would be able to see the nature of the Third Reich's crimes and to understand that a new age of international justice had dawned in 1945.

---

[4] Irmgard Hunt, *On Hitler's Mountain: My Nazi Childhood* (London: Atlantic Books, 2005), 236.

[5] Library of Congress, Washington DC, Eaker papers, I/30, intelligence sector Mediterranean Allied Air Forces, 'What is the German Saying?' [n.d. but late 1944], conversation of a German Rear-Admiral captured at Toulon, 28 August 1944.

[6] François Genoud (ed.), *The Testament of Adolf Hitler: The Hitler-Bormann Documents* (London: Cassell, 1961), 104, entry for 2 April 1945.

[7] Achim Kilian, *Einzuweisen zur völligen Isolierung NKWD-Speziallager Mühlberg/Elbe 1945–1948* (Leipzig: Forum, 1993), 7; Bessel, *Germany 1945*, 186–7.

There were evident ambiguities in this endeavour to create a new basis for penalizing war and political violence. Problems were raised by the presence of the Soviet Union as one of the prosecuting powers, also responsible for aggressive war and crimes against humanity, but these were not confronted by the Western powers. Bombing of civilians was not finally included in the indictment drawn up by the International Military Tribunal and confirmed in August 1945, since this had been a central feature of Western strategy and could not now be admitted to have been a crime. The trials were intended to go far beyond the twenty-one major criminals who sat in the dock in the Nuremberg court house on 20 November 1945. At Nuremberg there were twelve trials in all, involving 184 senior military, bureaucratic, industrial, and medical personnel.[8] In total the American occupation authorities tried 1600 people in 489 trials. In addition, there were a great many trials conducted by the German judicial authorities, reaching a total of 24,000 hearings in the British zone alone. Most of these were designed to confirm the defendants as active members of the National Socialist movement and subsequently to remove them from office and withdraw their voting rights. The overwhelming bulk of the 3.66 million German citizens who were subjected to 'de-Nazification' procedures were not prosecuted. But the whole process of reviewing, prosecuting, and punishing those deemed responsible for the regime's crimes was designed to place a distance between the pre-1945 world of racial violence and political oppression, and a new post-1945 world of democratic decency.[9]

For the German population the most visible line drawn under their past was the massive destruction of the urban environment through more than four years of Allied bombing. The obliteration of around one-half of the city area in Germany (and the widespread and random destruction meted out to many smaller towns and villages) helped to underpin the metaphorical sense of social and political reconstruction with an enforced physical programme of rebuilding. Indeed, it was the most obvious way in which the German people could help to create a new social environment for themselves and to focus on the future rather than the past. The Nuremberg city council was so successful at doing this that no objections were sustained against the decision to use stones from the demolished Jewish synagogue to build a monument to the city's bomb victims.[10]

The harrowing conditions of life imposed on millions of German city dwellers in the years after the end of the war meant that for many of them moving forwards was the only option. The physical loss of possessions, homes, and social networks made the search for the immediate past fruitless and the reconstruction of a different life unavoidable. In the decade after 1945 the initial term 'rebuilding' [*Wiederaufbau*] came to be replaced by the

---

[8] On the trials, see Donald Bloxham, *Genocide on Trial: War Crimes Trials and the Formation of Holocaust History and Memory* (Oxford: Oxford University Press, 2001).

[9] Norbert Frei, *Adenauer's Germany and the Nazi Past: The Politics of Amnesty and Integration* (New York: Columbia University Press, 2002), 9, 38–9; see too Konrad Jarausch, *After Hitler: Recivilizing Germans, 1945–1995* (New York: Oxford University Press, 2006), 46–55.

[10] Neil Gregor, *Haunted City: Nuremberg and the Nazi Past* (New Haven, CT: Yale University Press, 2008), 175–7.

concept of 'new construction' [*Neubau*], as a more authentic reflection of the process involved. More than two-thirds of the urban built environment in Germany was constructed after 1948.[11]

Political circumstances also accentuated the sense of a new beginning. The divisions that opened up between the Allied victors in the three years after 1945 created circumstances that made it impossible to restore a single unitary German state, even one shorn of its acquisitions after 1933 and reduced in size by the allocation of Prussian territory to the reconstituted state of Poland. The Western zones of occupation were needed as a bulwark against the further advance of Soviet communism; the Soviet zone was needed by the Soviet Union as a model of a 'progressive' Germany, linked with the other peoples' democracies in Eastern Europe in a defensive rampart against Western capitalism.

The remodelling of the political geography of Germany and Germans was completed with the forced expulsion of millions of ethnic Germans from Central and Eastern Europe during 1945–8. Around 13 million arrived in the zones of occupation, the overwhelming majority in the Western zones. This was a substantial fraction of the German population. Like the bombed populations, they had in many cases lost everything and had to begin from scratch. The Germany they entered was very different from the German Fatherland that had welcomed back German settlers in the war years to satisfy Himmler's fantasies of the racial reconstruction of the continent.

The Cold War and racial realities of Europe between 1945 and 1949 contributed to the idea that the two German states created in 1949, the Federal Republic in the West and the Democratic Republic in the East, were new experiments in democratic politics quite distinct from the legacy of a united Germany since 1871. There were, of course, evident continuities between the old Germany and the two new states, but it was difficult not to view the state-building in 1949 as a fresh trajectory and to see 1945 as a very real break with the German past. Historians have generally colluded with that view.[12] Very few books focus on German issues that cross the war period. Even Daniel Goldhagen, whose polemical book, *Hitler's Willing Executioners*, published in 1996, posited the idea that Germans had all been affected by a culturally embedded desire to eliminate the Jews that could be traced back centuries, argued that after 1945 German anti-Semitism evaporated in a wave of psychological reconstruction. This perception of a caesura in Germany's most damaging historical trend perhaps helps to explain the decision in 1997 to award Goldhagen the triennial 'Democracy Prize' of the *Blätter für deutsche und internationale Politik*.

---

[11] Jeffrey Diefendorf, *In the Wake of War: The Reconstruction of German Cities after World War II* (New York: Oxford University Press, 1993), xvii–xviii; Hartwig Beseler and Niels Gutschow (eds), *Kriegsschicksale Deutscher Architektur: Verluste-Schäden-Wiederaufbau*, 2 vols (Neumünster: Karl Wachlotz, 1988), I, xxxvii.

[12] See for example Mary Fulbrook, *The People's State: East German Society from Hitler to Honeker* (New Haven, CT: Yale University Press, 2008); Klaus Larres and Panikos Panayi (eds), *The Federal Republic of Germany since 1949* (London: Longman, 1996); Jan Palmowski, *Inventing a Socialist Nation: Heimat and the Politics of Everyday Life in the GDR, 1945–90* (Cambridge: Cambridge University Press, 2009).

Elsewhere in Europe also there was a powerful expectation that 1945 heralded a new age. The English peace campaigner Ruth Fry published privately a small pamphlet at the end of the year titled *1945: Annus Mirabilis*. She began by quoting the British poet Owen Seaman: 'To live in these great times and have your part/In Freedom's crowning hour/...I saw the powers of darkness put to flight/I saw the Morning break.' Fry called on her readers to see 1945 as a *tabula rasa*: 'Everything is smashed. We invoke a blank sheet of paper.'[13] It was possible, she continued, with an unfortunate choice of language, to build a 'brave new world'.

In Britain there had been active popular campaigns since the outbreak of war in 1939 for a postwar world in which a really effective international order could be constructed, and a world free from poverty and unemployment, unlike the world after 1918. The President of the League of Nations Union, Lord Robert Cecil, who had played an important role in drafting the covenant of the League in 1918, began in October 1939 drawing up proposals for a new world order to replace the one now defunct. The National Peace Council (NPC), the umbrella organization for all Britain's anti-war organizations, set up an emergency sub-committee on 'Peace Aims' even earlier, on 11 September 1939.[14] In March 1940 the NPC chairman, Cyril Joad, wrote to the American Under-Secretary of State, Sumner Welles, asking him to help in creating an enduring peace by negotiation, including Hitler's Germany. This was to be a peace, Joad continued, 'on the basis of a common justice and security for all nations'.[15] Progressive opinion in Britain spent the whole war period campaigning for some form of world government which would result, in the words of one petition, 'in a rising standard of life and potential happiness for all peoples'.[16] Victory in 1945 was hailed as the moment of opportunity to realize a progressive and democratic utopia. This teleology was later captured by historians. Both Angus Calder's *People's War 1939–1945* and Paul Addison's *The Road to 1945* are chronicles of a grand historical morality tale.

The arrival of peace in 1945 made it possible for the rest of Europe to share in the German sense of 'Hour Zero' as a point of irreversible departure. There was self-evidently a widespread desire for a changed and more stable Europe from the one that had plunged into economic crisis and war in the 1930s, and the decade following 1945 was a period of economic revival, political stabilization, and greater international collaboration, a reality reflected in much of the later historical writing on the long economic boom and the emergence of *détente*, both of which seemed rooted in the postwar experience. Moreover, for tens of millions of Europeans the war had abruptly intervened in their private world, usually for the worse, often dramatically, which placed a premium not necessarily on replacing what was lost but on constructing a new and more secure

[13] A. Ruth Fry, *1945: Annus Mirabilis* (privately printed, 1945), 2, 5.
[14] London School of Economics (LSE) archive, NPC papers, 2/5, minutes of special meeting of the Executive Committee, 11 September 1939.
[15] LSE archive, NPC 2/5, letter from Joad to Welles, 13 March 1940.
[16] Liverpool University special collections, Jones papers, D48/7 (i), Petition 'A First Step towards World Government'.

basis on which the private sphere might flourish. They wanted to see 1945 as a clear break and invested those hopes in their memory of the war's end. 'In peacetime,' wrote Ulrich Simon, a German–Jewish exile in Britain in 1945, 'individual destinies, released from the grip of wartime duties, assert their claims… Suddenly, we were all in a hurry to find a better life.'[17]

Much of the contemporary European history written since 1945 has focused on this divide as one that was historically meaningful. When Walter Laqueur wrote *The Rebirth of Europe* in 1970 his first two chapters were titled 'The New Political Map' and the 'New Balance of Power'. He concluded that far from collapsing under the accumulated shocks of decades of war and civil war 'Europe has shown a new vigour that has astonished friend and foe alike'.[18] Most textbook series on Europe also take 1945 as the break point. There appeared to be a chronological unity to the thirty years of war, revolution, and civil war from 1914 to 1945. The First World War and the Second World War were bookends to the interwar years of crisis. 'The Twenties were postwar, the Thirties were pre-war', wrote the poet Hubert Nicholson in his memoirs in 1941.[19]

Just as many Europeans turned their backs on memories of the 1930s, of ideological confrontation, economic crisis, state violence, and terror, so historians shared that rejection of a darker age. The prevailing sense in the 1930s of impending crisis, particularly of the inevitability of war, cast a deep shadow over years in which other advances in science, technology, economic management, and education promised a brighter future. The widespread perception of Europe in the age of war as decadent or politically diseased meant that little effort was devoted to constructing clear lines of historical continuity. For national histories where the recent past was enmeshed with political crisis and violence, there were obvious advantages in promoting historical narratives that recovered different values. This was true even for the Soviet Union, a victor in 1945. As Amir Weiner has argued, the Second World War became the foundation myth for the Soviet system and 1945 a clear break with the confused past of revolution, collectivization, and the terror. Although Soviet public history still invoked the revolution, the break in 1945 was nevertheless perceived by many Soviet people as a necessary closure with the past.[20]

There were three main strands to the contemporary history (and political analysis) that emphasized the discontinuities in Europe's post-1945 experience. The first was the dramatic shift in the economic fortunes of Europe, the second the apparent arrival of greater political stability on both sides of the Iron Curtain, and the third was the emergence of the cold war as a permanent reminder of the new political geography of Europe.

[17] Ulrich Simon, *Sitting in Judgement 1913–1963* (London: Society for Promoting Christian Knowledge (SPCK), 1978), 89.

[18] Walter Laqueur, *The Rebirth of Europe: A History of the Years since the Fall of Hitler* (New York: Holt, Rinehart and Winston, 1970), 10, 14, 403.

[19] Hubert Nicholson *Half My Days and Nights* (London: William Heinemann, 1941), 100.

[20] Amir Weiner, 'The Making of a Dominant Myth: The Second World War and the Construction of Political Identities within the Soviet Polity', *Russian Review* 55 (1996), 638–60.

Little of this process of stabilization was immediately evident in 1945, but the historical writing that emerged between the 1960s and the 1980s embraced the process in teleological terms, as if stabilization were directly caused by the outcome in 1945. The processes of stabilization were not, of course, accidental. They relied heavily on the capacity of Europe to recover the trajectory of sustained economic growth evident before 1914. It was understood at the time that perhaps the principal key to creating a new Europe was to embrace a different economic system from the ones that had been practised in pre-war Europe.

Much of the European left had before 1939 looked to the Soviet Union as an example of economic planning and social justice, though not necessarily as a practical model. Radical nationalists had looked to some form of 'New Order' economy based on a combination of autarkic trading blocs, colonial exploitation, and the substitution of what one German banker called in 1939 the principle of 'collective well-being' for the old economic egoism.[21] Conservative opinion had continued to favour old-fashioned free-market capitalism even though little case could any longer be made in the 1930s for unrestrained and unsupervised business activity. None of these prescriptions won much favour in Western and Central Europe after 1945; in eastern Europe the Soviet model was imposed piecemeal but willy-nilly. The British economist G. D. H. Cole summarized the failed options facing Europe from the pre-war world:

> A return to the old, *laissez-faire* type of capitalism is simply out of the question. A restoration of the pre-1939 type of capitalism, based on restrictive monopolies each claiming the support of its own State for a policy of economic nationalism, will mean general impoverishment, and will be destroyed by unemployment. A quasi-Fascist capitalism, resting on a nationalistic basis and using the State as an instrument for keeping the poor in order and maintaining economic activity by State-subsidised public works, will lead either to renewed war or to collapse under an unbearable burden of debt and popular unrest.[22]

For Cole and other socialists, the answer after 1945 was to introduce a higher degree of international collaboration, economic planning, state ownership, and welfare to ensure that the depression years would not be repeated. Even liberals like John Maynard Keynes, who was no friend to ideas of state ownership and direction, recognized that after 1945 some kind of new order was unavoidable and necessary.[23]

Much of the historical literature on European economic recovery has focused on West German revival. The gulf between the years of recession, poor trade, state restrictions, and planning for war in the 1930s and the booming consumer and construction sectors in the 1950s made it evident that something changed dramatically in 1945. The explanations for this success are well known. West Germany embraced a balance between state

---

[21] Bank of England archive, OV34, vol. 9, conversation with Dr Emil Puhl in Basle, 12 June 1939.

[22] G.d.h. Cole, *Europe, Russia and the Future* (London: Victor Gollancz, 1941), 53–4.

[23] The National Archive, T160/995, memorandum by Keynes 'Proposals to counter the German "New Order"', 1 December 1940: 'What we will offer,' wrote Keynes, 'is the same as what Dr Funk [German Economics Minister] offers, except that we shall do it better and more honestly.'

economic steering and neoliberal economic individualism, and then exploited the changed international economic climate of collaborative trade agreements and open commerce to embark on a remarkable and sustained export boom.[24] Volker Berghahn has argued that German industrialists after 1945 came to recognize that the established pre-war practices of cartel-building, price control, and market-share agreements were a barrier to re-entering the world market. Under pressure from the United States, something he calls the 'Americanisation of West German industry' took place, which helped to make German business more aware of the advantages of open competition and the disadvantages of a narrow conception of corporate defence.[25] The model of a mixed economy, with the state steering policy in collaboration with key interest groups, was extended to all of western Europe after 1945, whatever the political complexion. State ownership was introduced for key services or for vulnerable sectors, but the economic success story of Europe up to the 1970s was based essentially on a compromise between the socialist vision in 1945 and the neoliberal aspirations of the political centre and right.

This was a process often assumed to apply only to the non-communist half of Europe, yet the economic record of the Eastern bloc also shows a sustained boom after 1945. The imposition of the Stalinist model of economic development produced a very different kind of society from the West, but it also helped to overcome much of the endemic poverty and the broad inequalities that characterized much of eastern Europe before 1939 (not including the massive economic damage resulting from a war of scorched earth across much of the border region of the Soviet Union). Even allowing for socialist exaggeration, and recognizing the environmental costs and the surviving economic inequalities in communist society, the entire Soviet-dominated region experienced a wave of industrial growth, better welfare facilities, health reform, and the possibility of social mobility. In East Germany agriculture was collectivized and industry taken over into 'people's ownership' (over 92 per cent of East Germans worked for state enterprises by 1973); the social structure changed sharply, the large agricultural labour force declined from 30 per cent in 1949 to 12.8 per cent in 1970, while the industrial workforce increased from 27 per cent to 36.8 per cent, and the tertiary sector from 12 per cent to 17 per cent.[26] The reorganization of the economies of the Soviet bloc failed to provide the consumer opportunities that emerged in the West, but the gap between the two halves of Europe was not as wide in the first decades after 1945 as it was to become by the 1960s. The social wage in the Soviet system, even if it often amounted to poor services and inadequate

[24] The best account of the process is Anthony Nicholls, *Freedom with Responsibility: The Social Market Economy in Germany 1918–1963* (Oxford: Oxford University Press, 1994). See too James Van Hook, *Rebuilding Germany: The Creation of the Social Market Economy 1945–1957* (Cambridge: Cambridge University Press, 2004); Rebecca Boehling, *A Question of Priorities: Democratic Reform and Economic Recovery in Postwar Germany* (Oxford: Berghahn Books, 1996).

[25] Volker Berghahn, *The Americanisation of West German Industry, 1945–1973* (Leamington Spa: Berg, 1986).

[26] Statistics from Fulbrook, *The People's State*, 34–5.

welfare, did constitute a net addition for all households that had been almost entirely absent for the poorer fractions of the population before the Second World War.

The second strand in the story of Europe since 1945 has been the evidence of growing political stabilization. This was either created through voluntary collaboration between differing social classes and interest groups or imposed under the terms of the Soviet social model. Stabilization is of course a relative term. Europe in the generation after 1945 was divided between states ruled by dictatorships and states that were parliamentary democracies as it had been in the interwar years. There were insurgencies in Northern Ireland, the Basque region in Spain, and more distant insurgencies in the surviving colonial empires. The Soviet bloc practised widespread state terror and maintained concentration camps and political prisons for many years.

Nevertheless the exclusion or marginalization of political forces likely to create the instabilities of the pre-war era helped to create conditions for a relative stability. In West Germany, for example, both the Communist Party (KPD) and a number of fringe ultra-nationalist groups were banned under the terms of a constitution designed to give no platform to any organization which threatened its survival. In East Germany the bourgeois parties were either wound up or forced to join the 'Socialist Unity Party'; the prevailing political culture of anti-fascism ensured that there would be no revival of the nationalist milieu. In Italy and France, communism survived as a mass movement but participated in parliamentary politics and avoided revolutionary rhetoric. In Britain the election of the first majority Labour government in July 1945 helped to transcend the legacy of the 1930s and create a cross-party realignment in favour of a mixed economy and a social welfare state. In Western Europe political balance rested on the ability of the political elite to incorporate the major business and labour interest groups in the pursuit of economic expansion, which was rightly seen as the key to a stable politics and opened the way to more generous welfare and educational reforms.

The relative stabilization of European politics also rested on the third strand of the postwar historical experience, the absence of a major war. This outcome was not entirely predictable, but by the 1950s and the age of nuclear confrontation and mutual deterrence, a major conflict in Europe generated by European territorial ambitions and national rivalries, which had created the conditions for two world wars, was unthinkable. The shift in mentalities has seldom been given the historical attention it deserves, but 1945 was a critical turning point in the view Europeans took of their power position and international interests.[27] After 1945 the Soviet Union and the United States, with some hesitation on both sides, came to dominate the world order and to play a major part in shaping the political development of eastern and western Europe. The effect of the cold war was paradoxically a growing source of stability. The Soviet bloc united around the common defence of the peoples' democracies against the threat of international capitalism and imperialism; the West, first through NATO, then through growing economic and political collaboration sealed in the European Economic Community in 1957 and

---

[27] David Reynolds 'The European Dimension of the Cold War', in Melvyn P. Leffler and David S. Painter (eds), *Origins of the Cold War: An International History* (London: Routledge, 1995), 126–38.

the later European Union, understood that it had a common interest in avoiding conflict and containing or deterring the Soviet bloc. This did not mean that crisis was avoided, but it did make a major war unlikely and diverted national communities from expressing national interest in terms of chauvinistic antagonism or the desire for territorial aggrandizement or border revision.

The most remarkable break with the pre-1945 world was almost certainly the end of hundreds of years of European imperialism. The remaining colonial empires collapsed in the generation after 1945. The French wars for Vietnam and Algeria were the last throw of traditional imperialism and both failed. The unravelling of Europe's empires was accelerated by the hostility of both the United States and the Soviet Union. The Suez Crisis in 1956 was the point at which traditional imperial interests were finally discredited. European states lacked the means to sustain long wars in defence of empire, and also lacked widespread enthusiasm at home for doing so. More significant perhaps, as the recent historiography has illustrated, the final colonial conflicts were messy, violent, and involved harsh levels of European reprisal.[28] These echoes of the German or Italian 'dirty wars' of the 1930s and 1940s were unsustainable by liberal democracies. The territorial and cultural perception of 'empire' was fatally wounded in 1945 as a result of the efforts of Germany, Italy, and Japan to construct new imperial orders during the war.

The Cold War also had the effect of diverting historical attention and popular memory from the crises of the war and pre-war years. In the West the deteriorating relations with the Soviet Union merely substituted one dictator for another. The American president, Harry Truman, said in May 1947: 'There isn't any difference in totalitarian states...Nazi, Communist or Fascist...they are all alike.'[29] The concern with 'totalitarianism' differed from the attitude to dictatorship in the 1930s, when clear distinctions were usually made between Hitler and Stalin. It emerged from the growing awareness in the West of the apparently common character of the German and Soviet models of repression. Hannah Arendt, herself a refugee from pre-war Germany, famously analysed the components of totalitarianism in 1951. The effect was to help bridge the gap between the dictatorships of Hitler and Stalin by seeing them as varieties of a generic new authoritarianism.[30] The intellectual current in the West focused on the new science of 'Sovietology' to try to understand the nature of the new enemy. Fear of the Soviet Union replaced the fear of Hitler and the terms of the ideological war shifted. The effect was to focus the concerns of contemporary history and political science on the present danger and to gloss over the historical realities of the pre-1945 conflict, which had ended in a victory that made possible a new age and buried the menace of 'fascism'.

[28] See for example David Anderson, *Histories of the Hanged: Britain's Dirty War in Kenya and the End of Empire* (London: Weidenfeld & Nicolson, 2005).

[29] John L. Gaddis, *The Long Peace: Inquiries into the History of the Cold War* (New York: Oxford University Press, 1987), 36.

[30] Hannah Arendt, *The Origins of Totalitarianism* (London: Allen & Unwin, 1958). See the recent critical analysis in Michael Geyer and Sheila Fitzpatrick (eds), *Beyond Totalitarianism: Stalinism and Nazism Compared* (Cambridge: Cambridge University Press, 2009).

One result of this refocusing of threat was to avoid a serious evaluation of what had shaped the crisis leading to war and genocide and what the real circumstances, moral and physical, had been in the European area where both had been recently experienced. The amnesia expressed in German unwillingness to live any longer with their recent past in the years after the refounding of German states in 1949 was also reflected in a broader, non-German, desire not to confront the history of the 1930s and the war by reconstructing an honest narrative of the experience. For the historian this was also a problem of sources. Archives in Soviet bloc countries were largely closed to outside researchers as well as to the domestic historical establishment. Sources from Germany were scattered until the restitution treaties saw the slow return in the 1970s of originals from Britain and the United States. Other sources were generally closed until the 1970s or even later. As a result there was little serious European historical writing on the Holocaust until the 1980s. Gerald Fleming's *Hitler and the Final Solution*, published in 1985, was one of the first books to exploit archive resources other than those made available as a result of the postwar trials. Even more surprising, there was no serious history of the German concentration camps until the 1990s, and no academic research on the Soviet GULag system until the archives became partially opened in the late 1980s.[31]

This situation changed sharply in the late 1980s and the 1990s with the collapse of the Soviet bloc. Some archives had been opened before that, but after 1990 a flood of new research was made possible on the wartime period or on the Soviet Union in the 1930s and the Stalinist terror. The greater availability of research sources was not, however, the only explanation. The impact in Germany after unification in 1990 of a younger generation of historians willing to discuss the Holocaust in more than abstract terms, or to research the role of the armed forces and other elite groups, demonstrated a greater openness in dealing with the past. The 'Crimes of the Wehrmacht Exhibition', which opened in Hamburg on 5 March 1995, aroused strong views both for and against the proposition that ordinary German soldiers had engaged in atrocity alongside the SS, but it helped to set an agenda in which the blank historical spaces before 1945 could now be filled in.[32]

This was followed by extensive research on the survival and re-employment of former office holders in the Third Reich, which exposed the extent to which much of Germany's elite in the first decades of the two new states had been implicated in the criminal activities of the dictatorship.[33] This was partly a generational response. It is possible to argue

---

[31] Gerald Fleming, *Hitler and the Final Solution* (London: Hamish Hamilton, 1985). On the opening of GULag archives, Edward Bacon, *Stalin's Forced Labour System in the Light of the Archives* (London: Macmillan, 1994). On the concentration camps, Wolfgang Sofsky, *The Order of Terror: The Concentration Camp* (Princeton, NJ: Princeton University Press, 1999); Karin Orth *Das System der nationalsozialistischen Konzentrationslager: Eine politische Organisationsgeschichte* (Hamburg: Hamburger Edition, 1999).

[32] Hans-Günther Thiele (ed.), *Die Wehrmachtsausstellung: Dokumentation einer Kontroverse* (Bremen: Temmen, 1997).

[33] Frei, *Adenauer's Germany*, esp. chs 3–4. See too the discussion on continuities and confrontations in Jeffrey Herf, *Divided Memory: The Nazi Past in the Two Germanys* (Cambridge, MA: Harvard University Press, 1997).

that Germans who grew up with the Federal Republic in the 1950s and 1960s did not want to focus on the crimes of the dictatorship and those who perpetrated them, but instead wanted to claim a real 'new beginning' in 1949. The following generation, more secure with German democracy, wanted a more honest reckoning with the past. Yet this does not explain the wider cultural response in Europe to the new history, which also provoked a difficult and contested exploration of what many non-Germans did during the war as collaborators or perpetrators of atrocity. This culture, captured in the title of another of Daniel Goldhagen's books, *A Moral Reckoning* (this time on the failures of the Catholic Church to obstruct the genocide of the Jews), created new imperatives to represent the year 1945 not as a new beginning but as a reference point designed deliberately to obscure the grimmer realities before it.[34]

The ambiguity at the heart of 1945 (or 'Hour Zero') as a moment of closure and a new point of departure was evident at the time. There were uncertainties among British celebrations of 1945. George Orwell's *1984*, already worked out in the author's mind early in the war though only published in 1949, reflected his fear that victory would not end the growing march of state power, mind-numbing propaganda and endless wars.[35] In late 1945 Orwell wrote to his fellow author, Arthur Koestler, suggesting that since a third world war was likely in the near future, a campaign for 'psychological disarmament' should be launched to abate the hatreds and suspicions that gave rise to war. Koestler agreed and set out plans for a League for the Rights of Man to try to combat what he saw as a growing 'contempt for democratic traditions' in the Western states. His efforts to recruit the philosopher Bertrand Russell foundered on the latter's belief that atomic war might occur in two or three years' time, making any gestures for peace apparently pointless.[36]

Fear of atomic destruction also coloured the approach of the historian Arnold Toynbee, who shared little of the optimism of the left in Britain that victory would usher in a revived civilization. He thought atomic power brought civilization closer to the edge of destruction than ever before. His gloomy prognoses made him perhaps the natural choice when the Royal Institute for International Affairs in London, where he had been research director before the war, looked for a keynote speaker for a conference on 'The Passing of Europe' or 'The Passing of the Hegemony of the White Race' in early 1946.[37] The eventual emergence in Britain of a democratic and progressive consensus masked the extent to which confidence in victory was tinged with fear of disaster.

[34] Daniel J. Goldhagen, *A Moral Reckoning: The Role of the Catholic Church in the Holocaust and its Unfulfilled Duty of Repair* (New York: Vintage Books, 2002).

[35] University College, London, Orwell Archive, B/1, literary notebooks 1939/40, 36–7, 'The Last Man in Europe' synopsis.

[36] George Orwell, *Smothered under Journalism: 1946*, ed. Peter Davison (London: Secker &Warburg, 1998), 7–8; University of Edinburgh, Koestler Archive, MS 2345/2, Orwell to Koestler, enclosing draft of a petition, p. 1; draft proposal by Koestler for League for the Rights of Man, p. 1.

[37] Bodleian Library, Oxford, Toynbee papers, Box 39, Margaret Cleeve (RIIA) to Toynbee, 12 December 1945.

This ambiguity was much more marked in states which had suffered the full effects of occupation and destruction. In Italy the end of the war was in itself fraught with contradiction: for the Italian state, war had ended on 8 September 1943 with unconditional surrender to the Allies, but war had continued regardless on Italian territory because of the German occupation that followed Italian capitulation. Moreover, the founding in late 1943 of the Italian Social Republic (generally known as the Salò Republic, after the town on Lake Garda) meant that some Italians continued to fight at Germany's side as an Axis ally. Allied victory in Italy on 2 May 1945 had Italians on both sides, as co-belligerents with the United Nations and as Axis co-belligerents. The Italian public was temporarily caught, as Guido Crainz has put it, between 'hope and fear', between 'a heavy past and a very uncertain future.'[38]

There existed the same desire to try to eradicate the past that could be found in Germany, and the Allies encouraged a moral reckoning with those who had actively supported Italian Fascism both before and after 1943. But the work of the Allies had to be different in Italy, since the Italian state was formally an ally. An Allied Commission collaborated with the Italian authorities in purging the Italian state bureaucracy of fascists. Extraordinary courts were established (*Corti straordinarie di Assise*) to assess the degree of culpability. Some 23,213 state officials were investigated, 1879 were dismissed, and 671 compulsorily retired.[39] Leading fascists were arrested but far fewer were put on trial than in Germany. The Allied Commission wound up its activities on 31 March 1946 while the trial of the major war criminals was still going on at Nuremberg. Only in the last decades have historians begun to explore what this meant for postwar Italy, where bitter divisions have always existed between the legacy of the Resistance and of the fascist state. A neo-fascist *Movimento Sociale Italiano* was founded in December 1946 and thirty years later former fascists and neo-fascists had penetrated into many areas of Italian public life. By 1971, for example, around 95 per cent of Italy's senior civil servants had begun their careers before 1943 under the Mussolini dictatorship. The result was what Claudio Pavone has called 'the continuity of the state.'[40]

In France the ambiguity of victory was also shaped by wartime political realities. The Vichy regime established under Marshal Philippe Pétain in June 1940 was hailed by some of the population as an opportunity for a new beginning, and allegiance was seen as a test of patriotism. The Free French under Charles de Gaulle laid claim to be the true inheritors of the French state in 1940, but until French forces re-entered France in the summer of 1944 it was a claim that existed only on paper. French sympathies were not entirely with the conquering Allies; when de Gaulle entered Notre Dame Cathedral the day after the liberation of Paris he was fired at by a French sniper. The divided nature of liberated French society was expressed in a wave of violence directed at French fascists

---

[38] Guido Crainz, *L'Ombra della Guerra. Il 1945, l'Italia* (Rome: Donzelli, 2007), 9.

[39] Roy P. Domenico, *Italian Fascists on Trial, 1943–1948* (Chapel Hill, NC: North Carolina University Press, 1991), 267–8.

[40] Ibid., 224; Claudio Pavone, *Alle origini della repubblica: scritti su fascismo, antifascismo e continuità dello Stato* (Turin: Bollati Boringhieri, 1995), 140–3.

and collaborators with Vichy, many of whom had seen themselves only months before as true French patriots. In the summer of 1944 thousands of collaborators, perhaps as many as 15,000, were executed in informal acts of political revenge, the *épuration sauvage*.[41] The judicial authorities then intervened and out of 350,000 people investigated for collaboration, a further 1502 were executed.

Many major political figures who had sat in national and department bodies, or had been appointed to state offices under Vichy were barred from election or office, but thousands of other local councillors and municipal officials were allowed to remain.[42] This experience of liberation and victory has provoked decades of argument among historians about the nature of collaboration and resistance, and has continued to divide French opinion. The reaction to the trial during 1997–8 of the former secretary-general of the Gironde prefecture, Maurice Papon, accused of deporting Jews from Bordeaux, highlighted the difficulty in integrating Vichy into any consensual narrative of the recent French past. French opinion was divided over whether the case should have been brought at all, whether he was simply doing his job or was a real Holocaust perpetrator, or whether or not Vichy collaborators should have been brought back, as in Papon's case, into mainstream French politics. But not until the late 1960s and early 1970s had the real extent of Vichy cooperation with the German New Order been exposed, and not fully until the scholarship of the past dozen years.[43] France too suffered from the German problem of *Vergangenheitsbewältigung* [overcoming the past] with its own '*crise de l'histoire*'. Passing back through the 1945 two-way door remains a painful exercise.

One of the most sensitive areas in the story of pre-1945 France was official French treatment of the victims of the Spanish Civil War, 226,000 of whom fled to France during 1939 as victory for Franco's forces was finally secured. They were housed in rough camps until many returned to Spain. The approximately 25,000 who remained in September 1939 were placed in enclosures that closely resembled the concentration camps. These camps—with guards, barbed wire, dirty ill-kept barracks, endemic disease, and debilitating labour—were filled up not only with the Spanish refugees and former Republican soldiers, but with thousands of aliens, many of them Jewish, who had taken refuge in France from political and racial persecution.[44] Among them was the journalist Arthur Koestler, who recalled in *The Scum of the Earth*, his wartime account of the camp he was sent to at Le Vernet, that the prisoners, many of whom died, suffered neglect,

[41] Philippe Bourdrel, *L'épuration sauvage, 1944–1945* (Paris: Perrin, 2002), 535–9, 558; Jean-Paul Cointet, *Expier Vichy: L'épuration en France 1943–1958* (Paris: Perrin, 2008), 87–124. There is no final agreed figure on the number of those summarily executed, but most authors now favour a figure between 10,000 and 15,000.

[42] Olivier Wieviorka, 'Replacement or Renewal? The French Political Elite at the Liberation', in Andrew F. Knapp (ed.), *The Uncertain Foundation: France at the Liberation, 1944–47* (Basingstoke: Palgrave, 2007), 76–8; Andrew F. Knapp, 'France's "Long" Liberation, 1944–47', in ibid., 7–8.

[43] Richard J. Golsan, *Vichy's Afterlife: History and Counterhistory in Postwar France* (Lincoln, NE: University of Nebraska Press, 2000), 2–3, 11–12.

[44] Details on French camps from Anne Grynberg, *Les camps de la honte: les internés juifs des camps français 1939–1944* (Paris: Éditions la Découverte, 1991), 8–9, 40–52.

poor food, minimal medical care, and freezing temperatures with little protection. He thought Le Vernet 'the zero-point of infamy', though still a few degrees above Dachau.[45] In total, seven concentration camps were established for Spanish refugees in 1939 and a further 87 for alleged 'enemy aliens'.

Later, under Vichy, camps were also created for the internment or deportation of Jews living in France. The details of this camp system, like the camps and penal colonies established in Mussolini's Italy, have been the subject of serious scholarship only in the past twenty years, and remain a contested narrative.[46] The same is true of the terror imposed by the Franco regime after victory in the Civil War in March 1939 on all those opponents unfortunate enough to remain in Spain. As Dolores Silvestre has pointed out, a silence persisted about the repression even after the end of the Franco dictatorship.[47] The violent suppression of the anarchist, socialist, and liberal opposition, which resulted in 240,916 political prisoners by the end of 1940, and an estimated death toll of 50,000, went on across the whole period of the war, while the guerrilla warfare waged by anarchist groups concealed in the Pyrenees and other remote areas was not finally ended until the early 1950s, involving the death of around 5000 fighters and the torture and imprisonment of their families.[48] In this contest between the Spanish security forces and the residue of republican resistance, the year 1945 had little significance. Spain followed its own chronology, the harsh nationalist dictatorship disappearing only in 1975, when it at last became possible to reintegrate Spain into the mainstream of democratic and economically successful Western Europe.

The problem was also evident in the Soviet Union and the Eastern European bloc where the anti-fascist and anti-imperialist discourse made it possible to gloss over what was actually happening in Eastern Europe in 1945 and its immediate aftermath. For example the 'notes' of Daniil Kraminov, a Soviet war correspondent in 1945 when the war ended, published as late as 1985, were used to present the standard Soviet discourse on the end of the war and the collapse of the wartime alliance. He recalled meeting wealthy, well-dressed British and American officers in northern Germany after Hitler's suicide on 30 April 1945, 'who could not tell a self-propelled gun from a tank' and who were principally interested in taking over German industrial shares and re-establishing lines of capitalist communication:

> 'How come you are here?' thundered one of the newly created army majors from the large millionaire family of the du Ponts [to Kraminov] ... 'What are you doing here among the Allies—the British and the Americans?' 'We too are your allies,' one of us

---

[45] Arthur Koestler, *The Scum of the Earth* (London: Jonathan Cape, 1941), 103.

[46] On Italy see Carlo S. Capogreco, *I campi del duce: L'internamento civile nell'Italia fascista [1940–1943]* (Turin: Einaudi, 2004).

[47] Dolores Silvestre, *Clandestinos: El Maquis contra el franquismo 1934–1975* (Barcelona: Plaza Janés, 2002), 11.

[48] David Baird, *Between Two Fires: Guerrilla War in the Spanish Sierras* (Málaga: Maroma Press, 2008), 91–2; Antonio C. Sánchez, *Fear and Progress: Ordinary Lives in Franco's Spain 1939–1975* (Oxford: Wiley-Blackwell, 2010), 30–1.

reminded him. 'You apparently didn't know or have forgotten about it.' 'All alliances are temporary,' the young du Pont cut him short. 'And this alliance will soon come to an end.'[49]

Kraminov echoed the standard Soviet line that Soviet goodwill and Soviet good behaviour in 1945 were spurned by the return of reactionary and imperialist politics on the other side 'that undermined the anti-fascist coalition' and later 'launched the cold war'.[50] This is a line of argument that has not finally died out even after the collapse of the Soviet order.

It is now well known that Stalin would have taken much more in 1945 if he thought he could have got it. 'We toyed with the idea of reaching Paris', he told the French communist leader Maurice Thorez in 1947.[51] Soviet reactions were understandably opportunistic, not ideological. But the long period in which the standard Soviet story saw 1945 as a moment of decent communist triumph masked some very harsh realities, from the mass rape of German and Central European women by the Red Army (which was until recently almost entirely ignored even in Western historiography) to the savage counter-insurgency wars waged along the Soviet borderlands from 1944 until the late 1940s. While the Red Army was completing the rout of what was left of German forces in 1945, Soviet security men and military units were fighting pacification wars against armed resistance movements in the Baltic States, in eastern Poland, in the Ukraine, and Slovakia. These were areas that did not want to be under Soviet rule and the nationalist movements, themselves often divided, fought a desperate rearguard action against the new occupiers.

Almost nothing has been known of these conflicts until the archives became more readily available; the first major book on the Soviet pacification campaign was produced only in 2010, Alexander Statiev's *Soviet Counterinsurgency*. Using extensive new primary material, Statiev shows that between 1944 and 1946 some 132,900 'anti-Soviet' elements were killed in the borderland areas and 194,433 arrested.[52] Since 1990 more has been known of the fate of returning Soviet prisoners-of-war for whom 1945 was not a new beginning but a return to the 1930s habits of suspicion and irrational punishment. In the areas brought under the direct control of Soviet armed forces and security services, hundreds of thousands were rounded up and deported to camps in the Soviet Union. The real history of the Soviet victory in 1945 is one of savage reimposition of authority, thousands of deaths, mass deportation, and dispossession.

Through the thin membrane of 1945 there have been many other harsh truths that the former communist bloc has had to confront. Some of these involve complicity in the violence meted out to political groups and ethnic enemies in 1945 and the years

---

[49] Daniil Kraminov, *The Spring of 1945: Notes by a Soviet War Correspondent* (Moscow: Novosti Press, 1985), 75–6.

[50] Ibid., 118.

[51] Cited in John L. Gaddis, *The Cold War* (London: Allen Lane, 2005), 14.

[52] Calculated from Alexander Statiev, *The Soviet Counterinsurgency in the Western Borderlands* (Cambridge: Cambridge University Press, 2010), 110.

immediately following; some involve collaboration with the ambitions of Hitler's Germany, including participation in the Holocaust. The reaction to the book published in 2001 by the American scholar Jan Gross, which exposed the participation of a group of ethnic Poles in July 1941 in killing the Jewish inhabitants of Jedwabne, was predictably mixed.[53] The hostility aroused in Romania once the history of the wartime killing of Jews in Transnistria and southern Ukraine was firmly established was equally marked. In both cases the knowledge of participation in wartime atrocity involves difficult questions of memory and identity. For states keen to shed the residue of fifty years of communist domination, it was important to find a 'usable' history from the period beforehand, but at the same time it has been difficult to incorporate what often amounted to complicity in the crimes of the dictatorships. In Ukraine this has led to the paradox that Stepan Bandera, leader of the Ukrainian National Army in the war, fighting against Germans, Poles, and Russians, and hostile to the Jews, can be seen by some Ukrainians as a national hero in the pantheon of a post-communist state, despite his earlier reputation as a ruthless bandit.

All of these problems, throughout all of Europe, show the extent to which '1945' became a convenient alibi for a history that did not fit the idea of a new beginning, an end to violence and a stable and moral politics. The awkward questions raised by historians and journalists about that reality challenge a distorted or partisan view of the past whose survival is still sustained in current political and social discourses.

Beside the rediscovery of the complex reality of 1945 there are other obvious continuities that traverse the end of the war. For economic historians, historians of consumption, or cultural historians the divide does not mean a great deal. The narratives of material and cultural life, though affected by the temporary interruption of war, can be traced backwards and forwards without difficulty. Among the recent economic history of Germany has been an attempt to assess what the economy of the Third Reich contributed to the postwar economic boom.[54] This is to reverse the traditional narrative quite sharply, but there are evident links, not least in the survival of firms and individuals. The classic example is the career of the banker Hermann Abs who worked for Deutsche Bank during the Third Reich and participated in acquiring foreign shareholdings under the New Order. He was reinstated after the war and became one of West Germany's most respected and successful financiers.[55]

But there were many more individuals in German industry and commerce who spanned the dictatorship and contributed to the German economic revival. The most startling example of business continuity is the Volkswagen firm, first set up under the

---

[53] Jan Gross, *Neighbors: The Destruction of the Jewish Community in Jedwabne, Poland 1941* (Princeton, NJ: Princeton University Press, 2001). For the debate, see Anthony Polonsky and Joanna Michlic (eds), *The Neighbours Respond: The Controversy over the Jedwabne Massacre in Poland* (Princeton, NJ: Princeton University Press, 2004), particularly Bogdan Musiał, 'The Pogrom in Jedwabne: Critical Remarks about Jan T. Gross's *Neighbors*', 304–43.

[54] S. Jonathan Wiesen, *West German Industry and the Challenge of the Nazi Past, 1945–1955* (Chapel Hill, NC: University of North Carolina Press, 2001).

[55] Lothar Gall, *Der Bankier: Hermann Josef Abs. Eine Biographie* (Munich: C. H. Beck, 2004).

National Socialist Labour Front in 1938 following Hitler's insistent demand for a small, cheap family car, constructed during 1939–40 in Wolfsburg and then used as the site for the revival of the German car industry from 1947. By 1960 the firm had sold one million vehicles and exported cars in large numbers to British and American consumers who knew little or nothing about its political origins.[56] The legacy from pre-1945 was not in any sense a straightforward one, but it proved possible to sustain continuity and by adapting swiftly to changed external conditions.

There are also evident continuities with the Cold War. The difficulty of incorporating the Soviet Union into the prevailing international order after 1945 was nothing new. Something like a 'Cold War' also existed in the interwar years after the end of Western intervention in the Russian Civil War. Fears about Soviet ambitions and the spread of communism dominated considerations about managing the international order in Western capitals. The Soviet Union was invited to join the League of Nations in 1934 but survived only five years before being expelled for the war with Finland in 1939–40. When Hitler penned the strategic memorandum that formed the basis of the Second Four Year Plan launched in October 1936, his prime concern was the growing size of the Red Army and the threat that Bolshevism posed to European civilization.[57] There were those in the West who thought that it was better to turn Hitler against the Soviet Union as a shield against the spread of communism. It will be difficult for historians to claim Hitler as the first cold warrior, but the conflict with the Soviet Union, real or imagined, lasted the whole life of the dictatorship and was only sharpened, not caused, by Soviet success in 1945.

For historians, 1945 has become a permeable dividing line. In its own terms the history of that victory and its immediate aftermath is full of ambiguity and paradox. 1945 was neither a clean end nor a clean beginning. The historical weight it bears reflects more on the way in which the break was perceived and exploited at the time, as an opportunity to found a socialist Europe, or to build a better economy or to end the age of national and imperial rivalry. The year 1945 was filled with meaning by contemporaries and those meanings helped to shape collective memories and popular myths about what the break seemed to symbolize. A better case might be made today for 1917/18 as the real dividing line of the twentieth century, for the upheavals the Great War generated really shaped what was to happen over the following eighty years, including the blood-soaked decade between 1939 and 1949.

Even if 1945 retains its textbook neatness, it is perhaps time now for historians to write the history of 'Europe 1939–1949'. It is during the 1940s as a whole that the great majority of the continent's violent twentieth-century deaths occurred; the violence abated in 1945, but certainly did not end. The social, political, and ideological conflicts of pre-1945 survived into the years following the peace and make 1945 for the historian a messy,

---

[56] Walter H. Nelson, *Small Wonder: The Amazing Story of the Volkswagen* (London: Hutchinson, 1967), 218–26.

[57] On Hitler's obsession with Bolshevism, see Lorna Waddington, *Hitler's Crusade: Bolshevism and the Myth of the International Jewish Conspiracy* (London: I. B. Tauris, 2008).

contradictory, and unsatisfactory point at which to start or finish stages of European history. The rediscovery of progress in the 1950s was not an automatic consequence of the deadly decade that preceded it, but it brought the massive violence to an end and won back some of that lost trajectory of 1914.

Further Reading

Diefendorf, Jeffrey, *In the Wake of War: The Reconstruction of German Cities after World War II* (New York: Oxford University Press, 1993).

Domenico, Roy P., *Italian Fascists on Trial, 1943–1948* (Chapel Hill, NC: University of North Carolina Press, 1991).

Frei, Norbert, *Adenauer's Germany and the Nazi Past: The Politics of Amnesty and Integration* (New York: Columbia University Press, 2002).

Golsan, Richard J., *Vichy's Afterlife: History and Counterhistory in Postwar France* (Lincoln, NE: University of Nebraska Press, 2000).

Gregor, Neil, *Haunted City: Nuremberg and the Nazi Past* (New Haven, CT: Yale University Press, 2008).

Herf, Jeffrey, *Divided Memory: The Nazi Past in the Two Germanys* (Cambridge, MA: Harvard University Press, 1997).

Knapp, Andrew (ed.), *The Uncertain Foundation: France at the Liberation, 1944–47* (Basingstoke: Palgrave Macmillan, 2007).

Leffler, Melvyn P. and David S. Painter (eds), *Origins of the Cold War: An International History* (London: Routledge, 1995).

Sanchez, Antonio C., *Fear and Progress: Ordinary Lives in Franco's Spain 1939–1975* (Oxford: Wiley-Blackwell, 2010).

Statiev, Alexander, *The Soviet Counterinsurgency in the Western Borderlands* (Cambridge: Cambridge University Press, 2010).

Weiner, Amir, *Making Sense of War: The Second World War and the Fate of the Bolshevik Revolution* (Princeton, NJ: Princeton University Press, 2001).

Wiesen, S. Jonathan, *West German Industry and the Challenge of the Nazi Past, 1945–1955* (Chapel Hill, NC: University of North Carolina Press, 2001).

Zubok, Vladislav and Constantine Pleshakov, *Inside the Kremlin's Cold War: From Stalin to Khrushchev* (Cambridge, MA: Harvard University Press, 1996).

CHAPTER 3

EAST, WEST, AND THE RETURN OF 'CENTRAL': BORDERS DRAWN AND REDRAWN

CATHERINE LEE AND ROBERT BIDELEUX

RUDYARD Kipling's 'East is East and West is West and never the twain shall meet' has been proven wrong in respect of Europe.[1] Western Europe has not only met but also married Eastern Europe, even if there are rumours that it was a marriage of convenience, consummated in 'EU Europe'. Nevertheless, a significant outcome of the cohabitation has been the resurgence of debates about the status, location, and distinctiveness of 'Central Europe', the changing nature of borders and borderlands, and the emergence of 'new' East/West divides. This in turn has precipitated crises of identity for both Eastern and Western Europe; the boundaries, 'identities', purposes, and even the existence of the East, West, and Central Europes have been called into question. How, then, can we understand the changing positions and meanings of Eastern, Central, and Western Europe in the political, geographic, cultural, and symbolic cartography of postwar Europe?

Notions of Europe have manifested chameleon-like in many shapes and guises. This is perhaps a distinctive feature of Europe; as a presumed and self-ascribed continent, there is no clear and uncontested definition of its boundaries. In fact, 'there are several Europes, which become fleeting as one attempts to understand them too closely'.[2] It is much easier to agree on the general limits of North America, South America, or Australia, than it is to identify the places where Europe becomes Asia and vice versa. If there is no consensus on where Europe begins and ends, how then can we know where

[1] Rudyard Kipling, 'The Ballad of East and West', in *Collected Poems of Rudyard Kipling* (Ware: Wordsworth Editions, 1994), 245.

[2] Jacques Attali, *Europe(s)* (Paris: Fayard, 1994).

or what East, West, or Central Europe is, let alone understand what purposes these divisions might serve?

Many possible frames for conceptions of Europe have been put forth and argued for: history, geography, religion, culture, etc. However, ultimately, none of these frames is fully convincing,[3] and exceptions can always be found. Conceptualizing and constructing European geographies, physical and symbolic, is an ongoing preoccupation. This has contributed to an almost obsessive desire to put Europe in its place and to describe and demarcate Europe; a European Studies industry is flourishing in academia.[4] Since the Renaissance, Europeans have been preoccupied with notions of perspective, mental mapping, mathematical constructions of space, world maps as grids of mathematical coordinates, and the use of geography as a 'knowledge that could be exploited for religious, political, economic, and military purposes on a world stage'.[5] These ways of seeing and knowing have 'allowed the world to be divided up into a variety of grids' whereby 'global space was "hierarchized" and ordered into zones of greater or lesser significance',[6] cascading hierarchies and divisions not only around the world, but also throughout the Europes. Europe has been described as

> an intricate game of inclusions and exclusions, which still speaks of its . . . history of abuse and oppression . . . a history that has always been "Eurocentric" and selfish, and that has always known how to impose its own images of power.[7]

Nevertheless, notions of Europe and the configurations of European states and polities are not static. Europe has been conceptualized as a polycentric, de-centred, continually changing vortex with multiple identities, no original founding principles, and no fixed essence.[8] The Europes we think we see now are unlikely to have any more permanence or solidity than their predecessors.

TERRITORIAL RECONFIGURATIONS IN EUROPE AT THE CLOSE OF THE SECOND WORLD WAR

Trying to locate the constituent parts of Europe and to understand their complex relationships is akin to viewing a Jackson Pollock painting; countries have seemingly been dropped onto the map of Eurasia like viscous blobs of paint, and the viewer must try to

---

[3] Catherine Lee and Robert Bideleux, 'Europe: What Kind of Idea?', *The European Legacy* 14:2 (2009), 163–76.

[4] See Chris Rumford (ed.), *The Sage Handbook of European Studies* (London: Sage, 2009).

[5] John Headley, *The Europeanization of the World* (Princeton, NJ: Princeton University Press, 2008), 9–23.

[6] John Agnew, *Geopolitics: Re-Visioning World Politics*, 2nd edn (London: Routledge, 2003), 21–2.

[7] Marina De Chiara, 'A Tribe Called Europe', in Iain Chambers and Lidia Curti (eds), *The Post-Colonial Question: Common Skies, Divided Horizons* (London: Routledge, 1996), 232.

[8] Edgar Morin, *Penser l'Europe*, 2nd edn (Paris: Gallimard, 1990), 24–5, 37, 52–4, 69, 217.

make sense of the relationships. The close of the Second World War unleashed a seismic tremor of major territorial reconfigurations; borders were shifted dramatically, altering the ethnic compositions of Europe's states. Although the precise numbers are matters of considerable debate, the Second World War was accompanied by the killing of between five and six million European Jews (including 2.9 million Polish Jews); between 2.6 and 2.8 million non-Jewish citizens of Poland; between 650,000 and 736,000 non-Jewish Greeks; around 410,000 non-Jewish citizens of the Baltic States; approximately 537,000 non-Jewish Serbs and Montenegrins; 207,000 non-Jewish Croats; 86,000 Bosniaks (Bosnian Muslims); 30,000 non-Jewish Slovenes; 28,000 Albanians; between 200,000 and 600,000 Roma (Gypsies); between 320,000 and 530,000 non-Jewish Romanians; between 350,000 and 500,000 non-Jewish citizens of greater Hungary; between 200,000 and 230,000 non-Jewish Czechs and Slovaks; between six and eight million non-Jewish Germans and Austrians; and between fifteen and twenty million non-Jewish Russians, Ukrainians, and Belarusians.

Although the Holocaust against Europe's Jews has stood out as the most calculated and systematic dimension of Europe's ghastly bloodletting, it was not the largest single component. Indeed, because the Second World War was predominantly fought on the Eastern Front, almost 95 per cent of Europe's fatalities of war and genocide were in Central and Eastern Europe (including Germany and Austria). The number of Western European casualties was far smaller: the numbers of non-Jewish lives lost were just under half a million each for France, Italy, and the UK. Belgium lost 62,000, but Finnish and Dutch losses were relatively heavy at 97,000 and 197,000, respectively.

These mass killings, combined with the paramount role of the Soviet Union in the defeat of the Third Reich, led to substantial reconfigurations of the borders and ethnic compositions of European states. The major territorial changes carried out in Europe during 1945–8 included:

(i)   the incorporation of most of the territories which had formerly belonged to interwar Poland, Czechoslovakia, Hungary, and Romania, but which were inhabited predominantly by Ukrainians or Belarusians, into greatly expanded Soviet Socialist Republics of Ukraine and Belarus (ostensibly to bring territorial boundaries into closer correspondence with ethnic geography, but actually partly as the main fruits of the Soviet military victories during 1944–5);

(ii) the Soviet annexation of Bessarabia (renamed the Soviet Socialist Republic of Moldovia) and Bukovina, even though neither of these territories was inhabited by a Russo–Ukrainian ethnic majority (and Bukovina, unlike Bessarabia, had never previously been part of the Soviet Union or the Tsarist Empire);

(iii) the agreement between Roosevelt, Churchill, and Stalin at the Yalta Conference in February 1945 to relocate Poland massively westwards (at Germany's expense), as the major corollary of the large-scale westward expansion of the USSR, which was also agreed at Yalta;

(iv)   the incorporation of the port-city of Königsberg (renamed Kaliningrad) and parts of the interwar territories of the Baltic States into the Russian Federation (RSFSR), either on strategic grounds or for reasons of ethnic geography;

(v)   the transfer of the Vilnius region from Poland to the new Soviet Socialist Republic of Lithuania, mainly for reasons of ethnic geography;

(vi)   the restoration of northern Transylvania to Romania, mainly for reasons of ethnic geography;

(vii)   the restoration of the so-called Sudetenland and the Slovak–Hungarian borderlands to Czechoslovakia, partly for reasons of ethnic geography, but also partly for strategic reasons;

(viii)   the return of Vojvodina from Hungary to Yugoslavia, for reasons of ethnic geography;

(ix)   the return of South Dobrudja from Romania (which had annexed it in 1913) to Bulgaria (this occurred courtesy of the Axis powers in 1940, but was confirmed by the Allies in 1947);

(x)   the transfer of parts of the Friuli and Venezia Giulia border areas to Yugoslavia under the Paris Peace Treaties of 1947, and parts of Trieste's hinterland to Yugoslavia under the London Memorandum of 1954;

(xi)   the transfer of various partly Italian-inhabited islands in the Aegean and the Adriatic Seas to Greece or Yugoslavia;

(xii)   adjustments along the Greece–Yugoslavia border;

(xiii)   adjustments along the Albania–Yugoslavia border;

(xiv)   the partitioning of Germany into western and eastern zones of occupation, which soon evolved into separate states;

(xv)   the return of Alsace-Lorraine from Germany to France.

The demographic and territorial changes were smaller and less consequential in Western Europe than in Central and Eastern Europe, which, having borne the brunt of the war, also incurred the bulk of the wartime and postwar 'surgery'. Furthermore, although most of the border changes in Central and Eastern Europe were rationalized on the basis of ethnic geography, the decisions were often made for strategic reasons or so-called 'reasons of state', giving the inhabitants of the territories very little say in the matter. If they had been allowed to express free choices, many ethnic Ukrainians, Belarusians, and Moldovan Romanians might well have preferred to remain under Polish, Czechoslovak, Hungarian, or Romanian rule (instead of coming under direct Soviet rule). Where plebiscites were held, ostensibly to decide the future of territories or to ratify decisions made by Allied 'statesmen', the results may often have been rigged.

During the 1940s, the ethnic homogeneity of states in the eastern half of Europe was dramatically increased by the combined impact of: the large-scale redrawing of territorial boundaries, above all the westward expansion of the Soviet Union and the westward displacement of Poland; the extermination of over four million Central and East European and Balkan Jews, up to half a million Roma ('Gypsies'), and millions of non-Jewish Poles, Russians, Ukrainians, and South Slavs; the emigration of most of the surviving Central and East European Jews; and widespread 'ethnic cleansing' (mass expulsions and flight preceded or accompanied by widespread killing), including the expulsion or flight of thirteen to fifteen million Volksdeutsche from the eastern half of Europe to a truncated Germany during 1945–7.[9] Likewise, large numbers of ethnic Hungarians were expelled from Czechoslovakia and Romania to a truncated Hungary, while smaller numbers of ethnic Romanians and ethnic Slovaks were expelled from Hungary to Romania and Czechoslovakia, respectively.

These changes expedited the postwar socio-economic transformations of these regions, inasmuch as the German and Jewish communities had each comprised between 25 per cent and 40 per cent of the 'old' entrepreneurial and professional urban middle classes in the eastern part of Central Europe, and between 15 per cent and 30 per cent of the 'old' urban entrepreneurial and professional middle classes in much of the Balkans. In these regions, mass expulsion or extermination of Germans and Jews made it easier for nascent communist regimes to promote upward social mobility of millions of non-German and non-Jewish proletarians and peasants into the urban middle classes, who, under communist rule, were metamorphosed into white-collar 'intelligentsia' employed by the state. The drastic ethnic and territorial surgery carried out from above in the already brutalized and shell-shocked Baltic and Balkan states and the eastern parts of Central Europe between 1939 and 1946 greatly reduced potential societal resistance to the further large-scale social engineering and 'purges' enacted by communist dictatorships between 1946 or 1947 and 1953.[10]

Tim Snyder has highlighted the deeply intertwined roles of the Second World War, the Holocaust, and their immediate aftermaths, in rapidly and brutally destroying the hitherto strongly multi-ethnic and multi-denominational composition of towns in Poland, Lithuania, and Belarus, along with the relatively open, tolerant, and cosmopolitan conception of the political nation (associated with the still lingering heritage of the defunct Polish–Lithuanian Commonwealth, extinguished in 1795), thus paving the way for the emergence of more ethnically homogeneous towns, cities, nations, and states. In Poland,

> Polish communists, aided directly by Soviet forces and indirectly by Polish nationalists, completed a project of national homogenization in 1947. Withal we observe the line of continuity: from the Final Solution to partisan cleansings to communist cleansings to the establishment of communist rule.[11]

Equally dramatically, Vilnius, which had been part of interwar Poland but became the capital of the new Soviet Socialist Republic of Lithuania from 1945 onwards, was swiftly transformed from an overwhelmingly Polish and Jewish city into one with an ethnic

[9] István Deák, 'Introduction', in István Deák, Jan T. Gross, and Tony Judt (eds), *The Politics of Retribution in Europe: World War II and Its Aftermath* (Princeton, NJ: Princeton University Press, 2000), 4.

[10] Robert Bideleux and Ian Jeffries, *History of Eastern Europe*, 2nd edn (Abingdon: Routledge, 2007), 451–5, 464.

[11] Tim Snyder, *The Reconstruction of Nations: Poland, Ukraine, Lithuania, Belarus, 1569–1999* (London: Yale University Press, 2003), 1–8.

Lithuanian majority. In this way, 'the Second World War, the Final Solution, and Soviet deportations did incomparably more than the policies of inter-war Poland and Lithuania to homogenize populations.'[12]

Mass killing and ethnic cleansing of civilians belonging to minority groups were not exclusively the work of Soviet and Nazi German personnel. Between 1943 and 1947, Ukrainian nationalist partisans drove out or killed over 95 per cent of the ethnically Polish inhabitants of Volhynia and Galicia, as well as over 95 per cent of those Volhynian and Galician Jews who had escaped extermination at German hands; whereupon Polish militias and underground resistance groups retaliated by driving out or killing over 90 per cent of the ethnic Ukrainian inhabitants of the previously multi-ethnic eastern regions, which became Poland's new easterly and southerly borderlands.[13]

Similarly, the westward flight or expulsion of 6.6 million Germans from Poland's newly assigned 'Western Territories' in 1945 (soon to be replaced by millions of Poles from further east) resulted in tens of thousands of deaths.[14] The expulsion of about three million Germans from Czechoslovakia (comprising about a quarter of Czechoslovakia's population) also involved significant loss of German lives, albeit fewer than in Poland's new 'Western Territories'.[15] Significantly, the nearly 700 people executed in Czechoslovakia during the short interval between 'liberation' in May 1945 and the communist takeover in February 1948 exceeded the number of executions during the entire four decades of communist rule (from February 1948 to November 1989).[16] Nevertheless, such retribution was not confined to the eastern half of Europe. During 1945–46 there were also thousands of lynchings and hasty executions of fascists, 'collaborators', and alleged war criminals in Italy and France. As István Deák put it: 'For the first time in history, a whole continent made an attempt to settle accounts with its own political crimes and criminals'.[17]

THE GREAT HARDENING OF BORDERS

The drastic redrawing of European borders during 1945–48 was accompanied by major changes in their nature and meaning; 'Borders are not simply lines on maps where one jurisdiction ends and another begins. Borders are complex institutions shaping the

[12] Tim Snyder, *The Reconstruction of Nations: Poland, Ukraine, Lithuania, Belarus, 1569–1999* (London: Yale University Press, 2003), 91–2.

[13] Ibid., 191–204.

[14] Jan Gross, *Fear: Anti-Semitism in Poland after Auschwitz* (Princeton, NJ: Princeton University Press), 35; William Woods, *Poland: Phoenix in the East* (London: Penguin, 1972), 68; R.F. Leslie (ed.), *The History of Poland since 1863* (Cambridge: Cambridge University Press, 1980), 288.

[15] Derek Sayer, *The Coasts of Bohemia: A Czech History* (Princeton, NJ: Princeton University Press, 2000), 242–3; Benjamin Fromm, *National Cleansing: Retribution against Nazi Collaborators in Postwar Czechoslovakia* (Cambridge: Cambridge University Press, 2004), 2–3, 31.

[16] Fromm, *National Cleansing*, 2–3, 31.

[17] István Deák, 'Resistance, Collaboration and Retribution during World War II and its Aftermath', *Hungarian Quarterly* 35 (1994), 134.

nature of [the] polities they demarcate.'[18] Between the late 1940s and the late 1980s, a period often mistakenly regarded as coterminous with the Cold War (which actually began in 1918 rather than in the late 1940s),[19] European borders became harder and less porous, especially in the eastern half of Europe. The Iron Curtain, aptly labelled by Churchill in 1946, demarcated a forcibly bundled together Soviet bloc commonly referred to as 'Eastern Europe', which rapidly became hermetically sealed off from the rest of the world. 'Barbed wire, minefields, watchtowers and border guards with orders to shoot clearly marked the junction of East and West.'[20]

'Western Europe', which, like 'Eastern Europe', had not previously existed as a conceptually unified, geopolitical entity, was equally hurriedly and artificially devised and institutionalized in a top-down manner, over the heads of the wider public, through the Council of Europe, the European Communities, NATO, the OEEC-turned-OECD, and the 1947–51 Marshall Plan. Most Europeans were thus corralled into two mutually antagonistic armed camps. This drastically restricted contact, communication, and movement, not only across the Iron Curtain, but also between East European states.

Even though, among themselves, West European states rejected national seclusion and protectionism in favour of liberalized movement of goods (and later labour, capital, and services), most West European states, with the exception of Italy, initially resisted free movement of people.[21] Despite a brief interlude of liberalization of movement of people during the 1950s and 1960s, increasingly stringent border controls on immigration from outside Western Europe were developed from the mid-1970s onwards, raising the spectre of 'Fortress Europe'. The dramatic hardening of state borders from the late 1940s onwards represented a culmination of: (i) the rise of trade protectionism since the 1870s, which intensified greatly during the First World War and became more deeply entrenched during the interwar years; (ii) the systems of passports and other controls on movement of people introduced during the First World War and largely maintained thereafter; (iii) the controls on capital movements introduced during the First World War and largely maintained from then until the late 1980s; (iv) the gradual resurgence of European xenophobia and racism from the mid-1970s onwards;[22] and (v) a growing 'securitization' of immigration issues in Western Europe from the 1980s onwards.[23]

---

[18] Jan Zielonka, *Europe as Empire: The Nature of the Enlarged European Union* (Oxford: Oxford University Press, 2006), 3.

[19] See Robert Bideleux, 'Soviet and Russian Perspectives on the Cold War', in Alan Dobson, Shahin P. Malik and Graham Evans (eds), *Deconstructing and Reconstructing the Cold War* (Aldershot: Ashgate, 1999), 226–49.

[20] Lonnie Johnson, *Central Europe*, 2nd edn (Oxford: Oxford University Press, 2002), 9.

[21] Federico Romero, 'Migration as an Issue in European Interdependence and Integration: The Case of Italy', in Alan Milward et al., *The Frontier of National Sovereignty: History and Theory, 1945–92* (London: Routledge, 1993) 33–58.

[22] Robert Bideleux, 'Imigração, Multiculturalismo e Xenofobia na União Européia', in M. M. Tavares Ribeiro (ed.), *Europa em Mutação: Cidadania, Identidade, Diversidade Cultural* (Coimbra, Portugal: Quarteto, 2003), 243–61.

[23] See Jef Huysmans, 'The European Union and the Securitization of Migration', *Journal of Common Market Studies* 38:5 (2000); and Jef Huysmans, *The Politics of Insecurity: Fear, Migration and Asylum in the EU* (London: Routledge, 2006).

Europe's Borders Redrawn yet again in the Late 1980s and 1990s

In the late 1980s, Europe's geography began to quiver once more. In 1985, Mikhail Gorbachev became First Secretary (leader) of the Soviet Communist Party and began to introduce political openness (*glasnost*) and economic restructuring (*perestroika*) in the USSR and to indicate that the Soviet Union would no longer intervene militarily in its client states. These moves encouraged Soviet bloc countries to break loose, culminating in the fall of the Berlin Wall and the lifting of the Iron Curtain in November 1989, paving the way for German reunification in autumn 1990. After the failure of a military putsch by Soviet hardliners in August 1991, the Soviet Federation rapidly unravelled, and the Czechoslovak Federation split into two states in 1993.

The disintegration of the Soviet bloc also contributed to the violent break-up of the Yugoslav Federation. Slovenia and Croatia declared independence on 25 June 1991 although this only took effect after the expiry of a three-month moratorium brokered by the European Community. The resultant war between Serbia and Croatia (1991–5) claimed 22,000 lives. The Republic of Macedonia declared independence in September 1991, Bosnia followed suit in March 1992, and Montenegro and Serbia (which still controlled Kosovo) established a drastically downsized Federal Republic of Yugoslavia the following month. A federalized Bosnia and Herzegovina emerged out of the November 1995 Dayton Accords, which ended the Bosnia conflicts of 1992–5, in which about 105,000 people had perished. Finally, Montenegro seceded from its State Union with Serbia in June 2006, and Kosovo declared independence from Serbia in 2008. Former Yugoslavia had splintered into seven 'successor states': Slovenia, Croatia, Macedonia, Serbia, Montenegro, Bosnia and Herzegovina, and Kosovo.[24]

The Impact on European Borders of the EU and its 'Deepening' and 'Widening'

After experiencing the horrors of the Second World War, postwar Western Europe was marked by moves towards integration and cooperation. Belgium, France, Italy, Luxembourg, the Netherlands, and West Germany agreed to found the European Coal and Steel Community in 1950, and the European Economic Community in 1957. In 1973, the European Communities were enlarged to include Denmark, Ireland, and the UK. Greece joined in 1981, and Spain and Portugal followed in 1986. The 1985 Schengen

---

[24] Yugoslavia's disintegration is described in Robert Bideleux and Ian Jeffries, *History of Eastern Europe*, 519–25; and *The Balkans: A Post-Communist History* (Abingdon: Routledge, 2007), 183–580.

Agreement initiated preparations for a 'core Europe' of open borders without passport controls, while the 1986 Single European Act introduced the main legal and institutional foundations for a far-reaching and highly integrated single market. In 1990, former East Germany joined the European Community by the back door, as part of reunified Germany. The prospect of Germany re-emerging as Europe's hegemonic state and economy, combined with the demise of Europe's communist regimes between 1989 and 1991 and the dramatic proliferation of fully independent states in Europe after 1989, expanded the scope for European integration while also posing new challenges.[25] Thus, at Maastricht in 1991, the 'twelve' agreed to form a European Union (EU) embodying projects for deeper monetary union, political union, and a common foreign and security policy, starting in 1993. Faced with the possibility of being left out in the cold, Austria, Sweden, and Finland intensified their membership preparations during 1993–94 and joined the EU in 1995.

At Copenhagen in June 1993, the EU spelled out explicit membership criteria. Hungary and Poland submitted applications for EU membership in 1994, Slovakia, Romania, Latvia, Estonia, Lithuania, and Bulgaria followed suit in 1995, and the Czech Republic and Slovenia did so in 1996. In response, in July 1997, the EU Commission published its *Agenda 2000*, a more comprehensive and exacting set of preconditions for the admission of new member states, in the explicit expectation that the first wave of new accessions could occur in 2002–03. It also recommended that Poland, Hungary, the Czech Republic, Slovenia, Estonia, and Cyprus be invited to begin membership negotiations in 1998; this recommendation was ratified by the EU European Council in December 1997. In October and December 1999, in the wake of the Kosovo conflict, similar invitations were extended to the other candidates, including Turkey, but the envisaged date for the first wave of eastward enlargement was put back to 2004. In the event, two candidates (Romania and Bulgaria) were made to wait until 2007 and Turkey is in limbo, in danger of being required to wait indefinitely, while the other candidates were admitted on schedule in 2004.

The eastward enlargement of the EU, together with the disintegration of the former Yugoslav, Soviet, and Czechoslovak federations, has not merely rearranged Europe's formal and symbolic boundaries and extended the EU civil order eastwards. More fundamentally, it has ushered in a wider reconfiguration of the European order, including far-reaching changes in the nature, meaning, and implications of borders in the enlarged EU, and major extensions and strengthening of the EU's new supranational civil order.[26] While substantial restructuring and metamorphoses were likely results of these

---

[25] See Robert Bideleux and Richard Taylor (eds), *European Integration and Disintegration, East and West* (London: Routledge, 1996).

[26] Robert Bideleux, 'Introduction: Reconstituting Political Order in Europe, West and East', *Perspectives on European Politics and Society* 10:1 (2009), 3–16; 'Rethinking the Eastward Extension of the EU Civil Order and the Nature of Europe's New East-West Divide', *Perspectives on European Politics and Society* 10:1 (2009), 118–36; 'Post-Communist Democratization: Democratic Politics as the Art of the Impossible?', *Review of Politics* 71:2 (2009), 303–17.

changes, the emerging supranational civil order was, in principle, capable of moving either towards harder and more clear-cut borders in a vertically structured Europe, or towards softer and fuzzier borders in a less tidy, more horizontally structured, de-centred, 'postmodern', or 'neo-medieval' Europe.[27]

Since approximately 2002–3, some West European politicians, media, and public have expressed fears that eastward enlargement of the EU poses perceived 'threats' of increased crime, corruption, trafficking, migration, and job insecurity, and have there-fore demanded and expected that the EU's external perimeter borders should be hard-ened and made less porous, the 'Fortress Europe' syndrome. However, many of the perceived threats have been more illusory or alarmist than real, and smaller than feared. The UK, Ireland, and Sweden, the three countries that immediately opened their doors to a substantial wave of migrants from the eastern parts of Central Europe from 2004 onwards, experienced accelerated economic growth, increased job creation, reduced unemployment, and diminished crime rates between 2004 and 2007. Furthermore, the ethnic patchwork and borderland character of the Baltic region, the Balkans, and the eastern parts of Central Europe; the largely migration-induced, multi-ethnic, multicul-tural, and multiracial character of latter-day Western Europe; the 2004 and 2007 east-ward enlargement of the EU; the EU's ever deepening relations with current candidate countries and associated states; and the gradual development of the EU's Neighbourhood and Eastern Partnership policies towards countries lying immediately to the east and south of the EU, have, in practice, made it necessary for the enlarged EU to develop increasingly soft and porous borders, not just internally, as required by the Schengen agreement, but also along the EU's increasingly ill-defined and hard-to-police eastern and southern perimeters, Europe's 'eastern marchlands'.[28] The resultant flows of trade and networks of interdependence mean that a bricolage of overlapping relationships is developing. For example the rise of Turkey as a dynamic hub for trade, banking, air routes, pipeline networks, and student flows, combined with the development of organ-izations such as the Black Sea Economic Cooperation (since 1992), is challenging EU Europe hegemony and encouraging elasticity and dynamism.

Nevertheless, Europe's borders are far more controlled and controlling than those that existed prior to the First World War, that is, prior to the introduction of the elabo-rate systems of passports and visa requirements which came to be taken for granted as seemingly 'natural' and permanent features of the mid-to-late twentieth-century states system. The nature of the border regimes that have become obligatory in the EU's exist-ing member states, as well as in the European Economic Area and in any serious aspir-ant to EU membership, has acquired enormous significance for people from 'other' parts of the world. For many millions of people in Russia, Ukraine, Belarus, Moldova, the Caucasus, Latin America, and Africa, the questions of whether or not they can obtain

---

[27] Jan Zielonka, 'How Enlarged Borders Will Reshape the European Union', *Journal of Common Market Studies* 39:3 (2001), 509, 517–19.

[28] See also the similar but differently formulated perspectives in Zielonka, *Europe as Empire*, 1–6.

passports, visas, work permits, or full citizenship in or from any EU member states have become important determinants of life chances.

A key question is whether the EU should be merely a 'common space' within which to live, work, trade, and move freely, or whether it is or should become a more hierarchical, communitarian, primordial, and state-like entity, to be belonged to, identified with, and legally as well as militarily protected. The closer the EU moves to the latter model, the more rigid its external borders will become, and the more challenges this will pose for its relations with other parts of the world, especially for the immediately adjacent regions and countries. This is one of the EU's unresolved dilemmas, which is likely to be contested for decades because no easy answer is in sight.

LOCATING CENTRAL EUROPE

Logically, it would seem that Central Europe would lie between Western and Eastern Europe. However, the vagaries of history and the uncertain locations of Western Europe and Eastern Europe have meant that Central Europe has been a contested and ephemeral concept. After 1946, when the Iron Curtain bifurcated Europe, there was apparently little conceptual use for Central Europe. 'Eastern Europe' came to denote all those parts of Europe that were ensnared under Soviet domination. The idea of Central Europe was 'cherished between consenting adults in private, but from the public sphere it vanished'.[29]

This is not to say that the idea of Central Europe was abandoned during the postwar years. Rather, it assumed an a-geographic, dream-like quality, a tactical construct epitomized in Milan Kundera's essay, 'The Tragedy of Central Europe',[30] in which Central Europe is described as 'a culture or a fate' whose 'borders are imaginary and must be drawn and redrawn with each new historical situation'; a space 'situated geographically in the center—culturally in the West and politically in the East', 'locked within Germany and Russia'; a 'kidnapped Occident' cut off by the Yalta agreement, longing to reclaim its former intellectual and artistic status and to escape the 'disgusting East European brand'.[31] Kundera argues that 'the Jews in the twentieth century were the principal cosmopolitan, integrating element in Central Europe: they were its intellectual cement, a condensed version of its spirit, creators of its spiritual unity'.[32]

Kundera's essay was part of a discourse of both nostalgia and strategizing about the future of Central Europe which occurred in the 1980s, particularly among writers and

---

[29] Timothy Garton Ash, 'Does Central Europe Exist?', in *The Uses of Adversity, Essays on the Fate of Central Europe* (New York: Random House, 1989).

[30] Milan Kundera, 'The Tragedy of Central Europe', *New York Review of Books* 31:7 (26 April 1984), 33–8.

[31] Taras Wozniak, *East European déjà vu*, www.eurozine.com/articles/2004-06-25-wozniak-en.html, accessed January 2010.

[32] Kundera, 'The Tragedy of Central Europe', 35.

intellectuals in or from Czechoslovakia (e.g. Milan Kundera, Václav Havel, Miroslav Kusy); Hungary (e.g. György Konrád, Jenö Szücs, Peter Hanak, Ferenc Feher); Poland (e.g. Adam Michnik, Czesław Miłosz, Piotr Wandycz); and Croatia (Miroslav Krleža, Predrag Matvejevic). In their writings, Eastern Europe was where they did not want to be, whereas Central Europe was portrayed with longing, wistfulness, and Western credentials. Implicitly, they were protesting against the role of the February 1945 Yalta Conference in authorizing and constructing 'Eastern Europe' as a Soviet-dominated geopolitical entity.

The Hungarian, György Konrád (b.1933), wrote that 'Being Central-European is an attitude, a Weltanschauung, an aesthetic sensitivity for complexity, for the polyglot-ness of points of view... Being Central-European means, to consider variety as a value'. Yet he, too, acknowledged that Central Europe was more of an aspiration than a reality: 'By contrast with the political reality of Eastern Europe and Western Europe, Central Europe exists only as a cultural counterhypothesis.'[33] In 1987, the eminent Polish writer Czesław Miłosz (1911–2004) suggested that:

> Central Europe is an act of faith, a project... If you look at the real world, the world of borders and partitions and regional conflicts, then there is little reason to speak of 'Central Europe'. Once Europe was divided into so-called Eastern and Western Europe it became even harder to convince anyone that 'Central Europe' was more than a figment of someone's imagination. But I am attracted to what is frankly a utopian project, and I am supported in my faith by what I see as a largely common heritage, a whole range of unifying historical experiences, a common architecture in the major cities, and common religions, and cultural traditions. I can't define the geographical borders of our Central Europe, but clearly architecture might be one way of helping to define them... I'm probably on safer ground when I say that there is a certain feeling we have, when Poles, Czechs, Yugoslavs, Hungarians, and Lithuanians gather, that we share some common heritage.[34]

These authors were part of an attempt to 'reclaim' Central Europe's 'Western' prerequisites and distance it from the Soviet system by emphasizing the region's rich and diverse heritage, in what has been described as an attempt 'to construct or reconstruct a consciousness which emphasizes values other than those propagated by the [then] existing system, for this latter is seen as intellectually and morally bankrupt.'[35] Membership in a Central European club was thought to be a route out of the East and into the West, while largely ignoring the shady side of Central European history: 'after all', as Konrád noted, 'we Central Europeans began the first two world wars'.[36] Running parallel to the question,

---

[33] György Konrád, 'Is the Dream of Central Europe Still Alive?', in *Cross Currents: A Yearbook of Central European Culture* 5 (Ann Arbor, MI: University of Michigan, 1986), 109–21.

[34] Cynthia L. Haven, ed., *Czesław Miłosz: Conversations* (Jackson, MS: University Press of Mississippi 2006), 86–7.

[35] George Schöpflin and Nancy Wood (eds), *In Search of Central Europe* (Cambridge: Polity Press, 1989).

[36] Garton Ash, 'Does Central Europe Exist?'

Does Central Europe Exist?[37] were themes of losses, tragedies, and upheavals: narratives of a liminal space which had generated internal convulsions and been subjected to multiple 'penetrations'.[38]

These conceptions of 'Central Europe' bring to mind Salman Rushdie's notion of 'imaginary homelands' constructed by exiled or migrant diasporas.[39] Kundera and some of the other champions of 'Central Europe' were exiles cherishing idealized imaginings of their 'homeland', constructed as an antithesis to the grim, grey, banal realities of 'the Soviet bloc'. Other proponents of 'Central Europe' were trapped at home, unable to travel, but defiantly living in what has been called 'internal emigration', in an imaginary but nonetheless real homeland of their own construction. Václav Havel called it 'living in truth'.

With the demise of Europe's communist regimes during 1989–91, the term Central Europe emerged in the broader academic, social, and political discourses. The reacceptance of Central Europe into official international geopolitical parlance was heralded by the arrival of Central European departments in the US State Department and the British Foreign Office, and by Henry Kissinger's famous declaration in Warsaw in summer 1990: 'I'm delighted to be here in Eastern, I mean Central Europe.'[40] Since then, parts of Central Europe have been variously framed as in need of rehabilitation, reintegration, and reintroduction to 'Europe'. They are also held up as examples of successful marketization of former planned economies, though the global economic crisis, which manifested in 2008–09, has given pause to these convictions.

Nevertheless, the question of where or what is Central Europe stubbornly persists. It has been claimed that Central Europe encompasses the area that is considered Eastern by Western Europe, and Western by Eastern Europe. Ultimately, decisions about which countries to include in Central Europe have depended on the use to which the term is to be put; the implicit claims being made; and the historical, economic, political, or cultural reference points chosen. While it may be true that 'Historical memory, the presence of a past that is so remote that it bears little or no resemblance to the so-called realities of the contemporary world, is an important Central European attribute',[41] there have also been pragmatic political, social, cultural, and economic definitions of Central Europe.

Probably the broadest conception of Central Europe is embedded in the time zones. Central European Time (GMT + 1) and/or Central European Summer Time (GMT + 2)

---

[37] Ibid.

[38] The theme of tragedy appeared in Kundera's essay (1983–84) and in works such as Stephen Borsody's *The Tragedy of Central Europe: Nazi and Soviet Conquest and Aftermath* (New Haven, CT: Yale Concilium on International and Area Studies, 1980).

[39] Salman Rushdie, *Imaginary Homelands: Essays and Criticism, 1981–91* (London: Penguin/Granta, 1991).

[40] Quoted in Timothy Garton Ash, 'The Puzzle of Central Europe', *New York Review of Books* (18 March 1989).

[41] Lonnie Johnson, *Central Europe: Enemies, Neighbours, Friends,* 2nd edition (Oxford: Oxford University Press, 2002), 3.

is used in many countries. Even the UK toyed with the idea of joining this time zone when a Central European Time Bill was introduced in the House of Lords on 29 November 1994. Presently, the Central European (Summer) Time zones include: Albania, Andorra, Austria, Belgium, Bosnia-Herzegovina, Croatia, Czech Republic, Denmark (mainland), France, Germany, Gibraltar, Holy See/Vatican City, Hungary, Italy, Kosovo, Lichtenstein, Luxembourg, Macedonia, Malta, Monaco, Montenegro, the Netherlands, Norway, Poland, San Marino, Serbia, Slovakia, Slovenia, Spain (except the Canary Islands), Sweden, and Switzerland.[42] Despite the daily importance and sway of 'time', this definition of Central Europe would probably not be widely recognized or accepted.

The Central European Free Trade Agreement (CEFTA), on the other hand, highlights the role of the EU in the labelling of Central Europe. As a trade agreement between non-EU countries in Central and South-eastern Europe, the membership has changed over time from the original 1992 signatories of the Visegrád Group countries (Poland, Hungary, and the Czech and Slovak republics, at the time parts of the Czech and Slovak Federative Republic), adding Slovenia in 1996, Romania in 1997, Bulgaria in 1999, and Croatia in 2003. By 2006, because the original members of CEFTA had all joined the EU and thus left CEFTA, it was decided to extend CEFTA to Albania, Bosnia and Herzegovina, the United Nations Interim Administration Mission on behalf of Kosovo (UNMIK), Macedonia, Moldova, Serbia, and Montenegro. Accession of Ukraine has also been discussed. CEFTA has thus served as a forum for setting up free trade areas and an antechamber for EU membership.[43]

As countries become members of the EU, Central Europe is again redefined. The EU's Regional Development Fund (ERDF) programme, *Central Europe: Cooperating for Success* 'encourages cooperation among the countries of Central Europe' and 'promotes innovation, competitiveness, accessibility and environmental sustainability in Central Europe.' Here, the Central Europe 'cooperation area' encompasses the territory, or parts of the territory, of eight EU member states and the western border area of Ukraine including all or regions of: Austria, Czech Republic, Germany, Hungary, Italy, Poland, Slovak Republic, Slovenia, and the western border area of Ukraine. This definition is rather narrow, however, compared to the ways in which most academics have delineated Central Europe.

Perhaps the answer of a thirty-something-year-old Pole, now living in London, who was asked where or what he thought Central Europe was, whether Central Europe had a specific identity or culture, and whether he thought that he was Central European, can shed some light on the meaning of Central Europe:

> About Central Europe, it's an interesting question. I remember learning in Geography classes that the geographical centre of Europe is in Poland, not far from Warsaw. Because of this we were brought up to believe that we lived in Central Europe. So when I came to London I was very surprised to hear that I was from Eastern

---

[42] www.timeanddate.com/library/abbreviations/timezones/eu/cet.html, accessed January 2010.
[43] www.cefta2006.com, accessed January 2010.

Europe...the same applies to all my Polish friends. We didn't classify ourselves as Eastern European...For us Eastern Europe was the former Soviet republics like Belarus and the Russian area further to the east, because Europe stretches up to the Ural Mountains.

Now, having lived in London for over eight years I accept that I come from Eastern Europe and the image of Eastern Europe has changed. Now it seems to be more culturally- rather than geographically-based. Russia doesn't seem to be part of Europe probably because of its distinctiveness, even though they have an amazing cultural heritage. But maybe it's ignorance to some extent? I think it would be more correct to say that they are politically distinct rather than culturally.

If you ask people in Poland whether they live in Central or Eastern Europe, they almost invariably say Central Europe. Eastern Europe now has more to do with the borders of the EU rather than geographical Europe.

LOCATING EASTERN EUROPE, THE EU NEIGHBOURHOOD, AND EUROPE'S NEW EAST/WEST DIVIDE

Larry Wolff has argued that the notions of 'Eastern', 'Western', 'Northern', 'Southern' and 'Central' Europe, like the idea of 'Europe' itself, are implicitly relational concepts, mental constructs whose nature and significance depend on the location and self-identification of the perceiver. In Wolff's view, the idea of Eastern Europe was:

> not a natural distinction, or even an innocent one, for it was produced as a work of cultural creation, of intellectual artifice, of ideological self-interest and self-promotion...It was Western Europe that invented Eastern Europe as its complementary other half in the eighteenth century, the age of Enlightenment. It was also the Enlightenment, with its intellectual centers in Western Europe, that cultivated and appropriated to itself the new notion of 'civilization', an eighteenth-century neologism, and [Western European] civilization discovered its [East European] complement, within the same continent, in shadowed lands of backwardness, even barbarism. Such was the invention of Eastern Europe.[44]

Thus, Wolff has challenged the claims in Milan Kundera's 1983–84 essay, that the idea of Eastern Europe was a Soviet imposition on Central Europe.

> In 1989 there was a revolution in Eastern Europe, or rather a series of related revolutions in the different Eastern states...The division of Europe suddenly appeared to be over, erased, abolished, the halves all at once reunited as one continent...yet the shadow [of East/West division] persists...because the idea of Eastern Europe

---

[44] Larry Wolff, *Inventing Eastern Europe: The Map of Civilization on the Mind of the Enlightenment* (Stanford, CA: Stanford University Press, 1994), 4.

remains, even without the Iron Curtain. This is not only because the intellectual structures of half a century [of Soviet domination] are slow to efface themselves, but above all because that idea of Eastern Europe is much older than the Cold War.[45]

While there are claims that there are still East/West (and North/South) divides within EU Europe, it is the steady widening of the new East/West divide between EU Europe and its eastern neighbours that is the most disquieting.

The emergence and gradual eastward extension of the EU and its associated supranational civil order has set up a new separation between EU Europe and the Commonwealth of Independent States (CIS). In the immediate aftermath of the Cold War, Mikhail Gorbachev and his closest associates expressed hopes that Europe's East/West divide would be abolished by embedding the whole of 'the common European home' in an expanded civil order based on liberal democracy, liberal capitalism, limited government, unfettered and vibrant civil societies, and the rule of law. However, since then, democratization and the development of a new civil order have made very limited headway in the eleven post-Soviet states, loosely grouped together as the CIS (Armenia, Azerbaijan, Belarus, Kazakhstan, the Kyrgyz Republic, Moldova, Russia, Tajikistan, Turkmenistan, Ukraine, Uzbekistan). In these states, neoliberal capitalism has been installed in unequal and divisive forms, and civil society has been ensnared in paternalistic, clientelistic, and hierarchical structures and networks, while democratization has proceeded in strikingly illiberal and authoritarian directions.[46]

Consequently, Europe now exhibits an East/West divide between those states which do, and those which do not, participate in the new civil political order which was incubated in Western Europe from 1949 to 1989 and which, since the end of communist rule, has gradually been extended into other parts of Central Europe, the Baltic States, and the Balkans, but as yet has scarcely penetrated into the still relatively murky, unpredictable, Hobbesian CIS world. The most salient new East/West divide is based on a marginalization of Russia and the illiberal states clustered around it, which to varying degrees depend upon it for fuel, trade, transit, security support, and guest worker opportunities and remittances. Thus far, the EU has encompassed barely half of the inhabitants of Europe's post-communist states, and it is very conceivable, though not yet a foregone conclusion, that the rest (possibly including Turkey) will be left in limbo for a considerable time ahead, perhaps indefinitely.

Thus,

[45] Larry Wolff, *Inventing Eastern Europe: The Map of Civilization on the Mind of the Enlightenment* (Stanford, CA: Stanford University Press, 1994), 2–3.

[46] See Michael Emerson and Richard Youngs (eds), *Democracy's Plight in the European Neighbourhood* (Brussels: Centre for European Policy Studies, 2009); Bideleux, 'Rethinking the Eastward Extension', 118–36; Anders Aslund, *Russia's Capitalist Revolution: Why Market Reform Succeeded and Democracy Failed* (Washington, DC: Peterson Institute for International Economics, 2007); Andrew Wilson, *Virtual Politics: Faking Democracy in the Post-Soviet World* (New Haven, CT: Yale University Press, 2005); Andrew Wilson, 'Virtual Politics in the ex-Soviet Bloc', *Open Democracy* (17 July 2007).

the new context [of Eastern Europe] is determined first of all by the post-communist transformation of the former communist world. The first decade of this transformation separated former countries of Eastern Europe in two categories: 'winners' and 'losers'. The winners were granted entry tickets into the European Union and allowed to leave Eastern Europe; the losers have been told to stay in the Eastern European purgatory for an undefined time.

However, it is in the idea of Eastern Europe as a 'normal, but second-hand Europe', that the continuity with previous ideas of Eastern Europe can be seen. 'Eastern Europe is a second hand Europe to the extent that it tries to emulate ideas and practices that emerged in Western Europe, during large political and economic transformations in early modern and modern times'.[47] Eastern Europe comprises the places where EU-style political, economic, and social structures lap at the shores of former communist territories, but do not fully submerge them, that is, those parts of the EU that 'Brussels' considers to be economically, politically, or socially problematic, as well as the so-called EU Neighbourhood countries, which are 'of interest' but not (yet?) deemed to be eligible for EU branding.

Eastern Europe, in its new reduced form, is a very controversial and largely unfinished project. But then modernity and Europe are unfinished and controversial projects, too. To complete them, one has to integrate them: a divided Europe is no Europe. And this integration must be a two-way process in which both sides mutually recognize values and shortcomings of the other. One need not to be a prophet to foresee that this will take a long time.[48]

CONCLUSIONS

There is at least one major structural, as opposed to cultural–essentialist, difference between the 'eastern' and 'western' halves of Europe. The demise of Europe's communist regimes, combined with the resultant break-up of the Yugoslav, Soviet, and Czechoslovak federations, resulted in extensive ethnic homogenization of states and societies in the eastern half of Europe, further reinforcing the ethnic homogenization brought about by Nazism, the Second World War, the Holocaust, fascism, ethnic nationalist movements, and Stalinism during the 1940s. Indeed,

the spectacular reconfiguration of political space along national lines in Central and Eastern Europe and Eurasia has suggested that far from moving beyond the nation-state, history...was moving back to the nation-state...through the wholesale nationalization of previously multinational political space.[49]

[47] Yaroslav Hrytsak, *The Borders of Europe—seen from the outside*, www.eurozine.com/articles/2005-01-10-hrytsak-en.html, accessed January 2010.
[48] Ibid.
[49] Rogers Brubaker, *Nationalism Reframed: Nationhood and the National Question in the New Europe* (Cambridge: Cambridge University Press, 1996), 2–3.

As a consequence, states and societies in the eastern half of Europe have remained unflinchingly structured around principles and concepts of ethno-cultural homogeneity and the notion that each state is an 'ethnocracy', that is, the exclusive property of its dominant or titular ethnic group.[50]

Conversely, Western European states and societies have (like the USA, Canada, Australia, and New Zealand) become ever increasingly 'post-national', multi-ethnic, multi-denominational, multiracial, and multicultural, as a result of successive waves of immigration and the consequent need to devise frameworks capable of accommodating diversity and fostering peaceful and prosperous coexistence of diverse peoples; this has become one of the prime functions and *raisons d'être* of the EU. Thus, structurally, as 'ethnocracies', some Central European states still have much more in common with Balkan and CIS states than they do with Western European states, even if some of their intellectual spokespersons proclaim otherwise.

In the long run, however, it is very likely that reduced birth rates, incipient labour and skills shortages, and ageing populations will steadily increase the socio-economic pressure on states and societies in the eastern half of Europe to accept higher levels of immigration, diversity, and multiculturalism. It seems likely that states and societies in the eastern half of Europe will gradually harmonize with Western European policies, law, and pronouncements on these matters.

Thus, it may finally be time to discard outmoded conceptions of Western and Eastern Europe. Eastward enlargements of the EU since 2004 have meant that Europe's integration process has outgrown the project which originated and was brought to maturity in Western Europe between the 1950s and the 1980s. Moreover, the 2004 and 2007 enlargements of the EU, combined with EU commitments to eventual admission of the Western Balkan states, to seemingly unending membership negotiations with Turkey, and to European Neighbourhood, Eastern Partnership, and Mediterranean Union projects with the EU's eastern and southern neighbours, are slowly forcing Western European champions to acknowledge and come to terms with rival Central European, Baltic, Balkan, Eastern Orthodox, and even Muslim and Turkish conceptions of Europe and modernity. Central Europe, the Baltic, Balkan and Caucasus states, Turkey, Russia, Ukraine, Belarus, Moldova, and even Morocco (which submitted an application for EU membership in 1987) have implicitly or explicitly staked claims to defining or belonging to a post-western EU and/or 'greater' Europe, which has already far outgrown narrow and constricting geographical conceptions of Europe.[51] In this 'common market of ideas',[52] IT has aided the creation of a wide-ranging community in which Europe's smaller or weaker economies can participate on more equitable terms.

---

[50] The concept of the 'ethnocratic state' was coined during the 1930s by the Romanian nationalist Nicifor Crainic (1889–1972) in 'Programmul statului etnocratic', *Ortodoxie si etnocratie* (Bucharest: Cugetarea, 1938).

[51] Gerard Delanty, 'The Making of a Post-Western Europe: A Civilizational Analysis', *Thesis Eleven* 72 (2003) 8–25; and Delanty, 'Peripheries and Borders in a Post-Western Europe', *Eurozine* (August 2007), www.eurozine.com/articles/2007-08-29-delanty-en.html, accessed January 2010.

[52] Morin, *Penser l'Europe*.

The emerging post-Western Europe and EU has become too large and diverse to continue to be dominated by its six founder members plus the UK, the countries that have long been accustomed to calling the shots within the EU and to acting as the self-appointed 'European' representatives and 'voices' in the G8, the UN, and the major international financial institutions. The economic crisis which began in 2008–9 has substantially diminished their relative clout and influence. They are gradually being forced off their privileged pedestals, not only because of the inexorable resurgence of Asia, but also because a much 'greater Europe' is emerging from the EU chrysalis. Europe's hard divisions have become untenable. They are being replaced by a bricolage of Europes of networks, flows, exchanges, and aspirations.

FURTHER READING

Aslund, Anders, *How Capitalism Was Built: The Transformation of Central and Eastern Europe, Russia and Central Asia* (Cambridge: Cambridge University Press, 2007).

Bideleux, Robert, 'Reconstituting Political Order in Europe, West and East', and 'Rethinking the Eastward Extension of the EU Civil Order and the Nature of Europe's New East-West Divide', *Perspectives on European Politics and Society* 10:1 (2009), 3–16 and 118–36.

Bideleux, Robert and Ian Jeffries, *A History of Eastern Europe: Crisis and Change*, 2nd edn (Abingdon: Routledge, 2007).

Bideleux, Robert and Ian Jeffries, *The Balkans: A Post-Communist History* (Abingdon: Routledge, 2007).

Emerson, Michael and Richard Youngs (eds), *Democracy's Plight in the European Neighbourhood* (Brussels: Centre for European Policy Studies, 2009).

Falk, Barbara, *The Dilemmas of Dissidence in East-Central Europe* (Budapest: Central European University Press, 2003).

Johnson, Lonnie, *Central Europe: Enemies, Neighbours, Friends*, 2nd edn (Oxford: Oxford University Press, 2002).

Kirschbaum, Stanislav (ed.), *Central European History and the European Union: The Meaning of Europe* (Basingstoke: Palgrave Macmillan, 2007).

Lampe, John, *Balkans into Southeastern Europe* (Basingstoke: Palgrave, 2006).

Lee, Catherine and Robert Bideleux, 'Europe: What Kind of Idea?', *European Legacy* 14:2 (2009), 163–76.

Melegh, Attila, *On the East-West Slope: Globalization, Nationalism, Racism and Discourses on Central and Eastern Europe* (Budapest: Central European University Press, 2006).

Schöpflin, George and Nancy Wood (eds), *In Search of Central Europe* (Cambridge: Polity Press, 1989).

Snyder, Timothy, *The Reconstruction of Nations: Poland, Ukraine, Lithuania, Belarus, 1569–1999* (London: Yale University Press, 2003).

Wandycz, Piotr, *The Price of Freedom: A History of East Central Europe from the Middle Ages to the Present*, 2nd edn (London: Routledge, 2001).

CHAPTER 4

SPECTRES OF EUROPE: EUROPE'S PAST, PRESENT, AND FUTURE

LUIZA BIALASIEWICZ

'Europe has always been a term that designates what Europe *will be,* or would like to be, or should be. The figure of Europe has historically always been *a task*.'

Massimo Cacciari[1]

'European: he who is nostalgic for Europe.'

Milan Kundera[2]

THE relationship between past, present, and future has always been essential in defining European identity: what Europe was, where it 'began', and where it 'ended'. Presumed temporal divides have often served, indeed, as surrogates for spatial and political distinction. Ever since the late eighteenth century, the division of Europe into 'East' and 'West' bespoke not only a particular geography but also a particular temporal divide.[3] As Maria Todorova argued in her *Imagining the Balkans*, the 'East' came to be identified 'with industrial backwardness, lack of advanced social relations and institutions typical for the developed capitalist West, irrational and superstitious cultures unmarked by Western Enlightenment'. This, she suggested, 'added an additional vector in the relationship between East and West: time, where the movement from past to future was not

---

[1] Massimo Cacciari, 'Europa o filosofia', in Luigi Alici and Francesco Totaro (eds), *Filosofi per l'Europa* (Macerata: Edizioni Universita di Macerata, 2006), 21–33.

[2] Milan Kundera, *L' art du roman* (Paris: Gallimard, 1986).

[3] See Maria Todorova, *Imagining the Balkans* (Oxford: Oxford University Press, 1997) and Larry Wolff, *Inventing Eastern Europe: The Map of Civilisation on the Mind of the Enlightenment* (Stanford, CA: Stanford University Press, 1994).

merely motion but evolution from simple to complex, backward to developed, primitive to cultivated'.[4]

Although such explicitly colonial metaphors have (largely) disappeared, the habit of defining Europe and Europeans within a particular spatio-temporal matrix has tended to re-emerge in moments of geopolitical flux. For instance the transitions of the early 1990s were inscribed within a distinct understanding of the eastern and central Europe states as somehow 'delayed', 'not-yet-European',[5] having to 'learn' European mores and behaviours (social, political, economic).[6] Post 9/11 attempts at drawing lines in Europe, such as Donald Rumsfeld's evocation of 'New' and 'Old' Europes (on the eve of the invasion of Iraq) also rehearsed not only a geopolitical but also a spatio-temporal divide.[7]

In this chapter, I discuss changing understandings of Europe in (and through) time, stressing *how different understandings of Europe's relation to its past, present, and future have been reflected in radically different geopolitical visions for Europe.* This becomes particularly important as Europe begins to project itself as a global actor, invoking a distinctly European geopolitical imagination and vision of world order. As with all geopolitical imaginations, Europe's self- and other- understandings invoke particular constellations of past, present, and future. I will argue that contemporary visions of Europe's role in the world (in particular, the geographical imaginations of Europe's presumed 'spaces of responsibility') are inescapably bound up with certain historical shadows, but also rely in great part on distinct 'spectres' of a future to come.[8]

Over the past two decades (more or less since the demise of the cold war order), a number of leading European thinkers have attempted to trace the 'geo-philosophy' of the European idea focusing on the idea(l) of Europe as a *civitas futura*, as Italian philosopher and political theorist (and long-term Mayor of Venice) Massimo Cacciari defined it in his seminal *Geofilosofia dell'Europa*.[9] Cacciari is not the only contemporary European thinker to have described Europe in the future tense: Reinhart Koselleck has

---

[4] Todorova, *Imagining the Balkans*, 12. See also Slovenian anthropologist Bozidar Jezernik's *Wild Europe: The Balkans in the Gaze of Western Travellers* (London: Saqi, 2003).

[5] For a discussion, see Michael Burawoy and Katherine Verdery (eds), *Uncertain Transition: Ethnographies of Change in the Post-Socialist World* (Lanham, MD: Rowman & Littlefield, 1999) and Iver Neumann, *Uses of the Other: 'The East' in European Identity Formation* (Minneapolis, MN: University of Minnesota Press, 1999).

[6] Narratives of this presumed temporal–evolutionary divide re-emerged full force in the early 2000s, in the lead-up to the Eastern and Central European states' accession to the EU. See Merje Kuus, *Geopolitics Reframed: Security and Identity in Europe's Eastern Enlargement* (Basingstoke: Palgrave, 2006).

[7] Luiza Bialasiewicz and Claudio Minca, 'Old Europe, New Europe: For a Geopolitics of Translation', *Area* 37:4 (2005), 365–72.

[8] In the Derridean sense of 'spectrality' as 'the non-contemporaneity with itself of the living present'. See Jacques Derrida, *Spectres of Marx: The State of Debt, the Work of Mourning and the New International* (London: Routledge, 1994), xix.

[9] Massimo Cacciari, *Geofilosofia dell'Europa* (Milan: Adelphi, 1994).

also suggested that Europe is and always has been a *comunitas in itinere* that holds in the future tense the 'true' solution to its problems and contradictions.[10] For Koselleck, Europe is a concept that has always been bound to both 'experience' (*Erfahrung*) as well as 'expectation' (*Erwartung*). In Europe's (self-)imagination, Koselleck has argued, the two categories are not exclusive, but rather co-constitutive. While 'experience' is 'present past, the events of which have been incorporated and can be remembered', 'expectation' 'occurs in the present, while aiming at the future, at what is not yet. It is ... future made present—"presented" future'.[11]

The work of French sociologist and philosopher Edgar Morin offers a similar conception of Europe. In his *Penser l'Europe*, Morin suggests that Europe 'makes itself one', not in opposition to some external enemy, 'but rather in [permanent] struggle against itself';[12] in particular, against its past and its 'future to come'. Citing Czech philosopher Jan Patocka, Morin argues that what 'makes Europe uniquely Europe', is the awareness that 'the problem of History cannot be resolved. It must remain'.[13] Zygmunt Bauman's characterization of Europe as *An Unfinished Adventure* (the title of his 2004 book) also engages with the notion of a 'never-accomplished' Europe. He argues that the 'essence of Europe' has always tended to run ahead of the 'really existing Europe': 'it is the essence of "being a European" to have an essence that always stays ahead of reality, and it is the essence of European realities to always lag behind the essence of Europe'. Europe, he suggests:

> is the sole social entity that in addition to *being* a civilisation also *called itself* 'civilisation' and looked at itself as civilisation, that is as a product of choice, design and management thereby recasting the totality of things, including itself, as an in-principle-unfinished object, an object of scrutiny, critique, and possibly remedial action. In its European rendition, 'civilisation' (or 'culture') ... is a continuous process—forever imperfect yet obstinately struggling for perfection—of *remaking the world*.[14]

It is important to recognize the genealogy of such understandings of Europe as an ideal to come. Interwar appeals to Europe as a space–time of 'un-actualised possibility' (a continent forever in tension between its 'reality' and its 'ideality', as Paul Valéry

---

[10] See Reinhart Koselleck, *Futures Past: On the Semantics of Historical Time* (New York: Columbia University Press, 1985) and his *The Practice of Conceptual History: Timing History, Spacing Concepts* (Stanford, CA: Stanford University Press, 2002).

[11] Reinhart Koselleck, *Vergangene Zukunft: Zur Semantik geschichtlicher Zeiten* (Frankfurt am Main: Suhrkamp Verlag, 1979), 355. See also the discussion in Anders Schinkel, 'Imagination as a Category of History: an Essay Concerning Koselleck's Concepts of *Erfahrungsraum* and *Erwartungshorizont*', *History and Theory* 44:1 (2005), 42–54.

[12] Edgar Morin, *Penser l'Europe*, 2nd edn (Paris: Gallimard, 1990), 56.

[13] Ibid., 155. See also the analysis in Luiza Bialasiewicz, 'Europe as/at the Border: Trieste and the Meaning of Europe', *Social and Cultural Geography* 10:3 (2009), 325–42.

[14] Zygmunt Bauman, *Europe, An Unfinished Adventure* (Cambridge: Polity Press, 2004), 7–8, emphasis in the original.

imagined it[15]), as too ideas of Europe as a unique laboratory of/for peace are being replayed today, not only in philosophical reflection but also within Europe's own institutional attempts at political and geopolitical self-definition. Over the past decade, Europe has been variously characterized as a 'civilian' (or 'civil') power, a 'normative' power, a 'transformative power'[16]—*ideal* geopolitical imaginations that, nonetheless, increasingly exert *real* geopolitical effects. As Bachmann and Sidaway have argued, it is important to understand how such imaginations 'simultaneously internalise and occlude prior visions of Europe and European world roles';[17] precisely, I will suggest, by playing with distinct constellations of pasts, presents, and futures. In the next sections, I present three moments in the evolution of understandings of Europe as an ideal space–time: dreams of Europe in late-imperial Austria (and their contemporary hauntings); the Europe 'past its past' discourse in post-World War II European geopolitics; and, finally, post-cold war (and post-9/11) imaginations of Europe as a 'force for good'.

EUROPE, PAST: FROM HABSBURG MYTH TO EUROPEAN MYTH

This continent to which so many owe so much carries a great debt itself and it needs time to make up for its sins. We passionately wish to give it this time; a time in which one blessing after the other can spread itself over the earth; a time so victorious that no one in the whole world would ever have reason to curse the name of Europe again. Four men that I can't detach myself from have in my time belonged to this delayed, this real Europe.

Elias Canetti[18]

---

[15] See Paul Valéry, 'La crise de l'esprit' (1919) and 'Note, ou l'Européen' (1924), in *Variété. Essais quasi politiques* (Paris: Gallimard, 1957). Reprinted in Yves Hersant and Fabienne Durand-Bogaert (eds), *Europes. De l'Antiquité au XXe siècle. Anthologie critique et commentée* (Paris: Editions Robert Laffont, 2000). For a discussion, see Paul Lutzeler, *Der Schriftsteller als Politiker* (Stuttgart: Franz Steiner Verlag, 1997) and his *Kontinentalisierung. Das Europa der Schriftsteller* (Bielefeld: Aisthesis Verlag, 2007). Valéry's work has been an important source of inspiration for a number of contemporary European philosophers, including Jacques Derrida in *The Other Heading: Reflections on Today's Europe* (Bloomington, IN: Indiana University Press, 1992).

[16] See, among others, Veit Bachmann and James Sidaway, 'Zivilmacht Europa: a Critical Geopolitics of the European Union as a Global Power', *Transactions of the Institute of British Geographers* 34:1 (2009), 94–109; Thomas Diez, 'Constructing the Self and Changing Others: Reconsidering "Normative Power Europe"', *Millenium: Journal of International Studies*, 33:3 (2005), 613–36; Zaki Laïdi, *La Norme Sans la Force* (Paris: Presses de la Fondation Nationale des Sciences Politiques, 2005).

[17] Bachmann and Sidaway, 'Zivilmacht Europa', 106.

[18] Elias Canetti, in Sture Allen, *Nobel Lectures, Literature 1981–1990* (Singapore: World Scientific Publishing Company, 1994).

When Elias Canetti received the 1981 Nobel Prize for Literature, he cited 'Europe' as the most important source of his authorship. As Jeppe Ilkjaer notes, this may appear 'a surprising reference, [if] only because Canetti was born in a Jewish ghetto in the outskirts of the Ottoman Empire and carried a Turkish passport most of his life'. The 'Europe' Canetti alludes to, moreover, is a particular creature: as Ilkjaer points out, 'something [which is] behind schedule or not in time...something that falls behind without Canetti ever stating exactly what it is trying to reach'.[19]

Canetti's work has been the subject of countless critical studies highlighting his contribution in warning of the perils of modern totalitarian ideologies; of all attempts at enforced unity.[20] In his memoir *The Tongue Set Free: Remembrance of a European Childhood*, Canetti writes about his precocious awareness of the national passions that begin to pull apart the Ottoman Empire, an almost atavistic fear of the Empire's dismantling and the partitioning of people and territories that would necessarily follow. Europe figures powerfully in his work as both something that *precedes* the age of nationalisms— and as a future *to come*. Canetti's ideal imagination of Europe is detached, however, from any assumption of the existence—or superiority—of a singular 'European culture'. Europe, above all, is *a space–time of possibility*.

In great part, Canetti's understanding of Europe draws directly on the imaginations of the 'four men' that he cites as his most important influences in the Nobel acceptance speech: the writers Hermann Broch, Franz Kafka, Karl Kraus, and Robert Musil.[21] As some of the most perceptive analysts of the declining Habsburg Empire, the work of these authors focused on what they described in varying ways as the moment of twilight of European culture: to use Broch's terms, 'the dusk before the night'. Nonetheless, they also imagined its future transcendence. Indeed, in many of these works, 'Europe' and 'European culture' manifest themselves as stand-ins for the disintegrating Habsburg Empire or, more accurately, its myth.

As Claudio Magris has argued, the Habsburg myth always served a double, potent function, *both geopolitical and ideal*. The late-Habsburg literature to which Canetti appeals engages precisely this double dimension: on the one hand, these are narratives of disintegration, decline, dissolution, loss (of a centre, of particular values, of certainties, of the 'world of Security' described by Stefan Zweig,[22] and even of territory). On the

---

[19] Jeppe Ilkjaer, 'The Late Europe: Elias Canetti and the Ordering of Time and Space in *Auto Da Fe*', in Nele Bemong, Mirjam Truwant and Pieter Vermeulen (eds), *Re-Thinking Europe. Literature and (Trans)National Identity* (Amsterdam: Rodopi, 2008), 223.

[20] In particular, his *Crowds and Power* (*Masse und Macht*, 1960) and *Auto Da Fe* (*Die Blendung*, 1936). For a critical reassessment, see William Collins Donahue, *The End of Modernism: Elias Canetti's Auto Da Fe* (Chapel Hill, NC: University of North Carolina Press, 2001). See also Canetti's autobiographical trilogy: *The Tongue Set Free; The Torch in My Ear* and *The Play of the Eyes* (London: Picador, 1989).

[21] The works that Canetti appeals to in particular are Hermann Broch's (1931) trilogy *The Sleepwalkers*; Franz Kafka's (1926) *The Castle*; Karl Kraus's (1926) *The Last Days of Mankind* and Robert Musil's (1932) *The Man Without Qualities*.

[22] Stefan Zweig, *Die Welt von Gestern: The World of Yesterday* (Lincoln, NE: University of Nebraska Press, 1964).

other, however, the works of these writers are, as Magris notes, 'morality plays': describing a world that *was and should again be*, masterfully blending the literary and extra-literary, description and prescription, past, present, and future.[23] As Ilkjaer points out, neither Canetti nor the authors to whom he alludes speak directly 'of the creation of a European Utopia or a certain type of state; rather, the idea of Europe is a way to reflect, observe, and write in the absence of such a social and national order'.[24] *Europe, then, is evoked as an ideal space–time against which to set current failings; Europe becomes a foil to the absence of a certain ideal order.* In this sense, it becomes a direct descendant of the Habsburg myth.

As its foremost scholars have suggested, the Habsburg myth was not so much an alteration or deformation of reality or an attempt to extract some supposed metahistorical 'truth', but rather 'the sublimation of an entire society into a picturesque, safe and orderly fairy-tale world'.[25] The Habsburg myth was not only one which *derived* from an ideal space–time, but also one upon which that space–time was *actively built* in practice. Imperial Austria was a place and a time indelibly marked by what Franz Werfel would term its 'superior ideal': the attempt to reinstate 'God's reign upon the Earth, in the unity of all peoples'; the antithesis of 'the nation-state which is, in its very essence, demonic and, as such, idolatrous and menacing.'[26] The Austro–Hungarian Empire, Robert Musil's 'Kakania', presented itself as the rightful heir of the spirit of the Holy Roman Empire, embodying both the universalism of European culture and playing the role of mediator between East and West. Its paternalistic myth of 'the peoples' ran, moreover, counter to the very ideals upon which nationality and nationhood were founded. Emperor Franz Josef's invocation of *Meine Völker* thus served not merely as the symbol but also as the fundamental ideological basis of the imperial project—both its spiritual support and its propaganda tool in the struggle against the emergent ideal of the modern territorial nation-state.

Above all, the Habsburg vision provided an alternative vision of governance and community, opposing a dynastic ideal (a 'historical unity' representing an organic pluricultural, pluri-ethnic, and multinational totality, cemented by the legitimacy of the ruling house and a web of geopolitical alliances), to the emergent Prussian statist ideal, with its particularism, its romanticization of the one and only (German) *Volk*, its idealization of the ties of blood, soil, and belonging. As Franz Grillparzer (whose literary works were ordained by the Habsburg authorities as emblematic of the essence of the Austrian spirit—required reading in all imperial schools and adorning the shelves of every respectable bourgeois home) admonished in his 1848 drama *Libussa*, 'the itinerary of modern culture goes from humanity to bestiality passing through nationality'. As Magris has argued, the

---

[23] Claudio Magris, *Il mito absburgico nella letteratura austriaca moderna* (Turin: Einaudi, 1963).

[24] Ilkjaer, 'The Late Europe', 225.

[25] See Magris, *Il mito absburgico*; see also Jacques Le Rider, *Modernité viennoise et crises de l'identité* (Paris: Presses Universitaires de France, 1990) and his *Mitteleuropa: storia di un mito* (Bologna: Il Mulino, 1995).

[26] Franz Werfel, *Aus der Dämmerung einer Welt* (1936), 14.

Habsburg Empire asked of its subjects 'that they not only be Germans, Ruthenians, or Poles, but something more, something above'; it required 'a true *sacrificium nationis*'. It was a supranational ethico-cultural *oikumene* that strove to transcend the nation both as an exclusive territorial ideal and as the exclusive claimant of identity; it was the empire of many crowns and many languages which intoned together the *Gott erhalte*; the land where 'everyone was born *zwölfstimmig*—with 12 tongues, and 12 souls'.[27]

The disintegration of the Imperial project in 1918 is thus seen by many as the end of a world: Iain Bamforth recounts Joseph Roth's comment that the 1914–18 war was called a 'world' war 'not because the entire world had conducted it but because, owing to it, we all lost a world, our world'.[28] Nonetheless, in the realm of literature, this lost world is inscribed both as absence, but also as a space–time of expectation (in Koselleck's terms); a spectre of future possibility, as Derrida would have it.[29] The Habsburg author whose writings perhaps best express this tension is Robert Musil and it is not accidental that his work has received renewed prominence since the early 1990s, a time of profound European soul-searching with the demise of the Cold War order.[30] What is particularly interesting is that the renewed attention to Musil's work over the past two decades has come not only from literary critics but also from philosophers and social scientists, probing the political potential of Musil's writings and their lessons for the present day. The most important figure in this regard has undoubtedly been French philosopher Jacques Bouveresse, whose 1993 book *L'homme probable: Robert Musil, le hazard, la moyenne et l'escargot de l'histoire* (republished to great acclaim in 2004) engages with Musil not simply as a writer of fiction but, rather, as a philosopher of modernity. In particular, Bouveresse has stressed the author's contribution in imagining alternative futures—a task also taken up by a 2001 book by Jean-Pierre Cometti, *Musil philosophe*, that engages with the writer's notions of utopia, possibility,—and Europe.[31]

In his *Subject Without Nation: Robert Musil and the History of Modern Identity*, Stefan Jonsson attempts to distil the utopian ideal at the heart of Musil's oeuvre. The disintegrating (if not already lost) Danubian Empire described by Musil, he argues, is a space–time of

---

[27] Magris, *Il mito absburgico*, 70.

[28] See Iain Bamforth, *The Good European: Essays and Arguments* (Manchester: Carcanet Press, 2006), 40.

[29] Derrida, *Spectres of Marx*.

[30] The interest in Musil's work persists: in a recent survey among German critics, Musil's *The Man Without Qualities* (1930–1932) was voted as the most important work of German literature of the 20th century, and Karl Corino's biography of the writer has attracted great fanfare: *Robert Musil: Eine Biographie* (Hamburg: Rowohlt Verlag, 2003).

[31] Bouveresse has long insisted on the philosophical and 'cognitive' function of literature. Novels, according to Bouveresse, furnish unique ways of knowing; they are able to contribute in unique ways to the development of a 'moral imagination', much more than political theory. See Jacques Bouveresse, *L'homme probable: Robert Musil, le hazard, la moyenne et l'escargot de l'histoire* (Paris: Seuil, 1993) and his *La Voix de l'âme et les chemins de l'esprit* (Paris: Seuil, 2002); in English, his 'Robert Musil and the Destiny of Europe', *European Journal of Philosophy* 1:2 (1993), 200–23. Also, Jean-Pierre Cometti, *Musil philosophe: L'utopie de l'essayisme* (Paris: Seuil, 2001).

forfeited possibility. If Kakania is an empire without name or qualities, it is also a land of possibilities, a country where one speaks in a subjunctive mood, colouring every statement with a wish, and where one regards the nation as a fantasy rather than a reality.[32]

Citing Musil:

Naturally, that would have been the moment when a good Kakanian also could have answered the question of what he was by enthusiastically saying: 'Nothing!', meaning that Something, which is again set free to make of Kakania everything that was not yet there.[33]

As Jonsson argues,

Kakania's lack of national identity is affirmed as a negativity which, in its turn, is converted into possibilities. The Kakanian is Nothing, a site of lack which does not even have a name, but this nothingness really means a Something which can become Everything.[34]

He suggests, then, that we should transcend the imagination of Austria–Hungary in *The Man without Qualities* as simply a product of the author's nostalgia for a 'lost world': 'the images of Kakania are not descriptions of the Austro–Hungarian Empire as it once was but were produced by an intellect operating in an experimental mode'[35]—and as such *deeply political/geopolitical*. The role of interwar (mainly German-language) literature in imagining—and thus rendering possible/plausible—alternative political futures for Europe has been analysed in depth by Paul Michael Lutzeler in his *Der Schriftsteller als Politiker* as well as his more recent *Kontinentalisierung. Das Europa der Schriftsteller*. Lutzeler's argument (much like Bouveresse's) is that the discourse on/of Europe (*Europadiskurs*) that emerges from such writings is 'an ontological deep structure', a 'cultural sediment', a 'foundational tradition' that can be mobilized in times of crisis; that can serve as a very useful political grammar to 'weave Europe back together' in moments of disintegration or loss of purpose/meaning.[36]

In Lutzeler's interpretation, writers such as Musil, Hermann Broch, Karl Kraus, and Thomas Mann should thus be read *also* as 'geopolitical scribes',[37] whose imaginations of alternative worlds help make such worlds possible; whose (past) imaginations of geopolitical reality can have real political effects (in the present/future). It is interesting

---

[32] Stefan Jonsson, *Subject without Nation: Robert Musil and the History of Modern Identity* (Durham, NC: Duke University Press, 2000), 269.

[33] Robert Musil, *The Man Without Qualities*, trans. Sophie Wilkins and Burton Pike (New York: Knopf, 1995), 577.

[34] Jonsson, *Subject without Nation*, 269.

[35] Musil himself described literature as a 'vast experimental station for trying out the best ways of being human' (cited in Jonsson, *Subject without Nation*, 135).

[36] Lutzeler, *Der Schriftsteller als Politiker; Kontinentalisierung*.

[37] The term comes from Gearóid Ó'Tuathail, *Critical Geopolitics* (Minneapolis, MN: University of Minnesota Press, 1996).

to note that in Musil's case, it was not only his fictional writings that contributed to imagining other possible worlds, other possible Europes. Karl Corino's biography of the writer highlights Musil's various institutional roles as an active 'intellectual of statecraft':[38] from his post as the editor of military magazines intended to boost the patriotic spirit of the Imperial troops during the First World War, to his job in the post-1918 Austrian Republic's Foreign Ministry's press department, to his subsequent posting at the Ministry of Defence, where he was in charge of the 'intellectual training' of the Officer Corps. Musil also penned numerous essays specifically on the European question, imagining an 'ideal Europe able to transcend State and Nation'; a Europe whose past was also the way to its future.[39]

The reappearance of the myth of Imperial Austria in the 1990s as 'a world experiment which humanity failed to realize'[40] is worthy of note; in particular, the reasons for which in that moment of geopolitical flux this mythical space–time became 'so strangely attractive to Europeans who have seen their continent being dismembered by nationalism, fascism, Stalin's Iron Curtain, and Milosevic's ethnic cleansings'.[41] All through the 1990s, the Habsburg legacy enjoyed a buoyant revival across post-communist Eastern and Central Europe. In cities such as Budapest, Cracow, Ljubljana, and Prague, a revalorization of what passed as 'Imperial heritage' was the focus of numerous interventions into these cities' urban landscapes, and savvy tourism entrepreneurs promptly cashed in on the fashion for Empire.[42] The Habsburg model also enjoyed a revival, moreover, as a viable alternative for cross-national political organization following the collapse of the old walls. Indeed, a great number of the collaborative geopolitical initiatives born in Eastern and Central Europe soon after 1989 (such as the Visegrad Group or the Central European Initiative) drew their inspiration precisely within its memory.[43] As Predrag Matvejevic noted, for many Eastern and Central Europeans, 'the Habsburg legacy, especially in the early years of the transition, came to represent all that was true, good, beautiful and, above all, European'.[44] It was both an ideal past, a lost Arcadia, as well as a secret passage to an ideal (European) future, a 'hidden exit out of the intolerable present' (borrowing Jonsson's expression).

---

[38] Again, the term comes from Ó'Tuathail, *Critical Geopolitics*. See Corino, *Robert Musil: Eine Biographie*.

[39] See Robert Musil, 'Helpless Europe: A Digressive Journey' (original 'Das hilflose Europa oder Reise vom Hundertsten ins Tausendste', 1922), in Burton Pike and David Luft (eds) *Precision and Soul: Essays and Addresses* (Chicago, IL: University of Chicago Press, 1990).

[40] Jonsson, *Subject without Nation*, 270.

[41] Ibid., 220.

[42] See Luiza Bialasiewicz, 'Another Europe: Remembering Habsburg Galicja', *Cultural Geographies* 10:1 (2003), 21–44. François Fejtö's evocation of the Imperial past in his *Requiem pour un empire défunt* is illustrative in this regard: Fejtö paints 'an atmosphere of nonchalant cosmopolitanism' in which one would take the train to Vienna, Budapest, or Krakow, spend the weekend in Trieste or Fiume, check in at a hotel in Karlsbad to get a share of Western Europe, or go hiking in the Carpathian mountains to look for Dracula's dwelling, without even leaving the country. François Fejtö, *Requiem pour un empire défunt: Histoire de la destruction de l'Autriche–Hongrie* (Paris: Seuil, 1993).

[43] As Lee and Bideleux argue in their contribution to this volume.

[44] Predrag Matvejevic, *Mondo 'Ex'* (Milan: Garzanti, 1996).

This idealized return to a 'Europe past'—one that could serve as a paragon/parable for a (new) European future—marked nonetheless *a very important axiological and geopolitical shift in Europe's post-World War II self-understanding*, for this latter was presaged upon a very different relation to its (both real and ideal) past.

EUROPE, PAST ITS PAST: POSTWAR EUROPEAN GEOPOLITICAL IMAGINATIONS

Writing on Europe's security identity in the mid-1990s, Ole Wæver, one of the founders of the influential Copenhagen School of International Relations, argued that the geopolitical Other of Cold War Europe was its own past.[45] The dominant security discourse in Western Europe since the 1950s had been premised, he suggested, on a conception of danger bound to the 'threat of Europe's future becoming like Europe's past'. It was Europe itself that was Europe's fundamental Other—not 'the Turk, Russians, Moslems or the East'. *Unlike the articulations of difference found in most nationalist discourse, Europe's Other was differentiated in time rather than in space.* The geopolitical Other of contemporary Europe was, in other words, the threat of a return to its 'normal' pattern of political–territorial relations, based with a mosaic of (inherently belligerent and competitive) nation states, bound within an always tenuous balance of power. The idea that the European balance of power constituted a threat was a novel one: up to the twentieth century, the concept of the balance of power was seen, rather, as a uniquely European political virtue that assured stability and secured pluralism.[46]

Such a geopolitical framing had important implications for the constitution of European identity: as Wæver argued, the 'quintessentially European' was, in fact, a negation, with Europe defined by its breaking away from what was (presumably) typical of itself. The European project was thus less defined by a future realization of something 'typically European' than by a dialectical negation of what used to be 'all-too European'. In this sense, the ways in which Europe was being articulated against its past/present/future were quite distinct from the constellations inscribing most narratives of national identity (premised upon, as Slavoj Žižek had surmised some time ago in his characteristically caustic fashion, a Glorious Past and a Promising Future, whose actualization in the Problematic Present was only prevented from coming into being by Them).[47] In the

---

[45] See Ole Wæver, 'European Security Identities', *Journal of Common Market Studies* 34 (1996), 103–32; Ole Wæver, 'Security, Insecurity, and Asecurity in the West European Non-war Community', in Emmanuel Adler and Michael Barnett (eds), *Security Communities* (Cambridge: Cambridge University Press, 1998), 69–118.

[46] For a discussion, see Pim den Boer, 'Europe to 1914: The Making of an Idea', in Jan van der Dussen and Kevin Wilson (eds), *The History of the Idea of Europe: What is Europe?* (London: Routledge, 1995), 1–56.

[47] See Slavoj Žižek, 'Eastern Europe's Republics of Gilead', in Chantal Mouffe (ed.), *Dimensions of Radical Democracy: Pluralism, Citizenship, Community* (London: Verso, 1992); also, Gertjan Dijink, *National Identity and Geopolitical Visions: Maps of Pride and Pain* (London: Routledge, 1996).

case of postwar European geopolitical identity, *it was the break from the past that was being presented as Europe's central, most valuable characteristic.* Certain parts of Europe were, of course, seen as 'leaders' in this respect: in Wæver's words, places and events 'to be hero-ised and positivised as Europe's unique accomplishment'—and, moreover, to be presented as a model to the rest of the world.[48] I will say more on the transposition of the 'European model' to the rest of the world in the final section, but one more thing needs to be said about *the geopolitical effects* of such an understanding on the European project itself.

If preventing Europe's past from becoming Europe's future was the major threat facing post-World War II Europe, then European integration took on 'a security quality'—and had to be defended at almost any cost;[49] a highly compelling geopolitical imagination indeed. It is an imagination that maintained its potency long after the generation of politicians that grew up in the shadow of World War II had, for the most part, passed on. Looking at the rhetorical framing of European identity at the turn of the millennium, Barry Buzan and Ole Wæver noted the continuing resonance of Robert Schuman's vision of a 'European federation for the preservation of peace', with German Foreign Affairs Minister Joschka Fisher in 2000 pronouncing that:

> The core of the concept of Europe after 1945 was and still is a rejection of the European balance-of-power principle and the hegemonic ambitions of individual states that had emerged following the Peace of Westphalia in 1648, a rejection which took the form of closer meshing of vital interests and the transfer of nation-state sovereign rights to supranational European institutions...A step backwards, even just standstill or contentment with what has been achieved, would demand a fatal price of all EU member states and of all those who want to become members; it would demand a fatal price above all of our people. This is particularly true for Germany and the Germans.[50]

Nonetheless, since the end of the Cold War, the focus of such Euro-organizing efforts has shifted geographical location, with the European transcendence of its past being rewritten into a *new* geopolitical narrative of/for Europe. As Waever has argued, in such formulations, 'the war/peace = past/future formula' still remains the foundation of Europe's self-definition—only now 'the battleground [has] shifted to

---

[48] Certain other places/times of course took on the opposite function: for a discussion of the distinct place of Germany in the 'Europe past its past' discourse, see Thomas Risse and Daniela Engelmann-Martin, 'Identity Politics and European Integration: The Case of Germany', in Anthony Pagden (ed.), *The Idea of Europe: From Antiquity to the European Union* (Cambridge: Cambridge University Press, 2002), 287–316; Thomas Risse, *A Community of Europeans? Transnational Identities and Public Spheres* (Ithaca, NY: Cornell University Press, 2010); also, Maja Zehfuss, 'Remembering to Forget/Forgetting to Remember', in Duncan Bell (ed.), *Memory, Trauma and World Politics: Reflections on the Relationship between Past and Present* (Basingstoke: Palgrave, 2006), 213–30; Maja Zehfuss, *Wounds of Memory: The Politics of War in Germany* (Cambridge: Cambridge University Press, 2007).

[49] Wæver, 'Security, Insecurity, and Asecurity'. See also Barry Buzan and Ole Wæver, *Regions and Powers: The Structure of International Security* (Cambridge: Cambridge University Press, 2003).

[50] Cited in Buzan and Wæver, *Regions and Powers*, 361.

the outside.'[51] This is a key shift, for *it now allows the past to serve as a moral high ground for 'teaching peace'*. It is this rhetorical shift, Wæver argues, that has, for instance, allowed Great Britain to enter into the new geopolitical imaginary of/for Europe. The discursive weight of European integration as an antidote to Europe's past has always been of a different calibre in Britain from other European states, for a number of historical and political reasons. It is interesting to note, then, how British political leaders have begun to adopt a similar language in recent years, albeit applied to Europe's *external* role. Wæver cites the words of then Foreign Secretary Robin Cook during the Kosovo war:

> There are now two Europes competing for the soul of our continent. One still follows the race ideology that blighted our continent under the fascists. The other emerged fifty years ago out from behind the shadow of the Second World War. The conflict between the international community and Yugoslavia is the struggle between these two Europes. Which side prevails will determine what sort of continent we live in. That is why we must win.[52]

Europe now becomes the paladin that will save *others* from their past and that will show them the way to the future:

> The other Europe is the Modern Europe. It was founded fifty years ago, in the rubble that was left after the Second World War. We surveyed what was left of our continent. We saw the extermination camps, the piled bodies of the victims and the pathetic masses of survivors. And we made a promise. We vowed Never Again. It was on that pledge that we built the Modern Europe.[53]

Tony Blair's addresses the following year in Warsaw (October) and Zagreb (November) traced a very similar temporal geography:

> The 15 member states of the EU—countries that in the lifetime of my father were at war with one another—are now working in union, with 50 years of peace and prosperity behind us. And now, holding out the prospect of bringing the same peace and prosperity to the Eastern and Central European nations and even to the Balkan countries.[54]

The place of 'the Balkans' in this argument—as a place (in Europe?) where wars still do happen—is a crucial one. As Žižek, Todorova, and Jezernik have argued, the Balkan wars, though often inscribed as an example of the failures of the European project, have actually served to strengthen the 'security argument' underpinning European integration.[55] In this sense, the Balkans have continued to serve as 'Europe's ghosts' (see Robert

---

[51] Ole Wæver, 'The Temporal Structure of European Security Identity', paper presented at the Annual Meeting of the International Studies Association, Honolulu, March, 2005.

[52] Cited in Wæver, 'Temporal Structure'.

[53] Ibid.

[54] Ibid.

[55] See also Alex Jeffrey, 'Contesting Europe: The Politics of Bosnian Integration into European Structures', *Environment and Planning D: Society and Space* 26:3 (2008), 428–43.

Kaplan's well known characterization), reminding Europeans that war in Europe is still possible; reminding Europe of the risks of abandoning its 'pacific and pacifying' ideology.[56]

The Balkans are not the only site, however, where the role of the past in defining Europe's geopolitical present is being renegotiated in the post-Cold War era. As Eastern and Central European states have become fully fledged members of the European community, they too have complicated the 'Europe's past as its Other' discourse. The resistance of the 'New Europeans' to the mnemo-political authority of the West in delineating the contents—and (geo)political role—of postwar 'European history' has been seen by many observers as an important attempt at what Bell, Mälksoo, and others have termed an 'ideological decolonization'.[57] Nonetheless, the memorial militancy of states such as Poland has not only challenged Western Europe's rhetorical construction as a model for the whole of Europe (with Western Europe setting the rules of remembrance to the 'New Europeans', even after their formal acceptance into the EU). It has also forcibly re-exhumed many of the pasts that were supposed to have been forgotten or transcended. As Mälksoo has argued, recent Eastern European memory politics

> has not always struck a resonant chord among their Western counterparts who have attempted to form a common European identity by 'drawing a line' under World War II. Baltic and Polish memory politics have brought up the controversial and intensely debated comparison between Nazi and Stalinist regimes and their respective crimes, thus contesting the uniqueness of Nazi crimes and questioning the singularity of the Holocaust as *the* crime against humanity of the 20th century.[58]

This exhumation has been seen by many as, in many ways, challenging the progress of the European project,[59] despite calls in various quarters for a broader European historical consciousness as a precondition for solidarity within the enlarged European polity;[60] also because the unfreezing of memories in Eastern and South-Eastern Europe has brought forth some very unpleasant ghosts of Europe's past, as Stone compellingly argues in the final chapter of this volume.

---

[56] Robert Kaplan, *Balkan Ghosts* (New York: Vintage, 1994).

[57] Duncan Bell, 'Introduction: Memory, Trauma and World Politics', in Bell (ed.), *Memory, Trauma and World Politics*, 1–29; Maria Mälksoo, 'The Memory Politics of Becoming European: The East European Subalterns and the Memory of Europe', *European Journal of International Relations* 15:4 (2009), 653–80.

[58] Mälksoo, 'Memory Politics', 656.

[59] See Bell (ed.), *Memory, Trauma and World Politics*; also Richard Ned Lebow, 'The Memory of Politics in Postwar Europe', in Richard Ned Lebow, Wulf Kansteiner and Claudio Fogu (eds), *The Politics of Memory in Postwar Europe* (Durham, NC: Duke University Press, 2006), 1–39.

[60] Such as the 2008 declaration of a number of Eastern and Central European MEPs: see Wojciech Roszkowski, Gyorgy Schöpflin, Tunne-Väldo Kelam, Ģirts Valdis Kristovskis, and Vytautas Landsbergis, 'United Europe—United History: A Mission to Consolidate a Common Memory', Declaration by the Polish, Latvian, Lithuanian, and Estonian MEPs at the European Parliament Conference 'United Europe, United History', Tallinn, 22 January 2008.

Europe's post-World War II representation as a (geo)political community that had dispensed with the need for the Other to define its own self has, nonetheless, begun to mutate. In the next section, I discuss the evolution of European geopolitical imaginations in the post-Cold War era, noting in particular the role of the Iraq war in transforming Europe's visions of (and for) itself.

EUROPE'S FUTURE I: EUROPE AFTER THE IRAQ WAR

Commenting in a 2008 collection of essays on the 'Geopolitics of Europe's Identity', Russian political theorist Sergei Prozorov argued that 'the profound philosophico-political implications' of the 'Europe past its past' discourse were only now being fully grasped and invoked as a new geopolitical discourse for (what he saw as) an emergent 'European Empire'. To proclaim that the Other is history, he argued,

> is to pronounce history itself as the Other. In this way, contemporary Europe becomes a profoundly a-historical, or even an anti-historical project, more eschatological than teleological. According to this logic, all history is recast as a primitive period of error, madness and violence, whose transcendence ushers in a new order of freedom, security and justice that marks a veritable end of history.[61]

For 'what is this history that is presently "othered"?' he asked.

> It is nothing other than a history of spatial othering of the division of Europe into a plurality of sovereign states separated by territorial boundaries, which also have served as the boundaries of identity, containing particularistic political communities whose sovereign equality precluded the possibility of the existence of any over-arching political identity above them.[62]

The contemporary European project was simply constituted by a division of a different sort, Prozorov suggested:

> A strict boundary is drawn between the past age, in which boundaries of various kinds were constitutive of the necessarily particularistic identities, and the present moment, in which boundaries must be effaced in the project of the unbounded expansion of the universalist liberal–democratic identity. Moreover, this universalist identity apparently exists outside both space and time, since it no longer

---

[61] Sergei Prozorov, 'De-Limitation: The Denigration of Boundaries in the Political Thought of Late Modernity', in Noel Parker (ed.), *The Geopolitics of Europe's Identity: Centres, Boundaries, Margins* (Basingstoke: Palgrave, 2008), 27. See also Sergei Prozorov, *The Ethics of Post-Communism: History and Social Praxis in Russia* (Basingstoke: Palgrave, 2009).

[62] Prozorov, 'De-Limitation', 27.

practices spatial 'othering' and has dispensed with history in a temporal 'othering'.[63]

Crucially, such understandings of the European project carry with them concrete geopolitical implications that extend also beyond Europe, as Europe projects itself as a 'universal model' for the rest of the world still struggling with its pasts. The key moment marking this shift, Prozorov suggested, came with the Iraq war, *signalling a fundamental break in the postwar constitution of Europe's geopolitical identity—and its relation to its past.*

Prozorov was not the only one to make these points, of course, for a number of prominent European commentators had already advanced similar arguments on the eve of the war in 2003, from Etienne Balibar and Tzvetan Todorov, to Jacques Derrida and Jürgen Habermas. The invasion of Iraq was singled out by these commentators as a particularly important Euro-organizing moment for two key reasons. First, they argued, what the mass protests against the war made evident (beyond the sheer strength of feeling) was the crystallization, for the first time, of a European public opinion: the emergence, in practice, of a common 'European public sphere' (to cite Jürgen Habermas's assessment of the events).[64] The early European reaction against the war was also seen, however, as a strong stand against the American vision for the Middle East and the US's role in that part of the world and thus the emergence—here, too, for the first time—of *an alternative vision and geopolitical positioning for Europe.* Europe and the United States had long been geopolitical mirrors to each other, in a play of codependence and co-constitution ongoing since the end of the Second World War. What is more, the American role in liberating Europe had always been an important part of the 'Europe past its past' discourse.[65] The invasion of Iraq marked an important break in that relationship: *it was now Europeans that had to 'come to the aid of their American cousins'; that had to offer lessons in democracy.*[66]

But the war also revealed some breaks *within* the European whole. The most important was the divide that made itself apparent between a significant part of the public opinion in the countries of the EU15, and popular feelings within the 'New European' states in Eastern and Central Europe (to use Donald Rumsfeld's infamous characterization),

---

[63]   Ibid., 28.

[64]   Whose absence had long been bemoaned by theorists of the European project and political leaders alike: see Luiza Bialasiewicz, Stuart Elden and Joe Painter, 'The Constitution of EU Territory', *Comparative European Politics* 3:3 (2005), 333–63.

[65]   As Michael Smith has argued, the United States has long been involved in shaping the geographies—and geopolitical imaginaries—of European integration, with the 'Atlantic Europe' of postwar years very much an American creature. See Michal H. Smith 'European Integration and American Power: Reflex, Resistance and Reconfiguration', in David Slater and Peter J. Taylor (eds), *The American Century: Consensus and Coercion in the Projection of American Power* (Oxford: Blackwell, 1999), 136–48.

[66]   The expression comes from Timothy Garton Ash, 'American Blues', *The Guardian* (18 November 2004); 11; see also Daniel Levy, Max Pensky and John Torpey (eds), *Old Europe, New Europe, Core Europe. Transatlantic Relations after the Iraq War* (London: Verso, 2005).

where an important majority proclaimed themselves much closer to the American position than the 'Old European' one, with what was described by some commentators as a 'mixture of pragmatism and opportunism'.[67] Three Eastern and Central European states—the Czech Republic, Hungary, and Poland—were among the signatories of the famous 'United We Stand' Letter of Eight, pledging to support the American war effort. The characterization of the divide by then US Secretary of Defence Rumsfeld as that between a 'New Europe' (largely corresponding to the Eastern and Central European states, together with Britain, Denmark, Italy, Portugal, and Spain), willing to share the American burden and 'rise to the challenge' of the war, and an 'Old Europe' (most markedly, France and Germany), cowardly and weak in its convictions, may have been overly simplistic, but it did capture a fundamental break in the European family, and a very different set of attitudes towards the War on Terror. It is a divide that has persisted in the years that followed, marking not only divergent geopolitical understandings (and behaviours) on the part of some of the new EU member states, but also highlighting divergent national understandings of what Europe was—and what it was *for*. The ideal vision of Europe as a 'special area of human hope' evoked by the Constitutional Convention—a space where certain rights and values were assured to one and all—apparently did not mean the same thing across the now 25-member strong EU.[68]

One example is particularly revealing. In late November 2006, the European Parliament threatened to impose sanctions on Poland (including a possible suspension of Polish voting rights in the EU) if it continued to refuse to collaborate with an EU Parliamentary inquiry into the alleged web of secret CIA rendition flights and ghost prisons across Europe. Poland, along with Romania, was targeted in particular by the inquiry for supposedly having not only facilitated air transfers of imprisoned terrorists (something that a number of the 'Old European' states had done as well) but also for having provided interrogation and detention facilities for the CIA.[69] The EU Parliamentary inquiry took Poland to task especially for its failure to cooperate in the investigation: Warsaw declined to field any senior government ministers or MPs to answer the commission's questions and the Polish parliament explicitly decided not to hold an inquiry into the affair.[70] Continued EU pressure evoked public declarations from

---

[67] See the comments of former Polish dissident writer/journalist Adam Michnik, 'Noi, traditori dell'Europa', *La Repubblica* (8 April 2003), 17.

[68] See Bialasiewicz, Elden and Painter, 'The Constitution of EU Territory'. The extensive Eurobarometer surveys carried out in the years following accession (2006 in particular) highlighted in fact a wide divergence in attitudes on a series of moral and political issues between the 'New' and 'Old' EU states.

[69] As reported by Poland's largest daily newspaper *Gazeta Wyborcza*. See Marcin Gadziński, 'Polska na szlaku tortur CIA', *Gazeta Wyborcza* (27 November 2006); also, Stephen Grey, *Ghost Plane: The Untold Story of the CIA's Secret Rendition Programme* (London: Hurst & Co., 2006).

[70] When questioned by *Gazeta Wyborcza* in the days preceding the release of the results of the investigation, Minister and Deputy Chairman of the Parliamentary Defence Committee Przemysław Gosiewski declared the matter to be the exclusive domain of 'the appropriate national security bodies' (see the interview in Jarosław Gugała, 'Gosiewski: W Polsce nie było wiezien CIA', *Gazeta Wyborcza* (28 November 2006)).

representatives of the Polish right accusing 'totalitarian Europe' of 'bully tactics' (and counter-responses from other European MEPs branding Poland 'an American Trojan Horse in Europe').

We could say that, in this sense, broader geopolitical shifts simply allowed to come to the surface existing differences within Europe. At the same time, however, the 'geopolitical vertigo'[71] opened up by the War on Terror made *all* Europeans crucially aware of the need to define Europe's geopolitical identity and its world role in much clearer terms. Debates in the post-2001 period have focused, accordingly, on the question of how Europe's 'geopolitical difference' should be conceived; in the final section, I highlight some key voices in these debates.

Europe's Future II: A New European Promise?

'Europe...is a projection towards a world always on the horizon, always unattainable. The landscape of Europe is pure(ly) horizon...its history is pure(ly) horizon.'

Maria Zambrano[72]

'We are younger than ever, we Europeans, since a certain Europe does not yet exist.'

Jacques Derrida[73]

In their widely diffused intervention on the eve of the invasion of Iraq, Jürgen Habermas and Jacques Derrida argued that Europe could only define itself by defining a 'European model' that transcended the boundaries of Europe: 'a cosmopolitical order based on the recognition and protection of certain basic rights and the principles of international law...being European should also mean rejecting certain practices, certain violations *wherever* they occur'.[74]

Habermas's and Derrida's vision (and its later re-elaboration by the authors themselves as well as others) hinted at a radically new conception of Europe's geopolitical identity, one that was 'future oriented...defined by setting off towards the new, rather

---

[71] The term comes from Ó'Tuathail, *Critical Geopolitics*.

[72] Maria Zambrano, *La agonia de Europa* (Madrid: Editorial Trotta, 2000, orig. 1942).

[73] Derrida, *The Other Heading*, 7.

[74] Habermas and Derrida's original contribution appeared jointly in the German *Frankfurter Allgemeine Zeitung* and the French *Libération* on 31 May 2003 and was subsequently translated and re-printed in a number of other major European newspaper. This piece was followed by a series of editorials written by other leading European commentators, including Umberto Eco, Fernando Savater and Gianni Vattimo, again translated and published across Europe.

than pointing towards a perfect past'.[75] According to Wæver, in the Habermasian/ Derridean understanding, the key distinctive feature that Europe could bring to international affairs was not:

> some inner quality given by [its] history, but exactly an experience related to this negative identity: the experience of struggling over sovereignty's complexities, and thus being better prepared for the necessary conceptual innovations in international law and world order politics, compared especially to the US that pursues an unsustainable vision of sovereignty.[76]

The (successful) transcendence of its national past had made Europe, in other words, a unique geopolitical subject, a unique 'polity of the future', as Habermas and Derrida termed it.

Another important voice in the 2003 debates on rethinking the European geopolitical subject was French political philosopher Etienne Balibar. In his book *L'Europe, L'Amerique, La Guerre*, Balibar suggested that Europe must reject the essentialized geopolitical identities and civilizational divides inscribed by the War on Terror and reclaim, rather, its role as what he termed an 'evanescent mediator'. It was the role already ascribed to it by many outside of Europe, Balibar argued; those who saw in Europe the only possible alternative to American hegemony and the discourse of a 'clash of civilisations'. Europe could only be a mediator, Balibar suggested, because there is no—and there cannot be—a European identity that can be delimited, distinguished in essential fashion from other identities. This is because there are no absolute borders between a historically and culturally constituted European space and the spaces that surround it. Just as there are no absolute confines to those values, beliefs, and traditions that make up the 'European' inheritance: these, he argued, are present to various degrees, and in various 'reflections', throughout the world. The question then should not be one of tracing the contours of a European identity, but rather that of 'recognising Europe wherever it occurs'.[77]

Such an understanding of Europe has important consequences: it necessarily privileges, Balibar argued, practice over a singular identity; the deployment of 'European ideas', 'European ways of doing', rather than a 'European identity'. Balibar's ideas found close resonance in the work of a number of other authors. Tzvetan Todorov's notion of Europe as a *puissance tranquille* similarly invoked the European geopolitical subject as an 'evolving, becoming order', not 'prescribable but existing in practice'.[78] As Bertrand Ogilvie has noted, such theorizations challenged in a fundamental way the taken for granted ideas about sovereignty, politics, and power—and the spaces within which these are exercised. In Balibar's vision of the 'evanescent mediator', absence (or, better yet, a fading presence) becomes power of a different sort. Europe, in this reading, does not simply constitute itself as just another partner in a series of geopolitical strategies, but

---

[75] Wæver, 'The Temporal Structure of European Security Identity'.
[76] Ibid.
[77] Etienne Balibar, *L'Europe, l'Amerique, la guerre* (Paris: Editions La Découverte, 2003).
[78] Tzvetan Todorov, *Le nouveau désordre mondial* (Paris: Editions Robert Laffont, 2003), 42.

rather as a *realm of possibilities within which conflicts can be transformed*;[79] Europe seen, then, as *a mediator of (also others') pasts; as a laboratory for the resolution of conflict*.[80]

The idea of Europe as an 'exemplary' model for the world has, nonetheless, been most clearly elaborated in the work of the late Jacques Derrida, and it is with a brief consideration of his writings—and their influence—that I would like to close. In one of his final public addresses, in May 2004, Derrida made an impassioned plea for:

> a Europe that can show that another politics is possible, that can imagine a political and ethical reflection that is heir to the Enlightenment tradition, but that can also be the portent of a new Enlightenment, able to challenge binary distinctions and high moral pronouncements.[81]

In the address (entitled 'A Europe of Hope') Derrida summoned his audience to 'imagine a different Europe':

> I believe that it is without Eurocentric illusions or pretensions, without a trace of European nationalism, indeed without even an excess of confidence in Europe as it now is (or appears in the process of becoming), that we must fight for what this name represents today, with the memory of the Enlightenment, to be sure, but also with the full awareness—and full admission—of the totalitarian, genocidal and colonialist crimes of the past. We must fight for what is irreplaceable within Europe in the world to come so that it might become more than just a single market or single currency, more than a neo-nationalist conglomerate, more than a new military power.[82]

What was 'irreplaceable' within Europe, in Derrida's words, was precisely its ability to transform itself—and the world; here lay Europe's 'exemplarity' (the 'European Spirit' evoked by Paul Valéry). In *The Other Heading: Reflections on Today's Europe* published in 1992, Derrida wrote of the 'paradox' of this exemplarity that, to his mind, brought with it also a host of ethico-political responsibilities: responsibilities to that 'which has been promised under the name Europe' but also the duty to open up this legacy to 'what never was, and never will be Europe'.[83] The temporal dimension is of vital importance here. Elaborating his ideas further in 1994 in *Spectres of Marx: The State of the Debt, the*

---

[79] Bertrand Ogilvie, 'Sans domicile fixe. Entretien avec Etienne Balibar' *Le passant ordinaire* 43 (February/March 2003), 59.

[80] The ideal of Europe as mediator continues to resonate within the recent work of other theorists of the European project. In their best-selling book *Das kosmopolitische Europa* (Frankfurt/M: Suhrkamp Verlag, 2004); translated into English as *Cosmopolitan Europe* (Cambridge: Polity Press, 2007); and, interestingly enough, into French as *Pour un Empire Européen*, marking evidently different national understandings of what Europe is for... Ulrich Beck and Edgar Grande suggested that Europe can serve as a unique model for the world; can offer a 'unique historical lesson... namely, how enemies can become neighbours' (264). It can offer 'a global alternative to the American way, namely, a European way that accords priority to the rule of law, political equality, social justice, cosmopolitan integration and solidarity', (ibid.).

[81] Jacques Derrida, 'Une Europe de l'espoir', *Le Monde Diplomatique* (3 November 2004), 3.

[82] Ibid.

[83] Derrida, *The Other Heading*, 76–80.

Work of Mourning and the New International, Derrida suggested that a 'politics of responsibility' (here, Europe's) must extend also to the past and future. Justice is due not just to today's living, he claimed, but also to the dead—the victims of war, violence, extermination, oppression, imperialism, totalitarianism—and to the not-yet-born.

Derrida's reflections on responsibility and justice were articulated through the figure of the 'spectre' (upon which the title of this chapter draws). In Derrida's understanding, spectres are both those he termed *revenants* (those who return), and *arrivants* (those still to come). The present, he suggested, is unsettled as much by the return of the past as by the imminence of the future. Both temporal dimensions are an integral part of what Derrida terms 'spectrality', encompassing at once that which is no longer and that which is not-yet-present: as he put it, 'the non-contemporaneity with itself of the living present'.[84] In Derrida's formulation, the present 'is never free of vestiges of the past and stirrings of the future but rather constantly filtered through the structures of memory and anticipation'.[85]

According to Derrida, belief in the impermeable solidity (and contemporaneity) of the present has always been key to totalitarian ideologies: every regime would like to eternalize its present in order to rule out the possibility of its future disintegration and to erase the barbarity from which it sprang. Such regimes, he argued, fear spectres. In his attempt to sketch an alternative, 'exemplary', politics for Europe, Derrida thus invoked an ethico-political engagement with both past and future; with both 'memory' and 'anticipation'. His call for 'what is irreplaceable in Europe in the world to come'[86] thus appealed both to notions of Europe's unique 'inheritance'—and its 'promise'. For Derrida, what can be inherited from a European 'legacy' is only its promise: that which it defers, that which it postpones—and thus bequeaths to the future.[87] Indeed, the 'Europe to come' that Derrida calls upon is what he considers a 'paleonym': 'for what we remember—and for what we promise'. This, he argues, in no way weakens Europe's political/ethical potential: quite the contrary. It is only in its 'promise', in that which he terms the realm of 'im-possibility', that Europe's 'responsibility' can be exercised. For the exercise of (European) 'responsibility' in the realm of the possible becomes simply the execution of an (already given) programme; it is mere political technology, not politics itself.[88]

It is interesting that Derrida's call has being taken up by European political theorists in sketching out the 'real' spaces of Europe's responsibility (ethical, political, geopolitical).

---

[84] Derrida, *Spectres of Marx*, xix.

[85] See the discussion in Ross Benjamin and Heesok Chang, 'Jacques Derrida, The Last European', in Andrew Davidson and Himadeep Muppidi (eds), *Europe and Its Boundaries: Words and Worlds, within and beyond* (Lanham, MD: Lexington Books, 2009), 61; also, Silvano Petrosino, 'Scrivere "Europa" con una mano sola. Derrida e l'anticipazione', in Luigi Alici and Francesco Totaro (eds), *Filosofi per l'Europa* (Macerata: Edizioni Universita di Macerata, 2006), 206–17.

[86] Derrida, 'Une Europe de l'espoir'.

[87] Derrida, *Spectres of Marx*, 54.

[88] See the discussion in Silvano Petrosino, *Jacques Derrida e la legge del possibile* (Milan: Jaca Book, 1997).

In recent years (and in particular since the trans-Atlantic break following the invasion of Iraq), in their attempt to define the emergent European geopolitical subject, various political and legal scholars have emphasized the unique malleability of the European space of rights—and the political and geopolitical effects this carries. Scholars of international law such as Emmanuel Decaux have noted, indeed, that the 'exemplarity' of the contemporary EU space of rights comes from the fact that it allows (at least potentially) for claims to its law to come from and extend also to 'non-European' spaces, subjects, and events. The safeguarding of certain rights and values is opened up *also* to those not currently residing in the present territory of the Union; it is available (*in potentia*) to *all those who call upon 'Europe's promise'*; it extends also to the not-yet, 'im-possibly', European (to use Derrida's words).[89]

Writing in early 2010, sixty years on from the adoption of the European Convention on Human Rights, Decaux commented on the evolution of the Convention from its early days to its present incarnation within the EU's Charter of Fundamental Rights.[90] Beyond the new legal mechanisms now available for the enforcement of the Charter's provisions, what Decaux noted above all was the changing nature of the cases brought before the European Court of Human Rights (ECHR) over the past decade: cases that now not only increasingly extended beyond the territorial confines of the current EU-27, but that also stretched beyond the present day, with the Court being called upon to deliberate on events that occurred ten, twenty, even fifty years back.[91] I will cite just one example here, that I believe illustrates well the ways in which Europe is being asked to engage with its spectres—and make the seemingly im-possible possible.

In the spring of 2006, the families of Polish soldiers and intellectuals executed by Stalin's secret police in Katyń, in one of the Second World War's most infamous massacres, announced that they would take Russia to the ECHR in order to force a full disclosure of information about the killings. The massacre, perpetrated in April 1940, had been personally ordered by Stalin and took the lives of over 21,000 Polish officers, prominent intellectuals, writers, journalists, teachers, and civil servants. The victims were buried in mass graves, and the USSR authorities blamed the killings on the Nazi occupiers, going as far as reburying the bodies and bulldozing the evidence in order to deflect the blame

---

[89]   Emmanuel Decaux, 'Valeurs démocratiques communes et divergences culturelles', *Questions internationales* 9 (September/October 2004), 32–5.

[90]   Signed into law in Rome on 4 November 1950. See Emmanuel Decaux, 'La Convention Européenne des Droits de l'Homme', European Court of Human Rights/Cour Européenne des Droits de l'Homme, CEDH Working Paper, February 2010.

[91]   Over the past fifteen years, the European Court of Human Rights has seen a dramatic increase in cases, in particular from Eastern and Central European states, leading some commentators to note that it had become a *de facto* 'adjudicator of the transition': see Robert Harmsen, 'The European Convention on Human Rights after Enlargement', *International Journal of Human Rights* 5:4 (2001), 18–43. The most recent trend, however, has been a rise in claimants from countries in Europe's extended 'Neighbourhood': from states on the southern shores of the Mediterranean such as Morocco and Tunisia, to former Soviet republics such as Ukraine and Georgia (following the 2008 war, the ECHR received over 2000 claims filed by South Ossetian individuals against Georgia, and an analogous number of claims filed by Georgians against Russia).

from the NKVD. Katyń had long been a prominent marker of Polish suffering during the Second World War, but also of the humiliation of national memory in the forty years of communism when this, as too many other crimes perpetrated by the Soviets before, during and after the war, was simply unspeakable. The European Court was being asked to extend its juridical reach into time and space, to bring justice to events that took place seventy years ago; to bring the 'promise' of the Europe-to-come also to those who are no more.

FURTHER READING

Bauman, Zygmunt, *Europe, An Unfinished Adventure* (Cambridge: Polity Press, 2004).

Bell, Duncan (ed.), *Memory, Trauma and World Politics: Reflections on the Relationship between Past and Present* (Basingstoke: Palgrave Macmillan, 2006).

Derrida, Jacques, *L' autre cap* (Paris: Les Editions de Minuit, 1991) (translated as *The Other Heading: Reflections on Today's Europe* (Bloomington, IN: Indiana University Press, 1992)).

Derrida, Jacques, *Spectres de Marx. L' état de la dette, le travail du deuil et la nouvelle internationale* (Paris: Editions Galilée, 1993) (translated as *Spectres of Marx: The State of Debt, the Work of Mourning and the New International,* (London: Routledge, 1994)).

Geremek, Bronislaw and Robert Picht (eds), *Visions d'Europe* (Paris: Odile Jacob, 2007).

Hersant, Yves and Fabienne Durand-Bogaert (eds), *Europes. De l'Antiquité au XXe siècle. Anthologie critique e commentée* (Paris: Editions Robert Laffont, 2000).

Jonsson, Stefan, *Subject without Nation: Robert Musil and the History of Modern Identity* (Durham, NC: Duke University Press, 2000).

Lebow, Richard Ned, Wulf Kansteiner and Claudio Fogu (eds), *The Politics of Memory in Postwar Europe* (Durham, NC: Duke University Press, 2006).

Levy, Daniel, Max Pensky and John Torpey (eds), *Old Europe, New Europe, Core Europe: Transatlantic Relations after the Iraq War* (London: Verso, 2005).

Morin, Edgar, *Penser l'Europe*, 2nd edn (Paris: Gallimard, 1990).

Parker, Noel (ed.), *The Geopolitics of Europe's Identity: Centres, Boundaries, Margins* (Basingstoke: Palgrave, 2008).

Wæver, Ole, 'European Security Identities', *Journal of Common Market Studies* 34 (1996), 103–32.

CHAPTER 5

....

EUROPE AND ITS OTHERS: IS THERE A EUROPEAN IDENTITY?

....

LUISA PASSERINI

SOME HISTORICAL ANTECEDENTS

....

FOR centuries, forms of European identity were built up through contrasts and opposi-
tions,[1] creating various forms of orientalism and occidentalism. Europe's Other changed
from being an image of Asia, to one of Africa, and then to one of America—or of some
peoples of these continents, such as in various epochs Turks, Russians, and Chinese. The
European ambivalence towards its Others manifested itself in two different but indivisi-
ble relations: the area of concrete relations with non-European peoples (political, military, socio-economic, and missionary) through colonial expansion, and that of the
imagination, which created images not deriving from observation or experience but
from psychological projections.[2] The Other was therefore both the primitive, considered
as a holder of positive values with which to rejuvenate a corrupt civilization and a touchstone for the level of progress reached by Europe, and the savage to be exploited, converted, and 'civilized'. This very translation of customs and attitudes of Others into the
European languages—with their own metaphors, stylistic characteristics, and inertias—
was a form of assimilation, which took place through the accounts of travellers, mission-
aries, and anthropologists.[3]

The figure of the Other has also been projected onto the country that overtook Europe
on the road to modernity and progress, the United States. This projection was so strong

[1] Richard Mayne, *The Europeans: Who Are We?* (London: Weidenfeld & Nicolson, 1972).
[2] Ernest Henri Phillipe Baudet, *Paradise on Earth: Some Thoughts on European Images of Non-
European Man* (Westport, CT: Greenwood Press, 1965).
[3] Talal Asad and John Dixon, 'Translating Europe's Others', in *Europe and its Others: Proceedings of
the Essex Conference on the Sociology of Literature*, Vol. 1 (Colchester: University of Essex, 1984).

that it created in Europe persistent trends of anti-Americanism, which were often ways to either claim *ex negativo* forms of European identity or to express the crisis of this idea. It is for this reason that the concept of the West, which includes Europe and North America and particularly the United States, is ambiguous and conflictual, and that it exposes the aporiae and contradictions which have historically been at the basis of the European identity.[4] A part of the 'negative' patrimony constituted by the European representations of Others can be reversed to remind us that an implicit Europeanness did frequently become conscious—above all in the experiences of the strata of the population which were less or not at all intellectual—only through the experience of migration or travel to other continents.

The construction of a united Europe during the postwar period—from the founding of the European Economic Community in 1957 to the election in 1979 of the first European Parliament with universal suffrage and to the Maastricht Treaty in 1992—was accompanied by an increasing feeling of uncertainty over what represented the European specificity and what it meant to be European. The great histories of the idea of Europe and the collections of documents and examples of the European past published in the twenty years following the Second World War reflect a less problematic attitude towards the idea of a European specificity than the publications that appeared during the following decades.[5] It was indeed during the 1960s that 'Europeanness' began to be posed as a problem, together with the debate on 'identity', a term which had not been used much until the 1950s, and which began to be employed more frequently as a result of the new social, cultural, ethnic and regional movements. At the same time, a change in the conception of the Other was emerging: after the experience of Fascism and two world wars, new forms of the Other were found inside, in Europe's own history.[6]

In 1973, a declaration made by the European Community (as the Union was then called, when it was composed of nine members) and approved in Copenhagen, represented an attempt to define European specificity, which was in part affected by the debate on identity, while it was unable to avoid the contradictions of Eurocentrism. The Declaration on European Identity was based 'on the principles of the unity of the Nine', on their 'responsibilities with regard to the rest of the world', and on the 'dynamic nature of the construction of Europe.' Unity—even while admitting a diversity of cultures—answered the 'basic necessity to ensure the survival of the civilization which [the Nine] have in common.' European Identity, according to this document, should be based on a common heritage conceived as follows: the same attitudes towards life, converging to

---

[4] Dimitri D'Andrea, 'Europe and the West: Identity Beyond Origin', in Furio Cerutti and Enno Rudolph (eds), *A Soul for Europe*. Vol. 1, *A Reader*. Vol. 2, *An Essay Collection* (Leuven-Sterling, VA: Peeters, 2001), Vol. 2, 133–51.

[5] Federico Chabod, *Storia dell'idea d'Europa* (Bari: Laterza, 1961); Jean Baptiste Duroselle, *l'idée d' Europe dans l'histoire* (Paris: Denoel, 1965); Bernard Voyenne, *Histoire de L'idée européenne* (Paris: Payot, 1964); Denis De Rougemont, *Vingt-huit siècles d'Europe* (Paris: Payot, 1961).

[6] Thomas Diez quoted by William Biebuyck, 'Review Essay: The New European Imaginary', *European Journal of Social Theory* 12:2 (2009), 291–302.

build a society measuring up to the needs of individuals; the principles of representative democracy, rule of law, social justice and respect for human rights. 'An essential part' of European Identity was at that point represented by a common market based on a customs union, established institutions, as well as policies and machinery for cooperation.

In addition, while the first sections of the Declaration repeated presuppositions that were already familiar and acceptable in the main, the rest of it established a hierarchy of relations with the world. In the first place came the aim of intensifying ties with those European countries with which friendly and cooperative relations already existed; then came the aim of maintaining and strengthening the historic links with the Mediterranean and African countries, and with the Middle East. The 'close ties' with the United States—a country which shared the values and aspirations of a common heritage—were held to be 'mutually beneficial' and should be preserved 'on the basis of equality and in a spirit of friendship.' With Japan and Canada 'close cooperation and constructive dialogue' were foreseen; with the USSR and the countries forming the Eastern bloc, a policy of détente; with China 'exchanges in various fields'; with other Asian countries the extension of already existing commercial relations; with Latin America, and in particular with several countries in the same area, an increase in 'friendly' relations. As for 'the less favoured nations', the Nine declared the 'importance of the struggle against underdevelopment' through trade and financial aid. The last point announced that European identity 'will evolve as a function of the dynamic of the construction of a united Europe.'

It is not only the competitive and hierarchical nature of the Declaration which has been criticized, because in it relations with the rest of the world are organized according to a descending scale from 'equality and friendship' to 'aid', but also the concept of identity and its legitimizing use in this context has come under fire.[7] The potentially homogenizing character of the concept of identity has sometimes led to a preference for the terms 'identification' or 'subjectivity'.[8] Here the term will be used in order to illustrate the debate around it; thus its use intends to be critical and deconstructive, trying to avoid references to identity as a simple function or product of the European Union or as a basis for its legitimization.

The document cited exposes the dangers which are implicit in flattening the European identity on the idea (and the reality) of a united Europe; connections between the two exist, but each remains relatively independent of the other. The theme of a united Europe is in force in the political, social, economic and cultural fields, while identity refers to a field which is at the same time wider and narrower, which moves from everyday life in both its material and emotional aspects to 'high' and 'low' cultural forms, of the elites and the masses. The advantage of keeping separate the identity and the idea of Europe is that in this way the discourse on European identity is able to keep its distance from and to criticize the political projects and their realization.

---

[7] Lutz Niethammer, 'A European Identity?', in Bo Stråth (ed.), *Europe and the Other and Europe as the Other* (Brussels: Presses Interuniversitaires Européennes/Peter Lang, 2000).

[8] Respectively Homi Bhabha, 'The Third Space', in Jonathan Rutherford (ed.), *Identity: Community, Culture, Difference* (London: Lawrence & Wishart, 1990); and Luisa Passerini, *Storia e soggettività* (Florence: La Nuova Italia, 1988).

It is therefore useful to keep three levels of discussion distinct: (1) that of the concrete procedure of the unification of Europe, (2) that of the different ideas and ideologies regarding a united Europe, and (3) that of identity. Each of these levels is to some extent independent from the others; this does not, however, reduce the complexity of the relations between them but—on the contrary—increases it. For example, the link between the idea of a united Europe and the institutional reality of the European Union has at times been underrated, as if the latter were simply the result of the calculations of the member states so that they would be able to maintain their wealth and security. However, it has been rightly claimed that the current European construction is inexplicable if the federalist vision of the 'founding fathers' of Europe, Jean Monnet and his small group of technocrats, is not taken into account.[9] Perry Anderson also observed that ideas did indeed play a role in the history of European integration in as much as they were the expression of the political and intellectual elites, not of the popular masses, and that a European public opinion began to emerge as unanimous for the first time only after the collapse of the Soviet system, as an approval of the opening towards the Eastern bloc. All the same, this public opinion was that of the media, especially of the press, not that of the wider public or that of the electoral body, again underscoring the critical difference between the idea of a united Europe and European identity. The problem of the different topics therefore intersects with that of a potential European public sphere, where institutions, ideas, and ways of feeling can exist in various and connected ways.

Changes in the public sphere have had critical implications for the content of European identity. Research on the development of the public sphere in Europe, understood as a deliberative political space in which both government and civil society participate, has been related with the need for European political identity and therefore connected, given its small scale, with the study of elites.[10] However, new directions of research indicate an enlargement of the European public sphere, understood as a space characterized not by exclusion, but by inclusion, opening the way to a wide European sense of belonging. A potential European public sphere is in the process of being modified thanks to the vanishing of the boundaries between public and private that have been taking place in the last decades.[11]

Numerous efforts have been made during the second half of the twentieth century to find a foundation of European identity with specific contents that should distinguish it from the identities of other peoples and continents. The central example of this is the identification of Europe with modernity and progress, an equation which is as old as the Enlightenment. Today, however, Europe is no longer at the centre or the vanguard of

---

[9] Perry Anderson, 'The Europe to Come', *London Review of Books* 18:2 (1996), 3–8; Anderson, 'Under the Sign of the Interim', *London Review of Books* 18:1 (1996), 13–17.

[10] Juan Díez Medrano, 'The Public Sphere and the European Union's Political Identity', in Jeffrey T. Checkell and Peter J. Katzenstein (eds), *European Identity* (Cambridge: Cambridge University Press, 2009), 81–107.

[11] Etienne Balibar, *We, the People of Europe? Reflections on Transnational Citizenship* (Princeton, NJ: Princeton University Press, 2004). For the new developments, see Robert Frank, Hartmut Kaelble, Marie-Françoise Lévy and Luisa Passerini (eds), *Building a European Public Sphere: From the 1950s to the Present* (Brussels: Peter Lang, 2010).

modernity and this identification has lost its meaning, while maintaining its strong Eurocentric tone.

In reaction to the loss of old identifications, the trend has been not to search for one single value capable of organizing an entire cultural universe, but to choose a way by which to accumulate various specificities. One example of this is the attempt carried out at the beginning of the 1960s of analysing 'European ideas', which consisted in a series of concepts including modern science, Christianity, human rights, evolution, imperialism, the subconscious, youth revolt, and so on. Another of the many examples of this approach is the use of the epithets 'fragile, restless, contradictory, inconsistent' to connote the continent; faced with these adjectives, one can only ask to what other continents they could not also apply.[12] Today, 'only very few polities in the world do not include in their proclaimed self-understanding the notions of democracy, security, prosperity, a minimal set of rights of the population, and the maintenance and development of an "own" culture.'[13] The problem is that comparisons in which a clear definition of the second term is missing have been a constant characteristic of Eurocentrism, and definitions of identity based on such conceptions run the risk of reproducing rhetorical formulae which are either empty or suspect.

In the debate on European identity the insistence on European values has largely substituted the effort to indicate contents of identity, sometimes adding new values suggested by our times. 'Inwardness', 'the affirmation of ordinary life', and 'self-realization' have recently been indicated as core European values, together with others which have been traditionally considered such: diversity and rationality as well as 'freedom', 'toleration of difference', and a 'practical rationalism of world mastery'. These values are assigned to Europe as specific on the basis of the idea that the main source of European identity is the value of Christian civilization, although the European legacy is claimed to include Judaism, Christianity, Islam, Greek philosophy, Roman law, and humanism both religious and non-religious. It is not by chance that this position leads to the belief that the European Constitution should have included this type of declaration in its preamble, as proposed by the Polish writer Stefan Wilkanowicz.[14] This and similar positions are still based on an 'implausible idea of a morally superior European identity that transcends national ones', to use Gerard Delanty and Chris Rumford's terms. These authors

---

[12] The two examples are respectively from Erik Lund, Mogens Pihl and Johannes Sløk (eds), *A History of European Ideas* (London: Hurst, 1962); and from Richard Hoggart and Douglas Johnson, *An Idea of Europe* (London: Chatto, 1987).

[13] Volker Balli, 'An EU Self-Understanding of the European Union Revealed through Justifications of Political Actions', in Jessica Bain and Martin Holland (eds), *European Union Identity: Perceptions from Asia and Europe* (Baden-Baden: Nomos, 2007), 11–29, here 28.

[14] Hans Joas, 'The Cultural Values of Europe: An Introduction', in Hans Joas and Klaus Wiegandt (eds), *The Cultural Values of Europe* (Liverpool: Liverpool University Press, 2008), 1–21. The Eurocentrism of this position is all the more evident, as in the same collection Gudrun Krämer, in 'The Contest of Values: Notes on Contemporary Islamic Discourse', 338–56, argues that Islamists in their majority acknowledge no such stock of shared human values. A large-scale cross-national research project on values in European societies, the European Value Systems Study Group, was established in the 1970s and publishes a series of books based on their survey data (Brill, Leiden-Boston).

add that human rights have become an important expression of European identity, but a close look reveals a double standard in the EU, one for judging non-member states and another for judging the conduct of member states.[15]

This evokes the old and repetitive debate on the difference between national identities and European identities. So much has been written on this that it is more apt, rather than trying to summarise it, to resort to the ironical argument by Richard Robyn in reply to the question posed by Benedict Anderson about who would be willing to die for Comecon or the EEC rather than for their nations as happened in the past. Robyn counters, on the basis of a series of studies conducted in seven countries of Europe (the UK, Denmark, France, Germany, Italy, the Netherlands, and Sweden, through interviews with elites but also common folk, from day labourers to unemployed and retired), that these studies had difficulty in finding nationalists in Europe. He observes that Europeans may be less willing than in the past to die for their countries, while they may not be willing to die for Brussels either. However, he is confident that they may be willing to die for principles such as democracy, rule of law, multi-ethnic states and protection for minority rights, freedom of movement and trade, and peaceful cooperation among nations.[16] One could add that today there seems to be a widespread acceptance of the fact that national identities in Europe incorporate an implicit assumption of a European sense of belonging as well as vice versa, while it has lost meaning to measure European identity against national identities.

If a distance is established between the historical forms of European identity and those which are possible for the future, it becomes evident that the debate around European identity is polarised between two extremes, with many intermediate positions: one pole, oriented towards the present, points to the fragility and contradictions of the existing forms of European identity, while the other, oriented towards the future, resolutely assumes a normative position, indicating what European identity can and/or should be.

The debate on multiculturalism is part of this scenario. Multiculturalism has been suggested as the basis for an identity that could be recognised also by non-territorialized groups, such as foreigners or immigrants, and as the only possible basis for shaping a European political culture that could foster a European identity. While noticing that united Europe is de facto multicultural, Riva Kastoryano acknowledges that multiculturalism presents the risk of leading to a fracturing of European society into multiple identities and hints at the possibility that less loaded terms like pluriculturalism might be preferable, as long as they indicate an approach that could one day make the EU into a political space in which the paradoxes of democracy are negotiated.[17]

---

[15] Gerard Delanty and Chris Rumford, *Rethinking Europe: Social Theory and the Implications of Europeanization* (London: Routledge, 2005), 53 and 67.

[16] Robyn Richard, 'Introduction: National versus Supranational Identity in Europe' and 'Conclusion', in Richard Robyn (ed.), *The Changing Face of European Identity* (London: Routledge, 2005), 1–16, 227–35.

[17] Riva Kastoryano, 'Foreword' and 'Introduction: "Multiculturalism": An Identity for Europe?', in Kastoryano (ed.), *An Identity for Europe: The Relevance of Multiculturalism in the EU Construction* (New York: Palgrave Macmillan, 2009), ix–xv and 1–23.

A clear definition of this dilemma has been offered by Bassam Tibi, pointing at the difference between cultural pluralism understood as a state of mind related to a reality in which people of different cultures acknowledge and respect each other while sharing a cross-cultural consensus on basic values and norms, and multiculturalism as based on cultural relativism and denying the universal validity of norms and values.[18] Another criticism could be added for what concerns this second attitude: that, although multiculturalism proclaims absolute indifference of values between various cultural belongings, in practice it cannot avoid establishing hierarchies between cultures.

This issue of multiplicity in European identity has had many interpretations. An interesting one has been offered by Monica Sassatelli, according to whom multiplicity can be shifted from outside to inside the concept, in the sense that not only many European identities are available, but also each is in itself multiple, without any essentialist meaning.[19]

In conclusion, the problem of European identity accepts the solution offered with the formula of multiple identity only as a first approximation. In reference to Europeanness, it has been noted that the number and extension of currently possible cultural identities has increased: the identities based on gender and generation are vital, those based on class and religion continue to exercise their influence, but professional, civic, and ethnic identities have also proliferated and attract increasingly large groups all over the world. Human beings maintain a multiplicity of belongings which tend to push the national one into the background. In regard to this central problem, the concept of 'multiple identity' limits itself to underlining the quality of tolerance and to expressing some potentialities. It remains, however, conceptually undifferentiated and undefined, as does its correlate, multiculturalism. Both these terms and concepts lack a sufficiently explicit description of the power disparity between the subjects and the forms of subjectivity which they denote.

POLARIZATIONS AND EXTENSIONS

The polarization between different conceptions of European identity can be partially reconciled by distinguishing various types of collective identity. For instance, Michael Wintle has argued that it is erroneous to confuse the two separate issues of a European cultural identity, which is much richer, with a European identity as a political legitimator for a new modern state. So, he can conclude his analysis stating that there is a great deal of European identity in existence, in various forms and various places and in the

---

[18] Bassam Tibi, 'Between Communitarism and Euro-Islam: Europe, Multicultural Identities and the Challenge of Migration', in John Docker and Gerhard Fischer (eds), *Adventures of Identity: European Multicultural Experiences and Perspectives* (Tübingen: Stauffenburg Verlag, 2001), 45–60, here 53.

[19] Monica Sassatelli, *Becoming Europeans: Cultural Identity and Cultural Policies* (New York: Palgrave Macmillan, 2009).

minds of various groups. On the whole, however, he deems it to be the sort of cultural identity which can command a benign association or membership of a loose club. The kind of collective identity which provides political legitimacy for a modern state at the European level also exists, but for Wintle it is much scarcer and even more incomplete.[20]

Another form of conciliation has been proposed by Klaus Eder, who considers Europe as a candidate for a kind of

> postmodern identity construction where reflexivity and contingency of symbolic representations and the hard normative reality of legal exclusion together constitute a 'community', [...] an identity no longer disembedded from politics, no longer conceived as a higher order of reality than politics or something that 'underlies' politics. Identity becomes politics.[21]

However, these conciliatory efforts do not resolve the tension between the normative and empirical levels of European identity. The polarization is particularly evident in the debate on the connections between this concept and that of citizenship. There is no doubt that the existing level of European identification—in empirical terms—is no guarantee for a conception of citizenship which is wide enough to respond to the needs of present-day Europe, especially if the relationship is understood within the limits of national boundaries. Fiorella Dell'Olio disputes the assumption that citizenship requires identification at all, and that European citizenship in particular should function towards the formation of a European identity: 'as long as European citizenship is related to the idea of European identity, nationality will continue to function towards the establishment of national immigration policies, and nationality and citizenship will remain interchangeable.'[22] In contrast, Dell'Olio argues that the problem of identification can be confronted by adaptation and that 'compatibility' is achievable when governments devote more attention to the dynamics of change at the empirical level. For her, it is imperative to find a way of drawing individuals into a supranational sphere of 'legality' in order to make them aware not of a new identity but rather of progressive changes in the sphere of their new societal relationships.

However, the connection between European identity and citizenship becomes plausible when both concepts are interpreted with an orientation to the future and to what can be desirable in broad political terms for a post-national situation, and if citizenship is conceived as a new form that decouples territory from legal membership and implies a

---

[20] Michael Wintle, 'The Question of European Identity and the Impact of the Changes of 1989/90', in Jamal Shahin and Michael Wintle (eds), *The Idea of a United Europe: Political, Economic and Cultural Integration since the Fall of the Berlin Wall* (London: Macmillan, 2000), 11–30.

[21] Klaus Eder, 'Integration through Culture? The Paradox of a Search of a European Identity', in Klaus Eder and Bernhard Giesen (eds), *European Citizenship between National Legacies and Postnational Projects* (Oxford: Oxford University Press, 2001), 222–44, here 238. See also, in working towards reconciliation of the empirical and the normative, Ireneusz Pawel Karolewski and Viktoria Kaina (eds), *European Identity: Theoretical Perspectives and Empirical Insights* (Berlin: Lit Verlag, 2006).

[22] Fiorella Dell'Olio, *The Europeanization of Citizenship: Between the Ideology of Nationality, Immigration and European Identity* (Aldershot: Ashgate, 2005), 15.

type of trans-territorial membership based upon the rights of persons as persons.[23] This is a dimension which acquires meaning when territory is envisioned not along national lines, but rather as multidimensional and plastic. On this basis, it would be possible to recognize the Roma as Europeans, a non-territorial people who have been present in almost all the existing nation states in Europe since the fifteenth century. This approach envisages a link between territory and identity—and eventually citizenship—not only along national lines. However, it does not exclude attention to the empirical dimensions of identity, since it establishes a tension between them and a normative dimension.[24]

The case of the Roma is of particular interest for the study of European identity. There are indications that a sense of European identity is a recent development among their community.[25] According to the European Commission's report of 2004, The Situation of Roma in an Enlarged European Union, there are over ten million Roms and Romís in the EU today, who have faced discrimination and marginalization time and again. There are possible contributions that their worldview can make for shaping a new European identity: as an itinerant people in most of the European countries, the Roma have been able to maintain a sense of cultural identity without the need to have a specific territory, on the basis of processes of interaction. Some authors have claimed that not only have they maintained their identity, but they have also known how to combine this with other identities (national or European). A less optimistic view is presented by others, according to whom, under the auspices of the EU, with the help with the Soros Foundation and the World Bank, an invented Roma identity is progressively taking the place of real Roma people.[26]

The Roma are a case *éclatant*, but all intra-European migratory movements have posed the problem of nationals working in countries different from their own, who feel a double or triple loyalty to the country of origin (for instance Italy), the country where they work (for instance Germany), and the country where some of their relatives have established themselves (for instance the Netherlands). They may be said to nourish multiple identifications, and many would welcome recognition of this in terms of a multiple citizenship, which might well take the form of a European citizenship. The internal

---

[23] Yasemin Nuhoğlu Soysal, *Limits of Citizenship: Migrants and Postnational Membership in Europe* (Chicago, IL: University of Chicago Press, 1994).

[24] Mabel Berezin, 'Territory, Emotion, and Identity', in Mabel Berezin and Martin Schain (eds), *Europe without Borders: Remapping Territory, Citizenship, and Identity in a Transnational Age* (Baltimore, MD: Johns Hopkins University Press, 2003), 1–30.

[25] In slogans during protests against their eviction from camping sites in Italy as well as in replies to interviews conducted during the 2000s, Roma people claimed to be Europeans, a totally new claim in their culture. Luisa Passerini, 'From the Europe of Culture to the Europe of Cultures', in *L'Europa delle immagini/Images of Europe* (Florence: Alinari—24 Ore, 2008), 82–107.

[26] Respectively: Aitor Gómez and Rosa Valls, 'Romà's Contributions to European Identity', in Michael Kuhn (ed.), *Who is the European?—A New Global Player?* (Peter Lang: New York, 2007), 105–19; and, for a view on the risk of assimilation that makes the Roma invisible in a new way, Irène Bellier, 'Multiculturalization of Societies: The State and Human Rights Issues', in Gerard Delanty, Ruth Wodak and Paul Jones (eds), *Identity, Belonging and Migration* (Liverpool: Liverpool University Press, 2008), 134–51.

migrations from Central and Eastern Europe to the western parts of the continent have particularly shown that feelings of double and triple belonging have important implications for European identity.[27]

The developments in terms of population mobility and of demography require an enlarged concept of citizenship, not limited to its legal dimension, but rather extended to its cultural components. Today, the question of the relationship between citizenship and identity cannot be posed with reference only to the internal population movements in Europe, since it is especially the increasing immigration from outside Europe that has called into question old ideas of citizenship. While it is foreseen that Europe's ageing population will mean a labour shortage by 2020, it is also projected that by the year 2050 over 60 per cent of the populations of France, Germany, and Italy will be descendants of non-native-born persons.[28]

In this context,

> European citizenship is acquiring its own internal borders in the shape of the Other—the non-European, the Muslim and people who are marginalized. So a split is growing within the EU, between Europeans who can move around and live and work where they want and non-Europeans who need entry and residence visas.[29]

This implies a wide discrepancy between a European citizenship proclaimed with Eurocentric optimism, and the actual lack of rights that characterizes the state of many non-European migrants in Europe such as transnational workers, who are left to the arbitrary decisions of the nation states.[30] According to Rémy Leveau, this system has become even more discriminatory with the 1985 Schengen agreement, since by abolishing internal borders Europe raises with new urgency the question of an identity and a new positioning between 'Us' and 'Others'. Leveau points at a 'Europe of the policies' composed of national policy bureaucrats who decide on the granting of visas (in relation to consular services) as well as on clandestine immigration and rights of asylum.

---

[27] Luisa Passerini, Dawn Lyon, Ioanna Laliotou and Enrica Capussotti (eds), *Women Migrants from East to West: Gender, Mobility and Belonging in Contemporary Europe* (Oxford: Berghahn, 2007).

[28] UN's projections of 2000, quoted by Berezin, 'Territory, Emotion, and Identity', 27. See also Adrian Favell, 'Immigration, Migration, and Free Movements in the Making of Europe', in Checkell and Katzenstein, *European Identity*, 167–89.

[29] Rémy Leveau, Khadija Mohsen-Finan and Catherine Wihtol de Wenden, 'Introduction', in Leveau, Mohsen-Finan and Wihtol De Wenden (eds), *New European Identity and Citizenship* (Aldershot: Ashgate, 2002), ix–xv, here ix. See also Alison Brysk and Gershorn Shafir (eds), *People Out of Place: Globalization, Human rights, and the Citizenship Gap* (New York: Routledge, 2004), on the thinning of citizenship rights in a globalized situation.

[30] Chris Shore, 'Whither European Citizenship? Eros and Civilization Revisited', *European Journal of Social Theory* 7:1 (2007), 27–44. See also Marion Demossier, 'Introduction', in Demossier (ed.), *The European Puzzle. The Political Structuring of Cultural Identities at a Time of Transition* (New York: Berghahn, 2007), 1–12.

Procedures for democratic control are currently absent for all decisions that relate to access to community territory and regulation of borders.[31]

The effects of such policies on the image of Europe that is thus projected on new-comers, a relevant aspect of European identity, is certainly a negative one; this is particularly serious in the case of asylum seekers, who are often prevented from reaching borders, sometimes with the European states extending their jurisdiction in areas outside of the borders of Europe.[32]

Thus, a future-oriented position on European identity, however normative and visionary (in other terms, utopian) it can be, has the advantage of bringing to the forefront the urgency of change in the fields of membership, citizenship, and participation. This is most evident for what concerns the question of hyphenated identities. While some have denied that this phenomenon, so widespread in the USA, can ever reach meaningful dimensions in Europe, others have recognized that it is already going on at a national level: it is the case of Asian-British, Franco-Maghrebi, Turko-Germans. At a continental level it is most evident in the case of the many who choose to call themselves European Muslims, with a full awareness of the multiplicity of issues involved in such choice: 'religio-culturally I am a Euro-Muslim, ethnically I am a Damascene Arab, and politically I am a German citizen.'[33] While making such a statement, which rejects assimilation, Bassam Tibi has stressed the fact that any granting of minorities' privileges and communitarian rights to cultural and religious groups, rather than pursuing the political integration and the connected unfolding of a Euro-Islamic identity, would be counterproductive.

Such positions call not only for an extension of European identity within Europe, but also for a better interaction between European states and Islamic-Mediterranean states. For what concerns internal interaction, the auspice is for Europe to come up with a non-antagonistic view of Islam, including Islam as a legitimate component of European culture and identity, so as to create not only a higher level of integration within the continent, but also neighbourly aid-based relationships with the southern and eastern Mediterranean Muslim countries that many of the immigrants come from.

For what concerns inter-state relationships, a Euro-Mediterranean Partnership was created in 1995, and re-launched in 2008 as the Union for the Mediterranean. It includes the twenty-seven members of EU and sixteen partners around the Mediterranean and in the Middle East; it has six priority projects of ecological and commercial relevance. The viability of this enterprise calls for an emphasis on its cultural component, towards a Mediterranean cultural identity understood as a feeling of belonging to the same

---

[31] Rémy Leveau, 'Space, Culture, and Boundary: Projecting Europe Abroad', in Kastoryano, *An Identity for Europe*, 229.

[32] Vera Gowlland-Debbas, 'European Asylum Policies and the Search for a European Identity', in Lars-Erik Cederman (ed.), *Constructing Europe's Identity: The External Dimension* (Boulder, CO: Lynne Rienner, 2001), 213–29.

[33] Tibi, 'Between Communitarism', 58.

community, an identity still to be constructed.[34] However, this partnership does not address the issue of migration across the Mediterranean.

A specific issue within the Euro-Mediterranean scenario is the question of Turkey's accession to the Union. It is noteworthy that the great majority of the authors involved in the debate on European identity who mention this issue are in favour of the accession. Anthony Giddens, while noting that it was not obvious at all that Morocco's application for accession to the EU should be turned down, warns that the result of a denial of Turkey's accession could be a slowing of economic growth in the country, political polarization and an embittered society, one turning East rather than West. On the same line, others insist that 'Turkey represents a territorialized Islam coupled with secularization. Excluding Turkey from European multiculturalism would boil down to a Euronationalism that is likely to be as dangerous as nationalisms within Europe'.[35] All this shows how urgent and important an extension of the cultural components of Europeanness to Islam has become at a continental scale.

At the same time as 'outward' extensions of European identity are called for, it is worthwhile noting that some authors have underlined its 'inward' dimension on individual or personal grounds, making a plea for 'expressive individualism as a crucial element in the European legacy'.[36] Others have referred to the psychological aspect as a major component of the identification with the idea of Europe; or to the impact that the EU is having on personal identities; or to the fact that European identity exists in the context of the individual and may find favour or not depending on the perceived utility to the self and one's group.[37]

In this field, a new direction of research has emerged in the last twenty years, on the nexus between European identity and the discourse on love, exploring the historical relationships between political forms of identity and cultural attitudes in the field of emotions in Europe, and more specifically between the formation of identity in the European context, on the one hand, and the idea of courtly and romantic love, on the other. In the last two and a half centuries, it was claimed that the sense of belonging to Europe was characterized by a type of love considered unique both to the relationships between genders on the continent and to the type of civilization developed in Europe in the modern era. This sentiment, originating from the courtly love sung by the Provençal troubadours, was treated as if it evolved seamlessly into the feeling exalted by romanticism. Among its characteristics were the insurmountable distances between the lovers

---

[34] Stefania Panebianco (ed.), *A New Euro-Mediterranean Cultural Identity* (London: Frank Cass, 2003).

[35] Anthony Giddens, *Europe in the Global Age* (Cambridge: Polity 2007); Kastoryano, 'Foreword', xiii.

[36] Thomas Pedersen, *When Culture Becomes Politics: European Identity in Perspective* (Aarhus: Aarhus University Press, 2008).

[37] Respectively: Klaus Eder, 'Remembering National Memories Together: The Formation of a Transnational Identity in Europe', in Klaus Eder and Willfried Spohn (eds), *Collective Memory and European Identity: The Effects of Integration and Enlargement* (Aldershot: Ashgate, 2005), 197–220; Delanty and Rumford, *Rethinking Europe*; Sharon Millar and John Wilson, 'Introduction', in Millar and Wilson (eds), *The Discourse of Europe: Talk and Text in Everyday Life* (Amsterdam: John Benjamins, 2007), 1–16.

and most often a destiny of dissatisfaction and unhappiness, even in the case of recipro-
cated love. This love, stemming from private and personal spheres, was attributed a public function and was used as a distinctive characteristic of one civilization, the European
civilization, over African and Asian and indeed, also American civilization. Throughout
the second half of the nineteenth century, the formulation of the connection Europe/
Love in the context of European superiority lost the cosmopolitanism that had originally corrected its nationalism. Instead, it was stiffened into a concept of Europeanness
supported by imperial and colonial experiences, which at the same time tried to exclude
any influence from the Orient and Africa. This led to formulations of the relationship
between 'Europe and love' which were increasingly Eurocentric, if not racist, arguing
that the discourses and practices of love—in the form of romantic or other kinds of
attachment—were unique to Europeans and represented the superiority of gender relationships in Europe in respect to all other parts of the world.[38]

The Re-emergence of the Other in a Globalized Post-colonial Perspective

The process of globalization, which has relativized the nation state, has also led to the
interpenetration of the EU and other regions of the world. Thus it has suggested new
conceptions of regional identities, in a modified vision of the relationship between self
and other. In particular, this process has made obsolete a conception of the link between
identity and alterity as based on a necessary contrast. The present globalized and postcolonial situation of the world implies, from the point of view of subjectivity, that the
Other is indispensable not so much in order to represent the opposite of the subject, but
rather to represent its limit and its interlocutor in a continuous dialogue. Otherwise the
very concept of European identity becomes useless or even counterproductive, if it is
used to connote demarcation rather than solidarity with the Other.[39]

---

[38] Among the most important works that lay the foundation for the connection between Europe and
love are Carl Staples Lewis, *The Allegory of Love: A Study in Medieval Tradition* (Oxford: Oxford
University Press, 1936) and Denis De Rougemont, *Passion and Society* (London: Faber & Faber, 1956).
For a critical approach to the question: Luisa Passerini, *Europe in Love, Love in Europe: Imagination and
Politics in Britain between the Wars* (London: Tauris, 1999 and New York: NYU Press, 2000); Luisa
Passerini and Ruth Mas (eds), Special Issue of the *European Review of History* 11:2 (2004), on 'Europe
and Love – L'Europe et l'amour'; Luisa Passerini, *Love and the Idea of Europe* (Oxford: Berghahn, 2009).

[39] Bo Stråth, 'Belonging and European Identity', in Gerard Delanty, Ruth Wodak and Paul Jones
(eds), *Identity, Belonging and Migration* (Liverpool: Liverpool University Press, 2008), 21–37. The
proposal to substitute the notion of oppositional differentiation with that of positive distinctiveness of
one's group with respect to comparable others has been made by Furio Cerutti and Sonia Lucarelli
(eds), *The Search for a European Identity: Values, Policies and Legitimacy of the European Union*
(London: Routledge, 2008), who have applied their notion to the analysis of the relationship between
European political identity and EU's foreign policy.

The process of globalization has given new meanings to the idea of cosmopolitanism, no longer conceived along the abstractly universal lines that characterized the universalism of the Enlightenment. For Gerard Delanty and Chris Rumford, it is possible to conceive of European identity as a cosmopolitan identity, a form of post-national self-understanding embodied in the pluralized cultural models of a societal identity rather than understood as a supranational identity or an official EU identity in tension with national identities. These authors make the case for a normative conception of Europeanization as a cosmopolitan condition, allowing for the recognition of different cultures, the integration of minorities, the legal status of refugees, as well as problems of racism and discrimination, of sovereignty and of citizenship.[40]

This kind of cosmopolitanism refers to the transformation of cultural and political subjectivities in the context of the encounter of the local or national with the global, and is meant to be something more than the simple coexistence of difference in the sense of multiculturalism, and more than the motif of 'unity in diversity', which generally refers to the supposed coexistence of nation states and regions within the EU. In this perspective, becoming European is at the same time to become a part of the world.

This position must be framed in the wide debate about the existence of a European people or demos with a specific form of life. Most authors agree that such a demos does not exist for Europe and neither does an empirical identity referred to it. Thus, the new cosmopolitanism takes a distance from such presupposition, by stating that whether a European societal identity will emerge remains to be seen, and observing that a decisive factor will be the creation of a social project in which some of the defining values of European modernity can be realized in a new order of recognition.

The proposal of a cosmopolitan European identity is an important step in the direction of establishing a view of European identity that takes others into full account. A further decisive step is to develop a post-colonial perspective on European identity. This requires the recognition of the link between colonialism and decolonization, on the one hand, and the nexus of European integration/European identity, on the other, which have been largely ignored in both the scholarship on European identity and daily attitudes of ordinary Europeans.[41] This silence is connected with the need to continue projecting a positive European identity which does not acknowledge the dark sides of European history and with the persistent tendency to privilege a Eurocentric perspective. The need to project such a positive European identity might also be at the basis of the reluctance to approach colonialism as a European rather than a national experience.

---

[40] Delanty and Rumford, *Rethinking Europe*. It should be mentioned that, in the debate on European identity, some authors argue that the very idea of European identity fails to address the reality of a transnational, globalized, multicultural Europe, for instance Ralph Grillo, 'European Identity in a Transnational Era', in Demossier (ed.), *The European Puzzle*, 67–82.

[41] Peo Hansen, 'European Integration, European Identity and the Colonial Connection', *European Journal of Social Theory* 5:4 (2002), 483–98, here 485. On Europeans' racist attitudes in recent times, studied on the basis of travelogues through Europe, it is interesting to see John McLeod, 'European Tribes: Transcultural Diasporic Encounters', in Michelle Keown, David Murphy and James Procter (eds), *Comparing Postcolonial Diasporas* (New York: Palgrave Macmillan, 2009), 19–36.

Anthony Giddens has named this reluctance 'Euro-hypocrisy', as part of the European Union's failure to come to terms with the present and the opportunities that it offers for developing a more integrated European identity and a greater potential geopolitical influence.[42]

By contrast, Peo Hansen has reminded us of the fact that the four French Overseas Departments of Réunion, Guyana, Martinique, and Guadeloupe, as well as the Spanish possessions in North Africa, Melilla and Ceuta (which are not part of the EU's customs territory), are as much a part of the EU as are metropolitan France and Spain. Payments in these places are made in Euros, while Melilla and particularly Ceuta have come to serve as hubs in the EU's fight against illegal immigration from Africa. One should add that the inhabitants of the French colonies in the Pacific, of the Dutch and Danish Overseas countries and territories as well as of the Falkland Islands, all not fully integrated into the EU, carry 'European' passports. Thus the current EU stretches into Africa, South America, the Caribbean, and the Indian Ocean.

Hansen adds to these observations an important reflection on the peculiar role of the Algerian war between 1954 and 1962. Algeria formed at that time an integral part of metropolitan France and therefore it became, in the midst of the war, incorporated into the European Economic Community, the Treaty of Rome being signed in 1957: this means that not even a sizeable war fought inside the Community was able to impinge on the notion of European integration as a symbol of peace.

It is not by chance that one of the best historical interpretations of the vicissitudes of European identity, provided by Hartmut Kaelble, takes into due account the role of decolonization in this process.[43] Kaelble in fact includes, among the reasons for the fundamental change of European identities in the twentieth century, not only the experience of two world wars and the division of Europe after the Second, but especially decolonization, the decline of Europe as the centre of the world, and globalization: the overall change went into the direction of a European self-understanding centred around the concept of multiple modernities, no longer assuming the equation between Europe and modernity and its values. It must be noticed that the term adopted by Kaelble in his historical analysis is 'self-understanding', which is a more flexible and fluid—less liable to become fixed and reified—concept than 'identity'.

According to Kaelble, the feeling of European superiority that was widespread in Europe before World War I, was slowly given up in the half century after 1918 and in its place a feeling of inferiority arose. A new era gradually began around the 1960s and 1970s, when European self-understanding became more positive on the basis of new perspectives on Europe: as one civilization among other ones, all of them seen on equal terms; as a junior

---

[42] Giddens, *Europe*, 228.

[43] Hartmut Kaelble, 'European Self-Understanding in the Twentieth-Century', in Klaus Eder and Willfried Spohn (eds), *Collective Memory and European Identity: The Effects of Integration and Enlargement* (Aldershot: Ashgate, 2005), 17–35. See also Hartmut Kaelble, 'Identification with Europe and Politicization of the EU since the 1980s', in Checkell and Katzenstein (eds), *European Identity*, 193–212.

partner in a worldwide process of modernization led by the USA; and as a continent whose unity consisted in extreme internal diversity. European self-understanding became also more related to politics, around issues such as the stabilization of democracy and peace, a high standard of living brought about by a common market, and social security.

The value of this interpretation is that it points out that in the period following 1960, the relationship between Europe and the rest of the world changed fundamentally with the fall of the European colonial empires, with the definite end of Europe as the political and economic centre of the world, but also with the basic shift of Europe from the most important source of emigration to one of the most important immigration areas. Of course, also the rapprochement of European societies, economies, and politics in Western Europe had a place in this process.

A post-colonial perspective anchored in the globalization process has been absent from the wide debate on European identity sparked by an article by Jürgen Habermas and Jacques Derrida, published in German and French newspapers in 2003 in the wake of the Iraq war and following the mass demonstrations in many European cities in February of that year. According to Krishan Kumar, that debate illustrated the dangers and seductions of seeing European identity in terms of contrast with America, fuelling an anti-Americanism that ends up dividing Europe and not uniting it. Habermas and Derrida put the stress on the commonality of European values as a basis of its difference from the United States. But Kumar has noticed that Europe is not so different from the USA on questions such as religion, the legacy of the French revolution, the party system, the history of class consciousness, and class conflicts.

Altogether, the article by Habermas and Derrida showed a certain complacency, a self-congratulatory air, according to which even Europe's war-torn past can become a source of European superiority, the destructive legacy of Europe leading to the ban of capital punishment. The Europe they evoked appears like a 'small Europe' from the point of view of peoples in the global South, one which does not take into account that anti-war demonstrations occurred worldwide and thus signalled the emergence of a global public sphere.[44] Kumar rightly indicates that it is necessary for Europe to draw on the experience of other countries and other cultures—ambiguous as that may be—accumulated in the course of Europe's globalizing ventures since the fifteenth century, in order to find that reflective distance from themselves that Habermas and Derrida already took for granted.

In a globalized perspective, an issue which is significantly linked with European identity is whether a European memory exists or not. In a post-colonial light, this question must receive a paradoxical answer, in the sense of keeping open the tension between two positions: on the one hand, the recognition that the past of both Europe and Europeanness is discontinuous and contradictory, and there is no direct line from Aristotle to Maastricht, nor a collective European memory in a strict sense; on the other hand, that there is an ongoing Europeanization of commemoration, in the context of an institutionalization of public memory which is very partial, because it largely ignores dimensions of

[44] Krishan Kumar, 'The Question of European Identity. Europe in the American Mirror', *European Journal of Social Theory* 11:1 (2008), 87–105.

memory such as those connected with protest and popular movements. The danger of losing the tension between these two positions is serious. When Europe is defined as a shared cultural heritage continuously connecting the past and the present, through classical learning, Christianity, and the Enlightenment, it is easy to exclude the Judaic and Islamic worlds from this cultural community.[45] Ascribing a common destiny to a cultural, religious, and spiritual heritage amounts to projecting the image of a golden age of Europe onto the past, much along the lines followed by Novalis in his nostalgic evocation of an undivided Europe before the Reformation in *Die Christenheit oder Europa* (1799). At the same time, the Europeanization of memory also presents grave risks. The Shoah cannot be seen only in a European perspective, it must be framed within a global one, in which persecutions and genocides perpetrated by the Europeans in their own continent find many antecedents in colonialism and imperialism. A critical outlook is necessary towards the European past, aiming at the full recognition of the role of Europe's Others.

The variegated picture of the debate on European identity can suggest very different attitudes towards the future. Various authors suggest an optimistic view on the basis of recent developments. Michael Bruter, after a survey conducted in the UK, France, and the Netherlands, has found that a mass European identity has progressively emerged in the period 1970–2000, a political identity based on a civic conception regarding rights, duties, and symbolic civic attributes, and to a lesser extent on a cultural conception based on a shared heritage. Thomas Risse goes in the same direction, arguing that the sense of attachment to the EU among European citizens, elites, and ordinary people alike, is continuously increasing, leading to an emerging European demos as the democratic underpinning of the European polity.[46] At the opposite extreme we find the pessimistic view of Talal Asad, who sees the risk of Europe not being able to allow for multiple ways of life to flourish and therefore being 'fated to be no more than the common market of an imperial civilization, always anxious about (Muslim) exiles within its gates and (Muslim) barbarians beyond.'[47] There also exist many intermediate positions, like that held by David Green, who on the basis of his own survey data found that, in the same period considered by Bruter, 1970–2000, a European identity clearly exists and it is just as clearly a minority sentiment.[48]

Of course the destiny of European identity is largely linked with the destiny of the Union. On this topic, the gap between different judgements is even more pronounced, from the hopeful and universalising considerations of the 'European dream' to the various forms of Euroscepticism. It has been argued that, in a situation of faltering democracy and

[45] Talal Asad, 'Muslims and European Identity: Can Europe Represent Islam?', in Anthony Pagden (ed.), *The Idea of Europe: From Antiquity to the European Union* (Cambridge: Cambridge University Press, 2002), 209–27.

[46] Michael Bruter, *Citizens of Europe? The Emergence of a Mass European Identity* (New York: Palgrave Macmillan, 2005); Thomas Risse, 'European Institutions and Identity Change: What Have We Learned?', in Richard K. Herrmann, Thomas Risse and Marilynn B. Brewer (eds), *Transnational Identities. Becoming European in the EU* (Lanham, MD: Rowman & Littlefield, 2004), 247–71.

[47] Asad, 'Muslims and European Identity', 227.

[48] David Michael Green, *The European: Political Identity in an Emerging Polity* (Boulder, CO: Lynne Rienner, 2007).

accountability such as that of the EU, Europeanness should not be founded on an emotional attachment to it, but rather on the commitment to the rights and duties of a civic society which combines many demoi based on a hierarchy of identities (local, regional, and national).[49] At the same time, the need to go beyond market and currency unification has been stressed, as well as the need to give the Union a political and cultural character (on which a political identity can be based) of a 'soft, articulated' or postmodern type.[50] Meanwhile, new sources of identification for a wide public can be created at the level of the Union, if the ambition of the EU to be the leader on global changes in climate change can be put into practice with consistent efficacy. The recent efforts of the EU to be at the forefront of worldwide strategies to confront the threats of climate change hint towards just such a potential identity for the Union. But this future identity of planetary stewardship is contingent on technological and political expediency which to date is still quite uncertain.[51]

The final result will depend on whether it will be possible, at least for a consistent number of Europeans, to reformulate a sense of belonging to Europe in the light of the global developments. For this purpose it is useful to revisit in a new light some well known positions, first of all that of Jacques Derrida on the theme of European identity. 'Europe has always recognised itself as a cape of headland', in the sense that the first heading was Europe itself, a 'small sticking-out peninsula which wants to represent at all costs "men's progress" with respect to Asia' (Nietzsche). Moving to the other heading means renouncing the claim of being the vanguard of progress and centre of knowledge, and to accept finding one's position on the other side. 'I am not, nor do I feel, European in every part, that is, European through and through'; 'my cultural identity—that in the name of which I speak—is not only European, it is not identical to itself'; 'I feel European among other things', which means being among the others taking on roles that have traditionally been assigned to those who represented for many years the Other, such as Jews, women, and immigrants, and therefore taking sides with those who today are cast in the role of representing the Other. But Derrida's position should not be interpreted simply in terms of multiple identity, rather in terms of keeping the tensions between the criticism of a Eurocentric past and the openness to new forms of belonging.[52]

---

[49] Jeremy Rifkin, *The European Dream: How Europe's Vision of the Future Is Quietly Eclipsing the American Dream* (New York: Tarcher/Penguin, 2004); Dieter Fuchs, Raul Magni-Berton and Antoine Roger (eds), *Euroscepticism: Images of Europe among Mass Publics and Political Elites* (Opladen-Farmington Hills, MI: Barbara Budrichs, 2009); J.H.H. Weiler, *The Constitution of Europe: 'Do the New Clothes Have an Emperor?' and Other Essays on European Integration* (Cambridge: Cambridge University Press, 1999).

[50] Cerutti and Rudolph, *A Soul for Europe*, vol. 1, 27.

[51] David Buchan, *Energy and Climate Change: Europe at the Crossroads* (Oxford: Oxford University Press, 2009) and Andrew Holland, 'Learning from Europe on Climate Change', *Survival* 51:6 (2009–2010), 211–20; Denny Ellerman, 'The EU Emission Trading Scheme: A Proto-Type Global System?', in Joseph E. Aldy and Robert N. Stavins (eds), *Post-Kyoto International Climate Policy: Implementing Architectures for Agreement* (New York: Cambridge University Press, 2010).

[52] Jacques Derrida, *The Other Heading: Reflections on Today's Europe* (Bloomington: Indiana University Press, 1992), 20, 82–3. For a rereading of Derrida in this sense, see Michael Lister and Emily Pia, *Citizenship in Contemporary Europe* (Edinburgh: Edinburgh University Press, 2008).

Framing this perception in terms of the feminist tradition, Rosi Braidotti has written that the European identity has always been 'a notion fraught with contradictions' and has 'never been One', so that 'its alleged unity was at best a poor fiction'. At the roots of her own feeling of 'Europeanness' is therefore 'not the triumphant assumption of a sovereign identity but rather the disenchanting experience of dis-identifying myself with sovereignty all together': the Europe to which she feels she belongs is the place of possible forms of resistance to the systematic devaluation of the Other and to the destructive conflicts to which this leads. To be European today means positioning oneself within the historical contradictions of European identity and experiencing 'the political need to turn them into spaces of critical resistance to hegemonic identities of all kind.'[53] This remark can still be valid today, if the challenge it proposes is updated to the present situation of Europe in global and post-colonial perspective, as required by future-oriented forms of identity for the twenty-first century.

FURTHER READING

Balibar, Etienne, *We, the People of Europe? Reflections on Transnational Citizenship* (Princeton, NJ: Princeton University Press, 2004).

Berezin, Mabel and Martin Schain (eds), *Europe Without Borders: Remapping Territory, Citizenship, and Identity in a Transnational Age* (Baltimore, MD: Johns Hopkins University Press, 2003).

Delanty, Gerard and Chris Rumford, *Rethinking Europe: Social Theory and the Implications of Europeanization* (London: Routledge, 2005).

Derrida, Jacques, *The Other Heading: Reflections on Today's Europe* (Bloomington, IN: Indiana University Press, 1992).

Eder, Klaus and Willfried Spohn (eds), *Collective Memory and European Identity: The Effects of Integration and Enlargement* (Aldershot: Ashgate, 2005).

Hansen, Peo, 'European Integration, European Identity and the Colonial Connection', *European Journal of Social Theory* 5:4 (2002), 483–98.

Karolewski, Ireneusz Pawel and Viktoria Kaina (eds), *European Identity: Theoretical Perspectives and Empirical Insights* (Berlin: Lit Verlag, 2006).

Kastoryano, Riva (ed.), *An Identity for Europe: The Relevance of Multiculturalism in the EU Construction* (New York, NY: Palgrave Macmillan, 2009).

Kumar, Krishan, 'The Question of European Identity: Europe in the American Mirror', *European Journal of Social Theory* 11:1 (2008), 87–105.

Leveau, Rémy, Khadija Mohsen-Finan and Catherine Wihtol De Wenden (eds), *New European Identity and Citizenship* (Aldershot: Ashgate, 2002).

Pagden, Anthony (ed.), *The Idea of Europe From Antiquity to the European Union* (Cambridge: Cambridge University Press, 2002).

Stråth, Bo (ed.), *Europe and the Other and Europe as the Other* (Brussels: Presses Interuniversitaires Européennes/Peter Lang, 2000).

---

[53] Rosi Braidotti, *Nomadic Subjects: Embodiment and Sexual Difference in Contemporary Feminist Theory* (New York: Columbia University Press, 1984), 8–10.

PART II

PEOPLE

CHAPTER 6

··

ETHNIC CLEANSING

··

PHILIPP THER

When the war in former Yugoslavia erupted, the western media adopted the term 'ethnic cleansing' (in Serbian *'etničko čišćenje'*) as novel in their presentation of the atrocities committed there between 1991 and 1995. On track of the media, social scientists and historians also picked up the term. There has been a large array of publications about ethnic cleansing, ranging from introductory articles to profound monographs.[1] The geographical area, time periods and cases covered grew rapidly. Initially, most books about ethnic cleansing focused on former Yugoslavia, on the (former) Soviet Union, or Nazi Germany, and on the creation of the postwar order in Central and Eastern Europe.[2] There is also an increasing number of publications on non-European cases such as India, Palestine, or the Americas.[3] More recently, ethnic cleansing has been brought home to the West, where the idea of ethnic purity and population policy originated.[4]

[1] One of the first academic publications that used the term was Andrew Bell-Fialkoff's 'A Brief History of Ethnic Cleansing', *Foreign Affairs* 72:3 (1993), 110–21. Among the monographs are Norman M. Naimark, *Fires of Hatred: Ethnic Cleansing in Twentieth-Century Europe* (Cambridge, MA: Harvard University Press, 2001); Benjamin Lieberman, *Terrible Fate: Ethnic Cleansing in the Making of Modern Europe* (Chicago, IL: Ivan R. Dee, 2006); Stéphane Rosière, *Le nettoyage ethnique, terreur et peuplement* (Paris: Ellipses, 2006); This chapter is based upon Philip Ther, *Die dunkle Seite der Nationalstaaten. Ethnische Säuberungen im modenen Europa* (Göttingen: Vanndenhoek und Ruprecht, 2011).

[2] See for example Terry Martin, 'The Origins of Soviet Ethnic Cleansing', *Journal of Modern History* 70:4 (1998), 813–61; J. Otto Pohl, *Ethnic Cleansing in the USSR, 1937–1949* (Westport, CT: Greenwood Press, 1999). With respect to Nazi Germany, the focus was always on genocide, but books published in the 1990s showed the connections between Nazi resettlements, ethnic cleansing and the Holocaust. Götz Aly, *'Endlösung'. Völkerverschiebung und der Mord an den europäischen Juden* (Frankfurt/M: S. Fischer, 1995), and also the comparative chapter in Timothy Snyder, *Bloodlands: Europe between Hitler and Stalin* (New York: Basic Books, 2010), 313–38.

[3] On India, see especially Ian Talbot, 'The 1947 Partition of India and Migration: A Comparative Study of Punjab and Bengal', in Richard Bessel and Claudia B. Haake (eds), *Removing Peoples: Forced Removal in the Modern World* (Oxford: Oxford University Press, 2009). On Palestine and Israel, see especially the work by Benny Morris, *The Birth of the Palestinian Refugee Problem, 1947–1949* (New York: Cambridge University Press, 1987).

[4] See Eric D. Weitz, 'From the Vienna to the Paris System: International Politics and the Entangled Histories of Human Rights, Forced Deportations and Civilizing Missions', *American Historical Review* 113:5 (2008), 1313–43.

The fashionable status of the term ethnic cleansing in the media and academia has had the advantage that empirical knowledge has vastly increased. But there is the draw-back that sometimes the term has been overextended to cover any kind of inter-communal violence and time spans, when neither an ethnically exclusive definition of the nation nor modern administrations to carry out mass scale population movements existed.[5] Both preconditions of ethnic cleansing came into being only in the late nine-teenth century. This does not mean one should ignore earlier periods. In certain parts of the world, there were already earlier incidents of compulsory mass migration that spe-cifically targeted certain ethnic or religious groups; but they were driven by different motivations and categories.

The danger of overstretching the term can be avoided if a fairly narrow definition is provided. Ethnic cleansing is always directed at a particular group that is defined through its nationality and/or ethnicity. The goal of ethnic cleansing is to permanently remove a group from the area it inhabits. The power of deciding who is a part of this group rests upon the state or the institution that carries out the process of ethnic cleans-ing. Groups or individuals have no opportunity to declare a different ethnicity or to pre-vent their removal. Ethnic cleansing is always organized and therefore requires the existence of a modern administration which is usually operating in the framework of a state. There is a popular dimension to ethnic cleansing, because there are people needed to threaten with violence, to evict homes, organize mass transports, and to prevent the return of the unwanted. Nevertheless, ethnic cleansing is a modern, rationally planned administrative practice that needs to be steered from above. In this way, it can be distin-guished from inter-communal violence. A third defining element beyond the motiva-tion and the process is a spatial dimension. Ethnic cleansing always covers large areas and often large distances. The removal of a group is connected with a precise idea of the territory to where it can be sent, usually imagined as an external or 'true' national homeland.

This spatial dimension is also a first way to distinguish ethnic cleansing from geno-cide, which often happened on the spot if there was no territory where the enemy group could be brought to. Another way of distinguishing between ethnic cleansing and geno-cide is the primary intent. The main goal of ethnic cleansing was the removal of a group from a certain territory; the main intent of genocide the destruction and ultimate extinc-tion of a nation. The late Jan Havránek indicated the different outcomes by comparing the fate of the Czech Jews and the Bohemian Germans: the ethnic cleansing of the German minority mainly ended in 1945, after crossing the Bavarian or Saxonian border in poverty. The Jews were led through Theresienstadt to the gas chambers of Auschwitz.[6]

---

[5] See as an example for overstretching and unclear boundaries with other concepts: Daniele Conversi, 'Genocide, Ethnic Cleansing and Nationalism', in Gerard Delanty and Krishan Kumar (eds), *The Sage Handbook of Nations and Nationalism* (London: Sage, 2006), 320–33.

[6] Jan Havránek, 'Das tragische Jahrzehnt in Mitteleuropa', in Richard G. Plaschka, Horst Haselsteiner, Arnold Suppan and Anna M. Drabek (eds), *Nationale Frage und Vertreibung in der Tschechoslowakei und Ungarn 1938–1948: aktuelle Forschungen* (Vienna: ÖAW, 1997), xiii–xvii, here xvii.

Recent publications on genocide and the 1948 UN convention on genocide, if inter-preted from today's perspective, blur this distinction.[7] That results in a normative prob-lem. If the current trend of enlarging the scope of the term genocide continues, almost every modern war and many cases of inter-communal violence have to be acknow-ledged as having genocidal dimensions. But acknowledgement is a normative goal, not a scientific one, and it will ultimately result in the conflation of the Holocaust. Also for analytical purposes, it is better to distinguish between crimes and horrors. Genocide and ethnic cleansing, even if escalated into mass killing, resulted in a different kind of victimization as well as numbers and proportions of casualties.

Another important component of ethnic cleansing is the attempt to replace the cleansed population with new settlers and thus to homogenize the population until it reaches the aspired ethnic purity. Taking into account the other side of homogenizing practices also allows us to look beyond the immediate removal of people which is often taken as the end point in studies of ethnic cleansing. Furthermore, one can distinguish variants of ethnic cleansing. If it is carried out over existing or newly erected state bor-ders, it can often be termed 'expulsion', whereas if it is carried out within state borders, it is 'deportation'. Most cases of ethnic cleansing were based on international agreements, but there was also ethnic cleansing during wars, or in order to reach a fait accompli in view of expected contractual solutions. Summing up, one can define ethnic cleansing as a mass scale, violent, and permanent removal of an ethnically defined group from one territory to a perceived external homeland. Deportations within a state—as in the Soviet cases—were special in this regard because there was no vision of an external territory to which the cleansed population would be sent. Another similarity between deportation and genocide lies in the fact that the victim rates among deportees increased to almost 25 per cent (in the worst case, that of the Chechens), whereas even the most violent cases of trans-border ethnic cleansing resulted in a maximum loss of 10 per cent of the affected civilians, and was well below that margin in most cases. It still needs to be explored why some states treated deported minority groups worse than other states treated their sup-posed external enemies.

ORIGINS AND PRECONDITIONS
OF ETHNIC CLEANSING

Although ethnic cleansing became a catchword in the 1990s, one should not overlook the fact that its main component has a much longer history than the twentieth century. Leaving aside religious imaginations of purity, one can find the term 'cleansing' in all

---

[7] See Martin Shaw, *What is Genocide?* (Cambridge: Polity Press, 2007). For the discussion of genocide here I would like to thank Dirk Moses for his comments and insight.

major European languages and various historical sources from the early nineteenth century. The attribute 'ethnic' was absent, because that is a much more recent creation, but the spread of nationalism made it clear who and what needed to be cleansed. Hence, modern nationalism can be seen as a major precondition and obvious motive of ethnic cleansing.[8] The older and normatively grounded distinction between civic, or subjective, political, western, and hence basically 'good' nationalism, and ethnic, cultural, eastern, and therefore 'bad' nationalism, is not helpful for the discussion. A major step towards ethnic cleansing was the Darwinist turn in the late nineteenth century. According to the biologist concept of the nation, minorities were perceived as harmful to the organism or body of the nation.

A second precondition of ethnic cleansing was the concept of the modern nation state. Already in the Enlightenment one sees the conviction that a centralized, monolinguistic state would function better than the traditional empires. Second, the idea of popular sovereignty implied a different, much closer relationship between the state and the people it rules. There were no intermediary institutions as in feudal regimes, but direct accountability. If the people can hold their acclaimed or elected leaders to account, these leaders can ask for a different kind of loyalty. In the nineteenth century the idea of the nation state was connected with the expectation that the problem of ethnic diversity would solve itself through assimilation, with all subjects of a state eventually becoming French, German, Italian, etc. The first concrete proposals of ethnic cleansing came up when the liberal (and later Marxist) expectation of assimilation was proven wrong.

By and large, one can apply the rule that the later the nation-state formation occurred, the more contested and violent it was. Especially after World War I, the French centralized nation state was seen as the model of how to run a state. This brought the state almost automatically into conflict with minorities living in its territory. The very term 'minority problems', which can be found in numerous international discussions and conferences about the post-World War I order, already signifies who was seen as the culprit for Europe's major problems. Although additional conventions in the Paris peace treaties promised the protection of minorities in Central and Eastern Europe, the only minority right which was effectively put into practice was the 'right of option' to migrate to the external nation state in case of border changes, such as after the treaties of St Germain, Neuilly (1919), and Trianon (1920).[9] Moreover, in the treaties of Neuilly and Sèvres (1920) paragraphs concerning protection of minorities were already combined with provisions for their 'emigration'. On paper, the relocation was supposed to be voluntary, but the treaty of Neuilly was made compulsory when minorities resisted. Hence, over the course of time, the League of Nations gave emigration priority over protection in order to homogenize the newly created nation states. Often this has been explained by

---

[8] See Eric J. Hobsbawm, *Nations and Nationalism since 1780: Program, Myth, Reality*, 2nd edn (Cambridge: Cambridge University Press, 1992), 133.

[9] Eric Weitz's provocative thesis needs some addition to detail, but in principal he is right about the double face of the Paris peace treaties concerning the policy concerning national minorities.

a supposedly ethnic and violent character of nationalism in Central and Eastern Europe. But during 1918–19, the established Western European nation states avoided the acknowledgment of minorities altogether. These double standards contributed to the desire of the newly created 'minority states' to become 'real', i.e. homogenous nation states.[10]

A third pivotal factor was the development of *population policy*. Already in the late nineteenth century, European states (the German Empire being the first one) began to manipulate the demographic structures of contested border regions. At this time, and in the later policy of various nation states in the interwar period, the main means of homogenization was the settlement of additional groups. When borders changed, these groups were the first to be targeted as unwanted and forced to emigrate. The ethnic engineering depended upon precise statistics, population counts, and a clear-cut distinction between titular nation and minorities. Since the 1870s these statistics have been created all over Europe and brought to perfection even in countries which were commonly perceived as backward. As various population statistics show, every single soul and even newborn children were counted according to their nationality. Around the turn of the century, the British especially insisted on 'ethnological arguments' for drawing nation-state boundaries in post-imperial spaces such as South-Eastern Europe. In this way, national belonging was objectivized, and groups could be singled out for various measures. All of these factors can be summarized under the term of 'European modernity'.[11] The attribute 'European' is important, for it was in this continent where the first and so far most ethnic cleansing occurred.

PERIODS OF ETHNIC CLEANSING

In the history of ethnic cleansing in the twentieth century one can distinguish four major periods. The first one lasted from the Balkan Wars of 1912–13 until the aftermath of the Treaty of Lausanne in the mid–1920s. Compared to later ethnic cleansing the number of removed people was limited. But this period resulted in an international consensus, that ethnic cleansing is a means to stabilize the international order and single nation states. The second period began with the Treaty of Munich in 1938 and was continued under German hegemony over continental Europe until 1944. There were two kinds of ethnic cleansing; one under direct German occupation, the other carried out by the countries allied with Germany. The third period of ethnic cleansing resulted from the postwar order of Europe decided

---

[10] On treaties and resistance to them, see Carole Fink, *Defending the Rights of Others: The Great Powers, the Jews and International Minority Protection, 1878–1938* (New York: Cambridge University Press, 2004), 236–64.

[11] This thought is a continuation of Zygmunt Bauman, *Modernity and the Holocaust* (Cambridge: Polity Press, 1991). See also Amir Weiner(ed.), *Landscaping the Human Garden: Twentieth-Century Population Management in a Comparative Framework* (Stanford, CA: Stanford University Press, 2003).

at the Conference of Tehran and thereafter. This period, which brought by far the most numerous ethnic cleansing, also affected large areas beyond Europe, especially the Indian subcontinent and Palestine. The fourth period occurred in the first half of the 1990s, but it affected only the former Yugoslavia and some contested border regions in the former Soviet Union. In terms of numbers and area, the fourth period is of minor relevance compared to earlier ones. But it is important because it helped to create an international consensus against ethnic cleansing and even attempts to reverse previous flight and expulsion.

More recent books, such as Benjamin Lieberman's overview of ethnic cleansing, reach far back into the nineteenth century. Although it is true that hundreds of thousands of people were already expelled during the various wars against the Ottoman Empire in the Caucasus and in the Balkan peninsula, several aspects of modern ethnic cleansing were missing. The persecution of Muslims mostly occurred during wartime, when people could still attempt to escape to the woods and then return to their homes. For a long time, the newly created nation states in South-eastern Europe were too disorganized to carry out a consistent population policy through settling and unsettling. Moreover, the various postwar migrations of Muslims were driven not only by push, but also by pull factors, such as the Sultan's call to his Muslim subjects to come to the country where they could freely practise their religion.[12] The prominence of religion is a specific aspect of all the 'wars against the Turks', which brings them into the context of the *Reconquista* on the Spanish peninsula, or Habsburg policy in the areas reconquered from the Ottoman Empire in Hungary in the eighteenth century. Europe clearly has a tradition of persecuting Muslims. Nevertheless, one should not overlook the continuity of what happened in the Caucasus during 1860–64, in the Balkans 1876–78 and then again during and after the Balkan Wars of 1912–13. The violence, massacres, and expulsions were driven by an inconsistent mixture of fear of and contempt for 'the Turks', which had colonialist undertones.[13] In this way, the persecution of Muslims was decidedly modern and secular.

THE FIRST PERIOD OF ETHNIC CLEANSING (1912–25)

The Balkan Wars brought three major changes. Henceforth, ethnic distinctions clearly prevailed over the Christian–Muslim divide. The conflicts between ethnically defined Christian nations were as violent as the persecution of Turks. The ethnic cleansing was

---

[12] See Alexandre Toumarkine, *Les migrations des populations musulmanes balkaniques en Anatolie 1876–1913* (Istanbul: Isis, 1995). This book does not have the missionary zeal of proving the victim status of Muslims and is therefore superior to the English language publications by Justin McCarthy that are usually quoted regarding the persecution and expulsion of Turks.

[13] For the issue of colonialism and genocide see the edited volume by A. Dirk Moses (ed.), *Empire, Colony, Genocide: Conquest, Occupation, and Subaltern Resistance in World History* (New York: Berghahn, 2008).

more pervasive in total numbers and in regard to the proportion of minorities that were allowed to remain in their homes. The uprooting of unwanted minorities was combined with the resettlement of members of the titular nation. Especially near external borders, nation states carried out a population policy to demographically secure these areas. Hence, one could argue that the Balkan Wars marked the beginning of organized ethnic cleansing. Overall, up to 900,000 people had to leave their homelands permanently as a consequence of these two wars.[14] In 1914, Greece and the Ottoman Empire took up negotiations regarding a voluntary 'exchange of populations' across the Aegean Sea, which can already be seen as a precursor of the Lausanne treaty.[15]

The outbreak of World War I led to a preliminary decrease in forced migration between the Balkan peninsula and Asia Minor, because the borders were now closed and all the countries involved had other military and strategic priorities. But ethnic cleansing continued in other areas of Europe and on a larger scale. The Russian Empire deported one million Germans and Jews who lived near the front or along supply routes. Although these deportations were supposed to be only temporary and thus do not qualify as ethnic cleansing, they show how attitudes towards minorities had deteriorated. Although the Russian Jews and Germans did not pose any territorial threat, they were seen as potential traitors.[16] Similar attitudes and fears of further territorial dismemberment motivated the genocide of the Armenians in Ottoman Eastern Anatolia. In contrast to cases of ethnic cleansing, the Armenians were not expelled to their external homeland, but deported into the Syrian desert or semi-desert in the Anatolian highlands. This deportation into the void resulted in at least a million casualties and is commonly considered as the first genocide in twentieth century Europe. The Russian Revolution, the pogroms in the former Pale of Settlement, and the continued fighting in a broad zone from Lithuania in the north to Thrace in the south of Eastern Europe motivated millions of people to leave their homelands. Although this mass migration was not a planned ethnic cleansing, it further demonstrated how endangered were these minorities.

The persecution of Jews especially contributed to the establishment of collective minority rights in the Paris Peace treaties.[17] But these rights were only valid for the newly created or expanded nation states in Central and Eastern Europe. France especially carried out a very different policy in its newly acquired territories. In formerly German Alsace and Lorraine, the population was divided into four different categories, ranging

---

[14] This calculation is based upon Katrin Boeckh, *Von den Balkankriegen zum Ersten Weltkrieg. Kleinstaatenpolitik und ethnische Selbstbestimmung auf dem Balkan* (Munich: R. Oldenbourg, 1996), 257, 261; Elisabeth Kontogiorgi, 'Forced Migration, Repatriation, Exodus. The Case of Ganos-Chora and Myriophyto-Peristasis Orthodox Communities in Eastern Thrace', *Balkan Studies* 35 (1994), 15–45, here 21.

[15] On these negotiations, see Yannis G. Mourelos, 'The 1914 Persecutions and the First Attempt at an Exchange of Minorities between Greece and Turkey', *Balkan Studies* 26 (1985), 389–413, here 389, 391.

[16] Eric Lohr, *Nationalizing the Russian Empire: The Campaign against Enemy Aliens during World War I* (Cambridge, MA: Harvard University Press, 2003).

[17] See Fink, *Defending the Rights of Others*, 193–208.

from trustworthy French to Germans. Around 150,000 of the half million people belonging to category 'D' (which basically meant Germans) were pushed over the Rhine. Although this signifies that only a third of those presumed to be Germans were expelled, the French 'épuration' in Alsace set negative standards for the interwar period.[18]

Under the guidance of the western powers, another precedent was set at the Paris peace conference. In 1919, Bulgaria was forced to sign a peace treaty that included a convention about the 'reciprocal emigration' of the Greek minority in Bulgaria and the Bulgarian minority in Greece. Paradoxically, this provision was a part of the stipulation about minority protection.[19] The Treaty of Sèvres set up a similar provision for Greeks and Turks living on both sides of the future border in Asia Minor. Initially the convention of Neuilly did not result in mass migration because registration for emigration was on a voluntary basis. But the scenario changed with the arrival of refugees from Asia Minor. The Greek government purposely settled many refugees in the contested Greek borderlands with Bulgaria. This upset the local social and ethnic balance and added pressure for the so-called *Slavophonoi* to emigrate. When a commission of the League of Nations was called in to analyse the causes of the widespread local violence in 1925, it recommended that emigration should have priority over minority protection.[20] Subsequently 102,000 Bulgarians or around half of the Slavic speaking minority left Greece, and 53,000 Greeks left Bulgaria.

By then, the Treaty of Lausanne had set an even more ominous precedent. Under the auspices of the international community of states, Greece and Turkey agreed upon the compulsory exchange of minorities. All Muslims had to leave Greece, all Christians had to leave Turkey, with Western Thrace and Istanbul the only exceptions. Although Turkey is often blamed for this first case of ethnic cleansing, which covered almost the entire territory of two countries, it was Lord Curzon who set it on the agenda of the negotiations in Lausanne.[21] Moreover, Lausanne should be seen as a continuation of the Treaty of Sèvres, which also proposed mass migration over the future border. The main difference was the compulsory character and the fact that Greece (and indirectly its main patron state, Britain) had lost the war with Turkey. The borderline now ran along the shores of Asia Minor and not in its hinterland. The Treaty of Lausanne uprooted around 1.6 million people, and like the Treaty of Neuilly, it was not reciprocal or symmetrical.

---

[18] See Christiane Kohser-Spohn, 'Die Vertreibung der "Altdeutschen" aus dem Elsass 1918–1920', in Jerzy Kochanowski and Maike Sach (eds), *Die 'Volksdeutschen' in Polen, Frankreich, Ungarn und der Tschechoslowakei. Mythos und Realität* (Osnabrück: Fibre, 2006), 79–94.

[19] See the respective paragraphs of the treaty in H.W.V. Temperley (ed.), *A History of the Peace Conference of Paris, Vol. V. Economic Reconstruction and Protection of Minorities* (London: Oxford University Press, 1969), 317.

[20] On this commission, see Stelios Nestor, 'Greek Macedonia and the Convention of Neuilly', *Balkan Studies* 3 (1962), 169–84, here 181. On the entire situation, see the recent and very thorough study by Elisabeth Kontogiorgi, *Population Exchanges in Greek Macedonia: The Forced Resettlement of Refugees, 1922–1930* (New York: Oxford University Press, 2006).

[21] See *Lausanne Conference on Near Eastern Affairs 1922–23. Records of Proceedings and Draft Terms of Peace* (London: His Majesty's Stationery Office, 1923), 118.

Around three times as many Greeks left Asia Minor than Turks (officially Muslims) left Greece. Euphemistic terms such as 'exchange of populations' still helped to maintain a facade of a just, legal, and technical solution. As a result, Lausanne became an example that was quoted again and again in later periods of ethnic cleansing.[22]

It is often claimed that no such radical solutions were enacted in Central Europe. But in fact the 1924 Geneva Convention between Germany and Poland dealing with Upper Silesia also gave priority to migration over the protection of minorities. Around half of the minorities on both sides of the new border in partitioned Silesia used the 'right of option' to emigrate to their external nation state. In contrast to that, the creation of minority schools, language rights, and other stipulations that might have motivated the minorities to stay were put into practice only hesitantly or not at all. Only in the second half of the 1920s did migration recede and the new order of nation states was stabilized. By then, the Treaty of Lausanne had contributed to creating an international consensus that mass and compulsory population transfers were a last resort but a useful means of stabilizing the international order and single nation states.

Ethnic Cleansing under the Hegemony of Nazi Germany (1938–44)

The second period of ethnic cleansing began with the Munich Treaty in 1938. This treaty symbolizes the appeasement of Nazi Germany, which was allowed to annex the borderlands of Czechoslovakia. But the significance and consequences of the Munich Treaty go far beyond the case of the Sudeten Germans and the normative issue of appeasement. The four major European powers basically decided upon a new peace order for Europe. In future, states and societies should be separated by ethnic boundaries. Minorities had the choice to emigrate or to assimilate. Minority protection as a central element of the Paris peace treaties was abandoned, and only the 'right of option' was preserved. The groundbreaking character of the Munich Treaty is also shown by the fact that the four signatory powers stipulated additionally that Czechoslovakia and Hungary should agree upon a new border within three months. This new European order led to a first round of compulsory mass migrations, at first of around 190,000 Czechs, in 1939 of other additional nationalities.[23]

Adolf Hitler's ideas of 'European security' for the Central and South-eastern parts of the continent were based on similar premises: the creation of ethnic boundaries based on 'exchange of populations' or one-sided population transfers, which is what he

---

[22] Naimark, *Fires of Hatred*, 108–10.

[23] Jan Gebhart, 'Migrationsbewegungen der tschechischen Bevölkerung in den Jahren 1938–39, Forschungsstand und offene Fragen', in Detlef Brandes et al. (eds), *Erzwungene Trennung. Vertreibungen und Aussiedlungen in und aus der Tschechoslowakei 1938–1947 im Vergleich mit Polen, Ungarn und Jugoslawien* (Essen: Klartext, 1999), 11–22.

proposed in his Reichstag speech in October 1939.[24] While this speech has often been cited for its racist components, contempt for Poland, and its *Lebensraum* ideology, most of it was based on consensus reached in the Munich Treaty one year earlier.

Between 1938 and 1941 the German Empire reorganized Europe in two ways. In the areas it controlled directly as occupying power, it tried to vastly expand the German *Lebensraum* by expelling Poles, Slovenes, and other Slavic nations. There was also ethnic cleansing in the territories retrieved from France in the West. Jews in the occupied areas suffered other and even worse fates: mass shootings, deportation, and eventually industrialized killing in death camps. But the history of the Holocaust is left aside here in view of the specific attention it deserves. As Hitler announced in the aforementioned Reichstag speech, he had a vast scheme of population removals in mind in occupied Poland. In the much larger areas which were ruled by countries allied with Germany (that is Hungary, Croatia, Slovakia, Romania, and Bulgaria), Hitler's ideas of European security were put into practice by bilateral contracts for population exchanges or one-sided population transfers. Those countries had to organize their own ethnic cleansing.

Hitler's primary arena for ethnic cleansing carried out by Germans was the territory annexed from Poland. The initial idea was to eject the Polish population and to replace them with German 'resettlers'. This also was a major motivation for the various treaties with Italy, the Baltic States, the Soviet Union, and Romania about the resettlement of German minorities. When Hitler announced the first '*Heim ins Reich*' (home to the empire) plans in the summer of 1939, he still wanted to appear as a peace-loving statesman, who created a new European order through ethnic boundaries. As it turned out, the various German resettlers, who numbered around half a million,[25] were mostly transported to the 'Warthegau', the main area annexed from Poland in 1939. Shortly before and immediately upon arrival Poles were driven over the border to free apartments and farms for the German resettlers. All in all, around 365,000 Polish citizens were expelled from their homelands between the autumn of 1939 and spring 1941.[26]

Compared with the original plans of the Nazis, the numbers of people actually removed were small. The situation was similar in northern Slovenia, where according to the plans of Reinhard Heydrich, 260,000 Slovenes were supposed to be ejected, but eventually only 30,000 had to leave. The reasons for the limited ethnic cleansing were mostly practical. The Nazi authorities in the main part of occupied Poland, the *Generalgouvernement*, did not know what to do with the arriving expellees from the Warthegau and West Prussia. Since they could not provide shelter, food, and jobs, the occupation administration repeatedly protested against further mass migration. The

---

[24] The speech can be found at: http://www.reichstagsprotokolle.de/Blatt2_n4_bsb00000613_00067. html und -52.html, accessed July 2010.

[25] For statistics and ethnic cleansing during and after World War II, see the excellent collective monograph by Pertti Ahonen et al., *People on the Move: Forced Population Movements in Europe in the Second World War and its Aftermath* (Oxford: Berg, 2008), 19.

[26] On this case of ethnic cleansing, see Maria Rutowska, *Wysiedlenie ludności polskiej z Kraju Warty do Generalnego Gubernatorstwa 1939–1941* (Poznań: Instytut Zachodni, 2003).

second reason was the priority to keep the war economy intact and to prepare for the impending attack on the Soviet Union. The third reason was the priority of the destruction of the European Jewry, which reached another dimension after June 1941. As Götz Aly has shown, the organization of the Holocaust and mass ethnic cleansing of other European nations were sometimes linked in practice, for example in trains that carried Jews to the killing sites in the East, but then were also used to transport Poles and other groups for forced labour in the West.[27]

Although ethnic cleansing under direct Nazi rule remained limited in numbers, it should not be underestimated. In addition to the people pushed over the border of the *Generalgouvernement*, the German authorities deported 475,000 people from the Warthegau for forced labour. According to the various versions of the *Generalplan Ost* (General Plan East), the German government planned to remove up to 45 million people from Eastern Europe, 10 million from the annexed Polish territories alone. Had Germany won the war, some of these plans would have been put into practice and would have certainly resulted in another genocide. Moreover, the expulsion of Poles was accompanied by mass killings. Already during the attack on Poland, around 50,000 civilians were shot; resistance against the subsequent expulsions carried the death penalty.[28] Hence, the ethnic cleansing clearly had a genocidal aspect. This is especially true for later cases, such as in the area around Zamość, where the Nazi authorities deported around 110,000 Poles during 1942–43 in order to create an Aryan strip of settlement that reached from East Prussia to the Carpathians.

Aside from its extreme brutality, the Nazi ethnic cleansing was specific in its selection criteria. Not only the people who were removed but also the resettlers who were supposed to replace them were screened for racial characteristics. This turned out to be an obstacle for the planned Germanization of the annexed Polish territories and ultimately even slowed the ethnic cleansing of Poles.[29] Countries allied with Germany were less picky and, except for the Jews, used primarily national criteria of selection. Comparing the policy of Germany and its allies, one could label the Nazi policy as racial and not ethnic cleansing. Even that may appear as euphemistic in view of the mass killing of Poles. But still a distinction should be made. In the case of the Poles and other Slavic nations, the Nazis mainly targeted the social and political elites, not all classes, genders, and ages, as was the case with the Jews. Nevertheless, it is not easy to draw a line between genocide and ethnic or racial cleansing perpetrated by the Nazis. There was a gradual difference in the level of intent and a difference in the results, especially if one looks at victim rates. Whereas around 90 per cent of Polish Jews did not survive the war, almost 90 per cent

---

[27] For example, the single train transport that carried Jews, German resettlers and Polish expellees to and from the General Gouvernement, in Aly, '*Endlösung*', 260. On Nazi planning for an ethnically and racially clean *Lebensraum*, see also Isabel Heinemann, '*Rasse, Siedlung, deutsches Blut*'. *Das Rasse- und Siedlungshauptamt der SS und die rassenpolitische Neuordnung Europas* (Göttingen: Wallstein, 2003).

[28] See Czesław Madajczyk, *Die Okkupationspolitik Nazideutschlands in Polen 1939–1945* (Cologne: Pahl-Rugenstein, 1988).

[29] See Heinemann, '*Rasse, Siedlung, deutsches Blut*'.

of the non-Jewish Poles did. But even a death rate of more than 10 per cent, or including the Jews more than 20 per cent, is staggering and should not be used to downplay any of the individual and collective suffering of Poland.

The German policy of ethnic cleansing had far-reaching repercussions. Already in 1940, consensus emerged in Poland and Britain that the attempted Germanization of Western Poland would need to be reversed, and that there was no future for a German minority in Poland. The British journal *Fortnightly* wrote in 1940 with reference to the ethnic cleansing in Western Poland: 'Hitler has burned his boats . . . He is daily establishing precedents which cannot be forgotten when the reckoning comes.'[30] The ethnic cleansing also destroyed social connections within local societies. Peaceful coexistence of Germans with Poles in Poznań or other previously mixed cities and rural areas was precluded after the experience of German occupation.

In terms of numbers, the reordering of Europe through ethnic cleansing was much more effective in the areas ruled by the countries allied with Nazi Germany. As already mentioned, the Munich agreement contained a provision about the creation of an ethnic boundary between Slovakia and Hungary. This was put into practice in the First Vienna Accord (or Dictate, depending on the national viewpoint) in November 1938. Italy and Germany (France and Britain had dropped out due to rising tension with Nazi Germany) assigned parts of southern Slovakia to Hungary. More than 100,000 Czechs and Slovaks had to leave from there.[31] Once more, the arrival of refugees disturbed the local balance in the places of arrival. In late 1938 and early 1939, at least 50,000 Czechs were forced to migrate from Slovakia to the Czech lands, which were soon occupied by Nazi Germany.

The first Vienna Accord was followed by the second in the summer of 1940. This time a presumably ethnic boundary was set up in Transylvania, which was contested between Hungary and Romania. Around 370,000 Romanians and Hungarians who lived on the 'wrong' side of the new border had to get out.[32] Formally, the migrants took advantage of the 'right of option'; de facto most were forced to emigrate. In September 1940, Bulgaria and Romania concluded the Treaty of Craiova, which set up a new border in the contested Dobrudja: 61,000 Bulgarians who lived north of the new border and 100,000 Romanians who had resided in southern Dobrudja took part in a compulsory 'exchange of populations'. A similar solution had already been briefly proposed by the British ambassador in Bucharest before the outbreak of World War II.[33]

The ethnic reordering continued when Nazi Germany attacked Yugoslavia in April 1941. Nazi Germany was assisted by revisionist Hungary and Bulgaria. In the recovered

---

[30] Cited from Matthew Frank, *Expelling the Germans: British Opinion and Post-1945 Population Transfer in Context* (Oxford: Oxford University Press, 2008), 42.

[31] See Martin Vietor, *Dejiny okupácie južního Slovenska 1938–1945* (Bratislava: Vydavatelstvo Akadémie Vied, 1968), 42.

[32] Much information about this and other numerically smaller cases of ethnic cleansing is contained in Ralph Melville et al. (eds), *Zwangsmigrationen im mittleren und östlichen Europa. Völkerrecht—Konzeptionen—Praxis (1938–1950)* (Mainz: Zabern, 2008). On the various forced migrations in wartime and postwar Romania, see Dumitru Şandru, *Mişcări de populaţie în România (1940–1948)* (Bucharest: Editura Enciclopedică, 2003).

[33] On this proposal, see Frank, *Expelling the Germans*, 36–7.

Hungarian territories in the Vojvodina, at least 25,000 Serbs were immediately expelled to German occupied Serbia. Bulgaria, another state greatly diminished by the Paris peace treaties followed the Hungarian example. At least 110,000 Serbs were ejected from Vardar-Macedonia; a similar number of Greeks had to leave the Bulgarian zone of occupation in Thrace.[34] Ethnic cleansing by the revisionist countries, and also after June 1941 by Romania in formerly Soviet occupied Bessarabia and Northern Bukovina, had two components: one was retrospective and targeted the elites who had been settled by the interwar nation states that had profited from the Paris peace treaties. Hungary and Bulgaria basically removed everybody who was sent to the borderlands by the Czechoslovak, Yugoslav, Romanian, and Greek governments. The second element was proactive and future oriented. Hungary, Bulgaria, and Romania removed all people who could have guided irredentist national minorities in the future.

Ethnic cleansing in the German sphere of influence was connected with massive violence, mass killings, destitution, and hunger. Paradoxically, the number of affected people would have been many times larger had there not been the priority of attacking the Soviet Union. That is not only true for Nazi Germany, but also for its allies in Central and South-eastern Europe, all of whom had devised plans for an almost total removal of minorities from their territories. Although the cleansing remained limited, it created a permanent climate of fear and terror.

Another zone of violent conflict was the former South-east of Poland, where Ukrainian and Polish underground units had fought each other with great brutality since 1943. As a result, around 400,000 people escaped or were expelled until 1944, when a contractual solution was found under Soviet domination (see below). There was no direct German involvement in this case of ethnic cleansing, but the Holocaust set a negative example of how to deal with unwanted minorities, and Hitler's ideas of an order of homogeneous nation states in particular influenced the Ukrainian nationalist underground.

A special case in the German sphere of domination was the Independent State of Croatia (Nezavisna Država Hrvatska). There the goal to assimilate or remove all Serbs resulted in genocide. In early June of 1941, Nazi Germany and Croatia had agreed upon a chain of ethnic cleansings. Croatia would take in 170,000 Slovenes that were supposed to leave the parts of Slovenia which had been incorporated into the Reich; in turn, Croatia was allowed to remove as many Serbs. But matters had already spiralled out of control by the summer of 1941. The fascist Ustaša, who governed Croatia, were not able to organize the uprooting of the unwanted population and the transport. Consequently, the Croatian state mobilized criminals and the most radical nationalists to drive away the Serbs through maltreatment and symbolic killings.[35] Churches filled with people were set on

---

[34] On these statistics, see Joseph Schechtman, *European Population Transfers 1939–1945* (New York: Oxford University Press, 1946), 407; Björn Opfer, *Im Schatten des Krieges. Besatzung oder Anschluss— Befreiung oder Unterdrückung? Eine komparative Untersuchung über die bulgarische Herrschaft in Vardar-Makedonien 1915–1918 und 1941–1944* (Münster: LIT Verlag, 2005), 264–5.

[35] On ethnic cleansing in Croatia, see Jozo Tomasevich, *War and Revolution in Yugoslavia, 1941–1945. Occupation and Collaboration* (Stanford, CA: Stanford University Press, 2001), 380–416.

fire, people who could not swim were chased into the river Drina into Bosnia. The expel-lees arrived in Serbia plundered, maltreated, and malnourished. Because the German authorities in Serbia could not handle this humanitarian disaster and were afraid of a strengthening of the Serbian resistance, they closed the border. Subsequently the Ustaša turned the transit camps for Serbian settlers into concentration camps.

According to reliable calculations made by Croatian and Serbian historians, a mini-mum of 330,000 Serbs were killed during 1941–44 in the Independent State of Croatia, many of them in death camps.[36] Just to compare: during 1991–95, there were approxi-mately 100,000 victims on *all* sides of the war in Bosnia-Herzegovina.[37] Around the same number of Serbs was expelled to Serbia. These proportions and the mass killings demonstrate that this case of ethnic cleansing escalated into genocide. All in all, Hitler's vision of European security resulted in the ethnic cleansing of at least two million people in the countries allied with Germany.[38]

In creating a new European order, Nazi Germany was initially assisted by the Soviet Union. But in spite of all the recent literature on Soviet ethnic cleansing one should not forget that Stalin's priority rested upon social homogenization and persecution. The deportations of various minority groups between 1936 and 1941 were based either on military considerations (and sometimes security paranoia) or on the destruction of the social elites of the newly acquired western territories. Most affected were the Baltic countries and the former eastern territories of Poland, from which the NKVD deported 330,000 people. However, fewer than two-thirds of the deportees were Poles, which demonstrates again that social selection took priority over national, although in view of Stalin's anti-polonism, one can also see a combination of the two criteria.

After the attack by Nazi Germany, the Soviet Union changed its policy. Now it began with punitive and clearly ethnic deportations, which at first affected the Volga Germans. Soviet ethnic cleansing peaked in 1944 with the deportation of various Caucasian nations and the Crimean Tatars. But these measures were retrospective, based on accu-sations of treason and collaboration during the war. In contrast to the policy of European nation states, deportations were not based on the utopia of ethnic homogeneity of any territory within the Soviet Union. This might also explain why in view of the size and the population of the Soviet Union, and even more so compared to social cleansing, Soviet ethnic cleansing remained limited. Including the deportation of minority groups in the late 1930s, Stalin removed around 2.1 million people on ethnic premises.[39]

---

[36] See Tomasevich, *War and Revolution*, 738.

[37] These statistics were published by the Research and Documentation Center in Sarajevo. See its webpage at http://www.idc.org.ba/, accessed July 2010.

[38] The number is based on the following single national cases: 500,000 Serbs, 540,000 Romanians (however, 220,000 refugees from the territories annexed by the Soviet Union in 1940 could temporarily return), 280,000 Czechs and Slovaks, 120,000 Greeks, 150,000 Hungarians and 60,000 Bulgarians. Special cases are the 200,000 German settlers who came from the prewar territory of Romania, and the Jews from the countries allied with Germany who are dealt with below.

[39] On ethnic deportations, see the comprehensive volume by Pavel Poljan, *Ne na svoie vole. Istoria i geografia prinuditel'nych migracracii v. SSSR* (Moscow: Memorial, 2001).

Although ethnic cleansing in the period between 1938 and 1944 thus does not exceed six million people, it changed the ethnic map of Europe forever. The expulsions and deportations added to the already existing nationalist hatred, caused tremendous suffering, and made almost impossible a return to the status quo before 1938. Another and maybe the most important result of all these 'wars in the war' was that it confirmed the consensus of the Allies that peace in Europe could only be secured if it was based on ethnically homogenous nation states.

Ethnic Cleansing and the Postwar European Order (1944–48)

This consensus was officially expressed by Winston Churchill in his speech on the Future of Poland. In December 1944 he stated in the House of Commons: 'There will be no mixture of populations to cause endless trouble ... A clean sweep will be made.'[40] The British premier pointed to the 'success' of the Treaty of Lausanne and the manageability of large-scale population transfers. As Matthew Frank has shown, this speech and the following decisions taken at the conferences of Yalta and Potsdam were the result of a longer process of discussion. The principal decision, to remove the German minorities from postwar Czechoslovakia and Poland, had already been made in 1942, when the British government declared the Munich agreement of 1938 null and void.[41]

Yet this reversal only encompassed the border changes made then under the pressure of Hitler. The second element of Munich, that minorities should either assimilate or emigrate, remained intact. At the Tehran conference in 1943, the Allies decided to move Poland's borders westwards. The Poles who lived east of the future Polish–Soviet border were supposed to emigrate to postwar Poland, while as compensation the Germans should be ejected from the territories allotted to Poland.[42] In 1944 and 1945, the Allies continued to discuss the precise location of the Polish borders, which would determine the number of Poles and Germans who had to be removed. The result of these diplomatic deliberations, as in earlier cases, was an escalation of the territorial and demographic range of ethnic cleansing. While the plans of 1943 foresaw the transfer of between five and seven million Germans, in 1945 it was clear that at least 12 million should be removed.

---

[40] Winston Churchill, 'The Future of Poland. A Speech to the House of Commons, 15 December 1944', in Charles Eade (ed.), *The Dawn of Liberation: War Speeches by the Right Hon. Winston S. Churchill C.H., M.P.* (London: Cassell, 1945), 290–300, here 296.

[41] For a perspective focused more on the East Central European governments in exile, see Detlef Brandes, *Der Weg zur Vertreibung. Pläne und Entscheidungen zum 'Transfer' der Deutschen aus der Tschechoslowakei und aus Polen*, 2nd edn (Munich: Oldenbourg, 2005).

[42] The interdependence between the ethnic cleansing of Poles and Germans has been overlooked by Norman Naimark in his selection of case studies. For details, see Philipp Ther, *Deutsche und polnische Vertriebene. Gesellschaft und Vertriebenenpolitik in der SBZ/DDR und in Polen 1945–1956* (Göttingen: Vandenhoeck & Ruprecht, 1998).

These huge numbers attracted questions of the British and the US government about the feasibility of such unprecedented population movements.[43] But Stalin claimed that most Germans had already run away from the Red Army and that a very limited number was left in Poland. In addition, the main victor of World War II in Europe created a contractual solution for the Poles who still remained in the vast areas annexed by the Soviet Union. In September 1944 the communist puppet government in Lublin concluded 'evacuation treaties' with the Ukrainian, Belorussian, and Lithuanian Soviet Republics about the reciprocal exchange of minorities. Subsequently, 1.5 million Poles were moved westward, and 480,000 Ukrainians were moved from postwar Poland to the Soviet Union (another 150,000 who resisted were deported within Poland in 1947), whereas the number of affected Belorussians and Lithuanian was rather small.[44] All in all, 2.1 million Poles originating from the eastern territories arrived in postwar Poland—so far the largest single ethnic cleansing. The arrival of the Polish 'repatriates', as they were called in the spring of 1945, was often the starting point for expelling Germans.

Prior to the Potsdam conference, the Red Army, Poland, and Czechoslovakia attempted to create a fait accompli concerning the Germans. Especially near the postwar borders at the rivers Oder and Neisse, Germans were pushed out en masse from April to July of 1945. Simultaneously, the return of those who had fled from the approaching Red Army was prevented. The masses of expellees added to the chaos in the British, American and Soviet zones of occupation, which had already been flooded by war refugees (often both groups are lumped together, which is incorrect in view of motivations and the process of forced migration). The untenable situation motivated the Allies at the Potsdam conference to limit and control the ethnic cleansing. At the same time, they legalized the process by deciding upon the 'transfer' of all Germans who lived in Poland, Czechoslovakia, and Hungary. The stipulation for an 'orderly and humane' transfer never materialized, however. The living conditions of the Germans still residing in Poland and Czechoslovakia and the organization of transport improved only a little and after the British and American occupation authorities concluded agreements with Poland and Czechoslovakia at the beginning of 1946.[45] But even afterwards, many people arrived sick, maltreated, and badly traumatized.

---

[43] Frank, *Expelling the Germans*, 122.

[44] The ethnic cleansing of Poles is documented extensively in Stanisław Ciesielski, *Przesiedlenie ludności polskiej z Kresów Wschodnich do Polski 1944-1947* (Warsaw: Neriton, 1999). For the 'evacuation' of Ukrainians from Poland, see in English Orest Subtelny, 'Expulsion, Resettlement, Civil Strife. The Fate of Poland's Ukrainians, 1944-1947', in Philipp Ther and Ana Siljak (eds), *Redrawing Nations: Ethnic Cleansing in East-Central Europe, 1944-1948* (Lanham, MD: Rowman and Littlefield, 2001).

[45] On the way that ethnic cleansing of Germans was carried out in Poland, see the profound documentation by Włodzimierz Borodziej and Hans Lemberg (eds) '*Unsere Heimat ist uns ein fremdes Land geworden...*' *Die Deutschen östlich von Oder und Neiße 1945-1950. Dokumente aus polnischen Archiven*, 4 vols (Marburg: Herder Institut, 2000-2004) (there is also a Polish version of the documentation). On the ethnic cleansing of Germans from Czechoslovakia, see various works by Tomáš Staněk, among them *Odsun Němců z Československa 1945-1947* (Prague: Academia, 1991).

Stalin has often been accused of having been the mastermind behind these unprecedented ethnic cleansings. But all the 'Big Three' agreed that Europe's postwar order should be built upon homogenous nation states. This consensus was especially strong concerning the German minorities and their dissolution through compulsory migration. In its own sphere of influence, the Soviet Union pursued an ambiguous policy. When the Red Army occupied Transylvania, a region where mass ethnic cleansing had occurred during 1940–44, it stopped the Romanian army and paramilitary units from taking revenge against Hungarians. Around three-quarters of the 400,000 Hungarians who had fled from the front in the autumn of 1944 were allowed to return. The Red Army and Tito's National Liberation Army stopped widespread revenge against Hungarians and mass expulsions in the Vojvodina in early 1945. The country most fiercely advocating ethnic cleansing in Central Europe during 1945–46 was Czechoslovakia, which was still ruled by a mostly liberal and bourgeois government.[46]

However, the Soviet Union actively supported ethnic cleansing when it served its strategic aims. An example was the Polish–Ukrainian conflict, where the 'evacuation' of the minorities and the deportation of the Ukrainians remaining in Poland in 1947 helped to get rid of the Poles from the Soviet Union; these were likely to put up most resistance against the Sovietization of the newly acquired western territories, and to weaken the nationalist Ukrainian underground, which violently fought against the Red Army and the NKVD. The removal of the Germans also made Poland and Czechoslovakia dependent on Soviet military protection against German revanchism and thus preceded the Cold War set-up.

In Europe alone, the ethnic cleansing between 1944 and 1948 uprooted up to 20 million people. Many more were to follow in some of the British colonies, which became the main arena of ethnic cleansing during 1947–48. Around 12 million Muslims, Hindus, and Sikhs were violently removed or tried to escape at the last moment when India and Pakistan were separated. Again, the European concept of a modern nation state was pivotal. Pakistan was supposed to be a Muslim state, and the separation only made sense if the population was homogenized at least in religious terms. There had been partition plans for Bengal already in 1905, when Lord Curzon had served as viceroy. After World War I he proposed a neatly drawn borderline for Poles and Ukrainians, when in 1923 he chaired the Lausanne conference. This example shows that although Europe was the main area of ethnic cleansing in the twentieth century, the colonial experience and its application in Europe should be further studied. The British had also proposed the partition of Palestine between Jews and Arabs in 1937. Then, plans to move around 200,000 people, most of them Arabs, failed due to Arab resistance. But the Israeli–Arab war of 1948 created another opportunity to follow up on these earlier proposals. Again, the idea of a modern nation state could not be reconciled with the existence of a substantial ethnic minority. In both areas, there was also a long tradition of inter-communal violence which allowed ethnic cleansing to appear as a final means to create a stable nation state and lasting peace.

However, this consensus was shaken because of the massive suffering and chaos created by the post-World War II ethnic cleansing. Although Germany had few

---

[46] On Czechoslovak policy towards the Hungarian minority, see Štefan Šutaj, *Maďarska Menšina na Slovensku v Rokoch 1945–1948* (Bratislava: Veda, 1993).

sympathizers in 1945, the British and American public were appalled by the news from the areas of expulsion and the extreme misery in their zones of occupation. At the very least, the practicability of ethnic cleansing was questioned. The beginning of the Cold War also had a pivotal impact. Western powers (re)discovered the discourse of human rights and distinguished their ideas of western civilization from communist rule. Another important issue was the prevention of future genocide. Although population transfers were not viewed as immoral or let alone genocidal in the immediate postwar years, the UN convention against genocide in principle covered many aspects of ethnic cleansing, the singling out of one particular group for persecution, its removal from the territory it used to inhabit, and the destruction of material property and culture.[47] This is one of the reasons why ethnic cleansing eventually diminished in the postwar period.

In Europe there were only a few incidents, such as the 'Septembrianá' in Istanbul, when a massive pogrom forced the remaining Greeks in Turkey to leave, or after the partition of Cyprus when Greeks from the north of the island and Turks from the South migrated over the new border in 1975. But there was no more ethnic cleansing on the scale seen in postwar Europe or India. As a result of the 1968 movement, awareness of human rights issues and of the suffering of minorities further increased in the 1970s and 1980s. Due to the long period of peace in Europe after 1945, spectres of war also had receded into a distant past. So much greater was the shock when in the 1990s the breakdown of the Soviet Union and of Yugoslavia opened up another period of ethnic cleansing.

Epilogue: Ethnic Cleansing in Yugoslavia 1991–95

Although the pictures from the war in Yugoslavia were shocking, one should be careful about building up false continuities and analogies. In a historical perspective, one can indeed talk about 'a War of Yugoslav Succession',[48] where one side, the republics striving for independence, insisted on the existing boundaries of federative Yugoslavia, while Milošević and his allies wanted to change these boundaries by violent means in order to carve out as great as possible a sphere of power. Ethnic cleansing was a means to crush actual and potential resistance and to secure contested territories.

But the international context was radically different. There was no consensus for ethnic cleansing any more, but strong opposition against it. This is also true for non-Western states, which are often criticized for their human rights record. Moreover, Milošević was no new Hitler, as some western intellectuals suggested in the heat of the debate about the atrocities committed in Bosnia-Herzegovina. So far no master plan

---

[47] On the creation of the convention and how it was limited compared with Raphael Lemkin's earlier draft, see William A. Schabas, *Genocide in International Law: The Crime of Crimes*, 2nd edn (Cambridge: Cambridge University Press, 2009).

[48] For this term, see Naimark, *Fires of Hatred*, 139–84.

was detected in Belgrade that foresaw the ethnic cleansing of 'greater Serbia'. There is even some counter-evidence against plans of total cleansing, such as the continuing existence of ethnically mixed areas in Serbia proper, such as the Vojvodina and the Sandjak, and even within the war zone in northern and eastern Bosnia, such as the enclave of Bihać. When political power was undisputed, the authoritarian regime of Milošević tolerated the existence of subordinated minorities and of ethnic mixture. Of course, radical nationalists such as Vojislav Šešelj were already in 1991 very outspoken about the removal of all minority groups from contested areas, but the political elites that then carried out the ethnic cleansing in the breakaway parts of Croatia and Bosnia-Herzegovina only came to power shortly before or during the war. Hence, an explanation of this case of ethnic cleansing needs to focus on the course of events during 1991–92 and the subsequent escalation of violence to ethnic cleansing in various contested areas.[49]

In spite of all the suffering, one should keep an eye on the proportions of the war and the ethnic cleansing it involved. Recent calculations by the Research and Documentation Center (Istraživačko dokumentacioni centar) in Sarajevo reduced the number of casualties to around 100,000.[50] Moreover, among the war victims, Bosnian Serbs are only slightly under-represented in proportion to the entire population. But they were mainly victims of a different kind. While in Bosnia the Muslim victims who suffered most were by far mostly civilians, the Serbians mainly lost military combatants. That shows the asymmetry in warfare, in which well equipped Serbian soldiers and paramilitary units went into action against a Muslim population that could hardly put up armed resistance, thanks to the way the Yugoslav army was dissolved and because of the international weapons embargo on Bosnia-Herzegovina.

Another difference between previous periods of ethnic cleansing and the former Yugoslavia is that there have been attempts to reverse the effects and to repatriate the refugees. However, that policy has only brought limited results because many refugees do not see a future in the Republika Srpska. The sobering conclusion is that once the ethnic balance of an area has been violently changed, a return to the status quo is very difficult.

There were new and horrible proportions of this most recent case of ethnic cleansing in the twentieth century.[51] The refugees in Bosnia-Herzegovina numbered up to two

[49] There are numerous books about the former Yugoslavia, most of them written during or briefly after the war. For an in-depth analysis which includes a pre-history and a comparative perspective see Cathie Carmichael, *Ethnic Cleansing in the Balkans: Nationalism and the Destruction of Tradition* (New York: Routledge, 2002).

[50] Originally there was the claim that there had been 250,000 victims. See for the numbers published by the Center its webpage at http://www.idc.org.ba, accessed July 2010. There is extensive documentation in Serbo-Croatian language for all the casualties of the war. An overview can also be found on the web page of the Norwegian embassy, who sponsored the project at http://norwayportal. mfa.no/en/norveska/News_and_events/Society-and-Policy/rdc_bbd, accessed July 2010.

[51] On the course of ethnic cleansing, see Steven L. Burg and Paul S. Shoup, *The War in Bosnia-Herzegowina: Ethnic Conflict and International Intervention* (New York: M.E. Sharpe, 1999), 164–88; Naimark, *Fires of Hatred*.

million, almost half of the population. Most of the displacements were carried out in 1992 in a very short amount of time. This further demonstrates the increasing asymmetry between military might and civilian population in twentieth-century Europe. However, Serbian military power should not be overestimated. During 1991–92 Milošević had problems mobilizing people in support of his policy, and draft dodging was rife.[52] These problems and the general vacuum of power strengthened paramilitary units like the infamous 'Arkan Tigers', led by Željko Ražnatović, who did most of the dirty work of ethnic cleansing. Another factor in the mobilization were Serbian memories of World War II and a seemingly defensive nationalism, which was de facto very aggressive. Interviews with combatants after the war have shown that a major motive was the defence of the family or the neighbourhood, which according to propaganda was endangered by supposedly neo-fascist Croats and Islamist Bosnian Muslims.[53] The issue of memory has mostly been dealt with from a top-down perspective, pointing to the declaration of the 1986 memorandum of the Serbian Academy of Sciences, in which Serbia was presented as an eternal victim of history and nationalist neighbours.

A close look at the worst and most violent areas of ethnic cleansing also points to the validity of a bottom-up perspective. The first major massacre of the war in Croatia in 1991 occurred in Glina, the same city where the Ustaša first burnt an Orthodox Church full of people in the summer of 1941. Also in Eastern Bosnia, the expulsion and mass killing of Serbs during World War II had been especially horrendous. Moreover, the area around Srebrenica was the zone of fiercest military confrontation during the hot phase of the war in 1993. The Bosnian army temporarily regained large areas and persecuted the Serbs living there. Chasing out minorities cut off the support from enemy military units who, especially on the side of the Muslims, fought with a guerilla 'hit and run' strategy.[54]

Nevertheless, most of the ethnic cleansing in 1991 in Croatia and in 1992 in Bosnia was pre-emptive and not connected to changing front lines. Especially in northern Bosnia and along the most important railway routes and roads to Serbia proper, the purpose was to achieve lasting military and political domination. Still, this means that future research on ethnic cleansing in Croatia and Bosnia-Herzegovina will be confronted with numerous different regional and local arenas. In terms of time, one can distinguish a first phase of ethnic cleansing in late 1991 and 1992, which was supposed to mark the territory of the breakaway regions of Croatia and Bosnia-Herzegovina. Even after military domination had been achieved there was much violence including rape and mutilations.

---

[52] On problems of mobilization and the policy of demobilization, see Valère P. Gagnon, *The Myth of Ethnic War: Serbia and Croatia in the 1990s* (Ithaca, NY: Cornell University Press, 2004).

[53] See Natalija Bašić, 'Die Akteursperspektive. Soldaten und "ethnische Säuberungen" in Kroatien und Bosnien-Herzegowina (1991–1995)', in Ulf Brunnbauer, Michael G. Esch and Holm Sundhaussen (eds), *Definitionsmacht, Utopie, Vergeltung. 'Ethnische Säuberungen' im östlichen Europa des 20. Jahrhunderts* (Münster: LIT Verlag, 2006), 144–68.

[54] See the precise analysis of the war, including ethnic cleansing, in *Balkan Battlegrounds. A Military History of the Yugoslav Conflict, 1990–1995*, Vol. I (Washington, DC: Central Intelligence Agency, 2002), 142ff.

These crimes were often carried out in public in order to make the remaining minority population leave.

A second phase in 1993 was more connected to the military situation and strategic aims. The remaining minority population and the 'enemy population' in still contested areas were expelled in order to fortify the front lines and to prevent guerilla attacks. In this second phase central Bosnia and parts of Herzegovina were ravaged by the new Croat–Bosnian war. After a period of relative stability in 1994 a last round of ethnic cleansing occurred in 1995. Most affected was the Krajina in Croatia, where the Serbs were expelled by the Croatian army, and again in eastern Bosnia, where the Serbs aimed at dissolving the remaining Muslim enclaves in order to get as much territory as possible at a future peace conference. It was there where the worst massacre of the war occurred: the genocidal killing of 8000 Muslim men in and around Srebrenica. However, the fact that women and children were spared death marked a difference from numerous Nazi crimes and the Soviet deportations during World War II. By this crime against humanity, the worst one of this war and the only one internationally accepted as genocide, the leaders of the Bosnian Serbs wanted to demonstrate that eastern Bosnia was theirs. In spite of the international outcry, this strategy worked. The Dayton peace agreement allotted Srebrenica to the Republika Srpska. But it should be added that much research is still needed to analyse and explain the ethnic cleansing in former Yugoslavia. These are only preliminary findings which might be falsified when more archival documents become accessible, especially in Serbia and Croatia, which in 1995 expelled 250,000 Serbs from reconquered territories.

Will the international condemnation of the atrocities in Yugoslavia prevent future ethnic cleansing and genocidal acts like those in Srebrenica? Although there were around 10,000 casualties among the Albanians, maybe the history of Kosovo allows for such an optimistic reading of history. There, an international community of states intervened against a repetition of the Bosnian scenario. However, this could not prevent the persecution and exodus of the Serbian minority. Incidents like the war in Rwanda point to an even more pessimistic reading. Since ethnic cleansing is not accepted at the level of international politics any more, and is difficult for an individual state to organize because of its spatial dimension, the way out might be more mass killing on the spot, that is to say, the most blatant version of genocide.

FURTHER READING

Bessel, Richard and Claudia B. Haake (eds), *Removing Peoples: Forced Removal in the Modern World* (Oxford: Oxford University Press, 2009).

Borodziej, Włodzimierz and Hans Lemberg (eds) *'Unsere Heimat ist uns ein fremdes Land geworden….' Die Deutschen östlich von Oder und Neiße 1945–1950. Dokumente aus polnischen Archiven*, 4 vols (Marburg: Herder Institut, 2000–4).

Brandes, Detlef et al. (eds), *Erzwungene Trennung. Vertreibungen und Aussiedlungen in und aus der Tschechoslowakei 1938–1947 im Vergleich mit Polen, Ungarn und Jugoslawien* (Essen: Klartext, 1999).

Frank, Matthew, *Expelling the Germans: British Opinion and Post-1945 Population Transfer in Context* (Oxford: Oxford University Press, 2008).

Hryciuk, Grzegorz et al. (eds), *Wysiedlenia, wypędzenia i ucieczki 1939–1959. Atlas ziem polskich* (Warsaw: Demart, 2008).

Kontogiorgi, Elisabeth, *Population Exchanges in Greek Macedonia: The Forced Resettlement of Refugees, 1922–1930* (New York: Oxford University Press, 2006).

Lieberman, Benjamin, *Terrible Fate: Ethnic Cleansing in the Making of Modern Europe* (Chicago, IL: Ivan R. Dee, 2006).

Melville, Ralph et al. (eds), *Zwangsmigrationen im mittleren und östlichen Europa. Völkerrecht—Konzeptionen—Praxis (1938–1950)* (Mainz: Zabern, 2008).

Naimark, Norman M., *Fires of Hatred: Ethnic Cleansing in Twentieth-Century Europe* (Cambridge, MA: Harvard University Press, 2001).

Poljan, Pavel, *Ne na svoie vole. Istoria i geografia prinuditel´nych migracracii v SSSR* (Moscow: Memorial, 2001).

Rosière, Stéphane, *Le nettoyage ethnique, terreur et peuplement* (Paris: Ellipses, 2006).

Ther, Philipp, *Die dunkle Seite der Nationalstaaten. Ethische Säuberungen im modernen Europa* (Göttingen: Vandenhoeck und Ruprecht, 2011).

Ther, Philipp and Ana Siljak (eds), *Redrawing Nations: Ethnic Cleansing in East-Central Europe 1944–1948* (Lanham, MD: Rowman and Littlefield, 2001).

Weitz, Eric D., 'From the Vienna to the Paris System: International Politics and the Entangled Histories of Human Rights, Forced Deportations and Civilizing Missions,' *American Historical Review* 113:5 (2008), 1313–43.

CHAPTER 7

RESPONDING TO 'ORDER WITHOUT LIFE'? LIVING UNDER COMMUNISM

DAN STONE

'[W]hat we have here is simply another form of the consumer and industrial society, with all its concomitant social, intellectual, and psychological consequences. It is impossible to understand the nature of power in our system properly without taking this into account.'

Václav Havel[1]

INTRODUCTION: TERROR AND TRABIS

'TULIPS', the first story in György Dragomán's *The White King*, hits home with remarkable visceral impact. In restrained tones, the narrator, Djata, tells of his father's going away one morning with two 'colleagues' and how, more than half a year later, the child discovers, when the two men reappear at their apartment, that he is not working at a research institute but has been deported by the security police and is actually a forced labourer on the Danube Canal. Their threats to his mother provide an intimate counterpart to the structural violence of the coercive state that shapes the story. But most of the rest of the book is full of violent and touching stories of childhood among the Hungarian community in Romania. Brutal childhood games and developing relationships intermingle with the authorities' breathtaking indifference and hatred.[2] Terror was a reality for some of

[1] Václav Havel, 'The Power of the Powerless', in Havel, *Living in Truth*, ed. Jan Vladislav (London: Faber and Faber, 1987), 40. Many thanks to Scott Ashley, Paul Betts, Robert Bideleux, Cathie Carmichael, Becky Jinks, Rudolf Muhs, Anton Weiss-Wendt, and Christopher Wheeler who read at short notice an earlier draft of this hastily written chapter.
[2] György Dragomán, 'Tulips', in *The White King* (London: Black Swan, 2009), 7–21.

those who lived through communism, but so was the daily process of getting by, growing up, and making a living.[3]

Both during the Cold War, with the 1950s' theories of 'red fascism' and 'totalitarianism', and after 1989, when debates have been no less emotive, scholars and other political commentators have condemned communism for its bloody murderousness. The editors of *The Black Book of Communism* believe that communist regimes were responsible for between 85 and 100 million victims, while another estimate, revealing the difficulties of making such calculations with precision, reckons that the three cases of the Soviet Union, China, and Cambodia alone were responsible for between 21 and 70 million deaths.[4] Whatever the true figure, the numbers are shocking, far higher than those of victims killed by the Nazis.

But the long period of communist rule in Europe—from 1917 in the case of the USSR, and from the late 1940s in the case of the Soviet satellite states—cannot be summarized as no more than sustained and untrammelled violence. While terror was a key part of the establishment and maintenance of communist control, throughout the communist period people still lived, loved, played, worked, and died. This chapter asks: what was 'ordinary life' like in communist Eastern Europe? Can one talk of 'private life' in a political system that sought to eradicate the distinction between private and public? Although focusing on 'everyday life' runs the risk of 'normalizing' terror, the longevity of the communist regimes (in contrast to the 'mere' thirteen years of Nazi Germany) means that one can clearly distinguish periods of terror or upheaval from periods of 'normality'; indeed, 'normalization' was a term specifically used by the communists themselves in the late period (post-1968). Besides, as the historiography of Nazism shows, *Alltagsgeschichte* (the history of everyday life) need not lead one to focus only on the normal aspects of a society; rather it can help to explain how and why ordinary citizens coped with the pressures of living in societies that sought to enforce complicity and compliance, and how and why the communist regimes survived: certainly out of fear and the threat of violence, but also—again, as with the Third Reich, only less and less over time—because they partly won popular support.[5] It also helps to explain why communism collapsed, in a way that an emphasis solely on state security and terror cannot. Besides, in Soviet Russia, Ukraine, and Belorussia, there was no historical memory of democracy against which people could compare their current existence. This complex combination of identification, resentment, adaptation, and resistance can be summed up with the notion of 'terror and Trabis', for communist regimes were backed up with the threat of state violence, but the societies themselves were, especially by the 1970s, often shabby, shoddy, and drab, and functioned only because citizens imaginatively adapted

---

[3] See, for example, Slavenka Drakulić, *How We Survived Communism and even Laughed* (London: W.W. Norton, 1992).

[4] Stéphane Courtois et al., *The Black Book of Communism: Crimes, Terror, Repression* (Cambridge, MA: Harvard University Press, 1999); Benjamin A. Valentino, *Final Solutions: Mass Killing and Genocide in the 20th Century* (Ithaca, NY: Cornell University Press, 2004), ch. 4.

[5] See the essays in Michael Geyer and Sheila Fitzpatrick (eds), *Beyond Totalitarianism: Stalinism and Nazism Compared* (New York: Cambridge University Press, 2009).

what they had to hand in order to make it work, much like that symbol of East German progress and consumer happiness, the Trabant.

It does not suffice, therefore, to understand communism through the stock images of prison camps and empty shops. One must also bear in mind that, especially in the countries that had suffered under Nazi occupation (Czechoslovakia and Poland), there was considerable support for communism, especially in its early days, when the prestige of defeating fascism gave the regimes and their guarantor, the Red Army, immense power and a source of legitimacy that they fully exploited (although the Baltic States, which saw their independence crushed first by Nazi and then Soviet rule, which seemed like a return to the Tsarist Empire, offer a stark contrast). Furthermore, economic indicators suggest that, in terms of GDP (which masks individuals' spending power), Eastern Europe compared favourably with the West at least until the early 1960s. In other words, if we think of communism only in terms of the sinister manoeuvring of the takeovers and the ruthless suppression of opposition in the first postwar decades, and in terms of brave dissident activity, samizdat literature, and the 'alternative polis' in the later decades, we radically skew the picture in favour of an important, but strongly westernized narrative; one that omits to mention the vast majority of the population, who continued to live their 'normal lives', albeit within a very circumscribed framework. Communism was not experienced by those who lived through it simply as 'bad'; it was also the setting and shaper of their 'normal' lives. The same applies if we think of communism as 'a universe in a vacuum' characterized only by pain and suffering: this exoticization (or 'orientalism') feeds off and supplies stereotypes more than it accounts for people's real lives.[6] What is required instead is to approach the communist states not as a reflection of the western imagination but in terms of a complex history 'which comprehends the social as a psychically *and* socially organized formation', in Julia Hell's felicitous formulation.[7]

That said, and granted that the end of 'actually existing socialism' means that we can now historicize the ways in which people lived under the communist regimes, it does not follow that it is clear how we should describe, or even name, 'that society'. As Petya Kabakchieva notes, terms such as 'communism', 'socialism', 'real socialism', 'Soviet-type societies', 'state command economy', 'state capitalism', 'Stalinist totalitarianism', or just plain 'totalitarianism' each seem to imply different explanatory schemes. In some cases, particularly in the early post-1989 period, simply naming the regime worked as an explanation of it. More recently, understanding the specific nature of the communist regimes

---

[6] Compare Anna Funder, *Stasiland: Stories from Behind the Berlin Wall* (London: Granta Books, 2003) with Oliver Fritz, *The Iron Curtain Kid* (n.p.: Lulu.com, 2009). 'Universe in a vacuum' is from Funder, *Stasiland*, 157, whose character, Hagen Koch, goes on to explain this universe as 'complete with its own self-created hells and heavens, its punishments and redemptions meted out right here on earth. Many of the punishments were simply for lack of belief, or even suspected lack of belief. Disloyalty was calibrated in the minutest of signs: the antenna turned to receive western television, the red flag not hung out on May Day, someone telling an off-colour joke about Honecker just to stay sane'. Fritz (*Iron Curtain Kid*, 3), by contrast, writes that 'We citizens did not have to queue for absolutely everything, nor did we only communicate in hushed voices or were in constant fear of being randomly arrested'.

[7] Julia Hell, *Post-Fascist Fantasies: Psychoanalysis, History, and the Literature of East Germany* (Durham, NC: Duke University Press, 1997), 7.

has given rise to sophisticated studies in social and cultural history into, for example, consumption, design, sounds and noise in socialist states, the construction of communities, and the eking out of private space, cities, socialism as a 'society of networks', and the moulding of future socialist citizens through organizations such as the children's pioneers. The result, as Kabakchieva notes, is that 'Communism as an object is approached in its complexity and multidimensionality and, more importantly, there is an attempt to study it in its concrete manifestations, rather than in the mirror of abstract theories.'[8]

Still, one must make choices, and so I will henceforth talk of 'communism', not only to acknowledge the many non-communist varieties of socialist thought, but because the East European regimes themselves were governed by Leninist Communist Parties. And while one must of course note the local specificities of the Eastern European countries— their different national, imperial, economic, linguistic, religious, ethnic, and military traditions and histories—the premise of much of this literature, as of this chapter, is that one can profitably study communism as a project in its historical setting, and that the gross simplification required to synthesize these disparate strands into something more or less coherent can be tolerated, as long as one remains aware of the differences too. Although there are obvious exceptions to the main narrative—Romania or Albania in the 1980s, for example, or the Baltic States in the context of the mass deportations of the 1940s, which saw large percentages of their small populations replaced by ethnic Russians, or, in general, the many differences between the USSR and its Eastern European satellite states—there is enough common ground between the communist regimes of postwar Eastern Europe to warrant talking of them collectively.

Opposition, Accommodation, Enthusiasm

In the early days during and following the communist takeovers in Eastern Europe, societies were often quite markedly split between those who wanted to resist communism, even through the use of force, those who adapted and accommodated themselves to the regimes in the belief that there was no alternative, and the minority who enthusiastically supported the idea of building socialism and eradicating the vast inequalities that had characterized the region before World War II. In the states that became the Warsaw Pact in 1955, ultimate control lay with Moscow, and periods of Stalinism, de-Stalinization, 'normalization', and reform were dictated by Moscow. By contrast, in Yugoslavia, where Tito's Partisans had huge popular support, the new regime did not require the support of the USSR; indeed, Tito soon broke with Moscow altogether. Albania slipstreamed Yugoslavia—indeed, playing second fiddle to Tito was always Enver Hoxha's great paranoia—and here too, at least in the early years, communism had widespread support.

[8] Petya Kabakchieva, 'Rethinking Communism: Social Approaches to Comprehending "That Society" in Postcommunist Bulgaria', in Maria Todorova (ed.), *Remembering Communism: Genres of Representation* (New York: Social Science Research Council, 2010), 37–56, here esp. 37, 51.

In the early years, the regimes' social restructuring programmes created complicity among citizens, especially among those who were beneficiaries of the reallocation of private property.[9] In the period between the Great Patriotic War and the death of Stalin, for example, the Soviet Union employed a small army of informants to report 'non-political crimes', mostly the theft of state property, to the authorities. At the height of the campaign against the theft of state property, in 1947, more than 454,000 people were convicted.[10] The process of eradicating 'fascism', that is, all vestiges of private ownership of land and property, went hand in hand with the incorporation of the masses into the new system, as well as the emergence of the 'new class' of the *nomenklatura*, who grew more nepotistic, venal, and regime-dependent over time.[11]

As is well known, opposition to communism soon built up a head of steam, with major uprisings in East Berlin in 1953, Budapest in 1956, and Prague in 1968, and in 1956, 1970, and 1980–81 in Poland, as workers protested about the regimes' failure to meet their needs.[12] There is not the space to discuss these uprisings here, but suffice it to say that they were at once responses to official attempts to accelerate the construction of socialism and spurs to further efforts to achieve that aim, albeit in a more selective fashion that would not immediately alienate large sections of the population.[13] In Romania, the official response to the 1956 uprising in neighbouring Hungary was to bring to an end the 'zany' process of de-Stalinization, to consolidate Gheorghe Gheorgiu-Dej's grip on power, to hasten the Soviet troops' departure, which took place in 1958, and thus to facilitate the famed 'independent line' from Moscow.[14]

STABILITY AND THE TURN TO CONSUMERISM

But there is another side to this well known, Cold War-inspired narrative of communist repression, authoritarianism, and (later on) economic disaster. As the epigraph from Havel indicates, one way that the communist regime tried to legitimize itself was through encouraging consumerism, particularly after the death of Stalin and the East German uprising of June 1953. As several studies have recently documented, the Eastern Bloc

---

[9] Liviu Chelcea, 'Ancestors, Domestic Groups, and the Socialist State: Housing Nationalization and Restitution in Romania', *Comparative Studies in Society and History* 45:4 (2003), 714–40.

[10] James Heinzen, 'Informers and the State under Late Stalinism: Informant Networks and Crimes against "Socialist Property", 1940–53', *Kritika: Explorations in Russian and Eurasian History* 8:4 (2007), 789–815, here 796.

[11] Most famously examined in Milovan Djilas, *The New Class: An Analysis of the Communist System* (London: Thames and Hudson, 1957).

[12] Kevin McDermott and Matthew Stibbe (eds), *Revolution and Resistance in Eastern Europe: Challenges to Communist Rule* (Oxford: Berg, 2006).

[13] See the discussion in Corey Ross, *Constructing Socialism at the Grass-Roots: The Transformation of East Germany, 1945–65* (Basingstoke: Macmillan Press, 2000).

[14] See Johanna Granville, '"Ask for Bread, Not Peace": Reactions of Romanian Workers and Peasants to the Hungarian Revolution of 1956', *East European Politics and Societies* 24:4 (2010), 543–71.

economies kept pace with those of Western Europe for the first fifteen to twenty years after World War II. While the availability of consumer goods was nowhere near as widespread as in the West (although one should not forget that until the 1960s, owning a fridge or a vacuum cleaner, not to mention a car, remained the preserve of the fairly well-off in Western Europe), in a historically poor region, the mere fact that such things were now appearing is noteworthy. And even if the bare economic figures hid the fact that much of GDP was being spent on military, industrial, and other major infrastructural projects rather than on ordinary citizens' wants and needs, the communist countries could—and did—argue that they were able to increase living standards without their citizens having to endure the instability of living under capitalism.

Robert Bideleux points out in this volume that the inflexibility of Comecon's command structure was the cause of the Eastern Bloc's falling behind Western Europe, and that is surely right. But until that point—and to some extent even after it—there was some popular and elite support for a project to rebuild the eastern half of the continent according to functional, rational principles, with the aim of creating a fair society. This is not how things worked out, but it would perhaps be just too bitter to assert that 'what begins with a lie will remain a lie' as does the mother of Peter Kwinto, the main protagonist in Czesław Miłosz's novel *The Seizure of Power*.[15] That is an understandable statement from one who lived through those years, but it might be historically more accurate to admit that the communist takeover awoke great hopes and aspirations in many people, such as the fictional Kwinto himself. This was certainly true of many intellectuals, to whom Milan Kundera's notion of 'stalking a lost deed' might be more appropriately applied.[16] From architects and planners, such as the Dutchman Mart Stam, who wanted to revive a Bauhaus-style school in the Soviet zone of Germany, or the Yugoslav group EXAT 51, which promoted abstraction in the service of 'brotherhood and unity', to the participants in the 1948 World Congress of Intellectuals in Defence of Peace in Wrocław, there is no shortage of examples of those who hoped to realize the socialist dream of a utopian, planned society.[17]

In terms of art and design, this initial burst of enthusiasm for abstraction and modernism was swiftly overturned, as production rather than consumption became the order of the day and western style was condemned as bourgeois decadence. But a decade later, in an attempt to respond to workers' demands, things changed again. In the late 1950s, with Bierut replaced by Gomułka, Moda Polska, a range of ready-to-wear clothes shops, was launched in Poland, as was Sybille in East Germany. *Lada* fashion review appeared at the same time in Bulgaria. As David Crowley observes, modern design, advertising, textiles, music, ceramics, and enamel wares all suddenly took on

---

[15] Czesław Miłosz, *The Seizure of Power* (London: Abacus, 1985), 139.

[16] Milan Kundera, *The Book of Laughter and Forgetting* (London: Faber and Faber, 1992), 9.

[17] David Crowley and Jane Pavitt, 'Introduction', in Crowley and Pavitt (eds), *Cold War Modern: Design 1945–1970* (London: V&A Publishing, 2008), 17–18; Katarzyna Murawska-Muthesius, 'Modernism between Peace and Freedom: Picasso and Others at the Congress of Intellectuals in Wrocław, 1948', in Crowley and Pavitt (eds), *Cold War Modern*, 33–41.

western-style designs and became available in the name of a turn to consumerism.[18] Khrushchev set out his goals of creating 'communist-style consumer behaviour' in an apparent admission that the relentless pursuit of production had neglected citizens'— and especially women's—needs.[19] But how did the official turn to consumerism translate into a change in everyday life for citizens of communist states?

First, one should note that the pre-existence of private enterprise before collectivization meant that a thirst for consumerism was not entirely novel; what was new, in this mostly poor part of Europe, was the existence of goods other than pure essentials, as well as money to pay for them. Second, private enterprise not only survived the collectivization process— better in some regions than in others—but the strict regime that collectivization enforced on rural life meant that working to time and calculating labour and output in monetary terms was as much a part of communist life as it was of pre- and post-communism. As several anthropologists have noted, changes in perceptions of time wrought by communism—the need to work to timetables and to increase productivity and outputs on the one hand, and to stand in lines and endure intense boredom on the other—were different from perceptions of time under capitalism, but there were similarities nevertheless. Here one can profitably contrast 'Goulash communist' Hungary, where one scholar argues that the strict labour and financial controls of collectivization helped pave the way for capitalism after 1989, with Romania, where, in contrast to 'capitalist time' which is linear and ever accelerating, under Nicolai Ceauşescu time stood still, 'the medium for producing not profits but subjection, for immobilizing persons in the Party's grip'.[20]

In general, then, consumerism in Eastern Europe meant consumerism controlled by the Party for the purpose of developing communism. In Bulgaria, for example, the Eighth Congress of the Bulgarian Communist Party (BCP) of 1963 set out its vision of creating, in the long term in Bulgaria, a 'new socialist person'. This meant a process of homogenization, the standardization of citizens in terms of their behaviour and aspirations and their reshaping into citizens. The BCP stated its goal of developing the 'citizen of the socialist and communist society toward a high cultural level and elevated spiritual and material needs', including in this process a massive expansion in the range and availability of consumer goods.[21] And Khrushchev, rather awkwardly, argued at the CPSU's Twenty-Second Party Congress in 1961, that 'Personal ownership by the toiler of a large

---

[18] David Crowley, 'Thaw Modern: Design in Eastern Europe after 1956', in Crowley and Pavitt (eds), *Cold War Modern*, 128–53, here 130.

[19] Milla Minerva, 'Narratives and Images of Socialist Consumption: A Study of the Visual Construction of Consumer Culture in Bulgaria in the 1960s', in Todorova (ed.), *Remembering Communism*, 349–71, here 349. See also Mark Pittaway's chapter in this volume and Susan E. Reid, 'Cold War in the Kitchen: Gender and the De-Stalinization of Consumer Taste in the Soviet Union under Khrushchev', *Slavic Review* 61:2 (2002), 211–52.

[20] Martha Lampland, *The Object of Labor: Commodification in Socialist Hungary* (Chicago, IL: University of Chicago Press, 1995); Katherine Verdery, *What Was Socialism, and What Comes Next?* (Princeton, NJ: Princeton University Press, 1996), 57. As Granville notes ('"Ask for Bread, Not Peace"', 546–7), in Romania, after World War II, and continuing after 1956, the emphasis remained firmly on heavy industry; here there was no turn to consumerism.

[21] Minerva, 'Narratives and Images', 350–1.

number of things... is not at variance with the principles of communist construction as long as it keeps within reasonable bounds and does not become an end in itself.[22]

The turn to consumerism raised a fundamental problem: how could communist daily life be conceptualized as different from capitalist daily life if it too placed more emphasis on consumption than production? The answer lay in the *content* and *context* of material goods. As Milla Minerva explains, the placing of even as innocent an object as a vase in a room could take on unwelcome connotations of 'bourgeois viciousness' instead of 'socialist cosiness' if done wrongly. As Khrushchev went on to say, this sort of 'petty-bourgeois degeneration' means that 'the individual falls a prey to things and becomes a slave to them'.[23] 'Thus', Minerva writes,

> socialist daily life became a collection of exempla used to create the image of an appropriate socialist everyday life and to serve as practical instruments in the struggle to attain it, given the ability to inscribe every such detail in an ideological discourse.[24]

In Poland, residents' committees in apartment blocks (*komitety blokowe*) policed private space, and women's magazines offered a vision of the ideal home that stressed ideological conformity and the modelling of domestic life, a fact that acquired added poignancy given the communist regimes' inability to provide sufficient, not to mention decent, housing.[25] The new consumerism had to conform to, indeed to help in the construction of, the ideal communist citizen: well mannered, obliging, dedicated to the common good and to improving the public sphere, in contrast to the western consumer who was figured as individualist, inappropriate, and inauthentic.[26] At the same time, the adoption of western-style consumerism could be presented as the salvation of the 'progressive essence' of western bourgeois culture.[27] No wonder that the furniture designer,

---

[22] N.S. Khrushchev, 'Report of the Central Committee of the 22nd Congress of the Communist Party of the Soviet Union', in *Documents of the 22nd Congress of the CPSU* (New York: Crosscurrents Press, 1961), vol. 1, 131–2, online at: www.archive.org/details/DocumentsOfThe22ndCongressOfTheCpsuVolI, accessed November 2011.

[23] Ibid., 132.

[24] Minerva, 'Narratives and Images', 353.

[25] David Crowley, 'Warsaw Interiors: The Public Life of Private Spaces, 1949–65', in David Crowley and Susan E. Reid (eds), *Socialist Spaces: Sites of Everyday Life in the Eastern Bloc* (Oxford: Berg, 2002), 187–8. See also, in the same volume (207–30), Katerina Gerasimova, 'Public Privacy in the Soviet Communal Apartment', for an analysis of an institution that cannot easily be characterized as either private or public; and, more broadly, Steven E. Harris, 'In Search of "Ordinary" Russia: Everyday Life in the NEP, the Thaw, and the Communal Apartment', *Kritika: Explorations in Russian and Eurasian History* 6:3 (2005), 583–614.

[26] Paul Betts, *Within Walls: Private Life in the German Democratic Republic* (Oxford: Oxford University Press, 2010), ch. 4, argues that the SED consciously sought to reorganize domestic life as part of the project to build a model socialist culture. See also Betts' comments in 'The Politics of Post-Fascist Aesthetics: 1950s West and East German Industrial Design', in Richard Bessel and Dirk Schumann (eds), *Life after Death: Approaches to a Cultural and Social History of Europe during the 1940s and 1950s* (Cambridge: Cambridge University Press, 2003), 291–321, here 307–9.

[27] Greg Castillo, 'East as True West: Redeeming Bourgeois Culture, from Socialist Realism to *Ostalgie*', in György Péteri (ed.), *Imagining the West in Eastern Europe and the Soviet Union* (Pittsburgh, PA: University of Pittsburgh Press, 2010), 87–104, here 89.

Olgierd Szlekys, could say that in communist Poland, 'we have changed the forms of our life. We have moved part of private life to the houses of culture, to clubs and cafes which are places to meet comrades replacing, we say, the old salons'.[28]

Throughout the Eastern Bloc, the official turn to consumerism failed to meet people's needs and desires, especially as they grew increasingly aware of—or perceived— disparities between their own and Western Europeans' experiences of consumerism.[29] Here the so-called 'kitchen debates' of 1959—'perhaps the most dramatic instance of the more general politicization of material culture'[30]—when Khrushchev and Vice-President Nixon squared off over the meaning and quality of each system's kitchen appliances at the American Pavilion of the Moscow World Fair, are exemplary: they mark the high point of communist claims to be able to compete with the West and, in retrospect, the beginning of the West's outstripping of communism on these economic grounds (grounds which, it should be noted, were essentially the western ones of economic growth, consumer culture, and shopping as leisure. By competing on those terms, the communist countries were already acknowledging their inability to deliver much of what their citizens wanted).[31] As Greg Castillo notes, Khrushchev's competitive claims 'contradicted the Party's concurrent goal of inventing an alternative commodity culture based on temperance'.[32] The consequences of failing to live up to this promise were that people increasingly turning to a 'make-do and mend' philosophy, as well as to the black market, smuggling, hard currency, especially the Deutschmark and the dollar, and thus a correspondingly high instance of bribery and corruption in everyday business.

The new consumerism was only one way in which communism was going to be built, however. As David Crowley and Susan E. Reid observe, the Cold War period 'saw pervasive efforts to permeate not only places of work and public ceremony but also the most intimate spaces of the everyday with ideological meaning'.[33] This was as true of cinema, the radio, and football as it was of union or pioneer meetings. Cinema and radio could be used to inculcate the virtues of antifascism, though radio could also be used to inspire dissent, as when the broadcasts of Radio Free Europe's Voice of Free Hungary gave (false) hope to Nagy's supporters in 1956.[34] Sport was used to promote a cult of the body and

[28] Cited in Crowley, 'Warsaw Interiors', 188.

[29] See Rosemary Wakeman's chapter below.

[30] Betts, *Within Walls*, 266 n. 11. See also Ruth Oldenziel and Karin Zachmann (eds), *Cold War Kitchen: Americanization, Technology, and European Users* (Cambridge, MA: MIT Press, 2009); Susan E. Reid, 'The Khrushchev Kitchen: Domesticating the Scientific–Technological Revolution', *Journal of Contemporary History* 40:2 (2005), 289–316; Reid, 'Who Will Beat Whom? Soviet Popular Reception of the American National Exhibition in Moscow, 1959', in Péteri (ed.), *Imagining the West*, 194–236. More broadly, see Greg Castillo, *Cold War on the Home Front: The Soft Power of Midcentury Design* (Minneapolis, MN: University of Minnesota Press, 2010).

[31] See the excellent discussion in Mark Pittaway, *Eastern Europe 1939–2000* (London: Arnold, 2004), ch. 5.

[32] Castillo, *Cold War on the Home Front*, 170.

[33] David Crowley and Susan E. Reid, 'Socialist Spaces: Sites of Everyday Life in the Eastern Bloc', in Crowley and Reid (eds), *Socialist Spaces*, 3.

[34] René Wolf, *The Undivided Sky: The Holocaust on East and West German Radio in the 1960s* (Basingstoke: Palgrave Macmillan, 2010); Mark Pittaway, 'The Education of Dissent: The Reception of the Voice of Free Hungary, 1951–56', in Patrick Major and Rana Mitter (eds), *Across the Blocs: Exploring Comparative Cold War Cultural and Social History* (London: Frank Cass, 2004), 76–90.

physical fitness: 'Every person, in every place, should take part in sport once a week', declared Walter Ulbricht in 1959,[35] and the GDR devoted considerable resources to promoting sports in which competitors could win several medals, such as swimming, rowing, and athletics, though it neglected football. By contrast, the Hungarian national football team, captained by the exceptional Ferenc Puskás and led by its coach, Gusztáv Sebes, performed feats of individual sportsmanship that would have been regarded very suspiciously in any other sphere of communist life. Their exuberant displays, made on the basis of an innovative 4-2-4 formation, were forgiven on the basis that it propelled them to victory against every national team they played in 1952 and 1953, including, most famously, England at Wembley Stadium.[36]

And of course, people found that much of their 'private time' was accounted for, not only with work and obtaining life's necessities, but by the Party's attempts to inculcate socialist virtues into its citizens by engaging them in meetings and groups which pressed home the message, such as compulsory Marxism–Leninism in school, obligatory May Day parades, or communist 'invented traditions' such as Yugoslavia's Grandfather Frost. Children and youth were especially important here, with the Pioneers organizations central to the formation of a new communist consciousness, but in the process having to negotiate—in Eastern Europe, if not in the USSR—with young people's demands for spheres of autonomy and free expression. In Bulgaria, the Fatherland Front strove to construct the 'socialist way of life', with its leader (from 1974 to 1989), Pencho Kubadinski, explicitly claiming that it aimed to create the 'new man' and the 'socialist way of life'.[37] In the GDR the National Front and Cultural League, and in Hungary the socialist brigades played similar roles. All such organizations helped to establish and maintain the 'precarious stability' of the communist regimes, as did the ambivalent relationship to communism displayed by the region's churches, most of which collaborated with the regimes in return for some religious freedom, but which could also become centres of opposition.[38] Poland had one of the highest rates of church attendance in Europe by the 1970s; and in Croatia too, Catholicism took on the role of a sort of 'opposition'.

THE GREY YEARS

In the same way that avant-garde artists and architects who had hoped to deploy modernist principles in the building of socialism soon found that they had to renounce such 'bourgeois' decadence in the wake of the *Zhdanovshchina*, the Kremlin's reactionary

[35] Cited in Jutta Braun, 'The People's Sport? Popular Sport and Fans in the Later Years of the German Democratic Republic', *German History* 27:3 (2009), 414.

[36] David Goldblatt, *The Ball is Round: A Global History of Football* (London: Penguin, 2007), 341–6. Thanks to Scott Ashley for this reference.

[37] Ulf Brunnbauer, 'Making Bulgarians Socialist: The Fatherland Front in Communist Bulgaria, 1944–1989', *East European Politics and Societies* 22:1 (2008), 44–79.

[38] See Jeanette Z. Madarász, *Conflict and Compromise in East Germany, 1971–1989: A Precarious Stability* (Basingstoke: Palgrave Macmillan, 2003); Pittaway, *Eastern Europe*, 151.

cultural politics, so society as a whole was forced to shrink back into a narrowly circum-scribed range of permissible forms. At least officially, there was to be little deviance or room for expression that had not been approved by the Party, as the Brezhnev doctrine of defending the status quo ensured that room for manoeuvre in the sphere of daily life became increasingly restricted. The flow of consumer goods was rarely able to keep up with demand, and those who designed them saw their aspirations fail as shortages became the norm and the Brezhnevian focus on materialism and glossy consumer items replaced the notion of a rational society in which functional and aesthetically pleasing goods met people's needs. As Crowley nicely observes, 'Not only were the hopes of pro-ducing a rational world based on the principles of function and utility evaporating: the ambition of turning state socialism itself into a human design product was also being dashed.'[39]

The much-vaunted Khrushchev kitchen did not become a reality for most Russian women, and throughout the Eastern Bloc women spent more time in queues or hoping that they would find something to buy than engaging in selective consumerism. Technology too ended up in the doldrums, even though—at least in the case of Czechoslovakia and the GDR—there was a pre-existing industrial base and traditions of technological innovation. Thanks to central control and the fear of upsetting the status quo, new product development was stifled in favour of the continued manufacture of existing ones, and 'shortcomings in the system of planning and innovation' meant that, despite some notable successes in laser technologies or space optics, and despite the existence of what historians of technology call a 'consumption junction' (when consum-ers are able to make choices between competing technologies), the GDR suffered from a conflict between political decision making and technological innovation.[40] And the focus on heavy industry and 'socialist labour' meant that pollution was endemic, the environment was dangerously degraded (even before the Chernobyl accident, which further damaged the Soviet regime's reputation), and agriculture was seriously neglected, with the result that severe food shortages were common. Many people relied on their allotments and on their family links to the countryside for a supply of fresh food.[41]

The more the turn to consumerism failed, the more the regimes turned to celebrating the cult of anti-fascism, which was deliberately fostered as a social glue. As Roger Markwick notes, in the USSR the cult of the Great Patriotic War really took off only in

[39] Crowley, 'Thaw Modern', 151.

[40] Raymond G. Stokes, *Constructing Socialism: Technology and Change in East Germany 1945–1990* (Baltimore, MD: Johns Hopkins University Press, 2000). See also Stokes, 'Plastics and the New Society: The German Democratic Republic in the 1950s and 1960s', in Susan E. Reid and David Crowley (eds), *Style and Socialism: Modernity and Material Culture in Post-War Eastern Europe* (Oxford: Berg, 2000), 65–80, for the argument that there was a vicious circle as poor quality goods left workers unmotivated, meaning they produced inferior consumer and producer goods. On the 'consumption junction', see Karin Zachmann, 'A Socialist Consumption Junction: Debating the Mechanization of Housework in East Germany, 1956–1957', *Technology and Culture* 43:1 (2002), 73–99.

[41] For an example of the role played by alcohol, see Narcis Tulbure, 'Drink, Leisure, and the Second Economy in Socialist Romania', in David Crowley and Susan E. Reid (eds), *Pleasures in Socialism: Leisure and Luxury in the Eastern Bloc* (Evanston, IL: Northwestern University Press, 2010), 259–81.

the mid-1960s. And the collective memory being constructed by the regimes was highly selective, with its emphasis on the communist resistance and the people's overthrow of fascism. 'In virtually every site of Nazi terror', Mary Fulbrook reminds us, 'the fact that many victims were Jewish was disproportionately underemphasised.' Indeed,

> the empathy aroused by the concentration camp memorials in the GDR was abused, instrumentalized, distorted. It was deployed, not to open the way for an illumination of the past in all its fullness and contradiction, but rather to legitimize the present, to instil a sense of political commitment that was to be beyond valid questioning.[42]

This 'enforced consensus', if one can use this paradoxical term, meant that the official line was propagated all the harder as the conditions which helped this ideology to function increasingly disappeared: 'From a genuine fear of "fascists", "class enemies", and the like in the early years there developed a ritualised rhetoric or demonology, in which very few can have really believed any more.'[43] Still, anti-fascism continued to hold a powerful place in the minds of the regimes' citizens, even if fewer and fewer of them each year could remember the glorious days of 1945. No wonder that dark humour, especially at the expense of the *nomenklatura* and the police, became rife.[44]

At the same time, the communist regimes increasingly turned to nationalism. It is often assumed that nationalism emerged after 1989 to fill the political vacuum opened up by the demise of communism. In fact, the opposite is the case: nationalism did not cause the collapse of communism (which owed more to structural defects in the system) but it was one contributory factor. The fact that it already existed allowed nationalism rapidly to become the chief beneficiary of communism's collapse. The wars of Yugoslav succession are the clearest case of nationalism's successful rise, which took place despite the Party's official reproach, but secessionist movements in Chechnya and other areas of Russia and the CIS are direct heirs to the dangerous policy of using nationalism on a 'regional' basis while condemning it at the federal level of the Soviet Union.[45] At this policy's most extreme, in Romania, where the communist party had a tiny indigenous base until after World War II, nationalism, and by the 1970s and 1980s, national socialism in the strict sense (Norman Manea calls it 'camouflaged fascism'[46]), was cynically employed by a regime that had nothing else up its sleeve to appeal to the population in

---

[42] Mary Fulbrook, *German National Identity after the Holocaust* (Cambridge: Polity Press, 1999), 32, 33–4.

[43] Mary Fulbrook, *Anatomy of a Dictatorship: Inside the GDR 1949–1989* (Oxford: Oxford University Press, 1995), 27.

[44] See, for a famous example, Milan Kundera, *The Joke* (London: Faber and Faber, 1992).

[45] Rogers Brubaker, *Nationalism Reframed: Nationhood and the National Question in the New Europe* (Cambridge: Cambridge University Press, 1996), ch. 2; Yuri Slezkine, 'The USSR as a Communal Apartment: or How a Socialist State Promoted Ethnic Particularism', *Slavic Review* 53:2 (1994), 414–52. There are of course other factors that led to the wars in Yugoslavia and Chechnya, most notably historical memories of World War II and Tsarism. But these memories had been revived and instrumentalized, albeit often without official approval, since the late 1970s.

[46] Norman Manea, *On Clowns: The Dictator and the Artist* (London: Faber and Faber, 1994), 121.

the region least attracted to the lessons of 'antifascism' and communist internationalism. That it was backed up by intellectuals—many of whom went on to post-communist careers as radical right populists—is unsurprising in a country where the interwar intellectual elite was characterized by remarkably high and widely accepted levels of antisemitism and violent ultra-nationalism.[47]

Yet although the communist regimes left no sphere of life untouched, for most ordinary people their main problem under this late stage of stagnation was obtaining basic necessities, which is why so many turned to the black market and to their allotments. As Madarász rightly notes, although there was no shortage of grounds for tension between regime and society, 'To a mother searching for fresh fruit and vegetables for her children, small, everyday problems were of more immediate importance than the fundamental ones such as the undemocratic election process.'[48] East Germany was more than just a terror state, as recent research shows, with its focus on material culture, domestic interiors, visual culture, style, and design—all topics which deal with the paradox of 'privacy in an enclosed state'.[49] Even though the key geopolitical site occupied by the GDR during the Cold War remains central to the literature, and more scholarly and popular literature has been written on the Stasi than on any other aspect of the regime, the image of the mother hunting for food for her children suggests that the struggles of daily life occupied people's time more than any other consideration.[50]

Thus, in the late period of the Cold War (post-1968), we see a growing sense of inertia, or rather a grudging acceptance of one's inability to change the situation, following the crushing of the Prague Spring. This sense of accommodation was famously embodied in Havel's image of a greengrocer displaying the slogan 'Workers of the world, unite!' in his shop: Havel argued that the man had never given the meaning of the slogan a second thought, but displayed it because he had been given it by the enterprise headquarters, because that was how things had always been, and because he could be in trouble for not displaying it. 'It is', wrote Havel, 'one of the thousands of details that guarantee him a relatively tranquil life "in harmony with society", as they say.'[51] This then was the period of 'normalization', a term whose 'normalness' belies the fact that even the regimes did not really know what it meant.

[47] Brindusa Palade, 'The Romanian Utopia: The Role of the Intelligentsia in the Communist Implementation of a New Human Paradigm', *Southeast European and Black Sea Studies* 2:2 (2002), 93–100; Vladimir Tismaneanu, 'Understanding National Stalinism: Reflections on Ceauşescu's Socialism', *Communist and Post-Communist Studies* 32:2 (1999), 155–73; Katherine Verdery, 'Nationalism and National Sentiment in Post-socialist Romania', *Slavic Review* 52:2 (1993), 179–203. For background to Ceauşescu's ultra-nationalism, see Dragoş Petrescu, 'Community-Building and Identity Politics in Gheorghiu-Dej's Romania, 1956–64', in Vladimir Tismaneanu (ed.), *Stalinism Revisited: The Establishment of Communist Regimes in East-Central Europe* (Budapest: CEU Press, 2009), 401–22.

[48] Madarász, *Conflict and Compromise*, 142–3.

[49] The title of Betts' introduction to *Within Walls*, 1–18.

[50] Esther von Richtofen, *Bringing Culture to the Masses: Control, Compromise and Participation in the GDR* (New York: Berghahn Books, 2009); Patrick Major, *Behind the Berlin Wall: East Germany and the Frontiers of Power* (Oxford: Oxford University Press, 2010).

[51] Havel, 'The Power of the Powerless', 41.

Following the 1968 Warsaw Pact invasion of Prague, *normalizace* became the watch-word in Czechoslovakia, even among ordinary citizens. But as Paulina Bren notes, the fact that ordinary people used the term suggests that everything and yet nothing was normal after the Prague Spring. Still, the irony with which the word was initially used itself became normalized, as people increasingly used it 'to describe the society in which they now found themselves living and working'. It is also perhaps the apparent obvious-ness of this 'normalization' that accounts for the lack of scholarship on late commu-nism.[52] While work published at the time focused on the emergence of dissidents and organized dissent in groups such as Charter 77 in Czechoslovakia, the Prenzlauer Berg writers' groups in East Berlin, or Solidarity in Poland—which was far more widely known and politically effective[53]—this trend meant continuing to overlook most peo-ple's experience of daily reality under communism. Havel was right to say in 1975 that 'today's regime rests solely on the ruling minority's instinct of self-preservation and on the fear of the ruled majority', but that does not account for how people coped in this period of 'order without life'.[54]

Most people may not have been actively involved in dissident movements, but recent studies suggest that citizens became adept at 'playing the system', finding ways not only of adapting themselves to it that did not mean relinquishing all autonomy, but also get-ting the regime to respond to their demands. In the GDR, for example, while the state reached deeply into every sphere of life, it could not control everything. In fact, one can argue that the very attempt to control totally necessarily failed, inadvertently creating new zones of autonomy.[55] It seems unlikely, but one of the places where people felt most free from surveillance was in the cafés and bowling alley of the Palace of the Republic, the building which also housed the East German parliament.[56] Besides, until the end, the regime retained significant levels of support, precisely for those things the loss of which *Ossis* lamented after 1989: welfare, childcare, education, cheaply available culture

---

[52] Paulina Bren, *The Greengrocer and His TV: The Culture of Communism after the 1968 Prague Spring* (Ithaca, NY: Cornell University Press, 2010), 3.

[53] Padraic Kenney, *A Carnival of Revolution: Central Europe 1989* (Princeton, NJ: Princeton University Press, 2002). More specifically, see Robert von Hallberg (ed.), *Literary Intellectuals and the Dissolution of the State: Professionalism and Conformity in the GDR* (Chicago, IL: University of Chicago Press, 1996); Christian Joppke, *East German Dissidents and the Revolution of 1989: Social Movement in a Leninist Regime* (New York: New York University Press, 1994); John C. Torpey, *Intellectuals, Socialism, and Dissent: East German Opposition and Its Legacy* (Minneapolis, MN: University of Minnesota Press, 1995); David Ost, *Solidarity and the Politics of Anti-Politics: Opposition and Reform in Poland since 1968* (Philadelphia, PA: Temple University Press, 1990); Jouni Järvinen, *Normalization and Charter 77: Violence, Commitment and Resistance in Czechoslovakia* (Helsinki: Kikimora, 2009).

[54] Havel, 'Letter to Dr Gustáv Husák', in *Living in Truth*, 33.

[55] Jan Palmowski, *Inventing a Socialist Nation: Heimat and the Politics of Everyday Life in the GDR, 1945–1990* (Cambridge: Cambridge University Press, 2009), 9–10.

[56] Brian Ladd, *The Ghosts of Berlin: Confronting German History in the Urban Landscape* (Chicago, IL: University of Chicago Press, 1997), 58–9. In the absence of a 'civil society', perhaps there were few alternative places to meet. In an act of historical vandalism, the *Palast der Republik* was finally demolished between 2006 and 2008, to be replaced by a replica of the Imperial Palace that stood on the site until after World War II.

(the *Lumpenproletariat*, or underclass, was far smaller in communist Eastern Europe than in, say, the UK). It is salutary to be reminded that in struggling to walk a tightrope between buying people off with a reasonable standard of living but managing consumers' expectations, Brezhnev's policies contributed in no small measure to the survival of the USSR for another twenty-five years.[57] No one has put this ambivalence better than Alexei Yurchak, with his anthropologist's sensitivity to the structures of power and to people's emotional and personal encounters with them:

> Dichotomies such as oppression and resistance, truth and lies, official culture and unofficial culture, the state and the people, public self and private self overlook the complex meanings, values, ideals, and realities that constituted the Soviet system.... For great numbers of Soviet citizens, many of the fundamental values, ideals, and realities of socialism were of genuine importance, despite the fact that many of their everyday practices routinely reinterpreted the announced norms and rules of the socialist state.[58]

The Last Communist Generation

As Yurchak's analysis indicates, the last Soviet generation—and I think we can extend this analysis to include the last years of communism in Eastern Europe as a whole—existed both within and without the mental and physical spaces created by communism. Formal participation in the regime went hand in hand with its rejection and mental self-exclusion, paradoxical as that may seem. As with Yurchak's description of Soviet citizens acting 'as if' they accepted the regime, its rituals, and its expectations—attending Komsomol meetings, for example, but acting out the rituals on a 'pro forma' basis in order then to be better able to conduct other, meaningful work[59]—so citizens in the GDR seem to have done likewise. Even more striking, the East German regime has been described as acting 'as if' its citizens' formal assertions of loyalty were truthful, a claim which suggests some tension between the cynical clinging on to power and the aspiration, which none of the communist states ever abandoned, of creating new socialist human beings.[60] As Tony Judt nicely put it, the late-era communist regimes existed on the basis of the unspoken rule: 'we pretend to conform and you pretend to believe us.'[61]

For those who were children during the last decade or so of communist rule, looking back confirms many of Yurchak's claims, though perhaps not at the level of a child's consciousness. The historian Anton Weiss-Wendt, for example, who grew up in the small

---

[57] Reid, 'Cold War in the Kitchen', 252.

[58] Alexei Yurchak, *Everything Was Forever, until It Was No more: The Last Soviet Generation* (Princeton, NJ: Princeton University Press, 2006), 283.

[59] Ibid., 93.

[60] Palmowski, *Inventing a Socialist Nation*, 12.

[61] Tony Judt, *The Memory Chalet* (London: William Heinemann, 2010), 105.

town of Valdai, between Moscow and Leningrad, writes of the food shortages, the ingenuity his parents displayed in obtaining food and the rarely available shoddy goods, the dreariness of Soviet TV, the dull uniformity of Soviet apartments and of people's aspirations. But he also writes of children's play and youngsters' pranks, of collecting stamps, coins, and toy soldiers, and of friendships, in a universalizing manner. Still, as a young teenager Weiss-Wendt quickly became aware of the limits of such mischievousness. When he daubed anarchy signs around the school, Weiss-Wendt was lucky not to be denounced by his classmates to the School Director, who 'was beside herself with rage', and he concludes that schoolchildren only challenged authority 'insofar as the extremity of youth goes. In all other respects, the Soviet youth was a mere replica of the larger socialist society'. In the Pioneers, the children 'breathed ideology, without realizing', even if this did not preclude a fascination with heavy metal.[62]

In a way that a child could only have been dimly aware, if at all, this period of late communism is when we also witness the rise to prominence of new opposition movements, which gradually re-emerged following the ruthless suppressions of the 1950s and 1960s. But up until the last minute, even self-styled dissidents could hardly imagine the demise of the system they fought against. Miklós Haraszti went so far as to suggest that in the 'textbook model of a pacified post-Stalinist neocolony' that was Hungary, dissidents had become useful to the state: 'if dissidents have a place at all, that place is outside official culture, even if they are not in prison', he wrote. 'But in their isolation they have become predictable, and their numbers can be planned for systematically.'[63] Although Haraszti meant his book 'to be a denial of its own deliberate exaggerations', its pessimism was quite understandable.[64] It certainly had the merit of reminding people that a heroic model of dissidents bringing down the regimes can only ever be part of the story.

Besides, this image of 'inner emigration' or, in Havel's terms, a split between public compliance and 'living in truth', has been challenged. Bren suggests that, in late communism, 'Ordinary citizens did not, as has been argued so often, lead lives bifurcated by clear-cut public and private realms: a compliant public mask at work and a liberated self at home.' Rather, the reality was far more complex than this neat binary division would have us believe.[65] For example, when the Czechoslovak regime promoted the vision of 'self-realization' (*seberealizace*) and 'self-actualization' (*sebeaktualizace*) in the 1980s, many ordinary people chose to counter the 'the drabness of normalization' by choosing 'to self-realize as consumers'.[66] In other words, many acts of everyday life could

---

[62] Anton Weiss-Wendt, *Small Town Russia: Childhood Memories of the Final Soviet Decade* (Gainesville, FL: Florida Academic Press, 2010), 98, 103, 106 and ch. 14.

[63] Miklós Haraszti, *The Velvet Prison: Artists under State Socialism* (London: I.B. Tauris, 1988), 158, 161. The book was published in France in 1983 and in *samizdat* in Hungary in 1986.

[64] Haraszti, *The Velvet Prison*, 162.

[65] Bren, *The Greengrocer and His TV*, 7.

[66] Ibid., 189. See also Bren, 'Mirror, Mirror, on the Wall... Is the West the Fairest of Them All? Czechoslovak Normalization and Its (Dis)Contents', *Kritika: Explorations in Russian and Eurasian History* 9:4 (2008), 831–54.

be both 'system-critical and system-sustaining', to use Paul Betts's helpful formulation.[67] For all their differences, when one compares Bren's analysis with the recollections of Yurchak and Weiss-Wendt, one can see many commonalities in daily life across the Eastern Bloc, with formal conformity and gradually developing spheres of autonomy. Nevertheless, Prague in the 1970s and 1980s was not the same as Moscow, Bucharest, or 'small town Russia', and certainly not the same as Sarajevo, Dubrovnik, or Ljubljana, which suffered the paradoxical fate that the most open variety of communism was succeeded by the most vicious variety of post-communist ethno-nationalism.[68]

The exceptions to this image of a greying elite and an emerging countercultural scene are Romania and Albania, combining massive repression and poverty with a powerful police state. Outside of the Warsaw Pact and, in the case of Albania, allied to China between 1961 and 1978, the two countries may have been feted by the West for their independent stance vis-à-vis Moscow, but they adopted this position only to insist all the more strongly on their domestic Stalinist credentials.[69] With the absurd range of limitations and restrictions placed on people's lives, from the registration of typewriters to the required attendance at rallies and vast networks of informers and blackmailers, the state not only intruded unavoidably into everyday life but—with Hoxha and Ceaușescu having turned their countries into personal fiefdoms—many people were forced to turn to formal criminality simply in order to survive. As Vladimir Tismaneanu writes, Ceaușescu's Romania was

> a closed society, characterized by repression in all areas of human existence: property restrictions, hard labour and low wages, lack of freedom of movement, bureaucratic hurdles against emigration, violations of national minorities' rights, contempt for religious beliefs and persecution of religious practices, dramatic economic austerity, consistent cultural censorship, a crackdown on all dissenting views, and an all-embracing cult surrounding the president and his family that took its toll on the population's morale.[70]

Conclusion: Remembering Communism

To focus on everyday life under communism might seem frivolous at first glance. But if the communist states tried to legitimize themselves by encouraging consumerism, then the events of 1989 can to some extent be seen as 'consumerist revolutions'. For all the intellectual high-mindedness of the opposition, with its talk of human rights, it is striking—as news reports from the period attest—that for most East Germans, their first

[67] Betts, *Within Walls*, 226. Betts is here talking about GDR domestic photography of the 1970s and 1980s.

[68] See Cathie Carmichael's chapter below.

[69] For an excellent fictionalized account of Albanian–Sino–Soviet relations, see Ismail Kadare, *The Concert* (New York: Arcade Publishing, 1998).

[70] Vladimir Tismaneanu, *Stalinism for All Seasons: A Political History of Romanian Communism* (Berkeley, CA: University of California Press, 2003), 216.

taste of freedom meant the freedom to shop. But that in itself should not be seen as frivolous either: the ease with which Western Europeans can buy food and clothes, or
choose what style of jeans or what colour hair dye to buy, is so taken for granted that it is
often hard to grasp what it might mean were such privileges to disappear. Those who
had never enjoyed them were not engaging in trivialities by gawping at the shop fronts
on Kurfürstendamm. Yet after the euphoria, the true price of Western consumerism
soon became obvious and 'normal' life intervened yet again. Much of the history of post-
communism has been a confused story of finding stable alternatives to either 'actually
existing socialism' on the one hand and bandit capitalism on the other. The return to
power of one-party right-wing rule in Hungary in late 2010 shows that, for all the successes in the region, the correct formula has still not been found.

As the phenomenon of *Ostalgie* (nostalgia for the East, *Ost*) reminds us, some people
undoubtedly yearn for 'the static life of the communist present', which was supposedly
frozen in time. The fact that this German term is so widely used suggests that this is not
merely a response to the GDR being 'colonised' by the more powerful other Germany, but
a widespread 'homesickness' for lost markers of the quotidian. In the case of Romania,
which was untouched by the thaw of *glasnost* and *perestroika*, the fear of change was especially strong after 1989, but the communist years offered little by way of comforting memories. The result was confusion and, perhaps more so than elsewhere in the region (at
least until the rise of the populist radical right in post-financial crisis Hungary), the clearest expression of what Tismaneanu aptly called 'fantasies of salvation'.[71] But elsewhere,
Ostalgie has, ironically, become big business, as *Ostalikers* (practitioners of *Ostalgie*) end-
lessly recreate the communist regimes in a western-style, consumerist frenzy. *Ostalgie*,
Daphne Berdahl writes, 'in its many manifestations, meanings, and practices, has become
a highly visible cultural phenomenon in the actually existing post-Socialist landscape'.[72]

The phenomenon should not be condescendingly dismissed as an inevitable result of
'post-totalitarian blues', as the tough reality of life under capitalism has sunk in. Very few
who lived under communism miss the regimes. What they tend to recall through rose-
tinted spectacles are the things that people in general in late modernity tend to romanti-
cize: home, childhood, certain foodstuffs, clothes, music, the domestic and the
commonplace, the small anchors of everyday existence.[73] In other words, central to

---

[71] Oana Popescu-Sandu, '"Let's All Freeze Up Until 2100 or So": Nostalgic Directions in Post-
Communist Romania', in Maria Todorova and Zsuzsa Gille (eds), *Post-Communist Nostalgia* (New
York: Berghahn Books, 2010), 113–25. On 'fantasies of salvation', see Vladimir Tismaneanu's, Michael
Shafir's and D. Stone's ('Memory Wars') chapters in this volume.
[72] Daphne Berdahl, '*Good Bye Lenin!* Aufwiedersehen GDR: On the Social Life of Socialism', in
Todorova and Gille (eds), *Post-Communist Nostalgia*, 177–89, esp. 185–6.
[73] Betts, *Within Walls*, 229–30. See also Betts, 'Remembrance of Things Past: Nostalgia in West and
East Germany, 1980–2000', in Paul Betts and Greg Eghigian (eds), *Pain and Prosperity: Reconsidering
Twentieth-Century German History* (Stanford, CA: Stanford University Press, 2003), 178–207; Betts,
'The Twilight of the Idols: East German Memory and Material Culture', *Journal of Modern History* 73:2
(2000), 731–65; Daphne Berdahl, '(N)ostalgie for the Present: Memory, Longing, and East German
Things', *Ethnos* 64:2 (1999), 192–211. On nostalgia, see Peter Fritzsche, 'How Nostalgia Narrates
Modernity', in Alon Confino and Peter Fritzsche (eds), *The Work of Memory: New Directions in the
Study of German Society and Culture* (Urbana, IL: University of Illinois Press, 2002), 62–85.

post-communist memory politics is the idealized memory of 'normal life' under the communist regimes. Daily life under communism was hard, and by the 1980s it was harder than those who grew up in Western Europe could imagine. But while it is correct to remember communism in terms of terror, bleakness, and the suppression of personal liberty, Havel's concept of 'order without life' should be complemented by the existence of 'ordinary life of sorts'.

FURTHER READING

Apor, Balász, Péter Apor and E.A. Rees (eds), *The Sovietization of Eastern Europe: New Perspectives on the Postwar Period* (Washington, DC: New Academia Publishing, 2008).

Betts, Paul, *Within Walls: Private Life in the German Democratic Republic* (Oxford: Oxford University Press, 2010).

Bren, Paulina, *The Greengrocer and His TV: The Culture of Communism after the 1968 Prague Spring* (Ithaca, NY: Cornell University Press, 2010).

Castillo, Greg, *Cold War on the Home Front: The Soft Power of Midcentury Design* (Minneapolis, MN: University of Minnesota Press, 2010).

Crowley, David and Jane Pavitt (eds), *Cold War Modern: Design 1945–1970* (London: V&A Publishing, 2008).

Crowley, David and Susan E. Reid (eds), *Socialist Spaces: Sites of Everyday Life in the Eastern Bloc* (Oxford: Berg, 2002).

Crowley, David and Susan E. Reid (eds), *Pleasures in Socialism: Leisure and Luxury in the Eastern Bloc* (Evanston, IL: Northwestern University Press, 2010).

Oldenziel, Ruth, and Karin Zachmann (eds), *Cold War Kitchen: Americanization, Technology, and European Users* (Cambridge, MA: MIT Press, 2009).

Palmowski, Jan, *Inventing a Socialist Nation: Heimat and the Politics of Everyday Life in the GDR, 1945–1990* (Cambridge: Cambridge University Press, 2009).

Pence, Katherine and Paul Betts (eds), *Socialist Modern: East German Everyday Culture and Politics* (Ann Arbor, MI: University of Michigan Press, 2008).

Pittaway, Mark, *Eastern Europe 1939–2000* (London: Arnold, 2004).

Reid, Susan E. and David Crowley (eds), *Style and Socialism: Modernity and Material Culture in Post-War Eastern Europe* (Oxford: Berg, 2000).

Weiss-Wendt, Anton, *Small-Town Russia: Childhood Memories of the Final Soviet Decade* (Gainesville, FL: Florida Academic Press, 2010).

Yurchak, Alexei, *Everything Was Forever, until It Was No More: The Last Soviet Generation* (Princeton, NJ: Princeton University Press, 2006).

CHAPTER 8

....

THE SPECTRE OF AMERICANIZATION: WESTERN EUROPE IN THE AMERICAN CENTURY

....

PHILIPP GASSERT

By 1945, the spectre of Americanization had been haunting Europe for half a century. Starting with the Spanish–American War of 1898, European observers had tried to come to terms with what they increasingly perceived as an 'American menace'. Although some were concerned about an American military threat to European empires, most wrote about *l'américanisation du monde* as a challenge to European civilization.[1] With the US still struggling to establish colonial rule over the Philippine Islands, European observers began framing the 'American challenge' as a cultural and most of all economic threat to national independence. It was in the wake of the 1898 war that the German businessman Ludwig Max Goldberger coined the phrase the 'land of unlimited opportunities'. The British journalist William T. Stead for his part first wrote of what would turn out to be a hallmark term of the twentieth century: 'Americanization'.[2]

From the start European debates about Americanization were not limited to perceptions of US military, economic, and political power. As countless studies on the 'Americanization of Europe' have demonstrated, controversies about the impact of 'America' often served as a stand-in for a more fundamental reckoning with processes of

[1] Augustin Léger, 'L'américanisation du monde', *Le Correspondent* (25 April 1902), 221–53.
[2] Ludwig Max Goldberger, *Das Land der unbegrenzten Möglichkeiten: Beobachtungen über das Wirtschaftsleben der Vereinigten Staaten von Amerika* (Leipzig: F. Fontane, 1903); William T. Stead, *The Americanization of the World, or, the Trend of the Twentieth Century* (London: The Review of Reviews, 1902). Even though it mainly argued for an Anglo-American hegemony, Stead's book was soon translated into French (Paris, 1902) and German (Berlin, 1902). Everywhere the title struck a chord. It can therefore be seen as an anchor of pan-European debate.

modernization.[3] Beginning with the last decade of the nineteenth century, 'America' came to represent something larger. It was taken as a short cut for 'modernity', which can be defined as a social order that is built on mass production, mass consumption, mass culture, and mass politics. The US came to represent 'mass society's' most enduring prototype. As Stead pointed out in 1901, the 'melting' of particular ethnic identities into one new larger whole that allegedly was what was happening to immigrants caught in this 'crucible of nations' was a foreboding of a global trend towards the levelling of national particularities and the homogenization of humankind.[4]

During the interwar period 'Americanization' and 'Americanism' became household terms. The impact of World War I on European visions of America was huge. The US had tipped the balance in favour of the Franco–British alliance. This meant with regard to Weimar Germany that the 1920s 'America' debate was complicated by perceptions of Woodrow Wilson and Versailles peacemaking. Yet in the French and British cases too, transatlantic politics intersected with debates about cultural and economic penetration, when disappointment about the American political withdrawal ran high during the 1920s. Even though the US had temporarily given up on its global political mission, its impact in the fields of trade and culture could not be ignored. During the 1920s, Europeans were obsessed with the Fordist 'production miracle'. They worried about the inroads of Hollywood into European film markets.[5] Jazz, with its African–American roots, acquired the status of a forbidden fruit. This dreaded 'Americanization' now meant the transfer of specific American products and forms of cultural expression into European contexts.[6]

Once again, the debate shifted in the wake of World War II. In the US, Americanization still carried its original meaning of the blending of immigrant cultures into an envisioned 'American main stream'. In Europe as well as in Asia it continued to describe the transfer and import of 'American' cultural and economic ways into foreign contexts. Yet with the 1940s it became also linked to a specific set of US policies. Now, Americanization was no longer an anonymous process of cultural and economic 'penetration' or a stand-in for modernization. It resulted in part from US foreign policy and cultural diplomacy; it became a direct outgrowth of the political and economic hegemony of the US; it grew out of the propaganda wars that Washington was waging in order to win the hearts and minds of West Europeans in its Cold War struggles against the Soviet Union.

---

[3] For a good overview of recent scholarly findings with respect to various countries see Alexander Stephan (ed.), *The Americanization of Europe: Culture, Diplomacy, and Anti-Americanism after 1945* (New York: Berghahn Books, 2006).

[4] Stead, *Americanization*, 147.

[5] Mark Glancy, 'Temporary American Citizens? British Audiences, Hollywood Films and the Threat of Americanization in the 1920s', *Historical Journal of Film, Radio, and Television* 26:4 (2006), 461–84; Thomas J. Saunders, *Hollywood in Berlin: American Cinema and Weimar Germany* (Berkeley, CA: University of California Press, 1994).

[6] Mary Nolan, *Visions of Modernity: American Business and the Modernization of Germany* (New York: Oxford University Press, 1994); Egbert Klautke, *Unbegrenzte Möglichkeiten. 'Amerikanisierung' in Deutschland und Frankreich, 1900–1933* (Stuttgart: Franz Steiner Verlag, 2003).

Therefore, as Axel Schildt has proposed, 'Americanization from below'—that is, the autonomous societal processes of the adaption of American products, institutions, norms, values, icons, and 'ways of life' as part of intercultural transfer processes—was now accompanied by 'Americanization from above'—that is, the specific transatlantic linking of Western Europe to the Atlantic Alliance and North America.[7]

Anyone writing about 'Americanization' thus faces a triple challenge: First, 'Americanization' is not a static term. It obviously is a dynamic concept. Like other such cultural constructs it has a history and it means different things at different times. Second, although in the literal sense Americanization denotes that non-American (i.e. non-US) societies and cultures mimic or become similar to those of the United States, it is impossible to distinguish analytically such transfers (which inevitably go along with adaption processes) from general modernization. Third, not unlike 'modernization', 'Westernization', and 'globalization', Americanization has strong normative connotations. This limits its usefulness as an analytical tool for historians (which is why some have abandoned it altogether[8]). An amorphous fear of Americanization was often used to delegitimize a specific set of policies, or to criticize certain societal developments at home, or do both at the same time. Debates about the changing role of women in society, for example, were often couched in anti-American terms, even though the transformation of gender had little to do with actual influences emanating from the United States. Here, 'America' served as a semiotic tool (or icon) to communicate change, to make it comprehensible to contemporaries, and to argue for or against it. Europeans (and Asians for that matter) often externalized problems of their own by referring to an imagined space they called America.[9]

In the following chapter I will first analyse 'Americanization from above' as a specific set of policies linked to the US acquiring hegemonic status within the Western world beginning in the 1940s and lasting into the 1960s. I will continue in a second part with a discussion of 'Americanization from below', which cannot be delineated as easily as 'official', US government-induced 'Americanization from above'. There have been periods of increased and decreased Americanization 'from below'. It ebbed and flowed throughout the twentieth century. The initial period of sustained Americanization was the 1920s, when American film, music, and automobiles for the first time were conquering Europe. A second heyday of Americanization 'from below' started with the 'American occupation of Britain' and that of continental Europe during and after World War II. It peaked during the 1950s, when Western Europe experienced its breakthrough to consumer society. Young people now had the means and the leisure time to acquire

---

[7] Axel Schildt, 'Americanization', in Detlef Junker (ed.), *The United States and Germany in the Era of the Cold War. A Handbook, vol 1: 1945–1968* (New York: Cambridge University Press, 2004), 635–42.

[8] See for example David W. Ellwood, 'Containing Modernity, Domesticating America in Italy', in Stephan (ed.), *Americanization*, 253–76.

[9] Rob Kroes, 'American Culture in European Metaphors: The West as Will and Conception', in Rob Kroes, *If You've Seen One, You've Seen the Mall: Europeans and American Mass Culture* (Urbana, IL: University of Illinois Press, 1996), 1–42.

American products.[10] The 1950s and 1960s thus became the core period of voluntary Americanization 'from below'.

This postwar boom of Americanization dwindled during the second half of the 1960s. European popular culture was increasingly shaped by other influences, including that of British rock bands like the Rolling Stones and the Beatles, which in the beginning had themselves been affected by US models and who now were in turn influencing American and European musicians. The temporary ebb of Americanization during the 1970s reminds us that because of the criss-crossing of the Atlantic of cultural streams of influence, it often is more helpful to employ a model of circulation rather than conceiving of cultural exchange as a unidirectional experience. Since Europe and America have been in close communication throughout the nineteenth and twentieth centuries, it often is impossible to pinpoint the origins of a particular cultural item. Rather, we should conceive of Americanization as part of a dialogue among the cultures boarding the Atlantic.

Americanization 'from below' then experienced a third heyday during the 1980s and 1990s, when US fast food culture caught on with Europeans, MTV came to be broadcast on European TV channels, African–American rap music inspired European immigrant musicians, the internet led to a transformation of the media environment, and deregulation and privatization became popular models of industrial reorganization that (not unlike the fear of Fordism in the 1920s) were again debated with reference to an alleged Americanization. This third phase of Americanization was soon paralleled by the implosion of communism in Eastern and Central Europe, which gave American ways a new boost in Europe, even though the economic, military, and political hegemony of the United States had by now been seriously eroded. This third face of Americanization 'from below' was in part accompanied by renewed efforts of Americanization 'from above' (witness the role of US advisors in former communist countries) and lasted well into the first decade of the twenty-first century. It seems to have tapered off with recent developments in the Middle East and the further consolidation of the European Union.[11]

In the two final parts of this chapter I will discuss two concepts, which often come up within debates about Americanization. One is Westernization, a term which focuses on the intellectual history of the Western alliance (NATO), and anti-Americanism, which received much attention during the 1960s and 1970s, when leftist European critics of US imperialism were united with their American peers in protesting against the war in Vietnam; or during the 1980s, when the transatlantic peace movement grew increasingly concerned about nuclear weapons and the renewal of East–West tensions during the Reagan administration. More recently, anti-Americanism became a hot potato once again, when the United States and its allies embarked on another experiment in

---

[10]   Axel Schildtand Detlef Siegfried (eds), *Between Marx and Coca-Cola: Youth Cultures in Changing European Societies, 1960–1980* (Oxford: Berghahn Books, 2006).

[11]   Harm G. Schröter, *Americanization of the European Economy: A Compact Survey of American Economic Influence in Europe since the 1880s* (Dordrecht: Springer, 2005), 127–61.

aggressive nation building during the so-called war on terror in Afghanistan and Iraq. Yet at this point, anti-Americanism had changed into a phenomenon that has much more to do with American insecurities about the role of the United States in the world than Europeans defining themselves against a threatening American empire.[12]

FORGING THE AMERICAN CENTURY: AMERICANIZATION FROM ABOVE

When in February 1941 the American journalist and *Times* and *Life* editor Henry R. Luce scolded his isolationist compatriots for not living up to the fact that America was 'the most powerful and most vital nation in the world' and called them into action against German, Italian, and Japanese aggression, he made sure that his vision of an 'American century' was understood as something more profound than outright imperial dominance. Rather, he defined America's global mission as a democratic one, invoking Lincoln: 'of the people, by the people and for the people'. Reminding his audience that 'American jazz, Hollywood movies, American slang, American machines and patented products, are in fact the only thing that every community in the world, from Zanzibar to Hamburg, recognizes in common', America had already become 'the intellectual, scientific, and artistic capital of the world'. Yet this economic and cultural success now needed to be accompanied by the worldwide promotion of 'American ideals'. The latter was understood to be identical with 'all the great principles of Western civilization'. America should not only be the guarantor of private enterprise and open trade, an exporter of technical skills and cultural goods as well as the 'good Samaritan of the entire world', but also the 'powerhouse of the ideals of Freedom and Justice'.[13]

It was this expansive notion of an American Century that formed the core of the Americanization policies 'from above' that the US embarked upon at the end of World War II. Remaking the world according to American visions first of all implied a reordering of the world economy. Picking up where interwar governments (including those of the US) and the League of Nations had failed, the US was now firmly pushing a global free-trade regime. An international monetary system was created at Bretton Woods, with the IMF and the International Bank for Reconstruction and Development (later

---

[12] The recent transatlantic rows over anti-Americanism again underscore that 'Western Europe' obviously is too large a category to generalize about intellectual phenomena such as 'Americanization' that have touched a host of European cultures in specific ways at different times. Within the space limits of this essay I have drawn most of my examples from the British, French, and West German case. Furthermore, in constructing a Western European story about Americanization I needed to focus on easily identifiable general trends at peril of the particular experiences of Italy, the Benelux countries, Scandinavia, and a host of other nations, which all have their own imagined America. Obviously the French, Dutch, etc., views of America do not always conform to a general Western European model.

[13] Henry R. Luce, 'The American Century', reprinted in *Diplomatic History* 23 (1999): 159–71.

World Bank) as institutional anchors.[14] While still a joint venture of the United States, Great Britain, and the British Dominions (especially Canada), Bretton Woods marked the final arrival of American hegemony in the worlds of trade and finance. This American-style liberalization and multilateralization of world trade, however, was hindered by British, Dutch, French, and other imperial preference systems. It also met resistance on the ground in Germany, where things were complicated by the diverging interests of the four occupying powers.[15]

The 1947–8 Marshall Plan thus really made 'American concepts' of an open world economic order a political reality. In part it was a necessary reaction to the enormous economic problems that the huge US trade surplus had created in Europe. In part it was a corollary to the Truman Doctrine and the shift to containment. Yet in no small measure it also was an outgrowth of the liberalization policies, which had become institutionalized through GATT in 1947. The Marshall Plan, with its combination of sticks and carrots, led to a continued commitment of the United States to European economic integration.[16] While France and England first resisted again, the Marshall Plan also provided a basis for the reintegration of the future West Germany into a European and transatlantic (soon to be called 'Western') trade sphere. Although Germany was not the main beneficiary of Marshall Plan aid, the integration of its huge economic potential into the Western European economy through the Marshall Plan appealed to internationally experienced exile politicians such as Jean Monnet, who had been exposed to American models of economic reorganization while working in the United States during World War II. The Marshall Plan thus became a crucial first step towards European economic organizations through OECD and ECSC. Thus, European integration could be in part labelled an outgrowth of Americanization.[17]

The Marshall Plan also provided for a more specific form of Americanization through the transfer ('export') of American expertise, technology, and goods.[18] It also helped finance American trade with Europe. Therefore, it was popular with American entrepreneurs and politicians who feared the effects of a postwar depression. Yet these Americans goods and investments were eagerly sought by Europeans as well, who needed to reconstruct their war-torn infrastructure. West Europeans understood that without American machinery, trucks, technology, and most importantly know-how their economies would face severe difficulties in climbing back onto the path of

---

[14] Harold James, *International Monetary Cooperation since Bretton Woods* (New York: Oxford University Press, 1996).

[15] Volker R. Berghahn, *The Americanisation of West German Industry 1945–1973* (Cambridge: Cambridge University Press, 1986).

[16] David W. Ellwood, *Rebuilding Europe: Western Europe, America, and Postwar Reconstruction* (London: Longmans, 1992); Martin A. Schain, *Marshall Plan Fifty Years After* (Houndmills: Palgrave, 2001).

[17] Peter Duignan and L.H. Gann, *The Rebirth of the West: The Americanization of the Democratic World, 1945–1958* (Cambridge: Blackwell, 1992), 336–64.

[18] Matthias Kipping and Ove Bjarnar (eds), *The Americanisation of European Business: The Marshall Plan and the Transfer of US Management Models* (London: Routledge, 1998).

economic growth. Inevitably, however, Europeans were apprehensive when it came to symbolically charged imports such as Hollywood movies, jeans, and Coca-Cola. As Richard Kuisel has argued, during the 1940s and 1950s French industrialists eagerly embraced new American management and marketing methods. Yet most French, prodded by left-wing and communist politicians as well as by conservative defenders of 'Frenchness', were much less eager to accept American-style modernization when it came to popular culture and products geared towards conspicuous consumption.[19]

This 'Americanization from above' was by no means limited to economic expansion and trade liberalization. Starting in World War II, American politicians and diplomats also wanted to make sure that (in Luce's words) America was recognized as 'the powerhouse of the ideals of Freedom and Justice'.[20] The American Office of War Information (OWI), despite its origins in domestic propaganda, soon went beyond trying to convince Americans of the necessity of the war effort in Europe and Asia. After the landing of American troops in Britain in 1942 it also established a small reference library in London and financed travelling exhibitions to educate Britons about American life.[21] This was the kernel of a host of similar such programmes, which were later run throughout Western Europe, when during the Cold War the US government campaigned to immunize West Europeans against communism.[22] The idea was that increasing living standards and promoting economic recovery would not be enough. Western Europe would have to be made 'safe for democracy' by co-opting its elites. Through enrolling the next generation of leaders in transatlantic 'exchange' programmes (which in terms of the information flow were meant to be one-way streets), Europeans would learn 'how things were done, and why'.[23]

Fulbright became the institutional backbone of this cultural Americanization 'from above'. In its first year of operation in Britain, 257 American professors, teachers, and students were sent to Britain, whereas 237 Britons went to the US.[24] Many thousands would follow during the next two decades. Although Fulbright agreements were concluded with Asian countries, too, the programme was heavily tilted towards transatlantic exchange. American Fulbright grantees were expected to lecture Europeans on the history and culture of the United States, something few European students had been exposed to before. In turn, the European exchange personnel would study or teach at American universities in order to familiarize themselves with American-style democracy and 'democratic

---

[19] Richard Kuisel, *Seducing the French: The Dilemma of Americanization* (Berkeley, CA: University of California Press, 1993); see also Brian Angus Mckenzie, *Remaking France: Americanization, Public Diplomacy, and the Marshall Plan* (New York: Berghahn, 2005).

[20] Luce, 'American Century', 171.

[21] Hugh Wilford, 'Britain: In Between', in Stephan (ed.), *Americanization*, 23–43.

[22] See Nils Arne Sørensen and Klaus Petersen, 'Ameri-Danes and Pro-American Anti-Americans: Cultural Americanization and Anti-Americanism in Denmark After 1945', in Stephan (ed.), *Americanization*, 115–46, here 117–18.

[23] Quoted in Richard Pells, *Not Like Us: How Europeans Have Loved, Hated, and Transformed American Culture since World War II* (New York: Basic Books, 1997), 55.

[24] Wilford, 'Britain', 24.

methods' of teaching. Many came back as 'American Studies' professors, a new trans-disciplinary subject that was heavily underwritten by US government money and became slowly institutionalized at European universities.[25] Yet while Fulbright and the exchanges authorized under the 1948 Smith-Mundt Act clearly served as an instrument of the American offensive against the Soviet Union, it soon exported American dissent over racial discrimination and the Vietnam war to European colleges and universities.

One particular and sustained Americanization effort 'from above' was taking place in West Germany and Austria. Only here did the US have the feet on the ground and the institutional wherewithal to carry out a large-scale programme of the re-education, reorientation, and democratization of a European society.[26] This attempted transformation of West Germany into a 'little America' stretched from the de-cartelization of German industry (trust-busting after all was a time-honoured tradition of progressive US regulatory regimes, and the concentration of German industry was seen as one of the root causes of the failure of the Weimar Republic),[27] to the democratization of the political system, the liberalization of the public sphere, to the de-Nazification of individual Germans. Yet as the fruitless efforts to remake the German educational system (to mention one highly contentious example[28]) demonstrate, the US military's approach was inherently flawed. Imposing democracy 'from above' is tricky, especially if it is being carried out by a hierarchical and inherently undemocratic institution.

In most of Western Europe, Americanization 'from above' was limited to the immediate postwar period. After a new transatlantic and global institutional network had been created in the 1940s and 1950s, and with European economies back on track in the 1950s, the need to actively Americanize Europe withered away. This holds true for Germany too, where US democratization and Americanization 'from above' came to an end by the mid-1950s, after West Germany had regained its full sovereignty. While these earlier Americanization efforts may not have been as unsuccessful as critics have claimed, the ambivalent experiences of the US Army in Germany and Austria demonstrate that even under the best conditions 'Americanzation from above' faces severe limits. People can resist hegemonic efforts simply by walking away. This even holds true for the media, where Germans, because of their own traditions, were more drawn to the British (BBC) statist model than to the American, private one.[29] More successful were those

[25] Winfried Fluck, 'Inside and Outside: What Kind of Knowledge Do We Need? A Response to the Presidential Address', *American Quarterly* 59:1 (2007), 23–32.

[26] On Austria, see Reinhold Wagnleitner, *Coca-Colonization and the Cold War: The Cultural Mission of the United States in Austria after the Second World War* (Chapel Hill, NY: University of North Carolina Press, 1994); on Germany, see the numerous contributions in Junker (ed.), *United States and Germany*.

[27] Berghahn, *Americanisation of West German Industry*.

[28] James F. Tent, *Mission on the Rhine: Reeducation and Denazification in American-Occupied Germany* (Chicago, IL: University of Chicago Press, 1982).

[29] Christina von Hodenberg and Philipp Gassert, 'Media: Government versus Market', in Christof Mauch and Kiran Patel (eds), *The United States and Germany during the Twentieth Century: Competition and Convergence* (New York: Cambridge University Press, 2010), 234.

programmes that co-opted local elites. Here, as in the case of France, Great Britain, the Netherlands, and other European countries, exchange programmes did have an impact, as did the famous 'America houses' (i.e. American cultural centres and libraries) that sprang up throughout Germany. In all of these cases, however, Americanization entailed a conscious effort on the part of the Americanized. In the final analysis, the decision was theirs, what to pick and to choose from American programmes and products.

THE AMERICAN CENTURY TAKES ITS COURSE: AMERICANIZATION FROM BELOW

While Americanization 'from above' produced mixed records, the voluntary appropriation of American popular culture, lifestyles, and methods (Americanization 'from below') turned out to be a more durable phenomenon. When American GIs marched across Europe in 1944, but even before, starting with the 'American occupation of Britain', they brought with them habits that were soon to be emulated by young people all across Europe.[30] Popular American musical tunes, mostly swing, which in continental Europe had existed only in illegality during World War II, could now be heard from radios and corner bars that were frequented by American soldiers and local youth (frequently female). Obviously, by 1945 American film, music, and dance were not unknown to Europeans. Rather, already during the 1920s the African–American dancer and singer Josephine Baker had been revered and bedevilled. Hollywood had made its presence felt.[31] Even in Nazi Germany, American movies (sometimes pirated copies) were clandestinely shown almost until the end.[32]

Therefore, cultural Americanization 'from below' had a history in 1945. In that sense, the postwar decades continued where the 1920s had left off. As in the interwar period, youth and particularly working-class youth provided the main entry point for American popular culture. Like their American peers, young Europeans flocked to movie houses to watch Bill Haley's *Rock around the Clock*. They idolized Elvis Presley, Marlon Brando (*The Wilde One*), and James Dean (*Rebel without a Cause*). Images proliferated of male teenagers, clad in jeans, who were doing their best to use American slang expressions, or drove motor cycles, seemingly re-enacting what they had seen on screen in American movies. The release of *Blackboard Jungle*, which had caused youth riots in American cities, was dutifully accompanied by similar such phenomena in Britain, West Germany, and other parts of continental Europe.[33] In addition, the style of the American rebel

---

[30] David Reynolds, *Rich Relations: The American Occupation of Britain, 1942–1945* (London: HarperCollins, 1995).

[31] Frank Costigliola, *Awkward Dominion: American Political, Economic, and Cultural Relations with Europe, 1919–1933* (Ithaca, NY: Cornell University Press, 1984), 167.

[32] Michael Kater, *Different Drummers: Jazz in the Culture of Nazi Germany* (New York: Oxford University Press, 1992).

[33] Wilford, 'Britain', 32.

movies caught on. For example it was copied in German films such as *Die Halbstarken* (1956), whose main actor Horst Buchholz was billed as Germany's answer to James Dean.[34]

Dress was central to perceptions of an Americanized youth culture. As Uta Poiger, Kaspar Maase, and others have shown (again with respect to Germany) the 'shocking fashions', especially of female rock 'n' roll fans, made headlines east and west of the Iron Curtain. Reports on young male delinquents in communist East Germany, for example, featured girls with tight pants. Here, as in other parts of Europe, norms of female respectability and sexual passivity were allegedly being undermined by conspicuous dress codes and 'casual' behaviour. In Western Europe, the impact of US popular music as a perceived challenge to established order was further aggravated by class divisions. Upper middle-class kids listening to cool jazz did not endear themselves to their parents. Yet this form of self-Americanization 'from below' was seldom couched in the same alarmist terms as reports about the craze of lower class children letting loose to the tunes of rock 'n' roll. While similar debates and distinctions could be observed within the United States too, Europeans framed their coming to terms with a new mass consumer and youth culture as an unwelcome import from abroad.[35]

Predictably, this dreaded cultural Americanization led to charges that US popular culture was undermining 'European civilization'. All over Western Europe, critics made American imports responsible for youth not willing to conform to established standards and traditions. As had happened during the 1920s, European intellectuals perceived American influences as threatening to high cultural standards. Whether it was William Hoggart in Britain, who despised American 'gangster-fiction' as a form of pornography,[36] Walter Abendroth in West Germany, who compared the film and jazz craze of adolescents to the unleashing of hysteric mobs by the Nazis,[37] or Simone de Beauvoir and Jean-Paul Sartre in France who lamented the commercialization of life,[38] there was a strong sense among cultural critics that American-style consumer culture was leading to unwelcome social and political consequences and the 'end of Europe as we know it'.

This debate about 'Americanization from below' was not limited to youth and consumer culture. Another instance of voluntary Americanization through societal means was the adaption of American management methods, which was often furthered by direct investments of US firms in Europe. At their peak during the 1950s and 1960s, US corporations were responsible for about half of all foreign investments in the world.[39] It

---

[34] Uta Poiger, *Jazz, Rock, and Rebels: Cold War Politics and American Culture in a Divided Germany* (Berkeley, CA: University of California Press, 2000), 103.

[35] Petra Goedde, 'The Globalization of American Culture', in Karen Halttunen (ed.), *Blackwell Companion of American Cultural History* (New York: Blackwell, 2008), 246–62.

[36] Wilford, 'Britain', 32.

[37] Poiger, *Jazz, Rock, and Rebels*, 95.

[38] Richard J. Golsan, 'From French Anti-Americanism and Americanization to the "American Enemy"?', in Stephan (ed.), *Americanization*, 44–68, here 53.

[39] Lewis D. Solomon, *Multinational Corporations and the Emerging World Order* (Port Washington, NY: Kennikat Press, 1978), 9–12.

was during this heyday of American economic penetration—which would ebb during the 1970s—that the first business schools were founded in Europe, such as INSEAD near Paris.[40] While there is considerable debate regarding to what extent the transformation of European management and retailing cultures can be labelled 'Americanization',[41] invoking the American example was a strategy to push reforms on the shop floor and to improve the performance of European businesses (similar to the promotion of 'lean' Japanese production methods during the 1980s). This 'Americanization of business cultures' was accompanied by learning from US advertising methods—or the direct hiring of Madison Avenue advertising agencies.[42]

While 1950s discourses about Americanization often focused on youth and popular culture, by the mid-1980s Europeans were displaying more relaxed attitudes towards American-style popular music and film. With generational change, rock and pop had gone mainstream in Europe, too. US popular styles of expression were often mimicked by local artists and directors and thus had been successfully incorporated into European cultures. The discourse about Americanization partially shifted to new areas of contestation. Fast food became Americanization's *cause célèbre* during the 1980s and 1990s. Those seeking resistance against the 'American enemy' discovered McDonald's, which started to expand in Western Europe during the 1970s, pushing home-grown chains such as Wimpy to the side; or displacing 'traditional' fast-food dishes such as fish and chips (in Britain) or department store broilers (in Germany). Since McDonald's first European restaurants often opened in prime tourist locations such as Rome's Piazza di Spagna and were highly visible invaders into the monumental core of Europe's ancient cities, the burger chain was easily vilified as the cause of an alleged degradation of European food cultures.[43]

McDonald's was linked to discourses about globalization, which during the 1990s acquired an American tone.[44] Like modernization, globalization refers to large-scale processes of social and cultural transformation that are not particularly specific to any country or culture. One could even argue that in recent decades Europe has been more of a motor of globalization than the US, given its much greater exposure to world trade. Yet again, during the 1990s, with capitalism triumphant after the fall of communism, the US (and not Europe) served as the iconic model society that stood in for some larger

[40] Schröter, *Americanization*, 97–105.

[41] Paul Erker, '"Amerikanisierung" der westdeutschen Wirtschaft? Stand und Perspektiven der Forschung', in Konrad Jarausch and Hannes Siegrist (eds), *Amerikanisierung und Sowjetisierung in Deutschland 1945–1970* (Frankfurt/M: Campus, 1997), 137–45; Gareth Shaw and Louise Curth, 'Selling Self-Service and the Supermarket: The Americanization of Food Retailing in Britain, 1945–60', *Business History* 46:4 (2004), 568–82; Kipping and Bjarner (eds), *Americanisation*; Schröter, *Americanization*.

[42] Schröter, *Americanization*, 117–21.

[43] Philipp Gassert, 'The "Golden Arches": Image or Counter-Image of Europe?', in Benjamin Drechsel and Claus Leggewie (eds), *United in Visual Diversity: Images and Counter-Images of Europe* (Innsbruck: Studien Verlag, 2010), 225–37.

[44] Akira Iriye, 'Globalization as Americanization', in Bruce Mazlish, Chanda Nayan and Kenneth Weisbrode (eds), *The Paradox of a Global USA* (Stanford, CA: Stanford University Press, 2007), 31–48.

transformational experience. Critics of globalization could have chosen any trans-national corporation when staging protest demonstrations. Yet they often opted for US companies such as McDonald's to bring their political points across. McDonald's was a conspicuous target, because reports about the expansion of Western capitalism into former communist Eastern Europe and China were frequently visually underscored by images of the opening of a new McDonald's.[45]

With regard to Eastern Europe, this third wave of post-1990 Americanization 'from below' has been accompanied by renewed efforts of Americanization 'from above'. High-profile economic advisors who were American or had received their training at US universities (probably Chicago) were dispatched to Russia and the Baltic states with US government support or the support of US foundations. As in the postwar period, these experiments in Americanization 'from above' did not necessarily produce the hoped-for results and led, in the case of Russia, to a severe backlash against Western-style deregulation and privatization with 'external influences' serving as convenient scapegoats. Here, an old European story seems to have repeated itself. While consumers were choosing from American imports and making them conform to their own taste and standards (thus Russifying western popular culture), the alleged imposition of American models was at best producing ambivalent results. Also, the dogged Americanization efforts in Russia and later in Iraq demonstrate that other than in West Germany, Japan, Austria, and Western Europe right after 1945, the US no longer possessed such a commanding cultural and economic superiority that it could export its way of life to the same degree that had seemed possible under the specific circumstances of the first postwar decade.

BROADENING THE APPEAL OF THE AMERICAN CENTURY: WESTERNIZATION

The American impact on postwar Europe stretched beyond the realms of business and popular culture, or the outright imposition of US methods (as was briefly the case in occupied Austria and Germany). It was part and parcel of a larger intellectual and cultural reorientation, especially of continental European intellectuals towards the Atlantic, or rather, to be more specific, towards the Atlantic Alliance. While the term 'Westernization' is sometimes being used as synonymous with Americanization, it is usually reserved for processes of interaction among the political and intellectual elites of NATO member countries.[46] Its origins, however, stretch back to World War I, when for

---

[45] James L. Watson, *Golden Arches East: McDonald's in East Asia*, 2nd edn (Stanford, CA: Stanford University Press, 2006).

[46] This narrow definition obviously means something different from Westernization in the larger sense of the term, which refers to the global adaption of Western culture since the early modern period. For reasons of terminological clarity this process should be called 'occidentalization'.

all practical purposes the idea of the modern West was invented.[47] In Germany and countries further east (as well in the north of Europe) the term 'West' therefore has a particular meaning. Given Germany's traditional uneasiness about 'Western democracy' and its long-standing self-perception as a 'bridge between East and West', Westernization became a whiggish term for Cold War liberals in the Federal Republic. It highlighted the successful democratization of postwar Germany and the overcoming of Germany's 'special path'.[48]

For Western European Cold War intellectuals, Westernization was a way out of the conundrum that the old world was facing in the post-1945 period. Many were as uneasy about US as they were about Soviet propaganda.[49] There was considerable frustration among the elites of the former colonial powers (such as Britain, France, the Netherlands, Belgium, or Denmark), who had to come to terms with the fact that Europe had lost its once dominating position in the world. These nations now struggled to defend their cultural influences within their former imperial realms against this aggressive American modernizer, who wanted to make the 'Third World' safe for democracy. While France continued to fight for its civilizing mission abroad, Britain, as well as the Netherlands, and to a certain extent even Germany (which had lost its informal empire in Eastern Europe), came to accept that they were now playing second fiddle within the West. To varying degrees they invented or reinvented, polished, nurtured, and cherished their special relationship with the United States. This happened in part by building on and replacing older concepts of community (such as the Anglosphere that Stead and Bryce had once promoted) through exchange programmes and other efforts, that aimed at increasing interaction among 'Western' intellectual, cultural, and political elites.

The most famous (some say infamous) of these Westernizing networks was the Congress for Cultural Freedom (CCF). It was established during the 1950s as an anti-communist organization, ostensibly to counter Soviet inroads into Western European intelligentsia and immunize them against the totalitarian temptation. By bringing scientists, journalists, writers, philosophers, politicians, labour leaders, and clergy together, the CCF turned out to be a relatively moderate voice in the struggle for liberty in an illiberal age. While populist anti-communism ran amok in some quarters of the West, the CCF by contrast seemed to be a model voice for moderation as well as a body of detached and learned deliberation about what it meant to defend 'freedom'. Although it was later revealed that the CCF was secretly financed by the CIA,[50] few scholarly observers doubt that

---

[47] Michael Hochgeschwender, *Freiheit in der Offensive? Die Deutschen und der Kongress für kulturelle Freiheit* (Munich: Oldenbourg, 1998).

[48] Heinrich August Winkler, *Der lange Weg nach Westen*, 2 vols, 6th edn (Munich: Beck, 2005).

[49] Pells, *Not Like Us*, 66–7.

[50] In 1966 by the *New York Times*, see Christopher Lasch, 'The Cultural Cold War: A Short History of the Congress for Cultural Freedom', in Barton J. Bernstein (ed.), *Towards a New Past* (New York: Knopf, 1968), 322–59. For a more recent discussion see the contributions by W. Scott Lucas, Hugh Wilford, Ingeborg Philipsen, and Tity De Vries in Giles Scott-Smith and Hans Krabbendam (eds), *The Cultural Cold War in Western Europe, 1945–1960* (London: Frank Cass, 2003).

the CCF, whose conferences were stacked with famous centrist liberal, moderate social-democratic (or Labour), and moderate conservative intellectuals, such as Raymond Aron, Daniel Bell, Karl Jaspers, Arthur Koestler, Reinhold Niebuhr, Ignazio Silone, Stephen Spender, and others, was a mere front for American Cold War propaganda. The participants at the CCF's conferences and the contributors to its journals (*Encounter* in Britain; *Der Monat* in West Germany; *Preuves* in France) openly discussed the pitfalls of anti-communism and the frequent failures of the West to live up to its own professed ideals.[51]

In the scholarly literature, the concept of Westernization has been used to highlight processes of community building among Western allies beyond the embrace of a limited number of cultural products, which often acquire completely different meanings in different contexts. Other than Americanization, it highlights the construction of an international, 'Western identity', which is distinct from that of the hegemonic culture. Both North Americans and Western Europeans were to equal parts engaged in this endeavour, with both sides participating in the creation of a cultural and ideological system that they called 'The West'. Always nervous about an American return to 'isolationism', West Europeans set up institutions such as the Bilderberg Group, the Dutch Atlantic Institute, the Aspen Institute, or Atlantik-Brücke, that aimed at tying American elites to Europe.[52] Although mostly created by Europeans, these fledgling institutions would not have survived without US government or foundation money. The Ford Foundation was particularly active during the 1940s and 1950s in underwriting many of these European activities through its regular grant-making process.[53]

During the late 1950s and 1960s, Europeans increased their investment in these transatlantic community building efforts. While their principal orientation was towards the United States, the elites of those Westernizing countries also developed strong ties between each other. In the case of Germany, city partnerships with France are one prominent example, or the host of bilateral friendship organizations that existed between various European nations. To a certain extent, Westernization has been part and parcel of Europeanization, which could be conceived of as being opposed to Americanization, but for a long time was not. Westernization and its European corollary thus produced a level of institutional cooperation among European countries that did not have a historic precedent. To a lesser degree the same has been the case with respect to the Atlantic community, where military cooperation became institutionally most visibly

[51] Anselm Doering-Manteuffel, *Wie westlich sind die Deutschen? Amerikanisierung und Westernisierung im 20. Jahrhundert* (Göttingen: Vandenhoeck & Ruprecht, 1999).

[52] Valerie Aubourg, 'Organizing Atlanticism: The Bilderberg Group and the Atlantic Institute, 1952–1963', in Scott-Smith and Krabbendam (eds), *Cultural Cold War*, 92–105; Ludger Kühnhardt, *Atlantik-Brücke. Fünfzig Jahre deutsch-amerikanische Partnerschaft 1952–2002* (Berlin: Propyläen, 2002).

[53] Volker R. Berghahn, *America and the Intellectual Cold Wars in Europe: Shepherd Stone between Philanthropy, Academy, and Diplomacy* (Princeton, NJ: Princeton University Press, 2001).

entrenched, and has therefore had some Americanizing side-effects too.[54] Over the decades, Europeans have become more active in underwriting transatlantic exchange programmes or in financing institutions devoted to the promotion of transatlantic communication such as the Dutch Atlantic Institute or Germany's *Amerikahäuser* ('America Houses'). With the drying-up of US funding during the 1970s, they were transformed into German–American Institutes, which still promote topics related to the US, but are now no longer institutions of US propaganda abroad. Maintaining an interest in US civilization and culture, they have also led to a re-contextualizing of ideas and images of Americanization and the West.[55]

Compared to Americanization, Westernization therefore is at the same time the broader and the more specific concept. It is broader because it gives Europeans a more active role in the creation of an Atlantic community and in the shaping of the American (informal) empire after 1945. Even though I have pleaded for defining Americanization as something that involves an active participation on the part of the Americanized, Americanization still names a particular nation as the original source of what then becomes a French, German, or Italian item of popular culture. Yet Westernization is also more specific, because it normally refers to a process of intellectual and political community building whose sources reveal a much longer historical trajectory. Liberalism, with its origins in the transatlantic revolutions of the eighteenth century, was Americanized in the middle of the twentieth century. Yet as a political ideology it must be conceived of as a pan-Western exercise.

RESISTING THE AMERICAN CENTURY: ANTI-AMERICANISM

Finally, Americanization cannot be discussed without looking at discourses about the rejection of Americanization, which are often referred to as 'anti-Americanism'. Like Americanization, that term is tricky, because its analytical usefulness has been limited due to its normative meanings in daily political discourse and by its inherent historicity. The efforts of the Congress for Cultural Freedom or the Bilderberg group for example were often aimed at the ideological resistance that contemporary observers (as well as

---

[54] Thomas Maulucci and Detlef Junker (eds), *GIs in Germany: The Political, Social, and Cultural History of the American Military Presence, 1945–1990* (Cambridge: Cambridge University Press, forthcoming).

[55] Reinhild Kreis, 'Von der Reeducation zur Partnerschaft: Amerikahäuser und Deutsch-Amerikanische Institute in Bayern', in Christoph Daxelmüller, Stefan Kummer and Wolfgang Reinicke (eds), *Wiederaufbau und Wirtschaftswunder in Bayern* (Regensburg: Pustet, 2009), 186–95.

later scholars) labelled 'anti-Americanism'.[56] This may have entailed a critique of US foreign policy and its war effort in South-east Asia during the 1960s, which came under heavy criticism at home and abroad. Therefore, scholars have defined anti-Americanism as a normative, very general culturalist critique of an ideal typical (liberal–capitalist) modernity, which the US came to represent since around 1900. From this point of view, more specific criticisms concerning individual political actions of the US government or particular aspects of American society are not to be construed as anti-American just because they do not contain a wholesale rejection of things American.[57]

Hannah Arendt, Antonio Gerbi, or more recently in the wake of 9/11, Russell Berman and Andrei S. Markovits have argued that America is rejected 'as such' because this helps to create a certain idea of a unified Europe. In 1954, Arendt pointedly observed that a 'European ideology' was in danger of being built out of anti-American sentiments. For Markovits, anti-Americanism has now grown into a powerful pan-European idea: It has become 'an emotional, potent, and real moment of European identity formation'. Enmity towards the United States seems to hold this new and fractured European Community together. Anti-Americanism, Markovits claims, has now morphed into 'Europe's lingua franca', succeeding anti-communism as the new ideological anchor of Europe.[58] Yet even though Europeans are often as divided about America as they are about everything else, the recent fears about a resurgent anti-Americanism, which were running high in the wake of the 'war on terror' unleashed after 9/11, can draw on important antecedents.

Anti-Americanism was often motivated or ostensibly justified by (imagined or real) fears of Americanization. In the 1920s 'Americanism' was reviled by Marxists as well as fascist and national conservative ideologues, who created a pan-European language of resentment that resonated throughout the twentieth century. Both Nazis and Soviet communists, however, argued for a selective borrowing from America. Because they were impressed by the United States as an economic and technological powerhouse (and in the German case and that of Adolf Hitler by the continental expanse of the United States[59]), these anti-American ideologues often saw the US as a model from which they could learn something useful. At the same time they thought that they could out-

[56] Thomas W. Gijswijt, 'Beyond NATO: Transatlantic Elite Networks and the Atlantic Alliance', in Andreas Wenger, Christian Nuenlist and Anna Locher (eds), *Transforming NATO in the Cold War: Challenges Beyond Deterrence in the 1960s* (London: Routledge, 2007), 50–63.

[57] For definitions, see Philipp Gassert, 'The Anti-American as an Americanizer: Revisting the Anti-American Century in Germany', *German Politics and Society* 27:1 (2009), 24–38, here 27; Paul Hollander, *Understanding Anti-Americanism: Its Origins and Impact at Home and Abroad* (Chicago, IL: Ivan R. Dee, 2004), 9–14; and the numerous contributions to Brendon O'Connor (ed.), *Anti-Americanism: History, Causes, Themes*, 4 vols (Oxford: Greenwood Publishing, 2007).

[58] Andrei S. Markovits, *Uncouth Nation: Why Europe Dislikes America* (Princeton, NJ: Princeton University Press, 2007), 2.

[59] Detlef Junker, 'The Continuity of Ambivalence: German Views of America, 1933–1945', in David Barclay and Elisabeth Glaser-Schmidt (eds), *Transatlantic Images and Perceptions: Germany and America since 1776* (New York: Cambridge University Press, 1997), 243–64.

Americanize the Americans. These anti-liberal critics of America developed a fully fledged critique of American modernity by describing their (Socialist, Fascist, National Socialist) modernity as the more successful model in overcoming the economic and cultural crisis of the twentieth century.[60]

This selective borrowing 'from America' again highlights the paradoxical and ambivalent nature of Americanization. After 1945, few critics adhered consistently to anti-American or anti-western positions. As we have seen in the French and West German cases, from the immediate postwar well into the 1960s, moderate conservative critics hated US popular culture, yet they were willing to accept Marshall Plan money or willing to modernize businesses by learning from US corporations. European patriarchs such as Konrad Adenauer or Winston Churchill did not think highly of US cultural life, yet they were more than happy to realign their countries with the US in order to keep communism safely tucked away behind the Iron Curtain. Later, during the 1960s, the Left became highly critical of the Vietnam war effort. Yet it saw itself in an alliance with the American civil rights and anti-war movements, which also resisted US intervention.[61] Thus, many of these self-professed critics of the US openly displayed signs of Americanization, when their protest methods ('sit-ins', 'teach-ins', etc.) or their preferred means of cultural expression were shaped by US counterculture. Similar observations could be made with regard to the 1980s peace movement or 1990s opposition to globalization.

Ironies thus abound. As surveys of twentieth century anti-Americanism have demonstrated time and again, rejecting things American has often gone along with cultural Americanization. Even though negative images of the United States signified a critique of liberal, western-style modernity, the anti-Americans themselves were being shaped by the same forces of modernization they set out to combat. During the 1920s and 1930s, as well as during the 1950s, 1960s, and 1970s, anti-Americans frequently concurred with domestic American critics. They tried to 'learn from the enemy' by adopting arguments that were simultaneously voiced in domestic American contexts or by employing protest techniques that had originated in the US. European anti-Americans thus frequently have been anti-American 'with America'.[62] In the final analysis, the paradox that anti-Americanism was forced to acquire an American accent (and continues to do so within anti-globalization movements, even Islamic anti-Americanism today) is the most telling testimony to the power of American culture and civilization in Western Europe throughout the second half of the 'American century'.

---

[60] Jeffrey Herf, *Reactionary Modernism: Technology, Culture, and Politics in Weimar and the Third Reich* (New York: Cambridge University Press, 1986).

[61] With respect to Germany this paradox is now well researched; see Martin Klimke, *The Other Alliance: Global Protest and Student Unrest in West Germany and the US, 1962–72* (Princeton, NJ: Princeton University Press, 2009).

[62] Philipp Gassert, 'With America against America: Anti-Americanism in West Germany', in Junker (ed.), *The United States and Germany*, II, 502–9.

CONCLUSION

In conclusion I would like to highlight that even though scholars are uneasy about the virtues of Americanization as an analytical concept (with similar reservations regarding westernization and anti-Americanism, too), as a heuristic tool Americanization still carries some currency for historians. The very fact that terms like Americanization and Americanism (the staple of the interwar 'America' discourse) were ubiquitous in twentieth-century social and political language points to something significant in European history. With the United States of America rising to economic, cultural, and political dominance, beginning in 1900 and pertaining briefly during the period 1945–65, to hegemony within the West, its impact was too great to be ignored or belittled. While there is considerable agreement among scholars that Americanization is a process that involves two sides and includes a decision-making process on the part of the Americanized, the very fact that we are debating Americanization shows that Western Europe (and to a more limited extent the rest of Europe as well) was going through its 'American' era in the decades after World War II. Mostly voluntarily and sometimes involuntarily, Europeans appropriated models that had first been fully tested in the United States even though they may have originated in Europe, too. 'America' thus was their means to make sense of modern times.

FURTHER READING

Berghahn, Volker R. *America and the Intellectual Cold Wars in Europe: Shepherd Stone between Philanthropy, Academy, and Diplomacy* (Princeton, NJ: Princeton University Press, 2001).

De Grazia, Victoria, *The Irresistible Empire: America's Advance through Twentieth-Century Europe* (Cambridge, MA: Harvard University Press, 2005).

Doering-Manteuffel, Anselm, *Wie westlich sind die Deutschen? Amerikanisierung und Westernisierung im 20. Jahrhundert* (Göttingen: Vandenhoeck & Ruprecht, 1999).

Duignan, Peter and L.H. Gann, *The Rebirth of the West: The Americanization of the Democratic World, 1945–1958* (Cambridge: Blackwell, 1992).

Gassert, Philipp, 'The "Golden Arches": Image or Counter-Image of Europe?', in Benjamin Drechsel and Claus Leggewie (eds), *United in Visual Diversity: Images and Counter-Images of Europe* (Innsbruck: Studienverlag, 2010), 225–37.

Goedde, Petra, 'The Globalization of American Culture', in Karen Halttunen (ed.), *Blackwell Companion in American Cultural History* (New York: Blackwell, 2008), 246–62.

Hollander, Paul, *Understanding Anti-Americanism: Its Origins and Impact at Home and Abroad* (Chicago, IL: Ivan R. Dee, 2004).

Iriye, Akira, 'Globalization as Americanization', in Bruce Mazlish, Chanda Nayan and Kenneth Weisbrode (eds), *The Paradox of a Global USA* (Stanford, CA: Stanford University Press, 2007), 31–48.

Kroes, Rob, *If You've Seen One, You've Seen the Mall: Europeans and American Mass Culture* (Urbana, IL: University of Illinois Press, 1996).

Kuisel, Richard, *Seducing the French: The Dilemma of Americanization* (Berkeley, CA: University of California Press, 1993).

Pells, Richard, *Not Like Us: How Europeans have Loved, Hated, and Transformed American Culture since World War II* (New York: Basic Books, 1997).

Poiger, Uta, *Jazz, Rock, and Rebels: Cold War Politics and American Culture in a Divided Germany* (Berkeley, CA: University of California Press, 2000).

Schildt, Axel, 'Americanization', in Detlef Junker (ed.), *The United States and Germany in the Era of the Cold War. A Handbook, vol 1: 1945–1968* (New York: Cambridge University Press, 2004), 635–42.

Schröter, Harm G., *Americanization of the European Economy: A Compact Survey of American Economic Influence in Europe since the 1880s* (Dordrecht: Springer, 2005).

Stephan, Alexander (ed.), *The Americanization of Europe: Culture, Diplomacy, and Anti-Americanism after 1945* (New York: Berghahn, 2006).

CHAPTER 9

....

IMMIGRATION AND ASYLUM: CHALLENGES TO EUROPEAN IDENTITIES AND CITIZENSHIP

....

STEPHEN CASTLES

Introduction

....

MANY Europeans today perceive immigration as a major problem for society. Some claim that asylum seekers and low-skilled migrants are an economic burden and that ethnic diversity undermines the solidarity necessary for strong welfare states. Others link security discourses with suspicion of Islam and assert that Muslim residents are threats to security and public order. Above all, a widespread discourse portrays Europe's new found cultural and religious complexity as a challenge to historical models of national identity and citizenship. The power of anti-immigrant slogans in the media, politics, and popular discourse is indisputable.

Such concerns are far from new but they have grown sharply. The trigger for the perception of a 'migration crisis' was the end of the Cold War. Right-wing politicians and media predicted that 'millions of desperate migrants' from the East would 'swamp' west European welfare systems and drag down living standards. In fact, this did not happen: East–West movements in the 1990s were fairly modest and were driven partly by ethnic factors and partly by labour market demand.[1] Nonetheless, this period was a crucial

---

[1] The majority of East–West migrants were members of ethnic minorities moving to 'ancestral homelands', where they had a right to citizenship: ethnic Germans (*Aussiedler*) to Germany, Russian Jews to Israel, Bulgarian Turks to Turkey, and so on. See Dietrich Thränhardt, 'European Migration from East to West: Present Patterns and Future Directions', *New Community* 22:2 (1996), 227–42.

turning point in European perceptions of migration and ethnic community formation. It also marked an upsurge in social scientific interest in the theme.

In retrospect, the end of the Cold War was just the most obvious marker of a reordering of the world that opened the door to new forms of cross-border flows—of capital, commodities, ideas, and people. Neoliberal globalization created the conditions crucial to an upsurge and diversification of migration: a new global labour market based on differentiation and inequality; cultural capital in the form of knowledge of overseas opportunities disseminated through globalized media; and the technical means in the form of cheaper transport and new communications.[2] Europeans had to come to terms with important shifts, for which nothing (and least of all their political leaders) had prepared them: the metamorphosis of the labour migrants of the 1960s and 1970s into new and permanent ethnic minorities; increasing inflows of asylum seekers and migrants from all over the world; the globalization of markets for skills and qualifications, which led to increasing mobility both into and out of Europe; and the growing cultural and religious diversity of their cities.

To understand these trends and their meaning for European societies it is essential to examine the (often suppressed) history of migration, ethnicity, and racism that has always been closely interwoven with nation-state formation, colonialism, and modernity. The 'migration crisis' of the early 1990s reveals itself as just one of several crucial turning points in Europe's migration history. This chapter will focus on such epochal shifts. However, pre-1945 experiences will be summarized very briefly, and the emphasis will be on developments since the Second World War.

EUROPE'S FORGOTTEN HISTORY OF
ETHNIC DIVERSITY

In Western Europe, 'migration was a long-standing and important facet of social life and the political economy' from about 1650 onwards.[3] The centrality of migration is not adequately reflected in prevailing views on the past: as Noiriel has pointed out, the history of immigration has been a 'blind spot' of historical research in France[4]—especially in the canonic Braudelian view of the past. This applies equally elsewhere, as shown by 'historians' repeated neglect of the scale and impact of immigration on European societies from the Middle Ages onwards'.[5] Such neglect is not coincidental: nineteenth and

---

[2] Stephen Castles and Mark J. Miller, *The Age of Migration: International Population Movements in the Modern World*, 4th edn (Basingstoke: Palgrave Macmillan, 2009).

[3] Leslie Page Moch, 'Moving Europeans: Historical Migration Practices in Western Europe' in Robin Cohen (ed.), *The Cambridge Survey of World Migration* (Cambridge: Cambridge University Press, 1995). See also Moch, *Moving Europeans: Migration in Western Europe since 1650* (Bloomington, IN: Indiana University Press, 1992).

[4] Gérard Noiriel, *Le creuset français: Histoire de l'immigration XIXe–XXe siècles* (Paris: Seuil, 1988).

[5] Leo Lucassen, David Feldman and Jochen Oltmer (eds), *Paths of Integration: Migrants in Western Europe (1880–2004)* (Amsterdam: Amsterdam University Press, 2006).

early twentieth-century historians were conscious actors in the process of nation build-ing that was central to the democratic nationalism of the period. A leading French histo-rian pointed out in 1882 that *forgetting* was a crucial element in the creation of a nation.[6] Ernest Renan was referring to the importance of forgetting about the repression of minorities that had been an essential part of France's history of national expansion.

Similarly, the immigrant groups that played such an important part in providing the skills and labour needed for modernization had no place in nationalist accounts designed to foster the idea of homogenous and monocultural peoples. Curiously, European historians have been more interested in documenting European outflows to New World countries. It is only recently that a new generation of European historians (such as Bade, Noiriel, and Lucassen) have questioned the nationalist orthodoxy of the past.[7]

Immigration and the mixing of ethnic groups have been important in Europe for cen-turies. Britain is an obvious example, with influxes of successive groups of settlers and conquerors—Saxons, Danes, and Normans—paving the way for unification as a power-ful monarchic state. Expansion involved the forcible incorporation of Celtic peoples— the Welsh, Scots, and Irish—who were never willing to renounce their identities and languages. Britain today presents the paradox of a multi-ethnic nation state—a paradox that is looking increasingly shaky in view of rising regional nationalisms. This history of diversity has been constantly renewed: the Huguenot refugees of early modern times contributed to the rise of the woollen industry; Irish farmers, forced to emigrate by fam-ines caused by the practices of English colonial landlords, provided labour vital to the Industrial Revolution;[8] in the late nineteenth century, Jews fleeing the Russian pogroms were an important element in London's industrial and commercial growth. For centu-ries, immigrants have not only contributed labour, ideas, and energy—they have also served as scapegoats for problems and a legitimation for state surveillance and control.[9]

Every European country has a history of minority incorporation and immigration, and each of these histories is different. These histories cannot be told here, yet none of today's nation states can claim to fulfil the nationalist dream of homogeneity—either in the past or the present. Some of today's states still have indigenous minorities with dif-fering languages and lifestyles—such as the Sami in Sweden, Norway, and Finland. Other countries have territorially based minorities, some of whose members aspire to

---

[6] Ernest Renan, *Qu'est-ce qu' une nation? Et autres essais politiques* (Paris: Presses Pocket, Agora, 1992).

[7] Klaus Bade, *Migration in European History* (Oxford: Blackwell, 2003); Leo Lucassen, *The Immigrant Threat: The Integration of Old and New Migrants in Western Europe since 1890* (Urbana, IL: University of Illinois Press, 2005); Gérard Noiriel, *Immigration, antisémitisme et racisme en France (XIXe–XXe siècle)* (Paris: Fayard, 2007).

[8] J. A. Jackson, *The Irish in Britain* (London: Routledge and Kegan Paul, 1963); Friedrich Engels, 'The Condition of the Working Class in England', in *Marx Engels on Britain* (Moscow: Foreign Languages Publishing House, 1962).

[9] Robin Cohen, *Frontiers of Identity: The British and the Others* (London: Longman, 1994); Cohen, *Migration and its Enemies: Global Capital, Migrant Labour and the Nation-State* (Aldershot: Ashgate, 2006).

independence—Basques in Spain or Corsicans in France. In Eastern Europe, states that were held together by political ideologies and power during the Cold War have fragmented along ethnic lines—such as former Yugoslavia, the former Soviet Union, and Czechoslovakia.

For centuries, processes of nation-state formation have been concerned with managing cultural and religious diversity. Differing national models emerged in various European countries, and these models were to help to determine how states and the public reacted to immigrants after 1945.[10] For example the United Kingdom developed into a state that required political loyalty but could accept a certain level of cultural difference: a person's group identity could be Welsh or Scottish, Protestant or Catholic. However, this did not mean equality; regional cultures and minority religions were treated as inferior, and the fight for tolerance and equality continued for centuries. In France, the 1789 revolution established principles of equality and the rights of man that rejected group cultural identity; the 'Republican Model' was designed to include individuals as equal political subjects. In both Britain and France, however, it was the expansion of the state that created the nation—political belonging came before national identity.

Germany was different: it was not united as a state until 1871, and the nation came before the state. This led to a form of ethnic or folk belonging that was not consistent with incorporation of immigrants as citizens. In the Netherlands, religious conflicts were resolved through the principle of 'pillarization', which allowed social equality but separation of institutional structures for Protestants and Catholics. Belgium and Switzerland had their own institutional and cultural settlements to hold together groups with diverse languages and cultures.[11]

These differing approaches implied different relationships between society and nation, and between civic belonging and national identity. In Britain a person could be a full member of the society and political nation and yet belong to a distinct cultural or religious group. In France, civic identity required a unitary national identity. In Germany and Austria, national identity came first, and was the precondition for belonging as a citizen. Switzerland and Belgium rejected any influences that might upset their delicate balances. Only the Netherlands claimed to be tolerant of all forms of difference, but this principle was to be strongly challenged in the early twenty-first century.

All the European approaches had one thing in common: there was no openness to new forms of ethnic, cultural, and religious belonging imported by immigrants. Immigrants were either to be excluded from the nation (the German and Swiss model); assimilated at the price of cultural conformity within the national culture (the French approach); or assimilated into one of the accepted regional and religious groupings

---

[10] Stephen Castles and Alastair Davidson, *Citizenship and Migration: Globalisation and the Politics of Belonging* (London: Macmillan, 2000).

[11] By contrast, the white settler societies of the New World were built through the dispossession of indigenous peoples, and through immigration from Europe. Incorporation of immigrants as citizens was part of their national myths. This led to models of assimilation, such as the US image of the 'melting pot'. Of course, it was thought that only white people could be assimilated: Australia, New Zealand, Canada, and the USA all had racially selective immigration laws.

(Britain). When immigration started in the post-1945 boom, incorporation of the new-comers was not seen as a major issue. The numbers were not expected to be large, and there was a strong belief in the 'controllability of difference'—the idea that immigrants and new minorities would not bring about change in dominant social, cultural, and religious practices. This belief proved misguided, and Europeans are still struggling with the consequences.

Labour Recruitment: 1945–73

The migratory processes that were to lead to so much change in Europe started soon after 1945. In the immediate postwar years, it was widely believed that Europe was 'over-populated'. In the aftermath of the Great Depression of the 1930s and the devastation of the war, millions of people sought to emigrate, mainly to North and South America and Oceania. At the same time, millions of 'displaced persons' from Central and Eastern Europe, forced from their homes by warfare and forced labour recruitment, and then by the Cold War, had to be absorbed. The most significant influx was of some 12 million people into West Germany. In addition, through the 1950s and 1960s, independence of former colonies led to an exodus of former colonists and administrators, such as the 'pieds noirs' who migrated from Algeria to France, Dutch colonists and people of mixed ethnic background heading for the Netherlands from newly independent Indonesia, and British settlers bound for the UK from former African, Asian, and Caribbean territories. Despite these population increases, economic growth was so buoyant that by the 1950s labour shortages began to appear.[12] The response by employers and governments was to recruit migrant workers. This labour migration was of two main types.

First, virtually all Western European countries employed foreign workers. Some came of their own accord, but in many cases they were recruited as temporary labour (or 'guestworkers'). The legal and administrative arrangements varied.[13] Some countries, like France, Britain, and Sweden, were relatively open to family reunion and long-term stay. Others, such as the Federal Republic of Germany (FRG), Austria, and Switzerland, went to great lengths to prevent settlement, through 'rotation' of workers, that is, a constant circulation of short-term migrants. Germany established the most sophisticated guest-worker system, with a high degree of state control of the recruitment, working conditions, and rights of the migrants. At this time, immigration was mainly to Western European countries: Southern Europe, North Africa, Turkey, Finland, and Ireland

---

[12] Some economists argue that economic growth was actually in part due to the additional labour provided by the displaced persons. Thus, Germany's 'economic miracle' was partly to be explained by the very large labour reserves available at the time. See Charles P. Kindleberger, *Europe's Postwar Growth – the Role of Labor Supply* (Cambridge, MA: Harvard University Press, 1967).

[13] Stephen Castles and Godula Kosack, *Immigrant Workers and Class Structure in Western Europe* (London: Oxford University Press, 1973).

served as labour reserves for the industrial core countries, while Eastern and Central Europe were members of the Soviet Bloc, and imposed strict exit restrictions.

Second, colonial countries used labour from former or existing dependencies: the Caribbean and the Indian subcontinent for Britain, North and West Africa for France, and the Caribbean and Indonesia for the Netherlands. Generally there was no official recruitment: knowledge of work opportunities in the former metropole, together with the legal right of entry, was sufficient to start migratory chains. In the colonial period certain colonized peoples had been granted citizenship (or, in the British case, the status of 'subjects' of the Crown) as a form of ideological integration. This now facilitated the entry of much-needed labour, but it also meant that colonial workers could bring in dependants and settle.

In retrospect it seems curious that governments were so mesmerized by the economic benefits of migrant labour that they paid little attention to possible long-term impacts on the receiving societies. The governments of guest worker-recruiting countries such as the FRG were sure that their strict regulations would prevent family reunion and settlement, while former colonial powers seem to have convinced themselves of the feasibility of cultural and social assimilation. By the 1960s, in the light of economic decline and growing community relations problems, the authorities of the three former colonial powers were having second thoughts, and introduced restrictive laws (such as Britain's 1962 Commonwealth Immigrants Act) to stop immigration from former colonies. From then on, there was a convergence in status between guest workers and immigrants from former colonies.

By 1970 there were over 12 million immigrants in Western Europe, and the process of ethnic minority formation had become irreversible—although this had not yet become apparent to many policymakers. The 'oil crisis' of 1973 precipitated a reorientation. All the labour-importing countries of north-western Europe stopped recruitment in 1973 or 1974, except Britain, which had done so earlier. The recession of the mid-1970s was a major economic turning point, marking the end of the Fordist system of mass production in the old industrial countries. Migrant labour recruitment was replaced by capital outflows to new industrial areas in the global south. These in turn precipitated large-scale flows of workers, for instance from South Asia to the Gulf oil countries, and somewhat later from less developed parts of Asia to the new industrial tigers. Large-scale immigration to Western Europe seemed to be over, and governments expected guest workers to depart—a convenient way to export unemployment.

From Migrant Labour to Ethnic Minorities, 1974–89

The mid-1970s proved a major turning point for migration and diversity in Europe. Many migrant workers did leave, but these were mainly from countries such as Spain, Portugal, and Greece, which were soon to accede to the European Community. Those from more distant and impoverished origin countries, such as Turkey, Algeria, and Morocco, tended to stay. Soon, another type of immigration became important: family reunion; that is, the entry of spouses, children, and other relatives of earlier migrants. Between 1974 and the mid-1980s immigrant groups that had come to Western Europe to work took on more normal demographic patterns.[14] The predominance of young men waned, new families were formed, and the original immigrants aged. The consciousness of many immigrants changed from that of temporary sojourners to that of permanent residents. Social, cultural, and political associations were established, and networks of ethnic businesses and services emerged.

Central governments were slow to accept these new realities—partly because they were afraid of an electoral backlash from populations who had been told that immigration was a temporary economic expedient. The German and French governments both tried to limit inflows of migrants' spouses and children, but were forced to abandon such efforts through court actions: it soon proved that the constitutions and legal systems of democratic countries were a powerful counter to attempts by governments to restrict migrants' rights. Moreover, migrant workers had gained entitlements within European welfare states: even in the event of unemployment many were better off remaining in Europe than returning home to poor countries. By the mid-1970s, immigrants made up a substantial share of the population of most north-western European countries, ranging from 4 per cent to 8 per cent in Britain, France, Germany, and Sweden, with the largest share in Switzerland—nearly 17 per cent.

From the early 1980s, inflows of asylum seekers—that is, persons applying for recognition as refugees—to Western Europe began to grow. A refugee is a person recognized by a host state (or in some cases the United Nations High Commissioner for Refugees—UNHCR) as being in need of protection according to the terms of the 1951 UN Geneva Refugee Convention and its 1967 Protocol. Such recognition is only accorded to persons who are outside their country of citizenship and cannot return due to a 'well-founded fear' of individual persecution based on specific criteria laid down in the Convention.[15] Asylum seekers are persons applying for such recognition, and whose eligibility has not

---

[14] S. Castles, H. Booth and T. Wallace, *Here for Good: Western Europe's New Ethnic Minorities* (London: Pluto Press, 1984).

[15] The 1951 Convention was established to deal with the post-Second World War European displaced persons situation. It restricted protection to persons within Europe meeting the following criteria:

> as a result of events occurring before 1 January 1951 and owing to well-founded fear of being persecuted for reasons of race, religion, nationality, membership of a particular social group or political opinion, is outside the country of his nationality and is unable or, owing to such fear, is unwilling to avail himself of the protection of that country; or who, not having a nationality and being outside the country of his former habitual residence as a result of such events, is unable or, owing to such fear, is unwilling to return to it (1951 Refugee Convention Article 1A(2)).

The 1967 Protocol, designed to make the Convention fit the realities of the Cold War, dropped the spatial and temporal limitations of the original Convention, but maintained the restrictive conditions that refugees must have crossed an international border and have suffered individual persecution for the specific reasons mentioned above.

yet been determined. People displaced collectively by warfare do not, in principle, fall under the Convention, although they may be granted recognition as refugees under certain circumstances.[16] In the early Cold War period, most asylum seekers had come from communist countries. Welcoming refugees from the Hungarian Uprising of 1956 or the Prague Spring of 1968 had been a propaganda coup for the West, with broad public support. But now most asylum seekers came from Latin America, Asia, and Africa, and they were often fleeing the proxy wars of the East–West conflict, in which official Europe frequently sided with authoritarian regimes. Governments and population became increasingly reluctant to grant refugee status to such asylum seekers—a trend that was to become even stronger in the years that followed.

Immigrant and refugee families needed social infrastructure: housing, schools, medical services, and other public amenities. Educational authorities, social welfare agencies, and local authorities began to respond to new needs and problems. The guest worker system was dead, even where this was not officially acknowledged. European policymakers had to wake up to the need to permanently incorporate millions of migrants into their societies. From the 1980s, governments began to commission studies into 'the foreigner problem' (as it was called in Germany), 'race relations' (in Britain), 'minority issues' (Netherlands) or 'insertion' (France). Plans to deal with problems of housing, education, and community relations were developed. But governments remained reluctant to recognize immigrant communities as a long-term presence requiring new ideas on culture, identity, and citizenship. Strategies to deal with discrimination, structural disadvantage, and racism were slow to emerge. The apparent inability to face reality was most obvious in Germany: despite a report in 1979 by the prominent SPD politician Heinz Kühn, which called for recognition of foreign residents as permanent immigrants,[17] the constantly repeated dogma of all major political parties (except the Greens) until 1998 was: 'the German Federal Republic is not a country of immigration'.[18]

THE END OF THE COLD WAR AND THE GLOBALIZATION OF MIGRATION, 1990–2000

As already indicated, the 'migration crisis' of the early 1990s[19] was the most widely recognized turning point in Europe's recent migration history. It was generally attributed to the end of the Cold War, but in retrospect it is possible to see that the emergence of a

---

[16] See Arthur C. Helton, (2002) *The Price of Indifference: Refugees and Humanitarian Action in the New Century* (Oxford: Oxford University Press, 2002); Gil Loescher, *The UNHCR and World Politics: A Perilous Path* (Oxford: Oxford University Press, 2001); UNHCR, *The State of the World's Refugees: Human Displacement in the New Millennium* (Oxford: Oxford University Press, 2006).

[17] See Castles, Booth and Wallace, *Here for Good.*

[18] *Die Bundesrepublik Deutschland ist kein Einwanderungsland.*

[19] See Myron Weiner, *The Global Migration Crisis: Challenges to States and Human Rights* (New York: HarperCollins, 1995).

mono-polar power structure set the scene for a general reordering of global economics and politics, which in turn led to accelerated cross-border flows. This was not the 'end of history' celebrated by neoliberal commentators,[20] for it ushered in an era of major conflicts, and was in any case short lived: by 2008, in the wake of the global financial crisis, emergent powers were questioning US dominance. Nonetheless, this was a period of dramatic changes with regard to migration and its consequences for European societies.

The most immediate was the upsurge in asylum seeker entries and irregular migration. Asylum seeker entries to European OECD countries peaked at 695,000 in 1992 and then declined, only to reach new peaks by the late 1990s. Economic transformation, political upheavals, and ethnic conflicts all triggered forced migrations. The most dramatic flows were from Albania to Italy in 1991 and again in 1997, and from the former Yugoslavia during the wars in Croatia, Bosnia, and Kosovo. Many of the 1.3 million asylum applicants arriving in Germany between 1991 and 1995 were members of ethnic minorities (such as Roma) from Romania, Bulgaria, and elsewhere in Eastern Europe. The early 1990s was a period of politicization of asylum. Extreme-right mobilization, arson attacks on asylum seeker hostels, and assaults on foreigners were threatening public order.

European governments, fearful of a right-wing electoral backlash, reacted with a series of restrictions, which seemed to herald the construction of a 'Fortress Europe'.[21] The most dramatic changes to national legislation were in Germany and Sweden. The German Basic Law had granted a constitutional right to seek protection from persecution. After heated debates, the Basic Law was amended in 1993 to restrict this right. Sweden, long welcoming to refugees, also amended its law in the face of anti-asylum movements. Asylum-seeker entries dropped sharply in both countries. Several European countries introduced temporary protection regimes instead of permanent refugee status for people fleeing the wars in former Yugoslavia. European states introduced a series of 'non-arrival policies': citizens of certain states were required to obtain visas before departure; while 'carrier sanctions' compelled airline personnel to check documents before allowing people to embark. Countries bordering the EU were declared to be 'safe third countries', so that EU countries could return asylum seekers to these states if they had been used as transit routes.

European governments began to work together systematically in matters of border control and refugee determination procedures. The most visible results were the implementation of the Schengen Convention,[22] which, while tightening entry controls towards the outside, created a zone of free movement between a number

---

[20] Francis Fukuyama, *The End of History and the Last Man* (London: Penguin, 1992).

[21] Charles B. Keely, 'The International Refugee Regimes: the End of the Cold War Matters', *International Migration Review* 35: 1, 303–14.

[22] The Schengen Agreement was signed in 1985 by France, Germany, the Netherlands, Belgium, and Luxembourg, but did not come into force until 1990. It was incorporated into EU law by the 1997 Amsterdam Treaty. The Schengen Zone currently comprises some 25 states; the UK and Ireland opted out of Schengen's border control arrangements, but joined with regard to judicial and police cooperation.

of EU countries; and the Dublin Convention,[23] which laid down that a person could only apply for asylum in the first European country he or she had entered. Other measures included enhanced police cooperation and the establishment of an EU 'High Level Working Group' to recommend measures to enhance human rights and economic development in states bordering the EU in order to create a buffer zone.[24] As a result of these increasingly restrictive entry policies, refugees and asylum seekers often had to enter illegally (sometimes using the services of people smugglers). This gave rise to 'mixed flows' in which it became increasingly difficult for governments and the UNHCR to distinguish between refugees and irregular economic migrants.

At the same time, the old immigration countries of north-western Europe, which had adopted 'zero immigration policies' after 1974, experienced new waves of immigration. In the guest-worker period, most industrial countries had recruited systematically from a limited range of origin countries, often through bilateral agreements. Now migrants came much more spontaneously from near and far. The result was an ever greater diversity in the geographical, ethnic, and cultural backgrounds of migrant populations. Improved transport and communications facilitated movements not only from Europe's eastern and southern peripheries, but also from the Middle East, Asia, and Africa (while Latin America became a less significant source than in the era of the military regimes of the 1970s and 1980s). Italy, Spain, Portugal, and Greece, which had provided migrant labour for Europe's industrial core in the first decades after the Second World War, now themselves became immigration countries.[25] Most of entrants were undocumented, although periodic amnesties would later give many of them legal residence status, facilitating family reunion. By the mid-1990s, new immigration areas were also emerging in Eastern and Central Europe.[26] The Czech Republic, Hungary, Poland, and the Baltic states pulled in migrants from further east or from Asia and Africa.

A further important shift of the 1990s was the increasing public awareness that the migrations of the 1945–73 boom period, together with new migrations since the 1980s, were leading to large-scale settlement and ethnic community formation. Sometimes public opinion seemed better informed than official policies. In certain countries (notably the UK, Sweden, and the Netherlands) 'multicultural', 'minority', or 'diversity'

---

[23] The Dublin Convention was signed in 1990, but did not come into force until 1 September 1997, after being ratified by 13 European states: Belgium, Denmark, France, Germany, Greece, Ireland, Italy, Luxembourg, the Netherlands, Portugal, Spain, and the United Kingdom. Other states subsequently signed up. It was replaced in 2003 by the Dublin II Regulation, which, together with the EURODAC Regulation, established an EU fingerprint database of all unauthorized entrants to the EU.

[24] Stephen Castles, Sean Loughnaand Heaven Crawley, *States of Conflict: Causes and Patterns of Forced Migration to the EU and Policy Responses* (London: Institute of Public Policy Research, 2003).

[25] Russell King, 'Southern Europe in the Changing Global Map of Migration', in Russell King, Gabriella Lazaridis and Charalambos Tsardanidis (eds), *Eldorado or Fortress? Migration in Southern Europe* (London: Macmillan, 2000), 3–26.

[26] Claire Wallace and Dariusz Stola, *Patterns of Migration in Central Europe* (Basingstoke: Palgrave Macmillan, 2001).

policies were developed in the 1970s and 1980s, but in other immigration countries official policies and ideologies were largely based on a politics of denial. For instance
German leaders continued to declare that Germany was 'not a country of immigration'
until the federal election of 1998. After that, the coalition government of Social
Democrats and Greens at last introduced a new Citizenship Act, designed to make
descendants of immigrants into German citizens.[27] But the Christian Democratic opposition continued to resist change. Their reaction to Germany's attempts to attract Indian
IT professionals through a 'green card' scheme was the slogan *Kinder statt Inder*
(roughly: have children to keep the Indians out).

France continued to pursue its 'Republican Model' of 'insertion',[28] based on the idea
that turning immigrants and their children into citizens was a guarantee of equality and
rights.[29] Yet racism and processes of residential segregation and labour market exclusion
were rapidly leading to the emergence of a racialized underclass, concentrated in the
peripheral housing estates of the *banlieues*.[30] The official refusal to admit to the existence
of ethnic minorities, and the resulting ban on the monitoring of educational and occupational outcomes, helped to cement enduring inequality. Sporadic riots in the peripheral estates of Paris, Marseilles, and Lyons were dismissed as criminality or extremism,
and met by increasingly heavy-handed policing—paving the way for the youth revolts of
2005 and 2007.

By the turn of the millennium immigration had become a key political issue throughout Europe. In the UK, some politicians and sections of the media blamed asylum seekers for criminality, disease, and undermining the welfare state. In the Netherlands
undocumented immigration was a major recruiting theme for the populist *Lijst Pim
Fortuyn*. In Austria and Denmark liberal–conservative coalitions became dependent on
the support of anti-immigrant right-wing parties. In Southern and Eastern Europe,
despite these countries' short histories of immigration, populist movements centred on
immigration became politically influential. In Italy, Silvio Berlusconi came to power in
1994 on the basis of anti-immigrant alliances with the populist regional party *Lega Nord*
and the post-fascist party *Alleanza Nazionale* (he would repeat this successful strategy
again in 2001 and 2008).

[27] See Simon Green, *The Politics of Exclusion: Institutions and Immigration Policy in Contemporary
Germany* (Manchester: Manchester University Press, 2004).

[28] James F. Hollifield, 'France: Republicanism and the Limits of Immigration Control', in Wayne
Cornelius, Philip L. Martin and James F. Hollifield (eds), *Controlling Immigration: A Global Perspective*
(Stanford, CA: Stanford University Press, 2004), 183–214.

[29] S. Bouamama, A. Cordeiro and M. Roux, *La Citoyenneté dans tous ses États* (Paris: CIEMI
L'Harmattan, 1992); Alec C. Hargreaves, *Multi-Ethnic France: Immigration, Politics, Culture and Society*
(New York: Routledge, 2007); Catherine Wihtol De Wenden and Rémy Leveau, *La Beurgeoisie: les trois
ages de la vie associative issue de l'immigration* (Paris: CNRS Editions, 2001).

[30] Sophie Body-Gendrot and Catherine Wihtol De Wenden, *Sortir des banlieues. Pour en finir avec la
tyrannie des territoires* (Paris: Autrement, 2007).

THE EARLY TWENTY-FIRST CENTURY: FORTRESS EUROPE OR LABOUR MAGNET?

From 2000 migration movements again increased sharply. Annual inflows into European OECD countries (that is the EU plus Switzerland and Norway) were above 2 million for each year from 2000 to 2005. The biggest increases were in Southern Europe, but the UK also experienced substantial growth, while entries to Germany and France declined somewhat. The EU expansion of 2004 brought in ten new members (mainly in Eastern and Central Europe), creating a union of 25 states (the EU25), while the expansion of 2007 added Romania and Bulgaria (EU27). Most of the existing EU countries brought in transition measures to prevent large inflows, but many accession state nationals did move to seek work, especially in the UK, Ireland, and Sweden, which had not introduced entry restrictions.[31] However, despite official rhetoric giving priority to economic migration, the largest single immigration category in the great majority of European countries remained family reunion, which made up between one-third and two-thirds of all entrants.[32]

Asylum and other humanitarian entries, by contrast, were below 10 per cent of all inflows by the mid-2000s. Asylum entries for Europe as a whole rose from the late 1990s, peaking at 471,000 in 2001, but had declined to 243,000 by 2005[33] and continued to fall in subsequent years. Britain experienced considerable growth in asylum-seeker entries in the early 2000s. Campaigns by such popular newspapers as *The Daily Express, The Sun* and *The Daily Mail* claimed that asylum seekers were getting priority in housing allocation, as well as cars, jobs, and other privileges. Rather than providing leadership in exposing these myths, the Blair Labour Government did all it could to keep out asylum seekers. Other European governments—together with the USA and Australia—adopted similar approaches.

UN Refugee Commissioner Ruud Lubbers, appointed in 2001, had sought a reaffirmation of states' commitment to the 1951 Refugee Convention.[34] In response, many European politicians argued that the Convention had been introduced to deal with very different situations and was no longer appropriate for the globalized refugee flows resulting from decolonization and internal warfare in the global South. On the other hand, NGOs and refugee scholars pointed out that the Convention failed to provide protection for the large numbers of internally displaced persons (IDPs), as well as for people

---

[31] Home Office, *Accession Monitoring Report May 2004–September 2005* (London: Home Office, Department for Work and Pensions, HM Revenue and Customs, and Office of the Deputy Prime Minister, 2005).

[32] OECD, *International Migration Outlook: Annual Report 2007* (Paris: Organisation for Economic Cooperation and Development, 2007).

[33] OECD, *International Migration Outlook: Annual Report 2006* (Paris: Organisation for Economic Cooperation and Development, 2006).

[34] Ibid.; see also n. 15.

displaced by development projects (such as dams). The motivations for these critiques were very different: political leaders wanted to amend the Convention to reduce asylum seeker flows, while refugee advocates wanted an expanded Convention to cover groups lacking protection.

However, it became clear that, in the political climate of the early 2000s, any change to the Convention would mean a weakening of international protection. The UNHCR under Lubbers therefore developed the 'Convention Plus' programme, designed to reduce refugee flows by improving refugee protection in regions of origin and by addressing the developmental problems that precipitated violence and poverty.[35] European political leaders did then reaffirm their commitment to the Convention, but continued to do everything possible to make it hard for asylum seekers to enter their countries to apply for refugee status.

In 2003 Prime Minister Blair sought agreement from European leaders to set up 'off-shore processing' camps in countries such as Libya and Ukraine; the British 'new initiative' failed due to concerns about the human rights records of some such states. Deterrent measures were introduced, such as detention of asylum applicants, prohibition of employment, and exclusion from welfare payments. Asylum seeker entries to Britain did indeed fall from 103,000 in 2002 to just 28,000 in 2006, but the denial of a legal route to seek asylum pushed many people into irregular migration, as it was actually easier to live and work illegally than to make a claim for refugee status.

Fear of far-right mobilization may have been the motivation for tightening up asylum rules and demonizing immigrations, but the capitulation of centrist parties to racist claims probably actually strengthened the extremists. Asylum along with irregular immigration and employment became key political issues. In fact irregular migration was driven by the combination of unmet labour market demand for lower-skilled workers, differentials in potential income compared with poor countries of origin, and the failure of governments to introduce legal migration opportunities. The exact numbers are unknown—one of the more credible estimates put the irregular migrant population of the EU around 2005 at between 4.1 and 7.3 million.[36]

The political dilemma became ever more acute. On the one hand, it was increasingly clear that migration was of vital economic and demographic importance to Europe. On the other, public opinion was overwhelmingly negative about immigration. The old fears about loss of jobs and burdens on welfare systems were exacerbated by security scares following the terrorist attacks of 9 September 2001 in the USA, 11 March 2004 in Madrid, and 7 July 2005 in London. In the context of the wars in Afghanistan and Iraq, many people came to see Muslim minorities (numerous in France, Britain, Germany, and the

---

[35] Stephen Castles and Nicholas Van Hear, *Developing DFID's Policy Approach to Refugees and Internally Displaced Persons*. Report to the Conflict and Humanitarian Affairs Department (Oxford: Refugee Studies Centre, 2005); Stephen Castles and Nicholas Van Hear, 'Root Causes', in Alex Betts (ed.), *Global Migration Governance* (Oxford: Oxford University Press, 2011).

[36] Franck Düvell (ed.), *Illegal Immigration in Europe: Beyond Control* (Basingstoke: Palgrave Macmillan, 2005).

Netherlands) not only as a potential security threat, but also as a force undermining the national cultures and identities of European nations.

Governments struggled to manage this dilemma. The economic and demographic arguments for migration were persuasive, especially for employers and finance authorities struggling to maintain national industries in the face of global competition. By 2005, foreign-born workers made up a substantial share of the labour force: 25 per cent in Switzerland, 15 per cent in Austria and Germany, and around 12 per cent in other Western European countries. Migrants provided a new source of labour at a time when national workforces were stagnating or declining. From 1995–2005, migrants made up between one- and two-thirds of new employees in most Western and Southern European countries. Many migrants brought skills with them. In Belgium, Luxemburg, Sweden, and Denmark, over 40 per cent of the employed migrants who arrived from 1995 to 2005 had tertiary education. In France the figure was 35 per cent, and in the Netherlands 30 per cent. In many cases, migrant workers had higher qualification profiles than local-born workers. Only in Southern European countries did low-skilled labour migration predominate.[37]

Demographic factors were closely linked. According to a 2005 European Commission discussion paper, the population of the EU as a whole was likely to fall by 1.5 per cent from 457m in 2004 to 450m by 2050. However, the decline would be much greater in Germany (9.6 per cent), Italy (8.9 per cent) and the ten mainly Eastern and Central European 'Accession States' which joined the EU in 2004 (11.7 per cent). More serious still was population ageing. By 2050, a working age (15–64) population of 57 per cent would have to support 30 per cent of the population aged 65 and over. The Commission therefore called for a legal migration plan to meet labour needs at all skill levels, arguing that:

> In the short to mid-term, labour immigration can...positively contribute to tackling the effects of this demographic evolution and will prove crucial to satisfying current and future labour market needs and thus ensure economic sustainability and growth.[38]

However, European governments were reluctant to adopt such measures, for fear of a public backlash. The EU's migration plan therefore focused on attracting the highly skilled (even if this meant a brain drain for African and Asian countries of origin). In the face of fierce global competition for scarce skills in such areas as management, information technology, research and development, and health services, European governments differentiated their immigration policies to attract the highly skilled, while erecting barriers to the low-skilled. Yet low-skilled migrant workers were increasingly demanded by employers in areas unattractive to local workers, such as catering, cleaning, housework, health services, care of the elderly, the building industry, and garment manufacturing.

---

[37] OECD, *International Migration Outlook: Annual Report 2007*.

[38] CEC, *Communication from the Commission: Policy Plan on Legal Migration*. COM(2005)669 final (Brussels: Commission of the European Communities, 2005).

Since governments generally did not want to admit low-skilled migrant workers, labour was often provided by irregular workers, asylum seekers, ethnic minority women, and youth. Weak legal status, ethnic discrimination, social exclusion processes, and gender bias all combined to produce a new reserve of racialized labour, which formed the bottom rung in an increasingly polarized workforce.[39]

The global financial crisis of 2007–9 changed migration trends. Many Polish and other Eastern European workers left Britain and Ireland to return home. European countries sought to limit migration inflows, and in some cases tried to persuade migrant workers to leave. In the best known case, the Spanish government offered early pay-outs of social security contributions to workers who departed. This scheme was conspicuously unsuccessful, as most workers judged that their long-term chances were better if they stayed in Spain. In some countries hostility to new migrant workers led to strikes and demonstrations. Construction workers on oil refinery sites in Britain demanded priority for local workers. Although this demand was illegal under EU legislation, employers and the government did broker deals that partially met worker demands. However, by early 2010 it had become clear that the crisis had merely brought a brief interruption to long-term trends: migrant employment and remittances to families overseas remained resilient, and migration flows resumed as economic conditions improved. Moreover, much of migration is motivated by social and family considerations, which are not so susceptible to short-term economic trends.[40]

LIVING WITH DIVERSITY: MULTICULTURALISM AND SOCIAL COHESION

By 2005 the *foreign resident population* of European OECD countries totalled over 24 million persons—about 5 per cent of the total population. This figure refers only to people with foreign nationality, but in fact many immigrants do obtain the nationality of the country of residence. The *foreign-born population* figure includes such persons: in 2005 Europe had 39 million foreign-born residents—8 per cent of the total population.[41] But even this figure underestimates the immigrant contribution to European population, because it does not include children born to immigrant parents who acquire European nationalities by birthright.

Altogether, over half a century of immigration has transformed Europe's demographic and cultural make-up. Immigrants have come from all over the world, bringing with them a great variety of cultural practices, religions, and values. The effects are

---

[39] Carl-Ulrik Schierup, Peo Hansen and Stephen Castles, *Migration, Citizenship and the European Welfare State: A European Dilemma* (Oxford: Oxford University Press, 2006).

[40] For a collection of articles, papers and web links on the effects of the Global Financial Crisis on migration see: http://www.age-of-migration.com/uk/financialcrisis/index.html, accessed March 2010.

[41] Data from OECD, *International Migration Outlook: Annual Report 2007*.

particularly evident in Europe's cities, where immigrants have become concentrated. Throughout its history, Europe has been a place of movements and minglings, yet nineteenth-century nationalism embarked on the project of creating nation states based on myths of homogeneity and unitary national identities. Such ideals have been discredited by devastating wars and seem to have no place in a globalizing world. The enormous diversity brought about by immigration appears to make ideas of cultural homogeneity absurd. Yet recently, strong trends towards the reassertion of national identities as the basis of social cohesion have become evident. It is important to understand how and why this has happened.

A starting point is the gulf between the perceived economic benefits of migration and the popular fears of the social and political consequences. The era of neoliberal globalization since the late 1970s has brought a fundamental social transformation. For the old industrial countries, globalization has meant the closure of older industries, restructuring of labour forces, erosion of welfare states, and decline of traditional working-class communities. Many working people have experienced a devaluation of their skills and experience. Work has become more isolated and individualized, reflected in the weakening of trade unions and working-class culture. People with high educational credentials, marketable skills, and secure legal status enjoy unprecedented opportunities, while those who lack such attributes often have only a choice between unemployment and a succession of insecure, casual, and exploitative jobs. In a situation of insecurity, inequality, and individualization, the assertion of national identity has taken on a new significance. It appears as a form of resistance against globalization, but is in fact impotent against the economic and political processes that have brought rapid change. Yet the nostalgia for myths of homogeneity can act as a powerful force of exclusion against immigrants and ethnic minorities. The latter are not only visible signs of globalization, but are also vulnerable to populist sentiments and actions.

This helps to explain why there has been a backlash against multiculturalism in many European countries. From the 1970s to the early 1990s many countries had moved towards policies designed to recognize the cultural identities and social rights of minorities, as well as the role of the state in combating discrimination and racism. In some cases there were explicit multicultural policies (e.g. UK); in others terms such as 'immigrant policy' (Sweden) or 'minorities policy' (Netherlands) were used; in yet others the notion of 'integration of foreign fellow citizens' (Germany) were applied. France was an apparent anomaly, with its republican model, which mandated rejection of ethnic monitoring and non-recognition of immigrant cultures and communities. But even here there were surrogate minority policies under the euphemistic label of 'policy of the city'.

Since the mid-1990s this trend has been reversed. The stress in European political discourse was no longer on the recognition of minority cultures, but on integration, social cohesion, and 'national values'. In Britain, for example, critics of multiculturalism argued that it had failed to provide a unifying national identity. This was (explicitly or implicitly) linked to concerns about the integration and loyalty of Muslims, especially after July 2005. A citizenship test was introduced to promote knowledge of British society and values. Although government statements remained positive about the religious and cultural rights of minorities, a new pressure to confirm with mainstream cultural and behavioural patterns was evident.

In France, the centre-right government pledged to cut immigration and strengthen law and order. A law of 2004 forbade the wearing of Islamic headscarves and other 'conspicuous religious symbols' in public places such as schools. Interior Minister Sarkozy brought in policies of tougher policing in the *banlieues*. This exacerbated the marginalization of young people of immigrant origin. In autumn 2005, France experienced severe rioting, with nightly battles between police and youths, attacks on public buildings, hundreds of cars burnt out, and many people injured. The official response was to call for even tougher law and order measures. The Immigration and Integration Law of 2006—known as the *Loi Sarkozy*—included a new immigration policy, based on selection according to economic criteria (*immigration choisie*), mandatory 'integration contracts' (*contrat d'accueil et d'intégration*) for long-term residents, and policies of 'co-development' to link migration, return and development of countries of origin. This law was popular with French voters, and appears to have helped Sarkozy to become President of France in 2007. One of his first actions as President was to establish a Ministry of Immigration and National Identity. However, new riots in late 2007 showed that deep problems remained.

The Dutch Government also made sharp changes in policy,[42] while Germany, Sweden, and other countries moved in similar directions.[43] However, it is important to note that multiculturalist *discourses* have often declined more than actual multicultural *policies*: measures to recognize the social and cultural needs of immigrants and minorities have often changed little, even as public discourse has shifted. The realities of diverse populations and their different lifestyles and social needs make special measures essential, especially at the local level.

The backlash against multiculturalism has been interpreted in differing ways. A dominant approach is to draw attention to social disadvantage and marginalization of many immigrant groups—especially those of non-European origin—and to claim that ethnic minorities are to blame by clustering together and refusing to integrate. This is often linked to the idea of the incompatibility of Muslim values with modern European societies. In this interpretation, recognition of cultural diversity has had the perverse effect of encouraging ethnic separatism and the development of 'parallel lives'.[44] A model of individual integration—based if necessary on compulsory integration contracts and citizenship tests—is thus seen as a way of achieving greater equality for immigrants and their children. The problem for such views, however, is that the one country that has maintained its model of individual integration, France, is also experiencing dramatic problems, which came to a head with the youth riots of 2005 and 2007.

[42] Ellie Vasta, 'From Ethnic Minorities to Ethnic Majority Policy: Multiculturalism and the Shift to Assimilationism in the Netherlands', *Ethnic and Racial Studies* 30:5 (2007), 713–40.

[43] For details see Castles and Miller, *The Age of Migration*.

[44] Ted Cantle, *Community Cohesion: A Report of the Independent Review Team* (London: Home Office, 2001).

In contrast, proponents of multicultural and equality policies argue that economic, political, and social marginalization still experienced by many ethnic minorities in Europe actually reflects the unwillingness of destination societies to deal with two issues. The first is the deep-seated cultures of racism that are a legacy of colonialism and imperialism. In times of stress, such as economic restructuring or international conflict, racism can lead to social exclusion, discrimination, and violence against minorities. The second issue is the trend to greater inequality resulting from globalization and economic restructuring. Increased international competition puts pressure on employment, working conditions, and welfare systems. At the same time neoliberal economic policies encourage greater pay differences and reduce the capacity of states to redistribute income to reduce poverty and social disadvantage.

Taken together, these factors have led to a racialization of ethnic difference. Minorities often have poor employment situations, low incomes, and high rates of impoverishment. This in turn leads to concentration in low-income neighbourhoods and growing residential segregation. The existence of separate and marginal communities is then taken as evidence of failure to integrate, and this in turn is perceived as a threat to the host society. The result is a 'dual crisis' of national identity and the welfare state throughout Europe.[45] The attempt to resolve the crisis through racialization of minorities does not provide a solution. Rather, it threatens the fundamental values upon which democratic societies are based.

Further Reading

Bade, Klaus, *Migration in European History* (Oxford: Blackwell, 2003).

Banting, K.G. and W. Kymlicka (eds), *Multiculturalism and the Welfare State: Recognition and Redistribution in Contemporary Democracies* (New York: Oxford University Press, 2006).

Castles, Stephen and Mark J. Miller, *The Age of Migration: International Population Movements in the Modern World*, 4th edn (Basingstoke: Palgrave Macmillan, 2009).

Cohen, Robin, *Migration and its Enemies: Global Capital, Migrant Labour and the Nation-State* (Aldershot: Ashgate, 2006).

Düvell, Franck (ed.), *Illegal Immigration in Europe: Beyond Control* (Basingstoke: Palgrave Macmillan, 2005).

Hatton, T.J. and J.G. Williamson, *The Age of Mass Migration: Causes and Economic Effects* (Oxford: Oxford University Press, 1998).

Helton, Arthur C., *The Price of Indifference: Refugees and Humanitarian Action in the New Century* (Oxford: Oxford University Press, 2002).

Keely, Charles B., 'The International Refugee Regimes(s): The End of the Cold War Matters', *International Migration Review* 35:1 (2001), 303–14.

Lucassen, Leo, *The Immigrant Threat: The Integration of Old and New Migrants in Western Europe since 1890* (Urbana, IL: University of Illinois Press, 2005).

---

[45] This argument is developed in detail in Schierup, Hansen and Castles, *Migration, Citizenship and the European Welfare State*.

Moch, L.P., *Moving Europeans: Migration in Western Europe since 1650* (Bloomington, IN: Indiana University Press, 1992).

Noiriel, Gérard, *Immigration, antisémitisme et racisme en France (XIXe–XXe siècle)* (Paris: Fayard, 2007).

Swift, Jonathan, 'A modest proposal for preventing the children of poor people in Ireland from being a burden to their parents or country; and for making them beneficial to the public (1729)' in H. Davies (ed.), *Irish Tracts 1728–1733* (Oxford: Blackwell, 1955).

Torpey, J., 'Passports and the Development of Immigration Controls in the North Atlantic during the Long Nineteenth Century', in A. Fahrmeir, O. Faron and P. Weil (eds), *Migration Control in the North Atlantic World* (New York: Berghahn, 2003), 73–91.

Wang, G., *Global History and Migrations* (Boulder, CO: Westview Press, 1997).

Zolberg, A.R., A. Suhrke, and S. Aguayo, *Escape from Violence* (Oxford: Oxford University Press, 1989).

CHAPTER 10

GENDERING EUROPE, EUROPEANIZING GENDER: THE POLITICS OF DIFFERENCE IN A GLOBAL ERA

ULI LINKE

WHEN attempting to understand the cultural politics of gender in Europe after 1945, some readers will undoubtedly anticipate answers to the following set of questions: To what extent have the impact of the Cold War, the rise of feminism, the supposedly sexually liberated 1960s, the emergence of 'post-feminism', and the putative 'crisis of masculinity' changed attitudes towards gender and sexuality, and impacted on gender-related legislation? Such an approach to historical inquiry is intriguingly persuasive: it seeks to comprehend the present by a turn to the past as a chronological text, by assembling bits and pieces of official memory into a plausible narrative, an ordered sequence of events that logically unfolds through time into the present. But how can we decipher the European signposts of gender in this manner if the historical parameters as well as the constituent fields of power have become dramatically unstable? When proceeding with my research on these issues, it soon became clear that a succinct discussion about gender matters in contemporary Europe must follow a somewhat different trajectory.

During the past two decades, the political landscape of Europe has undergone dramatic change. The powerful matrix of global capitalism has deeply affected European nation forms, social ideologies, and political systems, as suggested by German (re)unification, the collapse of the Soviet regime, the war in the former Yugoslavia, and the subsequent formation of the European Union, including the ongoing Europeanization of post-socialist states. In this context, the historical fixity of borders, bodies, and spaces has been unmoored. The end of the Cold War furnished new possibilities for envisioning society, promoting major realignments of border regimes and fundamental transpositions in the topographic fabric of Europe's gendered imagination. In addition, the emergent entanglements of state and corporate interests not only changed the political contours of Europe but also altered the social conditions under which gendered imaginaries are brought to public visibility.

Under the conditions of European globalization, the cultural production of identities, bodies, and lifestyles has increasingly shifted to the market place, the terrain of advertising, fashion, and media. Culture industries manufacture national distinction by means of commodity desire and consumption. But the work of neoliberal economies, with their seductive promise of unlimited possibilities, is simultaneously defended as a state-protected privilege, a concession of citizenship reserved for European nationals. The political spaces of capitalism are closely guarded. Imaginaries of gender and race are called upon to authorize participation in the dreamworlds of prosperity. The formation of the European security state after 9/11 has intensified this process by giving rise to new border regimes, ethnic profiling, and militarized racism. From this perspective, the focus on gender in Europe by detour to the long-accepted master narratives of cold-war national history requires a critical reassessment. The impact of globalization, founded on a cohesive network of political, military, and corporate interests, has fundamentally shifted the parameters, discourses, and possibilities for negotiating gender-related matters in Europe.

How is gender configured in this globally transformed political space? In a post-national Europe, the reality of ethnic diversity and cultural pluralism has unravelled the idea of 'women' as a homogeneous or undifferentiated group. In the new Europe, women's studies includes a focus on ethnically diverse femininities.[1] The intensifying engagement with global scholarly debates and postcolonial theory has produced another feminist turn. Released from the phallocentric logic of the nation state, the category *woman* is no longer imagined as the 'second sex', a negatively marked 'other', whose difference can be reduced to the body. The very recognition that narratives of femininity are 'produced by political discourse' has had far reaching consequences for feminist scholarship, as Hillary Footitt suggests, including the rejection of the sexed binary male-to-female model.[2]

Such a paradigmatic shift in feminist thinking has been facilitated by the adoption of 'gender' as a conceptual tool: a gender-based inquiry examines how masculine and feminine life worlds are socially constructed and how hegemonies of male power can be altered or transformed. Subsequent research on gender relations, and women's lives, across Europe's multinational spaces reveals that the collusion of global economic restructuring and entrenched local traditions propagates old as well as new disparities.[3] Despite European reforms of education, welfare, and employment, gender segregation

---

[1] Gabrielle Griffin and Rosi Braidotti (eds), *Thinking Differently: A Reader in European Women's Studies* (London: Zed Books, 2002).

[2] Hilary Footitt, *Women, Europe, and the New Languages of Politics* (London: Continuum, 2002), 3, 5.

[3] Maria Dolors García-Ramon and Janice Monk, *Women of the European Union* (London: Routledge, 1996).

and gender inequalities persist. Whether in the private world of family life or in the public sphere, women's experiences as wives, mothers, workers, and sexual partners continue to be shaped by conventional gender expectations. Persistent cultural understandings of domestic work and childcare as female responsibilities have prevented women from full participation in flexible labour market opportunities.

How can these normative models be challenged? As a reformist entity, the European Union has positioned itself as a legal order against the unprecedented fluidity and instability of global power relations: the judicial system has become the 'Union's genetic code'.[4] Although founded on a political order sensitive to difference and social equality, as Clare McGlynn asserts, the quest for unity and uniformity tends to erode acceptance of otherness. In other words, Europe's preoccupation with judicial matters, which seeks to neutralize legal pluralism and minimize the incoherence of rights in political practice, produces unforeseen results: 'There is a tendency for the presence of rights to somehow construct the ideal rights-bearing citizen. This assertion of "ideal citizen" models, with its consequent marginalization and exclusion of the non-ideal, carries a particular resonance for feminists.'[5]

European family policy reforms provide an instructive example: by a focus on protecting women's reproductive capacity, the figure of the single, childless, or lesbian woman is rendered invisible.[6] While granting generous provision for maternity leave and maternal health care, such policy measures confirm prevailing gender expectations: men's exemption from domestic tasks is not challenged. In the family reform documents, 'women are presented as a homogeneous category without race, sexual orientation, ethnic origin, ability or any other life dimension.'[7] Women's distinguishing feature is the ability to produce children. Europe's legal intervention in the family aims to protect female procreativity as a matter of equal opportunity, thereby reifying women's traditional roles as mothers and caregivers. Although focused on enabling women's participation in the marketplace without infringing on maternal responsibilities, Europe's legal rights discourse does not prioritize gender equality. The reforms and provisions speak to political concerns about a demographic crisis, a shrinking European population, which is attributed to decreasing fertility rates among white women.

In what manner are these hegemonies of gender transformed when subjected to the regulatory mechanisms of the European Union? The formation of a united Europe requires normative standards for implementing binding policies: the rights of equality or prohibitions of sex-discrimination need to be enforceable across different nation states. Governed by efforts to avert a legitimation crisis, European unification proceeds by a turn to the global legal order: the supranational polity is stabilized by drawing on the repertoire of human rights laws and the 'universally valid' normative underpinnings

---

[4] Clare McGlynn, *Families and the European Union* (Cambridge: Cambridge University Press, 2006).
[5] Ibid., 9.
[6] Griffin and Braidotti, *Thinking Differently*, ch. 2.
[7] Emanuela Lombardo and Petra Meier, 'Gender Mainstreaming in the EU', *European Journal of Women's Studies* 13:2 (2006), 151–66; here 157, 158.

of legislation. Europe's interface with global legislative standards facilitates political integration. But at the same time, as Jo Shaw cautions, 'dominant ideologies about women, motherhood, family life, and the sexual division of labour' become European legal doctrine without critical attention to the diversity of women's experience or the privileged status of men.[8]

In contemporary Europe, gender politics are reconfigured by a global imaginary. But in this process, ethno-national and local machinations of race, sex, and nation remain uncontested.[9] The turn to global human rights is a legitimating practice: it advocates a pseudo-rational universalism that negates awareness of the existing hegemonies of gender inequality. In this manner, the sexual trafficking of girls and the treatment of women as refugees have gained attention as critical trans-border matters and national security issues rather than as formative fields of gender, democracy, and citizenship. A poignant example is the feminist-state alliance against female genital cutting in the United Kingdom: empowered by human rights laws, British parliament has prohibited the practice by criminalizing 'ritual' surgery and by encoding a European aesthetic of the 'normality' of women's genitalia.[10] Under the guise of 'protecting' female bodies, the 2004 Act engenders a form of institutionalized discrimination. The law is directed against 'woman of African origin', 'while permitting British women to have surgery to create "designer vaginas"'.[11] Despite the interface with global human rights norms, Europe's gendered imaginary remains exclusionary, governed by notions of impermissible difference.

This chapter examines the cultural politics of gender at the juncture of globalization, securitization, and Europeanization. In a most general sense, I inquire how Europeans have 'fashioned their distinction' in attempts to reconstitute themselves as global citizens in a multi-ethnic, post-imperial Europe.[12] More specifically, my research suggests that the European imaginary is a volatile construct, a formative identity staged against gendered machinations of difference: the 'veiled Muslim woman', the 'African refugee', or the 'Islamic terrorist' are figures of alterity that are forced to inhabit fields of gendered abnormality or sexual deviance, depending on the shifting ground of European identity.

If under late capitalism 'identification with a nation' or political regime 'presumes a simple, unambiguous process of subject-making', as Aihwa Ong proposed, then it is crucial to investigate 'how different modalities or regulations use gender stereotypes in configuring race, nation, and citizenship privileges'.[13] By a focus on the commoditization of white femaleness, the coercive normalization of Muslim masculinity, the 'liberation' of the veiled Muslim woman, and the eroticization of black men in white consumer fantasy,

---

[8] Jo Shaw, 'Importing Gender', *Journal of European Public Policy* 7:3 (2000), 406–31; here 407–8.

[9] R. Amy Elman (ed.), *Sexual Politics and the European Union* (Providence, RI: Berghahn Books, 1996).

[10] Moira Dustin, 'Female Genital Mutilation/Cutting in the UK', *European Journal of Women's Studies* 17:1 (2010), 7–23.

[11] Ibid., 17.

[12] Frederick Cooper and Laura A. Stoler (eds), *Tensions of Empire* (Berkeley, CA: University of California Press, 1997), 16.

[13] Aihwa Ong, 'Cultural Citizenship as Subject-Making', *Current Anthropology* 37:5 (1996), 737–51, 758–62; here 759.

my analysis of exemplary cases demonstrates how gendered imaginaries in Europe are forged by a complex dialogue with race, nation, capitalism, sex, and security.

Globalizing Europe: The Politics of Whiteness and the Allure of the 'White Woman'

Snapshot One: In London, New York, and Tokyo, financial investment opportunities are promoted by gigantic billboards in subway stations and airports featuring the German supermodel Claudia Schiffer. Seductively posed, her pale-white body is stretched horizontally across the visual frame: centered within a seamless back-ground-space of whiteness, she is casually positioned, reclined on her side. Her body's nudity, which reveals the immaculate smoothness of her legs and arms, is accentuated by the silky fabric of the German national flag that is tenderly draped across her torso. She is facing the camera, her head slightly propped up, framed by her arms and cascading blond hair. Lounging on the imperceptible ground, posed against and within a white screen, she extends an invitation as part of the global marketing campaign: 'Invest in Germany—Land of Ideas'. This advocacy of monetary investment in German business ventures is further articulated by a series of suggestive slogans: 'Discover the beauty of the deal.' 'Invest in Germany, boys.' 'Come on over to my place.' 'Follow your instincts.'[14]

How is gender made visible in these spaces of trans-border capitalism? Endorsed by government, commerce, and industry, the German marketing initiative is infused with erotic messages. The campaign designers envision international investors as male, as businessmen, whose lurid economic desires can be fulfilled by intimacy with the German nation as a female plaything. In this fantasy, transnational financial endeavours are crafted as intimate erotic encounters. Capital investment in Germany is presented as a sexual adventure. The white female body, positioned in unbounded white space, is offered up in the global marketplace as a sexual commodity in exchange for cash. Monetary transactions across international borders are evidently not tarnished by colour. Global capitalist space is safely imagined as a domain of (hetero-normative) whiteness. Although the white female figure inhabits this imaginary terrain, she is branded as a political subject: her body is enveloped by the German flag; she is marked as a national icon. Like a ventriloquist's doll, she gives corporal form and voice to the nation's desires.

---

[14] Land of Ideas: http://www.land-of-ideas.org/CDA/investment_promotion_cs,6359,0,,en.html, accessed February 2010.

In these advertisements, female erotic agency is less an assertion of feminist liberation than a demonstration of misogynist representation. Although offered freely, as an act of independent volition, the white woman's sexual being is appropriated as a national service, affirming her citizenship status. When transacted on behalf of the nation, white pornographic femininity is state sanctioned. Even in a global context, white femininity is entangled with the national order. In an interview, the German model explains her involvement in the campaign in precisely these terms:

> I feel it is an honor to be part of the Land of Ideas Campaign and to be honest I feel it is the least I can do for a country that has supported me so much... I immediately agreed to support the campaign... It's true that I'm now living very happily with my family in London... My lifestyle has forced me to be a citizen of the world but I can still identify with Germany as my homeland.... In reality I've felt a bit like an ambassador for Germany ever since the beginning of my international career.[15]

In this world of global financial markets, economic power is successfully promoted through the medium of white female signifiers. Images of the white European woman, displayed in various states of undress, are an effective marketing ploy in China, where she is ferociously desired as an icon of beauty, fashion, lifestyle, and consumer freedom.[16] In the twenty-first century, the white woman conquered Asian markets as a commodity ambassador to adorn urban commercial spaces, store displays, and billboards. In global consumer culture, even ice cream is marketed with representations of white femininity: identical images of her revealing body circulate across Japan, Korea, Singapore, Taiwan, and China, where she titillates the local imagination by indulging her lips, mouth, and tongue with the frozen delicacies. Signalling sexual availability within the bounds of gendered behaviour, the white woman incites consumer desire with promises of erotic intimacy: 'Love her'; 'Let your tongue travel'; 'Always like first time'.

Although whiteness and white femininity may appeal to a generalized desire for 'Western' modernity, in the above campaign for *Häagen-Dazs* ice cream, the link to Europe is encoded in the commodity. The brand name (created by Polish immigrants to New York City in 1967) mimics German and/or northern European product origin. While global marketing operates with generic signifiers of whiteness, consumer desire is harnessed by conjuring imaginative possibilities for possessing the white European woman. But this gender-encoded *and* racializing effect of global capitalism is rarely acknowledged.

How are such global machinations of gender, nation, and race produced and sustained in the centre of European space? What are the formative possibilities of 'whiteness' in this era of globalization? In Britain, BBC2 has introduced a new television series,

---

[15] See www.land-of-ideas.org, accessed February 2010.
[16] Louisa Schein, 'The Consumption of Color and the Politics of White Skin in Post-Mao China', in Roger Lancaster and Michaela di Leonardo (eds), *The Gender/Sexuality Reader* (New York: Routledge, 1997), 473–82.

which is shown under the contentious title *White Season*.[17] First released in 2007, the series includes documentaries about how members of 'the white working class in Britain' (including male labourers, single mothers, adolescents, and elderly couples) share a growing sense of erasure, of 'becoming invisible' in an increasingly multi-ethnic society. The programme voices British anxieties about being a white minority in neighbourhoods, schools, and jobs. Sentiments of erasure have promoted a recuperation of white legitimacy. In Germany, commercial image makers have likewise identified 'whiteness' as the new trend colour. This determination was made in 2006 by the executive of an advertisement firm in Hamburg, who publicized his assessment of the media's prevailing colour preferences in a widely disseminated article.[18] In his essay 'Trend Colour White: The New Simplicity', the author proclaims that whiteness 'signifies a new simplicity'. It is 'pure, honest, rational'; 'in an era of uncertainty', whiteness is 'a contemporary liberation from that which is coloured'; it 'symbolizes clarity, purity, superiority and intelligence'. The author's assertions are illustrated by a portrait photo of a sensuous female head, sculpted from plaster or white marble. Chosen as the physical embodiment of the author's narrative claims, the white woman's face transports the idealized whiteness into the iconography of race. By implication, blackness is devalued, relegated to the antithetical space of the mentally and emotionally inferior. According to this colour scheme, whiteness connotes rational intellect, while blackness inhabits the body and is equated with raw physicality, signifying a 'premodern' masculinity. These articulations are an imprint of what Frantz Fanon has characterized as Europe's 'attempt to decerebralize' the black colonial subject, thereby creating inferior 'natives'.[19]

Such a gendered racial imaginary is reified by the recruitment of black male athletes from Africa and the Americas for white European entertainment. In this capitalist, profit-driven enterprise, the sports arena emerges as a carceral zone for the enactment of public rituals of degradation. Strategically essentialized as performative bodies, reduced to their physicality, black soccer players are 'spit upon, jeered with racial remarks and mocked with monkey noises, [with] banners that reflect neofascist and racist beliefs, and the tossing of bananas or banana peels, all familiar occurrences during matches'.[20] The crass dehumanization of black men in the European soccer stadium by spectators and officials continues despite the threat of heavy penalties. In response to these anti-black sentiments, Adebowale Ogungbure, a Nigerian–German professional player, stated: 'I'm a human [being], too. They don't spit on dogs. Why should they spit on me? I felt like a nobody'.[21] In these contact zones, the public denigration of black male bodies is intertwined with a visual culture that perpetually normalizes white privilege.

[17] See www.bbc.co.uk/white/, accessed February 2010.

[18] Alexander Hahn, 'Trendfarbe Weiß: die neue Einfachheit', *Slogans.de* (1 June 2006), online at: www.slogans.de/magazine.php?Op=Article&Id=35, accessed February 2010.

[19] Frantz Fanon, *Toward the African Revolution* (New York: Grove Press, 1988), 53.

[20] Jere Longman, 'Surge in Racist Mood Raises concerns on the Eve of the World Cup', *The New York Times* (4 June 2006), online at: www.nytimes.com/2006/06/04/sports/soccer/04racism.html?_r=1&oref=slogin, accessed February 2010.

[21] Ibid.

In response to these racist practices, political activists have launched publicity cam-paigns to promote the message that the nation also includes black people. Such strat-egies include anti-racist banners that visually reclaim black men and white women as equal members of the European community.[22] A similar initiative was pushed by a thirty-million-euro campaign titled 'You are Germany', which was sponsored by leading media industries.[23] The initial phase of the project, which ended in 2006, was launched to enhance the national self-esteem of ordinary Germans by promoting their identifica-tion with well known public figures, including black athletes, ethnic musicians, and minority artists. But the promotion of German nationalism by rendering non-white subjects hyper-visible was unsuccessful. After 2006, the campaign shifted its focus onto the propagation of white children as the iconic future of the European community. Nevertheless, images of a multi-ethnic and multicultural Europe are increasingly circu-lated in the commercial marketing of consumer products, revealing 'multiculturalism as a logic of late capitalism'.[24] Although such ads are strategic insofar as diversity and erotic exoticism are transported into a consumable commodity, they likewise 'affirm that the peculiar synonymity of the terms European and white cannot continue'.[25] But even in these visual proclamations of social inclusion, black masculinity is positioned at the fringe, presented spatially and sexually as a 'modern primitive'.

Some commercial images pursue a more disturbing visuality. In 2006, a German advertising campaign for a detergent (Persil) proclaimed that 'only genuine whiteness creates happiness' by featuring white babies. In the ads, whiteness and babies were visu-ally equated and promoted as a desirable product: happiness. Billboards with the white baby image and slogan were displayed in the central shopping districts of various German cities.[26] During the campaign, the company website further advertised its prod-uct with slogans such as 'whiteness is the color of joy' and 'what is truly white should remain so beautifully white'; the website was likewise saturated with white-baby images. A white infant is by implication conceived by white mothers and fathers. The advertise-ments fabricate an idealization of the white German family, and white parenting in par-ticular.[27] When placed in the context of current public debates about declining birth rates in Germany, and a shrinking white European population, these images gain an added relevance.

[22] Martin Kött, 'Afrodeutsche', Exil-Club.de (29 January 2004), online at: www.exil-club.de/dyn/9.asp ?Aid=67&Avalidate=328914821&cache=63938&url=55972.asp, accessed February 2010.

[23] The original project mentioned here is no longer shown on the site: www.dubistdeutschland.de, accessed February 2010.

[24] See the Berlin billboard ads: http://en.wikipedia.org/wiki/Langnese, accessed February 2010; Ong, 'Cultural Citizenship as Subject-Making', 759.

[25] Paul Gilroy, 'Migrancy, Culture, and a New Map of Europe', in Heike Raphael-Hernandez (ed.), Blackening Europe (New York: Routledge, 2004), xi-xxii; here xii.

[26] Simon Müller 2006, 'Stuttgart – Rassismus', online at: www.flickr.com/search/?q=Persil&w=41894 187404%40No1, accessed February 2010.

[27] The site mentioned here no longer exists (http://news.persil.de/anti-grau/). But even the revised and updated home pages and related info-sites from 2008 continue to promote the product with this motif of white mothers and babies (see http://www.persil.de/100jahre_03_01.php, accessed February 2010).

How is the popular assertion of a 'white Europe' contested or propagated by state officials? My research suggests that gendered notions of race are encoded in the ways in which the European Union configures and imagines its population. The phantasmatic 'whiteness' of the people of Europe is protected by a governing apparatus that seeks to obscure or diminish the presence of 'blackness'. Consequently, the actual size of the black community in European space is difficult to assess. Official estimates are conjectures, mere approximations, based solely on *immigrant* statistics. Following those figures, black Europeans constitute a highly visible although surprisingly small minority population:

> According to research by the European Union...it is roughly estimated that...there are about 300,000 [blacks in Germany]. In France...people of African descent constitute about 1 million. And in the United Kingdom, the Afro-Caribbean population is about...880,000.[28]

European Union records suggest that Europe's black population is numerically insignificant and therefore inconsequential. Although the European Commission acknowledged in 2007 that 'it is likely that these figures are under-estimates of the extent of migration flows between countries' because they exclude 'clandestine migration (such as illegal immigrants or human trafficking)',[29] the statistical disappearance of black Europeans, here explained by criminalizing the vanishing subaltern, is much more problematic.

The magnitude of the numerical erasure of black presence is suggested by current United Nations' documents, in which the international migrant population in Europe is assessed at 64 million.[30] Corresponding demographic figures reveal that close to a third of these 'immigrants in Europe' are from Africa and the Caribbean. This data would suggest a seven-fold differential in the approximate size of the black community when compared to the minimalist estimate produced by the European Union: 3 million versus the UN estimate of 20 million. But even these numbers are misleading. With an exclusive focus on *immigrants and immigration*, the demographic figures erase the reality of blackness among Europe's nationals and citizens. Such statistical estimates work by exclusion. State sponsored racial census counts are prohibited by the European Union.[31]

---

[28] Clarence Lusane, *Hitler's Black Victims* (New York: Routledge, 2003), 251; Eurostat, *European Social Statistics: Migration* (Luxembourg: Office for Official Publications of the European Communities, 2002).

[29] G. Schäfer, M. Feith, M. Fritz, A. Johansson-Augier and U. Wieland (eds), *Europe in Figures: Eurostat Yearbook 2006–07* (Luxembourg: Office for Official Publications of the European Communities, 2007), 75.

[30] United Nations, *International Migration and Development, Report of the Secretary-General* A/60/871 (2006), 1–90; here 29, table 2: www.unhcr.org/protect/PROTECTION/44d711a82.pdf, accessed February 2010. In contrast to European Union statistics, this figure not only includes the narrowly defined bureaucratic figure of the 'immigrant' but short-term migrants, reunited family members, spouses, refugees, and other foreign residents, who are excluded from the EU statistical roster. The United Nations Recommendations on Migration Statistics suggest that the migrant stock be measured in terms of foreign-born and foreign populations.

[31] Jo Goodey, 'Racist Violence in Europe', *Ethnic and Racial Studies* 30:4 (2007), 570–89; here 583–4.

While the 2007 EU anti-discrimination directive makes prominent mention of race to criminalize racism, according to Jo Goddey, the 'data collection practices in England and Wales' are at present at the forefront of legislation and policy implementation; among other Member States, the population's ethno-racial composition remains unreported as well as unrecorded.[32] Although the prohibition against racial data collection is anti-discriminatory in intent, designed to expunge the biometric registers of Nazi persecution from bureaucratic memory, European population statistics are configured by a new discourse of race. What are some of the truth claims embedded in the manufacture and dissemination of this 'official' knowledge?

Black presence is presumed to enter Europe from *outside*: from the Caribbean Islands, Africa, the 'developing' world, and the 'global south'. In this statistical universe, immigrant bodies are inferentially blackened (or whitened) on the basis of national origin. According to this procedure, colour is erroneously ascribed as an essential geographical trace. It is however absurd to categorically assume, as Clarence Lusane points out, 'that an immigrant from South Africa or Jamaica is black' and 'to believe that one from the United States or Canada is white'.[33] Such a vision of human bodies branded by space and invariably marked by a geopolitical territory not only belies the histories of globalization, hybridity, and mobility, but recuperates colonial fantasies of white entitlement. Writing race onto the world map is clearly a political project. The symbolic charting of racial zones across the globe, which relies on the ontological coupling of nature, race, and space, is crucial for our understanding of contemporary European population politics. A white Europe imagined without blacks, following David Theo Goldberg, 'serves as the subliminal text for the raceless state': a body politic conceived as benign (female), civilized, Christian, and white.[34] In Europe's phantasmatic production of race, blackness is affixed to the peripheries of a global cartographic project that strives to *see* the citizen subjects of a united Europe as intrinsically white.

It is no coincidence that the statistical yearbooks produced by the European Community not only diminish the presence of black people in numerical terms but also imagine the 'people in Europe' as white citizen subjects. The statistical erasure of blackness is enmeshed with a visual record. Europe's population statistics are illustrated with an assortment of photographs of white babies.[35] The images reveal a pattern: each photo depicts a single white infant cradled, held, embraced, kissed, or cuddled by a white woman—a young mother, a grandmother, a female medical caregiver. While the accompanying statistical figures and narratives speak about Europe's 'declining fertility rate'

---

[32] Ibid, 571, 575.

[33] Lusane, *Hitler's Black Victims*, 251.

[34] David Theo Goldberg, 'Racial Europeanization', *Ethnic and Racial Studies* 29:2 (2006), 331–64; here 339–40.

[35] See M. Copers, V. Guillemet, A. Johansson-Augier, G. Kyi and M. Radulescu (eds), *Eurostat Yearbook 2004: The Statistical Guide to Europe* (Luxembourg: Office for Official Publications of the European Communities, 2004); G. Schäfer, S. Cervellin, M. Feith and M. Fritz (eds), *Europe in Figures: Eurostat Yearbook 2005* (Luxembourg: Office for Official Publications of the European Communities, 2005), 61, 67, 71; Schäfer et al., *Europe in Figures: Eurostat Yearbook 2006–07*.

and 'fewer children' (messages repeated as truth claims in the captions), the photos provide a record of women's sensuous, loving, devotion to white children. The fearful message of the demographic projections (white Europeans as an endangered species) is
countered by a suggested solution: the need for more white offspring. The recuperation
of apocalyptic visions regarding Europe's anticipated white depopulation is simultaneously infused by a fabricated fear of blackness.

The demographic analysis of the 'People in Europe', as published in the EU statistical
yearbook in 2005, concludes with an untitled photo of babies in a hospital setting: in the
centre, six cribs with white infants; on the outer edge, positioned on either side, two
cribs with black infants; a population graph is superposed on the photo.[36] Interpreted in
context, based on the statistical data presented in the preceding text, the visual message
is uncompromisingly clear: in Europe, one out of four babies born is black. The unsettling implications of the numerical decline of Europe's white population are enhanced
by a visual focus on the multiplication of black children. Europe's statistical imagination
conjures and affirms cultural anxieties about the disappearance of a white European
future by a focus on diminishing birth rates among white mothers and the disproportionate fertility of the black female body. From this perspective, the statistical diminution of blacks in Europe may be no accident. Indeed, it articulates 'Europe's repressed,
denied, and disavowed blackness'.[37] The preoccupation with immigration and female
reproductivity, as Paul Gilroy asserts, implicates the European Union in the explicit construction of a 'white fortress', a 'bleached, politically fortified space'.[38]

EUROPEANIZING EUROPE: CONTESTED
MASCULINITIES AND THE 'VEILED MUSLIM
WOMAN'

Snapshot Two: In Bulgaria, a European Union state since 2007, the trope
of the *Muslim woman* has promoted intense debates about the public
frontiers of gendered subjectivities. As in France, where Islamophobia is
implicated in the controversial ban on the Muslim headscarf in public
schools, Bulgaria has considered 'legal regulations on the wearing of
religious symbols' by women. Similar controversies about the 'hijab' have
emerged in Holland, Belgium, Italy, and Germany, where the admissibility
of 'conspicuous' religious clothing in public schools and secular institutional
spaces has come under consideration by lawmakers. In Bulgaria, however,
when several Muslim schoolgirls filed complaints with the national

[36] See Schäfer et al., *Europe in Figures: Eurostat Yearbook 2005*, 79.
[37] Gilroy, 'Migrancy, Culture, and a New Map of Europe', xii.
[38] Paul Gilroy, *Between Camps: Nations, Cultures and the Allure of Race* (London: Penguin, 2000),
247; Gilroy, 'Migrancy, Culture, and a New Map of Europe', xii.

Commission of Protection Against Discrimination, the court's ruling merely affirmed the local headmaster's right to enforce existing school uniform codes. In those cases, where such dress codes were already in place, Muslim schoolgirls were mandated to continue their public education 'bareheaded', a decision judged to 'promote gender equality'. In other instances, where no such uniform codes were evident, the commission ruled that the schoolgirls were free to wear whatever clothing they desired. By empowering local institutions and by rejecting the turn to national legislation, post-socialist Bulgaria has managed to safeguard the public deportment of Muslim female bodies from state intervention.

This judicial approach is remarkably different from the course of action taken in other Western European countries, where the public demeanor of Muslim women is socially monitored and legally restricted. In Bulgaria, Muslims are citizens, political subjects with long-standing claims to membership in the national community: 'Unlike in Germany, Britain or France, Bulgaria's Muslims have been living in the country for hundreds of years, a legacy of the Ottoman Empire'. The religious attire of Muslim girls is thereby less entangled in debates about immigration, national security, and the resistance of ethnic minorities to integrate or 'westernize'. While not completely disengaged from Europe's neocolonial or imperialist imagination, including ethno-religious intolerance, the headscarf debates in Bulgaria are differently encoded by economic rationality: secondary education in Bulgaria depends on tuition-paying students and the continuous enrollment of Muslim girls in public schools is judged a critical issue.[39]

Why has the Islamic female body been so vigorously pushed into the centre of political attention? Spectacularized by media, commodified by political discourse, and scrutinized in public debates, the figure of the Muslim woman has emerged as a global symbol of modernity's female double. In Europe's orientalist imagination, the public sight of veiled female bodies invokes fantasies about polygamy, arranged marriages, honour killings, female genital cutting, domestic confinement, and other imagined affronts to European sensibilities regarding gender roles and sexual mores. The practice of female veiling is interpreted as an outward sign of the patriarchal reach of Islam, which prevents Muslim women from shedding their non-modern cultural allegiance and inhibits their ability to become modern European subjects. This Europeanizing logic negates the meanings attached to the veil by Muslim women themselves, who wear it as a dense signifier of distinction, social standing, devotion, and protection. The use of the veil or some other form of head-body-covering has historically been regarded as a liberating device: as a means of 'portable seclusion', it grants women the freedom of mobility.[40]

[39] Example and quotes from Kristen Ghodsee, 'The Headscarf Debate in Bulgaria', *Anthropology News* (May 2009), 31–2.

[40] Lila Abu-Lughod, 'Do Muslim Women Really Need Saving?' *American Anthropologist* 103:4 (2002), 783–90; here 785.

Since a conventional 'cover' enables Muslim women to freely move about in public, it makes little sense that they should suddenly desire to denounce or abandon this article of clothing. But in Europe, in the volatile terrain of national border security and anti-immigration sentiments, this practice has been encoded with different meanings. Interpreted in political terms as a barrier to cultural integration and as an embodied sign of oppression, the practice of female concealment has become a battleground—a criminalized site—for disciplinary intervention.

Seen through the affective resonance of a global security lockdown, Europe's Muslim women are linked to an intrusive, negative 'immigrant' presence that needs to be diminished or controlled. Under such conditions, marked by a politics of fear and fluctuating demands for border fortification, divergent images of dangerous alterities are assembled to create a unitary figure: the Muslim–Arab–Other. This iconic template presents a montage of diverse tropes: the 'immigrant', the 'terrorist', the 'enemy-outsider'. Criminalized as icons of global instability, disorder, and terror, Muslims are stripped of their right to belong. In the European Union, as suggested by the Bulgarian case, this imaginative turn against Muslim minorities is however not completely synchronized. Global anxieties are variously galvanized in different countries. In Germany, the figure of the Islamic Other is given life by anti-Turkish sentiments, a racial formation energized by memories of postwar economic reconstruction, 'guest' worker recruitment programmes, and the desired impermanence of a mobile ethnic labour force. Anti-Islamic politics in France are nourished by resentments against Muslim immigrants from North Africa, whose precarious status as a racial minority in the centre of Europe is an effect of the aftermath of French colonial violence. In the Netherlands, the figure of the Muslim is populated by Indonesian immigrants, whose citizenship rights are entangled with their status as descendants of slave labourers in Dutch plantation colonies. In each of these cases, the ethnographic life of Muslim communities has been shaped by political histories, societal memories, and demographic realities. But such local complexities are globally unremembered, replaced by a singular, non-temporal, spatially mobile template: the Muslim Other. The negated icon can thereby subsume salient ethnicities, 'drawing together West Indians, Africans, South Asians into a blackening singularity as uninvited immigrant presence'.[41] Reified by global ideologies, the construct of the Islamic Other furnishes a distorted lens for assessing difference and alterity.

In Europe's securocratic world, public space is continuously monitored for tangible signs of difference: otherness is to be identified, governed, and normalized. Restrictive measures concerning the 'ostentatious' display of religious symbols have been adopted by France: Muslim girls are prohibited from wearing the Islamic headscarf to school. While officially contested as a non-western religious emblem that has inserted itself into European secular space, the veil or headscarf is also an intensely gendered, racially marked signifier. When encountered in public, worn by schoolgirls or women, it provides a visual affirmation of the presence of Muslim communities in Europe, in the

---

[41] David Goldberg, *The Threat of Race* (Malden, MA: Blackwell, 2009), 179.

national interior. But this hyper-visibility and recognizability of the contested Other in everyday life has intensified the push to de-islamicize public space. Accordingly, the 'conspicuous' assertion of ethno-religious difference, which is firmly encoded on the Muslim female body, has been declared a national threat, resulting in the denouncement of the symbolic stand-in: the veil, the headscarf, and similar garments. The attempt to legally prohibit such notable signs of difference may serve a legitimating or restorative function for the political order, especially when the state's capacity to protect sovereign space is called into question. In addition, one could speculate that after 1945, in remembrance of the visual tactics of persecution deployed by the Nazi regime, the 'branding' of ethnic minorities (even if self-imposed) is deemed politically intolerable. But the push to criminalize the figure of the 'veiled Muslim woman' is an even more complex matter.

Embedded in political fantasies about national security, terror, and border protection, as Achille Mbembe observed, Europeanness 'is imagined as an identity against the Other.'[42] Tangible alterities or figures of difference (the veiled Muslim woman, the Arab terrorist, the black immigrant) occupy a strategic place in the determination of Europeanness and the articulation of the corresponding fields of whiteness. These 'largely unspoken racial connotations' of national belonging in Europe, as Stuart Hall observes, are encoded by a cultural logic of othering that promotes either assimilation or exclusion.[43] Distinction is manufactured along a narrow register that 'accords differing groups cultural normativity or deviance.'[44] In this volatile terrain, the European nation state is 'caught between the need to enforce sameness and the fear of absolute difference, with no middle ground.'[45] What modalities of gender and what machinations of othering are deployed by Europe's border regime when assessing residence or citizenship privileges for Muslims? Based on postulates of dangerous masculinities and subservient femininities, the European security state executes its protective mission by cutting deeply into the social fabric of Muslim alterity: the domestic unit, the family, and the community of kin.

The sovereignty of the European Union 'is founded on the principles of liberty, democracy, respect for human rights, and fundamental freedoms' (Article 6.1, Treaty on European Union). Although the family unit is thereby 'protected' by law, and the reunification of family members across international borders is guaranteed, even 'enshrined' in legal codes, the European concept of kinship is restrictive: 'polygamy is not recognized.'[46] Enacted in October 2003, the directive sends a clear message to the global community of Muslims, the principal protagonists in Europe's orientalist imaginary. The Europeanization of a single family form criminalizes those marriage practices that

---

[42] Achille Mbembe, 'Necropolitics', *Public Culture* 15:1 (2003), 11–40; here 23.

[43] Stuart Hall, 'A Question of Identity (II)', *The Observer* (15 October 2000), online at: www.guardian. co.uk/uk/2000/oct/15/britishidentity.comment1, accessed February 2010.

[44] Ong, 'Cultural Citizenship as Subject-Making', 759.

[45] Leora Bilsky, 'Muslim Headscarves in France and Army Uniforms in Israel', *Patterns of Prejudice* 43:3–4 (2009), 287–311; here 306.

[46] Council Directive 2003/86/EC [CNS/1999/0258].

deviate from the normative monogamous model: additional wives and children are barred from entering Europe. By encoding unacceptable kinship types in immigration laws, the European security state has the 'capacity to define who matters and does not, who is *disposable* and who is not'.[47] In compliance with corresponding integration measures, non-sanctioned reproductive practices and concepts of family life have to be abandoned at the border. These legal stipulations reveal a procedure of social engineering: by minimizing family units and by criminalizing marriage forms, the anticipated multitude of Muslim immigrants in Europe is judicially limited.

In these judicial borderlands, the term 'polygamy' appears as a code word for European notions about the erotic world of the Muslim harem. Seen through the distorted lens of orientalism, the Islamic family is imagined as an ensemble of young sensuous females controlled by the sexual desire of a powerful male. This fantasy is further elaborated by the binding prohibitions against infant betrothal, wife capture, female seclusion, and other sexual perpetrations attributed to Muslim masculinity. Taken together with the legal restrictions placed on family membership, kinship ties, and marital practices, such judicial renderings suggest that social solidarities propagated by the Islamic male cannot be tolerated. By reifying popular truth claims about the sexual pathologies of Muslim masculinity, the European Union has created a defensive legal system that seeks to dismantle families and kinship units. As per legal mandate, Muslim men are forced to abandon their female kin. By negating the men's responsibilities as a father, husband, and brother, Europe's restrictive border laws disrupt the conventional definition of men as protectors of women. In this judicial universe, Muslim women become invisible: their status as a legal persona is recognized solely by their link to men—as wives (by marriage) or as daughters (by descent). In these documents, female subjects are rendered legally mute. In attempts to subdue contested Muslim masculinities, the European security state has instituted a gender-biased legal system.

Why is the figure of the 'veiled Muslim woman', who is invisible and voiceless in border law discourse, pushed into the political field of vision in Europe? The centrality of Muslim men in immigration law and Muslim women in public discourse requires further consideration. Leora Bilsky's analysis of 'citizenship as mask' provides a useful conceptual tool.[48] In the European Union, as in other nation-state systems, the legal persona is defined by 'citizenship', which secures the 'dimensions of political equality'. The corresponding metaphor of the 'mask' exposes the artificiality of this postulate. The right to belong, as Bilsky suggests, is defined by specific requirements of 'concealment' or 'disclosure': legal subjectivity may be differently encoded in different subjects. A black person, for instance, is 'not offered the protection of the mask and thus remains exposed, not able to re-present his or her body in public'.[49] Such a radical fixture of personhood by colour suggests that citizenship status is also encoded by extra-legal dimensions. In the

---

[47] Mbembe, 'Necropolitics', 27.
[48] Leora Bilsky, 'Citizenship as Mask', *Constellations* 15:1 (2008), 1–39.
[49] Ibid., 7.

European national imaginary, the very mask of citizenship is racialized. Whiteness *is* the mask of national belonging, rendering all European subjects metaphorically equal under the 'white' signifier. How do those individuals regarded as 'outsiders' become European? To secure entry into Europe's political space or to acquire the semblance of cultural citizenship, persons of Muslim backgrounds are forced to undergo a process of reconditioning. In contrast to 'blackness', Islamic otherness is perceived as a cultural artefact that can be reformed or concealed.

Europeanization follows a gendered protocol of coercive integration. Muslim masculinity is de-Islamicized, forcibly excised or contained by legal means. Muslim women undergo a similar process of gender reformation. According to Bilsky,

> we can interpret the demand directed at the Muslim girls in France to unveil as a demand to cover their difference (their religious dress code) by 'uncovering', to arrive at school without a hijab. The demand is not to negate their religious belief, but only to cover its conspicuous representation, to cover its public manifestation.[50]

Muslim females are rendered 'European' by an act of concealment: artefacts of ethnic identity cannot remain visibly apparent on the body. The insignia of difference must be removed or obscured so that public claims to legal status cannot be contested. Europeanness is confirmed by appearance. Such practices of 'cultural citizenship' or 'social processes of whitening', as Aihwa Ong points out, are monitored by public officials to ascertain whether a person's 'embodiment of culturally correct citizenship and privilege' has been successful.[51] The Europeanization of Muslim women not only prohibits the public assertion of ethnic difference but also demands a refashioning of femininity under cultural capitalism.

The forcible unveiling of the Muslim woman's body in European nation states, as in France or Germany, suggests that integration or assimilation requires compliance with the practices of western consumer culture. Minority women are rendered 'white' or socially acceptable when they embody the sexualizing regimes of commoditization. Muslim women's emancipation is linked to sexual objectification, a central trope of global consumer capitalism. In order to become 'European', the veiled Muslim woman must trade in social respectability for bodily allure. Given the coded eroticism of women's hair, as Bronwyn Winter suggests, the hijab or veil, like the headscarf, is in fact 'a hypersexualizing marker'.[52] But in capitalist Europe, the very practice of concealment—the hiding of a woman's hair or the covering of the female form—signifies an act of defiance. This defiance is presumed at several levels: a rebellious turn against individuation, consumer compliance, and liberation (which are the hegemonic requirements of capitalist culture). These understandings are vocalized in European political discourse as concerns about Muslim women's problematic or incomplete integration. Interpreted as a rejection of Europeanness, the adornment of the female headscarf is read as a public

---

[50] Leora Bilsky, 'Muslim Headscarves in France and Army Uniforms in Israel', 299.
[51] Ong, 'Cultural Citizenship as Subject-Making', 745.
[52] Bronwyn Winter, *Hijab and the Republic* (Syracuse: Syracuse University Press, 2009), 26–7.

gesture of allegiance to an ethnic community perceived as intrusive, dangerous, and male dominated.

Seen through European eyes, Muslim women's conformity to female dress codes under Islam are 'racializing' practices: an ethnic 'un-whitening' of cultural citizenship. Since the women are not regarded as independent agents, Muslim men are collectively blamed for their resilient refusal to uncover. This view is pervasive in European public debates about legal intervention. In 2004, in France, 'the meaning of the veil was taken to be self-evident, as representing the subordination and discrimination of women under Islam'.[53] In Germany, news headlines in 2009 declared that the Muslim girls' headscarf causes political offence as 'a symbol of men's claim to power over women'. The inclusion of Muslim women in Europe's civilizing project is simultaneously a rejection of the stigmatized Islamic male.[54] As Muslim women are harnessed for European integration, Muslim masculinity is diminished: the men's authority over female kin is challenged. Imagined as sexual deviants and misogynist agents (linked to a popular fascination with polygamy, female genital cutting, and domestic violence), Islamic males are situated outside the boundaries of 'civilized' society. By devaluing these 'men of colour' and by rescuing the oppressed and victimized females from 'the pathologized sexuality of these subaltern figures', the normative masculinity of the European state (as embodied by police, judge, border guard, lawmaker, and politician) is upheld.[55]

European machinations about the oppressed female victim, who wears the male-imposed headscarf as a 'native embodiment of deviant sexual norms', makes Muslim women 'ripe for salvation' by white intervention.[56] In the European imaginary, as articulated by French, Dutch, or German public debates, Muslim girls 'need saving'. The legal ban on wearing the headscarf, an act of coercion by the state against Muslim women, is presented as a civilizing, liberating endeavour. In this process of forced integration, Muslim females are pitted against the orientalized figure of the negated Islamic male: Europeanization, by unveiling, means to embrace the prescribed gender roles and normalized sexualities, as a docile (white) citizen subject, in Europe's capitalist security state.

GENDERING EUROPE: CONSUMER CAPITALISM AND BLACK MALE SEXUALITY

Snapshot Three: In Sweden, at the turn of the 21st century, retrieved from the hidden archives of the wax cabinet and anatomical museum, the remains of a black male body are put on display in Stockholm by the National Historical Museum. Transformed into a commodity form, the

---

[53] Bilsky, 'Muslim Headscarves in France', 305.

[54] Katherine Pratt Ewing, *Stolen Honor: Stigmatizing Muslim Men in Berlin* (Stanford, CA: Stanford University Press, 2008).

[55] Ong, 'Cultural Citizenship as Subject-Making', 745.

[56] Ibid., 746.

exhibited body parts are the skin of a flayed African and his severed sex-organ. Brought to public visibility among an assortment of the erotic, sensational, and grotesque, and displayed like a hunter's trophy, 'fully stretched out' on a 'door-size wooden panel,' 'and nailed to its constituent planks, the skin of a black African "native".' And next to it, amputated from the once living body, a few inches long, 'a Negro penis.' Not an authentic wax replica, but the real dismembered native. He has been reduced to the insignia of difference: his black skin (race) and his genital (sexuality).

The exhibit is greeted with silence in Swedish public discourse, in a society whose nationals imagine their society above all as tolerant, progressive, egalitarian, and generous. No media outrage, no protests are stirred in Stockholm by the exhibit's expropriation of racist imagery from colonial discourse, when the African body and black masculinity were treated as a negative object to affirm the civilizational superiority of the Swedish audience a century earlier. Perhaps the image appeases popular anxieties about the presumed 'excessive sexual desires of blacks', which is encased in stereotypes about 'their sexual abuse or rape of white Swedish women.' In the exhibit, used as a visual exemplar, the African male has been tamed: his sexuality has 'been conquered, colonized, disciplined, and brought under control, nailed down and rendered impotent.' How is such an installation reconcilable with the European treatise on human rights and social justice?[57]

In European colonial and fascist imaginaries, black men were often visualized as predatory figures with an uncontrolled lust for white women. Fears of miscegenation or racial interbreeding saw black men as a threat: as potential rapists. But such racial stereotypes have not completely disappeared from European visual culture.[58] Phallocentric racism, which is obsessed with the sexual prowess of black men, appears in material artefacts, visual representations, and everyday discourse. What changes can we observe in the depictions of black male bodies in the new Europe? When black masculinity is eroticized in contemporary European culture, it is often through contact with a white woman. Consider this title page of a Berlin paper: 'Below the headline "Blacks in Berlin: Beautiful and Coffee-Brown" is an African man in a tiger-skin. A white woman embraces him from behind... The article was part of a series entitled "We're Getting Some Colour".'[59] But in such media images, 'getting some colour' can also be read in terms of white women's sexual appetite for black bodies. Images disseminated by major fashion or cosmetic industries seek to attract female consumers by showing white women in a pleasurable, even lustful, embrace with a black man. The ads deploy the fantasy of erotic contact with

[57] Example, paraphrased text and quotes from Allan Pred, 'Unspeakable Spaces', *City & Society* 13:1 (2001), 119–59.

[58] Michelle Wright and Antje Schuhmann (eds), *Blackness and Sexualities* (Berlin: LIT Verlag, 2007).

[59] May Opitz, 'Racism Here and Now', in May Opitz, Katharina Oguntoye and Dagmar Schultz (eds), *Showing our Colors* (Amherst, MA: University of Massachusetts Press, 1992), 125–44; here 141.

the black male body to create a sensuous, emotional, and confident female agent: she never surrenders but dominates her source of pleasure. In contemporary European consumer culture we thus observe a concurrent depiction of female desire for black maleness, 'signaling an ambivalent fascination with something that is both alluring and threatening'.[60]

Interestingly, in a 2006 advertisement campaign, AfroPort, a German organization for the promotion of African culture, decided to capture its members' economic mobility with a related image. The image is titled 'Having Arrived!' Against a blurry urban canvas, we see a black businessman, smartly dressed in an elegant suit with tie, walking in close body contact next to a pretty blond businesswoman, animatedly talking to her, looking at her; she seems engaged, laughing in response to his remarks.[61] 'Having arrived'—being a success—is here signified by the black man's ability to engage the rapture of a white woman. Although clearly shown to inhabit the signs of middle-class status, the black man's turn to whiteness is offered as a visual validation of his socio-economic achievement. Such a presentation of black masculinity both departs from and recuperates European anxieties about the 'specters of racial mixture'.[62]

This might in part explain why black masculinity is often miniaturized, thereby rendered safe. In addition to the small figurines of black men as entertainers, musicians, and servants that are offered for sale, we encounter the miniaturized black male in ads for consumer products, brand names for beer, pharmacies, hotels, restaurants, and cafés. In these visual fantasies, we see a problematic persistence of European colonial images of the 'African' and 'Moor' as eager helpers, often rushing to provide their services. In Berlin, the hotel Sarotti-Höfe advertises its business with a wall painting that covers the entire facade of the building: the mural depicts the Sarotti company's logo, an orientalized Moor, resembling the Arabian nights 'eunuch' servant, who is imagined as a black man-child, dressed in a turban, pump pans, and pointed slippers.[63] In such images, which represent men of colour as miniatures, the threatening dimensions of black sexuality are stripped by diminution and sometimes infantilization.

Representations of the black man as a child or 'boy', a humble servant, are symbolic forms of emasculation, images that signify lack of power by machinations of dependence, servitude, and subordination. In such images, black masculinity is stripped of violent sexual agency. This phantasmatic strategy persists in contemporary marketing. European sports ads are a case in fact. On the rarest of occasions, when a black male is inserted into the image, he is visually truncated, made physically smaller. This is apparent in a 2005 German television commercial promoting Adidas shoes. Titled 'impossible is nothing', the advertisement targets consumer desire by metonymically linking the shoe's promise of enhanced physical agility to possibilities of the athletic body—shown

[60] Christian Rogowski, 'Triumph der Negerkultur über die weiße Zivilisation' (2005), online at: www.best.uni-Mainz.de/modules/AMS/article.php?storyid=145, accessed February 2010.

[61] Afro Port, 'Bildanzeige Beispiel A: Angekommen' in *afroport.de* (2008), online at: www.afroport.de/as_werbung.php, accessed February 2010.

[62] Campt 'Converging Specters of an Other Within', 83.

[63] See www.hotel-sarottihoefe.de/hotel.bilder.html?lang=de, accessed February 2010.

by featuring members of the German national soccer team. But here, among the staged assemble of soccer players, the black athlete is shown sitting on the side, on the margins: he is spatially and physically dominated by the towering (standing) white male athletes, his teammates. Although his muscular arms and legs are exposed, his physicality poses no threat and therefore may be safely desired, and consumed.

This same principle operates in the manufacture of food products, whereby black sexuality can be sensuously tasted, ingested, enjoyed. European consumer culture offers up black male bodies in the form of candies and sweets—especially as licorice and chocolate. The consumption of blackness, or black masculinity, ranges from miniature black licorice penises and licorice African heads to the notorious 'Moor's head' (*Mohrenkopf*), also termed 'Negro's kiss' (*Negerkuss*): a chocolate-covered confection with a white marshmallow filling. These phallic-looking constructs, sometimes anthropomorphized—decorated as 'human heads'—are offered in restaurants, cafes, bakeries, and in stores. In response to anti-racist protests, many German companies have renamed this product 'foam kiss' or 'chocolate kiss', thereby retaining the erotic branding. But the conventional designation 'moor's head' continues on menu items, in bakeries, on price tags, store advertisements, printed receipts, and vernacular identifications. In 2009, the Swiss company Dubler vouched to forever retain the contested designation 'Moor's head' as a product label.[64] In Europe, among the most popular brands of this confection is 'Super Dickmann's', which fabricated a 'Negro's kiss' that vertically expands in the microwave oven. The description on the packaging leaves no doubt as to the phallic nature of the product: 'Man, he is super big. *He* grows and grows'. The consumption of this black phallus is visually and sensually displaced to the mouth. In German media culture, we often see white women pleasurably devouring the black sweetness. The symbolics of the 'negro kiss' transports white erotic fantasies into an act of sensuous consumption. Yet even in these seemingly innocent practices of oral incorporation, black masculinity is violated by its reduction to a single trace: severed from the male body, the black phallus is forced to participate—perform—in these enactments of racist sexual fantasy. In such instances, black masculinity is reduced to an emblematic sign that is given one performative function: to enhance white (female) pleasure in the phantasmatic contact zones between Europe and Africa.

Concluding Reflections

The promise of national distinction by racial exclusivity contradicts conventional understandings of globality. A globalized world, marked by 'reform' and 'openness', is said to unsettle old identities and unlock new imaginaries.[65] From such a perspective, the

---

[64] See www.dubler.net/produkte.htm, accessed February 2010.
[65] Arjun Appadurai, 'Grassroots Globalization and the Research Imagination', in Arjun Appadurai (ed.), *Globalization* (Durham, NC: Duke University Press, 2001), 1–20; here 3.

European racial state is regarded as a matter of the past. Racism in Europe is presumed to belong to colonial history, an era that ended with fascism in 1945. This historical past with its carceral spaces of race, sex, and gender is opposed to the present, which is conceived as a world without frontiers, as 'a world of flows' and 'liquid' social forms.[66] Accordingly, processes of globalization have been analysed by recourse to metaphors of fluidity, flexibility, and liquidity, rather than gendered fortification or racial closure. The global order comes into view through the possibilities and signs of motion: mobile populations, permeable borders, transnational flows of capital, and the traffic of culture across space or time. As such, the historical fixity of borders, bodies, and identities appears to have been radically altered, suggesting a progressive weakening of political units: the disempowerment of nation states. Such visionary models of the decline of state power and the end of racial thinking have been expounded further.

With a focus on the geopolitics of globalization, Michael Hardt and Antonio Negri deployed the term 'empire' to describe the delocalized and decentred system of transglobal control: the world empire operates as 'a non-place' of power in a universal terrain.[67] The impact of empire on global life is said to be dramatic: as sovereignties, borders, and territories are reconstituted and negated, imaginaries based on place attachment are rendered meaningless. In a world without borders, social constructions of difference cannot be spatially anchored. Following this logic, the global empire is to produce a deterritorialized world that lacks interior vantage points or centre-spaces of privilege from which salient others can be imagined, marginalized, and excluded. According to Hardt and Negri, the unbinding of economic space evaporates the logic of gendered, racial, and sexual difference. But global transformations are never so simple, never so uniform. The political realities of globalization reveal a different trajectory.

Globalization has not produced a singular or unified world order. The global empire does not operate as a single-space economy, 'as a non-contradictory, uncontested space' in which all strands of social life are perfectly synchronized.[68] In a global world, as Arjun Apadurai observed, 'objects, persons, images, and discourses—are not coeval, convergent, isomorphic, or spatially consistent. They are in...relations of disjuncture.'[69] Political forms, cultural identities, social lives, and economic interests engage global possibilities along different, sometimes contradictory, trajectories. On the ground, globalization operates with a flexible fixity. Capitalist imperatives, subjectivities, and the manufacture of elusive authenticities may intersect to produce 'counterintuitive' results, as John and Jean Comaroff propose in *Ethnicity, Incorporated*: 'Cultural identity, in the here-and-now, represents itself ever more as two things at once: the object of choice and

---

[66] See Arjun Appadurai, *Modernity at Large* (Minneapolis, MN: University of Minnesota Press, 1996) and Zygmunt Bauman, *Liquid Modernity* (Cambridge: Polity Press, 2000).

[67] Michael Hardt and Antonio Negri, *Empire* (Cambridge, MA: Harvard University Press, 2000), 210.

[68] Stuart Hall, 'The Local and the Global', in Anthony D. King (ed.), *Culture, Globalization, and the World-System* (Minneapolis, MN: University of Minnesota Press, 2000), 19–39; here 32.

[69] Appadurai, 'Grassroots Globalization', 5.

self-construction, typically through the act of consumption, *and* the manifest product of biology, genetics, human essence.'[70]

Under globalization, ethno-racial and gendered logics can be reclaimed for profit. Likewise, the imaginative geography of a 'white Europe' or the sense of Europeanness, as my research suggests, may be reconfigured by elements both known and unconventional: forged by recourse to space, by signifiers of gender, nation, and race, and by new consumer practices. Under a global consumer capitalism, the 'whiteness' of Europe has come to be imagined and defended as a lifestyle. Europeanness is reclaimed, enacted, and consumed in ontological space by placing emphasis 'on conjuring affect, itself ever more a commodity, by aesthetic means'.[71] While culture can perform the work of race or gender, drawing on variable aesthetic and affective repertoires, the emergent volatility of white Europeanness is stabilized by recourse to border regimes, anti-immigrant legislation, and, most recently, discourses of national security.

In light of these developments, my analysis of Europe's Europeanization of gender takes account of how the politics of immigration, national belonging, and citizenship are governed by neoliberal security issues: racial exclusivity, inserted into the political terrain of the biosocial (gender, family, sexuality) has 'become a critical affair of state'.[72] In Europe, as in other imperialist nation states, we observe new forms of border protection, surveillance, and anti-black and anti-Muslim violence that seek to counter the effects of globalization. When critically examining these political realities, we need to acknowledge that the 'vision of a decentered empire', as Nicholas Mirzoeff observes, 'has come to be overtaken by a more familiar model of empire controlled by a concrete nation state'.[73]

Militarization, policing, and state intervention are deployed in attempts to securitize Europe. Such a politics of space, with its regime of borders, camps, and racial terror, is emblematic 'of the renewed desire of nation states to restrict global freedom of movement to capital and deny it to people'.[74] This is an important observation. The management of white Europeanness and black Islamicized alterities by producing racial boundaries, sexual deviancies, and gendered hierarchies is *not naturally* propagated. The negation or integration of racialized, sexualized, and gendered Others in Europe's presumed white spaces is sustained by state intervention.

FURTHER READING

Bowen, John R., *Why the French Don't Like Headscarves: Islam, The State, and Public Space* (Princeton, NJ: Princeton University Press, 2008).
——, *Can Islam be French?* (Princeton, NJ: Princeton University Press, 2009).

[70] John, L. and Jean Comaroff, *Ethnicity, Inc.* (Chicago, IL: University of Chicago Press, 2009), 1.
[71] Ibid., 16.
[72] Jean Comaroff, 'Beyond Bare Life', *Public Culture* 19:1 (2007), 197–219; here 214.
[73] Nicholas Mirzoeff, *Watching Babylon* (New York: Routledge, 2005), 145.
[74] Ibid., 146.

Bunzl, Matti, *Anti-Semitism and Islamophobia: Hatreds Old and New in Europe* (Chicago, IL: Prickly Paradigm Press, 2007).

Elman, Amy R., *Sexual Equality in an Integrated Europe* (New York: Palgrave Macmillan, 2007).

Fehrenbach, Heide, *Race after Hitler: Black Occupation Children in Postwar Germany and America* (Princeton, NJ: Princeton University Press, 2005).

Linke, Uli, 'Body-Shock: The Political Aesthetics of Death', *Social Analysis* 54:2 (2010), 80–98.

Linke, Uli, 'Technologies of Othering: Black Masculinities in the Carceral Zones of European Whiteness', in Manuela Ribeiro Sanches, Fernando Clara, João Ferreira Duarte, and Leonor Pires Martins (eds), *Europe in Black and White* (Chicago: Intellect, The University of Chicago Press, 2011), 123–41.

Mandel, Ruth, *Cosmopolitan Anxieties: Turkish Challenges to Citizenship and Belonging in Germany* (Durham, NC: Duke University Press, 2008).

Pred, Allan, *Even in Sweden: Racisms, Racialized Spaces, and the Popular Geographical Imagination* (Berkeley, CA: University of California Press, 2000).

Roth, Silke (ed.), *Gender Politics in the Expanding European Union* (New York: Berghahn Books, 2008).

Ticktin, Miriam, 'Sexual Violence as the Language of Border Control', *Signs: Journal of Women and Culture in Society* 33:4 (2008), 863–89.

Ware, Vron, *Who Cares About Britishness?* (London: Arcadia Books, 2007).

CHAPTER 11

1968: EUROPE IN TECHNICOLOUR

MARTIN KLIMKE

In February 1969, after much soul searching, the German philosopher Theodor W. Adorno finally agreed to publish a new edition of the *Dialectic of Enlightenment* together with his colleague, Max Horkheimer, at the Institute for Social Research at the University of Frankfurt. In the planned prologue to the book, he included the worldwide youth revolt as a reason for his change of heart:

> [Y]oung people at least have set out to resist the transition to the totally adminis-
> tered world which is not being accomplished seamlessly, but by means of dictator-
> ships and wars. The protest movement in all the countries of the world, in both blocs
> as well as in the Third World, testifies to the fact that wholesale integration does not
> necessarily proceed smoothly. If this book assists the cause of resistance to achieve
> a blind consciousness that illuminates and that prevents people from submitting to
> blind practice out of despair and from succumbing to collective narcissism, that
> would give it a genuine function.[1]

Adorno's legendary disapproval of student activists in Frankfurt and his criticism of the protest movements in general notwithstanding, he felt that the activists of 1968 could obstruct the path towards the all-encompassing regulation and rationalization of modern life, which, he feared, fundamentally alienated human beings everywhere. A new edition of his work was supposed to help them overcome the perceived spiritual void of modern industrial society. Although the edition never materialized, many student activists at the time demanded precisely the cultural resistance that Adorno desired. They advocated individual and collective emancipation from the constraints of modern industrial society

---

[1] Theodor W. Adorno to Max Horkheimer, February 1969, quoted in Detlev Claussen, *Theodor W. Adorno: One Last Genius* (Cambridge, MA: Harvard University Press, 2008), 338. For Adorno and the Frankfurt School's relationship to the student movement, see Wolfgang Kraushaar (ed.), *Frankfurter Schule und Studentenbewegung: Von der Flaschenpost bis zum Molotowcocktail*, 3 vols (Hamburg: Rogner & Bernhard, 1998).

and pursued a utopian vision of post-materialistic values to effect fundamental social and political transformations—in the societies in which they lived and the world at large. Especially in Europe, this vision remains the most striking historical legacy of the events of 1968.

Indeed, the 'children of Marx and Coca-Cola' continue to haunt us. Even after more than four decades, the events of the tumultuous year 1968 still mesmerize and polarize Europe, both culturally and politically.[2] Although prominent representatives of the continent's student revolt have called for people to 'forget 68', Europeans have entered the historicization and memorialization process for this period with vigour.[3] By no means simply innocent bystanders in this analytical and commemorative boom, historians have, however, only just begun to paint a comprehensive picture of what transpired during the European 'sixties' and to discover the limits of the metaphorical shorthand '1968' for encompassing the many dimensions of the decade's social transformations. Their scholarly accounts in recent years have transcended the focus on well known protagonists and supposed capitals of the revolt, opened up a variety of new locations and topics, and utilized fresh methodological approaches to situate the protest movements of these years in a broader history of postwar Europe.

Combining the extensive theoretical discussions with the detailed empirical reconstructions of 1968, this article outlines the major political, social, economic, intellectual, and cultural perspectives in the narratives of this period. It takes a pan-European view, paying particular attention to the local specificity of 1968 in all parts of the continent, while also tracing the influence of national, transnational, and global factors.

Causes and Contexts of 1968 in Europe

Among the causes and contexts of the social movements, acts of dissent, and youthful revolts that are commonly subsumed under the cipher '1968', the Cold War and the division of Europe after 1945 usually enjoy pride of place, although these were by no means the only influences. The rapid demographic changes after World War II were probably the primary force that shaped the context in which the opposition of the young was to unfold. The postwar baby boom reached its climax in 1947, placing an unprecedented strain on education systems across Europe throughout the 1960s, although its intensity varied (and was not always justified by the actual numeric increase of young people) by country. This population growth coincided with a massive economic upswing in many Northern and Western European countries that reached into all segments of society and proved particularly beneficial to the lower middle and working classes.[4]

---

[2] The phrase refers to an intertitle in the film *Masculin, féminin* (1966), dir. Jean-Luc Godard.

[3] Daniel Cohn-Bendit, Stéphane Paoli, and Jean Viard, *Forget 68* (La Tour d'Aigues: Aube, 2008).

[4] Axel Schildt and Detlef Siegfried (eds), *Between Marx and Coca-Cola: Youth Cultures in Changing European Societies, 1960–1980* (New York: Berghahn Books, 2006), 18. For a statistical overview, see ibid., 17–20.

With this upswing, the economic hardships of the war years and the immediate post-war period gave way to material improvements and prosperity on a previously unknown scale. With fewer work hours and more vacation days, people enjoyed a slew of new leisure and entertainment activities. Major advances in transportation and communication, such as an increase in the private ownership of automobiles and television sets, improved mobility and connectivity, fundamentally changing people's lifestyles. These changes magnified the 'growing "visibility" of youth' in society so that the young generation not only became a powerful target audience in the new consumer society but also advanced as an active force in it. Cosmetics, fashion, records, as well as record players and tape recorders, became attainable markers of a subculture of teenagers, who started to set social trends and fulfil their desires for individualization with their increasing purchasing power.[5]

In the education system, this generational cohort encountered institutions that were in no way prepared for this demographic expansion. In many European countries, educational reforms in the late 1940s and 1950s had created a system of mass secondary education that enabled greater social mobility and channelled an ever-growing pool of young people from all social strata towards university. Whereas higher education had been an elite privilege before World War II, it now became a system of mass education. Entrance examinations were widely abolished and enrolment soared. Across the continent, the share of university students among twenty- to twenty-four-year-olds rose from 7 to 14 per cent between 1960 and 1970, and by 1978 had reached 24 per cent.[6] Packed lecture halls, overwhelmed administrators, and a growing gulf between elitist professors and frustrated students were the consequences.

To be sure, in many European countries, students still constituted a privileged minority. And an even smaller minority of these took an interest in political issues that they translated into activism. Yet what came to be known as the 'New Left' composed of student activists in the second half of the 1960s was, in fact, the cognitive offspring of a transnational movement whose intellectual origins lay in late 1950s Europe. It had deep roots in a firmly established network of international pacifists who had protested the atom bomb since the early 1950s, particularly via national organizations such as the Campaign for Nuclear Disarmament in Great Britain and international organizations such as the International Fellowship of Reconciliation, the International Confederation for Disarmament and Peace, and the World Peace Council.[7] It was in this context that

[5] For discourses on the young generation in postwar France, see Richard Ivan Jobs, *Riding the New Wave: Youth and the Rejuvenation of France after the Second World War* (Stanford, CA: Stanford University Press, 2007).

[6] Schildt and Siegfried, *Between Marx and Coca-Cola*, 19.

[7] On the impact of the peace movement for the events of 1968, see Michael Frey, 'The International Peace Movement', in Martin Klimke and Joachim Scharloth (eds), *1968 in Europe: A History of Protest and Activism, 1956–1977* (New York: Palgrave Macmillan, 2008), 33–44. For contextualization, see also Lawrence S. Wittner, *The Struggle against the Bomb*, 3 vols (Stanford, CA: Stanford University Press, 1993, 1997, and 2003); Holger Nehring, *The Politics of Security: West European Protests against Nuclear Weapons and the Cold War* (Oxford: Oxford University Press, forthcoming 2012).

the idea of a New Left first bore fruit in the United Kingdom, fostered in no small part by the dramatic events of 1956: Khrushchev's denunciation of Stalin, the Soviet invasion of Hungary, and the Suez Crisis, in which the United Kingdom and France displayed their full imperialist might in attacking Egypt alongside Israel.

In the aftermath of these events, the group of thinkers associated with the *New Left Review*, including Stuart Hall and Raymond Williams, pioneered and disseminated a new theoretical agenda. Emancipating themselves from a purely class-based analysis of modern industrial society, this group outlined a more complex picture of the social and cultural forces responsible for materialism, apathy, and the competitive mindset of post-war capitalism. Their position comprised a fundamental criticism of the Cold War stale-mate between the superpowers, Western anti-communism and nuclear deterrence policy, as well as an emphasis on an anti-bureaucratic socialist internationalism that defied both party doctrine and dogma.

The young generation eagerly took up this new agenda. Much to the dismay of their parent organizations, socialist youth associations from France, West Germany, the UK, the Netherlands, Norway, and Belgium, among others, were the first to establish an organizational infrastructure for channelling this burgeoning movement into a more permanent transnational network at the congress of the International Union of Socialist Youth (ISUY) in Vienna in 1960. This development fostered the rise of the French *Nouvelle Gauche* in France, the Italian *Nuevo Sinistra* in Italy, the West German *Neue Linke*, and eventually led to the foundation of the *International Socialist Journal* in 1964.[8]

Flanking these intellectual expressions of dissatisfaction with the status quo were developments in the cultural and artistic arena that would prove no less influential for the events of 1968. Across the Atlantic, the emergence of pop-cultural rebels such as rock 'n' roll stars Bill Haley and Elvis Presley, as well as their cinematic counterparts James Dean and Marlon Brando, had already inspired the 'first transnational youth revolt' in the late 1950s, whose European offshoots were decidedly working-class-based and hedonistic.[9] Recognizable by a particular 'proletarian' style with a preference for jeans and black leather jackets, the Dutch *nozem*, Italian *teppisti*, and German *Halbstarken* stunned their national audiences and, just like the British Teddy boys, sparked wide-

---

[8]   The most formative national journals for the New Left were: *New Reasoner, Universities and Left Review, New Left Review* (UK); *Socialisme ou Barbarie, Arguments, International Situationniste* (France); *Problemi del Socialismo, Quaderni Rossi, Classe Operaia* (Italy); *neue kritik, Kursbuch* (West Germany). For recent introductions into the British New Left, see Madeleine Davis, 'The Origins of the British New Left', in Klimke and Scharloth (eds), *1968 in Europe*, 45–56; Holger Nehring, '"Out of Apathy": Genealogies and Meanings of the British "New Left" in a Transnational Context, 1956–1962', in Martin Klimke, Jacco Pekelder, and Joachim Scharloth (eds), *Between Prague Spring and French May: Opposition and Revolt in Europe, 1960–1980* (New York: Berghahn Books, 2011), 15–31. For the British New Left, see also Lin Chun, *The British New Left* (Edinburgh: Edinburgh University Press, 1993); Michael Kenny, *The First New Left: British Intellectuals after Stalin* (London: Lawrence and Wishart, 1995).

[9]   Gerd-Rainer Horn, *The Spirit of '68: Rebellion in Western Europe and North America, 1956–1976* (Oxford: Oxford University Press, 2007), 23–7.

spread debates about juvenile delinquency and the moral decay of the young. The articulations of beat poets Allen Ginsberg, Jack Kerouac, and William Burroughs served as literary manifestation of this rebellious attitude. These writers transformed their alienation from society into a withdrawal from its conventional hierarchies and values. Suffused with nonconformity and hunger for spiritual fulfilment, their works, like *Howl* (1955) and *On the Road* (1957), became instant classics and objects of subcultural allure.

In contrast to this approach, the Situationist International, a heterogeneous band of artists and intellectual bohemians founded in 1957, offered a radical theoretical critique of modern society. Influenced by the existentialism of Sartre and Camus, this conglomerate of various artist groups subscribed to the ideas of Dadaism, surrealism, and the Lettrist International. It constituted a truly European network of avant-gardists that included Guy Debord from France, Asger Jorn from Denmark, and Raoul Vaneigem from Belgium, among others. Their dissent transcended traditional Marxism by focusing on the totality of everyday life. Viewing contemporary society as a spectacle that constrained individual creativity and as a place where art had become a mere capitalist commodity, Situationists sought to restore imagination and raise consciousness through provocative and experimental actions that subverted daily routines and rituals. Many of their techniques would later become part of the standard repertoire of the Dutch *Provos*, the West German *Kommune I*, and other student and countercultural activists across Europe and North America.[10]

Advances in media and communications technologies made possible all of these trends and discourses to transcend national boundaries. With the triumph of television, the growth of international satellite communications, and fresh emphasis on visual codes in periodicals, mass media became a catalyst for the nearly synchronic and increasingly globalized dissemination of ideas long before 1968. Moreover, it provided activists with unprecedented opportunities to promote their causes, mobilize their peers, and strategically provoke scandals to generate public attention.[11] Naturally, the national impact of these phenomena varied substantially across European countries. What is remarkable, however, is that protest events in the United States provided a rich source of inspiration and were observed with great interest across the continent despite its diverse local idiosyncrasies. The efforts of African–American civil rights activists such as Rosa Parks, Martin Luther King, Jr, or the Freedom Riders exercised an enormous influence on European youth, serving as examples for direct action and civil disobedience. The Free Speech Movement at the University of California, Berkeley, also resonated among

---

[10] For an introduction, see Thomas Hecken and Agata Grzenia, 'Situationism', in Klimke and Scharloth (eds), *1968 in Europe*, 23–32. See also Christopher Gray, *Leaving the 20th Century: The Incomplete Work of the Situationist International* (London: Rebel Press, 1998); Tom Mcdonough, *Guy Debord and the Situationist International: Texts and Documents* (Cambridge, MA: MIT Press, 2002).

[11] See the pioneering work by Kathrin Fahlenbrach, *Protest-Inszenierungen: Visuelle Kommunikation und kollektive Identitäten in Protestbewegungen* (Wiesbaden: Westdeutscher Verlag, 2002). See also Todd Gitlin, *The Whole World is Watching: Mass Media in the Making and Unmaking of the New Left* (Berkeley, CA: University of California Press, 1980); Rolf Werenskjold, 'The Dailies in Revolts', *Scandinavian Journal of History* 33:4 (2008), 417–40; Meike Vogel, *Unruhe im Fernsehen: Protestbewegung und öffentlich-rechtliche Berichterstattung* (Göttingen: Wallstein, 2010).

student peers on the other side of the Atlantic with its critique of the increasing economic influence of the university and the lack of democratic participation in university affairs, as well as in society. Yet the issue that galvanized students across Europe and provided a unique connection to their American counterparts was the US war in Vietnam.

The 'Third World' liberation movements and the legacies of European colonialist policies had already been on the agenda of European student activists in the first half of the 1960s with regard to Cuba, the Congo, South Africa, and especially Algeria, fostered by the presence of African, Asian, and South American immigrants and students in European societies and on European campuses.[12] But it was the American-led war in Southeast Asia that became a symbol of imperialist oppression and the nemesis of the 'Free West'. Starting in 1965, growing opposition to the war in the United States, including the burgeoning teach-in movement, served as a role model to unite anti-war activists around the world. As the Vietnam conflict escalated, students across Europe, regardless of their local situation, came to regard the Viet Cong as international icons embodying the uncompromising struggle against the all-powerful, globally operating forces of imperialism.

THE DIFFERENT FACES OF 1968 IN EUROPE

Of course, local circumstances determined the nature of dissent in each European country and the extent to which it could be articulated. In East Germany, the authorities had swiftly quelled the worker's uprising in 1953 with the help of Soviet forces. The riots in Poland in the summer of 1956 and the Hungarian revolt in the autumn had met a similar fate.[13] Despite a brief post-Stalinist thaw under Khrushchev, activists in most communist countries had to frame their opposition carefully to avoid harsh state repression and possible imprisonment.

Czechoslovakia was the exception rather than the rule in this respect. The Prague Spring was a liberalization effort initiated from above with long-lasting repercussions throughout the Eastern bloc.[14] As an experiment in the democratic modernization of communism from within, the events of 1968 in this country consisted of a reform project directed at the political system, a social movement seeking civil liberties, as well as an

[12] See, for example, Jim House and Neil Macmaster, *Paris 1961: Algerians, State Terror, and Memory* (Oxford: Oxford University Press, 2006).

[13] See Gary Bruce, *Resistance with the People: Repression and Resistance in Eastern Germany, 1945–1955* (Lanham, MD: Rowman and Littlefield, 2003); Charles Gati, *Failed Illusions: Moscow, Washington, Budapest, and the 1956 Hungarian Revolt* (Stanford: Stanford University Press, 2006); Pawel Machcewicz, *Rebellious Satellite: Poland, 1956* (Stanford, CA: Stanford University Press, 2009).

[14] For the Prague Spring and Czechoslovakia in 1968, see Kieran Williams, *The Prague Spring and Its Aftermath: Czechoslovak Politics, 1968–1970* (Cambridge: Cambridge University Press, 1997); Jan Pauer, 'Czechoslovakia', in Klimke and Scharloth (eds), *1968 in Europe*, 163–78; Günter Bischof, Stefan Karner and Peter Ruggenthaler (eds), *The Prague Spring and the Warsaw Pact Invasion of Czechoslovakia in 1968* (Lanham, MD: Lexington Books, 2010).

often overlooked expression of Slovak striving for national emancipation. After World War II, the Czech Communist Party (KPC) became the strongest political force in the country, and, from 1948 to 1955, it presided over a rigorous Sovietization of all segments of society. Some two million people became victims of its brutal campaign of economic collectivization and political and religious persecution. De-Stalinization efforts and the perceived need for a 'scientific and technical revolution' at the beginning of the 1960s produced a variety of openings in the cultural sphere, allowing non-conformist western ideas such as critical theory, existentialism, and structuralism, among others, to influence local Marxist philosophy and doctrine. Intellectuals, writers, and artists, in particular, began to challenge the regime's cultural authority, openly clashing with the party at the Fourth Writers' Congress in 1967. At the same time, the Slovak Communist Party, led by Alexander Dubček, was able to establish a national power base from which it successfully capitalized on economic uncertainties as well as long-term political disillusionment and yearning for change. At the turn of 1967–68, it replaced the party leadership of Antonin Novotný and ushered in an eight-month period of domestic reform.

The declared goals of these transformations were economic innovations, a greater focus on consumer goods, as well as the democratization of the workplace, the party, and the government. The separation of powers, the rehabilitation of the victims of Stalinist terror, independent courts, and individual freedom and other human rights were also major points on this ambitious agenda. To be sure, the new party leadership never intended neutrality or a departure from the Warsaw Pact system as a result of these policies. Its strategy was to create a free and open public sphere in which to launch a democratic modernization in lockstep with and safeguarded by the party itself. The famous June 1968 '2000 Words' manifesto by prominent writers and intellectuals underscored their general support and loyalty to the government despite their criticism. A student movement that shared most of these goals, but also attempted to set up its own representative organizations outside the Communist Party, also fostered this transition to a civil society.

The reactions of other Warsaw Pact members, most notably of the Soviet Union, East Germany, Poland, Bulgaria, and Hungary, to developments in Czechoslovakia were much less enthusiastic. Their leadership considered the reforms a major threat to socialism and their own domestic stability. Although not completely unexpected, their implementation of the military option to solve the 'Czechoslovakian problem' came as a shock. The invasion of 21 August 1968 conjured up bitter memories of the Nazi invasion thirty years earlier and generated a broad and peaceful civil resistance movement across the country that confused the occupying military forces and unmasked the nature of Soviet communism in the court of global public opinion once and for all. Dictates from Moscow and the gradual retraction of achieved liberties by the reformers themselves buried the dream of any 'socialism with a human face' under the subsequent 'normalization' period launched by the new party leadership of Gustáv Husák.[15] It also cemented

---

[15] See Paulina Bren, *The Greengrocer and His TV: The Culture of Communism after the 1968 Prague Spring* (Ithaca, NY: Cornell University Press, 2010).

the ideological division of Europe and served as a constant reminder of the consequences of any deviations from the orthodoxy of the Kremlin, which would not tolerate utopian illusions about a third path between capitalism and the Kremlin's brand of socialism.

Although its leadership was markedly reserved with regard to the liberalization efforts of the Prague Spring, neighbouring Poland had to come to terms with an internal power struggle, a left-wing critique from the young generation, and also domestic calls for greater democratization.[16] In 1956, the Polish October and the return to power of Władysław Gomułka as the new First Secretary of the Communist Polish United Workers' Party (PZPR) had brought only a short-lived liberalization of the communist system, which had been imposed on the country with the help of the Soviet army after World War II. The situation in Poland was complicated by conflicts between the state and the Catholic Church, a hostile government attitude towards intellectuals and artists, as well as economic decline. In addition, a power struggle among opposing nationalist, revisionist, and nationalistic factions within the upper ranks of the PZPR further aggravated the situation. Particularly the latter, heavily anti-Semitic faction around Minister of the Interior Mieczysław Moczar provided an outlet for younger party members eager for advancement. It launched its first anti-Semitic campaign in the wake of the 1967 Six-Day war in order to oust its political adversaries. In a widely publicized speech, Gomułka himself promoted these efforts by referring to Polish Jews as a 'fifth column'.

The events of the 'Polish March' of 1968 gave further traction to those seeking a liberalization of the system. In March 1964, a group of prominent writers and artists voiced their dissatisfaction with the cultural and political realities of post-1956 Poland in a letter to Prime Minister Jósef Cyrankiewicz. In the following November, two young intellectuals named Jacek Kuroń and Karol Modzelewski, each with a history of advocating for greater liberalization and more democratic socialism in Poland, attempted to publish an 'Open Letter to the Party'. Exasperated by these initiatives, the authorities sentenced Kuroń to three and Modzelewski to three and a half years in prison. Through a faction of the Union for Socialist Youth called 'Komandosi' and their fellow student leader at Warsaw University, Adam Michnik, their letter was smuggled to Western Europe and in May 1968 became one of the most widely read texts among activists at the Sorbonne, with French student leader Daniel Cohn-Bendit famously identifying himself as 'Kuroń-Modzelewski' before a Paris judge.

The issue galvanizing Polish students in 1968, however, was the PZPR's ban on a play by the nineteenth-century writer Adam Mickiewicz at the Warsaw National Theatre for its supposed anti-Soviet tendencies. Its last performance on 30 January triggered student demonstrations demanding 'independence without censorship' and was followed by a petition to the Polish parliament on 16 February to lift the ban. An extraordinary

---

[16] Jerzy Eisler, 'March 1968 in Poland', in Carole Fink, Philipp Gassert and Detlef Junker (eds), *1968: The World Transformed* (Cambridge: Cambridge University Press, 1998), 237–52; Stefan Garsztecki, 'Poland', in Klimke and Scharloth (eds), *1968 in Europe*, 179–87.

convention of the Warsaw branch of the Polish Writers' Union, which had last met this way in 1922, seconded these demands. The situation escalated when, on 4 March, the students Adam Michnik and Henryk Jabłonski were expelled and the Polish militia, with the help of voluntary reserve units, forcefully broke up a peaceful demonstration in the courtyard of Warsaw University on 8 March, beating up many of its participants. The incident elicited a wave of student riots and strikes across Poland that seemed threaten the social and political stability of the country. A government propaganda campaign with explicit anti-Semitic overtones ensued, targeting students, intellectuals, and writers, and blaming the crisis on Jewish agitators. Student activists countered these claims with slogans such as 'Democracy and Freedom' and 'The Press is Lying'. A 'Declaration of the Student Movement' from 28 March even went so far as to demand the abolition of all censorship, the establishment of independent trade unions, and an independent judicial branch, including the creation of a constitutional court, thereby crossing by far 'the line between revisionism and revolution'.[17]

Despite the support of the Catholic Church, the brutality of the Polish militia and its voluntary reserve units had successfully suppressed any further expression of dissent by the end of March. More than 2700 people were arrested, trials and purges set in, and 300 people were imprisoned. In a 19 March speech to workers, Gomułka personally singled out Michnik and Kuroń, together with other writers and intellectuals, as instigators of the conflict. The first secretary also condemned Zionism and promoted the emigration of Polish Jews to Israel. In the following months, the government conducted anti-Semitic purges in its own ranks, the universities, the armed forces, and the media and publishing sectors. It is estimated that about 15,000 people of Jewish origin were forced to leave the country. Kuroń, Modelewski, and others were imprisoned, and many students were expelled from university. Although Gomułka was able to stabilize his position at the party's Seventh Plenum of the Central Committee in July 1968 despite persistent attacks on his leadership that year, he could not soften the fundamental blow that this crisis dealt to communism in Poland.

In non-aligned Yugoslavia, by contrast, the governing League of Communists of Yugoslavia (LCY) initially even welcomed the worldwide eruption of student protests in 1968 as a confirmation of its own political agenda. The ruling party had allowed critical discussions and grassroots initiatives to develop on an informal level since the mid-1960s. Despite their increasingly open criticism, workers' strikes and a critical student press never departed from the official ideological framework. Student activists in Yugoslavia were mainly driven by a desire for greater democratization and a widening gap between party programme and political and social reality. Influenced by their peers in East and West in their rejection of both Stalinism and liberal capitalism, their slogan was 'Down with the Red Bourgeoisie!'[18]

---

[17] Garsztecki, 'Poland', 183.

[18] Želimir Žilnik, 'Down with the Red Bourgeoisie!', in Philipp Gassert and Martin Klimke (eds), *1968: Memories and Legacies of a Global Revolt* (Washington, DC: German Historical Institute, 2009), 181–7.

When in June 1968 students at Belgrade University went on strike, occupied campus buildings, and proclaimed a 'Red University of Karl Marx', the authorities were nonetheless shocked about their loss of control over this kind of grassroots activism. As chairman and state president, Josip Tito feared 'the volcanic explosion of discontent' could potentially cause party officials to 'fly from [their] chairs'.[19] As a consequence, Yugoslav officials countered this domestic wave of dissent with rhetorical concessions and a gradually escalating campaign of repression in the aftermath of the Soviet invasion of Czechoslovakia. Their main targets were critical university associations, such as the famous 'Praxis' group at Belgrade and Zagreb Universities, as well as student media and action committees. Despite the flare-up of conflict at Belgrade University in June 1970 and at Ljubljana University in May 1971, party officials successfully confronted a final challenge to their political leadership by crushing the 'Croatian Spring' at the end of 1971. This last conflict, however, raised the spectre of the national question as a far greater challenge to the stability of Yugoslavia than the New Left ever posed.

An ambivalent position between East and West also shaped Romania's reaction to the events of 1968.[20] In this case, it was the government of Nicolae Ceaușescu, Secretary-General of the Romanian Communist Party, which skilfully navigated between ideological blocs. Ever since the 1950s, Romania had pursued a strategy of emancipation from the Soviet Union. The withdrawal of Soviet troops in 1958, Romania's neutrality in the Cuban Missile Crisis in 1963, and a 1964 party declaration signalling equal distance to Beijing and Moscow fostered an increasing break from Russian language and culture as the dominating forces in Romanian society. Ceaușescu's rise to power in 1965 and a host of reform efforts aimed at broadening the appeal of the party sustained this course. His sympathies with the Prague Spring and his support for the course pursued by the Czechoslovakian leadership even led to a Treaty of Friendship, Collaboration, and Mutual Assistance between the two countries a mere five days before the Soviet invasion.

When the Russian tanks entered Prague on 21 August 1968, Ceaușescu's reaction was swift and forceful. From the balcony of the party's central committee headquarters in Bucharest, which would become the site of his downfall in 1989, he condemned the invasion as 'a grave error and great danger for peace in Europe [and] worldwide Socialism'. Flanked by the entire state and party leadership, Ceaușescu decried it as a contradiction

---

[19] Quoted in Boris Kanzleiter, '1968 in Yugoslavia: Student Revolt between East and West', in Klimke et al. (eds), *Between Prague Spring and French May*, 84. See also Ralph Pervan, *Tito and the Students: The University and the University Student in Self-Managing Yugoslavia* (Nedlands, WA: University of Western Australia Press, 1978).

[20] Corina Petrescu and Serban Pavelescu, 'Romania', in Klimke and Scharloth (eds), *1968 in Europe*, 199–207; Corina Petrescu, 'Performing Disapproval toward the Soviets: Nicolae Ceaușescu's Speech on 21 August 1968 in the Romanian Media', in Klimke et al. (eds), *Between Prague Spring and French May*, 199–210. See also Dennis Deletant, *Romania under Communist Rule* (Iași: Center for Romanian Studies in cooperation with the Civic Academy Foundation, 1999); Vladimir Tismaneanu, *Stalinism for All Seasons: A Political History of Romanian Communism* (Berkeley, CA: University of California Press, 2003).

of Marxist–Leninist principles, called for its end, and defended the doctrine of national self-determination. In a clear warning to Moscow, he vowed to defend the Romanian homeland, labelling the intervention 'a shameful moment in the history of the revolutionary movement'. Although he returned to the official rhetoric of friendship and solidarity with Moscow only four days later, his defiant posture galvanized popular support, channelled national sentiment, and boosted the party's standing in its struggle for domestic legitimacy.[21]

As events in these countries demonstrated, 1968 in Eastern Europe was characterized by a complex dynamic of liberalization efforts from above and below, the preservation of the national communist project and relationship to Moscow, as well as concerns about the stability of the domestic political system. Students and other members of the younger generation were often a crucial factor in these developments, but by no means their sole initiators or main agents. In Western Europe, on the other hand, youth was most often the driving force behind the developments of 1968.

In France, it was the students who initiated the so-called *évènements* of the French May. Despite its iconic status, 1968 in that country only started on 22 March of that year with the occupation of campus buildings at the University of Nanterre. It came about as a result of the actions of two student groups comprised of Trotskyites, Maoists, and anarchists, namely, the *Enragés* and what later came to be known as the Movement of 22 March. Although extremely heterogeneous in their ideological orientations, both groups favoured an action-oriented strategy that mobilized a large number of Nanterre students frustrated with the shortcomings of the university system and the reform plans of the French government. These activists engaged in calculated direct actions that were designed as provocations, that is, violations of existing rules and regulations, in order to bring disciplinary measures against the students. The university's measures, in turn, triggered solidarity demonstrations at the Sorbonne, which elicited a police intervention in the university courtyard.

This intervention of security forces on campus property enraged students and set in motion a spiral of student mobilization and government response, ending with the closure of the Sorbonne and violent clashes between demonstrators and the police in the Paris Latin Quarter from 3 to 10 May. In conscious reference to the Paris Commune in 1871 and the liberation of Paris from the Nazis in 1944, students built barricades during the night of 10 to 11 May, demanding the release of their peers arrested during a previous demonstration, the reopening of the Sorbonne, and the withdrawal of the police. When the French minister of the interior, overwhelmed by this escalation of events, ordered the security forces to move in and remove the barricades early on the morning of 11 May, he only exacerbated an already tense situation. The excessive use of force during the

---

[21] Quoted in Petrescu, 'Performing Disapproval', 206. See also Mary Ellen Fischer, *Nicolae Ceauşescu: A Study in Political Leadership* (Boulder, CO: L. Rienner Publishers, 1989); Dennis Deletant, *Ceauşescu and the Securitate: Coercion and Dissent in Romania, 1965–1989* (Armonk, NY: M.E. Sharpe, 1995); Mihai Retegan, *In the Shadow of the Prague Spring: Romanian Foreign Policy and the Crisis in Czechoslovakia, 1968* (Iaşi: Center for Romanian Studies, 2000); Dennis Deletant and Mihail E. Ionescu (eds), *Romania and the Warsaw Pact, 1955–1989: Selected Documents* (Bucharest: Politeia-SNSPA, 2004).

'Night of the Barricades' and the subsequent raid prompted labour unions to call for a twenty-four-hour general strike in solidarity with the students. Even Prime Minister Pompidou's offer that night to accept student demands could not prevent 7.5 to 9 million workers across the country from going on strike in the following days, occupying, for example, the Renault car factories.

Although far removed from the anti-authoritarian and anti-imperialist impetus behind the students' actions, the workers protested against authoritarian structures in industry and demanded a greater say in company decisions, climaxing in the call for *autogestion* or self-management. As spontaneous expressions of dissatisfaction mod-elled after the students' call for greater democratization of university structures, the workers' actions were neither coordinated nor controlled by union officials. Indeed, the communist-oriented General Workers Union (CGT) dismissed their goals and strate-gies, attempted to prevent contact between students and workers, and even took over negotiations with the government to resolve the conflict. A negotiated settlement called the Grenelle Agreements was reached on 27 May. It provided financial compensation and formalized a series of union rights, but the workers represented in general assem-blies nonetheless rejected it. As a consequence, the strike continued both in the factories and the universities. The national standstill created an alternative public space for artis-tic imagination, political debate, and the articulation of utopian ideas, all of which emerged in an atmosphere bursting with the excitement of the moment.

This festival of the senses came to an abrupt halt with the reaction of the established political system. Prime Minister Pompidou's strategy of appeasement and accommoda-tion was counterbalanced by the initiative of President de Gaulle, who went on the polit-ical offensive—first with the announcement of a referendum, then with the dissolution of parliament and a call for new elections in June. De Gaulle's calculation was to rely on the framework of the regulated democratic process to outmanoeuvre the protest. The absence of a unified political opposition and alternative to de Gaulle eventually led to a victory of the governing coalition and gradually dissolved the energy and broad appeal of the student and workers' movement by the end of the year.

In Italy, the events of 1968 ran a very different course.[22] Their origins lay, among other things, in the death of the socialist student Paolo Rossi, who was killed during a conflict between left-wing and neo-fascist students in April 1966. This incident, which was fol-lowed by a wave of protest across Italy, brought the situation at the University of Trento—where students had already occupied the university at the beginning of the year—into the public eye. In opposition to the democratic deficits of the traditional central student organization (*Unione nazionale universitaria rappresentativa italiana*, UNURI), these students relied on alternative modes of representation and decision making to voice

---

[22] See Robert Lumley, *States of Emergency: Cultures of Revolt in Italy from 1968 to 1978* (London: Verso, 1990); Luisa Passerini, *Autobiography of a Generation: Italy, 1968* (Hanover, NH: University Press of New England, 1996); Jan Kurz and Marica Tolomelli, 'Italy', in Klimke and Scharloth (eds), *1968 in Europe*, 83–96; Stuart J. Hilwig, *Italy and 1968: Youthful Unrest and Democratic Culture* (Basingstoke: Palgrave Macmillan, 2009).

their demands for university reform. In this context, activists interpreted Rossi's death as a manifestation of Italy's repressive society, which they detailed in the 'Manifesto for a Negative University'. Over the course of 1967, opposition to government plans for university reform and to the war in Vietnam coalesced across the country. In February, students occupied the University of Pisa. In November, their peers at the Catholic University of Milan followed suit. In the following months, the protests spread to Florence, Genoa, Rome, and Naples, among other cities. By the spring of 1968, Italian universities almost came to a standstill. Classes were held only on an irregular schedule, if at all. Alternative curricula, general assemblies, political workshops, study groups, and demonstrations, were the norm.

With the 'Battle of Valle Giulia' at the University of Rome on 1 March 1968, violence became a vital component of students' protest repertoire, when demonstrators directly attacked the police. Street battles with local authorities or political rivals on the right ensued in the following weeks. For a brief period, the student movement advanced as an independent political force that dominated the nation's headlines as it took its protest outside the university, also in an effort to connect to the working class in the industrial centres of the North. This shift, however, diverted students' attention from their original objectives, thereby weakening their base. Protest activities at university decreased, and classes resumed in the fall of 1968, relegating the protests to a few local centres, where they gradually dissipated in the first half of the 1970s.

In West Germany, 1968 also represented the climax of a protest movement that had been active since the mid-1960s.[23] Student activists here were driven by the lack of democratic participation at university, an 'emergency legislation' bill that threatened to vastly expand executive powers at the expense of parliament, and a fundamental opposition to the war in Vietnam being fought by its NATO ally, the United States, which had a strong military presence in the Federal Republic. Concentrated in West Berlin and Frankfurt, mostly under the banner of the German Socialist Student League (SDS), these student activists maintained close contacts with their US counterparts and were influenced, in both theory and practice, by the American civil rights, anti-war, and Black Power movements.[24] Ideologically, these activists drew on the early writings of Marx, the minority theory of German *émigré* Herbert Marcuse, the voluntarism exposed by Hungarian philosopher Georg Lukács, and an infatuation with the liberation movements of the 'Third World' and the writings of Che Guevara, Frantz Fanon, and Régis Debray. The West German movement was also characterized by the Kommune I, a vibrant countercultural avant-garde and anti-authoritarian commune in West Berlin. The group's provocative actions, colourful attire, and active agenda of sexual liberation effectively fused situationist techniques, media manipulation, and political existentialism to garner public attention.

[23] Nick Thomas, *Protest Movements in 1960s West Germany: A Social History of Dissent and Democracy* (Oxford: Berg, 2003); Martin Klimke, 'West Germany', in Klimke and Scharloth (eds), *1968 in Europe*, 97–110.

[24] Martin Klimke, *The Other Alliance: Student Unrest in West Germany and the United States in the Global Sixties* (Princeton, NJ: Princeton University Press, 2010).

The key event for the movement in West Germany occurred on 2 June 1967, when the demonstrating student Benno Ohnesorg was fatally shot by a plain-clothes policeman during the visit of the Iranian head of state, Rehza Palewi, to West Berlin. Similarly to their Italian peers in the case of Paolo Rossi, West German activists saw Ohnesorg's killing as emblematic of authoritarian structures in their society and the latent violence of the state. The lingering legacies of the Nazi past and the attempted assassination of student leader Rudi Dutschke on 8 April 1968 further nourished this perception.[25] The growth and popularity that the movement experienced from mid-1967 onwards, however, ebbed dramatically with the ratification of the emergency laws by the West German parliament on 30 May 1968 and the upcoming summer break at the universities. The lack of a coherent national strategy, ideological infighting, and the emerging women's movement contributed to an organizational faltering of the SDS and a splintering of the student movement as a whole into a variety of political factions with varying degrees of strength at the local level.

In contrast to the Eastern European examples, the protest movements in France, Italy, and West Germany, although they faltered organizationally, underwent a political diversification, transformed themselves into single-issue movements, and continued to exercise an indirect influence on society in general in the following decades, as well as direct influence on local issues. Most dramatically, in the case of the West German Red Army Faction, the Italian Red Brigades, the French *Action Directe*, and the British Angry Brigade, a minority of activists resorted to terrorism to achieve their goals, frequently dominating headlines in the following decade and disproportionately overshadowing the manifold legacy of 1968 in these countries.[26]

RESEARCH PERSPECTIVES

Yet even a dichotomous East–West perspective on 1968 as outlined by the previous cases does not do justice to the variety of experiences on the continent. Recent historiography has sought to establish a more nuanced image of pan-European developments. This

---

[25] On the impact of the Nazi past, see Philipp Gassert and Alan E. Steinweis (eds), *Coping with the Nazi Past: West German Debates on Nazism and Generational Conflict, 1955–1975* (New York: Berghahn Books, 2006); Hans Kundnani, *Utopia or Auschwitz? Germany's 1968 Generation and the Holocaust* (New York: Columbia University Press, 2009).

[26] David Moss, *The Politics of Left Wing Violence in Italy, 1969–1985* (London: Palgrave Macmillan, 1989); Raimondo Catanzaro (ed.), *The Red Brigades and Left-Wing Terrorism in Italy* (London: Printer, 1991); Michael Dartnell, *Action Directe: Ultra-Left Terrorism in France, 1979–1987* (London: Frank Cass, 1995); Tom Vague, *Anarchy in the UK: The Angry Brigade* (London: AK, 1997); Jeremy Varon, *Bringing the War Home: The Weather Underground, the Red Army Faction, and Revolutionary Violence in the Sixties and Seventies* (Berkeley, CA: University of California Press, 2004); Dorothea Hauser, 'Terrorism', in Klimke and Scharloth (eds), *1968 in Europe*, 269–80; Ingrid Gilcher-Holtey, 'Transformation by Subversion? The New Left and the Question of Violence', in Belinda Davis et al. (eds), *Changing the World, Changing Oneself* (New York: Berghahn, 2010), 155–70.

approach also takes into account the repressive regimes in Southern Europe. In Portugal, for example, students contested the governments of Prime Ministers Salazar and Caetano through an anti-capitalism and anti-imperialism movement that was connected to student movements in other countries. It was imbued with a specific sense of urgency due to the country's own drawn-out colonial wars, for which dissenting students were frequently drafted as punishment. Culturally, student criticism in Portugal voiced an increasingly hostile attitude towards conservative Catholic morality. It also expressed affinity for a new informality while revealing burgeoning connections to the international counterculture.[27]

In Greece, 1968 was shaped by a military coup of colonels and the abolition of the democratic process in April 1967. Since students were unable to articulate any form of dissent at the universities, a violent and underground resistance movement gained increasing support. Its members viewed their anti-regime activities as a liberation struggle in union with the 'Third World'. It would take the student occupation of the Polytechnic School of Athens on 14 November 1973 and a brutal police raid before the repressive regime of the junta could finally be ousted—in August 1974—and the country's transition to democracy could proceed.

In Spain, students opposed the dictatorship of General Franco by various means throughout the 1960s, calling for the formation of independent student organizations and clashing violently with the police at the University of Madrid in March 1968. In subsequent months, they engaged in mass demonstrations, boycott of classes, occupation of university premises, and the smashing of Franco portraits. Although the government declared a state of emergency in 1969 and suspended *habeas corpus*, the student riots, in combination with the Basque separatist movement and workers' strikes, substantially weakened the system, which eventually collapsed after Franco's death in 1975.[28]

Other European countries not usually associated with the iconic events of 1968 also experienced serious, but commonly overlooked, forms of domestic unrest. In Belgium, the dominance of the French language at the Flemish university in Leuven triggered major protests among Flemish students. The ensuing conflict not only had a strong nationalist current but its escalation also brought down the Belgian government —the only case of protest-induced resignation of the head of a national government in Europe during the events of 1968.[29] Similarly, the Netherlands, the Scandinavian countries,

[27] See David L. Raby, *Fascism and Resistance in Portugal: Communists, Liberals and Military Dissidents in the Opposition to Salazar, 1941–1974* (Manchester: Manchester University Press, 1988); Miguel Cardina, 'On Student Movements in the Decay of the Estado Novo', *Portuguese Journal of Social Science* 7:3 (2008), 51–164; Idem, *A tradiçao da contestação: resistência estudantil em Coimbra no marcelismo* (Coimbra: Angelus Novus Editora, 2008); Idem, *A esquerda radical* (Coimbra: Angelus Novus, 2010).

[28] On the experience in both countries, see Kostis Kornetis, '1968 in Spain and Greece', in Klimke and Scharloth (eds), *1968 in Europe*, 253–66; Dimitris Asimakoulas, 'Translating "Self" and "Others": Waves of Protest under the Greek Junta', *The Sixties* 2:1 (2009), 25–47; Eduardo Romanos, 'Anarchism, Franco's Dictatorship and Postwar Europe: High-Risk Mobilization and Ideological Change', in Hara Kouki and Eduardo Romanos (eds), *Protest Beyond Borders: Contentious Politics in Europe Since 1945* (New York: Berghahn Books, 2011), 140–57.

[29] Louis Vos, 'Belgium', in Klimke and Scharloth (eds), *1968 in Europe*, 153–62.

Northern Ireland, Turkey, and East Germany have recently received growing scholarly attention.[30]

This expanded historiographical and geographical perspective has been facilitated by, among other things, the firm recognition of the transnational nature of the events of 1968. Student activists easily transcended national boundaries, exchanging ideas during mutual visits, or adopting protest techniques from each other. Rudi Dutschke, for example, met with students at the Charles University in Prague in April 1968, when he spoke there, and the French activists Alain Krivine and Daniel Bensaïd brought the strategy of limited rule breaking with them to Paris from the International Vietnam Congress in West Berlin in February 1968.[31] Student activists were drawn to the same intellectual sources, shared an international language of dissent, and even came together for joint international seminars and conferences, such as an annual international summer school on the Yugoslavian island of Korcula, an international conference in Ljubljana in August 1968, or the International World Youth Festival in Sofia in September 1968. Despite vastly different national conditions, activists were ideologically unified on a basic level through shared anti-authoritarian and anti-capitalist orientations, a distrust of both

---

[30] For the Netherlands, Sweden and Denmark see: Rimko Van Der Maar, *Welterusten mijnheer de president: Nederland en de Vietnamoorlog 1965-1973* (Amsterdam: Boom, 2007); Thomas Ekman Jørgensen, *Transformation and Crises: The Left and the Nation in Denmark and Sweden, 1956-1980* (New York: Berghahn Books, 2008); Tity De Vries, 'Resisting the Sixties: A Dutch Reaction in Global Perspective', in Dubinsky et al. (eds), *New World Coming*, 97-105. For Northern Ireland, see Bob Purdie, *Politics in the Streets: The Origins of the Civil Rights Movement in Northern Ireland* (Belfast: Blackstaff Press, 1990); Niall Ó Dochartaigh, *From Civil Rights to Armalites: Derry and the Birth of the Irish Troubles* (Cork: Cork University Press, 1997); Simon Prince, *Northern Ireland's '68: Civil Rights, Global Revolt and the Origins of the Troubles* (Dublin: Irish Academic Press, 2007); Simon Prince and Lorenzo Bosi, 'Writing the Sixties into Northern Ireland and Northern Ireland into the Sixties', *The Sixties* 2:2 (2009), 145-61. Among the few titles available in English on Turkey are Joseph Z. Szyliowicz, *A Political Analysis of Student Activism: The Turkish Case* (Beverly Hills, CA: Sage Publications, 1972); Jacob M. Landau, *Radical Politics in Modern Turkey* (Leiden: Brill, 1974); Ahmet Samim, 'The Tragedy of Turkish Left', in Ertuğrul Ahmet Tonak and Irvin Cemal Schick (eds), *Turkey in Transition: New Perspectives* (New York: Oxford University Press, 1987). For works in Turkish see, for example, Turan Feyizoğlu (ed.), *Türkiye'de Devrimci Gençlik Hareketleri 1960-1968* (Istanbul: Belge Yayınları, 1989); Bedri Baykam, *68'li yıllar: eylemciler* (Ankara: İmge Kitabevi, 1998); Gün Zileli, *Yarılma: 1954-1972* (İstanbul: İletişim Yayınları, 2002); Idem, *Havariler: 1972-1983* (Cağaloğlu, İstanbul: İletişim, 2002). On East Germany see Timothy Brown, 'East Germany', in Klimke and Scharloth (eds), *1968 in Europe*, 189-98; Eckard Jesse, 'Das Jahr 1968 und die Bürgerbewegung in der DDR', *Forschungsjournal Neue Soziale Bewegungen* 21:3 (2008), 87-95.

[31] For the general argument, see Richard Ivan Jobs, 'Youth Movements: Travel, Protest, and Europe in 1968', *American Historical Review* 114:2 (2009), 376-404. For individual examples, see Paulina Bren, '1968 East and West: Visions of Political Change and Student Protest from across the Iron Curtain', in Gerd-Rainer Horn and Padraic Kenney (eds), *Transnational Moments of Change: Europe 1945, 1968, 1989* (Lanham, MD: Rowman and Littlefield, 2004), 119-35; Petr Kopecký, 'Czeching the Beat, Beating the Czech: Ginsberg and Ferlinghetti in Czechia', *The Sixties* 3:1 (2010), 97-103; Belinda Davis, 'A Whole World Opening up: Transcultural Contact, Difference, and the Politicization of New Left Activists', in Davis et al. (eds), *Changing the World, Changing Oneself*, 255-73. For general transnational approaches to 1968, see Horn, *The Spirit of '68*; Kostis Kornetis, '"Everything Links"? Temporality, Territoriality and Cultural Transfer in the '68 Protest Movements', in Ada Dialla, Vangelis Karamanolakis and Kostis Kornetis (eds), *Historicizing 1968 and the Long Sixties,* special issue, *Historein* 9 (2009), 34-45.

Western liberal democracy and orthodox Soviet communism, and solidarity with liberation movements of the so-called Third World, whose philosophies they emulated and sought to apply to their own national contexts.[32]

The most striking scholarly advances have been made in situating 1968 in a cultural history of Europe. Whether it be the avant-gardist antecedents of the student activists of the late 1960s or countercultural role models such as the Situationist group SPUR or the Amsterdam Provos, the intertwinement of culture and politics, often in transnational contexts, has became the hallmark of most recent studies on the 1960s.[33] This field of inquiry has come to include music, fashion, emotions, drug experiences, and social experiments, as well as transformations in sexual habits, gender roles, and their representations. Recent historiography illuminates how a global popular culture of protest emerged throughout the decade and came to represent individual emancipation and notions of freedom, and how the authorities in various countries reacted to the political connotation of these new symbolic forms and lifestyles.[34]

[32] On the impact of the Third World, see Ingo Juchler, *Die Studentenbewegungen in den Vereinigten Staaten und der Bundesrepublik Deutschland der sechziger Jahre* (Berlin: Duncker & Humblot, 1996); Tina Mai Chen, 'Third World Possibilities and Problematics: Historical Connections and Frameworks', in Karen Dubinsky, Susan Lord, Sean Mills and Scott Rutherford (eds), *New World Coming: The Sixties and the Shaping of Global Consciousness* (Toronto: Between the Lines, 2009), 412–32; Karen Stellerbjerregaard, 'Guerillas and Grassroots: Danish Solidarity with the Third World, 1960–1979', in Klimke et al. (eds), *Between Prague Spring and French May*; Ingrid Gilcher-Holtey, 'The European 1960/70s and the World: The Case of Regis Debray', in Klimke et al. (eds), *Between Prague Spring and French May*, 269–82; Samantha Christiansen and Zachary Stanley (eds), *The Third World and the Global Sixties* (New York: Berghahn Books, forthcoming 2012); Quinn Slobodian, *Foreign Front: Third World Politics in Sixties West Germany* (Durham, NC: Duke University Press, forthcoming 2012).

[33] For an introduction to this field, see Martin Klimke and Joachim Scharloth (eds), *1968: Handbuch zur Kultur und Mediengeschichte der Studentenbewegung* (Stuttgart: Metzler, 2007). On the avant-garde and countercultural groups, see Niek Pas, 'Subcultural Movements: The Provos', in Klimke and Scharloth (eds), *1968 in Europe*, 13–22; Mia Lee, 'Gruppe Spur: Art as a Revolutionary Medium during the Cold War', in Timothy Brown and Lorena Anton (eds), *Between the Avant Garde and the Everyday: Subversive Politics in Europe, 1958–2008* (New York: Berghahn Books, 2011), 11–30; Niek Pas, 'In Pursuit of the Invisible Revolution: Sigma in the Netherlands, 1966–1968', in ibid, 31–43. For individual case studies with regard to the role of culture in 1968, see Stefan Backius, 'Popular Culture as a Tool for Change: Rural Working-Class Theatre in Sweden', in Dubinsky et al. (eds), *New World Coming*, 196–208; Angela Bartie, 'A "Bubbling Volcano": Edinburgh, the Festivals, and a Cultural Explosion', in ibid., 209–18; Timothy Brown, '"1968" East and West: Divided Germany as a Case Study in Transnational History', *American Historical Review* 114 (2009), 69–96; Martin Klimke and Joachim Scharloth, 'Utopia in Practice: The Discovery of Performativity in Sixties' Protest, Arts and Sciences', in Dialle et al. (eds), *Historicizing 1968 and the Long Sixties*, 46–56; Malgorzata Fidelis, 'Red State, Golden Youth: Student Culture and Political Protest in 1960s Poland', in Brown and Anton (eds), *Between the Avant Garde and the Everyday*, 145–53.

[34] Dagmar Herzog, *Sex after Fascism: Memory and Morality in Twentieth-Century Germany* (Princeton, NJ: Princeton University Press, 2005); Detlef Siegfried, *Time is on My Side: Konsum und Politik in der westdeutschen Jugendkultur der 60er Jahre* (Göttingen: Wallstein, 2006); Robert P. Stephens, *Germans on Drugs: The Complications of Modernization in Hamburg* (Ann Arbor, MI: University of Michigan Press, 2007); Detlef Siegfried, 'Music and Protest in 1960s Europe', in Klimke and Scharloth (eds), *1968 in Europe*, 57–70; Idem, *Sound der Revolte: Studien zur Kulturrevolution um 1968* (Weinheim: Juventa, 2008); Anna Pelka, 'Youth Fashion in 1950/60s Poland: From Oppositional Tool to Political Manipulation', in Kathrin Fahlenbrach et al. (eds), *The Establishment Responds: Power, Politics, and Protest since 1945* (New York: Palgrave Macmillan, 2012), 197–210; Jakob Tanner, 'Motions and Emotions', in Klimke and Scharloth (eds), *1968 in Europe*, 71–80.

To situate the events of 1968 in the broader history of postwar Europe, the inclusion of reactions of other social and political actors, such as political parties, government bureaucracies, churches, trade unions, and the media is certainly indispensable.[35] As part of a larger examination of the impact of decolonization on the Cold War in general and the aforementioned processes in particular, the connections and imaginaries that linked European activists to their counterparts, or revolutionary movements across the globe warrant further investigations. Likewise, an analysis of the 'afterlives' of 1968 (Kristin Ross) and the role these events played in the politics of memory in Europe as a whole and in individual countries is vital for showing the various transformations '1968' has undergone since the actual historical events.[36] Only then will we be able to evaluate whether 1968 represented a turning point for Eastern Europe's transition to democracy in 1989, whether it was a fundamental democratization and liberalization of many societies in Europe, or, as Adorno had hoped for in 1969, a victory of the imagination over the alienation of modern society.[37]

FURTHER READING

Anton, Lorena and Timothy Brown (eds), *Between the Avant Garde and the Everyday: Subversive Politics in Europe, 1958–2008* (New York: Berghahn Books, 2011).

Bischof, Günter, Stefan Karner and Peter Ruggenthaler (eds), *The Prague Spring and the Warsaw Pact Invasion of Czechoslovakia in 1968* (Lanham, MD: Lexington Books, 2010).

Bracke, Maud, *Which Socialism? Whose Détente? West European Communism and the Czechoslovak Crisis, 1968* (New York: Central European Press, 2007).

Capdevielle, Jacques and Henri Rey (eds), *Dictionnaire de mai 68* (Paris: Larousse, 2008).

De Groot, Gerard J., *The Sixties Unplugged: A Kaleidoscopic History of a Disorderly Decade* (Cambridge, MA: Harvard University Press, 2008).

Hilwig, Stuart J., *Italy and 1968: Youthful Unrest and Democratic Culture* (Basingstoke: Palgrave Macmillan, 2009).

---

[35] Promising beginnings: Maud Bracke, *Which Socialism? Whose Détente? West European Communism and the Czechoslovak Crisis, 1968* (Budapest: Central European University Press, 2007); Kimmo Rentola, 'The Soviet Communist Party and 1968: A Case Study', in Dubinsky et al. (eds), *New World Coming*, 56–67.

[36] Elizabeth Peifer, '1968 in German Political Culture, 1967–1993: From Experience to Myth', PhD thesis, University of North Carolina at Chapel Hill, 1997; Kristin Ross, *May '68 and Its Afterlives* (Chicago, IL: University of Chicago Press, 2002); Gassert and Klimke (eds), *1968: Memories and Legacies*; Ingo Cornils and Sarah Waters (eds), *Memories of 1968: International Perspectives* (Bern: Peter Lang, 2010).

[37] See Belinda Davis, 'What's Left? Popular and Democratic Political Participation in Postwar Europe', *American Historical Review* 113:2 (2008), 363–90; Helmut Fehr, 'Von 1968 bis 1989: Die Studentenproteste als Kristallisationspunkt für eine neue politische Generation in Ostmitteleuropa', *Forschungsjournal Neue Soziale Bewegungen* 21:3 (2008), 96–105; Paul Hockenos, *Joschka Fischer and the Making of the Berlin Republic: An Alternative History of Postwar Germany* (Oxford: Oxford University Press, 2008); Hanco Jürgens et al. (eds), *Eine Welt zu gewinnen! Formen und Folgen der 68er Bewegung in Ost- und Westeuropa* (Leipzig: Leipziger Universitätsverlag, 2009).

Horn, Gerd-Rainer, *The Spirit of '68: Rebellion in Western Europe and North America, 1956–1976* (Oxford: Oxford University Press, 2007).

Jørgensen, Thomas E., *Transformation and Crises: The Left and the Nation in Denmark and Sweden, 1956–1980* (New York: Berghahn Books, 2008).

Klimke, Martin and Joachim Scharloth (eds), *1968 in Europe: A History of Protest and Activism, 1956–1977* (New York: Palgrave Macmillan, 2008).

Klimke, Martin with Jacco Pekelder and Joachim Scharloth (eds), *Between Prague Spring and French May: Opposition and Revolt in Europe, 1960–1980* (New York: Berghahn Books, 2011).

Marwick, Arthur, *The Sixties: Cultural Revolution in Britain, France, Italy, and the United States, c.1958–c.1974* (New York: Oxford University Press, 1998).

Prince, Simon, *Northern Ireland's '68: Civil Rights, Global Revolt and the Origins of the Troubles* (Dublin: Irish Academic Press, 2007).

Ross, Kristin, *May '68 and Its Afterlives* (Chicago, IL: University of Chicago Press, 2002).

Schildt, Axel and Detlef Siegfried (eds), *Between Marx and Coca-Cola: Youth Cultures in Changing European Societies, 1960–1980* (New York: Berghahn Books, 2006).

Thomas, Nick, *Protest Movements in 1960s West Germany: A Social History of Dissent and Democracy* (Oxford: Berg, 2002).

PART III

BLOCS, PARTIES, POLITICAL POWER

CHAPTER 12

MAKING POSTWAR
COMMUNISM

MARK PITTAWAY

THE Soviet Union's victory in the Second World War offered both Moscow and Communists Europe-wide the opportunity to break out of the isolation that had afflicted them during the interwar years. With the end of the war in Europe on 7 May 1945, the Soviet front line traversed Central Europe from Germany's Baltic Coast in the north to the Yugoslav–Italian border in the south. Tito's Communist Partisans emerged victorious in a conflict in Yugoslavia that was a war of liberation against occupying powers, and a bitter civil war among Yugoslavs. The Greek People's Liberation Army (ELAS), led by the Communists, ended the war in control of swathes of Greek territory, while a resistance movement with substantial Communist participation played a central role in the liberation of northern and central Italy. A wartime swing to the left produced an upsurge in support across the European continent for Communist parties, first visible in Sweden's September 1944 elections where they polled 10.44 per cent of the vote. Aided by the prestige of the Soviet Union, and Communist participation in the resistance, early postwar elections revealed this to be a pan-European phenomenon; they took 40.17 per cent in the Czech Lands and 30.28 per cent in Slovakia in the May 1946 Czechoslovak parliamentary elections; 26.23 and 28.26 per cent in the October 1945 and November 1946 elections in France; 18.93 per cent in the June 1946 elections in Italy; and 16.95 per cent in Hungary in November 1945. Even in the Low Countries their performance varied between 10.6 per cent polled in the Netherlands in May 1946, and 13.5 per cent won in Luxembourg the previous October, while in Scandinavia they peaked at 12.5 per cent in Denmark in the same month.

By the mid-1950s the enhanced influence of Communism had been both consolidated and contained. The Soviet Union was established as both continental and global superpower, while allied socialist regimes ruled Albania, Bulgaria, Czechoslovakia, East Germany, Hungary, Poland, and Romania. This had come at a price, for Yugoslavia had left the Soviet orbit. Furthermore, widespread popular protest that shifted in spring 1953 from Bulgaria, Czechoslovakia, and East Germany to Poland, and most catastrophically

Hungary by the end of 1956, underlined the precarious legitimacy and stability of these regimes. In Western Europe the spectacle of the suppression of the Hungarian Revolution by the Red Army, at a time when de-colonization dominated the political agenda on the left, weakened Communist parties, exacerbating the impact of the early Cold War. Outside France and Italy, Communist parties, though powerful, ceased to constitute a viable alternative to established politics across the west of the continent, having lost much of the moral authority won during the Second World War.

Explaining the paradoxical consolidation and containment of Communism's influence across the continent is fundamental to grasping the contours of politics in Europe during the postwar period. The dominant strand in the historiography that approaches such an explanation is informed by the perspective of international history. It seeks to explain the breakdown in the wartime alliance between Great Britain, the United States, and the Soviet Union, and its impact on the states of Central and Eastern Europe. This body of historical writing concentrates on the role of the Soviet Union in postwar development across the continent.[1] Following the opening of the archives in the eastern half of Europe during the early 1990s, a range of studies has highlighted the diverse routes that individual nation states in the region took at the end of the 1940s towards dictatorship. National political actors, including Communist parties, possessed considerable agency.[2] This stress on the interaction between processes that occurred at the level of the great powers and national Communist parties has been extended geographically to explain the behaviours and roles of Communist parties west of the divide through the middle of Europe that emerged in 1948 and 1949.[3]

This work has underlined the role of Communism as not being merely an extension of the power of the Soviet Union, but as a political and social movement embedded within the fractures of national political cultures. These conclusions point to a multifaceted and nuanced explanation of Communism's role within the history of the immediate postwar period in Europe. Communism interacted with military and diplomatic struggles over the continent, and internal political struggles within the reconstructed states of Europe from the Soviet Union to the Atlantic coast. It was embedded in and

[1] See Mervyn P. Leffler and David S. Paynter (eds), *The Origins of the Cold War: An International History*, 2nd edn (New York: Routledge, 1994); David Reynolds (ed.), *The Origins of the Cold War in Europe: International Perspectives* (New Haven, CT: Yale University Press, 2005).

[2] Bradley F. Abrams, *The Struggle for the Soul of the Nation: Czech Culture and the Rise of Communism* (Lanham, MD: Rowman and Littlefield, 2004); Melissa K. Bokovoy, *Peasants and Communists: Politics and Ideology in the Yugoslav Countryside* (Pittsburgh, PA: University of Pittsburgh Press, 1998); Vesselin Dimitrov, *Stalin's Cold War: Soviet Foreign Policy, Democracy and Communism in Bulgaria, 1941–48* (Basingstoke: Palgrave Macmillan, 2008); Benjamin Frommer, *National Cleansing: Retribution against Nazi Collaborators in Postwar Czechoslovakia* (Cambridge: Cambridge University Press, 2004); Padraic Kenney, *Rebuilding Poland: Workers and Communists, 1945–1950* (Ithaca, NY: Cornell University Press, 1997); Norman Naimark, *The Russians in Germany: A History of the Soviet Zone of Occupation, 1945–1949* (Cambridge, MA: Harvard University Press, 1997); Gareth Pritchard, *The Making of the GDR 1945–53: From Antifascism to Stalinism* (Manchester: Manchester University Press, 2000).

[3] See especially Robert Mencherini, *Guerre Froide, grèves rouges. Parti communiste, Stalinisme et luttes sociales en France. Les grèves 'Insurrectionelles' de 1947–1948* (Paris: Éditions Syllepse, 1998).

expressed the aspirations, demands, and tensions of postwar societies. There were tensions too between Communism's role as a movement demanding greater social justice, and the culture of non-participatory, bureaucratic Stalinism that spread from Moscow, with its drive to subordinate Communist politics to the interests of the Soviet regime.

No history of postwar Communism can be written without paying adequate attention to its evolution in power within the Soviet Union both during and preceding the Second World War. The political practice of Stalinism emerged from the tensions and struggles within the Communist Party that followed Lenin's death. Ideological struggles over how the Soviet state coped with realizing the goals of the Revolution in circumstances of international isolation were resolved by Stalin's focus on 'building socialism in one country'. The state was strengthened against potential external threats through a programme of rapid industrial modernization. It built on the 'civil war' state inherited from the early years following the revolution by driving forward repression against political opponents, and 'class enemies'.

The political practice of the years of the First Five-Year Plan represented a renewal of social revolution, after years of drift under the New Economic Policy. Productive labour in the state sector was promoted; private sector activity was curbed, and revolutionary rhetoric proclaimed the creation of a new socialist, modern industrial state. Central planning through which economic activity, production, and consumption was coordinated bureaucratically was introduced, while 'socialist primitive accumulation' that drove rapid economic growth through raiding the agricultural population as both source of cheap labour and of capital for investment was pursued at enormous human cost, which reached its most intense in Ukraine, where millions starved during 1932–33. The real wages of urban workers plummeted, yet unemployment was eliminated, allowing household incomes to stabilize, as many of the politically loyal were promoted off the factory floors to staff the economic planning apparatus. The large cities and new industrial centres like Magnitogorsk were flooded with impoverished migrants from rural areas.

As a new social structure struggled to consolidate itself during the mid-1930s, Stalin and his security apparatus applied the logic of the 'civil war' state and its concern with apparent 'internal enemies' to the party and state bureaucracy that had expanded dramatically during the years of the First Five-Year Plan. The party was purged in 1933, initiating a prolonged period of bloodletting within the party and state elite, fuelled by the murder of Sergei Kirov in 1934. It gathered force during the mid-1930s and culminated in the wave of political trials which expanded in their scope beyond the Soviet elite in 1937 and 1938. The purges were directed from above and driven from below, for from the Kirov murder onwards the state deployed strategies of revolutionary mobilization throughout the lower levels of the security apparatus and in factories, collective farms, and offices across the country, to identify enemies.

In a newly industrialized society racked by class tension, the state emphasized mobilization and the agency of those subordinate groups who embraced the regime's ideology of revolutionary mobilization of building the future against the past through purging enemies. Consequently, the purges escalated. At their culmination during the Great Terror in 1937–8, 1.7 million people were arrested, and just under 700,000 executed. The chaos that resulted throughout the party, the government apparatus, the military and economic leadership, led Stalin to stabilize his regime through closing off the routes through which further purges could be driven from below, as the authorities de-emphasized Stalinism's 'populist' dimensions and placed greater stress on unquestioned, authoritarian bureaucratic control in everyday life, as they retreated from the excesses of the Terror. It was the more rigidly bureaucratized Stalinism that emerged from the stabilization of 1939–40, with its hostility to popular radicalism that would shape not only the Soviet Union after the Second World War, but would play a central role in structuring relations between Moscow, Europe's other Communist parties, and their grass roots.[4]

Stalinism was reforged by the Soviet Union's experience of total war from 1941. Moscow's truce with Berlin under the Molotov–Ribbentrop pact led to a failed attempt to subjugate Finland—a disastrous enterprise that revealed the weaknesses of the Red Army as a fighting force—and territorial expansion through the subjugation of the Baltic States, the occupation of Moldova, and the *Kresy* from Poland.[5] The weaknesses of the Red Army were again immediately visible after the launch of the German attack on the Soviet Union in June 1941, as the insurgent German forces encircled Leningrad in September and threatened Moscow by November. They were aided by the brittleness of support for the Soviet regime, not only in the new western border regions occupied during 1940, but also in much of the rural west of the Soviet Union, where opposition to collective farming undermined Moscow's authority, and in Ukraine, where memories of the famine of 1932–33 and continued hardship were a potent political factor. Yet the German advance did not occur without facing considerable resistance, as Red Army troops, aware of the brutality shown by the German forces to prisoners-of-war, showed progressively less willingness to capitulate as the conflict went on, and formed partisan units to harry occupying forces behind their lines. Furthermore, by the end of 1941 the German advance had been stopped at Moscow.

The pressures of survival during the precarious situation for the Soviet Union that persisted throughout 1942 reinforced the non-participatory, bureaucratic Stalinism that emerged during 1939–40. The Red Army was modernized with the support of Lend Lease provided by the United States; then the Germans were defeated at Stalingrad, leading to the long offensive that led to Berlin in spring 1945. The war's transformation of Soviet society was fundamental to reconstituting Communism as a political movement, as well as to the regime. The war fought on the territory of the Soviet Union 'became radicalized into a war of all-out extermination.'[6] Germany's offensive was conceived as

---

[4] My discussion here owes much to Cynthia V. Hooper, 'Terror from within: Participation and Coercion in Soviet Power, 1924–1964' (PhD thesis, Department of History, Princeton University, 2003), especially 233–41.

[5] Jan T. Gross, *Revolution from Abroad: The Soviet Conquest of Poland's Western Ukraine and Western Belorussia* (Princeton, NJ: Princeton University Press, 1988); Geoffrey Swain, *Between Stalin and Hitler: Class War and Race War on the Dvina, 1940–1946* (London: Routledge, 2004), 17–46.

[6] Mark Edele and Michael Geyer, 'States of Exception: The Nazi-Soviet War as a System of Violence, 1939–1945', in Michael Geyer and Sheila Fitzpatrick (eds), *Beyond Totalitarianism: Stalinism and Nazism Compared* (New York: Cambridge University Press, 2009), 349.

imperialist conquest through which the German state would destroy the Soviet Union, and create *Lebensraum* for an expanded German empire, that rested on 'a new ethnographic order' in which Slavic peoples would be subordinate within a racialized political order. It was also conceived as a crusade against Communism.

Thus the launch of Barbarossa underpinned an escalation in the radicalization of Nazism; radicalization that had already been visible in its brutal attempts to restructure occupied Poland on 'racial lines'. Ideological vision interacted with practice to drive descent into barbarity. Not only was war conducted with little restraint, but the dynamic of a conflict where the German military advanced rapidly and became increasingly overextended, while the Nazi regime's commitment to protect, as far as possible, living standards at home at the expense of those in newly occupied territories, shaped a regime of vicious exploitation of the population and territories of the western Soviet Union. Even during the early stages of the war, limited partisan violence had provoked disproportionate retaliatory violence against civilians, and as the prospect of German victory became ever more distant, its rule became progressively more brutal, and material exploitation of land and people escalated dramatically. In areas where support for the Soviet regime was weak prior to 1941, such as in Ukraine, famine conditions in Kiev and the major cities combined with the extreme brutality and racism of the occupation forces to turn the population against the Germans.[7]

Radicalization into 'a war of outright extermination' was also a consequence of the Soviet regime's casting of the conflict as an extreme version of a defensive war against 'the war of extermination with the peoples of the USSR' launched by Hitler.[8] In so doing it was able to both draw on and recast pre-existing traditions of revolutionary mobilization against enemies, both 'internal' and 'external', that had been central to Soviet political culture since the Civil War. To stem the Red Army collapse during the first months of the war, deserters and their families were labelled 'internal' enemies, as family members of soldiers who went missing were imprisoned, in order to inculcate the notion that to 'defend every inch of Soviet soil, right to the last drop of blood for our towns and villages' was a patriotic duty.[9] Given the sheer scale of the suffering brought by the war—between 26 and 27 million excess deaths, and almost generalized hardship and hunger—propaganda that mobilized the population to hate its external, German enemy, such as Ilya Ehrenburg's exhortation to the army to 'kill the German. If you have killed one German, kill another. There is nothing jollier than German corpses', fell on fertile ground.[10]

The war touched Soviet society not just through the scale of death and hardship, but also through that of mobilization. Over 34 million Soviet citizens served in the military between 1941 and 1945, emptying not only the cities, but also the countryside—from

---

[7] Karel C. Berkhoff, *Harvest of Despair: Life and Death in Ukraine under Nazi Rule* (Cambridge, MA: The Belknap Press of Harvard University Press, 2004), 205–31.

[8] Quoted in Geoffrey Roberts, *Stalin's Wars: From World War to Cold War, 1939–1953* (New Haven, CT: Yale University Press, 2006), 109.

[9] Catherine Merridale, *Ivan's War: The Red Army, 1939–1945* (London: Faber & Faber, 2005), 98; Edele and Geyer, 'States of Exception', 367.

[10] Quoted in Merridale, *Ivan's War*, 159.

where 60 per cent of recruits came—of adult males. The factories producing for the war effort filled with women; female workers made up 41 per cent of workers in 1940, 53 per cent by 1943. The need to ensure efficient industrial production to support military conflict at the front increased the prestige of managers and technical experts in the factories, further enhancing the turn towards authoritarian stabilization that had characterized politics since the end of the Terror.[11] Mobilization led to a recasting of Soviet patriotism, in which the defence of the homeland and the more politically abstract struggle against fascism were embedded. Within this recast Soviet patriotism, notions of 'internal' and 'external' enemies were embedded deeply. It proved deeply exclusive of those nationalities such as Crimean Tartars and Volga Germans who were labelled 'enemy' groups collectively responsible for the collaboration of some of their number, or in the case of the latter group, punished with deportation in August and September 1941 on the basis of ethnic association alone. It greatly aided the accommodation of Soviet identities with other hegemonic, particularly Russian national identities that had been visible during the 1930s.

The recasting of Communism around notions of 'socialist patriotism', and the defence of the homeland against a fascist aggressor was fundamental to the renewal of 'popular front' ideology, buried by the Molotov–Ribbentrop pact in 1939, across Europe after 1941. From the moment of the German attack, the war was not just about the patriotic defence of the Soviet homeland, but as far as Stalin was concerned, it was to ensure the 'enslaved peoples of Europe' would be liberated from the Nazi yoke. The Comintern placed emphasis not on socialist revolution but 'the struggle against national oppression, against the enslaving occupying regimes, about national liberation' in its message to individual parties across Europe.[12] With German occupation, a common European experience of brutality and material exploitation by the occupiers that affected disproportionately subordinate social groups most likely to support left-wing political alternatives formed the basis for a renewal of Communism. This process of renewal was uneven and reflected both the severity of given occupation regimes, and the role that Communist parties had played within pre-war political cultures in the states concerned.

Outside those parts of Poland ruled by Hans Frank's Generalgouvernement and the western Soviet Union, the experience of occupation and internecine conflict was at its harshest in south-eastern Europe, where it was met by the broadest degree of Communist mobilization. In Yugoslavia the state was dismembered after its collapse in the face of the Germans in 1941. The former Yugoslavia was divided into Italian and German occupation zones; northern Slovenia was incorporated into Germany; and collaborationist states were established in Serbia and Croatia, the latter of which pursued a campaign of genocide not only against Jews, but the 1.9 million Serbs who lived on its territories. Given economic collapse, endemic brutality, and harsh conditions in the cities, widespread partisan mobilization resulted.

---

[11] John Barber and Mark Harrison, *The Soviet Home Front, 1941–1945: A Social and Economic History of the USSR in World War II* (London: Longman, 1991), 94–119.

[12] Quoted in Martin Mevius, *Agents of Moscow: The Hungarian Communist Party and the Origins of Socialist Patriotism 1941–1953* (Oxford: Clarendon Press, 2005), 27.

Yugoslavia's Communists drew on limited support that stemmed from mobilization in the cities during the period of the royal dictatorship in the late 1930s. Their strength as a fighting force, and appeal to a population weary of protracted ethnic conflict, enabled them, following Italy's exit from the war in 1943, to achieve a commanding position across the west of the country, though not in Serbia, where they faced the Serbian non-Communist, or Chetnik resistance. In Greece, defeat at the hands of the Germans in 1941 led to the occupation of the country by Bulgarian, German, and Italian forces, with civil control nominally exercised by a puppet government in Athens, as most of the pre-war political elite chose exile over collaboration. Occupation in turn led to famine, and starvation conditions in cities from the winter of 1941, and severe hyperinflation thereafter.

Radicalization induced by occupation, and the Greek Communist Party's (KKE) embrace of popular front principles, allowed the party to recover from its effective destruction at the hands of the security forces of the Metaxas regime. As militant resistance increased, and occupation forces became ever more brutal in their response, the KKE achieved a dominant position in the National Liberation Front (EAM), the unified body that acted as the political leadership of the resistance. Its military wing, ELAS, grew enormously in strength and effectiveness, subordinating much of the country to popular, partisan-based revolutionary rule so that by mid-1944, according to one British officer 'Greece today forms two separate countries, occupied and unoccupied'.[13]

Italy's protracted exit from the war with Mussolini's overthrow in September 1943, the subsequent German occupation and armed conflict between them and the Allies, combined with the creation of the Italian Social Republic, produced a bitter civil war in northern and central Italy. Partisan warfare was coordinated by the Committee of National Liberation (CLN), in which all parties who sought anti-fascist renewal after two decades of Mussolini's rule cooperated. Entrenched initially in peripheral 'liberated zones' across the north, the numbers of partisans grew and their influence spread—in autumn 1944 there were between 20,000 and 30,000; 80,000 by March 1945; 130,000 on the eve of liberation the following month, and 250,000 immediately after.[14]

Across the Alps in France, the stress of Moscow on 'national liberation' enabled the renewal of the French Communist Party (PCF). It was able to rely on the memory of the 'popular front' to reconstruct the social base built in the industrial north, the Paris suburbs, and the Rhone delta in 1936 through the war years. This reconstruction was fed by the privation and repression in industrial areas, such as that which followed the May–June 1941 miners' strikes in Nord-Pas de Calais. Immediately after Barbarossa it met the call from Moscow for armed resistance in both Vichy and the zones of German occupation, forging its armed groups into *Francs-Tireurs et Partisans Français* in February 1942. True to the spirit of a struggle for 'national liberation' it joined the National Council of the Resistance (CNR) with the Gaullists and other anti-fascist parties in 1943.

---

[13] Quoted in Mark Mazower, *Inside Hitler's Greece: The Experience of Occupation, 1941–44* (New Haven, CT: Yale University Press, 1993), 265.

[14] Santo Peli, *Storia della Resistenza in Italia* (Turin: Einaudi, 2006), 139.

Given its superior organization in industrial areas, 'liberation' was met with an upsurge in radical activism, as across the south of the country, in an echo of the activism that had met the 'popular front' election victory eight years before, its militants founded workers' councils in many factories.[15] The experience of occupation in the Czech regions of Czechoslovakia, named the Protectorate of Bohemia-Moravia, was fundamental too in creating the base for the Communist Party (KSČ), given growing anti-German hatred among Czechs following the reprisals for the assassination of Reich Protector, Richard Heydrich, by members of the resistance flown in from London in May 1942; alienation from the western powers due to the sense of betrayal at Munich; and the increased prestige of the Soviet Union. Longer working hours, deteriorating food supplies, falling real wages, and despotic management in factories as war progressed contributed to the situation.

With military victory in 1945, the substantial gains made by Communists in a number of newly 'liberated' countries across Europe, and direct Red Army conquest of the eastern half of the continent, the power of the Soviet Union over the continent was greatly enhanced. Stalin envisaged the Soviet Union playing a central role in postwar Europe, and extending its influence over the countries it occupied, famously telling the Yugoslav Communist, Milovan Djilas, in April 1945 that 'this war is not like those of the past; whoever occupies a territory imposes their own social system upon it. Everyone imposes their system as far as their army can reach. It cannot be otherwise.'[16] This has sometimes been taken to mean that Stalin's intentions at the end of the war were exclusively aggressive, expansionist, and imperialist, and his initial cooperation with the western powers was merely cynical manipulation designed to hide his designs. The evidence, however, suggests that there was nothing that resembled a grand plan to create socialist dictatorships across Central and Eastern Europe at the point of the fall of Berlin.

First, the Soviet regime faced huge challenges in consolidating its authority on its own territory that needed to be overcome before it was able to convert the fruits of victory into permanent geopolitical strength. In the Baltic States, Belarus, and Ukraine the Soviet regime faced armed nationalist resistance that prevented the consolidation of Moscow's authority, while more seriously it faced the challenge of rebuilding in a climate of extraordinary human loss and material devastation that absorbed the regime's energies. Second, Stalin believed that the end of fascism had created an opportunity for the spread of socialism through means other than revolution, telling Yugoslav and Bulgarian Communists in January 1945 that 'we have to forget the idea that the victory of socialism could be realized only through Soviet rule. It could be presented by some other political systems—for example by a democracy, a parliamentary republic and even by constitutional monarchy.'[17]

---

[15] Stéphane Courtois and Marc Lazar, *Histoire du Parti Communiste Français* (Paris: Presses Universitaires de France, 2000), 213.

[16] Milovan Djilas, *Conversations avec Staline* (Paris: Gallimard, 1962), 127.

[17] Quoted in Roberts, *Stalin's Wars*, 236.

The interests of Communist parties across Europe were subordinated to the Soviet Union's moderate foreign policy goals that were pursued within the framework of the wartime alliance. First among its goals was the neutralization of Germany as a potential source of future military threat to the Soviet Union over the long term. The second was to establish a buffer zone running down its western border, which could serve as the basis of future containment of Germany, through which friendly regimes, though not fully-fledged state socialist ones, would be established in the Central and Eastern European region; special emphasis was placed on Poland and Romania. In these 'peoples' democracies', states that conformed explicitly to the formula of a state committed to social reform and anti-fascism would be guaranteed, if necessary, by Soviet military force. In order to ensure the cooperation of its wartime allies and believing in the inevitability of the victory of socialism through means other than revolution across Europe, Stalin urged moderation on Communist parties. The formula of anti-fascist 'national liberation' was extended into peacetime through the creation of coalitions of all anti-fascist forces in each state to pursue economic reconstruction based on mixed economies, retribution against members of the previous regimes, and social reform. It was in this context, at least for the time being, that the goals of Communist parties were supposed to be pursued.

Not all Communist parties accepted demands from Moscow for moderation. This was especially the case in Yugoslavia and Albania, where Communist-led partisan armies had won wars of 'liberation' on their territories. Josip Broz Tito at the helm of the Yugoslav party was not prepared to rule in any genuine coalition and shaped a policy of building Communist power through a 'popular front from below'. This involved transforming the Unitary People's Liberation Front, which had acted as the political organ of the partisans, into the People's Front, which was a vehicle under exclusive Communist control. In Yugoslavia, but also in Albania, this Communist controlled umbrella organization carried out a strategy of building a 'popular front from below'. A revolutionary state was created that both cleansed society of 'fascists', eliminated political opponents, and sought immediate social transformation. It was legitimated by elections in late 1945, nominally won by these anti-fascist fronts in both countries that, in practice, sealed single-party rule.

Attempts by Greece's Communists to orchestrate a state based on the 'popular front from below' were frustrated when British troops fought and defeated ELAS on the streets of Athens in December 1944; until the outbreak of civil war in 1946 they consented to becoming junior partners in a popular front coalition. In Bulgaria, the arrival of the Red Army and the arrival in power of a 'popular front' Fatherland Front government in September 1944 energized the grassroots of Bulgarian Communists, and their partisans, as they attempted to pursue the policy of 'popular front from below' at local level, initiating a radical purge of local administrations and security services. The party leadership was restrained by Moscow who wanted a 'popular front' government of all fascist forces, and who were disturbed that the radicalism of the Communists would disrupt their plans. As Traicho Kostov, one of the party's leading lights, pointed out in

March 1945 'the Soviet army would have put an end' to any attempt to 'establish Soviet power' in autumn 1944.[18]

Outside south-eastern Europe Communist parties and their supporters had difficulty in grasping and following Moscow's moderate line, in part because of their own revolutionary aspirations, but also because of the powerful expectations of social change that their wartime renewal as a movement had generated. In Hungary, while the Hungarian Communist Party (MKP) cooperated in a coalition which contained other anti-fascist parties, including the conservative Smallholders, in its propaganda its leaders expressed open admiration for the radicalism of the Yugoslavs in overturning immediately established governing practices.[19] Grassroots Communists were radical too, and their supporters impatient in demanding retribution against fascists and other social measures, such as land reform in agriculture, and public ownership and workers' control in industry. In Hungary, as the MKP was organized, it incorporated many underground Communists into its ranks who, motivated by the memory of the Soviet Republic that ruled the country for 133 days in 1919, were bemused at the party's opposition to immediate socialist revolution. The security services of the new state spent considerable time repressing those within the organizing party who refused to toe the line. Occasionally, some of these activists engaged in their own acts of revolutionary violence.[20]

In Italy the party leadership, who both lacked the support of a Soviet occupation force and were pessimistic regarding the chances of a left-wing majority without bourgeois allies, needed no persuading of the virtues of moderation. Yet in its areas of strength, like the Emilian countryside surrounding Modena, the political violence between 'fascists' and 'anti-fascists' that characterized the period of liberation, and which reached back to the agrarian conflicts in the region in the 1920s, continued into peacetime, aggravating relations between the Communists and their Christian Democrat partners, who accused them of orchestrating continuing violence.[21]

Even as the violence and chaos of the immediate postwar months subsided and state orders stabilized across Europe, Communism's moderate line forced it to contain the expectations of its supporters that radical change would result. This was especially marked in economic policies where Communist parties in both east and west expected their working-class supporters to defer demands for raised living standards and greater social justice in the interests of supporting the reconstruction effort. Through campaigns such as France's 'battle for coal' and policies such as those in Czechoslovakia, where the autonomy of factory councils set up during 'liberation' were restrained, managerial authority was asserted, and the egalitarian wage systems created in 1945 were gradually replaced with performance-based ones as production proceeded, working-class

---

[18] Quoted in Dimitrov, *Stalin's Cold War*, 74.

[19] Zoltán Ripp, 'Példaképből Ellenség. A Magyar Kommunisták Viszonya Jugoszlaviahoz, 1947–1948', in Éva Sztandeisky, Gyula Kozák, Gábor Pataki and János M. Rainer (eds), *A fordulat évei. Politika. Képzőművészet. Építészet* (Budapest: 1956-os Intézet, 1998), 45–62.

[20] Mária Palasik, 'A gyömrői gyilkosságok és következményeik, 1945–1946', *Valóság* 4 (1995), 58–67.

[21] Guido Crainz, *L'Ombra della Guerra. Il 1945, l'Italia* (Rome: Donzelli Editore, 2007), 101–9.

demands were sidelined.[22] Given the very real penury in industrial areas this generated a culture of semi-official protest across Europe that strained the party's pro-reconstruction line.

Perhaps the most serious social obstacles to Stalin's moderate line were the limits of Communist support and the persistence of anti-Communism within European societies. Almost everywhere in Europe, with the partial exception of the Czech Lands, the notion of a Communist-led 'democracy' only enjoyed the support of a minority of the electorate; in Czechoslovakia, even in Slovakia, a majority voted for the conservative Democratic Party in the 1946 elections. Across the continent, as broader continuities in political culture reasserted themselves, the suspicion of and opposition to Communism from supporters of bourgeois and religious parties was strong. In western Hungary, the November 1945 parliamentary elections were won decisively by the conservative Smallholders' Party on the basis that a vote for the party would mean 'the Soviets will be forced to leave the country, if they vote for the communists, they'll stay forever'.[23] In areas of significant partisan activity, such as the region of north-eastern Italy surrounding Trieste contested between the Italian Resistance, Yugoslav partisans, and the German occupiers, even prior to the end of the war, the occupation authorities' use of anti-Communist propaganda had been effective in ensuring the cooperation of the conservative and the propertied.[24]

The lack of support and the strength of anti-Communism were especially serious in those areas that had been incorporated into the Soviet Union in 1940, and from which the Soviets had been driven in 1941. In the Baltic States reincorporation into the Soviet Union after 1945 and pacification were long and protracted processes characterized by widespread armed resistance in all three republics; a collectivization campaign marked by waves of deportation, and industrialization supported by inward migration from Russia.

In Poland, resistance to Nazi rule had been dominated by the non-Communist Home Army who profoundly distrusted the Soviet Union, and Polish Communists. This distrust was exacerbated by Red Army inaction during the German suppression of the Warsaw Uprising in 1944. With Stalin determined to ensure a pliant regime in Poland as a key plank of his 'buffer zone', the Communists enjoying only minority support and facing both political opposition from the Polish Peasants' Party (PSL) and armed resistance from the Home Army, and the likelihood that the PSL would win free elections, the Communists, in control of the police and security state, consolidated their hold on power through fraudulent elections in January 1947.

---

[22] Peter Heumos, 'State Socialism, Egalitarianism, Collectivism: On the Social Context of Socialist Work Movements in Czechoslovak Industrial and Mining Enterprises', *International Labor and Working-Class History* 68 (2005), 48–51.

[23] Mark Pittaway, 'Making Peace in the Shadow of War: the Austrian-Hungarian Borderlands, 1945–1956', *Contemporary European History* 17:3 (2008), 354.

[24] Gianmarco Bresadola, 'The Legitimizing Strategies of the Nazi Administration in Northern Italy: Propaganda in the Adriatisches Küstenland', *Contemporary European History* 13:4 (2004), 425–51.

In Romania, of similar strategic importance to Stalin, the Communists were even weaker, with a tiny membership before Romania switched sides in August 1944 and the Red Army overran the country. A 'popular front' government of Communists and Social Democrats was formed with the 'historic' parties of the right, the National Peasants, and National Liberals. Amid the reluctance of the traditional political elite to accept the anti-fascist measures the Soviets demanded, or the social reform in a deeply unequal society that was advocated by the left, politics polarized quickly. The Communists, Social Democrats, and another left-wing organization, the Ploughmens' Front, formed the National Democratic Front (FND), which opposed the National Peasants and National Liberals. Relying on Soviet backing amid riots as Communists took to the streets across the country a government headed by FND politician, Petru Groza, took power in February 1945. Opposed by the 'historic' parties and not recognized by the western allies until February 1946, the FND government resembled a 'popular front from below' administration, consolidating its support with a radical land reform in 1945, and sealing its hold on power with rigged elections in November the following year.

The use of blatantly undemocratic tactics in countries of central strategic importance to Stalin, such as Poland and Romania, to secure pliant regimes, was an important stimulant to Europe's slide into the first Cold War, exacerbating anti-Communist fear continent-wide. Red Army occupation policies and practices in countries such as Germany, Hungary, and Austria, also played similar roles. In Hungary, Soviet support in creating a political police force under the effective control of the local Communists was vital in allowing them to wage a campaign to neutralize the victorious Smallholders' Party after its victory in November 1945 and re-establish MKP control over the 'popular front' government by summer 1947.

In Germany's Soviet Zone of Occupation the logistical support offered by the occupying forces was central in forcing through the merger between Communists and Social Democrats to create the Socialist Unity Party (SED) in the zone, which would become the ruling party of the German Democratic Republic in 1949. Equally, however, the Red Army presence, especially in Germany and former Axis allies, where wartime propaganda about the need to defend 'civilization' against 'Bolshevism' had left a deep imprint on the population, undermined support for Communist parties. The wave of violence and rape that accompanied the arrival of the Red Army across Romania, Hungary, Austria, Germany, and Slovakia, motivated in part by the anger and desire for revenge on the part of a Red Army who had witnessed the destruction of their own homeland, was deeply corrosive of support for Communism, and acted as the basis for a private 'anti-Communist' memory in many of these territories which outlasted even the Cold War.

The dismantling of industrial plants, a process that was hugely significant in the Soviet Zones of Occupation in both Austria and Germany, undermined the potential support for Communism, as it ran counter to their insistence on the need for 'reconstruction'. The expulsion of millions of ethnic Germans from Central and Eastern Europe during the late 1940s as part of an attempt to hold Germans collectively 'guilty' for the crimes of

Nazism, at the insistence of the Soviet Union and the region's Communist parties, reinforced anti-Communist attitudes in Austria and Germany well into the Cold War.

The fragile political constellation of international, national, and social factors that shaped Communism's role in early postwar Europe fed the progressive polarization of politics continent-wide during the late 1940s and the breakdown of the wartime alliance. Distrust of the western allies towards the Soviet Union was sparked by the undemocratic tactics used by Communists in Bulgaria, Poland, and Romania to secure their power in the face of limited support and domestic political polarization. In Greece, 1945 and 1946 were marked by growing left–right polarization, and finally the Communists announced the formation of a partisan army in October 1946 to bring about Communist revolution. Bitter civil war which lasted until 1949, in which the government and the right were supported first by the United Kingdom, and then the United States, led to over 80,000 deaths and massive displacement, which resulted in defeat for the Communists. In a deteriorating international climate Communist parties in Hungary and Czechoslovakia became more openly radical, using their control over domestic security services and mobilization of their supporters to neuter anti-Communist opposition and consolidate their control over the political system.

The support of the United States for the nationalists in the Greek Civil War was combined with more assertive steps from Washington to bolster anti-Communist forces across Europe during 1947. The announcement of the Marshall Plan, through which the United States offered a programme for the economic reconstruction of Europe, accelerated the process of international polarization, especially as the Soviet Union and Communists across Central and Eastern Europe rejected its terms. Communists were expelled from the French and Italian governments in 1947, while Stalin abandoned his moderate line of 1945, and instructed Communist parties to shift to the pursuit of 'popular front from below' policies through the foundation of the Cominform at Szklarska Poręba in Poland in September 1947. Across the eastern half of Europe, Communists eliminated opposition parties where they still existed during 1947 and 1948, and enforced 'fusions' with Social Democratic parties to give them a monopoly over the political representation of the labour movement. In Czechoslovakia the Communists seized power eliminating democratic institutions after non-Communist members walked out of the government in February 1948. The breakdown of the wartime alliance and the climate of polarization resulted in Germany in outright crisis over Berlin, and the formation of two German states in 1949.

As political polarization spread across the continent, and the dichotomy between Soviet interests and the nature of Communism as a movement shaped the ways in which it was contained internationally, this interacted with the domestic pressures on Stalin's regime within the Soviet Union. The sacrifices of the war years and mass mobilization around the patriotic defence of the Soviet homeland had generated expectations of change and improvement that would be brought with victory. The millions who returned home from active service abroad brought an awareness of the wider world that provided a language that enabled criticism of hardship at home. How dangerous this could be for the regime was illustrated by the comment of one veteran that 'people abroad live well, because there is private property and everything belongs to the people'.[25]

The Soviet state was scarcely able to meet these expectations. This was due to the scale of economic devastation, in turn intensified by population loss, and the long-term legacy of hunger that had persisted throughout the war years. As a consequence of the failure of the 1946 harvest, 1947 was a year of severe hardship for Soviet citizens, and even though 1948 brought improvement, the period was bleak. The regime's practice was dominated by the spirit of bureaucratic, authoritarian Stalinism which demanded sacrifice from the population in the interests of reconstruction, with no outlets for popular participation. Draconian controls were imposed on labour, which eroded the difference between the free and the imprisoned. Given both the deteriorating international climate and the destabilizing impact of the expectations for change brought by the war and growing contact with the West during the war years, the regime increasingly turned to isolationist rhetoric and offensives against 'cosmopolitanism' among the intelligentsia.

Yet this turn did not represent a turn back to the radical and chaotic mobilization of the Great Terror, but instead represented the heyday of the non-participatory, bureaucratic Stalinism that emerged during 1939–40. Public culture celebrated petty bourgeois values, while repression was highly selective, and government moved forward with more respect for bureaucratic regularity than before 1938. The consolidation of a repressive, bureaucratic Stalinism was enabled by the hunger and exhaustion of a population anxious for recovery and who feared a further war, given the deteriorating international situation. Yet among the population there were frustrated expectations, which were not to re-emerge until the thaw of the mid-1950s.[26]

With Communist parties in leading positions in governments across the eastern half of Europe by mid-1948, the practice of bureaucratic, authoritarian Stalinism within the Soviet Union also characterized relations between Communist parties internationally. Given the deterioration of the international climate, those Western European parties deemed to have been seen as too accommodating to their bourgeois partners, like those in France and Italy, had been castigated for being so at Szklarska Poręba. Yet parties that contravened Soviet interests in pursuing their revolutionary goals were also condemned. It was Yugoslavia's support for the Greek Communists' civil war effort, and Tito's parallel attempts to rally the support of his south-eastern Communist neighbours for Greece, in contravention of Moscow's more moderate line, and which was prepared, in line with wartime agreements, to leave Greece within the western sphere of influence, that provoked the first major split in Communist ranks. Yugoslavia's refusal to accept Moscow's foreign policy lead sent Tito initially into international isolation; over the following

---

[25] Mark Edele, 'More than just Stalinists: The Political Sentiments of the Victors 1945–1953', in Julianne Fürst (ed.), *Late Stalinist Russia: Society between Revolution and Reinvention* (London: Routledge, 2006), 177.

[26] Elena Zubkova, *Russia after the War: Hopes, Illusions and Disappointments, 1945–1957* (Armonk, NY: M.E. Sharpe, 1998), 101–9; Yoram Gorlizki and Oleg Khlevniuk, *Cold Peace: Stalin and the Soviet Ruling Circle, 1945–1953* (Oxford: Oxford University Press, 2004), 45–120.

years its struggle to survive in the face of hostility from Moscow led it to build during the 1950s the first post-Stalinist socialist state in the region.[27]

Stalin disciplined the party leaderships of the states within the bloc, where some party activists were deemed to have fallen under 'Titoist influence', with a series of show trials, endorsed by loyal party leadership, but coordinated by the Soviet security forces, which led in 1949 to the trials and executions of the Albanian and Hungarian former Interior Ministers, Koçi Xoxe and László Rajk, and Bulgarian former deputy Prime Minister, Traicho Kostov. Yet while restraining ruling parties in Central and Eastern Europe in questioning the primacy of Soviet interests, he also released them to expand internal security services, and launch drives against internal political opponents, especially the organized Christian churches, and those who had supported bourgeois political parties immediately following the war. The new dictatorships also began to overtly 'construct socialism', launching their own drives against the individual ownership of agricultural land, opening the door to collectivization and radical nationalization in industry and commerce. During the initial stages of 'socialist construction' in 1948 and early 1949, as living standards began to rise slightly after the penury of the immediate postwar years, it was welcomed by the social groups that supported Communist parties, but had been frustrated by their moderation in economic and social spheres.

Groups such as left-wing industrial workers would be disappointed. Mobilization was limited, and the dictatorships that were formed across the Soviet bloc were local versions of the non-participatory, bureaucratic Stalinism at its apogee at the turn of the 1950s in the Soviet Union. Even the ways in which socialism was constructed in Central and Eastern Europe were subordinated in conception to the foreign and security policies of the Soviet Union. Between the onset of the Berlin crisis in 1948 and the outbreak of the Korean War in 1950, Stalin became progressively more concerned about war with the West in Europe; the industrialization drives launched in a series of economic plans across the region that commenced in 1949 and 1950 were based on the rapid build-up of heavy industrial sectors designed to supply armaments. They rested too on strategies of 'socialist primitive accumulation' which, though more moderate than that introduced during the Soviet Union's first five-year plan, still generated penury and unrest in rural areas, and large-scale migration from agriculture to industry.

Intensified production and performance-based wages combined with the introduction of campaign-based mobilizations, such as the Stakhanovite movement, pioneered in the Soviet Union, led to worsening working conditions in industry. Cuts in real wages together with mounting food shortage created by a crisis of production in agriculture caused by a combination of social tensions generated by collectivization drives and the impact of 'socialist primitive accumulation' on rural living standards impacted on urban areas. With widespread chaos in production generated by the bottlenecks created by rapid industrialization in non-market conditions, labour shortage, and widespread, though submerged, working-class protest, the regimes were in crisis by 1953.

---

[27] Geoffrey Swain, 'The Cominform: Tito's International', *Historical Journal* 35:3 (1992), 641–63.

West of the divide that ran through the middle of Europe after 1949, anti-Communism was consciously used to cement the authority and legitimacy of bourgeois, yet democratic polities. This was at its most visible in the April 1948 elections in Italy, where the campaign mobilized impressive numbers, beyond the 1.1 million registered members of the eventually victorious Christian Democrats, or the 2.1 million who belonged to the Communists and their Socialist allies. Mass mobilization, and the use of propaganda and cinema by both sides, represented a marked modernization and democratization of political culture. Yet the election in terms of its messages was fought on a Cold War terrain, as the left found themselves outflanked by a modernized right-wing politics that stressed both traditional themes of religion and protection for the family against the menace of Communism, along with the less traditional ones of a future of freedom and plenty guaranteed by aid from the United States.[28] The promise of Marshall Aid and economic reconstruction under American auspices underpinned and supplemented more traditional forms of anti-Communist suspicion sharpened by the polarization that accompanied the onset of the Cold War.

As early as 1949, West Germany's future Federal Chancellor, Konrad Adenauer, was able to use his opposition to the threat of 'a socialist economy' not only against the tiny Communists, but also against the far larger Social Democrats.[29] In this climate too, where substantial numbers of workers supported Communists, protest could be tarred with an anti-Communist brush. This happened as early as 1947 when protest at the increase in tram fares in Marseilles sparked a wave of working-class protest countrywide at low living standards that was labelled by the Interior Minister, Jules Moch, as an attempt at Communist 'insurrection' and defeated. The ability of employers to use anti-Communism to break Communist affiliated unions and break down Communist organization and support became a regular theme of industrial politics in Italy throughout the 1950s. By the middle of the decade it was clear that across most of Western Europe, Communism was relegated to the status of a marginal political force, outside of France and Italy. While it attracted considerable electoral support in both countries, even there the dream of a socially radical government that rested on the principles of a 'national liberation' led by Communists was effectively dead, though both parties continued to draw on their role in the resistance and anti-fascism in French and Italian collective memory to shape for themselves a role as legitimate national political actors.

In France by 1956 the PCF polled 23.56 per cent of the vote in legislative elections, below its 1946 election peak, but nevertheless a substantial tally. Yet its support remained concentrated in industrial regions or those rural areas, like Allier, with a Communist tradition, allowing it to retain a place within the French public sphere as the 'party of the working class'.[30] In Italy, the Communists polled 22.6 per cent in 1953 and grew at each

---

[28] Edoardo Novelli, *Le Elezioni del Quarantotto. Storia, strategie e immagini della prima campagna elettorale repubblicana* (Rome: Donzelli Editore, 2008), 81–97.

[29] Eckart Conze, *Die Suche nach Sicherheit. Eine Geschichte der Bundesrepublik Deutschland von 1949 bis in die Gegenwart* (Munich: Siedler, 2009), 112.

[30] Julian Mischi, *Servir la classe ouvriére. Sociabilités militants au PCF* (Rennes: Presses Universitaires de Rennes, 2010), 11–31.

election thereafter, peaking in 1976, carving out an institutionalized role within national politics; yet this stabilization combined with a crisis of activism as their working-class membership in industrial centres fell sharply in the mid-1950s.[31]

East of the Iron Curtain, Communism's resurgence thanks to the Second World War had fizzled out by the mid-1950s. Though state socialist regimes emerged consolidated from the crisis that followed Stalin's death in 1953, the political project on which it rested was ossified. Within the Soviet Union itself non-participatory, bureaucratic Stalinism was in deep crisis by 1953, as the regime sat on a cauldron of frustrated expectation. The collective, post-Stalin leadership and then Nikita Khrushchev were forced to liberalize, but to do so cautiously in order to avoid outright social explosion. The risks incurred were illustrated by the violent reactions to the news of Khrushchev's denunciation of Stalin at the 20th Congress in February 1956, as it seeped into the public realm: 'there had taken place many incidents of public destruction of portraits, busts and monuments of Stalin'.[32] The regime was forced to manage the extent of permitted discussion to preserve existing political structures.

Outside the Soviet Union, the wave of popular protest immediately following the death of Stalin beginning with riots in Plovdiv in Bulgaria, Plžen in Czechoslovakia, and then across the German Democratic Republic in spring 1953, illustrated both deep-seated material frustration and the lack of legitimacy socialist dictatorship enjoyed among the working class. The events in Poznań in June 1956 and the outbreak of the Hungarian Revolution in October, which was only suppressed through the intervention of the Red Army, were far more damaging. In Hungary especially, the outright lack of legitimacy of the regime was underlined in full view of international opinion. While force allowed Communists to occupy political power, in Hungary, as in the rest of the region, building a functioning regime required a policy of pacification that rested especially on addressing the material concerns of the population, particularly industrial workers, and buying their accommodation with the political system.[33]

While the political settlements across the Soviet bloc, variable as they were, ensured the completion of socialist construction through the completion of agricultural collectivization everywhere other than Poland, and brought increases in living standards during the 1960s, they rested on a retreat in that they emphasized a consolidation of existing structures of power and political relations, rather than an attempt to innovate and drive forward change. In this way they masked the decay of the Communist political project, which would not become fully apparent until the 1980s.

[31] Guido Crainz, *Storia del Miracolo Italiano. Cultura, identità, trasformazioni fra anni cinquanta e sessanta* (Rome: Donzelli Editore, 2005), 36–42.

[32] Polly Jones, 'From the Secret Speech to the Burial of Stalin: Real and Ideal Responses to De-Stalinization', in Polly Jones (ed.), *The Dilemmas of De-Stalinization: Negotiating Cultural and Social Change in the Khrushchev Era* (London: Routledge, 2006), 50.

[33] Mark Pittaway, 'Accommodation and the Limits of Economic Reform: Industrial Workers during the Making and Unmaking of Kádár's Hungary', in Peter Hübner, Christoph Kleßmann and Klaus Tenfelde (eds.), *Arbeiter im Staatssozialismus: Ideologischer Anspruch und soziale Wirklichkeit* (Cologne: Böhlau Verlag, 2005), 453–71.

Further Reading

Abrams, Bradley F., *The Struggle for the Soul of the Nation: Czech Culture and the Rise of Communism* (Lanham, MD: Rowman and Littlefield, 2004).

Dimitrov, Vesselin, *Stalin's Cold War: Soviet Foreign Policy, Democracy and Communism in Bulgaria, 1941–48* (Basingstoke: Palgrave Macmillan, 2008).

Frommer, Benjamin, *National Cleansing: Retribution against Nazi Collaborators in Postwar Czechoslovakia* (Cambridge: Cambridge University Press, 2004).

Gorlizki, Yoram and Oleg Khlevniuk, *Cold Peace: Stalin and the Soviet Ruling Circle, 1945–1953* (Oxford: Oxford University Press, 2004).

Jones, Polly (ed.), *The Dilemmas of De-Stalinization: Negotiating Cultural and Social Change in the Khrushchev Era* (London: Routledge, 2006).

Mevius, Martin, *Agents of Moscow: The Hungarian Communist Party and the Origins of Socialist Patriotism 1941–1953* (Oxford: Clarendon Press, 2005).

Pittaway, Mark, *Eastern Europe 1939–2000* (London: Arnold, 2004).

Roberts, Geoffrey, *Stalin's Wars: From World War to Cold War, 1939–1953* (New Haven, CT: Yale University Press, 2006).

Swain, Geoffrey, 'The Cominform: Tito's International', *Historical Journal* 35:3 (1992), 641–63.

Zubkova, Elena, *Russia after the War: Hopes, Illusions and Disappointments, 1945–1957* (Armonk, NY: M.E. Sharpe, 1998).

CHAPTER 13

....

EUROPE'S COLD WAR

....

JUSSI M. HANHIMÄKI

IN 1945 much of Europe was in rubble, following an orgy of violence and genocide unprecedented in recorded history. This alone provides one explanation for the phenomenal rise of Soviet and American power in Europe after the Second World War: with Germany in ruins, France largely excluded from the victors' table, and Britain in no condition to play a major role in continental Europe, there were, ultimately, only two major powers capable of exercising predominant influence over the old continent. And given the ideological differences, material capabilities, security interests, and contrasting personalities of those in power, it was no wonder that any possibility of cooperation between Moscow and Washington vanished after the common objective of defeating the Axis powers had been achieved. While the Cold War may not have been inevitable, it would have been difficult to avoid.[1]

Over subsequent decades Europe was dramatically transformed. The loss of empires, the process of economic (and to a lesser extent political) integration, and the Cold War political division of Europe dramatically shaped the continent and its role in the world. Whereas Europe had earlier been at the centre stage of international relations, it gradually became a sideshow—an object of policy by the postwar superpowers, the United States and the Soviet Union, rather than the cockpit of international relations it had been for centuries. With Moscow's influence dominant in the East and Washington's power decisive in the West, the traditional great powers of Europe (France, Britain, Germany) were but shadows of their former selves. To a large extent the Cold War was a struggle *for Europe* waged in large part *by non-Europeans*.[2]

According to the above, admittedly oversimplified, understanding of post-1945 European history, Europe's Cold War can easily be divided into three periods. The early Cold War—roughly from 1945 to the early 1960s—saw the division of the continent and

---

[1] For a colourful and brief account of the state of Europe in 1945, see Tony Judt, *Postwar: A History of Europe Since 1945* (New York: Penguin, 2005), 13–40.

[2] Reflected in the titles of several overviews of Cold War Europe, such as: William I. Hitchcock, *The Struggle for Europe: The Turbulent History of A Divided Continent, 1945–2002* (New York: Doubleday, 2003).

the erosion of Europe's global influence with the demise of the great empires of Great Britain and France. There was the creation of NATO and the Soviet imposition of its domination over Eastern Europe. The second period—from the early 1960s to the mid-1970s—saw the rise of détente and the stabilization of the Cold War balance of power in Europe in the shadow of an ongoing Soviet–American nuclear arms race. The last period, from the mid-1970s to the late 1980s, saw continued globalization of the Cold War and, during 1989–91, the astonishingly rapid erosion of Soviet power. Cold War in Europe thus ended with a victory for the United States; as a unipolar post-Cold War era began, Europeans continued to play, at best, supporting roles to the American hyper-power that had won what one scholar calls the 'struggle for the soul of mankind'.[3]

Such a straightforward chronology—a narrative of the rise, maturity and erosion of the Cold War—is, however, only part of Europe's Cold War. For while Europe was undoubtedly divided for several decades into two hostile blocs dominated by one extra-European power (the United States) and one 'Eurasian' power (the Soviet Union), the traditional narrative often downplays the influence that the Europeans themselves—East and West—had on the unfolding of events. The loss of formal empires, for example, did not equal the loss of influence. In fact, far from being merely victims or passive bystanders, various European powers played key roles at each stage of the Cold War. As numerous historians have shown over the past two decades, manipulation, dependency, and yielding of influence were never unidirectional processes. Instead, the Cold War order produced interdependencies that often allowed the 'weaker' Europeans to exercise significant influence over the dominant powers. This was evident at all stages of the Cold War. Or, as John L. Gaddis sums it up, 'the "superpowers" during the Cold War were not all that "super"'.[4]

It is impossible to review all of Europe's Cold War here. Yet, in order to illustrate the complexity of this era in European history, I will focus on three general themes that reflect some of the ongoing debates among historians. First, I will explore the evolution of transatlantic relations during the Cold War, with particular emphasis on Geir Lundestad's well known thesis about 'empire by invitation'.[5] I will then turn to the other side of the Cold War divide and evaluate the supposed omnipotence of the Soviet Union over its client states. Last, I will briefly examine the cracks in the Iron Curtain – the evolution of relations between, beneath, and beyond the two blocs in Europe. I will further maintain that the peaceful ending of Europe's Cold War was as a result of the complex web of intra-bloc and inter-bloc relationships that had undermined the rigidity of the bipolar 'superstructure' of the international system for decades prior to the revolutions of 1989.

---

[3] Melvyn P. Leffler, *For the Soul of Mankind: The United States, the Soviet Union, and the Cold War* (New York: Hill & Wang, 2007).

[4] John L. Gaddis, 'On Starting All over again: A Naïve Approach to the Study of the Cold War', in Odd Arne Westad (ed.), *Reviewing the Cold War: Approaches, Interpretations, Theory* (London: Frank Cass, 2000), 30.

[5] The argument was originally developed in Geir Lundestad's 'Empire by Invitation? The United States and Western Europe, 1945–1952', *Journal of Peace Research* 23 (1986), 263–77.

EMPIRE BY INVITATION? AMERICA'S EUROPE

The enhanced American role in Western Europe after World War II represented both a dramatic reversal of US foreign policy as well as virtual surrender of traditional European powers of their pre-eminent positions in world affairs. In some ways this was quite humiliating. In the immediate postwar years many European countries depended on American aid simply to feed their populations. Whether proud nationalists or life-long imperialists, West European leaders found no alternative to their postwar dilemmas than to accept American economic aid and, ultimately, an American security guarantee. Behind this lay a myriad of concerns, yet one was perhaps foremost among them all: the spectre of communism.

While anti-communism sometimes acquired irrational features (as in the form of McCarthyism in the United States) its influence in postwar Europe should not be underestimated. In the UK, a recent book claims, anti-communism 'became an integral part of British Cold War strategy'.[6] Ideological affinity between the United States and many Western European countries—an anti-communist but also anti-totalitarian Atlanticism—was indeed a key building block for the postwar transatlantic community. In terms of domestic European politics this meant, simply, that such disparate political organizations as the Christian Democrats in Italy and Germany, the Gaullists in France, and even the various Social Democratic parties in Scandinavia, saw eye to eye on one issue: they viewed the potential ascent of the extreme left to power—be it in their respective countries or in nations nearby—as a dangerous scenario.[7]

At the origins of such European concerns were hard facts. The Red Army was in control of the eastern half of the continent. Various national communist parties in Western Europe—most notably in Italy and France—made spectacular gains at the ballot box, reflecting a general shift towards the left throughout Western Europe. Even such respected wartime leaders as Winston Churchill suffered an electoral defeat in 1945. National economies that had not fully recovered from the international economic crisis of the 1930s had been seriously damaged by the war. Millions of Europeans had been rendered homeless. Indeed, much of 'liberated' Europe was downtrodden, politically unstable, and vulnerable to further upheaval. Without reassurance against external— real or imagined—security threats and economic assistance that would boost postwar

---

[6] Andrew Defty, *Britain, America and Anti-Communist Propaganda, 1945–1953* (London: Routledge, 2004), 1.

[7] For example: Alessandro Brogi, *A Question of Self-Esteem: The United States and the Cold War Choices in France and Italy, 1944–1958* (New York: Praeger, 2001); William I. Hitchcock, *France Restored: Cold War Diplomacy and the Quest for Leadership in Europe, 1944–1954* (Chapel Hill, NC: University of North Carolina Press, 1998); Patrick Major, *The Death of the KPD: Communism and Anti-Communism in West Germany, 1945–1956* (Oxford: Clarendon Press, 1997); Jussi Hanhimäki, *Scandinavia and the United States: An Insecure Friendship* (New York: Twayne's, 1997). On the role of refugees from Soviet-occupied Europe, see Anna Holian, 'Anticommunism in the Streets: Refugee Politics in Postwar Germany', *Journal of Contemporary History* 45:1 (2010), 134–61.

reconstruction, a return to stability was difficult to conceive. It was in such conditions that the role of the United States became critical for the reshaping of Western Europe.[8]

The key goals of American policy in Europe are easily identifiable: to restore and strengthen capitalism; minimize left-wing influence; and prevent the Soviet Union from extending its influence to Western Europe. By 1947, to counter the Soviet Union's supposedly expansionist goals, Washington evoked the Truman Doctrine and unveiled the Marshall Plan. Two years later came the first Berlin crisis, the foundation of NATO, and the formal creation of two separate German states. Many West European countries saw the continued presence of American troops (in Germany the number would not go below 250,000 until after 1989). In Europe, the basic structure of the transatlantic relationship that would last throughout the Cold War was essentially already in place by the late 1940s.[9]

Simultaneously, Western Europe's global presence rapidly declined. The wave of decolonization began with the British departure from India and (forced) Dutch exit from Indonesia in the 1940s. In the 1950s and 1960s this trend continued further as, among other developments, the French left Indochina and Algeria, the Belgians granted independence to the Congo, and the UK's African empire was extinguished. The 1956 Suez crisis left London and Paris humiliated. By 1968 the British announced that they were removing remaining troops from the Middle East. Finally, in 1975 the longest lasting colonial empire collapsed as Portugal withdrew from Angola, Mozambique, and Cape Verde. The demise of Europe's global presence was all but complete, not to be countered by the sentimental attachment of certain Europeans to their former holdings, be it in the form of the British Commonwealth or the idea of a Francafrique.[10]

---

[8] See Judt, *Postwar*, 129–64.

[9] It is impossible to list all books and articles that address these issues in detail. Useful summaries can be found in Marc Trachtenberg, *A Constructed Peace: The Making of the European Settlement, 1945–1963* (Princeton, NJ: Princeton University Press, 1999), 34–65; W.R. Smyser, *From Yalta to Berlin: The Cold War Struggle over Germany* (New York: St Martin's Press, 1999), 53–104; David Reynolds (ed.), *The Origins of the Cold War in Europe: International Perspectives* (New Haven, CT: Yale University Press, 1994). On the continued presence of US troops in Europe, see Hubert Zimmermann, 'The Improbable Permanence of a Commitment: America's Troop Presence in Europe during the Cold War', *Journal of Cold War Studies* 11:1 (2009), 3–27.

[10] Some interesting accounts on the end of European empires include: Nicholas White, *Decolonisation: The British Experience* (London: Longman, 1999); John Darwin, *The End of the British Empire: The Historical Debate* (Oxford: Oxford University Press, 2006); Peter Clarke, *The Last Thousand Days of the British Empire: The Decline of a Superpower, 1944–1947* (New York: Penguin, 2008); W. Taylor Fain, *American Ascendance and British Retreat in the Persian Gulf Region* (New York: Palgrave Macmillan, 2008); Raymond Betts, *Decolonization* (London: Routledge, 2004); Philip C. Naylor, *France and Algeria: A History of Decolonization and Transformation* (Miami, FL: University Press of Florida, 2000); P.L. Pham, *Ending 'East of Suez': The British Decision to Withdraw from Malaysia and Singapore* (Oxford: Oxford University Press, 2010); James Fiscus, *The Suez Crisis* (New York: Rosen, 2008); Frances Gouda with Thijs Zaalberg, *American Visions of the Netherlands East Indies/Indonesia: US Foreign Policy and Indonesian Nationalism, 1920–1949* (Amsterdam: Amsterdam University Press, 2002); Kathryn C. Statler, *Replacing France: The Origins of American Intervention in Vietnam* (Lexington, KY: University of Kentucky Press, 2007).

Thus it is no wonder that the Cold War relationship(s) between the United States and its West European allies has often been described as one of dependency. Europeans simply needed American money and American security guarantees more than the other way around. In this regard the argument that the United States–West European relationship after World War II represented an empire by invitation strikes a chord. The Marshall Plan, for example, originated with an 'invitation' for the Europeans to present a recovery plan for the Americans to consider funding. Many participated in the early stages of such negotiations; in the end, the Soviets declined and pressured countries under Moscow's influence to reject participation as well. But many West Europeans were more than happy to join in, reaping the dual benefits of membership in a collective defence organization and reconstruction assistance.[11]

Dominant though the United States was, its power was limited. Throughout the Cold War, the transatlantic relationship was filled with tensions and conflicts that can be viewed both as a continuation of an uneasy pre-war transatlantic relationship as well as a particular feature of the Cold War transatlantic community. National interests, economic prerogatives, and cultural peculiarities did not vanish despite the broad structure of a bipolar international system. In particular, three broad points should be kept in mind.

First, the United States may well have been the senior partner in NATO but its influence on the other member states' foreign and security policy had strict limits. The cooperation rarely extended beyond the NATO area itself. The French and British action in Suez in 1956 was an early and extreme example of how some Europeans still acted without paying much attention to the American reaction (or Cold War considerations). To be sure, prior to Suez, the Americans had given assistance to the French effort in Indochina in the early 1950s and most Europeans had lined up with the United States in the Korean War. But by the 1960s it was clear that when it came to the use of military force, America's global Cold War policies received little direct West European support. When the United States asked for European support in an 'out-of-area' military conflict—such as Vietnam—its NATO partners saw no need to express alliance solidarity by sending troops to South-east Asia. While expressing sympathy with the American position, Europeans—including the British—refused persistent US calls for joint action. Vietnam was America's war and, eventually, America's disaster.

Nor did the United States find the tools to create a common Atlantic front in the Middle East. The 1973 October war and, in particular, the oil crisis that accompanied it, split the Atlantic community in two. West Europeans, concerned over the flow of oil from the region, were weary of taking a stand that might have caused their vital oil imports to be impeded. Those that did side with the United States' position and assist in the airlift of arms to Israel—such as the Netherlands—paid for it dearly.[12]

[11] For a sample of the various debates over the impact of the Marshall Plan, see the essays in John Agnew and J. Nicholas Entrikin (eds), *The Marshall Plan Today: Model and Metaphor* (London: Routledge, 2004).

[12] For a summary of these disputes, see Geir Lundestad, *The United States and Western Europe Since 1945: From 'Empire' by Invitation to Transatlantic Drift* (New York: Oxford University Press, 2003), 142–67. See also Francine McKenzie, 'GATT and the Cold War: Accession Debates, Institutional Development, and the Western Alliance, 1947–1959', *Journal of Cold War Studies* 10:3 (2008), 78–109.

While out-of-area issues were the primary source of tension and conflict in the trans-atlantic relationship, the economic dominance of the United States in 1945 also proved short-lived. By the time Marshall Plan aid ended in 1952, European recovery was already a fact of life; in the decade that followed, Western Europe gradually emerged as a rival. European integration—that was spurred on by US policies in the 1950s—eventually produced an economically healthy European community. When the British finally joined the EEC in 1973, *Time* magazine heralded the emergence of 'America's New Rival'.[13] While trade wars were not *a la mode*, from the 1960s onwards the transatlantic economic relationship was constantly soured by a series of disputes over tariffs and bickering over international trade rules that made agreements within the context of GATT increasingly difficult to conclude. Nevertheless, investment flows remained extremely high and it is difficult to escape the fact that trade disputes—be they characterized as 'wars' or not—were ultimately driven mainly by domestic political needs.[14]

Third, transatlantic ideological affinity always had its limits. In the United States a Cold War consensus may have been briefly broken down as a result of the Vietnam war, yet the resurgence of conservatism that was spearheaded by Ronald Reagan in the early 1980s struck a marked contrast with continental Europe's internal left–right divisions. In brief, socialism retained its appeal throughout most European NATO countries— Great Britain under Margaret Thatcher being a chief exception—throughout the Cold War, but was at best a fringe movement in the United States. In general terms this meant that even most conservatives in Europe preferred welfare state capitalism to the more stringent individualism prevalent in the United States; in contrast many American observers considered Western Europe a Scandinavian style nanny state writ large. It was partly due to such cultural and ideological differences that the United States (through the State Department, the United States Information Agency, even the CIA) expended a great deal of effort in the field of cultural diplomacy.[15]

None of this is to say that there was no community of values and interests. The Cold War institutional arrangements and shared concern over the security threat presented by the Warsaw Pact made most Europeans accept American global leadership without much protest. But even at the height of the Cold War, transatlantic cooperation had its limits and individual countries—or groups of countries—never blindly lined up behind Washington. The Cold War transatlantic relationship was one of a united community in constant conflict. This presented a stark contrast with the situation on the other side of the Iron Curtain.

[13] 'Europe: America's New Rival', *Time* (12 March 1973).

[14] See Lundestad, *'Empire' by Integration: The United States and European Integration* (New York: Oxford University Press, 1998), 58–98; and the essays in Piers Ludlow (ed.) *European Integration and the Cold War: Ostpolitik-Westpolitik, 1965–1973* (London: Routledge, 2007).

[15] For example: Frances Stonor Saunders, *Who Paid the Piper? CIA and the Cultural Cold War* (London: Granta, 2000); Volker Berghahn, *America and the Intellectual Cold Wars in Europe* (Princeton, NJ: Princeton University Press, 2001); Gilles Scott-Smith, *The Politics of Apolitical Culture: The Congress for Cultural Freedom, the CIA, and Postwar American Hegemony* (London: Routledge, 2002).

UNIFORMITY AND THE POWER
OF THE WEAK: THE SOVIET BLOC

While the United States was not in a position to establish and maintain an unquestioned hegemony over Western Europe after World War II, the situation on the other side of the Iron Curtain was different. Not only did the Red Army occupy most of the countries that became, in 1955, the Warsaw Pact (WP), but the immediate postwar years saw a rapid takeover of power by local communist parties, a trend completed by the February 1948 coup d'etat in Czechoslovakia. In the late 1940s and early 1950s a series of purges and executions confirmed that the local elites from Romania to Poland were loyal to the 'centre' in Moscow. An organization for economic cooperation, the COMECON, was established in 1949 to control trade and industry in the Soviet bloc. Following the Soviet model, Eastern Europe's agriculture was partially collectivized. Police forces, armies, and internal security services were closely linked to the USSR's central command, even to the extent that East European officials' uniforms were modelled on those worn by their counterparts in the USSR. All in all, the late 1940s and early 1950s saw a clear move towards conformity behind the Iron Curtain.

But while the Soviets often acted like ruthless imperialists, the uniformity and conformity within the Warsaw Pact area was always a relative phenomenon. As in Western Europe, national interests did not vanish despite the talk of socialist unity, and resistance to external domination lived on. While Eastern Europeans rarely resisted Soviet domination outright they constantly manipulated their positions of weakness. But perhaps most importantly for the ultimate outcome of the Cold War, the governments supported by the Soviet Union failed to gain the internal legitimacy that would have allowed a solid Eastern Bloc to emerge.

There were repeated challenges to Soviet domination. Some were in the form of outright defections. Already in 1948 Tito's Yugoslavia had made clear that the idea of a monolithic communist bloc was a fantasy invented in the minds of conservative western ideologues. That it was the Soviets who, after Stalin's death, approached the Yugoslavs was in itself testament to the limits of Soviet power. That the reconciliation proved short-lived—a development discussed in detail in Svetozar Rajak's new book—only underlines the lack of ideological and political appeal that would continue to undermine the USSR's claims for global leadership of a socialist bloc. In decades to come Yugoslavia's key role in the Non-aligned movement represented another type of challenge to the broader notion of a bipolar world order.[16] As such it was different from—but not necessarily any more significant than—Albania's defection to the Chinese camp.

---

[16] Svetozar Rajak, *Yugoslavia and the Soviet Union in the Early Cold War: Reconciliation, Comradeship and Confrontation, 1953–1957* (London: Routledge, 2010). See also Jeronim Perovic, 'The Tito-Stalin Split: A Reassessment in Light of New Evidence', *Journal of Cold War Studies* 9:2 (2007), 32–63.

While the Soviet–Yugoslav confrontation was relatively bloodless and devoid of the actual use of military force, other events dramatically exemplified the continuous resistance to Soviet domination inside the bloc itself. In 1953 riots in East Germany could only be countered by the use of force; eight years later the Soviets responded to their clients' demands by building a wall that would separate Berlin—and stem the brain drain from the GDR to the FRG—for the remainder of the Cold War.[17] In 1956 Soviet troops intervened in Hungary following that country's attempt to move away from the recently founded Warsaw Pact. What western observers called freedom fighters were duly defeated by a superior force.[18] But the unrest continued. In 1968 Warsaw Pact troops moved into Prague to crush the famed 'Prague Spring'—symbolized by a reformist government aiming to give socialism a 'human face'. But even such an apparent show of Soviet bloc unity in face of a potential renegade nation was challenged by the fact that one of the most brutish of East European governments—Nicolae Ceaușescu's Romania—refused to take part in the intervention. The Romanian dictator had already initiated a foreign policy course that included independent approaches to the main adversaries of the Soviet Union: the United States *and* the People's Republic of China.[19]

And then there was Poland. From the early days of the Cold War, Polish communist leaders took advantage of their country's special position to maintain a degree of independence. In 1956, the Polish unrest—not dissimilar in origins and content to that in Czechoslovakia—did not result in Soviet intervention but actually strengthened the autonomy of the reformist leader, Władysław Gomułka. In the 1980s the Solidarity movement acted as a harbinger of the end of socialism not only in Poland but in much of the Soviet bloc. The Warsaw Pact may have been named after the Polish capital but the Poles themselves played a central role in destroying it.[20]

It is, in fact, difficult to talk about alliance solidarity within the Soviet bloc. To be sure, most Warsaw Pact countries joined in 'punishing' the Czech reformists in 1968. Yet, as numerous historians have shown in recent years, the uniformity that was supposedly constructed east of the Iron Curtain was to a large extent a fantasy. National rivalries—such as

---

[17] An excellent document collection on the 1953 uprising is Christian Ostermann (ed.)'s *Uprising in East Germany, 1953: The Cold War, the German Question, and the First Major Upheaval Behind the Iron Curtain* (Budapest: Central European Press, 2003). For a narrative analysis of East Germany in the early Cold War, see Gareth Pritchard, *The Making of the GDR, 1945–1953* (Manchester: Manchester University Press, 2004). On the Berlin Wall crisis, see Hope Harrison, *Driving the Soviets up the Wall: Soviet-East German Relations, 1953–1961* (Princeton, NJ: Princeton University Press, 2003) and Gerhard Wettig, *Chruschtschows Berlin-Krise 1958 bis 1963: Drohpolitik und Mauerbau* (Munich: R. Oldenbourg, 2006).

[18] Charles Gati, *Failed Illusions: Moscow, Washington, Budapest and the 1956 Hungarian Revolt* (Stanford, CA: Stanford University Press, 2008); Paul Lendvai, *One Day That Shook the Communist World: The 1956 Hungarian Uprising and Its Legacy* (Princeton, NJ: Princeton University Press, 2008).

[19] Surprisingly little has been written about Romania in the Cold War. See: Mihai Retegan, *In the Shadow of the Prague Spring: Romanian Foreign Policy and the Crisis in Czechoslovakia* (Iași: Institute for Romanian Studies, 2000); J.F. Harrington and B.J. Courtney, *Tweaking the Nose of the Russians: Fifty Years of American-Romanian Relations, 1940–1990* (Boulder, CO: East European Monographs, 1991).

[20] Vojtech Mastny and Malcom Byrne, *A Cardboard Castle? An Inside History of the Warsaw Pact, 1955–1991* (Budapest: Central European University Press, 2005).

those between Poland and East Germany—were constant and became increasingly evident whenever the Soviets flirted with bloc-wide reform (as in the aftermath of Stalin's death in 1953 or, more obviously, within the context of Gorbachev's ascendancy in the 1980s).[21]

If holding the Warsaw Pact was difficult, building a functioning socialist community—Warsaw Pact Socialism[22]—proved ultimately impossible. Although there are relatively few histories of COMECON/CMEA and of Soviet foreign economic policy in general, they tend to agree on a few salient facts. First, the chief goal of Moscow's economic policies in the early Cold War was not to create an integrated trade system but one that had a clear unchallenged centre (from early on, bilateral agreements between USSR and its client states took precedence over multilateral agreements, making Soviet policy almost mercantilist). While COMECON introduced, in 1959, a charter heralding the idea of an 'internationalist socialist division of labour', this effort faltered in the early 1960s as East European countries—particularly Romania—held on to the principle that each country should retain the right to determine its internal economic policies. The addition of extra-European countries into the COMECON (Mongolia, Cuba, and Vietnam) and increased East–West trade in the 1960s and 1970s further undermined the socialist integration project in Eastern Europe.[23] In fact, over time Soviet policies had a counterproductive end result: rather than unity, they created dissent and a craving for an opening to the West. While Stalin may have succeeded—however violent his methods—in building socialism in one country, his successors were ultimately unable to repeat the experiment on a broader scale.

Moreover, throughout much of the Cold War the Soviets subsidized their Warsaw Pact allies, mainly in the form of cheap energy exports. At the basis of such subsidies may have been the need to 'pacify' dissent by according the national leaderships within the Soviet bloc a concrete reason for continuing to submit to Moscow's unquestioned leadership. But as Vladislav Zubok has observed: 'what emerged was a model of economic interdependence imposed on reluctant East European allies by Moscow and generously financed from vast Soviet economic and natural resources'.[24]

In the end, two general trends undermined Soviet bloc unity throughout the Cold War. First, unlike in Western Europe where fear of a potential Soviet (or Warsaw Pact) invasion held a forceful grip on much of public opinion, East Europeans did not always

---

[21] Mastny and Byrne, *A Cardboard Castle?* See also Sheldon Anderson, *A Cold War in the Soviet Bloc: Polish-East German Relations, 1945–1962* (Boulder, CO: Westview, 2000).

[22] Harriet Friedmann, 'Warsaw Pact Socialism: Détente and the Disintegration of the Soviet Bloc', in Allen Hunter (ed.), *Re-Thinking the Cold War* (Philadelphia, PA: Temple University Press, 1998), 213–31.

[23] Ian Jackson, 'Economics', in Geraint Hughes and Saki Dockrill (eds), *Palgrave Advances in Cold War History* (New York: Palgrave Macmillan, 2006), 175–6.

[24] Vladislav Zubok, 'The Soviet Union and European Integration from Stalin to Gorbachev', *Journal of European Integration History* 2:1 (1996), 89. David R. Stone, 'CMEA's International Investment Bank and the Crisis of Developed Socialism', *Journal of Cold War Studies* 10:3 (2008), 48–77; Henry W. Schaefer, *Comecon and the Politics of Integration* (New York: Praeger, 1972); Philip Hanson, *The Rise and Fall of the Soviet Economy* (London: Pearson, 2003); Adam Zwass, *The Council for Mutual Economic Assistance: The Thorny Path from Political to Economic Integration* (Armonk, NY: M.E. Sharpe, 1989).

see the capitalist West as their only, or even primary, external security threat; East Europeans were equally concerned about Soviet and—later on—Warsaw Pact interventions. This inherent tension made internal Warsaw Pact politics inherently paranoid. Second, in Eastern Europe there was limited support internally for political and economic integration. Both trends stood in stark contrast to the state of affairs in the West and, over time, seriously undermined the construction of a unified Soviet-led bloc.

BETWEEN AND BEYOND THE BLOCS: THE GRADUAL EROSION OF EUROPE'S COLD WAR DIVISION

Although the lack of alliance solidarity and ideological affinity was evident throughout the Warsaw Pact area, this relative discontent does not alone explain the eventual collapse of the Cold War system. Nor does it explain the biggest surprise of the end of the Cold War: the (relatively) peaceful nature of the transformation from one world order to another. To be sure, the general disillusionment of Soviet bloc citizens, the role of Mikhail Gorbachev (and maybe that of Ronald Reagan), all played an important role in bringing about the end of the Cold War in Europe. But to fully understand the revolutions of 1989 and the rapid chain of events that prompted the relatively peaceful disintegration of the Soviet bloc, one needs to emphasize the limits of the division of Europe. While the Iron Curtain was a fact of life for over four decades, it was not an impenetrable barrier. Historians have uncovered much evidence to show that a constant and gradually increasing movement of goods, ideas, and people undermined the rigidity of the bipolar order. While the East and West in Europe were politically divided, transnational forces and currents during the Cold War built the foundation for a relatively rapid and successful post-Cold War pan-European integration following the collapse of the Iron Curtain.

Penetrating the Iron Curtain through psychological warfare and cultural diplomacy was, in fact, a continuous objective of US Cold War policies. In the past two decades Walter Hixson, Scott Lucas, Kenneth Osgood, Arch Puddington, and Giles Scott-Smith, among others, have reconstructed the continuous American effort to influence Soviet bloc public opinion during the Cold War. Even at the height of the Cold War, 'soft power'—as we have more recently come to call it—was an important component in American Cold War policy.[25] In addition to such conscious government-supported

---

[25] Walter Hixson, *Parting the Curtain: Propaganda, Culture and the Cold War, 1945–1961* (New York: Palgrave Macmillan, 1997); Scott Lucas. *Freedom's War: The American Crusade against the Soviet Union* (New York: New York University Press, 1999); Kenneth Osgood, *Total Cold War: Eisenhower's Secret Propaganda Battle at Home and Abroad* (Lawrence, KS: University of Kansas Press, 2006); Arch Puddington, *Broadcasting Freedom: The Cold War Triumph of Radio Free Europe and Radio Liberty* (Lexington, KY: Lexington University Press, 2000); Giles Scott Smith, 'Confronting Peaceful Coexistence: Psychological Warfare and the Role of Interdoc, 1963–72', *Cold War History* 7:1 (2007), 19–43.

propaganda as the various cultural exhibitions inside the Soviet bloc, many historians have further reconstructed the attractiveness of western (American) consumer culture, ranging from blue jeans to household gadgets and popular music.[26]

While much of this literature tends to be centred on the United States and American culture—on how American government or other 'westerners' targeted the Soviet bloc—scholars have also recently begun to unearth the grassroots changes that took place within the Soviet bloc countries during the Cold War. What has emerged is a far more complex picture of societies in constant transformation; a direct contrast to the simplified picture of uniformity occasionally disturbed by a few nationalistic eruptions. The idea that the Soviet Union, for example, was morphed by Stalin's policies into a vast geopolitical space best described as 'half gulag, half tank' until the arrival of Mikhail Gorbachev in the Kremlin no longer appears to be a close approximation to the reality of life inside the USSR. There were plenty of countercultures in operation throughout the Cold War era.[27]

What is still missing in Cold War literature, however, is a truly transnational examination of Europe's Cold War. With few exceptions—such as Jeremi Suri's *Power and Protest*—international historians have yet to focus on the social and cultural similarities across the Cold War's political boundaries. But that such similarities existed is suggested—although the explicit nature of such linkages remains a matter of conjecture—by Suri's work on the origins of détente. By describing the connections between policy and protest from the Berkeley riots to the Prague Spring, from the Paris strikes to massive unrest in Wuhan, China, Suri maintains that the simultaneous growth of distrust and disillusion in nearly every society left a lasting legacy of global unrest, fragmentation, and unprecedented public scepticism towards authority. At the state level détente—of which the easing of East–West relations in Europe was a major part—was an attempt to preserve, rather than change, the existing order. Whether one accepts Suri's thesis in its entirety or not, it is difficult to argue against his assertion that large parts of the general public—East and West—were simply fed up with the existing constraints that the Cold War international system placed upon their lives.[28]

While Suri's book focused on social movements spearheaded by the activities of what can broadly be called the global sixties generation, a new edited volume takes yet a broader view of the decade that is increasingly seen as pivotal to the overall development of the Cold War. *The Shock of the Global*—a collection of essays by a group of renowned historians like Charles Maier and Niall Ferguson—has as its core argument what another

---

[26] For example: Penny von Eschen, *Satchmo Blows up the World: Jazz Ambassadors Play the Cold War* (Cambridge, MA: Harvard University Press, 2004); Michael Krenn, *Fallout Shelters for the Human Spirit: American Art and the Cold War* (Chapel Hill, NC: University of North Carolina Press, 2005); Timothy Ryback, *Rock Around the Bloc: A History of Rock Music in Eastern Europe and the Soviet Union* (Oxford: Oxford University Press, 1990).

[27] Martin Walker, *The Cold War: A History* (New York: Henry Holt & Co., 1993).

[28] Jeremi Suri, *Power and Protest: Global Revolution and the Rise of Détente* (Cambridge, MA: Harvard University Press, 2003).

book more recently referred to as the 'rise of the rest'. For the 1970s saw perhaps some of the greatest global structural upheavals of the entire Cold War era. The breakdown of the postwar Bretton Woods system and the advent of floating currencies and free capital movements shook the international economy, while the rise of non-state actors and transnational issues from environmental protection and population control to human rights activism became major forces. In international politics the image of a bipolar order was challenged not only by détente but by the launching of two great revolutions that would have repercussions in the twenty-first century: the Iranian theocratic revolution and the Chinese market revolution. Moreover, the late 1970s saw the beginning of the rise of the Asian 'tiger economies' (Hong Kong, South Korea, Singapore, and Taiwan).[29]

While the world was transformed, Europe suffered. The popular image was one of a stagnant continent, burdened by high inflation, record unemployment (the stagflation phenomenon), and growing energy costs. There is no denying these facts. In Southern Europe, for example, inflation reached double figures and inched dangerously close to the 10 per cent mark in countries such as France. The oil crisis of 1973 brought home to West Europeans the stark reality of their dependence on Middle East resources. In Eastern Europe, economies that had—even admitting unreliable counting techniques—been growing at record rates in the 1950s and 1960s, suddenly came to a virtual standstill, made worse by the rising cost of Soviet energy imports and accumulation of debt to Western Europe. East Europeans were, as Harriet Freedman puts it, 'caught in the scissors of deteriorating terms of trade with both the USSR and the West'.[30]

But in other ways Europe did not stand still in the 1970s. The continent's economic troubles were to some extent only relative: several decades of almost uninterrupted economic growth, buoyed by cheap energy, could not be sustained indefinitely. More importantly in Cold War terms, the 1970s saw an increase in East–West contacts in Europe. In the 1980s these linkages would play a significant role in discrediting the Cold War system in Europe and in bringing about an end to Europe's postwar division.

Indeed, much ink has recently been spilled on debating the impact of the 1975 Conference on Security and Co-operation in Europe (CSCE). It has become commonplace to argue that the agreements signed in Helsinki in August 1975 produced a revolutionary outcome by eroding Soviet domination in Eastern Europe. After several years of painstaking negotiations, representatives from thirty-five countries (all European countries save Albania, as well as the United States and Canada) gathered in Helsinki to sign the Helsinki Accords, the final outcome of the CSCE. Divided into three major 'baskets', the Helsinki Accords were a remarkable series of documents that dealt with virtually all aspects related to pan-European security issues. Basket I, for example, included provisions about the 'inviolability of borders', while Baskets II and III dealt with such issues as

---

[29] Niall Ferguson, Charles S. Maier, Erez Manela, and Daniel Sargent (eds), *The Shock of the Global: The 1970s in Perspective* (Cambridge, MA: Harvard University Press, 2010). 'The rise of the rest' is a phrase trumpeted in Fareed Zakaraya, *The Post-American World* (New York: W.W. Norton, 2008).

[30] Friedmann, 'Warsaw Pact Socialism', 229.

economic and cultural relations and human rights. In short, the CSCE extended far beyond the 'traditional' security issues of borders into economic and human security.[31]

Even as the thirty-five countries prepared to sign the Helsinki Accords, however, different interpretations emerged. Most Soviet leaders assumed, and many in the West disapprovingly feared, that Basket I, which defined the 'inviolability of borders', was equal to a multilateral acknowledgement of the legitimacy of Soviet control over Eastern Europe. Defenders of the treaty, however, pointed out that the Soviet and East European acceptance of the human rights provisions in Basket III would, in turn, act as a significant boost to the various dissident and pro-democracy groups in the Soviet bloc who had traditionally been heavily suppressed. Similarly, while many West Germans feared that the CSCE's notion about inviolability of borders translated into a permanent division of Germany, others took heart from the fact that the CSCE did approve the possibility of a 'peaceful transformation of borders'. By encouraging cultural and economic exchanges as well as by emphasizing such principles as freedom of movement, the CSCE became an agent of transnationalism. In time, the 'Helsinki effect'—as one scholar calls it—led to the erosion of the Soviet bloc from within.[32] By becoming the manifesto of various dissident movements in Eastern Europe and the Soviet Union, the CSCE's Basket III indeed had a corrosive effect within the Soviet bloc. Merely two years after the signing of the Helsinki Accords, dozens of so-called Helsinki Groups had been established with the specific purpose of monitoring human rights abuses within the Soviet bloc. The 1975 CSCE thus commenced a decade-and-a-half-long process during which men like the future Czech President, Vaclav Havel, challenged, eventually successfully, totalitarian rule in Eastern Europe.[33]

If the Helsinki process accelerated the end of the Cold War in Europe, it was one of recent history's greatest unintended consequences. For most historians would acknowledge that in 1975 the CSCE provided no road map for the tearing down of the Iron Curtain; no direct line exists between 1975 and 1989. If anything, Europe's Cold War ended as a result of a complex set of processes—economic and political integration foremost among them—unfolding within, across, and beyond the blocs that undermined the bipolar order erected in the aftermath of World War II.[34] Moreover, as transnational history suggests, the rigidity of that order was perhaps never nearly as encompassing as

[31] For a recent overview of the road to Helsinki, see Andreas Wenger, Vojtech Mastny and Christian Nuenlist (eds), *Origins of the European Security System. The Helsinki Process Revisited, 1965–1975* (Oxford: Oxford University Press, 2008).

[32] Daniel C. Thomas, *The Helsinki Effect: International Norms, Human Rights and the Demise of Communism* (Princeton, NJ: Princeton University Press, 2001).

[33] Even in the last few years much has been published on these issues. See the essays in Oliver Bange and Gottfried Niedhardt (eds), *Helsinki 1975 and the Transformation of Europe* (Oxford: Oxford University Press, 2008); Poul Villaume and Odd Arne Westad, eds, *Perforating the Iron Curtain: European Détente, Transatlantic Relations, and the Cold War, 1965–1985* (Copenhagen: Museum Tusculanum Press, 2010).

[34] Frederic Bozo, Marie-Pierre Rey, N. Piers Ludlow and Leopoldo Nuti (eds), *Europe and the End of the Cold War: A Reappraisal* (London: Routledge, 2008).

the rhetoric of the many cold warriors had suggested.[35] For how does one otherwise account for the greatest surprise of the late 1980s: the lack of a 'big bang'? What kind of world order was it that could simply wither away in a span of a couple of years—perhaps one with relatively few long-term consequences?

FROM COLD WAR EUROPE TO TODAY'S EUROPE

From the perspective of 2012 the Cold War seems almost as distant as Charlemagne. The physical reminders of the long division are gone, with pieces of the Berlin Wall to be found scattered around the globe. In Europe communism is an ideological oddity that one can find on obscure web sites or fringes of college campuses. To be sure, the ideological divisions of the Cold War—and the various political, cultural, and other representations thereof—sometimes resurface in debates about globalization and its pitfalls. Instead of a divided Europe, we have the ever larger European Union (EU), an ever growing benevolent empire (a civilian superpower) of sorts.[36] What is sometimes lost within this bird's-eye view, however, is the simple fact that the EU is in part a by-product of the Cold War.

Most importantly, it is impossible to conceive European integration without the Cold War. To be sure, it can be argued that those participating in the process did so—and continue doing so—mainly in order to safeguard their specific national interests. Yet whether one views the process that began with the unfolding of the Marshall Plan as 'true' integration or not, the fact remains that the participating countries did give up certain vestiges of their national sovereignty to a set of supranational bodies. That this process has continued since the end of the Cold War suggests that something appealing has taken place. Imperfect though the EU undoubtedly is, the remarkable fact is that it has managed to unite Europe peacefully and, so it seems, on a more long-term basis than the armies of Napoleon or Hitler ever could. While this hardly means the end of the American era, as one author has put it, Europe emerged from the Cold War more stable, more united, and more prosperous than ever before.[37]

Well, maybe not. For what is very difficult to lose sight of even today is the continued existence of one of the Cold War's major institutional frameworks: the North Atlantic Treaty Organization (NATO). Like the EU, NATO has grown. While it searches for new missions and rationales—in peace enforcement and peacekeeping missions and in such

---

[35] Matthew Evangelista, *Unarmed Forces: The Transnational Movement to End the Cold War* (Ithaca, NY: Cornell University Press, 1999).

[36] See: John McCormick, *The European Superpower* (Basingstoke: Palgrave Macmillan, 2006); Jan Zielonka, *Europe as Empire: The Nature of the Enlarged European Union* (Oxford: Oxford University Press, 2006).

[37] Charles Kupchan, *The End of the American Era: U.S. Foreign Policy and the Geopolitics of the Twenty-First Century* (New York: Vintage, 2003).

out-of-area issues as Afghanistan—the alliance may be on its way to transforming from a regional defence organization into a more globally active security player. Lord Ismay's much cited Cold War dictum, that NATO was created 'to keep the Soviets out, the Americans in and the Germans down' seems ill-suited to the NATO of the twenty-first century. But only just. Today's NATO still keeps the Russians out (and concerned) and makes sure the Americans remain involved in European security arrangements. And because of this NATO also keeps the Europeans—not just the Germans—'down'.[38]

It has become clear on several occasions in the post-Cold War era that NATO retains the ability to irritate its original nemesis, Russia. Whether the question is NATO enlargement or America's new nuclear strategy that would include installations in former Warsaw Pact countries, commentators tend to be eager to declare either the emergence of a 'new Cold War' or argue that beneath the surface disagreements, Russian–American relations are actually on a solid basis. For Europeans (East and West) and Americans, such events as the August 2008 Russian–Georgian war elicit fears of a resurgent Russia, prompted by its new-found oil wealth into restoring the empire lost when the Soviet Union disintegrated.[39] But whichever way the arguments about a possible revival of Cold War-like tensions flow, one thing most commentators tend to take for granted: Europe ultimately matters little in the grand chessboard of twenty-first century global politics. For in 2012, hardly a day goes by without the familiar complaints about an EU that punches way below its potential weight, or about individual European countries that try to yield an influence beyond their relative significance only to be either considered mere appendices of American power or, perhaps even worse, ignored.

There is no denying that the EU in international affairs is far less significant than the sum of its parts might suggest. But this in itself is a legacy of the Cold War. By setting in motion the processes of continent-wide integration of broadly like-minded nations, the Cold War's long-term impact on Europe was twofold. First, it fostered a community of states that has institutionalized and internalized a socio-economic model on an amazingly wide, if still uneven, scale. One might describe the European model as a convergence of the two Cold War extremes (with a definite tilt towards the American model), rather than an enthusiastic embrace of free market capitalism. More remarkable, the EU has managed this without producing the type of cultural homogeneity that was labelled 'Americanization' during the Cold War and has been dubbed globalization thereafter.

---

[38] For a recent analysis of NATO's staying power, see Wallace J. Thies, *Why NATO Endures* (New York: Cambridge University Press, 2009). See also James Goldgeier, *The Future of NATO*, Council of Foreign Relations Special Report no. 51 (February 2010); and the essays in Basil Germond, Jussi M. Hanhimaki and George-Henri Soutou (eds), *The Routledge Handbook of Transatlantic Security* (London: Routledge, 2010).

[39] On contrasting views about United States and Russia since the Cold War, see James Goldgeir and Michael McFaul, *Power and Purpose: U.S. Policy Toward Russia after the Cold War* (Washington, DC: Brookings, 2003); Edward Lucas, *The New Cold War: How the Kremlin Menaces both Russia and the West* (New York: Palgrave Macmillan, 2008). On the Georgian war: Ronald D. Asmus, *A Little War That Shook the World: Georgia, Russia, and the Future of the West* (New York: Palgrave Macmillan, 2010).

Second, the Cold War era loss of empires and the decades-long dominance of extra-European powers in international affairs relegated Europe (and individual European countries) to the role of an 'active observer', opinionated yet rarely influential. Few would deny that the former development has a beneficial side to it. As to the latter, it is a logical consequence of the institutional arrangements necessary for the successful integration of a group of countries that still regard each other as 'foreign'. Or to put it simply: it remains difficult for the Finns and the Portuguese—or the Bulgarians and the Irish—to accept the idea that it is important that they have a similar outlook on the conflicts in the Middle East or the flow of illegal immigrants into the EU area. It is a safe bet that in this regard, the Europe that emerged from the Cold War will remain a work in progress.

FURTHER READING

Berghahn, Volker, *America and the Intellectual Cold Wars in Europe* (Princeton, NJ: Princeton University Press, 2001).

Bozo, Frederic, Marie-Pierre Rey, N. Piers Ludlow and Leopoldo Nuti (eds), *Europe and the End of the Cold War: A Reappraisal* (London: Routledge, 2008).

Evangelista, Matthew, *Unarmed Forces: The Transnational Movement to End the Cold War* (Ithaca, NY: Cornell University Press, 1999).

Ferguson, Niall, Charles S. Maier, Erez Manela and Daniel Sargent (eds), *The Shock of the Global: The 1970s in Perspective* (Cambridge, MA: Harvard University Press, 2010).

Germond, Basil, Jussi M. Hanhimäki and George-Henri Soutou (eds), *The Routledge Handbook of Transatlantic Security* (London: Routledge, 2010).

Hanhimäki, Jussi M., Benedikt Schoenborn, and Barbara Zanchetta, *Transatlantic Relations since 1945: An Introduction* (London: Routledge, 2012).

Hitchcock, William I., *The Struggle for Europe: The Turbulent History of a Divided Continent, 1945–2002* (New York: Doubleday, 2003).

Leffler, Melvyn and Odd Arne Westad (eds), *The Cambridge History of the Cold War*, 3 vols (Cambridge: Cambridge University Press, 2010).

Lundestad, Geir, *The United States and Western Europe since 1945: From 'Empire' by Invitation to Transatlantic Drift* (New York: Oxford University Press, 2003).

Mastny, Vojtech and Malcolm Byrne, *A Cardboard Castle? An Inside History of the Warsaw Pact, 1955–1991* (Budapest: Central European University Press, 2005).

Thomas, Daniel C., *The Helsinki Effect: International Norms, Human Rights and the Demise of Communism* (Princeton, NJ: Princeton University Press, 2001).

Trachtenberg, Marc, *A Constructed Peace: The Making of the European Settlement, 1945–1963* (Princeton, NJ: Princeton University Press, 1999).

CHAPTER 14

THE WESTERN EUROPEAN WELFARE STATE BEYOND CHRISTIAN AND SOCIAL DEMOCRATIC IDEOLOGY

IDO DE HAAN

INTRODUCTION

ONE of the most striking features of Europe's postwar history is the emergence of the welfare state. Even though the first social policies had already been introduced in the 1880s, and while many of the organizational forms that became entrenched after 1945 were initiated in the first half of the twentieth century, the size and impact of the postwar welfare state was unprecedented. Even more remarkable was the widespread consensus with which structural social and economic reforms were implemented. The deep political and social rifts of the 1920s and 1930s and the lack of trust in democratic means to overcome these confrontations had been replaced by the acceptance of an interventionist state and parliamentary democracy as the way to solve conflicts about the way in which this state distributed social goods.

The connection between the welfare state, and social and political peace was even more intricate: 'The Western European state was increasingly detached from any doctrinal project', while 'the rise of the welfare state had defused the old animosities', as Raymond Aron stated at the Milan Congress for Cultural Freedom in 1955, where western intellectuals had declared the end of ideology. As Tony Judt summarized in his influential study, *Postwar*, 'the provision of administration and services replaced revolutionary hopes and economic despair as the chief concern of voters (who in many places now included women for the first time): governments and political parties responded accordingly'.[1]

---

[1] Tony Judt, *Postwar: A History of Europe since 1945* (London: William Heinemann, 2005), 256 and 384.

This swift and consensual growth of the welfare state is also remarkable because most western European countries were governed by conservative governments, or coalition governments in which Social Democrats had to share power with conservative Christian Democrats and Liberals. They all seemed to have supported and stimulated the emergence of the postwar welfare state, which Tony Judt, following a widespread usage, framed as 'the Social Democratic Moment' in European postwar history.[2] This leads to a series of questions: why did the welfare state in 1945 start such an unprecedented career? Why was there so little controversy about it? And more specifically, why did conservative governments accept, and even contribute to the development of a state and social order that appeared to be deeply tainted by socialist ideals?

Explaining the Model/Models of Explanation

To start with the last question: this only is a paradox when the welfare state is perceived as a social democratic project. This 'social interpretation of the welfare state' is still widely supported. It is often reinforced by the idea that the United Kingdom is the originator of the postwar welfare state, and the Scandinavian countries, or even more specifically Sweden, the purest model of the European welfare state.[3]

The social interpretation of the postwar welfare state has a prima facie plausibility. According to this interpretation, the postwar welfare state was a reaction both to the authoritarian pre-war social legislation as well as to the totalitarian 'warfare state'. The pre-war social legislation was generally an instance of social policy from above, following the authoritarian model of Bismarck's legislation of the 1880s, and not the result of substantial socialist mobilization.[4] Initially, German legislation functioned as an example for social policy elsewhere, notably in the United Kingdom and France.[5] Yet the German example lost much of its appeal in the interwar period. In Germany itself, these

---

[2] Judt, *Postwar*, 360–89.

[3] An example of the reduction of the history of the welfare state in the British case is offered by Michael Freeden, 'The Coming of the Welfare State', in Terence Ball and Richard Bellamy (eds), *The Cambridge History of Twentieth Century Political Thought* (Cambridge: Cambridge University Press, 2003), 7–44; for the Swedish model, see Kurt Samuelson, 'The Swedish Model and Western Europe 1945–1988', *Journal of International Affairs* 41:2 (1988), 363–84; for a critique on both perspectives, see Peter Baldwin, 'The Scandinavian Origins of the Social Interpretation of the Welfare State', *Comparative Studies in Society and History* 31:1 (1989), 3–24.

[4] See Jens Alber, *Vom Armenhaus zum Wohlfahrtsstaat. Analysen zur Entwicklung der Sozialversicherung in Westeuropas* (Frankfurt/M: Campus Verlag, 1982), 133–4.

[5] Peter Hennock, 'The Origins of the British National Insurance and the German Precedent 1880–1914', in W.J. Mommsen and Wolfgang Mock (eds), *The Emergence of the Welfare State in Britain and Germany* (London: Croom Helm, 1981), 84–106; Allan Mitchell, *The Divided Path: The German Influence on Social Reform in France after 1870* (Chapel Hill, NC: University of North Carolina Press 1991).

policies were expanded by the Weimar regime and became increasingly criticized for leading to a *Wohlfahrtsstaat*, a term with a distinctively negative ring in the conservative and Nazi rhetoric of the 1920s and 1930s. This is not to say that the Nazi regime did not implement social policies; it did, but with geopolitical and racist motives, to strengthen the German *Volksgemeinschaft* and to ensure its support in the war against 'Judeo-Bolshevism'.[6] For other countries, this was sufficient reason to reject the German example completely. When the notion of the welfare state was introduced into British public discourse by Archbishop Temple in 1941, it was deliberately used to distinguish it from the German 'warfare state'. Moreover, the Atlantic Charter of 1941 and the Beveridge report of 1942, with their stress on freedom from want and individual right, functioned as important sources of inspiration in the plans for a postwar welfare state drafted by the governments in exile in London and the first postwar governments.[7]

Yet Britain was the only country which in the first years after the war had a Labour government that was able to implement its plans for a welfare state. It did so on the basis of pre-war social legislation that was more developed than anywhere else. But it was also a welfare state that came under conservative attack and was rejected more forcefully than anywhere else after Margaret Thatcher's assault on the 'nanny state'.[8] Its demise might be one of the reasons why after the 1970s the British example was replaced by the Swedish model. In any case, 'the British experience is unrepresentative of Western Europe as a whole.'[9] Without the British example, much of the social interpretation of the welfare state, including the Scandinavian model, becomes unconvincing.

In most European countries outside Scandinavia, the welfare state came about under the wings of government coalitions dominated by Christian Democrats. Only in the Scandinavian countries did social democratic governments reign more or less continuously. But in Germany the Christian Democratic Union (CDU) was in power between 1949 and 1969, between 1982 and 1998, and has been since 2005. In Belgium, Christian Democrats dominated in coalition governments from the end of the 1940s until the end of the 1990s. In the Netherlands, the first coalition without Christian parties since 1917

---

[6] Götz Aly, *Hitlers Volksstaat. Raub, Rassenkrieg und nationaler Sozialismus* (Frankfurt/M: S. Fischer, 2005). For an overview of the debate on social policy in Nazi Germany, see Ian Kershaw, *The Nazi Dictatorship: Problems and Perspectives of Interpretation*, 4th edn (London: Hodder Arnold, 2000), 161–82.

[7] H. G. Hockerts, 'German Post-War Policies against the Background of the Beveridge Plan: Some Observations Preparatory to a Comparative Analysis', in Mommsen and Mock (eds), *The Emergence of the Welfare State in Britain and Germany*, 315–39. For the Netherlands, see Kees Schuyt and Ed Taverne, *1950: Prosperity and Welfare* (Assen: Koninklijke Van Gorum, 2004), ch. 3; for France, see Pierre Rosanvallon, *L'état en France de 1789 à nos jours* (Paris: Seuil, 1990), 184–6; Olivier Dard, 'Théoriciens et praticiens de l'économie: un changement de paradigme', in Serge Bernstein and Pierre Milza (eds) *L'année 1947* (Paris: Presses de la Fondation Nationale des Sciences Politiques, 2000), 75–114.

[8] Stuart Hall and Martin Jacques, *The Politics of Thatcherism* (London: Lawrence and Wishart, 1983); Richard Vinen, *Thatcher's Britain: The Politics and Social Upheaval of the 1980s* (London: Simon and Schuster, 2009).

[9] Peter Flora and Arnold J. Heidenheimer, 'The Historical Core and Changing Boundaries of the Welfare State', in Peter Flora and Arnold J. Heidenheimer (eds), *The Development of Welfare States in Europe and America* (New Brunswick, NJ: Transaction, 1990 [1982]), 21.

was established in 1994, with Christian Democrats returning to power in 2002. Also, in Italy, Christian Democrats were in power until the disintegration of the political system and the emergence of the Second Republic in the early 1990s. However, in Italy the main contender against the Christian Democrats was the Communist Party, while other left-wing groups were strongly divided. In this respect, Italy resembled France, yet there the conservatives were Gaullist, while a more progressive Christian Democratic Mouvement Républicain Populaire (MRP) was part of a centrist coalition that ruled during the entire Fourth Republic. Only in 1981, Social Democrats led by François Mitterrand won a presidential majority, soon to be shared, and finally to be handed over to the Gaullists again.

It is therefore tempting to replace, or at least to expand, the social interpretation by a Christian Democratic interpretation of the welfare state, and to argue that the welfare state needs to be understood as the result of the dominance of Christian Democratic parties. In this perspective, Christian Democracy emerges as a 'distinctive political actor', with a programme that cannot be subsumed under a vague kind of conservatism, but is defined as 'social capitalism', centred around the idea that conflicts of social and economic interests 'can and must be reconciled politically in order to restore the natural and organic harmony of society'.[10] This argument fits into the attempt to define various trajectories of state formation, or 'varieties of capitalism'. This approach is most influentially applied to the welfare state by Gösta Esping-Andersen, who in *The Three Worlds of Welfare Capitalism* distinguished a liberal, conservative, and social democratic type of welfare state.[11]

All of these typologies need to take into account one of the most remarkable characteristics of the postwar welfare state: its post-ideological character. Even when the results that welfare states produce can be evaluated in ideological terms—as liberal, conservative, Christian or social democratic—their constitution and development does not need to be, and very likely cannot be, explained by ideological convictions alone. Instead, a number of other models of explanation have been suggested in the social science literature on the development of the welfare state.[12]

Some of these texts focus on the economic pressures resulting in the development and restructuring of welfare states.[13] Although productivity, wealth, and the available tax base are evidently preconditions that enable or limit the development of welfare state arrangements, the reaction to these preconditions still seems to depend very much on the paradigm within which reactions are formulated. In the postwar era, these paradigms are generally identified as

[10] Kees Van Kersbergen, *Social Capitalism: A Study of Christian Democracy and the Welfare State* (London: Routledge, 1995), 2.

[11] Gøsta Esping-Andersen, *The Three Worlds of Welfare Capitalism* (Cambridge: Polity Press 1990); Peter A. Hall and David Soskice, *Varieties of Capitalism: The Institutional Foundations of Comparative Advantage* (Oxford: Oxford University Press, 2001).

[12] For an overview, see Jill Quadango, 'Theories of the Welfare State', *Annual Review of Sociology* 13 (1987), 109–28; Norman Ginsburg, *Divisions of Welfare: A Critical Introduction to Comparative Social Policy* (London: Sage, 1992); Robert Goodin and Deborah Mitchell (eds), *The Foundations of the Welfare State*, 3 vols (Cheltenham: Edward Elgar, 2000).

[13] Harold L. Wilensky, *The Welfare State and Equality: Structural and Ideological Roots of Public Expenditures* (Berkeley, CA: University of California Press, 1975).

'Keynesian' for the period between 1945 and 1980, and 'Hayekian' for the period after 1980—from a policy in which social security legislation aims to sustain demand in times of economic crisis, to a model in which social security is perceived as a disturbance of the market, and needs to be reduced in times of crisis, both to lower the tax pressure and to stimulate private initiative. As Peter Hall has demonstrated, the shift in these paradigms involves learning processes that are informed by practical experiments, the trial and error of policy failures and successes, yet are also conditioned by the structure of the state and its relation to society and the orientation of the government.[14] In that sense, ideology is inevitable, yet these considerations also point to a third approach, focusing on social and political relations.

The conceptualization of these relations is very diverse. One aspect leads back to the question of which political parties were dominant. The relevance of these party coalitions is not obvious, since political parties of the same background have a very diverse impact in different countries. For instance there are substantial differences between welfare state arrangements in Germany, Italy, and the Netherlands, despite the fact that Christian Democrats dominated in all three countries. Also Social Democrats, when in power, did not always bring about the same results.[15] There are various explanations for these differences. One is of course that parties have to operate in widely varying government coalitions. For instance, there are indications that it is not so much Left or Catholic power as such that explains the level of welfare spending, but the intensity of their competition, which results in higher welfare spending by Social Democrats when in power.[16] Yet another reason might be that similar parties in different countries represent very different constituencies. The specific form of the welfare state then needs to be explained in terms of the social interests, groups, or classes that compete for welfare goods.[17]

Other analyses stress the institutional context within which welfare states develop. An important aspect of that context is the structure and capacity of the state actually to carry out welfare policies, which appears to depend among other things on the measure of insulation of executive power from party and parliamentary pressures, as well as on

[14] Peter A. Hall, 'Conclusion: The Politics of Keynesian Ideas', in Peter A. Hall (ed.), *The Political Power of Economic Ideas: Keynesianism across Nations* (Princeton, NJ: Princeton University Press, 1989), 361–91; Peter A. Hall, 'Policy Paradigms, Social Learning, and the State: The Case of Economic Policy Making in Britain', *Comparative Politics* 25:3 (1993), 275–96.

[15] Evelyne Huber, Charles Ragin and John D. Stephens, 'Social Democracy, Christian Democracy, Constitutional Structure, and the Welfare State', *American Journal of Sociology* 99:3 (1993), 711–49; Francis G. Castles (ed.), *The Impact of Parties: Politics and Policies in Democratic Capitalist States* (London: Sage, 1982); Gøsta Esping-Andersen, *Politics against Markets: The Social Democratic Road to Power* (Princeton, NJ: Princeton University Press, 1985); Van Kersbergen, *Social Capitalism*.

[16] Harold L. Wilensky, 'Leftism, Catholicism, and Democratic Corporatism: The Role of Political Parties in Recent Welfare State Development', in Flora and Heidenheimer (eds), *The Development of Welfare States in Europe and America*, 345–82.

[17] Peter Baldwin, *The Politics of Social Solidarity: Class Bases of the European Welfare State 1875–1975* (Cambridge: Cambridge University Press, 1990). For a more abstract approach to these issues, see Robert E. Goodin, *Reasons for Welfare: The Political Theory of the Welfare State* (Princeton, NJ: Princeton University Press, 1988).

the role and learning processes of bureaucrats.[18] Another aspect is related to channels for the mediation of interests between state and society. Characteristic of welfare states is that this mediation takes place not only through political parties, but that it is embedded in a wide variety of social institutions which together make up a (neo-)corporatist social and political structure. At the time social scientists and historians began to analyse this structure, from the mid-1970s onwards, it was already in decline—demonstrating the Hegelian insight that Minerva's owl only flies at dusk.[19] Since then, a great number of studies on corporatism have been published, often focusing on the institutional legacies on which corporatist structures are built. Some of these are projected back into a very long history of late medieval guild structures.[20] Others stress the organizational structures that emerged in the nineteenth century, both culturally in the form of church organizations and voluntary associations, and economically, for instance in the form of vocational training.[21]

A final aspect is the relation between state and nation. The sociologist Peter Katzenstein has argued that smaller states are more vulnerable to the waves of international economic conjunctures and therefore generate ideologies of social partnership and cooperative institutions. However, the strength of solidarity seems to depend not just on size, but also on the entrenchment of national identities.[22] In general, it is striking that welfare states emerged after a fifty-year period of increasing ethnic homogeneity in Europe, often as the result of very violent policies. Postwar welfare states rest on the solid foundations of culturally homogeneous nations. They are in general highly exclusive

[18] Ellen Immergut, *Health Politics: Interests and Institutions in Western Europe* (Cambridge: Cambridge University Press, 1992). Hugh Heclo, *Modern Social Politics in Britain and Sweden* (New Haven, CT: Yale University Press, 1974); see also Daniel P. Carpenter, *The Forging of Bureaucratic Autonomy: Reputations, Networks, and Policy in Executive Agencies, 1862–1928* (Princeton, NJ: Princeton University Press, 2001).

[19] Philippe Schmitter, 'Still the Century of Corporatism?', *Review of Politics* 36:1 (1974), 85–131; Harold L. Wilensky, *The 'New Corporatism', Centralization and the Welfare State* (London: Sage, 1976); Philippe Schmitter and Gerhard Lehmbruch (eds), *Trends towards Corporatist Intermediation* (London: Sage, 1979); Suzanne Berger, *Organizing Interests in Western Europe: Pluralism, Corporatism, and the Transformation of Politics* (Cambridge: Cambridge University Press, 1981).

[20] This is characteristic of much of the literature on 'pillarization', which is often related to an age-old 'consociational' tradition. See Hans Daalder, 'The Consociational Democracy Theme', *World Politics* 26:4 (1974), 604–21; Arendt Lijphart, *The Politics of Accommodation: Pluralism and Democracy in the Netherlands* (Berkeley, CA: University of California Press, 1968); Rudy B. Andeweg and Galen A. Irwin, *Governance and Politics of the Netherlands*, 2nd edn (Basingstoke: Palgrave Macmillan, 2005); Gerhard Lehmbruch, *Proporzdemokratie: Politische System und Politische Kultur in der Schweiz und Oesterreich* (Tübingen: Mohr, 1967); Jürg Steiner, *Amicable Agreement versus Majority Rule: Conflict Resolution in Switzerland* (Chapel Hill, NC: University of North Carolina Press, 1974).

[21] See Colin Crouch, *Industrial Relations and European State Traditions* (Oxford: Clarendon Press, 1993); Kathleen Thelen, *How Institutions Evolve: The Political Economy of Skills in Germany, Britain, the United States, and Japan* (Cambridge: Cambridge University Press, 2004).

[22] Peter Katzenstein, *Small States in World Markets: Industrial Policy in Europe* (Ithaca, NY: Cornell University Press, 1985); John L. Campbell and John A. Hall, 'National Identity and the Political Economy of Small States', *Review of International Political Economy* 16:4 (2009), 547–72.

and based on very sharp distinctions between citizens with social rights, and foreigners, immigrants, and denizens who cannot appeal to those rights.[23]

These considerations point to the conclusion that the postwar welfare state and its, at least initially, uncontroversial acceptance, cannot be related only to its social or Christian Democratic roots. The various trajectories that European welfare states have followed are related to economic preconditions and social and political relations that stem from previous institutional legacies and varying relations between state, society, and nation. Yet welfare states not only emerged under conditions already existing, but they also produced unintended consequences, which after the 1970s initiated another round of welfare state reforms, again to be explained in terms of anterior circumstances and unintended outcomes.

ANTECEDENTS

In terms of antecedents of the postwar European welfare states, three aspects stand out: the social question after 1870; the contested nature of state intervention in the first decades of the twentieth century; and the reconstruction of polities after the institutional vacuum created by World War II. After half a century in which *laisser faire* had become the leading economic ideology, around 1870 the social question was raised not only to address the inequality and exploitation a market society generated, but also to offer an alternative to the predominantly liberal conception of politics as a civilized parliamentary debate on constitutional issues. While the pace of economic growth slackened after 1870, there was a growing awareness that it was not just the political constitution of the state, but the organization of society that was at stake. It inaugurated the expansion of all kinds of social organizations, which generally began with mutual benefit associations and cooperatives, later to be followed by trade unions, syndicates, chambers of labour, and the like. They all expressed the objective of creating, or maybe even recreating, a corporative structure that Europe had lost after the French Revolution.[24]

There were huge differences between these intermediary bodies. One dimension of difference was the extent to which they would function as vessels for social struggle, or form the framework for collaboration between workers and employers. The French syndicates could be seen as the prototype of combative organizations, which tried to put

[23] Yasemin Nuhoglu Soysal, *Limits of Citizenship: Migrants and Postnational Membership in Europe* (Chicago, IL: University of Chicago Press, 1994); Will Kymlicka and Keith Banting, 'Immigration, Multiculturalism and the Welfare State', *Ethics and International Affairs* 20:3 (2006), 285–304; Will Kymlicka and Keith Banting (eds), *Multiculturalism and the Welfare State: Recognition and Redistribution in Contemporary Welfare States* (Oxford: Oxford University Press, 2006).

[24] See Jonathan Sperber, *Europe 1850–1914: Progress, Participation and Apprehension* (Harlow: Longman, 2009), 137–42, 366–7; Anthony Black, *Guild and State: European Social Thought from the Twelfth Century to the Present* (New Brunswick, NJ: Transaction, 2003), 220–36; Alex R. Vidler, *A Century of Social Catholicism 1820–1920* (London: SPCK, 1964).

pressure on employers by organizing strikes. Trade unions in other countries sometimes aimed at class collaboration, at times even in terms of employer membership. A crucial factor determining the collaborative nature of social organizations was religion. Trade unions established in regions with a strong political presence of religious groups, such as the Low Countries, Germany, and Austria, were inspired by notions of class collaboration presented by Pope Leo XIII in his encyclical *Rerum Novarum* (1891) and in the social thought explored in the Protestant Social Congresses of the 1890s. In many cases, representation of social interests also became institutionalized in Chambers or Councils of Labour, which around 1900 became the first instances of corporatist structures.[25]

A second aspect of development towards the postwar welfare state was increased state intervention. The German social legislation of the 1880s is only one example of this. Most European states developed an intimate interest in the physical and mental well-being of their population, generally in the context of war. Just as the Boer War had sparked initiatives to increase 'national fitness' in the United Kingdom, so the French defeat by Germany in 1871 initiated policies to strengthen the population. Elsewhere policies were also developed to stimulate a healthy citizenry. These policies were generally informed by eugenicist and racist concerns about the declining birth rate among the middle classes and the degeneration of the working classes. As a result, in the first decades of the twentieth century a network of organizations had already come about aimed at the care of women and children: antenatal clinics, child-care centres, inoculation and school milk programmes, and from the 1930s onwards also maternity support and universal child allowance.[26]

Scandinavian countries were frontrunners in these developments, but they also occurred elsewhere.[27] An important impetus was the First World War, not just in the sense that it reinforced concerns about the strength of the nation, but also because wartime emergency legislation allowed states to develop policies for the distribution of raw material, food, and labour, which greatly contributed to the power of the state.

The legislative initiative of the state also played an important role in the emergence of intermediary bodies, demonstrating that the development of these bodies and state

[25] On Germany, see Ralph Henry Bowen, *German Theories of the Corporative State, with Special Reference to the Period 1870–1919* (New York: McGraw-Hill, 1947); for France, see Steven L. Kaplan and Philippe Minard (eds), *La France, malade du corporatisme? XVIIIe-XXe siècles* (Paris: Belin, 2004); Alain Chatriot, *La démocratie sociale à la française. L' expérience du Conseil National Économique 1924–1940* (Paris: La Découverte, 2002); for Belgium, see Dirk Luyten, *Ideologisch debat en politieke strijd over het corporatisme tijdens het interbellum in België* (Wetteren: Koninklijke Academie van Wetenschappen, 1996).

[26] See Roger Cooter (ed.) *In the Name of the Child: Health and Welfare 1880–1940* (London: Routledge, 1992); Daniel Pick, *Faces of Degeneration: A European Disorder c.1848–c.1918* (Cambridge: Cambridge University Press, 1989); A.R. Aisenberg, *Contagion: Disease, Government and the 'Social Question' in Nineteenth-Century France* (Stanford, CA: Stanford University Press, 1999); Paul Weindling, *Health, Race and German Politics between National Unification and Nazism, 1870–1945* (Cambridge: Cambridge University Press, 1989).

[27] Roman Lundqvist, 'Construction(s) of Swedish Family Policy 1930–2000', *Journal of Family History* 33:2 (2008), 216–36.

activity was not a zero-sum game. States enabled corporatist institutions, yet the latter also provided a solution to the growing criticism of the state's lack of expertise in governing society, by outsourcing complex social issues to semi-state, or even completely independent social bodies. In this way, a corporatist structure emerged in the 1920s, which greatly contributed to the reconsolidation of social relations that had been uprooted by World War I.[28]

Moreover, agreements such as the German Stinnes-Legien Pact of 1918, the French Matignon Pact of 1936, and the 1938 social pact of Saltsjöbaden between Swedish workers and employers gave workers an acknowledged position in negotiations on labour conditions, while they also established their acceptance of a capitalist economy, held in rein by these agreements. Yet these social pacts also fuelled the debate about the extent to which the state should actually play a role in regulating social and economic relations. This became an increasingly politicized issue in the 1930s when the fascist model of a corporatist state professed an autonomous role for workers and employers, but as the Palazzo Vidoni Agreements of 1925 had already demonstrated, in practice aimed at the incorporation of their organizations in the fascist state. Against this model, Catholics promoted a neo-medievalist corporatism, in which workers and employers collaborated independently from the state. Social Democrats increasingly rejected these corporatist arrangements, and were instead inspired by ideas about large-scale state planning proposed by John Maynard Keynes in the UK, Jules Moch, André Philippe, and Marcel Déat in France, Hendrik de Man in Belgium, and Jan Tinbergen in the Netherlands.[29]

Despite these debates, Catholics and Social Democrats also had a lot in common. Neither Catholics nor Social Democrats had high hopes about the ability of the liberal state to bring about the necessary reforms, and they agreed about the need for social organization and economic intervention during the economic crisis of the 1930s. Both had to compete with Fascism and Nazism which had excluded them in practice in Germany and Italy, but also with Communism, which was a major opponent to the Social Democrats, if not politically, as in France, than at least intellectually, and in the context of resistance to the Nazi threat also increasingly in practice. These parallel political, ideological, and intellectual interests thus drew Catholics and Social Democrats together. Actually, the first Roman-Red coalitions had already been established in Belgium and the Netherlands during the second half of the 1930s.

The emergence of the postwar welfare state was, thirdly, a product of the institutional breakdown at the end of the Second World War of Western European polities and their reconstruction in the first decade after 1945. The experience of the economic crisis of the 1930s had already undermined many social and political certainties, but the German occupation, terror, and persecution led to the abolition of political parties, the disruption

---

[28] Charles S. Maier, *Recasting Bourgeois Europe: Stabilization in France, Germany and Italy in the Decade after World War I* (Princeton, NJ: Princeton University Press 1988 [1975]).

[29] Martin Conway, *Catholic Politics in Europe 1918–1945* (London: Routledge, 1997), 6–7, 38–42; Donald Sassoon, *One Hundred Years of Socialism: The West European Left in the Twentieth Century* (London: Fontana, 1997), 60–73.

of governmental structures, and the disintegration of social relations. As a result, many perceived the social and political landscape as a *tabula rasa*. The notion that society and politics had to be created anew stimulated radical proposals for a postwar order. How this should be done was debated in resistance circles and by the governments in exile, and in the Dutch case also by prominent pre-war leaders held hostage by the Germans in the camp of Sint-Michielsgestel.[30]

During the first months and years after the German defeat, immediate needs necessitated quick choices that were crucial for the development of the postwar states. In the first place, large-scale state intervention became widely accepted as a necessary instrument to bring about urgent economic measures. This contributed to an already widespread preference for a stronger executive power. Yet the criticism of parliamentary democracy for which executive power was presented as an alternative in the 1930s, was muted at the end of the war. The failure of Charles de Gaulle to establish a radical presidential system in France was but one example demonstrating how parliamentary democracy returned as the best way to hold dictatorial tendencies in check. This was reinforced by the fact that all postwar governments needed to establish their legitimacy after a years-long interruption of constitutional rule, and generally tried to create this by organizing general elections.

The outcome of these elections showed that the majority of the population was averse to radical reform. The political parties that promised social peace and order won the day. It inaugurated a period for which Konrad Adenauer's campaign slogan in the West German elections of 1957, 'No experiments', was emblematic. The exclusion of radical parties—the remnants of Nazism, but more importantly Communist parties—was also demanded by the Allied forces and effectively realized under American pressure, by the stick of occupation in Germany, and the carrot of the Marshall Plan in the rest of Europe. The main concern in all this was to establish social peace, based on an obedient working class, a moderate elite, and private and public austerity as preconditions for economic recovery. As a result, at the end of the 1940s, all switches were set for a consensual and centrist Europe.[31]

The struggle for the political centre was dominated by conservatives, generally Christian Democrats versus Social Democrats. Both party formations went through a reorientation, but with different results in the different countries. In contrast to their reactionary positioning of the pre-war period, Christian Democrats after 1945 embraced human rights as well as democracy—a position that was legitimated by the radio speech of Pius XII at Christmas 1944, in which he abandoned a long-standing aversion against

[30] See Andrew Shennan, *Rethinking France: Plans for Renewal (1940–1946)* (Oxford: Oxford University Press, 1989); Els Witte, J. C. Burgelman and P. Stouthuysen (eds), *Tussen restauratie en vernieuwing. Aspecten van de naoorlogse Belgische politiek (1944–1950)* (Brussels: VUB Press, 1990); Martin Conway and Peter Romijn (eds), *The War for Legitimacy in Politics and Culture 1936–1946* (Oxford: Berg, 2008); Nele Beyens, *Overgangspolitiek. De strijd om de macht in Nederland en Frankrijk na de Tweede Wereldoorlog* (Amsterdam: Wereldbibliotheek, 2009).

[31] Mark Mazower, *Dark Continent: Europe's Twentieth Century* (London: Allen Lane The Penguin Press, 1998), chs 6, 7.

democracy by describing it as 'the "natural" political form which came closest to the Church's thinking'.[32] Within the Christian Democratic parties, there were attempts to push into an even more progressive direction, for instance by Adenauer, who initially argued in favour of a Christian Socialism, to be united in a broadly constituted and religiously neutral 'Labour Party', modelled after the British example.

Yet fear of Communism, as well as the Marxist perspective to which most Social Democrats still clung, drew the majority of Christian Democrats away from Christian Socialism. Instead, in the *Königsteiner Beschlüsse* of February 1947, the CDU embraced a *soziale Marktwirtschaft*, in which the dominance of private capitalism was abolished, yet the creative initiative of the individual was preserved within a corporatist economic order. The same pattern can be discerned in Italy, where Alcide De Gasperi initially set the Democrazia Cristiana (DC) on a manifestly anti-capitalist track, which soon became more conservative, without rejecting the 'social capitalism' it had embraced to claim the political centre. Only in France, where de Gaulle dominated the right flank of the political spectrum, did the MRP sustain a progressive orientation, inspired by the 'personalist' ideology of Emanuel Mounier, which emphasized that liberation was to be found in the connectedness of human beings. This connectedness was primarily defined by labour, and personalists therefore criticized capitalist individualism for destroying the human community by an exploitative approach to labour.[33]

Also, Social Democrats went through a period of reorientation, motivated by the desire to broaden their basis of support from the working class to the people at large. This meant a more positive stance towards the nation, but more importantly the rejection of the class struggle as a central dogma. In the Low Countries, Social Democrats had already in the 1930s replaced Marxism by the reformist 'planism' of De Man. After 1945, they participated in coalitions with Christian parties, with which they compromised on the policies aimed at social justice and security for all. This was similar to Austria, where the *Sozialistische Partei Österreichs* (SPÖ) embarked on a long-term collaboration with the Christian Democratic Party.

Yet other social democratic parties were more hesitant to revise the main tenets of Marxism. The *Sozialdemokratische Partei Deutschlands* (SPD) had for a long time maintained a fortress mentality, due to its suppression in the Nazi era, and political marginalization in the first decade of the FRG. Only with the Bad Godesberg Programme of 1959

---

[32] Paolo Pombeni, 'The Ideology of Christian Democracy', *Journal of Political Ideologies* 5:3 (2000), 298.

[33] David Hanley (ed), *Christian Democracy in Europe: A Comparative Perspective* (London: Pinter, 1994); Emiel Lamberts (ed.), *Christian Democracy in the European Union (1945–1995). Proceedings of the Leuven Colloquium, 15–18 November 1995* (Leuven: Leuven University Press 1997); Gerd-Rainer Horn and Emmanuel Gerard (eds), *Left Catholicism 1943–1955: Catholics and Society in Western Europe at the Point of Liberation* (Leuven: Leuven University Press, 2001); Michael Gehler, Wolfram Kaiser and Helmut Wohnout, *Christdemokratie in Europa im 20. Jahrhundert* (Vienna: Böhlau, 2001); Thomas Kselman and Joseph A. Buttigieg (eds), *European Christian Democracy: Historical Legacies and Comparative Perspectives* (Notre Dame: University of Notre Dame Press, 2003); Michael Gehler and Wolfram Kaiser (eds), *Christian Democracy in Europe since 1945* (London: Routledge, 2004).

did it explicitly reject the class struggle, nationalization, and the communist utopia as the end-goal of socialism, embracing instead reformist policies aimed at creating social justice and welfare for all. In this, the SPD followed the same trajectory as the British Labour Party. During the long period of electoral defeats in the 1950s, the leadership of Hugh Gaitskell and Anthony Crosland failed to convince their party to abandon common ownership as its ideological baseline. In France, the Section Française de l'Internationale Ouvrière (SFIO) competed with the Communists for the ideological leadership of the Left, which made it difficult to abandon Marxism. The same situation persisted in Italy, yet there it was the Partito Comunista Italiano (PCI) which developed its own revisionism when Moscow loosened its ideological grip as a result of de-Stalinization after 1956.[34]

However, despite the persistent Marxist rhetoric of class struggle and socialization of the means of production as the royal road to socialism, the social democratic parties followed their electorate in its practical desire for work under acceptable conditions and for a fair wage, and protection against the vagaries of the market and the misfortunes of life. Just like the Christian Democrats had moved towards an acceptance of democracy and socialism, Social Democrats basically accepted private property and the accumulation of private wealth as a fact of life. Moreover, both agreed on labour as the central category of social order, and drew on the pre-war experience of corporatist interest mediation to argue that the institutionalized negotiation between labour and capital was the best way to ensure acceptable working conditions and protection against sickness, unemployment, and old age.

CHARACTERISTICS OF WELFARE STATES

The welfare states as they emerged after 1945 shared a number of basic characteristics. All created a mix between direct payments of cash benefits, indirect benefits through tax credits, as well as direct provision of services. As Esping-Andersen has argued, the core business of welfare states is therefore de-commodification, that is, 'the degree to which individuals, or families, can uphold a socially acceptable standard of living independently of market participation'.[35] The distribution of benefits has been organized in a wide variety of ways, based on various criteria, and administered by an even more varied number of institutions, ranging from private insurance companies, trade unions, companies, collaborative funds of workers and employers, to semi-state pension funds, and state agencies with a varying range of executive autonomy. Although the variation is great, there are four dimensions within which a division has emerged between more restricted and conservative welfare states, and more expanded welfare with a social democratic character.

---

[34] Sassoon, *One Hundred Years of Socialism*, 189–273.
[35] Esping-Andersen, *The Three Worlds of Welfare Capitalism*, 37.

A first dimension is the criterion on which entitlements are based. While a basic drive to develop a more expanded welfare state was freedom from want, the welfare states after 1945 generally responded not only to bare needs, but were founded on a combination of returns on contribution and universal right. The Scandinavian countries with a predominantly social democratic government generally offered universal rights to services, financed by a highly progressive tax system. Yet they also emphasized solidarity and reciprocity, which required welfare claimants not only to contribute to social insurance schemes, but also to accept paid labour as the way to express this solidarity. As a result, Scandinavian welfare states were generally more conducive to high labour participation than the more conservative examples as in Germany. The latter were generally more committed to the protection of the family—who therefore could reckon with larger transfer payments—and averse to a strict enforcement of equal treatment, as a result of which the labour participation of women remained low.[36] However, all welfare states depended upon full male employment, not just because workers had to pay premiums, and a high number of unemployed would burden the system beyond repair, but most importantly because labour under fair conditions was perceived as the social basis of self-respect, at least for men.

A second dimension of ordering postwar welfare state regimes is their redistributive effects, or more generally, the impact they have on social stratification. Social democratic welfare states were strongly redistributive and aimed 'at protecting the largest possible portion of the population with generous benefits for low- and medium-income groups'. In contrast, the Christian democratic welfare state 'is segmented, and it tends to reproduce social inequalities, not reduce them. Different occupational groups have different insurance schemes, with different contribution requirements and different benefits.'[37]

The typology of welfare states has generally been based on these first two dimensions—criteria for distribution and redistributive effects. Feminist critics of the welfare state literature have argued that the distribution of in-kind care, in terms of unpaid care by women within families and the related availability of child care and care for the elderly, creates a different typology of welfare states. By addressing the dimension of care, welfare states can be distinguished by states that strengthen traditional gender relations, as in the breadwinner model that prevails in Germany and the Netherlands, and those states that give women more opportunities in the labour market, such as France and the Scandinavian countries.[38] From this perspective it is clear that welfare states are more than machines for the redistribution of wealth through financial transfers, but also institutions providing the facilities that contribute to education, personal

---

[36] Johan Jeroen De Deken, 'Christian Democracy, Social Democracy and the Paradoxes of Earnings-related Social Security', *International Journal of Social Welfare* 11 (2002), 22–39.

[37] Huber, Ragin, and Stephens, 'Social Democracy, Christian Democracy, Constitutional Structure, and the Welfare State', 740.

[38] Jane Lewis, 'Gender and the Development of Welfare State Regimes', *Journal of European Social Policy* 2:3 (1992), 159–73; Jane Lewis (ed.), *Gender, Social Care and Welfare State Restructuring in Europe* (Aldershot: Ashgate, 1998).

development, health, well-being, and, according to some, even happiness. As a result, welfare states have pursued increasingly ambitious goals, not only in terms of the regulation of individual behaviour within households, but also by proposing social and cultural programmes that had to contribute to altogether new social relations. One particular aspect of these policies was regional development programmes that combined economic development with community development, social work, and the dissemination of culture.[39]

A final dimension concerns the various ways in which these social arrangements have been governed. In 1945 economic emergency and the need for quick measures created an atmosphere in which large-scale nationalization of core sectors of the economy became imaginable. In Germany, 40 per cent of coal and iron production, 60 per cent of energy production, 75 per cent of aluminium production, and more than half of the banks were in state hands. Similarly in France, coal, steel, energy, and banks, but also insurance companies, the car industry, and airlines were nationalized. In Italy, the Instituto per la Recostruzione Industriale, set up by Mussolini to combat the economic depression by nationalizing major parts of Italy's industry, continued to dominate core sectors after 1945.

Such nationalization can hardly be interpreted as an indication of social democratic planning frenzy. The French and German nationalizations were carried out by centrist and conservative governments, while the social democratic leadership in Sweden largely refrained from nationalization, just like the postwar governments of the Netherlands or Belgium.[40] It appears that size of the country and strength of the state are better explanations than political orientation for the emergence of interventionist states. However, in all Western European countries, the role of the state increased strongly, as is indicated by the rise in public expenditure (government expenditure plus social transfer expenditure). Expressed as a percentage of the gross domestic product (GDP) between 1950 and 1975, it rose least in France, from 28.4 per cent to 42.4 per cent, and most in the Netherlands, from 27 per cent to 54.3 per cent. Scandinavian figures were close to the Dutch extreme, while other Western European countries scored somewhere in between France and the Netherlands. If social transfer expenditures in the same period are considered separately, the increase is even more dramatic, with the lowest range increase in Germany, from 12.4 per cent to 16.7 per cent of its GDP; and the Netherlands again the highest with an increase from 6.6 per cent to 26.1 per cent of its GDP.[41]

Not all of this expenditure contributed to the growth of the state per se. In many countries, there emerged corporatist political arrangements, in which representation

---

[39] A. de Swaan, *In Care of the State: Health Care, Education, and Welfare in Europe and the USA in the Modern Era* (Cambridge: Polity, 1988); Michael Storper and Allan J. Scott (eds), *Pathways to Industrialization and Regional Development* (London: Routledge, 1992).

[40] Judt, *Postwar*, 266, 362; see also Hubert Bonin, *Histoire économique de la IVe République* (Paris: Economica, 1987), 80–5.

[41] Jürgen Kohl, 'Trends and Problems in Postwar Public Expenditure Development in Western Europe and North America', in Flora and Heidenheimer (eds), *The Development of Welfare States in Europe and America*, 310, 317.

of social interests, negotiations and settlements of social disputes, and in some cases also the administration and even the formulation of public law was in the hands of bipartite (labour and capital) or tripartite bodies (including government representatives). Again, the emergence of these neo-corporatist arrangements built on pre-war institutional foundations, leading to a variation between more elaborate corporatist institutions in Scandinavia and the Netherlands, and much less developed arrangements in Italy and, especially, France, where industrial relations remained tense. While corporatist bodies on the national level were less developed in Germany, the law on *Mittbestimmung* (workers co-determination) of 1950 contributed to negotiated trade-offs between labour and capital at the shop-floor level. As such, these lower level bodies also contributed to social peace.[42] Regardless of the question of whether it was the state itself or independent social bodies by which social transfers and public provisions were arranged, their growth contributed to the emergence of a new class of professionals. Their pivotal role contributed to a system in which political disagreements were transformed into technical problems, to be solved through expert judgment instead of by political stand-off. Also in this sense 'welfare capitalism, as it unfolded in Western Europe, was truly post-ideological.'[43]

(Un)intended Consequences

The welfare states had a substantial impact on the lives of European citizens. Some of the effects were as intended, yet there were also unintended consequences, which undermined the social and political bases of the welfare state. First of all, welfare states contributed to the dramatic social changes that took place in postwar Europe. Although the relative weight of agriculture had already been declining for a much longer period, the welfare state, notably the regional development plans and community work, functioned as a lubricant for the large-scale transformation of the countryside. Instead of a rural society, the postwar world became a largely sub-urban world, populated by people who increasingly earned their living with the mass production of consumer goods, which they now also were able to obtain. The most remarkable expansion was in the services sector, education and care, which were directly related to the growth of the welfare state. Their activity also had a crucial impact on the health and well-being of citizens. Improved care, ranging from free milk to cash allowances for children, led to substantially lower infant mortality, while improved medical services and health insurance extended life expectancy. Within twenty-five years, the postwar welfare state had made the needs and wants of the 1930s and 1940s into something of the past, not just for a happy few but for all members of the community. Despite the continued relevance of

---

[42] Crouch, *Industrial Relations and European State Traditions*, 176–232.
[43] Judt, *Postwar*, 362.

class distinctions, the overriding effect of the welfare state had been that social stratification played a decreasing role in the distribution of life chances and created a world in which individual choices would become the basis of the distribution of social goods—just as welfare state de-commodification had aimed to do.

From the early 1970s onwards, sociologists began to observe the disappearance of the working class and a concomitant change in social and political preferences, which they framed from a critical Marxist point of view as the *Verbürgerlichung der Arbeiterklasse* and the loss of the revolutionary potential of the working classes, yet from a more liberal point of view as the emergence of a widespread middle-class mentality. It indicated that the cultural homogeneity of European societies increased—we are all middle-class individualists now—while social and political conflicts became more opaque, since the fault lines along which political conflicts had been arranged were disappearing. Others observed the emergence of a new post-materialist frame of mind, enabled by a welfare state that satisfied immediate material needs and gave room (and subsidies) to pursue more refined ambitions. Part of this analysis came from conservative critics, who feared that a welfare state would stimulate expectations of universal entitlements to an ever increasing number of goods, just like the old poor relief based on charity had invited laziness and profiteering among the poor. Yet also more progressive critics started to criticize the welfare state for its lack of genuine solidarity, the emergence of a new ruling class of technocratic experts, and the suspicion that the authentic complaints of the working classes were bought off with meaningless consumer goods.[44]

This criticism emerged at a moment in the early 1970s when the economic foundations of the welfare state began to show deep cracks. The oil crisis of 1973 introduced a period when the Keynesian recipe for economic crises in the form of government spending to stimulate demand and to keep unemployment down lost its attraction, thereby undermining an important economic rationale for the welfare state. Western European economies went through a period of de-industrialization and a slowdown of economic growth, rising unemployment combined with continued inflation. As a result, social relations became more tense, not just in Britain, where Margaret Thatcher steered towards a head-on collision with the trade unions, but even in Sweden and the Netherlands, where collective agreements between unions and employers became hard to attain around 1980. Despite the harsh measures that were taken to 'roll back the state', government spending continued to go up, partly because of the growing claims to

---

[44] This analysis was presented by various authors. Relevant titles are Daniel Bell, *The Cultural Contradictions of Capitalism* (London: Heinemann 1976); Ronald Inglehart, *The Silent Revolution: Changing Values and Political Styles among Western Publics* (Princeton, NJ: Princeton University Press, 1977). A more conservative interpretation is presented by Helmut Schelsky, *Die Arbeit tun die anderen: Klassenkampf und Priesterherrschaft der Intellektuellen* (Opladen: Westdeutscher Verlag, 1975); for a Leftist criticism see Jürgen Habermas, *Legitimationsprobleme im Spätkapitalismus* (Frankfurt/M: Suhrkamp, 1973); André Gorz, *Adieux au prolétariat: au delà du socialisme* (Paris: Galilée, 1980); Claus Offe, *Contradictions of the Welfare State* (London: Hutchinson, 1984).

unemployment benefits. It created an atmosphere in which the welfare state was increasingly considered to be 'ungovernable'.[45]

These transformations had a strong impact on the position of the main political parties. Christian Democracy had always stressed that family life, membership of the church and other social organizations, and labour were the social bases of self-respect that the welfare state had to protect. Yet postwar welfare states had created individual choice and moral liberties, which undermined not just the ideological basis but also the organizational footing of more conservative welfare states. Welfare states incorporated professionalized social organizations, while also turning institutions for social work, care, schools, and hospitals from bulwarks of Christian social power into subsidized fortresses of professional interest. As a result, Christian Democratic parties in the Low Countries and Germany lost important channels for interest mediations, party recruitment, and electoral mobilization, while in Italy the even more intricate clientelist connections between the DC, social organizations and individual clients lost their legitimacy once they came to be viewed as corrupt abuse of public means for private interests. While the Italian Christian Democratic party collapsed completely, the other Christian Democratic parties went through a period of reorientation. Part of their survival strategy was defined by a pragmatic profile as crisis managers. The Dutch Christian Democrat Ruud Lubbers, Prime Minister between 1982 and 1994, presented a 'no-nonsense' response to the economic crisis of the 1980s in the form of welfare state reform. Also Helmut Kohl, the German CDU *Bundeskanzler* between 1982 and 1998, presented himself as the manager of transition, both of the welfare state and towards a unified Germany. The reforms Christian Democrats proposed were generally 'liberal-communitarian' in nature, that is: inspired by Hayekian arguments about the state as a burden to prosperity, but legitimated with the aid of the communitarian political philosophy of Amitai Etzioni and others, who revived the neo-Thomist ideology of social responsibility on which Christian ideas about social capitalism had been based.[46]

Social Democracy also went through a period of reorientation, after it lost much of its electoral support in the early 1980s. According to many commentators at the time, this was the natural consequence, or even the ironic result of the success of Social Democracy in establishing the welfare state. It had obliterated the working class base of social democratic parties, created new preferences and identities that fitted the new social

[45] Michael Crozier, Samuel P. Huntington and Joji Watanuki, *The Crisis of Democracy: Report on the Governability of Democracies to the Trilateral Commission* (New York: New York University Press, 1975); Mancur Olson, *The Rise and Decline of Nations: Economic Growth, Stagflation and Social Rigidities* (New Haven, CT: Yale University Press, 1982); Juhana Vartiainen, 'Understanding Swedish Social Democracy: Victims of Success?', *Oxford Review of Economic Policy* 14:1 (1998), 19–39.

[46] Martin Seeleib-Kaiser, Silke Van Dyke and Martin Roggekamp, *Party Politics and Social Welfare: Comparing Christian and Social Democracy in Austria, Germany and the Netherlands* (Cheltenham: Edward Elgar 2009), 159–63; Steven Van Hecke and Emmanuel Gerard (eds), *Christian Democratic Parties since the End of the Cold War* (Leuven: Leuven University Press, 2003); Michael Fogarty, 'How Dutch Christian Democracy Made a New Start', *The Political Quarterly* 66:3 (1995), 138–55; Amitai Etzioni, *The Moral Dimension: Toward a New Economics* (New York: Free Press, 1988).

movements of feminists, ecologists, gay and peace activists better than the old social movements of organized labour, while also exhausting the utopian potential that social democratic parties historically had been able to mobilize.[47] However, not all Social Democrats suffered in the same way: at the same time as they lost support in Germany and the Low Countries, they won the 1981 presidential elections in France under the leadership of François Mitterrand, who inaugurated a series of social policies—reducing the working day and retirement age, raising wages and benefits, as well as the announcement of nationalizations—which seemed to indicate Social Democracy was not beaten.

However, Mitterrand's U-turn of June 1982, in which prices and wages were frozen, state spending was cut, and nationalization reversed, inaugurated a period of 'cohabitation' in which power was shared between Left and Right. In other parts of Europe, the image was even more mixed: most social democratic parties followed Tony Blair's Third Way towards New Labour. The parties united in the Socialist International in 1989 and published the Stockholm Declaration in which the abolition of capitalism was no longer a goal. It inaugurated a period in which Social Democrats embraced the market as the most efficient way to allocate goods, while the excesses of a market society now had to be contained by responsible citizenship instead of large-scale social programmes. It led to a paradoxical situation at the end of the 1990s, when Social Democrats held government positions in almost all European countries, while taking the lead in the most drastic reforms the welfare state had ever experienced.[48]

The nature of these reforms varied between the countries of Western Europe, but they shared some basic characteristics. One recurring aspect was the privatization of services such as railways, hospitals, postal and telecommunication services, and the retreat of government from many other areas of public services under the catchphrase of deregulation and new public management. The basic assumption of these reforms was that the market, rather than the state, is better able to allocate goods and services; and that state intervention should be considered a disturbance of market processes. Therefore the role of the state had to be limited, but also the state should incorporate market mechanisms such as price incentives and decentralization of financial responsibility, in order to improve the efficiency of policy output.

Another aspect of welfare state reforms was the reduction of social entitlements, in terms of the period for which one can claim support, the age of retirement, or the level of payments. The rationale for these reforms was not just reduction of financial pressure on the state, but also the idea that welfare states tended to discourage labour participation. In response to the 'jobless growth' many welfare states experienced in the 1990s, policies

---

[47]   Adam Przeworski and John Sprague, *Paper Stones: A History of Electoral Socialism* (Chicago, IL: University of Chicago Press, 1986); Jürgen Habermas, *Die neue Unübersichtlichkeit. Kleine politische Schriften V* (Frankfurt/M: Suhrkamp, 1985).

[48]   Sassoon, *One Hunderd Years of Socialism*, 730–54; Herbert Kitschelt, *The Transformation of European Social Democracy* (Cambridge: Cambridge University Press, 1994); René Cuperus and Johannes Kandel (eds), *European Social Democracy: Transformation in Progress* (Amsterdam: Wiardi Beckman Stichting, 1998); Anthony Giddens, *The Third Way: The Renewal of Social Democracy* (Cambridge: Polity, 1998).

were proposed that would stimulate labour participation. Limits to social entitlements were part of these policies, but so were initiatives aimed at the 'flexibilization' of the labour market, not just in terms of decreased protection against lay-offs, but also by way of liberalization of wage policies and the lowering of the minimum wage. A final aspect of the transition 'from welfare to workfare' was the expansion of social care for children and the elderly, in order to stimulate especially female labour participation in particular.[49]

Although welfare state reforms have generally been perceived as an indication of the strength of neoliberalism or of a shift 'from Keynes to Hayek', the productivist nature of many of these reforms, stressing the priority of work over welfare, was not very different from the tight connection to paid labour that characterized the social democratic welfare states of Sweden or the Netherlands. Family policies too were not altogether new, but had been a pivotal part of the Christian Democratic welfare state of the 1950s and 1960s.[50] What is different, however, is the clear break with the tendency towards greater equality that characterized the western European welfare states until the 1980s. Not only have inequalities increased, but the social democratic parties, which traditionally supported egalitarian policies, voiced little protest against the growing inequality.[51]

Instead, new foci of protest have formed around radical populist parties both from the left, as with Die Linke in Germany or the Socialistische Partij in the Netherlands, yet the same 'welfare chauvinism' also contributed to the growth of radical right-wing and xenophobic populist parties, such as the Vlaams Blok in Belgium, the ÖVP in Austria, and the populist leaders Pim Fortuyn and Geert Wilders in the Netherlands. These political protests indicate that the corporatist mechanisms that once contributed to a consensual expansion of the welfare state now function less effectively. Even if there are indications that corporatist negotiations have contributed to relatively peaceful implementation of welfare reforms (and the lack of such mechanisms in states like France to a *société bloquée* that is unable to reform), the force of populist protest indicates that these reforms are introduced into a society that is much less consensual than were those in which the postwar welfare state initially emerged.[52]

[49] Frank Nullmeier and Friedbert W. Rüb, *Die Transformation der Sozialpolitik. Vom Sozialstaat zum Sicherungsstaat* (Frankfurt/M: Campus Verlag, 1993); Paul Pierson, 'Coping with Permanent Austerity: Welfare State Restructruing in Affluent Democracies', in Paul Pierson (ed.), *The New Politics of the Welfare State* (Oxford: Oxford University Press, 2001),410–56; Peter Taylor-Gooby, 'Paradigm Shifts, Power Resources and Labour Market Reforms', in Peter Taylor-Gooby (ed.), *Ideas and Welfare State Reform in Western Europe* (Basingstoke: Palgrave Macmillan, 2005), 12–29.

[50] Gøsta Esping-Andersen, 'Welfare without Work: The Impasse of Labour Shedding and Familialism in Continental European Social Policy', in Esping-Andersen (ed.) *Welfare States in Transition: National Adaptations in Global Economies* (London: Sage, 1996), 66–87.

[51] OECD, *Growing Unequal Income Distribution and Povery in OECD Countries* (Paris: OECD, 2008); Tony Judt, *Ill Fares the Land* (London: Allen Lane, 2010).

[52] Frans van Waarden and Gerhard Lehmbruch (eds), *Renegotiating the Welfare State: Flexible Adjustment through Corporatist Concertation* (London: Routledge, 2003); Jelle Visser and Anton Hemerijck, 'A Dutch Miracle': Job Growth Welfare Reform and Corporatism in the Netherlands (Amsterdam: Amsterdam University Press, 1997); Michel Crozier, *La société bloquée* (Paris: Seuil, 1971); Hanspeter Kriesi et al., *West European Politics in the Age of Globalization: Six Countries Compared* (Cambridge: Cambridge University Press, 2008).

Again, these reforms indicate that the history of the welfare state can hardly be analysed in terms of social democratic and conservative or Christian Democractic political dominance. Welfare states emerged and were transformed in the context of institutional and social relations, as a result of which the centre of ideological convergence may have shifted from a more progressive equilibrium in the 1950s to a more liberal or conservative point after 1980. Yet welfare state regimes have showed considerable variation, both between states and in time, so that it is difficult to speak of the welfare state as the social democratic moment in postwar history, or, for that matter, of a Christian Democratic moment.

Welfare states were the product of a particular constellation of forces emerging at the end of the Second World War, just as their reform is the consequence both of the various trajectories of the development of welfare states and the institutional, social, and ideological forces that emerged at the end of the 1970s. In the process, both the egalitarian basis, as well as the consensual acceptance of the welfare state, came under pressure. The current welfare states are a contested and in some cases even despised product of Europe's postwar history.

Further Reading

Baldwin, Peter, *The Politics of Social Solidarity: Class Bases of European Welfare States 1875–1975* (Cambridge: Cambridge University Press, 1990).

Castles, Francis G. et al. (eds), *The Oxford Handbook of the Welfare State* (Oxford: Oxford University Press, 2010).

Castles, Francis and Deborah Mitchell, 'Identifying Welfare State Regimes: The Links between Politics, Instruments, and Outcomes', *Governance* 5 (1992), 1–26.

Crouch, Colin, Klaus Eder and Damian Tambini (eds), *Citizenship, Markets, and the State* (Oxford: Oxford University Press, 2001).

De Swaan, Abram, *In Care of the State: Health Care, Education, and Welfare in Europe and the USA in the Modern Era* (Oxford: Oxford University Press, 1988).

Esping-Andersen, Gøsta (ed.), *Welfare States in Transition: National Adaptations in Global Economies* (London: Sage, 1996).

Kersbergen, Kees van, and Philip Manow (eds), *Religion, Class Coalitions and the Welfare State* (Cambridge: Cambridge University Press, 2009).

Manow, Philip, 'Electoral Rules, Class Coalitions and Welfare States, or how to Explain Esping-Andersen with Stein Rokkan', *Socio-Economic Review* 7 (2009), 101–21.

Scruggs, Lyle A. and James P. Allan, 'Social Stratification and Welfare Regimes for the Twenty-first Century: Revisiting the Three Worlds of Welfare Capitalism', *World Politics* 60:4 (2008), 642–64.

Svallfors, Stefan (ed.), *The Political Sociology of the Welfare State* (Stanford, CA: Stanford University Press, 2007).

CHAPTER 15

THE TRUTH ABOUT FRIENDSHIP TREATIES: BEHIND THE IRON CURTAIN

DOUGLAS SELVAGE

THE basic, legal building blocks for the Soviet sphere of influence during the Cold War were the bilateral 'Treaties of Friendship, Cooperation, and Mutual Assistance' between the states of East Central Europe and the Soviet Union. The treaties shared certain common characteristics. All were concluded for a period of twenty years. At the centre of the friendship treaties was an alliance clause, in which both sides promised to come to each others' aid in the event of an armed attack. Germany was the main potential enemy, but the treaties also applied to any state allied with it or any third state in general—most importantly, the United States.[1]

However, the treaties came to embody and represent much more—namely, the limited sovereignty of the states of East Central Europe. A second major provision of the treaties, a commitment not to enter into any alliances or coalitions directed against each other, meant in practice that the states of the region were forbidden from entering into any alignment or international organization not approved by the Soviet Union. This provision, when combined with the commitment to defence against countries from which at least some of the East Central European states saw no threat, suggested more of a protectorate arrangement. That is, the states of East Central Europe had limited sovereignty in international affairs. The characteristic declaration in all the friendship treaties of 'mutual respect for independence and sovereignty', equality in relations, and 'non-intervention in internal affairs' confirmed exactly the opposite.[2] Moscow's regular intervention in the internal affairs of the

---

[1] Robert L. Hutchings, *Soviet-East European Relations* (Madison, WI: University of Wisconsin Press, 1987), 17; Boris Meissner (ed.), *Das Ostpakt-System* (Frankfurt/M: Alfred Metzner Verlag, 1955), 19.

[2] Jörg K. Hoensch, *Sowjetische Osteuropa-Politik, 1945–1975* (Kronberg im Taunus: Athenäum Verlag, 1977), 31.

East Central European states suggested a redefinition of 'sovereignty', equality, and 'non-intervention'. The contrast between the wording of the friendship treaties and actual practice confirmed the limited sovereignty of the Soviet bloc states.

This chapter traces the evolution of the East Central European states' limited sovereignty from the origins of the friendship-treaty system during World War II through to its final reformulation in the mid-1970s. In terms of the Soviet bloc friendship treaties, one can speak of three periods. The first began with the establishment of the system of friendship treaties under Soviet dictator Joseph Stalin, 1943–1948, and ended with his death in 1953. This period witnessed the construction of the Soviet sphere of influence in Europe. A second period began after Stalin's death in 1953 and the eventual assumption of power by Soviet leader Nikita S. Khrushchev. Khrushchev's toleration of greater autonomy for the communist states, his attempts at multilateralism, his de-stalinization campaign, and the ensuing rift between the USSR and the People's Republic of China (PRC), all threatened to transform the friendship-treaty system. Khrushchev's removal ushered in a third and final period for the friendship-treaty system under his successor, Leonid Brezhnev. Under Brezhnev, Moscow sought, with some degree of success, to exploit the earlier friendship treaties' renewal in the 1960s and 1970s and the GDR's integration into the bilateral system to re-stabilize the Soviet bloc. The system of bilateral treaties remained in place until the Revolutions of 1989 and the collapse of the Soviet Union in 1991.

STALIN'S BILATERAL FRIENDSHIP TREATIES AND THE CONSOLIDATION OF A SOVIET BLOC (1943–49)

Between 1943 and 1947, Stalin's Soviet Union undertook what became the initial round of friendship treaties between itself and three other victims of German aggression during World War II: Czechoslovakia, Poland, and Yugoslavia.

What was Stalin's goal in concluding and promoting this initial round of friendship treaties? During World War II, he had made clear to his British and US allies his desire to have 'friendly' postwar governments along the USSR's western borders in order to defend against any resurgence of German aggression. The text of the friendship treaties suggested the minimum, basic terms of such friendship; the Soviet Union's neighbours should cooperate with it to prevent renewed German aggression, avoid any alliances or alignments hostile to it, and agree to pursue economic and cultural cooperation. On the surface, such terms would have been unobjectionable in and of themselves to the West. Such terms did not seem to conflict with the Franklin D. Roosevelt administration's idea of an 'open' Soviet sphere of influence in East Central Europe.[3]

---

[3] Melvyn Leffler, *For the Soul of Mankind* (New York: Hill and Wang, 2007), 46.

However, Soviet practice at the end of World War II and immediately thereafter suggested a much less 'open' sphere of influence, one in which the sovereignty of Moscow's western neighbours in international and domestic affairs would be strictly limited. First, while the treaties forbade its neighbours' entering into any alliance or alignment directed against the USSR, it did not specify that Moscow considered any alignment in East Central Europe that excluded it to be 'unfriendly'. In the case of Poland and Czechoslovakia, Moscow opposed the alignment inherent in the agreement of January 1942 between their respective Governments-in-Exile, which provided for cooperation in foreign, defence, economic, and financial policy after World War II. The Soviet–Czechoslovak treaty of 1943 effectively trumped this arrangement. It was concluded two months after Moscow had severed its relations with the Polish Government-in-Exile; the protocol providing for Poland's accession suggested that the agreement of 1942 between Poland and Czechoslovakia was open to renegotiation. Moscow had broken off relations with the London Poles because they had dared to call for an investigation by the International Red Cross into the mass murder of Polish officers at Katyń, a Soviet war crime that Moscow had falsely laid at the feet of the Nazis. Similarly, in January 1948, Moscow publicly opposed the plans of communist leaders Josip Broz Tito of Yugoslavia and Georgii Dimitrov of Bulgaria to establish a federation or confederation of Balkan states. Instead, Yugoslavia, Bulgaria, and Albania concluded friendship treaties with each other and—with the exception of Albania—with Moscow.[4] In other words, Moscow curtailed the sovereignty of its friendship-treaty allies in international affairs.

More significantly, the case of Poland suggested as early as 1945 that Moscow's friendship-treaty allies also faced limitations in their domestic sovereignty. Moscow concluded the Polish friendship treaty with its own, Lublin government for Poland, which had been expanded at US and British insistence after Yalta to include some London Poles. The treaty was also concluded after the Warsaw uprising of August to October 1944, during which the Polish partisans of the Home Army (AK), loyal to the Polish Government-in-Exile, had fought to wrest control of the Polish capital from the Nazis. During the two-month uprising, the Red Army had halted its advance just outside the city; the Soviets not only failed to provide effective support but also limited the ability of the US and Great Britain to do so. Tens of thousands of Poles died or were deported by the Nazis.[5] Given this larger context, Stalin's declaration upon the conclusion of the Soviet–Polish friendship treaty that it constituted a 'prerequisite for the independence of the new, democratic Poland . . . its power, its prosperity' suggested a major redefinition of 'independence', 'democracy', and 'power'.[6]

One key element of state sovereignty is territorial integrity; also in this regard, Moscow compelled its friendship-treaty allies to compromise their sovereignty. It

---

[4] Piotr S. Wandycz, *Czechoslovak-Polish Confederation and the Great Powers, 1940–43* (Bloomington, IN: Indiana University, 1956) 67–8, 92–9; Meissner, *Ostpakt-System*, 15–16.

[5] Andrzej Paczkowski, *The Spring will be Ours* (University Park, PA: Pennsylvania State University Press, 1995), 121–30.

[6] Stalin's speech, 21 April 1945, in Meissner, *Ostpakt-System*, 26–7.

successfully pressured Czechoslovakia to cede the Carpatho-Ukraine to the USSR, and Poland's post-Yalta government signed over one third of Poland's pre-war territory.[7] Moscow did, in return, successfully support at the Potsdam Conference in 1945 Poland's expansion at Germany's expense up to the Oder and western Neisse Rivers. However, when the US declared in 1946 that the Oder-Neisse line was subject to adjustment as part of a final German peace settlement, Moscow settled for a public rebuff. It refused to sign a treaty with Poland guaranteeing the border.[8] Poland's communist leader, Władysław Gomułka, later called the open border question a 'leash' that Moscow used to keep Poland in line.[9] Likewise, Stalin pressured Poland and Czechoslovakia to sign their own friendship treaty despite an ongoing dispute between the two states about their mutual border.[10] As a result, the Polish–Czechoslovak friendship treaty, concluded on 10 March 1947, did not resolve the border dispute.[11] It was not officially resolved until 1958, five years after Stalin's death, in a new treaty between Warsaw and Prague.[12] At least until 1958, the border question remained yet another 'leash' in Moscow's relations with its neighbours.

Economic agreements between the USSR and its friendship-treaty allies further compromised their domestic sovereignty. This was perhaps not surprising in the case of Germany's former allies in the second round of friendship treaties—Romania, Hungary, and Bulgaria—which continued to pay reparations to the USSR until the early 1950s. Still, the sums were quite high, and the three states also had to agree to the establishment of joint enterprises in which the USSR's interests predominated.[13] Poland, the first country to fight Nazi Germany and ostensibly a Soviet ally after 1941, successfully rebuffed Soviet demands for joint enterprises. Instead, it had to agree to provide the USSR throughout its occupation of Germany with 12 million tons of coal per year at a price of $1.22 per ton, less than the actual cost of mining the coal. The coal was the price that Poland paid for the 15 per cent of the Soviet reparations from Germany that it had been granted at the Potsdam Conference.[14]

---

[7] Ibid., 9–20.

[8] Jan Ptasiński, *Pierwszy z trzech zwrotów* (Warsaw: Krajowa Agencja Wydawnicza, 1983), 123–4.

[9] Mieczysław Rakowski, 'Dziennikarz i polityczny emisariusz między Warszawą a Bonn', in Friedbert Pflüger and Winfried Lipscher (eds), *Od nienawiści do przyjaźni* (Warsaw: ISP-PAN, 1994), 175–7.

[10] Letter of the Soviet Government to the Governments of Poland and Czechoslovakia, 26 July 1946, in T.V. Volokitina et al., *Vostochnaia Evropa v dokumentakh rossiĭskikh arkhivov, 1944–1953* (henceforth, *VEDRA*), T. 1: 1944–1948, Document 164.

[11] 'Treaty of Friendship and Mutual Aid between the Republic of Poland and the Czechoslovak Republic', 10 March 1947, United Nations Treaty Collection: http://treaties.un.org/doc/Publication/UNTS/Volume%2025/volume-25-I-365-English.pdf, accessed April 2010.

[12] Agreement concerning the final demarcation of the State frontier between Poland and Czechoslovakia, 13 June 1958, ibid.: http://untreaty.un.org/unts/1_60000/10/23/00019116.pdf, accessed April 2010.

[13] Zbigniew K. Brzezinski, *Soviet Bloc* (Cambridge, MA: Harvard University Press, 1967), 125.

[14] Memorandum of Conversation, 24–25 May 1957, Archiwum Akt Nowych (AAN), sygn. 2627, 254–6; Andrzej Paczkowski (ed.), *Tajne dokumenty Biura Politycznego, 1956–1970* (London: 'Aneks', 1998), 76.

The question of how 'friendly' the Soviet Union's western neighbours would have needed to be in order to please Stalin—that is, whether the compromises to their sovereignty already in place at the beginning of 1947 would have sufficed—will never be answered with 100 per cent certainty due to the intervention of the Cold War. It seems likely, however, based on the Polish example and the behaviour of the Red Army and the Soviet intelligence services in East Central Europe that Moscow would have continued to undermine the sovereignty of its western neighbours, including those allied against Nazi Germany in World War II.

In 1947, the US decided to contain the expansion of communism with the Marshall Plan and Truman Doctrine. Stalin responded by tightening and formalizing Soviet rule over East Central Europe, as reflected in the establishment in September 1947 of the Communist Information Bureau (Cominform) to oversee the communist parties of Europe, and the Prague coup of February 1948. Communists ended their participation in coalition governments throughout the region and assumed one-party rule.

It was against this backdrop that Stalin's Politburo ordered the Soviet foreign ministry in October 1947 to integrate Germany's former World War II allies—Bulgaria, Romania, and Hungary—into the existing friendship-treaty system. This second round of friendship treaties, unlike the first, served merely to confirm the signatories' existing subordination to Moscow.[15] After Stalin expelled Yugoslavia from the Cominform, all friendship-treaty ties between the East Central European states and Belgrade were severed.[16] Yugoslavia was thus expelled from the Soviet bloc.

The system of bilateral friendship treaties formed the Soviet alliance system under Stalin; together, they constituted the Soviet bloc. They demonstrated Stalin's preference for bilateralism in relations with Moscow's allies. No multilateral consultations took place between the states or parties of the communist bloc between the last summit session of the Cominform in November 1949 and the Nineteenth Party Congress of the Communist Party of the Soviet Union (CPSU) in 1952. After Tito's expulsion, the Cominform focused primarily on attacking the Yugoslav leader; his political survival served to discredit the multilateral body, which Khrushchev finally disbanded in 1956.[17] Similarly, the multilateral Council for Mutual Economic Assistance (Comecon), established at Soviet behest in 1949, met only once under Stalin and served as a mechanism for the Soviet planning agency (Gosplan) to coordinate the production of the Soviet bloc states at least until Stalin's death in 1953.[18] After 1949 and at least until Stalin's death in 1953, all ties between the states of East Central Europe ran directly or indirectly through Moscow.

Under Stalin, the informal ties between the ruling communist parties assumed much greater importance than the formal ties embodied in the friendship treaties. These informal ties further limited the sovereignty of the now communist states: worship of

---

[15] Brzezinski, *Soviet Bloc*, 111. For the text of the directive from the Soviet Politburo, 14 October 1947, see *VEDRA*, Document No. 245.

[16] Meissner, *Ostpakt-System*, 17.

[17] Brzezinski, *Soviet Bloc*, 112, 117.

[18] Hoensch, *Sowjetische Osteuropa-Politik*, 31.

Stalin and emulation of his cult of personality by each regime; ideological conformity to the CPSU; oversight and reports on local regimes by Soviet ambassadors; the widespread presence and virtual domination of Soviet advisors in the security forces of the Soviet bloc states; the recommendations of Gosplan and other Soviet economic ministries in the economic realm; and the Red Army's presence in some communist states.[19] The formal relations between the communist states assumed importance again only after 1956, when Khrushchev implemented limited reforms and dismantled some of the more onerous informal controls.

KHRUSHCHEV: EROSION OF THE FRIENDSHIP-TREATY SYSTEM AND INTEGRATION OF THE GDR

Because the existing Soviet bloc friendship treaties were not subject to renewal for twenty years, they formally became an issue only in the final years of Khrushchev's rule (1956–64). Nevertheless, Khrushchev did much to transform the relations underlying the paper architecture of the friendship treaties—namely, by granting the communist states of East Central Europe greater sovereignty. This transformation ran parallel to his reform policies at home, dubbed 'de-stalinization' in the West.

Under Khrushchev, the states of East Central Europe moved from having almost no sovereignty to having limited sovereignty. After Moscow's adoption of the New Course in its foreign and economic policies in 1953, the People's Democracies were permitted to negotiate and argue with each other—and eventually the USSR—about bilateral economic relations. Representatives of the Comecon states began to meet on a regular basis, and real debates about economic cooperation took place. Even more significant was the increased political autonomy of the Soviet bloc states in the wake of Khrushchev's 'Secret Speech' to the 20th CPSU Party Congress in March 1956. Khrushchev's criticism of Stalin's cult of personality and admission of the ideological fallibility of the CPSU undermined two of the fundamental informal devices for control over the bloc's communist parties. Then, on 30 October, the Soviet Government issued a 'Declaration on the Principles of Development and Further Strengthening of Friendship and Cooperation between the Soviet Union and Other Socialist States'. Moscow proclaimed it 'urgent to review, together with the other socialist states, the question of the expediency of the further presence of USSR advisors' in the communist states.

Subsequently, Soviet advisors were withdrawn from key positions in the armies and intelligence services of the communist states. They either returned to Moscow or assumed—at least formally—a purely advisory role as liaisons. The Soviet declaration also expressed a willingness 'to review with the socialist countries...the question of

---

[19] Brzezinski, *Soviet Bloc*, 136.

Soviet troops stationed on [their] territory'. The USSR subsequently signed bilateral agreements with the Soviet bloc states regarding the status of Soviet forces on their territory. The agreement with Poland's communist government, for example, stipulated that Soviet forces should not engage in manoeuvres without Warsaw's permission. In 1958, Khrushchev even agreed to withdraw Soviet forces from Romania.[20]

Still, there were limits on the sovereignty of Moscow's Soviet bloc allies, as the Soviet declaration of 30 October 1956 made clear. It noted the existence of unrest in Hungary and declared Moscow's intention to intervene militarily.[21] In both Hungary and Poland, initial efforts at de-stalinization, combined with years of repression and economic difficulties, had sparked popular movements in 1956 that threatened to overwhelm their respective communist regimes. In the case of Poland, Gomułka had returned to power after his purge and house arrest to pursue a 'Polish road to socialism', which entailed an abandonment of the forced collectivization of agriculture, greater toleration for the Catholic Church, and increased freedom in the cultural sphere. Despite Soviet disapproval of his policies, Gomułka had succeeded in maintaining communist rule in Poland and sworn his regime's fealty to Moscow. In Hungary, reform communist leader Imre Nagy proved unable and later unwilling to maintain the communist party's monopoly on power in the face of popular revolt. The Soviets intervened militarily, crushed the Hungarian Revolution, and eventually imprisoned and executed Nagy.[22]

Moscow justified its intervention after the fact by citing Hungary's plans to leave the multilateral alliance established by Moscow in 1955: the Warsaw Treaty Organization (WTO), popularly known in the West as the Warsaw Pact. The Pact itself was a multilateral friendship treaty; its formal title was 'Treaty of Friendship, Cooperation and Mutual Assistance'.[23] Did Khrushchev intend to replace the bilateral friendship-treaty system with the Warsaw Pact?

The early history of the WTO suggests that this was not the case. The Soviets established it in hasty response to the real or alleged threat posed by the West's decision to integrate the Federal Republic of Germany (FRG) into the North Atlantic Treaty Organization (NATO) in 1955. At the time of the Warsaw Pact's establishment, there were no plans for a military organization. In fact, as conceived by Moscow, the WTO was open to accession by any European state, was purely defensive, and was intended (at least in terms of propaganda) to constitute the basis for an all-European security system. Moscow and its allies repeatedly stressed their willingness to dissolve it in return for NATO's dissolution. Moscow could make such an offer, Western statesmen noted, because its system of bilateral friendship treaties would have remained in place while

[20] Ibid., 172–6, 229–31; Hutchings, *Soviet-East European Relations*, 18–21; 'Declaration by the Soviet Government', 30 October 1956, ena.lu/declaration_soviet_government_moscow_30_october_1956-3-7496, accessed April 2010.

[21] 'Declaration by the Soviet Government'.

[22] Ivan T. Berend, *Central and Eastern Europe, 1944–1993* (Cambridge: Cambridge University Press, 1996), 120–6.

[23] For the text of the treaty, see Yale Law School, Avalon Project, http://avalon.law.yale.edu/20th_century/warsaw.asp, accessed April 2010.

NATO, the backbone of the Western alliance, would have disappeared. Nevertheless, the WTO did provide the Soviets with a legal rationale for maintaining their troops in East Central Europe, as the declaration on the eve of their invasion of Hungary showed. By the 1960s, it became the main structure for command and control of the Soviet bloc's armies and thus somewhat more equivalent to NATO.[24]

Although all the bilateral friendship treaties remained in place under Khrushchev, the underlying relations between Moscow and the Soviet bloc states had changed. They had not achieved the 'independence and sovereignty', equality in relations, and 'non-intervention in internal affairs' inscribed in the treaties, but they had attained more sovereignty than under Stalin. Relations were more complex, not only due to the addition of the new multilateral structure of the Warsaw Pact and the activation of Comecon, but also due to the varying degrees of de-stalinization among the communist states. While Poland and Hungary—despite the mass repressions in the wake of the Soviet invasion in 1956—would move the furthest away from the Stalinist model in economic and political affairs, other communist states simply toned down the cult of personality, ended some of the worst repressive practices of the period, and quietly rehabilitated some victims. Otherwise, they sought to avoid any public or even private discussion of past errors. These states included Czechoslovakia, the GDR, and Bulgaria. Other states—that is, Albania and Romania—in the bloc effectively rejected Khrushchev's changes and continued the old system; they followed a 'national Stalinist' path.[25]

THE PEOPLE'S REPUBLIC OF CHINA AND THE FRIENDSHIP-TREATY SYSTEM

However, the most important 'national Stalinist' state, the People's Republic of China (PRC) was not within the Soviet bloc, The PRC was also a friendship-treaty ally of the Soviet Union: on 14 February 1950, the USSR and the PRC had signed a 'Treaty of Friendship, Alliance and Mutual Assistance'. Despite the replacement of the term 'cooperation' with 'alliance', the Sino–Soviet treaty followed closely to Moscow's friendship treaties with the Soviet bloc both in its wording and content. It was also a military alliance; it also forbade entry into any alliance or alignment directed against either party, and it announced the intention of both sides to engage in economic and cultural cooperation. Japan replaced Germany as the potential enemy, along with any allied country—that is, the United States. One difference between the Sino–Soviet friendship treaty

---

[24] Vojtech Mastny, 'The Warsaw Pact as History', in Vojtech Mastny and Malcolm Byrne (eds), *A Cardboard Castle?* (Budapest: Central European University Press, 2005), 2–4; Hutchings, *Soviet-East European Relations*, 22–4.

[25] Berend, *Central and Eastern Europe*, 126–8, 156.

and the Soviet bloc treaties was its duration: thirty years, rather than twenty, along with an automatic renewal every five years as long as neither side renounced it.[26]

The context of the Sino–Soviet friendship treaty also bore similarities to the Soviet bloc treaties. There was an element of Soviet dominance and humiliation. Chairman Mao Zedong of the Chinese Communist Party (CCP), who travelled to Moscow in December 1949, two months after the CCP's victory in the Chinese civil war, waited in Moscow for over a month before negotiations began on the treaty. In the end, the Chinese communists had to sign off on concessions previously made by China's Nationalist government to Stalin, including mining, oil, and railroad concessions in Manchuria and Xinjiang—joint enterprises again—and a continuation of the Soviet leases of Dalian Harbour and the naval base at Lushun (Port Arthur).[27]

Still, there were significant differences between the Sino–Soviet friendship treaty and the Soviet bloc friendship treaties. The PRC had more room for manoeuvre in international affairs. It resisted Soviet attempts to integrate it more closely into the Soviet bloc during the 1950s. Article 1 of the Sino–Soviet friendship treaty stated that the two sides 'declare their readiness, in a spirit of sincere cooperation, to participate in all international actions that serve to safeguard peace and security in the entire world'.[28] The phrasing suggested a more equal relationship than the Soviet bloc friendship treaties. An early test of the alliance came in 1950 with the Korean war, during which the USSR and the PRC provided assistance to communist North Korea. However, in the end, Stalin left it to Mao to decide whether to order Chinese troops into North Korea to save the communist regime. He did so, and the war ended in 1953 in stalemate with an armistice.[29]

The Sino–Soviet friendship treaty thus marked a more equal partnership than the Soviet bloc friendship treaties. At the same time, talk in the West of a 'monolithic Sino–Soviet bloc' neglected the underlying tensions that had already existed under Stalin—tensions that the PRC downplayed due to its dependence on Moscow.

Ironically, it was under Khrushchev, who did much to end the humiliations of Stalin, that Sino–Soviet relations eroded and came to a final breach. During a visit to Beijing in the autumn of 1954, Khrushchev agreed, among other things, to return the Soviet share in joint enterprises to China; promised a long-term credit of 420 million rubles; and announced the withdrawal of Soviet forces from Lushun (Port Arthur).[30] Thus began a short-lived 'golden age' in Sino–Soviet relations, whose high watermark came at the Moscow conference of world communist parties in 1957. Despite initial, strenuous opposition from the Polish and Yugoslav communists, the conference approved, at China's insistence, a declaration affirming the leading role of the Soviet Union, 'the first and mightiest' communist state.[31]

---

[26] Meissner, *Ostpakt-System*, 160.

[27] Chen Jian, *Mao's China and the Cold War* (Chapel Hill, NC: University of North Carolina Press, 2001), 52–3; Lorenz M. Lüthi, *Sino-Soviet Split* (Princeton, NJ: Princeton University Press, 2008), 37.

[28] Meissner, *Ostpakt-System*, 166.

[29] Jian, *Mao's China*, 54–61.

[30] Meissner, *Ostpakt-System*, 159–60; Lüthi, *Sino-Soviet Split*, 39.

[31] Hutchings, *Soviet-East European Relations*, 21.

At the same time, at the Moscow conference, Mao voiced his opposition to Khrushchev's policy of peaceful coexistence with the West. More significantly, he opposed Khrushchev's ideological reforms and sought to maintain his own 'cult of personality' at home.[32] Although both Moscow and Beijing initially sought to conceal and minimize their ideological differences, by 1961, their problems became public, not least of all through Albania's vocal and public alignment with Beijing. After 1961, Moscow stopped inviting Albania to Warsaw Pact meetings; Albania was effectively kicked out of the Eastern alliance.[33]

Romania, another national Stalinist state, skilfully exploited the rift between Moscow and Beijing to assert its sovereignty. After failing in its role of self-proclaimed mediator between Moscow and Beijing in early 1964, it issued a declaration calling for a restoration of unity between Moscow and Beijing on the basis of 'national independence and sovereignty, equality and mutual advantage'—principles that Romania now applied to its own relations with Moscow. Although Romania, the declaration had read, was willing to cooperate with 'all socialist lands' (that is, including China), it would also defend its sovereignty against any encroachment by supranational organs—most importantly, the Comecon or the Warsaw Pact.[34] After 1964, Romanian obstruction became a standing feature of both bodies.[35]

Khrushchev and the Soviet–GDR Friendship Treaty (1964)

It was against this backdrop of disarray that Khrushchev decided in 1964 to conclude a friendship treaty with the GDR. This raises not only the question of why Khrushchev decided to do so in 1964, but also why Moscow waited so long. After all, the GDR had been in existence for fifteen years, since 1949.

Stalin had not wanted to conclude any agreement with the GDR that would have underlined its sovereignty or suggested that Germany's division was final. He wanted to leave the issue of German unification officially open. At the very least, he hoped to lay the blame for Germany's division on the West and to forestall the FRG's political and military integration in the Western alliance. At most, he sought a unified, neutral, demilitarized Germany that would have been open to Soviet influence. Thus, the GDR was integrated into the Soviet bloc only on an informal basis: through the Treaty of Zgorzelec

---

[32] Lüthi, *Sino-Soviet Split*, 50–1.

[33] Berend, *Central and Eastern Europe*, 127–9; Mastny, 'Warsaw Pact', 16–17.

[34] Dionisie Ghermani, 'Die nationale Souveränitätspolitik der SR Rumänien, 1. Teil', *Untersuchungen zur Gegenwartskunde Südosteuropas*, 17 (Munich: R. Oldenbourg Verlag, 1981), 36–46, 82–3; Henryk Różański, *Spojrzenie na RWPG* (Warsaw: Państwowe Wydawnictwo Naukowe, 1990) 161, 165–6, 171–3, 179–82.

[35] Berend, *Central and Eastern Europe*, 131–4.

(1950) with Poland, in which it recognized the Oder-Neisse line as the final Polish–German border; and through a series of bilateral declarations with the other Soviet bloc states. The GDR also became a member of the Comecon.[36]

In contrast, Khrushchev sought to compel the West to recognize the GDR and accept a two-state solution to the German question. This led him in 1958 to spark the Berlin Crisis. Basically, Khrushchev demanded that the West agree to conclude peace treaties with both German states, the GDR and the FRG, on the basis of the existing postwar borders and with a ban on either state's access to nuclear weapons. Western forces should also leave West Berlin, which would become a demilitarized 'free city'. If not, Khrushchev would conclude a separate peace treaty with the GDR and hand over all Soviet control functions in occupied Berlin to the GDR. The West would then face the choice of either recognizing the GDR's sovereignty at its border checkpoints or else sparking a third world war.[37]

In the end, Khrushchev's gambit failed. The West was willing to negotiate, but it refused to give in to Soviet demands. The GDR had to settle for construction of the Berlin Wall, which ended the stream of refugees to the capitalist FRG and thus helped to shore up the GDR's borders and its economy. Khrushchev also decided not to conclude the separate peace treaty that he had promised the GDR. Several of Moscow's allies warned that they could not survive the West's planned response: an economic embargo against the entire Soviet bloc.[38]

It was partly in order to make good the resulting damage to the GDR and to the international prestige of the USSR that Khrushchev agreed to an East German proposal to conclude a bilateral friendship treaty in 1964. Such a treaty would underline Moscow's recognition of the GDR's sovereignty, along with its commitment to a two-state solution to the German problem. At the same time, the treaty would not infringe upon western interests in Berlin. In the treaty, the GDR agreed to recognize the separate status of West Berlin; previously, the GDR had hinted that West Berlin should eventually become part of the GDR.[39]

However, Khrushchev had other, ulterior motives for concluding the treaty with the GDR. On 11 June 1964, one day before its signing, he explained to East German leader Walter Ulbricht that the friendship treaty was 'not least of all a point of departure for his normalization campaign towards West Germany'.[40] After the Cuban Missile Crisis (1962) brought the world to the brink of a nuclear war, Khrushchev had begun to move towards a relaxation of tensions with the West. Contributing to his decision were Moscow's growing tensions with China. A turning point came in 1963 with Moscow's conclusion

---

[36] Meissner, *Ostpakt-System*, 18–19.

[37] John Lewis Gaddis, *We now Know* (Oxford: Clarendon Press, 1997), 129–31; Vladislav Zubok and Constantine Pleshakov, *Inside the Kremlin's Cold War* (Cambridge, MA: Harvard University Press, 1996), 197–8.

[38] Hope M. Harrison, *Driving the Soviets up the Wall* (Princeton, NJ: Princeton University Press, 2003), 221–2; Douglas Selvage, 'The End of the Berlin Crisis', *Cold War International History Project (CWIHP) Bulletin* 11 (1999), 220.

[39] Daniel Kosthorst, 'Sowjetische Geheimpolitik in Deutschland?', *Vierteljahrshefte für Zeitgeschichte* 44 (1996), 268.

[40] Ibid., 271.

of the Limited Test Ban Treaty with the US and Great Britain. One of Moscow's goals in concluding the treaty had been to increase international pressure on Beijing to abandon its nuclear bomb programme.

By this point, Khrushchev, it seems, was more worried about Beijing than Bonn. There were grounds for concern; China had publicly called into question its borders with the Soviet Union and had begun massing troops along them. To the chagrin of Gomułka, who—like Ulbricht—kept close watch for potential Soviet backsliding on the German question, Khrushchev seemed willing to take the next step and to conclude a nuclear non-proliferation treaty with the US that would not have explicitly banned West German 'access' to nuclear weapons through NATO's planned multilateral nuclear force (MLF). Privately, the Soviet leader began to speak more and more about the possibility of a 'new Rapallo' with the FRG. Both Ulbricht and Gomułka feared fundamental concessions. While the Soviet–East German friendship treaty awaited ratification by the Supreme Soviet, Alexei Adzhubei, Khrushchev's son-in-law and editor-in-chief of *Izvestiya*, visited West Germany in the summer of 1964. In private conversations, he hinted at potential Soviet concessions at Soviet and East German expense and even hinted that China's nuclear programme was of greater concern to Moscow than West German access to nuclear weapons—a confirmation of Gomułka's fears. Poland provided the Soviet Presidium with a transcript of Adzhubei's comments, and Khrushchev's opponents used it to help justify his removal from power in October 1964.[41]

BREZHNEV'S RECONSOLIDATION OF THE SOVIET ALLIANCE SYSTEM

Khrushchev's successor as CPSU General Secretary, Leonid Brezhnev, sought to reduce or eliminate the accumulated tensions in Moscow's relations with its allies and to reconsolidate the Soviet alliance system. The impending expiration and renewal of most of the friendship treaties in the mid- to late 1960s presented such an opportunity. Shortly after Brezhnev assumed power, the Supreme Soviet ratified the Soviet–East German friendship treaty, and within a year, the USSR signed a new friendship treaty with the People's Republic of Poland. Although the USSR did not explicitly recognize the Oder-Neisse line—Gomułka's desideratum since at least 1948—in its new treaty with Poland, it did proclaim its readiness to defend the border by name. Moscow's ratification of the two friendship treaties, along with its submission of a draft non-proliferation treaty to the UN that would ban alliance nuclear forces (and thus West German 'access' to nuclear weapons through NATO), suggested that the USSR had returned to its hard line on the German question of 1955 to 1963. That is, any normalization of relations with Bonn

---

[41] Douglas Selvage, 'The Warsaw Pact and Nuclear Nonproliferation, 1963–1965', *CWIHP Working Paper* 32 (2001), 2–12.

would require the FRG's recognition of the Oder-Neisse line, its recognition of the GDR, and its renunciation of access to nuclear weapons in any form.[42]

However, the Soviet bloc's relations with the FRG quickly became a matter of contention once again, and this affected, in turn, the evolution of the bloc's friendship-treaty system. The international constellation remained in place that had led Khrushchev to seek a rapprochement with the West—most importantly, Moscow's rift with China. Relations grew only worse after Mao launched the 'cultural revolution' in 1966, during which anti-Soviet proclamations and demonstrations reached fever pitch. The final straw came during the Vietnam war. 'Although the Sino–Soviet military alliance had been in dire straits for many years', Lorenz Lüthi writes, 'by 1966 it effectively died over diplomatic and military strategy in Vietnam'.[43] The death became official, though, only in 1979, when Beijing announced its intention not to renew its friendship treaty with Moscow.[44]

At the same time, the FRG began its first halting steps towards a new *Ostpolitik*. In 1966, Bonn offered to conclude renunciation-of-force agreements with the GDR's Warsaw Pact allies and to establish diplomatic relations with them. While Poland, Czechoslovakia, and the GDR responded with demands that the FRG recognize the status quo in Europe, the other Warsaw Pact states demonstrated an openness to improved relations.

It was against this backdrop that Ulbricht proposed to Brezhnev in the autumn of 1966 the GDR's further integration within the friendship-treaty system. In order to blunt Bonn's diplomatic offensive, he proposed that the GDR conclude friendship treaties with Poland and Czechoslovakia, along with other measures.[45] When Brezhnev raised Ulbricht's proposal with Gomułka, the Polish leader voiced support for the idea—indeed, he claimed it as his own. However, he offered two reservations. First, the treaties between Poland, Czechoslovakia, and the GDR, he said, should do more than provide bilateral support for the GDR. They should also serve, he said, to strengthen economic integration between the three states. The GDR's firm economic integration within the Soviet bloc, a longstanding demand of Gomułka, would help preserve Germany's division—for Gomułka, the key to communist Poland's security.[46]

Second, Gomułka also suspected that Moscow sought to create a situation in which the 'northern-tier' states of the Warsaw Pact—Poland, the GDR, and Czechoslovakia—would preserve a hard line against Bonn, and the 'southern-tier' states—Romania, Bulgaria and Hungary—could move ahead and normalize relations with the FRG for the sake of credits and increased trade. As the other communist states began to put out feelers to Bonn, Poland stalled its negotiations with the GDR over a friendship treaty. Gomułka insisted that Moscow compel the other Warsaw Pact states to accept three

[42] Ibid., 14; Michael J. Sodaro, *Moscow, Germany and the West* (Ithaca, NY: Cornell University Press, 1990), 67; Alexander Uschakow, 'Der erneuerte Bündnisvertrag zwischen der Sowjetunion und Polen vom 8. April 1965', *Osteuropa-Recht* 12 (1966), 299.

[43] Lüthi, *Sino-Soviet Split*, 338.

[44] See Soviet note, 5 June 1979, in Stiftung Archiv der Parteien und Massenorganisationen der ehemaligen DDR im Bundesarchiv (SAPMO BA), DY 30, J IV2/2.035-64 (Büro Axen), 17.

[45] Memorandum, Second Part, 10 September 1966, SAPMO BA, J IV 2/201-735.

[46] Paczkowski, *Tajne dokumenty 1956–1970*, 407, 418–21.

preconditions for diplomatic relations with Bonn: recognition of the existing borders, including the Oder-Neisse line; recognition of the GDR *de facto*; and Bonn's renunciation of access to nuclear weapons in any form.

Romania's establishment of diplomatic relations with Bonn on 31 January 1967, and Gomułka's dire warnings, finally led the Soviets to act. In February 1967, the foreign ministers of the Warsaw Pact states gathered in Warsaw, where Gomułka, with the backing of the Soviet Union and the GDR, succeeded in pushing through his three conditions for diplomatic relations between the remaining Warsaw Pact states and Bonn. The blunting of Bonn's diplomatic offensive opened the path for the conclusion of the friendship treaties between Poland, the GDR, and Czechoslovakia. The treaties, which stressed the states' respective demands vis-à-vis Bonn, were dubbed an 'iron triangle' in the West. The three states had allegedly joined together—successfully—to prevent any further normalization of relations between their allies and Bonn.[47]

In fact, the 'triangle' consisted of mere paper. The weakest link in the triangle was the CSSR. At the signing of Prague's new friendship treaty with the GDR on 17 March 1967, Czechoslovak communist leader Antonin Novotný publicly declared that it was not directed against any third state—that is, the FRG. Shortly thereafter, Prague renewed its contacts with the FRG, and although it did not establish diplomatic relations, it did agree to exchange trade missions with the FRG in August. As part of the agreement, Prague recognized that West Berlin was economically a part of the FRG. Ulbricht, denouncing Prague for allegedly breaking with the spirit of the Warsaw agreement, re-called the GDR's ambassador to Czechoslovakia.

Despite the East German leaders' gratitude to Gomułka for his success in blocking Bonn's diplomatic offensive, relations between the GDR and Poland quickly soured after the signing of their friendship treaty on 14 March 1967. In September, Ulbricht vetoed various economic agreements that the GDR had negotiated with Poland, along with language that simply spoke of a 'higher stage' of economic cooperation between the two states. Relations between Poland and the GDR, especially in the economic realm, would not improve significantly until 1972, after both Gomułka and Ulbricht had fallen from power.

THE BREZHNEV DOCTRINE OF LIMITED SOVEREIGNTY AND THE FRIENDSHIP-TREATY SYSTEM

The invasion of Czechoslovakia in 1968 by the states of the Warsaw Pact, except Romania, marked a watershed in Brezhnev's policy towards Moscow's allies. Some Western observers saw the 'iron triangle' at work—allegedly, the efforts of Novotný's successor,

---

[47] See, for example, Hutchings, *Soviet-East European Relations*, 33.

Alexander Dubček, to normalize relations with Bonn and perhaps even establish diplomatic relations led Ulbricht and Gomułka to push for the invasion. Indeed, both Gomułka and Ulbricht had been observing Prague's contacts with Bonn with growing concern, and both did push for military intervention. However, as noted above, the CSSR had not considered itself bound by an 'iron triangle' even under Novotný. Gomułka's main concern in the spring of 1968 was not Prague's relations with Bonn, but the real and potential 'spillover' of the 'Prague Spring' into Poland. More importantly, it was Moscow—not Warsaw and East Berlin—that ultimately decided on military intervention.

Despite the propaganda of the five invading Warsaw Pact states—Romania refused to participate—it was not West German 'infiltration' of the CSSR that sparked the decision to intervene. The real reason found expression in Brezhnev's speech to a plenum of the Polish Central Committee in November 1968. He began with a formal reaffirmation of the sovereignty of communist states, echoing the language of Moscow's friendship treaties with the socialist states. 'Socialist states', he declared, 'stand for strict respect for the sovereignty of all countries. We resolutely oppose interference in the affairs of any states and the violation of their sovereignty'. However, he quickly added:

> When external and internal forces hostile to socialism try to turn the development of a given socialist country in the direction of the restoration of the capitalist system, when a threat arises to the cause of socialism in that country...this is no longer merely a problem for that country's people, but a common problem, the concern of all socialist countries.

That is, the domestic sovereignty of the Soviet bloc states was limited; they could not engage in reforms that threatened the cause of 'socialism' as interpreted by Moscow. Western observers discerned in Brezhnev's speech, along with similar pronouncements from Moscow, a 'Brezhnev Doctrine'. Arguably, the Soviet leader merely reaffirmed the longstanding, open secret of the satellite states' limited sovereignty. He did, however, signal Moscow's intention to reassert communist orthodoxy under the guise of 'socialist internationalism' after years of relative neglect under Khrushchev.[48]

The limited sovereignty of Czechoslovakia found expression in a renewed friendship treaty with the USSR in the summer of 1970. The treaty constituted 'the most elaborate and ambitious statement of the Soviet interpretation of socialist internationalism' under Brezhnev. It spoke not only of the 'internationalist duty of the socialist countries' to defend their 'socialist gains', but also contained provisions to strengthen the 'unity and solidarity of all countries of the socialist commonwealth', to promote an 'international socialist division of labour', 'socialist economic integration', 'all-round cooperation', and a 'drawing together' of the Soviet bloc states. All subsequent friendship treaties between the Soviet bloc states, except with Romania, contained similar

---

[48] Matthew J. Ouimet, *Rise and Fall of the Brezhnev Doctrine in Soviet Foreign Policy* (Chapel Hill, NC: University of North Carolina Press, 2003), 67.

references.[49] The friendship treaties thus marked the reconsolidation of communist orthodoxy under Brezhnev.

The one exception to Brezhnevian orthodoxy—even as it maintained Stalinist orthodoxy at home—was the Socialist Republic of Romania. Having refused to participate in the invasion of Czechoslovakia in 1968, Romania also rejected the ideas of a 'socialist commonwealth' of states, socialist economic integration, and the Brezhnev Doctrine of limited sovereignty. This stance found expression in the renewed Soviet–Romanian friendship treaty of July 1970. The commitment to mutual defence applied only to external aggression; there was no talk of an 'internationalist duty' to 'defend socialist gains'—that is, a commitment to military intervention in the case of domestic 'counterrevolution'. Similarly, the Soviet–Romanian treaty spoke of economic cooperation, not 'socialist economic integration', and there was no talk of a 'drawing together' of the socialist countries. Rather than stressing the 'internationalist duties' of the socialist countries, the emphasis in the Soviet–Romanian treaty was on national rights: 'sovereignty and national independence, equality, and non-interference in…internal affairs'. Romania succeeded in placing similar clauses in its subsequent friendship treaties with the other Soviet bloc states.[50]

Some in the West hoped that a relaxation of tensions between East and West—the détente of the 1970s—would lead the Soviet Union to move gradually away from the Brezhnev Doctrine. The Soviet bloc states could then assert their sovereignty in a fashion similar to Romania or even Yugoslavia. Many in the West spoke of the ultimate 'Finlandization' of the Soviet bloc states—that is, that they might assume the status of Finland, a non-communist state with 'friendly' relations to Moscow.[51] In February 1948, Finland had concluded its own friendship treaty with the USSR in lieu of the formal military alliance that Stalin had been demanding.

Although Finland's friendship treaty with the USSR bore similarities to those of the Soviet bloc states, it contained significant differences. First, it provided for mutual consultations only in the event of an attack on Finland or on the USSR through Finland 'by Germany or any state allied with the latter'. Prior consultations or preventive military action were not part of the treaty. Second, the Finnish–Soviet treaty was valid for ten years, rather than twenty; however, it was subject to automatic renewal every five years unless either side renounced it. Third and most importantly, Moscow explicitly recognized 'Finland's desire to remain outside the conflicting interests of the Great Powers'— that is, Finland's neutrality. The treaty, including the provision recognizing Finland's neutrality, remained the basis for Finnish-Soviet relations until the Soviet Union's collapse in 1991.[52]

---

[49] Ibid., 162, 166.

[50] Ibid., 162–3.

[51] Jason Lavery, *History of Finland* (Westport, CT: Greenwood Press, 2006), 137–9. On 'Finlandization' see, for example, Douglas Selvage, 'Transforming the Soviet Sphere of Influence?', *Diplomatic History* 33:4 (2009), 683.

[52] Lavery, *History of Finland*, 137; Meissner, *Ostpakt-System*, 19.

Such hopes proved to be illusory, however. Finland had always represented an exception in Soviet policy; it had not made Stalin's list of countries to be included in the friendship-treaty system in October 1947.[53] The détente between East and West culminated in the Final Act of the Conference on Security and Cooperation in Europe at Helsinki in August 1975. The USSR interpreted the results of the conference, along with the treaties that they signed with the FRG as a result of Chancellor Willy Brandt's 'new Ostpolitik', as constituting recognition of its sphere of influence in East Central Europe. This also found expression in the friendship-treaty system.

In 1977, the GDR concluded a new round of friendship treaties with its allies that dropped any and all references to a potential unification of Germany and underlined the 'inviolability' and 'immutability' of the existing borders in Europe. The new treaties contained the same 'socialist commonwealth' clauses adopted in all the friendship treaties—except those with Romania—concluded after 1970.[54] The era of détente thus proved not to be the era of 'Finlandization' but of 'real existing socialism' as defined by the Soviet Union. It would remain so until a new and final wave of reform undertaken by Soviet General Secretary Mikhail S. Gorbachev, who renounced the Brezhnev Doctrine and condemned the Soviet bloc states to be free. The result was the end of communist rule in East Central Europe and the ultimate collapse of the Warsaw Pact, the Soviet sphere of influence, and the friendship-treaty system.

Summing up, the friendship treaties between the USSR and the states of East Central Europe served as the basic legal building blocks for the Soviet sphere of influence in East Central Europe from 1943 to 1991. For the most part, they played little role in structuring the policies of their signatories and the relations between them; they served merely to confirm the political status quo—most importantly, the East Central European states' subordination to the USSR—in part through a vigorous denial of such subordination. The friendship treaty with the greatest influence upon developments in East Central Europe, it turned out, was the Sino–Soviet Treaty of Friendship and Alliance. Its erosion and ultimate collapse helped pull national Stalinist Albania out of the Soviet orbit and provided the necessary preconditions for Romania's manoeuvrings within the Warsaw Pact. Romania's limited success in expanding its sovereignty found expression, in turn, in its final round of friendship treaties with its Soviet bloc allies.

The only state beneficiary of the Soviet bloc friendship-treaty system was the GDR, which successfully exploited its integration to underline its equality with the other communist states in the 1960s and to stress its international recognition in the 1970s. Otherwise, the system served merely to underline the limited sovereignty of the Soviet bloc states, whether in the original Stalinist formulation or in the less restrictive Brezhnevian synthesis of the 1970s. They also served, especially in the Stalinist era, to paper over exploitative bilateral arrangements to the USSR's benefit; the repressive activities of Soviet occupation forces, including Soviet intelligence services; and the more important tools of informal domination through local communist parties.

[53] *VEDRA*, Document No. 245.
[54] Hutchings, *Soviet-East European Relations*, 162–6.

FURTHER READING

Berend, Ivan T., *Central and Eastern Europe, 1944–1993: Detour from the Periphery to the Periphery* (Cambridge: Cambridge University Press, 1996).

Brzezinski, Zbigniew K., *Soviet Bloc: Unity and Conflict*, rev. and enlarged edn (Cambridge, MA: Harvard University Press, 1967).

Hutchings, Robert L., *Soviet-East European Relations: Consolidation and Conflict* (Madison, WI: University of Wisconsin Press, 1987).

Jian, Chen, *Mao's China and the Cold War* (Chapel Hill, NC: University of North Carolina Press, 2001).

Kosthorst, Daniel, 'Sowjetische Geheimpolitik in Deutschland? Chruschtschow und die Adschubej-Mission 1964', *Vierteljahrshefte für Zeitgeschichte* 44 (1996), 257–93.

Lavery, Jason, *History of Finland* (Westport, CT: Greenwood Press, 2006).

Lüthi, Lorenz M., *Sino-Soviet Split: Cold War in the Communist World* (Princeton, NJ: Princeton University Press, 2008).

Mastny, Vojtech, 'The Warsaw Pact as History', in Vojtech Mastny and Malcolm Byrne (eds), *A Cardboard Castle?* (Budapest: Central European University Press, 2005), 1–74.

Meissner, Boris (ed.), *Das Ostpakt-System* (Frankfurt/M: Alfred Metzner Verlag, 1955).

Ouimet, Matthew J., *The Rise and Fall of the Brezhnev Doctrine in Soviet Foreign Policy* (Chapel Hill, NC: University of North Carolina Press, 2003).

Selvage, Douglas, 'The Warsaw Pact and Nuclear Nonproliferation, 1963–1965', *Cold War International History Project Working Paper* 32 (2001).

Selvage, Douglas, 'Poland, the GDR, and the "Ulbricht Doctrine"', in M.B.B. Biskupski (ed.), *Ideology, Politics and Diplomacy in East Central Europe* (Rochester: University of Rochester Press, 2003), 227–41.

Selvage, Douglas, 'The Treaty of Warsaw: The Warsaw Pact Context', in David C. Geyer and Bernd Schaefer (eds), *Bulletin of the German Historical Institute, Supplement 1 (2003): American Détente and German Ostpolitik*, 67–79.

PART IV

RE-CONSTRUCTION: STARTING AFRESH OR REBUILDING THE OLD

CHAPTER 16

....

A CONTINENT BRISTLING WITH ARMS: CONTINUITY AND CHANGE IN WESTERN EUROPEAN SECURITY POLICIES AFTER THE SECOND WORLD WAR

....

LEOPOLDO NUTI

INTRODUCTION—IT'S A JUNGLE OUT THERE?

....

SINCE the end of the Second World War, Europe has known an unprecedented period of peace that has profoundly altered the political landscape of the continent. The role of military institutions in most European states has changed remarkably, losing the centrality it enjoyed for centuries. Yet at the same time for much of the post World War II era this peace has been accompanied by frightening preparations for a global nuclear war—in the 1960s NATO planned to deploy in Western Europe 7000 tactical atomic warheads of different yields—and by a number of recurrent crises which repeatedly threatened the stability of the postwar order. Nor should one neglect the fact that two European powers—France and Britain—still field respectively the third and fifth largest nuclear arsenals in the whole world. How should these two trends be reconciled, and what, if any, causal connections can be established between the two?

Has Europe really entered a post-Hobbesian, neo-Kantian world where war is forever banned, as claimed by Robert Kagan in a notorious essay published shortly before the bitter transatlantic dispute about the invasion of Iraq?[1] Have the Europeans learned from their experience in two world wars, as James Sheehan has argued, to relegate the military to the margins of their society because they 'hate going to war'?[2] This chapter will address the issue by canvassing the post World War II evolution of Western European defence and security policies, as well as by looking at the role of nuclear weapons in European security and at the shifting perceptions of war in European public opinion and mentality. It will hopefully demonstrate how the concept of a sharp postwar break with the past does not apply to the history of European security policies. Rather, the post-1945 period should be seen as one in which multiple narratives overlap following different timelines, and fragments of the old mentality coexist side by side with the new one.

THE FORMATIVE YEARS, 1945–55

In retrospect, the history of European security after the end of the Second World War seems to have followed a clear pattern. The Western European states—winners and losers alike—learnt from their previous mistakes and hastened to devise new formulas for cooperating and integrating, thereby merging their efforts and looking for a common solution to cope with the problems of the postwar era. So did the United States, whose policymaking elite tried to redress the errors committed after the First World War and searched for the best possible way to avoid a relapse into isolationism and to commit themselves firmly to the stabilization of Europe.

This straightforward narrative, however, needs some additional qualifications. First of all, if the common learning from previous mistakes certainly played a role in taming the virulent nationalism and militarism that had plunged Europe into two world wars in 30 years, as well as in pushing the Western European governments towards some form of cooperation, what really forced them to coalesce was the impending threat of a Soviet political hegemony over the continent, combined with sudden spurts of fear for an actual military invasion. Beginning from 1947, if not earlier, the increasing tensions of the Cold War revealed the stark realities of the imbalance of power in the heart of the continent and caused an unprecedented transformation in the way European security was perceived in the western half. Sometimes exaggerated, sometimes real, the perception of a Soviet menace provided the main impulse that forced Western Europeans to coordinate their security policies and above all to look for American help. The early steps of the construction of the new Europe, therefore, cannot be understood outside of the Cold War framework: before the Soviet threat started looming over the horizon, whatever impulses there were to promote European integration and cooperation achieved very limited results.

---

[1] Robert Kagan, 'Power and Weakness', *Policy Review* 113 (June–July 2002), 1–22.
[2] James Sheehan, *The Monopoly of Violence: Why Europeans Hate Going to War* (Boston, MA: Houghton Mifflin Company, 2007).

Second, there was little unanimity of intent in the West European capitals about what to do. Since its very beginning, as a matter of fact, the history of postwar European security was fraught with a number of ambiguities. If one were to judge from the ambitious declarations released by the High Contracting Parties at the time of the signature of the Brussels Treaty on 17 March 1948, the governments of Belgium, France, Great Britain, Luxembourg, and the Netherlands signed that treaty of mutual defence not just to set up an alliance, but to achieve nothing less than the unity and progressive integration of Europe. Behind these lofty statements, however, there was a remarkable difference of intentions among the signatories.[3] French Foreign Minister René Bidault, for instance, did not exclude the possibility that the Brussels treaty might provide a general framework for the efforts of European federalists to promote a truly integrated Europe. The British government, on the other hand, was much more reluctant to tie the difficult construction of a European security structure to a set of somewhat abstract theoretical speculations. As British Foreign Minister Ernest Bevin aptly summed up his government's point of view on 22 January 1948:

> It is easy enough to draw up a blueprint for a United Europe and to construct neat looking plans on paper. While I do not wish to discourage the work done by voluntary political organizations in advocating ambitious schemes of European unity, I must say that it is a much slower and harder job to carry out a practical programme which takes into account the realities which face us, and I am afraid that it will have to be done a step at the time.[4]

Nor did the differences among the Europeans stop there, as there were also some crucial divergences about the kind of relationship to be developed with the United States. There can be little doubt that by 1947–48 most Western European states were avidly looking to extract a US commitment to their defence, as Geir Lundestad has made clear with his thesis on an 'empire by invitation'.[5] And yet, even if the Truman administration did receive a steady stream of requests from across the Atlantic to step up and fill the strategic void that emerged in the heart of Europe after the war, there was no particular harmony of intention among the Europeans about the role the US should play. The French government seemed mostly interested in immediate military assistance for its armed forces and in an ironclad guarantee about an American intervention to protect France and the status quo in Europe from any return of hegemonic ambitions across the Rhine.[6]

---

[3] John Young, *Britain, France and the Unity of Europe, 1945–1951* (Leicster: Leicester University Press, 1984); Anne Deighton and Eric Rémacle (eds), *WEU, 1948–1998: From the Treaty of Brussels to the Treaty of Amsterdam*, (Brussels: Institut Royale des Relations Internationales, 1998).

[4] David Gowland and Arthur Turner, *Britain and European Integration 1945–1998: A Documentary History* (London: Routledge, 2000), 9.

[5] Geir Lundestad, 'Empire by Invitation? The United States and Western Europe, 1945–1952', *Journal of Peace Research* 23:3 (1986), 263–77.

[6] Pierre Guillen, 'France and the Defence of Western Europe: From the Brussels Pact (March 1948) to the Pleven Plan (October 1950)', in Norbert Wiggershaus and Theodore G. Forster (eds), *The Western Security Community, 1948–1950: Common Problems and Conflicting National Interests during the Foundation Phase of the North Atlantic Alliance* (Oxford: Berg, 1993).

The British, on the other hand, seemed to have nurtured a somewhat schizophrenic design, namely to lure the US into the defence of Europe to balance the Soviet hegemony—Ernest Bevin was supposed to have defined the Brussels pact as the bait to bring the US into Europe by calling it 'the sprat to catch a mackerel'—while at the same time using American assistance as a stop gap measure of limited duration to restore their depleted power, until they could be back on their feet and take the lead of a vaguely social-democratic Western European third force.[7]

Similar discrepancies can also be found among the other minor European powers that eventually entered the Atlantic pact: all welcomed the US guarantee, but with very different goals in mind. Norway for instance would have probably preferred a Scandinavian pact to an Atlantic one, if it had been compatible with some form of indirect American assistance;[8] while Italy would have been happier with the continuation of the low-profile military assistance it had received from the US since 1947, rather than having to face the domestic turmoil that would necessarily be unleashed by the parliamentary debate necessary to ratify any formal military commitment.[9]

The final outcome of the process through which Western Europe and the United States defined a common security framework, therefore, was influenced not only by the invitations extended to the US by the Europeans, but also, and above all, by American reactions. The Truman administration played a crucial role in shaping into a coherent design the uncoordinated cacophony of demands that came from across the Atlantic. While it cannot be denied that an invitation was issued, it should also be made clear that once it was accepted it was the guest, and not the hosts, who defined most of the rules and the basic pattern of the new transatlantic security system.

Thus the US quickly assumed the leadership of Western European security and defined its structure. Once the Atlantic Pact was signed on 4 April 1949, however, the process that shaped the transatlantic relationship turned out to be far more complex, in turn, than the US simply imposing its hegemonic will and corralling the requests of its unruly European partners into a rational framework. When the Truman and Eisenhower administrations pushed on with their attempt to structure the new-born Atlantic institution into an efficient military machine, they ran into a number of puzzling contradictions. In September 1950, shortly after the outbreak of the Korean War, the Truman administration tabled its demand for an increase in Europe's contribution to the costs of conventional armaments, only to discover that its own partners by and large preferred the US to foot the bill for any major rearmament effort. By mid-1952, it was already clear that the major NATO conventional rearmament conceived in Washington was running

---

[7] Geoffrey Warner, John Kent, and John Young are among the historians who have stressed the 'Third Force' dimension of Bevin's foreign policy: see a general discussion in Oliver Daddow, *Britain and Europe since 1945: Historiographical Perspectives on Integration* (Manchester: Manchester University Press, 2004), 125–33.

[8] Helge Pharo, 'The Cold War in Norwegian and International Historical Research', *Scandinavian Journal of History* 10:3 (1985), 163–89.

[9] Leopoldo Nuti, *L' esercito italiano nel secondo dopoguerra, 1945–1950. La sua ricostruzione e l'assistenza militare alleata* (Rome: Ufficio storico SME, 1989).

to a standstill, and that there were clear limits as to what the Western Europeans were willing to pay for their own defence.

Nor was it any easier to persuade the Allies to follow what in Washington seemed the only logical course if one was to strengthen Western defence in order to deter any possible Soviet aggression in the heart of Europe. When the Truman administration proposed to rearm West Germany, the suggestion ran up against strong French opposition, even after first Truman, and later Eisenhower explicitly gave their full support to the idea that such rearmament should be safely ensconced in the protective framework of a European community, which might help to emasculate any possible German nationalist or militarist impulses.

It is impossible here to retell the full story of the failed attempt to build a European Defence Community, with all its twists and turns.[10] Suffice it to say that a number of European statesmen, including President Eisenhower and his Secretary of State, John Foster Dulles, had come to believe that a Federalist solution would not only solve the riddle of German rearmament but also create the basis for building a political Europe. Such a solution, in turn, would provide the best antidote to any further Soviet attempt to expand its influence across the continent and therefore would ease the American commitment to prop up European security. Once such a Europe was built, Eisenhower said, the US could 'sit back and relax somewhat'.[11] But it was not to be, as the proposal to permit German rearmament and the creation of a European Defence Community (EDC) within a European Political Community was simply too much for many Europeans to stomach—with France leading the way to its final rebuttal in August 1954.

The consequences of the setback were paramount for the definition of a European security identity. First of all, the failure of the EDC had a dramatic impact on the process of European integration, steering it away from political and security issues and reorienting it towards the economic dimension it would retain as its main field for almost another forty years. A second consequence, moreover, was the growing marginalization of Europe inside the Atlantic alliance, as the failure to build up a reliable and partly independent European pillar within the alliance meant that European security would have to rely more and more on the American guarantee. In short, the failure of the EDC entailed the relegation of Western Europe to the role of junior partner inside the transatlantic security system.

This marginalization of Europe was further compounded by the parallel evolution of American strategy. Reluctant to shoulder the whole burden of the huge conventional rearmament conceived in the aftermath of the Korean invasion, the US increasingly relied on its nuclear build-up to protect its security and that of its allies. When the Eisenhower administration formally adopted the theory of massive retaliation, it also

---

[10]   Michael Creswell and Marc Trachtenberg, 'France and the German Question, 1945–1955', *Journal of Cold War Studies* 5:3 (2003), 5–28; see also the comments by Charles Cogan, Mark S. Sheetz and William I. Hitchcock in the same issue.

[11]   267th Meeting of the National Security Council, 21 November 1955, in *Foreign Relations of the United States, 1955–1957*, vol. IV, *Western European Security and Integration*, 348–9.

made the entire defence of the West dependent on the credibility of its nuclear threat as the best way to prevent possible Soviet aggression. As Marc Trachtenberg has convincingly argued, however, for Eisenhower the adoption of a strategy centred on the nuclear threat was also predicated on the successful construction of the EDC: both had been conceived for the purpose of reducing the American burden in the defence of Europe, while somehow rebalancing the structure of the Atlantic alliance.[12]

The failure of the EDC, however, left only the US nuclear threat as the main guarantee of European security, thereby making it the central pillar in the architecture of transatlantic defence for the whole time of the Cold War. Nor did the subsequent creation of the Western European Union (WEU) in October 1954 really modify the pattern of the growing marginalization of Europe inside the Atlantic alliance. The birth of the WEU did certainly solve the problem of providing for German rearmament, thereby preventing it from becoming a serious threat to Western European stability. It did not, however, make any other substantial contribution to the shaping of an effective European security system. The WEU remained all along a secondary institution providing at best a conveniently inconspicuous forum for confidential consultation among the Western Europeans in times of crisis.

To sum up, by the mid-1950s European security had defined those basic features that would remain more or less constant until the end of the Cold War.[13] While by the late 1940s it had become clear that the US would play a large role in the definition of Western European security, the final shape of the transatlantic relationship was not entirely spelled out until 1954–55, when a number of alternative solutions—conventional rearmament, a Federated Europe—had been tried out and failed. The fact that European security came to rely more and more on the threat to use American nuclear weapons, however, had some unexpected consequences for European identity. In the following years, Western Europeans came to enjoy a pattern of defence and security which was relatively inexpensive from the economic point of view and enabled them to concentrate a large part of their resources on their own economic growth, even if this entailed making their security largely dependent on an external guarantor. On the other hand the US, albeit at a very heavy economic cost, remained the central element of Western European security. The European emphasis on integration in the economic field, therefore, was partly the unintended consequence of a series of failures to achieve more ambitious goals as well as of the dialectical process between Europe and the US.

A second important consequence of this security arrangement was its inherent instability, as it was based on a wasting asset, namely American technological superiority in the nuclear field, which sooner or later was bound to be matched by the Soviet Union. While the threat of nuclear annihilation to keep the Soviets in check might have retained

---

[12] Marc Trachtenberg, *A Constructed Peace: The Making of the European Settlement, 1945–1963* (Princeton, NJ: Princeton University Press, 1999).

[13] Anne Deighton, 'The European Security and Defence Policy', in Joseph H. H. Weiler, Iain Begg and John Peterson, *Integration in an Expanding European Union. Reassessing the Fundamentals* (London: Blackwell, 2003), 274–5.

some credibility as long as the US enjoyed a straightforward superiority, it quickly lost it as the USSR built up its own nuclear arsenal. The security of Western Europe, therefore, came to rest essentially on the very precarious willingness of the US to risk a nuclear holocaust in order to protect its allies or, as some observers caustically defined it, on a bluff. No wonder that the central element of this strategy—control of the American nuclear arsenal—became the main bone of contention between Washington and its allies.[14]

Nevertheless, what is important to stress here is that the arrangement lasted, in spite of all its drawbacks and precariousness. It did so because it satisfied a large number of exigencies all at once: the American nuclear guarantee allowed the Europeans to concentrate on their domestic growth, ensured a certain degree of protection against the Soviet Union, and it also made sure that West Germany's amazing economic and political recovery would remain safely ensconced in a European framework supervised by the US.

REVERSING THE TREND?

This fragile balance was repeatedly called into question by both sides, but the failures of the repeated attempts to change it confirm the remarkable stability of the compromise. The US tried time and again to persuade the Western Europeans to step up their defence budgets and strengthen NATO's conventional forces. Burden sharing, as it was first conceived by the Kennedy administration in the early 1960s, would serve many purposes at once: (1) it would raise the threshold of the need to resort to nuclear weapons, by giving NATO the alternative of being capable of fighting a prolonged conventional war, rather than plunging straight ahead into a full-blown nuclear confrontation at the first sign of a Soviet move; (2) it would relieve the US economy of the pressure of supporting Western European security by making the Europeans pay for a larger share of their own defence; and (3) it would also conveniently reduce the strain on the dollar as well as the gap in the US balance of payments if the Western Europeans could be persuaded to purchase American-made conventional armaments.[15]

In order to achieve these goals, a number of agreements were eventually reached by the Kennedy and Johnson administration through the so-called offset negotiations, but they did not modify to any substantial extent the informal division of labour worked out in the first half of the 1950s. By the late 1970s, therefore, US President James Carter tried once again to persuade his recalcitrant NATO allies to raise their defence expenditures to 3 per cent of their national GDP in order to give some credibility to the Alliance's conventional forces. His efforts, however, met the same fate as those of his predecessors.

---

[14] David N. Schwartz, *NATO's Nuclear Dilemmas* (Washington, DC: Brookings Institution, 1983).

[15] Hubert Zimmermann, *Money and Security: Troops, Monetary Policy, and West Germany's Relations with the United States and Britain, 1950–1971* (Cambridge: Cambridge University Press, 2002), 97–143.

Western Europe security remained largely dependent on the US nuclear guarantee for most of the Cold War.

Nor were the European attempts to stake out a more independent position any more successful in redressing the inequalities inside the Alliance. At least as early as 1961 the French President, Charles de Gaulle, began to envisage a possible framework for closer Western European political cooperation that would reformulate the basic tenets of the security and defence policies of its participants.[16] Under the so-called Fouchet plan, de Gaulle twice tried to foster a project which would reduce Europe's strategic dependence on the United States, eventually replacing the American nuclear guarantee—which de Gaulle regarded as no longer credible after the Soviets had achieved strategic parity with the Americans—with closer Western European cooperation in the security and defence fields. De Gaulle's initiatives, however, were repeatedly thwarted by the reluctance of his possible partners to trade the American guarantee, questionable as it may have been, with an even more questionable French one. By the mid-1960s, the frustrated French president would be forced to resize his ambitions and limit his goals to sabotage any attempt at strengthening the existing European and transatlantic structures, rather than trying to replace them with those of his own design. Eventually, his main achievement was the withdrawal in March 1966 of France from the Atlantic Alliance's integrated military structure. After de Gaulle's resignation in 1969, any further attempt to build an autonomous European pillar inside the alliance—let alone a truly independent Western European defence system—remained somewhat dormant for the rest of the Cold War, a *sotto voce* theme running through the history of the alliance without ever fully materializing in a concrete project.

EMPIRES, DECOLONIZATION AND NUCLEAR ISSUES

No description of the evolution of the postwar Western European security policies would be complete without mentioning the end of the colonial empires and the military nuclear programmes of the main Western European states. Both issues seem to follow a different timeline from the establishment of the security arrangement described in the previous paragraph, as they do not show any major break with the past but a remarkable continuity, at least until the mid-1960s. Both reveal a strong attachment to a national, rather than collective—let alone European—vision of security, as well as the persistence of an inclination to use force, if necessary, to safeguard the national interest. Finally, an analysis of these issues sheds an additional light on the complex web of relations between

---

[16] Frédéric Bozo, *Two Strategies for Europe: De Gaulle, the United States, and the Atlantic Alliance* (Lanham, MD: Rowman and Littlefield, 2001); Maurice Vaïsse, *La grandeur: politique étrangère du général de Gaulle, 1958–1969* (Paris: Fayard, 1998).

Western Europe and the United States, as it shows the incapacity to achieve a satisfactory level of transatlantic coordination in both fields.

The literature on the decolonization of the two major European empires, the British and the French, usually underlines the difference between the two processes, comparing the bloody conflicts fought by the French with the relatively smoother British process of adaption to new realities. What concern us here, however, are not the differences but the similarities in the attitudes of both countries. Both Paris and London attached remarkable importance to their imperial possessions and above all they both displayed a willingness to use force—sometimes discreetly and sometimes not—to retain their control. Britain may have avoided the bloodbaths of Indochina and Algeria, thereby sparing its domestic political system all the dramatic consequences these disasters had on French political stability; nevertheless, it fought its own fair share of colonial conflicts, from the Mau-Mau rebellion in Kenya to the communist insurgency in Malaya, ending up with the anti-Indonesian confrontation in the mid-1960s. All these campaigns clearly point to continuities with the longstanding British tradition of imperial small wars fought in far-flung territories and show the persistence of a security mindset which, although *also* affected by the perception of the Soviet threat, cannot be framed exclusively in Cold War terms.

The wars of French decolonization reveal a similar, if not stronger, attachment to imperial possessions and a willingness to use military force to retain their control that lasted well into the early 1960s. Far from gracefully accepting that colonial rule was now an artefact of the past, France devoted a large portion of its armed forces to extra-European duties, since the Empire was perceived as crucial to the recovery of the great power status lost in the summer of 1940. The paradoxical result of the bitter struggle in Indochina, however, was to make France even more dependent on American assistance, both in Europe and in the colonies, as the conflict ended up being subsidized almost entirely by the US. It was only after de Gaulle accepted the loss of Algeria that the French government rethought its strategic outlook and reshaped its armed forces accordingly.

Nor was the attachment to the colonies an exclusively Franco–British prerogative. The Dutch government was ready to go to war to retain control of Indonesia, and even the defeated Italians tried as hard as they could to hold on to whatever fragments of their ramshackle empire the Allies might be willing to leave them. Deprived by the peace treaty of most of its colonies, the Italian government carried on long negotiations to retain at least some of them, and it was only in 1949, after all its efforts failed, that Italy discovered anti-colonialism as a new tool for its foreign policy.

While the Dutch and the Italians solved their colonial legacies early on, in both the British and the French cases the turning point of their colonial history does not seem to coincide with the major watershed in their security policies represented by the Atlantic Pact and the shaping of the transatlantic security bargain described in the previous section. While the Suez crisis in 1956 might have been the tocsin of the end of the imperial era, France and Britain continued to use force to protect their areas of influence well into the 1960s. For France, the turning point might have been the 1962 Evian agreements that gave Algeria its hard-won independence, while for Britain the last major colonial military effort was probably the *confrontasj* against Indonesia ending in 1966. The Wilson government's decision to drop its commitments 'East of Suez' between 1967 and 1971 was really the turning point in British imperial history, even if the implementation of that decision was in itself a long drawn out affair. Nor should the 1960s be regarded as the time of a clear-cut conclusion of both countries' inclination to use force in their former spheres of influence and colonial possessions, as can be clearly seen by the French Foreign Legion's repeated engagements in Africa—such as Operation Manta against Libya in the early 1980s—or the British war against Argentina for retaining control of the Falkland Islands in 1982.

It is also important to emphasize how these legacies of their colonial past affected the Western Europeans' relations with the United States, as they show a different picture from the one described in the previous section. While the US and Western Europe succeeded in working out a precarious arrangement for the defence of Europe, they failed to strike a similar agreement for the rest of the world. In spite of some halting attempts to do so, and of some sporadic and troublesome episodes of cooperation, the disastrous impact and bitter legacies of such events as the French defeat at Dien Bien Phu in 1954 and the joint Anglo–French debacle at Suez two years later clearly testify to the difficulties of extending the transatlantic security arrangement outside of Europe. The result of these failures was that NATO remained focused on the protection of Western Europe rather than becoming the global western alliance that some of its founders had envisaged, and that 'out-of-area' issues remained largely a matter of national concern with little or no coordination among the Allies. A decade later, the US war in Vietnam would dramatically confirm it.

The strong attachment of most Western European governments to their imperial pasts must be seen in parallel with the interest they displayed towards nuclear weapons. A quick survey of the main European military nuclear programmes reveals several common features, namely the difficulty in establishing a mutually satisfactory arrangement with the United States and the persistence of a strong, nationally-oriented, security mindset. Great Britain and France had already started their nuclear programmes before the war, and Britain in particular had played a significant role in the development of the Manhattan project. When the Truman administration adopted the McMahon Act in 1946 and terminated wartime nuclear collaboration with the British, the Labour government led by Clement Attlee did not hesitate to launch its plan for an independent nuclear arsenal. Whether foreign secretary Bevin really declared, 'We've got to have this thing over here, whatever it costs... we've got to have the bloody Union Jack flying on top of it', or, more prosaically, 'we could not afford to acquiesce in an American monopoly of this new development' he was undoubtedly aware of the political implications of the new weapon.[17] Thus Britain started its own programme in 1947, tested its first nuclear bomb in 1952, and its first H-bomb in 1957. British defence planners also played a significant

---

[17] Ian Clark, *Nuclear Diplomacy and the Special Relationship: Britain's Deterrent and America, 1957–1962* (Oxford: Clarendon Press, 1994), 24.

role in elaborating the conceptual basis of deterrence theory in the early 1950s with the 1952 Defence White Paper.

The British nuclear programme was conceived to bolster the UK's status as an independent player on the world stage, but also to persuade the US to resume the wartime collaboration. Recent research in this field shows the deep attachment of most British postwar governments to their independent programme as a symbol of the nation's independence and great power status, *and* to the fruits of their atomic collaboration with the US, which was eventually resumed after the US modified the McMahon Act.[18]

The French case has a similar multifaceted dimension, but its historical development has gone through different phases. While De Gaulle is reported to have expressed his understanding of the political implications of nuclear weapons as early as 1944,[19] and an atomic energy commission (CEA) was created shortly after the end of the war, in the early aftermath of the war nuclear research in France did not have an exclusively military focus and there was no clear plan to build a bomb. Then in December 1954 the Mendes–France cabinet adopted a formal decision to start planning for a French atomic weapon. That the decision was made shortly after the conclusion of the negotiations for the formation of the WEU and the rearmament of West Germany clearly shows the implicit rationale behind the French government's thinking. A French nuclear bomb was meant above all to keep France a step ahead of Germany in the political and military realm, in order to perpetually freeze the balance of power between the two countries. At the same time, at least during the mid-1950s, a French bomb was also conceived as the main tool to participate in the decision-making process of NATO strategy. It was, in other words, still an Atlantic bomb, particularly if the US was willing to share its nuclear secrets with its allies. If, on the other hand, Washington was not willing to cooperate, France might support a European nuclear weapon as long as it would allow it to retain the leadership of any nuclear effort in continental Europe. In 1957–58, in fact, the Gaillard government sponsored the idea of a Franco–Italian–German consortium to produce modern weapons, including nuclear ones.[20]

With the passing of time, however, this possible multilateralization of the French nuclear programme became increasingly difficult to reconcile with 'the imperatives of national sovereignty'.[21] Eventually it was abandoned with the return to power of de Gaulle, who conceived a French bomb as the ultimate guarantee of the country's more independent attitude in international relations. The *force de frappe* quickly became the cornerstone of De Gaulle's project for the transformation of his country's foreign policy,

---

[18] Ken Young, 'A Most Special Relationship: The Origins of Anglo-American Nuclear Strike Planning', *Journal of Cold War Studies* 9:2 (2007), 5–31.

[19] Bertrand Goldschmidt, *Les rivalités atomiques, 1939–1966* (Paris: Fayard, 1967), 87–9.

[20] Georges-Henri Soutou, *L' alliance uncertaine. Les rapports politico-stratégiques franco-allemands, 1954–1996* (Paris: Fayard, 1996), 55–121; Leopoldo Nuti, *La sfida nucleare. La politica estera italiana e le armi atomiche* (Bologna: Il Mulino, 2007), 131–69.

[21] Jean Delmas, 'Military Power in France, 1954–1958', in Ennio Di Nolfo (ed.) *Power in Europe? Vol. II, Great Britain, France, Germany and Italy and the Origins of the EEC, 1952–1957* (Berlin: De Gruyter, 1992), 238–53.

and in the following years it acquired a symbolic status which went beyond the military and strategic value attributed to it by French nuclear strategists.

The losers of World War II shared with the winners a similar perception of nuclear weapons as ultimate status symbols. The main difference between France and Britain on the one hand, and West Germany and Italy on the other, was that the winners openly launched into their military nuclear programmes while the losers seem to have been reluctant to engage in a national effort, concentrating their energies and aspirations on achieving nuclear status through a multilateral approach. Both countries were among the staunchest supporters of NATO's nuclear sharing projects in the late 1950s and the early 1960s, and both were among the strongest opponents of the Non-Proliferation Treaty exactly because they saw it as a reversal of the previous American attitude to allow its European allies to have a 'finger on the nuclear trigger'. While expressed differently from France and Britain's, therefore, the attitude of the West German and Italian policy-makers reveals the same attention to the political implications of military force, and in particular of nuclear power, as the ultimate element in defining the hierarchy among the major powers of the postwar international system.[22]

A New Mentality?

When combined with reliance on the US as the key guarantor of European security, these aspirations to achieve nuclear status or to retain as many fragments as possible of the old empires provide a complex picture of the role of military force in the postwar mentality of the Western Europeans. Clearly many pieces of the traditional mindset coexisted side by side with the new elements forced upon the Europeans by the realities of the Cold War. This precarious balance between old and new had begun to shift conspicuously by the 1960s, when a number of factors noticeably changed the perception of war and military force throughout Western European societies.

A first major alteration was the gradual achievement of strategic parity by the Soviet Union, which called into question the validity of the American nuclear guarantee. This forced the US to search for some sort of accommodation with the USSR, particularly after the Berlin and Cuban crises between 1958 and 1962 demonstrated the dangers of a full-blown nuclear confrontation between the two superpowers. As the Kennedy and Johnson administrations moved from an antagonistic stance towards some form of engagement with Moscow, it became clear that eventually this would entail the acceptance of the European status quo and the division of Germany. In turn, for Western Europe this meant the necessity to start looking for some additional, or alternative, instruments to provide its own security.

[22] Catherine Kelleher, *Germany and the Politics of Nuclear Weapons* (New York: Columbia University Press, 1975); Nuti, *La sfida nucleare*.

On the one hand, betting the survival of one's country on American willingness to risk a nuclear holocaust raised the stakes of a game that many in Europe seemed reluctant to keep playing; on the other, the Europeans felt the need to start looking to the Soviet Union for some sort of direct accommodation, rather than relying exclusively on whatever bilateral arrangement might be reached by the superpowers. The beginning of détente, in other words, weakened the transatlantic security arrangements that had been established in the previous decade; and even if they eventually survived, they lost part of the political significance they had previously acquired. A purely military concept of security, relying on the use of an unthinkable force, began to look increasingly outdated.

Another crucial role in altering the Western European consideration of war was played by the growing US involvement in Vietnam. While it may be too much to infer that the war in Indochina opened a cultural divide about the use of force between Western Europe and the United States (after all, the war caused an even harsher cultural confrontation inside American society), there is no doubt that with the passing of time the images of the conflict pushed many Europeans to call into question the pattern of security provided by the Cold War and loosened the transatlantic bond that had been forged in the early post war years. Besides, the protest against the war was not only one of the causes of the rebellious outbursts that took place all over Western Europe around 1968, but it also acted as one of the catalysts for a generational rebellion that had its roots in the domestic problems of each Western European country. Wilfried Mausbach for instance has convincingly argued that in the case of West Germany the protest was the ultimate result of the quest of a new generation to come to terms with unsolved issues of the recent German past.[23]

Revulsion against the Vietnam war also affected the image of the United States as an increasingly irresponsible leader of the West. By 1970, 49 per cent of the French population doubted the capacity of the Americans to act wisely over international issues, and 39 per cent of them thought the US was a more serious threat to peace than the Soviet Union (25 per cent), albeit less than Communist China.[24] The CIA itself wrote a perceptive description of the impact of the war as far as 'respect for US leadership was concerned':

> Especially in Europe, something has been lost which will take time to recover; because of the widespread belief, even among those who support us, that the US has blundered and refuses to recognize its blunder, the US will have greater difficulties in procuring support for its policies... A longer lasting damage to US influence would come from disillusionment, especially among European intellectuals and

[23] Wilfried Mausbach, 'Auschwitz and Vietnam: West German Protest against America's War during the 1960s', in Andreas W. Daum, Lloyd C. Gardner and Wilfried Mausbach (eds), *America, the Vietnam War and the World: Comparative and International Perspective* (Cambridge: Cambridge University Press, 2003).

[24] Jacques Rupnik and Muriel Humbertjean, 'Images of the United States in Public Opinion', in Denise Lacorne, Jacques Rupnik and Marie-France Toinet (eds), *The Rise and Fall of Anti-Americanism: A Century of French Perception* (London: Macmillan, 1990).

youth, with US morality...Rightly or wrongly, it has been highly critical of both [the bombing and the correctness of the US intervention], and this will plague us for many years to come.[25]

To quote the CIA once again, the war probably 'accelerated the process' of the decline of US influence in Western Europe. The changing of the European attitude towards military security, therefore, was not a direct, immediate result of the war, but a slow, gradual consequence of a chain of events. The negative impact of Vietnam on European public opinion coincided with the coming of age of the new generation of baby boomers and with the economic downturn of the late 1960s, as well as with an overall effort to redesign the international system according to a different pattern from that of the Cold War. While the American military commitment in Vietnam grew, the whole structure of the transatlantic association was as a matter of fact undergoing a serious redefinition that affected in depth the nature of the relationship between Washington and its allies, reinforcing their fears of a downsizing of their importance for US foreign policy. The combination of all these different factors was bound to have a profound impact on the way Western Europeans perceived their own security and defence policies.

THE LAST YEARS OF THE COLD WAR

By the early 1970s the first signs of shifting attitudes in Western Europe became more perceptible during the negotiations for the Conference on Security and Cooperation in Europe (CSCE). Requested by the USSR as an additional multilateral instrument to confirm the political status quo in Europe, the conference was approached by Washington and by the European allies from different perspectives. While Nixon and Kissinger regarded it as a minor episode on the main road to a détente which they both conceived as strictly regulated by the superpowers, for Western European diplomats involved in its negotiations the CSCE was perceived as an opportunity to practise a different kind of diplomacy which downsized the importance of military factors and emphasized cultural exchanges and the protection of human rights as new dimensions of international relations.

The Third Basket of the Helsinki Act which in August 1975 concluded the CSCE negotiations, therefore, was seen as the first step in a new, distinctively European approach to the conduct of diplomacy and was regarded at the time as a possible alternative to the militarized confrontation of the previous years. It might be too much to infer that it was a result of the cultural transformation engineered by the turmoil of the late 1960s and by the revulsion inspired by the Vietnam war, but it was definitely a contribution that reflected the search for envisaging new patterns of European security.

---

[25] CIA , *The Vietnam Situation: An Analysis and Estimate*, ch. XIV, *Implications of the Vietnam War for the US international Position*, 23 May 1967, pp. 5–6, in Declassified Documents Research System (DDRS), 1989, f. 196, doc. 3235.

In the following years, however, Europe wavered between new and old approaches. To begin with, there were repeated contrasts with the US on how to implement the protection of human rights in Eastern Europe; after 1977 it was the Carter administration, and not the Western Europeans, who advocated a serious campaign to defend those rights across the Iron Curtain. Having finally accepted détente with all its pros and cons, the Europeans seem to have been quite reluctant to jeopardize its fruits in order to challenge the repressive regimes of the Soviet bloc.

At the same time, however, the Western Europeans were not ready to discard entirely their traditional security policies established over the past thirty years: on the contrary, by the mid-1970s a number of Western European statesmen had voiced their concerns about the possible consequences for Europe if the military balance of power between the blocs was not preserved. In particular, the German Chancellor, Helmut Schmidt, clearly displayed his personal unease about the consequences of the strategic parity between the superpowers, as sanctioned by such bilateral agreements as those defined by the Strategic Arms Limitation Talks—SALT I, and the first draft of the SALT II—which set a ceiling for the number of strategic nuclear weapons each side could field. That parity, Schmidt argued in a famous speech at the IISS in London in October 1977, was to be enforced also at the so-called sub-strategic, or theatre, level (weapons with a range in excess of 500km), and the Soviet Union should be persuaded to reduce its conventional and theatre nuclear forces. Otherwise failure to do so would seriously affect the European balance of power, with the gravest consequences for the future of détente itself and the stability of the continent.

These concerns eventually led NATO to adopt a plan for the modernization of its own theatre nuclear forces in order to match the new Soviet ones. In December 1979, the North Atlantic Council decided that if the Soviet Union would not halt the deployment of its new missiles and withdraw at least some of them, NATO would field a new generation of nuclear weapons in Western Europe.[26]

The dual track decision opened up a new major crisis that almost entirely spanned the following decade. With such flashpoints as the Soviet invasion of Afghanistan (1979) and the coup in Poland (1981) in the background, there was an escalation of tension that reached a climax in 1983, the year when negotiations with the Soviet Union were stalled and the deployment of the new NATO weapons was implemented. It was one of the most dangerous years of the whole Cold War and in the last months of the year there were a number of dangerous accidents which generated a veritable 'war scare' in the Soviet bloc.

This last major military confrontation in the history of the Cold War provides yet another example of the complexities of European security. The NATO decision in itself was the result of a protracted transatlantic debate about the best possible modernization of the alliance's nuclear arsenal and it was reached only after a major flop in 1978 had prevented NATO from enforcing a somewhat similar project, the deployment of the so-called neutron bomb (technically, the Enhanced-Radiation Weapon, or ERW). It was

---

[26] Leopoldo Nuti, 'The Origins of the 1979 Dual Track Decision: A Survey', in Leopoldo Nuti (ed.), *The Crisis of Détente in Europe: From Helsinki to Gorbachev, 1975–1985* (London: Routledge, 2009), 57–71.

also conceived in such a way as to leave open the door to negotiations with the USSR that would make the deployment unnecessary—hence the name 'dual track decision'—in order to make it more palatable to a European public opinion, which had grown accustomed to the climate of détente and was quite reluctant to return to the harsh confrontations of the past.

As a matter of fact, the decision was hotly contested by European public opinion and the early 1980s saw the emergence of a new generation of pacifist movements, shaped by the experiences of the 1960s and opposition to the Vietnam war and heavily influenced by the mentality of the New Left, that filled the streets of Western Europe with hundreds of thousand of people. By the late 1970s, according to data provided by Lawrence Wittner, in most NATO countries the majority of the population opposed the deployment of the new weapons, even if they did not call into question the existence of NATO itself.[27] If there ever was a time during the Cold War when a peaceful European identity came to the fore, this was it. This swelling pacifist movement, however, did not affect the decision-making process in Western European countries, as the missiles were eventually deployed by the end of 1983, revealing the existence of a major gap between the governments' perceptions of security and that of their publics' opinions, which lasted almost until the end of the Cold War.

Conclusions

Tempting as it may be to see the emergence of a clear pattern, it seems difficult to frame the whole postwar period as a single entity in which Western Europe progressively abandoned its traditional military approaches to security and gradually adopted a new set of rules of behaviour. It seems more fitting to describe the post-1945 era as a time when a number of unprecedented innovations drastically altered the way European statesmen and citizens alike used to think of their national defence and security policies, at the same time leaving in place some of the old habits.

The first major break with the past was certainly represented by the arrival of the US on the European scene, as it pushed Europeans towards a limited multilateralization of their security policies. Clearly this implied a certain downsizing of the importance of the domestic military institutions, whose role now became less relevant for their countries' security than in the past. By the mid-1950s the new transatlantic arrangement had by and large succeeded in setting up a system which combined elements of collective security and mutual defence. Yet it did not entirely replace the century-old mentality of unilaterally preserving and enhancing a country's own status and security in the international system, be it through the retention of the old colonial empires or by developing national nuclear arsenals.

[27] Lawrence Wittner, *Toward Nuclear Abolition: A History of the World Nuclear Disarmament Movement 1971 to Present* (Stanford, CA: Stanford University Press, 2003), vol. 3, 64–71, 149.

Thus the narrative of a straightforward transformation of the concept of security from the national to the multilateral level must be integrated and corrected with the plain fact that the Western European governments continued for most of the postwar era—and even up to today—to frame their security policies through the prism of national interests. Nor should the emergence of a strong pacifist inclination in European societies be confused with the actual political choices of their governments, even if since the 1970s it is possible to detect in the foreign policies of many Western European states clear signs of the search for alternative security patterns that emphasize political and economic dimensions over the military one.

Far from emerging from the Cold War with a distinct security identity, Western Europe throughout the long confrontation with the Soviet bloc featured a mixed bag of different, and sometimes contradictory, experiences and approaches—multilateral and national, traditional and innovative—which left a much more complex legacy than the peace-loving Europe scorned by Kagan or praised by its admirers.

FURTHER READING

Clark, Ian, *Nuclear Diplomacy and the Special Relationship: Britain's Deterrent and America, 1957–1962* (Oxford: Clarendon Press, 1994).

Deighton, Anne and Eric Rémacle (eds), *WEU, 1948–1998: From the Treaty of Brussels to the Treaty of Amsterdam* (Brussels: Institut Royale des Relations Internationales, 1998).

Gosha, Christopher and Maurice Vaïsse (eds), *La guerre du Vietnam et l'Europe, 1963–1973* (Brussels: Bruylant, 2003).

Heuser, Beatrice, *Nuclear Mentalities? Strategies and Beliefs in Britain, France and the Federal Republic of Germany* (London: St. Martin's Press, 1998).

Kaplan, Lawrence S., *The Long Entanglement: The United States and NATO after Fifty Years* (New York: Greenwood, 1999).

Lundestad, Geir, *The United States and Western Europe since 1945. From 'Empire by Invitation' to Transatlantic Drift* (Oxford: Oxford University Press, 2005).

Nuti, Leopoldo (ed.), *The Crisis of Detente in Europe: From Helsinki to Gorbachev, 1975–1985* (London: Routledge, 2009).

Schwartz, David N., *NATO's Nuclear Dilemmas* (Washington, DC: Brookings Institution, 1983).

Sheehan, James, *The Monopoly of Violence: Why Europeans Hate Going to War* (Boston, MA: Houghton Mifflin, 2007).

Soutou, Georges-Henri, *L' alliance uncertaine. Les rapports politico-stratégiques franco-allemands, 1954–1996* (Paris: Fayard, 1996).

Trachtenberg, Marc, *A Constructed Peace: The Making of the European Settlement, 1945–1963* (Princeton, NJ: Princeton University Press, 1999).

Wenger, Andreas, Vojtech Mastny and Christian Nuenlist (eds), *Origins of the European Security System: The Helsinki Process Revisited, 1965–75* (London: Routledge, 2008).

CHAPTER 17

'*LES TRENTE GLORIEUSES*': FROM THE MARSHALL PLAN TO THE OIL CRISIS

NICHOLAS CRAFTS AND GIANNI TONIOLO

THE French economist Jean Fourastié called them '*les trente glorieuses*'. The Germans and the Italians, bewildered by their winning the peace after losing the war, coined the words *Wirtschaftswunder* and *miracolo economico*. No matter how the thirty-odd years after the end of the Second World War were characterized by Europe's various cultures, they stand out as the period of most rapid economic growth in the Continent's history. After losing ground for about a century to the United States, Europe vigorously caught up with the productivity leader, while at the same time managing to reduce the gap between the richest and the poorest European countries. In retrospect, the years between the late 1940s and the early 1970s are seen as a Golden Age, when the foundations of future prosperity were established on firm ground.

This chapter assesses the most relevant features of Europe's extraordinary growth during the 'glorious thirty', and tries to explain why, after all, there was nothing 'miraculous' about them. In doing so it takes a broad perspective of Europe as a single region within the world economy, although divided into two areas by an 'iron curtain'.

'*LES TRENTE GLORIEUSES*': FACTS TO BE EXPLAINED

After a surprisingly rapid reconstruction, Western Europe's real GDP per head of population grew about twice as fast as the secular rate.[1] Eastern Europe enjoyed the most rapid economic growth in the history of planned economies for a comparable length of time.

---

[1] Nicholas Crafts, 'The Golden Age of Economic Growth in Western Europe, 1950–1973', *Review of Economic History* 47:3 (1995), 429.

Between 1950 and 1973, the real per person GDP of Western Europe (29 countries) increased at an annualized rate of 4.1 per cent, against a secular (1870–1998) growth rate of 1.7 per cent, outperforming all other world regions except Asia.[2] The performance of the centrally planned Eastern European countries (3.8 per cent per annum) was not much below that of the capitalist western side of the continent. The Soviet Union grew at a yearly average rate of about 3.4 per cent (see Table 17.1).

Table 17.1 Levels and Rates of Growth of Real GDP/Person in European Countries ($1990GK and average % per year)

	1950	1973	1950–1973
Switzerland	9064	18,204	3.08
Denmark	6943	13,945	3.08
UK	6939	12,025	2.42
Sweden	6739	12,494	3.06
Netherlands	5971	13,081	3.45
Belgium	5462	12,170	3.54
Norway	5430	11,324	3.24
France	5271	13,114	4.04
West Germany	4281	13,153	5.02
Finland	4253	11,085	4.25
Austria	3706	11,235	4.94
Italy	3502	10,634	4.95
Czechoslovakia	3501	7041	3.08
Ireland	3453	6867	3.03
USSR	2841	6059	3.29
Hungary	2480	5596	3.60
Poland	2447	5340	3.45
Spain	2189	7661	5.60
East Germany	2102	5753	4.47
Portugal	2086	7063	5.45
Greece	1915	7655	6.21
Bulgaria	1651	5284	5.19
Yugoslavia	1551	4361	4.59
Romania	1182	3477	4.79
Albania	1001	2273	3.62
United States	9561	16,689	2.45

Sources: Groningen Growth and Development Centre (GGDC) (2007), Total Economy Database at http:// www.ggdc.net/databases/ted.htm; for West Germany, Statistiches Bundesamt Deutschland (2007), Volkswirtschaftliche Gesamtrechnungen der Lander VGR d L: Bruttoinlandsprodukt 1991 bis 2007 at http://www.vgrdl.de/Arbeitskreis_VGR/tbls/tab.01.asp.

[2] Between 1950 and 1973, the following annual growth rates were realized: Japan 8.05 per cent, other Asia 4.09 per cent, Western offshoots (USA, Canada, Australia, and New Zealand) 2.44 per cent, World 2.93. Angus Maddison, *The World Economy: A Millennial Perspective* (Paris: OECD, 2001).

The relative dynamics of these growth rates implies that, for the first time since the beginning of 'modern economic growth', Europe managed to catch up with the United States, the productivity leader.[3] In 1950 the 572 million Europeans (including those living in the Soviet Union) enjoyed a per person GDP that was only one-third that of the United States, in real terms roughly similar to today's Latin America. By the end of the Golden Age, a larger population (720 million) enjoyed an income per person 2.3 times higher than twenty-three years earlier and about one-half that of the United States. Western Europe's GDP *per caput*, in 1950 less than one-half the United States, reduced the gap markedly and, by 1973, stood at almost 70 per cent of the United States' level (see Table 17.2).

Growth was not uniform across countries. A remarkable convergence process took place whereby countries with low initial income levels grew faster than average.[4] With few exceptions (notably Ireland) initially poorer western countries grew faster than the more developed ones. Some centrally planned eastern economies (Bulgaria, Yugoslavia, and Romania) grew faster than some of the more 'advanced' market economies, even though their convergence was on average less satisfactory than in the case of low-income capitalist economies (so that this period in Eastern Europe's economic history is sometimes described as a Silver Age). Overall, the income gap between Eastern and Western Europe widened by about three percentage points, slowing down but not reversing a divergence trend that had been in place since the nineteenth century.[5] At the end of the 'Silver Age' in 1973, all centrally planned countries except Czechoslovakia were poorer

Table 17.2 Relative levels Real GDP/Person (US = 100) and Growth Rates of (average % per year)

	Western Europe	Eastern Europe	Russia/USSR		Western Europe	Eastern Europe	Russia/USSR	USA
1820	95.9	54.5	54.7					
1870	80.2	38.5	38.6	1820–1870	0.98	0.63	0.63	1.34
1913	65.3	32.0	28.0	1870–1913	1.33	1.39	1.07	1.82
1950	47.9	22.1	29.7	1913–1950	0.78	0.60	1.76	1.61
1973	68.5	29.9	36.3	1950–1973	4.06	3.81	3.35	2.45
2005	67.5	23.5	20.8	1973–2005	1.86	1.14	0.14	1.91

Sources: Groningen Growth and Development Centre (GGDC) (2007), *Total Economy Database* at http://www.ggdc.net/databases/ted.htm; A. Maddison (2006), *Historical Statistics of the World Economy, 1-2005 AD* at http://www.ggdc.net/Maddison/oriindex.htm.

[3] Simon Kuznets, *Modern Economic Growth: Rate, Structure and Spread* (New Haven, CT: Yale University Press, 1966).

[4] A process known by economists as β-convergence. Nicholas Crafts and Gianni Toniolo, 'Postwar Growth: An Overview', in Nicholas Crafts and Gianni Toniolo (eds), *Economic Growth in Europe since 1945* (Cambridge: Cambridge University Press, 1996), 4–7.

[5] In 1950 GDP per capita of Eastern Europe (excluding the Soviet Union) stood at 46 per cent of Western Europe; it fell to 43 per cent twenty-three years later.

than Ireland, then the poorest country in Western Europe. The USSR was always a long way below the United States in terms of real GDP per person and managed to realize only a limited catch-up process (from about 28 per cent in 1913, to 30 per cent in 1950, and 36 per cent in 1973).

In Western Europe, the rate of growth of output per hour worked was even more spectacular than that of GDP per person, because of a decline in the average number of hours worked per capita and per worker, which also contributed to welfare gains. Convergence with the US in product per hour worked was therefore faster than in GDP per capita. Thus for instance in 1950, an hour worked in Italy produced on average only 38 per cent of an hour worked in the United States; the ratio jumped to 74 per cent by the end of the Golden Age. Reliable data on output per hour worked in Eastern Europe are not available but estimates for the whole of the Soviet Union (1958–73) point to an annual growth rate of only 2.8 per cent compared to 7.1 per cent and 5.5 per cent per annum in Italy and West Germany respectively. This implies, as we shall see, different sources of GDP growth in centrally planned and market economies.

If the number of hours worked over the year by each worker decreased, total employment rose. Immediate postwar unemployment was rapidly reduced: by the early 1960s, full employment prevailed throughout the western part of the continent, in many countries for the first time in history.[6]

Relevant welfare indicators such as life expectancy at birth and infant mortality also improved throughout the Continent (Table 17.3) with initially less well performing countries, particularly in the East, catching up with the advanced north-west.

Taking into account increases in life and leisure time enjoyed by the average European during the Golden Age, we estimate the growth rate of an 'augmented GDP per person' by imputing a value of time and leisure.[7] The results of the exercise (Table 17.4) show considerably higher welfare gains from life expectancy and leisure in Western Europe than either the USA or the USSR.

Welfare growth was also inclusive, in that its benefits spread to an increasingly large number of people.[8] If a common pattern in postwar income distribution cannot be easily detected, Scandinavia, France, and Germany, as well as Eastern European countries, show a trend towards a more egalitarian distribution of incomes up to the end of the 1970s.[9] The trend was favoured by both fiscal policies (direct taxes became more

---

[6] By definition, full employment is attained in centrally planned economies but it is impossible to measure the extent of disguised unemployment.

[7] We use a version of the method proposed by Dan Usher, *The Measurement of Economic Growth* (Oxford: Blackwell, 1980), which is set out in full in Nicholas Crafts, 'The Human Development Index and Changes in Standards of Living: Some Historical Comparisons', *European Review of Economic History* 1 (1997), 299–322.

[8] Income distribution statistics are fraught with problems. In particular, international comparisons of such measures as the level of Gini coefficients should be taken with caution.

[9] See Anthony Atkinson, *The Changing Distribution of Earnings in OECD Countries* (Oxford: Oxford University Press, 2008), 53–67; Andrew Leigh, 'How Closely Do Top Income Shares Track Other Measures of Inequality?', *Economic Journal* 117 (2007), 619–33.

Table 17.3 Life Expectancy at Birth and Infant mortality (deaths per 1000 in the first year of life)

	1950	1973	1950	1973
Austria	65.7	70.5	66	24
Belgium	67.5	71.4	53	18
Denmark	71.0	73.6	31	12
Finland	66.3	70.7	44	11
France	66.5	72.4	52	15
(W) Germany	67.5	70.6	55	23
Greece	65.9	72.3	35	24
Ireland	66.9	71.3	46	18
Italy	66.0	72.1	64	26
Netherlands	72.1	74.0	25	12
Norway	72.7	74.4	28	12
Portugal	59.3	68.0	94	45
Spain	63.9	72.9	64	20
Sweden	71.8	74.7	21	10
Switzerland	69.2	73.8	31	13
UK	69.2	72.0	30	17
Albania	55.2	67.7	124	n.a
Bulgaria	64.1	71.2	95	26
Czechoslovakia	65.9	70.0	78	21
East Germany	67.0	71.2	72	16
Hungary	63.9	69.9	86	34
Poland	61.3	70.4	108	28
Romania	61.1	69.0	117	38
Yugoslavia	58.1	68.4	119	44
United States	69.0	71.3		
Russia/USSR	64.1	68.6	81	26

Sources: N. Crafts, 'The Human Development Index and Changes in Standards of Living: Some Historical Comparisons', *European Review of Economic History* 1 (1997), 299–322; United Nations, *Demographic Yearbook* (New York: UN, 1957); United Nations, *World Population Prospects* (New York: UN, 1988); B.R. Mitchell, *International Historical Statistics: Europe 1750–1993*, 4th edn (Basingstoke: Macmillan, 1998).

progressive) and social transfers (government spending in social security, health, and education).[10] The comprehensive structure of social protection that goes under the name of the welfare state is one of the main features of this period, and, as we shall see below, authors such as Eichengreen also see it as part of a triangular deal (government–firms–trade unions) for consensus building on long-term productivity growth.

Rapid growth entailed rapid structural change. Since the share of total output or total labour force in agriculture is negatively correlated with GDP per person, only 5 per cent,

---

[10] For an excellent comparative survey see Peter H. Lindert, *Growing Public: Social Spending and Economic Growth since the Eighteenth Century* (Cambridge: Cambridge University Press, 2005).

Table 17.4 Growth Rates of Augmented GDP/Person: Western European
Countries, United States and USSR (% per year), 1950–1973

	GDP/Person	Leisure	Longevity	Augmented GDP/P
Austria	4.94	0.71	0.43	6.08
Belgium	3.54	0.87	0.35	4.76
Denmark	3.08	0.52	0.23	3.83
Finland	4.25	0.32	0.40	4.97
France	4.04	0.76	0.53	5.33
West Germany	5.02	0.59	0.28	5.89
Greece	6.21	0.14	0.58	6.93
Ireland	3.03	1.05	0.40	4.48
Italy	4.95	0.13	0.55	5.63
Netherlands	3.45	0.66	0.17	4.28
Norway	3.24	0.68	0.15	4.07
Portugal	5.45	0.78	0.78	7.01
Spain	5.60	0.24	0.81	6.65
Sweden	3.06	0.74	0.26	4.06
Switzerland	3.08	0.25	0.41	3.74
UK	2.42	0.31	0.25	2.98
United States	2.45	0.08	0.21	2.74
Western Europe	4.12	0.46	0.43	5.01
USSR	3.35	0.09	0.40	3.84

Source: Authors' own calculations.

8 per cent, and 12 per cent of GDP was produced by the so-called primary sector respectively in Great Britain, Belgium, and West Germany c.1950. The share of value added of agriculture over GDP was somewhat higher in France (15 per cent), Austria (17 per cent), Czechoslovakia (18 per cent), and Denmark (21 per cent). In the least developed southern and eastern economies, agriculture still made up a large part of the economy (around 25 per cent in Spain and 30 per cent in Greece, Hungary, Italy, Portugal, Yugoslavia, Bulgaria, and over 35 per cent in Poland). By the early 1970s, the contribution of agriculture to GDP in the former countries had been dramatically reduced to about 8 per cent in Italy, 10 per cent in Spain, and 17 per cent in Greece and Hungary.

This process underscores the massive reallocation of resources, notably labour, from lower to higher productivity sectors (mainly manufacturing) that took place during the Golden Age. Perhaps the most impressive case of all is that of Italy, whose agricultural sector shed 61 per cent of its labour force, or over five million workers. But other national cases are similar: 4.3 million workers (58 per cent of the initial labour force) left the French countryside, so deeply rooted in national politics and culture. In West Germany, the exodus involved 51 per cent of the workforce (2.1 million), and in Spain forty-three per cent (2.3 million). Even in the United Kingdom, where the number of agricultural workers had been relatively low since at least the eighteenth century, the Golden Age was characterized by a reduction of 35 per cent of the agricultural labour force.[11] It is difficult to overstate the social, cultural, and political implications of such a rapid transfer of so many people from country to town; they are discussed in other chapters of this book.

Macroeconomic stability stands out among the main features of the Golden Age. Cyclical fluctuations were mild—no European country experienced a decline in GDP between 1950 and 1970. No episodes are recorded of systemic financial crises, even when currency crises occurred. In most countries price inflation was somewhat higher than in the 1990s and 2000s but it nevertheless remained stable at relatively low levels until the late 1960s.

EXPLANATIONS OF THE GOLDEN AGE

As for other defining moments in economic history, such as the Industrial Revolution and the Great Depression, research on the causes of the Golden Age never cease—scholars continue to discuss and disagree. Nonetheless, a longer term perspective and the emergence of more comprehensive theories allows for increasing explanatory convergence.[12]

A satisfactory explanation of the Golden Age should answer the following three questions: (1) What explains the Golden Age? That is, why did the whole of Europe rapidly catch up with the productivity leader in the thirty-odd years after the Second World War rather than before or afterwards? (2) Why did the Golden Age come to an end? (3) What accounts for relative success and failure of individual countries or regions during the Golden Age?

Western Europe had endured two world wars and the interwar depression, a period sometimes referred to as the Second Thirty Years War, which affected its economy much more severely than that of the United States.[13] In 1950 many countries' incomes were well below the levels predicted by a continuation of pre-1914 trends. Peace, cooperation, recovery from depression, and the correction of policy errors such as the disastrous protectionism of the interwar period had the potential to deliver a phase of rapid growth.

---

[11] Data are from Brian R. Mitchell, *International Historical Statistics: Europe 1750–1993*, 4th edn (Basingstoke: Macmillan, 1998).

[12] For recent reviews of the contemporary explanations of the Golden Age, see Crafts, 'The Golden Age of Economic Growth in Western Europe, 1950–1973', in Crafts and Toniolo (eds), *Economic Growth in Europe* (Cambridge and New York: Cambridge University Press, 1996) 1–37; Gianni Toniolo, 'Europe's Golden Age, 1950–73: Speculations from a Long-Run Perspective', *Economic History Review* 51 (1998), 252–67; Peter Temin, 'The Golden Age of European Growth: A Review Essay', *European Review of Economic History* 1 (1997), 127–49.

[13] Charles H. Feinstein, Peter Temin and Gianni Toniolo, *The World Economy between the World Wars* (Oxford: Oxford University Press, 2008); Peter Temin, 'The Golden Age of European Growth Reconsidered', *European Review of Economic History* 6 (2002), 3–22.

The architects of the second postwar settlement did not repeat the mistakes made at Versailles. Better institutions and cooperative international policies promoted many of the conditions that augmented growth by enhancing 'social capability' and 'technological congruence', at a time when American technology became more appropriate in a European context.[14]

The relative importance of these factors varied over time, as is revealed by cross-country comparative analysis.[15] In the 1950s, countries with greater potential for postwar reconstruction (e.g. West Germany) grew faster than others. Both in the 1950s and early 1960s, countries with large agricultural sectors (e.g. Italy) performed relatively well by transferring resources from low- to high-productivity sectors. After 1965, shifts in capital-to-labour ratios and technology gaps took centre stage in engineering growth.[16]

Slowly but steadily, trade liberalization and movement towards multilateral payments and currency convertibility raised income levels not only by promoting more efficient resource allocation but also by enhancing technology transfer, competition, and the realization of both internal and external economies of scale. Technology transfer played a relevant role in helping Europe to reduce the technology gap with the United States.[17]

Improvements in resource allocation play an important role in explaining the Golden Age. Rapid productivity advance in agriculture was predicated on the transfer of surplus labour from small-scale family farms to manufacturing occupations.[18] Broadberry showed that structural change strongly increased labour productivity growth with a major impact in Italy and Spain and a quite considerable one in France and West Germany.[19]

[14] Moses Abramovitz and Paul David, 'Convergence and Delayed Catch-Up: Productivity Leadership and the Waning of American Exceptionalism', in Ralph Landau, Timothy Taylor and Gavin Wright (eds), *The Mosaic of Economic Growth* (Stanford, CA: Stanford University Press, 1996), 21–62.

[15] Temin, 'The Golden Age of European Growth Reconsidered'.

[16] Terrence C. Mills and Nicholas Crafts, 'After the Golden Age: A Long-Run Perspective on Growth Rates that Speeded up, Slowed down and still Differ', *The Manchester School* 68:1 (2000), 68–91.

[17] In the postwar European conditions, American technology was particularly cost-effective. Richard Nelson and Gavin Wright highlight the codification of technological knowledge and the enhancement in European technological competence based on growing investments in human capital and research and development in 'The Rise and Fall of American Technological Leadership: The Postwar Era in Historical Perspective', *Journal of Economic Literature* 30 (1992), 1931–64. Bart Verspagen provides some quantitative evidence of the importance of improvements in European technological competence in promoting catch-up in 'Technology Indicators and Economic Growth in the European Area: Some Empirical Evidence', in Bart van Ark and Nicholas Crafts (eds), *Quantitative Aspects of Post War European Economic Growth* (Cambridge: Cambridge University Press, 1996), 215–43. See also Jakob B. Madsen, 'Technology Spillover through Trade and TFP Convergence: 135 Years of Evidence for the OECD Countries', *Journal of International Economics* 72 (2007), 464–80.

[18] Charles Kindleberger, *Europe's Postwar Growth: The Role of Labor Supply* (Princeton, NJ: Princeton University Press, 1967).

[19] Steven N. Broadberry, 'How Did the United States and Germany Overtake Britain? A Sectoral Analysis of Comparative Productivity Levels, 1870–1990', *Journal of Economic History* 58 (1998), 375–407.

A striking hypothesis to explain enhanced social capability in postwar Western Europe has been advanced by Eichengreen. He argued that the high investment rates which allowed for the successful exploitation of opportunities to catch up were facilitated by social contracts that sustained wage moderation by workers in return for high investment by firms.[20] In Eichengreen's view, high postwar investment rates were possible if both capitalists and workers agreed to defer part of current compensation (dividends and wages) in return for future gains. Such an agreement is difficult to sustain given the sequence of the required commitments: if liquidity is needed for new investments then workers must exercise moderation *now* in order for capitalists to invest *later*. Once wage restraint is obtained, however, capitalists are better off reneging on their agreement to invest and paying out dividends instead. Some form of social contract therefore needs to take place between the two social groups to overcome the dynamic inconsistency problem, rendering both groups better off.

Eichengreen argues that several of the social and economic institutions that emerged in most European countries after the Second World War can be thought of as mechanisms to enforce this agreement. European postwar labour market institutions derived, with more or less substantial adjustments, from those developed earlier, particularly during the 1930s when most democratic countries came to share 'with fascism a concern for building strong organisations and for finding new organisational forms that were neither free-market nor state-socialist'.[21] In the immediate postwar years it seemed, for a moment, that the whole of Europe would converge on a model of industrial relations based on 'tight tripartite co-operation'.[22] If labour market institutions in individual countries developed along somehow different lines, a widespread conviction remained, both to the right and to the left of the political spectrum, that labour market regulation was desirable.

The forms of such regulation differed from country to country, but everywhere wage moderation was one of its main objectives. In Scandinavia, Austria, and Switzerland there was a tightening of the web that bound governments and unions together. In Belgium and the Netherlands 'the government was much more of an active partner in forcing the social partners into forms of co-operation'.[23] In the early 1950s, the newly-born Federal Republic of Germany gave workers the right to elect one-third of their company's supervisory board as well as work councils that were legally bound to cooperative relations with the employers. In all of the above-mentioned cases, labour market institutions had their roots in pre-war developments. They all aimed at introducing explicit or implicit pacts between labour and capital, sometimes labelled as co-determination, where the government acted as a more or less visible broker.

---

[20] Barry Eichengreen, *The European Economy since 1945: Coordinated Capitalism and Beyond* (Princeton, NJ: Princeton University Press, 2007).

[21] Colin Crouch, *Industrial Relations and European State Traditions* (Oxford: Oxford University Press, 1992), 155.

[22] Ibid., 177.

[23] Ibid., 179.

France and Italy are the outliers in this pattern. No official institutions were created to manage a bargaining structure based on co-determination. In practice, however, even in these more confrontational systems the government acted as broker between workers and employers' organizations, sustaining wage moderation.[24] French governments continued in their pre-war practice of exercising tight ministerial controls over wages and working conditions. Both in France and in Italy, direct government intervention in wage setting by nationalized companies operating in the technologically advanced sectors provided guidance and moderation to private-sector industrial relations. As for small business, informal agreements were set in motion at local community level whereby job security was traded for wage moderation. The existence of a large supply of labour and, particularly in Italy, the moderation of the communist-led trade unions contributed to the result.

Not every Western European country tried or succeeded in implementing the corporatist recipe. This was notably the case in the United Kingdom and Ireland which, possibly also for this reason, grew more slowly than their scope for catch-up might have allowed.

Wage moderation per se is likely to have been an important element for the initial kick-off of rapid growth and for its long-term sustainability, and coordinated (rather than centralized) wage bargaining had a significant positive effect on both investment and growth before 1975 (but not afterwards).[25]

To sum up: rapid growth in the Golden Age was partly based on opportunities to recover from earlier adverse shocks and policy errors. Changes in labour market institutions and incentive structures were crucial in enhancing Europe's social capability for growth, allowing both capital-to-labour ratios and productivity gaps with the United States to be substantially reduced.

GROWTH IN EASTERN SOCIALIST ECONOMIES

Throughout the period covered in this chapter, Europe was divided along the lines—soon nicknamed the Iron Curtain—broadly drawn at a Crimean sea resort in February 1945. The division of Europe was not only political and military but also economic. Central planning of the economy, first introduced in the Soviet Union in 1928, was exported to Eastern European countries occupied by the Red Army. The state directed every productive activity as if the economy were a gigantic mega-company, setting prices, imposing investment and production targets, reallocating resources among sectors and between investment and consumption. In other words, 'producers had no

---

[24] Toniolo, 'Europe's Golden Age'.
[25] Gilmore Oisin, *Corporatism and Growth Since 1945: Testing the Eichengreen Hypothesis*, MSc Thesis, University of Warwick, 2009, supervised by N. Crafts.

connection whatsoever with the market and were totally dependent on central orders regarding the assortment, technological parameter, and quality of their product'.[26]

Needless to say, this simple characterization of a centrally planned economy overlooks both its evolution and the specific features it assumed in individual countries, particularly those where, over time, cracks surfaced in the system and the political and economic debate focused on what reforms were feasible without changing the main tenets of a socialist economy. After breaking with Stalin in 1948, Yugoslavia introduced a system whereby firms were largely independent of central government, and operated under a management elected by workers' council (a system similar to western-type cooperatives). With the passing of time, more rapidly after a new wave of reforms set in from 1965 onward, prices were progressively liberalized, as was, to a certain extent, foreign trade. The Yugoslav system looked attractive to neighbouring socialist countries. After the 1956 revolution, the Hungarian government opened a season of prudent reforms which slowly introduced a measure of price flexibility and allowed some room to private initiative. Poland changed its agricultural policy, somehow improving the incentive structure. In the 1960s, Czechoslovakia tried to experiment with rather radical economic reforms which inevitably gave rise to demands for political reforms as well, prompting a crushing intervention by Moscow in 1968.

Over the Silver Age, the various eastern countries slowly came to develop their own idiosyncratic forms of socialist economies which, in the extreme case of Yugoslavia, radically differed from Soviet Russia's blueprint.[27] These differences, together with the specific features of the pre-war economies and societies, of factor endowment and geography go a long way in explaining the relative performance of individual countries in catching up with the more advanced west. Unfortunately, no recent comprehensive comparative economic assessment of Eastern Europe's Silver Age has yet appeared.

Data on Table 17.1 broadly reflect the current consensus on Soviet Russia's and Eastern Europe's growth during the Silver Age. Consensus was not easy to reach—statistical compilations were rife with problems of definition, data availability, ideological prejudices, and political manipulation. In the 1950s serious western scholars feared that Russia's industrial output might soon overtake that of the United States, and data were possibly inflated by US official agencies to stress the need for investment in space and military technology. It was only in the second part of the 1980s that *glasnost* finally prevailed.[28] In the past two decades, as Soviet archives were opened to the public, a new generation of western scholars was able to make credible estimates of Soviet growth.

---

[26] Ivan Berend, *An Economic History of Twentieth-Century Europe* (Cambridge and New York: Cambridge University Press, 2006), 159.

[27] See Ivan Berend, *Central and Eastern Europe, 1944–1993: Detour from the Periphery to the Periphery* (Cambridge: Cambridge University Press, 1996); Berend, *An Economic History*; and Eichengreen, *The European Economy*.

[28] For a review of the technical and informational problems faced by western researchers on the Soviet economy, see Gur Ofer, 'Soviet Economic Growth 1928–1985', *Journal of Economic Literature* 25 (1987), 1767–833. For a discussion of the reliability of current estimates of Soviet national income, see Appendix A in Robert C. Allen, *Farm to Factory* (Princeton, NJ: Princeton University Press, 2003).

Their aggregate assessment is summarized in Table 17.1, which shows that the thirty-odd years following the end of the war witnessed a period of unprecedented growth in Eastern Europe.

Driven by a robust increase in private and public consumption, welfare gains accrued to all strata of society. Socialism introduced generalized free education and health care and forms of social security in societies hitherto unaccustomed to such universal benefits. Full employment, if at low wages, was achieved for the first time in history. It is a small wonder that these policies initially created a consensus for the new regimes. As noted by Eichengreen, 'The Prague Spring of 1968 may have featured wide-ranging discussions of economic reform, but it was rank-and-file workers who were least willing to contemplate radical reform.'[29]

The Soviet Union also grew rapidly from 1928 to the early 1970s. Peacetime output growth might have been higher during the pre-war period and slightly 'less impressive during the post-war period.'[30] On the other hand, private consumption—a better indicator of welfare than GDP—grew faster between 1950 and 1973 (3.8 per cent per annum) than before the war (2.9 per cent per annum in 1928–40).[31]

A long-run assessment of the performance of centrally planned economies must take into account the catch-up factor, as their starting income level in 1945–50 was lower than that of most Western European countries. Allen maintains that from 1928 to 1970, the Soviet Union 'exceeded the catch-up regression', doing better than all other large countries but Japan.[32] On the other hand, the catch-up performance of most Eastern European countries in the Golden Age does not 'compare favourably to that of low income western countries such as Austria, Italy, Spain and Greece but also with West Germany and France'.[33] Nevertheless, up to the 1970s, communist Europe's growth was exceptionally high by the region's historical standards. Given the geographical and cultural proximity of the two halves of the Continent and the time coincidence of rapid growth despite such different economic institutions, one cannot rule out the hypothesis that common factors might explain high growth both east and west of the Iron Curtain.

Allen argued rather persuasively that, beginning with the 1928 Five Years Plan, 'a rise in the investment rate caused rapid growth [in the Soviet Union] as surplus labour was put to work. By the 1950s, structural unemployment was eliminated and growth slowed as capital accumulation ran into diminishing returns.'[34] However, signs of a serious

[29] Eichengreen, *The European Economy*, 161.

[30] Ofer, 'Soviet Economic Growth', 1777; Allen, *Farm to Factory*.

[31] Laurie R. Kurtzweg, *Measures of Soviet Gross National Product in 1982 Prices: A Study Prepared for the Use of the Joint Economic Committee, Congress of the United States* (Washington, DC: US GPO, 1990), 89–91.

[32] Allen, *Farm to Factory*, 6–7, 216–17.

[33] Nicholas Crafts and Gianni Toniolo, 'Aggregate Growth 1950–2005', in S. Broadberry and K. O'Rourke (eds), *The Cambridge Economic History of Modern Europe* (Cambridge: Cambridge University Press, 2010), vol. 2, 296–332.

[34] Allen, *Farm to Factory*, 192.

retardation in productivity growth slowdown did not appear until the 1970s.[35] Investment continued to generate growth as long as surplus labour in low-productivity agriculture could be drawn to industry. 'The era of high-speed growth ended, however, when surplus labour was exhausted. Thereafter capital accumulation failed to generate growth.'[36] A similar explanation was used by Kindleberger to account for rapid growth in the least developed Western European countries. More generally, we have seen that resource allocation underpinned by structural change plays a relevant role in explaining postwar growth.

However, while total factor productivity (TFP)[37] growth takes a central place in explaining Western Europe's Golden Age, the 'model' of Soviet and Eastern European growth was largely based on high investment/GDP rates. Relatively low TFP growth in the East was not the result of inadequate volumes of investment in human capital and research; by the 1970s, the latter was high by world standards, at around 3 per cent of GDP. Rather, the problem stemmed from incentives to innovation at the firm level. This can be viewed as a case of 'social capability'. The planning system rewarded managers who achieved production targets in the short term rather than those who found ways to reduce costs or improve the quality of output over the long term. The balance of risk and reward was inimical to organizational and technological change and the 'kicking foot' of competition was absent.[38] In addition, the slowdown in eastern growth was also due to diminishing returns on investment, in economies that disproportionately relied upon factor inputs rather than total factor productivity growth.

Setting the Stage: 'Reconstruction'

If, to a good extent, the story of the Golden Age can be told in terms of catch-up to the productivity leader driven by American technology in an institutional context that promoted 'social capability for growth', what unleashed Europe's dormant Prometheus in the first place? In other words, why only in the second half of the 1940s could Europe finally exploit its potential for growth and regain part of the ground lost to the productivity leader over a century of modern economic growth?

---

[35] Mark Harrison, 'Trends in Soviet Labour Productivity, 1928–85: War, Postwar Recovery, and Slowdown', *European Review of Economic History* 2 (1998), 171–200.

[36] The investment/GDP ratio roughly doubled between 1950 and the early 1970s to just under 30 per cent and the capital stock grew at about 8.5 per cent per year in this period. Ofer, 'Soviet Economic Growth'; Allen, *Farm to Factory*, 193.

[37] Total factor productivity (TFP) measures the amount of total output (product) not accounted for by input of productive factors (essentially labour and capital). TFP is due to technical progress and improvements in the organization of the production process (including economies of scale). It is brought up in this context to highlight the lesser efficiency of the Soviet economy, relative to the economies of Western Europe.

[38] Joseph Berliner, *The Innovation Decision in Soviet Industry* (Cambridge, MA: MIT Press, 1976).

History meets economics in trying to answer this question, largely by focusing on the differences between the first and second 'post-war settlements'.[39] The Versailles Peace Conference had a divisive impact on international political and economic relations that resulted in instability, crippled cooperative efforts to counter the Great Depression, and led to the Second World War. Several of the factors leading to Europe's productivity slowdown between 1914 and 1945, the Second Thirty Years War, can be traced back to the short-sighted Versailles Treaty. The mistakes of 1919 were not replicated after 1945. The reparation burden was mild, aid was provided for reconstruction, the United States sustained European cooperation, a slow but steady movement to freer trade was set in motion, and a (temporarily) stable international monetary system was put in place.

Against this backdrop, economic historians have primarily focused on two issues: the impetus provided by reconstruction to longer term growth; and the role of the Marshall Plan.

Reconstruction can be defined either as recovery of the pre-war's income *level* or as the return of the economy to its long-term growth trend. The latter concept was first proposed by Janossy.[40] In this view, 'reconstruction' lasted until the late 1960s, by and large coinciding with the Golden Age itself. This interpretation of 'reconstruction' turns out to be a version of catch-up growth discussed above, stressing 'wartime destruction and dislocation', which generated a unique potential for reconstruction growth'.[41]

In what follows we refer to reconstruction in the narrower definition, confined to the 1945–50 time span. Even using this definition, 'reconstruction' stimulated longer term growth, much beyond 1950.

By the end of 1945, GDP of the defeated European countries had fallen back to early twentieth-century levels, that of France to late nineteenth century. Reconstruction took place at an unexpectedly fast pace. Between 1949 and 1951, the whole continent had returned to income levels equal to those of the best pre-war years. In the process, several conditions for sustaining growth (even if at slower pace) over the long run had been put in place.

The very process of physical reconstruction entailed the substitution of old for new infrastructure and production plants, the latter incorporating state-of-the-art American technology now easily obtainable (it was actually actively sought after by ad hoc official 'missions' visiting the United States to that end). The process itself, therefore, increased long-term productivity growth. As argued by Eichengreen and Ritschl, rapid reconstruction was possible because, in spite of massive strategic bombing, productive capacity had not been heavily disrupted.[42]

'Reconstruction' was one of those rare periods in history when substantial institutional changes become politically feasible. If it is impossible to quantify the economic

[39] Feinstein *et al.*, *The World Economy*.

[40] Ferenc Jánossy, *The End of the Economic Miracle* (White Plains, NY: IASP, 1969).

[41] Támas Vonyo, 'Post-War Reconstruction and the Golden Age of Economic Growth', *European Review of Economic History* 12 (2008), 239.

[42] Barry Eichengreen and Albrecht Ritschl, 'Understanding West German Economic Growth in the 1950s', *Cliometrica* 3:3 (2009), 191–219.

impact of restored democracy in Germany, Italy, and Austria, and the creation of the Fourth Republic in France, it is hard to argue that these changes did not create the prerequisites for a livelier and more open economic environment. Decolonization was set in motion, notably with India's independence, unwinding empires that had long been a drag on national resources. The labour market institutions mentioned above began to be put in place in the reconstruction years.

The role of American aid to Europe has been the subject of substantial research and much disagreement. In large parts of Eastern (including Russia) and Southern Europe the first phase of reconstruction was assisted by rapid intervention of the United Nations Relief and Rehabilitation Administration (UNRRA). Between 1945 and 1947, UNRRA aid came in the form of food, clothing, medical supplies, raw materials, farming machinery, and other essential equipment. By June 1947, UNRRA had spent about $2.8 billion in Europe. 'Thus the annual UNRRA expenditure per capita [in the countries involved] was at least as much as the later Marshall plan in Western Europe' and it covered 'a substantial part of the cost of imports for the major recipients in 1945–47'.[43]

The European Recovery Program (ERP) better known as the Marshall Plan, operated between 1948 and 1951. Overall, it provided $13 billion of aid from the United States to Western Europe. The Marshall Plan was traditionally seen as the engine that allowed reconstruction to take place and therefore kicked off the Golden Age. This view has been radically challenged, first by Milward.[44] It is now generally agreed that the direct effects were of modest quantitative importance in kicking off rapid growth. Impact on growth was possibly about 0.2 per cent per annum.[45] There is also little reason to think that the alleviation of supply bottlenecks mattered much either.[46]

In order to argue that Marshall Plan had nonetheless substantial effects, one has to look at indirect channels. De Long and Eichengreen suggest that it was highly successful in promoting a structural adjustment of the European economy, mainly working through well designed conditionality that changed the environment in which economic policy was made both by strengthening commitments to the market economy and trade liberalization and also by facilitating social contracts that underpinned high investment.[47] In other words, Marshall Plan conditionality made 'the advantages of the co-operative equilibrium suddenly clear'.

[43] John Killick, *The United States and European Reconstruction* (Edinburgh: Edinburgh University Press, 1997), 62–3.

[44] Alan Milward, *The Reconstruction of Western Europe* (Berkeley, CA: University of California Press, 1984).

[45] Crafts and Toniolo, 'Aggregate Growth 1950–2005'; Francisco Alvarez-Cuadrado and Mihaela I. Pintea, 'A Quantitative Exploration of the Golden Age of the European Growth', *Journal of Economic Dynamics and Control* 33:7 (2009), 1437–50.

[46] Barry Eichengreen and Marc Uzan, 'The Marshall Plan: Economic Effects and Implications for Eastern Europe and the Former USSR', *Economic Policy* 14 (1992), 13–76.

[47] Bradford De Long and Barry Eichengreen, 'The Marshall Plan: History's Most Successful Structural Adjustment Program', in Rudiger Dornbusch, Wilhelm Nalling and Richard Layard (eds), *Postwar Economic Reconstruction and Lessons for the East Today* (Cambridge, MA: MIT Press, 1993), 189–230.

The creation of the OEEC (later OECD), one of the conditions imposed by the United States, was intended as a forum to coordinate the distribution of ERP aid to the individual recipient countries. As the first cooperative European institution, it helped to ease postwar international relations at a time when the war wounds were still bleeding.

The economic historian is reluctant to enter the volatile field of social psychology. It is difficult, however, to overlook the u-turn from interwar American isolationism contained in Marshall's commencement speech at Harvard in June 1947. Regardless of its quantitative importance, the Marshall Plan unequivocally signalled Washington's firm commitment to Europe. If it is impossible to prove that the new international stance of the United States produced a 'boost to Europe's morale' and generated a climate of optimism conducive to rapid reconstruction, it is less difficult to argue that the Marshall Plan created most of the political and economic conditions for an early transfer of American technology to Europe.[48]

TRADE AND THE PROCESS OF EUROPEAN INTEGRATION

Autarky was one of the legacies to Europe of the Second Thirty Years War. At the beginning of the reconstruction, not only were complex panoplies of barriers to trade and capital movements in place, but each individual economy had somehow adjusted to autarkic production, with all the attendant corporate and bureaucratic vested interests. Moreover, everywhere foreign exchange reserves had been wiped out, particularly in the defeated economies, making it impossible for Europe to immediately honour the pledge to currency convertibility it made upon joining the Bretton Woods agreements. Trade was necessarily limited to bilateral agreements, substantially amounting to barter. Policymakers faced the daunting task of restoring multilateral trade and currency convertibility as preconditions to long-term growth.

The slow but steady process of Western European economic integration was deliberately kicked off by the United States at the time of launching the Marshall Plan. As noted by Reinalda, the programme was politically sold to the American electorate not only 'as a means of preventing Europe from coming under communist control' but also 'as a step in the direction of a new, more united Europe'.[49] In his Harvard speech, Secretary of State Marshall explicitly invited Europe to join forces to produce a common programme of aid requirements. America exercised strong leadership on the OEEC in the first couple of years of its existence, promoting Western European cooperation.

---

[48] Volker R. Berghahn, 'The Marshall Plan and the Recasting of Europe's Postwar Industrial Systems', in Eliot Sorel and Piercarlo Padoan (eds), *The Marshall Plan: Lessons Learned for the 21st Century* (Paris: OECD, 2009), 33.

[49] Bob Reinalda, *Routledge History of International Organizations: From 1815 to the Present Day* (London: Routledge, 2009), 407.

The 1948 Agreement for Intra European Payments and Compensations (IEPC) was the first step away from bilateral (barter) trade, oiled by the allocation of American dollars to multilateral settlements. It was followed in 1950 by the creation of the European Payments Union (EPU). Even if scholars disagree on whether or not it constituted the most efficient road towards currency convertibility, the EPU certainly promoted cooperation.[50] Managed by the only cooperative institution created in 1930—the Bank for International Settlements—the EPU provided the structure for automatically offsetting bilateral balances and for multilaterally settling the remaining claims in gold or dollars (out of an ad hoc American allocation). Crucially, the EPU extended credit to debtor countries out of a pool created from surplus balances. Multilateral settlements provided the framework for rapid European trade growth in the 1950s.

The year 1951 saw the birth of the European Coal and Steel Community (ECSC).[51] Its economic impact was negligible but its institutional novelty cannot be overrated. For the first time, nation states surrendered part of their sovereignty to a supranational institution. The European Economic Community (EEC) followed in the ECSC's tracks in 1957. In 1960, seven states which had not participated in the EEC created the less ambitious European Free Trade Association (EFTA).

In tune with progressive trade and payments liberalization between 1950 and 1973, Western European trade grew at an annualized rate of 8.36 per cent.[52] Trade is expected to raise income levels, by allowing for a more efficient allocation of resources: one of the reasons for pre-war Europe's sluggish growth was indeed the inability of each area to exploit its comparative advantages. In addition to this, trade impacted growth through greater investments, additional technological transfer, productivity-enhancing competition, and economies of scale. In particular, the increased integration of the European market was a factor that sped up technology transfer, helping Europe to reduce the technology gap with the United States.[53]

While it is most likely that progressive trade liberalization, after two decades of autarky, had a positive impact on Europe's growth during the Golden Age, the benefits deriving from the creation of the EEC and EFTA are neither self-evident nor easy to measure. Badinger estimated the impact of the EEC on growth to be as large as 1 per cent per year between the late 1950s and the early 1970s.[54] Other scholars are more cautious.

---

[50] Barry Eichengreen, *Reconstructing Europe's Trade and Payments: The European Payments Union* (Manchester: Manchester University Press, 1993).

[51] On the history of the ECSC, see Dirk Pieter Spierenburg, *The History of the High Authority of the European Coal and Steel Community: Supranationality in Operation* (London: Weidenfeld and Nicolson, 1994).

[52] Maddison, *The World Economy.*

[53] While US technology was particularly cost effective in the European context, as late as the 1980s even the most technologically advanced European countries were still obtaining over 40 per cent of their technological progress from American research. See Jonathan Eaton and Samuel Kortum, 'International Technology Diffusion: Theory and Measurement', *International Economic Review* 40:3 (1999), 537–70; Madsen, 'Technology Spillover'.

[54] Harald Badinger, 'Growth Effects of Economic Integration: Evidence from the EU Member States', *Review of World Economics* 141 (2005), 50–78.

Boltho and Eichengreen argue that, while a rough guess indicates that the customs union may have boosted the GDP of the original six members by 5 per cent by the mid-1970s, not all of these gains can be attributed to the Common Market since, in its absence, the participating countries might have found other ways of liberalizing trade. In their opinion, a counterfactual second-best economic and institutional arrangement would have emerged in the absence of the Rome Treaty of 1957, increasing GDP by about 3 to 4 per cent by the mid-1970s, leaving the 'true' impact of the EEC to just a total 1 to 2 per cent (i.e. a negligible contribution to the annual growth rate). Counterfactual has proven a useful intellectual tool to measure the impact of technical innovations. It works best when *ceteris paribus* assumptions are credible. This may not be the case of complex institutional changes likely to impact on other institutions and to affect behaviours and expectations.

The postwar international and domestic compromises between various conflicting interests resulted in such institutions as the OEEC, the EPU, and eventually the EEC bringing down the average European tariff protection from 30 per cent in 1931 (and a much higher level in 1944) to less than 9 per cent in the mid-1970s. In doing so, these institutional tools also shaped the social, political, and institutional landscape in a much deeper way than it was possible to anticipate in the early 1950s.

In accounting for the effect of trade liberalization on growth, Baldwin suggests that a 'domino effect' should be taken into account whereby regional free-trade agreements trigger tariff-lowering reactions from outsiders.[55] Thus, he argues, the creation of the EEC, or rather De Gaulle's refusal to admit the United Kingdom to it, produced both the British-led EFTA and an acceleration of multilateral tariff cutting within the GATT 'Kennedy round' as well as other regional free trade agreements (for example between Australia and New Zealand). All this, in turn, had positive feedbacks on Europe trade.

The Eastern Bloc opted out of the Marshall Plan. Instead, in 1949 the Soviet Union created an organization for regional trade integration (Comecon) that aimed at realizing Stalin's goal of 'two separate capitalist and socialist world markets'.[56] Comecon resulted largely in regional autarky, absorbing from 60 per cent to 75 per cent of Eastern European countries' foreign trade, mostly with the Soviet Union. This boosted a 10 per cent annual increase in international trade between 1950 and 1973. After Stalin's death in 1953, Khrushchev introduced mild reforms based on 'socialist division of labour' aiming at better taking advantage of individual countries' comparative advantages. An International Bank for Economic Cooperation and a multilateral clearing-house (reminiscent of the European Payments Union) were established, making the payment system (based on the clearing system pioneered by Germany in the 1930s) more efficient.

---

[55] Richard E. Baldwin, 'Multilateralising Regionalism: Spaghetti Bowls as Building Blocs on the Path to Global Free Trade', *World Economy* 29:11 (2006), 1451–518.

[56] Ivan Berend, *An Economic History of Twentieth Century Europe* (Cambridge: Cambridge University Press, 2006), 166.

WESTERN EUROPE AND THE INTERNATIONAL MONETARY SYSTEM

In the immediate postwar era, it was crucial for Western Europe not only to recreate a system of intra-European multilateral trade and, eventually, of free capital and labour movements, but also to re-establish economic relations with the rest of the world that were as open as possible. European participation in the GATT has already been mentioned. Of paramount importance, not least for the negative role played in exacerbating the Great Depression, the memory of which still loomed large in the late 1940s, was the issue of international payments. The Bretton Woods agreement envisaged a system of fixed exchange rates based on the gold-convertible dollar as the main currency for the settlement of international transactions. It was a modified version of the gold standard in which the visible hand would basically replace the automatic adjustment mechanism that supposedly kept the classical gold standard viable. The visible hand took the form of central banks' and the International Monetary Fund's activism, and required a considerable degree of international cooperation.

During the 1950s, as we saw, the complex system of controls on foreign exchange transactions was progressively simplified and relaxed. Within Europe, the EPU was the main instrument in recreating conditions for lowering the transaction costs of multilateral trade. Internationally, once the Korean War increased the supply of international dollars, the International Monetary Fund supervised a system of exchange rates in a context of inconvertible currencies.[57] Since an immediate postwar 'big-bang' of free mobility for goods and factors of production did not look like a feasible option, progressive liberalization was the realistic approach to the problem.

Once current account currency convertibility was introduced in 1959, the Bretton Woods rules fully applied—individual currencies were convertible in dollars and the latter in gold, on demand from central banks only.[58] The system rested on an implicit pact whereby the United States would supply sufficient international liquidity (dollars) for international settlements without jeopardizing price stability, and Europe would accept a US balance of payments deficit as the indispensable channel for the creation of such liquidity. Since trade was growing about twice as fast as GDP, the supply of international money (largely dollars) had to grow equally rapidly resulting in a decrease of the gold/dollar reserve ratio (given the slow and erratic growth of gold supply) and a swelling of US balance of payments deficit. By the late 1950s, as observed by the Belgian

---

[57] Harold James, *International Monetary Cooperation since Bretton Woods* (Oxford: Oxford University Press, 1996).

[58] For a discussion of how the Bretton Woods system worked, see Barry Eichengreen, *Globalizing Capital: A History of the International Monetary System* (Princeton, NJ: Princeton University Press, 1996).

economist Triffin, it was already clear that the system could not survive indefinitely.[59] It lasted as long as intense US–European cooperation held, and collapsed thereafter.

Cooperation rested on a credible (if implicit) commitment by surplus European countries to avoid converting their dollar balances into gold. In 1961, the Bretton Woods system suffered its first serious crisis, which was overcome by a series of swaps of gold for dollars by some European countries to the United States. Thereafter, European and North American cooperation took the form of a 'Gold Pool' that operated in the free market for the yellow metal to keep its price close to the US official price of thirty-five dollars per ounce.[60] General Agreements to Borrow (that is, for mutual support in case of balance of payments crises) were also signed.

Intensive cooperation of this kind allowed the Bretton Woods system to survive for another decade. An important factor in limiting the size and impact of currency crises in the 1960s was also found in controls of international capital movements and in tight regulation of the banking system by domestic monetary authorities. Both resulted in forms of 'financial repression' that limited financial innovation as well as in less-than perfect international equalization of interest rates.

Cooperation towards the production of a public good (in this case a stable monetary system) is notoriously fraught with a collective action problem: while all participants have an interest in the success of the joint enterprise, each of them individually has an interest in freeriding on the efforts made by other participants. The fragility of the arrangement was increased by the participants' growing divergence in the definition of the conceptual framework for cooperation and by mounting disagreements in assessing the costs borne by each country.[61] In particular, Gaullist France felt that balance of payments deficits not only allowed the United States to live permanently above its means at the expense of Western Europe, but were also responsible for an undesirable 'invasion' of American capital. The postwar beneficiary effects of such an 'invasion' were all but forgotten. On the other hand, the American government and public opinion felt both that the county's deficit was due to expenses for common defence to which Europeans did not sufficiently contribute and that the 'burden' of owning the main reserve currency unduly constrained domestic policymaking at a time when the combined needs of the Vietnam war and the Great Society required an expansionary monetary and fiscal policy and, therefore, a larger external deficit. The publication in 1967 of *Le défi américain* by Servan-Schreiber[62] somehow symbolized the change in transatlantic relations that had taken place since the early post-war. With the end of the Gold Pool in 1968, the crumbling of the whole Breton Woods edifice was only a matter of time. It is possibly a

[59] Robert Triffin, *Europe and the Money Muddle* (New Haven, CT: Yale University Press, 1957).

[60] For details on the so-called Gold Pool, and generally on transatlantic cooperation in the 1960s, see Gianni Toniolo, *Central Bank Cooperation at the Bank for International Settlements* (Cambridge: Cambridge University Press, 2005), 350–436; Barry Eichengreen, *Global Imbalances and the Lessons of Bretton Woods* (Cambridge, MA: MIT Press, 2007), 35–72.

[61] Eichengreen, *Global Imbalances*, 64–5.

[62] Jean Jacques Servan-Schreiber, *Le défi américain* (Paris: Denoël, 1967).

coincidence, but nevertheless a highly symbolic one, that the Golden Age and the Bretton Woods system ended more or less simultaneously.

The End and the Long-Term Impact
of the Golden Age

The Golden Age came to an end sometime between 15 August 1971, when the dollar was taken off gold, and 16 October 1973, when OPEC announced its first decision to steeply raise oil prices. Cracks in the wall became visible in the late 1960s, not only with the end of transatlantic monetary cooperation but especially with the big wage pushes of 1968–69 that signalled the weakening of the tacit moderation pacts that had been in place since the late 1940s. High growth continued until the early 1970s, after which time it suddenly set on a secular trend which characterized both the pre-Great War *belle époque* and the last quarter of the century (with a gentle further slowdown in the 1990s). Although the lower income countries continued to grow faster than average, in Western Europe as a whole catch-up stalled, with real GDP per person at only about two-thirds of the American level. Western European countries, however, continued to close the labour productivity gap with the United States.[63]

To a great extent, the Golden Age was brought to an end by the weakening of the transitory factors that had been behind its origin and sustainability for quarter of a century. The long-term boost from postwar reconstruction was exhausted, diminishing returns to investment slowly set in, and the scope for catch-up was reduced as the distance from the leader narrowed. At the institutional level, the Eichengreen wage moderation/high investment equilibrium did not generally survive the turbulence of the 1970s, a time when union militancy and union power rose considerably, as did labour's share in aggregate value added, and the rewards for patience fell in a world of greater capital mobility, floating exchange rates, and higher inflation. Other hitherto successful economic institutions such as French and Italian public enterprises either tended to sclerosis or became captive of vested political interests. More generally, the whole model of coordinated–regulated capitalism, in its various forms, was less capable of delivering economic growth in contexts which henceforth would rely more on innovation than imitative ingenuity, as Eichengreen himself has emphasized. The institutional and regulatory legacy of the Golden Age, however, turned out to be difficult to reform, as its very success had created large constituencies in favour of the status quo. In addition, for reasons not yet entirely clear, productivity growth suddenly and simultaneously also slowed down in the United States, creating a less dynamic Atlantic environment.

---

[63] Nicholas Crafts, Ian Gazeley and Andrew Newell (eds), *Work and Pay in Twentieth-Century Britain* (Oxford: Oxford University Press, 2007).

It was in Eastern Europe, however, that slower growth produced the most acute problems, so much so that, at the end of the 1980s, they triggered a momentous tide of regime change. The Soviet economy suffered from problems that, in a sense, were similar to those of Western Europe but on a much larger scale. By the 1970s, Soviet growth was undermined by rapidly diminishing returns that reduced the capital deepening associated with the constant investment rate of a little under 30 per cent of GDP.[64] The situation was exacerbated by a decline in TFP growth that turned negative in the 1970s. The incentive structures used by the Soviet leadership to motivate managers and workers were a complex mixture of rewards, punishments, and monitoring. Each of these became increasingly expensive over time, threatening the viability of the system. Product innovation drove up monitoring costs that also inhibited moves from mass to flexible production.

It is only possible to speculate on the long-term economic and social legacy of '*les trente glorieuses*'. In 1973, the average citizen of Western Europe's twenty-nine countries was 2.5 times better off than he/she had been only twenty-three years earlier. Never, before or afterwards, was economic well-being raised so significantly in less than a generation. Citizens of Eastern Europe did only marginally worse; those of the initially poorer Western European countries improved their lot faster than Europe's average. These extraordinary aggregate achievements meant not only higher and more equally distributed consumption but also the allocation of a considerable amount of resources to the creation of social overhead capital and the diffusion of education, arguably with favourable longer term effects on the economy and society at large. Rapid growth, in a context of fairly low government debt to GDP ratios and a relatively young population, made it possible for governments to create generous systems of universal health care and social security. In the long run, the promises of social transfers made during the Golden Age, while positively impacting welfare, locked governments into the high taxation–high expenditure equilibrium that characterize the economic history of Europe to the present day. Government spending, already high by historical standards at onset of the Golden Age, was over 60 per cent greater by the end of it.[65] It would increase further in subsequent decades.

If, as Blaise Pascal claimed, 'All men seek happiness. This is without exception', then one should perhaps wonder to what extent the Golden Age permanently increased if not happiness, so difficult to define, at least the self-assessed life satisfaction of Europeans.[66] In 1974, Easterlin established the homonymous paradox whereby, while higher incomes closely correlate with life satisfaction within countries, the same was apparently not true across countries. He claimed that average GDP per person does not account for between-countries differences in average life satisfaction. However, recent research, based on

---

[64] The data constructed for the analysis in Allen's *Farm to Factory* show that the capital-stock growth rate fell from 7.4 per cent per year in the 1960s to 3.4 per cent per year in the 1980s, and the scope for raising the investment rate was constrained by defence expenditure (16 per cent of GDP).

[65] OECD, *Public Expenditure Trends* (Paris: OECD, 1978).

[66] Blaise Pascal, *The Thoughts of Blaise Pascal* (London: George Bell & Sons, 1905), 94.

much larger databases and more sophisticated statistical techniques, finds not only that there is a positive relationship between income and happiness across countries but that there seems to be a positive over time relationship as well for Europe (but not for the US). Europe seems to do better than its transatlantic cousins at enjoying income growth. Over time, a 1 per cent increase in GDP per person lifts the average life satisfaction in a given country by 0.4 per cent.[67] If this is true, then we might assume that an important legacy of the Golden Age was to make by 1973 the average European about twice as satisfied with his/her life than he/she was in 1950.

FURTHER READING

Armstrong, Philip, Andrew Glyn and John Harrison, *Capitalism since World War II: The Making and Break-Up of the Great Boom* (London: Fontana, 1991).

Berend, Ivan, *Central and Eastern Europe 1944–1993: Detour from the Periphery to the Periphery* (Cambridge: Cambridge University Press, 1996).

Berend, Ivan, *An Economic History of Twentieth-Century Europe* (Cambridge: Cambridge University Press, 2006).

Boltho, Andrea (ed.), *The European Economy: Growth and Crisis* (Oxford: Oxford University Press, 1982).

Broadberry, Steven and Kevin O'Rourke (eds), *The Cambridge Economic History of Modern Europe*, vol. 2 (Cambridge: Cambridge University Press, 2010).

Crafts, Nicholas and Gianni Toniolo (eds), *Economic Growth in Europe Since 1945* (Cambridge: Cambridge University Press, 1996).

Eichengreen, Barry, *The European Economy since 1945: Coordinated Capitalism and Beyond* (Princeton, NJ: Princeton University Press, 2006).

Neal, Larry, *The Economics of Europe and the European Union* (Cambridge: Cambridge University Press, 2007).

Schulze, Max-Stephan (ed.), *Western Europe: Economic and Social Change since 1945* (London: Longman, 1999).

van der Wee, Herman, *Prosperity and Upheaval: The World Economy, 1945–1980* (New York: Viking, 1986).

---

[67] Betsey Stevenson and Justin Wolfers, 'Economic Growth and Subjective Well Being: Reassessing the Easterlin Paradox', *Brookings Papers on Economic Activity* 1 (2008), 1–102.

CHAPTER 18

EUROPEAN INTEGRATION: THE RESCUE OF THE NATION STATE?

ROBERT BIDELEUX

INTRODUCTION

THE relationship between European integration and the nation-state has long been hotly debated. This chapter argues that EU Member State governments have pursued European integration (i) as a 'security project' or 'peace project' designed to secure durable and mutually advantageous reconciliation, peaceful coexistence, and 'interlacing' of states, societies and economies, primarily to 'rescue' the European states system from its hugely damaging fractious, fissiparous, conflict-inducing, and beggar-my-neighbour tendencies; and (ii) as a way of empowering or capacitating these states, economies and societies, and safeguarding their perceived requirements and interests. Europhobic claims that EU Member States have actively promoted and collectively locked themselves into a self-damaging project designed to supersede, erode, and weaken their own power(s), interests, aspirations and prerogatives do not survive close scrutiny. The relationships between European integration, nations and states have been 'positive-sum' games (rather than 'zero-sum games'). Even though the most tangible institutional and legal embodiments of European integration have been economic, these economic 'means' have largely been ways of attaining political and security-oriented 'ends'. The frameworks of common rules, policies and supranational law and institutions which Europhobes continually denounce as dangerous and/or unwarranted encroachments and limitations on 'national' freedom, democracy, customs and diversity have been consensually negotiated and implemented by elected governments engaged in prudent endeavours to make peace, prosperity, liberal democracy, the rule of law, fundamental rights and freedoms, inter-state cooperation, and the effective autonomy of states as secure and resilient as possible, in conditions of ever-increasing interdependence. They are, on balance, more enabling and empowering than disabling, restrictive or disempowering. This has been especially important to smaller, poorer, and weaker European states. The EU has also helped to support and safeguard (rather than imperil) small and sub-state nations and minority languages and cultures, thereby nurturing and conserving (rather than threatening or dissolving) Europe's rich heritage of ethno-cultural diversity. Successive EU enlargements and the 2009 Lisbon Treaty have further strengthened European states and the confederal ('intergovernmental') nature of the EU order.

Logically, however, the EU can only continue to play its indispensable positive roles in supporting, safeguarding, and strengthening the effective autonomy of its Member States so long as it does not develop in ways or directions which seriously restrict, impair or encroach upon the effective autonomy of those states. Unfortunately, the momentous economic crises of 2008–12 have cruelly exposed not only the deep structural flaws and hazards inherent in the high-risk EU project for Economic and Monetary Union (EMU), but also the alarming degrees to which EMU (far more than any previous EU project) can only be kept viable and sustainable by developing quite draconian disciplinary and enforcement mechanisms which (if they were to be fully accepted and implemented by all eurozone members) would seriously restrict, impair and encroach upon the (hitherto indispensable) substantial autonomy and freedom of action of Member States, thereby violating or transgressing fundamental functional and prudential constraints on European integration and placing the future of the EU as a whole seriously in jeopardy.

VIRTUES OF ALAN MILWARD'S *EUROPEAN RESCUE OF THE NATION-STATE* METAPHOR

Many (mostly British) 'Europhobes' and 'Eurosceptics' regard European integration as a nefarious conspiracy to subvert the nation-state, national sovereignty and liberal parliamentary democracy, and to suppress Europe's rich heritage of diverse cultures, identities, traditions, customs and ways of life, by subjecting the EU Member States to a rigid, soulless, technocratic, authoritarian, and monolithic uniformity within an emerging 'European super-state', which in turn is often demonized as an embryonic Orwellian 'Big Brother' state centred on Brussels. Less stridently, many European integration specialists and many 'European federalists' have routinely assumed that European integration is a zero-sum game, that 'more Europe' necessarily means 'less nation-state', and that 'more supranationalism' must in practice diminish state autonomy and sovereignty.

Rejecting claims that European integration has been inimical or antithetical to nations, states and 'national' interests, Alan Milward's *The European Rescue of the Nation-State* (1992; henceforth ERNS)[1] argues that the relationship between European integration and the nation-state has been mutually beneficial and supportive (2–5); and that European integration was launched, not in opposition to the nation-state, but as 'an integral part' of the postwar reconstruction, reassertion and 'rescue' of six key West European nation-states, following the various military defeats, occupations, blood-letting, devastations, and political and economic collapses which they had suffered between 1914 and 1945 (3–4). European integration has consistently been carried out by elected governments, with the aim of strengthening their own and their country's capabilities, effective autonomy and perceived interests (2–5, 8–12, 18–19). Without the European Community (EC), the West European nation-state 'could not have offered to its citizens the same measure of security and prosperity which it has provided and which has justified its survival' (3); and the Keynesian welfare-statist political consensus on which this 'rescue' depended required 'the surrender of limited areas of national sovereignty to the supranation' (4). Nevertheless, 'Integration was not the supersession of the nation-state by another form of governance . . . but was the creation of the European nation-states for their own purposes'; and 'there has surely never been a period when national government in Europe has exercised more effective power and more extensive control over its citizens than that since the Second World War' (18). The derogations of national sovereignty to the European Communities after 1950 were 'one aspect of the successful reassertion of the nation-state as the basic organizational entity of Europe' (428).

Many analysts of European integration have assumed that there are clear-cut either/or choices between intergovernmentalism and federalism, and between 'wider' and 'deeper' integration, but in practice these have mostly *complemented* one another.[2] Much of the progress towards 'deeper' European integration has been achieved by intergovernmental means; each 'widening' of European integration has generated fresh pressures for further 'deepening'; and, each time that further 'deepening' has been initiated by new intergovernmental bargains (treaties), additional *supranational* processes or dynamics of integration have been set in motion, often taking that 'deepening' considerably further or faster than the original instigators intended. The particular directions of EU development have stemmed, not just from conscious premeditated plans and designs, but also in large measure from the unforeseen implications of pragmatic responses to practical problems, unexpected events and challenges, and short-term perspectives and expediencies.

---

[1] In this chapter, all page references to Alan Milward's *The European Rescue of the Nation-State* (London: Routledge, 1992) refer to the second edition, published in 2000.

[2] Peter Poole, *Europe Unites: The EU's Eastern Enlargement* (Boulder, CO: Praeger, 2003), 3–7; and Christopher Preston, *Enlargement and Integration in the European Union* (London: Routledge, 1997), 8.

IMPORTANT LIMITATIONS OF ALAN MILWARD'S *ERNS* THESES

Rejecting influential claims that Europe's experiences of fascism and World War II and the conspicuous incapacity of Europe's nation-states system to cope with these disasters had resulted in a widespread groundswell of popular support for supranational 'European federalism',[3] ERNS claims that the sentiments most commonly engendered by resistance to fascism and enemy occupation were 'patriotism and even nationalism'; that 'the idea of a peacefully united Europe' was far less potent and pervasive than 'the idea of resurrecting the conquered nations'; and that advocates of a supranational 'federal' polity for Europe were 'of little importance or influence in the political life of their own countries' and 'had practically no influence on the negotiations' that formed the European Communities during the 1950s (16). ERNS also argues that Jean Monnet and Robert Schuman, the two catalytic progenitors of European integration, were primarily architects of French *national* reconstruction (16); and that the French state pursued European integration chiefly as 'an attempt to restore France as a major national force by creating an integrated area in Western Europe which France would dominate', while the new German Federal Republic embraced it 'precisely in order to establish itself as the future German nation-state' (17).

In a sequel to ERNS, Milward claims that 'the national interests which have underlain the process of integration are made up of positions taken by interest groups which are themselves compromises in consensus-building at a micro level before they become part of the greater compromise represented by a national policy.'[4] However, Milward's very British and somewhat Eurosceptical view of 'the nation-state' as a maximizer of national self-interest, largely conceived in narrowly socio-economic terms, inadequately explains how the calculus of 'national' socio-economic self-interest changed the political behaviour of voters, parties and governments. The rhetoric of 'the national interest' has often been a smokescreen for diverse competing or conflicting *sectional interests*. These frequently *claim* to represent 'the national interest', while actually representing class, regional, sectoral, gender, ethnic and religious interests and aspirations; and they have rarely cohered sufficiently to be the drivers of state policy and/or European integration. Far from being *nationalist*, the interests and rhetoric that drove (West) European integration from the 1950s to the 1990s emphasized the need to 'pool' national sovereignty and curb and guard against political and economic nationalism.

---

[3] Walter Lipgens, *A History of European Integration, 1945–1947*, Vol. 1, *The Formation of the European Unity Movement* (Oxford: Oxford University Press, 1982); Walter Lipgens and W. Loth (eds), *Documents on the History of European Integration*, Vol. 3 (Berlin: European University Institute Series, 1988); Altiero Spinelli, 'The Growth of the European Movement since World War II', in C. G. Haines (ed.), *European Integration* (Baltimore, MD: Johns Hopkins University Press, 1957), 40–63; and Alberto De Bernardi and Paolo Ferrari (eds), *Antifascismo e identità europea* (Rome: Carocci editore, 2004).

[4] Alan Milward et al., *The Frontier of National Sovereignty* (London: Routledge, 1993), 190.

Milward's emphasis on the primacy of 'national interests' sits uncomfortably with his strong emphasis on the primacy of economics, as *national interests involve much more than narrowly economic considerations.* Moreover, ERNS also repeatedly conflates or confuses *the state-as-country* with *the state-as-bundle-of-institutions*, often employs these very different usages interchangeably (a common malpractice!), and treats the growth in the power(s) and technical/organizational capabilities of the state-as-bundle-of-institutions since 1945 as evidence of 'the reassertion of the nation-state' (most explicitly on p. 18), even though this notion obviously concerns states-as-countries.

ERNS does acknowledge the *political* and *security* concerns and motives of the 'founding fathers' of the European Communities:

> The basis of the rescue of the nation-state was an economic one, and it follows that the Europeanization of its rescue had also to be economic. The interdependence of European states was, however, by no means purely economic. The single greatest problem within that interdependence was political, the future of Germany, as it had been in 1848, in 1864, in 1870, in 1914, and since 1933. No European rescue of the nation-state was of any validity, unless it also offered a solution to this problem. Although…the European rescue of the nation-state was necessarily an economic one, it is at the point where that economic rescue intersected with the problem of Germany's future in Europe that the common policies of the European Community developed. [44–45]

Consequently, 'some national policies aiming at national reassertion had to be internationalized in order to make them viable, and… where they intersected with the fearful question of the future of Germany, the reinvigorated nation-state had to choose the surrender of a degree of national sovereignty to sustain its reassertion' (45).

Nevertheless, ERNS seriously underplays the *relative* importance of *non-economic* factors. François Duchêne, who worked as Jean Monnet's assistant from the early 1950s to the early 1960s, became Monnet's most insightful and authoritative biographer, and shared the values and outlook of the founders of the European Communities, offered a more cogent account of their thinking and motives:

> The key was… the security needs of the continental neighbours of the new postwar Germany and especially of France, the only state placed to launch a new policy. Germany was still the potential hegemonic power in Europe outside the USSR and might have reached a bilateral accommodation with it. The risks of a third bid for such domination had to be removed. This could not be assured by insurance policies, which had failed between the wars, but only by a basic political process designed to supersede the old national rivalries. This demanded that everyone be equal before new rules, and that 'European' bodies should have the power to take decisions without national bias. Supranationality followed, not only to reach effective decisions, but to guarantee the levels of trust to implement them. This was agreed first for the ECSC then the Common Market, both expressing the same policy of absorbing Germany into a new European civil system via unity.[5]

[5] Letter from François Duchêne to Robert Bideleux, 2 February 1994.

The paramount concerns of the founders of the European Communities were to embed Franco-German reconciliation and (West) German economic, political and military recovery within a robust and not easily reversible framework that would be non-threatening to Germany's neighbours and Germany itself. European integration was central to the Phoenix-like 're-emergence of the separate states of Continental Europe after the cataclysm of total war', and to restoration of 'their control of their own destiny.'[6] The *means* chosen were obviously *economic*, but, as Duchêne repeatedly assured me, the *ends* had much less to do with economics than with *security, peace-building, and politics*. Unions or leagues of states have most often come into being as 'security communities', motivated primarily by security concerns, including fears of actual or potential external enemies and hegemons; and confederal union has long been one of the 'classic forms of relationship that states adopt to guarantee or underwrite their continued existence as states.'[7] Talk of a limited *union of economies* may have helped to sell a *union of states* to wider publics. However, if the goals of the ECSC, EEC and EC had really been *primarily economic and welfarist* (as ERNS argues*), it would not have been necessary to endow them with the elaborate supranational institutional trappings of a nascent (West) European federation*: (i) the ECSC's High Authority, precursor of the Commission of the EEC and the EU; (ii) an Assembly, which the 'founding fathers' intended to evolve into a directly-elected European Parliament; and (iii) a Court of Justice, designed to uphold and interpret a far-reaching supranational legal order, which is still unique to the EU. All of this was far more appropriate to an *embryonic European federal polity* than to a mere *economic union*. The minimalist economistic European Free Trade Area (EFTA, established in 1960) was just as successful as the EEC in promoting integration and prosperity based upon increasingly barrier-free movement of goods, services, labour and (eventually) capital.[8]

The fact that France had been humiliatingly defeated and partly occupied by Germany in three successive wars since 1870 was what finally persuaded France's proud and nationalistic elites of the need to 'swallow' some national pride and sovereignty and enmesh France, Germany, Italy and Benelux within a robust and durable *union of states* capable of containing, 'domesticating' and counterbalancing German scientific, military and economic might and its scarcely diminished potential to dominate Europe; and these political and security concerns were in large part shared by the leaders of Italy and Benelux.[9] *The extreme experiences of fascism, defeat,*

[6] Tony Judt, *Postwar: A History of Europe since 1945* (London: Heinemann, 2005), 5–7.

[7] Murray Forsyth, *Unions of States* (Leicester: Leicester University Press, 1981), 204ff; Karl Deutsch, *Political Community and the North Atlantic Area* (Princeton, NJ: Princeton University Press, 1957); Karl Deutsch, *France, Germany and the Western Alliance* (New York, NY: Charles Scribner, 1967).

[8] Loukas Tsoukalis, *The New European Economy*, 2nd edn (Oxford: Oxford University Press, 1993), 21–2.

[9] See Robert Bideleux, 'Introduction: European Integration and Disintegration', and François Duchêne, 'French Motives for European Integration', in Robert Bideleux and Richard Taylor (eds.), *European Integration and Disintegration: East and West* (London: Routledge, 1996), 1–21 and 22–35.

occupation and collapse during two successive World Wars were indeed what induced these hitherto strongly nationalistic countries to accept considerable 'pooling' of their 'national sovereignty'. Conversely, Adenauer's nascent German Federal Republic, having soberly recognized that Germany's two colossal drives for hegemony over Europe had ultimately been disastrous for everyone (Germans included), circumspectly accepted European integration and the implicit voluntary limitation and 'pooling' of national sovereignty as a much more propitious, peaceful, non-antagonistic, and durable European framework within which to (re)build a new Germany capable of securely locking up and transcending its hegemonic 'inner demons' and the terrible sufferings and traumas which the Second and Third Reichs had inflicted on Europe.

Milward's *economistic* account of European integration and his scathing dismissal of 'European federalism' and 'the European saints' (on 15–17, 318–44) reflect characteristically British ways of (mis)understanding the origins of 'the Common Market', as most Brits persisted in calling it long after other Europeans had stopped doing so; and an unwarranted belittling of the non-economic ideals, values, bonds and goals which most Continental European politicians and analysts have much more accurately perceived to be *at the heart* of the European integration project. Significantly, no other scheme of regional integration anywhere else in the world has managed to achieve anything as ambitious and far-reaching as the EU's unique supranational institutions, systems and legal order: the directly elected Parliament; the Court of Justice; the Commission; the Single Market; the eurozone; and the huge and complex system of supranational rules, regulations and law.[10] Claims that the European Communities were established primarily in pursuit of ('national') economic and welfarist goals shed *some* light on their main *outcomes* and long-term *'historical significance'*, but very little on the main *motivations* of 'the founding fathers', most of whom espoused 'European federalist' *political* and *security-oriented* conceptions of the project's *finalités* (long-term goals).[11]

Overall, ERNS fails to do justice to the broader political, security and 'identitarian' motives and dimensions of European integration. Furthermore, since ERNS was first published in 1992, the nature of 'European rescues of the nation-state' (especially the characteristics of the states to be rescued) has been transformed by greatly intensified globalization, the rise of neoliberalism, the resurgence of Asia, the two-stage instauration of the eurozone (monetary union) in 1999–2002, and momentous enlargements of the EU in 1996, 2004 and 2007.

---

[10] Robert Bideleux, 'El Mercosur y la Unión Europea: Cómo se comparan dos modelos de intregración regional?', in Raul Bernal-Meza (ed.), *Economía mundial y desarrollo regional* (Buenos Aires: Nuovohacer Grupo Editor Latinoamericano, 2005), 163–83.

[11] Documented in Bideleux and Taylor (eds.), *European Integration and Disintegration*, 1–35.

BEYOND MILWARD'S EUROPEAN RESCUE
OF THE NATION-STATE THESES

The ERNS metaphor continues to offer valuable insights into the 'positive-sum' nature of relationships between European integration and European nations and states, but the extent and implications of these relationships have been much more far-reaching than ERNS suggests.

In 1982, in his seminal essay conceptualizing '*embedded liberalism*' as the basis of the post-1945 order in the West, John Gerard Ruggie highlighted the ways that the Hungarian sociologist Karl Polanyi (from whose *The Great Transformation* [1944] Ruggie derived the concept of 'embedded liberalism') and the British economist John Maynard Keynes had publicly argued that the rise of European fascism and Communism had made it politically and socially untenable for the post-World War II West to return to the pre-1914 classical laissez-faire liberal orthodoxies. By 1940, both Polanyi and Keynes had concluded that the forthcoming postwar (and post-fascist) reconstruction of the Western liberal democracies would have to eschew those orthodoxies, in order to put forward socio-economic programmes that could upstage and outbid potent fascist and Stalinist promises of social protection, economic welfare and full employment; and that liberal democracy and liberal capitalism would therefore have to be reconstituted on the basis of radically new conceptions of 'political authority as a fusion of power with legit-imate social purpose' and of 'the appropriate role of authority vis-à-vis the market', thus heralding 'a fundamental reordering of the relationships between domestic political authority and economic processes.'[12] This line of reasoning has been developed further by Mark Mazower and Alessandro Roncaglia.[13] Ruggie also pointed out that Ernst B. Haas had argued (long before Milward) that 'the very fact of the welfare state propels its leaders to cooperate with one another [internationally] to a greater extent than any pre-vious socio-political forms did, if doing so is necessary to satisfy the everyday needs and demands of their domestic constituents.'[14]

Far from being antithetical to the nation-state, the era of European integration (1950s-2000s) has been 'the "golden age" of the national-democratic welfare state.'[15] The successes of West European integration from 1947 to the 1970s were made possible by judicious combinations of Keynesian state intervention, counter-cyclical macroeco-nomic policies, welfarism, strong labour unions, and liberalization of international movement of goods and labour (albeit not yet services or capital) between West

---

[12] John G. Ruggie, *Constructing the World Polity* (London: Routledge, 1998), 62–76.

[13] Mark Mazower, *Dark Continent: Europe's Twentieth Century* (London: Allen Lane, 1998); and Alessandro Roncaglia, *The Wealth of Ideas: A History of Economic Thought* (Cambridge: Cambridge University Press, 2005), 387.

[14] Ruggie, *Constructing the World Polity*, 1.

[15] Stefano Bartolini, *Restructuring Europe* (Oxford: Oxford University Press, 2005), 116.

European states.[16] This fertile combination of 'J.M. Keynes at home and Adam Smith abroad' was central to the 'embedded liberalism' of the post-1945 Western order.

Furthermore, William Wallace has cogently argued that, without clearly drawn borders and lines of jurisdiction, states cannot function in efficient, predictable, responsible and accountable ways; and that, without efficient, predictable, and clearly defined Member States, the EU cannot do so either.[17] Far from eroding, weakening, superseding or being antithetical to the nation-state, the systems, structure, and functioning of the EC/EU have strongly depended upon the tenacious persistence and saliency of robust and clearly demarcated Member States.

The dependence of successful regional integration on the continued existence of robust and autonomous states was most fully brought home to me when I investigated and analysed the reasons for the *intrinsic inability* (and not just circumstantial failure) of Comecon (CMEA, the Soviet-dominated 'Council of Mutual Economic Assistance') to *successfully* integrate the Soviet bloc states between 1949 and 1989.[18] Comecon was unable to flourish precisely because the imprisonment of its Member States within the hegemonic, hub-and-spoke, largely non-marketized, inherently bilateral, and vastly asymmetrical (patron-client) power-relations of the Soviet bloc precluded any far-reaching potential for genuine and largely self-generating *multilateral* trade, payments and integration between countries. Ironically, Comecon always formally insisted on the untrammelled sovereignty of its Member States, even though (or *because*) their sovereignty was largely phoney. This was its most fatal defect. Its dismal forty-year existence teaches us that, in order to maximize trade, investment, cooperation, division of labour, trust, and integration between economies and societies and make these as mutually advantageous as possible, the participants need to be *economically and politically autonomous, free-standing* and *juridically-equal partners*; and relations between them have to be *multilateral*. This is not merely *desirable*, but a *sine qua non* for successful regional integration.

Thus, if it is to be successful, regional integration *cannot afford to threaten 'the nation-state'* (and thus, logically, ought not to be expected to do so). *It heavily depends upon the establishment and maintenance of 'complex multilateralism' and the liberty, autonomy, integrity and equal juridical standing of the participating states*. Regional integration can only flourish in forms that *maintain or enhance* (rather than diminish) the autonomy, integrity, capabilities, viability and sovereignty of the participating states, and it can *only* be accomplished easily and effectively between highly marketized and self-supporting economies operating within the sort of multilateral trading and payments environment

[16] Tsoukalis, *The New European Economy*, 19–32.

[17] William Wallace, 'Where Does Europe End? Dilemmas of Inclusion and Exclusion', in Jan Zielonka (ed.), *Europe Unbound: Enlarging and Reshaping the Boundaries of the European Union* (London: Routledge, 2002), 83. See also Lee and Bideleux's chapter in this volume.

[18] Robert Bideleux, 'The Comecon Experiment', in Bideleux and Taylor (eds), *European Integration and Disintegration*, 174–204.

that the architects of the post-1945 order in the West built through the Bretton Woods institutions, the Marshall Plan, the Organization of European Economic Cooperation (the OEEC, forerunner of OECD), the European Payments Union, and even NATO. Without these (largely US-funded!) *prior* achievements in promoting multilateralism and resurrecting an autonomous Western European states system after 1945, the regional integration that flourished in Western Europe during the 1950 to 1973 boom would simply not have been feasible, as Alan Milward cogently argued in his earlier (and in this respect sounder) book on *The Reconstruction of Western Europe, 1945–51* (1984). Loukas Tsoukalis and John Gillingham have provided further support to these important perspectives.[19]

For even profounder reasons than those adduced by ERNS, European integration can only flourish in 'state friendly' forms. 'EU Europe' is *functionally and inherently obliged* to remain, in de Gaulle's apt terminology, '*l'Europe des états*'. (De Gaulle rarely, if ever, spoke of '*l'Europe des patries*. Claims that he did are apocryphal.) Any attempt to abandon or supersede genuinely *autonomous, pluralist and multilateral* monetary, trading, and states systems would soon cause European integration to 'seize up'. While this cannot absolutely guarantee the continued autonomy, liberty, integrity, viability, and juridical equality of EU Member States (nothing on Earth can do that!), it does offer the strongest-possible assurance that the wide-ranging autonomy, integrity, liberty, and juridical equality of EU states (both as countries and as bundles of institutions) is genetically 'hardwired' into the long-term viability of European integration.

Furthermore, the regional and international associations and shared frameworks of rules, laws, common policies and institutions within which most of the world's formally democratic states increasingly operate (but which many nationalist, left-wing, right-wing, and libertarian critics of such associations and their rules, common policies and international regimes misleadingly denounce as menacing or unwarranted encroachments and limitations on the autonomy, freedom, democracy, customs, and diversity of states) are primarily *self-binding mechanisms* which have been voluntarily and consensually devised, negotiated and implemented by such states, in prudent endeavours to render democracy, fundamental rights and freedoms, prosperity, state effectiveness, state autonomy, inter-state cooperation, and the rule of law as stable and secure as possible. Even though the governance structures and institutions of the EU undoubtedly suffer from much-publicized 'democratic deficits', and even though the EU's vast size renders it very difficult to further democratize these inevitably rather remote ('Olympian') and technocratic structures and institutions, they nevertheless help to strengthen and uphold legal, institutional, and economic frameworks which provide valuable additional support for the long-term effectiveness, viability, and survival of the formal (and also in many ways quite limited and remote) forms of representative

---

[19] Tsoukalis, *The New European Economy*, 14–15; and John Gillingham, *European Integration: 1950–2003: Superstate or New Market Economy?* (Cambridge: Cambridge University Press, 2003), ch 2.

liberal democracy which exist at the state and sub-state levels in the individual EU Member States. Although many leftists, Thatcherites and nationalists rant against alleged EU 'encroachments' and 'restrictions' on the liberty, democracy and autonomy of the Member States, these limitations are analogous to the forms of 'limited government' and 'rule of law' which all liberal regimes rely on to limit and regulate the exercise of power and help safeguard fundamental liberties.

In an increasingly 'globalized' and 'regionalized' world, countries participate in international associations and organizations primarily in order to *maximize* their political, economic or military viability, stability, and security, as well as their *effective* state capacity and state autonomy vis-à-vis external environments that are otherwise largely beyond their control. Formal liberal democracies have voluntarily negotiated and accepted frameworks of stable and binding inter-state rules and law in prudential endeavours to attain *at least a modicum of indirect collective control* over external pressures and environments which they would not be able to deal with as effectively without such frameworks; and to help to empower and safeguard one another by making the arenas in which they operate more stable, predictable, and calculable, and hence more manageable. In effect, supranational rules, organizations and common policies serve as 'traffic codes', 'traffic cops', 'traffic lights' and 'road maps', which help to keep international flows of goods, services, information, people, and capital moving as smoothly as possible along their respective 'highways' towards ascertainable destinations, while minimizing the potential for 'traffic hold-ups', 'pile-ups', and 'collisions'. Even if the EU framework mainly reflects or embodies the interests and aspirations of the largest and strongest Member States (which is very debatable, as EU systems of representation and 'qualified majority voting' are weighted in favour of the smaller Member States), the resultant increases in contextual stability and in routinized and predictable civil conduct generally offer far greater security, safeguards, and calculability to smaller, poorer, and weaker Member States than would the major alternatives: 'might is right' and 'the law of the jungle', or the unconstrained exercise of brute power by Europe's biggest and strongest countries.

England's Europhobes, whose country has not experienced enemy occupation since 1066 and all that, seem blissfully unaware of this—in contrast to most citizens of many Continental European states, whose forebears have repeatedly experienced brutal military occupations. Indeed, the commonest motivations for forming or joining rule-based unions of states and supranational frameworks of rules and law have been to help weak, insecure, poor, small or medium-sized countries cope with difficult or menacing external political, economic and military pressures.[20] These are the prime reasons why so many such countries have either joined or are striving to join the EU.

[20] Forsyth, *Unions of States*, passim; and Terry Nardin, *Law, Morality and the Relations of States* (Princeton, NJ: Princeton University Press, 1983).

> Far from relinquishing their power and identity, states are increasingly using col-
> laborative power arrangements to create more real control over their economies
> (and indeed over security). As such, these new coalitions should be seen as gambits
> for augmenting rather than shedding state capacity.[21]

States, both as countries and as bundles of institutions, increasingly seek to make themselves indispensable catalytic partners in strategic coalitions, whether of states alone or
states plus firms, and:

> the most successful states will be those which can augment their conventional
> [home-grown] power resources with collaborative power: engaging others...to
> form cooperative agreements and "consortia" for action'; and for such states 'build-
> ing or augmenting state capacity, rather than discarding it, would seem to be the
> lesson of dynamic integration.[22]

The development of inter-national, inter-governmental and supranational organizations should therefore be seen 'as attempts by nation-states to keep their power.'[23]

In any case, the colossal power of hugely inegalitarian global capitalism threatens the democratic autonomy and sovereignty of European states and nations far
more than the EU does. Neoliberal capitalism and intensified globalization have
greatly augmented the largely unaccountable power of 'finance capitalism' and
transnational companies, relative to mere countries, labour, trade-unions,
churches, clubs, and other voluntary civil associations and communities of people;
and such developments have increased social atomization and inequalities far more
than the relatively corporatist, protective, and socially-conscious EU has done.[24]
The EU offers its Member States and their citizens the most promising institutions,
legal frameworks and common policies for regulating and counterbalancing neoliberal global capitalism by maintaining at least a modicum of substantive European
control and regulation of what occurs within Europe. The EU's existence helps its
Member States *collectively* to exercise far more effective and extensive jurisdiction
over their economies and societies than they would if the EU did not exist. In this
admittedly limited sense, EU membership *augments* (rather than diminishes) its
Member States' democratic control and scrutiny of European affairs, *even though*
the EU's vast size, complexity and diversity structurally predetermine that it can
only function as a relatively remote, technocratic, elitist and undemocratic
organization.

---

[21] Linda Weiss, *The Myth of the Powerless State* (Ithaca, NY: Cornell University Press, 1998), 204–9.

[22] Weiss, *The Myth of the Powerless State*, 209–12.

[23] Neil MacCormick, *Constructing Legal Systems: 'European Union' in Legal Theory* (Frankfurt/
M: Springer, 1997), 434.

[24] Anthony Giddens, Patrick Diamond and Roger Liddle (eds), *Global Europe, Social Europe*
(Cambridge: Polity Press, 2006), 1–3; Andrew Glyn, *Capitalism Unleashed* (Oxford: Oxford University
Press, 2006), 168–75.

EU 'Rescues' of Small and Sub-state Nations, Languages, Cultures and Minorities

The relationship between European integration and sub-state or small-state nations and nationalism has proven to be far less embattled and antagonistic than had been anticipated in the 1950s and 1960s. Especially since the doubling of EU 'structural funds'[25] in the late 1980s and the EU's espousal of a 'Europe of the Regions' during the 1990s, sub-state nationalist, autonomist and regionalist parties such as the Scottish National Party (SNP), Plaid Cymru, and Catalonia's Convergencia i Unio have effectively combined quests for greater recognition and autonomy with broad support for European integration, as encapsulated in SNP calls for Scottish 'independence in Europe'.[26] While becoming increasingly adept at using the EU's institutions, regional policies, and 'Committee of the Regions' to augment their visibility, roles and room for manoeuvre in wider EU arenas,[27] most sub-state nationalist parties have developed increasingly variegated interpretations of the principle of self-determination, becoming less insistent on immediate independent statehood and more prepared to bide their time and develop intermediate or transitional solutions.[28] Most strikingly, Convergencia i Unio has projected 'commitment to European integration as a buttress to Catalan autonomy within Spain', and on the whole 'tension between nationalist ideology and European integration is denied by the nationalists themselves.'[29] The EU's institutions, arenas, level playing fields, and supranational civil order have also assisted many more public figures from the smaller European states and sub-state nations to rise to far greater international prominence and influence than they would have done without the EU's existence.

During the 2000s, admittedly, West European sub-state nationalist and regionalist movements expressed considerable disappointment with the limited results of 'Europe of the Regions', especially the non-emergence of an EU-wide regional tier and system of governance.[30] However, the EU and quests for EU membership have contributed very

---

[25] EU transfer payments, designed mainly to promote regional development and social regeneration.

[26] Peter Lynch, *Minority Nationalism and European Integration* (Cardiff: University of Wales Press, 1996).

[27] John McGarry and Michael Keating (eds), *European Integration and the Nationalities Question* (Abingdon: Routledge, 2006); and Charlie Jeffery (ed.), *The Regional Dimension of the European Union* (London: Routledge, 1997).

[28] Michael Keating (ed.), *Regions and Regionalism in Europe* (Cheltenham: Edward Elgar, 2005); W. John Hopkins, *Devolution in Context: Regional Federal and Devolved Government in the European Union* (London: Cavendish Publishing, 2002); Michael Keating, *The New Regionalism in Western Europe* (Cheltenham: Edward Elgar, 1998); and Michael Keating, *Plurinational Democracy* (Oxford: Oxford University Press, 2001).

[29] Claire Sutherland, 'Another Nation-building Bloc? Integrating Nationalist Ideology into the EU and ASEAN', *Asia Europe Journal* 3:2 (2005), 145.

[30] Anwen Elias (ed.), 'Whatever Happened to Europe of the Regions? Revisiting the Regional Dimension of European Politics', special issue of *Regional and Federal Studies* 18:5 (2008), 483–635.

substantially to the development of significant tiers and systems of regional governance and representation and autonomy for sub-state nations/ethnic minorities in post-communist Hungary, Slovakia, Poland, Romania, Macedonia, and Bosnia and Herzegovina.[31]

EU membership *has not been dissolving national cultures and identities 'like lumps of sugar in a cup of coffee'*, in the manner that the Europhobic Czech President Vaclav Klaus has repeatedly predicted since 1994.[32] Far from fostering or imposing increased cultural uniformity or homogenization, the EU has promoted and provided valuable recognition and considerable publicity and financial and infrastructural support for national cultures, ethno-cultural rights, ethno-cultural pluralism/diversity, non-discrimination, mutual respect, anti-racism, more level playing fields, freer circulation of people and ideas, a benchmark Charter of Fundamental Rights and Freedoms, and minority rights, languages, cultures, communities, schools, broadcasting, histories and monuments.[33] Significantly, ethnic minority groups, movements and parties increasingly look primarily to Brussels and the EU (rather than to local intra-state channels, representation and institutions) for recognition, support, protection of rights, non-discrimination, and ethno-cultural justice. This is among the EU's greatest triumphs.

EU State-Building and 'Rescues of the Nation-State' in the Post-Communist East Central European, Baltic and Balkan Regions

The main benefits of EU membership, arising from its *enduring transformative potential*, are not fully captured by a superficial short-term economic calculus. EU membership and quests and preparations for membership have *cumulatively reshaped structures of*

---

[31] Michael Keating and James Hughes (eds), *The Regional Challenges in Central and Eastern Europe* (Bruges: College of Europe Publications, 2003).

[32] Mats Braun, 'Understanding Klaus: The Story of Czech Eurorealism', *EPIN Working Paper* (Prague) 26 (November 2009), 2.

[33] Cultural and linguistic dimensions and implications of European integration are interestingly explored in Peter Kraus, *A Union of Diversity: Language, Identity and Polity-Building in Europe* (Cambridge: Cambridge University Press, 2008); Riva Kastoryano (ed.), *An Identity for Europe: The Relevance of Multiculturalism in EU Construction* (Basingstoke: Palgrave Macmillan, 2009); Jane Warren and Heather M. Benbow (eds), *Multilingual Europe: Reflections on Language and Identity* (Newcastle: Cambridge Scholars Publishing, 2008); Jeffrey Checkel and Peter Katzenstein (eds), *European Identity* (Cambridge: Cambridge University Press, 2009), among others.

power, opportunity, constraints and incentives. This has helped to promote, strengthen and entrench more rule-governed political and economic conduct, the rule of law, more strictly limited government (in the liberal sense), and fundamental rights and freedoms, as frameworks within which representative liberal democracy and liberal capitalism are most likely to survive and flourish. By increasing cross-European economic, social and geographical mobility, EU membership has been a crucial 'passport' to (transformative) unrestricted access to EU-wide product, capital and labour markets, and to major educational, business, networking and funding opportunities. In the countries that joined the EU in 1981, 1986, 2004 and 2007, as well as in the Western Balkans and Turkey since 2000, the requirements of EU membership have gradually promoted: more strongly entrenched rule of law; increased rule certainty and predictability; 'more level playing fields'; movement from strongly 'vertical' (hierarchical, clientelistic, patrimonial) power-relations to increasingly 'horizontal' and law-governed civil ones; and the 'administrative and judicial capacity' needed to cope with very complex, extensive and exacting membership requirements, including implementation of over 80,000 pages of EU legislation, rules, policies and membership obligations (the *acquis communautaire*'). Struggles to satisfy the requirement that new EU entrants must have 'functioning market economies' capable of withstanding the competitive pressures and requirements of the Single Market and absorbing and complying with the rules and obligations of EU membership, have required increased rule certainty, clarity, consistency and calculability. This in turn has helped to integrate and harmonize dispersed/marketized/decentralized decision-making and to consummate the transformation of former command economies into more rule-governed and predictable civil economies and civil societies.[34]

The large and commodious EU order has offered the most promising overarching framework for defusing and overcoming the tensions, grievances, minority issues, economic problems and geopolitical vulnerabilities that have dogged the mostly small, poor, and weak East Central European, Baltic, and Balkan nations and countries. These problems, which helped to drag their inhabitants (and hundreds of millions of other people) into two World Wars, *cannot be resolved or overcome within the cramped confines of the nation-state, which has been one of the main problems to be solved, rather than a solution to such problems.* Most of these countries are too small or poor to offer adequate markets and capital and material inputs for their main industries, which were long stunted or constrained by being 'boxed into' constricted national markets dominated by local monopolists. They cannot flourish without secure, unimpeded access to wider and

---

[34] See: Robert Bideleux, 'The Southern Enlargement of the EC: Greece, Portugal and Spain', in Bideleux and Taylor (eds.), *European Integration and Disintegration*, 127–53; Robert Bideleux and Ian Jeffries, *A History of Eastern Europe* 2nd edn (Abingdon: Routledge, 2007), 574–614; Robert Bideleux and Ian Jeffries, *The Balkans: A Post-Communist History* (Abingdon: Routledge, 2007); Heather Grabbe, *The EU's Transformative Power: Europeanization through Conditionality in Central and Eastern Europe* (Basingstoke: Palgrave Macmillan, 2006); Frank Schimmelfennig and Ulrich Sedelmeier (eds), *Europeanization of Central and Eastern Europe* (Ithaca, NY: Cornell University Press, 2005).

freer markets. These states (in both senses) have long been 'ethnocracies', in that they are seen as 'belonging' collectively and exclusively to their dominant ethnic groups. Incorporation into the EU's strongly law-governed and anti-discriminatory civil association and legal order, within which legal safeguards for fundamental rights and freedoms (including minority rights) are increasingly entrenched and all ethnic and religious groups are minorities (albeit some much more so than others!), offers these nations and states the most dependable framework for peaceful, profitable and equitable coexistence, as well as the most promising ways 'to free human beings from the bondage of ethnic collectivism—that source of all strife and enslaver of human individuality.'[35] These are the deepest reasons why so many such countries have striven or are still striving to be 'rescued' by EU membership.

All of this has augmented the EU's 'soft power' over these countries, especially in the Balkans, where the EU has increasingly looked and acted like a development agency with unusually broad remits and deep pockets, offering enticing financial and technical assistance or 'sweeteners' and promoting or financing increased administrative and judicial capacity, while sometimes withholding EU transfer payments or imposing fines to penalize blatant non-compliance with EU precepts and regulations.[36] While some have considered the EU's quasi-colonial tutelage over these countries to be profoundly irksome and humiliating, others have regarded the quest for EU membership as the most potent driver of much-needed political, economic and cultural change[37] and as 'the best conflict resolution mechanism that Europe has ever had.'[38]

Since 2007 critics have claimed that, once post-communist states have securely entered the EU, the pressures and incentives for these states (in both senses) to continue to persevere with difficult, painful, but 'progressive' restructuring and reform evaporates, and they start 'backsliding' or reverting to 'bad old ways.'[39] It has increasingly been alleged that some post-communist states were admitted into the EU prematurely, too leniently, or on false pretences, and even that the EU was tricked into admitting a country (Romania) whose rulers had little intention of changing their ways.[40]

However, such critiques tend to underestimate the far-reaching degrees to which EU membership changes structures of power, opportunity, constraints and incentives. After all, three of the six countries that launched the European Communities in 1950–52 either

[35] Vaclav Havel, 'The Hope for Europe', New York Review of Books (20 June 1996), 40.

[36] See Bideleux and Jeffries, The Balkans, 581–91; and updates in Adam Fagan, Europe's Balkan Dilemma (London: I. B. Tauris, 2010).

[37] On the resultant pressures, tensions, incentives and penalties in the Balkan post-communist states, see Antoaneta Dimitrova (ed.), Driven to Change: The European Union's Enlargement Viewed from the East (Manchester: Manchester University Press, 2004); Bideleux and Jeffries, The Balkans; International Commission on the Balkans, The Balkans in Europe's Future (Sofia: Centre for Liberal Strategies, 2005); Elisabeth Pond, Endgame in the Balkans (Washington, DC: Brookings Institution, 2006); and Fagan, Europe's Balkan Dilemma.

[38] György Schöpflin, 'The Slovak-Hungarian "Cold War"', euobserver.com (14 January 2009).

[39] Jacques Rupnik, 'Is East Central Europe Backsliding?', Journal of Democracy 18:4 (2007), 17–63.

[40] Tom Gallagher, Romania and the European Union: How the Weak Vanquished the Strong (Manchester: Manchester University Press, 2009).

had perpetrated or were deeply complicit in the most notorious mass genocide in world history just one decade previously. Crucially, EU membership and the increasingly arduous struggles to attain it greatly enhance both the rewards for playing by new rules and the explicit and implicit penalties for non-compliance, with major consequences for actual structures of power, opportunity, incentives, constraints, and conduct. The fact that *the combined GDP of the EU's ten post-communist Member States still amounts to less than 8 per cent of the overall EU GDP* (at official exchange rates) means that the strongly vertical or hierarchical (patron-client) structures of power, opportunity, incentives and constraints inherited from Communist regimes in these formerly very 'boxed in' economies and societies must gradually become hugely outweighed by the structures of power, incentives, opportunity and constraints prevalent in the much vaster, richer and more competitive market economies of the 'EU-15' (the pre-2004 members), in which (admittedly still very powerful) *vertical* power-relations and power-structures are increasingly counterbalanced by more *horizontal* ones (including the EU's much-trumpeted 'level playing fields' and its unique supranational civil legal order).

Reassuringly, despite the severity of the 'Great Recession' of 2008–09, all of the new and prospective EU Member States have continued (at least formally) to uphold liberal democratic modes of governance, very open market economies, and the rules of the Single Market, and have largely resisted nationalist, protectionist, and authoritarian temptations, in striking contrast to the swift and widespread recourse to government by decree, beggar-my-neighbour protectionism, and authoritarian nationalism or fascism in these same countries during the tumultuous interwar era. Their commitments to liberal democracy, open economies and open societies appear (thus far) to have passed the very stern tests imposed by the Great Recession of 2008–9 and the eurozone crises of 2010–12. (The most likely exception is the right-wing nationalist Fidesz government elected in Hungary in April 2010, which has lost no time in generating serious grounds for concern, but it could yet resume the more liberal paths of its predecessors.) Inasmuch as EU membership may have strengthened the will, incentives, confidence and capacity of formerly 'recidivist' states to withstand and deal with severe crises in relatively open, liberal and democratic ways, this could come to be seen as the most extraordinary 'EU rescue of the nation-state'.

Transformations of the States in Need of 'Rescue': 'Embedded Neoliberalism'

Many pundits have assumed that supranational market forces, transnational corporations and supranational 'finance capitalism' will eventually overpower or supplant states and nations. Even the US National Intelligence Council has postulated that by 2025 the familiar 'world of states' will have been largely eclipsed by a 'world of networks'.[41] If this occurs, the EU probably *would* supersede the nation-state as Europe's main locus of governance, and claims that European integration strengthens and safeguards the nation-state would lapse. However, rumours of the imminent death of the (nation-)state have repeatedly turned out to be exaggerated. Instead of meekly 'withering away', states have displayed remarkable capacities to reinvent themselves and operate in new ways, and *'l'Europe des états'* has survived.

Nevertheless, since the 1980s, the meteoric rise of formidable economic competition from East and South Asia, the post-Vietnam resurgence of the USA, intensified globalization, and the global ascendancy of neoliberalism have considerably transformed the nature and functions of states and the environments in which they operate. The EU has endeavoured to meet these challenges through the 'Single Market' programme initiated in 1985–86; the 1985 Schengen Agreement on border-free movement (implemented during the 1990s); the 'Lisbon Strategy' launched in 2000; the 'Growth and Jobs Strategy' launched in 2005; and the 'Europe 2020 Strategy' launched in 2010. These strategies have both responded and contributed to the growing importance of transnational companies, far-reaching internationalization and relocation of production and control, and exponential growth of cross-border flows of information, ideas, knowledge, technology and money. Protective and interventionist Keynesian, social democratic, or Christian democratic welfare states, presiding over 'Fordist' economic systems amenable to varied forms and degrees of hierarchical top-down state regulation, *dirigisme* and corporatism, have given way to the enhanced 'flexibility' of neoliberal *'competition states'*, while emphasis has shifted from macroeconomic demand management to microeconomic 'supply-side economics', whose chief function is to position increasingly 'post-Fordist' economies to maximum advantage in fiercely rivalrous global markets.[42] These markets are more 'rivalrous' than 'competitive', in that widespread *oligopoly* and cross-border, inter-firm and state-firm *cooperation* often involves *more collusion than competition*.

The EU has sought to reconcile EU citizens to globalized capitalism by promoting relatively robust and extensive regulatory governance at the supranational EU level, while supporting the maintenance of free trade-unions and relatively comprehensive systems of rights, social protection, health insurance and pensions, primarily at the 'national' level. This combination is best characterized as 'embedded neoliberalism'.[43] EU-wide frameworks of consensual regulation and rule-setting are widely preferred to the anarchic free-for-alls of full-blown neoliberalism, yet 'social Europe' has remained

[41] National Intelligence Council , *Global Trends 2025: A Transformed World* (Washington, DC: US Government Printing Office, November 2008), iv, x, 1, 81, 84–90. Available online at: www.dni.gov/nic/ NIC_2025_project.html

[42] Philip Cerny, *The Changing Architecture of Politics* (London: Sage, 1990); and Philip Cerny, 'Paradoxes of the Competition State', in *Government and Opposition* 32:2 (1997), 251–74.

[43] Incisively and illuminatingly analysed in Bastiaan van Apeldoorn, Jan Drahokoupil and Laura Horn (eds), *Contradictions and Limits of Neoliberal European Governance: From Lisbon to Lisbon* (Basingstoke: Palgrave Macmillan, 2009).

largely confined to non-discrimination policies arising from EU commitments to free movement of labour, gender equity, and civil equality, with little attempt to foster an EU-wide welfare state.[44]

The EU and 'the Nation-State' after the Lisbon Treaty of 2009

Europhobic opponents of the 2009 Lisbon Treaty have often fulminated against what they see as the latest in a long series of EU encroachments on the autonomy and sovereignty of the nation-state. However, it is somewhat naïve to suppose that states as jealous of their 'national' sovereignty as the UK, France, Germany, Denmark and Sweden would have ratified a treaty designed to seriously reduce or dilute their still considerable (and in many ways enhanced) *effective* autonomy, powers, capabilities and sovereignty. European integration is still mainly about *empowering and capacitating EU Member States, not emasculating them*. The new posts of president of the European Council and EU foreign minister (both chosen by and responsible to the governments of the Member States) have further eclipsed the EU Commission, whose independence, power(s) and capacity to lead the EU and promote allegedly 'federalist' agendas have diminished steadily since its halcyon years under Jacques Delors (1985–94); and EU agenda-setting, gate-keeping, and external relations are now very firmly under the collective control of the elected governments of the Member States.[45] Thus the 2009 Lisbon Treaty (like the 1997 Treaty of Amsterdam and the 2000 Treaty of Nice) represents a '*rebalancing*' of the EU in favour of its Member States. Even though successive treaties have steadily increased the proportions of EU decisions and legislation *formally* subject to so-called 'qualified majority voting', in practice the vast majority of EU decisions, laws, and policies continue to be adopted by unanimous 'common accord' between EU governments.[46] Whether these are positive or retrograde trends is a moot point. So long as European democracy continues to be overwhelmingly *national* in focus and underpinnings, it is tempting to portray any 'repatriation' of powers and responsibilities and any strengthening of EU 'intergovernmentalism' as expansions of the scope for democratic control and accountability in EU governance. However, such changes could merely increase

[44] Mark Kleinman, *A European Welfare State? European Union Social Policy in Context* (Basingstoke: Palgrave Macmillan, 2001).

[45] Piotr M. Kaczynski, 'The European Commission: 2004–09: A Politically Weakened Institution?', *European Policy Institutes Network Working Paper* 23 (May 2009), 1–9.

[46] Elizabeth Bomberg, John Peterson and Alexander Stubb (eds), *The European Union: How Does It Work?*, 2nd edn (Oxford: Oxford University Press, 2008), 53, 56.

'executive empowerment', the autonomous power of governments to govern over the heads of 'the people' (whether the embryonic *demos* of the EU as a whole or the separate *demoi* of the individual Member States), further reinforcing the EU as a confederal and elitist 'cartel of governments'. Fortunately, the overarching EU polity also furnishes and upholds institutions, frameworks, codes, and policies which mostly enhance fundamental rights and freedoms, the rule of law, limited government, and the scope and efficacy of democracy and governance at the state and sub-state levels. By creating a diffuse, decentred, law-governed and increasingly rights-based EU polity, attained more by iterative trial-and-error than by premeditated design, EU represents an ingenious solution to 'the most crucial problem of political organization, namely how to limit the "popular will" without placing another "will" above it.'[47]

THE 'GREAT RECESSION' OF 2008–09 AND THE EUROZONE CRISES OF 2010–12: THE END OF THE 'EUROPEAN MIRACLE'?

For centuries, Europe's vaunted dynamism and the liberties, relative prosperity and free-standing survival of most of its states have rested upon the maintenance of a *rule-governed multiplicity of competing states* and *the absence of a hegemon*. Through shifting and balancing alliances and the emergence of an increasingly robust system of international law, successive bids for hegemonic domination of Europe have been thwarted (Charlemagne; Charles V and his son Philip II; the Habsburgs again during the 1618–1648 War; Napoleon; and Hitler), permitting the survival of a pluralistic European states system in which 'wrong-headed and incontrovertible systems-wide decisions could not be imposed [on Europe as a whole] by some central authority.'[48] A fresh version of this 'European miracle' has come about through the combination of the EU's unified Single Market for goods, services, labour and capital (operating under the overarching jurisdiction of an increasingly robust and elaborate supranational legal order) with the maintenance of the vital autonomy and liberties of its Member States and the absence of a 'federal' political union.

Until 2009, the pursuit of Economic and Monetary Union (EMU) without a corresponding 'federal' political union was routinely presented as a major source of EU strength. However, the eurozone crises that began in early 2010 quickly made that com-

---

[47] Friedrich Hayek, *Law, Legislation and Liberty* (London: Routledge, 1982), Vol. 1, 6.
[48] E. L. Jones, *The European Miracle* (Cambridge: Cambridge University Press, 1981), 106–23; 2nd edn (1987), 104–26.

bination look more like *a potentially fatal source of rigidity, incapacity and weakness,* rather than resilience. There are grave doubts as to whether the EU and the eurozone have sufficient flexibility, agility, and central power and resources to deal with these crises.

In addition, spiralling EU expenditure on structural, cohesion, and agricultural policies, combined with much-publicized fiscal, monetary, accounting, or regulatory laxity in various Member States from 2000 to 2008, has fuelled mounting worries that the EU and (even more crucially) the eurozone have not devised sufficiently stringent and robust rules and disciplinary mechanisms to control or deal effectively with widespread and often flagrant rule-breaking and 'freeriding' problems and the profound tensions and contradictions within 'embedded neoliberalism',[49] all of which have been most cruelly exposed by the successive crises of 2008–12. The disciplinary and enforcement problems of the eurozone became obvious in 2003–05, when first France and then Germany exceeded the 3 per cent of GDP budget deficit limit with impunity and were in no hurry to comply. That signalled to the Southern eurozone members that such limits were unlikely to be strictly enforced or, if they were, that this would invite accusations of double standards.

So long as European integration was largely confined to 'negative integration' (elimination of barriers to free movement of goods, services, people, and capital), there was much more complementarity and mutual reinforcement than tension or contradiction between European integration and the still extensive autonomy and freedom of action of EU Member States. This is what made successive EU 'rescues of the nation-state' possible. However, the further the EU has travelled down the road of 'positive integration' (involving centralized allocation of substantial resources and decisions on how to share them out), the stronger and the less tractable have been the potential tensions and contradictions between the EU and its Member States, and between pursuit of full economic union and the almost complete absence of political union. These have left the EU and the eurozone *much less capable of dealing sufficiently swiftly and decisively with large external and/or asymmetric economic shocks, and much less able to pursue strongly redistributive or counter-cyclical economic policies, than is the case for fully-fledged political federations,* such as the USA, Canada, Brazil, India and Australia. By its very nature, moreover, the eurozone is lumbered with a dysfunctional 'one-size-fits-all' monetary policy.

During 2010–12 the eurozone repeatedly came close to breakdown. This was *not* primarily attributable to the alleged profligacy, indiscipline, regulatory laxity or 'freeriding' of Greece and/or Ireland. Since Greece's GDP and Ireland's GDP amounted to only around 2.3 per cent and around 1.2 per cent of EU GDP respectively (at market prices and exchange rates), their economies were too small to have been the chief causes of the crises that erupted in the vast eurozone economy in 2010. The major causes of these crises have been that: (i) EU and eurozone accounting, disciplinary and enforcement

[49] van Apeldoorn et al. (eds), *Contradictions and Limits of Neoliberal European Governance*, chs. 1 and 2.

mechanisms have been (and may well remain) too vague and too weak to play their requisite roles; and (ii) Germany has been very reluctant to discharge (or even comprehend) the crucial roles of lender, importer and spender of last resort, which the hegemon in any international monetary-cum-trading regime has to fulfil if that regime's long-term viability is to be assured.

The reasonably successful operation of the international gold standard from the 1850s to 1914 and of the Bretton Woods system during the 1950s–60s (and, conversely, the breakdown of those international monetary regimes during the 1930s and early 1970s) highlighted the high degrees to which *the viability of international monetary-cum-trading regimes depends upon the willingness and ability of a hegemon to act as the major importer, investor, spender and lender of last resort*, in order to facilitate and/or bankroll economic adjustments among weaker or ailing participants. During the 1930s, the world's main international monetary-cum-trading regime broke down in large part because the UK was no longer able to play this role, while the USA was not yet ready to take over the UK's former role.[50] The German government, parliament, and public seem dangerously reluctant to fully understand and accept the nature and scale of the eurozone's systemic flaws and of the hegemon's responsibilities, and thus have increasingly floundered vis-à-vis the eurozone's problems and crises. This poses one of the major threats to the EU's continued capacity to 'rescue' nation-states—and thereby survive.

However, at the landmark European Council meeting in Brussels on 16–17 December 2010, all twenty-seven EU Member States agreed to add important institutional and rule changes to Article 136 of the Treaty on the Functioning of the European Union, in an endeavour 'to safeguard the stability of the euro area as a whole'. It was also formally agreed that, with effect from 1 January 2013, a permanent European Stability Mechanism would supersede the temporary emergency European Financial Stability Facility (fund) and European Financial Stabilization Mechanism adopted to deal with the economic crises of 2010 in Greece and Ireland; that all bailouts would be 'made subject to strict conditionality'; and that further EU legislation would beef up the eurozone's Stability and Growth pact and 'economic governance', to allow the imposition of mandatory (IMF-style) 'stringent economic and fiscal adjustments' on recipients of bailouts, as well as structural reforms and 'effective and rigorous economic surveillance, which will focus on prevention and... substantially reduce the probability of a crisis arising in the future', and to render private creditors liable to negotiated debt-restructuring, including (by an EU 'qualified majority decision') 'a legally binding change in the terms of payment (standstill, extension of maturity, interest-rate cut and/or haircut) in the event that the debtor is unable to pay'.[51]

---

[50] Charles P. Kindleberger, *The World in Depression, 1929–1939* (London: Allen Lane/Penguin, 1973), 28, 292–305; and Barry Eichengreen, *Golden Fetters: The Gold Standard and the Great Depression, 1919–1939* (New York: Oxford University Press, 1992), 4–28, 187–221, 392–9. Patricia Clavin, *The Great Depression in Europe, 1929–1939* (Basingstoke: Macmillan, 2000), 44, has objected that 'Teamwork, not hegemonic leadership, was what made the gold standard work.' However, effective hegemonic leadership often rests on promoting or eliciting effective teamwork.

[51] 'Conclusions of the European Council, 16–17 December 2010', EUCO 30/10, Brussels: European Council, 17 December 2010, 1–2, 6–12.

It remains to be seen whether all seventeen eurozone members will fully accept and implement the severity of eurozone rule-tightening and the draconian penalties for non-compliance and 'freeriding' needed to assure the eurozone's long-term viability. However, *if such a strong and intrusive regime were to be fully implemented, the implicit large reductions of state autonomy and freedom of action would represent a huge departure from the pivotal mutually-beneficial equilibrium and complementarity between the EU and the autonomy of its Member States, which has been indispensable to the great successes of European integration from 1952 to 2008.*

IRISH AND 'SOUTHERN' DISCOMFORT

Furnishing fully repayable interest-bearing loans ('bailouts') to seriously insolvent economies can postpone their 'final reckonings' for a few years, but, as was most horrifically demonstrated by the Third World debt crises of the 1980s and 1990s, this often results in massive escalations of their external indebtedness, while locking them even more deeply into the webs of obligation that got them into such dire straits in the first place. Thus, although many pundits and politicians have assumed that the eurozone's survival hinges on whether it can mobilize enough resources to 'bail out' its most crisis-stricken members, the opposite could prove to be the case. Such 'rescues' are often much more beneficial to the creditors than to the debtors. 'Bailouts' could foster additional 'moral hazards' and 'freeriding' (Germany's chief concern), but, unless accompanied by large 'write downs', 'hair-cuts' or 'negotiated defaults', *they could also greatly increase the total external indebtedness of the 'bailed-out' countries, thereby exacerbating (rather than alleviating) their longer-term cash-flow/solvency problems.* This is most immediately pertinent to Greece, Ireland, and Portugal, but could also become so for Spain or Italy as well.

The relative strength of the euro, combined with the eurozone's relatively strict rules and their own varyingly 'corporatist' traditions, has made it increasingly hard for these countries to compete successfully in global markets and to attract as many tourists as they did before joining the eurozone. Between 1999 and 2008 they experienced substantial appreciation of their real exchange rates and serious loss of international competitiveness (see Table 18.1), while most of the former Deutschmark zone countries (especially Germany) had the opposite experience:

This contributed to a decade-long 'money illusion' of economic prosperity in the so-called 'PIIGS' (Portugal, Ireland, Italy, Greece and Spain), based upon cheap imports, unaccustomedly low interest rates, credit booms, inflated real estate prices, high prices for their exports and tourism services, and apparently diminishing economic disparities vis-à-vis Europe's most advanced economies. However, all of this steadily reduced the

Table 18.1 Real Exchange Rate Appreciation (%), 1999–2008[52]

'PIIGS'		Former Deutschmark Zone	
		Netherlands	5
Ireland	21	Belgium	4.5
Spain	14	France	−0.5
Greece	10	Austria	−1.0
Portugal	6	Finland	−2.0
Italy	4.5	Germany	−3.0

international competitiveness of their export and tourism sectors and the sustainability of their economic 'bubbles'.

As in the 1950s–1990s, these countries need to periodically restore their international competitiveness via intermittent currency devaluations, but membership of the eurozone (rashly self-imposed for short-term gain or non-economic status enhancing reasons) precludes this. Swift restoration of their international competitiveness by emulating the draconian 15–25 per cent 'internal devaluations' undertaken by the Baltic States in 2008–09 would probably evoke too much internal social resistance to be politically feasible.[53] The interests of Ireland and the Southern eurozone countries might therefore be best served by withdrawing from the eurozone as soon as this can be done in an orderly manner. Otherwise they face the likelihood of decades of economic austerity and slow growth—far too high a price to pay for continued membership of the eurozone club and seats at the 'high table'.

BACK TO THE DEUTSCHMARK ZONE?

The more Northerly eurozone countries are a relatively integrated, cohesive, highly developed, and cyclically synchronized group of economies. For them, a smaller monetary union (resembling the old Deutschmark zone, which also included Denmark and

[52] Stephanie Flanders, 'Thinking the Unthinkable', BBC News, 11 February 2010, accessed 19 December 2010, available online at: http://www.bbc.co.uk/blogs/thereporters/stephanieflanders/2010/02/thinking_the_unthinkable.html

[53] The Baltic States reduced wages, salaries, public spending and pensions by 15–25 per cent across the board in 2008–09, as a way of cutting costs and budget deficits, restoring their international competitiveness, and promoting export-led recovery, while keeping their currencies firmly tied/pegged to the euro. In mid-2010 Estonia was offered eurozone membership with effect from January 2011. Despite Estonian public opinion being soundly opposed to this, Estonia did join at the start of 2011.

Sweden) may be economically sustainable. Their higher degrees of economic convergence, synchronization, and fiscal and monetary discipline would reduce the need for further restrictions or encroachments on their autonomy, to sustain the viability of such a union. These economies appear to have been marching closely in step with one another since the early 1980s, and this seems likely to persist. Nevertheless, such a union would have drawbacks. Germany's even more hegemonic position within a smaller grouping might assist its synchrony, convergence and discipline, but it could rankle with those people in France and the Low Countries who were originally drawn to EMU partly to escape or dilute German dominance of the Deutschmark zone. Moreover, the more stringent eurozone rules adopted in 2010–11 may unduly restrict the economic manoeuvrability of highly indebted economies (notably Belgium).

The Heart of the Matter

Until the establishment of the eurozone in 1999–2002, the EU and its precursors developed in ways that were not merely *compatible* with the maintenance of considerable Member State autonomy and freedom of action, but in many ways *required, depended on and further reinforced it*. Even EU citizenship has been conceived and developed in ways that have not supplanted or encroached upon citizenship of Member States. On the contrary, EU citizenship is predicated on citizenship of a Member State, which is thus guaranteed to retain its primacy.

Admittedly, the rules and requirements of the Common Market and the subsequent Single Market *have* limited the freedom of action of Member States in certain respects (for example, by precluding beggar-my-neighbour protectionism). *On balance*, however, EU membership has expanded and strengthened (rather than weakened) the *effective* autonomy and freedom of action of its Member States; and this has been indispensable to the successes of European integration.

During the 1990s debates on the feasibility of EMU, there were many prescient warnings (mostly Anglo-American) that EMU could only be viable and sustainable in the long term if it was buttressed by stringent rules, disciplinary mechanisms and enforcement mechanisms which (to be effective) would entail major curtailments of the autonomy and freedom of action of the participating countries, especially in the economic domain, not least because the EU states collectively lack(ed) several key attributes of an 'optimal currency area'. For example, despite formal freedom of movement, workers do not in practice move as easily and readily ('freely') *between* (or even *within*) EU countries as they do between US, Indian or Brazilian states or Canadian provinces. The EU also has much less wherewithal and scope to engage in counter-cyclical and redistributive policies than is the case for any fully-fledged federation, mainly because the EU's chief paymasters have never allowed EU expenditures to reach (let alone exceed) the chosen ceiling: 1.27 per cent of EU GDP.

Debates on the eurozone's viability and chances of survival have also given too little attention to the fact that *international monetary unions and regimes have rarely survived for very long*, and have been acutely prone to breakdown during global and/or regional economic recessions and to exacerbation and international transmission of recession and breakdown. Indeed, a classic study of the gold standard concluded that its rigid mechanisms and rules, which strikingly foreshadowed those of EMU, substantially prolonged the 1929–39 Depression and magnified its international transmission.[54] This makes it all the more reckless and irresponsible for the EU to have turned monetary union into 'a central part of European integration'.[55]

EMU is more likely to promote implosion of the European economy and states system (possibly with echoes of the disintegration of the Soviet and Yugoslav Federations) than European stability, prosperity and further EU 'rescues' of the nation-state. Embarking on the EMU experiment has been a colossal gamble and blunder. It would be prudent to discontinue or at least downsize this deeply flawed project while it is still feasible to do so in an orderly and controlled manner, before the EMU 'Titanic' hits even bigger 'icebergs' bearing names like Spain and Italy....

Naturally, the enormous costs and loss of face involved in downsizing or dismantling the eurozone may well encourage current eurozone members (and even the EU as a whole) to repeatedly use the 'bail-out' funds and mechanisms approved in 2010–11 to maintain the status quo and postpone the day of reckoning for as long as possible. However, the longer this continues, the greater the danger that the euro(zone) as a whole will collapse, with vastly more damaging 'backwash effects' on the EU as a whole (and on non-EU countries that heavily depend on the EU).

It would be much wiser to start an orderly retreat from this foolhardy experiment with the economic wellbeing of over 320 million people, and to recognize that this need not mark 'the end of the road' for European integration. Valuable and viable 'widening' and 'deepening' of the EU can still take place on other very important fronts, notably further 'eastward enlargements' of the EU (incorporating dynamic Turkey as well as several much weaker Western Balkan countries) and the development of sorely needed common environmental policies. There could even be an EU 'rescue' of the 'European social model', as advocated by the late Pierre Bourdieu.[56]

The heart of the matter, as seen by an ardent Europhile, is that European integration should only be pursued in forms that can be made to work and be sustained in the long term. Among other things, successful European integration has indispensably involved and depended upon the preservation and reinforcement of substantial autonomy and freedom of action for EC and EU Member States, not least in the economic domain.

---

[54] Eichengreen, *Golden Fetters*, xi–xii, 3–28.

[55] The wording used in the 'Conclusions of the European Council, 16–17 December 2010', 11.

[56] Pierre Bourdieu, *Firing Back: Against the Tyranny of the Market* 2 (New York, NY: The New Press, 2001), 26–7.

Monetary union, like any other far-reaching departure from this pivotal requirement, places this greatest of all regional integration projects seriously in jeopardy. Further integration of Europe can take place most successfully in other ways, ones that do not encroach so heavily and dangerously on state autonomy.[57]

Postscript, January 2012: The 'bailouts', institutional reforms, and rule changes put forward by eurozone governments during 2010–11, treated *symptoms* of the potentially terminal eurozone crisis (primarily sovereign debt problems), but largely ignored the *root causes*: the unsustainability of a 'one-size-fits-all' exchange rate and interest rate for seventeen economies with *widely divergent* international competiveness, productivity change, and structural malleability, and of monetary union without commensurate fiscal/political union. The euro looked increasingly beyond rescue.

FURTHER READING

Apeldoorn, Bastiaan van, Jan Drahokoupil and Laura Horn (eds), *Contradictions and Limits of Neoliberal European Governance: From Lisbon to Lisbon* (Basingstoke: Palgrave Macmillan, 2009).

Bartolini, Stefano, *Restructuring Europe* (Oxford: Oxford University Press, 2005).

Bideleux, Robert, 'Reconstituting Political Order in Europe, West and East', and 'Rethinking the Eastward Extension of the EU Civil Order and the Nature of Europe's New East-West Divide', *Perspectives on European Politics and Society* 10:1 (2009), 3–16, 118–36.

Bomberg, Elizabeth, John Peterson and Alexander Stubb (eds), *The European Union: How Does It Work?*, 2nd edn (Oxford: Oxford University Press, 2008).

Gillingham, John, *European Integration, 1950–2003: Superstate or New Market Economy?* (Cambridge: Cambridge University Press, 2003).

Kleinman, Mark, *A European Welfare State? European Union Social Policy in Context* (Basingstoke: Palgrave Macmillan, 2001).

Majone, Domenico, *Dilemmas of European Integration: The Ambiguities and Pitfalls of Integration by Stealth* (Oxford: Oxford University Press, 2005).

Mariscal, Nicolás, *Teorías politicas de la integración europea* (Madrid: Tecnos, 2003).

Milward, Alan, *The European Rescue of the Nation-State*, 2nd edn (Abingdon: Routledge, 2000).

Ruggie, John Gerrard, *Constructing the World Polity: Essays on International Institutionalization* (London: Routledge, 1998).

Schmidt, Vivien, *Democracy in Europe: The EU and National Polities* (Oxford: Oxford University Press, 2006).

Wiener, Antje and Thomas Dietz (eds), *European Integration Theory*, 2nd edn (Oxford: Oxford University Press, 2009).

---

[57] Many thanks to Dan Stone for his many patient and constructive comments on successive drafts of this chapter, and to Catherine Lee for providing numerous leads and ample doses of healthy scepticism.

CHAPTER 19

··

A RESTRUCTURED ECONOMY: FROM THE OIL CRISIS TO THE FINANCIAL CRISIS, 1973–2009[1]

··

IVAN T. BEREND

CREEPING ECONOMIC CRISIS AND ITS EXPLOSION: THE LATE 1960S AND 1970S

WORLD WAR II was a watershed in European history. The devastated and decimated continent was divided into two isolated eastern and western halves, hostile and living under the threat of nuclear war. However, during the quarter of a century that followed the war, Western Europe enjoyed the most spectacular prosperity in history. While the population of Western Europe increased by less than 20 per cent, the Gross Domestic Product rose by 286 per cent. As an average, roughly two and a half times more goods and services were available for every citizen. A prosperous consumer society emerged with a majority of people having comfortable housing, mechanized households, cars, and long vacations abroad.

The twelve countries of the region increased the value of their exports nearly six and a half times, from $115,087 million to $730,235 million (at constant prices). In 1950, a west European worker, as an average, produced $5.82 value per hour; by 1973, this was $16.37 value, thus labour productivity increased 2.8-fold. The western half of the old continent, already relatively rich before World War I, had never experienced such affluence. Economists explained that depression and economic crisis were things of the past.

---

[1] This study is based on my book, *Europe Since 1980* (Cambridge: Cambridge University Press, 2010).

Economic cycles supposedly no longer existed. In mid-October 1973, however, a dramatic event ended European prosperity.

The Arab oil-exporting countries made a political decision against the West by introducing an oil embargo, increasing prices. The cost of a barrel of oil jumped from $2.70 in 1973 to $9.76 by 1974, and then to $12, and generated a sharp worldwide price increase. Six years later a second oil crisis followed and, between 1973 and 1980, led altogether to a tenfold increase in oil prices. Inflation reached a two-digit rate in the West and was combined with an increasing trade deficit, since the price of imported goods, mostly raw materials, increased 20 per cent more than export prices did.[2] Fast economic growth stopped from one day to the next. The twelve advanced European countries (later the EU-12) saw annual growth decline from 4.8 per cent between 1960 and 1973, to 0.5 per cent during the first half of the 1980s.[3] Unemployment increased tenfold in West Germany and then remained high during the entire 1980s, at between 5 and 12 per cent. In some countries, such as Spain, it reached 20 per cent.[4] Countries lost control of inflation, which reached an average of nearly 10 per cent per year in Western Europe and nearly 20 per cent in Mediterranean Europe.

The feelings associated with the forgotten Great Depression and cyclical economic development, all of a sudden replaced growth-cum-consumption euphoria. However, both oil crises had extra-economic origins. Both were the consequences of local or regional political crises. The first exploded as the consequence of the Arab-Israeli War (the so-called Yom Kippur War), when Syria and Egypt attacked Israel, followed by the political punishment of the Israel-friendly West by the oil embargo, while the second oil crisis was a consequence of the Iranian Islamic Revolution.

However, it soon turned out that the roots of the crisis were much deeper, and that the politically ignited oil crisis simply made the crisis manifest. Most paradoxically, the postwar prosperity in Europe undermined itself, and paved the way for a deep economic crisis. Virtually full employment, the lack of a labour reserve that entered and left the labour market, as well as a shortage of labour, which initiated the employment of guest workers and immigration, made labour's position strong. Workers' attitudes changed. The unions launched mass strikes for higher wages. The postwar social partnership between employees and employers ended, and class confrontation reappeared. Collective self-restraint that helped to overcome postwar decline disappeared. A race between wages and prices initiated a wage-price spiral in West Germany, France, Italy, and several other countries from the late 1960s.[5]

---

[2] Angus Maddison, *Two Crises: Latin America and Asia 1929–38 and 1973–83* (Paris: OECD, 1985), 13.

[3] Instead of nearly 5 per cent annual growth in Germany before 1973, growth rates dropped to 1.6 per cent between 1974 and 1983. In the Netherlands growth declined from 5 to 1.4 per cent per annum in the same period.

[4] Unemployment rate was nearly 14 and 13 per cent in the Netherlands and Britain.

[5] A contract in 1969 stipulated a 19 per cent wage increase in Italian industry. In France, wages rose more quickly than GDP every year between 1968 and 1973. Social expenditures steeply increased in postwar Europe: by 14 times in Italy, 7 times in France, 6 times in Sweden, and 4 times in Western Europe as a whole. Public spending grew from 30 to 50 per cent of GDP in Italy. The western countries spent 40 to 50 per cent of GDP on welfare expenditures.

Prices also soared and required the introduction of rigorous fiscal measures to regain control in June 1972.[6] In West Germany, the *rate* of wage increases doubled during the 1970s. Inflation gradually emerged during the period of high prosperity and full employment, and became significant between 1968 and 1973. As Andrea Boltho explains, 'the success of the 1950s and 1960s had laid the preconditions for at least some of the failures of the 1970s.'[7] High prosperity paved the way for its end in the form of over-investment and over-production. The gross capital stock per employee in France, West Germany, the Netherlands, and Britain increased nearly threefold between 1950 and 1973. As one chronicler noted:

> Tremendous over-investment [took place] in the traditional industrial sectors of the modern consumption economy during the 1960s, causing massive overcapacity...the enormous investment in the secondary and tertiary sectors, held out the prospect of a shortage of foodstuff, raw materials and energy. The turning of the terms of trade in favour of primary producers from the beginning of the 1970s came as a result of this growing imbalance.[8]

The economy became overheated: industrial output in the advanced West increased by 10 per cent, and the price of energy and raw materials increased by as much as 63 per cent in 1972–1973. The rate of inflation in West Germany reached 7 per cent that year, i.e. before the oil crisis. Excessive growth and skyrocketing consumption led to the saturation of consumer goods markets. As part of this trend, exports also became more difficult, and their growth slowed. Mass production, a key factor for prosperity, became less and less sustainable. Between 1965 and 1973, the aggregate manufacturing profitability of the seven wealthiest countries of the world declined by 25 per cent.[9]

In the middle of this changing economic trend, the postwar Bretton Woods agreement, which created economic stability by fixing exchange rates for the West, collapsed in 1971.[10] Because of its accumulating deficit, the United States first devalued the dollar, which was the de facto international currency, and then abolished its exchange rate for gold. Fixed exchange rates and control of the financial markets were eliminated. Stability, the basis of mass production, dramatically weakened. Keynesian stimulation of demand did not stop recession, but rather provoked wage compensation and increased inflation.[11] Creeping economic crisis was joined with an unexpected political crisis in Western Europe. In

---

[6] OECD, *Structural Adjustment and Economic Performance* (Paris: OECD, 1987), 129.

[7] Andrea Boltho, *The European Economy: Growth and Crisis* (Oxford: Oxford University Press, 1982), 28.

[8] Herman Van der Wee, *Prosperity and Upheaval: the World Economy 1945–1980* (Berkeley, CA: University of California Press, 1986), 90.

[9] Robert Brenner, 'Uneven Development and the Long Downturn: Advanced Capitalist Economies from Boom to Stagnation, 1950–1988,' *New Left Review,* Special Issue, (May-June, 1998), 138.

[10] In August 1971, the Nixon administration practically ended dollar convertibility. This shocked the international monetary system and led to uncertainty.

[11] Barry Eichengreen, 'Institutions and Economic Growth: Europe after World War II', in Nicholas Crafts and Gianni Toniolo (eds), *Economic Growth in Europe since 1945* (Cambridge: Cambridge University Press, 1994), 61.

March 1968, riots began at French universities. Events culminated in May with general university strikes, occupations, and mass demonstrations by 1 million people. Street battles rattled the Latin Quarter, and special military headquarters were established for operations. Workers occupied factories, and 2 million of them went on strike and achieved substantial wage increases. The Paris events ignited massive echoes in several other countries, most of all in Italy and West Germany. The *Rote Armee Fraktion* (an urban guerilla force) and the bloody actions of the Baader-Meinhof group in Germany, as well as the activities of the Italian *Brigate Rosso* in Italy (such as the occupation of the Fiat factory in Milan, bombing of landmark monuments, attacks against banks, and the Piazza Fontana bombing that killed sixteen people and wounded ninety) signalled the end of an era. Bombing, kidnapping, and the executions of kidnapped politicians and business leaders scarred Italy and West Germany between 1968 and the 1970s.

Nothing worked as normal any longer. Economic growth stopped, prices and unemployment sharply increased, and Keynesian demand-side economics—which held that economic crisis could be coped with by increasing demand and strengthening the purchasing power of the population through job creation and state investments—was not able to cure stagnation and to prevent decline. In fact, it generated even higher inflation. The Philips curve, the classic 'law' of economics, describing the inverse relationship between inflation and unemployment, such that increasing inflation decreases unemployment and *vice versa*, stopped working, as inflation and unemployment rose together. Between 1950–73 and 1973–83, consumer prices in the leading western economies more than doubled from an annual average increase of 4.2 to 9.4 per cent. In the Mediterranean region, they more than quadrupled from 4.0 to 18.4 per cent. World price levels had also more than doubled. Unemployment, averaging 2 to 4 per cent in Western and Mediterranean Europe between 1950 and 1973, jumped to 12 per cent and hit more than 7 million people.[12] What followed was a sudden slowing down and then a decline in economic growth, accompanied by high inflation and unemployment. The Belgian mining industry declined by half, construction by one-third. In ten west European countries, employment in the three ailing industrial sectors dramatically decreased between 1974 and 1985: in the iron and steel industry to 58 per cent, in textiles to 62 per cent, and in shipbuilding to 28 per cent.[13]

The coal output of Belgium, Britain and France combined decreased by 40 per cent. By the early 1980s, the combined textile production of Belgium, West Germany, France, Italy, the Netherlands, and Britain dropped to less than half of the production levels of the 1960s.[14] At its lowest point, industrial output had declined by 13 per cent. The International Monetary Fund was unable to maintain the liquidity of the international

---

[12] Angus Maddison, *Monitoring the World Economy 1820–1992* (Paris: OECD, 1995), 84.

[13] Based on OECD, *Structural Adjustment,* 236 (unweighted average of Austria, the three Benelux countries, Britain, France, Germany, Italy, Norway, and Sweden).

[14] Wolfram Fischer, Jan A. van Houtte, Herman Kellenbenz, *Handbuch der Europäische Wirtschafts- und Sozialgeschichte vom Ersten Weltkrieg bis zum Gegenwart* (Stuttgart: Franz Steiner, 1987), vol. 6, 117, 135.

banking system. Severe austerity measures became unavoidable and closed the circle. This odd pairing of stagnation *and* inflation led to the introduction of a new economic term: *stagflation*.

It soon turned out that besides the deeper roots that went back to the 1960s, the real causes of the decline were also much deeper than the transitory oil crisis. What happened was a phenomenon typical of the market economy, best described and analysed by the Austrian-born Harvard economist, Joseph Schumpeter, who called it 'structural crisis'. He explained:

> Industrial revolutions periodically reshape the existing structure of industry by introducing new methods of production…new forms of organization…new trade routes and markets to sell in. While these things are being initiated we have brisk expenditure and "prosperity" predominates…and while those things are being completed…we have the elimination of antiquated elements of the industrial structure and "depression" predominates. Thus there are prolonged periods of rising and falling prices, interest rates, employment and so on, which phenomena constitute parts of the mechanism of this process of recurrent rejuvenation of the productive apparatus.[15]

In this interpretation, the 'whole set of technological changes' or industrial revolutions are what generates pressure for adjustment. Those firms and industrial branches that represent the old technologies and methods, and are unable to change, will in time disappear. Readjustment is difficult and requires a relatively longer period, especially because countries and companies are unable immediately to satisfy the demands for investments, credits, and new skills. This causes a period of economic turmoil and depression. The significant slowdown and destruction are, nevertheless, 'creative', as the way is cleared for new technologies and methods. New leading sectors emerge, based on new technologies and organizational principles, and the whole process brings about a restructuring of the economy. When most sectors of the economy have completed the transformation, a new wave of prosperity follows. This entire process is thus inherent in the market system and in free market competition. However, extra-economic factors, such as wars and political upheavals, also contribute to this process as happened in the late 1960s.

The recession of the 1970s, which lasted until the early 1980s, clearly exhibited the signs of a structural crisis. The old postwar leading sectors literally collapsed: in eight west European countries, employment in the iron and steel, textile, and shipbuilding industries dropped to 59, 61, and 37 per cent of their pre-recession levels, respectively.[16] The share of traditional industries—i.e., construction and building materials, iron and steel, traditional engineering, wood, paper, textile, and clothing—in the gross value added of total industry declined by 40 per cent in West Germany between 1970 and 1980. During the decade after 1973, exports slowed to roughly one-third and one-half of the

---

[15] Joseph Schumpeter, *Capitalism, Socialism and Democracy* (London: Allen & Unwin, 1976), 67–8.
[16] OECD, *Structural Adjustment*, 236.

growth rates of the decade before 1973.[17] The stagflation from the mid-1970s was thus not accidental, but a characteristic long-term cyclical phenomenon.

A new technological revolution gradually transformed the economy. What happened is comparable to the British Industrial Revolution in importance. As two hundred years before, technological revolution also had a history several decades long. Its beginning went back to World War II, when the first mainframe computer started decoding German military communications at the end of 1943. The other most visible invention of the time was the atomic bomb, or the ground-breaking use of nuclear energy. The revolution in electronics had advanced after World War II with the invention of the transistor, and then the first silicon integrated circuit in 1958.

> Mass production of chips with thousands of transistor circuits reduced the price drastically... Since the mid-1960s the chip has become increasingly an internal part of the 20th century civilization... The chip made possible reliable computers, personal computers, lap computers, and calculators. It also made possible digital watches, increased efficiency in automobiles, control robots, and... communications. The chip has made possible cellular telephones, satellite communications... electronic mail... home banking and many other new technologies.'[18]

The transistor and the chip created the real foundation of the computer revolution that gradually gained ground and opened a new age of communication and in everyday life by the appearance of the personal computer in 1974,[19] and by the World Wide Web in 1991. The electronics revolution gained an ever-greater momentum in the last third of the century. Most important was the new age of telephony, crowned by the digital cellular revolution of the 1980s that itself generated an unending series of inventions.

Europe was hit especially hard by the structural crisis, because its rapid postwar development was based, as Barry Eichengreen underlined, on an *extensive development model*, i.e. on increased capital and labour input and imported existing technology. The labour force increased by an average of 1 per cent per annum, partly by using 'imported' Turks, Portuguese, Italian, North African, and Yugoslav temporary 'guest workers'. The extensive development model would not have been possible without the importation of the existing stock of technological knowledge, transferred from the friendly United States during the Cold War decades.

The sources of extensive development and its institutional framework, however, dried up and became inappropriate by the early mid-1970s. 'The same institutions of coordinated capitalism that had worked to Europe's advantage in the age of extensive growth now posed obstacles to successful economic performance.'[20] Western Europe, already facing strong challenges, arrived at a turning point.

---

[17] Angus Maddison, *The World Economy in the 20th Century* (Paris: OECD, 1989).

[18] Edward N. Singer, *20th Century Revolution in Technology* (Commack, NY: Nova Science Publisher, 1998), 76, 77.

[19] Ibid., 93–106.

[20] Barry Eichengreen, *The European Economy since 1945: Coordinated Capitalism and Beyond* (Princeton, NJ: Princeton University Press, 2007), 6–7.

THE IDEOLOGICAL CONSEQUENCES: NEOLIBERAL REVOLUTION, DE-STATIZATION AND DEREGULATION

The dual economic and political crises of the 1960s and 1970s, together with rising globalization, when employment became uncertain as jobs were outsourced, and investments shifted to low-wage countries,[21] generated a major change in the cultural-ideological environment of the western world. The sudden change generated doubts, and harsh critiques about the unintended negative side effects of postwar policies and institutions. A significant group of liberal, left-wing intellectuals became deeply disappointed and turned against their former ideas with neophyte vehemence. Genuine traditional conservatives, pushed aside after the war, re-emerged and became influential again. In a situation of global competition, slowdown, and declining income, they challenged redistributive welfare systems and the achievement of social harmony by neo-corporatist intervention as 'unaffordable'. Dominant Keynesian economics with its strong belief in state intervention and regulation was declared to be the problem, not the solution. These ideologies found a social base in a post-industrial society where the growing majority of white-collar employees and the middle class replaced the old class structure.

The entire concept of rationalism and the Enlightenment, which dominated social thinking and actions since the eighteenth century, was vehemently questioned. Belief in historical progress and the power of human actions to influence and push it ahead—the basic idea of Enlightenment and a popular concept of postwar Europe—lost ground and was replaced by scepticism about the possibility of understanding the world and historical truth. Disappointment generated relativism and nihilism. Left-leaning parties—communists, socialists, and left-liberals—lost their self-confidence and the belief in a politics they had previously regarded as successful. Their identity crisis undermined their organizations. The Left became fragmented and disorganized, and their mass parties lost the masses. This environment became the hotbed of a rising new political culture and ideology, a new zeitgeist from the 1970s and 1980s on. From that time, neoliberalism emerged, triumphantly rejecting Keynes and negating the role of state. It merged with the rising neoconservatism or the new Right, and a whole set of postmodern culture and ideology. The cultural–ideological arena became the main battlefield.

Neoliberal economics became the most powerful new ideological trend. The return to a simplified classical liberal school in an extreme way not only dethroned Keynesian economics, but also offered a new comprehensive ideological political base, which was later often called market fundamentalism. The prophets of this new zeitgeist were Ludwig von Mises and Friedrich

---

[21] Terence Ball and Richard Bellamy (eds), *The Cambridge History of Twentieth-Century Political Thought* (Cambridge: Cambridge University Press, 2003), 365.

Hayek of the Vienna School of Economics, and Milton Friedman, and other members of the neoliberal Chicago School of Economics. An ideological war erupted and led to the victory of deregulation, privatization, and unrestricted free markets as the only solutions in a free society in the grips of cut-throat global competition. Both Hayek and Friedman connected laissez-faire policy with social and political principles. Undisturbed, they claim, self-regulating markets guarantee social and individual freedom and prosperity. Freedom of the individual and freedom of the market, they argue, are inseparable prerequisites of each other. State intervention, on the other hand, is *The Road to Serfdom*, as the title of one of Hayek's books proclaims.

For Friedman, state intervention was the real cause of economic trouble because, he claims, it disturbs market automatism and undermines freedom. A self-regulated market has a strong corrective automatism. He advocates the privatization of various governmental functions to increase efficiency. Moreover, he argues, a self-regulated market is able to provide healthcare, pensions, and various kinds of insurance. Welfare institutions represent brutal intrusions upon personal freedom; it is like 'sending a policeman to take the money from somebody's pocket'. He recommended making radical tax cuts and introducing a flat tax rate of around 16 per cent for everybody, reducing government expenditures drastically by privatizing nearly everything, as well as making families and individuals responsible for their own schooling, health care, and pension schemes. He argued for 'a free, competitive, private-market educational system' and 'a high natural rate of unemployment' as a prerequisite of a dynamic and progressive economy.[22]

As they returned to old ideas, neoliberalism's new twin ideology, *neoconservatism*, arose. Neoconservatives maintained that the postwar 'values of modernity are irreparably corrupt', even 'hostile', and offered a 'total critique' of them.[23] In their view, the system had become 'ungovernable'; the postwar decades had resulted in the 'inflation of expectations' about what could be expected from the state. The ideas of liberal intellectuals had undermined the basic principles and moral basis of capitalism; and postwar profane political culture had to be replaced by religion to re-establish social cohesion, and the culture of obedience, service, duty, and faith.

The neoconservatives also reinterpreted social justice. Egalitarian ideas became 'destructive and counterproductive' in their interpretation. Rather, 'inequality is the inevitable (and beneficial) outcome of individual freedom and initiative.' 'Human nature' explains inequality and serves as its legitimization. The balance between equality and freedom in the social state was broken, they claimed: it had been distorted towards an equality that undermined the self-assurance of private ownership and replaced it with the fear of ownership. In short, liberal democracy

---

[22] Milton Friedman, *The Program for Monetary Stability* (New York, NY: Fordham University Press, 1959); Friedman, *Inflation: Causes and Consequences* (New York, NY: Asia Publishing House, 1963); Friedman, *The Optimum Quantity of Money and Other Essays* (Chicago, IL: Aldine Publishing Co., 1969); Friedman, *The Tax Limitation, Inflation and the Role of Governments* (Dallas, TX: Fisher Institute, 1978).

[23] Richard Wolin, 'Introduction', in Jürgen Habermas, *The New Conservatism: Cultural Criticism and the Historians' Debate* (Cambridge, MA: MIT Press, 1989), xxiii.

commits suicide.[24] These victorious ideas strongly dominated the last decades of the twentieth century and paved the way for the conservative political revolution of Ronald Reagan and Margaret Thatcher. Domestic political party formations were partly rearranged along these lines.

During the 1980s, the burgeoning neoliberal ideology seriously questioned both of the two peculiar postwar institutions that distinguished the European model: the mixed economy and the welfare system. The mixed economy, established by major wartime and postwar nationalizations, created a 20 to 25 per cent state-owned sector in the Western European economies. The state sector, which worked in a market environment and acted accordingly, played a strategic role in modernization and economic growth during the postwar decades. However, neoliberals attacked the state-owned sector as a parasite and inappropriate in the new global environment. Privatization became a universal agenda. The first steps were taken by Thatcher: several services covered by the Ministry of Defence and the National Health Service (in its 2000 hospitals) were contracted out to private companies in Britain. By 1985, the government had privatized nearly a dozen major state companies: among them, the North Sea Oil licenses and part of the stock of British Petroleum, followed by major assets of British Aerospace, Associated British Ports, British Gas, and British Telecom. Altogether, they transferred more than £5 billion and 400,000 jobs from state to private ownership.

In Mitterand's France, 53 per cent of the assets of French companies were in public hands after the unique nationalization wave of the early 1980s. But the July and August 1986 privatization bills placed thirteen major companies in private hands in nine months. Another nine months and all the nationalized companies were re-privatized. In post-Franco Spain, where a huge part of the economy was state-owned, a privatization wave began in 1984, and 350 industrial firms and ninety-two banks, and then the Instituto Nacional de Industria, the huge holding company with 700 industrial and banking interests, were taken over by private firms in two years. Italy also privatized a dozen major firms of the traditional state sector, including Alitalia, Autostrada, Banco di Roma, and Elsag.[25] Europe eliminated one of the main characteristics of its postwar economic model: the mixed economy. Although the welfare system was attacked and curbed, and the pension system radically reorganized, it was saved and the European social model was preserved, albeit in altered form.

Besides eliminating the state sector, Europe adjusted to the new situation by abolishing a large number of economic regulations, including the control of the financial market, and several forms of state interference that had dominated the entire postwar period of prosperity. It turned instead towards the neoliberal, American-type laissez-faire system. The main economic trend, the transformation from a regulated to an unregulated

[24] Walter Leisner, 'Demokratie, Selbstzerstörung einer Staatsform', cited in Iring Fetscher (ed.), *Neokonservative und 'Neue Rechte'. Der Angriff gegen Sozialstaat und liberale Demokratie in den Vereinigten Staaten, Westeuropa und der Bundesrepublik* (Munich: C.H. Beck, 1979), 108.

[25] J-J. Santini (ed.), *Les privatisations à l'étranger: Royaume-Uni, RFA, Italie, Espagne, Japon* (Paris: La Documentation française, 1986).

market system, was an interrelated 'western' phenomenon that actually emerged first in the United States, followed closely by Britain and then the Western European countries. The deregulation process began in 1971 with the collapse of the Bretton Woods system, the fixed international exchange rate policy, and of control of international money movements. The advanced countries entered into vast international financial transactions. Their foreign assets and liabilities increased by fivefold during the 1990s, and they doubled in the single decade between 1998 and 2008.

The United States, followed by Britain and gradually the western half of the continent deregulated their banking system.[26] *The Economist,* looking back from 2008, evaluated these steps in the most positive way: because of 'financial deregulation...freer markets produced a superior outcome. Unencumbered capital would flow to its most productive use, boosting economic growth ...'[27] Indeed, deregulation increased flexibility for relocating resources from crisis-ridden areas to emerging sectors of the economy. America's envied growing advantage in coping with the crisis of the 1970s and early 1980s lay not simply in its technology, but in its flexible financial system that provided incentives and helped employ new technology.

The entire banking and financing industry changed radically. The separation of commercial and investment banking, a regulation introduced during the Great Depression, was abolished. Banks increased their liabilities (loans) far beyond their assets (deposits). Their capital was far from sufficient to repay deposits if some financial panic pushed people or institutions to withdraw their deposits. Insurance companies also performed banking activities, and the most flexible financial institutions, the hedge funds, began playing a crucially important role in investment. Their activities clearly illustrate the deregulated financial markets. Among the big hedge funds, the 'billion dollar members' of the 'club', 120 had their headquarters in New York, 65 in London. In 2007, 370 new hedge funds were established in Europe. In the summer of 2008, the hedge fund business, worth more than $2.68 trillion, had financed most of the start up companies and technological development that had occurred since 1980. They attracted huge amounts of capital by offering spectacular profits. Hedge funds performed lucrative investments for their investors for a 20 per cent to 40 per cent performance fee, deducted from the capital gain. However, if the investment failed, the fund did not share the loss, but the investors bore the cost. This rule transformed the hedge funds' investment activities into reckless gambling. The fund managers were strongly interested in the gain, but did not suffer from the losses, a system which encouraged wild speculations. When the German government initiated regulation of the hedge funds before the financial crisis, the British government and the American administration blocked any regulatory measures. In the five years before 2008, hedge funds gained 47 per cent profit from investing in Central and Eastern Europe.

---

[26] Paul Krugman, *The Return of Depression Economics and the Crisis of 2008* (London: Penguin Books, 2008).

[27] *The Economist* (11 October 2008), 10. I used this study in discussing the transformation of the international financial markets in the next pages as well.

Bond markets that were national became international: countries issued bonds and sold them to other countries to manipulate interest rates. One of the flexible financial innovations allowed by an unregulated market was the securitization of credits, which entirely transformed commercial lending. Creditors (mortgage loans, credit card loans, student loans, corporate loans, car loans, etc.) performed this transaction by pooling their assets, issuing securities, and selling their existing loans to an investor in this form. The borrowers gradually paid back the fully amortized securities in the specified term. Selling these assets became legal in the mortgage business in the 1970s United States, but from 1985–86 they were used broadly and became part of the victorious Anglo-Saxon deregulated financial system.

Securitizing credits increased money circulation; the company that issued the loan did not have to wait until the borrowers repaid it, sometimes in 3 to 30 years, but sold it, received cash, increased its liquidity, and could issue new credits and gain new profits. Besides, they could report the transaction as new earnings that attracted investors and opened the door for easier access to credit. The lending companies transferred the risk to other companies. By 2005, the amount of securitized credits in the United States amounted to $8.06 trillion. Household debt, which accounted for 80 per cent of the disposable income of borrowers in 1986, reached 140 per cent by 2007. However, the indebtedness of British households was even greater. Deregulated financial markets offered the advantage of more flexible and risky financial activities, which mostly earned higher profits and resulted in cheap credit for the economy.

One of the most innovative new characteristics of the financial market was the derivatives business. Traders—first of all commercial and investment banks and insurance companies—bought and sold future contracts, future commodity trade, and future options on shares, bonds, currencies, and interest rates. These transactions aimed to avoid risk by selling or buying at an assumed (forecasted) price, to eliminate future changes in exchange or interest rates or commodity prices. In Germany, the leading banks established a Derivate Forum in 2004 to provide risk ratings. Because of this trading practice, banks ended their traditional practice of assessing the creditworthiness of their clients. The derivatives business thus served risk management, but it was itself at the same time a major risk, involving speculation about future prices, exchange rates, and interest rate movements. In other words, this business became a form of gambling, based on assumed future price movements. It might offer huge profits as well as huge losses, according to real price and rate formations. According to the Bank for International Settlements, the world's derivates trade increased from $75 trillion in 1997 to $600 trillion in 2007. To evaluate these astronomical figures, it is noteworthy that the 1997 figure was already equal to two and a half times the world's global GDP. It thus became impossible for any single company, or even a single nation, to handle the potentially huge losses.

Deregulation and the flexible financial market worked and helped to cope with the crisis of the early 1980s. Neoliberal ideologues and economists, as well as governments under their influence, celebrated the success. They did not worry about possible negative consequences, since they blindly believed in the self-correcting mechanism of the market. The warning they often made was just the opposite: not to interfere, not to destroy the market mechanism that would, if necessary, correct itself and solve all the emerging problems.

The blind neoliberal belief in self-regulating markets and the withdrawal of state regulations helped prosperity in the short-run, and gave a huge spurt to globalization. Internationalization has had a long history in Europe. However, the transition from the 1970s to the 1980s was the real watershed for its breakthrough. Globalization emerged as a new policy that replaced colonialism for the leading economic powers, but it had an objective economic base in the new technological and corporative-managerial revolution. The end of the Cold War division of Europe in 1990 created a new, and even more favourable political environment for further globalization, opening large new markets and resources in the significantly enlarged laissez-faire system. During the 1980s and 1990s, Western Europe therefore entered a radically transformed era of economic globalization. Europe—besides North America and Asia—emerged as the strong third pillar of the global system. International trade increased three and a half times from $1.7 trillion in 1973 to $5.8 trillion by the end of the century. In 1970, nearly 9 per cent of the world's gross products were exported, but, by 2001, this was already more than 16 per cent. Daily financial transactions amounted to $15 billion in 1973 but increased to $1.3 trillion by 1995. This amount was fifty times higher than the value of world trade.[28] This was the time when advanced countries, exploiting the achievements of the communication revolution, established subsidiaries all over the world and supported a policy of eliminating trade barriers, strengthening competitiveness by outsourcing workplaces, and establishing a new division of labour. Multinational companies became dominant in the world economy by monopolizing most of the industrialized innovations, as well as 75 per cent of the world trade in manufactured goods. The stock of Foreign Direct Investments (FDI) abroad increased to $2.5 trillion by 2004, and advanced countries began investing into each other. Outsourcing production allowed the advanced countries to concentrate on service and high-tech industries, as well as on research and development. Adjustment to globalization provided the exit from the economic crisis of the 1970s and early 1980s and opened a new paradigm of economic development for the West.

By 2004, Europe had become the most globalized region, and Belgium the most globalized country, of the world. According to the Swiss KOF globalization index, which assesses the economic, social and political aspects of 122 countries, the first 16 of the most globalized countries are European, with a score of between 80 and 92 out of 100. Among the first twenty countries, only four—including the United States and Canada—are non-European.

Inspired by the transformation of the world system, thirty years after the Treaty of Rome, the European Community introduced its first major revision with the Single European Act, implemented in the summer of 1987. Instead of a united Western Europe as a defence against

[28] Maddison, *World Economy*, 127, 362; OECD, *Structural Adjustment*, 273.

war, the Act declared that the Community protects the common interests of its member countries by creating a common market with the free movement of goods, people, services, and capital. The realization of these ambitious goals was assisted by 282 detailed measures. 'As regards research and technical development', Article 130F of the agreement set out the objective 'to strengthen the scientific and technological basis of European industry and to encourage it to become more competitive at international level.' Jacques Delors summed up as follows: 'History is accelerating and we should make it with her.'[29]

The integration process shifted into high gear: in December 1991, the Maastricht Treaty led to the establishment of the European Union, which was served by a common currency and a central bank within a decade. Development of a common foreign policy, citizenship, and a European constitution sped the integration process during the 1990s towards the goal of an 'ever closer union'. In this environment, even before the total collapse of the Soviet Bloc, Jacques Delors, the President of the Commission of the Community, launched a further major process in a speech in Bruges in October 1989:

> The Twelve [member countries] cannot control history but they are now in a position to influence it once again. They did not want Europe to be cut in two at Yalta and made a hostage in the Cold War. They did not, nor do they close the door to other European countries.... The present upheavals in Eastern Europe are changing the nature of our problems. It is now merely a matter of when and how all the countries of Europe will benefit from ... the advantages of a single market.[30]

In this international environment, a window of opportunity opened for the former Soviet Bloc countries to join the new world system that helped the countries' democratic transformation and stabilization, as well as their introduction of functioning market economies. Meanwhile it also offered the opportunity for Western Europe to give a better answer to the challenge of globalization. The European Union countries gained an unprecedented chance to establish their economic backyard in Central and Eastern Europe. They outsourced a great part of their expanding car industry to the former communist countries, they owned more than 80 per cent of their banking assets, and gained a huge share of their 100 million people market.

RESTRUCTURING THE ECONOMY

Adjusting to the new requirements of the world economy was difficult. How to counterbalance the sharp decline of the old sectors? Replacing them with new industries representing the latest word in technological development was not a simple task. The Western

---

[29] Activities of the European Union: Summaries of Legislation (www.europa.eu/scadplus/treaties/singleact_eu.htm-31K-).

[30] Jacques Delors, 'Address by Mr Jacques Delors, Bruges, 17 October 1989', in Brent F. Nelsen and Alexander Stubb (eds), *The European Union: Readings on the Theory and Practice of European Integration* (Boulder, CO: Lynne Rienner, 1998), 59.

European core, as an OECD analysis found in 1987, was suffering from structural rigidities, and could not keep up with modern technology. Because of slow adjustment, Europe's position in intensive research and development branches significantly worsened after 1973.[31] The slow structural-technological adjustment was clearly expressed by Europe's losing ground to international competition in technology-intensive products. Around the mid-1980s, European companies had only a 9 per cent world market share in computer and data processing products, 10 per cent in software, 13 per cent in satellites and launchers, and 29 per cent in data transmission services.[32]

After the stagflation of the troubled 1970s and early 1980s, however, Western Europe made great progress in adjusting to the requirements of the new technological regime and the globalized world economy. They had to turn towards their own innovation base and establish competitive modern high-tech sectors. Investment in information and communication technology (ICT) doubled between 1980 and 2005, and in some countries, it nearly quadrupled. Sweden, Finland, and Britain exhibited especially impressive performance in this area. During the 1980s, the United States had a huge advantage, which increased their total investment in ICT to 24 per cent by 1992, compared to the European Union-15 countries' average of only 13 per cent in cutting edge technology, hardly more than half of the American investment share. By 2003, the average European investment increased to 17 per cent, but Sweden and Finland (each nearly 27 per cent) and Britain (22 per cent) approached the 27–29 per cent American share.[33]

Accordingly, modern high-tech sectors emerged only gradually in Europe. Their share of manufacturing output increased in Finland from 3.6 to 5 per cent and in France from 12 to 13 per cent, as well as increasing somewhat in Belgium and Germany. More successful was the adjustment in technological modernization and the renewal of traditionally strong medium–high-tech industries. The country leading this trend was Germany. The output of medium–high-tech branches—motor vehicles, engineering, and chemicals—increased from 32 to 41 per cent of total industrial output in Germany, and to about one-third of the industrial output in several other west European countries.[34] Through renewed technology, product differentiation, and specialization, they were able to lower the cost of production and conquering markets that were less saturated and less competitive. These medium-level R&D-intensive sectors significantly increased their exports.[35]

---

[31] OECD, *Structural Adjustment*, 203.

[32] Ibid., 213.

[33] OECD, *Factbook: Economic, Environmental and Social Statistics* (Paris: OECD, 2007), 155. Investment rates in general recovered from a severe decline—from a 5.6 per cent annual increase before 1973, to an annual decrease of 0.6 per cent between 1973 and 1980—and again reached a 5.7 per cent increase per year in the second half of the 1980s.

[34] OECD, *Structural Adjustment*, 254. During the 1980s, the share of medium–high-tech industries increased from 29 to 34 per cent in France, from 29 to 32 per cent in Italy, from 20 to 25 per cent in Holland, and from 30 to 37 per cent in Belgium.

[35] Ibid., 215.

As a clear sign of structural adjustment, the output of the ICT sector made good progress in Europe. The income share of this sector tripled between 1980 and 1996. In 1980, it stood at only one-third of the U.S. level, but by 1996 it had reached one-half of it, signalling that capital stock in the most modern technology branches was accumulating in Europe. This had an important impact on output growth: during the first half of the 1990s, ICT contributed less than a third to growth, but during the second half of the decade, it contributed one-half. At the turn of the century, Europe lagged only about five years behind the United States in the diffusion of modern technology. The output of the ICT sector in Western Europe reached more than 4 per cent of GDP. Only Ireland, at nearly 8 per cent, and Sweden and Finland, at nearly 6 per cent each, were around the American level of almost 7 per cent of GDP. In another clear sign of modern structural changes, even though job creation was weak and slow during the 1990s, 75 per cent of net job creation during the second half of the decade occurred in high-tech sectors whose work force was at least 40 per cent comprised of individuals with tertiary education.

By 2004, high-tech exports from the European Union-15 nearly matched the Japanese level: 23 per cent of total exports, compared to 24 per cent for the Japanese. This remained behind the United States, for whom high-tech exports comprised 33 per cent of the total. Regarding medium–high-tech exports, Europe's share increased to 47 per cent, while only 44 per cent of total exports from the United States were in this category. Although somewhat later than the United States, Europe closely followed modern technological and structural changes around the turn of the century.[36]

Western Europe was consequently able to counterbalance the decline of the old sectors with a rapid increase in the modern sectors, that is, it was able to cope with the structural crisis. For example, consumer price inflation, which reached roughly 10 to 14 per cent in Western Europe, dropped to 3–5 per cent in the second half of the 1980s and thereafter. The Western European economy was consolidated. Private consumption also almost recovered and increased by 3–4 per cent annually. After a series of years of negative figures, fixed capital formation regained the pre-Oil Shock dynamism of 6–8 per cent increases annually. In the late 1980s, industrial production in Germany increased by 4–6 per cent per annum, and it increased in Western Europe as a whole by 2–4 per cent. The increase in GDP also returned to a solid 2.5 to 3.5 per cent annual growth rate.[37]

Technological transfiguration was also closely connected with a major structural change, often called the service revolution. Occupational structure clearly expressed the dramatic decline of the agricultural population, the decrease in industrial employment, and the enormous increase in service employment. At the end of 2006, twelve western member countries of the European Union employed, on average, slightly more than 4

[36] Commission of the European Communities, *European Economy* (Brussels: European Commission, 2000), 37, 108–9, 115, 117.

[37] United Nations *Economic Survey of Europe* (New York, NY: UN, 1991).

per cent of their active population in agriculture, and almost 29 per cent in industry. All of these countries experienced a service revolution: this sector employed roughly one-third of the active population after the war, half of them in the early–mid 1970s, and roughly 70 per cent by 2005. This share reached three-quarters of the active population in quite a few countries, including Belgium, Denmark, France, Norway, Sweden, Switzerland, and Britain. The service sector produced roughly half of the total value added in the 1970s, but it became the leading sector of the western economies around the turn of the twenty-first century, producing nearly three-quarters of total value added.[38]

The structural changes in occupation, and the considerably increased contribution of services to the GDP, also reflected increased productivity in agriculture and industry, which produced more value with far fewer employees and thus freed a greater part of the labour force to work in other sectors of the economy. On the other hand, these changes also clearly placed the service revolution, brought on by a more sophisticated division of labour, at centre stage. During the last decades of the twentieth century, several functions were separated from manufacturing: research, design, accounting, transportation, and various other activities were taken over by specialized service companies serving several firms with increased efficiency. In Silicon Valley-type industrial agglomerations, several service companies settled to serve dozens of high-tech companies. Several functions that were parts of agricultural or industrial production before became independent services, provided by specialized service companies. Technological-structural transformation strongly contributed to a further advance of labour productivity, which increased in Western Europe by more than fivefold. Ireland, one of the formerly backward European countries, increased productivity by more than sevenfold after the 1980s.[39]

Around the turn of the century, however, growth slowed down again; a new oil crisis temporarily skyrocketed prices to $150/barrel in the summer of 2008. The new oil crisis, however, was not the real cause of gathering economic clouds. Mid-2008 became the scene of a major international financial crisis that started in the United States and spread throughout the world. It was mostly the backlash of deregulation and reckless financial gambling. As noted before, flexible, deregulated financial markets had a major and positive role in coping with the crisis of the 1970s-80s. In reality, however, the question was not *whether*, but *when* the negative effects would become dominant. Since the 1980s, local crises have actually accompanied the transformation of international financing in Mexico, Asia, and Russia, as well as in the bursting of stock market and housing market bubbles. George Soros, one of the main winners in, and experts on, the unregulated financial markets, actually warned of the danger in 1998: 'market fundamentalism...put financial capital into the driver's seat....Market forces, if they are given complete

---

[38] Based on OECD, *Science, Technology and Industry Outlook* (Paris: OECD, 2000), 63; *World in Figures* (London: The Economist, 2008).

[39] Maddison, *World Economy*, 351.

authority... produce chaos and could ultimately lead to the downfall of the global capit-alist system.'[40] Indeed, global crisis and the collapse of financial systems, on a scale unheard of since the Great Depression, arrived in 2007–08 in the United States, and spread to Europe and throughout the world in 2008–09. Hedge funds that gained a for-tune from investments lost 57 per cent of their invested money in 2008. As Keynesian economics and practice failed after the 1970s crisis, neoliberal economics and policy failed in 2008–09. The circle was closed, and a new orientation and adjustment began.

FURTHER READING

Berend, Ivan T., *An Economic History of Nineteenth Century Europe* (Cambridge: Cambridge University Press, 2006).

Berend, Ivan T., *Europe Since 1980* (Cambridge: Cambridge University Press, 2010).

Boltho, Andrea, *The European Economy: Growth and Crisis* (Oxford: Oxford University Press, 1982).

Brenner, Robert, *The Boom and the Bubble: The US in the World Economy* (London: Verso, 2002).

Krugman, Paul, *The Return of Depression Economics and the Crisis of 2008* (London: Penguin, 2008).

OECD, *Measuring Globalization: The Role of Multinationals in OECD Economies* (Paris: OECD, 1999).

Rhode, Paul W. and Gianni Toniolo (eds), *The Global Economy in the 1990s: A Long-Run Perspective* (Cambridge: Cambridge University Press, 2006).

Soros, George, *The Crisis of Global Capitalism: Open Society Endangered* (New York: Public Affairs, 1998).

Stiglitz, Joseph E., *Globalization and Its Discontents* (New York, NY: W.W. Norton, 2002).

Williamson, John, 'The Washington Consensus Revisited', in Louis Emmerij (ed.), *Economic and Social Development into the XXI Century* (Washington, DC: Inter-American Development Bank, 1997).

[40] George Soros, *The Crisis of Global Capitalism* (New York, NY: Public Affairs, 1998), xx, xxvii.

CHAPTER 20

....

VEBLEN REDIVIVUS: LEISURE AND EXCESS IN EUROPE

....

ROSEMARY WAKEMAN

MASS consumption and leisure are among the most fascinating and thought-provoking challenges for twentieth-century historians. The concepts are riddled with theoretical controversy, the historical evidence is tricky, and the boundaries of study notoriously vague. From the perspective of the early years of the twenty-first century, consumption and leisure are at the core of existence. It is difficult to imagine a time when these practices were not essential to people's lives. Yet historically, they are a recent phenomenon, associated with the late nineteenth and twentieth centuries. It was precisely the initial phases of mass consumerism that prompted Norwegian–American economist Thorstein Veblen to warn of the consequences of 'conspicuous consumption' and misguided materialism in his 1899 *The Theory of the Leisure Class*. In Veblen's estimation, new-money leisure classes could dress up their pretensions and social status with a wasteful display of commodities.

Veblen was one of many theorists critical of the new culture of consumption by the early years of the twentieth century, Sigmund Freud, Max Weber, and Werner Sombart also among them. But they were swimming against the consumerist tide. By the 1920s, Europe was shifting from a bourgeois to a Fordist mode of mass production with goods available to broad sectors of the working population. Europe's venerable department stores were offering women easy-to-wear 'flapper' fashions. Chain stores as well as new forms of marketing and advertising were spectacularizing commodities. André Citroen scandalously advertised his brand name in electric lights cascading down the Eiffel Tower. Companies such as Dutch Unilever and Braun were experimenting with mass consumer research. Avant-garde artists at the Bauhaus were churning out designs for mass produced household goods from tea sets to cradles. European consumers purchased toasters from the German AEG Works and vacuum cleaners from Electrolux. Crystal radios and gramophones were staples of prewar European domestic life, while early television sets with cathode ray tubes were going into commercial production by the 1930s. The BBC was transmitting programmes to between 25,000 and 40,000 homes before the service was suspended in September 1939. In the same respect, middle- and working-class families were already enjoying organized leisure activities and packing their bags for vacation in the years before the war. In emulation of long-established elite travel to fashionable resorts and watering holes, holidays were increasingly associated with travel away from home and work. Seaside resorts were all the rage among the salaried masses.

The changeover to a culture of consumption was not seamless. The depression of the 1930s and World War II were economically disastrous. Bourgeois taste and the cultural power of elitist consumption practices were maintained by time-honoured business strategies, protectionist barriers, and simply by the low wages endured by European workers. Historians have been quick to point to these obstacles. For these reasons, mass consumption and leisure have largely been associated with the post-World War II 'age of affluence' and the thorny influence of Americanization. Nonetheless, European practices were more than just a matter of following the all-encompassing logic of consumption and entertainment emanating from the colossus across the Atlantic. Europe developed its own consumption styles and regimes within the context of its national political economies.

The continuities across the twentieth century were not just impediments. Diverse local and regional consumer markets, different ideas about work and play, the customs of small-scale retailing, and state-sponsored consumer programmes all acted as alternatives to the model of US consumer capitalism. European consumption took place through a multifaceted process of diffusion, resistance and acceptance, local appropriation, and the juxtaposition of routines and habits. A whole host of consumer leagues and cooperatives, labour unions, business associations, and government agencies mediated a specifically European style of consumer identity and citizenship. Consumer politics and the relationship between civil society and the market were complex, contentious, and distinctive to the politics of modernization in each nation, in both East and West. The diversity of these trajectories stands out as a defining feature of European leisure and consumer culture.

Despite the early precedents set before the debacle of World War II, for the overwhelming majority of Europeans at mid-century, disposable income to consume was unheard of. Notwithstanding the postwar economic miracle and the 'affluent society', in the 1950s the majority of people in Europe still lived frugally on tight budgets. Rationing was not fully lifted until the mid-1950s. A decent apartment remained an elusive dream for many a young married couple. Food remained the main expenditure in household budgets.

Against this backdrop of scarcity, US companies flooded Europe with advertisements about the American way of life. Tantalizing exhibitions such as the *Salon des Arts Ménagers* in Paris or the 1951 Festival of Britain in London extolled the consumer living standards achieved under American-style capitalism. Coca-Cola, Kellogg, and Kraft Foods set up business in Europe and hawked American-style soft drinks, cornflake cereal, and mayonnaise. They were among a multitude of American companies breaking into the European market. The public relations campaign and consumer advertising were weapons of the Cold War. European workers would be turned into consumers. They would form the first line of defence against communism. The Marshall Plan pushed the Western European economy towards mass consumption as part of this ideological and material struggle. Europe was viewed as a *tabula rasa*, eager to adopt the American version of modern life. Nevertheless, the reaction to American goods ranged from willing acceptance to outright hostility.

Consumption practices began to change dramatically in the late 1950s and early 1960s. The years of scarcity were left behind as consumers rushed to fulfil material aspirations and pent-up dreams of a better life. These years witnessed the development of a confident, prosperous working class based on urban living, full employment, and the social partnership negotiated with postwar capitalism. There was more disposable wealth than ever before. Even though prices rose almost constantly, in Western Europe average real wages and purchasing power rose ahead of them through the mid-1950s and 1960s. Increased social services such as free medical care and pensions, education, subsidized public housing, and transportation helped create a degree of security and comfort for broad ranges of working people that had never before been achieved. As incomes rose, personal consumption was equated with happiness. It became commonplace for consumers to turn to credit to satisfy immediate desires. For war weary Europeans tired of poverty and rations, consumption offered a new kind of social respectability and quality of life. They navigated through a complex array of merchandise in which choice was mediated through the language of advertisement and marketing.

Magazines such as France's *Elle* and *Constanze* in West Germany featured glossy advertisements for beauty aids and the newest sewing machines and electric mixers available to the efficient housewife. Free *Housewife's Films* toured Sweden introducing the newest domestic products. The first IKEA catalogue appeared in Sweden in 1951. Unilever marketed its Lux Toilet Soap throughout Western Europe. Domestic consumerism was the new barometer of quality of life. A survey conducted by the *Financial Times* found that from 1957 to 1959 alone, the number of British households owning a television set increased 32 per cent, with washing machines by 54 per cent, and with refrigerators by 58 per cent.[1] The refrigerator was the premier object of desire—a must for the modern home. It quickly became the norm in European households as a symbol of cleanliness and hygiene. As consumers acquired Frigéco, Brandt, and Bosch refrigerators, daily shopping was forsaken for weekly food expeditions to the new self-service supermarkets. Shoppers wandered through a dizzying array of foods and examined price tags.

It heralded a modern, time-saving shift in household consumption practices. In the UK, Tesco opened its first self-service supermarket in 1954. Carrefour (one of the largest

---

[1] Cited in Dominic Sandbrook, *Never Had it So Good: A History of Britain from Suez to the Beatles* (London: Little, Brown, 2005), 596.

supermarket–department store chains in the world by the twenty-first century) opened its first sales outlet in suburban Annecy in 1957. The Monoprix chain, which started as a grocery store in Rouen in 1932, switched to self-service in 1950 and then to large-scale suburban supermarkets. France had over 1800 supermarkets by the end of the 1960s. By 1965 West Germany had more than 53,000 self-service shops, among which were the Konsum retail chain and Aldi supermarkets. Only seven supermarkets existed in the Netherlands in 1961: there were 520 ten years later.[2]

These new distribution strategies moved consumerism downward socially and out-ward beyond Europe's big cities. People everywhere in Western Europe could pick from an abundance of brand-named canned, frozen, and high-priced food items temptingly offered on supermarket shelves. Attractive packaging became a medium of communica-tion. Advertised, instantly recognizable pre-packaged goods spoke directly to the cus-tomer. In 1964, the first jar of Nutella, the Ferrero Company's rebranded chocolate, almond, and hazelnut spread, left the factory in Piedmont and became an instant suc-cess. Chain restaurants such as Nordsee, which expanded to 300 outlets in West Germany and Austria in the 1950s and 1960s with its Nordsee Quick meals, catered to fast-paced modern lifestyles. The sleek silhouette of the Italian Autogrill restaurant and filling station chain hovered over Italian highways from 1959, when owner Mario Pavesi inaugurated the first model along the Autostrada del Sole at Fiorenzuola. The Autogrills became a classic symbol of consumerism in Italy.

Owning a private vehicle was a central feature in this vision of consumer bliss. Between 1950 and 1964 the number of motorcycles and scooters in Italy rose from 700,000 to 4.3 million.[3] The Italian Vespa motor scooter (designed by Piaggio engineer Corrado D'Asciano) was an unprecedented success in mass consumerism. By 1960, one million had already been sold. A car was the ultimate luxury. Annual car shows such as the Paris *Salon d' automobiles* drew thousands of aficionados. European films were filled with speeding open-air sports cars and luxury sedans. The French Citroen DS, or *Déesse* (Goddess) became a mythic image of sleek. Affordable cars such as the VW Beetle, the Renault 4CV, British Leyland's Mini, and the Italian Fiat 500 were emblematic symbols of a new freedom and trouble-free affluence shared by the working classes. Italians owned 5.5 million cars by 1965. British car ownership, especially of the Austin A30 and the Morris Minor, rose to 8 million by 1964 and then reached 11.5 million by the end of the 1960s. Motor scooter and car companies launched vast advertising campaigns that included the formation of social clubs, mass rallies, long-distance tours and races.

    [2] These statistics are given in James B. Jeffreys and Derek Knee, *Retailing in Europe: Present Structure and Future Trends* (London: Macmillan, 1962), 106; and Wolfgang Disch, *Der Grosse- und Einzelhandel in der Bundesrepublik Deutschland* (Cologne: Opladen, 1966), 60 as cited in Victoria de Grazia, 'Changing Consumption Regimes in Europe, 1930–1970', in Susan Strasser, Charles McGovern and Matthias Judt (eds), *Getting and Spending: European and American Consumer Societies in the Twentieth Century* (Cambridge: Cambridge University Press, 1998), 79.

    [3] Guilio Mazzocchi, 'Come si viveva prima, durante e dopo', *I Problemi di Ulisse* 83–7 (1979), 74, as quoted in Stephen Gundle, *Between Hollywood and Moscow: The Italian Communists and the Challenge of Mass Culture, 1943–1991* (Durham, NC: Duke University Press, 2000), 80.

Thousands of scooterists converged on Brighton for the National Lambretta Club's annual rally. In the 1960s and 1970s, vehicles were deeply embedded in the image of the modern young European. The Vespa motor scooter or French Renault was a sign of progress and a passport to the future.

Undeniably, young Europeans were the main agents of change. They upended Veblen's theory that consumption preferences 'trickle down' from social elites. Youth culture and the category of 'teenager' was in good part an invention of consumer capitalism. Teenagers heralded the arrival of commodity culture and a seemingly classless consumer society. But public education was also a powerful force for cultural convergence for the bumper crop of children growing up in the 1950s and 1960s, as were the full employment and high wages that boosted buying opportunities for young workers even in unskilled jobs. In the 1950s, versions of the brooding teenage delinquent emerged in London as 'teddy boys', the *blouson noirs* in France, and the *Halbstarkers* in Germany and Austria. Long hair and sideburns, black leather jackets, cowboy boots were the essential, and expensive, new look.

Consumerism was staged by the young people of Europe as a formula for their own identity. There was an extension of informality in family and social relations, a conflation of the 'public' with 'personal', a merging of consumption with display. Commodity culture was carried in magazines, in radio and on television, and in film to youthful audiences of millions across Europe who absorbed the same images, shared the same values, and collectively engaged with the same icons and objects of desire. Teenagers, especially adolescent girls, poured surplus cash into clothes, inexpensive cosmetics, the new rock 'n' roll music, and inspired a cornucopia of commercial leisure and personal products. The allure and seductive appeal of commodities privatized and materialized dreams. Even if in actuality teenage culture was largely working class rather than classless, the ideals passed on through identification with any social class or family were diffused, if not out-and-out rebelled against. In their place, consumer capitalism produced and marketed collective desires that perpetually reinvented themselves and became a universalized set of signs, a language of value explicitly associated with adolescent youth. They signified both an affluent avant-garde and a slavish consumerism: signatures of the high living standards enjoyed during the age of prosperity.

By the 1960s, postwar baby boomers, their morals and lifestyle dominated the mass media. Advertisements, first in catalogues and magazines, then on commercial radio and television, stimulated desire and expectations through coded references to consumer identity. From motorbikes and vinyl records to the trendy fashions, graphics, furniture, and personal accessories of the 'pop sixties', youthful Europeans demanded artefacts that provided them with generational style. Shopping became fun.

Although the hedonism and permissiveness of the 'swinging sixties' appeared threatening, as a cultural revolution they were a radical adaptation to affluence and consumer society. Standards of beauty, cleanliness, personal attributes, autonomy were determined by consumer culture and market relations. In the early 1960s, it was the Italian-inspired 'Mods' that captured the youthful imagination. It became hip to drink cappuccino, wear Italian-made suits, and zip around town on an Italian Vespa. The cool continental, puffing on Gauloise cigarettes, replaced the American imagery of youth. Mod was a matter of commodity selection. They indulged in a 'furious programme' of clothes, accessories, and hairstyles in an attempt to use leisure and consumption as codes for the self.[4] Swinging London replaced Paris as fashion vanguard. Michelangelo Antonioni's steamy 1966 film *Blow Up* became a Mod masterpiece. The explosion of the London scene and the pop music and imagery of the Beatles spearheaded the British Invasion—not only to the US but to the rest of Europe. Rebel rock counterculture became cheap, mass produced glamour. Mary Quant's miniskirt established King's Road in London's Chelsea district as street-scene cool. Beauty was a mass commodity sold by supermodel Twiggy. Ordinary objects were aestheticized and sold as ciphers of modern trendsetting.

By the 1960s modern households were equipped with 'princess' telephones, colour television sets, and stereo record players, with an endless stream of the latest knick-knacks and domestic paraphernalia glamourized in the mass media. Pop art was rooted in everyday life and in a kitschy tongue-in-cheek consumerism. Its techniques were absorbed into advertising and packaging as the new form of smart, savvy commercial art. Op art crossed over into psychedelic home decor. Experiments with moulded plastics created cheery, fluid furniture in vibrant colors. Danish designer Verner Panton's inflatable chairs were all the rage. Terence Conran's first Habitat store opened in Chelsea in 1964, and sold a modern populist aesthetic for everything from lamps to pasta storage jars. Italian designer Ettore Sottsass turned the Olivetti 'Valentine' typewriter into the ultimate in chic. Sleek appliances, radios and record players designed by Dieter Rams for Braun were the signature of sophisticated taste. The 'art of living' well and comfortably became the shared aspiration of millions who followed the dream of trouble-free consumption.

Consumerism was driven by the godheads of celebrity. The aura of glamour around film stars and celebrity spectacles fed the dreams of spending and pleasure, and penetrated into everyday life. Wealthy ostentation and consumerism were essential to the stardom performed in film, on television, and in the pages of fan magazines. Although these fantasies were associated with the highly polished, manufactured image of Hollywood, Europe invented its own allure. The cult of Mediterranean beauty produced Sophia Loren and Gina Lollobrigida among a host of Italian stars who kept Europeans and Americans flocking to the box office in search of things Italian. A sexy voluptuousness became the newest fashion trend. Brigitte Bardot gave new meaning to the image of Frenchness.[5] Women functioned in new public roles as the symbols, creators, and consumers of mass culture. The raw material of Pop Art was drawn from upfront sexual themes that focused on the body, especially the female body, as subversive seduction. Adored by millions, 'Latin lovers' Marcello Mastroianni and Rossano Brazzi proved that male sexuality claimed as much celebrity on the silver screen.

---

[4] Dick Hebdige, *Hiding in the Light* (London: Routledge, 1988), 110–11.

[5] See David Forgacs and Stephen Gundle, *Mass Culture and Italian Society from Fascism to the Cold War* (Bloomington, IN: Indiana University Press, 2007), and John Gaffney, *Stardom in Postwar France* (New York: Berghahn, 2007).

For Marxist intellectuals Georg Lukács, Max Horkheimer, and Theodor W. Adorno, the consumer had fallen under the spell of capitalist production and was made captive to fabricated needs. Capitalist industry produced, steered, and disciplined consumer identity. It perpetually deceived the consumer with the very thing that it perpetually promised. 'Amusement under late capitalism', Adorno and Horkheimer wrote in their 1947 *Dialectic of Enlightenment* 'is the prolongation of work'. For Herbert Marcuse, the individual is subordinate to an oppressive compulsion to consume. The critique of consumer society continued in the 1960s with French sociologist Henri Lefebvre and Italian sociologist Francesco Alberoni, who argued that the consumer was entirely an invention of capitalism. The ultimate denunciation was that of Guy Debord and the Situationists, who defiantly drifted outside the capitalist spectacle of consumption, refusing to be fooled by its allure. French cultural critic Jean Baudrillard drew on semiology to argue that consumption entails the active manipulation of signs and images that eventually float free in an endless profusion of simulacra. But it was difficult to argue with material comfort and prosperity. Alongside these pessimistic interpretations of 'false needs' and the psychologically manipulative character of consumerism inherent in theories of mass culture, scholars also looked to the social implications and the changes wrought in the class structures of European society. French sociologist Pierre Bourdieu argued that commodities formed part of a class communication directly related to lifestyle, both desired and actual. Taste and consumption had become constituents of social class definition.

By the late twentieth century, scholars such as Bourdieu moved away from regarding consumer culture as homogeneous and instead focused on the process of consumption and its emotional and aesthetic satisfactions. Consumer culture created complex public and social relations. It tended to differentiate. Consumers responded and used goods in different ways. This complicated relationship to commodities is perhaps best exemplified by the reception of the McDonald's fast food chain in France. From its arrival in 1979, France became McDonald's second biggest market after the United States. While French families regularly feasted on Big Macs, the chain's popularity made it a hated symbol of global capitalism and the continuous target of protests. Consumption becomes a creative act, even in something as venerable as the Eurovision Song Contest. Begun in 1956 by the newly founded European Broadcasting Union, the song contest is one of the most enduring popular television events in the world. Millions of viewers voted via electronic media for Finnish monster-clad heavy-metal rock band Lordi in 2008 and handed them the victory. This subversive pick by a youthful consumer public transformed a moribund musical ritual into a cultural pop extravaganza.

If by the 1960s and 1970s Western Europeans were reflecting on the deleterious effects of conspicuous consumption, Eastern Europeans were still coveting the possibilities of buying. In the East, the Soviet Union and its satellites initially emphasized production and planning. Consumer goods were seen largely as collective commodities and offered little by way of diversity or quality. Under state socialism consumption was centrally controlled. Work, bread, and housing for everyone were paramount. Cheap food and everyday merchandise was available at State-owned supermarkets and department stores, which began converting over to self-service at about the same time as the West. But cars, television sets, refrigerators, and fashion clothing were in short supply, costly and beyond the reach of average families. Buying high-end goods remained the privilege of Politburo elites. Nonetheless consumer displays and advertising in both West and East were crucial to the Cold War rivalry between the two economic systems. Eastern Europe was never a closed society. Eastern Europeans looked longingly across the Iron Curtain at the cornucopia in the West. A divided Germany and especially a divided Berlin were on the frontlines in this Cold War battle for the hearts and minds of the citizen–consumer.

West Germany experienced an unprecedented influx of American goods, from nylon stockings to American music and films, as part of the *Wirtschaftswunder* promotion of the American way of life. Western products were omnipresent in East Germany through hard-currency retail outlets (Intershops), on western television commercials, and in homes. Until the construction of the Wall in August 1961, a constant stream of teenagers flowed back and forth between East and West Berlin. American popular culture provided models of dress and behaviour for young people on both sides of the Iron Curtain. Through illicit copies of their records, music fans in Prague heard the Beatles as early as Londoners did. The Rolling Stones played to hysterical crowds in Warsaw in 1967.

Young Eastern Europeans turned rock and pop music into a voice of opposition against the dreary repression. John Lennon's 'Give Peace a Chance' became their political anthem. Black-market traders on the streets of Warsaw and Budapest served wailing rock 'n' roll wanabes. Mods and chic young consumers paid small fortunes for Italian raincoats, American jeans, jazz and rock albums, and cigarettes. In official state circles, rock music and western youth culture were undermining socialist values. But semi-illegal rock concerts and rampaging fans were an inspired form of political resistance, while the flood of images of consumer capitalism 'beyond the iron curtain' fuelled desires.

In an effort to build social support, state governments increasingly cultivated a consumer orientation and moved towards coordinating and regulating the design and production of household goods. As historian Tony Judt has suggested, individual consumption became key to the socialist system, just as it was for its capitalist rival in the West. Access to consumer opportunities and improved living standards, along with a measure of liberalization under 'goulash Socialism', were crucial to normalization after the 1956 Hungarian uprising, and then again after the Prague Spring of 1968. However, historians see East European consumerism as more than a way to maintain political control. A distinctive socialist version of the Good Life had surfaced in the most prosperous of East European societies by the late 1960s and 1970s. Stores were well stocked with merchandise advertised on state television. The new intelligentsia were fashionably dressed, their city flats comfortably decorated, and their subsidized vacations expected. Stylish young models with cigarettes and portable radios set the tone in 1960s advertising under socialism. Domestic life was an escape from authoritarianism. Dreams of freedom were in the 'golden years' of the 'Sixties' traded for Kristall refrigerators, Praktica cameras, Schwalbe mopeds and Trabant cars. Home-grown GDR rock groups such as the Puhdys and Karat became icons.

East Germany and Czechoslovakia were key Soviet gateways for consumer goods, but the glow of consumer society reached provincial capitals throughout Eastern Europe. The social scene in cities was still limited by the lack of bars, restaurants, and private shops. But a scaled-down socialist style of fashion consciousness and domestic comfort was attainable.[6] This did not necessarily mean a liberalization of politics. Despite the too-easy association of the two, especially in the West, consumer and citizen are not the same. Eastern Europeans made a Faustian bargain with repressive regimes. They could enjoy material comforts, but they could not participate politically. Market dynamics and consumerism do not automatically lead to democratization, as the hard fought struggle for political rights in Eastern Europe attests.

After the fall of the Berlin Wall in 1989, the spread of material progress and the commercialization of leisure and consumption began shifting social and political relations in the countries of Eastern Europe. The reunification of Germany and indeed of Europe involved a fight for individual freedom and prosperity based on consumption. With the Wall demolished, young East Berliners drove their Trabants to the Kurfürstendamm to gaze at the window displays. Hundreds of thousands poured down the boulevard, rushing in and out of stores. They plunged into the world of consumer capitalism. The number of food retail outlets in Eastern Europe immediately zoomed up as privatization catered to pent-up demand. Foreign chains moved in to take over feeble companies. Dutch Ahold bought out the Czech Mana supermarket chain. Carrefour quickly moved into Poland, the Czech Republic, and Hungary. Tesco entered the Czech Republic and Slovakia in 1996 by buying the former Prior department stores. By 2002, Tesco had 144 stores in the Czech Republic, Hungary, Poland, and Slovakia and employed a staff of forty thousand around the region.[7]

The privileged classes under communism splintered as the first post-communist young adults embraced privatization and defined themselves increasingly around consumerism. Those with money became western-style 'leisure omnivores'.[8] Poster shops tore down their portraits of Marx and Lenin and replaced them with Madonna and Michael Jackson. Fast food was the new cuisine. East European hipsters rented weekend villas on the Adriatic coast and went to Trieste and Graz to buy Nike sneakers, Levi's, and Benetton pullovers. New SUVs replaced old Fiats and Trabants. Cable TV hookups, computers, and the newest electronic devices defined social chic. Expenditures on recreation and culture more than doubled in Lithuania and Estonia, Hungary and Slovakia.

Young people took part in the marches and street demonstrations that brought down the communist regimes in Eastern Europe, but in the 1990s and early years of the

---

[6] See Susan E. Reid and David Crowley (eds), *Style and Socialism: Modernity and Material Culture in Post-War Eastern Europe* (Oxford: Berg, 2000).

[7] BBC News online (5 December 2002). http://news.bbc.co.uk/1/hi/business/2515903.stm, accessed March 2010.

[8] Ken Roberts, Sue Povall and Jochen Tholen, 'Farewell to the Intelligentsia: Political Transformation and Changing Forms of Leisure Consumption in the Former Communist Countries of Eastern Europe', *Leisure Studies* 24 (2005), 123.

twenty-first century, disillusion with democratic politics set in. Cynicism with government became the new norm. Even as pro-nationalist movements fragmented the political geography of Eastern Europe, privatization allowed individuals to decouple their own life chances from any national agenda. The dream of freedom was increasingly imagined as the right to private leisure and consumption.

By the end of the twentieth century, the great icons of the European department store tradition such as Harrods, Galeria Kaufhof, Galaries Lafayette, and El Corte Inglés vied for designation as the largest outlets, while clothing retailers Marks & Spencer and H&M, Zara, Benetton, and cosmetics chain Sephora were international conglomerates. Small independent stores and specialized chain retailers maintained a remarkable degree of popularity among consumers, especially in Southern Europe. Far from being an urban pursuit, consumerism spread out to Europe's suburbs and their vast shopping malls. Malls are social magnets for Europeans of all social strata. Consumption is symbolic and shopping a leisure-time performance in which people move through a spectacle of opulence and luxury. Mall space is a theatre of desire, a stage for the social performance of buying. Gateshead's MetroCentre near Newcastle upon Tyne, and Westfield London are among the largest shopping malls in Europe. With shops and restaurants, multiplex theatres and family entertainment, and a host of consumer services, they are the latest in shopping–leisure entertainment. Sociologist Mike Featherstone argues that there are common features emerging between shopping centres, malls, theme parks, and tourist experiences.[9] Madrid's glamorous Xanadú mall includes a 250 metre ski slope for customers looking for the latest in fun. Metropolitan areas throughout Eastern Europe enjoyed a late century boom in multiplex theatres and consumer entertainment venues. Delta City in New Belgrade and the Polus Centre outside Budapest are among the largest shopping malls in Eastern Europe.

THE CULTURE OF LEISURE

In *The Theory of the Leisure Class*, Veblen equated free time and consumption with the decadent display of social status; and like many intellectual elites of his day differentiated true needs from false wants. However, theorists coming to grips with consumer society in the first half of the twentieth century rapidly shifted their view of free time to the prospect, along with high wages, of absorbing the unlimited potential of industrialism and solving the problem of overproduction. Free time, according to Gary Cross in his history of consumer culture,[10] was the opportunity for the discretionary spending necessary for mass production and market expansion. In the context of the postwar 'age of affluence', leisure and free time became one of the most potent markets for consumption and services and one of the most intricate semiotic structures of consumer culture.

---

[9]   Mike Featherstone, *Consumer Culture and Postmodernism*, 2nd edn (Los Angeles: Sage, 2007), 101.
[10] Gary Cross, *Time and Money: The Making of Consumer Culture* (London: Routledge, 1993).

Its value may be surmised from the extraordinary investment in new technologies associated with play, leisure, and recreation, and the power of the sports and tourism industries.

A weekend day of rest, holidays, and the right to leisure were already acknowledged as basic entitlements in most countries before World War II, and the working week had already dropped from 50 to 48 hours, and then even to 40 hours in a few countries on the continent during the depression. In 1936, France introduced the 40-hour working week and paid holidays as part of Popular Front reforms. The Communist Party provided organized leisure activities and vacations, as did both fascist Italy and Nazi Germany through the *dopo lavoro* and *Kraft durch Freude* programmes. But if leisure and mass tourism were already a part of European life before World War II, it is without doubt a phenomenon of the second half of the twentieth century. Working hours generally fell to 42 or 44 hours across Europe in the 1950s.

The five-day working week was introduced in Eastern Europe in the 1960s. By then, most employees in Europe were entitled to two weeks paid vacation plus holidays, while three weeks was the norm in Norway, Sweden, Denmark, and France. In the early 1970s, the number of working hours in Europe declined even further. The power of labour unions in defending the welfare state, public pensions, and worker rights in the face of the oil crisis and recession of the 1970s in part explains the continued fall in working hours. Reducing the working week was a strategy for keeping everyone employed—a position that was reinforced by left-leaning and socialist governments. The slogan 'work less-work all' echoed throughout Europe. A 35-hour working week was introduced in France in 2000, while 37 to 39 hours was the average across Europe.

Economists such as Olivier Blanchard worried that Europe had fallen into a 'leisure trap' and forsaken future income for a relaxing life.[11] Others argued that high tax rates made work less rewarding and leisure a better alternative. The causes may have been multiple, but the result was a late twentieth-century surge in the democratization of free time. By 2004, Germany and Italy had the highest number of paid holiday and vacation days (39 days). The average European worked 20 per cent less than their American counterpart. Far from having a subsidiary quality in relation to work, the notion of free time became a way of life. The result was the development of a distinct postmodern European culture of leisure. Fun, play, and fantasy became integral to lifestyle expectations.

Consumption and Television

Leisure became a landscape of conspicuous consumption. It was television more than any other factor that introduced people to the new world of things. Television programmes circulated a discourse of consumerism and the good life, and made

---

[11] Olivier Blanchard, 'The Economic Future of Europe', *Journal of Economic Perspectives* 18 (2004), 3–26.

consumption practices visible. Television programming resumed in England in 1946 and some 10 million television sets graced British homes by 1958. West Germans tuned into television broadcasts from 1952. French television resumed just after the Liberation and in Italy in 1952, but both countries remained suspicious of the new medium. Although early European television followed the American model of broadcasting, it also differed in important ways. First, the networks were national entities, state-controlled, and tended towards middle-brow culture and family entertainment. Programming was strongly influenced by national identity. Second, the inspiration for programming often came from national radio, theatre, and variety shows. ITV in Britain inaugurated commercial programming and television advertising in 1954, while commercially-driven networks came later in other countries. A European context for television watching was developed quite early with the launch of Eurovision in June 1954 and the Europe 1 network in January 1955, which gave national networks a shared body of taped and live broadcasts. Hundreds of thousands of Europeans stood transfixed in June 1953, watching the coronation of Elizabeth II flicker on television screens. It was many people's first major television experience.

Television produced familiarity and the intimacy of domestic life. Lifestyle and class tastes, the way people should decorate their homes, what they should wear, how they should 'keep up' socially all were portrayed by entertainment programming that was generally aimed at women. The 1950s French docu-drama *si c' était vous* (*If It Were You*) explored contemporary family life. The British soap opera *The Grove Family*, which first appeared in 1954, carefully constructed modern identities for an ordinary lower-middle class family. In the first episode of the popular 1960s British sitcom *The Likely Lads*, the two working-class characters were seen arriving home from a holiday in Spain.[12] The phenomenally successful Mod television programme *Ready, Steady, Go* provided cues to the latest fashions of Carnaby Street and King's Road in London. The single most successful and popular British programme of the 1960s was *Coronation Street*, which reached audiences in excess of 20 million. The characters and daily life of this stereotypical district of the northern industrial cities explored how the traditional working class faired in the age of affluence.

Gradually, second and third channels were added to national line-ups. The channel RAI2 appeared in Italy in 1961, while a second German channel (ZDF) joined ARD in 1963. France's ORTF added a second channel in 1964, when a full 42 per cent of French households owned a television set. By the 1960s, American entertainment series and soap operas were being dumped on to European television at rock-bottom prices. As television viewers from Budapest to Dublin tuned in to episodes of *Dynasty* and *Baywatch*, the influence of Hollywood image-making and American media machines became unprecedented, as did the reaction against Americanization. By 1988, 22 per cent of French, 13 per cent of British, and 6 per cent of Italian broadcasting consisted of American programmes. Even production styles and the personalization of news

---

[12] Rob Turnock, *Television and Consumer Culture: Britain and the Transformation of Modernity* (London: I.B. Tauris, 2007), 149.

mirrored the American example. In 1997, the European Union finally attempted to stem the influence of global entertainment by regulating a quota of European broadcasts on television.

But rather than focusing exclusively on American cultural imperialism, historians now interpret the circulation of media programming as a complex form of interaction and mutual construction. Productions such as Britain's 1960s *That Was the Week That Was* and *Monty Python's Flying Circus*, as well as France's *La Bebete Show*, were at the forefront of inventiveness. Within a few years of its first broadcast on Dutch television in 1999, *Big Brother* had been adopted with nationally specific variations in countries throughout Europe, and the Netherlands continued to be a source for European programming.[13] The Columbian telenovela *Ugly Betty* (*Yo soy Betty, la fea*) became *Verliebt in Berlin* in a 2005–07 German adaptation of the phenomenally successful programme, while in Eastern Europe the original series had mythic status. And in general, Italy, Spain, and Portugal preferred Latin American programming to American imports.

Even the socialist GDR began broadcasting televised advertisements as early as 1959 and continued until commercials were banned in 1976. By the early 1970s, nearly every Eastern European home had a television set. Television under communism featured predictable, propagandistic, cultural programming. National-day parades, and the first cosmonauts in space were grandiose television events. But Eastern Europeans initially watched Finnish television and then pirated broadcasts from across the Iron Curtain such as the extraordinarily successful West German reality crime show *Aktenzeichen XY... Ungelöst* (Case XY... Unresolved). By the 1970s, televisions in Eastern Europe were tuned to well known American and BBC series. In terms of popular programming, the biggest traffic across the frontiers were British serials. The most successful of these, action series such as *Doctor Who* or *The Avengers* were aired to devoted fans across the continent. The fall of communism opened television viewers to the full range of talk shows, soap operas, and serials, both in international and local formats. The first private television station in post-communist Europe, TV Nova, began operations in Czechoslovakia in 1993. The 1995 Media Law opened the way to commercialization and a new breed of Eastern European media conglomerates such as Poland's TVN or Romania's ProTV. By the early twenty-first century, Eastern Europe was hit with the reality show craze as Slovakians and Hungarians sat mesmerized by *Pop Idol* and *Who Wants to be a Millionaire*.

MEDIA AND SPORTS

Sports claimed a prominent place on television and in leisure life throughout Europe in the second half of the twentieth century and beyond. Association football is the sport of millions. Its popularity rose steeply in the aftermath of World War II, when attendance

---

[13] Cited in Jonathan Bignell and Andreas Fickers, *A European Television History* (Oxford: Wiley-Blackwell, 2008), 14.

at matches reached their peak. From the onset, television magnified national sports as mass entertainment. By the mid-1950s, both BBC and ITV were offering sports magazines and Saturday afternoon sports coverage, while European Cup matches were shown continent-wide by Eurovision. The 1966 broadcast of the English World Cup victory over Germany at London's Wembley Stadium catapulted what had been a working-class spectator sport into a symbol of a new classless society. But the rise of football hooliganism in the 1970s and 1980s undid these idealistic claims. Young firm members threw aside their working-class origins and turned to designer sportswear to distinguish themselves from their rivals, while the media glamourized hooligan lifestyles. Italian *ultrà* groups besieged matches with their political flags, banners, and chants. Football fans collectively constructed charismatic national identities and emotional bonds. AC Milan and Real Madrid were fantasy images of power and media-driven jingoism. The match between Dinamo Zagreb and Red Star Belgrade in March 1990 ended with rioting and exacerbated tensions in the Yugoslav wars.

Interpretations of the football phenomenon and its 'sense of belonging' are legion. The 1998 World Cup victory by France was heralded as a great moment of social unity as French and North Africans linked arms in street celebrations. For others, football was a platform for pan-Europeanization, or a form of consumer identity linked tightly to global media. Manchester United legend David Beckham became a turn-of-the-century global sensation with his multiple brand personalities worth millions. Audiences worldwide tuned their television channels to the 2006 World Cup and watched fabled French footballer Zinédine Zidane head-but Marco Materazzi for verbal insults and hand the Italians the victory. Highly ritualized and increasingly tied to spending, football became a multi-million dollar consumer industry dependent on the deep allegiance and rituals of millions of devoted fans. Football has the highest global television audience in sport. Media and marketing rights to club football, hosting European and world cup championship matches, set off bidding wars between potential sponsors. The tight relationship between consumerism and sport was evidenced in 2009 in the top ranking of Adidas, Nike, and Puma brands as the football sponsors most recognized by fans. Advertisers invested millions in spots during television matches.

The deregulation of the media industry in the late 1980s and 1990s split up the big national networks and opened up television viewing to private channels and commercialization. Commodities were made the primary spectacle in evermore extravagant advertising. Television, video, computers, the internet, and eventually mobile electronic devices and mp3 players, expanded media consumption and entertainment exponentially. By the end of the twentieth century, global conglomerates such as Bertelsmann AG, Vivendi Universal, and Rupert Murdoch's News Corporation were locked in ruthless battle over the flow of information and advertising. Their interests spread from film production and book publishing to music and television, with untold profits generated from spin-off merchandise such as video games. The control of information by a small number of media giants called into question the very nature of democracy and citizenship. The Berlusconi family's Fininvest media empire controlled Italy's largest film production and publishing companies, the A.C. Milan football team, and a cluster of television networks.

Fininvest's televised advertising, showgirl and sports spectacle, was instrumental to the victory of his right-wing Forza Italia alliance and in creating a new tele-visual politics.

Although the internet was initially heralded as a counterbalance to this concentration of media power, the European Commission's decision against Microsoft and its monopoly practices in 2007 was evidence of the struggle between the global media industry and European interests. Fears about internet colossus Google led to a European Commission investigation of privacy issues around the buy-up of small-scale European competitors. Nonetheless, the most popular websites in Europe in 2007 were Google, Microsoft, and Yahoo. In a tracking survey carried out in April 2007, there were more Europeans than Americans online during the day. In 2009, the European Commission issued yet another call to arms against global media dominance, urging its member states to start digitizing books as a 'pro-European' answer to Google's overpowering control of information.

Tourism

Tourism emerged from the ashes of World War II as one of the best prospects for European economic recovery and for providing relief for restive, war-weary Europeans only too happy for a few days of holiday respite. Enormous marketing campaigns were launched to persuade citizens that touristic representations were vital to their national way of life. International travel restrictions were lifted, heritage sites restored as potential tourist attractions, the hotel industry modernized, and aggressive advertising campaigns launched that turned Europe into touristic theatre. In Britain, for example, the campaign emerged as the successor to wartime propaganda in equating tourism with patriotism. The venerable Thomas Cook travel agency promoted foreign holidays by showing information films at town halls throughout the country. The tourist industry fashioned an imaginary of European distinctiveness and heritage as a prized commodity essential to prosperity.

A new mobility provided by air, rail, and car transport made this possible. Coach companies blossomed as did cheap rail and airline services. Airlines such as West Germany's Lufthansa worked hand-in-hand with state Tourist Offices to encourage travel and sightseeing in stereotypical German places. By the mid-1950s, 30 million travellers were already crossing European frontiers every year, and in 1966 their number exceeded a hundred million. Domestic tourism was even more extensive. During the months of July and August the highways, train stations, and airports of Europe were scenes of mass migration of unprecedented historic proportions. Vacation and travel were accepted as essential to personal replenishment and fulfilment. Holidays became, according to John Urry, 'almost a marker of citizenship, a right to pleasure'.[14] Free time became the opportunity to consume places and activities. Travel and leisure became a matter of consumer choice.

---

[14] John Urry, *The Tourist Gaze: Leisure and Travel in Contemporary Societies* (London: Sage, 1990), 27.

Economy hotels and bed-and-breakfast establishments mushroomed across Europe. Standardized hotel chains dotted the highways. The first Novotel highway hotel was opened near Lille in northern France in 1967 by Paul Dubrule and Gérard Pelisson, a former head of market research at IBM-Europe. The first no-frills Ibis hotel opened in 1974 outside Bordeaux. Cheap and cheerful holiday camps featuring an assortment of sports and recreational activities sprang up for working- and middle-class families. Billy Butlin's inexpensive seaside holiday camps in England and Ireland were immensely popular in the 1950s and 1960s. Club Méditerranée or Club Med welcomed vacationers to its first resort in the Balearics in 1950. Started in 1968 as part of a Dutch camping and sporting goods business, the Center Parc resort chain, with 'holiday villages' throughout Western Europe, offered carefully controlled family-friendly recreational experiences.

Eastern Europe remained hermetically sealed off to foreign tourists during the Stalin era and eastern Europeans themselves remained trapped behind the Iron Curtain. But subsidized trade union, company, and cooperative holiday camps offered vacations not unlike Billy Butlin's. By the early 1960s, the border with Eastern Europe was gradually being opened. Yugoslavia's Adriatic Coast opened to foreign tourists in 1963. In 1966, Czechoslovakia welcomed nearly three million tourists and Hungary nearly two million tourists. A vast European-wide market in holiday packages, tour programmes, and touristic commodities from leisure clothes to camping equipment signalled the transformation of leisure practices into consumption. Interest in the outdoors became a veritable mass movement, with hundreds of thousands of people flocking to campsites with their cameras, tents, and gear. The number of campers in the GDR for example rose from 172,000 in 1959 to 500,000 in 1970.[15] Millions of people entertained themselves with boats and water craft on Europe's rivers, lakes, and coastal waters. Nature itself became a leisure-time commodity.

After deregulation, the low-cost revolution in airline services made travel even more enticing. Freddie Laker's Laker Airways began its hugely popular Skytrain service between London and New York in 1977. It was a forerunner of Richard Branson's Virgin Atlantic airline and a host of other no-frills carriers that collapsed distance and travel costs across Europe and beyond. Easyjet and Irish carrier Ryanair led the way in the 1990s. By the early years of the twenty-first century, over one hundred budget carriers flew to a dizzying array of cities and towns from Norway to Cyprus, from Portugal to the Ukraine. High-speed rail service provided travel alternatives for landlubbers. An early German version reaching 200 km/hour appeared in 1965 at the International Transport Fair in Munich, while 'Le Capitole' between Paris and Toulouse was the first French high-speed line. Beginning in 1981, the French *Train à Grande Vitesse* (TGV) technology was adapted by numerous countries as well as for the opening of the Channel Tunnel and EuroStar service.

---

[15] Anne Kaminsky, '"True Advertising Means Promoting a Good Thing through a Good Form"': Advertising in the German Democratic Republic', in Pamela E. Swett, Jonathan Wiesen and Jonathan R. Zatlin (eds), *Selling Modernity: Advertising in Twentieth-Century Germany* (Durham, NC: Duke University Press, 2007), 282.

In 2007, the tourism industry was directly responsible for 5 per cent of the European Union members GDP and employed between 7 and 8 million people. The most frequent use of the internet by Europeans was to book travel and holiday accommodation. Nearly 90 per cent of the 458 million tourists in Europe were Europeans themselves, with Americans far behind at 6 per cent.[16] France was the most visited country in the world with 79 million visitors in 2008, representing some 11 per cent of GNP. The touristic identities of individual European nations became systematized by state policy and the tourism industry. National history and memory, a portrait of 'authentic' national culture were all increasingly interpreted through the lens of touristic and heritage narrations and sites, food, crafts, and culture consumable by visitors. The historic districts of Europe's cities were refashioned in a visitor economy of safe, picturesque backdrops for the consumption of leisure. Cities throughout the continent vied for designation as an official European Union 'capital of culture' as a catalyst for their tourism and leisure industries. Ethnic neighbourhoods became a form of vicarious travel, a localized ethnoscape of exotica to consume. The everyday spaces of Europe were turned into place-consumption while national identity and the 'likability' or courteousness of the French or Germans were produced through tourism as commodities. As Victoria de Grazia has argued, consumer culture thus produces social and political meaning and acts on the nature of citizenship.[17]

The Citizen–Consumer

The second half of the twentieth century gives scholars every reason for pause in assessing the intertwining of citizen and consumer. Is Veblen's analysis worth resurrecting in the age of leisure and excess? Snared by luxury, seduced by ease, and tricked by consumer culture's egoistic flatteries, has Europe's 'leisure class' gone soft and succumbed to political acquiescence? Has genuinely democratic citizenship been traded for a culture of abundance at shopping malls and supermarkets? Or has the pursuit of consumer abundance been less a Faustian bargain than a logical, straightforward connection to dreams of a better life? Consumption and leisure had a marked egalitarian effect. Traditional class boundaries were broken down. Consumer behaviour was no longer shaped by social class but by lifestyles that cut across social hierarchies. Class boundaries seemed to dissolve in a new set of gender, generational, and pluralist categories and in the absorption with individuality and its display. In 2006, consumers were brandishing a total of 715 million bank cards throughout the EU, while 360,000 ATMs made quick

---

[16] European Union, *European Travel Commission Factsheet* (Brussels: European Travel Commission, May 2007).

[17] Victoria de Grazia, 'Introduction', in Victoria de Grazia with Ellen Furlough (eds), *The Sex of Things: Gender and Consumption in Historical Perspective* (Berkeley, CA: University of California Press, 1996), 21.

cash available for purchasing desires. The majority of credit loans were for personal consumption.[18] The politics of cultural belonging was based on consumerism as much as on class or national identity.

Undeniably, the evolution of the citizen–consumer lies in the intersection between civil society, the state, and the marketplace. States—whether communist or capitalist—came to see mass consumption and leisure as vital to political power. In the process, the consumer gained unprecedented influence in contemporary Europe. Perhaps for these reasons, historians have increasingly focused on the way consumers themselves co-produced new technologies and products from washing machines to cars, from radios and televisions to computers. The media industry helped to deeply politicize consumerism and consumer rights and elevated them to the level of state affairs. Consumer culture played a central role in the shaping of the European Union and European identity. Part of the European social contract involved admission to a robust mass consumer and leisure industry as the citizen–consumer negotiated a political exchange in which a highly technocratic, regulatory Europe was accepted for the price of an affluent society. Consumer safety for example was behind the 'beef wars' of the late 1990s and the decision by the European Union to ban imports of American hormone-treated beef. Consumer panic over mad cow disease (bovine spongiform encephalitis, or BSE) in 1999 and 2000 led to an EU veto of British beef exports. Harmonization guidelines for one after another commodity from the Cassis Ruling in 1979 to standards for French Camembert have been fought out in high-profile battles between member states and the EU in the name of consumer interests.

A possessive individualism is equated with citizenship, which itself is defined as consumer participation. Individuals are free to project their own meaning onto commodities, and their public identities are equated with performing their distinctive appropriation of goods. According to sociologist Adam Burgess, people do not want to do consumption merely for simple gratification or to reinforce identity: they also want to watch and *pursue* it.[19] Young people throughout Europe share computers, personal digital assistants (PDAs), and internet access. Some 100 million Europeans logged on to the Facebook social networking site in 2009. Video games are a top leisure activity. The right of entry to a 'European audiovisual and consumer space' is imagined as the new cultural bond.

Yet as the dynamic fluidity across social and cultural boundaries has increased, new distinctions have emerged and indeed are provoked by mass culture and consumption. Self-expressive identity politics has created an unending appropriation of material objects as ciphers of difference and diversity. The mutual operation of common identity and difference, entitlement and marginalization, are what distinguish consumer culture. Better educated Europeans had the greatest access to consumption and leisure. They are

---

[18] Eurostat, *Consumers in Europe 2009* (Luxembourg: Publications of the European Communities, 2009), 35.

[19] Adam Burgess, 'Flattering Consumption: Creating a Europe of the Consumer', *Journal of Consumer Culture* 1 (2001), 93.

international in perspective and more likely to identify with cities and urban culture than any particular country. For the most privileged young Europeans, brandishing the newest electronics and fashions purchased over the internet, indulging in gentrified hipsterism and international travel have become a way of life.

Those that are excluded from the IT revolution and consumer society are the newly dispossessed. Ten of the European Union's twenty-five member states reported that in 2006 fewer than half of all households owned a computer, and fewer than half had an internet connection. Generational differences are stark. Young Europeans spend far more on consumer and leisure products than did their parents and grandparents. National and regional differences in consumer and leisure practices remain wide. In 2003, household expenditures on recreation and culture were highest in the United Kingdom, then Austria and the Czech Republic. They were lowest in Ireland and Portugal.[20] Household expenditures in Luxembourg were ten times higher than those in Romania.[21] Fewer than one-third of East Europeans could afford an annual holiday, although they spend vast amounts of money on consumer goods. Desperation still haunts Europe's poorest countries in the East. These divisions are hidden by a social life in which everything has become cultural. According to Frederic Jameson, material objects and leisure practices have created a 'depthless culture' that is saturated with images, signs, and messages.[22] These were the greatest challenges for European civic life at the beginning of the twenty-first century.

FURTHER READING

Bignell, Jonathan and Andreas Fickers (eds), *A European Television History* (Oxford: Wiley-Blackwell, 2008).

Bigsby, C.W.E. (ed.), *Superculture: American Popular Culture and Europe* (London: Paul Elek, 1975).

Carter, Erica, *How German Is She? Postwar West German Reconstruction and the Consuming Woman* (Ann Arbor, MI: University of Michigan Press, 1997).

Castillo, Greg, 'Domesticating the Cold War: Household Consumption as Propaganda in Marshall Plan Germany', *Journal of Contemporary History* 40:2 (2005), 261–88.

Crew, David F., *Consuming Germany in the Cold War* (Oxford: Berg, 2004).

Daunton, Martin and Matthew Hilton (eds), *The Politics of Consumption: Material Culture and Citizenship in Europe and America* (Oxford: Berg, 2001).

Gundle, Stephen, *Between Hollywood and Moscow: The Italian Communists and the Challenge of Mass Culture, 1943–1991* (Durham, NC: Duke University Press, 2000).

Mitter, Rana and Patrick Major (eds), *Across the Blocs: Cold War Cultural and Social History* (London: Routledge, 2004).

---

[20] OECD, *OECD Factbook 2006: Economic, Environmental and Social Statistics* (Paris: OECD, 2006), 213.

[21] Eurostat, *Consumers in Europe 2009*, 65, 68.

[22] Frederic Jameson, *Postmodernism, or, the Cultural Logic of Late Capitalism* (Durham, NC: Duke University Press, 1992), 388.

Pence, Katherine and Paul Betts (eds), *Socialist Modern: East German Everyday Culture and Politics* (Ann Arbor, MI: University of Michigan Press, 2008).

Poiger, Uta G., *Jazz, Rock and Rebels: Cold War Politics and American Culture in a Divided Germany* (Berkeley, CA: University of California Press, 2000).

Reid, Susan E. and David Crowley (eds), *Style and Socialism: Modernity and Material Culture in Post-War Eastern Europe* (Oxford: Berg, 2000).

Schildt, Axel, and Detlef Siegfried (eds), *Between Marx and Coca-Cola: Youth Cultures in Changing European Societies, 1960–1980* (New York: Berghahn, 2006).

Schissler, Hanna (ed.), *The Miracle Years: A Cultural History of West Germany, 1949–1968* (Princeton, NJ: Princeton University Press, 2001).

Strasser, Susan, Charles McGovern and Matthias Judt (eds), *Getting and Spending: European and American Consumer Societies in the Twentieth Century* (Cambridge: Cambridge University Press, 1998).

PART V

FEAR

CHAPTER 21

'GENTLEMEN, YOU ARE MAD!': MUTUAL ASSURED DESTRUCTION AND COLD WAR CULTURE

P.D. SMITH

'The more one thinks about the implications of a nuclear policy, the more absurd and dangerous it all becomes.'

Tony Benn[1]

INTRODUCTION

IN the year after the bombing of Hiroshima and Nagasaki, the historian and critic Lewis Mumford made a dramatic attack on the insanity of the nuclear age. 'We in America', he wrote, 'are living among madmen. Madmen govern our affairs in the name of order and security.' According to Mumford, the modern superweapon society, for all its technological supremacy, was unable to recognize the looming disaster. People were sleepwalking towards the abyss of atomic war:

> The madmen have taken it upon themselves to lead us by gradual stages to that final act of madness which will corrupt the face of the earth and blot out the nations of men, possibly put an end to all life on the planet itself.[2]

---

[1] Tony Benn, *Out of the Wilderness: Diaries 1963–67* (London: Hutchinson, 1987), entry for 3 April 1957.

[2] Lewis Mumford, 'Gentlemen: You are Mad!', *Saturday Review of Literature* (2 March 1946), cited in Kai Bird and Lawrence Lifschultz (eds), *Hiroshima's Shadow: Writings on the Denial of History and the Smithsonian Controversy* (Stony Creek, CT: Pamphleteer's Press, 1998), 284–7.

Mumford's article, entitled 'Gentlemen: You are Mad!', was published at a time when most Americans credited the atomic bomb with ending World War II and saving the lives of many US soldiers. But the shockwaves from the bombs that destroyed Hiroshima and Nagasaki reverberated throughout the world in the following years. As the arms race accelerated in the 1950s, people were forced to come to terms with the idea that, for the first time in history, humankind was able not just to wipe out entire cities at the touch of a button, but to end life on earth. To quote one science fiction story of the period, the Cold War became the era of the 'alphabet bombs': first there was the A-bomb, then the H-bomb, and after that came the scientists' ultimate gifts of destruction—the C-bomb (cobalt bomb) and the N-bomb (neutron bomb).[3]

As the superpowers built up their arsenals and the fear of nuclear technologies grew, so people became increasingly hostile towards their inventors: the scientists. Scientists had signed a Faustian pact with what President Eisenhower termed the military–industrial complex and it seemed to many observers that in the Cold War the notion of progress itself was increasingly compromised. At the start of the twentieth century, scientists had been viewed as saviours, heralds of a coming technological utopia. Now their genius seemed to be directed solely at transforming the laws of nature into new and more destructive weapons. Bertholt Brecht summed up the dilemma facing Cold War science and society in his great play *Leben des Galilei* (1955). As the father of modern physics looks into the distant future, he sees a time when the scientists' shouts of *Eureka!* will be greeted by 'a universal cry of horror' because people have learnt that, rather than improving the lot of humanity, science now leads to ever more terrible weapons of mass destruction.[4] As a result, in popular film and fiction during the Cold War, scientists were more likely to be depicted as Strangelovean madmen than saviours.

War had traditionally been viewed as the continuation of politics by other means, an idea first expounded in the nineteenth century by the Prussian general and war theorist Carl von Clausewitz. This notion had made war socially acceptable—even useful. But the atomic bomb changed that. As H.G Wells had predicted in his novel *The World Set Free* (1914), in which he coined the phrase 'atomic bomb', war in an age of superweapons became mutual suicide. Instead, atomic-age politicians and strategic analysts introduced the concept of deterrence. Jonathan Schell—author of the hugely influential 1982 study of nuclear weapons *The Fate of the Earth*—has argued that the effect of deterrence was to create 'terror on a mass scale without actually using force'. The fear of annihilation was the only thing preventing war: 'The battles that *could not* be fought physically were to be fought out instead on psychological terrain.'[5]

The Cold War arms race created and served to maintain what Churchill termed 'the balance of terror'. By the end of the 1960s, both the US and the USSR had more than

[3] Fritz Leiber, 'Coming Attraction' (1950), in James Gunn (ed.), *The Road to Science Fiction, Vol. 3: From Heinlein to Here* (New York: Mentor, 1979), 173.

[4] Bertolt Brecht, *Leben des Galilei* (Frankfurt/M: Suhrkamp, 1972), Scene 14, 126. See P.D. Smith, *Metaphor and Materiality: German Literature and the World-View of Science 1780–1955* (Oxford: European Humanities Research Centre, 2000), 265ff.

[5] Jonathan Schell, *The Unconquerable World: Power, Nonviolence, and the Will of the People* (London: Allen Lane, 2004), 52.

enough nuclear weapons to withstand a first strike and still be able to retaliate. The superpowers had reached the point of 'assured destruction', to use US Secretary of Defense Robert McNamara's 1968 phrase. It was critic Donald Brennen who added 'mutual' to this concept and created the memorable acronym that aptly sums up the politics and strategy of the Cold War: MAD.[6] This essay explores how mutual assured destruction was reflected and refracted in European culture and society from 1950 to 1985 and shows how film and fiction played a key role in highlighting the potential effects of MAD—a global nuclear holocaust.

The Doomsday Decade: 1954–64

By summer 1949, President Truman had given up on postwar attempts to secure international control of atomic energy. Instead, he said, 'we must be strongest in atomic weapons'.[7] Until 6 October 1949, the President had not even heard of the hydrogen bomb. But the successful Soviet test of an atomic bomb in 1949 and lobbying by scientists such as Edward Teller soon convinced him that this was the new winning weapon that America needed to have in its arsenal. The arms race had begun.

Many scientists, some of whom had been involved in the Manhattan Project, were disturbed by the prospect of a nuclear arms race. If the project to build the hydrogen bomb was successful, Einstein warned in 1950, then 'radioactive poisoning of the atmosphere and hence annihilation of any life on earth has been brought within the range of technical possibilities'.[8] Einstein's apocalyptic warning was splashed across nearly every front page. In France the paper *Aurore* printed a startling headline across three columns: 'wherever it falls the H-bomb will obliterate all human life for a thousand years'.[9] You didn't need Einstein's brain to work out that Europe would be the battlefield of World War III. As the *New Statesman* put it, 'the British people know perfectly well that, even if America and Russia might survive an atomic war, Britain and Western Europe would not'.[10]

In his Nobel acceptance speech in 1950, William Faulkner captured the mood of atomic anxiety perfectly: 'there are no longer problems of the spirit. There is only the question: When will I be blown up?'[11] These concerns, dismissed by *Time* magazine as 'hydrogen hysteria', were also emerging in popular culture.[12] The classic Boulting

[6] Joseph M. Siracusa, *Nuclear Weapons* (Oxford: Oxford University Press, 2008), 68.

[7] Truman, July 1949; quoted in Richard Rhodes, *Dark Sun: The Making of the Hydrogen Bomb* (New York: Touchstone, 1996), 363.

[8] 'Einstein Sees Bid to "Annihilation" in Hydrogen Bomb', *New York Times* [hereafter *NYT*] (13 February 1950), 1.

[9] Cited in Harold Callender, 'Paris Fears Race for Super-Weapon', *NYT* (15 February 1950), n.p.

[10] 'The Logic of the H-bomb', *New Statesman* 39 (4 February 1950), 117.

[11] William Faulkner, *Essays, Speeches and Public Letters*, ed. James B. Meriwether (New York: Modern Library, 2004), 119.

[12] 'Hydrogen Hysteria', *Time* (6 March 1950), 88.

brothers film *Seven Days to Noon* (1950) reveals both the growing anxieties about atomic war and a feeling that scientists had betrayed the ideals of their discipline. Professor Willingdon, a British scientist who worked on the Manhattan Project, disappears from his government research establishment together with an atomic bomb. Willingdon threatens that, unless the British prime minister agrees to stop building atomic weapons, he will destroy central London. The professor is tormented by the thought that atomic war will mean the 'total destruction of mankind'.[13] He has also lost faith in science: 'When I was a young man I saw in science a way of serving God and my fellow men. Now I see my life's work used only for destruction. My dream has become a nightmare.'

The idealism of the early years of the twentieth century, when scientists were hailed as saviours of humankind, was long gone. Cold War films were quick to reflect the growing suspicion of scientists. The stock-in-trade character of the mad scientist was as old as cinema itself. But in the 1950s, more subtly flawed scientists began to appear in the movies. They included scientists such as Dr Edward Morbius in *The Forbidden Planet* (1956) and the sinister Dr Carrington in *The Thing* (1951), who is even prepared to sacrifice human lives in the cause of science. Such scientists were the antecedents of that most famous Cold War cinematic scientist—Dr Strangelove.

In contrast to popular movies, Cold War public information films sought to reassure audiences by glossing over the true horror of nuclear war. In *Atomic Alert* (1951) viewers were told that 'the chance of your being hurt by an atomic bomb is slight'.[14] In private, scientists and statesmen were rather more concerned. Within weeks of the first atomic bombs being dropped, the new British prime minister, Clement Atlee, admitted in a personal memorandum that:

> It is difficult for people to adjust their minds to an entirely new situation . . . Even the modern conception of war to which in my lifetime we have become accustomed is now completely out of date . . . it would appear that the provision of bomb-proof basements in factories and offices and the retention of ARP [Air Raid Precautions] and Fire Services is just futile waste . . . The answer to an atomic bomb on London is an atomic bomb on another great city.[15]

Atlee's foreign secretary, Ernest Bevin, was more outspoken: 'We've got to have this thing over here, whatever it costs. We've got to have the bloody Union Jack on top of it.'[16] The Royal Air Force received its first atomic bombs in 1953, the year Queen Elizabeth II was crowned. As Atlee had predicted, deterrence was now accepted as the only defence against atomic attack.

In the same year that the RAF began carrying atomic bombs, Her Majesty's civil servants calculated the effects of a nuclear attack on the United Kingdom. They assumed that the aerial assault would consist of 132 bombs of the type dropped on Nagasaki, targeted

[13] John and Roy Boulting, dir., *Seven Days to Noon* (London Films, 1950).

[14] *Atomic Alert* (Encyclopaedia Britannica Films, 1951) [no dir.].

[15] Clement Atlee, 'Memorandum by the Prime Minister', 28 August 1945, PRO, CAB 130/3; cited in Peter Hennessy, *The Secret State: Whitehall and the Cold War* (London: Penguin, 2003), 46.

[16] Ernest Bevin's comment was made during discussions in the Cabinet Committee on Atomic Energy on 25 October 1946; see Hennessy, *The Secret State*, 48.

on major cities and facilities. The result would be 1,378,000 of the Queen's loyal subjects dead and 785,000 seriously wounded. London would lose 422,000 of its citizens. During the whole of World War II, Britain had suffered 440,000 military and civilian dead.

America successfully tested its first thermonuclear device in 1952. On 1 March 1954, an improved version was detonated on Bikini Atoll in the Marshall Islands. The Los Alamos scientists who designed it expected a yield of 5 megatons. Instead it exploded with the power of 15 million tons of TNT, making it the biggest bomb ever tested by the United States. The fireball expanded to four miles wide. Without warning, radioactive fallout began raining down on the nearly ten thousand personnel of the naval task force gathered in the Pacific to observe the test, code-named Bravo. The test cast a vast radioactive pall over thousands of miles of the Pacific Ocean. But the rest of the world might never have heard about what happened were it not for what occurred two weeks later. A Japanese tuna fishing boat, the *Fukuryu Maru* ('Lucky Dragon'), returned early to its homeport of Yaizu. All twenty-three crew members were suffering from a mysterious illness. It turned out to be radiation sickness. They had been fishing 90 miles east of the Bravo test, several miles outside the exclusion zone.

What especially 'alarmed the world' about this 'thermonuclear monster', as the American press labelled the Bravo H-bomb, was the invisible yet lethal fallout from the explosion.[17] In spite of the warnings four years earlier from Albert Einstein and other scientists about radioactive poisoning of the atmosphere, the word 'fallout' had scarcely been mentioned. Now the papers were full of stories describing how the fishermen had been 'burned by fall-out'.[18] As Daniel Lang wrote in the *New Yorker*, Bravo 'was the shot that made the world fallout-conscious'.[19]

Despite frequent reassurances from the Atomic Energy Commission, the public in America and around the world began to wake up to the threat posed by this new, invisible killer. In November 1954 one of the most famous atomic movies of the Cold War opened in Tokyo: *Gojira*, better known in the West as *Godzilla*. According to Tomoyuki Tanaka, the film's producer, *Gojira* was about 'the terror of the Bomb. Mankind had created the Bomb, and now nature was going to take revenge on mankind.'[20] *Gojira* was an instant box-office success in Japan where 32 million people had signed a petition against the H-bomb in 1954. Audiences who knew better than any nation on earth what a nuclear weapon could do, watched in total silence. Many left the cinema in tears.

On his return from the Bravo test site, AEC chairman Lewis Strauss boasted to reporters that they could now make an H-bomb 'as large as you wish'. According to Strauss 'any city' could now be wiped out by an H-bomb.[21] Strauss clearly hoped to reassure his fellow

[17] Hanson W. Baldwin, 'H-Bomb Fall-out Poses New Defense Problems', *NYT* (20 February 1955), IV, 10.

[18] Lindesay Parrott, 'Japan to Survey Radioactivity of Sea around the Bikini Tests', *NYT* (17 April 1954), n.p.

[19] June 1955, in Daniel Lang, *From Hiroshima to the Moon: Chronicles of Life in the Atomic Age* (New York: Simon & Schuster, 1959), 369.

[20] Tomoyuki Tanaka, quoted in William Tsutsui, *Godzilla on My Mind: Fifty Years of the King of Monsters* (New York: Palgrave Macmillan, 2004), 18.

[21] [Anon], 'H-Bomb Tests End; Called a Success', *NYT* (14 May 1954), 5.

Americans that they were winning the arms race. Instead, many asked: 'But at what price?' By 1954, the hands of the Doomsday Clock on the cover of the *Bulletin of the Atomic Scientists*—the Cold War's most graphic depiction of how close the world was to nuclear Armageddon—stood at two minutes to midnight. With the Bravo H-bomb test, the world entered its most dangerous years.

Within days of the Americans exploding the biggest bomb the world had yet seen a high-level meeting of civil servants and top scientists took place in London. The man in charge of building the British atomic bomb, mathematician Sir William Penney, briefed them on the hydrogen bomb projects of the Soviet Union and the United States as well as describing to the assembled Whitehall mandarins what would happen if even a modest five-megaton bomb were dropped on their city. If such a bomb exploded above Nelson's Column in Trafalgar Square, everything and everyone from the Houses of Parliament and Downing Street in the south (including the room in which they were all sitting) to Soho in the north would be instantly vaporized. Beyond that, buildings would be totally destroyed up to three miles away and badly damaged up to seven miles. The Prime Minister, Winston Churchill, was appalled. It was, he said, 'the most terrible and destructive engine of mass warfare yet known to man'.[22] Nevertheless, at Cabinet later that year, he still argued that Britain needed to be armed with H-bombs, or risk losing 'influence and standing in world affairs'.[23]

A month after the Bravo H-bomb test, a headline in the *New York Times* declared: 'now most dreaded weapon, cobalt bomb, can be built'. In his article, William Laurence (the only journalist allowed access to the Manhattan Project during World War II) explained how a thermonuclear bomb with a shell of cobalt around the fission and fusion devices would create a lethal radioactive cloud when it exploded.[24] A giant cobalt ship bomb exploded offshore could potentially wipe out an entire continent. This article drew shocked responses from around the world. The following day, the London *Times* reported Laurence's article prominently. Beneath it was a report on the worsening condition of the twenty-three Japanese fishermen exposed to radioactive fallout after the H-bomb test at Bikini on 1 March. Media stories about the cobalt bomb—a theoretical possibility in nuclear weapons design that no country has ever admitted building— reflected widespread public anxiety at this time regarding fallout and the development of ever more terrible weapons of mass destruction. From 1954, the reports of a cobalt doomsday weapon would feature regularly in newspapers around the world. In fiction and film, such as Stanley Kubrick's *Dr Strangelove*, it also became a powerful symbol of the suicidal nature of the Cold War arms race and mutual assured destruction.

Two days before Christmas 1954, the philosopher and mathematician Bertrand Russell, who had been imprisoned in World War I for his pacifism, gave a BBC radio talk

[22] Macmillan Diary, 26 January 1955; quoted in Hennessey, *The Secret State*, 52.

[23] Winston Churchill, 8 July 1954, PRO, CAB 128/27, quoted in Hennessey, *The Secret State*, 58.

[24] William L. Laurence, 'Now Most Dreaded Weapon, Cobalt Bomb, Can Be Built', *NYT* (7 April 1954), 4. The idea of a cobalt bomb was first described publicly by Leo Szilard in 1950. See P. D. Smith, *Doomsday Men: The Real Dr Strangelove and the Dream of the Superweapon* (London: Allen Lane, 2007).

in what the *Times* described as 'the solemn, urgent tones of Cassandra'. Russell voiced people's unspoken fears: 'Is our race so destitute of wisdom, so incapable of impartial love, so blind even to the simplest dictates of self-preservation,' he asked, 'that the last proof of its silly cleverness is to be the extermination of all life on our planet?'[25]

The broadcast struck a chord with the public and Russell received many letters of support. Encouraged, he decided to approach leading scientists to add their names to a joint statement warning about the dangers of thermonuclear war. In February 1955, Russell wrote to the world's most famous scientist: Albert Einstein. A lifelong anti-militarist, Einstein was immediately enthusiastic and promised to sign the statement. Russell received Einstein's signed copy on 18 April—the day the world learned of the great physicist's death. On 9 July 1955, Russell held a press conference in Caxton Hall, central London, to announce the publication of what became known as the Russell–Einstein Manifesto. It called on governments, the general public, and scientists to confront the dangerous situation that was facing the world:

> We are speaking on this occasion, not as members of this or that nation, continent, or creed, but as human beings, members of the species Man, whose continued existence is in doubt.... Almost everybody who is politically conscious has strong feelings about one or more of these issues; but we want you, if you can, to set aside such feelings and consider yourselves only as members of a biological species which has had a remarkable history, and whose disappearance none of us can desire. We shall try to say no single word which should appeal to one group rather than to another. All, equally, are in peril, and, if the peril is understood, there is hope that they may collectively avert it. We have to learn to think in a new way.[26]

In 1955, Russell's call for a new way of thinking about the nuclear issue made a huge impression on a student at the Moscow State University. His name was Mikhail Gorbachev. Thirty years later, the new Soviet leader would reiterate Russell's words and lead the world into a new era of disarmament that would end the Cold War.

The Russell–Einstein Manifesto received widespread media coverage around the world. In Britain there had been growing opposition to the development of atomic weapons from pacifist groups as well as trade unions and some Anglican bishops. However, for the Labour Party the nuclear issue became a deeply divisive matter in the coming decades. Although anti-nuclear Labour MPs fiercely attacked the Churchill government's decision to develop the H-bomb in March 1955, the executive of the Labour Party eventually endorsed the British bomb. But individual Labour MPs, such as Fenner Brockway and Anthony Wedgwood Benn (who were involved in founding the Hydrogen Bomb National Campaign in April 1954), began organizing protest against nuclear weapons in general and the British nuclear deterrent in particular.

In March 1955, a poll found that 54 per cent of people were in favour of Britain developing the H-bomb, and 32 per cent opposed it. However, in common with other

---

[25] '1954—Portrait of the Year', *Times* (1 January 1955), 11.
[26] 'The Russell–Einstein Manifesto', in Reiner Braun et al. (eds), *Joseph Rotblat: Visionary for Peace* (Weinheim: Wiley-VCH, 2007), 263.

Europeans most Britons were appalled by the idea of ever using such a weapon. A survey conducted for the US government in February that year found that 71 per cent opposed using nuclear weapons in response to an attack on Europe with conventional weapons. Two months later, 67 per cent opposed first use in any circumstance. These attitudes were echoed across the continent. West Germans were shocked to learn in 1953 that atomic cannon had been deployed on their territory. In 1955, a mere 15 per cent said they wanted nuclear weapons used to defend West Germany against an invasion. In June that year, 88 per cent said they wanted to ban the bomb, a desire expressed in opinion polls throughout Europe.[27]

After the 'Bravo' H-bomb spread fallout across the Pacific, nuclear testing became an issue of increasing concern for Europeans. US intelligence reports from Britain mention that when a new series of nuclear tests was announced for 1956, 'the press as a whole expressed varying degrees of repugnance to the idea', with considerable 'concern for the possible genetic effects of radiation'. By the end of 1956, 72 per cent of Britons wanted their politicians to work for an international agreement to halt H-bomb tests.[28] Across Europe, prominent intellectuals added their voices to the chorus of concern about fall-out. In 1957, Albert Schweitzer described it as 'a catastrophe for the human race', a view endorsed by the Pope.[29]

Despite the clear opposition of Europeans, nuclear testing continued. By the end of 1958, America, the Soviet Union, and Britain had detonated 307 devices, most in the atmosphere. Britain's first thermonuclear test, in May 1957, provoked a public outcry. At the beginning of that year, the National Council for Abolition of Nuclear Weapon Tests had been formed with the support of leading cultural figures such as Russell, E. M. Forster, Julian Huxley, and Henry Moore. Within a year this had become the Campaign for Nuclear Disarmament, the most influential anti-nuclear movement of the Cold War. At its public launch on 17 February 1958, there were speeches from public intellectuals including the author J. B. Priestley, Labour MP Michael Foot, and historian A. J. P. Taylor, who encouraged the audience to attend political meetings and shout 'Murderer!' at politicians. According to opinion polls that year, 72 per cent of British people supported global nuclear disarmament.[30] However, from the outset, one of CND's core objectives was unilateral disarmament and this remained a controversial and less popular aim throughout the movement's history.

The Aldermaston march of Easter 1958 was organized by the Direct Action Committee against Nuclear War with the full support of CND. It began with a rally in Trafalgar Square that, despite the rain, attracted 5,800 people. Afterwards thousands spent four days marching 52 miles to the Atomic Weapons Research Establishment at Aldermaston. It was on this historic march that artist Gerald Holtom's classic anti-war symbol—the

[27] Lawrence S. Wittner, *Resisting the Bomb: A History of the World Nuclear Disarmament Movement 1954–1970, The Struggle Against the Bomb* (Stanford, CA: Stanford University Press, 1997), vol. 2, 17, 19.

[28] Ibid., 17.

[29] Albert Schweitzer, 'Declaration of Conscience', broadcast 23 April 1957; quoted in Wittner, *Resisting the Bomb*, 31.

[30] Wittner, *Resisting the Bomb*, 47, 50.

circle with a broken cross—first appeared on placards and banners. Based on the sema-phore symbols for *n* and *d* from the words nuclear disarmament, Holtom's design would become an instantly recognized emblem of opposition to nuclear war around the world.

In the 1940s and 1950s, fiction writers played an important role in thinking the unthinkable—to use the infamous phrase of nuclear theorist Herman Kahn. After the atomic bombing of Hiroshima and Nagasaki, the Pentagon moved swiftly to confiscate and suppress images of the victims of America's new superweapon. Fiction writers stepped into the vacuum, describing what no one was allowed to see: what would hap-pen when the Cold War turned hot and the dreaded mushroom clouds started rising on the horizon. Through narratives of human suffering, their texts brought alive for people the doomsday threat hanging over the world. Novels about a future nuclear war—such as Philip Wylie's *Tomorrow!* (1954), Pat Frank's *Alas, Babylon* (1959), Walter M. Miller's *A Canticle for Leibowitz* (1959), and Mordecai Roshwald's *Level 7* (1959)—were no longer regarded as mere science-fiction fantasies, but became international bestsellers. The most famous of these was by British-born author Nevil Shute. His novel *On the Beach* (1957) sold 100,000 copies in its first six weeks. By the 1980s it had sold more than four million copies, an astonishing total and more than any other novel about nuclear issues.

Set in 1963, Shute's novel depicts a world dying a slow and creeping death caused by fallout from a war fought with cobalt bombs. The novel centres on the only part of the globe not yet affected by radioactivity, Melbourne in the far south of Australia. Shute examines how people behave when faced with the inescapable reality that within nine months—when the cobalt-60 fallout finally reaches them—they will all be dead. 'It's just too big a matter for mankind to tackle', says one character. Indeed, Shute depicts people reacting fatalistically to what lies ahead: 'It's not the end of the world at all. It's only the end of us. The world will go on just the same, only we shan't be in it. I dare say it will get along all right without us.'[31]

For Shute and for many readers, the stoicism of his characters and their attempt to continue a normal life, right up to the very end, was deeply poignant. It captured per-fectly the mood of powerlessness that many people did indeed feel in the 1950s, as they faced the awesome possibility of a global nuclear holocaust that might end life on earth. Shute's moving human story cut through the Cold War propaganda and confronted peo-ple with what could actually happen if deterrence failed. The film version of 1959, star-ring Gregory Peck, Ava Gardner, and Anthony Perkins, became one of the most popular nuclear movies of all time and left audiences around the world 'stunned or weeping'.[32] Nobel prize-winning chemist Linus Pauling said after watching the film 'it may be that . . . *On the Beach* is the movie that saves the world'.[33] At a time when the top secret US *Emergency Plans Book* (1958) estimated that one in five Americans would die in a nuclear

[31] Nevil Shute, *On the Beach* (London: Heinemann, 1957), 40, 89.

[32] Spencer R. Weart, *Nuclear Fear: A History of Images* (Cambridge, MA: Harvard University Press, 1988), 218.

[33] Jerome F. Shapiro, *Atomic Bomb Cinema: The Apocalyptic Imagination on Film* (New York: Routledge, 2002), 23.

attack, novels and films brought home to people the urgency of the situation and helped swell the ranks of anti-nuclear organizations such as CND.

The beginning of the 1960s saw a dramatic increase in anti-nuclear activism in Europe and beyond. In 1960, 40,000 joined the Aldermaston march. The direction of the march had now been reversed, culminating in a rally at Trafalgar Square. That year the square was packed with 100,000 people, the largest popular protest in Britain since the Chartist demonstrations of 1848. CND went from strength to strength. In 1962, 150,000 attended the final rally at the end of the Aldermaston march. CND counted among its supporters key members of Britain's intellectual and cultural elite, including John Osborne, Doris Lessing, Vanessa Redgrave, Robert Bolt, Michael Tippett, Benjamin Britten, and Iris Murdoch. CND's core supporters were predominantly middle class, with women and students being particularly active in the movement. According to Lawrence S. Wittner, who has written the definitive history of the global anti-nuclear movement, 'nuclear disarmament activism helped spawn a rambunctious "youth culture" that scandalized more conventional members of British society'. Peggy Duff, secretary and chief organizer of CND from 1958 to 1967, agrees: 'they were slightly crazy, but not so crazy as the world they were trying to change'.[34] CND and its sister groups across Europe sowed the seeds of 1960s youth culture as well as preparing the ground for environmentalist activism in later decades. CND's campaigns were hugely successful and emulated by protest movements around the world. West Germany, in particular, witnessed vast demonstrations in this period. In polls across Europe the numbers who wanted to ban the bomb grew steadily in the late 1950s and early 1960s.

In September 1961, the Soviet Union shocked the world by resuming its programme of atomic tests, which the superpowers had suspended in 1958 largely as a result of widespread public concern about the dangers of fallout, particularly of strontium-90. According to the press, Moscow blamed 'the threatening attitude of the United States and its allies in the Berlin dispute' for its decision.[35] That year the notorious Berlin Wall had been built, dividing the city (said *Time*) like 'a monstrous guillotine'.[36] On 30 October 1961, the Soviets detonated the largest nuclear weapon ever tested, the *Tsar Bomba*, 'King of Bombs'. The western press described it as 'Khrushchev's monster'.[37] Its potential yield was an enormous 100 megatons but for the test it was limited to 50 megatons. On the same day, Khrushchev wrote a chilling letter to the British Labour Party warning that in any future war the United Kingdom 'may be among the first to experience the destructive power of nuclear blows'.[38] The presence of American nuclear-armed bombers and Britain's own H-bombs (supplied to the RAF this year) made this green and pleasant land a certain target for Soviet weapons, including the new 100-megaton bomb.

---

[34] Wittner, *Resisting the Bomb*, 194.

[35] Seymour Topping, 'Moscow Cites Berlin Tensions—Boasts of Superbomb Project', *NYT* (31 August 1961), 1.

[36] 'Berlin', *Time* (8 September 1961), 26.

[37] 'Superbomb', *Newsweek* (30 October 1961), 44–5.

[38] James Feron, 'Britain is Atomic-War Target, Khrushchev Warns Laborites', *NYT* (31 October 1961), 14.

Each day the newspapers were full of stories about the threat of nuclear Armageddon. It was at this time that Stanley Kubrick began reading the best-selling nuclear thriller *Red Alert* by British author Peter George, an active member of CND. It would become the basis for the film that depicted the insane logic of the Cold War better than any other—*Dr Strangelove or: How I Learned to Stop Worrying and Love the Bomb*.

In Britain, *Red Alert* had been published in 1958 as *Two Hours to Doom* under the pen name, Peter Bryant. It describes how World War III might be started by a maverick military commander. Terminally ill and suffering from depression, General Quinten (the psychotic General Jack D. Ripper in Kubrick's film) orders his B-52 bombers to attack the Soviet Union. But what he does not realize is that the Soviet Union has secretly built a doomsday machine using cobalt bombs beneath the Urals. Any nuclear attack on their country automatically triggers the device, the ultimate symbol of the precarious Cold War balance of terror.

In the novel, the world escapes the nuclear apocalypse. But Kubrick's film has a darker conclusion. *Dr Strangelove* ends with an awesome display of mushroom clouds erupting across the face of the earth, as the cobalt bombs of the Soviet doomsday machine explode. News footage of H-bomb tests is accompanied by British forces' favourite Vera Lynn singing 'We'll Meet Again'. The brutal reality—fully understood by the film's audience in 1964—was that there would be no reunions after World War III. Nuclear war could have only one outcome: mutual annihilation.

Despite Peregrine Worsthorne in the *Sunday Telegraph* likening Kubrick's portrayal of Americans to Soviet propaganda, the film was hugely popular with moviegoers who 'ringed the block' at the Columbia cinema in London.[39] Ticket sales were 25 per cent higher than for any other film the Columbia had shown. For Lewis Mumford, Kubrick's masterstroke was to make Dr Strangelove 'the central symbol of this scientifically organized nightmare of mass extermination'. Mumford thought that the tragedy of the age they were living in was eloquently expressed by the manic figure of this fanatical, ex-Nazi rationalist, a composite character inspired by Cold War scientists such as Edward Teller, Wernher von Braun, Herman Kahn, and John von Neumann: 'This nightmare eventuality that we have concocted for our children is nothing but a crazy fantasy, by nature as horribly crippled and dehumanized as Dr Strangelove himself.'[40]

Mumford rightly described Kubrick's masterpiece as a crucial moment in the culture of the Cold War. For people all over the world, Dr Strangelove came to personify the sinister alliance of science and power politics that made it possible to annihilate millions at the touch of a button. Dr Strangelove's logic could transform acts of inhumanity into practical solutions, his rhetoric clothed barbarity in sweet words of reason, and his think tanks—such as the 'Bland Corporation', aka RAND—used computers to transform lives into numbers. For numbers, as Herman Kahn once said, are something you can think the unthinkable about. But in the 1960s, a new generation began to reject a life reduced to numbers and to look for answers beyond science and rationality. This generation—

---

[39] [Anon.], 'Debate over *Strangelove* Film Echoes Happily at the Box Office', *NYT* (10 February 1964).
[40] Lewis Mumford, ' "Strangelove" Reactions', *NYT* (1 March 1964), II, 8.

the people who queued around the block to see *Dr Strangelove*—no longer felt comfortable with the easy postwar certainties that their parents had accepted without question. For those who grew up in an age haunted by the Strangelovean cobalt bomb, the old ways of looking at the world seemed to lead to a dead end—to mutual assured destruction.

Protest and Survive: 1964–85

After world leaders stepped back from the brink of nuclear Armageddon during the Cuban Missile Crisis in 1962, public concern about the Bomb declined significantly. It seemed as though the superpowers had stared into the abyss and realized that they were not prepared to press the doomsday button after all. The following year Khrushchev signed the Limited Test Ban Treaty. CND rightly regarded it as a victory for public protest, a view echoed later by McGeorge Bundy: 'what produced the treaty was steadily growing worldwide concern over the radioactive fallout from testing'. The atmospheric test ban was, he claimed, 'achieved primarily by world opinion'.[41]

Despite this success, after 1963 CND's membership fell dramatically and the Aldermaston march was abandoned as an annual event in 1964. Across Europe the anti-nuclear movement went into a similar decline. In 1959, 64 per cent of Americans had told pollsters that nuclear war was the nation's most urgent problem. Six years later that figure had dropped to 16 per cent. By the early 1970s, the atomic bomb was 'no longer an editorial topic for local newspapers or a conversation piece at dinner tables', claimed an American sociologist. It was a 'dead issue'.[42] According to Robert Jay Lifton, 'psychic numbing' and denial played a major role in the fall-off of support for the protest movements. One young person summed it up in 1965: 'If we lived in fear of the bomb we couldn't function.'[43] Frustration and fear had created doomsday fatigue. Ironically, in the same period as anti-nuclear activism declined, nuclear arsenals were increasing dramatically until US and Soviet arsenals reached the point of mutual assured destruction.

Although the fear of nuclear weapons faded from people's minds during the late 1960s and early 1970s, it didn't disappear. How could it? The Bomb was now an intrinsic part of Cold War culture. Nuclear fear re-emerged with a vengeance in the late 1970s and early 1980s. The neutron bomb (an enhanced radiation weapon that killed people while minimizing damage to property), and the deployment of intermediate-range nuclear missiles in Eastern and Western Europe raised anxieties anew. In 1974, a mere 200 people had taken part in the Aldermaston march and 2000 attended the final rally. By contrast,

---

[41] McGeorge Bundy, *Danger and Survival* (New York: Random, 1988), 460–1; quoted in Wittner, *Resisting the Bomb*, 467.

[42] Peyton Lyon, *Canada in World Affairs 1961–3* (Toronto: Oxford University Press, 1968), 78; cited in Wittner, *Resisting the Bomb*, 447.

[43] Quoted in Wittner, *Resisting the Bomb*, 451.

in October 1980, a rally organized for UN Disarmament Week attracted 80,000 demonstrators. It was, said the *Times*, 'the second coming of CND'.[44]

Across Europe, the decision by NATO leaders to deploy cruise and Pershing II missiles brought people on to the streets in unprecedented numbers. In the UK, Prime Minister Margaret Thatcher's decision in 1982 to replace the submarine-launched Polaris nuclear-armed missile system with Trident missiles played a major role in the revival of CND's fortunes. Another factor was the election of Ronald Reagan. The new American president referred to the anti-nuclear movement as 'a suicide lobby' and called, not for more negotiations with the Soviet Union, but 'strategic superiority'.[45] During the presidential campaign he championed a number of new weapons systems, including the B-1 bomber, Trident, the MX 'Peacekeeper' missile, and the neutron bomb. The former Hollywood actor's credits included *Murder in the Air* (1940), a film about an 'Inertia Projector', a ray gun that destroys planes in mid-air. In the film an American admiral claims that by 'making the United States invincible', this superweapon 'promises to become the greatest force for world peace ever discovered'.[46] It was possibly with this film in mind that President Reagan described the neutron bomb as 'the dreamed of death ray weapon of science fiction', and 'the ideal deterrent weapon'.[47]

Reagan instigated a dramatic escalation of the arms race and raised anxieties amongst Europeans. In 1981 he speculated about a nuclear war limited to Europe. Two years later he referred to the Soviet Union as an 'evil empire' and commented: 'I find myself wondering if we're the generation that's going to see [Armageddon] come about.'[48] In the same year he gave the go-ahead for the Strategic Defense Initiative, popularly known as 'Star Wars', a far-fetched project for space-based weapons systems proposed by the father of the H-bomb, Edward Teller, that most scientists believed was unachievable. CND was quick to capitalize on Reagan's unpopularity on the eastern side of the Atlantic. His actions and opinions, generally supported by the British prime minister, alienated many Europeans on both sides of the Iron Curtain. One CND poster captured the public mood. It depicted Reagan and Thatcher embracing like Rhett and Scarlett at the end of *Gone with the Wind*. Behind them rose a mushroom cloud and the slogan read: 'She promised to follow him to the end of the earth. He promised to organise it.'

From 1983 to 1985, CND membership rose from 75,000 to 100,000, the largest membership of any political organization in Britain apart from the Conservative Party. Its October 1983 rally of 400,000 in Hyde Park was the largest demonstration up to that date in British history. In February that year as many as 49 per cent of people thought a nuclear war was likely. Later that year, 70 per cent said US policies had increased the risk

---

[44] Lawrence S. Wittner, *Toward Nuclear Abolition: A History of the World Nuclear Disarmament Movement, 1971 to the Present, The Struggle against the Bomb* (Stanford: Stanford University Press, 2003), vol. 3, 65.

[45] Ibid., 112–13.

[46] Quoted from Christopher Frayling, *Mad, Bad and Dangerous? The Scientist and the Cinema* (London: Reaktion, 2005), 173.

[47] Wittner, *Toward Nuclear Abolition*, 113.

[48] Ibid., 120.

of war. In West Germany, a mere 15 per cent expressed approval for the deployment of cruise and Pershing II missiles. In October 1983 rallies held in four West German cities brought over a million people on to the streets. According to Wittner, 'the antinuclear campaign had become the largest extraparliamentary movement in the history of the Federal Republic'. Petra Kelly, Chair of the Green Party, spoke for many: 'We...have little time left to stop the nuclear madness... We are a country which can only be defended in the atomic age at the price of its total destruction.'[49] Across Europe—in Rome, Oslo, Paris, Vienna—Europeans demonstrated in unprecedented numbers. In 1984, polls found that in six out of seven NATO countries a majority believed that 'US policies have increased the risk of war'.[50]

Popular culture responded to heightened public anxieties about nuclear issues, as it had in the 1950s and 1960s. In fiction, Russell Hoban's powerful novel *Riddley Walker* (1980) offered a haunting vision of a world blasted back to the stone age by its own advanced weaponry. *When the Wind Blows* (1982), a poignant graphic novel by Raymond Briggs, satirized civil defence advice such as the British government's *Protect and Survive* (1980). This booklet, together with the accompanying TV and radio programmes, had a widespread impact on popular culture in Britain at this time, although not in the way the authorities had intended. Indeed E. P. Thompson immediately produced a parody entitled 'Protest and Survive'. Patrick Allen, the narrator of the *Protect and Survive* TV programmes, featured in some mixes of the *Frankie Goes to Hollywood* pop song 'Two Tribes' (1984), the title of which is itself derived from the *Mad Max* series of post-apocalyptic films (1979–85). The *Protect and Survive* booklet was also lampooned in an episode of the popular BBC sitcom *The Young Ones* in 1982. Rather than reassuring the public, British civil defence advice convinced many that there was indeed no defence against nuclear war, something fiction writers had been saying for the last forty years.

Chas Newkey-Burden, author of *Nuclear Paranoia*, was 11 when he saw the BBC film *Threads*. The 1984 film was a realistic depiction of the effect of a nuclear attack on the city of Sheffield. Afterwards he was physically ill. The next morning he rang CND and formed a youth branch. 'I was utterly consumed by a fear of nuclear war', he writes, and suggests that many CND marchers were like him more 'petrified than political'. The British novelists Ian McEwan and Martin Amis (whose 1987 collection *Einstein's Monsters* directly addresses the nuclear issue) both recall watching and being impressed by the film. The *Daily Express* thought it was 'brilliant, informative and shattering'. The *Financial Times* described it as an 'awful warning'. Afterwards CND received thousands of phone calls. The organization had prepared information packs describing the effects of a nuclear attack to send out to worried viewers. A survey of Sheffield residents found that of those who had been neutral regarding nuclear weapons, half said they were more in favour of disarmament after watching the film.[51]

[49] Ibid., 144–5.
[50] Ibid., 168.
[51] Chas Newkey-Burden, *Nuclear Paranoia* (Harpenden: Pocket Essentials, 2003), 8, 58–9.

In 1985, to mark the fortieth anniversary of the Hiroshima and Nagasaki bombings, the BBC screened *The War Game*. A hard-hitting docudrama directed by Peter Watkins, this film had originally been commissioned in 1965. However, the Director General of the BBC, Sir Hugh Greene, refused to show it on the grounds that it was 'too horrific for the medium of broadcasting'. Privately Watkins was told that if it were shown the BBC expected thousands of people to commit suicide. The film was indeed disturbing and shocking. Using simulated newsreels and street interviews it depicts the effect of a nuclear attack on Kent with three single-megaton bombs. As *Gojira* and *On the Beach* had shown, such nuclear films and fictions could have a powerful impact on audiences. It has been estimated that half the adult population of America watched *The Day After* (1983), which depicted a nuclear attack on Lawrence, Kansas, and Kansas City, Missouri, a record for a TV film.[52] Booklets on the issues raised by the film were distributed to half a million people and teach-ins were organized across America. Even President Reagan watched *The Day After* and according to the film's director Nicholas Meyer it made a deep impression on the hardline president. After Reagan met Gorbachev at Reykjavik in 1986 to agree the terms of the landmark INF Treaty, Meyer recalls, 'I got a telegram from his administration that said, "Don't think your movie didn't have any part of this, because it did."'[53]

In the 1980s, as the temperature of the Cold War plummeted and nuclear war seemed imminent, a change in leadership in the Soviet Union suddenly transformed the relationship between the superpowers, ushering in a new era of trust. In October 1985, just after he became leader of the Soviet Union, Mikhail Gorbachev addressed the French Parliament. He told them bluntly that humankind faced 'self-destruction'. It was time, declared the leader of one of the world's most powerful nuclear nations, 'to burn the black book of nuclear alchemy'. Gorbachev said that they had to make the twenty-first century one 'of life without fear of universal death'. Using a phrase that echoed the words of Russell and Einstein thirty years earlier, Gorbachev called for 'new thinking' to halt the arms race.[54] He had been a student in 1955 when the Russell–Einstein Manifesto was published. Now their call for a new way of thinking to deal with the nuclear issue spoke powerfully to Gorbachev at this time of renewed tension. The leader of the Soviet Union had finally realized that 'the arms race, just like nuclear war, is unwinnable'.[55]

This change of heart at the top of the Soviet state opened the floodgates to progress on arms control, progress many had thought impossible. On 6 August 1985, the anniversary of the bombing of Hiroshima, Gorbachev instigated a unilateral moratorium on nuclear testing. Then, in January of the following year, he put forward an ambitious blueprint for the abolition of nuclear weapons by 2000. This proposal paved the way for the landmark

[52] Chas Newkey-Burden, *Nuclear Paranoia*, 50–1; Shapiro, *Atomic Bomb Cinema*, 186–91.

[53] 'Fallout from *The Day After*', 19 November 2003, online at: http://www.lawrence.com/news/2003/nov/19/fallout_from. Accessed 12 November 2008.

[54] Wittner, *Toward Nuclear Abolition*, 370–1.

[55] Gorbachev, *Perestroika* (New York: Harper & Row, 1987), 138; quoted in Wittner, *Toward Nuclear Abolition*, 371.

Intermediate-Range Nuclear Forces Treaty (INF) of 1987, the first treaty to eliminate an entire class of nuclear weapons—including the ground-launched Pershing II, cruise, and Soviet RSD-10 Pioneer (SS-20) that had proved so unpopular in Europe. Gorbachev's new thinking on the nuclear issue represented the beginning of the end of both the Cold War and the era of mutual assured destruction.

CONCLUSION

The threat from nuclear weapons has certainly not disappeared in the twenty-first century, but the two superpowers have now acknowledged that the policy of mutual assured destruction was unsustainable. According to Wittner, the progress of the 1980s was only possible thanks to the public protests of the previous thirty years:

> as millions of people poured into the streets of Sydney and New York, Amsterdam and Moscow, Budapest and London, bearing the nuclear disarmament symbol, it became the largest grassroots movement in world history—one which exemplified, through its global nature, the gradual emergence of a world community.[56]

However, as I have argued, the new thinking on nuclear weapons also owed much to attempts by writers and film-makers to imagine the unimaginable: a global nuclear holocaust. Films and fictions from *On the Beach* to *The Day After* played a major role in convincing people that the logic of MAD was deeply flawed and that mutual assured survival was what world leaders should be working towards. Or, as Albert Camus said just days after the bombing of Hiroshima, 'peace is the only battle worth waging'.[57]

FURTHER READING

Bird, Kai and Lawrence Lifschultz (eds), *Hiroshima's Shadow: Writings on the Denial of History and the Smithsonian Controversy* (Stony Creek, CT: Pamphleteer's Press, 1998).

Braun, Reiner, Robert Hinde, David Krieger, Harold Kroto and Sally Milne (eds), *Joseph Rotblat: Visionary for Peace* (Weinheim: Wiley-VCH, 2007).

Brians, Paul, *Nuclear Holocausts: Atomic War in Fiction 1895–1984* (Kent, OH: Kent State University Press, 1987).

Caufield, Catherine, *Multiple Exposures: Chronicles of the Radiation Age* (London: Penguin, 1990).

Franklin, H. Bruce, *War Stars: The Superweapon and the American Imagination* (New York: Oxford University Press, 1988).

Frayling, Christopher, *Mad, Bad and Dangerous? The Scientist and the Cinema* (London: Reaktion, 2005).

---

[56] Wittner, *Resisting the Bomb*, 473.
[57] Albert Camus, 'After Hiroshima: Between Hell and Reason', *Philosophy Today* (Spring 1988), in Bird and Lifschultz (eds), *Hiroshima's Shadow*, 260–1.

Hennessy, Peter, *The Secret State: Whitehall and the Cold War* (London: Penguin, 2003).

Newkey-Burden, Chas, *Nuclear Paranoia* (Harpenden: Pocket Essentials, 2003).

Rhodes, Richard, *Dark Sun: The Making of the Hydrogen Bomb* (New York: Touchstone, 1996).

Smith, P.D., *Doomsday Men: The Real Dr Strangelove and the Dream of the Superweapon* (London: Allen Lane, 2007).

Weart, Spencer R., *Nuclear Fear: A History of Images* (Cambridge, MA: Harvard University Press, 1988).

Winkler, Allan M., *Life under a Cloud: American Anxiety about the Atom* (New York: Oxford University Press, 1993).

Wittner, Lawrence S., *The Struggle against the Bomb*, 3 vols: *One World or None; Resisting the Bomb; Toward Nuclear Abolition* (Stanford, CA: Stanford University Press, 1993–2003).

CHAPTER 22

WHAT WAS NATIONAL STALINISM?

VLADIMIR TISMANEANU

INTRODUCTION

As a political variety within Leninism, different from what is usually called national communism, national Stalinism systematically opposed any form of liberalization, let alone democratization. Reactionary and self-centered, it valued autarky and exclusiveness. It adhered to a militaristic vision both domestically and internationally. National Stalinism clung to a number of presumably universal laws of socialist revolution and treated any 'deviation' from these as a betrayal of class principles. It voiced political anguish and played on sentiments of national isolation, humiliation, and panic. It frequently tempted Leninist elites in countries where the pre-Stalinist radical left had been weak or virtually non-existent, or where the regime's legitimacy derived from external sources (for example Romania, Albania, to some extent the GDR under Erich Honecker). National Stalinism was a symptom of degeneration. It was narcissistic and anachronistic; it valued uniformity and exploited tribalist resentment and primordialist allegiances. Its goal was the achievement of the Leninist utopia, even at the cost of generalized poverty. The fundamental values of such a regime are: political voluntarism, sectarianism, radicalism, cult of hierarchy and authority, scorn for parliamentary democracy, and constitutionalism. In the present article, I will first analyse what I consider the origins and the model for national Stalinism. I will then concentrate on four cases amongst Eastern European countries in the post-Stalin era. Two of them, Romania and Albania, I label as archetypical examples, while the others, Bulgaria and Poland, are taken as representative only within limits of this particular type of communist regime. The latter, however, reveal certain features that bring them closer to the nationally integrative forms of Stalinism rather than to its institutional variants (for example, Erich Honecker's GDR, or Gustav Husak's Czechoslovakia).

The blueprint for this type of system was Stalin's Russia from the mid-1930s until the dictator's death. In the words of Robert C. Tucker, Stalin was 'a Bolshevik of the radical right, who blended his version of Leninism with Great Russian nationalism'.[1] He labelled Stalinism as 'Russian National Bolshevism'.[2] Stalin formulated the theory of socialism in one country which became the main justification for his autocratic dictatorship. Stalin imposed his iron will on the party and the whole country, banning and persecuting any form of opposition. He pursued the policies of breakneck industrialization, forced collectivization of agriculture, and complete regimentation of culture. In the 1930s, Stalin unleashed mass terror against workers, peasants, members of the party, army, and intelligentsia. To ensure his absolute power, Stalin relied on the secret police and other institutions of terror, including concentration and labour camps (Gulag). The Stalinist genocidal policies resulted in the deaths of millions of innocent people. Following the Soviet victory over Hitler in World War II, Stalin imposed Soviet-style regimes in East and Central Europe.[3] By the time of his death, in March 1953, Stalin was the supreme leader of the Soviet Bloc and of the world communist movement.

In contrast to Lenin, for Stalin the complete, irreversible victory of socialism in Russia was not contingent upon the success of proletarian revolutions in the West. He developed Lenin's vision of the predestined revolutionary party under the guidance of which the advent of a classless society would become reality. To achieve this goal no measure was too harsh and no sacrifice too high. 'There is no fortress we Bolsheviks cannot storm,' Stalin used to say. In the Soviet experiment, the Marxian principle of social unity was transformed into Lenin's 'unity of will', which, under Stalin, became what Erik van Ree called 'the organic theory of the party'. If, in Lenin's case, the idea of unity was a solution against factionalism, for Stalin it was an instrument for 'the *Gleichschaltung* of the member minds'. In the midst of his struggle for supremacy, in December 1923, Stalin stated that it was wrong to see the party only as 'something like a complex of a whole series of institutions with lower and higher functionaries'. Instead, it was a 'self-acting [*samodeiatel'nyi*] organism'. He described it as 'actively thinking' and 'living a lively life'. The vision of the revolutionary leading body combined with the imposition of the practice of repentance for one's past incorrect political views (at the Fifteenth Party Conference in 1927) opened the door to murderous campaigns of removing the sores from the party organism so that the latter wouldn't fall ill.[4] The struggle for sustaining and furthering the Bolshevik miracle turned into fighting against the degeneration of

---

[1] Robert C. Tucker, *Stalin in Power: The Revolution from Above 1928–1941* (New York: W.W. Norton, 1990), xv. The author wishes to thank Bogdan Cristian Iacob, a graduate student in the History Department, Central European University (Budapest), for the enthusiastic and competent research and editorial assistance in the completion of this article.

[2] See Robert C. Tucker, interview with George Urban in G.R. Urban (ed.), *Stalinism—Its Impact on Russia and the World* (London: Maurice Temple Smith, 1982), 151, 170.

[3] See Vladimir Tismaneanu (ed.), *Stalinism Revisited: The Establishment of Communist Regimes in East-Central Europe* (Budapest: Central European University Press, 2009).

[4] For the whole argument see Erik van Ree, 'Stalin's Organic Theory of the Party', *Russian Review* 52:1 (1993), 43–57.

the body politic. Thus, he established absolute control of the party bureaucracy (*nomenklatura*) over society, imposed a centrally planned economy, heavy industrialization, collectivized agriculture, and smashed any form of dissent (both within and outside the party).

Stalin's 'revolution from above' lasted between 1929 and 1934 and resulted in the complete transformation of Soviet society. During the 1930s, the Communist Party lost any autonomy and became a mere vehicle to expand Stalin's absolute power. Stalin's speeches and articles were treated as revealed truths. As the symbol of the party, Stalin was seen as infallible and worshipped as humanity's greatest genius. In 1936, Stalin proclaimed the victory of socialism in the USSR and promulgated a new Constitution, hailed by his propaganda as 'the most democratic in the world'. The contrast between the professed ideals and the repressive practices could not be greater. In theory, the USSR was a community of free nations and its citizens were granted the greatest freedoms. In reality, the secret police were controlling every walk of life and basic freedoms were denied. In theory, the state was bound to wither away, as maintained by the Marxist tenet. In practice, the bureaucratic government apparatus grew exponentially. Internationally, Stalin used the Comintern to pursue Soviet foreign policy goals. He claimed that the touchstone of proletarian internationalism was unconditional solidarity with the USSR and asked communists throughout the world to approve of every twist and turn in Soviet policies. Those who refused were labelled traitors and were eliminated through permanent purges.

Stalinism represented the ideology of the party and state bureaucracy and meant a resolute break with the initial internationalism of the Bolshevik revolution. As mentioned earlier, during his reign Stalin espoused many themes of the traditional Russian chauvinism typical of great powers. Authors such as Terry Martin and David Brandenberger emphasize a neo-traditionalist turn in process of building socialism in one country and explain how 'Soviet patriotism' became an apology for national authenticity, pride, and loyalty. At the same time, the Soviet Union, 'a state with no ambition to turn itself into a nation-state—indeed with the exact opposite ambition', did become a site of large-scale ethnic cleansing.[5]

Moreover, the society was a hierarchy on the basis of 'Stalinist *soslovnost*', that is, 'in terms of their relationship to the state rather than, as with Marxist classes, in terms of their relationship to each other'.[6] This whole array of developments originated in Stalin's development of a new, non-class, 'popular' form of mobilization. As David Priestland pointed out, 'the unified *narod*, now no longer divided by class, embodied socialism, and was to achieve heroic feats in the struggle against largely external enemies'.[7] Subsequently, the USSR itself became 'the avant-garde of the international communist

---

[5] Terry Martin, *The Affirmative Action Empire: Nations and Nationalism in the Soviet Union, 1923–1939* (Ithaca, NY: Cornell University Press, 2001), 341.

[6] Sheila Fitzpatrick, 'Ascribing Class: The Construction of Social Identity in Soviet Russia', in Sheila Fitzpatrick (ed.), *Stalinism: New Directions* (London: Routledge, 2000), 20–47, here 39.

[7] David Priestland, *Stalinism and the Politics of Mobilization: Ideas, Power, and Terror in Inter-War Russia* (Oxford: Oxford University Press, 2007), 249.

movement and the dynamic centre of world politics'.[8] What this 'mutation' tells us, though, is that the ultimate aim of Stalin's policies *remained* communism. Even his cult of personality functioned as 'a unifying mechanism', 'a personification of socialist state-building'.[9] In 1941, he warned the authors of the commissioned *Short Course of Political Economy* that 'If you search for everything in Marx, you'll get off track…In the USSR you have a laboratory…and you think Marx should know more than you about socialism.'[10] His 'creative' approach to the founding fathers' political thought (that is, Marx and Lenin) would later become the *modus operandi* emulated by the national Stalinist party leaders in Eastern European countries.

Stalinism cannot be explained only through reference to the peculiar conditions pertaining in building socialism in an economically backward and isolated country. It was the Bolshevik hyper-centralized, militaristically sectarian, and extremely authoritarian system that made possible Stalin's rise to the pinnacle of power. For Stalin the principle of *natsionalizatsiia*, that is the idea of national consolidation through state building, was fundamental. The all-Union culture acquired a template by making essential the Soviet–Russian hybridization of the polity according to which particularisms of Soviet peoples were harmonized into a meta-narrative of Great Power heritage that legitimized the accomplishments of building socialism in one country. At the same time, Stalin left the mark of his personality on the nature of the system: obsessed with treason, subversion, and enemies, he created a political culture based on suspicion and terror. In short, one could simply say: 'Without Stalin, no Stalinism'. His legacy was the model of a self-contained hyper-personalized regime. Stalin considered himself (and asked his followers to support this belief) as the greatest Marxist–Leninist theorist. In fact, he was a cynical pragmatist and master manipulator who used theory to legitimize his unchecked hold on power.

ROMANIA

The ambivalence of the Romanian Communist Party (RCP)'s 'independent line' (beginning under Gheorghe Gheorghiu-Dej and later developed and intensified under Nicolae Ceauşescu) was deeply rooted in the excruciating anxiety of the Romanian communist elite that reforms would unleash political unrest and jeopardize the party's monopoly on

---

[8] Erik van Ree, 'Stalin as Marxist: The Western Roots of Stalin's Russification of Marxism', in Sarah Davies and James Harris (eds), *Stalin: A New History* (Cambridge: Cambridge University Press, 2005), 159–80, here 172.

[9] David Brandenberger, 'Stalin as Symbol: A Case Study of the Personality Cult and its Construction', in Davies and Harris (eds), *Stalin*, 250. For his discussion of national Bolshevism, see David Brandenberger, *National Bolshevism: Stalinist Mass and the Formation of Modern Russian National Identity, 1931–1956* (Cambridge, MA: Harvard University Press, 2002).

[10] Both quotations from Stalin are from Ethan Pollock, 'Stalin as the Coryphaeus of Science: Ideology and Knowledge in the Post-War Years', in Davies and Harris (eds), *Stalin*, 283, 280.

power. This explains Gheorghiu-Dej's post-1960 autonomist course, in fact a symbolic camouflage meant to justify his reluctance to engage in Khrushchevite de-Stalinization.[11] Under Ceaușescu, the RCP reasserted its commitment to developing a 'mass movement regime' through steady infusions of zeal and political fervour.[12] On the one hand, Ceaușescu emphasized the party's monopoly on power, the need to preserve collective ownership of the means of production, and the historical competition with the capitalist West. On the other, his rhetoric was unabashedly chauvinistic, implicitly anti-Hungarian and anti-Semitic, and obsessed with the need to establish a perfectly 'homogenous' ethnic community.

There is a growing tendency to dismiss the Romanian experiment in autocracy as a historical anomaly, irrelevant to the general development of Soviet-style regimes. The truth, however, is that Ceaușescu exacerbated and carried to an extreme certain characteristics of the Stalinist political culture within the particular Romanian conditions. In other words, Ceaușescu's socialism could be seen as totalitarianism Romanian-style, a combination of Stalinism, Third World-ism, and Byzantinism that at certain moments reached out to significant strata of the population beyond the party and Securitate bureaucracies. Romanian communism could never fully overcome its pariah genealogy. Lacking a mass base, dominated by foreigners, fractured, and pathetically impotent, the interwar RCP was, moreover, treated contemptuously by the Comintern. Ceaușescu's success within the Romanian communist elite and his victory over potent rivals in the struggles that followed Gheorghiu-Dej's death in March 1965 were foreshadowed, predetermined, and facilitated by the party's history of unmitigated commitment to the exclusive logic of Stalinism. Generations of Romanian communists had treated their nation as a pawn to be manoeuvred. With the exception of Enver Hoxha's Albania, Romania was the only communist state in Eastern Europe to adamantly resist the shock waves of the Twentieth Congress of the CPSU and Khrushchev's denunciation of Stalin's cult.

The 'paranoid style' in Romanian Leninist politics was rooted in an underdog mentality, problematic national credentials, long subservience to Moscow as the Mecca of proletarian internationalism, and deep distrust of anything smacking of democratization or liberalization. This complex manifested itself not only in the RCP's inordinate concern with authenticity and genealogy, but also, on a more general level, in the endless fixation on national identity and historical predestination among the Romanian intelligentsia, communist, non-communist, and anti-communist alike. This pariah syndrome (a term I owe to Kenneth Jowitt) is perhaps the main explanation for Ceaușescu's grotesque behaviour during the last decade of his reign. Both in theory and in practice, Ceaușescu's reign was a desperate attempt by a beleaguered elite to win domestic authority and international recognition by emphasizing precisely the quality it had most conspicuously lacked for most of its history: national prestige and influence.

---

[11] See Vladimir Tismaneanu, 'The Ambiguity of Romanian National Communism', *Telos* 60 (1984), 65–79. In that article I started to elaborate on the main features of what I would later call national Stalinism.

[12] I am developing Robert C. Tucker's argument from 'On Revolutionary Mass-Movement Regimes' in *The Soviet Political Mind: Studies in Stalinism and Post-Stalinist Change* (New York: Praeger, 1963), 3–19.

Combined with limited domestic liberalization from above, this distancing from Moscow offered the increasingly self-confident new wave of party bureaucracy an ideological underpinning. Ceauşescu's supporters were his protégés during the late 1950s and early 1960s, middle-aged apparatchiks who took themselves seriously as exponents of a national managerial class on the way up. The elimination of the Stalinist old guard provided them with long-expected opportunities to climb the ladder of power. Many of these party and government bureaucrats identified with the autonomist (allegedly anti-Soviet) promises on the first stage of Ceauşescu's rule and participated eagerly in the consolidation of the new general secretary's personal power, among them Maxim Berghianu, János Fázekas, Ion Iliescu, Ion Ioniţă, Paul Niculescu-Mizil, Cornel Onescu, Gheorghe Pană, Vasile Patilineţ, Ion Stănescu, Virgil Trofin, and Ilie Verdeţ.[13] All of them had worked in the 1950s and early 1960s under Ceauşescu's guidance. Later, as Ceauşescu realized that under his shield, this party apparatus group envisaged semi-reformist, potentially destabilizing strategies, he backed down and restored a superannuated, extremely rigid, ideologically dominated leadership pattern.

The Conducător's xenophobic outbursts, romanticization of Romania's archaic past, identification with mythological Thracian-Dacian chieftains and despotic feudal princes, fascination with organic corporatism, and rehabilitation of militaristic and ethnic symbols had deeper sources than Ceauşescu's personal psychology—they originated in the RCP's problematic relationship with Romanian cultural traditions and patterns. Following Gheorghiu-Dej's obstinate anti-Khrushchevism, Ceauşescu pursued a policy of constant rejection of any genuine reforms, a line of neo-Stalinist, autarchic retrenchment that included elements of nepotism, kleptocracy, and corruption characteristic of Brezhnevite 'neotraditionalism'. Starting in the late 1950s, and evolving in a convoluted and sometimes perplexing way, which made it increasingly self-centred and self-enclosed, Romanian domesticism turned out to be a 'conservative' (almost 'reactionary') political strategy devised to preserve and enhance precisely those values, symbols, and institutions questioned by the proponents of 'socialism with a human face', from Imre Nagy and Alexander Dubček to Mikhail Gorbachev. The ambivalence of Romanian communism therefore stemmed from the contrast between its patriotic claims in challenging the Kremlin and its refusal to overhaul the Soviet-imposed Leninist model of socialism.

The Ninth RCP Congress became one of the founding myths of Ceauşescu's cult. It represented the point at which the most important ideological and political options of Nicolae Ceauşescu's socialism were defined. Among these were: the thesis of the social and ethnic homogenization of the Romanian nation; the stress on industrialization and the maximum use of domestic resources; the view of the party leader as a symbol of monolithic unity of the party and the people; active neutrality inside the world communist movement; re-establishment of cordial relations with some Western communist parties, especially the Spanish and Italian ones, in an effort to strengthen a joint strategy

---

[13] For a complete analysis of the power dynamics within the Romanian Communist Party and of Nicolae Ceauşescu's policies, see Vladimir Tismaneanu, *Stalinism for All Seasons: A Political History of Romanian Communism* (Berkeley, CA: University of California Press, 2003).

in opposition to Moscow's hegemonic manoeuvres; and the rhetoric of internal democracy, associated with the image of Ceauşescu as the champion of legality, justice, ethics, and socialist equity. At this Congress, Ceauşescu formulated one of the most defining principles of his regime:

> For a long time to come the nation and the State will continue to be the basis of the deployment of socialist society. The development of the nation, the consolidation of the socialist State comply with the objective requirements of social life; not only does this not run counter to the interests of socialist internationalism, but, on the contrary, it fully corresponds to these interests, to the solidarity of the working people, to the cause of socialism and peace. The development and flourishing of each socialist nation, of each socialist state, equal rights, sovereign and independent, is an essential requirement upon which depend the strengthening of the unity and cohesion of the socialist countries, the growth of their influence upon mankind's advance toward socialism and communism.[14]

However, the year 1968 was perhaps crucial in determining the future of Romanian national Stalinism and its evolution into 'dynastic socialism'. For Ceauşescu and his associates, the Prague Spring's failure served to justify the dogma of the indefectible unity of party, leader, and nation. The party's leader was simultaneously the main doctrinaire, the visionary genius, and the 'architect of the national destiny'. The slogan 'Partidul, Ceauşescu, România' was ubiquitous at the time and would be deployed extensively until the very end. Ceauşescu's 21 August speech condemning the Warsaw Pact's military intervention in Czechoslovakia emphasized first and foremost the unity of the party leadership and the symbiotic relationship between party and people. But it also reassured the party Old Guard that criticizing the Soviet invasion would not result in any deviation from the orthodox line:

> We stand here before you as communists and antifascists who survived the jails, who faced death, but who never did betray the interests of the proletariat, the interests of our people. Rest assured comrades, rest assured citizens of Romania that we will never betray our motherland, we will never betray the interests of the people.[15]

Both the population's and the foreign observers' infatuation with the regime's foreign policy misled many into ignoring the true dynamics within the Romanian communist regime: a budding personality cult, a re-strengthening of party, security and propaganda controls; a new cultural orthodoxy (signalled by the mini-Cultural Revolution, Chinese-style, 1968–1972), a sort of updated Zhdanovism; and last but not least, a propensity to an 'I do it my way' attitude soon to turn into fully fledged autarchy.

Under Ceauşescu, Romanian communism never departed from the despotic rules instituted by the Bolsheviks after 1921 and perfected during Stalin's reign: the elimination of any form of intraparty democracy, bureaucratic centralism, and the omnipotence

---

[14] Nicolae Ceauşescu, *Report at the Ninth Congress of the Romanian Communist Party* (Bucharest: Editura Politica, 1965), 60.
[15] *Scânteia* (22 August 1968).

of the general secretary. Ceauşescu could not accept factional struggles and had a milita-ristic view of the party's role and structure. Since party and leader were identical in his mind, the cult of the party implied the deification of the leader. Byzantine rituals of glo-rification were interspersed with claims to Marxist–Leninist orthodoxy, while humble underlings competed in eulogizing the Conducător's valour and 'clear-sightedness'. Enver Hoxha apart, no other Eastern European leader in the post-Stalin era managed to engineer such a systematic, theatrical cult of personality. Romania exemplified the enduring nature of the crucial contradictions of Stalinism, namely, that between the accumulation of all political power in the leader's hands and his failure (inability) to ensure a competent decision-making process. An aggravating circumstance was Ceauşescu's belief that what might be called political magic, or ideological shamanism, could replace common sense, that both human will and reality were infinitely flexible, ready to be moulded according to his own utopian blueprints.

ALBANIA

As already mentioned, the case of Albanian communism, despite obvious differences, is strikingly similar to the Romanian one. The Party of Labour in Albania (PLA) (until 1948 the Communist Party of Albania) and its leader Enver Hoxha boasted a psycho-political and historical pedigree similar to the RCP and its late leader Ceauşescu. Indeed, the PLA came to power as a result of its military victory against the other political forces in Albania and it strengthened itself during the partisan movement in World War II. Nevertheless, the PLA developed a similar pariah syndrome to that of the RCP because of its initial status of vassal party to Josef Broz Tito's League of Communists in Yugoslavia. Enver Hoxha's entire political career was fundamentally defined by his permanent strug-gle for political survival. He was always searching for a political sponsor, from Yugoslavia to the Soviet Union and China. He unflinchingly extolled the Stalinist principle of the 'besieged fortress', consequently pursuing ever deepening isolationism, while 'making ideology the permanent gloss on his brand of socialism and perpetuating class struggle within the country'.[16] Ultimately, as one scholar stressed, 'both Albanian external isola-tion and internal totalitarianism under Enver Hoxha had to be understood as a political strategy to ideologically homogenize and socially reconcile (or rather, "force together") internal, divergent forces for the sake of national unity'.[17] The Albanian leader never let the PLA's dramatic shifts in stipendiary foreign affairs within the communist movement

---

[16] Paulin Kola, *The Myth of Greater Albania* (New York: New York University Press, 2003), 130.

[17] Stephanie Schwandner-Sievers, 'Narratives of Power: Capacities of Myth in Albania', in Stephanie Schwandner-Sievers and Bernd Jürgen Fischer (eds), *Albanian Identities: Myth and History* (Bloomington, IN: Indiana University Press, 2002), 17; see also Arshi Pipa's illuminating essay, 'The Political Culture of Hoxha's Albania', in Tariq Ali (ed.), *The Stalinist Legacy: Its Impact on 20th Century World Politics* (Harmondsworth: Penguin Books, 1984), 435–64.

bring about relaxation of his repressive Stalinist system. As Joseph Rothschild noted, from this point of view, were 'the goals of the Albanian regime in seeking an end to satellite status and a recovery of national autonomy ... analogous to those of Romania'.[18]

Enver Hoxha as a leader was a mixture between a traditional chieftain and a Bolshevik bureaucrat. He was a diehard dogmatic, obsessed with the Stalinist principle of permanent purge as a means of political consolidation and authority building, a springboard for newcomers and time servers. The purges were bound to secure the human basis for effective control over society. Zbigniew Brzezinski synthetically listed a long time ago the main objectives of the purge: 'the cleansing of the party, the restoration of its vigour and monolithic unity, the elimination of enemies, and the establishment of the correctness of its line and the primacy of the leadership'.[19] Hoxha refined his Enverism not through revolutionary, permanent struggle against foreign invaders or 'imperialism', but through a continuous, ruthless, and bloody battle within and against the party (or better put, those individuals or factions that hindered his total control of power). According to Miranda Vickers, Hoxha, just like Stalin did with the Old Guard of the Bolshevik party, by the mid-1950s had already eliminated all the members of the original Albanian Central Committee.[20] For him, unreformed Stalinism was 'politically functional as well as ideologically warranted' (Rothschild). Therefore, his objectives in power never changed, but were:

> to maintain and strengthen the grip of the ruling Communist Party, under his leadership, on Albania and on all aspects of life in the country; to modernize Albania in accordance with the Stalinist Soviet model; and to preserve the independence and territorial integrity of Albania.[21]

Albania experienced a series of ideological offensives very similar to the mobilizational campaigns in Romania. In both cases, the mini-cultural revolutions were expressions of the Leader's consolidation or reassertion in power. After its break with Moscow and realignment with China, Hoxha, through his proxy and eventual successor, Ramiz Alia, called for the cleansing of 'the nation's superstructure' and of the remaining 'bourgeois traces and influences', and for vigilance against the infiltration of 'revisionist ideas' from abroad. Until 1969, this campaign was characterized by

> a series of initiatives to reduce the size of the bureaucracy, abolish military ranks and reintroduce political commissars into the armed forces, improve the status of women and expand their participation in the work force, narrow the salary differentials for all categories of workers, achieve the total collectivization of agriculture and reduce the size of collective farm private plots, and destroy the institutional church

[18] Joseph Rothschild and Nancy M. Wingfield, *A Political History of East Central Europe since World War II*, 3rd edn (New York: Oxford University Press, 2000), 178.

[19] Zbigniew Brzezinski, 'The Pattern of Political Purges', *Annals of the American Academy of Political and Social Science* 317 (1958), 79–87.

[20] Miranda Vickers, *The Albanians: A Modern History* (London: I.B.Tauris, 2006).

[21] Nicholas Pano, 'The Process of Democratization in Albania', in Karen Dawisha and Bruce Parrott (eds), *Politics, Power, and the Struggle for Democracy in South-East Europe* (Cambridge: Cambridge University Press, 1997), 291.

and the practice of religion. By 1969, when the Ideological and Cultural Revolution had run its course, it had—at least outwardly—achieved the majority of its object-ives. Some 15,000 former bureaucrats were now 'gainfully employed in productive labour'; the 'military reforms' had been implemented; the Albanian version of the women's liberation movement had resulted in an increase of female representation in all sectors of the economy and all levels of education as well as in a national consciousness-raising campaign to eliminate discriminatory practices against women; and Albania had the distinction of being the only officially designated athe-ist state in the world.[22]

After a brief period of limited relaxation and openness from 1970 to 1972, during which Hoxha pursued a cautious rapprochement with Tito, by 1974 he was already reinstituting Stalinist orthodoxy in society and over its intellectuals.[23] In 1979, upon the defeat of the 'Shanghai group' and the rehabilitation of Deng Xiaoping, Hoxha broke with his 'bigger brother', China. He focused his policies on two directions: a dual strategy of economic self-reliance while simultaneously intensifying relations with virtually all states other than the two superpowers, that is, a form of Third-World-ism.

In the late 1960s, after the Soviet-led intervention in Czechoslovakia, Hoxha despised Ceauşescu's 'independent line' because of his obsession with making an impression on Western countries and leaders, his 'dependence on capitalist aid...his allegiance to Tito...and his nationalist, chauvinistic and anti-Stalinist policies'.[24] But by the 1980s, Romania and Albania were two peas in the same pod. No wonder that writer Fahri Balliu states that

> no movie could have had a greater impact and weight than the reel of Ceauşescu and his wife, Elena's, execution. Those images horrified Nexhimije [Enver Hoxha's widow and the heir of his power and influence after the leader's death]. The execution of the two convinced her and Ramiz Alia [Hoxha's official successor] to design a strategy to counter the changing times.[25]

In their last phase, both regimes ultimately relied both on family members (or an extended clan) and on an ideology that served more as a repressive *simulacrum*, rather than a mobilizing, unifying weapon. They were cases of 'familialization of communism' (Kenneth Jowitt) advocating a highly patrimonial pseudo-modernity.

BULGARIA

Todor Zhivkov's rule in Bulgaria (1956–1989) produced its own synthesis of quasi-nationalism and enduring Stalinist practices, but despite employing at times an organic, ethnocentric conception of the socialist nation, it never accompanied these efforts with

---

[22] Pano, 'The Process of Democratization in Albania', 292–3.
[23] Fahri Balliu, *Sinistra Doamna* (Bucharest: Humanitas, 2009), 181.
[24] Kola, *Myth of Greater Albania*, 145.
[25] Balliu, *Sinistra Doamna*, 230.

an anti-Soviet self-determination. In reality, the Kremlin's tutelage provided the checks and balances necessary for avoiding the extremes reached in Hoxha's Albania or Ceaușescu's Romania. First and foremost, in contrast to these two previous cases, Zhivkov's regime derived its political legitimacy from the momentous revelations of the twentieth CPSU congress. Indeed, in 1956, Zhivkov engineered the elimination of his former patron, the Comintern veteran Vulko Chervenkov, from the top party position. At the April 1956 plenum, the foundation myth of Zhivkov's pretence to being the embodiment of a new face of communism was created. Only after the Soviet twenty-second Congress (1961) and the purge of Anton Yugov (prime-minister at the time), however, did Zhivkov manage to consecrate his triumph within the Bulgarian Communist Party (BCP). He was a skilful communist bureaucrat whose commitment to liberalization was perfunctory. When Khrushchev was ousted in October 1964, Zhivkov immediately tried to ingratiate himself with the new Soviet leadership headed by Leonid Brezhnev and Aleksei Kosygin. His power remained fragile, and in the spring of 1965 a conspiracy composed of communist veterans and high ranking army officers almost managed to topple him. After defeating them, Zhivkov chose to found the very existence of his regime on unconditional support for the Soviet Union.

Nevertheless, Todor Zhivkov succeeded in creating a functional, sustaining synthesis between internationalism (presupposed by its condition of subservient satellite) and latter-day nationalism. Similarly to Hoxha and Ceaușescu, his identity-driven narrative was based upon the glorification of the state-building principle and the gradual but extensive rehabilitation of what the BCP perceived as 'progressive' traditions of the country's past and (political) culture. Just like his above-mentioned South-Eastern European colleagues, Zhivkov found his own version of Bulgarian ethno-genesis (the triadic theory of the mix between Thracian, Protobulgarian, and Slavic)[26] that allowed him to claim in 1981 a historical validation of no less than 1300 years. As one scholar already emphasized, this new addition to the official communist doctrine was 'unambiguously status quo nationalism'. The party leadership advocated a socialist patriotism that attacked the perceived 'national nihilism' of the 1950s and boasted 'high national esteem'. The latter supposedly meant 'a healthy respect for one's historical achievements, and pride "of having been able to contribute something to the world."'[27] Last but not least, through the efforts of Lyudmila Zhivkova (Minister of Culture and *eminence grise* until her death in 1981), one can also notice the persistence of the Leninist myth of the New Man:

> the idea of developing man according to the laws of Beauty has become a high social ideal. We ourselves must defend this idea, the high perspective and aim which man has now before him, by creating the public and social atmosphere essential for the

[26] In the case of Albania, the party leadership, in tone with its autarchic ideology, claimed an Illyrian origin of the national community, appropriate for the new breed of revolutionary Albanians. See Vickers, *The Albanians*, 196.

[27] Maria Todorova, 'The Course and Discourse of Bulgarian Nationalism', in Peter Sugar (ed.), *Eastern European Nationalism in the Twentieth Century* (Washington DC: American University Press, 1995), 92–5.

continual discovery and development of the creative abilities inherent in each human individual, by creating the conditions that allow each person to be able to defend his sacred evolutionary right to form himself as a complete personality, to perfect himself and to harmonize his relations with other human individuals and with the reality he lives in, to globalize and universalize his consciousness.[28]

In conclusion, the Bulgarian communist state was transformed into the bearer both of the 'state idea'[29] and of the democratic, 'genuine', folk-based physiognomy of the national community. Under the pressure of the Gorbachevite wave of reforms, Zhivkov's version of limited national Stalinism did turn openly xenophobic in the mid-1980s. In 1984, he launched a policy to 'rename' the Turks in Bulgaria. By 1989, this campaign had reached its boiling point causing exactly the opposite result from that anticipated by the party leadership. The ethnic Bulgarians rejected this typical Stalinist practice of scapegoating for the sake of achieving homogenization and mobilization. Just like in Romania, Albania, and, as we shall see, in Poland, this method of rule was an attempt by Stalinist elites to preserve their power through manipulation of ethnic passions and frustrations. It avoided modernization and reforms by creating a general sense of national danger and resorting to patriotic fundamentalism rather than traditional Marxist universalism.[30]

POLAND

In Poland, we can observe an intermediary situation where Władysław Gomułka's initial national communist regime, because of pressures from within and outside the Polish United Workers' Party, almost transmogrified into a national Stalinist system. During World War II, the Communist Party re-emerged as a political force active in anti-Nazi resistance. At the time, the party's main leader was Gomułka, but in 1949 he was ousted by the more powerful Muscovite faction headed by Bolesław Bierut, Hilary Minc, and Jakub Berman. After 1956, as de-Stalinization gathered momentum in the Soviet Union, the Polish communist elite started to split between those favourable towards liberalization and the Stalinist fundamentalists for whom there was no need to renounce any of the traditional dogmas.

---

[28] Speech by Lyudmila Zhivkova, 'Unity of the Past, the Present, and the Future', 13 October 1978, in Sugar (ed.), *Eastern European Nationalism*, 66.

[29] Similarly to the historiographical paradigm of the Nation purported by the RCP's 1974 Political Program (at the XIth Party Congress), in Bulgaria the party sponsored and encouraged the appropriation of the Revival and of its legacy, 'but not without first translating it in terms of revolution (social and increasingly national)... This was argued using the Leninist precept that the proletariat and its party are successors of all democratic traditions of the past, regardless of their origin, the progressive legacy of the bourgeoisie included.' See Roumen Daskalov, *The Making of a Nation in the Balkans: Historiography of the Bulgarian Revival* (Budapest: CEU Press, 2004), 244–6.

[30] Michael Shafir, 'Xenophobic Communism: The Case of Bulgaria and Romania', *RFER*, RAD Background Report/112 (Eastern Europe), 27 June 1989, 3.

Domesticism, or the temptation to emphasize the distinctive peculiarities of the Polish road to socialism, was fighting a moribund version of Stalinist pseudo-internationalism. Gomułka had been released from his forced residence in 1954, and the charges against his alleged 'nationalist' deviation were forgotten. The chasm between reformers ('liberal doves') and dogmatics ('conservative hawks') further widened, making Gomułka's return to power a pressing condition for the party's very survival. Because of his persecution under the Bierut regime, he enjoyed popularity and could clean the party's tarnished image. Edward Ochab, a veteran communist who succeeded Bierut as the party leader in March 1956, decided to step down and endorsed Gomułka's candidacy during a tempestuous Central Committee meeting on 19 October. In spite of Soviet reservations, Gomułka was elected First Secretary of the party and announced the establishment of the 'Polish way to socialism'. The new leader insisted on the need for autonomy in domestic policy and reassured the Soviets that Poland would remain a loyal ally within the Warsaw Pact. However, he was convinced that Poland's alliance with Moscow was indispensible for the country's integrity, especially in the light of potential West German territorial claims. When the West German Chancellor, Willy Brandt, pursued a policy of reconciliation with Poland, Gomułka faced an uneasy situation: the absence of a threat from a revanchist neighbour. He was no longer able to use the external enemy as a means of strengthening his hold on the country and within the party.

Moreover, he refused to recognize the party's responsibility for the economic morass and continued to cling to the dogmas of the central plan. The innovations Gomułka permitted resulted in a softening of domestic repression, a slowdown in industrial investments, and greater tolerance for intellectual and artistic experimentation. He did not pursue an out-and-out break with Stalinism. At most, his dream was to rejuvenate the system, not to replace it. At soon as he consolidated his power within the communist hierarchy, Gomułka proceeded to curb spontaneous development from below and to restore the party's overall control over society. In 1957 he unleashed a purge against Marxist revisionist intellectuals, whom he accused of trying to undermine the socialist order. Freedom of the press, a Polish reality of the previous year, was severely curtailed.[31] By the late 1960s, Gomułka had started to champion Brezhnev-style conservatism. In 1968, Gomułka called for an ideological offensive that would lead to 'complete victory of socialist consciousness in the hearts and minds of the working class, of all working people, and of the entire nation'. As his closest advisor, chief ideologue Zenon Kliszko, said in 1966, 'the problem of political democracy in our country...to a high degree concerns the continuing struggle between the socialist and capitalist forces, *kto kogo*'.[32] Nevertheless, in contrast to leaders such as Hoxha or Ceauşescu, Gomułka did not become an anti-Soviet Stalinist, as he never attempted to challenge the Kremlin's hegemony.

[31] See Raymond Taras (ed.), *The Road to Disillusion: From Critical Marxism to Postcommunism in Eastern Europe* (Armonk, NY: M. E. Sharpe, 1992).

[32] Quoted in Wlodzimierz Rozenbaum, 'The March Events: Targeting the Jews', *Polin: Studies in Polish Jewry* 21 (2009), 65–6.

The Polish communist leader was attacked from within the party by a new, radical–nationalist faction composed mainly of people who had spent the war years in the communist underground—the Partisans. Their leader was General Mieczysław Moczar, Minister of Internal Affairs by 1964, and Chairman of the Union of Fighters for Freedom and Democracy (ZBoWiD). In his bid for power, Moczar made use of xenophobic arguments, charging Gomułka with leniency in his dealings with an alleged 'imperialist-Zionist conspiracy'. Simultaneously, the Partisans were targeting the proponents of political and economic reforms, whom they accused of trying to rock the boat of socialism. Moczar's ideology consisted of rabid anti-Semitism combined with intense hatred of liberalism and democracy. According to Andrzej Wróblewski, Moczar represented 'a type of populist socialism, based on the primitive class hostility toward the Jews, whom he knew from his early days in Lodz, when a Jew meant a capitalist'.[33] Or, as Zbigniew Brzezinski more generally remarked in 1965, '[the] emerging new Polish communist elite resembles the pre-World War II extreme right-wing groups in Poland more than it resembles either its Comintern-reared Stalinist predecessors or the earlier, internationalist founders of the Polish Communist Party'.[34]

The social turmoil of the 1968 'March events' expedited the collapse of Gomułka's strategy of stabilization. Both Edward Gierek and Moczar accused Gomułka of 'complacency with revisionism' and asked for an exemplary repression of the student movement that had erupted at the University of Warsaw in March. The fact that some of the student leaders were of Jewish origin and came from old communist families became a propaganda theme for the Moczarites. The fight between Gomułka and Moczar continued the following year: the former tried to mobilize the workers on his behalf, while the latter intensified his vicious anti-intellectual and anti-Semitic activities. A new spectre was invented in the time-honoured tradition of Stalinist chauvinism, always obsessed with the 'internal enemy'. Instead of recognizing the political causes of the students' protest, they preferred to blame a mythological 'Zionist-revisionist plot' for having fomented the unrest. On 19 March 1968, Gomułka delivered a speech to party activists in which he divided Jews into three groups: 'patriotic Jews', 'Zionists', and those who were neither Jews nor Poles but 'cosmopolitans'. The latter aimed to 'avoid those fields of work where the affirmation of nationality is indispensable'.[35] He added, however, that 'the sole criterion for evaluating a citizen of our nation is his attitude towards socialism and towards the interests of our state and its people'.

But neither Gomułka nor either of his challengers (Moczar or Gierek) could provide a clear-cut project of a new 'socialist fatherland' in Poland. Here lies the main reason why this case can only be interpreted as an intermediary form of national Stalinism. Despite the anti-cosmopolitan, anti-revisionist, and anti-Semitic thrust of the official propa-

---

[33] Quoted in Jerzy Eisler, '1968: Jews, Antisemitism, Emigration', *Polin: Studies in Polish Jewry* 21 (2009), 48.

[34] Rozenbaum, 'The March Events', 63.

[35] See Dariusz Stola, 'The Hate Campaign of March 1968. How Did It become Anti-Jewish?', *Polin: Studies in Polish Jewry* 21 (2009), 31.

ganda, despite the pogrom-like atmosphere, the party leadership was in disarray. These developments themselves were the result of power struggles among various factions in the search for supremacy. The 'war games' within the Polish *nomenklatura* ultimately ended in 1970, when Gomułka was replaced by Gierek, who, after toning down his own anti-Zionist declarations, proposed a technocratic solution to the country's deepening structural crisis.[36]

The radical results of these tribulations, however, indicated the fundamentally Stalinist political culture of Polish communism. When faced with an identity crisis it created an internal enemy in order to rediscover its heroic mission. It pursued a form of socialist offensive in order to reassert its 'charismatic impersonalism' (Kenneth Jowitt). Polish historian Dariusz Stola gives an excellent diagnosis of the state of the facts, when:

> portraying the dissident students and intellectuals as aliens—Jews, bloodstained Stalinists or their sons, arrogant members of the establishment, and so forth—certainly contributed to alienating them from the masses. Jewish communists seem to have been the best scapegoat available, against whom the party could direct popular frustration and anger for its past crimes, recent misdeeds, and constant absurdities of the regime...Pointing at Jewish communists, their Polish (ex)comrades could absolve themselves and imply that after the purge, a better, purely Polish socialism would come.[37]

As Marxism–Leninism was faltering, nationalism came to the fore: '"ethnic background" was item 3 on the personal questionnaire for those within the party *nomenklatura*, right after date and place of birth. The fact that "social background" (class) was two spaces below represented a new hierarchy enforced in the party.'[38] In Poland, the imperatives of political unity and of calming social unrest under circumstances of a succession crisis reasserted, through officially sponsored anti-Semitism, two fundamental features of national Stalinism: communist xenophobia and anti-cosmopolitanism.[39]

CONCLUSION

Despite the differences among them, what do all of these four regimes in Eastern Europe have in common? First of all, they are all children of the twentieth Congress of the CPSU. Their identity and future evolution was defined by the Tomist emancipation (the

---

[36] See the chapter 'The 1968 and 1970 Crises and the Fall of Gomulka', in *It All Began in Poland...1939–1989* (Warsaw: Institute of National Memory, the Polish Ministry of Culture, and the European Solidarity Centre, 2009), 108–15.

[37] Stola, 'The Hate Campaign', 35.

[38] Marcin Zaremba quoted in Eisler, '1968', 61.

[39] See Audrey Kichelewski, 'A Community under Pressure: Jews in Poland, 1957–1967', *Polin: Studies in Polish Jewry* 21 (2009), 159–86.

emphasis on regime individuality) brought about by Khrushchevism.[40] At the same time, their domestic profile was fundamentally marked by their inability to complete the de-Stalinization process. This brings us to our second point: the true nature of all four of them was revealed under the pressure of the 1968 Prague Spring. For Hoxha and Ceaușescu, the events in Czechoslovakia offered an opportunity to reassert domestic dominance and legitimacy while employing the spectre of Soviet intervention as a catalyst of national unity and revolutionary mobilization. In Poland, however, Gomułka's unwillingness to make good the spirit of the October 1956 reform movement and failure to develop an anti-Soviet (anti-hegemonist) line, forced him into a dangerous political game with Moczar and Gierek. He tried to attain stability and supremacy by means of exclusionary policies towards the Jews (anti-Semitism masquerading as anti-Zionism and de-Stalinization)[41] and the perceived revisionists.

In Bulgaria, the year 1968 consecrated Zhivkov's party line: gradually overarching integrative nationalism at home simultaneously with total allegiance to the Soviet Union's neocolonial practices. And third, they all, although to different degrees, relied on the leadership cult as both a supplement to and personification of the Party's charismatic impersonalism. In Poland it took the form of Gomułka's image as resurgent national communist leader, a World War II hero. His supremacy was indeed challenged on similar grounds by Moczar. The myth of his demiurgic mission was ultimately subverted by political failure, economic crisis, and appeal to violence against the population. Zhivkov built his cult on the image of the enlightened leader of the communist bureaucracy, the spearhead of the *nomenklatura* dictatorship. Despite the high profile role of his daughter within the regime's ideological establishment, it is unlikely that he wished to follow the path of dynastic socialism.

In Albania and Romania, the cult of personality was one of the fundamental instruments for reaffirming the messianic role of the Party. Just as in the case of the USSR, when the Soviet state and the Russian core became under Stalin the foremost agents of

---

[40] Kenneth Jowitt, *New World Disorder: The Leninist Extinction* (Berkeley, CA: University of California Press, 1992).

[41] Anti-Semitism seems to be a specific ideological pathology of Stalinism. From the late 1930s through the Doctors' Plot in the early 1950s, it was a recurrent state policy within 'the first workers' state'. It famously made its appearance during the Eastern European purge trials (e.g., the cases of Rudolf Slánský being the most notorious). Moreover, Poland is not the only one of the four cases discussed here that pursued formal and informal anti-Jewish policies. In Romania, by the beginning of the 1960s a strange situation had appeared: 'a continuous process of marginalization [within the party and in leadership positions] that was accelerated in the 1970s and 1980s—which, paradoxically, was accompanied by an improvement in the status of Jewish community life'. The end result of these practices was quite similar to that of Poland: emigration of the Jews and the homogenization of the nation. Leon Volovici argues that Ceaușescu's nationalist doctrine viewed the voluntary departure of the German and Jewish populations as 'the best and most profitable way both to remove "foreigners" from positions of influence and to "ameliorate" the country's ethnic mix...Romanian Jewry attained a favoured minority status whose main privilege, paradoxically, was the freedom to leave.' See Leon Volovici, 'Romanian Jewry under Rabbi Moses Rosen during the Ceaușescu Regime', in Ezra Mendelsohn (ed.), *Jews and the State: Dangerous Alliances and the Perils of Privilege* (Oxford: Oxford University Press, 2003), 181–92.

socio-economic progress in the world, in Romania and Albania, Ceauşescu and Hoxha triggered a dizzying upward spiral of political, economic, and cultural struggle for self-realization and systemic insulation on the world stage. The achievement of the latter was proof of the successful modernity projects of their versions of communism. At the same time, in the late stages of both regimes, the myth of the leader, under circumstances of ideological disenchantment of the elites and the population, transmogrified into a 'familialization of communism' (Ken Jowitt aptly spoke about 'socialism within one family').

All in all, what fundamentally distinguished Albania and Romania from Bulgaria and Poland was that their attempt to find 'a national path to socialism' simultaneously meant the organic, ethnocentric re-imagination of the community, the continuous external assertion of and gyrations in an 'independent line' from the Moscow centre, and the permanent commitment to Stalin's 'revolution from above'. They remained committed to crash industrialization, state ownership of all means of production (including the countryside), and the creation of the New Man.

In conclusion, I would argue that the essential characteristic of national Stalinism is that it preserves the original belief in the validity and importance of implementing Stalin's civilizational blueprint. The latter was founded upon a secular eschatology (Marxism–Leninism), a radical vision of the world (capitalist encirclement and the touchstone theory of socialist internationalism), and, ultimately, an alternative idea of modernity (based on anti-capitalism, state managed collectivism, and the principle of the sharpening of the class struggle) self-identified as infallibly righteous.[42] Hoxha and Ceauşescu not only 'indigenized Marxism' (that is, 'incorporated categories of Marxism–Leninism into arguments in which ethnic or national questions had priority')[43] with the aim of preserving their hold on state and party power; they also reconstructed and altered the entire history and development of their nations in accordance with the radical goals and totalizing imperatives of Stalinism.

FURTHER READING

Brandenberger, David, *National Bolshevism: Stalinist Mass Culture and the Formation of Modern Russian National Identity, 1931–1956* (Cambridge, MA: Harvard University Press, 2002).

Daskalov, Rumen, *The Making of a Nation in the Balkans: Historiography of the Bulgarian Revival* (Budapest: Central European University Press, 2004).

[42] Stephen Kotkin, *The Magnetic Mountain* (Berkeley, CA: University of California Press, 1995), 225–37; Stephen Kotkin, '1991 and the Russian Revolution: Sources, Conceptual Categories, Analytical Frameworks', *Journal of Modern History* 70:2 (1998), 384–425, and 'The State—Is it us? Memoirs, Archives, and Kremlinologists', *Russian Review* 61 (2002), 35–51. For further commentary of this view see also Astrid Hadin, 'Stalinism as a Civilization: New Perspectives on Communist Regimes', *Political Studies Review* 2 (2004), 166–84.

[43] Katherine Verdery, *National Ideology under Socialism: Identity and Cultural Politics in Ceauşescu's Romania* (Berkeley, CA: University of California Press, 1991), 139.

Dragovic-Soso, Jasna, 'Saviours of the Nation': Serbia's Intellectual Opposition and the Revival of Nationalism (London: Hurst, 2002).

Epstein, Catherine, The Last Revolutionaries: German Communists and Their Century (Cambridge, MA: Harvard University Press, 2003).

Gluchowski, Leszek W. and Antony Polonsky, Polin. Studies in Polish Jewry. 1968 Forty Years after, vol. 21 (Oxford: The Litman Library of Jewish Civilization, 2009).

Kola, Paulin, The Myth of Greater Albania (New York: New York University Press, 2003).

Paczkowski, Andrzej, The Spring Will Be Ours: Poland and the Poles from Occupation to Freedom (University Park, PA: Pennsylvania State University Press, 2003).

Tismaneanu, Vladimir, Fantasies of Salvation: Democracy, Nationalism, and Myth in Post-Communist Europe (Princeton, NJ: Princeton University Press, 1998).

Tismaneanu, Vladimir, Stalinism for All Seasons: A Political History of Romanian Communism (Berkeley, CA: University of California Press, 2003).

Tucker, Robert C., Stalin in Power: The Revolution from above, 1929–1941 (New York: Norton, 1990).

van Ree, Erik, The Political Thought of Joseph Stalin: A Study in Twentieth-Century Revolutionary Patriotism (London: RoutledgeCurzon, 2002).

Verdery, Katherine, National Ideology under Socialism: Identity and Cultural Politics in Ceauşescu's Romania (Berkeley, CA: University of California Press, 1991).

CHAPTER 23

....

COLONIAL FANTASIES
SHATTERED

....

MARTIN EVANS

'Hong Kong soon fell, and the Singapore garrison surrendered even though it outnumbered the Japanese forces by three to one. So was nailed down the coffin of the British Empire, though the corpse was the only one not to know it was dead, and continued to kick for many years to come.'

J.G. Ballard, 'The End of My War' (*Sunday Times*, 20 August 1995)

J.G. BALLARD was born in the Shanghai International Settlement in China in 1930 into a privileged colonial milieu with a chauffeur, a nanny, and servants.[1] Within his autobiography, interviews, and 1984 novel *Empire of the Sun*, Ballard brilliantly captures this closed world of imperial wealth and racial hierarchy that looked down upon Asians as inferiors.[2] Ballard remembers how his parents and their entourage took it for granted that the International Settlement would always be protected by British power, boasting that any war against Japan would be over in a matter of weeks.

This arrogance was shattered first by the attack on Pearl Harbor on 7 December 1941, second by the Japanese occupation of International Settlement in Shanghai one day later, and finally by the fall of Singapore on 15 February 1942. Singapore was *the* symbol of the British Empire's strength in Asia and the fact that it was overrun in seven days was a blow of incalculable proportions. This was the biggest ever defeat suffered by a British-led force and, as 80,000 Australian, British, and Indian soldiers were ushered into captivity at gunpoint, the image of imperial invulnerability was gone forever: a consequence

---

[1] The Shanghai International Settlement was established in 1842 by the British as a gateway to China after the first opium war.

[2] The two novels that draw upon his experience in Shanghai and post-1946 Britain are *Empire of the Sun* (London: Gollanz, 1984) and *The Kindness of Women* (London: HarperCollins, 1991). His autobiography was published in 2008 as *Miracles of Life* (London: Fourth Estate, 2008).

that was self-evident in the Shanghai International Settlement where Allied nationals wore numbered armbands and then, like Ballard and his family in early 1943, were put into an internment camp.

When Ballard arrived in Britain in 1946, he confronted a country in denial where large numbers still subscribed to this imperial fantasy: a paradox for Ballard because to his eyes Britain, with rationing, had the look of a defeated nation:

> The whole country seemed at complete variance with its situation. Everyone believed that Britain was still a world power ruling a world empire, with an obligation to maintain large forces at every point of the Atlas. Even in the 1960s, people were still debating whether Britain should maintain forces east of Suez.[3]

Ballard witnessed at first hand the collapse of the British Empire in Asia: an experience that framed all his subsequent fiction writing from in *The Drowned World* in 1962, through to *Crash* in 1973 and *Kingdom Come* in 2006. Yet, the danger in Ballard, particularly when he is remembering from the perspective of the 1980s, is to see a straight line from Singapore to the end of empire. All too easily, the historical complexities can be smoothed out into a narrative of inevitable imperial decline, when in fact the opposite was true. 1945, as this chapter will show, was not a moment of imperial defeat, but of imperial reassertion for Belgium, France, the Netherlands, and Britain, each of which saw their futures as global, colonial entities.

EMPIRE

At the most basic level, empire means, as Robert Aldrich has argued, the 'rule by a particular group in a political centre over a diverse and different set of other, often distant countries and peoples, generally as a result of military conquest.'[4] By this measure empire has been one of the most enduring forms of political organization.[5] Throughout Africa, the Americas, Asia, and Europe, it has dominated the historical landscape for more than 2000 years, even if empire cannot be reduced to one design. This makes the contemporary world of nearly 200 nation states a recent phenomenon, barely sixty years old. So, to go back to 1914 is to enter a time where imperial polity was the norm in the shape of the Austro-Hungarian, Belgian, British, Dutch, German, Italian, Ottoman, Portuguese, Russian, Spanish, and US empires.

---

[3] J.G. Ballard and Danny Danziger, 'The Worst of Times', *The Independent* (16 December 1991), 2.

[4] Robert Aldrich, 'Introduction: Imperial Overview', in Robert Aldrich (ed.), *The Age of Empires* (New York: Thames and Hudson, 2007), 7.

[5] On this debate about the place of empire in world history see Linda Colley, 'The Difficulty of Empire: Present, Past and Future', *Historical Review*, 79:207 (2006), 367–82; John Darwin, *After Tamerlane: The Global History of Empire* (London: Allen Lane, 2007); Jane Burbank and Frederick Cooper, *Empires in World History* (Princeton, NJ: Princeton University Press, 2010).

The First World War led to the destruction of the Austro-Hungarian, German, Ottoman, and Russian empires: a process that became political fact when the 1919 Versailles Peace Conference redrew Europe's map in terms of the nation state.[6] However, Versailles did not signal an end to extra-European empires. On the contrary, Belgium, Britain, and France underlined the legitimacy of their imperial missions, adding territories from the German and Ottoman Empires under the auspices of the newly established League of Nations.[7] Nor did the Versailles settlement prevent the emergence of new ambitious empire makers, as the 1920s and 1930s saw the arrival of Fascist Italy, Militarist Japan, and Nazi Germany on the international scene.

These last three were destroyed by the Second World War, while the USA divested itself of the Philippines, the country's one major colony, in 1946. Leaving aside the question of whether the Soviet Union has to be understood as an imperial phenomenon, this meant that the only colonial entities left standing were the seafaring empires of Western Europe: Belgium, Britain, France, Netherlands, Portugal, and Spain. These had emerged from the fifteenth century onwards when, blocked by Ottoman power in the Mediterranean, Portugal, and Spain, followed by the English, the Dutch Republic, and France, expanded outwards through the Atlantic to West Africa, the Americas, and Asia to establish global networks of colonies and trading posts based upon naval power.

By 1945 these empires were all in a very different shape. Portugal and Spain, neither of whom were belligerents in the Second World War, had been in a state of long imperial decline. The Portuguese Empire was reduced to its colonies on the African coastline, East Timor, and the enclaves in India and Macau, while the Spanish Empire comprised just African territories: Spanish Morocco, Gulf of Guinea, and Spanish Sahara.[8] The British Empire was the largest, followed by France, both of which extended to the four corners of the globe. The Dutch Empire was made up of Indonesia in Asia and Surinam in the Caribbean, while Belgium's imperial possessions were focused upon Africa in the shape of the Belgian Congo, Rwanda, and Urundi.

Out of these six countries only Belgium, Britain, and France had been participants in the 'age of empire' at the end of nineteenth century: the mad dash for colonies in competition with Germany, Italy, Russia, and the USA motivated by economics, nationalism, and ideas of a civilizing mission. Yet, whatever their relative power, in 1945 these six countries still controlled whole swathes of the world: a pattern of imperial domination that they thought would be unending. Why these six Western European overseas empires disappeared by the mid-1970s is my focus and in answering this question the

---

[6] On this see Margaret Macmillan, *Peacemakers: The Paris Peace Conference of 1919 and Its Attempt to End War* (London: John Murray, 2001).

[7] In the Middle East, Mesopotamia (which became Iraq in 1932), Palestine and Transjordan (which became Jordan in 1946) were administered by the British, and Syria and Lebanon by the French. In Africa Ruanda-Urundi was administered by Belgium; Tanganyika by the British; while Cameroun and Togoland were split into British and French-administered territories.

[8] On Portugal see Jill Dias, 'Portugal: Empire-building in the Old World and the New', in Aldrich (ed.), *The Age of Empires*, 68–91; and on Spain see J. H. Elliot, *Empires of the Atlantic World: Britain and Spain, 1492–1830* (London: Yale University Press, 2007).

chapter is divided into part one which will analyse the '1945 moment'—a point of imperial reassertion not decline; part two which will outline how, in the new era of the welfare state, these empires tried to reform between 1945 to 1960 in order to win the 'hearts and minds' of the local populations; while part three will examine the aftermath of empire.

The 1945 Moment

On Tuesday 8 May 1945 across Algeria towns and cities witnessed Muslim crowds brandishing British, American, Soviet, French, and Algerian flags, and placards with the slogans 'For the liberation of peoples, long live free and independent Algeria!', 'Down with colonialism', 'Long live the Atlantic Charter', and 'Long live Messali Hadj!', the nationalist leader having been deported by the French on 23 April 1945. Looking to the United Nations Conference, which had begun on 25 April in San Francisco, they wanted to show that Algerians existed and were ready to take their place amongst the nation states of the world.

These demonstrations produced a tense atmosphere, but for the most part there were no major confrontations. In the town of Sétif, in eastern Algeria, populated by 32,000 inhabitants, it was different, however. There local Algerians were incensed by the fact that the Swiss-owned Compagnie Genevoise was using fifteen thousand hectares of the best land in the area for export crops, while they were coping with near famine conditions. Added to this, within Sétif Algerian nationalism was widespread, leading to a mood of confrontation during the 'Victory in Europe' celebrations on 7 May. For many Algerians the end of the war in Europe was the sign for a general uprising and on the following day 8000 demonstrators assembled outside the main mosque at 9.15 am, then marched down Avenue Clemenceau to lay a wreath at the war monument. Some were armed and when gendarmes waded into the crowd to seize nationalist banners, the demonstration descended into violence. Fleeing into the side streets and towards the market, some demonstrators set upon Europeans, killing twenty-one and wounding a further forty-nine.[9]

By late morning this violence ignited an uprising throughout the western part of the Constantine department and over the following three days 102 Europeans were killed. In response the French authorities proclaimed a state of siege in Constantine and despatched a 10,000-strong force to quell the uprising. In the ensuing three weeks these troops, comprising Foreign Legion, Moroccan, and West African units, flushed out all the insurgents in a pitiless fashion, burning down houses, carrying out summary executions and systematically humiliating prisoners. Once suppressed, the French government quickly sought to turn the page on the violence, claiming that 1500 had been killed in the operation. In contrast the *New York Times* talked of between 7000 and 20,000

---

[9] On Sétif see Annie Rey, *Aux Origines de la Guerre d'Algérie* (Paris: La Découverte, 2002) and Jean-Louis Planche, *Sétif 1945* (Paris: Perrin, 2006).

dead, while, since independence in 1962, Algerian estimates have never been less than 45,000.[10]

The intensity of this violence and counter-violence has to be understood in terms of the specificity of Algeria, which was invaded by France in 1830 and then annexed as sovereign French territory, under the control of the Ministry of the Interior. This particularity was reinforced by the arrival of European settlers from France, Italy, Malta, and Spain, most of who were poor whites that populated the coastal towns and cities, while a tiny handful of rich settlers created a lucrative export economy based on wine, cork, and alfalfa. In 1889, to mark the centenary of the French Revolution, adult male settlers were given French citizenship that enshrined a divide between the voting European minority and the non-voting Arab and Berber majority. This majority suffered material and cultural dispossession on a huge scale, producing anger that manifested itself in rebellion and vandalism of settler property before giving rise to a new political factor: modern Algerian nationalism. This first flowered amongst the emigrant Algerian community in Paris during the mid-1920s, but took root in Algeria itself during the 1930s, particularly in the eastern part of the country, which was always the most recalcitrant to French rule. The Amis du Manifeste de la Liberté (AML), founded in March 1944, was the first mass Algerian nationalism organization whose membership, soon numbering 100,000, were impatient for confrontation with colonial rule: a key factor in the May 1945 violence.

At the same time, Algeria has to be placed in a wider historical context. Sétif was not an isolated incident. It was part of a general challenge to European colonial rule that was evident elsewhere in the French Empire, in Indochina, Lebanon, and Syria, in Dutch Indonesia and in the British Empire in Asia in Burma, India, and Malaya. What, therefore, were the contours of this 1945 global moment?

The first strand of the 1945 moment was the enduring fragility of European rule. In this respect the 'rise of the West' from the fifteenth century onwards must not be overplayed. At this point there was a significant shift in power towards the far western tip of the Eurasian landmass. But this global expansion was not an unstoppable machine that flattened all before it. By the time of the 'age of Empire' in the forty years before 1914, Portugal and Spain were already in terminal decline and played no part in Western imperialism's high point. And even then colonial rule was always contingent, limited and, in the mad dash for territory, potentially overextended. Furthermore, as Christopher Bayly has underlined, non-Europeans were 'not passive recipients of Western bounty, or, alternatively, simply the West's supine victims. Their reception and remoulding of Western ideas and techniques for their own lives set limits to the nature and extent of their domination by European power-holders.'[11]

So, although a significant competitive advantage accrued to Western European powers and their overseas colonists, it is vital to remember that Africans and Asians retained dynamism and initiative in significant areas of cultural, economic, and social life.

[10] Martin Evans, *Algeria: France's Undeclared War* (Oxford: Oxford University Press, 2012).
[11] C.A. Bayly, *The Birth of the Modern World* (London: Blackwell, 2004), 3.

Moreover, by 1914 the rise of Japan and the beginnings of extra-European nationalisms ensured that Europe's lead had been seriously curtailed.

Many of these limitations were imposed by the combination of demography and geography. In Algeria the European population remained at around one million during the first four decades of the twentieth century, while the Muslim population leapt from four million to seven million, jumping up to nine million by the mid-1950s. Large parts of this Muslim population retreated into the east of the country and the interior mountains. The result was that in the Constantine department that bordered Tunisia, nine times the size of its mainland equivalent, French authority was skin deep: a pattern of superficial rule equally apparent in vast tracts of the Belgian Congo and British India.

These inherent weaknesses were magnified by the impact of the Second World War, the second aspect of the 1945 moment. For Belgium, France, and the Netherlands, Nazi occupation meant that the lines of imperial power from Western Europe were badly damaged: a factor that was made worse in South-East Asia when the breathtaking Japanese onslaught in 1942 led to the fall of Dutch Indonesia and British Malaya, Burma, and Singapore. Initially presenting themselves as liberators to the local populations, the Japanese dismantled the colonial presence by interning Europeans, using them as forced labour and removing all signs of their rule. So, when Japan surrendered on 15 August 1945 there was a vacuum. If the old imperial powers were going to reimpose their power, this would involve force, and in some cases a second colonial conquest.

Such weakness was at the root of French violence in Sétif. Painfully aware of France's exclusion from decisions over the postwar settlement by the 'big three'—Britain, the USA, and the Soviet Union—de Gaulle wished to project an image of French strength, which is why, on leaving Algiers for Paris in August 1944, he gave orders to suppress Algerian nationalism. Fearful that large parts of the French Empire were about to be put under a United Nations trusteeship, Sétif was part of a general reassertion of French rule throughout the empire, which, in combination with the repression of nationalist demonstrations in Syria on 8 May and the dispatching of troops to Indochina, sent a clear signal to Britain, the Soviet Union, and the USA about France's recovery of great-power status.[12]

This weakness of the old imperial powers was inseparable from the next strand of the 1945 moment: the emergence of nationalism within empires during the first half of the twentieth century. By 1945 the undisputed star of Algerian nationalism was Messali Hadj and to trace his political journey is to understand the forces that shaped nationalism throughout European Empires.[13] Born in 1898 in Tlemcen near the Moroccan border, he was conscripted into the French Army during the First World War: an experience that transformed his political horizons by bringing him into contact with the ideas of the French Left, the 1917 Russian Revolution and President Woodrow Wilson's call for a

[12] Friction between Britain and France was evident in Lebanon and Syria at this point since Britain was demanding that both countries, French possessions, be brought under British military authority. De Gaulle initially thought that there was a link between Syria and Algeria. In an interview with *The Times* in September 1945, de Gaulle sought to repair the rift by emphasizing common imperial interests.

[13] Benjamin Stora, *Messali Hadj* (Paris: Hachette, 2004).

new international system based on national self-determination. Furthermore, the final demise of the Ottoman Empire led Messali to believe that Islam's torch would now be taken up by the 'rise of the Arabs'.[14]

Returning to France after 1918, Messali forged links with French Communist Party that were instrumental in forming the North African Star in Paris in July 1926: the first political party committed to Algerian independence. By the late 1920s Messali, in quest for political independence, distanced the North African Star from the Communist Party and in October 1930 Messali launched a monthly paper in French: *El-Ouma*. By choosing this title, Messali explicitly situated the Algerian struggle within the wider transnational Muslim community (*umma*). This Islamic dimension was further strengthened when Messali met Emir Shakib Arslan in Geneva at the end of 1935. Since 1921, Emir Shakib Arslan had been the unofficial representative of Syria and Palestine at the League of Nations in Switzerland where he had become an outspoken proponent of pan-Arab and pan-Islamic solidarity through an intellectual review published in French, *Arab Nation* (*La Nation Arabe*). In conversation with Messali, Arslan reiterated the importance of these two themes, along with the need to resist the French policy of divide and rule across North Africa, which sought to identify the Berber populations and ethnically different to Arabs: three ideas that framed the invention of national symbols, songs, and political gestures.[15]

In this manner the making of Algerian nationalism was a creative dynamic. The combination of transnational ideas, pan-Arabism and communism, and new models of political action (organized parties, meetings, the press, and mass demonstrations) opened up the space for the 'imagining' of national communities, which found a willing audience amongst a population suffering from unemployment, overcrowding and famine; processes that were equally prevalent in British Burma, India, and Malaya, Dutch Indonesia and French Indochina and where nationalists too looked to the end of the Second World War as a moment of national assertion.

In large part this assertiveness was encouraged by the political impact of the Atlantic Charter, the fourth strand of this 1945 moment. Signed on 26 August 1941 by President Franklin Delano Roosevelt and Winston Churchill, the Charter was a statement for a new world order based upon anti-Nazi values, although the USA did not enter the Second World War until December 1941. At the Charter's core was the recognition of the 'rights of all peoples to choose their form of government under which they will live' and on 1 January 1942 the Charter was endorsed by representatives of 26 Allied nations, calling themselves the United Nations, including the exiled governments of the occupied European colonial powers.[16] But in framing the Charter, Churchill was clear that

[14] Ibid., 31.

[15] In Morocco Marshal Lyautey courted the Berber populations, arguing that they were different from the Arabs. The Berber Dahir (Decree) of 1930 inscribed customary law, and not the sharia, within the Berber-speaking areas.

[16] The other seven principles were no territorial gains to be sought by the British or the USA; territorial adjustments to be in accord with the wishes of the people concerned; trade barriers to be lowered; global economic cooperation and the advancement of social welfare; the objective of a world free of want and fear; freedom of the seas; the disarmament of aggressor nations and common postwar disarmament.

self-determination only applied to occupied Europe. For him it was not a charter for the liquidation of the British Empire.

These subversive implications were as obvious to anti-colonial nationalists, a perspective that Roosevelt himself encouraged. During the British and US landings in Algeria and Morocco in November 1942, US planes dropped thousands of leaflets, adorned with the American flag and Roosevelt's picture, addressed to the peoples of French North Africa in the following terms: 'We come to your country to free you from the grip of conquerors who seek to deprive you of your sovereign rights, your religious freedom and the right to lead your way of life in peace.'[17]

Although Roosevelt made no public commitment to end French rule in North Africa, nationalists in Algeria, Morocco, and Tunisia quickly made his language of self-determination into their own. When, in 1943 and 1944, they demanded independence, they all did so in terms of the Atlantic Charter: political rights that became an international idiom with the establishment of the United Nations in April 1945.

The final strand of the 1945 moment was the existence of wider historical patterns that transcended the Second World War. This aspect was not immediately obvious, principally because, given the significance of victory over Germany and Japan, it was easy to see 1945 as an end moment. Indeed, these wider patterns would only become really apparent in retrospect when the decolonization process was over. But, as Bayly and Harper have argued, in terms of Asia the Second World War must be situated within a much broader process: the Great Asian War which, in their opinion, began in 1931 and only ended with the end of European empires.[18] Likewise in Algeria, Morocco, and Tunisia, although undoubtedly accelerated by the Second World War, the contestation of colonialism was already in play and must be traced back to the beginnings of French rule in the nineteenth century.[19]

All of these five factors were present in 1945 or, in the case of nationalism, would become present in the next fifteen years, although their particular impact varied from empire to empire, and then, within each empire, from territory to territory. In Dutch Indonesia, for example, much of the archipelago was only lightly governed, despite over 100 years of imperial rule, and in the first part of the twentieth century this power was confronted with the rise of an Indonesian nationalism fashioned by communism and pan-Islamic ideas. By the 1930s Sukarno, a secular nationalist, had emerged as the leading figure of the movement and it was he who, given the way in which the Japanese occupation dismantled Dutch power, declared Indonesian independence on 17 August 1945, two days after the Japanese surrender. At this point the country witnessed a surge in

[17] Marvine Howe, *Morocco: The Islamist Awakening and Other Challenges* (New York: Oxford University Press, 2005), 70.

[18] Christopher Bayly and Tim Harper, *Forgotten Wars: The End of Britain's Asian Empire* (London: Allen Lane, 2007). See also Christopher Bayly and Tim Harper, *Forgotten Armies: The Fall of British Asia, 1941–1945* (London: Allen Lane, 2004).

[19] Evans, *Algeria: France's Undeclared War*. See also Benjamin Stora, *Algeria 1830–2000: A Short History* (Ithaca, NY: Cornell University Press, 2001) and Sylvie Thénault, *Histoire de la guerre d'indépendance algérienne* (Paris: Flammarion, 2005).

nationalism in the form of demonstration, flag-waving and graffiti, some of which was couched in the language of the Atlantic Charter. But the Dutch government was determined to reimpose colonial rule because Indonesia was seen to be the precondition for the country's future as a 'medium power'.[20] On this basis the Dutch authorities, backed up by the newly freed Dutch settlers, looked to the British army to suppress Indonesian nationalism, which it duly did.

DEVELOPMENTAL COLONIALISM AND IMPERIAL CITIZENS

Although events in Algeria and Indonesia represented a challenge to colonial rule, none of the governments in Brussels, the Hague, London, or Paris anticipated the collapse of their empires. In official thinking their respective futures were as imperial states, even if there was recognition that the old colonial status quo was unacceptable. What emerged, therefore, was a reformist strand of thinking that sought to transform the colonial relationship into a cooperative partnership in keeping with the new world of human rights and the welfare state. Colonial policy makers became involved in a new engagement with the colonized populations that wished to recognize the latter's aspirations, albeit within in a context of continued colonial sovereignty.

This shift underlines how Western European imperialism was not a single ideology, but one where concepts of 'race' intermingled with notions of 'civilizing mission' and the 'white man's burden'. Within this spectrum post-1945 represented a liberal variant that bubbled with new projects about economic development and layered sovereignty.[21]

This reformist thinking was clearest in France where the 1946 Fourth Republic Constitution announced a new federal arrangement with the overseas territories: the French Union. The constitutional blueprint for the French Union was introduced by Marius Moutet, the Socialist Party Minister for Overseas France, in 1945 where he accepted that the impact of the Second World War, the Atlantic Charter, as well as past errors in colonial policy meant that change was necessary.[22] Now, he argued, France had an opportunity to establish a liberal policy that would be an example to the world and on this basis the final 1946 Constitution underlined that the French Union was 'formed by France and overseas countries and based on equality of rights and obligations without distinction of race or religion'. Within this schema no concession was given to independence, but discrimination was ended and the local populations empowered through a

---

[20] Martin Shipway, *Decolonization and Its Impact: A Comparative Approach to the End of the Colonial Empires* (London: Blackwell, 2008), 88.

[21] Burbank and Cooper underline that it was this interventionist variant that collapsed in the 1950s and 1960s. Burbank and Cooper, *Empires in World History*, 413.

[22] *Commission de la Constitution: Comptes Rendus Analytiques de l'Assemblée Constituante Élue le 21 octobre 1945* (Paris: Imprimerie de l'Assemblée Constituante, 1946), 258–9.

series of local assemblies, as well as various levels of representation in parliament and the French Union Assembly. In short the French Union was a balance that claimed to be more democratic, while maintaining French sovereignty: the basis of a third international bloc that would rival the USA and the Soviet Union.

In Britain, the new Labour Government also accepted that change was inevitable within the imperial sphere. This was clear from the way civil servants in the Colonial Office talked about the need to transfer power at the level of *local* government in Africa. Such gradualism, they believed, would allow London to control the direction of change by upholding Britain's wider geostrategic interests and cutting away the ground from more radical anticolonial movements. As Frederick Pedler, a senior civil servant in the African Division in the Colonial Office, explained in an internal memorandum on 1 November 1946:

> What is needed now is a vigorous policy of African local government which will progressively democratise the present forms and bring literates and illiterates together, in balanced and studied proportions, for the management of local finances and services. Failing this we shall find the masses apt to follow the leadership of demagogues who want to turn us out very quickly.[23]

This increased political participation was to be accompanied by increased development in Africa which, the Labour Government hoped, would be a panacea to Britain's precarious economic position: an argument underlined by Sir Stafford Cripps, the Minister for Economic Affairs, in a speech to colonial governors on 12 November 1947:

> It is the urgency of the present situation and the need for the Sterling Group and Western Europe both to maintain their economic independence that makes it so essential that we should increase out of all recognition the tempo of African economic development. We must be prepared to change our outlook and our habits of colonial development so that within the next 2–5 years we can get a really marked increase of production in coal, minerals, timber, raw materials of all kinds, and foodstuffs and anything else that will save dollars or will sell in a dollar market.[24]

By establishing a reinvigorated empire in alliance with a rejuvenated Western Europe, Ernest Bevin, Labour's Foreign Secretary, hoped to create a British-led bloc that would equal the USA and the USSR.[25]

In contrast, Belgian and Dutch plans were of a different scale. Both countries saw their colonies as essential to economic rebuilding. Both saw them as an expression of national identity. But neither country saw their imperial possessions as the basis of a 'third force' to compete with the Cold War superpowers, even if they too adopted a reform perspective. Already in 1942 the Dutch government-in-exile in London had declared the creation of a Commonwealth in which the Netherlands, Indonesia, Surinam, and Curaçao in the

---

[23] R. Hyam (ed.), *The Labour Government and the End of Empire, 1945–1951* (London: HMSO, 1992), vol. 1, 117–18.

[24] Ibid., 300. The sterling area's dollar deficit that in the immediate post-1945 period was running at a staggering £600 to £700 million a year.

[25] Nicholas J. White, *Decolonisation: The British Experience since 1945* (London: Longman, 1999), 11–12.

Caribbean 'will participate, with complete self-reliance and freedom of conduct for each part regarding its internal affairs but with readiness to render mutual assistance.'[26] This Commonwealth, the declaration underlined, would be based upon racial equality. Equally, Brussels now talked of a Belgian-Congolese Federation that could lead to some form of independence, albeit in some unspecified time in the future. But again this new arrangement was tempered by greater economic control in the interests of the Belgian nation state. So, when officials unveiled a ten-year plan of £183 million investment for the Federation, this was to facilitate more mining production, which itself rose by 60 per cent by the mid-1950s.

In these ways the late 1940s and early 1950s witnessed a new type of colonial state: one that claimed to be liberal while deploying force to defend what were seen to be key geo-strategic interests. So, talk of rights and empowerment stood side by side with surveillance, censorship, prison, and repression when local populations rejected these liberal policies in the name of nationalism.

THE END OF EMPIRES: PALESTINE, LEBANON, SYRIA, AND SOUTH-EAST ASIA

These reformed empires were predicated on a simple belief: to survive in the post-1945 world, Belgium, Britain, France, and the Netherlands had to have a global reach. Yet, it rapidly became obvious that these global pretentions posed enormous economic difficulties. In August 1945 Britain was so bankrupt—Lord Keynes talked ominously of 'a financial Dunkirk'—that the Labour Government was obliged to negotiate a new $3.75 billion loan from Washington.[27] Then over the next twelve months the Atlee Administration admitted to the USA that it could not prop up the Greek Government in its war against communist insurgents. It was a defining moment in twentieth-century history. The USA was being asked to take up the cause of anti-communism and on 12 March 1947 President Truman announced that it was USA policy 'to help free peoples who are resisting subjugation by armed minorities or outside pressure.'[28] Three months later, the Truman doctrine was backed up by economic aid, organized by his secretary of state, George Marshall, and dispensing $12,500 million to 16 participating countries. The Cold War proper had begun with enormous implications for the old colonial powers, because the USA was now the dominant power in the Western Alliance. This shift was evident in the fact that Belgium, France, and the Netherlands were all major recipients of Marshall Aid and, given this level of economic problems, it was difficult to see how they, or Britain, had the resources to reimpose colonial control: a reality that was clear

[26] Shipway, *Decolonization and Its Impact*, 100.

[27] R. Hyam (ed.), *The Labour Government and the End of Empire, 1945–1951* (London: HMSO, 1992), vol. 2, 5.

[28] Harry S. Truman, 'Special Message to Congress on Greece and Turkey: The Truman Doctrine', 12 March 1947, http://www.trumanlibrary.org, accessed July 2011.

from the way in which France was forced out of Lebanon and Syria in 1946, followed by Britain's ignominious withdrawal from Palestine in the face of competing claims of Arab and Jewish nationalism in mid-1948.

In Asia, too, the threads of empire quickly began to unravel. In India, the Indian National Congress was the most significant national movement within the European empires.[29] By the late 1930s power was within its grasp of Indian National Congress, but the outbreak of the Second World War led to a clampdown and the leading figures of Indian nationalism— Mahatma Gandhi and Jawaharlal Nehru—were imprisoned. Even so, by 1945 it was obvious that Indian nationalism was too powerful and the colonial administration too weak to make British rule a feasible option. The question was what sort of exit. Nehru wanted a unified nation state that would take its place on the world's stage, while the All-India Muslim League pushed for a federation. In the end the two could only agree on one solution: partition into two separate nation states in August 1947: India and Pakistan; a process that also saw independence accorded to Burma and Ceylon in 1948.

In India Britain undoubtedly wished to leave as quickly as possible, despite the fact that this disengagement was marked by enormous intercommunal violence.[30] In contrast, in Malaysia the British remained. There the aim was to defeat a communist led insurgency, win local 'hearts and minds' and produce an independent state, the Malaysian Federation established in 1957, which would be part of the British sphere of influence. Post-colonial influence was now the name of the game and here the new Conservative Government, elected in 1951, followed the lines prescribed by their Labour predecessors, namely the transformation of the Commonwealth, established with the 'white' Dominions in 1931, into a multiracial entity that accepted these Asian countries as equal members.[31]

In Indochina, France became engaged in what was essentially a war of reconquest, although in June 1949 the Fourth Republic recognized Vietnam, along with Cambodia and Laos, on the basis that all three remained with the French Union.[32] By early 1954 this war-effort was being financed by the USA, who did not want the region to fall to the communists. But by this point the blunt truth was that the French had little support beyond the cities. Defeat at Dien-Bien-Phu in May 1954 left the French with no choice than negotiation: a humiliation which stemmed from the fact that the French had underestimated nationalist sentiment among the Indochinese and the capacity of the communists, led by Ho Chi Minh, to rally the majority of Indochinese behind a successful guerrilla war.

The other big European force in South-East Asia was the Netherlands. Pouring 170,000 troops into Indonesia, the Dutch looked for support from the USA in the name of anti-communism. Washington, however, did not equate Indonesian nationalism with

[29] On this see C.A. Bayly, *The Origins of Nationality in South Asia: Patriotism and Ethical Government in the Making of Modern India* (Oxford: Oxford University Press, 2001).

[30] By March 1948 violence and displacement had reached unprecedented levels. Some 180,000 Punjabis had died of whom two-thirds were Muslims moving westwards, while 6 million Muslims and 4.5 million Hindus and Sikhs were refugees.

[31] White, *Decolonisation*, 33–5.

[32] On Indochina see Nicola Cooper, *France in Indochina: Colonial Encounters* (Oxford: Berg, 2001) and Martin Shipway, *The Road to War: France and Vietnam, 1944–1947* (Oxford: Berghahn, 1996).

communism. On the contrary, the Truman Administration perceived Dutch action as strengthening pro-Soviet sentiment in the region with the result that the USA put great pressure on the Netherlands, threatening to suspend Marshall Aid. Thus isolated, the Dutch had little option but to concede independence in 1949, at which point the Dutch East Indies became the new state of Indonesia.

Significantly, the emergence of these countries transformed international politics: a shift that took on a concrete meaning in April 1955 with the Conference at Bandung in Indonesia. Lasting eight days, attended by twenty-three countries, including China, India, and Vietnam, and accounting for half of the world's population, the discussions, dominated by Nehru, emphasized that these new countries were pawns of neither old-style imperialism nor the Cold War. Instead this non-aligned movement would be a force for good and the final communiqué called for a new global politics based on the United Nations Charter. Making an explicit link between Nazism and colonialism, the Bandung countries also declared their support for the rights of Algeria, Morocco, and Tunisia to national self-determination, in effect setting off a chain reaction that challenged European imperialism everywhere.

Blueprints for Africa

For Britain and France the loss of their South-East Asian colonies did not mean the end of the imperial idea. Instead blueprints for a liberal policy now focused upon Africa where the keywords were cooperation and development. Within Britain's African colonies, this strategy had an open-ended feel at the beginning of the 1950s. The idea was to transfer power to internal self-government, which would encourage greater political participation while carefully defending Britain's international geostrategic interests. However, with political elites following decolonization in South-East Asia, this reform opened the door to parties who wanted to run their territory's *national* institutions. This process became apparent first in the Gold Coast, where the election victory of 1951 paved the way to independence six years later (as Ghana), then in Nigeria. In each case British officials accepted this transition while seeking to retain British influence through the drawing up of constitutions and the entry of these countries into the multiracial Commonwealth. However, when British officials thought they were losing control of the process, repression was the response. This was the case in Kenya where the Mau-Mau uprising, a movement drawn from the Kikuyu people, led to the imposition of a state of emergency between October 1952 and December 1959, which resulted in internment, torture, and the forced relocation of entire villages.[33]

---

[33] On Kenya see David Anderson, *Histories of the Hanged: Britain's Dirty War in Kenya and the End of Empire* (London: Weidenfeld and Nicolson, 2005); Daniel Branch, *Defeating Mau Mau, Creating Kenya: Counterinsurgency, Civil War and Decolonisation* (Cambridge: Cambridge University Press, 2009); Caroline Elkins, *Britain's Gulag: The Brutal End of Empire in Kenya* (London: Cape, 2005).

In France, the vision of a Franco–African entity stretching from Paris to the French Congo was at the heart of the Socialist Party-led Republican Front Government elected in January 1956. Speaking to journalists in Paris on 9 January 1957, Guy Mollet, the Prime Minister, underlined that this 'Eurafrican' community would be based upon cooperation and mutual independence. Moreover, a reformed Algeria, that empowered Algerians within the context of French sovereignty, would be the lynch pin of this bloc uniting Africa and the European Economic Community:

> France is negotiating at this time with her European partners for the organization of a vast common market, to which the Overseas Territories will be associated. All of Europe will be called upon to help in the development of Africa, and tomorrow Eurafrica may become one of the principal factors in world policy.
>
> Isolated nations can no longer keep pace with the world. What would Algeria amount to by itself? On the other hand, what future might it have, as one of the foundations of the Eurafrican community now taking shape?[34]

The foundation for the 'Eurafrica' bloc had been laid the previous May with the reforms for French Africa pushed through by Gaston Defferre, the Overseas Minister. For him, this devolution of powers to the local territories was superior to the British model in the Gold Coast because it was based upon the principle of continuing political and technical partnership within an overall French umbrella; a claim underlined by Defferre in an interview on 22 March 1957:

> To concede purely and simply, as Britain has done, independence to these territories, withdrawing our civil servants, our technicians, doing away with our investment, is to doom the populations of the overseas territories to insurmountable difficulties (perhaps) for them and to regression in certain domains... This system seems to me to be more realistic, more certain, more in line with the interests of the populations of overseas territories than the system employed by the English in the Gold Coast.[35]

These arguments were used by the Republican Front government to justify the intensification of repression in Algeria against the Front de Libération Nationale (FLN), which had been engaged in violent struggle against French rule ever since November 1954. But they were also part of a wide geostrategic vision. A French-led 'Eurafrica', the Republican Front argued, would preserve French power standing in face of communism, pan-Arabism, and rival British and US imperialisms.

However, by the mid-1950s, French plans were being challenged from two directions. On the one hand, Black African leaders in the late 1940s and early 1950s were campaigning for equality of wages and benefits with the French mainland: the realization of a genuinely equal French Union, which had rapidly mounting cost implications for France

---

[34] 'Guy Mollet, 'Statement by Premier Mollet on 9 January 1957'. The speech was translated into English by the French Embassy at the United Nations and became the first document in a 'Dossier on Algeria' which put the French case and was widely distributed at the United Nations. 'Dossier on Algeria', Guy Mollet Archive, OURS, APO 6, 11.

[35] *L'Express* (22 March 1957), 6.

that Defferre's reforms tried to offset through decentralization.[36] On the other hand, violent nationalist movements in North Africa had forced the Fourth Republic to concede independence to Morocco and Tunisia in March 1956, while simultaneously trying to defeat the FLN rebellion in Algeria. In each case repression had embroiled France in controversies over torture and human rights abuses, but in particular in Algeria where defeat of urban FLN operatives during the 'Battle of Algiers' between September 1956 and October 1957, led to the 'disappearance' of 3024 prisoners.[37]

SUEZ 1956

As Britain and France tried to control events in Africa, their power was further undermined by a pivotal event in post-1945 history: the 1956 Suez Crisis. Administered as a British protectorate from 1882, Egypt had regained independence in 1922, although Britain effectively recolonized the country during the Second World War. After 1945 the monarchy remained closely allied to the British: a stance that provoked popular hostility and led to King Farouk's overthrow by army officers in 1952. Within the coup, Colonel Gamal Abdel Nasser emerged as the country's new undisputed leader. Preaching a message of pan-Arab nationalism, he called on Arabs to stand up against Britain and France, a stance that led him to annex the Suez Canal Company in July 1956. Given that the canal was a vital economic artery, carrying two-thirds of Western Europe's oil from the Persian Gulf, and given that the French Government saw Nasser as the hidden hand behind the FLN, Egyptian nationalization provoked an aggressive response from Britain and France who, in a secret alliance with Israel, concocted a plan to retake the canal and destroy Nasser. Both Mollet and Eden, the Conservative Prime Minister, presented Nasser as a fascist-style threat, but the actual Suez Operation itself ended in ignominious failure.

Israel attacked Egypt on 29 October, but when British and French forces entered Egypt on 5 November, ostensibly on the deception that they were going to restore peace, international condemnation was unanimous. In the White House, newly re-elected President Dwight Eisenhower was furious. By running counter to his plan to construct an anti-communist alliance within the Middle East and North Africa, Britain and France had put their own imperial interests above those of the NATO alliance. They had handed a propaganda victory to the Communist Bloc, which cast itself as a defender of Arab rights against 'Western Imperialism' and, worse still, with the world's attention diverted, Suez provided the Soviet Union with the unique opportunity to crush the Hungarian revolution and reimpose a pro-Moscow regime in Budapest.

---

[36] Frederick Cooper, *Decolonization and African Society: The Labor Question in French and British Africa* (New York: Cambridge University Press, 1996).

[37] On this see Raphaëlle Branche, *La Torture et l' armée française pendant la guerre d' Algérie* (Paris: Gallimard, 2001).

In reply Eisenhower refused to guarantee the supply of US petrol to replenish that of the Gulf, lost through the canal's closure, and allowed a run on sterling to develop: two weapons that forced Eden to give way on 6 November, followed by Mollet shortly after. Equally, within the United Nations, the US resolution calling for an immediate ceasefire won resoundingly with sixty-four to five in favour: a crucial moment for the Vice-President, Richard Nixon, because: 'For the first time in history, we have showed independence of Anglo–French policies towards Asia and Africa that seemed to us to reflect the colonial tradition. That declaration of independence has had an electrifying effect throughout the world.'[38]

POST-SUEZ

Suez was a moment of revelation; one that demonstrated the limitations on British and French imperial power. Yet it did not produce immediate colonial disengagement. Britain and France continued to pursue their imperial commitments, through a combination of reform and repression, while grappling with the changing realities of the Cold War, the establishment of the European Economic Community in May 1957, the cost of the welfare state, and the emergence of the Western European economic miracle.

In Britain, Eden, tarnished by Suez, was replaced by Harold Macmillan in 1957 who sought to rebuild the alliance with the USA in a way that would allow Britain to defend its geostrategic interests in Africa and the Middle East. At the same time, in continuing with Eden's thoroughgoing review of British spending commitments at home and abroad, Macmillan asked for officials to draw up a profit and loss account for each colony.[39] Soon Macmillan was coming to the conclusion that colonies were a drain on resources, particularly with the ongoing conflict in Kenya. Moreover, he increasingly took the view that in the Cold War context empire was counter-productive because in the global battle for 'hearts and minds', imperial possessions gave the Soviet Union a stick with which to beat Britain. These ideas were encapsulated in his groundbreaking 'Winds of Change' speech given on 3 February 1960 to a silent South African parliament in Cape Town. Signalling that African nationalism was a fact, and that for the other major European power in Africa colonialism was now at an end, Macmillan declared: 'We must all accept this fact, and our national policies must take account of it.'[40] The key question was which side the uncommitted peoples of Asia and Africa would swing to: 'Will they be drawn into the Communist camp? Or will the great experiments in self-government that are now being made in Asia and Africa, especially within the

---

[38] Keith Kyle, *Suez* (London: Weidenfeld and Nicolson, 1991), 149.

[39] On this see Frederick Cooper, *Africa since 1940* (Cambridge: Cambridge University Press, 2002), 76–84.

[40] Harold Macmillan, 'The Winds of Change', in Simon Heffer (ed.), *Great British Speeches* (Chester: Quercus Publishing, 2007), 214–18.

Commonwealth, prove so successful, that the balance will come down in favour of free-dom and order and justice? The struggle is joined, and it is a struggle for the minds of men.'[41]

For Macmillan the issue in 1960 was about managing a transition to national inde-pendence that would ensure the best strategic advantage, both in terms of Britain's nar-row interests and the wider global struggle against communism. Without doubt, therefore, Macmillan's speech was a landmark moment. He had served notice on the Empire even if his speech contained no precise timetable.

Within France, too, Suez did not immediately alter policy. The Republican Front con-tinued with the conflict in Algeria in combination with plans for a 'Eurafrican' bloc. At one level, though, Suez was another blow to the Fourth Republic, which imploded in May 1958 in the face of revolt by settlers and the army in Algiers: a crisis that led to the return to power of General de Gaulle. By establishing a Fifth Republic based upon a strong presidential system, de Gaulle hoped to find a solution to Algeria. Initially he fol-lowed the lines prescribed by the Fourth Republic, which sought to chart a third way solution that rejected the FLN *and* settler extremism. This legacy was self-evident in the huge investment programme unveiled by de Gaulle in October 1958, which aimed to dramatically improve Algerian lives through health care for women, education, and industrialization.[42] De Gaulle hoped to win Algerians over to a French solution, but European intransigence, combined with massive nationalist demonstrations in Algeria in December 1960, convinced de Gaulle that negotiation was the only option: a process that led to Algerian independence in July 1962.

This shift stemmed from the fact that de Gaulle saw Algeria as a drain on resources, telling journalists on 11 April 1961: 'Algeria is costing us, this is the least that one can say, much more that it brings into us.'[43] But it was also due to his personal prejudices. In March 1959 de Gaulle confided to Alain Peyrefitte that he did not see how France could absorb 10 million Muslims, who would become 20 million and then 40 million.[44] For him the cultural difference was insurmountable, meaning that France would no longer be 'a European people of a white race, Greek and Latin culture and Christian religion'.[45] And, then finally, there was de Gaulle's inability to construct a Franco–African entity within which a reformed, pro-French Algeria, could be anchored. Here again de Gaulle followed the Fourth Republic's 'Eurafrica' concept, offering each territory an option in a 1958 referendum: independence or membership of the French Community. Only Guinea voted for complete separation, yet during the following year this Community dissolved. In part this was because de Gaulle's failure to convince Washington of the case for a

[41] Ibid., 215.

[42] On this see Ryme Seferdjeli, '"Fight with us, women, and we will emancipate you": France, the FLN and the Struggle over Women during the Algerian War of National Liberation 1954–1962', PhD thesis, London School of Economics, 2005 and Neil Macmaster, *Burning the Veil* (Manchester: Manchester University Press, 2010).

[43] De Gaulle, *Discours et messages* (Paris: Plon, 1970), vol. 3.

[44] Alain Peyrefitte, *C'était de Gaulle* (Paris: Fayard, 1994), vol. 1, 68.

[45] Ibid.

Franco–African entity, this time in the guise of a French-led wing of NATO based upon Africa and the Mediterranean.[46] Instead, President Eisenhower, during an official visit in September 1959, reiterated the USA's anti-colonial tradition. But it was principally because of the strength of nationalism. By 1960 the African elites, looking to the example of Ghana, wanted national sovereignty.[47]

Given that Britain and France were the two dominant imperial powers, their actions set the international tone from which Belgium was unable to cut itself off. Thus, although Brussels had increased investment and talked of Belgian-Congolese Community, this reforming scenario was overtaken by events in January 1959 when large-scale riots announced the arrival of a new factor: Congolese nationalism. This was a shock for the Belgian Government which, unable to control the situation, conceded independence eighteen months later: a sudden unravelling that further reinforced 1960 as a tipping point. This was the moment when the political leaders in Western Europe finally accepted that empires, even reformed empires, belonged to the past. This had not been the view from 1945, but in the ensuing years this model lost out because politicians in Belgium, Britain, France, and the Netherlands had to confront the strength of anti-colonial nationalism; the full cost implications of these models; and the new realities of the Cold War, whereby Washington was unwilling, from Suez onwards, to support colonial entities that allowed the Communist World to take the moral high ground.

New Future Visions

The transition to independence now became the framework as the 'Winds of Change' played out across the remaining colonies, principally during the early 1960s but also into the 1970s: a two-sided process whereby Belgium, Britain, France, and the Netherlands surrendered sovereignty to new nation states that claimed to represent a people. Decolonization, therefore, marked a crucial stage in a much wider process—the transformation of the globe from a world of empires into one of nation states, each in principle equal members of the United Nations, bound together by international law.

For the Belgian and Dutch governments, the search for a post-imperial role had a double effect. It turned them inward, as the logic of empire gave way to the much narrower logic of the nation state, and outward, since these nation states were firmly anchored within the European unification process. Their political and economic futures were seen to be within the European Economic Community: a gateway to modernization and prosperity that would more than compensate for the end of empire. In contrast this process

---

[46] On the Cold War context and the Algerian war see Irwin Wall, *France, the United States and the Algerian War* (Berkeley, CA: University of California Press, 2001) and Matthew Connelly, *A Diplomatic Revolution: Algeria's Fight for Independence and the Origins of the Post-Cold War Era* (Oxford: Oxford University Press, 2002).

[47] Tony Chafer, *The End of Empire in French West Africa* (Oxford: Berg, 2002).

was much more complicated for the political elites in Britain and France, because for them their empires had been measures of great-power status. The loss of empire could not be equated with loss of this status and this meant finding different future visions that would conceal this basic reality. One future vision was the nuclear option.

For both British and French governments accession to the nuclear club was hugely important. It showed the world that both countries had not been left behind by the superpowers. Even if their status had clearly diminished during the 1950s, and even if their nuclear arsenals could never rival the USA and Soviet Union, possession of nuclear weapons meant that their voices could not be ignored within the Cold War. This in turn fed into a much wider future vision, namely modernization as both British and French governments seized on the notion of the 'white heat of technology': technical expertise that would maintain both countries as world leaders, exemplified by the 1962 joint Franco–British project to build the Concorde supersonic passenger plane.

Equally, governments in Britain and France underlined another future vision: the consumer economy.[48] The late 1950s and early 1960s was when the Western European economic miracle really became visible. 'You have never had it so good', Macmillan told electors in 1959; a reference to the rising living standards that transformed the focus of society away from empire and into one defined by the consumption of cars, refrigerators, and televisions. The final future vision was the nation state.[49] During the 1960s and 1970s both Britain and France put in place tight restrictions on immigration from the former colonies, in effect replacing imperial citizenship with one closely aligned to nation-state borders.[50]

At the same time, the British and French governments pursued policies that allowed them to project images of international power. The two countries jealously guarded their respective seats on the United Nations Security Council, a legacy of their roles in the victorious Second World War alliance which was underpinned by imperial power. Over US power, however, they took opposite directions. Macmillan sought to repair the damage of Suez through the development of the 'special relationship'; one where Britain would hand over the baton of Anglo-Saxon power to the USA while retaining a huge cultural influence becoming, in Macmillan's words, like the Greeks in the Roman Empire. De Gaulle meanwhile took a hostile stance. Still angry at way in which the USA had not backed his vision of a French-led NATO, de Gaulle condemned the Vietnam War, withdrew France from the NATO Command Structure in 1966 and blocked British entry to the EEC on the grounds that Britain would be a Trojan horse for US interests; an application that he also opposed on the grounds that Britain, unlike France, had not properly decolonized.

---

[48] Kristin Ross, *Fast Cars, Clean Bodies: Decolonization and the Reordering of French Culture* (Cambridge, MA: MIT Press, 1995).

[49] Todd Shepherd, *The Invention of Decolonization: The Algerian War and the Remaking of France* (Ithaca, NY: Cornell University Press, 2006).

[50] In Britain the Commonwealth Immigration Act of 1962 put controls on immigration from the Commonwealth that were further tightened in 1968 and 1971. France effectively closed the borders to the former colonies in the wake of the 1973 oil crisis.

As regards the former colonies in Africa, France sought to maintain influence through a secretive policy, pursued by the shadowy Jacques Foccart, which built up networks of relationships with African rulers. This was complemented by an economic strategy based upon the Franc zone, covering all the ex-colonies in Sub-Saharan Africa and giving France privileged commercial access, in combination with Sahara oil and gas extraction, which was dominated by French companies until nationalization by the Algerian Government in 1971. By contrast during the 1960s the intellectual and institutional impetus for the Francophone movement, extolling shared French values of language and culture, came from Senghor in Senegal and Bourguiba in Tunisia, with France only becoming fully involved after the election of the Socialist Party leader, François Mitterrand, in May 1981 as *Francophonie* became a way of opposing Anglo-Saxon globalization.

With Britain the idea of empire was replaced by the notion of the Commonwealth. Like *Francophonie*, the Commonwealth emphasized a common linguistic heritage but this had a stronger institutional basis with the establishment of the Commonwealth Institute in London in 1962.[51] And it was within this Commonwealth framework that the two throwbacks to empire were resolved; the first Rhodesia, where whites, denying the black majority a meaningful political role, had declared unilateral independence in 1965, which became Zimbabwe in 1980; and the second South Africa, which withdrew from the British Commonwealth in 1960 and continued with racial segregation, but accepted the end of the apartheid system with free elections on 27 April 1994.

Spain and Portugal

Within this decolonization process the two exceptions were Portugal and Spain. They could not insulate their territories from decolonization, but the timeframe was different because the Cold War calculus was different. The USA did not want to challenge Portugal or Spain for fear of destabilizing them, either domestically or in Africa, and aiding the advance of communism.

In the case of Portugal, a NATO country and recipient of Marshall Aid, empire was the price of Portuguese adherence to international anti-communism. For Salazar, imperial possessions provided prestige as well as raw materials and markets that were a buffer against economic uncertainty. This meant that the 1950s were years of imperial expansion. Thousands of Portuguese settlers left for the dominions in search of opportunities they did not have at home. Yet, the spread of African nationalism was unstoppable and as a result Portugal became bogged down in a series of colonial wars that began with Angola in 1961, followed by Guinea in 1963 and Mozambique in 1964.[52] These conflicts endured, however, because they were in effect proxy wars where the USA supported Portugal

[51] The building housed a permanent exhibition on the countries of the Commonwealth.
[52] Goa was annexed by India in 1961.

against movements that were pro-Soviet. Their abrupt end in 1974 was due to revolution in Portugal itself, led by army officers who saw colonial wars as unwinnable. The new left-wing government immediately changed policy and recognized the independence of all its colonies, except for Macau, which was only returned to China in 1999.[53]

Franco's Spain was not a NATO member, but became a recipient of USA aid in 1953. This drew Spain into the anti-communist camp, but the country's colonies were not a major issue because by this point all that remained of the Spanish Empire was small African enclaves. Unlike with Portugal these never became settler colonies. They were in effect backwaters whose role was to be a frontier against Africa. Consequently, Spanish decolonization, beginning with Spanish Morocco in 1956, followed by Gulf of Guinea in 1968 and Spanish Sahara in 1975, never assumed Portuguese dimensions.

By the mid-1970s, therefore, Portugal and Spain, the first to establish overseas empires, were the last to lose them. And, like the other four countries, they abandoned imperial conceptions of themselves in favour of a future vision that was more national and more European; a process facilitated by their double entry into the EEC in 1986.

AFTERMATH

Although empire has ended, each of these countries is conditioned by the aftermath of empire. This is clear from how immigration from ex-colonies has altered their social make-up. To compare Paris in 1945 with Paris in the twenty-first century, is to see how France has been transformed from a largely white country into a multicultural society, but one where the long legacy of colonial racism still defines much of the way in which French citizens of North African descent are perceived in contemporary France.[54] This aftermath is also obvious in the way in which the Right has an attempted to dispense with colonial guilt. In 1988, for example, Margaret Thatcher, the British Conservative Party Prime Minister, in a major speech, was unequivocal about how 'Europeans... and yes without apology had civilized much of the world.'[55] While in France in 2005, a law called on the positive aspects of French colonial rule to be taught in schools and universities, despite the ongoing controversy over torture in Algeria.[56]

Finally, the aftermath is clear from shifting perceptions of international power. Arguably the demise of the six seafaring empires marks the end of the ascendency of

---

[53] Currently, the Azores and Madeira archipelagos are the only territories overseas that remain politically linked to Portugal.

[54] On the relationship between colonialism and racism see Max Silverman, *Deconstructing the Nation: Immigration, Racism and Citizenship in Modern France* (London: Routledge, 1992).

[55] Margaret Thatcher, 'Bruges Speech', 20 September 1988, http://margaretthatcher.org, accessed July 2011.

[56] Martin Evans and Raphaëlle Branche, 'Where Does Colonial History End?', in Robert Gildea and Anne Simonin (eds), *Writing Contemporary History* (London: Hodder, 2008), 145–67.

the western end of the Eurasian landmass that dominated the world between 1500 and the mid-twentieth century. Confronted with decolonization in combination with the rise of the USA and USSR, these countries found solace in the European Economic Community. This decline was then disguised by the collapse of the Soviet Bloc in 1989–1991 and continued European integration. But this spectre has returned with the 2011 Eurozone crisis and the rise of new countries such as Brazil, India, and, most significantly, China, which takes us back to J. G. Ballard and *Empire of the Sun*. For him, internment in a Japanese prisoner of war camp destroyed the myth of European invincibility forever, something that an eleven-year-old like himself, brought up on tales of imperial derring-do, found hard to accept. It showed that 'the British Empire was based upon bluff, in many ways a brilliant one, but that bluff had been called.'[57] And, out of the wreckage of empire Ballard's novel describes a transformation in the Chinese mindset in 1945. Now, they are determined to rise up and cast off imperial domination. There is a new mentality which, Ballard hints, will have enormous consequences for the future.[58] In this way the novel encapsulates an embryonic moment: the beginning in the shift of power from Western Europe to the Pacific Rim, which has been one of the defining contours of Europe since 1945.

FURTHER READING

Aldrich, Robert (ed.), *The Age of Empires* (New York: Thames and Hudson, 2007).

Anderson, David, *Histories of the Hanged: Britain's Dirty War in Kenya and the End of Empire* (London: Weidenfeld and Nicolson, 2005).

Bayly, Christopher, and Nick Harper, *Forgotten Wars: The End of Britain's Asian Empire* (London: Allen Lane, 2007).

Branch, Daniel, *Defeating Mau Mau, Creating Kenya: Counterinsurgency, Civil War and Decolonisation* (Cambridge: Cambridge University Press, 2009).

Burbank, Jane, and Frederick Cooper, *Empires in World History* (Princeton, NJ: Princeton University Press, 2010).

Chafer, Tony, *The End of Empire in French West Africa* (Oxford: Berg, 2002).

Cooper, Frederick, *Decolonization and African Society: The Labor Question in French and British Africa* (New York: Cambridge University Press, 1996).

Darwin, John, *Britain and Decolonisation* (London: Macmillan, 1988).

Evans, Martin, *Algeria: France's Undeclared War* (Oxford: Oxford University Press, 2012).

Shipway, Martin, *Decolonization and Its Impact: A Comparative Approach to the End of the Colonial Empire* (London: Blackwell, 2008).

White, Nicholas J., *Decolonisation: The British Experience since 1945* (London: Longman, 1999).

---

[57] J. G. Ballard, 'The End of My War', *Sunday Times* (20 August 1995), 2.

[58] On the final page of *Empire of the Sun*, the young boy Jim notes how ordinary Chinese react in silent disgust when they are insulted by American and British sailors.

CHAPTER 24

AFTER THE FEAR WAS OVER? WHAT CAME AFTER DICTATORSHIPS IN SPAIN, GREECE, AND PORTUGAL[1]

HELEN GRAHAM AND ALEJANDRO QUIROGA

'Memory transforms the past into a future possibility.'

Hannah Arendt

INTRODUCTION

WHAT Spain, Greece, and Portugal have in common in the twentieth century is the manner in which their internal processes of change—rural to urban, agrarian to industrial—were intervened and inflected at crucial moments and with enduring effect by the force of international political agendas. Cold War fears caused the western allies to support repressive regimes on the southern boundaries of 'free' Europe. In both Spain and Greece, these international priorities determined the eventual outcomes of civil wars, guaranteeing the survival into the post-1945 era of traditionalist polities and elites, which in the preceding decades had come under domestic challenge to countenance levelling social and political reform. In the case of Portugal, too, international calculations

---

[1] For reasons of space and target readership, sources in languages other than English have been excised here—except when they are being directly quoted. The further reading includes some of the most important, non-English secondary works used. Readers may contact the authors for full endnotes: h.graham@rhul.ac.uk; alejandro.quiroga@ncl.ac.uk

ultimately proved decisive; crucial to the survival of the viscerally change-resistant Salazar dictatorship in its existing form after 1945, an era that was otherwise to be defined by European decolonization, was the tacit acceptance in the West that the Portuguese empire would remain in place. Without the empire as both economic resource and safety valve, Salazar would have been unable to insulate metropolitan Portugal so 'effortlessly', or for as long, against urban and industrial change. As it was, violence within the metropolis remained for a long while 'marginal', mainly inflicted by the political police, *Polícia Internacional e de Defesa do Estado* (PIDE) on an urban activist minority, while hundreds of thousands migrated abroad to circumvent poverty. The extremes of violence were, meanwhile, decanted to Portugal's colonies, until, in April 1974, in a singular inversion of the usual role of armies in the Southern European dictatorships, a disaffected officer class triggered a political revolution in the metropolis. This was 'colonialism come home' in reverse thrust, and, ultimately, the price paid for Salazar's high-risk, brutalizing strategy in the colonies.

In neighbouring Spain, by contrast, the twentieth-century oligarchic elites never had a real or substantive empire to fall back on. The Francoist coalition that achieved military victory in 1939 thus had a greater awareness of the need to develop the country economically, but, like Salazar, it too was determined to avoid political and cultural change and used the idea of empire as a metaphor to justify and enact repression in the metropolis. But ensuring social control in Spain, even within the straitjacket of the much more actively interventionist, if not also explicitly totalitarian, Francoist dictatorship would require greater levels of overt violence. In the decade immediately following Franco's victory, state-led violence continued to be perpetrated in Spain on a scale so vast and with an intensity so socially pervasive—in effect the regime continued to wage war against defeated sectors of society—that the phenomenon requires a qualitatively different analysis; one that ultimately means that Spain's mid-twentieth-century trajectory cannot be satisfactorily theorized within the conventional 'southern Mediterranean model' of authoritarian and 'developmentalist' regimes operating in largely rural and demobilized societies (because 1930s Spain was already a substantially mobilized society). Francoism also stands out because of the lasting toxicity of its original legitimating strategy, which actively created tens of thousands of perpetrators and maintained their ideological mobilization throughout the four decades of the regime, giving rise to an afterlife of violence that still burns the social and political landscape of twenty-first-century Spain.

Cold War agendas were adopted in Spain, Portugal and Greece as preventive instruments against social change, as well as being strategies to guarantee political support, and much-needed economic aid, from western power actors. In the same way, the on- and offshore gulags of all three Southern European states served a dual function between the 1940s and 1960s. Indeed, the fear-driven discourse of anti-communism itself, for all that its origins were evidently coterminous with the Russian revolution, has always been a rallying cry and a form of mobilization deployed against indigenous constituencies bearing agendas of social and cultural change. In Greece, the legislation used in the 1950s to repress and exclude communists was first enacted in the 1920s, and then deployed throughout the interwar period. Many leftist political prisoners were the same people across the interwar period and through the 1940s and 1950s. By the 1960s in all three countries, the fearful imaginaries of traditionalists still saw a disguised form of communism in the 'godlessness' of Americanization, social liberalization, and anti-puritanism—since these were the forces now threatening to sweep away a certain conception of 'eternal' Spain, Portugal, and Greece founded on the pillars of religion, the military, and a rigidly hierarchical society.

One of the acute paradoxes of this ideological bid for stasis was the effect it wrought upon the sense of time as experienced by many of the politically and socially marginalized—whether the rural landless and urban workers, the constituencies defeated in the Spanish and Greek civil wars, or many of Portugal's migrants of the late 1950s and 1960s who also set off travelling because they did not 'fit'. 'Stasis' propelled them into living in the future, away from a stagnant present of sacrifice and labour. But, particularly in the case of Greece and most especially Spain, they were also being distanced from a past that, far from resembling the immobilist ideal of regime rhetoric, contained the 'dangerous' memories of other social and political possibilities. Indeed, that sense of danger in the past underscores one of the key functions of the postwar order in Greece and Spain: to inflect or reconfigure memories of earlier egalitarian projects for social change with a sense of ineradicable danger and risk for those who participated in them or even 'remembered' them.

The illusion—or delusion—of stasis would finally be exploded by the radical energy of the April 1974 revolution in Portugal. Fuelled by the military's anger at being trapped in a colonial war it could not win, the revolution sounded the death knell for the Colonels' attempt to reinforce barriers against internal social change in Greece, via the quasi-imperial venture of *enosis* ('union' with Cyprus), as well as calling time on any form of Francoism 'after Franco'. The events in Portugal had a shock value that helped reconfigure the perceptions of international power brokers: most especially the US, which, in spite of tirelessly declaiming 'free world' rhetoric, seemed unperturbed by the persistence into the 1970s of the dictatorial and authoritarian polities it had long patronized in the south. But the spectre of revolution brought directly to its attention the internal urban shifts and industrial transformations undergone by Spain, Portugal, and Greece since the 1940s beneath the ideological canopy of 'stasis' propagated by their governing orders.

This chapter adopts a tripartite structure (1945: survival; 1970s: transition; after 1989: memory) in order to explore why, how, and with what consequences Southern European political establishments with clear Nazi links or empathies not only survived the collapse of Hitler's new order, but were also able to persist as dictatorial and authoritarian regimes into the 1970s. It then interrogates the nature of the subsequent transitions to parliamentary democracy, paying particular attention to the continuities. For it is these that explain the impact, ongoing in Spain today, of the continental reckoning with the European 'postwar' opened up in 1989 by the collapse of the communist bloc. Not least, this reckoning has also raised the broader historical (and historiographical) question of why the Southern European dictatorships were easily overlooked for so long in narratives of postwar history. Much of this chapter provides an implicit argument and evidence of why this was so. But to conclude this introduction, we will tackle the question head-on.

The post-World War II states of Southern Europe constitute a central anomaly. They were partners in the western alliance against communism, but they were 'uncomfortable' and awkward ones. Not only did they fail to fit the mythic grand narrative of a 'national resistance to fascism as generator of parliamentary democracy' that proved so useful for nation-building in post-1945 Western Europe, but these three states replicated the structural violence and coercion of the Cold War enemy, which meant that they actively undermined the idea of western political superiority and civility. And while western historians were not necessarily bound by this narrative, it nevertheless exerted considerable cultural influence and at least in part explains why the experience of Greece, Portugal, and (especially) Spain—at once liminal and central to the history of the 'West'—have been for so long passed over in historical accounts of the postwar continent. From a twenty-first-century perspective, with that western mythic narrative everywhere under strain, one might have expected the story of what these three ruling orders were, *and of what each did to their own citizens and subjects*, to have come sharply into focus. However, it is remarkable, even today, how few Western European or North American commentators understand the brutality beneath the burlesque of Southern European dictatorship.

1945: Survival

(i) Unleashing fear

> 'We ourselves are the war.'
>
> Freikorps diary

In September 1940, the victorious Franco dictatorship removed the legal nationality of thousands of exiled Spanish Republicans incarcerated in prisoner-of-war camps in German-occupied France, opening the way for their deportation to the Nazi concentration camps where 10,000 of them died. This decision, along with Spain's wartime provision to Germany of key materials, labour, and reconnaissance and intelligence facilities, exemplified the regime's commitment to the core values of Hitler's new order in Europe. In May 1945, as the Thousand Year Reich met its end in a Berlin bunker, included among its praetorian guard were Spanish fascist paramilitaries of the Falange, now encadred in the Waffen-SS. Franco had finally and reluctantly to accept that the future to which he was ideologically committed was dead, and with it the hopes he had clung to of acquiring Spain's 'lost' empire in the slipstream of Nazi victory.

But inside Spain, Franco went on forging his own *Volksgemeinschaft*, no less brutal or absolute in practice for not being racially based, and conceived in its way too as an 'imperial' endeavour to secure a rigid political and social hierarchy that had earlier been challenged by the pluralist and cosmopolitan values associated with Spain's urban centres. The exceptional virulence of the Francoist project was at least partly due to its having been born in war. In its name, the regime murdered and incarcerated its own nationals on a scale that outdid anything that the Nazi state had undertaken within its pre-1938 borders. Between 1936 and the end of the 1940s Francoist forces were responsible for killing over 150,000 people, who were either extrajudicially murdered, or executed after summary military 'trials'. Around a million men, women, and children passed through prisons and work camps or suffered other forms of preventive detention/punitive regime.[2] These included the workings of Franco's autarkic economic policy, a major tool of revenge and reconfiguration, centring on the operation of a huge black market—as a consequence of which some 200,000 starved to death between 1939 and 1945.[3]

Singular too in the Spanish case was the very high level of social complicity in state violence. Seeking to consolidate itself, the Franco regime exhorted 'ordinary Spaniards' to denounce neighbours, friends, and family members who had been on the losing side in the civil war. Denunciation triggered mass military trials, making citizens across the land responsible for the proceedings that led to the killing, torture, and imprisonment of tens of thousands of their compatriots.[4] Thus a western order that retrospectively mythologized its opposition to Nazism as opposition to the camp universe, and which denounced this too as the ultimate offence of Stalinism, patronized a regime in Spain that was, like the Soviet Union's, based on mass murder and the gulag. For Francoism, like Stalinism and Nazism, can best be defined as a regime that was at war with its own society. Until its very end in 1975 it perpetuated the civil war division of Spaniards through discourse and discriminatory practices. It is this unremitting, reiterative, and Manichean quality in Francoism, combined with very high levels of social complicity, that explains its peculiarly poisonous and abiding afterlife into the twenty-first century.

For the western allies, their knowledge of Franco's murderousness was inconvenient. Britain, especially, believed that any alternative would be weak and 'disordered', so, for the sake of Cold War *realpolitik*, the terror had to be ignored. More problematic was squaring this with the strong currents of anti-Franco public opinion in Europe. As a result, the institutional re-integration of Spain was lower key than that of Salazar's Portugal or the conservative postwar order in Greece. Spain was excluded from Marshall

---

[2] Helen Graham, 'The Memory of Murder: Mass Killing and the Making of Francoism', and 'Franco's Prisons: Building the Brutal National Community in Spain', in Helen Graham, *The War and its Shadow: Spain's Civil War in Europe's Long Twentieth Century* (Brighton/Portland/Toronto: Sussex Academic Press, 2012), chs 2 and 6 respectively.

[3] Michael Richards, *A Time of Silence: Civil War and the Culture of Repression in Franco's Spain* (Cambridge: Cambridge University Press, 1998), 7; Paul Preston, 'Spain 1945–85', in Andrew Graham with Anthony Seldon (eds), *Government and Economies in the Postwar World* (London: Routledge, 1991).

[4] Peter Anderson, *The Francoist Military Trials: Terror and Complicity 1939–1945* (London: Routledge, 2009).

Aid, and a diplomatic embargo enacted. However, by 1953 Spain had got its own US aid package, which underwrote the dictatorship and led Franco himself to declare: 'at last I have won the Spanish civil war'.[5]

The survival of the Portuguese dictatorship in the post-1945 period is more straightforward to explain than the survival of Franco's. True, in the 1930s Salazar had given his regime some fascist drapery, creating a single party, a militia, and organizations for women's and youth mobilization. He also promoted an ultranationalistic and imperialistic discourse in schools and at public ceremonies;[6] but ideological enlistment remained a minority 'urban event'. Would-be fascists were comforted by the existence of a real empire, while Salazar took good care not to disturb the depths of the rural demobilized majority. While the dictator hailed the Nazis for their social project, the risks of such an alignment for the Portuguese empire saw him opt for a 'collaborationist neutrality' with the allies in 1943. There were Portuguese volunteers for Hitler too, but they were much more isolated from regime thinking and interests than were their Spanish equivalents. Salazar's pre-1945 collaboration facilitated the incorporation of the Portuguese regime into the western camp early in the Cold War. Portugal received Marshall Aid and became a founding member of NATO in 1949.

Salazar also used fear as a way of controlling the population. But he had no need for a project like Franco's; the level of political mobilization inside Portugal was far lower, and his regime had come to power peacefully. Nevertheless, with the fresh memory of some big urban strikes in the 1940s, Salazar put in place a wide-ranging network of repression. Its hub was the much-feared political police, PIDE, which, along with the army and new judicial institutions, took aim at the major threat—urban dissidence. As in Spain, not only were those deemed 'subversive' imprisoned, tortured, and killed, but they were also excluded from education and professional employment in both the public and private sectors.[7] Physical and economic repression thus operated in tandem.

In Greece the royalist forces victorious in the civil war of 1946–1949 were, formally, a constitutional government. But they also pursued brutal policies. Their target was the defeated side in the civil war—for, as in Spain, these were groups that had allied themselves with options for social change. Given, too, that the articulating forms for this earlier social mobilization were, broadly speaking, communist, Greek conservatives were facilitated in their domestic repressive aims by emergent geopolitical imperatives. The country's position in the Balkans, as the frontline against the nascent eastern bloc, brought a level of US support—announced by the Truman Doctrine in March 1947— that was sufficient to win them the civil war (Greece too would be admitted to NATO by

---

[5] Juan Pablo Fusi, *Franco* (London: Unwin Hyman, 1987), 80; Paul Preston, *Franco* (New York: HarperCollins, 1993), 622–3.

[6] Nuno Luís Madureira, 'Cartelization and Corporatism: Bureaucratic Rule in Authoritarian Portugal, 1926–45', *Journal of Contemporary History* 42:1 (2007), 90, 94. David Corkill and José Carlos Pina Almeida, 'Commemorations and Propaganda in Salazar's Portugal: The Mundo Português Exposition of 1940', *Journal of Contemporary History* 44:3 (2009), 381–99.

[7] Manuel Loff, 'Los regímenes autoritarios', in Hipólito de la Torre Gómez (ed.), *Portugal y España contemporáneos* (Madrid: Marcial Pons, 2000), 150.

1951, even though it was not an Atlantic country). For the allies, fear of social revolution and of communist subversion in Greece had become indistinguishable and led them to ignore their conservative clients' ideological affinities with, and (sometimes) their material links to, the Nazi occupiers.

For the same reasons, little external pressure was applied to bring collaborators to account in Greece. The state apparatus—civil service, security forces, and the courts—all remained in the hands of the pre-war conservative establishment, again often with dubious wartime links.[8] As in Portugal and Spain, US advisers took over the training of the secret police which, also just like their Iberian counterparts, had previously been trained by Nazi operatives. The Greek military, sealed like Spain's in a sociological cocoon of nostalgic rightism, acquired a huge influence in Greece's long-running quasi-imperial dispute with Turkey over Cyprus, which had become entrenched over the years. This structural continuity explains the gap between the constitutional form of postwar government in Greece and its authoritarian substance: the legal framework, consolidated by Metaxas and utilized by the Nazis, was not altered. The decrees of the 1930s and 1940s went on being used to surveil and subdue all groups who bore the possibility of change in post-1945 Greece.[9]

Here, too, the coalition, emerging victorious from the civil war, used military trials and prison camps as a brutal form of state- and nation-making, in each case generating 'community aliens' as an explicit category. Although a smaller operation than in Spain, it was still considerable.[10] In both countries too, a raft of other apartheid policies were effective in stigmatizing and marginalizing defeated constituencies. Franco's recasting of Republicans as 'anti-nation' and 'barbarian', to be excluded from all but manual employment and denied access to higher education and civic participation generally, was echoed in postwar Greece where the government created a so-called certificate of 'national mindness'[*ethnikofrones*], an official document stating the bearer had no 'leftist sympathies'. Its withholding would debar a person from university or civil service employment, but equally a municipal cleaning lady could lose her job if her brother had gone to the mountains to fight the Germans. The result was a disciplinary model that, as elsewhere, 'worked' not just for the stigmatized sectors, but for the whole of society.

The exclusionary process in Greece, despite its smaller scale, was violent and destructive in one way that makes it unique. Unlike Spain and 'neutral' Portugal, Greece had an explicit history of indigenous anti-fascist and patriotic wartime resistance to violent Nazi occupation, which had taken the form of guerrilla warfare. But Greek conservatives actively set about reconfiguring their own national resistance history by stigmatizing it

---

[8] John O. Iatrides, 'Greece at the Crossroads, 1944–1950', in John O. Iatrides and Linda Wrigley (eds), *Greece at the Crossroads: The Civil War and its Legacy* (University Park, PA: Pennsylvania State University Press, 1995), 22–3.

[9] Ibid., 24.

[10] Official data gives 50,000 prisoners/deportees – 40, 000 to remote islands, 17,000 death sentences and 3000 executions. Figures exclude Makronisos 'reeducation' camp. There were political prisoners until 1974: Mogens Pelt, *Tying Greece to the West: US-West German-Greek Relations, 1949–1974* (Copenhagen: Narayana Press, 2006), 43.

as 'communist subversion'. (The Greek Communist Party was banned in 1947, along with other parties deemed to be of a leftist persuasion.) They did this because it seemed impossible to extract the resistance tradition from its progressive associations. The usefulness of the Cold War was that it gave those opposing domestic change an unassailable alibi. Ideologies of social change had become 'tainted', apparently indelibly, as 'communism'—the tyranny of the geopolitical enemy.

Instead of anti-fascism, the postwar orders in Spain, Portugal and Greece used as ideological cement an ultra-nationalism that was both virulently anti-communist and explicitly founded on religion—whether Catholic or Orthodox. Among small-town populations and rural smallholders, familiar religious values gave comfort, but also inspired awe. The authorities took care, nevertheless, to ratchet up fear by implementing widespread censorship that also maintained rural dwellers in ignorance. A traditional notion of order was thus reinforced, along with a respect for hierarchy. Religious values of this kind were of course explicitly divisive, in Spain especially, where 'National Catholicism' was practised by the dictatorship to 'sanctify' the punishment of Republican prisoners. Some could 'redeem' their sentences as forced labourers, which demonstrates Francoism's historic function—of not blocking but of mediating change. Traditionalist Catholic values justified new forms of social disciplining and the extraction of economic value for national modernization. In Portugal and Greece, rulers still aimed more straightforwardly to build barriers against change by fostering conservative social values through the Churches.[11] But whenever cultural awe proved insufficient, then the Greek political establishment could always fall back upon the direct violence of the 'shadow state' [*parakratos*] to end the argument. This group of paramilitary anti-communist organizations with their origins in German occupation and civil war operated well into the 1960s, intimidating or killing those deemed to be troubling the political and social order.

(ii) Developmentalism as Survival?

> 'It had all changed so much, so fast... What was happening to them in real life was like when they were watching a movie and lost the thread... and couldn't work out how much time had elapsed in between the frames or connect the immediate past with the present racing past them.'
>
> Antonio Muñoz Molina, *El jinete polaco* (1991)

Franco understood that industrialization and economic growth would transform the fabric of society. But the economic disastrousness of his autarkic policies, pursued for

---

[11] António Costa Pinto and Maria Inácia Rezola, 'Political Catholicism, Crisis of Democracy and Salazar's New State in Portugal', *Totalitarian Movements and Political Religions* 8:2 (2007), 358–68.

reasons of domestic politics in the 1940s, provoked a looming state bankruptcy that forced him to embark from the 1950s on economic liberalization. This was sealed by the agreement with the US, which provided military material and financial support in return for allowing American bases on Spanish soil. It saw Spain opened up to international investors, triggering the beginning of a massive industrial expansion.[12] The intensity of this internal transformation would make Francoism more complex. Although the dictator and his old guard never ceased to view Spanish and world politics through a crude lens of conspiracy, once Franco's governments had adopted policies to privilege the emergent white collar managerial sectors of the 1960s, turning them into a support base for the regime, then they inevitably had to incorporate, if ambivalently, a notion of developmentalism as a further legitimizing force, in a way that was not replicated in either Portugal or Greece.

The situation in 1960s Spain was far more 'mobile' than in metropolitan Portugal or in Greece. The massive internal demographic change that accompanied the shift to an industrial base broke up what had historically been the reservoirs of social support for both revolution and traditionalist reaction—the rural landless of Spain's deep south and the smallholding peasantry of the centre-north, respectively. Both were atomized to become the new urban workers of Spain's second industrial revolution. The scale and speed of this process in Spain was brutally disorienting, as the Muñoz Molina epigraph conveys. It ripped apart the social fabric, provoking enduring cultural and psychological effects that have still not been adequately reckoned by today's scholars. The 'time of the poor' during the 1960s was an 'escape forward'. The 'better times' of economic modernity were proffered to 'fill' the void of a lost and 'dangerous' culture. This fear-induced autism was perhaps the Franco regime's most generalized cultural product. Nevertheless, migration, combined with the emergence of urban managerial sectors loyal to Franco, both worked—temporarily at least—to stabilize the regime.

In Portugal, in contrast, the continuing existence of an empire in Asia and Africa (including the discovery of oil off the coast of Angola) provided a buffer against economic uncertainty. This allowed Salazar, with the backing of landowning and commercial elites, to entertain lower levels of development (living standards were well below those of Spain and even Greece) and thus to conserve a relatively more stable and controllable social structure. A direct consequence of this 'static metropolis' was the 'recolonization' of the 1950s and 1960s, as thousands of Portuguese settlers left for the dominions, seeking opportunities they could not find at home. Even larger numbers migrated elsewhere in Europe, allowing Salazar to displace structural unemployment in much the same way as was occurring with Spain and Greece.

While Greek economic and urban development occurred in the 1960s on a significant scale, outstripping Portugal's, it did not compare with the accelerated change occurring

---

[12] Borja de Riquer, 'Social and Economic Change in a Climate of Political Immobilism', in Helen Graham and Jo Labanyi (eds), *Spanish Cultural Studies* (Oxford: Oxford University Press, 1995), 259–71; also Preston, 'Spain', in Graham and Seldon (eds), *Government and Economies*; Gabriel Tortella, *The Development of Modern Spain* (Cambridge, MA: Harvard University Press, 2000).

inside Spain.[13] Most of the US aid received was channelled into military objectives, while Greece's 'excess' population sought its fortune abroad. Even so, the balance between urban and rural populations was virtually reversed between 1951 and 1971, from 38 per cent and 48 per cent, respectively, to 53 per cent and 35 per cent, a shift accompanied by an increase in small service-sector businesses.[14] This eventually brought progressive political forces to power in elections in 1963 and again in 1965, convincing conservatives, backed by a military with the habit and expectation of rule, that shock tactics would be required to pull Greece back from 'apocalypse'. Greeks, unlike the Spanish and Portuguese, could vote for change. However, the army stood ready to prevent democratic forms being invested with democratic content.

The impetus for army intervention in April 1967 was to forestall the return of another progressive government likely to take too permissive a line on Cyprus. But at root the Colonels sought to block change at home in Greece. In a familiar discourse, they claimed to be foiling a communist coup, and acting in the name of 'the traditional values of Helleno-Christian civilization'.[15] The murderous reality was that they purged army officers who were considered to be 'disloyal', school and university teachers, doctors, lawyers, and anyone deemed a political dissident, while shadow state operatives killed some of them. Brutality notwithstanding, the Colonels' anti-communism meant they maintained at least the tacit support of the US and Greece's other NATO allies.

Similar geostrategic fears had also led the US to bankroll Portugal's military expenditure—with the increasing importance of Africa in the Cold War chessboard. The army grew massively through conscription. By 1974 one in four Portuguese males of military age was serving in the armed forces and of those, one in four was stationed overseas. By the 1970s some 50 per cent of Portugal's national expenditure was on maintaining this army which, with secret US support, was engaged in a losing war against national liberation movements in both Mozambique and Angola, the key colonies that were by then propping up Portugal's economy. This bloated army constituted the other face of a static metropolis and recalled what has been the historic dilemma of the Iberian states—the choice between war and domestic reform.

1970S: TRANSITIONS

'Forgetting is full of memory.'
Mario Benedetti

This dilemma in its 1970s variant would be resolved from outside, for the most significant factor in the Southern European transitions to constitutional democracy was the

---

[13] From 1940 to 1965, industrial production in Greece increased fivefold, driven by foreign investment. With an average growth rate of 6 per cent from 1957 to 1966, Greece *outperformed all European countries, except Spain.* Richard Clogg, *A Concise History of Greece*, 2nd edn (Cambridge: Cambridge University Press, 2002), 145–6.

[14] Ibid., 143–6, 152.   [15] Ibid., 163–4.

recession crystallizing with the oil crisis of 1973. Recession acted as a catalyst for existing discontents, producing an intensification of social mobilization in Portugal, Greece, and Spain. Military reactions too played a crucial role—although in diametrically opposed ways. Above all, this new configuration made international actors, especially the US, gradually reassess the political expedience of continuing to prop up the Southern European dictatorships now that they were becoming increasingly internally delegitimized. This was not only among the popular classes and dissident constituencies who had always borne the brunt of their repressive actions, but also among conservative urban middle classes and domestic power elites, precisely because the regimes were no longer able to guarantee either economic prosperity or internal social order. As the crisis made itself felt in inflation and unemployment (the latter exacerbated by returning economic migrants), so the erupting strikes and demonstrations saw events accelerate—although we should be wary about retrospective assumptions that the 'relatively bloodless' aspect of the ensuing transitions was a structural 'given'. In all three, but especially Portugal and Spain, the risk of large-scale violence was present throughout.

Of the three, Spain exhibited the greatest disparity between a dynamic society and a fossilized regime. Accelerated development had shored up Franco in the short to medium term. Ultimately however the cultural transformation thus generated, combined with the society's expectations of increasing material wealth—which the regime was already struggling to fulfil when the oil crisis of 1973 capsized all hope of so doing—provoked a latent crisis of legitimacy. The political situation was blown apart by the assassination in December 1973 of Franco's closest confidant, the acting head of the government, Admiral Luis Carrero Blanco, who was killed by an ETA bomb. Given that Franco was already seriously ill, this immediately plunged the regime's future into uncertainty. The situation was especially acute because Franco's regime, unlike Salazar's, still had the backing of most of the army—and 100,000 members of the Falange, the single party of the dictatorship, were still permitted to carry guns.[16] Again unlike Salazarism, Francoism possessed wider social support: Spain's habitual *uneven* development exacerbated matters, as Franco's apocalyptic propaganda fed the fears of small-town conservatives, including small businesses, now facing economic recession and thus even more dependent on regime preferment and patronage to survive. The potential for a bloodbath was thus great, something which is often 'forgotten' in prevailing accounts.

The Portuguese dictatorship faced a similar challenge by the 1970s—able to offer neither economic well-being nor social peace and in consequence suffering its own crisis of legitimacy. It too had relaxed its economic policy in the 1960s (though not, notably, political repression), thereby generating more inward foreign investment and higher living standards. When growth was suddenly cut short by the oil crisis, responsibility was perceived to be the regime's and as a result, in metropolitan Portugal, it was up against escalating social protest fuelled both by economic hardship and political alienation.

[16] Paul Preston, *The Triumph of Democracy in Spain* (London: Routledge, 1990), 57.

In the months before the revolution of April 1974, 100,000 workers went on strike and thousands of university students organized sit-ins nationwide. The dictatorship reacted by expanding repression and granting extra powers to the political police, now called the DGS (*Direcção Geral de Segurança*). The security forces crushed worker demonstrations and student occupations, closing clubs and cultural associations in an attempt to stifle dissent. Like Franco, Salazarism resorted to violence until the very end. But unlike in Spain, the death penalty was not used in the metropolis. Francoism, which had colonized its own metropolis, executed its opponents right up to the end. The Portuguese equivalent of this deadly force still resided in its colonies, although it was about to make a spectacular return to the metropolis.

The war in Africa had reached huge levels of violence and outright atrocity. Even official reports recorded that for Angola alone between 1963 and 1970, 26,000 people were taken prisoner, routinely tortured, used as human guinea pigs for mine detection, and most of them later shot.[17] Increasingly, these atrocities were being exposed, including through the efforts of the Catholic Church in Portugal. Abroad too there was lobbying against Portuguese companies. But it was the Portuguese army, caught up for thirteen years in a bloody unpopular struggle that they knew to be unwinnable, that eventually proved decisive. Colonial frustrations channelled through the army would be the factor dictating the singular course of Portugal's transition, investing it—albeit temporarily—with a revolutionary elan. On 25 April 1974 officers of the *Movimento das Forças Armadas* (MFA) entered Lisbon atop tanks, and, unopposed, ended Salazar's *Estado Novo* virtually with one blow. In fact, they did even more, for what happened in Portugal profoundly influenced events in Greece. Similarly, the MFA coup concentrated the minds of reformist Francoists to take the initiative early, the better to control the process of change.

The US was caught off guard by the events in Portugal, partly because of other foreign crises, but mostly because it was turned inward upon its own domestic problems (culminating in near presidential impeachment after the Watergate scandal). Its apparent paralysis meant that the transition process in Portugal happened without any real input from Washington. Indeed the US failure to grasp the seismic nature of what was supervening became more than clear three months later, when, in July 1974, the Greek Colonels, faced by mounting economic discontent at home and seeking to drum up support, staged a coup in Cyprus. They imposed the ultra-right-wing journalist and convicted murderer Nicos Sampson as the new dictator, whereupon the US came close to recognizing him. But the Turkish invasion of the northern part of the island, provoked by this clumsy and violent bid to enforce *enosis*, led the Americans to a rapid strategic recalculation. The events were an embarrassment for NATO, especially the Colonels' refusal to allow US mediation between Greece and Turkey, both NATO members. Blind to their weakness, the Colonels still saw an imperial venture in Cyprus as a 'magic bullet' that could undo the effects of social change in Greece. They thus insisted on a military counter-response to the Turkish invasion. It turned into a shambles, with many senior

[17] Loff, 'Los regímenes autoritarios', 151.

officers refusing to obey. This loss of confidence by military elites inevitably meant the end of the road for the dictatorship, which collapsed on 24 July 1974. Just like its counterparts in Spain and Portugal, it found itself no longer able to guarantee either economic prosperity or social peace. For all the US government's initial ambivalence over Greece, it had no real interest in propping up the Salazar regime since, with Portuguese military disaffection running high, the dictatorship no longer offered any solution to American strategic concerns in the guerrilla war against Soviet-backed forces in Angola and Mozambique; but nor, given its radical tenor, did the MFA-led revolution augur a palatable replacement.

It was clearly Salazar's own long-running immobilist strategy, maintained into the 1970s, that gave the Portuguese revolution its highly explosive quality—the confluence of any number of things staved off for too long. Radicalized officers and angry conscripts from the colonial campaigns were a returning fireball that struck the petroleum of mass landlessness in Southern Portugal, added to which was the anger of new urban sectors—industrial workers suffering poor living and labour conditions and also poorly paid, along with almost equally disaffected urban service sectors. This mounting mobilization had also seen the growth of the Portuguese Communist Party (PCP), which, having become the main force of the democratic opposition, came to the fore to collaborate with the MFA.

But what gave the revolution of April 1974 its compelling force was the MFA itself, which remained throughout both the engine and limit-maker. The initial revolutionary impetus of the coup, and the sheer angry energy inhabiting the MFA, brought to its fore the junior officers, many of whom were politically radicalized by their experiences in the colonial war to the extent of becoming political sympathizers with the eclectic Marxism of the African independence movements. The days following the coup in Lisbon saw tanks with their gun barrels adorned with red carnations, as popular supporters of the revolution flooded the streets. Beneath the carnations and carnival, the MFA and PCP drove forward serious structural change, nationalizing the banking system and promoting agrarian reform. The revolution's radical élan also meant that in Portugal not only were the institutions of dictatorship dismantled—the single party, the official youth organization and, above all, the hated political police (PIDE/DGS)—but there was also a purge of the regime's other personnel (including civil servants and some conservative army officers), as well as of civilian collaborators—something that would not occur in Spain or Greece. Indeed, in Portugal the purges extended further, encompassing industrialists and entrepreneurs: panic spread like wildfire through Portugal's economic elites,[18] giving conservative reformists in Spain and Greece pause for serious strategic thought.

If the US seemed paralysed in the face of Portuguese events, not so the Greek conservative establishment. Its leading light, Constantine Karamanlis, who had led postwar conservative governments from 1955 until 1964, saw the writing on the wall and with

---

[18] António Costa Pinto, 'Political Purges and State Crisis in Portugal's Transition to Democracy, 1975–76', *Journal of Contemporary History* 43:2 (2008), 310–20.

speed and daring, returned from his Paris exile to make a reverse 'constitutional coup'. This was accepted grudgingly even by the Greek army. Karamanlis' actions were possible because of the widespread fear among Greece's conservative establishment, and also its economic elites, some parts of which had supported the 1967 coup, that in the dangerous vacuum following the Colonels' discredit and fall, they were potentially vulnerable to a scenario like the one playing out in Portugal.[19] Their fears in July 1974 shaped events, even though, looking back, military attitudes remain the crucial *difference* between the Portuguese and Greek cases.

Benefiting from Karamanlis' speed, which gave the opposition no time to organize, his conservative forces won the elections in November 1974 with 54.5 per cent of the vote. Therefore, unlike Portugal, no new political class took control in Greece (although the monarchy was jettisoned) and no entrepreneurs were sanctioned for collaboration. Karamanlis did release all political prisoners and legalize the Communist Party prior to the elections, as another establishment insider, Adolfo Suárez, would do later in Spain— also using speed as a weapon against the extreme right, just as he would use his insider knowledge to steal an electoral march over the left. Suárez, unlike Karamanlis, would have to pact with the left, because he needed its support against die-hard Francoist sectors, especially those in the army with a still bullish sense of their own possibilities— something the Cyprus debacle had ripped away from their Greek counterparts.

The new Greek government did not, however, punish the crimes of the dictatorship other than symbolically. Judicial proceedings were restricted to the leaders of the 1967 coup.[20] No other servant of the state had to answer for human rights violations committed under the Colonels or before. Post-transition Greece became a multi-party parliamentary democracy, but this did not translate into the democratization of the state. As in post-Franco Spain, there was a continuity of state personnel, civil servants, and security forces that lasted for over a decade and, in terms of institutional culture, for much longer. In contrast, in Greece there was an appearance of greater justice because the Colonels were put on trial, while in Spain the Franco state remained untouchable. Suárez's October 1977 amnesty was loaded in plain sight: it forgave those who imprisoned and tortured political dissenters, as it 'forgave' their victims. Suárez's interlocutors on the democratic left accepted the deal because it was the price of transition in a country where a still largely pro-Francoist military establishment risked having the last word.

In Portugal, reversing the revolution was made easier by an intensifying economic crisis, further exacerbated by the return of a million destitute Portuguese refugees from the colonies, which were now on the fast track to independence. The presence inside Portugal of a deeply conservative small peasantry in the north, still *in situ*, unlike their

[19] Stylianos Hadjiyannis, 'Democratization and the Greek State', in Ronald H. Chilcote (ed.), *Transitions from Dictatorship to Democracy* (New York: Taylor and Francis, 1990), 138–9.

[20] Nicos D. Aliviziatos and P. Nikiforos Dimandoros, 'Politics and the Judiciary and the Greek Transition to Democracy', in James McAdams (ed.), *Transitional Justice and the Rule of Law in New Democracies* (Notre Dame, IN: University of Notre Dame, 1997), 27–60.

Spanish equivalents, combined with the mainly conservative *retornados*, provided a domestic coalition of forces that offered appalled western power brokers an opportunity to defuse the revolution, assisted too by the deep internal fissures within the revolutionary coalition. Crucially, a more conservative faction emerged inside the MFA. These officers were nationalists of a new sort, disgusted at the dictatorship for insisting on unfeasible colonial wars that undermined the *patria* when what the new times required was Portugal's redefinition. Backed by the socialists, these MFA moderates oversaw a gradual return to civilian control. By April 1976 there was a new democratic constitution and slowly the remnants of MFA radicalism were purged from Portugal's constitutional arrangements.

By April 1976 Spain's transition was also underway, the death of Franco in November 1975 removing both the real and the symbolic impediment to change. Under the tutelage of Suárez, a one-time Falangist civil governor, the dismantling of the dictatorial institutions was negotiated with startling speed by December. Suárez bargained the political support of the democratic left—socialists and communists—against their legalization, a prison amnesty, and a set of promised structural economic reforms—though these latter never materialized. While socialists and communists both supported Suárez, creatively pressuring him to prove his democratizing credentials, Suárez relied on fast footwork, his inside knowledge of the system, and his talents as a wheeler-dealer to keep the extreme right at bay. Given the continuing power of Francoist loyalists—collectively known as the 'bunker'—Suárez's daring outstripped that of Karamanlis. The continuing presence of a reform-accepting king who was also Commander-in-Chief of the armed forces, and whom the bunker still saw as a guarantee of Francoist continuity, also assisted Suárez, who was thus able to speed through his reforms 'under cover'. In a sense, the transition in Spain was more difficult than the others, yet also easier because, already by the late 1960s, it was a society 'in waiting', both for its urban and cultural diversity, but also because its most dynamic business sectors were already looking to Europe as a guarantee of continuing opportunities for growth.

Nor was it only in Spain that EEC membership played a key role in stabilizing the new constitutional system on an economically and socially more conservative base. In Greece and Portugal too, integration to the EEC as a marketplace was presented not only positively as the seal of democratic consolidation, but also negatively as an 'antidote' to resurgent civil conflict. Once again, fear was being mobilized as a means of limiting change: in Portugal from 1976 the constitutional governments dismantled the MFA's revolution by reversing agrarian reform and re-privatizing industry and commerce, and justified themselves in the name of democratic normalization and European integration. In Greece too, Karamanlis used his pro-EEC policies as an electoral device against socialists and communists—who initially opposed integration. In the late 1970s, heading up his 'new' conservative party, Karamanlis bluntly—and revealingly—stated his determination to industrialize the country and to 'Europeanize' the Greeks 'by force if necessary'.[21]

---

[21] Christopher, M. Woodhouse, *Modern Greece: A Short History* (London: Faber and Faber, 1986), 315.

Significantly too, in none of the new Southern European democracies was there ever a reckoning with the old terror. In Portugal, the revolution had seen popular assaults on the headquarters of the hated political police, on the censors' HQ, and on other state agencies associated with Salazar's repressive machinery. However, only a minority of PIDE/DGS operatives ever stood trial and even then they received minor sentences. In Greece and Spain there was no release of surveillance files. Pre-transition Greece had possessed more citizen-informers per head of population than the DDR, and the Portuguese dictatorship deployed similar levels to Greece.[22] While the more bureaucratic and impersonal forms of Greek surveillance likely made them less psychologically damaging than in East Germany, the result was the same in both cases—discrimination and social apartheid.[23] Ordinary Greeks were policing and informing on their compatriots for the usual web of ugly motives— ideological and otherwise—that are to be found wherever forms of everyday terror obtain. The citizen–informer statistic is noteworthy too for what its very obscurity and unexpectedness tell us about our asymmetrical images of western and eastern totalitarianism.

While these observations do not diminish the value of constitutional reform and the emergence of multi-party democracy in Southern Europe, the problem is that these transitions stopped short, at the stage of technical superstructural change. While essential, this could not constitute a sufficient prerequisite for a healthy pluralist democracy in the medium to long term. For, in the end, democracy requires not just a form or system, but a participatory content or practice, and the key to this practice is the cultivation of an active civil society. Instead, the modes of Southern European transition resembled a nineteenth-century politics of notables—arrangements made between political elites (even if these sometimes included oppositional forces) where the result, if not the express objective, was to contain already occurring forms of mass political mobilization, revolutionary or otherwise. It is also thus unsurprising that the cultural concomitant of this transitional model was an exhortation to look forward, not back— encapsulated in the PSOE's slogan 'for change' during the landscape-changing elections of October 1982. We can read these at least in part as a re-inscription of the 'flight forward' that had underpinned the upheavals of migration and industrialization from the 1960s onwards.

Indeed one could argue that the 'promise' of EEC entry itself was offered to the populations of Southern Europe in the 1980s not just as providing economic growth and a (post-crisis) future of consumerist plenty, but also, implicitly, as a substitute for any unpredictable and potentially destabilizing engagement with the 'difficult past'. So EEC criteria saw not only the disappearance from the political agenda of redistributive

---

[22] Pelt, *Tying Greece to the West*, 44; Kenneth Maxwell, *The Making of Portuguese Democracy* (Cambridge: Cambridge University Press, 1997), 69–70.

[23] Minas Samatas, 'Studying Surveillance in Greece: Methodological and Other Problems Related to an Authoritarian Surveillance Culture', *Surveillance & Society* 3:2–3 (2005), 181–97 (189 for comparative observations).

structural reform—witness the uneven outcome of Spain's Moncloa Pacts—but also promoted cultural and social demobilization. This continued to ensure invisibility within the historical reckoning for the murderous basis of post-World War II western 'stability' and 'plenty'—whether the gulag in Spain, or the high social cost (one should probably call it structural violence) of mass migration from all Southern European societies, or carnage in Portugal's colonial territories, or extrajudicial murder and the 'disappeared' in Cyprus.

On this reading, the managerial modes of the 1970s transitions—which in the end supervened in Portugal as well as Greece and Spain—were models posited not as alternatives to resurgent civil war, but as alternatives to democratic memory itself. By this we mean a publicly circulating understanding of the past that encompasses in full the human stories of the cost of historical change. If one accepts this as an ethical baseline, then working through the 'difficult past' is also an integral part of an inclusive and fully participatory democracy. At its simplest, then, the western transitions remained unfinished into the 1980s because the postwar 'selves'/histories that underlay them were still un-reckoned, as Benedetti's epigraph resonantly recalls. There was no basis on which to make the transition at all—if by this we mean a process of deepening democratic culture in the everyday lives of citizens (or indeed of creating citizens through the exercise of those faculties). This suspended state was in part attributable to the Cold War effect of 'freezing time'. The transitions of the 1970s and early 1980s were still part of that older political and psychological landscape, which is why a key function of the post-1989 memory wave has been to 'open up the past' in Southern Europe—particularly in Spain, whose full-blown memory wars are the most spectacular examples of the unfinished business of the transitions.

AFTER 1989: MEMORY

'For violence is not just a "mode" of civil warfare that dissipates thereafter, it can be an enduring consequence too. It can leave an indelible track which saturates social relationships, vitiating the fabric of psychic and emotional life.'

Reflections on Michael Taussig's *Law in a Lawless Land,* 2003

'Luckily for you my son, we stopped being afraid a long time ago in Spain.'

Pedro Almodóvar, *Carne Trémula,* 1997

For as long as the Cold War division of Europe held, it impeded the reckoning with Southern Europe's 'difficult past' in mainstream politics and the media. Thus, as late as the 1980s, when Andreas Papandreou's successor social democratic administration

(PASOK) sought to promote national reconciliation by rehabilitating the anti-fascist tradition and recognizing Greek communists as part of the national resistance movement, they were opposed by the conservatives of New Democracy (ND) who accused Papandreou of 'fomenting discord among Greeks'.[24] Intranational disagreements over how to interpret past events are a reality, but the accusation was a coded warning: manipulating the old fear, the ND was reminding everyone that, as far as they were concerned, those memory wars had already been won and neither PASOK nor anyone else had the right to challenge the status quo. This dynamic could be seen in the 1985 elections too when PASOK accused the ND's leader Konstantinos Mitsotakis of collaborating with the Nazis. The ND retorted that a PASOK election victory would mean either another civil war or another military coup.[25] One could read this interaction flatly as 'the continuing influence of the civil war as a component in contemporary party political battles', but there is a deeper significance in the unevenness of the exchange. The ND's response glanced past PASOK's claim, to issue a threat: if you insist on revisiting these questions, then the result will have to be violence.

Even with the Cold War freeze, those Greek, Spanish, and (to a lesser extent) Portuguese constituencies who bore the brunt of this past through suffering it in their own lives were able to enact commemoration, as many had been doing for years, either in private spaces or ceremonies, or indeed in other countries and hemispheres for the civil wars (especially Spain's), produced an exile that crossed the European and American continents. An ideological freeze however did block any wider dissemination or understanding of the experiences of these memory communities within their respective national arenas—for that required willing interlocutors, something in relatively scarce supply prior to 1989. It was the fall of the Berlin Wall and communism that, by destroying the symbolic charge of Cold War discourse, created these interlocutors en masse.

But the immediate focus post-1989 was quite naturally on the overthrow of communist regimes in Central and Eastern Europe, and the exposure of their thoroughgoing and everyday tyrannies. So there seemed little in the immediate aftermath to unsettle the non-reckoning still prevalent in Southern Europe. Indeed, the status quo appeared initially confirmed by an emergent conservative revisionism that undertook direct comparisons between 'fascist' and communist dictatorships, representing them as analogous and thereby sanitizing non-communist forms of totalitarianism, without ever confronting or properly analysing what the fascist pasts of most European countries had actually *meant*, and at whose cost. (This kind of revisionism also led to some notorious instances of obviating historical context and chronology, for example, in the revisionist 'equating' of the violent actions of the Italian anti-fascist resistance with those of the Social Republic.) In terms of its tactical goal too, this discourse blended imperceptibly into another, more familiar one, urging people to 'overcome the past' by resolutely *not*

[24] David Close, 'The Road to Reconciliation? The Greek Civil War and the Politics of Memory in the 1980s', in Philip Carabott and Thanasis D. Sfikas (eds), *The Greek Civil War: Essays on a Conflict of Exceptionalism and Silences* (Aldershot: Ashgate, 2004), 257–78.

[25] Close, 'The Road to Reconciliation?', 257, 278.

looking back, and which thus resonated strongly with earlier notions of the necessary 'flight forward' into economic development and away from 'terror'. To this end, the old fear was still sometimes pressed into service too: in 1986 in Spain, when socialist Prime Minister Felipe González sought to turn around the national vote and bring in a referendum result in favour of Spain's NATO membership, he virtually constituted a new national audience *in fear*, as he warned that the cost of not 'moving on' would be civil conflict, national failure, and apocalypse.

The precedent for this flight from the past had been clearly set in Spain with the so-called 'pact of silence', on which the technical transition and amnesty of the late 1970s was founded. Yet in spite of it, the cunning of civil society asserted itself slowly but unmistakeably from the margins, with the first tentative commemorations in the early 1980s of the extrajudicially murdered victims of Francoism, a wave of films explicitly about the civil war, memoirs of political prisoners, and the first accounts of deportees to Nazi concentration camps, which it had been impossible to publish in Spain prior to the 1980s. Also, as early as 1977, the now iconic comic strip *Paracuellos* appeared, provocatively named—for Paracuellos, the village outside Madrid where the Republicans shot military and civilian prisoners during the wartime siege of the capital, constituted a major plank of the Francoist martyrology. In the comics, Paracuellos is a state orphanage in the same location in the 1940s, where a group of impoverished children, sometimes from Republican families, but always from the urban and rural poor, endure the petty tyrannies and everyday barbarism of Franco's new order, as it taught them their station in life.

From these early cultural beginnings, the excavation of the difficult past grew apace across the decade and into the 1990s. Perhaps its most remarkable feature was an outpouring of detailed, empirical works by historians—some professional, but many more working entirely outside academia. From forgotten, often mouldering, documentation in local archives they produced a record of the Francoist repression, naming the dead from municipal registers and cemetery lists and thereby recreating a history for which the analogous sources in state repositories no longer existed. By the new millennium this expanding historical record was both driving, and being further driven by, the labours of a burgeoning memory movement rooted in civil pressure groups, who demanded the exhumation of the Republican 'disappeared' from the common graves that lie all across Spain, so that the remains could be identified and reburied by family and friends.[26] This grassroots movement predated the international tectonic shift of 1989, but that shift would bring it centre stage in Spain, making available an increasingly mainstream audience nationwide; in turn this provoked a series of fierce memory wars, which continue to rage.

These memory wars are not only greater in scale and intensity than anything occurring in Greece or Portugal, as might be expected from the larger scale of Francoist repression; they are also qualitatively unique. The reasons for this are complex to

---

[26] Helen Graham, *The Spanish Civil War: A Very Short Introduction* (Oxford: Oxford University Press, 2005), 140–4.

untangle. Certainly the lack in Spain, unlike in Greece, of any 'screen', or 'alibi' of foreign occupation is one important factor explaining their singular power and intensity. (Portugal in this respect is out of the comparison, having never experienced modern war on its metropolitan territory.) What is ultimately at stake is political legitimacy measured against the depth of social hurt done. The Spanish case involved the most extensive social damage and yet, at the same time, Francoism retained—arguably still retains—legitimacy well into present times. Franco was never defeated in any war. Moreover, the longevity of the dictatorship, the unparalleled opportunities it had to shape cultural memory and/or public perceptions *for forty years*, and also the retrospective sense of the smoothness of Spain's 'pacted' transition, all explain the residual legitimacy of Francoism, and not only among ideological supporters.

At the same time, the consolidation of a constitutional system in Spain has allowed the safe resurgence of an older cultural memory borne by a Republican nation, forged in the 1930s, in war and afterwards in exile, as the memory of a different future. These memories—plural, not singular—have become intergenerational 'memories' too, for it is young Spaniards who predominate in the civic movement to excavate the mass graves of Republicans. They lie, thus, under 'the grandchild's gaze', and, as such, the issue is no longer only one of an unquiet past (i.e. of emotional closure for the victims' families), it has also become a litmus test for participatory democracy in Spain today. The historical memory law of 2007, for all its limitations, does provide for a state census, for counting the dead and the disappeared, which builds on the numerous civic projects already in train for naming all those who were traduced by the dictatorial state, including the thousands of Republican Spaniards deported, at the Franco regime's behest, to Nazi camps. This memory work is consolidating a new dimension of contemporary democratic practice—as a *constitutional pact between the living and the unquiet dead*. It remains controversial, producing bruising confrontations in the arena of civil society—a space which Francoism sought, but ultimately failed, to annihilate, but which is still today shaped by the mind games of the dictatorship. But the civic memory movement remains hugely empowered, above all by its ability to call things by their rightful name. To date it has confronted what Franco's state did to the defeated, unpicking its poisonous 'discourse of barbarians'. But that process will only be complete the day it also unravels its identical twin, the 'discourse of martyrs', thus disenthralling the 'victors' too from the spell of a malevolent state.

This full-on broaching of the issues is what makes the Spanish case different, although that does not in itself explain the relative lack of public stocktaking in Greece of what brutal state- and nation-building cost those excluded in its name. Less even again do the ghosts of 'distant' colonial violence seem to disturb daily politics in Portugal today. The reason the violent past remains 'closer' in Spain is partly the absence of the aforementioned 'screen memory'; but mainly it is because of the unprecedented way in which the violence and 'prison universe' once inhabited every inch of the metropolis, was enshrined at the heart of dictatorial legitimacy, and was ceaselessly reiterated by the Franco regime. By the same token, a live Republican memory at once transmits, and is a testimony to, how much was lost in Spain.

In Greece, in contrast, where the postwar polity was, if vindictive, nevertheless relatively less monolithic, one could argue that the *outright political and military humiliation* of the Colonels, faced by 'imperial' defeat in Cyprus, made the subsequent work of 'disenthralling' much easier than in Spain. Greece has thus been able leap a stage and achieve potentially more sophisticated forms of national reconciliation because there has come about a generalized understanding that there is no need for, *nor can there be*, a single agreed narrative representing 'the truth of the past'. Instead, the emphasis has been on correcting perceived injustices and allowing the free circulation of differing interpretations of that past within a democratic environment.[27] Books dealing with the memory of the civil war flooded the market throughout the 1990s, as, in academic studies, a new trend emerged focusing on local histories of wartime, or questions of ethnic or gender identity therein.[28] The new approaches of younger scholars were polemical and often fruitful in that they challenged assumptions, enabling the war to be seen 'against the grain'. But there is a danger inherent in such fragmentation—that it also serves as a screen to avoid talking about what fascist totalitarianism did and with what consequences.

In Greece, too, there are still clear democratic deficits, as manifest, for example, in the 1980s debate over the fate of police surveillance files identifying citizen-informers. In real terms it was an impoverished 'non-debate' which drowned in party politics without ever addressing the huge ethical and political implications of opening—or not opening—the files. In the end, these files are presumed mainly burned in 1989 (or digitized?).[29] We can now see that the decision to open the DDR files turned out to be almost unique in the Central/Eastern European context. While in Spain, as in Greece, the 'evaporation' of surveillance files (they remain sealed in the AGA (State Archives) in Alcalá de Henares, near Madrid) is facilitated by the lack of concern exhibited by succeeding mainstream generations not only towards past abuses of state power but also towards current issues of state management of personal data.[30]

The issue of surveillance files is a thorny one, and as such it epitomizes the real dilemma of openly confronting the difficult past—because it means acknowledging the extent of 'everyday barbarism', the complicity of ordinary nationals in the repression of their compatriots. But the price of not confronting it has likely fed a galloping political passivity. Recent research by political scientists suggests that the failure to investigate, and/or the rapid rehabilitation of regime personnel, especially security police, has fomented civic disengagement and an uncritical acceptance of the prevailing 'order', as well as (especially in Southern Europe) the continuation of rampant

---

[27] Peter Siani-Davies and Stefanos Katsikas, 'National Reconciliation after Civil War: The Case of Greece', *Journal of Peace Research* 46:4 (2009), 559–75.

[28] Nikos Marantzidis and Giorgos Antoniou, 'The Axis Occupation and Civil War: Changing Trends in Greek Historiography, 1941–2002', *Journal of Peace Research* 41:2, (2004), 228–9.

[29] Samatas, 'Studying Surveillance in Greece', 194.

[30] Ibid., 187–95; the folly of this unconcern in Spain is also a major theme in Isaac Rosa's novel *El vano ayer* (Barcelona: Seix Barral, 2004).

political clientelism, and the viewing of political and state questions cynically as part of a *Systemzeit*.[31]

In turn, these attitudes have eased the rapid rise in the 1990s of forms of ultra-nationalism that—in Southern Europe, just as in the Centre and East—depend on an absence of knowledge about the recent past. In Portugal, opinion movements related to the victims of the dictatorship remain relatively marginalized, whereas the commemoration of the twentieth anniversary of the revolution in 1994 saw the beginning of a concerted attempt by former regime personnel and new-generation conservatives to rehabilitate the Salazar dictatorship as efficient, patriotic, and even 'gentle'. In 1999 José Hermano Saraiva, a former Minister of Education, declared Salazar was 'a true anti-fascist', while General Kaúlza de Arriaga, part of the Portuguese high command in Africa, publicly denied that the well documented massacre of Wiriamu (Mozambique) had ever happened.[32]

But as in Spain, so too in twenty-first-century Portugal there is now, post-dictatorship, a civic space in which such pronouncements can be refuted and their underlying assumptions contested. In 2005 the first civic association for the preservation of historical memory appeared, *Não apaguem a memória* (don't switch memory off). This called for the preservation of symbolic buildings (especially those of the PIDE/DGS), the foundation of a National Museum of the Resistance, the creation of monuments dedicated to the political prisoners, and a more complete treatment of the dictatorship's policies and crimes in school textbooks. Writers, sculptors, painters, and filmmakers too have begun to focus on the dictatorship's last years, especially the colonial wars. In so doing, they have begun the work of 'disremembering' the dictatorship, by unravelling the links Salazar made between Portuguese national identity and the country's imperial past.[33]

CONCLUSION

The post-World War II polities in Spain, Portugal, and Greece have now begun to be adjudged, including in terms of their complex relationship to the violence of 'empire'. Greek autocrats, Salazar, and Franco all consistently criminalized those of their citizens who had been actively anti-Nazi. From 1989 onwards, a gradual, if often uneven, 'thaw' has occurred, thus permitting a democratic stocktaking, long after the technical transitions. As the fear retreated, other stories of the war and its long aftermath of uncivil

---

[31] See studies cited by Irene Pimentel, 'A memória pública da dictadura e da repressão', *Le Monde Diplomatique*, 8 February 2007 (Portuguese Edition), online at: http://pt.mondediplo.com/spip.php?article146, accessed August 2010.

[32] Manuel Loff, 'Esquecimento, revisão da História e revolta da memoria', in Iva Delgado et al., *De Pinochet a Timor Lorosae. Impunidade e Direito à Memória* (Lisbon: Fundação Humberto Delgado/Edições Cosmos, 2000), 196–7.

[33] Ellen W. Sapega, 'Remembering Empire/Forgetting the Colonies: Accretions of Memory and the Limits of Commemoration in a Lisbon Neighborhood', *History and Memory* 20:2 (2008), 18–38.

peace have emerged into the democratic public sphere. But how this might develop is an open question: there is never a fixed point for historical assessment, and as ultra-nationalism goes from strength to strength in zones of Europe central and eastward, then it reverberates back on these processes of historical recuperation in the south. Nationalist conservatives in power in Poland have claimed Franco as a kindred spirit, while simultaneously denouncing Polish International Brigaders who fought for the democratic Spanish Republic. Indeed, there can be few clearer indications that the reckoning with the difficult past is not only incomplete but also unpredictable than the small advert which appeared on 13 December 2009 in *La Razón*, Spain's nationwide Catholic daily newspaper, *and without any ensuing polemic in the political mainstream*: it was a fulsome commemorative death notice to SS-Aufseherin Irma Grese, sentenced at the Belsen trial and executed on that day in 1945, which read—'your death was unjust and unnecessary and you deserve to be commemorated. I hope to see you one day in Heaven, with your sweet smile. *Hasta siempre*.'[34]

FURTHER READING

Aguilar, Paloma, *Memory and Amnesia: The Role of the Spanish Civil War in the Transition to Democracy* (Oxford: Berghahn, 2002).

Casanova, Julián, Francisco Espinosa, Conxita Mir and Francisco Moreno Gómez, *Morir, matar, sobrevivir. La violencia en la dictadura de Franco* (Barcelona: Crítica, 2004, 2008).

Castillo, Michel del, *Tanguy, Histoire d' un enfant d' aujourd'hui* (Paris: Gallimard, 1957). (English translation, *A Child of Our Time* (New York: Alfred A. Knopf, 1958)).

Costa Pinto, António, *Salazar's Dictatorship and European Fascism. Problems of Interpretation* (New York: Columbia University Press, 1995).

Delgado, Iva, Manuel Loff, António Cluny, Carlos Pacheco and Ricardo Monteiro (eds), *De Pinochet a Timor Lorosae. Impunidade e direto à memoria* (Lisbon: Edições Cosmos, 2000).

Graham, Helen, *The War and its Shadow. Spain's Civil War in Europe's Long Twentieth Century* (Brighton/Portland/Toronto: Sussex Academic Press, 2012).

Graham, Helen, 'The Uses of History', in Helen Graham, *The Spanish Civil War: A Very Short Introduction* (Oxford: Oxford University Press, 2005), 138–50.

Graham, Helen and Jo Labanyi (eds), *Spanish Cultural Studies. An Introduction* (Oxford: Oxford University Press, 1995).

Juliá, Santos (ed.), *La memoria de la guerra y del franquismo* (Madrid: Taurus, 2006).

Kalyvas, Stathis N., *The Logic of Violence in Civil War* (Cambridge: Cambridge University Press, 2006).

Labanyi, Jo, 'Memory and Modernity in Democratic Spain: The Difficulty of Coming to Terms with the Spanish Civil War', *Poetics Today* 28:1 (2007), 89–116.

Labanyi, Jo (ed.), *The Politics of Memory in Contemporary Spain*, special issue of *Journal of Spanish Cultural Studies* 9:2 (2008).

Lewis, Norman, *Voices of the Old Sea* (London: Hamish Hamilton, 1984).

Mazower, Mark (ed.), *After the War was Over: Reconstructing the Family, Nation and State in Greece 1943–1960* (Princeton, NJ: Princeton University Press, 2000).

[34] http://observatorioantisemitismo.fcje.org/?m=200912, accessed August 2010.

Molinero, Carme et al. (eds), *Una inmensa prisión. Los campos de concentración y las prisiones durante la guerra civil y el franquismo* (Barcelona: Crítica, 2003).

Moreno Julià, Xavier, *La División Azul. Sangre española en Rusia, 1941–1945* (Barcelona: Editorial Crítica, 2004).

Papadakis, Yiannis, *Echoes from the Dead Zone: Across the Cyprus Divide* (London: I.B. Taurus, 2005).

Pimentel, Irene, *Víctimas de Salazar: Estado Novo e Vigilância Política* (Lisbon: Esfera dos Livros, 2007).

Preston, Paul, *The Spanish Holocaust* (London: HarperCollins, 2012).

Richards, Michael, 'Grand Narratives, Collective Memory, and Social History: Public Uses of the Past in Post-war Spain', in Carlos Jerez Farrán and Samuel Amago (eds), *Unearthing Franco's Legacy: Mass Graves and the Recovery of Historical Memory in Spain* (Notre Dame, IN: University of Notre Dame Press, 2010).

Rodrigo, Javier, *Cautivos. Campos de concentración en la España franquista, 1936–1947* (Barcelona: Crítica, 2005).

Rosa, Isaac, *El vano ayer* (Barcelona: Seix Barral, 2004).

Roudometof, Victor, *Collective Memory, National Identity, and Ethnic Conflict: Greece, Bulgaria, and the Macedonian Question* (Westport, CT: Praeger, 2002).

Sánchez Cervelló, Josep, 'El nudo gordiano del régimen: Marcelo Caetano y la cuestión colonial', *Espacio Tiempo y Forma*, Serie V. *Historia Contemporánea* 19 (2007), 103–14.

Voglis, Polymeris, 'Political Prisoners in the Greek Civil War, 1945–1950: Greece in Comparative Perspective', *Journal of Contemporary History* 37:4 (2002), 523–40.

CHAPTER 25

....

WHAT COMES AFTER COMMUNISM?

....

MICHAEL SHAFIR

Two things are certain in life: the first is death and the other is uncertainty. The corps of 'sovietologists' to which this author once belonged is nowadays largely a corpse. This is because it so miserably failed to predict the death of its object of observation. The reasons for that failure are manifold, but one of them stands out in particular: 'mainstream' political science (with all its institutional benefits, not least among them academic tenure) had run out of patience with 'oddities' that allegedly belonged to the 'outdated' disciplines of 'area studies'. A related factor was the effort to 'leave behind' the 'totalitarian model', as the world was perceived to be growing into a convergent complexity.[1] Unwisely, we complied and died.

Twenty years on, a plethora of coroners agree on some of the pathological findings while disagreeing on others—mostly on what precipitated the patient's death. Not ours, but our former patient's. Neither the identity nor the location of that patient is clear by now. Was it communism or socialism that succumbed in 1989?[2] Was communism dead in 1989, when the 'Sinatra Doctrine' ('each does it his own way') replaced the Brezhnev Doctrine in East Central Europe?[3] Or did the patient agonize until the official

---

[1] For a harsh, but mostly fair, indictment of 'sovietology', see Walter Laqueur, *The Dream that Failed: Reflections on the Soviet Union* (Oxford: Oxford University Press, 1994), 77–130.

[2] Compare, for example, Archie Brown, *The Rise &Fall of Communism* (London: Bodley Head, 2009) with Katherine Verdery, *What Was Socialism and What Comes Next?* (Princeton, NJ: Princeton University Press, 1996) or Valerie Bunce, *Subversive Institutions: The Design and Destruction of Socialism and the State* (Cambridge: Cambridge University Press, 1999).

[3] For instance J. F. Brown, *Surge to Freedom : The End of Communist Rule in Eastern Europe* (Durham, NC: Duke University Press, 1991); Gale Stokes, *The Walls Came Trembling Down* (Oxford: Oxford University Press, 1993); Timothy Garton Ash, *The Magic Lantern: The Revolutions of '89 Witnessed in Warsaw, Budapest, Berlin and Prague* (New York: Vintage Books, 1993); Harald Wydra, *Communism and the Emergence of Democracy* (Cambridge: Cambridge University Press, 2006).

dismemberment of the Soviet Union in 1991?[4] To be sure, there are some remarkable attempts to combine the collapse in both locations, indeed to see it as interconnected.[5] Still, many questions remain. Why did the Soviet model (or at least the ideology on which it claimed to be based and to function) prove so attractive to intellectuals East and West, even after its shadowy side emerged for all but the blind to see?[6] Indeed, why is it still attractive, whether this is openly acknowledged or not?[7]

Most tricky of all: does communism have a future, and if yes, in what form or format? Twenty-seven countries share a communist past in Europe and Asia. Of the surviving five, not all would pass the 'Leninist test'. Having identified six 'defining features' of communist systems (the monopoly of power of the Communist Party; democratic centralism; non-capitalist ownership of the means of production; the dominance of a command economy, as distinct from a market economy; the declared aim of building communism; and the existence of, and sense of belonging to, an international communist movement[8]), Archie Brown concludes that twenty years on, the last two features have 'most completely disappeared'. China is described by Brown as being a 'hybrid system', where the party still retains a monopoly of power and democratic centralism is applied, but where the economy is 'so far removed from Communist orthodoxy' as to justify its description as 'party-state capitalism'. As for the 'aspiration to build Communism, 'it has been put so far ahead into the unknowable future that it is perfectly obvious that this task is not on the long-term agenda' of the Chinese leadership.

As in China, in the remaining five countries where communism survives as a ruling ideology, the party's leading role and democratic centralism continue to be exercised in North Korea, Laos, and Vietnam, as well as (on the American continent) in Cuba. However, these states 'differ greatly in the extent to which they still possess the defining features of a Communist system economically'. In any case, the picture is vastly different from that of the 1980s, when communism was still ruling over half of Europe.[9] Yet back in 1994, Walter Laqueur warned against the 'mistake to bury Communism too early'. 'There is the temptation', he added, 'to assume that, like Lucifer, Communism has fallen, never to hope again'. Yet in 'one guise or another', its heritage could be with us for a long

---

[4] Robert V. Daniels, *The End of the Communist Revolution* (London: Routledge, 1993); Martin Malia, *The Soviet Tragedy: A History of Socialism in Russia, 1917–1991* (New York: The Free Press, 1994), 405–520; Richard Pipes, *Russia Under the Bolshevik Regime* (New York: Vintage Books, 1995), 502–12; Laqueur, *The Dream that Failed*, 50–77, 131–62; Richard Sakwa, *The Rise and the Fall of the Soviet Union 1917–1991* (London: Routledge, 1999), 410–80.

[5] Leslie Holmes, *Post-Communism: An Introduction* (Cambridge: Polity Press, 1997); Stephen White, *Communism and Its Collapse* (London: Routledge, 2001); Brown, *The Rise & Fall of Communism*.

[6] François Furet, *Le passé d'une illusion: Essai sur l'idée communiste au XX siecle* (Paris: Éditions Robert Laffont, 1995); Richard Pipes, *Communism; A History of the Intellectual and Political Movement* (London: Phoenix Press, 2002).

[7] See Alex Callinicos, *The Revenge of History: Marxism and the East European Revolutions* (University Park, PA: Pennsylvania State University Press, 1991); Slavoj Žižek, *Did Somebody Say Totalitarianism? Five Interventions on the (Mis)use of a Notion* (London: Verso, 2001); Michael E. Brown, *The Historiography of Communism* (Philadelphia, PA: Temple University Press, 2009).

[8] Brown, *The Rise and Fall of Communism*, 105–14.

[9] Brown, *The Rise and Fall of Communism*, 603–7.

time. Whether 'as left-wing or right-wing populism', he predicted, attempts might be made 'to restore it or at least to salvage some of its major components'.[10] What is more, this might not be the worst scenario. The 'extinction' of Leninist regimes, according to Ken Jowitt, created a 'Genesis-like' situation, where chaos dominates. The international communist movement (an independent variable, for all its faults) might be replaced by the dependent and unpredictable variable of 'movements of rage'.[11] The scenario was produced nearly a decade before the collapse of the Twin Towers in New York.

Not that we lacked other scenarios. Following the initial euphoria epitomized by Francis Fukuyama's misplaced neo-Hegelianism,[12] there were numerous variations of 'it's the economy, stupid!'—paradoxically enough just as deterministic in predicting a democratic institutional outcome as a result of privatization as Marxists had been in expecting 'superstructure' to reflect the socialized means of production. Yet no one has yet come up with a plausible explanation for the fact that the former Yugoslavia, undoubtedly one of the most economically developed former communist states, 'produced the bloodiest of all transitions, spawning four (or more) full-scale wars'.[13] For accuracy's sake, one must mention that some 'transitologists' were from the start more sceptical than others as to the primacy of the economy in particular, and the 'one-way street' to democratization in general. This was best illustrated by the subtitle of the final tome (out of five volumes) on transitions from authoritarian rule.[14] But it is just as significant that the discussion of 'uncertain democracies' did not refer to the communist states, where *annus mirabilis* 1989 was just three years off. By the time more general comparative studies on transitions were launched, authors were making a clear distinction between 'completed democratic transitions' on the one hand, and 'consolidated democracies' on the other. Under consolidated democracy, it was pointed out, one met a 'political situation in which ... democracy has become "the only game in town"'.[15]

What is meant here are, of course, the institutional, or 'formal rules of the game'. It would hardly be suitable to engage here in disputes concerning 'substantial' or 'participatory' democracies, since formal rules are a *sine qua non* condition for the functioning of 'real' democracies. And it has been the weakness, the disregard, or the absence of such formal rules that has raised questions concerning 'what comes after communism'.

This is not tantamount to claiming that nothing of importance changed after 1989 or 1991. If the collapse of communism was produced by the cumulative effect of a

---

[10] Laqueur, *The Dream that Failed*, viii, 48–9.

[11] Ken Jowitt, *New World Disorder: The Leninist Extinction* (Berkeley, CA: University of California Press, 1992), 272, 275–7, 279, 283.

[12] Francis Fukuyama, *The End of History and the Last Man* (New York: Avon, 1993).

[13] Charles King, 'Postcommunism: Transition, Comparison, and the end of "Eastern Europe"', *World Politics* 53:1 (2000), 155.

[14] Guillermo O'donnell and Philippe C. Schmitter, *Transitions from Authoritarian Rule: Tentative Conclusions about Uncertain Democracies* (Baltimore, MD: Johns Hopkins University Press, 1986).

[15] Juan J. Linz and Alfred Stepan, *Problems of Democratic Transition and Consolidation: Southern Europe, South America, and Post-Communist Europe* (Baltimore, MD: Johns Hopkins University Press, 1996), 4, 5. See also Bruce Parrott, 'Perspectives on Postcommunist Democratization', in Bruce Parrott and Karen Dawisha, *Politics, Power, and the Struggle for Democracy in South-East Europe* (Cambridge: Cambridge University Press, 1997), 1–39.

many-faced crisis of legitimation, as Leslie Holmes convincingly argues,[16] it surely reflected and affected above all the teleological capability of communism to serve as an 'external role model'. But whereas Holmes refers to external role models only in connection with the emulation (and its ending) of the Soviet system by East European political leaderships, what is meant here by this notion is the delegitimation of Marxism on a global scale. Its intensity, however, was certainly higher in places that had only recently experimented with that model. The net result, as shown by Andrew Janos, has been the replacement of one 'international regime' (the communist) by another (the capitalist system).[17] What that meant in practice is that post-communist successor leaderships and their local competitors (regardless of their former beliefs and allegiances) strove to distance themselves both domestically and internationally from the former teleological legitimation. In turn, this produced the phenomenon called by Peter Evans 'institutional monocropping'; but this highly dubious endeavour of 'institutional export', Grigore Pop-Eleches points out, is highly unlikely to last long, since it ignores the importer's socio-economic, cultural, and political development.[18] (That in the long run such delegitimation might turn out to have been only a temporary phase of history is of no concern here, for we know from John Maynard Keynes that in the long run we are all dead.)

The empty room left by the former teleological delegitimation had to be filled by some new content, however. As Claus Offe has pointed out,[19] the 'social and political forces' emerging 'in the aftermath of state socialism' could be envisaged as being 'split among three centres of gravity': those whose referential 'positive history' is directed towards a '("golden") pre-Communist past'; those who (without necessarily seeking to redeem it as a political system) direct their affective attachments to 'the ("better aspects" of the) Communist past, with the security, equality and authoritarian-paternalistic protection offered by it'; and finally, those belonging to the category seeking to achieve a '"better future"' through 'the emulation of Western-style democratic capitalism'. In between these three main centres of gravity one may find 'all kinds of synthetic hybrids':

> The strongest of these hybrids is an ideological alliance of the two pasts, which amounts to an appeal to statist-authoritarian protection cum national pride and ethnic patriotism. Second comes the nationalist-liberal hybrid, an alliance of the economic modernizers with the patriotic or regionalist conservatives. Least strongly developed and least auspicious is the liberal-social democratic alliance, which would retain some transformed welfare state guarantees of the old regime while combining it with the economic institutions of democratic capitalism.[20]

---

[16] Holmes, *Post-Communism*, especially 42–58.

[17] Andrew Janos, 'From Eastern Empire to Western Hegemony: East Central Europe under Two International Regimes', *East European Politics and Societies* 15:2 (2001), 221–49.

[18] Grigore Pop-Eleches, 'Between Historical Legacies and the Promise of Western Integration: Democratic Conditionality after Communism', *East European Politics and Societies* 21:1 (2007), 142–61. Peter Evans's article 'Development as Institutional Change: The Pitfalls of Monocropping and Potentials of Deliberation', *Studies in Comparative International Development* 38 (2004), 30–52, is cited on 156.

[19] Claus Offe, *Varieties of Transition: The East European and the East German Experience* (Cambridge, MA: MIT Press, 1997), 186.

[20] Ibid., 187.

We thus come to the problem of legacies. Which legacies affect post-communist systems has been an issue under debate since shortly after the fall of the Old Regimes. Offe pointed out that post-communist regimes are faced with a 'dilemma of simultaneity', amounting to a 'triple transition': the process of having to cope concomitantly with unconsolidated borders, democratization, and property redistribution.[21] To that dilemma, as I pointed out some time ago, one must add an additional one, that is 'merely' double, not triple: can some of these states overcome their communist and authoritarian past without relying on precedents that hardly render themselves to idealization, such as anti-communist (but hardly democratic) regimes?[22]

Which factors influenced the prevailing options? Jeffrey Kopstein and David Reilly provided an intriguing answer to this question: proximity to the West. The two authors wrote that as early as 1995 it became 'possible to see two very different (and stable) postcommunist outcomes' of transitions, 'one increasingly "Western" and the other decidedly not'. This suggested a 'spatially dependent nature of the diffusion of norms, resources, and institutions that are necessary to the construction of political democracies and market economies in the postcommunist era'. A synthetic table in their article showed that states placed at the closest distance from the West (35–500 miles) scored highest on a six-year (1993–98) political reforms record. These included (in descending order of spatial proximity) Slovakia, Hungary, the Czech Republic, Croatia, Slovenia, Bosnia-Herzegovina, Poland, and Macedonia. The highest score (10) in this group was registered by Hungary, the Czech Republic, and Slovenia, and the lowest (−1) by Croatia. The second group included states distanced from the West by between 501 and 1000 miles. Lithuania scored highest in this category (10) and Belarus lowest (−7), followed by Bulgaria, Latvia, Romania, Estonia, Moldova, Ukraine, and Albania. In the group of countries distanced 1001–1500 miles, Armenia scored highest (6), followed by Georgia (5) and Russia (4). Finally, all states placed in the group distanced 1501–4080 miles with the exception of Mongolia (+9) and Kyrgyzstan (+2) had negative records, ranging from −9 (Turkmenistan and Uzbekistan) to −6 (Azerbaijan), −3 (Kazakhstan), and −2 (Tajikistan). Records measured over a five-year period (1995–99), on the other hand, showed that 'distance from the West is not a substantively significant influence on economic reform'.[23]

Aside from wondering why Albania (a short boat-ride away from Italy) should be placed in the group of countries distanced from the West by over 500 miles, Kopstein and Reilly's conclusions were obviously nullified by subsequent developments. Examples are numerous; suffice it to mention that a country ruled by a populist–nationalist coalition as Slovakia was after 2006 would hardly qualify for high scoring on political reforms (unless these mean regression as well), nor would Hungary under Viktor Orbán's

---

[21] Ibid., 36–7.

[22] Michael Shafir, 'Anti-Semitism in Post-communist East Central Europe: A Motivational Taxonomy', in Andrei Corbea-Hoisie et al., *Umbruch im östlichen Europa* (Innsbruck: Studien Verlag, 2004), 57.

[23] Jeffrey S. Kopstein and David A. Reilly, 'Geographic Diffusion and the Transformation of the Postcommunist World', *World Politics* 53:1 (2000), 1–37.

government (1998–2002), or Poland under the joint steering of the Jarosław and Lech Kaczyński twins (2006–07); and what about Alyaksandr Lukashenka's Belarus, geographically closer to the West but politically not very different from Turkmenistan?[24]

In their thought-provoking article, Kopstein and Reilly brought into discussion the question of legacies, relying mainly on Herbert Kitschelt and his associates' volume on post-Communist Party systems. While other authors have often wondered which legacies 'count' in post-communism (those of communism itself or the ante-communist heritage), it is Kitschelt's merit to have pointed out that the modes of communist rule have been in turn influenced by historical antecedents. It logically follows that in post-communism both legacies will be reflected and impact the social and political system. He distinguished between three types of communist rule. In 'patrimonial communism' one finds a reliance 'on vertical chains of personal dependence between leaders in the state and party apparatus and their entourage, buttressed by extensive patronage and clientilist networks'. In patrimonial communism 'political power is concentrated around a small clique or an individual ruler worshiped by a personality cult'. In 'extreme cases, such regimes give rise to the "sultanistic" rule of an individual and his family', Kitschelt added, relying on Linz and Stepan's book on transitions and the consolidation of new democracies.[25] Regimes of patrimonial communism emerged

> in historical settings where a traditional authoritarian regime, assisted by compliant religious leaders, ruled over societies of poor peasants…weak cities, a thin layer of ethnic pariah immigrant entrepreneurs and merchants, a small and geographically concentrated industrial working class, and a corrupt coterie of administrators, dependent on the personal whims of the ruler.

The second type of communism is the 'national-accommodative'. It included regimes 'with more developed formal rational-bureaucratic governance structures that partially separated party rule and technical state administration'. These regimes 'evidenced a greater propensity to permit modest levels of civil rights and elite contestation at least episodically, while relying more on cooptation than repression as ways to instil citizens' compliance'. One dealt here with societies that 'emerged from semi-democratic and semi-authoritarian inter-war polities with rather vibrant political mobilization around parties and interest groups'. They had 'already undertaken significant steps toward industrialization' before the oncoming of communist rule, but

> were saddled with inefficient state bureaucracies over-staffed by the offspring of a state-centered educated middle stratum unable to find work in private business. In these settings, urban-rural conflicts were particularly salient and congealed around intense party divisions, while industrial class conflict played a comparatively minor role in the crystallization of political divides.

Finally, in what Kitschelt designates as 'bureaucratic-authoritarian' communism, forces belonging to the opposition 'encountered a much harsher and more hostile climate than

---

[24] Parrott, 'Perspectives on Postcommunist Democratization', 7.
[25] Linz and Stepan, *Problems of Democratic Transition and Consolidation*, 51–4.

in national-accommodative communism, but for different reasons than in patrimonial communism'. One dealt here with a type of governance that 'came closest to the totalitarian model of a party state with an all powerful, rule-guided bureaucratic machine governed by a planning technocracy and a disciplined, hierarchically stratified communist party' that relied on 'a tier of sophisticated economic and administrative professionals who governed a planned economy that produced comparatively advanced industrial goods and services'. It must be emphasized, however, that 'Bureaucratic professionalism and strict party discipline…were inimical to political bargaining with and mutual accommodation to potential outside challengers.' According to Kitschelt's (ideal-type) typology,

> Bureaucratic-authoritarian communism occurred in countries with considerable liberal-democratic experience in the inter-war period, and early and comparatively advanced industrialization, and a simultaneous mobilization of bourgeois and proletarian political forces around class-based parties beginning in the late-nineteenth century.[26]

It follows not only that the 'extrication paths'[27] from communism were different, but so were the systems from which the extrication itself occurred. Archie Brown's six defining features notwithstanding, one hardly dealt here with (to employ Rothschild's terminology) a *return* to diversity, but rather with its continuation.[28] It is against this background that the actions and reactions of actors making up the post-communist mosaics must be analysed. To get as full an image as possible, the level of analysis should ideally include general international trends and reactions to them ('globalization and its discontents' might be a good starting point); regional factors (kin-states and their attitude towards 'diasporas', irredentism, but also 'empire traditions'); actors performing at local and cross-border level (civil societies, 'uncivil' societies, intellectuals, and their perceived and self-perceived political role); pre-and post-communist constitutional design (to what extent did Soviet, Yugoslav, and Czechoslovak federal constitutional design encourage the dismemberment of those entities and what role does that design play under post-communism); and of course personality impacts—all of these elements being grasped while addressing a plethora of ante-communist legacies as well. This is an overwhelming agenda not only for a short article, but also for a thick tome.

In face of such complexity, one might alternatively choose to proceed impressionistically; that is to say, to choose as 'dependent variable' the most salient aspects of those listed above, concentrate on providing examples illustrating that saliency from as many

---

[26] Herbert Kitschelt et al., *Post-Communist Party Systems: Competition, Representation, and Inter-Party Cooperation* (New York: Cambridge University Press, 1999), 21–6.

[27] On extrication and the ensuing path-dependency see Alfred Stepan, 'Paths toward Redemocratization: Theoretical and Comparative Considerations', in Guillermo O'donnell, Philippe C. Schmitter and Laurence Whitehead (eds), *Transitions from Authoritarian Rule: Comparative Perspectives* (Baltimore, MD: Johns Hopkins University Press, 1986), 64–84, 170–4.

[28] Joseph Rothschild and Nancy M. Wingfield, *Return to Diversity: A Political History of East Central Europe since World War II* (New York: Oxford University Press, 2000). On the continued importance and influence of diversity after the extrication point, cf. Paul Blokker, 'Post-Communist Modernization, Transition Studies, and Diversity in Europe', *European Journal of Social Theory* 8:4 (2005), 503–25.

places as possible and attempt to determine which are the 'independent variables' that produce the phenomenon.

This is precisely what Vladimir Tismaneanu did in a volume whose subtitle (*Democracy, Nationalism and Myth in Post-Communist Europe*) implicitly addresses many of the issues mentioned above. The volume's main title (*Fantasies of Salvation*) bears witness to the centrality of legacies and their continuity, and for any informed reader immediately recalls the 'palingenetic' dimension that Roger Griffin identified as the essential element of fascism.[29] A foremost role in forging and propagating the mass acceptance of palingenesis, as some of the foremost scholars of fascism and Nazism emphasize, has been played by intellectuals or, as Yehuda Bauer called that category, 'lumpenintellectuals'.[30] Tismaneanu makes that role into the main thesis of his book, just as he attributed to intellectuals the main role in the 'reinvention of politics' that brought about the dismissal of the Old Regime.[31]

Because intellectuals had played a prominent role in forging and in supporting dissent and opposition under communism (wherever it occurred, which was by no means universal), there was a natural initial inclination to expect that they would play the same role in the process of democratization. Those who did so had knowingly or not opted to ignore the fact that intellectuals had played a no less central role in forging and disseminating authoritarian patterns of thought and political behaviour (whether fascist or Marxist) just as they ignored the blurred traditional distinction between that category and politicians, typical of latecomers to modernization. And whatever else post-communism might be, it is also a belated and renewed attempt at modernization. Alongside Tismaneanu, many have now rediscovered that modernization has its no less traditional opponents among the local intelligentsia and political entrepreneurs, sometimes merged into a single personality, at other times mutually reinforcing each other.[32]

Tismaneanu distinguishes between 'two main strands of thought' among intellectuals in post-communist states: 'the once widely acclaimed but now increasingly marginalized "Westernizing" liberals and the resurgent xenophobic, nativist right'. Against the background of pre-communist 'anti-Enlightenment, ethnocentric forces in the pre-communist period, and the ways in which they were co-opted and even officially encouraged in many of these countries during the late communist stage', the resurrection of such forces is perceived to be 'a grim omen for the future'. The author warns that 'The anti-capitalist and anti-democratic sentiments, including paternalistic, corporatist and populist nostalgias, could coalesce in new authoritarian experiments.'[33] He attributes

---

[29] Roger Griffin, *The Nature of Fascism* (London: Routledge, 1994).

[30] Yehuda Bauer, *Rethinking the Holocaust* (New Haven, CT: Yale University Press, 2001), 32.

[31] See Vladimir Tismaneanu's *Reinventing Politics: Eastern Europe from Stalin to Havel* (New York: The Free Press, 1992).

[32] See Slavenka Drakulic, 'Intellectuals as Bad Guys', *East European Politics and Societies* 13:2 (1999), 271–7; Andrew Baruch Wachtel, *Making a Nation, Breaking a Nation: Literature and Cultural Politics in Yugoslavia* (Stanford, CA: Stanford University Press, 1998), and 'Writers and Society in Eastern Europe, 1989–2000: The End of the Golden Age', *East European Politics and Societies* 17:4 (2003), 583–621.

[33] Vladimir Tismaneanu, *Fantasies of Salvation: Democracy, Nationalism and Myth in Post-Communist Europe* (Princeton, NJ: Princeton University Press, 1998), 4–5.

these tendencies to both ante-communist and communist legacies acting at one and the same time. They have a 'dual nature'. Post-communist nationalism, he writes, 'rejects the spurious internationalism of communist propaganda and emphasizes long-repressed national values', but at the same time 'it is a nationalism rooted in and marked by Leninist-authoritarian mentalities and habits, directed against any principle of difference and primarily against those groups and forces that champion pro-Western, pluralist orientations'.

While the 'first direction is related to the global tendency toward rediscovery of ancestry, roots, and autochthonous values', the second 'perpetuates and enhances collectivistic communist and pre-communist traditions by denying the individual the right to dissent, sanctifying the national community and its allegedly providential leader, and scapegoating or demonizing minorities for imaginary plots and betrayals'.[34] It follows that under post-communism, the 'mythologies of salvation are ideological surrogates' whose 'principal function is to unify the public discourse and provide the citizen with an easily recognizable source of identity as a part of a vaguely defined ethnic (or political) community'. They favour a 'politics of anger and resentment', capitalizing on the 'legitimate aspirations and grievances' that are the effect of transitions. These new mythologies 'indulge in self-pity'. Croatians, Lithuanians, Poles, Russians, Slovaks, Serbs, Ukrainians, Romanians, all perceive themselves as 'having been the ultimate victims of communism (and of Western betrayal)'. It is a 'longing for lost certitudes' that 'explains the growing nostalgia for the pre-communist national and cultural values, the resurrection of the messianic myth of the Nation (the People as One) and the burning belief in its regenerative power'.[35]

Tismaneanu brings ample documentation to support his thesis, and specific case studies further evince his argument. To take but one example: Russia's evolution in both internal and foreign policy on the eve and in the aftermath of the USSR's collapse can be explained to a great extent as a continuation of the clash between Westernizers and the different streams of thought feeding authoritarianism,[36] such as Slavophilism, Euroasianism, and combinations thereof.[37] One could say we are dealing here with what

[34] Ibid., 7.

[35] Ibid., 7–8.

[36] See Robert D. English, *Russia and the Idea of the West: Gorbachev, Intellectuals and the End of the Cold War* (New York: Columbia University Press, 2000).

[37] See Vera Tolz, 'The Radical Right in Post-Communist Russian Politics', in Peter H. Merkl and Leonard Weinberg (eds), *The Revival of Right-Wing Extremism in the Nineties* (London: Frank Cass, 1997), 177–202, and 'Conflicting "Homeland Myths" and Nation-State Building in Postcommunist Russia', *Slavic Review* 57:2 (1998), 267–94; Heikki Patomäki and Christer Pursiainen, 'Western Models and the "Russian Idea": Beyond "Inside/Outside" in Discourses on Civil Society', *Millennium-Journal of International Studies* 28:1 (1999), 53–77; Wayne Allensworth, *The Russian Question: Nationalism, Modernization and Post-Communist Russia* (Lanham, MD: Rowman and Littlefield, 1998); Judith Devnin, *Slavophiles and Commissars: Enemies of Democracy in Modern Russia* (London: Macmillan, 1999); Susanna Rabow-Edling, *Slavophile Thought and the Politics of Cultural Nationalism* (Albany, NY: State University of New York Press, 2006); Marlène Laruelle, *Russian Eurasianism: An Ideology of Empire* (Baltimore, MD: Johns Hopkins University Press, 2008).

Stephen White termed the 'cultural limits of transition'. The same element largely explains the 'personalist dictatorships' of the former Soviet republics of Central Asia.[38] Former President and current Premier Vladimir Putin's policies have been defined as an 'overmanaged democracy', which is a '"hybrid regime" combining elements of high state centralisation with the gutting of democratic institutions and their systematic replacement by *substitutions* that are intended to serve some of their positive functions without challenging the incumbent leader's hold on power' (emphasis in the original).[39] Such hybrid regimes are particularly prone to appeal to the past in order to justify the present. As Harald Wydra has argued,

> In search for a structuring principle of Russian history, Yeltsin's and Putin's leadership has focused identity-formation on the reaffirmation of the imperial legacy such as in the reburial of the last tsar in late 1998 or the re-establishment of the melody of the Soviet national anthem.

Thus, 'Putin's project of rejecting any myth of Russia's path as permanently deviant from the normal course of development associated with the West is compensated for by his attempt to turn Russia into a "normal" country', which in and of itself is but a 'mythical construct' retrieving a 'variety of national symbols, whose mythologisation is essential to attenuate Russia's permanent contradiction with itself'.[40]

Whether explicitly or implicitly, several authors have contested Tismaneanu's approach. One of the main objections concerns nationalism and its role in ante-communist and post-communist systemic change. Valerie Bunce for example has claimed that 'nationalism is wanton. It can couple with a wide variety of regimes'.[41] This may well be so, but wantonness may tell us more about those regimes than about nationalism.

Based on the perspective of 'imperial legacies', Bunce argues that in the wake of the Second World War, the 'Soviet bloc' was made up of two components: an 'internal empire and [an] external empire composed of semisovereign nationally defined units'. The former component, in her view, included 'not just the Soviet ethnofederation, but also the Yugoslav and, after 1968, the Czechoslovak ethnofederations'.[42] In both imperial components, she writes, one found

---

[38] Stephen White, *Russia's New Politics: The Management of a Postcommunist Society* (Cambridge: Cambridge University Press, 2000), 288–92.

[39] Nikolai Petrov, Marsha Lipman and Henry E. Hale, 'Overmanaged Democracy in Russia: Governance Implications of Hybrid Regimes', *Carnegie Papers,* Russia and Eurasia Program 106 (February 2010), online at: www.carnegieendowment.org/files/overmanaged_democracy_2.pdf, accessed April 2010.

[40] Wydra, *Communism and the Emergence of Democracy,* 238.

[41] Valerie Bunce, 'The National Idea: Imperial Legacies and Post-Communist Pathways in Eastern Europe', *East European Politics and Societies* 19:3 (2005), 412. Cf. her 'Comparative Democratization: Big and Bounded Generalizations', *Comparative Political Studies* 33:6/7 (2000), 712–13, 719; Stefan Auer, 'Nationalism in Central Europe: A Chance or a Threat for the Emerging Liberal Democratic Order?', *East European Politics and Societies* 14:2 (2000), 213–45; Alan Renwick, 'Anti-Political or just Anti-Communist? Varieties of Dissidence in East-Central Europe and Their Implications for the Development of Political Society', *East European Politics and Societies* 20:2 (2006), 286–318, particularly 294, 299.

[42] Bunce, 'The National Idea', 427, 428.

a growing belief on the part of publics, nations and opposition (and sometime communist) leaders that the boundaries of their republics, their states, and the Soviet bloc, the coercive monopoly of the centre at home and the Soviet Union within the region, and the multiple and interlocked regimes that governed these units were *all* illegitimate.[43] (Emphasis in the original.)

Nationalism, according to Bunce,

did not just multiply sovereign claims, generate conflict, and undermine democracy in ethnofederal settings, it also liberated states, united people in a common cause, and supported democratic governance…This is because the revolutions of 1989 were not just rebellions against illegitimate regimes; they were also *nationalist* revolutions against Soviet domination.[44] (Emphasis in the original.)

While few would challenge this argument, much of its force withers away when juxtaposed with Holmes's definition of post-communism as emerging from the 'double-rejective' revolutions of 1989–91. The first rejection, according to this perspective, 'was of what was perceived to be external domination' by the Soviet Union in the case of East Central Europe and by Russia and Serbia respectively in the case of the USSR and former Yugoslavia. The 'second rejection', however, concerns the rebuttal of 'communism as a system of power' and (just as important) advocacy of what that system should be replaced with, which was far from clear, being for many 'a deduced, not an induced, concept'. Thus,

many citizens of the formerly communist world tended at the time of the collapse of communist power and in the immediate aftermath to assume that if something had long been criticized by the communists, then it was probably what was now needed.[45]

And this assumption extended to pre-communist authoritarian regimes, though not exclusively to them. Second, Bunce's exemplifications of democratic regimes emerging from nationalist impulses are in themselves arguable on two main grounds: first, she tends in this article to equate market reforms and privatization with political liberalism and democratization, explaining both in terms of a nationalist consensus said to have existed in the Polish immediate post-communist transition. Neither equation is, however, valid, since market economies are by no means incompatible with semi-democracies or authoritarianisms of, for example, the 'Asian "tigers"' of precisely those transition years. And far from pursuing liberalism in the *political* sense of the word, the Polish reformers of the immediate post-communist years actually neglected and even rejected precisely the civic liberal aspects that had propelled them to power.[46] The Baltic States are another case in point. While no one would deny the role played by nationalism in those state's pioneering role in the USSR's collapse, there are grounds to doubt that the

---

[43] Ibid., 429.

[44] Ibid., 433.

[45] Holmes, *Post- Communism*, 14–15.

[46] See David Ost, *The Defeat of Solidarity: Anger and Politics in Postcommunist Europe* (Ithaca, NY: Cornell University Press, 2005), 98, 112, 192–3.

exclusivist policies pursued vis-à-vis the Russian minority in Estonia and Latvia, or the handling of sensitive issues in the Nazi collaborationist past in the three countries are matters of secondary importance when examining democratic consolidation.[47]

The major imputation that could be brought against Tismaneanu's book is the equation of the democracy-undermining trends he surveys with populism. The second chapter of the volume discussed 'the Leninist debris' in terms of 'waiting for Peron', while the third chapter groups 'vindictive and messianic mythologies' under the same category with 'post-communist nationalism and populism'. This is heuristically challenging, but does not pass the test of closer examination.

As I have argued elsewhere,[48] what distinguishes historical populism from post-communist neo-populism is the anti-systemic nature of the former versus the latter's systemic nature. That does not make neo-populism necessarily democratic, but hinders it from openly displaying its undemocratic nature and objectives. The causes of this difference are to be sought both in the 'international democratic regime' that prevailed after 1989, with both external and internal impacts. Andrew Janos, who employed the distinction between populism and neo-populism, missed, I believe, its central point. Janos distinguishes between three traditions that have influenced the 'strategic choices' made by post-communist political elites: the liberal/civic tradition, the technocratic tradition, and the neo-populist one.[49] As he formulates it, however, the 'neo' in populism resides in continuity, rather than in change. It refers to such aspects as the cultivation of a self-centred apprehensive perception of 'the Other' and of a globalizing world and to the cultivation of 'the symbols of the victim and the weak'.

There is very little 'neo' here for anyone familiar with the history of East Central Europe, indeed with the history of European radicalism in general. For the 'neo' to become relevant, it seems to me that the distinction should rather introduce a different dimension: that of Sartorian 'systemic' and 'anti-system politics'.[50] In the post-1989 context, politics in East Central Europe simply cannot be successfully conducted if openly admitting an 'anti-systemic' telos. 'In present-day Central Europe, unlike in Europe of the 1930s, there is no ideological alternative to democracy', Ivan Krastev writes, adding that the 'streets of Budapest and Warsaw today are flooded not by ruthless paramilitary formations in search of a final solution, but by restless consumers in search of a final sale'.[51] In turn, Jacques Rupnik observes that Eastern Europe's populists (or rather

[47] Linz and Stepan, *Problems of Democratic Transition and Consolidation*, 401–33; Leonidas Donskis, 'Between Identity and Freedom: Mapping Nationalism in Twentieth-Century Lithuania', *East European Politics and Societies* 13:3 (1999), 474–500; Andres Kasecamp, 'Extreme-Right Parties in Contemporary Estonia', *Patterns of Prejudice* 37:4 (2003), 401–14; Efraim Zuroff, 'Eastern Europe: Anti-Semitism in the Wake of Holocaust-Related Issues', *Jewish Political Studies Review* 17:1 (2005), 63–79.

[48] Michael Shafir, 'From Historical to "Dialectical" Populism: The Case of Post-Communist Romania', *Canadian Slavonic Papers* 50:3–4 (2008), 425–70.

[49] Andrew Janos, 'Continuity and Change in Eastern Europe: Strategies of Post-Communist Politics', *East European Politics and Societies* 8:1 (1994), 1–31.

[50] Giovanni Sartori, *Parties and Party Systems: A Framework for Analysis* (Cambridge: Cambridge University Press, 1979), 132–3, *passim*.

[51] Ivan Krastev, 'The Strange Death of the Liberal Consensus', *Journal of Democracy* 19:4 (2007), 58.

neo-populists) 'are not anti-democratic (indeed they claim to be the "true voice of the people" and keep demanding new elections and referenda) but anti-liberal.'[52] Yet neo-populist anti-liberalism does not imply the rejection of a market economy.

That is not to claim that there are no 'anti-system' parties, organizations, or personalities in post-communism. There are plenty of them, and we shall yet dwell on the difference between neo-populists and the anti-system radical right. However, in one way or another, even those belonging to the latter category are conscious of the fact that such an admission would transform them into pariahs within, and particularly outside, their own political community. Neo-populists are different from both interwar populists and from the earlier populists of the socialist or *völkisch* shades. Unlike their predecessors, they no longer denounce the 'evils' of capitalism, only the 'rapaciousness' of capitalists who allegedly forgot where they stemmed from. In neo-populism, there are 'virtuous' and 'corrupt' capitalists, and the former engage in self-sacrifice by entering politics allegedly against their own personal interests. The image the neo-populists pursue is, as Cas Mudde pointed out, that of 'reluctant politicians' where politics is presented as being a 'necessary evil' in a self-sacrificing posture. Hence, neo-populists are, at least in appearance, 'systemic'. Not only do they not claim, as their predecessors did, 'system destructive' objectives, but, on the contrary, the claim is made that they do so in order to safeguard genuine democracy. The claim, as Mudde writes, is built upon a rigid dichotomy of the 'pure people' whom they reluctantly took upon themselves to represent, versus 'the corrupt elite'.[53] The dichotomy is at the core of the very definition of populism Mudde would eventually provide:

> [P]opulism is understood as a thin-centred ideology that considers society to be ultimately separated into two homogenous and antagonistic groups, 'the pure people' versus 'the corrupt elite', and which argues that politics should be an expression of the *volonté générale* (general will) of the people...In the populist democracy, nothing is more important than the 'general will' of the people, not even human rights or constitutional guarantees...[54] (Emphasis in the original.)

This definition is very much in line with that provided by Daniele Albertazzi and Duncan McDonnell, who portray the populists as pitting 'a virtuous and homogenous people against a set of elites and dangerous "others" who are together depicted as depriving (or attempting to deprive) the sovereign people of their rights, values, prosperity, identity and voice'.[55] The assumption of the people's 'homogeneity' and the 'dangerousness' of 'others' is an essential feature of the radical right populists; but not all populists are necessarily radical right.

---

[52] Jacques Rupnik, 'Populism in Eastern Central Europe', *Eurozine*, www.eurozine.com/articles/2007-09-10-rupnik-en.html, accessed April 2010.

[53] Cas Mudde, 'In the Name of the Peasantry, the Proletariat and the People: Populisms in Eastern Europe', *East European Politics and Societies* 15:1 (2000), 37.

[54] Cas Mudde, *Populist Radical Right Parties in Europe* (Cambridge: Cambridge University Press, 2007) 23.

[55] Daniele Albertazzi, Duncan McDonnell, *Twenty First Century Populism: The Specter for Western European Democracy* (London: Palgrave Macmillan, 2007), 3.

None of the above rules out elements of continuation from populism to neo-populism. It is striking, however, that these elements are often denied when the neo-populists are confronted with uncomfortable parallels drawn by either domestic opponents or foreign political critics. Furthermore, not only is the democratic dress-up considered to be inevitable, but neo-populists are particularly gifted in mobilizing support via the self-transmogrification into the very personal embodiment of popular grievances or those of influential segments in their societies. This category is large and of different ideological persuasions, but would include such political parties and leaders (in country alphabetical, rather than chronological order) as Boyko Borisov's Citizens for European Development of Bulgaria (GERB); Hungary's Viktor Orbán and his Alliance of Young Democrats-Hungarian Civic Party (FIDESZ-MPP); Poland's Law and Justice (PiS) party headed by the Jarosław and Lech Kaczyński twins; Romania's Liberal-Democratic Party (PDL) whose de facto leader is incumbent President Traian Băsescu; the Yedinaya Rossiya (United Russia) party of Vladimir Putin; and Slovakia's SMER headed by Premier Robert Fico. All these parties and leaders were at one point or another ready to forge formal and informal coalitions with anti-system parties on the right or left spectrum of the political map, or with both, as in PiS's case.

With the possible exception of Cas Mudde,[56] experts (whether on the region or on Western Europe) concur that modern populists tend to support a market economy. Nowhere is this better illustrated than in Herbert Kitschelt and Anthony McGann's famous 'winning formula' of right-wing Western parties, which is grounded on assembling 'a significant voter constituency' that is based not only on 'authoritarian and ethnocentric and even racist messages' but also on a choice of 'economic free market appeals'. According to the two authors, 'Parties that feature only racist and authoritarian positions but fail to highlight and embrace their commitment to free markets appeal only to modest segments of blue-collar and lower white-collar electorate' but 'If they also include free market slogans, they additionally attract small independent businesspeople such as shopkeepers, family farmers, and craftspeople.'[57] Mudde would argue with some justification that his rejection of economic liberalism as a trait of neo-populism refers only to the populist radical right parties and not to populism or neo-populism in general.

One is stepping here on a dangerous definitional trap that has taken (and is likely to continue taking) many victims. Briefly stated, neither are all populist members of the radical right family, nor are all right wingers populist. Failure to make the distinction explains in part why populism has become a 'dirty political word', standing in for such 'niceties' as 'ethnic radicalism', 'paranoia' and their likes—in fact for what Tismaneanu calls 'fantasies of national salvation'.[58]

According to Mudde, there are three core elements of the populist radical right: nativism, authoritarianism, and populism. His definition of populism has been cited above.

---

[56] Mudde, Populist Radical Right Parties, 119–37.

[57] Herbert Kitscheltand Anthony McGann, *The Radical Right in Western Europe* (Ann Arbor: University of Michigan Press, 1997), vii–viii.

[58] Tismaneanu, *Fantasies of Salvation*, 54.

By 'nativism' he understands '*an ideology, which holds that states should be inhabited exclusively by members of the native group ("the nation") and that nonnative elements (persons and ideas) are fundamentally threatening to the homogenous nation-state*' (emphasis in the original).[59] Finally, adopting Theodor Adorno and his Frankfurt School's definition, authoritarianism is said to be 'a general disposition to glorify, to be subservient to and remain uncritical toward authoritative figures of the ingroup and to take an attitude of punishing outgroup figures in the name of some moral authority'.[60]

Populist radical right parties seem to have adjusted to democracy, although

> Populist radical right democracy is fundamentally at odds with liberal democracy because of its monism, most strongly expressed in its nativism and populism. Consequently, the more liberal a democracy is, the more antisystem the populist radical right will be. Similarly, we can posit that the more ethnic and plebiscitary a democracy, the more pro-system the populist radical right... In conclusion, then, while the populist radical right does not constitute a fundamental challenge to the democratic procedural system itself, clear tensions exist between its interpretation of democracy and liberal democracy... At the core of this tension is the distinction between monism and pluralism: whereas populist radical right democracy considers societies to be essentially homogenous collectives, liberal democracy presupposes societies to be made up of groups of fundamentally different individuals. [61]

This indeed *is* so, which makes even stranger Mudde's rejection of the Sartorian systemic-non-systemic distinction on grounds that 'if one wants to use the term populist Radical Right in a (nearly) universal way, i.e. not limiting it to liberal democracies, the antisystem criteria cannot be included in the definition'.[62] Yet on the same page that carries this quote, Mudde writes: 'populists will defend an extreme form of majoritarian democracy, in which minority rights can exist only as long as the majority supports them. Similarly, constitutional provisions are valid only as long as they have majority support'. And, above all, 'the practice shows that once in power the populist Radical Right clearly follows these ideas. This has led to some serious (attempts at) infringements of constitutionally protected liberal rights (e.g. in Austria, Croatia, Italy and Slovakia.)' What are such infringements if not anti-systemic?

The distinction between radical right anti-systemic post-communist political parties and neo-populist systemic parties is essential. It shows (and this is valid not only for the former communist states, but for some Western democracy as well) that a state of what I would describe as 'permanent liminality' including both democratic and anti-democratic elements is possible.

Although attempts were made to classify non-democratic post-communist political formations according to their main line of legatee descent,[63] until recently no notable

---

[59] Mudde, *Populist Radical Right Parties*, 18.   [60] Ibid., 22.

[61] Ibid., 156, 157.   [62] Ibid., 156.

[63] See Michael Shafir, 'The Mind of Romania's Radical Right', in Sabrina Ramet (ed.), *The Radical Right in Central and Eastern Europe Since 1989* (University Park, PA: Pennsylvania State University Press, 1999), 213–32, and 'Reds, Pinks, Blacks and Blues: Radical Politics in Post-Communist East Central Europe', *Studia Politica* 1:2 (2001), 397–446.

effort was made to establish concomitantly a spatial distance between these two categories as well. Authors have usually concentrated on either one of these aspects, occasionally combining it with other dimensions, such as organizational structures.[64] Viewed from this perspective, an article authored in 2009 by Lenka Bustikova and Herbert Kitschelt is clearly an important contribution to making possible the distinction between neo-populist post-communist formations and political parties that belong to the radical right spectrum, despite the fact that no such distinction is to be found in the tract itself. There are no grounds to assume that the boundaries of such permanent liminality stop at the gates of the rightist family of parties. As will be shown in at least one case, that of Slovakia, the liminality crosses the border and applies to the leftist side of the spectrum; and Slovakia is by no means a singular exception.

Utilizing the three temporal legacies that Kitschelt and his associates proposed back in 1999, namely those of national-accommodative communism, bureaucratic-authoritarian, and patrimonial communism (see above), the article examines the effect of welfare retrenchment on the electoral support mobilized by these parties in the 2000s. Contrary to previous claims,[65] the study assumes that reforms of social policy (in themselves critically essential once free markets and privatization become general policies) have a turbulent potential for the new democracies that part with the communist universal welfare system and may thus encourage conflicts on which radical right parties might thrive. Legacies, Bustikova and Kitschelt write, are 'deep, durable causes that affect the potential for radical right wing politics across the post-communist region'; they 'create the base-line for patterns of party competition, shape partisan politics, and thus mold a proximate cause of radical right mobilization'. Economic grievances, 'when matched with ethnic and socio-cultural attributes of party competition', might be turned into a powerful means of mobilization.[66]

Where the prevailing legacy is that of national accommodative communism (the Baltic States, Croatia, Hungary, Poland, Slovenia, and Slovakia), the early differentiation of the major political formations on both sociocultural and social policy compensation kept at bay the losers of the reform, which limited the electoral success of extremist rightist parties. Under the legacy of bureaucratic-authoritarian communism (the Czech Republic and to some extent the former German Democratic Republic) one deals with a mutually exclusive polarization between the remnants of the former communist regime and an uncompromising anti-communist side. With each of the two sides having a strong electoral base, in post-communist times unreformed communist parties that reject any weakening of the welfare state continue to be successful in elections.

In the case of patrimonial communist regimes (Albania, Bulgaria, Macedonia, Moldova, Romania, Russia, Serbia, and Ukraine) on the other hand, one deals with

---

[64] For instance Michael Minkenberg, 'The Radical Right in Postsocialist Central and Eastern Europe – Observations and Interpretations', *East European Politics and Societies* 16:2 (2002), 335–62.

[65] Mudde, *Populist Radical Right Parties*.

[66] Lenka Bustikova and Herbert Kitschelt, 'The Radical Right in Post-communist Europe: Comparative Perspectives on Legacies and Party Competition', *Communist and Post-Communist Studies* 42:4 (2009), 460.

communist successor parties that often forge 'red-brown' alliances with extreme rightist parties, enunciating authoritarian and exclusionary appeals often combined with anti-market positions. Where this is combined with the rapid dismantling of the welfare state, it falls on fertile breeding ground for the emergence of radical right postures. The authors also show that ethnic composition plays an important role in radical right mobilization and that, paradoxically enough, the larger the ethno-cultural minority in a country, the smaller the chance of the radical right to mobilize such support.

Bustikova and Kitschelt's potential distinction between neo-populist and radical right parties comes best to fore in the case of national accommodative category. They write that in those countries 'moderate right wing parties have incorporated exclusionary appeals into their programmatic agenda, thus further reducing the options for the successful entry and endurance of the radical right'.[67] This is best shown by a table in the article illustrating the proximity to and at the same time the difference between radical right parties and 'nearby' rightist competitors on two main dimensions: that of the 'socio-cultural' grid (with its two categories of exclusive–inclusive nationalism and traditionalist versus liberal–secular and cosmopolitan culture) and that of the distributive economic policy positions (in turn measuring spending on one hand and privatization on the other as categories).[68] The table demonstrates that neo-populist formations such as the Hungarian FIDESZ-MPP is closest to extreme rightist Justice and Life Party (MIÉP); that in Poland the Law and Justice Party (PiS) is closest to the extremist League of Polish Families (LPR); and in Croatia the Croat Democratic Union (HDZ) matches with the positions of the extreme right Croatian Party of Rights (HSP).

On closer inspection, however, this is far from being that simple. First, the table shows that in the cases of Slovenia, Lithuania, and Estonia, extremist formations place themselves in the vicinity of Christian Democratic, rather than the neo-populists. In the case of Slovakia, the extremist Slovak National Party (SNS) entered into a coalition with the neo-populist SMER, but SMER evolved to neo-populism coming from the left, rather than the right wing of the political spectrum. What is more, cooperation and alliances with the radical right were also encountered within the legacy of patrimonial communism, as demonstrated by the Russian red-brown issue alliance between the Communist Party of the Russian Federation (KPRF) under Gennady Zyuganov with different shades of the radical right, ranging from those supportive of a return to an autocratic monarchy to fascists, or by the Romanian 'red quadrangle' of the first half of the 1990s.

These alliances are not 'unnatural' as has often been claimed. Individualism, parliamentarianism, and democracy have long been joint enemies for both sides and I believe Bustikova and Kitschelt err by not including in their analysis legacies that go beyond communism. None of these caveats eliminates the validity of other points they make in connection with the legacy of patrimonial communism, where 'unreformed communist parties set against economic and political liberalization, regardless of whether they kept their communist labels or adopted some other party names'. The successors of communist regimes in these countries confronted 'a highly inexperienced, diffuse, disorganized pro-market and

---

[67] Ibid., 460.   [68] Ibid., 471.

pro-democratic opposition' incapable, even where it briefly came to power as in Albania, Bulgaria, or Romania 'to effectively govern a process of economic and institutional reform'. As a result, 'Where this situation did not yield an outright return to dictatorial rule, like in Belarus, inconsistent, partial economic reforms without capitalist institution building took a heavy toll on the economies.' Furthermore, the situation was 'exacerbated by the virtual collapse of social security, as pensions devalued, educational and medical services deteriorated and former state enterprises reneged on their social service provisions'.

In countries such as Bulgaria, Romania, Moldova, or Serbia, where successor parties were eventually forced to implement social democratic reform strategies, the outcome was the discrediting of market reforms, leading to increased support for 'new social-protectionist populist parties'. Where the communists did not return to power under a social democratic guise 'as in Russia, it was not liberal democrats who could take advantage of this situation, but non-partisan technocratic government cadres who increasingly manipulated electoral processes through "parties of power." '[69]

A considerably serious problem, however, is posed by the static temporal implications of the article. While it may be true that FIDESZ-MPP for a short time 'reduced the options for the successful entry of the radical right MIÉP to endure' in Hungary's political life, this did not hinder the eventual appearance of the far more radical Movement for a Better Hungary (Jobbik) party, a formation that successfully ran in the 2009 elections for the European parliament and entered the legislature in 2010. There are two further implications deriving from this danger of a static approach. The first might be labelled 'who does the counting'? In other words, what some (for reasons touching on either an attempt to transform cultural into political capital or intellectual metamorphosis, or both) would describe as mere 'conservatism',[70] those who share liberal values might perceive as (at best) 'standing by' extremism or taking political advantage of it,[71]

---

[69] Ibid., 465.

[70] Compare, for instance, George Schöpflin, *Politics in Eastern Europe* (Oxford: Blackwell, 1993), 292–9, with the same author's 'Hungary's Elections: The Dilemma of the Right', *RFE/RL Newsline* (29 April 1998), online at: www.rferl.org/content/article/1141646.html, accessed April 2010; 'New-Old Hungary: A Contested Transformation', *East European Perspectives* 4:10 (2002), online at: www.rferl.org/eepreport/2002/05/10-150502.html, accessed April 2010. See also György Schöpflin, 'Democracy, Populism, and the Political Crisis in Hungary', *Eurozine* (5 July 2007), online at: www.eurozine.com/articles/2007-05-of-schopflin-en.html (accessed April 2010) vs Thomas Von Ahn, 'On the Aims of Discourse', *Eurozine* (6 July 2007), online at: www.eurozine.com/articles/2007-06-12-vonahn-en.html, accessed April 2010.

[71] See, for example, Eric Beckett Weaver, *National Narcissism: The Intersection of the Nationalist Cult and Gender in Hungary* (Oxford: Peter Lang, 2006); Csilla Kiss, 'From Liberalism to Conservatism: The Federation of Young Democrats in Post-Communist Hungary', *East European Politics and Societies* 16:3 (2003), 739–63; Myra Waterbury, 'Internal Exclusion, External Inclusion: Diaspora Politics and Party-Building in Post-Communist Hungary', *East European Politics and Societies* 20:4 (2006), 483–515; Agnes Rajacic, 'Populist Construction of the Past and Future: Emotional Campaigning in Hungary between 2002 and 2006', *East European Politics and Societies* 21:4 (2007), 639–60; Thomas Von Ahn, 'Democracy on the Street? Fragile Stability in Hungary', *Eurozine* (5 July 2007), online at: www.eurozine.com/articles/2007-05-07-vonahn-html, accessed April 2010; Michael Shafir, 'Hungarian Politics and the Post-1989 Legacy of the Holocaust', in Randolph L. Braham and Brewster S. Chamberlin (eds), *The Holocaust in Hungary: Sixty Years Later* (New York: Columbia University Press, 2006), 257–90.

particularly if those who do the counting also happen to be at the 'receiving end' of (in the Hungarian case) Jobbik's unconcealed anti-Roma racism and anti-Semitism. Similarly, to place the Latvian Fatherland and Freedom Party (LNNK) among the non-radical right might be fine for some, but would raise an eyebrow among others, who do not take kindly to that party's turning of the Latvian Legionnaires' participation in World War II as members of the Waffen SS into national heroes and thus indulge in self-victimization.

Neither does the apparently neat partitioning of the legacy of national accommodative versus patrimonial communism always lead to the same outcome. In fact, the opposite argument might be made with the same justification: not only do economic reforms and privatization not pre-empt a surge in the popularity of extreme right parties; they might encourage it. The latter argument has been powerfully made by David Ost for Poland, but might also be extended to other former communist countries. According to Ost, the intellectual leading core of Solidarność became exclusively preoccupied with the economic aspects of the transition, neglecting its social costs and becoming suspicious of its former power base: the workers. It thus neglected any but the economic aspects of liberalism, and gradually abandoned political civism to the right and the far right, which cunningly combined its own values (as defined by Bustikova and Kitschelt's 'grids', I would add) with the posture of defending those paying the immediate highest costs of the economic transition, successfully mobilizing what initially appeared to be a social class beyond its reach. Viewed from this perspective, Ost does not consider the 'politics of anger' to be as negative a phenomenon as did Tismaneanu, but rather self-defensive politics.[72] That the populist Polish Samoobrana RP (Self-Defence of the Republic of Poland) managed to enlist enough popular support to become part of the Jarosław Kaczyński cabinet in 2006–07 should be taken as both a confirmation and a warning. While the electoral base of Samoobrana was rural rather than urban, and while the party and its leadership excelled in the corruption it exclusively attributed to others, its 'politics of anger', verging occasionally on what Jowitt called 'rage', was symptomatic.

If Ost is right (and there are plenty of indications that he might be elsewhere in the former communist world in the wake of the current world economic crisis), one wonders to what extent the ideological hegemony of capitalism is as lasting as it seemed to be twenty years ago. In Poland itself the left wing seems to benefit from a 'transfusion of young blood', inconceivable two decades earlier.[73]

But it is hard to say whether a return to the neo-populist 2005–07 governance is to be ruled out in a not-too-distant future. The neo-populists excel in exploiting the existence and resentment of corruption, and if there is one common trait shared by all former communist countries, regardless of any other differences, it is the universality of that malady, whose roots are to be sought in the transition 'from plan to can'.[74] Whether as

[72] Ost, *The Defeat of Solidarity*, 94–120.

[73] See Dan Bilefsky, 'Polish Left Gets Transfusion of Young Blood' *The New York Times* (12 March 2010), online at: www.nytimes.com/2010/03,13/world/europe/13iht-poland.html, accessed April 2010.

[74] Verdery, *What Was Socialism*, 212.

'velvet corruption', as it has been called in the Czech case, the 'kelptocracy' of the Balkans or the 'sultanistic despoilment' of Central Asia, corruption breeds self-appointed 'defenders of the people' (often enough from among its champions) and decisively contributes to the permanent liminality that is likely to accompany the post-communist world for many a decade, if not a century. Liminality, it should be recalled, makes different futures all likely, and therefore all just as unlikely. What comes after communism, then? Life; a permanency of which, it will be recalled, is uncertainty.

FURTHER READING

Alexander, James, *Political Culture in Post-Communist Russia: Formlessness and Recreation in a Traumatic Transition* (New York: St. Martin's Press, 2000).

Ekiert, Greggorz and Stephen E. Hanson (eds), *Capitalism and Democracy in Central and Eastern Europe: Assessing the Legacy of Communist Rule* (Cambridge: Cambridge University Press, 2003).

Fish, Steven, 'Post-Communist Subversion: Social Science and Democratization in East Europa and Eurasia', *Slavic Review* 58:4 (1999), 794–823.

Hollander, Paul H., *Political Will and Personal Belief: The Decline and Fall of Soviet Communism* (Ann Arbor, MI: Edwards Brothers, 1999).

Meseznikov, Grigorij, Olga Gyarfasova and Daniel Smilov, *Populist Politics and Liberal Democracy in Central and Eastern Europe* (Bratislava: Institute for Public Affairs, 2008).

Petocz, Kalman (ed.), *National Populism and Slovak-Hungarian Relations 2006–2009* (Samorin-Somroja: Forum Minority Research Institute, 2009).

Schmitter, Phillippe C., 'A Balance Sheet of the Vices and Virtues of "Populisms"', *Romanian Journal of Political Science* 7:2 (2007), online at: http://www.eui.eu/Documents/ DepartmentsCentres/SPS/Profiles/Schmitter/PCSBalanceSheetApr06.pdf.

Schöpflin, George, 'Culture and Identity in Post-Communist Europe', in Steven While, Judy Batt and Paul Lewis (eds), *Developments in East European Politics* (London: Macmillan, 1993), 16–35.

Staniszkis, Jadwiga, *Post-Communism: The Emerging Enigma* (Warsaw: Institute of Political Studies, Polish Academy of Sciences, 1999).

Szabados, Krisztián, 'Back by Popular Demand', Demand for Right Wing Extremism (DEREX) Index (Budapest: Political Capital Policy Research Institute), 11 June 2010.

Vujacic, Veljko, 'From Class to Nation: Left, Right, and the Ideological and Institutional Roots of Post-Communist "National Socialism"', *East European Politics and Society* 17:3 (2003), 359–92.

CHAPTER 26

BROTHERS, STRANGERS AND ENEMIES: ETHNO-NATIONALISM AND THE DEMISE OF COMMUNIST YUGOSLAVIA

CATHIE CARMICHAEL

IN the forty-five years after the Second World War that Communist Yugoslavia existed, judgements as to the success of the experiment differed widely. Unlike the first royalist Yugoslav state, which had been dominated by the Serbian Karadjordjević Dynasty, the new country eventually gave recognition to all nationalities within the limits of its own authoritarian ideology. The creation of the second Yugoslavia united Bosnian Muslims, Albanians, Serbs, Montenegrins, Macedonians, Croats, and Slovenes with significant Hungarian, Roma, Italian, and Turkish minorities into a single, nominally Leninist state. What united it was the charismatic authority of its wartime leader Josip Broz Tito and a very large and politically significant army.[1] Communist Yugoslavia brought together people with wide historical experiences and levels of social and infrastructural development varied widely. It was a state without a single language, although the Slavonic variants were similar and often mutually intelligible. In its attempts at standardization in 1954, the Communists decided that 'work will proceed on the common terminology for all spheres of economic, scholarly and cultural life' and 'Serbo-Croat' was forged on the foundations of more than a century of literary collaboration.[2]

In many respects the Communists had faced an almost insuperable task in overcoming the mutual radicalization and distrust between the 'nations' that belonged in the new

---

[1] John B. Allcock, *Explaining Yugoslavia* (London: Hurst, 2000), 270.

[2] Robert D. Greenberg, *Language and Identity in the Balkans* (Oxford: Oxford University Press, 2004), 30.

state. In particular popular culture abounded with tales and sayings about lack of trust and the impossibility of friendship between peoples.[3] Bato Tomašević bitterly recalled wartime collaboration in Plevlje and how some 500 Cetinje Partisans 'were mown down in the streets by a storm of machine-gun fire from the curtained windows and walled courtyards of the Moslem houses where the Italians were concealed'.[4] To overcome that mistrust, the Communist Partisans invented a 'noble lie',[5] namely that the problems of the region were due to foreign invasion and threats and that the Yugoslav peoples had deep fraternal bonds that transcended their religious differences. While this might have been true of the Partisans themselves, their actual combatants during the war had more often been local nationalists (Ustaša and Serbian nationalist Četniks (*Četnici*)) than Germans or Italians.

The Ustaša, led by veteran radical and terrorist Ante Pavelić, were intent on destroying Serb civilization in Croatia and Bosnia during the Second World War.[6] After the establishment of an enlarged fascist 'Independent State of Croatia', which also encompassed Bosnia, they followed the Third Reich's direction on the elimination of Jews and Roma, but were primarily concerned with the Orthodox peoples. Hercegovina, with its minority Catholic population was regarded as Croat land and they targeted Serbs living there and elsewhere in the new state in order to create a more homogenous polity. On 24 July 1941 Eugen Dido Kvaternik, chief of the Ustaša's internal security said to Branko Pešelj of the Croatian Peasant Party:

> I know that you believe and expect the English to win the war. I agree with you; I too believe that the English will win the war in the end, but there will be no Serbs left in Croatia then. In other words, whoever wins the war will have to accept the situation as he finds it.[7]

Ustaša gangs carried out the genocide so rapidly in the early summer of 1941 that some Serbs reported their actions to the authorities, largely because they could not believe that these actions could be sanctioned by a legitimate government.[8]

Muslim Ustaša trained by the SS carried out atrocities against Serbs in 1943 and 12,000 men volunteered to join the Handžar (Simitar) division of the SS.[9] Serb nationalist

---

[3] Mistrust between the Bosnian nationalities during the Second World War is well documented in the memoirs of Rodoljub Čolaković, *Zapisi iz oslobodilačkog rata*, 3 vols (Zagreb: Naprijed, 1961).

[4] Bato Tomašević, *Life and Death in the Balkans: A Family Saga in a Century of Conflict* (London: Hurst, 2008), 176.

[5] Djordje Stefanović, 'From Genocide to Brotherhood and Unity: Bosnia-Herzegovina, 1941–1943', Association for Study of Nationalities 12th World Convention, Harriman Institute, Columbia University, New York, April 2007.

[6] Vladimir Dedijer, *The Yugoslav Auschwitz and the Vatican: The Croatian Massacre of Serbs during World War II* (Buffalo, NY: Prometheus Books, 1992).

[7] Tomislav Dulić, *Utopias of Nation: Local Mass Killing in Bosnia and Herzegovina, 1941–42* (Uppsala: Acta Universitatis Upsaliensis, Studia Historica Upsaliensia, 2005), 100.

[8] Aleksa Djilas, *The Contested Country: Yugoslav Unity and Communist Revolution 1919–1953* (Cambridge, MA: Harvard University Press, 1991), 121.

[9] Francine Friedman, *The Bosnian Muslims: Denial of a Nation* (Boulder, CO: Westview, 1996), 124.

Četniks posed a simultaneous threat to Muslim life[10] in the Independent State of Croatia and laid waste to ancient towns such as Foča.[11] In addition to their extreme anti-Islamic beliefs, they mocked their Communist Partisan opponents as 'Stalin's bastards', shouting out 'Where's Moša to help you now?'[12] Tomislav Dulić has calculated that approximately 75 per cent of Jewish and Roma communities of the Ustaša state died as 'victims of fascism' and up to 17 per cent of Serbs, 6 per cent of Croats, and 9 per cent of Muslims, many of the latter killed by Četniks.[13]

The Communists faced enormous problems of reconstruction once they had defeated the Axis and its local collaborators. Bridges, roads, and railway lines had been destroyed and over one million people killed. In 1941 there had been 150,000 sheep in Bosnia and by 1945 this number had dwindled to only 8000.[14] The survivors were frequently traumatized by the violence they had witnessed and exhausted by overwhelming personal loss. Bato Tomašević went with his mother in search of his brother Duško, who had been killed by Četniks. He eventually identified his brother's skull from the filling in one of the molars.[15] The historian Vladimir Dedijer, who later played a key role in creating the cult of Tito's personality,[16] remembered being 'pulled toward the dark forest' by his dead friend Lola Ribar and wife Olga, who lost an arm before finally succumbing to her wounds, awaking from terrifying dreams in tears.[17] It was with the joint sentiment of triumph over adversity and grief that the second Yugoslavia was founded.

After the break with the Soviets in 1948, which rocked them to the core, the Yugoslav Communists veered on an uneasy path between centralization and republican autonomy.[18] For many of them, an intellectual schism with Stalin had probably occurred somewhat earlier,[19] but the leadership was probably given a short-term patriotic boost by its expulsion from Cominform, as Nikita Khrushchev was later to observe.[20] Tito's

---

[10] Nusret Šehić, *Četništvo u Bosni i Hercegovini (1918–1941). Politička uloga i oblici djelatnosti Četničkih udruženja* (Sarajevo: Akademija nauka i umjetnosti Bosne i Hercegovine, 1971).

[11] Adil Zulfikarpašić with Milovan Djilas and Nadežda Gaće, *Bošnjak* (Zürich: Bošnjački institut, 1994), 56.

[12] Tomašević, *Life and Death*, 241. The taunt refers not only to the prominent Jewish Partisan Moša Pijade, but also to the Biblical Moses.

[13] Tomislav Dulić, 'Mass Killing in the Independent State of Croatia, 1941–1945: A Case for Comparative Research', *Journal of Genocide Research* 8:3 (2006), 273; Vladimir Dedijer, *Genocid nad muslimanima 1941–45, Zbornik documenta i svjedočenja* (Sarajevo: Svjetlost, 1990).

[14] Morgan Philips Price, *Through the Iron Curtain: A Record of a Journey through the Balkans in 1946* (London: Sampson Low, 1949), 63.

[15] Tomašević, *Life and Death*, 352–3.

[16] Vladimir Dedijer, *Josip Broz Tito: Prilozi za biografiju* (Zagreb: Kultura, 1953).

[17] Vladimir Dedijer, *The Beloved Land* (London: MacGibbon and Kee, 1961), 338.

[18] Sabrina P. Ramet, *Nationalism and Federalism in Yugoslavia 1962–1991*, 2nd edn (Bloomington, IN: Indiana University Press, 1994).

[19] See for example the memoirs of Milovan Djilas, *Conversations with Stalin* (New York: Harcourt, Brace and Co, 1962).

[20] 'Tito had behind him a state and a people who had had a serious education in fighting for liberty and independence, a people who gave support to its leaders', Nikita Khrushchev, ' "Secret Speech" of 1956', in Robert V. Daniels (ed.), *A Documentary History of Communism in Russia: From Lenin to Gorbachev* (Burlington, VT: University of Vermont, 1993), 257.

closest advisor Edvard Kardelj, sincerely believed in the principle of 'national self-determination', which meant that that the initial 1946 Yugoslavian Constitution was closely modelled on the Soviet one of 1936. He was responsible for drawing up internal boundaries, favouring a compromise between historical settlement and new realities. The Slovenian republic was given three Adriatic port towns, Koper, Izola, and Piran, historically occupied by ethnic Italians, most of whom had fled or been pushed out by force at the end of the war. Bosnia-Hercegovina was allowed to keep one coastal town, Neum, despite the fact that it bifurcated coastal Croatia and had an overwhelming majority of Croats living there in 1946. Although other elements of Soviet ideology were eventually jettisoned in favour of local experiments such as 'workers' self-management' and a 'non-alignment' in foreign policy, the republics defined in the internal borders of the state until its collapse and beyond. It was the Soviet-style system of republics that weakened the state more than any other single factor, primarily because nationalists could remember the war and alternative ideologies and wanted different borders.

The borders between the new Communists republics of Montenegro, Croatia, Serbia, and Bosnia had been fundamentally unstable since the 1870s and remained a potential nationalist tinderbox even after the Partisans' defeat of the Četniks. In 1878 the Treaty of Berlin had allowed the Habsburg Monarchy to administer the formerly Ottoman Bosnia. They faced considerable opposition from the local Orthodox and Muslim populations leading to rebellions in 1878 and 1882, which were brutally repressed.[21] Both Serbia and its neighbour Montenegro, which had gained part of Hercegovina in 1878, had wanted to prevent further Habsburg incursions. The Serbs considered the Orthodox people of Bosnia to be an 'unredeemed' part of their nation and this is the core of the ideology that later defined the Četnik movement.

Eventually Muslims were pacified by the Habsburg authorities, but the Serbs remained fundamentally opposed to their rule. In 1914, during a state visit to Sarajevo, the heir to the Habsburg crown Franz Ferdinand was assassinated by a Bosnian Serb Gavrilo Princip. Within the monarchy, a hate campaign was waged against the Serbs as they blamed the Belgrade government for Princip's terrorism and used the assassination as an excuse to declare war and commit widespread atrocities against their neighbours. Possibly one quarter of the Serb population perished during the First World War from starvation, disease, and war injuries.[22] After the collapse of the Habsburgs at the end of 1918, Muslims became the focus of local nationalist plans for expulsion. Large landed estates were broken up, which led to poverty among the formerly rich Muslim landowners.[23] Political crises and the breakdown of authority led to further attacks on Muslims in the 1940s. The genocide in Bosnia in the 1990s can largely be attributed to a revival in Četnik nationalist ideas from the period between the 1870s and 1940s.

---

[21] John R. Schindler, 'Defeating Balkan Insurgency: The Austro-Hungarian Army in Bosnia-Hercegovina, 1878–82', *Journal of Strategic Studies* 27:3 (2004), 528–52.

[22] Mark Cornwall, 'Introduction', in Andrej Mitrović, *Serbia's Great War 1914–1918* (London: Hurst, 2007).

[23] Zulfikarpašić, *Bošnjak*, 27–9.

Despite strong leadership in the years before Tito's death in 1980, many observers noted marked differences between the ethnic and religious groups and the general absence of 'Yugoslavs'. American William Lockwood noted that ethnic demarcation amongst men in Bugojno in Central Bosnia could be discerned by hats in the mid-1970s.[24] The older Muslims wore a maroon fez while the younger ones preferred a beret and the Catholics had a soft knitted cap or skullcap. In contrast, the Orthodox wore a fur hat (*šubara*) or more importantly a communist-style worker's cap (*titova kapa*), an indication of support for the regime and continuity with the Partisan traditions of the 1940s (and inferring less-warm regime support from the other groups). A decade or so later in Sarajevo, Cornelia Sorabji observed that there was quite a profound level of ignorance among Muslims of Sarajevo about both Orthodox and Catholic culture.[25] Adil Zulfikarpašić suggested that much vaunted Bosnian tolerance and respect were accompanied by a lack of interest in the habits of other religions.[26] Of course, the existence of difference did not necessarily equate to hostility, but it did become a clear political problem once Communist hegemony had gone in 1990.

The regime's policy of mutual respect and interdependence between nationalities (*bratstvo i jedinstvo*) was closely adhered to by official bodies. The national football team normally had to have a player from each nation, regardless of whether that would improve their sporting chances. Army conscripts were sent to other republics to build up their sense of Yugoslav patriotism. Tito took great care to remind Yugoslavians to 'guard brotherhood and unity as the apple of their eye'.[27] In some respects the 1990s war in Bosnia has been seen as a clash between 'intolerant' ethnic nationalism and 'tolerant' multinationalism,[28] but this would be a misleading dichotomy. In Bosnia there was a blurring between religious and national identity in a very dynamic and fluid overall situation before the 1990s. During the Communist period, all manifestations of national identity were tightly policed by the regime, which might give an impression of living in peace, but it was always a kind of controlled harmony.

The Communists also showed little respect for traditional culture and religion when they came to power. Alojzije Stepinac, Archbishop of Zagreb was put on show trial to highlight the collaboration between the Roman Catholic Church and the Croatian fascist Ustaša. Muslim material culture was often levelled under the guise of modernization. Munevera Hadžišehović recalled that after the war in Prijepolje '(t)hree Muslim graveyards, a *turbe* (tomb), and a mosque in the town were destroyed so that new

---

[24] William G. Lockwood, *European Moslems: Economy and Ethnicity in Western Bosnia* (New York: Academic Press, 1975), 49.

[25] Cornelia Sorabji, 'Muslim Identity and Islamic Faith in Sarajevo', PhD thesis, University of Cambridge, 1989, 208. On Muslim–Catholic relations in Bosnia before the 1992 war see also Tone Bringa, *Being Muslim the Bosnian Way* (Princeton, NJ: Princeton University Press, 1995).

[26] Zulfikarpašić, *Bošnjak*, 41.

[27] Vjekoslav Perica, *Balkan Idols: Religion and Nationalism in Yugoslav States* (Oxford: Oxford University Press, 2002), 101.

[28] Francine Friedman, *Bosnia and Herzegovina: A Polity on the Brink* (New York: Routledge, 2004), 82.

buildings could be constructed'.[29] Initially Muslims were not named as a separate ethnic category, but during the 1970s the regime relaxed its attitudes towards other faiths, which allowed both Christians and Muslims to invest in new religious buildings and the Catholics even built a pilgrimage site in Medjugorje, Hercegovina.[30] Somehow there remained glimmers of another world in which tolerance and mutual respect between the nations and peoples existed, which even survived the nationalist surge of the 1990s. Medical doctor Svetlana Broz collected a remarkable series of stories about neighbours who helped each other during the Bosnian War,[31] a phenomenon also noted by the ethnographer Dunja Rihtman-Auguštin.[32] Muslims living in what James Ron has called the 'Serbian core' were generally left alone during the entire Bosnian war, as were over 100,000 Kosovars living in Belgrade in 1999.[33]

Despite the Communist regime's attempts to create a unified culture, nationalist discontent occasionally surfaced. In Croatia between the late 1960s and 1971, there was something of a revival of interest in the literary language and a rejection of Communist cultural homogenization. Although this was ruthlessly suppressed, some economic liberalization took place, which allowed Croatians to make modest profits from international tourists. Yugoslavs frequently worked abroad as *Gastarbeiter* in West Germany and invested their hard currency in homes, many of which were burnt down during the war in the 1990s. Apparent prosperity was short-lived. There was a severe economic crisis in the 1980s after regime borrowing in the previous decades. In 1987 there were 1500 strikes involving 365,000 workers caused by low wages and rampant inflation. By 1986 young people experienced an average of a three-year wait for a job and the situation was worse for graduates.[34]

One of the preconditions for the growth of extreme ideologies is often the gap between expectations and reality and nationalism became something of an alternative career for underemployed Yugoslavs after the death of Tito. In 1984, a young Bosnian Serb academic Vojislav Šešelj was imprisoned for 20 months after writing material that was deemed excessively nationalist by the regime.[35] His case, which was regarded at the time as a miscarriage of justice by Amnesty International, raised the profile of alternative Četnik beliefs that had previously been suppressed and demonized through literature and films.[36] After the rise of Slobodan Milošević in 1987, he was able to flaunt his views

---

[29] Munevera Hadžišehović, *A Muslim Woman in Tito's Yugoslavia* (College Station, TX: Texas A&M Press, 2003), 112.

[30] Élisabeth Claverie, *Les guerres de la Vierge. Une anthropologie des apparitions* (Paris: Gallimard, 2003).

[31] Svetlana Broz and Laurie Kain Hart (eds), *Good People in an Evil Time: Portraits of Complicity and Resistance in the Bosnian War* (New York: Other Press, 2004).

[32] Dunja Rihtman-Auguštin, 'O susjedima', in Božidar Jakšić (ed.), *Tolerancija* (Belgrade-Zemun: Biblioteka XX vek, 1999), 151–64.

[33] James Ron, *Frontiers and Ghettos: State Violence in Serbia and Israel* (Berkeley, CA: University of California Press, 2003), 73–4.

[34] Barbara Jančar, 'Ecology and Self-Management: A Balance Sheet for the 1980s', in John B. Allcock, John J. Horton and Marko Milivojević (eds), *Yugoslavia in Transition* (Oxford: Berg, 1992), 351–2.

[35] Robert J. Donia, *Sarajevo: A Biography* (Ann Arbor, MI: University of Michigan Press, 2006), 245.

[36] See for example the response of his supporters published as Vojislav Šešelj, *Pravo na istinu* (Belgrade: Multiprint, 1988).

quite openly in Serbia. On the television programme *Minimaxovizija* in 1991, he told the audience 'Where is Bosnia-Hercegovina? It is a Serbian land.'[37] The audience laughed politely, still nervous perhaps at the open flaunting of views associated with Četnik Stevan Moljević, who had been jailed by the Communists after the war.

During his long career as Tito's second-in-command, Kardelj had displaced internal rivals in the Communist hierarchy, particularly Aleksandar Ranković, whose policies were associated with Belgrade centralization.[38] Kardelj was the moving spirit behind the 1974 Constitution, which changed the status of Serbia within the Communist Federation and provoked an angry backlash in that republic. In particular, Serbs were angry that Vojvodina and Kosovo, which had both previously been part of the Serbian republic were given fresh status as 'autonomous regions' and had most of the privileges of discrete republics. After 1980, less restraint was shown about their public manifestations of nationalism although it was always rumoured that these ideas had been kept alive at the private level.

Popular nationalist fears were stirred up by the media,[39] the Orthodox Church and by academics, articulated in the draft Memorandum of the Serbian Academy of September 1986, a sophisticated critique of the Communist legacy as well as a strident 'defence' of the Serbs within the Confederation.[40] In particular the status of Serbs in Kosovo concerned the authors of the memorandum and they borrowed the term 'genocide' from the author of a recent text on the subject to describe the putative fate of that community.[41] Between 1961 and 1981, over 110,000 thousand Serbs had left Kosovo, especially as their status in the region was seen to have declined after the fall of Ranković in 1966.[42] By the mid-1980s, the newspapers in Serbia had begun to publish wild stories about violent and/or sexual attacks on Serbs by Albanians.[43] These myths may have helped to lay the foundations for the events of the 1990s in Bosnia, where sexual violence was widely carried out against Muslim women.

The rise in Serbian nationalism has often been attributed to Milošević, who came to power within the League of Communists after outspoken remarks on Belgrade television about Kosovo's Serbs in 1987, but the growth of such ideas predated his ascendency by several years. What he did do was to make the beliefs of a small number of radicals more widely acceptable, ending the Communist ideological hegemony on the national question. At the time of his rise to power, the Yugoslavian economy had begun to decline and this downturn was accompanied by a profound loss of confidence in existing state

[37]   http://www.youtube.com/watch?v=xIRMJMLyenw, accessed December 2009.

[38]   Mitja Velikonja, *Religious Separation and Political Intolerance in Bosnia and Herzegovina* (College Station, TX: Texas A&M Press, 2003), 223.

[39]   Mark Thompson, *Forging War: The Media in Serbia, Croatia, Bosnia and Hercegovina* (Luton: University of Luton Press/Article 19. International Centre against Censorship, 1999).

[40]   Jasna Dragović Soso, *Saviours of the Nation? Serbia's Intellectual Opposition and the Revival of Nationalism* (London: Hurst, 2002), 176–95.

[41]   Dimitrije Bogdanović, *Knjiga o Kosovu* (Belgrade: Srpska akademija nauka i umetnosti, 1985).

[42]   Viktor Meier, *Yugoslavia: A History of its Demise* (New York: Routledge, 1999), 32.

[43]   Wendy Bracewell, 'Rape in Kosovo: Masculinity and Serbian Nationalism', *Nations and Nationalism* 6:4 (2000), 563–90.

structures. However without nationalist agency, conflicts would not be perpetuated for generations and the charismatic authority of individuals is crucial.[44] The foundation of a new nationalist party, *Srpska demokratska stranka* (SDS), in 1990 with offshoots in Serbia, Montenegro, Krajina, and Bosnia also helped to increase communication between Serbs in different parts of the state with key nationalists such as the writer Dobrica Ćosić in Belgrade.

Elsewhere in Yugoslavia, there was also clear discontent with the Communist state. In 1982, the journal *Nova revija* first appeared in Ljubljana, stating that its authors were inspired by the Polish *Solidarność*. In 1987, they issued 'contributions to the Slovene National Question,'[45] with 'overtly secessionist tones.'[46] The following year, journalists, including the future Prime Minister Janez Janša, writing for the maverick party youth journal *Mladina* were charged with handling confidential Yugoslav army documents. The trial of the four reflected 'the enormous gulf in opinion between Slovene society and the Yugoslav military'[47] and sharpened a process of rejection of the Communist state apparatus. In 1989 democratic parties began to organize openly and when the League of Communists finally collapsed in January 1990, a coalition of democratic parties (DEMOS) was elected. At the end of that year, the new government held a plebiscite on independence, which was overwhelmingly endorsed and moved towards full independence in the early summer of 1991. The Yugoslav National Army initially tried to prevent this move, but with no politicians in the rest of the federation willing to fight Slovenia, the independence of the small Alpine state was recognized internationally within a few months. The southernmost republic of Macedonia also departed from Yugoslavia later that year, without significant opposition except from neighbouring Greece.

When the Croatian government also announced independence from Yugoslavia in the early summer of 1991, their situation was far more difficult than in Slovenia or Macedonia. They did not actually control the parts of the republic that had been formed into a 'Serbian Autonomous Region' during the previous months.[48] During the following months, until the United Nations brokered a peace and division of Croatia in January 1992, Serbs centred on the town of Knin drove out Croats from the Krajina and parts of Slavonia and Dalmatia. The historic Adriatic port of Dubrovnik was repeatedly shelled from the sea and its hinterland attacked. Much of the damage inflicted appeared to be from 'malice'[49] rather than for defined military objectives. Serbs living in Zagreb came under pressure to leave the capital and relations between the two peoples deteriorated,

---

[44] Siniša Malešević, *Ideology, Legitimacy and the New State: Yugoslavia, Serbia and Croatia* (London: Frank Cass, 2002), 87–90.

[45] Jože Pučnik et al., 'Prispevki za slovenski nacionalni program', *Nova revija* 57 (1987).

[46] Dragović Soso, *Saviours of the Nation?*, 163.

[47] James Gow and Cathie Carmichael, *Slovenia and the Slovenes: A Small State in the New Europe* (London: Hurst, 2000), 152.

[48] James Gow, *The Serbian Project and its Adversaries: A Strategy of War Crimes* (London: Hurst, 2003).

[49] Paul Theroux, *The Pillars of Hercules: A Grand Tour of the Mediterranean* (London: Hamish Hamilton, 1995), 243.

with Serbs often dubbed 'Srbo-Četnici' by the Croatian media.[50] According to Vitomir Belaj, very negative essentialist stereotypes of Serbs circulated through the medium of jokes in Croatia in the autumn of 1991.[51] Similarly, the mawkish words of a Croatian pop song 'E, moj druže beogradski' from the war period can be interpreted in terms of 'revenge':

> O my Belgrade friend, we will meet again near the Sava. And you will know me and you will shoot. I will not even aim and will pray to God that I miss you. But in the end I will not miss. I will mourn you and close your eyes. Oh, I was so sad because I lost my friend.[52]

The new government in Croatia was not especially careful in the early 1990s about its association with the past and the legacy of the fascist Ustaša. Across Croatia, local monuments were named after Ustaša minister and literary figure Mile Budak, one of the 'offensive phenomena' that provoked a sad response from local Jewish communities.[53] Official literary Croatian was purged of 'Serb' words, 'echoing the practices of the Pavelić regime'.[54] President Franjo Tudjman welcomed the exodus of Serbs from Krajina in 1995[55] and harboured war criminals who had been active in Hercegovina in 1993. Some of his cabinet members, including Defence Minister Gojko Šušak, had clear links with the far right. Fifteen years after the signing of the Dayton Treaty, sections of the Croatian public still show vivid public support for accused war criminals such as General Ante Gotovina.[56]

Perhaps more important to Tudjman's political project was the idea of the martyrdom of the Croatian people during the war of 1991–5, which also allowed the Catholic Church to increase its influence and public profile in everyday life. Atrocities committed by Serb paramilitaries certainly led to a general sense of righteous indignation and victimhood.[57] During the autumn of 1991, the Slavonian town of Vukovar was reduced to rubble by paramilitaries and the Yugoslavian National Army (JNA). On the other hand, the destruction of the town was presented as 'theatre' to Red Star Belgrade

---

[50] Dunja Rihtman-Auguštin, *Ulice moga grada. Antropologija domaćeg terena* (Belgrade: Biblioteka XX vek, 2000), 19.

[51] Vitomir Belaj, 'Jokes about the Serbs, Autumn 1991', *Etnološka stičišča* 5 & 7 (1997), 49.

[52] Tatjana Pavlović,'Women in Croatia: Feminists, Nationalists and Homosexuals', in Sabrina P. Ramet (ed.), *Gender Politics in the Western Balkans: Women and Society in Yugoslavia and the Yugoslav Successor States* (Pennsylvania, PA: Penn State University Press, 1999), 144. On Croatian rock music, see also Catherine Baker, *Sounds of the Borderland: Popular Music, War and Nationalism in Croatia since 1991* (Farnham: Ashgate, 2010).

[53] Sabrina P. Ramet, *Nihil Obstat: Religion, Politics, and Social Change in East-Central Europe and Russia* (Durham, NC: Duke University Press, 1998), 178.

[54] Cathie Carmichael, ' "A People Exists and That People Has Its Language": Language and Nationalism in the Balkans', in Stephen Barbour and Cathie Carmichael (eds), *Language and Nationalism in Europe* (Oxford: Oxford University Press, 2000), 238.

[55] James Gow, *Triumph of the Lack of Will: International Diplomacy and the Yugoslav War* (London: Hurst, 1997), 43.

[56] Pål Kolstø, 'Bleiburg: The Creation of a National Martyrology', *Europe-Asia Studies* 62:7 (2010), 1163.

[57] Dubravka Ugrešić, *The Culture of Lies* (University Park, PA: Penn State Press, 1998), 100.

supporters. 'Utilising the football stadium as the perfect venue to brandish the spoils of war, a group of (Arkan's paramilitary) Tigers in full uniform held aloft consecutive road signs: "20 miles to Vukovar", "10 miles to Vukovar", "Welcome to Vukovar".[58] Croatian independence had triggered a Serb rebellion at a time when many Serbs across Yugoslavia had been radicalized over the Kosovo issue. The element of trauma due to the suppression of memory from two world wars amongst Serbs should not be under-estimated. Fear of Islamic encroachment stemmed from the years of Ottoman oppression, the legacy of earlier genocides and the Iranian revolution of 1979 making Serbs vulnerable to cynical nationalist politicians.[59]

The demise of Communism had led to a fraught examination of the numbers killed in the Second World War and symbolic reburials of their bodies, often led by the Orthodox Church.[60] Many observers have analysed the historicized nature of Serbian nationalism.[61] Michael Sells observed that in the 1990s, Serb paramilitaries transformed themselves into different figures and actually wore ski masks or painted their faces: 'Before he put on the mask, the militiaman was part of a multi-religious community...Once he put on the mask, he was a Serb hero; those he was abusing were *balije* or Turks, race-traitors or killers of the Christ-Prince Lazar.'[62] In some Serbian nationalist circles, indicted war criminals remain figures that command respect, joining a pantheon of earlier 'heroic' figures such as the Četnik leader Draža Mihailović, who was executed by the Communists in 1946.[63]

Events in Bosnia after 1991 resembled the deteriorating circumstances in Croatia that had led to fighting and ethnic cleansing. Serb nationalists in the SDS led by Radovan Karadžić threatened the 'Muslims' led by President Alija Izetbegović in a parliamentary session with 'hell' if it left Yugoslavia.[64] In April 1992, his government called a referendum on independence, which was boycotted by almost one third of the population of the republic, largely on the instruction of the SDS. Of those who did vote, over 99 per cent opted for full independence. The referendum emphasized the depth of the chasm between Serb nationalists and the supporters of Izetbegović's government. Despite the fact that they had failed to carry the support of even a minority of the Serb population with them, the Bosnian government went ahead, declared independence

---

[58] Richard Mills, ' "It all ended in an unsporting way". Serbian Football and the Disintegration of Yugoslavia', *International Journal of the History of Sport* 26:9 (2009), 1188.

[59] Bette Denich, 'Dismembering Yugoslavia: Nationalist Ideologies and the Symbolic Revival of Genocide', *American Ethnologist* 21:1 (1994), 367–90.

[60] Katherine Verdery, *The Political Lives of Dead Bodies: Reburial and Postsocialist Change* (New York: Columbia University Press, 2000).

[61] Ivan Čolović, *Bordel ratnika. Folklor, politika i rat* (Belgrade: Biblioteka XX vek, 1993); Ivo Žanić, *Prevarena povijest. Guslarska estrada, kult Hajduka i rat u Hrvatskoj i Bosni i Hercegovini 1990–1995. Godine* (Zagreb: Durieux, 1998).

[62] Michael Sells, *The Bridge Betrayed: Religion and Genocide in Bosnia*, 2nd edn (Berkeley, CA: University of California Press, 1998), 77.

[63] Sabrina P. Ramet, 'The Denial Syndrome and its Consequences: Serbian Political Culture since 2000', *Communist and Post-Communist Studies* 40:1 (2007), 50.

[64] Florence Hartmann, *Milošević: La diagonale du fou* (Paris: Denoël, 1999), 247.

and promptly faced Serb military resistance as they took over the northern and eastern parts of the country.

Serb nationalists argued that independence was illegal without the support of all three 'constituent' nationalities of Bosnia and that they would be in the majority had they not been subjected to genocide in the past. Claiming to be in defence of their national rights, Serb paramilitary troops murdered civilians often leaving their bodies on display. Backed by an armed wing of the SDS, the Bosnian Serb Army (VRS), commanded by Ratko Mladić, took over large areas and set up prison camps using weapons from the Yugoslavian People's Army.[65] The government remained in Sarajevo, which was subjected to shelling and sniper attacks. Their supporters fled into the towns such as Goražde, Srebrenica, and Žepa often living without safe transport, medical supplies, or food. In their attempts to destroy the Muslims as an ethnic group within the regions of Bosnia that they claimed, armed Serb extremists committed acts that were designed not only to kill individuals, but also to destroy morale and break community cohesion such as gang rape and torture.[66] Rather than breaking people down, atrocities against Bosnian Muslims actually reinforced a sense of group identity.[67]

Izetbegović appealed to the International Community to help him defend the state. During the early stages of the war, a UN embargo on importing armaments had crippled his government's ability to defend itself. It is possible that international ineptitude made the fate of Bosnia worse and delayed the Bosnian government's military successes. Internationally supported peace treaties such as the one set forward by Cyrus Vance and David Owen in 1993, which proposed dividing Bosnia into ethnic 'cantons', may have speeded up the ethnic cleansing of some regions to make Serb and Croat claims stronger and actually made the conflict worse. Attempts to end the fighting tended to emphasize wholly erroneous notions of 'ancient hatreds' between peoples and failed to understand that the war was actually being fought to revise the 1946 borders in favour of Serbs (and subsequently Croats) and to reverse Tito's Yugoslav experiment. Apparently emboldened by plans to divide the Bosnian state, Croat Defence Council paramilitaries (HVO) began targeting Bosnian Muslims in Hercegovina in 1993.

After the United Nations Protection Force intervened in June 1992, many Bosnian Muslims were confined to so-called 'safe areas' in the Eastern towns. Under the terms imposed by the United Nations they were also disarmed, leaving the people of Srebrenica completely dependent on others to defend them. In 1995, the Bosnian government began to reverse the military stagnation of the previous three years and the

---

[65] The high incidence of criminal actions led to the establishment of the International Criminal Tribunal for the former Yugoslavia (ICTY) to punish breaches of international law, which was convoked in The Hague in 1993.

[66] Caroline Kennedy-Pipe and Penny Stanley, 'Rape in War: Lesssons of the Balkan Conflicts in the 1990s', in Ken Booth (ed.), *The Kosovo Tragedy: The Human Rights Dimension* (London: Frank Cass, 2000), 67–84.

[67] Manus I. Midlarsky, 'Systemic War in the Former Yugoslavia', in David Carment and Patrick James (eds), *Wars in the Midst of Peace: The International Politics of Ethnic Conflict* (Pittsburgh, PA: University of Pittsburgh Press, 1997), 62.

Croatian government retook the areas of that republic that had been occupied by Serbs.[68] As the rebel Serbs were pushed out of Krajina and failed to take strategically crucial Bihać in Western Bosnia despite huge losses, their military tactics became more desperate and the army more demoralized.[69] Inadequate protection from Dutch UN troops in July 1995 led to the surrender of the 'safe haven' of Srebrenica to Mladić and the slaughter of almost the entire Muslim male population of about 8000. Sensing imminent intervention by Serbia, the Americans brokered the Dayton Peace Treaty in 1995, which split the administration of Bosnia-Hercegovina into the Serbian controlled Republika Srpska and Federation Territory, controlled primarily by Muslims and Croats. Although the creation of a Serbian section of Bosnia might have seemed like the culmination of Četnik ambitions, the Serbs lost their historic populations in Croatia in 1995 leading to widespread recriminations within the nationalist ranks.[70] Furthermore in 2006 the Montenegrins, who most nationalists regard as the 'salt of Serbdom', severed formal links with Serbia and opted for independence. The Serb population of Kosovo is also less than half of its pre-1990 number. The implementation of the Dayton Treaty has been administered by a European Union High Representative, a unique arrangement that has now been renewed beyond its original mandate. Bosnia is governed through a highly 'complex' set of political rules.[71] Over 100,000 people died as a result of the war, most either in the summer of 1992 by Serb paramilitary groups or during the siege of Sarajevo. By far the highest number of individuals killed were Muslims, although over 25,000 Serbs and about 8000 Croats also died. Bosnia's Muslims were also heavily displaced.

Stephen Saideman has suggested that by supporting nationalists in Croatia and Bosnia, the Serbian state left itself vulnerable to secessionist movements, which is what effectively occurred in Kosovo after 1998.[72] The issue of Kosovo remained untouched at Dayton even though the constitutional rights of the region had been revoked in 1989. Thereafter, until 1999, the region was effectively run from Belgrade without significant cooperation with the vast majority of Kosovars.[73] In 1992, 80 per cent of the region's population voted for independence in 1992 by a margin of 98 per cent. This vote, which had been boycotted by the region's Serbs, was also ignored internationally. This situation was cut short by the formation of a guerrilla group that called itself the Kosovo Liberation Army (KLA). Ironically the strategy of armed resistance adopted by the KLA had

---

[68] Marko Attila Hoare, *How Bosnia Armed: The Birth and Rise of the Bosnian Army* (London: Saqi Books, 2004).

[69] Phillip Corwin, *Dubious Mandate: A Memoir of the UN in Bosnia, Summer 1995* (Durham, NC: Duke University Press, 1999), 202.

[70] Milisav Sekulić, *Knin je pao u Beogradu* (Bad Vilbel: Nidda Verlag, 2000).

[71] Sumantra Bose, *Bosnia after Dayton: Nationalist Partition and International Intervention* (London: Hurst, 2002), 1.

[72] Stephen M. Saideman, 'Explaining the International Relations of Secessionist Conflicts: Vulnerability versus Ethnic Ties', *International Organization* 51 (1997), 742.

[73] Shkëlzen Maliqi, *Kosova: Separate Worlds: Reflections and Analyses 1989–1998* (Priština: Dukagjini, 1998).

similarities to the formation of Serbian Autonomous Regions in Croatia and Bosnia in the early 1990s.[74]

The KLA provoked violent clashes with the Serb authorities and increasingly found support within the Kosovo's Albanian community. In 1998, one of its founders, Adem Jashari and his entire family were killed by the police, a massacre that led to an international backlash. The Belgrade government received a number of ultimatums from an International Community led by the NATO countries in France in 1999, which were primarily designed to avoid another Bosnia. Milošević was unable to abandon Kosovo because of nationalist tenacity amongst his supporters and an insistence that Kosovo was 'Serbia'. He was also unable to withstand NATO airpower. During the first half of 1999, the Yugoslav Army (VJ) committed atrocities against the Albanians in order to depopulate Kosovo, as had already happened in Bosnia and parts of Croatia. The Yugoslav Army killed over 10,000 Kosovars during the campaign of air strikes upon Serbia and Montenegro in 1999 and up to 500 non-Kosovar citizens of the Federal Republic of Yugoslavia (FRY) were also killed by NATO. After the surrender of the FRY and the introduction of United Nations (UNMIK) administration, the Kosovars returned to their damaged homes, beginning a process of revenge against local Serbs and Roma and as many as 700 were killed that year. Serbs left over the following years leading to a further decline in their numbers until Kosovo's independence in 2008. The declaration precipitated a Serb backlash in areas in the north of the country, particularly in the town of Mitrovica.

It has remained difficult to discuss genocide and crimes against humanity in fair historical context within parts of Croatia, Serbia, and enclaves within the Croat–Muslim Federation, Republika Srpska, and Montenegro. A lack of contrition and repentance in some circles does not bode well for future relations between Balkan states, despite general aspirations to join the European Union. Some public figures remain amongst the most overtly extreme in Europe and thus it has proved notoriously difficult to unsettle this worldview among a still large nationalist milieu. Serb nationalists have often accused those who disagreed with them with 'treachery'. In May 1999, the then opposition politician Zoran Djindjić, who was later assassinated for his part in the removal of Slobodan Milošević to the ICTY was accused by state-controlled television as being a 'traitor' and 'fifth columnist'.[75] The Serbian Radicals, a far-right party, won almost 29 per cent of the votes cast in the January 2007 parliamentary elections. In May 2008, after the declaration of Kosovo's independence in the previous February, the Serbian Radicals received a slightly higher percentage of votes, which gives us an insight into the ability of the far right to reinvent itself in the twenty-first century.[76]

[74] Keiichi Kubo, 'Why Kosovar Albanians Took up Arms against the Serbian Regime: The Genesis and Expansion of the UCK in Kosovo', *Europe-Asia Studies* 62:7 (2010), 1135–52.

[75] Slobodan Antonić, 'Poslednje greške i pad Slobodana Miloševića', *Reč: Časopis za književnost i kulturu i društvena pitanja* 62:8 (2001), 168.

[76] Djordje Stefanović, 'The Path to Weimar Serbia? Explaining the Resurgence of the Serbian Far Right after the Fall of Milošević', *Ethnic and Racial Studies* 31:7 (2008), 1195–221.

In many respects the areas that had once been part of Yugoslavia changed beyond recognition between 1990 and 2010 and are unlikely ever to be linked in a political sense except as part of the European Union. Rather than repudiating the Communists per se, the Yugoslav peoples (or at least the most vocal nationalists) rejected the state structures and ideologies of 1945–90 and reverted to many of the former nationalist beliefs. Paradoxically at a time when much of Europe appeared to have jettisoned the extreme nationalism of the first half of the twentieth century, a small number of Croat and Serb radicals reinvented it in the 1980s. Because of the revival of irredentist values and the violence that accompanied it, the collapse of Yugoslavia differed rather markedly from the end of the other Communist states in Eastern Europe. School and university curricula were rewritten and the once compulsory course 'History of the Yugoslav Peoples' replaced by nationalist variants. In cases where there was no money to purchase new textbooks, paragraphs were simply blocked out with dark ink to suit local purposes.[77] A longing for the past is not unknown in the region, although it is possible to overstate the actual importance of 'Yugonostalgia'.[78] There has been a notable recrudescence in 'traditional' forms of identity such as the Muslim veil, which was banned by the Communists in the 1950s.[79] As a result, the memory of 'brotherhood and unity' has become dimmer with time and been replaced by new essentialist nationalisms that appear to be 'historical' but are very much traditions invented at the expense of the lived experience.

FURTHER READING

Calic, Marie-Janine, *Geschichte Jugoslawiens im 20. Jahrhundert* (Munich: C.H. Beck, 2010).

Garde, Paul, *Vie et mort de la Yougoslavie* (Paris: Fayard, 2000).

Magaš, Branka, *The Destruction of Yugoslavia: Tracking the Break-up, 1980–90* (London: Verso, 1993).

Mills, Richard, 'Velež Mostar Football Club and the Demise of "Brotherhood and Unity" in Yugoslavia, 1922–2009', *Europe-Asia Studies* 62:7 (2010), 1107–33.

Pavlowitch, Stevan K., *Hitler's New Disorder: The Second World War in Yugoslavia* (London: Hurst, 2008).

Rusinow, Dennison I., *The Yugoslav Experiment, 1948–74* (London: Hurst, 1977).

Silber, Laura and Allan Little, *The Death of Yugoslavia* (Harmondsworth: Penguin, 1995).

Swain, Geoffrey, *Tito: A Biography* (London: I.B. Tauris, 2010).

Thompson, Mark, *A Paper House: The Ending of Yugoslavia* (New York: Pantheon, 1992).

Woodward, Susan L., *Balkan Tragedy: Chaos and Dissolution after the Cold War* (Washington, DC: Brookings Institution, 1994).

---

[77] Ann Low-Beer, 'Politics, School Textbooks and Cultural Identity: The Struggle in Bosnia and Hercegovina', *Paradigm: Journal of the Textbook Colloquium* 2:3 (2001), online at: http://faculty.ed.uiuc. edu.westbury/paradigm/, accessed January 2010.

[78] Zara Volčič, 'Yugo-nostalgia: Cultural Memory and Media in the Former Yugoslavia', *Critical Studies in Media Communication* 24:1 (2007), 21–38.

[79] Špela Kalčić, *Nisem jaz Barbika: oblačilne prakse, Islam in identitetni procesi med Bošnjakinjami v Sloveniji* (Ljubljana: Filozofska fakulteta, oddelek za etnologijo in kulturno antropolologijo, 2007).

PART VI

CULTURE AND HISTORY

CHAPTER 27

THE COUNTRYSIDE: TOWARDS A THEME PARK?

HUGH D. CLOUT

THE KALEIDOSCOPE OF RURAL EUROPE

WHEN World War II came to an end, most Europeans were hungry and all would experience food rationing for several years. As well as being a place of leisure for a minority, Europe's diverse countryside was essentially the locus of work and production. Despite imports from many parts of the globe, the continent's farmers were required to generate increasing quantities of foodstuffs, just as their forebears had done since sedentary agriculture began. At mid century, most farms were small and were worked by the families that owned or rented them, however large estates employing landless workers were found in some areas. For most farmers, work was hard and incomes low, with rural living conditions generally lagging behind those in towns and cities. Mechanization was rare except in lowland England and northern France. As in earlier decades, large numbers of country dwellers moved in the 1950s to town and cities and to new employment opportunities in factories and offices. Human labour was gradually replaced by machinery on farms, where the 'productivist' model, that aimed to intensify food output, reigned supreme. It would remain predominant until the final decades of the century when overproduction of farm goods gave rise to major challenges, in Western Europe at least. Some analysts advocated that substantial areas should be taken out of agricultural use. Thereafter, a new 'post-productivist' philosophy came into play, with sustainable use of resources and diversification of rural activities as its keynotes. By the dawn of the twenty-first century, Europe's agriculture had been reshaped dramatically since policy makers viewed rural space as more than a resource base of crops, animal products and timber. Indeed, many town dwellers saw the countryside as a backdrop for leisure and recreation, and as a place of consumption rather than of production.

The landscapes of rural Europe are highly varied and its many regions have experienced different changes and also different degrees of change since 1945.[1] The countryside is almost like a toy kaleidoscope that produces a remarkable array of patterns when subjected to the slightest movement. Local aspects of climate, soil, terrain, settlement, landscape, farm structure, labour input, mechanization, and countless other features may be thought of as the coloured pieces in this imaginary kaleidoscope. Mountainous terrain in the Alps, Carpathians, Pyrenees, and Tatra contrasts with low-lying countryside around the estuaries of great rivers in the Low Countries and also with areas of openfield and nucleated villages across the plains of Northern Europe (Figure 27.1). Enclosed landscapes, with hedgerows, permanent pastures, and dispersed farms characterize the Atlantic fringes of the continent, and irrigated farmland around the Mediterranean forms yet another rural milieu.[2] These seemingly timeless landscapes had, of course, been retouched across the centuries but change was generally slow until after 1945 when agricultural activities were modernized and mechanized.[3] Political regimes in Southern and Eastern Europe promoted land reform, which was followed by widespread collectivization in the Communist states.

Farmers in many parts of Western Europe transformed their activities during the third quarter of the century, applying large quantities of fertilizers, pesticides, and other chemicals to the soil, and mechanizing many aspects of work formerly undertaken with human or animal labour. Adoption of the modest tractor was soon followed by acquisition of other machines, of ever greater size and power. Since about 1990, the 'productivist' imperative to generate more food to feed hungry mouths was replaced in parts of Western Europe by the 'post-productivist' challenge of diversifying how farmland and other rural resources might be used in sustainable ways to avoid expensive food surpluses whilst defending fragile habitats.[4] Between 1980 and 2000, numbers of woodland birds, which reflect biodiversity, declined by one-tenth across Europe and common farmland birds declined by half due to inputs of agricultural chemicals and pesticides, and destruction of habitats.

Car ownership had been the privilege of only small sections of society at mid century, however all that changed in the years ahead as the total number of cars rose from 7.5 million in 1950 to 235 million in 2009—a thirtyfold increase. Mass mobility made many parts of the countryside easily accessible to growing numbers of town dwellers in search of leisure and recreational opportunities in the great outdoors. As a result, new perceptions of rural resources were introduced that were very different from those focused on food and timber.[5] Conversion of farm houses into second homes for city people, opening of country estates to visitors, and development of winter sports facilities in mountain areas reflect such new perceptions, as does the arrival of foreigners to settle in 'unspoiled'

[1] Hugh Clout, 'The Recomposition of Rural Europe', *Annales de Géographie* 100 (1993), 714–29.
[2] René Lebeau, *Les grands types de structures agraires dans le monde* (Paris: Masson, 1969); Jan Meeus, 'Pan-European Landscapes', *Landscape and Urban Planning* 31 (1995), 57–79.
[3] Robin Butlin and Robert Dodgshon, *Historical Geography of Europe* (Oxford: Oxford University Press, 1998); Clifford Smith, *An Historical Geography of Western Europe, 1500–1840* (London: Longman, 1978).
[4] David Pinder, *The New Europe: Economy, Society and Environment* (Chichester: Wiley, 1998), 341–57.
[5] Placide Rambaud, *Société rurale et urbanisation* (Paris: Seuil, 1969).

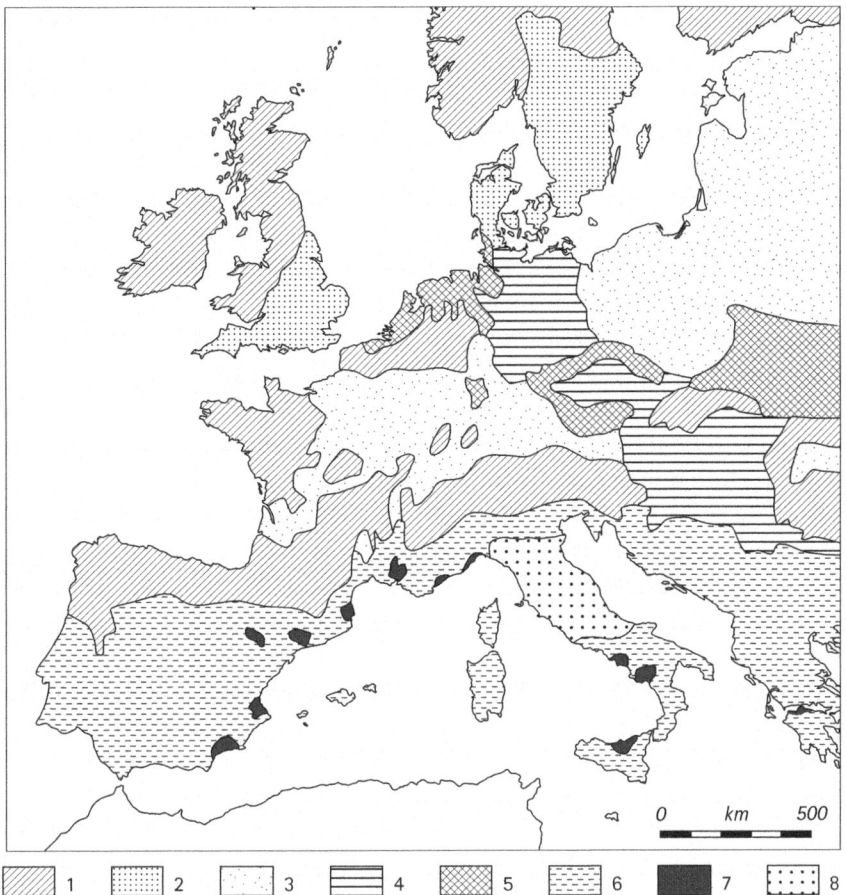

FIGURE 27.1 European Rural Landscapes

Source: simplified from Lebeau, 1969. 1. Enclosed landscape, dispersed settlement, much permanent grass; 2. Former open fields, grouped settlement, subsequent enclosure and some settlement dispersion; 3. Open fields, grouped settlement, much arable (recent changes in East-Central Europe); 4. Open fields transformed in some formerly communist states; 5. Linear settlements in polder land or in forests; 6. Mediterranean open fields, tree crops, mainly grouped settlement with some dispersion; 7. Irrigated areas, horticulture; 8. Mixed landscape of cereal plots, vines, olives and tree crops, including cork oak.

countryside.[6] Some new arrivals in the European countryside are facilitated by the availability of low cost air fares, but the withdrawal of such services would reduce the attractiveness of many distant locations at a stroke. Rising rates of car ownership, new roads, and expanding information networks also made accessible stretches of countryside increasingly attractive for suburbanization and long-distance commuting.[7] Some

---

[6] Henry Buller and Keith Hoggart, *International Counterurbanization: British Migrants in Rural France* (Aldershot: Avebury, 1994).

[7] Bernard Kayser, *La renaissance rurale* (Paris: Armand Colin, 1989).

commentators have argued that information and communications technology (ICT) is now leading to 'the death of distance' and is diluting the power of spatial constraints.

At weekends and holiday periods, city dwellers flood out to enjoy a 'countryside experience', thereby generating new sources of income for some people in the rural economy but also creating problems for others, for example as house prices escalate beyond the financial reach of many local folk.[8] In addition to temporal and spatial dimensions of change there is a highly important social register in rural Europe. The countryside has become contested territory, with manifest 'winners' and 'losers'.[9] During the second half of the century, many rural areas continued to experience outmigration and depopulation, with their remaining residents suffering problems of service depriva-tion after population numbers fell below economic thresholds for keeping open schools, shops, medical services, and other facilities.[10] For the affluent, often with several cars in the household, these issues can be resolved through personal mobility, but problems remain intense for poor and elderly carless residents.[11]

Rapid urbanization and industrial growth since 1945 has covered substantial stretches of rural Europe with bricks, concrete, and tarmacadam. Nevertheless, more than four-fifths of the continent's land surface is still under crops, grass, trees, or scrub at the end of the first decade of the twenty-first century, with such 'rural' forms of land use being overwhelmingly dominant in remote areas of Scandinavia, the Baltic States and north-ern Scotland, where population densities are below 15 persons per km^2. As well as sup-plying foodstuffs, timber and water, and providing space for hunting and other traditional pursuits, rural Europe is being called upon to accommodate many other functions.[12] Concern to conserve land, soils, and vegetation led to the designation of national parks and nature reserves in each European country, but in the last couple of decades responsibility has also been placed on farmers and foresters to manage their land resources with the interests of future generations in mind rather than working to satisfy short-term needs.[13] Despite many changes in the rural 'kaleidoscope', most of the food consumed in Europe is still produced in its own surprisingly diverse countryside, and the continent is now a large net exporter of food in the early twenty-first century. On the other hand, there is a disturbing and unsustainable trend to import commodities over great distances from other parts of the globe, clocking up frightening numbers of 'food miles' to allow Europeans to eat whatever they want, whenever they want through-out the year.

[8] J. Terry Coppock, *Second Homes: Curse or Blessing?* (Oxford: Pergamon, 1977); Bertrand Hervieu and Jean Viard, *Au bonheur des campagnes* (La Tour d' Aigues: Editions de l' Aube, 2001).

[9] Andrew Flynn and Philip Lowe, *The Contested Countryside* (London: UCL Press, 1994); Hugh Clout, 'The European Countryside: Contested Space', in Brian Graham (ed.), *Modern Europe: Place, Culture and Identity* (London: Arnold, 1998), 287–309; Doris Schmied, *Winning and Losing: the Changing Geography of Europe's Rural Areas* (Aldershot: Ashgate, 2005).

[10] Keith Hoggart, Henry Buller and Richard Black, *Rural Europe: Identity and Change* (London: Arnold, 1995).

[11] Alexandre Pagès, *La pauvreté en milieu rural* (Toulouse: Presses Universitaires du Mirail, 2004).

[12] Birgit Elands and Soren Praestholm, 'Landowners' Perspectives on the Rural Future and the Role of Forests across Europe', *Journal of Rural Studies* 24 (2008), 72–85.

[13] José Bové and François Dufour, *The World Is Not For Sale* (London: Verso, 2001).

In our increasingly consumer-orientated world, many rural landscapes and cultural features have been invested with new meanings and values. 'Heritage' now occupies an important place in survival strategies to sustain fragile local economies, which are of course changed subtly and sometimes dramatically in the process.[14] Some analysts argue that in our urbanized continent, where agriculture occupies less land than half a century ago, rural space is becoming a 'décor' or backdrop against which the aspirations of spatially mobile town dwellers are performed.[15] A few commentators even maintain that the countryside is becoming a kind of 'theme park' for the enjoyment of the urban majority in which some farmers are little more than 'park keepers' being paid to make farmed landscapes 'attractive' for urban visitors.[16] 'Ghost villages', many of whose dwellings have been converted into second homes and are fully inhabited only at holiday times, certainly contribute to the 'theme park' idea embraced by the title of this chapter. This provocative argument contains more than a grain of truth but it may be overstated. New trends in the global food market in the early twenty-first century, especially the rising demand for food and the enrichment of diets in the rapidly urbanizing and industrializing economies of South and East Asia, pose profound challenges for food production in Europe and elsewhere across the world. As global food networks continue to develop, it is very likely that the continent will need not only to feed its own inhabitants, but also to assist the survival of those in developing portions of the world. In addition, the physical resource base is changing as global warming takes effect. Temperature zones and crop belts are shifting northwards across Europe and the retreating polar ice cap raises the threat of productive farmland—as well as major cities—sited in low-lying coastal areas becoming submerged if adequate defensive works are not put into place.

Employing only 5 per cent of the European workforce and generating 2 per cent of the total domestic product, agriculture is now a very small element in the European economy but it remains a major user of land, despite the cultivated surface having contracted in recent decades.[17] Nonetheless, it has commanded great attention among policy makers. Memories of wartime food shortages and postwar rationing remained strong for many years after World War II and doubtless fuelled the expensive drive towards 'productivist' agricultural systems. In addition, family farming retained a symbolic significance as a repository of core values in many European nations. Even now, farmers are willing to stage disruptive demonstrations to ensure that their case is not overlooked in the corridors of power, especially in Brussels. Whilst fully acknowledging that the countryside kaleidoscope is greater than its agricultural components, this chapter will chart how the food economy has been managed since 1945, explore how the Common Agricultural Policy (CAP) evolved from being concerned with food to embracing rural affairs, and then look at the challenge of countryside management in which many activities are in competition.

[14] David Herbert, *Heritage, Tourism and Society* (London: Pinter, 1995); Jean-Pierre Husson, *Envies de campagne* (Paris: Ellipses, 2008).

[15] Bertrand Hervieu and Jean Viard, *L' archipel paysan* (La Tour d' Aigues: Editions de l' Aube, 2001).

[16] Denis Chevallier, *Vives campagnes: le patrimoine rurale, projet de société* (Paris: Autrement, 2000).

[17] Emmy Bolsius, Gordon Clark and Jan Groenendijk, *The Retreat: Rural Land Use and European Agriculture* (Utrecht: Royal Dutch Geographical Society, 1994).

POSTWAR AGRICULTURAL RECOVERY

By 1945, land had fallen out of cultivation only in the most battle-scarred places in Europe, but agriculture had deteriorated in many areas as livestock were killed, buildings damaged, and land subjected to poor farming techniques. By contrast with such experience in mainland Europe, food production in the United Kingdom had been refashioned through 'dig for victory' campaigns that brought agriculturally 'marginal' land, such as playing fields and gardens into productive use during, and immediately after, the war.[18] Once peace was restored, the main agricultural challenge in Europe was to generate more food for the continent's citizens who had to endure rationing for several years, although the hardships of some were eased by the 'black market' that flourished in many areas. Recovery was rapid in Western and Southern Europe where most states regained pre-war levels of food output by 1950.[19] Revival took longer in Eastern Europe, where livestock losses were severe and fighting and enforced movements of population disrupted farming. Very harsh winters and summer droughts (1945–48) made things worse, and were followed by new upheavals associated with land reform and collectivization. Major contrasts in agricultural development were apparent at mid century (Table 27.1), however the family—or 'peasant'—farm, on which the household provided virtually all the labour input, was the predominant form of agricultural operation across the European mainland. By contrast, large mechanized farms were widespread across lowland England and the northern plains of France, and large estates employing landless labourers were found in parts of Southern Europe.

Governments across the continent made major investments in the 1950s and 1960s to enhance agricultural production and reorganize farm structures, thereby banishing the spectre of food shortages. In Western Europe these funds came in the form of price-support measures and technical assistance, whilst in Eastern Europe they were associated with collectivization and subsidies for producers and consumers. Achievements varied substantially, but in parts of Western Europe remarkable advances in food production were made, including use of highly productive and resistant crop strains, improved breeds of livestock, new fertilizers, chemicals and machinery. During the 1950s, Europe's average wheat yields rose by a half (the highest rate of increase of any major region of the world) and the number of tractors tripled whilst combine harvesters increased fivefold. As a result of all these changes, less land and fewer farm workers were needed to produce a given quantity of food. In varying degrees throughout the continent, rising agricultural productivity was dovetailing into urban industrialization, and was contributing to widespread rural–urban

---

[18] Brian Short, Charles Watkins and John Martin (eds), *The Front Line of Freedom: British Farming in the Second World War* (Exeter: British Agricultural History Society, 2006).

[19] Hugh Clout, *Agriculture* (London: Macmillan, 1971).

Table 27.1 Agriculture in Europe (excluding the USSR) in 1950 (%).

	Total area	Arable area	Total population	Agricultural workforce	Agricultural production
United Kingdom	4	4	12	2	9
Northern Europe*	24	8	5	4	8
France	10	13	10	8	17
Central Europe^	8	8	20	11	19
Eastern Europe~	18	28	22	28	21
Southern Europe#	36	39	31	47	26

* Denmark, Finland, Iceland, Ireland, Norway, Sweden
^ Austria, Belgium, West Germany, Luxembourg, the Netherlands, Switzerland
~ Albania, Bulgaria, Czechoslovakia, East Germany, Hungary, Poland, Romania
# Greece, Italy, Portugal, Spain, Yugoslavia
Source: United Nations, Economic Survey of Europe since the War (Geneva, 1953, p. 164)

migration on a daily or a permanent basis.[20] It was widely believed that the end of the peasantry was in sight.[21]

A revolution of rising expectations was unleashed as newspapers, radio, and eventually television penetrated the European countryside to depict the attractions of urban living and the incomes that city work could provide. Younger members of many farming families perceived life in the countryside in negative terms, realizing that villages and hamlets lacked the range of shops, colleges, services, and entertainments that only larger concentrations of population could provide. However, the transition from farming and rural life to factory work and urban living did not always involve a sharp break; the two apparently opposing situations could coexist. In many areas, 'worker-peasants' acquired full-time urban jobs but continued to live on their family farms from which they commuted on factory 'workdays'.[22] Their holdings were farmed at evenings and weekends, with family members providing assistance. Beyond the relative stability of the worker-peasantry, official policies encouraged further growth in agricultural productivity, and led to drastic changes not only in the size and layout of fields and farms, but also in the ecological composition of the countryside in many regions. Harmful side effects of agricultural modernization, such as soil erosion, accelerated runoff, soil compaction, acidification, accumulation of pesticides, and reduced species diversity among plants and animals, were not appreciated until much later when negative effects on food quality gave rise to widespread scares in European society.

[20] Anthony Champion, Counterurbanization: The Changing Pace and Nature of Population Decentralization (London: Arnold, 1989).

[21] Henri Mendras, La fin des paysans (Paris: Futuribles, 1967).

[22] Samuel Franklin, The European Peasantry: The Final Phase (London: Methuen, 1969).

Agricultural Change in Eastern Europe

During the interwar years, many large properties with land were confiscated through land reform legislation which reallocated land to peasant farmers. In 1939, agriculture continued to employ a large share of the workforce of Eastern Europe and, despite the survival of some great estates, was characterized by farms below 5 ha that lacked capital and machinery. Between 1945 and 1948 more land reform was carried out by Communist regimes to win support from farmers.[23] The resulting, slightly enlarged, holdings still relied on family labour and were inappropriate for introducing scientific techniques or machinery. Serious food shortages followed these changes in land holding. Communist governments soon introduced industrialization policies that required large quantities of labour to be released from family farming. This transformation was accompanied by agricultural collectivization between 1948 and 1952. The timing and approach varied from country to country, but a distinction could be drawn between state farms, owned and financed by national authorities and whose workers were state employees, and collective farms, owned by their members. Both types of enterprise were subject to the exigencies of national economic planning. Members of collectives retained small patches of land (usually under 0.5 ha), often kept a few livestock, and produced crops for family consumption and for sale on local markets. Not surprisingly, farmers tried to resist the changes associated with collectivization that undermined their traditional ways of life but were not supported by adequate state investment for farm modernization. By 1952 much of Eastern Europe was in agrarian crisis and the drive to collectivize decelerated. Agricultural employees worked with little enthusiasm on the collectives, preferring to devote time and energy to their private plots.

Despite challenges and reversals, collectivization was implemented throughout Eastern Europe by the early 1960s. Straightforward collectives predominated in Albania, Bulgaria, and Romania where collectivization had been rapid, whilst modified forms were found in Czechoslovakia, East Germany, and Hungary, where the process had encountered fierce resistance. In Poland, collectivization had been started in 1950 but was reversed in 1956 enabling many family holdings to survive in a peasant system. Large estates were kept intact as state farms in west-central Poland and in areas acquired from Germany, but across most of the country land reform permitted a slight enlargement of existing farms. In Yugoslavia, land reform had been introduced in 1945 but was overtaken by collectivization three years later; however this was discontinued in the early 1950s because of farmer opposition. With 85 per cent of the agricultural surface in the hands of family farmers in 1965, agricultural conditions in Poland and Yugoslavia differed profoundly from those in neighbouring countries. By the late 1960s, collective farms throughout Eastern Europe were in need of major investment for modernization

---

[23] György Enyedi, 'The Changing Face of Agriculture in Eastern Europe', *Geographical Review* 47 (1967), 358–72; Clout, *Agriculture*, 27–39.

and mechanization to produce more food for domestic consumption and for trade in the Eastern Bloc. Despite bold statements in national plans, agriculture received far less attention than planned industrialization. Necessary links between farms, suppliers of equipment, and fertilizers were rarely achieved, and marketing processes were inefficient when compared with Western European countries. Private plots continued to provide essential supplies of fresh food.

AGRICULTURAL CHANGE IN WESTERN EUROPE

The main objective in the postwar farm policies of Western European nations was to increase food supplies. Other targets included raising farmers' incomes, which lagged behind industrial wages, and keeping food prices at reasonable levels for consumers. With the exception of the United Kingdom, farms were too numerous, small, and fragmented, and the professional training of many family farmers was poor. National governments introduced measures to raise farm incomes by supporting commodity prices, to promote cooperatives for purchasing fertilizers and machinery, for marketing farm products, and to provide advisory schemes. In 1955, at least half of Western Europe's farmland had been in need of plot consolidation. Structural schemes varied from rearrangement of scattered plots into compact holdings to ambitious programmes embracing soil fertilization, construction of new roads and farmhouses, clearance of rural slums, and provision of industrial buildings in the countryside. Long-established farmers saw these schemes as revolutionary, but they merely rearranged the existing rural mosaic and rarely faced up to the challenge of farm enlargement. By 1960, farms below 10 ha still made up more than 70 per cent of holdings in ten Western European countries. During the ensuing decade, special funds were introduced to encourage elderly farmers to retire, and to release land for incorporation into adjacent holdings. Parallel measures helped others to leave farming for new jobs and trained younger people before they entered farm work. In addition, schemes for reorganizing settlements, and building replacement farmhouses out in their fields rather than in congested villages, were implemented in West Germany and the Netherlands.

Land reform was carried out in Italy and Greece, where the political objective of winning support among farmers and agricultural labourers accompanied the economic aim of reorganizing farm structures. Interwar governments in Italy had failed to address rural poverty in the south and on the islands, with sympathies for Communism increasing when soldiers returned after 1945. Land reform was introduced in 1950 to expropriate large estates, provide new farms for landless labourers, and enlarge existing smallholdings.[24] As well as creating work for a new property-owning democracy, land reform also sought to increase food production. Expropriation generally involved poor,

[24] Russell King, *Land Reform: The Italian Experience* (London: Butterworth, 1973).

extensively cultivated land that had to be deep-ploughed, fertilized, and in places irrigated before new farmers could move in. Land reform proved to be costly, and its impact varied from success on irrigated lowlands to failure on arid uplands where new farms were soon abandoned. Critics argued that investment to bring in industrial employment opportunities would have been more appropriate, advocating 'exogenous development' whereby the main forces for rural progress were to be found beyond the 'backward' countryside. The same commentators pointed to the impossibility of generating decent incomes from many new farms, and insisted that fragmentation of rural property ran counter to farm enlargement elsewhere in Western Europe.

THE COMMON AGRICULTURAL POLICY
OF THE EUROPEAN UNION

When the European Economic Community was established on 1 January 1958, farming employed one-fifth of the working population of the six founder states and contributed 8 per cent of the total domestic product. On 25 March 1957, the Treaty of Rome had stipulated the need to devise a Common Agricultural Policy to increase farm productivity through technical progress, provide a fair standard of living for farmers, stabilize food markets, and guarantee reasonable prices to consumers.[25] With their own agricultural policies in place, member states found it difficult to put Community interests before their own. Protracted discussions focused on the need to improve marketing and farm structures, increase food trade among members of the Six and with other countries, avoid food surpluses, encourage specialization, reduce subsidies, improve the rate of return on capital and labour, encourage rural industrialization, and allocate special aid to very poor agricultural regions. The tension between some of these objectives was evident, and not until January 1962 were agreements reached on a marketing policy for many farm products, enabling the CAP to go ahead. Agriculture commissioner Sicco Mansholt encouraged further discussions to promote modernization. The CAP soon became the most expensive of the Community's activities, and accounted for 80 per cent of budgetary expenditure by 1970. High guaranteed prices boosted production not only of goods in demand, but also of many in surplus. Large sums were simply poured into the agricultural fund to shore up domestic prices, destroy surpluses of perishable fruit and vegetables, and store vast quantities of butter and milk products. Critics described how 'grain mountains' and 'wine lakes' were being produced by the Community's subsidized farmers.

In 1968, Mansholt had presented the '1980 Agriculture Programme', which revealed that two-thirds of holdings in the Six were under 10 ha apiece, and 80 per cent were 'marginal' judged by technical and economic circumstances at the time.[26] He argued that

---

[25] Brian Hill, *The Common Agricultural Policy* (London: Methuen, 1984).
[26] Hugh Clout, *A Rural Policy for the EEC?* (London: Methuen, 1984).

new measures should be introduced to reduce the number of farmers and farm workers by nearly 5 million by 1980, to enlarge farm sizes by reducing their number, and to bring supply and demand into balance. Alternative forms of rural employment should be created, elderly farmers be paid to retire, and young people trained to help rejuvenate the much smaller agricultural workforce. Guaranteed commodity prices should be slashed to discourage surpluses and the agricultural surface of the Six reduced by at least 5 million ha that would be converted into national parks, nature reserves and woodlands.[27] Associations defending family farmers reacted angrily, and national governments expressed reservations, however a moderate version of Mansholt's plan was accepted in 1970. When Denmark, Ireland, and the United Kingdom joined the European Economic Community (EEC) two years later, his initial project had been reduced to three European directives concerning farm modernization, abandonment of holdings, and training of farmers. Not until the 1980s did the influence of the traditional farming lobby start to wane, enabling further CAP reforms to take place.[28] Environmentalists gradually gathered support, especially in northern member states where ecological concerns were well established, but it was the issue of costly overproduction that tipped the balance in favour of change. In 1984, a quota on dairy production was introduced, and four years later a ceiling was set for expenditure on all agricultural funding. By this time, Greece (1981), Portugal, and Spain (1986) had entered the EU, adding to the number of impoverished family farmers and also giving rise to new forms of competition for producers on irrigated land in southern France and Italy.

FROM FOOD TO COUNTRYSIDE

In 1992, the commissioner for agriculture, Ray MacSharry, introduced new reforms to restrain Europe's growing production of food and to create a freer market in agricultural goods. Financial support for cereals and beef was reduced, 'set-aside' payments were introduced for farmers who withdrew land from crop production, and new measures were established to limit livestock numbers, to assist elderly farmers to retire, and to encourage rational afforestation of former farmland. Entry of Austria, Finland, and Sweden to the EU in 1995 added new challenges of rural management in northern and alpine environments. 'Agenda 2000' reforms put MacSharry's ideas into action and advanced a more holistic view of the countryside. The CAP was separated into two sections—or 'pillars'—to support agricultural production but also to assist rural management by diversifying employment, setting up producer groups, supporting young farmers, and encouraging the elderly to quit farming. Special projects were introduced in 'less favoured areas' and across territory subject to environmental constraints. Such

[27] Bolsius, Clark and Groenendijk, *The Retreat.*
[28] Commission of the European Communities, *The Future of Rural Society* (Brussels and Strasbourg: CEC, 1988); John Marsh, *The Changing Role of the CAP* (London: Belhaven, 1991).

terrain was typically mountainous, but also included places threatened by land abandonment where farming was necessary to conserve cherished landscapes, and to protect stretches of coastline for tourism. 'Agri-environment' schemes to promote sustainable development became compulsory in each member state, and market support prices on cereals, milk and dairy products, beef, and veal were reduced. EU agriculture ministers agreed to redirect subsidies from the first to the second 'pillar' through a process of 'modulation', and to 'decouple' subsidies to farmers from the production of particular quantities of foodstuffs. In 2007, the European Agricultural Guarantee Fund was set up to finance the first 'pillar', and the European Agricultural Fund for Rural Development to support the second. In addition, 'single farm payments' were introduced that were subject to conditions of 'cross compliance' whereby farmers had to pay due regard to sustainable management, food safety, and animal health and welfare. Memories remained of foot and mouth disease and of 'mad cow disease' (bovine spongiform encephalopathy) of 2003.

On 1 May 2004, Europe's new policy for farming and the countryside had to confront major new challenges as ten more countries joined the EU.[29] The number of farmers in the enlarged Union rose from 7 million to 11 million, the agricultural surface grew by 30 per cent, and the volume of crop production increased by 15 per cent. The difference between the last two figures reflected the low productivity of farming in East-Central Europe. Seven of the new entrants had experienced collectivization and subsidization for both producers and consumers of food.[30] When political and economic regimes changed after 1989, these state subsidies were removed thereby exposing agriculture to market forces. In addition, a complicated process of decollectivization and land reform began. Identifying former owners and matching them with pre-collectivization parcels proved extremely difficult. These problems slowed down land reform and frustrated owners wishing to work their land. Crop production and livestock rearing were disrupted, and some plots fell out of use until ownership was resolved. Some collectives were subdivided into their pre-existing holdings that were allocated to former members. Others were reorganized into joint stock companies, little different from collectives. Those in a third group, typically in remote areas with harsh environmental conditions, were abandoned; livestock were slaughtered and former members had to migrate to urban places to find work. Now exposed to market forces, farmers in Eastern Europe had to face up to the kinds of change experienced by their Western counterparts. Some farms, regardless of size, adapted successfully to market requirements; others managed to survive but provide little more than a subsistence living for their, often elderly, occupants; and the remainder were amalgamated with adjacent farms, converted to woodland, or simply degenerated to scrub.

[29] Irina Ramniceanu and Robert Ackrill, 'EU Rural Development Policy in the New Member States: Promoting Multifunctionality?', *Journal of Rural Studies* 23 (2007), 416–29. EU enlargement in 2004 involved Cyprus, Czechoslovakia, Estonia, Hungary, Latvia, Lithuania, Malta, Poland, Slovakia and Slovenia. In 2007, Bulgaria and Romania entered the EU; Croatia, Macedonia and Turkey are official candidates for membership.

[30] Pinder, *New Europe*, 359–78.

In 2002, EU members agreed that agricultural expenditure should not increase in real terms up to 2013. This decision required a cut in funding of 5 per cent to existing members to accommodate the ten states joining in 2004, and a reduction of 8 per cent following the entry of Bulgaria and Romania in 2007. Intending members were allocated special assistance to support farming, and upon entry had immediate access to price-support measures on farm products. Direct farm payments are being phased in to bring agricultural funding into line with the EU norm. A 'temporary rural development instrument' operated until 2006 in the new member states, providing funds to encourage elderly farmers to retire, to promote agri-environment schemes and rational afforestation, and to subsidize farmers in less favoured areas and mountainous terrain. As well as benefiting from measures available elsewhere in the EU, the new members receive special funding to help modernize farms, support cooperatives, provide technical assistance, and improve standards of animal welfare and food safety.

In its various manifestations, the CAP has been subject to profound criticism. Opponents question why farmers should receive financial support that is denied producers in other economic sectors. They show how this massively expensive preferential treatment led to overproduction, and required costly stockpiling of surpluses. Price intervention was also blamed for creating artificially high food prices, whilst subsidies contributed to a 'Fortress Europe' phenomenon that distorted competition on the world market for food. Most policy makers in Europe declared their concern to protect family farms but for many years CAP support favoured larger, market-responsive holdings, such as those with vast fields of sugar beet in northern France or expanses of oil-seed rape stretching far into the distance in eastern England. After reform in 2003, this situation came to an end, with payments being linked directly to farm size. Critics also argued that Europe's expansion of food output was achieved through massive application of fertilizers and pesticides with serious ecological consequences. These problems were tackled by the revised farm payment scheme that emphasizes environmental issues and requires observation of ecological regulations.

Despite all these changes, many commentators still believe that the CAP remains unsustainable. Following the 2004 enlargement, the EU contained almost 15 million farmers who made up 5 per cent of the workforce but contributed only 2 per cent of the total domestic product, and was composed of holdings that averaged 17 ha in size. In recent years the EU has been obliged to control agricultural expenditure and has reduced payments to long-standing members. By virtue of the size of its farming sector, France was traditionally a net beneficiary from the CAP, but now makes a net contribution to the agricultural budget, although still receiving the largest share of farm funding paid to an individual member state. The fact that Poland alone contains two million family farms, averaging 10 ha apiece—which will have to confront the kinds of challenges that their French counterparts faced half a century ago—indicates the magnitude of new problems facing the CAP. Membership of the EU has opened up new markets for larger Polish farms but, at the same time, has exposed them to harsh competition from more efficient producers elsewhere in Europe.

Towards a Sustainable Countryside?

Changing patterns of trade, concern over costs of supporting farmers, worries about food quality and animal health, the challenge of sustainability, and the need to retain viable economies in the countryside have reconfigured the CAP, and have shifted the attention of policy makers away from food to wider issues of rural management.[31] At last, the holistic significance of the countryside to European life is being appreciated, and the need to diversify activities both within and beyond agriculture has been recognized. Since the early 1990s, the EU has assisted job creation by promoting rural tourism and craft activities, and has allocated funds to subsidize services and activities to help keep communities alive in the countryside and thereby avoid further depopulation. The LEADER (*Liaison Entre Actions de Développement de l'Économie Rurale*) funding initiative of the EU operated from 1991 to 2007 and was very responsive to local initiatives for creating and sustaining rural employment.[32] These monies have been complemented by EU aid for regional development and by programmes that individual member states target on specific rural problems. Increasingly, emphasis is placed on finding ways to energize local agents, such as community organizations, producer cooperatives, informal local networks and individual households. This 'endogenous' model of rural development draws on local initiatives, with 'neo-endogenous' approaches emphasizing the creative and supportive role of area-based partnerships, external business support agencies, and voluntary organizations. It is now widely accepted that rural localities cannot operate autonomously and should take advantage of external influences operating in our increasingly connected and globalized world.[33]

'Pluriactivity' has become one of the watchwords of rural Europe—growing numbers of farming families adding new elements to their portfolio of activity as they seek to make a decent living, rather as worker-peasants continue to do. Some farming families have incorporated new forms of livestock rearing or cropping, such as rare breeds or organic production, enabling them to run their holdings full time and to make a profit so long as demand holds up. However, only 4 per cent of Europe's farm land is used for organic production (rising to 11 per cent in Austria and Latvia), and in periods of economic recession the market for expensive organic foodstuffs may well decline, thereby demonstrating the vulnerability of this tactic. Many farmers have incorporated non-agricultural activities into the farm profile, such as providing bed-and-breakfast accommodation for visitors, 'farm shops' to supply wholesome, locally-grown food, or have encouraged members of the family to bring in off-farm incomes from jobs in factories or offices.[34] Others support their farm businesses with income from sources such as

---

[31] Commission of the European Communities, *The Future of Rural Society*.

[32] B. Korf and E. Oughton, 'Rethinking the European Countryside', *Journal of Rural Studies* 22 (2006), 278–89.

[33] Lois Labrianidis, *The Future of Europe's Peripheries* (Aldershot: Ashgate, 2004).

[34] Henri Mendras, *Voyage au pays de l' utopie rustique* (Arles: Actes Sud, 1979).

investments or pensions. Right across the European continent, farming is being integrated into local rural economies in ever more complicated ways but it remains vulnerable to competitive forces associated with globalization and to downward fluctuations in the world economy.[35]

In the early years of the twenty-first century, the fundamentalist belief that agriculture is dominant in rural life is being questioned, and attitudes to the countryside are changing. 'Post-productivist' thinking has firmly placed sustainability and nature conservation on the farming agenda, as well as the traditional objective of generating supplies of food.[36] National parks and nature reserves have been established for a combination of scientific and aesthetic reasons in response to a wide range of interest groups. However, the term 'national park' is used in different ways in various European countries, sometimes being applied to very remote, uninhabited areas where nature conservation is the prime objective, but in other contexts embracing territory that is farmed, accommodates green tourism, and thereby supports a local population.[37] An inventory of special protection areas was established in 1998, originating from the European Commission's 1992 Directive on the Conservation of Natural Habitats and of Wild Fauna and Flora. Member states are required to conserve an array of representative areas and habitats thereby contributing to a basic network for nature conservation, known as 'Natura 2000', right across the continent. Following the EU Birds Directive, they also identified special protection areas for threatened and migratory species. Unlike earlier times, 'nature' is now being cherished rather than tamed. Wetlands and moorlands that would have been 'improved' for growing food in the past are protected and acclaimed as special areas of natural interest. The ecological folly of uprooting hedgerows, reclaiming marshes, felling farm woodland, and applying great quantities of chemicals to the soil, which characterized 'productivism', is increasingly recognized; land management is becoming increasingly sustainable.

Countryside features, including vernacular buildings, habitats and whole landscapes, that had simply been taken for granted by earlier generations of Europeans, have been reappraised in recent decades, with visitors from the city realizing their potential for exploitation and enjoyment.[38] Redundant farm buildings, land commanding pleasant views, accessible lake shores, banks of fishing rivers, and countless other landscape elements are being seen as 'commodities' to be purchased at sums beyond the financial

---

[35] Pinder, *New Europe*, 341–78.

[36] David Vail, Knut-Per Hasund and Lars Drake, *The Greening of Agricultural Policy in Industrial Societies* (Ithaca, NY: Cornell University Press, 1994); Anne Buttimer, *Sustainable Landscapes and Lifeways* (Cork: Cork University Press, 2001); Geoff Wilson, 'From Productivism to Post-productivism . . . and Back Again? Exploring the (Un)changed Natural and Mental Landscapes of European Agriculture', *Transactions of the Institute of British Geographers* 26 (2001), 77–102; Lewis Holloway, 'Managing Sustainable Farmed Landscapes Through "Alternative" Food Networks', *Geographical Journal* 172 (2006), 219–29.

[37] Pinder, *New Europe*, 455–76; Ingo Mose, *Protected Areas and Regional Development in Europe* (Aldershot: Ashgate, 2007).

[38] Rambaud, *Société rurale*.

reach of ordinary country people. Rural places tend to be seen not so much as interlocking components for food production, but are perceived in a completely different way that recognizes them as discrete purchasable 'goods' set in a green environment.[39] Castles, landscaped parks, manor houses, medieval abbeys, market halls, and 'unspoiled' villages all have their value in the realm of cultural consumption and contribute spatial markers that link vineyards, cheese farms, battle sites, and a host of other components in themed itineraries for the enjoyment of visitors in the countryside. For example, designation of *Appellation d'Origine Contrôlée* (AOC) vineyards began in France in the early twentieth century as a means of protecting the wine industry from adulteration and fraud. Recently, AOC or 'protected designation of origin' ('protected food name') status has been extended to other countries and to other traditional products, notably cheese.

The traditional *pays* or 'natural regions' of old Europe have been rediscovered as appropriate units for rural management and others have been invented, being associated with the spatial settings of works of fiction or with the landscapes used as backdrops in popular television series. Territorial identities, along with a vast array of appropriate *produits du terroir*, are being repackaged and marketed by tourism offices, with rural regeneration in mind.[40] As well as being vulnerable to economic fluctuations, commodification is also socially discriminating. Winners include those who acquire second homes or retirement cottages; losers are ordinary rural people who discover that affordable homes in the countryside are impossible to find in particularly attractive areas.[41] The fragility of the whole situation is illustrated by the fact that large numbers of British homeowners in rural France sold their properties and moved back to the UK as a result of the punitive rate of exchange between sterling and the euro in 2009.

It is, of course, impossible to predict the future but it seems clear that Europe's countryside will continue to accommodate a wide array of functions that interlock in different ways from place to place across a continent that displays enormous rural diversity from the Western Isles of Scotland to the Danube delta, and from Sicily to Arctic Scandinavia. Despite homogenizing processes of economy, lifestyle and popular consumption over recent decades, differences in climate, terrain, settlement, landscape, and population density remain highly significant across Europe; nonetheless four 'types' of countryside may be recognized.

1) Pressure on rural land close to major cities and tourism resorts will grow in order to accommodate suburban expansion and facilities for urban dwellers, such as airports, golf courses, entertainment complexes, and theme parks. Many villages in such

[39] Brian Garrod, Roz Wornell and Ray Youell, 'Reconceptualizing Rural Resources as Countryside Capital', *Journal of Rural Studies* 22 (2006), 117–28.

[40] Michel Rautenberg, *Campagne de tous nos désirs* (Paris: Maison des Sciences de l'Homme, 2000); Sarah Blowen, Marion Demossier and Jeanine Picard, *Recollections of France: Memories, Identities and Heritage in Contemporary France* (Oxford: Berghahn, 2000).

[41] Nicholas Gallent and Mark Tewdwr-Jones, *Rural Second Homes in Europe* (Aldershot: Ashgate, 2000); Nicholas Gallent, Alan Mace and Mark Tewdwr-Jones, *Second Homes: European Perspectives and UK Policies* (Aldershot: Ashgate, 2005).

locations will become commuter settlements and prices of property will rise to urban levels, with negative implications for poorer members of local society. Oil prices will, of course, have an important role to play in determining how far such peri-urban countryside, which is heavily dependent on car-based mobility, will extend in the future. Some stretches of farmland in the urban shadow will continue to be used intensively for growing fruit and vegetables, whilst others will be converted to nature reserves, sites for farm-based recreation, 'horsiculture', and other 'playground' activities.

2) Further away from major concentrations of population, sections of farmland will continue to produce large quantities of food. In the postwar decades, these areas bore the brunt of productivist farming associated with mechanization and large applications of chemicals and fertilizers. Their farmed landscapes became 'blandscapes', as they were stripped of hedgerows, copses and other 'redundant' features, with the single objective of ever more efficient food production in mind. These areas will most probably continue to be farmed intensively as global demand for food increases. However, in line with current agricultural and rural policy, as well as environmental thinking, their land resources will be used more sustainably and their landscapes will become more variegated, with some fields being converted to nature reserves, woodland, and low-intensity farming activity.[42]

3) Agricultural uses may continue to decline in hilly and middle-mountain areas that have undergone many decades of depopulation. Part-time farming, rural tourism, and other manifestations of diversification are already established in such stretches of 'deep countryside'. Provided that capital is available for non-essential investment, a sizeable proportion of the farm buildings across such terrain may continue to be converted into second homes, retirement cottages, and holiday properties thereby reinforcing 'theme park' characteristics. Further designation of conservation areas will enhance the appeal of these hilly areas with attractive views for 'consumption' by visitors, and development of green tourism will be injected into local survival strategies. Some farmers will indeed be 'park keepers' who work the land and raise livestock in traditional ways that appeal to visitors in an age of commodification and consumerism. Visual changes in these stretches of hilly terrain, such as the installation of wind farms—particularly numerous in north-western Spain—will continue to provoke opposition from sections of the conservation lobby, despite the virtues of this form of sustainable energy production. However, such a scenario is by no means certain since this third type of European countryside may well be called upon to perform a greater productive role should the rapidly changing international market for food, coupled with terrestrial outcomes of global climatic change, impose significant adjustments on the world map of food production. Abandoned field boundaries and farm walls in mid Wales, and derelict terraces across Mediterranean Europe remind us that such stretches of deep countryside were cultivated more intensively during phases of population growth in past centuries.

---

[42] Joks Janssen and Luuk Knippenberg, 'The Heritage of the Productive Landscape: Landscape Design for Rural Areas in the Netherlands, 1954–85', *Landscape Research* 33 (2008), 1–28.

4) Finally, residential densities in high mountain areas and the most remote rural areas will remain low, and the few people who remain will continue to experience intense difficulties with respect to service provision. Information technology may offer a solution to some of the challenges that they confront, however broadband coverage is often poor across thinly populated terrain where demand is slight, and will remain so. ICT has spread at various speeds, with the UK currently in the lead and the countries of Southern and Eastern Europe at the bottom of the table of adoption. Rural teleworking, telemedicine, tele-education, and teleconferencing remain in their infancy. Few stretches of remote countryside have succeeded in attracting efficient fibre optic links and digital exchanges. Incomers have been the most adept users of ICT, whereas established rural residents tend to lag behind. Age and infirmity will prevent some elderly residents from taking advantage of technological fixes to overcome the discipline of distance. Access to the wider world by means of a computer will never replace the local shop or the delivery of food and other essential goods to the door. These remote rural areas will continue to be perceived and protected as wilderness country, whose plants, animals, and habitats are of great significance to biodiversity and the gene pool. However, their snowy slopes and the lure of the great outdoors have attracted ski resorts and other manifestations of winter tourism that support the local economy on a seasonal basis but, at the same time, cause harm to the natural environment.[43] Further developments of this kind, which respond to the recreational aspirations of urban Europeans, will depend on the availability of capital for non-essential expenditure.

Early in the twenty-first century, the European countryside continues to experience important changes in landscape, economy, and society that are the latest outcome of many interacting processes that operate at different scales, from the local, through the national and European, to the global. Changes in the world economy, affecting employment, incomes, and oil prices, will condition the pace with which city dwellers continue to invade the countryside and consume its 'commodities'. Climatic changes will affect the environmental potential of specific areas of Europe to grow particular crops, and rising sea levels may well lead to the loss of low-lying agricultural areas along coasts and estuaries, notably around the North Sea and the Baltic, thereby exerting greater pressures for food production on higher land. Moves towards a 'healthy diet', comprising more fruit and vegetables and fewer meat and dairy goods, will have landscape implications by reducing the amount of high quality pasture land whilst increasing the growing surface under polythene tunnels. The changing global market for food products and the rate of population growth and economic development, coupled with the propensity to eat richer diets, in distant regions such as East and South-East Asia are already having implications for the appearance of Europe's countryside. In the future, it is not inconceivable that the 'post-productivist' trend away from intensive food production may be

---

[43]   Reto Soliva, 'Envisioning Upland Futures: Stakeholder Responses to Scenarios for Europe's Mountain Landscapes', *Journal of Rural Studies* 24 (2008), 56–71.

relaxed. Nonetheless, the 'post-productivist' message has been proclaimed and Europe's farmers are aware of their responsibilities as stewards of the continent's fragile resources. Even if they have to increase the volume of food they produce in the future, one must hope that this will be accomplished with due regard to sustainability, and that appropriate techniques will be employed to avoid the kind of ecological damage that occurred in recent decades. Provided that the global economy recovers in the years ahead, it is very likely that more stretches of Europe's countryside will assume 'theme park' characteristics for the enjoyment of urban visitors; however numerous inter-related processes within world food systems and the changing global environment will mean that many rural areas will escape this scenario during the coming half century.

FURTHER READING

Buller, Henry, and Keith Hoggart, *International Counterurbanization: British Migrants in Rural France* (Aldershot: Avebury, 1994).

Champion, Anthony, *Counterurbanization: The Changing Pace and Nature of Population Deconcentration* (London: Arnold, 1989).

Chevallier, Denis, *Vives campagnes: le patrimoine rural, projet de société* (Paris: Autrement, 2000).

Clout, Hugh, *A Rural Policy for the EEC?* (London: Methuen, 1984).

Franklin, Samuel, *The European Peasantry: The Final Phase* (London: Methuen, 1969).

Hill, Brian, *The Common Agricultural Policy* (London: Methuen, 1984).

Hoggart, Keith, Henry Buller and Richard Black, *Rural Europe: Identity and Change* (London: Arnold, 1995).

Labrianidis, Lois, *The Future of Europe's Rural Peripheries* (Aldershot: Ashgate, 2004).

Lebeau, René, *Les grands types de structures agraires dans le monde* (Paris: Masson, 1969).

Mose, Ingo, *Protected Areas and Regional Development in Europe* (Aldershot: Ashgate, 2007).

Pinder, David, *The New Europe: Economy, Society and Environment* (Chichester: Wiley, 1998).

Rambaud, Placide, *Société rurale et urbanisation* (Paris: Seuil, 1969).

Schmied, Doris, *Winning and Losing: The Changing Geography of Europe's Rural Areas* (Aldershot: Ashgate, 2005).

CHAPTER 28

···

HERITAGE AND THE RECONCEPTUALIZATION OF THE POSTWAR EUROPEAN CITY

···

G.J. ASHWORTH AND BRIAN GRAHAM

THE sinking on its maiden voyage of the White Star liner, *Titanic*, early on 15 April 1912 with the loss of 1517 lives, has become, perhaps, the most famous shipwreck in history. It seems an unpropitious symbol around which to base the regeneration of the city of Belfast as it emerged from almost three decades of conflict but, at the heart of the plans for its future lies the 'Titanic Quarter', where the customary detritus of post-industrial capitalism—signature building, apartments, penthouses, hotels, interactive entertainment and public art—will provide the 'finest in European-style urban living'.[1] The Quarter occupies the site of Harland and Wolff's shipyard where the *Titanic* was built and which, at its height, employed a workforce in excess of 30,000. The material remains of the shipyard, its drawing office and some docks, together with the two gigantic cranes that still dominate the Belfast skyline, now constitute the 'heritage' of the Titanic Quarter. Meanwhile, in Berlin, once again the capital city of a Germany reunified in 1990, an 'emerging memory district' marks numerous events in the city's complex and brutal recent history.[2] The major sites include: the Museum Island on the River Spree; the highly contested Memorial to the Murdered Jews of Europe sited close to Norman Foster's reconstructed Reichstag with its iconic dome, and the Brandenburg Gate; Daniel Libeskind's Jewish Museum where the artefacts of a vanished people survive; the 'Topography of Terror' site at the old Gestapo headquarters; and the remnants of the Berlin Wall (generally marked on the ground by a cobbled line) together with the populist

[1] www.titanic-quarter.com/tqdevelopmentsdetail.php?CID=1&ID=1, accessed 16 November 2009.
[2] Karen E. Till, *The New Berlin: Memory, Politics, Place* (Minneapolis, MN: University of Minneapolis Press, 2005), 9.

'Checkpoint Charlie' museum. But this use of the past is selective: in 2008, the *Palast der Republik*, the parliament building of the German Democratic Republic, was demolished (although, at the time of writing, the hallmark statue of Marx and Engels that stood in front of the *Palast* still survives).

Despite their marked differences, Belfast and Berlin demonstrate a trait that, since the mid-1970s, has become a defining characteristic of European cities, namely the repositioning of the contemporary urban area through representations of its past. This is the most recent stage in the genesis of postwar European cities which, since 1945, have undergone an, as yet incomplete, process of radical restructuring that has changed not merely the outward physical appearance of morphologies, buildings, and spaces but, more fundamentally, the ways in which cities are used and, ultimately, their meanings for those that use them. The restructuring has been driven by several factors: the necessities of the physical rebuilding of war-shattered cities after 1945; functional revitalization in response to economic change; ideological change most especially in Central and Eastern Europe; and, finally, by fundamental changes in political and social expectations about what cities were expected to deliver. Urban decision makers in the immediate postwar period were faced with a fundamental choice. On the one hand, they could seek to preserve those material structures that had survived while reconstructing those that had been lost so as to recreate the pre-war city and, by implication, the pre-war society that had inhabited it. On the other, they could seize the fortuitous possibility of creating new cities, often literally from the rubble of the old, to house a new and hopefully better society in structures that marked a clear aesthetic and functional break with a discredited past. During the period immediately following 1945, the choice, perhaps unsurprisingly, tended towards the latter. As typified by Rotterdam, Coventry, or Plymouth (among many examples), city centres destroyed or badly damaged by aerial bombing were unashamedly rebuilt in an international modernist style that made little or no reference to the past. The economic and political imperative behind city centre reconstruction was the assertion that the city was 'back in business', ready to embrace the future and reject the past. In the United Kingdom, Crawley, the original government-sponsored New Town (1948), was the first of many throughout Europe in which new building on a *tabula rasa* was to house and help shape a new society freed from the constraints of the old cities from which the populations were drawn.

In time, of course, this economic functionalism and architectural modernism was not to achieve a complete hegemony. All Western European countries had legislation, mostly dating to before World War I, to protect individual designated monuments. In numerous cities, elements of the old were not only preserved but also incorporated into the new as typified by the hybrid rebuilding of Coventry Cathedral or the *Kaiser-Wilhelm-Gedächtniskirche* in Berlin, expressing an idea of progress from the ruinous old to the rational new. In several cities and even countries, a contrasting course to modernism was adopted although on a continental scale, such examples were exceptional. Most notably, as in Warsaw and Gdańsk (formerly Danzig), the city centres of Poland, deliberately and almost completely destroyed, were rebuilt in replica as were a few German gem-cities such as Rothenburg ob der Tauber.

More commonly, the primary roles of the newly reconstructed cities, their accompanying suburbs, and New Towns were threefold: to accommodate new urban functions, including the offices of the service economy which was replacing the factories of the industrial sector as the prime urban economic driver; replacement of slums by ergonomically designed high-rise housing; and, eventually, accommodating the space requirements for free accessibility to urban space by private motor vehicles. It was this last requirement, however, that proved the catalyst in slowing, stopping and eventually reversing the modernist trend although there were many other factors, both negative and positive. Often, the new districts and towns did not deliver the social satisfactions and functional efficiencies that they had promised. More positively, by the last quarter of the twentieth century, both historicity and culture in general were being viewed, not as non-essential luxuries but as environmental assets and economic resources. This was reflected in the reframing of conservation legislation during the 1960s and 1970s throughout Western Europe, which shifted the focus from the protection of buildings to the enhancement of historic areas. The 'paradigm shift' was marked by the publication in the UK of Colin Buchanan's immensely influential report for the Ministry of Transport, *Traffic in Towns* (1963). This demonstrated clearly that the unlimited accommodation of the motor vehicle would necessitate the complete reconstruction (in practice demolition) of traditional cities and was not feasible in historic towns. Buchanan pointed to the need for urban planning to place restrictions on car use while providing much better public transport. Nevertheless, it took the building of urban motorways around and even through major European cities in the early 1970s, most notably in London and Paris, to bring home the costs of accommodating the car. There was a turning point, which might perhaps be identified in Western Europe as by 1973–75, but also in North America, when there was a re-evaluation, often supported by public protest, and even eventual cancellation of such transport schemes. The modernist project had reached its apogee and since then, has been reversed.

What has emerged, instead, is this seeming paradox of a model of a postwar European city that, like Belfast and Berlin, has self-consciously historicized. At one level, cities remain the centres of the continent's national and regional economies while the bulk of Europeans are urban dwellers. At another, however, the European urban landscape has become a focus for the constant invocation and acknowledgement of the past and is marked by the ubiquitous refurbishment or even reconstruction of the materiality of the past. Landscape has come to be seen as a 'text…a signifying system through which a social system is communicated, reproduced, experienced and explored.'[3] Urban landscapes have become sites of memory and representations of identity and are often used essentially as 'stage sets' for political and ideological spectacles. Thus, in November 2009, for example, the Brandenburg Gate acted as the visual focus of the celebrations to

---

[3] James Duncan, *The City as Text: The Politics of Landscape Interpretation in the Kandyan Kingdom* (Cambridge: Cambridge University Press, 1990), 17.

mark the twentieth anniversary of the collapse of the Berlin Wall. But urban landscapes also constitute a powerful economic resource in that the European city has become a keystone in cultural tourism while the historically referenced landscape is also used to 'sell' places. The overall aim of this chapter is to explore how European cities have been reconceptualized since 1945, not just as places to live and work, but as sites of memory and culture embodied within this matrix of interlinked social and economic processes.

The discussion is framed through the lens of heritage. Although this is often presented as a vague, even meaningless word, heritage is seen here as having a very precise definition, referring to the 'ways in which very selective past material artefacts, natural landscapes, mythologies, memories, and traditions become cultural, political, and economic resources for the present.'[4] In constituting the meanings placed upon the past and the representations that are created from them, heritage is thus present-centred, infusing the past with present purposes.[5] As such, however, heritages are open to constant revision and change and also may be both sources and outcomes of social conflict. Thus the heritage of the European city since 1945 has interconnected with the reframing of postwar national identities and expiation for, and rewriting of, history to accommodate the legacies of World War II. During the Cold War it was used to underpin the legitimacy of new states, boundaries and ideological mindsets. Later, the collapse of Marxist-Leninism and the further reframing of national identities after 1989 promoted another wholesale renegotiation of meanings and their representations in the urban landscapes, a process that still continues today in the former Eastern Europe.[6]

All heritages involve a deliberate selection from the infinity of the past whether conveyed through material relics such as buildings, landscapes, and monuments or through memory and tradition. Conceptually, heritage can take the form either of adapting historical landscapes, monuments, and buildings to present needs and incorporating them into the present landscape or, conversely, of inserting into that landscape new structures which reference the past's relevance to the present. Heritage therefore includes but is broader than processes of museumification. If heritage is a mentality—a way of seeing and knowing—then it is a contemporary cultural construct whose meanings vary between groups and individuals and change through time. This may be a source of contestation as the same objects carry different meanings for different social groups at the same time, such discordance or lack of agreement or consistency as to the meaning of heritage being known as 'dissonance'.[7]

As briefly noted earlier, heritage also has two distinct sets of uses, which, while overlapping, also contribute to the idea of dissonance. The first encompasses a variety of

---

[4] Brian Graham and Peter Howard (eds), *The Ashgate Research Companion to Heritage and Identity* (Aldershot: Ashgate, 2008), 2.

[5] David Lowenthal, *The Heritage Crusade and the Spoils of History* (Cambridge: Cambridge University Press, 1996), xv.

[6] See for example Monika Murzyn, 'Heritage transformation in Central and Eastern Europe,' in Graham and Howard (eds), *The Ashgate Research Companion to Heritage and Identity*, 315–46.

[7] John E. Tunbridge and G.J. Ashworth, *Dissonant Heritage: Managing the Past as a Resource in Conflict* (Chichester: Wiley, 1996).

social and political uses that interconnect with the realm of identity and its sense of communal membership but also exclusion of those who do not qualify. Heritage thus interconnects with questions of identity and with processes of social inclusion and exclusion, lifestyle, diversity, and multiculturalism/pluralism.[8] Lowenthal argues that within this context, the past validates and legitimates the present by conveying a sense of timeless values and continuity that underpin senses of social belonging.[9] These latter are often grounded in representations of place, which are, in turn, used to legitimate peoples' claims to those places. But place images are not usually explicable in terms of a single dominant ideology—peoples, identities, images, and motivations 'are all just too plural to be reduced simplistically in this way'.[10] Consequently, European cities are places of complex, overlapping and ambiguous messages, not least because most 'were plurally encoded by socially pluralist societies and are now also decoded pluralistically' due to migration.[11] Much of the iconography of the city is not decoded at all, less because it is intelligible but because of its irrelevance to contemporary multicultural urban societies.

The second set of uses of heritage is concerned with its role as an economic resource. While by no means all tourism can be classified as 'cultural' in the sense that it consumes heritage experiences, or the products of the creative industries, it is difficult to consider any form of tourism utterly devoid of culture in the wider sense of the representation and imaging used to sell tourism destinations. In this regard, the recent global growth of heritage and culture-based tourism represents a 'major shift in... tourism demand' towards a tourism that is place-specific, that is where the uniqueness of the place itself is the tourism product rather than any generic quality.[12] In Europe, as elsewhere, cities provide this place-specific product and consciously attempt to differentiate themselves from others, generally using heritage as a powerful instrument of such differentiation. This has become very important economically because increased disposable income and markedly enhanced access to transport have induced behavioural changes in European attitudes to mobility. In particular, the advent of so-called low cost airline transport, most particularly since 1990, has notably increased the range of accessible heritage cities and thus the competition between them for tourism and culture-related inward investment.[13]

Consequently, the realms of culture have become increasingly 'economized' and whereas culture was once seen as a merit good purchased from the surplus earned by the

---

[8] For a full discussion of heritage and identity, see G.J. Ashworth, Brian Graham and J.E Tunbridge, *Pluralising Pasts: Heritage, Identity and Place in Multicultural Societies* (London: Pluto Press, 2007).

[9] David Lowenthal, *The Past is a Foreign Country* (Cambridge: Cambridge University Press, 1985).

[10] G.J. Ashworth and Brian Graham, 'Senses of Place, Senses of Time and Heritage', in G.J. Ashworth and Brian Graham (eds) *Senses of Place: Senses of Time* (Aldershot: Ashgate, 2005), 4.

[11] G.J. Ashworth, 'The Conserved European City as Cultural Symbol: The Meaning of the Text', in Brian Graham (ed.) *Modern Europe: Place, Culture and Identity* (London: Arnold, 1998), 261–86; see 69.

[12] Timothy Dallen and Stephen W. Boyd, *Heritage Tourism* (Harlow: Prentice Hall, 2003), 10.

[13] Brian Graham, 'New Air Services: Tourism and Economic Development', in Anne Graham, Andreas Papatheodorou and Peter Forsyth (eds), *Aviation and Tourism: Implications for Leisure Travel* (Aldershot: Ashgate, 2008), 227–37.

economy, it has now become a resource for economic development. Economy and culture, once regarded as 'self' and 'other', are held 'to be linked, co-constitutive or seamlessly intertwined'.[14] Meanwhile, modern economies increasingly produce, circulate, and consume cultural commodities. There is ample evidence that cultural innovation and the promotion of cultural industries can be linked to the growth of cities and to wider regional development. Rather curiously, however, tourism is essentially elided from Florida's highly influential concept of the 'creative city'. He focuses instead on the competitive capacities of cities and regions to attract highly mobile creative capital, the basis of the knowledge economy, arguing that 'place is the key economic and social organising unit of our time'[15] with 'place' being a synonym for city. Similarly, the essentially urban characteristics of 'Tolerance and diversity clearly matter to high-technology concentration and growth.'[16]

The concept of the creative city overlaps with, but is separate from, that of the 'tourist-historic' city.[17] Florida argues for cosmopolitanism and tolerance as the cornerstones of the creative city while the tourist-historic city is the ultimate beneficiary of diversifying both the pasts it can sell and the workforce collectively motivated to sell them. The cause-and-effect relationships between the cultural economy and regional or city innovation and growth are, however, ambiguous and difficult to measure, particularly when similar strategies are employed by multiple cities and regions to achieve similar ends. While there are sound reasons for qualifying the cliché of the 'Guggenheim effect'—in which the regeneration and transformation of the grim, decayed industrial city of Bilbao is attributed to the catalyst of an internationally recognizable signature building, Gehry's Guggenheim Museum (opened 1997)—the key point is that the model is 'believed' to be effective and therefore acts as a talisman supporting the self-esteem of residents and a place image attractive to exogenous investment. Unsurprisingly the model has been continuously emulated elsewhere and heritage in its widest sense has become fundamental to the branding of European cities as they struggle to assert their distinctiveness from others.

As a result, the postwar European city functions as an artefact of identity, continuously being rewritten in response to social and political change, but is also a commodified culture, geographical brand, and marketing symbol for economic objectives, not least tourism, common processes which would seem to result in two quite contradictory outcomes.[18] On the one hand, the search for the unique, whether for external competitive advantage or internal citizen identification, would seem to stress a distinctive

---

[14] Noel Castree, 'Economy and Culture are Dead! Long Live Economy and Culture', *Progress in Human Geography* 28 (2004), 204–26, esp. 206.

[15] Richard Florida, *The Rise of the Creative Class* (New York: Basic Books, 2002), xix.

[16] Richard Florida, *Cities and the Creative Class* (London: Routledge, 2005), 137.

[17] G.J. Ashworth and J.E. Tunbridge, *The Tourist-Historic City* (London: Belhaven Press, 1990); G.J. Ashworth and J.E. Tunbridge, *The Tourist-Historic City: Retrospect and Prospect of Managing the Heritage City* (Oxford: Pergamon, 2000).

[18] See Brian Graham, 'Heritage as Knowledge: Capital or Culture?', *Urban Studies* 39:5–6 (2002), 1003–17.

individuality. Conversely, the similarity of the forces, reactions, and objectives would seem to tend towards the homogeneous and generic. Furthermore, the problem of interpretation is rendered more complex in that the nature of 'European' and 'Europeanness' is being worked out across an interplay of scales. On one hand, there is a diffusion of state-based power and competencies, as state sovereignty is challenged by the emergent European Union (EU) polity. On the other, there is a strengthening of state-based orders, a buttressing of national government and a return to nationalism and its identity iconography.[19] One repercussion of globalization in Europe has been to accentuate the importance of the sub-national scales as particular regions and metropoles have benefited to the exclusion of others, leading to a postwar economic geography of Europe that is defined less by national boundaries than by regional ones. As Clark and Jones observe, 'the inherent tension between states and the supranational political project of building "Europe" arises precisely because Europeanization processes are both supportive of yet transcend national territory-government-power bases.'[20] Simultaneously, Europe's cities have become culturally more diverse places as migration both internal within the EU and from external sources has created new dimensions of cultural complexity and hybridity. Optimists, such as Ulrich Beck, point to a cosmopolitan vision of Europe that is transformative and transgressive, a counter-image to the 'territorial prison theory of identity, society, and politics' that informs national stereotyping and heritage selection. Among others, a guiding principle of cosmopolitanism is that it embodies the '*mélange* principle' in which 'local, national, ethnic, religious, and cosmopolitan cultures and traditions interpenetrate, interconnect, and intermingle.' Beck sees cosmopolitanism as a sense of boundarylessness but does admit to a resurgence of 'introverted forms of nationalism' that are consciously resistant to cosmopolitanism and globalization,[21] the sense of boundarylessness sitting alongside a longing for the re-establishment of old boundary lines and a resurgence in many countries of ethno-nationalism. Within the contextual framework provided by heritage as an instrument for the reshaping of the postwar European city, this interplay of the local, national, European, and global scales acts as a structure of interpretation through the remainder of the chapter.[22]

Heritage is often regarded as intrinsically specific and local, the history of each place being necessarily different and distinctive; thus the transformation of that history into heritage will encourage the production of a unique place inhabited by a unique people.

[19] Julian Clark and Alun Jones, 'The Spatialities of Europeanisation: Territory, Government and Power in "EUrope"', *Transactions of the Institute of British Geographers* 33 (2008), 300–18.

[20] Clark and Jones, 'Spatialities of Europeanisation', 313.

[21] Ulrich Beck, *Cosmopolitan Vision* (Cambridge: Polity Press, 2006), 7.

[22] An excellent set of case studies of European heritage, largely in an urban context, is to be found in the three volumes published by the HERMES project: Sebastian Schröder-Esch (ed.), *Practical Aspects of Cultural Heritage: Presentation, Revaluation, Development*, (HERMES Vol. I: Weimar: Bauhaus-Universität Weimar, 2006); Sebastian Schröder-esch and Justus H. Ulbricht (eds), *The Politics of Heritage and Regional Development Strategies: Actors, Interests, Conflicts* (HERMES Vol. II: Weimar: Bauhaus-Universität Weimar, 2006); Dieter Hassenpflug, Burkhardt Kolbmüller and Sebastian Schröder-Esch (eds), *Heritage and Media in Europe: Contributing Towards Integration and Regional Development* (HERMES Vol. III: Weimar: Bauhaus-Universität Weimar, 2006).

This perspective assumes not only that heritage is intrinsically a local phenomenon but also that heritage can be used as an instrument for the creation and expression of the unique character of localities, a belief that underlies many policies for the management of European cities for diverse markets. In very competitive markets heritage is employed to endow places with a place-product centred on a 'unique selling point' which is used to brand the city and differentiate it from its competitors, in the eyes of the potential consumer. The generic urban product acquires the added value of the distinctive brand. The creation and promotion of a local place-bound heritage is not the only way to do this but it is among the most widespread and effective strategies. The three instruments most commonly used throughout Europe in long-term city branding strategies are: personality association; the signature building; and hallmark events.[23]

Personality association occurs when an individual, usually from the past, with whom people can identify, is associated deliberately with a particular place.[24] In this way the attributes of the personality are transferred to the place and, above all, the individuality of the person supports the individuality of the place. Designers, architects, and artists are especially favoured in such branding because of the physical, visible, and internationally intelligible nature of their work, which, if possible, should be typified by a recognizable distinctiveness if not eccentricity. The very successful branding of Barcelona as 'city of Gaudí' has many precursors, parallels, and later imitators, with varying impact and longevity. Vermeer's Delft, Macintosh's Glasgow, Goethe's Weimar, and Kafka's Prague are all cases where the city is inseparably associated with a memorable and preferably idiosyncratic architectural style or design of an individual, a particular writer, or possibly a school of individuals. Rather more than 'x lived here' marketing, this is branding to the extent that it becomes all but impossible to conceive of the place without the person and vice versa, with the representations of each acquiring some of the attributes of the other.

The signature building is the deliberate use of the visual qualities of a building, design, or even urban district as an instrument of place-branding and is a commonplace strategy in the marketing of the European city, not least because local government and planning agencies have considerable control over the appearance of the urban physical environment. Signature buildings may be either historic edifices, now monumentalized, or newly constructed structures. One expression of this is the flagship building,—which is not a new idea as can be testified by the 'Seven Wonders' of the ancient world— designed not only to accommodate notable public functions but more importantly to convey, through its very presence, statements about the political leader and government that erected it. For example, François Mitterrand's *Bibliothèque Nationale de France* in Paris, which opened in 1995, is more a flagship for general policies and ideas rather than

[23] G.J. Ashworth, 'The Instruments of Place Branding: How is it Done?', *European Spatial Research and Policy* 16: 1 (2009), 9–22.

[24] G.J. Ashworth, 'Personality Association as an Instrument of Place Branding: Possibilities and Pitfalls', in G.J. Ashworth and M. Kavaratzis (eds), *Towards Effective Place Brand Management: Branding European Cities and Regions* (Cheltenham: Edward Elgar, 2010).

the rather utilitarian functions that it performs. To be successful the architecture of a flagship building must be notable and noticeable; it matters little if it is aesthetically liked but matters much that it is seen and talked about. Secondly, the artistic creator of the building is almost as important as the building itself. The architect or designer (as in Norman Foster, Richard Rogers, or Santiago Calatrava) should be as renowned and instantly recognizable as the creation. On a wider scale a flagship building can be used as a centrepiece of broader cultural and economic revitalization, a process that could be labelled 'Guggenheiming' after the centrepiece museum in Bilbao. The purpose of these techniques is to gain instant international recognition, the building becoming the city's signature (or in cinematic terms the location-shot) in a highly competitive marketplace to attract mobile capital and consumer expenditure in the knowledge economy. There is hardly a European city that has not discovered or created such iconic structures in the attempt to be distinctive in this inter-urban global competitive arena and acquire some unique advantage in the struggle to become a recognized centre of creativity and culture.

The third commonly encountered instrument of branding in the European city is the use of temporary or recurrent hallmark cultural events. The city identifies both with the activity and also demonstrates its capacity to host it. Various European cities host both long-standing cultural festivals (as typified by Salzburg, Edinburgh, Venice, or Bayreuth) and also compete for exceptional honorific designations, as, for example, designation as 'European City of Culture' or 'Capital of Culture' (the terminology changed from former to latter in 1999). Conceived, ostensibly, to bring people together, this EU scheme has been prominent in obtaining funds for cultural and tourism initiatives at the local city scale, although the meaning attached to 'European' in the title remains vague and unexpressed. Success or otherwise seems largely to be calculated at the local scale, it being claimed, for example, that some £178m in tourism income was generated by Liverpool's designation as a 2008 European Capital of Culture.[25] Cultural events are favoured largely because of their visibility and the wide acceptability of cultural products as merit goods adding value and desirable brand attributes to a place but there are numerous other possibilities including sporting events, commercial fairs, and even political rallies or international 'summit' meetings.

All three techniques, which, in Europe, are generally applied in combination and as part of wider urban strategies, are intended first to establish global recognition of the local individuality of cities through global media attention and public interest and, secondly, to convey associations of cultural creativity. However, although much early place marketing and promotion was directed at attracting new exogenous investment, customers, or residents, cities must also be 'sold' to their existing inhabitants and users. A sense of local pride or 'civic consciousness' was seen as not only desirable in itself but also as a precondition for successful external marketing, an identification with the local

---

[25] Patrick Wintour, 'In Liverpool's Footsteps: Now Every City can Aim to be Britain's Capital of Culture', *Guardian* (7 January 2009), 11.

being one apparently paradoxical response to globalization. In Europe, heritage, and specifically what can be termed the 'heritagization' of urban public space, was in part a reaction to a decline in the actual importance of localities and in part an essential pre-requisite for the realization of the opportunities for local development. The self-consciously created historic city is an important vehicle for such self-marketing and also a highly visible symbol of its operation. Local residents are confronted in the daily life of the city with an observable non-rejectable public good, evident in the buildings and spaces of the historic city.

National governments have also recognized that heritage may be expressly used to encourage and strengthen an identification of people with localities. Typical of such pol-icies is the Dutch 'Belvedere' programme which was launched in 1999 as a joint initiative of four government departments in a quite explicit attempt to discover, map, protect, and promote landscapes and cityscapes that possess and foster 'local identity'. Such pro-grammes assume that a single local identity exists in cities, passively awaiting discovery and expression, and that localism can be evoked through heritage in order to mitigate some of the less welcome effects of an inexorable globalization.[26]

Vernacularism can be viewed as a self-conscious and deliberate expression of local-ism. It stresses the unofficial, non-professional, non-elite, creativity of local areas and local people. It is strongly linked to the concept of 'folk', the idea of the 'common people' leading 'everyday lives' and to the idea of 'craft', which asserts an opposition not only to industrialized production but also to 'art' produced by a self-consciously separate artis-tic caste. As a political and artistic movement, vernacularism parallels the rise of the modern industrial world and can be viewed as a reaction to it through a conservative nostalgia for a vanished, vanishing, or even imagined idealized pre-modern society. The conserved historic city has adopted many vernacular elements drawn from the folk museum movement associated with Artur Hazelius who established the first such exam-ple at Skansen, Stockholm, in 1891.[27] It is a short step from the deliberately assembled museum town to the vernacular museumification of existing towns and districts. The distinction between town and museum has become blurred and the vernacular may merge with national and even international styles. Vernacularization may have origi-nated as defence against modernist internationalism but it has become little more than a fashionable global eclecticism. The paradox is of course, as with the historic city more generally, that such vernacular design elements first introduced to express local differ-ence become widely imitated and diffused and thus part of a new recognizable global style, composed of imported elements divorced from the localities and societies that originally produced them.

---

[26] G.J. Ashworth and Marie-Jeannette Kuipers, 'Conservation and Identity: A New Vision of Pasts and Futures in the Netherlands', *European Spatial Research and Policy*, 8:2 (2001), 55–65.

[27] Paul Oliver, 'Re-presenting and Representing the Vernacular: The Open Air Museum', in N. Alsayyad (ed), *Consuming Tradition, Manufacturing Heritage: Global Norms and Urban Forms in the Age of Tourism* (London: Routledge, 2001), 191–210.

Turning to the next stage in the spatial hierarchy, the national, in almost all European countries heritage is principally created, financed, and managed by national government agencies. The content selected from the stock of physical relics, memories, and past associations for preservation, memorialization, and interpretation, is the near exclusive responsibility of national governments pursuing officially mandated national policies. The explanation for this attempted 'nationalization of the past' can be sought in the political ideology of nationalism and the dependence of the state for its legitimation upon the creation of the imagined entity 'nation', a process which Smith refers to as the creation of the 'authorized heritage discourse'.[28] The city accordingly becomes a local reflective variant of this national heritage, a process which is reflected in three different ways.

First, there is the handful of cases when a national government has deliberately created a city to serve as an administrative capital and thus visible symbol of the authority and legitimation of that government as it seeks to create a unity from culturally diverse immigrant or indigenous populations. The best examples are European settler cities in the former colonial societies beyond Europe. The longer history of state formation in Europe largely precludes clear examples of this form of the national city although it is worth remembering that many European cities originated or owe their development and importance, at least in part, as national seats of government and were designed to reflect and project that status. Madrid, for example, emerged as the administrative centre of Castilian Spain in the sixteenth century, its pre-eminence marked in the cityscape by monumental planning and architecture.

Secondly, if nations have created the heritage city, then there should be recognizable national schools or styles of heritage city planning and design that suppress or incorporate the local into a national archetype. Hence, favoured historical periods, buildings, or conservation practice may be recognizable in the contemporary urban fabric of the European city. The stress upon the seventeenth century in the Netherlands, the eighteenth and nineteenth centuries in France, and the high Victorian age in Britain reflects not just the availability of resources but also a search for a legitimation of the national entity conferred by a 'golden age'. Equally, there are the techniques of painstaking replication of an idealized 'Jagiellonian' urbanism (typified by Cracow) that is the self-styled 'Polish School' of conservation;[29] the lavish set piece 'palatial' style of the French cloning of Paris's Place des Vosges or mansard roofs in many provincial town centres; or the fussy detailed domesticity of Dutch *monumentenzorg* practice.[30] The 'German School' has created and reproduced in numerous urban conservation projects a rediscovered German 'vernacular' style which is not only an artistic reaction to 'modernism' as an international architectural style but also an assertion of a new national confidence after a generation's submission to international political dominance in the immediate postwar period.[31]

[28] Laurajane Smith, *The Uses of Heritage* (London: Routledge, 2006).
[29] A. Milobedzski, *The Polish School of Conservation* (Krakow: International Cultural Centre, 1995).
[30] Roger Kain, *Planning for Conservation: An International Perspective* (London: Mansell, 1981).
[31] John Soane, 'The Renaissance of Cultural Vernacularism in Germany', in G.J. Ashworth and Peter J. Larkham (eds), *Building a New Heritage: Tourism, Culture and Identity in the New Europe* (London: Routledge, 1994), 159–77.

Thirdly, there is the 'epitome argument'. Here elements of a local vernacular are appropriated as national design symbols with particular cities serving as exemplars to be more or less reproduced nationally. In the Netherlands, the local place-specific characteristics of the seventeenth-century Holland trading town, popularized as the 'Vermeer' style, has seen Delft replicated in regions with quite different characteristics and histories. Delft has become the Dutch heritage archetype. In reaction to this 'Hollandization', encouraged through the second half of the twentieth century by the centralized national heritage agencies, the southern provinces of the country are developing a 'Burgundian' style in cities such as Maastricht, Roermond, and s'Hertogenbosch; and in the north, a 'Hanseatic' style which, of course, merely exchanges a national stereotype for a regional one that links, more widely, with the cities of North Germany, Scandinavia and the Baltic coast. Rothenburg ob der Tauber in Bavaria evolved in the course of the nineteenth century from a by-passed medieval market town to an iconic expression of a romantic national identity of the new Germany, carefully reconstructed after 1945 as the epitome of Germanness.[32] Smaller towns such as Stow-on-the-Wold in England, Adare in Ireland, Ribe in Denmark, or Evora in Portugal have become successful national archetypes despite the reality that the actual design features iconized in this way were regional rather than national and often highly place-specific rather than nationally typical.

Although the national scale remains pre-eminent, not least because heritage legislation is nationally defined, the postwar European city—as we have noted in the cases of Belfast and Berlin—also reflects the continual social and political change in the meaning of the national. This is perhaps most marked in the former Eastern Europe, the countries there having repositioned themselves, first in the wake of World War II and then the collapse of Marxist-Leninism at the end of the 1980s. In Warsaw, for instance, post-socialist revisionism reflects resurgent Polish nationalism, the 'old town' reconstructed to re-enact that destroyed in 1943–4 (and inscribed as a World Heritage Site in 1980), now standing at the centre of a swathe of post-socialist memorialization marking not just Polish suffering at the hands of the Nazis, the martyrdom of the Warsaw Rising of 1944 but also the Soviet culpability in war crimes such as Katyn Forest and its postwar oppression of the Polish people.

This engagement with the dramatic changes of postwar European history also emphasizes the European dimension to the culture and heritage of the continent's cities. The assertion that cities located in the continent of Europe are recognizably European can be argued less from the history of their evolution as such than from the history of their conservation. First the idea of ascribing value to past built environments and then preserving them originated in the nation states of Europe. The urban conservation movement began in the second half of the nineteenth century and received its organizational and legislative structures in the first half of the twentieth century in the countries of

[32] Joshua Hagen, *Preservation, Tourism and Nationalism: The Jewel of the German Past* (Aldershot: Ashgate, 2006).

northern Europe.[33] It spread subsequently to the Mediterranean, Eastern Europe and beyond, resulting in broadly similar organizational structures, legislation, and practice and thus conserved heritage cities. Arguably, therefore, if the postwar European city exists as an idea, then it is composed of conserved urban forms and the idealized urban lifestyle that these contain. Such an archetype was created, not by a few thousand years of an essentially unique urban historic experience, but by around a hundred years of a continentally standardized conservation planning. The process was European in that although, of course, other continents have distinguished urban histories and architectural creativity, urban conservation was a European idea which diffused later elsewhere, most usually first to cities of European settlement overseas.[34] This has numerous implications some of which are commercial, in that European cities today are the product leaders in the cultural and heritage tourism industries, and others political, in that 'world heritage' and its international institutions, such as UNESCO represent little more than European conservation concepts and practice extended onto a world stage.

Neither of these arguments, however, justifies the existence of a specifically European dimension in contemporary conserved cities in the sense of expressing a distinctive and self-conscious continentalism as opposed to localism or nationalism. Such a European city might exist in two senses, the first of which can be quickly dismissed. There is a small group of contemporary cities, or parts of cities, which house the institutions of European organizations or which might be associated with events and personalities connected to such institutions. The centres of the EU, Strasbourg, Luxembourg City and, above all, Brussels might be expected to symbolize the 'European movement' (together with the European Central Bank in Frankfurt and the sites of the various 'treaties', as in Rome, Maastricht, Nice, or Lisbon). However, unexceptional office blocks, housing the officials of the EU's many mundane agencies, lack any popular resonance. The EU has not created symbolic cities that compete with the national showcase cities for popular identification, enthusiasm, or visitation.[35]

Secondly, a postwar European city might exist as a reflection of a common Europe-wide historical experience and common set of contemporary problems, needs, and expectations. As a result it might be expected that the cities of Europe would appear distinctively European because they share a European history. Continent-wide events, trends, and fashions, from Roman imperial rule, through the Renaissance, Reformation, industrialization to post-Fordist consumerism should be evident in varying degrees in cities from the Urals to the Atlantic. If a commonality of history has been sufficient to shape a contemporary European city, then the common features must be more influential than the local, regional, national, and global dimensions. Patently they are not and,

---

[33] Brian Graham, G.J. Ashworth and J.E. Tunbridge, *A Geography of Heritage: Power, Culture and Economy* (London: Arnold, 2000).

[34] For a wider discussion, see Ashworth and Tunbridge, *Tourist-Historic City: Retrospect and Prospect*, ch. 9.

[35] G.J. Ashworth and Brian Graham, 'Heritage, Identity and Europe', *Tijdschrift voor Economisch en Sociale Geografie*, 88 (1997), 381–8.

consequently: Bristol has in many ways more in common with Boston than with Munich; Glasgow with Montreal rather than Kiev; Reggio Calabria with Tunis rather than Stockholm. The concept of a European city is either so particular as to be largely irrelevant or so general as to be effectively global.

In the postwar European city as described above, heritage may well have been used in pursuit of local or even national identity but the instruments applied in the pursuit of such goals are themselves neither local nor national. Rather, they constitute what is inherently an international phenomenon and part of a wider economic, political, and cultural globalization. It can be argued that heritage is a process that is intrinsically global even if its application and even motivation is local or national. Much heritage planning is a local perception and reaction to globally apparent problems and trends.[36] Cities throughout Europe have been endeavouring to express their unique individuality for reasons, and using instruments, that are broadly comparable and aimed at similar goals. The reconceptualization of the European city since 1945 has been created by the cooperative actions of numerous individual and corporate actors in a coalition of interests. Many of these were local but, equally, many were not and the argument here is that almost all such actors, regardless of their local associations, had a strong motive for global networking. The addition of tourism, which is as a matter of course a global phenomenon in its demands and facility supply, the expectations of visitors, and the satisfaction of these, further encourages globalization.[37]

Throughout Europe, the creation of the heritage city, its monuments, historic districts, attractions, and symbolisms is a high risk enterprise in which public and private venture capital is invested in expectation of a return at least as high as alternative possibilities. The safe maxim has been and always will be to identify what has worked previously or elsewhere and replicate it. This applies to the choice of consumer markets being targeted, the mix of functions to be included, uses of historicity to add atmosphere, the balance of new and conserved old forms and structures, and the techniques of promotion and branding. Such standardization is not only a feature of the private sector but also evident among public-sector policy makers. Architects and designers, town planners, and local politicians all have an interest in minimizing risk, whether financial, professional, or political, through global networking, interaction, and ultimately repetition.

The result in the heritagization of the European city, especially since the 1970s, is a replication complete to the detailing of materials, signage, and street furniture, which can be caricatured as an 'off the peg' heritage. This is typified in the projection of a 'European' image, by cobblestones, 'period' litter bins, traffic bollards and lamp standards, hanging flower baskets, and heritage signage. This 'catalogue heritage' is, however, only a visible indication of a much deeper standardization, justified under the rubric of

---

[36] N. Alsayyad (ed.), *Consuming Tradition, Manufacturing Heritage: Global Norms and Urban Forms in the Age of Tourism* (London: Routledge, 2001).

[37] P. Boniface and P.J. Fowler, *Heritage and Tourism in the Global Village* (London: Routledge, 2003).

'best practice'. There is an inherent tendency for investors to reiterate previously profitable financial structures, developers to imitate previously successful plans, local planners and politicians to approve what has already been approved elsewhere, marketing consultants to repeat previously effective campaigns, and even architects and urban designers to replicate previously lauded forms and designs.

Consequently, there are many examples of what can be termed cliché heritage in European cities. In their first manifestation, these strategies may have been original, exciting, and experimental but are now replicated throughout the continent to the point where they no longer express the sense of the locally distinctive identity that was the intention of their creators. Many such clichés can be recognized in urban heritage development. The use of now redundant quayside buildings and piers to create a linear waterfront recreation, residential, and leisure facility incorporating historic buildings and associations and commonly associated with other components such as 'festival' and 'craft' marketplaces, originated in the United States, most specifically in Boston, Baltimore, and San Francisco, in the 1970s. As in Belfast's rather tardy waterfront renaissance, the concept has rapidly disseminated through almost every waterfront city in Europe and elsewhere. The pedestrianized and heritagized shopping street typified by appropriate street furniture, shop type design, and leisure shopping activity, often in conserved buildings, is found from Elm Hill, Norwich, the 'Shambles', York, Böttcherstrasse, Bremen, to Stokstraat, Maastricht. The 'plaza mayor' was originally a feature of Spanish cities in which a combination of architecturally imposing facades accommodating publicly accessible shopping or catering facilities, enclosed an open-air 'happening' space. It has now migrated from its Mediterranean origins to a climatically less sympathetic Northern and Central Europe where the dubious attraction of an outdoor cafe culture is now reinforced by bans on smoking. To this could often be added the 'Ramblas' inspired by Barcelona's eponymous linear pedestrian boulevard which combines some aspects of the park with 'happening space' for commercial, leisure, and entertainment activities. The Mediterranean 'fishing harbour' with its quayside promenade, lined with fish restaurants, and boats as décor accessory and tourism facility and preferably enhanced by some heritage harbour structure of castle, customs house, mole or lighthouse, has been replicated not only around the Mediterranean but also along the Atlantic, North Sea and Baltic coasts of Europe. Similarly, the medieval 'old town' provides a predictable array of retailing and food outlets, irrespective both of its location in Europe and the point that, in their physical fabric, many of the continent's 'old towns' date only to the era of postwar reconstruction.

Other examples abound. The 'artists' colony' is the deliberate use of a previous, and often long vanished, association of a place with creative artists for environmental enhancement and commercial opportunity. The original uniqueness of Paris's Montmartre, has evolved into the stereotypical, predictable creative district where arts and crafts (often mass-produced outside Europe altogether) are merged into a saleable product with a distinctive cultural atmosphere. The 'signature museum', or other public cultural buildings such as opera houses or theatres, was described earlier as an instrument for establishing local individuality, restoring local self-confidence and promoting a new externally marketable brand, especially in cities needing economic or social renewal. Although the structures themselves are usually new and often designed to be deliberately and provokingly anti-historicist, they are often used as part of heritage districts and as statements of the general importance of culture to the place concerned. They have, however, become a *de rigueur* addition to almost any city and have thus lost the impact made originally by a Paris *Beaubourg* (otherwise the Pompidou Centre) or Stockholm and Helsinki's Houses of Culture. Arguably, the contemporary European city has become a pastiche assembled though a selection of one or more of these well known, 'off the shelf' cultural and heritage developments, seasoned with only a minimal addition of local historical or cultural flavour through local events, artefacts, or place associations. Present day European cities are becoming less local, national, or even 'European' as economies and cultures globalize in the service of citizens and consumers of the global city.

Finally, in respect to this discussion of the globalization of the postwar European city, it is worth mentioning the ambivalent role of the world agencies officially charged with the recognition, designation, protection, and management of 'world heritage'. The agencies of UNESCO (especially the World Heritage Centre and its expert advisory groups, ICOMOS, ICOM and IUCN) reflect the paradoxical nature of the culture and economy of postwar European cities. It might be thought that place-bound heritage would represent an intrinsically local history and culture. However, the much sought after World Heritage Site designation tends to encourage the establishment of a set of heritage sites in Europe and around the world, many of which are cities displaying similar characteristics. The European World Heritage List is dominated by city centres and urban buildings, Spain, for example, having no less than thirteen *Ciudades Patrimonio de la Humanidad* or world heritage cities. The trend towards the homogeneous is encouraged by the stimulation and transfer of 'best practice' and the internationalization of expert knowledge, frequently coupled with UNESCO approved site management plans that again tend towards a uniformity of approach. Conversely, UNESCO remains a forum for national representation rather than world government. This is demonstrated especially clearly in the national conflicts, agreements, and compromises that govern World Heritage Site selection. The places designated represent those national choices and priorities, often quite deliberately made to symbolize and project perceived national characteristics.[38]

In sum, therefore, it has been argued here that the cities of Europe have been reinvented in the period since 1945 in response to economic, social, and cultural change. The scalar taxonomy used here is one simple and convenient way of linking place with people and seems to point to four possibilities. Is the postwar European city essentially a collection of recognizably individual cities, linked only by their chance location within one continent? Does it merely express the attributes of the nation state, so that the most important characteristic of a city is that it is German, Italian, or whichever? Is the

[38] See Graham et al., *Geography of Heritage*, ch 11.

adjective 'European' the most fundamental taxonomic determinant in a world in which the European city offers a fundamentally different urban experience to the North American or East Asian city? Finally, have the myriad aspects of globalization resulted in a type of European city that is fundamentally similar in all but its trivial detailing? It may be that an affirmative answer can be given to all four questions. There is an inherent contradiction summarized in the idea of the European city being an arena for the simultaneous search for the three basic attributes of distinctiveness, balance, and universality, with heritage playing a decisive role in all three incompatible goals.

First, competition between the cities has led to a continuous embellishment, expansion, and differentiation of the heritage product, rapidly consumed by tourists and residents alike. Such a process is ultimately self-perpetuating as each city attempts to increase the distinctiveness of its heritage in similar ways among the limited range of possibilities. The most popular optional 'add-ons' are the 'tourist-historic waterfront', medieval old town, 'ethnic' district, festival calendar, sanitized 'red light' district, and the gentrified 'urban village'; all devised to be different but ultimately becoming the same.

Secondly, there has been an evident attempt in many European countries to construct a more representative heritage in response to an increasing social and cultural pluralism and therefore a heritage city that includes a wider selection from the varied social, ethnic and racial composition of society.[39] This is a response both to the political and social demands within European societies for a heritage that represents the currently un- or under-represented. It is also a reaction to the demands of tourism for more product variety and the requirement that tourists, themselves socially varied, can identify with their own heritage presented abroad. Heritage is thus ascribed an instrumental role in a search for a 'balanced' heritage city. This may be a chimera as 'balance' is, at best, changing and, at worst, indefinable but the attempt itself, and the expectations that underlie it, are important in the contemporary European city.

Finally, not only is the planning of the heritage city becoming more clichéd but also the heritage itself is becoming meaningless to the extent that it conveys no meaning other than a simple idea of antiquity. Increasingly, the conserved European city is not related specifically to, or representative of, any selected historical time period, artistic style, political message, or even locality. It is just instantly recognizable as heritage, a property in itself, rather than a vehicle for conveying any further messages. This universalization can be seen in artefacts and design features such as the Victorian cast iron street lamp, the carriage lamp exterior door light, granite paving setts, hanging flower baskets, and even the use of a pseudo-Gothic script on signage. Together this semiology creates a near ubiquitous non-place-bound code conveying a generalized and non-locally specific historicity. The simultaneous search for distinctiveness and universality has resulted in the reconceptualization of a postwar European city that that symbolizes the idea of antiquity or tradition, without reference to any particular age or locality. As

---

[39] See Ashworth et al., *Pluralising Pasts,* for a full discussion of multicultural heritage.

such, it can be argued that generic heritage is creating a placeless vernacularism in contemporary European cities, which is dissonance free, inoffensive, and all-inclusive. It evokes almost universal feelings of continuity, familiarity, well-being, and reliability. In consequence, the local has become globally accessible and the global locally obtainable as localism has become divorced from locality. It is thus that the postwar European city is, perhaps, no more than a reflection of these selfsame characteristics in European society especially since the 1970s.

FURTHER READING

Ashworth, Gregory J., Brian Graham and John E. Tunbridge, *Pluralising Pasts: Heritage, Identity and Place in Multicultural Societies* (London: Pluto Press, 2007).

Beck, Ulrich, *Cosmopolitan Vision* (Cambridge: Polity Press, 2006).

Benton, Tim (ed.), *Understanding Heritage and Memory* (Manchester: Manchester University Press and Open University, 2010).

Graham, Brian, Gregory J. Ashworth and John E. Tunbridge, *A Geography of Heritage: Power, Culture, Economy* (London: Arnold, 2000).

Graham, Brian, Peter Howard (eds), *The Ashgate Research Companion to Heritage and Identity* (Aldershot: Ashgate, 2008).

Harrison, Rodney, *Understanding the Politics of Heritage* (Manchester: Manchester University Press and The Open University, 2010).

Lowenthal, David, *The Heritage Crusade and the Spoils of History* (Cambridge: Cambridge University Press, 1998).

Smith, Laurajane, *Uses of Heritage* (London: Routledge, 2006).

Till, Karen, *The New Berlin: Memory, Politics, Place* (Minneapolis, MN: University of Minnesota Press, 2005).

West, Susie, *Understanding Heritage in Practice* (Manchester: Manchester University Press and Open University, 2010).

CHAPTER 29

THE POSTCOLONIAL CONDITION

ROBERT J.C. YOUNG

THE phrase, 'the postcolonial condition', is usually invoked with respect to the particular state as well as common circumstances of the many colonies that were freed from colonial rule during the second half of the twentieth century and are now living on in the legacy of colonialism.[1] Those conditions are hardly the same everywhere, but the historical impact of colonial rule in its various forms remains a feature of everyday life, whether at the level of institutions, law, economy, education, language, cultural production, or even old repainted postboxes, for all formerly colonized countries. Although European countries were by no means the only imperial masters (Japan, the Ottoman Empire, Russia, the United States, should also be included), postcolonial conditions all over the world remain very substantially the product of European rule, given the extent of the European empires. If the postcolonial condition is for the most part a European product, it is so in more ways than one, for it also pertains to Europe itself. While the rest of the world gradually frees itself from its postcoloniality, as it earlier freed itself from the shackles of colonialism, it is the Europe from which colonialism came that remains caught within the postcolonial condition: for this reason the idea of 'the postcolonial' has had most currency in Europe. Postcoloniality remains Europe's enduring condition, a colonial effect of belatedness that continues to link colony and metropole under its common shadow. A collective postcolonial situation still binds Europe to much of the rest of the world, stretching over all barriers constructed between 'the continent' and the continents of Asia and the global South.

Europe is subject to the postcolonial condition in a number of ways. I am going to leave the term 'postcolonial' with a simple historical reference here. Although it will accumulate further meanings in the course of this essay, the historical meaning remains the

---

[1] Peter Geschiere, 'Is There "A" Postcolonial Condition?', *The Salon* 1 (2009), 23–5.

foundation of them all, and all those that follow are conditional on it.[2] The general assumption when speaking of the postcolonial condition is that 'condition' in this context refers to a manner or state of being, and the postcolonial condition is therefore something that requires diagnosis and a cure. The word 'condition' can suggest a positive state, as when we talk about an athlete being 'in condition', or more typically a negative one, as when we talk about someone being 'out of condition', or, 'in a bad condition', which suggests that the person requires treatment, or bears a scar that may be closed, or still weeping, that remains either way as a discernible and inextinguishable trace. The term 'condition' itself comes from the Latin *condicere* to speak with, agree, from *com* + *dicere*, a speaking together. The basis of an agreement is made on a condition, in the sense of the phrase 'terms and conditions', that is, a stipulation, part of a bargain, something whose fulfilment depends on that condition being achieved. Grammatically, this means a clause that begins with an 'if', as in, 'if this... then that', just as in logic where a condition refers to a proposition on which the truth of another proposition depends. Finally, as a verb, to condition also means to accustom a person or persons to something. A speaking together, then, an agreement with a condition, a state of being, and an accustomizing of people to something: the postcolonial condition in Europe involves all these.

How can Europe ever be more than 'post' to its history of colonialism? At what point will Europe emerge from its own shadow that it cast so forcefully and violently over the rest of the world? It was not just that Europe annexed far-away territories and made them its colonies. Colonialism also joined Europe to the world: around the globe, territories became part of Greater Britain or Greater France, so that all continents were drawn in towards the European homeland. In that process, the barriers between Europe and the world beyond broke down such that Europe itself became globalized. This universalization of Europe was not undone at the time of decolonization: its languages and institutions were already spread everywhere, while its interests of capital remained, as did those of its foreign policy. Besides, the world was already in Europe. That was the condition that was not bargained for. While Europeans assumed that the proposition was 'if colonialism, then gold, and Christian conversion', the colonies' condition was 'if colonialism, then transculturation of commodities, cultures, and people'. If colonialism, in other words, then immigration—of Europeans to their colonies, and of non-Europeans to Europe: 'we are here because you were there'. The postcolonial condition means that there is no longer a fundamental distinction between Europe and the rest of the world. Eurocentricity has, certainly in its original form, become impossible, because Europe is no longer centric to itself. The cost of decolonization has involved the loss of Europe's own cultural autonomy, combined with a lingering memory of its own lost colonial past, the insistent repetition of a history that refuses to dissolve while it continues to play itself out in the present. The 'postcolonial' marks the fact that the concession of sovereignty to the colonized did not produce a clean break, so much as generated a working through and re-memorization of the past and the present. At the same time, rather less obviously, the postcolonial condition marks an unfulfilled transition, the

---

[2] Robert J. C. Young, *Postcolonialism: An Historical Introduction* (Oxford: Blackwell, 2001).

moment of temporalization, of deferment and delay, before Europe moves from the untimely status of being caught between the past and the future, postwar, postmodern, postcolonial, without ever yet having emerged into a new era of its own, into a fully self-defined present.[3]

When will Europe emerge from the temporality of the clause that begins with the conditional 'if'? The postcolonial condition is both symptomatic and names an indicator that recurs across the European body: the colonial has not been entirely overcome. The symptoms are not hard to detect, but what is the condition for the passing of postcoloniality? What can bring it about and allow Europe to move beyond it?

THE SPACE OF HISTORY

If we think of the twentieth century in Europe as involving an extended period of war that began in 1914 and ended in 1945, then the century falls almost neatly into two, the period of war, and the period of peace.[4] And yet, few of the victors of that war experienced an extended peace after 1945. The imperial war may have ended in Europe but its aftershocks continued to explode across the furthest reaches of Europe's empires. Each part of the imperial war had finished with its own condition of postcoloniality: the dismemberment of the empires of the vanquished. The First World War concluded with the dismantling of three empires, the German, the Austro-Hungarian and the remnant of the Ottoman Empire that had survived the nineteenth century. All other empires continued more or less uninterrupted, indeed they promptly ingested the territories of the defeated imperial powers, not anticipating that the break-up of the German and Ottoman empires would have their own postcolonial effects. Despite Woodrow Wilson's principles of self-determination, and the many activist groups that travelled to Versailles in 1919 to claim independence for their countries or their peoples, the victors insisted on the spoils of war that had always formed part of their original war aims—the appropriation of more colonial territory, together with the people who inhabited it, passed from one owner to another like chattels. The Second World War ended in turn with the enforced dismemberment of two more empires: the Italian and the Japanese, together with the Third Reich's short-lived empire of the Greater Germany in Europe. This time, however, a majority of Italian and Japanese territories were given independence. Even the Philippines, which had been occupied by the Japanese in 1941–2, and which had originally declared its own independence in 1898, the same year in which the United States of America had purchased it from Spain for $20 million, was finally ceded independence by the USA on 4 July 1946.

---

[3] Sandro Mezzadra and Federico Rahola, 'The Postcolonial Condition: A Few Notes on the Quality of Historical Time in the Global Present', *Postcolonial Text* 2:1 (2006), online at: http://journals.sfu.ca/pocol/index.php/pct/article/viewArticle/393, accessed June 2010.

[4] Patrick Deer, *Culture in Camouflage: War, Empire, and Modern British Literature* (Oxford: Oxford University Press, 2009).

In 1945, the conditions for the survival of the world's empires were very different from 1919 when the victorious empires had confidently continued to overreach themselves. Humiliated by a defeat that baffled the public, shorn of its colonies in 1919, and refused the demand for their return in the 1930s, within a short space of time Germany would go on to turn almost the whole of Europe into its colony. Aimé Césaire was not the first but certainly the most influential of those who pointed out that Fascism was essentially the deployment of colonial techniques—concentration camps, genocide, militarization—for the first time within Europe itself (though some might wish to instance Ireland at this point). Finding itself finally prey to the monster of colonial rule that it had itself created, ending the war either freed from Nazi rule or in submission to the new Soviet Empire, Europe would then have to re-emerge from its own postcolonial condition.

Each war had been concluded with its own condition of postcoloniality, that is, the dismemberment of the empires of the vanquished. The anomaly was that those making this postcolonial stipulation exempted themselves from it. That was the bad luck of those colonies that had formerly been part of the empires of the European victors, and had generally fought on their behalf. So France celebrated its liberation from Nazi rule by refusing its own colonies the postcolonial condition, beginning with the Sétif massacres which formed the reprisals for the 'disturbances' that began the very day that the Algerians, like the French, were celebrating VE day. The Algerians quickly discovered that the liberation of France was not to be extended to Algeria. In making that decision, defeated but now liberated France condemned itself to seventeen years of further war and political instability. The depth of an undiminished imperialist and racialized thinking was illustrated by the determination of the newly liberated European nations to reinstate their colonial empires. Aided by the British and American armies, the French promptly quashed independence movements in former colonies in Algeria, Madagascar, and Vietnam, while the Dutch attempted less successfully to do the same in Indonesia. Britain behaved rather differently, abandoning some of its colonies with unseemly haste. Having already promised independence to India in return for support during the war, Britain duly liberated its mightiest colonial possession, but at the cost of huge human suffering and death. In August 1947, India, together with Pakistan joined the USA, Ireland, and much of Latin America, in the ranks of postcolonial nations. Ceylon followed the following year, the same year in which Britain also simply withdrew from its Versailles-authorized Palestine Mandate, abandoning an intractable problem to an apparently interminable conflict. Once it had released its most conflictual colonies of India, Ireland and Palestine, British politicians did not, however, anticipate that the rest of its empire would follow suit.

One aspect of the European postcolonial condition was the refusal to recognize its overall historical inevitability even as the decolonization process was taking place, a slow dismemberment that in some ways compares to that of the Ottoman Empire in the nineteenth and early twentieth centuries. There was some reason for this: Truman had asserted the right to self-determination in 1919, but had been easily outmanoeuvred by Lloyd George and Clemenceau who engineered the expansion of their empires to the largest extent in their history. Despite the activities of a committed anti-imperialist

Third International trying to foment World Revolution, the only major colony to achieve independence between the wars was Ireland, which technically was not even a colony at all. So the European powers had been very successful for the first half of the twentieth century in maintaining their empires in the face of calls to self-determination. What they failed to see was that their relatively easy defeat by the Germans in Europe and by the Japanese in the East had, in the eyes of the world, altered international perceptions forever, above all the myth of invincible imperial power and the powerlessness of people of colour. The long-term effect of German and Japanese imperial expansion in the mid-twentieth century was the end of imperialism itself, certainly in its European form. By 1945, as a result of the war, the world political scene had been completely transformed into a new dialectic of power between the USA and the USSR, both of which, in different ways, were ostensibly committed to the idea of independence from imperial rule. In 1949 they were joined by China, also a postcolonial anti-imperialist nation, even if, in the very next year, it itself recolonized neighbouring Tibet.

Europe itself began in 1945 as a decolonized continent. Its own new postcolonial condition implied a stipulation that it too should also decolonize, should hand back sovereignty to the territories of its empires, a wholly reasonable quid pro quo in the eyes of the colonized. However, it then took much of the rest of the century for Europe to cede independence to its many colonies. There was a persistent reluctance to let imperial possessions go, fuelled by imperial ideologies and nostalgia, and an inability to accept the implications of the end of empire. As a result, the postcolonial condition was subject to an almost indefinite deferment. In that sense, the states of postwar Europe only gradually transformed themselves into a postcolonial situation, consistently refusing the stipulation that would allow Europe to emerge in its own time not mediated by the postcolonial. The European empires were only dismembered bit by bit, in the face of persistent uprisings and anti-colonial wars, and in fact are technically not yet defunct: there are many colonies still in existence, even within 'Europe', such as Gibraltar, while beyond its geographical boundaries we find Ceuta and Mellila, Martinique, Guadeloupe, Réunion, French Polynesia, even France's Clipperton Island off the shores of Mexico— all, in different senses, part of Europe (Réunion, in the Indian Ocean, was the first 'European' country to use the Euro). Europe is both a geographical continent and an entity that stretches around the world. These islands and landfalls are the remnant, the rump of empire. But they are not the only reason why Europe remains in a state of unfulfilled postcoloniality.

Whereas its own postcoloniality with respect to the Nazi empire was instituted within the space of two years, the postcolonial condition produced by the decolonization of the European empires was a much more long drawn-out affair. If we begin with Indian independence in 1947 and end with the return of Macao and Hong Kong to China in 1997, we can see that the whole of postwar Europe for the second half of the twentieth century has been scarified by the decolonization process. In some countries, such as France and Portugal, anti-colonial struggles came to affect and even overturn the governments that were in place. When the bulk of Western European colonies had been liberated, the last major territories being the Portuguese colonies that became independent in 1975, so at the end of the next decade the Soviet Union released its European and most of its other colonies after 1989. As smaller and smaller countries achieved sovereignty, all over Europe, nationalist activists from nations such as the Basques, or the Scots, also used the overarching framework of the EU to agitate for independence or secession. The whole of the second half of the twentieth century thus involved a narrative of Europe slowly putting itself in a postcolonial condition in a process that even now seems unending, and this perhaps provides one explanation of the preference for 'post' epithets—for marking the present time as a process of transition, of crossing over from the past without a clear sense of the identity of the present or the future.

And yet much of the identity of the present state of things internationally remains very recognizable—since the geography of the world is effectively a European invention—not only the shape of the individual nation states that reflect their particular colonial histories, but the invention of the nation state itself as the basis of the world political system. Europe absent-mindedly facilitated the world of nation states that arose after 1945, and remains determined by the world beyond its borders, which it has created for, aside from anything else, an ever-expanding global capitalism sees no reason to remain tied to particular nation states. In their own way, too, in a dialectical response, the anti-colonial struggles could be said to have created the globalized world. The protracted decolonization process has meant that the anti-colonial movements too became a long-standing condition of European politics, and their processes remain a persistent feature of its political life. The anti-colonial struggles formed part of an extended history of struggles against the West, not just to free themselves from its political control, but to break out of the confines of the hierarchies of coloniality. The larger battle was to assert coevalness as human beings and as human societies, to make the colonial no longer 'other' to the metropolis.[5] The colonized societies wanted not only sovereignty and autonomy, they also wanted equality, to be recognized as fully human.

CULTURAL PRODUCTION

The dilatory deferment of decolonization from 1945 produced a form of temporality in Europe that turned decolonization into a semi-permanent postcolonial condition. If the first stipulation that followed Europe's own decolonization in 1945 was that it should decolonize its empires, the second was that it should also decolonize itself, beginning with the cultural and racial ideologies that had been developed to sustain imperial rule. It was a question of decolonizing laws, institutions, and education, as well as the mind, and realizing that the postcolonial condition has never been static, but has always been a dialectical process, a state of translation. Historically, that translation has always proved to be a two-way activity, not only the European states translating themselves as colonies

[5] Johannes Fabian, *Time and the Other: How Anthropology Makes Its Object* (New York: Columbia University Press, 1983).

across the rest of the world, New Amsterdam, New Caledonia, New England, New Hebrides, New Jersey, New Orleans, New Spain, New York, New Zealand...but more unexpectedly finding themselves being translated by the colonies. This transculturation, brilliantly described by the Cuban anthropologist Fernando Ortiz in 1941 in his work *Cuban Counterpoint*, began several centuries ago with the introduction of tobacco, tea, chocolate, tomatoes, and potatoes, which transformed European social habits;[6] in the eighteenth century, it emerged at a significant cultural level with the first major writings of Orientalism, which may be described as the European fascination with the super-civilized of the eighteenth-century world;[7] in the nineteenth and early twentieth centuries, it was repeated in a different way in the attempt to undo a perceived European decadence and degeneration through a grasping of the so-called primitive in contemporary art and other systems of thought. Despite much cultural traffic, up to that point there were relatively few actual visitors and travellers to Europe from the expanding European colonies around the globe; in the postwar period, those earlier cultural transpositions were followed by the people of the former colonies who soon transformed the cultures of Western Europe far more dramatically than the commodities that had preceded them. The centuries-long trajectory by which the European nation state attempted to unify itself with respect to its people, its language, its religion, and its literature, was undone within the space of fifty years and refashioned into an ethnoscape of multiple and diverse peoples, languages, and cultures that stretch across the oceans in the same way as Europeans themselves had done for the centuries during which they spread out across the globe in a medley of extraordinary diasporas. For Paul Gilroy this represents the kernel of what he calls British and European 'postcolonial melancholia':

> I should emphasize that I do not see the larger mechanism at work here as something uniquely relevant to Britain. The modern histories of numerous other European countries, particularly Belgium, France, Spain, Italy, and the Netherlands, might also be used to construct equivalent arguments amidst the wreckage of their colonial extensions and the injustices of their inconsistent responses to immigration. These analyses would be based upon their obvious difficulties in acknowledging the pains and the gains that were involved in imperial adventures and upon the problems that have arisen from their inability to disentangle the disruptive results supposedly produced by an immigrant presence from the residual but potent effects of lingering but usually unspoken colonial relationships and imperial fantasies.[8]

While I would agree with Gilroy that there is a dialectical relation between the end of empire, immigration, and attitudes to immigration, I do not see Europe being caught significantly in the kind of imperial nostalgia that he suggests. The majority of people in Europe today were not even alive during the high imperial moment, and empire does

---

[6] Fernando Ortiz, *Contrapunteo cubano del tabaco y el azúcar (advertencia de sus contrastes agrarios, económicos, históricos y sociales, su etnografía y su transculturación)* (La Habana: J. Montero, 1941).

[7] Raymond Schwab, *The Oriental Renaissance: Europe's Rediscovery of the East 1680–1880* (New York: Columbia University Press, 1984).

[8] Paul Gilroy, *After Empire: Multiculture or Postcolonial Melancholia* (London: Routledge, 2004), 109.

not have a huge continuing valency. What remains more urgent is the legacies of empire that emerge in the conditions of immigration. Even these are more complicated than Gilroy allows—for his list is notable for its exclusion of Germany, which on the one hand precipitated the decolonization process, and on the other hand has its own issues around immigration, particularly with respect to Turkey, a country that it never colonized. In certain respects, Europe has begun to accede to its own postcolonial condition, which marks the remarkable transformation of Europe in the face of immigration, and its submission to the slow osmotic processes of cultural translation even if for all parties this has also involved encounters with modalities of resistance to translation. Politically, socially and intellectually, the anti-colonial fight against inequality, against racism, against cultural hierarchy, has been fought within Europe in the postcolonial era by the subaltern subjects of the developing world who had migrated there.

That battle was ceded relatively easily. In fact, European culture has for long been so deeply imbricated with other cultures, from Arabic numerals and Gothic arches in medieval times, to the influence of Japanese and Chinese artists on Europe in the nineteenth century, to that of Indian sculpture on early twentieth-century modernists, such as Jacob Epstein and Eric Gill, or African masks on Ernst Ludwig Kirchner, Henri Matisse, Amedeo Modigliani and Pablo Picasso in the twentieth century, that by 1945 it was ready to assimilate and adjust further just as non-Western cultures were embracing forms of European modernity. Encouraged by state cultural institutions, today contemporary artists and writers have created a new milieu in which crossing borders, transgressions across boundaries, creolization and cultural hybridity, have become characteristic forms of cultural self-expression. Artists have always worked at the cusp of what it means to be human in a particular period. Contemporary artists signal the humanity as well as the inhumanity of their era, articulating the dialectics of the experiences of their time, showing how hybridity and cultural translation form new identities and take others away, in processes of productivity and loss. They have developed a new language through which they rehearse and articulate the mingled and mangled transactions of the postcolonial age, signalling through continuous experimentation the range of pain and of satisfaction that such processes can produce. Modernism's impersonality has been replaced by the cult of personality and identity as individual artists explore the paradoxical pains and pleasures of their own complex cultural and ethnic affiliations. The repeated transformations of postcolonial time mean that artists are more often reflecting on their own experiences and mutating identities, trying to make meaning of social, political and technological change, than trying to transform older perceptions of the world in order to make it new. The problem now is not that perception has gone stale, but that the world itself has been made new and few know how to account for what we see. Modernism's 'poetics of impersonality' was a different kind of response to the beginnings of this accelerating transformative situation, seeking refuge in stasis and constancy in the face of political and economic instability. Today's artists have moved in the other direction, offering a poetics and politics of personality. Many artists today maintain an activist stance in their art, addressing either the politics of the self and the body first articulated by Frantz Fanon with respect to the lived experience of racism in

Black Skin, White Masks (1952),[9] or working through the politics of the self in order to signal and reach out to all those other selves in transit who have to submit to the same circumstances of difficult adaptation to alien cultures.

In the literary sphere, these issues were broached most successfully and influentially by Salman Rushdie, whose work has been dedicated to a political aesthetic of mixture and the impure from his first novel *Grimus* (1975) onwards, and has provided a rich repository of ideas about the rewriting of dominant modes of history, and the formation of new transcultural forms through contemporary immigrant culture. His work both enabled the explosion of postcolonial writing on the European literary scene, and, at the same time, has been foundational for the best-known contemporary postcolonial critic, Homi K. Bhabha, whose own writings, at once political and poetic, have in turn become a touchstone for cultural theorists and artists alike, and dominated the remarkable development of postcolonial theory across Europe since the 1990s.[10] Bhabha moved discussions of the postcolonial condition away from the older confrontational language of colonizer and colonized to emphasize their mutual dependence and imbrication, a situation that Bhabha found depicted most subtly in the writings of V.S. Naipaul. Bhabha also extended the purview of postcoloniality to the situation of the European metropolis, now transformed by the presence of immigrants from the former colonies. Their situation, Bhabha argued, was not simply one of assimilation, but rather of a double translation—translating themselves into the forms of the host culture, while at the same time, translating the host culture also into their own cultural idiom. Though liminally placed, the postcolonial migrant becomes the marker of the transforming world of contemporary modernity.

POSTCOLONIAL THEORY AND ISLAM IN EUROPE

Postcolonial theory has been the voice of the radical cultural change that has accompanied European decolonization, reversing the former imperialist emphasis on cultural and racial hierarchy, and undoing what Frantz Fanon called the Manichaean division of colonial territories and peoples into colonizer and colonized.[11] Where there was separation, we now find mixture. Since its inception with Edward Said's *Orientalism* in 1978, postcolonial thinking has come to dominate cultural and institutional practices.[12] Postcolonial theory has been taken up in almost every discipline in the humanities and social sciences, from anthropology to medieval studies to theology; emphasis on the

---

[9] Frantz Fanon, *Black Skin, White Masks* (London: Pluto, 1986 [1952]).
[10] Homi K. Bhabha, *The Location of Culture* (London: Routledge, 1994).
[11] Frantz Fanon, *The Wretched of the Earth* (London: MacGibbon & Kee, 1965 [1961]).
[12] Edward W. Said, *Orientalism: Western Representations of the Orient* (London: Routledge & Kegan Paul, 1978).

history of cultural interaction, the multiplicity of languages, peoples and cultures, and earlier historical traditions of tolerance, has become ubiquitous in academia. At the centre of this extraordinary transdisciplinary migration is the fact of the contemporary social experience of migration in Europe itself. Any analysis of the development of postcolonial theory in Germany, Greece, Italy, and Spain, even, against all resistance until recently, in France, shows that the interest in such work is less a concern with the revaluation of colonial history (a focus that dominates postcolonial writing in formerly colonized countries such as India) than with the reformation of European culture in the face of immigration, with particular emphasis on the histories, often repressed in nationalist eras, of ethnic, linguistic and religious minority cultures. Governments, the European Union, and their many agencies have actively encouraged this dramatic reconstruction of European identity by generously funding academic and cultural activity of this kind.

This cultural work transforming the postcolonial condition of Europe continues, but it received a dramatic setback with the political reactions that followed the 9/11 attacks on the USA in 2000. At this point, a different trajectory of the twentieth century, focusing on the Israel–Palestine conflict in the Middle East, together with events such as the Iranian Revolution in 1979, and the invasions of Afghanistan, was thrown into a stark visibility. The Caribbean model of creolization and hybridity, championed so effectively by Jamaican-born British cultural theorist Stuart Hall, and adapted without too much difficulty to Britain's own earlier models of integration with respect to the Irish and other Catholics, and to Jews, in the nineteenth century, no longer seemed universally appropriate.[13] The fact that Salman Rushdie, the best-known advocate for the new hybrid cultures of Europe, had come into conflict with Muslims across the world with the publication of *The Satanic Verses* in 1988, was transformed from what at first sight seemed like a particular incident about the conflict of artistic and religious values, into a symptomatic and indicative historical marker. What had been little noticed was that Islam itself had also been changing, losing its many heterogeneous or syncretic traditions in the face of a new ultra-orthodox and amply funded Wahhabi Islamism promoted from Saudi Arabia or an Iranian Shiite militancy.[14]

The events of 9/11 brought the conflict between the new cultural language of hybridity and the language of the pure, of Islam, together with the historical grievance of the history of Western imperialism in the Middle East. Here we return to the story of the appropriation of the Ottoman Empire by Britain and France after the First World War. Al-Qaeda's international terrorist campaign against all those Western powers, particularly but not exclusively the United States of America, involved in the various countries of the Islamic domain, has been their chosen means for achieving their declared object of sovereignty and autonomy in the Middle East. Appropriating Islam for its own political purposes, Al-Qaeda has affiliated itself with the still active anti-colonial tradition of armed struggle, which came into its own in the period of

[13] See Robert J.C. Young, *The Idea of English Ethnicity* (Oxford: Blackwell, 2008).
[14] Olivier Roy, *Globalized Islam: The Search for a New Ummah*, 2nd edn (New York: Columbia University Press, 2004).

reluctant European decolonization in the second half of the twentieth century.[15] The Saudi Arabian leader of Al-Qaeda, Osama Bin Laden, also explicitly traced the origins of Al-Qaeda's grievance back to the dismemberment of the Ottoman Empire in 1919 and the Deposition of the Caliphate by the new National Assembly of Turkey on 3 March 1924. Already by 1919, the French and British occupation of Istanbul had produced the 'terrorist' or military response of the Khilafat Movement across Asia Minor and, particularly, India, and in some respects Al-Qaeda represents a modern recreation of this transnational campaign.

During the nineteenth century, the European powers took comparatively little interest in the Middle East, other than as a staging post to India. The major European involvement in the Middle East was the product of a quite specific colonial history that developed after Winston Churchill changed the fuel for British battleships from coal to oil after 1912.[16] Britain had been able to use its own resources for coal, but it lacked any oil. British, US and French attempts to control resources in Persia and the Middle East dominated the region from that point. The present essay is not the place to try to assess the role of the Balfour Declaration of 1916 in that particular history, but its implementation certainly made Western involvement more complex and Arab reaction more profoundly alienated. The transformation that 9/11, and the subsequent London and Madrid bombings, brought about in Europe meant that the cultural work of hybridization continued, but was supplemented and reinforced by a military anti-terrorist arm and the resumption of Euro–American imperialism with the invasions of Afghanistan and subsequently Iraq, together with the ongoing threats to invade Iran. At the level of social and cultural politics, the new forms of Islam are fundamentally opposed to the cultural discourses of hybridity, which is both why Islamism resists assimilation and why the contemporary left-liberal secularist thinking of postcolonial theory developed as a powerful and influential response to the postcolonial conditions of the 1908s and 1990s remains culturally alien and ineffective.

The postcolonial condition in Europe therefore has now moved to marking the continued unresolved presence of the after-effects of a specific colonial history. Largely absent in postcolonial theory, reconsideration of the identities of Islam is more advanced among artists and in everyday cultural practices and human interaction. Here Europe has once more rediscovered an older tradition, namely its centuries-long history of interaction with Islam and Muslim peoples. This perspective emerged in a new and definitive way at the moment of European opposition to the US/British invasion of Iraq. Despite apocalyptic right-wing warnings in the USA and from some politicians in Europe claiming that a sleeping Europe is being taken over by Islam unawares,[17] Europe

---

[15] Robert J.C. Young, 'Fanon and the Turn to Armed Struggle in Africa', *Wasafiri* 44 (2005), 33–41.

[16] 'British and French Agreement on Oil in the Near and Middle East, 24 April 1920', in Louis L. Snyder (ed.), *The Imperialism Reader* (Princeton, NJ: D. Van Nostrand, 1962), 376–8.

[17] Bruce Bawer, *While Europe Slept: How Radical Islam Is Destroying the West from Within* (New York: Doubleday, 2006); Melanie Phillips, *Londonistan: How Britain Has Created a Terror State within*, 3rd edn (London: Gibson Square, 2008). The best known European anti-Islamist is the Netherlands politician Geert Wilders.

has discovered that, perhaps uniquely, it can turn to the resources of its long historical interaction with Islam, and indeed its own Islamic history, particularly in Andalucía. The proportion of Muslims, affiliated to a wide variety of sects, in the overall European population means that a unique milieu is being developed. Europe's new postcolonial condition could be said to comprise a positive or reversed version of what has happened in the twentieth century in India (or in Cyprus), where centuries of integration between Hindu, Islamic and Christian cultures have been remorselessly unwound in the name of nugatory nationalisms. What remains unresolved is the historical legacy of Europe's now largely forgotten attempt to colonize Turkey with the Treaty of Sèvres of 1920 which led to the Turkish War of Independence of 1919–23. Turkey was the only country that successfully resisted the terms imposed by the Allies at the end of the First World War. Where they succeeded outside Europe has become the basis for all contemporary problems in the Middle East. Having created the problem, Europe has a moral duty to help to resolve its own postcolonial legacy that figures in the Israeli–Palestinian conflict. With respect to the failed partitioning of the Treaty of Sèvres, the possibility of one other political move that could have reaffirmed the older tolerant traditions practiced at times in Spain and elsewhere between Christians, Muslims and Jews has been widely debated. The accession of Turkey to the European Union would, in a certain sense, have marked the end of the European postcolonial era by undoing the geographical boundaries of the European landmass while at the same time undoing the legacy of the imperialist ambitions of Britain, France, Greece and Italy on Turkey at the time of the First World War. Turkey's accession to the European Union would have signalled assent to a new condition, that is, to the possibilities of a new political beginning that would open up a time no longer marked by the 'post' and the postcolonial: a new time that would emerge from a speaking together that would bring about the accustomization of all to a new political and cultural state of being in Europe and in those countries that lie at its borders. It seems likely, however, that that moment has already passed: Germany and France have effectively ended the possibility of Turkish accession, as a result of which Turkey, with a resilient economy, has now began to focus its attention eastwards rather than westwards. It remains to be seen whether this will help to facilitate the resolution of Europe's colonial legacy in the Middle East and enable Europe itself for the first time to go beyond its fractured postcolonial condition.

Further Reading

Balibar, Etienne, *We, the People of Europe? Reflections on Transnational Citizenship* (Princeton, NJ: Princeton University Press, 2004).

Benhabib, Seyla, *The Rights of Others: Aliens, Residents and Citizens* (Cambridge: Cambridge University Press, 2004).

Bhabha, Homi K., *The Location of Culture* (London: Routledge, 1994).

Chakrabarty, Dipesh, *Provincializing Europe: Postcolonial Thought and Historical Difference* (Princeton, NJ: Princeton University Press, 2000).

Gilroy, Paul, *After Empire: Multiculture or Postcolonial Melancholia* (London: Routledge, 2004).

Mcleod, John, *Postcolonial London: Rewriting the Metropolis* (London: Routledge, 2004).

Mezzadra, Sandro and Federico Rahola, 'The Postcolonial Condition: A Few Notes on the Quality of Historical Time in the Global Present', *Postcolonial Text* 2:1 (2006), online at: http://journals.sfu.ca/pocol/index.php/pct/article/viewArticle/393

Modood, Tariq, *Still Not Easy Being British: Struggles for a Multicultural Citizenship* (London: Trentham Books, 2010).

Said, Edward W., *Orientalism: Western Representations of the Orient* (London: Routledge & Kegan Paul, 1978).

Young, Robert J.C., *Postcolonialism: An Historical Introduction* (Oxford: Blackwell, 2001).

CHAPTER 30

....

POSTWAR ART, ARCHITECTURE, AND DESIGN

....

STEFAN MUTHESIUS

INTRODUCTION: HOW RELEVANT IS THE TERM 'POSTWAR ART'?

....

THERE is no doubt that planners, architects, and designers, or anybody involved with creating works addressed to the public, would have testified to the overwhelming importance of a comprehensive sense of a new postwar world, most definitely for the first twenty years after 1945. It was a period which followed what appeared as the 'zero hour', marking the end of the most terrible war in history. There was a sense of a new beginning which aimed at 'making good' what the war had destroyed and pacifying the evils of dictatorship. But not only that; the 'reformers' aimed higher, at creating a world which was 'better' than any known before, and even the pre-war years in those countries which had not been under a dictatorship, such as Britain, were held to have been gravely deficient. Indeed, the aims were often little short of creating utopia. Naturally, these feelings were strongest in the countries directly affected by the war, that is, most of the European countries and North America, in other words, 'the West'. But almost all other countries also took part in this 'renewal', chiefly under the banner of 'modernity', a term to which we will return below; for many in those decades 'postwar' and 'modernity' were synonymous.

After the mid-1960s, however, the term 'postwar' has to be used with caution. One has to remember that twentieth-century art as a whole was characterized by a constant demand for innovation. By 1970 some of the younger artists felt that much 'new' painting and sculpture of the preceding decades did not in fact represent anything new but merely formed a continuation of trends that had been around since the 1920s or even earlier. Architects and town planners were beginning to doubt the value of the grand utopian schemes of the 1950s and 1960s, if they did not already condemn them outright. Product design entered a new phase, declaring the avant-garde of the 1950s as simplistic. The 'brave new world spirit' of the previous decades was now viewed with much scepticism. Postwar can from now on only be usefully applied to those works which make a direct reference to the war, such as monuments to the Holocaust.

The term 'postwar European art' is more complex when we consider art geographically. Within a global context it is in fact now difficult to mark out a coherent body of works with the label 'European' art. Such a term would make sense when talking about the Middle Ages or the Early Modern period, meaning the sixteenth to the beginning of the nineteenth century. But already by the late nineteenth century, the artistic borders of Europe had become diffuse; thus to speak of European Art in the later twentieth century is highly problematic. This claim is of course directly related to the postwar political situation itself: much of Europe was, and still is, closely tied in with North America. A more relevant term for the main body of art studied here is of course 'Western'. And this brings us also to the massive dividing line, which from 1946 onwards, cut right though Europe. The 'Iron Curtain' seemed to mark the eastern border of Western art and a world of anti-Western art beyond. Thus all standard Western histories of postwar art concentrate on the art produced in Western Europe and the USA.

As the decades proceeded, that term Western also had to be expanded, as the art that mattered and became widely known increasingly came from all parts of the world. All this formed part of a continuous process that began with colonialism, became stronger in the nineteenth century, but may be said to have reached a plateau by the later twentieth century. One only needs to consider the day-to-day new architecture of large towns: their office blocks or housing blocks take part in the same style worldwide, regardless of ethnicity or political system. By the mid- to later 1960s most of the major communist bloc countries joined in with Western art, too. As regards labels for art forms, one now ought to use 'world' or 'international'. Indeed, the chief architectural style of the twentieth century received the moniker 'international style' as early as 1932. The term international style is less appropriate for the fine arts and perhaps least relevant of all when it comes to product design.

All of this also means that those who did not want to follow the international style, which, to reiterate, is an extension of Western, would be classified as retrograde or purely 'local', and as such, inferior. Only in the last decade or two has recent non-Western art received more attention by Westerners, and a new stress on the indigenous become widespread, for instance in the case of 'hybrids', such as art created in Africa or Asia partly affected by modern Western art. Naturally, all this has hardly contributed to a firmer definition of 'European art'. Finally, there are now also inward-looking trends within each European country, with regard to what has come down from the past. This is enshrined in the term 'heritage', which is usually given a strong national sense.[1]

---

[1] See the chapter by Graham and Ashworth, this volume.

This whole discussion may seem unnecessary in the face of the one key term: 'modern'. Postwar art meant modern art—if it was not modern it simply did not count as art, for the advanced art critic as well as for most public institutions, such as virtually all major art museums. This would hold true most emphatically of architecture. (In this context 'modern', 'modernism', and 'modernist' are taken to refer to the same trends, whereas 'modernistic' and '*moderne*' refer to earlier subspecies of the style and are avoided here.) 'Modern' meant, first of all, that all other styles, such as the period styles of Stalinism, were condemned by the modernist critics. As with all major discourses, we witness a circular process: that which was not modern simply did not enter the discussion on art, and subsequently was totally omitted from history textbooks. Hence this chapter, too, deals predominantly with modernism.

The term modern for art and especially in architecture was and is of course tied in with the wider notion of modernization, especially in the context of new technology. In this sense modernism is a term which, even now, and for the foreseeable future, has a universal validity which we would find hard to question or to transcend. On the other hand, modern in our context also has a much narrower definition, as 'designed in modern style'. And that style has since been superseded; since the 1980s, art has entered into a period which is (for want of a more sophisticated or original term) labelled 'postmodern' and thus modern is now treated as a historical style. Such a history was presented in 2006 by an exhibition held in the Victoria and Albert Museum that started with the seemingly intriguing question, 'What was Modern?'

POSTWAR

Our first question is: what was new immediately after World War II? If there was one further keyword that applied to both politics and art after 1945 it was 'freedom'. The Nazis had prohibited the creation of modern art (some painters were placed under a '*Malverbot*'; they were not allowed to paint), and looted, destroyed, or sold what modern art they found. During the same years, Stalin quashed the new Soviet avant-garde. Both reintroduced 'traditional', that is mainly realist art. In the case of the Soviet Union this doctrine remained in power until at least the mid-1950s and in some of the satellite states, such as the GDR and China, it lasted until the 1970s and beyond.

As with politics, the artistic iron curtain helped to solidify the notion that there was an art specific to the 'Free World'. For many of the modernists this meant simply a return to what they had done in previous decades, before the Nazi diktat. Realism was frowned upon by almost all western avant-garde artists. Many present-day art historians, however, take a somewhat different view as regards all of these evaluations. For a start much nineteenth-century realism was itself revalued, and by the 1960s a new avant-garde kind of realism, under the label 'Pop' had begun to challenge the supremacy of abstract art (see below). No historian would try and argue away Nazi and Soviet repression in the field of culture, nor would one try and deny the many similarities between the arts of the two dictatorships; nevertheless, art historical explanations have diversified.

There has been a new stress on the broader European origins of Nazi art; for instance in French monumental sculpture of the early 1900s, Socialist Realism had deep and very specific roots in older Russian art, including nineteenth-century socio-critical realism and naturalism as well as in the European classical tradition. This, in the face of a new direct use of classical forms in prominent American architecture of the 1980s (Charles Moore and others), could no longer be held a sin. Lastly, paralleling the statement that Stalin was an essential help in removing Hitler, his art and architecture can be taken as a celebration of the end of war misery in the same way as the optimistic rhetoric of western 'free art'. Eastern period decor apart, both sides shared the same enthusiasm for a rapid modern rebuilding of all cities, and especially for building as many dwellings as possible. It is, of course, this very optimism which now appears dated, but those doubts apply just as much to the western modernism of the 1940s–60s.

For the art historian, the style of socialist realism is in most cases instantly recognizable in the way its personages appear simultaneously to be working hard and enjoying themselves. There is often a festive radiance that is rendered with a pervasive lightness. Sculptures, invariably used to heighten the effect of buildings, tend to be over-heavy versions of old classical models.

As regards rebuilding, the Soviet bloc, as in the West, put considerable emphasis on town planning. Streets had to be widened to cope with the anticipated increase of traffic, as well as for the frequent parades; and dwellings had to be given light and sun. All parts of Europe, West and East, shared a condemnation of the nineteenth-century dense urban block dwellings with their narrow courts; they also shared, to some extent, a distaste for uncontrolled suburbanization. It is important to recall that many members of the architectural profession in Western Europe, and even more among the town planners, especially in Britain, but also in France and Italy, belonged to left-wing parties. The difference lay in the décor.

Stalinists condemned the look of what they saw as bourgeois and capitalist forms, and harked back to neoclassicism. In the occupied countries, Stalinism devised a new formula, 'socialist in content, national in form', which allowed for certain variation in the external decor, such as for Poland a kind of parapet, that is decor on the edge of the roof, taken from the Polish Renaissance. To this day the city centres of the capitals Moscow, Warsaw, and former East Berlin are dominated by the monumental buildings of that area, either lining the major arteries of the city centres or standing as isolated monuments, such as the Palace of Culture in Warsaw (1951). However, by 1955–60 this phase had already come to an end. Subsequent architecture and design in Soviet bloc countries joined with western modes, in the international modern style. Ironically, this did not earn the eastern countries much recognition in the West and it is still the Stalinist splendour which is most noted.

The West's deep conviction of having achieved freedom in art cannot be understood without the spectre of Nazi dictatorship and the emerging Cold War polarity. More recent scholarship has, however, drawn attention to the way in which all more notable architecture was dominated by a small band of protagonists and institutions. In the years immediately after the war the USA called the shots, because it had the means and because it found itself in the position of helping the Europeans. And that meant picking up where Europe had left itself at the point of the onset of fascism. As far as Nazism was concerned, the USA could now appear as having safeguarded the pre-1933 modernist achievements, especially in the collections of the Museum of Modern Art in New York and by providing a home and teaching positions for Germany's chief modernists, Walter Gropius and Mies van der Rohe. They never returned permanently to Germany, but they did leave their mark there. One of Mies's crowning commissions, as well one of the chief public monuments in the Free City of West Berlin, was his Neue Nationalgalerie. Its modernist characteristics can be summed up with a rare directness: its construction consists eminently of steel and glass and all forms of the building, in its plan and in its details, are reduced to a square.

One may say that this architecture, too, comes across as monumental, though of course in a totally different way from that of the Stalinist avenue across the Wall. Walter Gropius, by contrast, represented the other side of modernist architecture, established as a central doctrine in the 1920s: 'functionalism'. The architect should never think of giving a formal or monumental impression but should reveal on the outside the detailed practical planning of the inside. To catch the sun in the kitchens was the main aim of the curved southern front of the housing block Gropius designed for Berlin's Internationale Bauausstellung of 1957.

The most internationally famous of all architectural careers was that of the Swiss–Parisian architect Le Corbusier. Having kept a low profile during the Vichy regime, his practice took off after the war, when he became involved with some of the world's most prestigious projects, such as the New York headquarters of the United Nations of 1949. Eventually his work spanned nearly the whole globe, including a new city in India (Chandigarh, 1950s). In France his most influential work was a large block of public housing called *Unité d'Habitation* at Marseilles (1946–52). Here too, function appeared the main issue: new types of flats, elaborate facilities for children and much else, combined with, if not a monumental, then a heavy look, an arresting pattern of the walls and frames all in raw concrete. Like no other modernist, Le Corbusier achieved a convincing combination of striking architectural planning and a devotion to serve the general population with the great reputation of an artistic individual.

With regard to this first phase of postwar modern architecture, European countries differed somewhat from each other. In Germany most architects of the postwar decade had been brought up in the 1920s and early 1930s and some of them had trained at the Bauhaus. Modernism did not quite produce the impact it did in Britain. On the whole it produced a more sober and uniform new image of the countless rebuilt towns and cities. In Holland the interruption of 1940 to 1945 proved much less decisive; in the Scandinavian countries there appeared no gap at all between the 1930s and 1950s. Swedish welfare state architecture from the 1940s served as a model for many countries. In Italy the situation again differed markedly, as fascism had never condemned modernism entirely and there was a continuation of what was called 'rationalism', meaning much the same as functionalism. Both terms essentially entailed an ethos, namely that architecture should be reticent rather than showy, and that a building's ability to function well in practical terms was the chief, if not exclusive, aim of all architecture and design—an ethos which from the 1970s onwards was increasingly held to be simplistic.

British architects in particular lapped up the message of Le Corbusier's Marseille block and it became one of the models for the vast new campaign for public housing (social housing, or in Britain, 'council housing'). The London County Council's own architects, in turn, considered themselves the 'best architectural department in the world'. British clients who had so far been lukewarm towards modernism and who in the 1930s had often considered modern design as a fad for the rich now held it to be the most suitable expression of the new welfare state ethos, for housing but also for schools and any other public building. The 'free' modern style, and not the classical style and its ordering effects which had been prevalent in Britain until the late 1930s, symbolized the liberation from all the evils of dictatorships, as well as of what appeared the squalor of nineteenth-century industrial towns.

Of rather greater significance during the early postwar decades was the challenge of providing the millions of dwellings needed after destruction. Arguably this was the most important area where postwar politics and social issues were linked to artistic issues. To reach beyond the grind of mere production, the normality of churning out numbers, architects teamed up with town planners; many modernists, such as Le Corbusier, insisted that there was no real separating line between the two professions. The new down-to-earth utopia of the postwar planners was not only that of 'form' and 'space', but of a creating the frame for a psychologically and socially satisfying life. The belief, on the part of many designers, that architecture could achieve this, was very strong. Such planning could be applied to projects of any size: to a large town; to any more specific groups of buildings, such as a town centre; to any kind of space that served to gather people, such as a university or a kindergarten (for example the famous Amsterdam Orphanage by Aldo van Eyck of 1960–61); or to the ubiquitous small housing estates. The social–sociological keyword for bringing people together was 'community'.

The communist countries of Europe embarked on their post-1945 rebuilding only a few years later than the West. By that time, the 1950 Stalinist diktat of monumentalizing urban architecture had led to blocks of 'ordinary' dwellings characterized by a splendour never seen before, such as Berlin's Stalinallee (later Karl Marxallee, now Frankfurter Allee, mainly by Hermann Henselmann, 1949–61). On the other hand, these blocks conform to modernist principles in that we no longer see the old urban kind of back yard, but a stretch of greenery instead.

Arguably, the new all-comprehensive British welfare state's plans and actual built work was even more ambitious than the communist bloc's housing programmes, which at that time remained at the stage of showpieces. British planners aimed at nothing less than the transformation of the whole country. Based on the model of Ebenezer Howard's 'Garden City' idea of 1900, they wanted to clear up both inner urban squalor and avoid the endless outward spread of suburbs. Their chief concept was that of the 'New Towns', in effect satellite towns, many of them around London, each fitted out with a complete town centre and all social and shopping facilities (such as Harlow New Town, 1946 onwards).

DESIGN

There had been a time when modern art was meant to comprise all art forms. In the 1920s, the European movements of De Stijl, the Bauhaus, and the Russian Constructivists strove to create the total or universal work of art which comprised colour, surface, and space, and which, more importantly, should comprise our total environment. At the time this kind of desire appeared utterly utopian, but considering some of the many extravaganzas of world architecture of the last twenty or so years, presented at the end of this account, this original desire of modernism may appear to have been fulfilled. But important immediate applications of the great utopian vision may be found in a new field of artistic activity, which developed mainly out of modernist architectural circles, namely product design.

The belief was cultivated, especially by the Bauhaus, that the talents of the artist or architect could be used to produce objects serving daily life which function well and which at the same time are beautiful. The convinced functionalist would declare that these articles are beautiful precisely because they function well, and because this functioning is not 'disguised' by any additional decor. The key architects of the twentieth century, such as Mies von der Rohe and Le Corbusier, had begun to produce designs for furniture in the 1920s and these objects continued to be icons of modernity in the postwar decades. Originally the architects had intended them for the interiors of their own buildings, but now they could be bought individually and they served as signs of high-class modernity in many homes and offices. A small number of designers took modern designs of all kinds of objects for the home as their starting point and arrived at the architecture of the house as the end product, notably in the case of the Californian couple Charles and Ray Eames.

By the 1970s probably the majority of new furniture produced in western countries could be labelled at least as mildly modern. This could be rated as a success of which the pioneers of the 1920s could only have dreamt. Naturally, this kind of design was mass or machine produced; what was really new was the attachment of positive values to the term 'industrial design'. After the war, quasi-public organizations sprang up, in West Germany the *Rat für Formgebung*, meaning exactly the same as the name of its British equivalent, the Design Council; they acted as preachers and watchdogs, condemning everything that did not fit the functionalist formula. They were joined by a number of commercial firms which staked their claim on '*gute Form*' or 'good design', that is, modernist design.

From the 1950s Braun electrical goods proudly advertised themselves with the name of their chief designer, Dieter Rams. These objects appeared above all sober, with precise geometrical contours and matt surfaces, whereas in the slightly later Italian movement, under designer Ettore Sottsass, the firm Alessi went for rather more upmarket products, stressing inventiveness and the elegance of shiny surfaces. By the 1970s the doctrine of functionalism was weakening and the watchdogs faded away, and with it the ethos, the idea of subjecting all product design to functionalist controls. Expensive products had always been elegant and this could be considered the equivalent to 'good design'. The modernist term 'design', though, kept its importance in the proliferating wording of 'designer', now belonging to sales rhetoric, although the designer's name is hardly ever mentioned.

PAINTING AND SCULPTURE

The atmosphere of a liberated Western Europe, the removal of Nazism from Germany, and of the occupation from France and the Benelux countries led first of all to a new sense of togetherness under the banner of modern art. Most of the eminent painters who worked in Germany before 1933, such as Paul Klee and Wassily Kandinsky, had emigrated and then died before 1945. Their German successors after 1945 did not reach nearly the same kind of fame. But France regained its position as the innovator of all new movements. At the same time, all the movements that had been superseded kept some validity, with the result that a plethora of 'isms' proliferated. Basically, though, every artist was entirely in charge of his or her own style. All this substantially reduced the impact of academy or college teaching; rather, small groups of artists would associate themselves with a small, influential private gallery which itself radiated exclusivity (e.g. René Drouin), almost all of which were situated on the Left Bank of the Seine.

As it had done for a century or more, Paris still drew artists from all parts of Europe. Paris was further fortified as the world centre of modern art by the fact that the greatest innovators of the key years 1906 to 1914 were still very much around. Exhibitions soon after the war of the work of Braque and Picasso, as well as of Fernand Léger, consolidated their position once again. Picasso, in particular, rapidly assumed the role of the world's most famous painter. Utter radicalism and abstraction had been their trademark, but there was enough of figurative and symbolic meaning in their paintings to appeal to the more moderately-minded modern client.

A complex issue was the political involvement of the western artists. One has to remember once more that modernists tended to side with the left. Picasso in particular had been on the side of Republican Spain in the 1930s. After 1945, he fraternized quite heavily with Soviet communism by travelling to propaganda events such as the Congress of Intellectuals in Defence of Peace in Wrocław in 1948, although that did not mean that Soviet socialist realism in any way affected his work—all of which in the end only served to reaffirm the gap between East and West. Modern art, it was assumed, could only be found in the West. However, few were aware at that time of the fact that western modern art, too, was propagated and instrumentalized by politics, as in the case of the CIA-supported Congress for Cultural Freedom in West Berlin in 1950.

Another major trend that survived the war was surrealism. Again, those who had started in the 1920s now flourished anew, such as Salvador Dali and Max Ernst, each of them easily recognized through his own version of the doctrine: Dali with his hyper-realistic details, Ernst through the mystical imprecision of his phantasmagorias.

Every new movement had to be more radical than the all previous ones, as well as bringing something entirely new. The newest postwar 'ism' was 'tachisme', characterized by sketchy, light dabs of paint (for example Nicholas de Stael). At the same time, we now note in the works of Wols (Alfred Otto Wolfgang Schulze), Jean Fautrier, and Jean Dubuffet a disdain for abstract art, that is, for those painters using clean lines and geometric exactitude. Instead, masses of paint of unsightly colours are smeared on the canvas, often, especially in Dubuffet's canvasses, incised with drawings suggesting the work of a child or a mentally ill person.

Britain held its own position for the first two postwar decades in a way however that found little attention outside. The war years had not played any particular role and there had always been a sense of artistic freedom, side by side with much artistic conservatism. Those movements in London that tried to associate themselves with the Paris avant-garde never really succeeded. Instead, home grown expressionism became more popular, for example in the work of Graham Sutherland, which played with abstraction as much as with symbolism. The strongest work was that of Francis Bacon, working from the late 1940s onwards. Concentrating on figures and faces, he then disfigured it all, somewhat in the manner of the Parisian *art brut* just mentioned, but lending it all a more disturbing psychology, often culminating in subhuman expressions of sheer bestiality. A later follower, in the sense of concentrating on figures and lightly distorting them, was Lucian Freud, who remained active and highly influential until his death in July 2011.

The latter two names put British modernism finally on the world art map, but they were outdone by another artist from roughly the same circle, not a painter, but a sculptor. Henry Moore's fame matched that of Turner and Blake in the previous century. In his case, mid-1930s surrealism and primitivism as well as a fascination with objects of nature such as large pebbles or flint stones led to forms which mostly represented an enigmatic figure, always executed in smooth stone or metal with a matt, but smooth, surface. These semi-abstract forms were instantly recognizable, not just by the connoisseurs and critics, but by a much wider public, too. Moore's fame spread throughout the world, so much so that sculptures of his can be found in front of many major public buildings across the world, as, for example, next to the UNESCO building in Paris (1957). With Moore, by the 1960s, we thus reach the stage when modernism found widespread acceptance on the part of the onlooker, and widespread recognition by all kinds of institutions. Likewise, Moore and many of the artists mentioned here quite quickly found their works hanging in publicly supported museums. Indeed, Moore represented an 'acceptable face of Modernism'.[2]

---

[2] D. Hopkins, *After Modern Art* (Oxford: Oxford University Press, 2000), 68.

However, by that time the western image of the heroic artist who innovated and who placed himself (the number of woman artists in this particular context is very small) outside and above all previous art movements had definitely passed over to the USA. It is impossible to write a history of the succession of new trends in art from now on without the USA. Now it was the New York school with its abstract expressionism and minimalism, not the École de Paris which took the top place in exhibitions. A branch, or derivative, of minimalism was 'Land art', one of the most ambitious art forms in which abstract forms were created out of nature's formation, such as stones, or earth heaps. One of its most prominent members was the British sculptor Richard Long. All this was backed by a renewed idea of art for art's sake, by the narrowest formal definition of art, as 'pure', as contentless, as utterly opposed to 'academic' realism, or 'kitsch', in the writings by the American critic Clement Greenberg.

And yet, already by the later 1950s, new developments were afoot, which undermined most of the trends of fine art that have been investigated here. At the same time, the art world operated on an ever grander scale. Art vastly enlarged its modes of existence. Many objects were too bulky, or they existed as once-only performances, or even only as descriptions on paper. The old categories 'painting' and 'sculpture' ceased to have much meaning.

The venue of the small gallery and its intimate circles lost its importance. Large international exhibitions, such as the Biennale in Venice, and a new venue (from 1955), the Documenta in Kassel, made works known, and to a much wider public than before. Avid private collectors, such as the Saatchi Brothers in London also played a major role. Photographs of art works or performances assumed an ever greater importance, for often it is the only record we have. With some exaggeration one may conclude that art in the sense of painting hanging on a wall is now something thoroughly old fashioned, and that includes abstract painting.

What were the main components of these steps to widen 'art'? Crucial was the work of Marcel Duchamp, who from the 1920s oscillated between Paris and New York. He was the first major artist for whom the traditional notion of a painting, possibly in an attractive frame, containing a finite figuration, whether figurative or abstract, was of no significance. Duchamp's starting point was the object itself, preferably an everyday object, which was then torn and alienated from its normal sphere, like his famous 'urinal' of 1917. These ideas were taken up by the Dada movement around 1920 and soon by the surrealists. Surrealism had come to an end by the 1940s, with the major exception of René Magritte's work, presenting a magic and always ordered, single-joke kind of presentation. Instead, Duchamp's, who was active into the 1960s, and Dada's concept of the 'objet trouvé' (the 'found object'), rose to new prominence. These objects, of the most diverse kinds, were then assembled in complex concoctions and lastly given an opaque name usually suggesting some kind of mysterious action.[3]

Can one speak here of a new realism? There was certainly a turn away from abstraction and a widening of interest in all facets of contemporary life. The surest way of

---

[3] Ibid., 40.

avoiding the banal or sentimental was, according to Greenberg in his essays from the late 1930s onwards, to paint abstract forms. But to the new 'realists', there was no bar to what could be picked up. In fact, after a long phase of art's detached purity and political and social aloofness, we enter a new phase of response to and involvement with the contemporary world, with contemporary mass production and mass consumption.

One medium that could be included now was photography, which most modernists treated as painting's other. Andy Warhol's fame with assembling photos of soup cans swept the art world in the 1960s. It somewhat overshadowed earlier English efforts to comprehend the common modern urban world, the first 'Pop' movement in the 1950s. In fact, a fascination had set in with the imagery of advertising, its exaggerated female beauties, and its shiny chromium-plated objects. Now it was the Europeans, first the British, who began to cherish what they saw as typical US mass culture, the streamlined auto shapes, the sparkling kitchen with all its new gadgets. Here a blow was struck not only at the 'serious' content of high art, but at all the attempts to create the pure 'functional' design mentioned above. The modern environment, certainly the newer American one, was full of fun and exaggerations. Richard Hamilton thematized these forms and themes, truncated them and mixed them up in a surrealist manner in his paintings of the mid- to later 1950s.

Together with Nigel Henderson, Eduardo Paolozzi, and others, Hamilton pursued his search for popular art in the London 'Independent Group'. They were followed by two other English artists, David Hockney and Peter Blake, who, however, both returned to the normal kind of easel paining, whereby Hockney sanitized and abstracted the 'pop' subject matter, while the latter went into more and more colourfully presented details of common life, extending the meaning of pop from a high art movement into the 'popular' in a much wider sense. The kind of popularity enjoyed by Hockney and Blake was quite at variance with the atmosphere of exclusivity traditionally cultivated in Paris.

Some artists went further and tried to mediate between art and life in more direct forms. 'Happenings' and 'Fluxus' events were new art forms, in which brief stage-set actions metaphorizing and symbolizing everyday events (for example in the USA Jim Dine's *The Car Crash* of 1960, or Wolf Vostell's happenings in Germany in the early 1960s); especially important were the attempts to involve the audience in these performances. A further development of performance art was 'Body Art' where the centre was taken by the artist him/herself (in Germany Rebecca Horn, in Italy Piero Manzoni), involving manipulations of their own bodies and their clothes; a later example is the 'work' of the French female artist Orlan.

The field of media constantly expanded in other directions. Video art involved devising abstract TV programmes or the manipulation of existing programmes, as in the work of the Korean, Nam June Paik, who was active in many countries around the world. Related was the preoccupation with serialization, with the multiplication of the same, or the slightly altered photograph, in the work already mentioned of Warhol and, in Europe most famously, by Gerhard Richter. These works, too, thematize issues of the contemporary world, for instance the way in which modern mass production and mass reproduction is held to lead to a blurring of the image. Such images are then elaborately recreated and thereby manipulated by the painter. As with 'Pop' all this may be taken as a new kind of celebration of the everyday; it may elevate to a value notion which previous modern art hated, such as the superficial. Some artists though did use the 'new media', especially those stemming from photography, for socio-critical analysis of the capitalist commercial world, especially the British artist and theoretician Victor Burgin with his mock advertisements.

Finally, the possibility arose of leaving out altogether the physical work of art, the actual end product of an artistic conception, even any sketches and even the *objet trouvé*. In the 'conceptual art' movement it was sufficient to present a verbal description. The process of conception and deliberation itself constituted the work of art. In Britain, from 1968, the *Art & Language Journal*, produced by the group of the same name, marked such an attempt, using complex discursive and often obtrusive deliberations.

AFTER THE 1970S

From the 1980s onwards it becomes virtually impossible to assign specific locations or national designation to any major new art movement, or for that matter, to the person of the artist. No artist would be content with being exhibited in his or home region—all of which of course attests to the health of the art scene as a whole, the commercial health of it all, one may add, although one may also add that many artists held teaching positions in the most renowned art schools. For British artists, the intense collecting of the Saatchi Brothers, who created their own public art gallery, cannot be overlooked, creating a special sphere suspended between commercial dealing, private collecting, and museum display.

There was, however, an old division of outlook between Europe and the USA, and that lay in social and political conscience. In the later 1950s, the Western European links between avant-garde art and socialism were revived. A group calling itself the Situationist International came together in Paris in 1957. Instigated by the writer Guy Debord, it was concerned with the life of the city, not primarily to view it as picturesque and amusing but, from the perspective of the early Marx, recognizing the drudgery and alienation inherent in modern town planning. Somewhat similarly, the English Independent Group drew attention to the images and issues of urban daily life. But this movement was hardly concerned with planning and building; in fact, it foreshadowed the conservationism of the American sociologist Jane Jacobs in the 1960s. In Italy, however, the similarly inspired Arte Povera movement of the mid-1960s did construct happenings which 'exposed' the habits of the modern art market and many tropes of traditional art history.[4]

But the culmination of all the movements dealt with so far can be found in the work, and one should add, in the personality, of Joseph Beuys, who worked internationally

[4] Ibid., 171.

from his base at the Düsseldorf Art Academy from the 1950s to the 1980s. His was an intense concentration on himself as a quasi-actor on a stage which he created for himself for each event. Many of those art actions were related to his own experiences, notably to those of severe existential importance during the war. At the same time he continuously advocated a kind of populism in which everybody could be his or her own artist. With his background as a sculptor, he experimented with diverse materials, with hard and awkward metal and stone, but also with unstable substances such as felt and wax, and with any kind of found objects, preferably dusty and aged ones, including, even, dead animals. In his performances he would maintain the closest bodily contact with his objects, meditating and acting like a shaman proffering poetic explanations of the very bases of being.

Postmodernism

To identify 'trends' or 'styles' and to try and put them in some kind of 'order', becomes an ever more difficult task. 'Postmodernism' appears to sanction this state of affairs by declaring the complete arbitrariness of the sign. The major terms cherished by modernism, such as 'significance', 'expression', or 'espressiveness', and the value of 'depth', have now lost their use. What we do notice is a constant widening of issues, groups of persons, and countries. Only some of them can be noted here. First, the questioning and erosion of old gender specificities. As traditionally in art, for many centuries central modernism had been male dominated. But now there were far more women artists who often took up new issues of feminism, for example Mary Kelly, an American working in Britain, who carefully recorded in a psychoanalytically-thematized series of graphics and collages her early relationship with her baby son.

Globalization notwithstanding, there was the occasional resurgence of vaguely formulated national groups. German painters, such as Sigmar Polke, Georg Baselitz, and Marcus Lüpertz harked back to the turbulent work of early twentieth-century German expressionism. Anselm Kiefer's huge canvases contain deep and ponderous mysteries, conjuring up, albeit in a sarcastic or taunting way, the wilds of ancient German forests, not even stopping short of reminiscing on Hitler's Reich Chancellery (in 'Shulamit', 1983).

In England, the group yBa (young British artists) was launched, largely with the help of the Saatchis, and centred round the flamboyant works of Damian Hirst, with his dead animals preserved in formaldehyde. Finally, the fall of the Soviet bloc governments brought about a much more differentiated view of the effects of political regimes on art. During the 1960s to 1980s, artists in those countries had made their own contributions to the trends discussed here. West Germans now began to admire the vitality of the 'realism' of the 'Leipzig School', Poles the photographic installations of Zofia Kulik and the films of Katarzyna Kozyra.

The art form which crystallizes most of what has been going on in the last forty years, or which at least can serve as a convenient label, is 'installation', underlining, literally, that the object, or objects, have been attached to a given location. We witness a 'shift from a stress on the art object to its physical location as defining points', whereby location means invariably the museum or exhibition venue, which is where everybody has guaranteed access, and often even the right to participate.[5] There have been occasional attempts to locate small-scale installations 'live' in towns, such as the film-maker Peter Greenaway's 'The Stairs 1 – Geneva' of 1995, a temporary erection of small, slightly elevated frames up which one could climb and experience a framed and thus a structured view of an urban scene.

BACK TO ARCHITECTURE

In the years after the war, as was indicated above, the chief effort was to provide mass housing, with a great number of new planning solutions being tried out. From the early to mid-1950s onwards, many younger architects took up completely new notions of the town or the city, many of them directed diametrically against the core values of classical modern. Le Corbusier's plans for grand urban agglomerations, as well as the newer socialist/communist grand avenues were essentially devised for movement, including propaganda marches. Today they serve very well for fast vehicular traffic.

But from the mid-1950s, the idea of 'urban' began to mean a new longing for concentration, for smallness rather than grandeur. 'Community' somewhat changed its meaning from a political–social concept of a contented town to a much narrower focus on the gathering of people in a town square or in a school hall. From the early 1960s a new type of building came to the fore, the complete campus for higher education. This was a worldwide phenomenon, but Britain excelled with its seven new universities: Sussex, Warwick, Kent, York, Essex, Lancaster, and East Anglia. One way to create 'community' was to separate pedestrian from vehicular traffic. This helped to create what were called small 'nodes', or points where people were able to meet. Key theorists in the 1950s of the 1950s in matters of this kind of planning were Alison and Peter Smithson.

From the 1920s into the 1950s, utopia meant the grand layout of vast cities, rationally planned; now, by comparison, the focus was myopic, the small meeting place, with the aim not merely of providing rational–'functional' practical facilities (this was now taken for granted), but of serving the mental well-being of all inhabitants. In France this was to some extent paralleled by the Situationist movement.

Related too was the British group Archigram, working from the early 1960s. Making use of the most advanced constructional technologies and social mores, such as huge steel frames, and employing the concept of extreme mobility, Archigram designed vast city networks of an enormous height and density within which the freely movable units

---

[5] Ibid., 228.

of dwellings or other types of functions were accommodated. All this was then garnered with elements of pop, with scraps of popular culture. Here architects moved very close to the international artistic avant-garde mentioned above. Just as the younger fine art artists held 'traditional' modern methods of geometric abstract figuration on canvas in contempt, so the younger architects looked down upon old modern 'functionalism', with its endless repetition of plans and forms. Of course, virtually all of Archigram's ideas remained on paper, but nevertheless it at least strongly influenced one major building, perhaps the key building of its decade, the Paris Pompidou Centre (by the Italo-British team of Piano and Rogers).

From the 1970s, the architects' and planners' attitudes to housing and the urban environment changed yet again. In conjunction with popular disenchantment with so much modern architecture, planners now began to advocate, in Britain at least, but soon in many other Western countries, the validity of much older patterns of housing, such as the terraced house; the postwar public housing ethos, certainly as regards large blocks of flats, had come to a definite end. The reasons for this were complex: the new desire for intimacy would condemn anything large and straight and high. Moreover, many of the large public housing blocks increasingly served as concentrations of difficult tenants and thus many blocks were now associated with bad housing.

From the later 1970s onwards the interest and the focus of architectural art shifted considerably. General consumption/knowledge about new architecture became mainly tied to a number of names of star architects. As in the field of fine art, 'western' now meant a competition between USA and Europe. While in the 1950s and 1960s it appeared that the main US practitioners, that is, the generation following that of the old European masters (who in many cases had been their teachers), were in the lead; indeed, there are far more notable buildings designed by American architects in Europe than European architect-designed buildings in the USA.

But by the end of the century Europeans caught up as regards the worldwide spread of their activities. The most notable names are Norman Foster and Richard Rogers from Britain (of Pompidou-fame), and lately Zaha Hadid, the world's most prominent woman architect, an Iraqi working from London; the Swiss firm Herzog & De Meuron and the Dutchman Rem Koolhaas. Each of these names stands for some particular qualities, for certain kinds of forms, and for a preference for one or other material or method of construction. Foster and Rogers excel with their daring constructions in glass and metal, while Hadid practises an architecture of vast curvatures; the Swiss pair show smooth and often opaque exteriors, and Koolhaas has a way of 'creating life' through using unexpected diagonals. The term 'signature architecture' is often used, pinpointing both the fact that a known designer has been employed and the way in which the designer's style can easily be recognized.

A type of building that was most definitely developed in the USA, and constitutes that country's most important contribution to world architecture, was of course the skyscraper. Here, Europe has caught up in the last three decades or so, with Norman Foster's designs prominent in London, Frankfurt, and Hong Kong. By virtue of all being very different from each other in shape, Foster thus greatly helped in promoting the move away from the earlier international modern mode of creating the same kind of sleek glass box for every locality.

For the last twenty years, most of the postwar years' burning debates about social architecture or about choice of style appear to have evaporated. The architect, or better the architectural team, is deemed to provide for the psychological, the social/sociological requirements; in one word, the 'functional' side of the building according to a vast body of professional knowledge. In addition there are new demands for ecological control and energy saving. It is understood that many new buildings now require advanced engineering. All this is now taken for granted by the client and by the public. 'Architecture' starts beyond that. The building has to provide individual solutions for all these factors. The chief characteristic of today's architecture is indeed diversity of appearance. This is achieved mainly though the diversity of construction methods and the endless possibilities in the combination of materials, brick, wood of all kinds, plastics in ever new versions, glass, steel and other metals, reinforced concrete; the architect does his or her best to emphasize, to bring out the particular visual qualities of each material.

One remnant of an earlier modernism is a taste for the combination of steel and glass, combining smoothness and shininess of surface with elegance of lines. Moreover, a glass building always looks clean, it never looks old or 'used'. But our desire for the new may be juxtaposed with the desire for a look that suggests that the building has stood solidly for a long time, where brick and wood are used instead. Much of the smaller bespoke architecture in Britain follows the latter values.

In the end, one may ask: does it make sense to speak of a European art and architecture today? This question is asked in the sense of: do art and architecture, originating in Europe, impact on the rest of the rest of the world? The answer is: it still does, but not nearly as much as in the eighteenth to mid-twentieth centuries. A very different way of putting the questions is: to what extent is there a European art vis-à-vis that of each individual nation? Here the answer would require a precise examination of each of those countries and their comparison. Of late, nobody has undertaken such a work. The likely outcome is, however, not going to be very conclusive at all.

FURTHER READING

Ashton, Dora, *The New York School: A Cultural Reckoning* (Berkeley, CA: University of California Press, 1992).

Bayley, Stephen, *Twentieth Century Style and Design* (London: Thames & Hudson, 1986). Catalogues of the Exhibitions: Documenta, Kassel, 1955 onwards. Catalogues of Exhibitions: Documenta, Biennale, Venice.

Hewison, Robert, *Culture and Consensus: England, Art and Politics since 1940* (London: Methuen, 1995).

Jencks, Charles, *The Language of Postmodern Architecture*, 6th edn (New York: Rizzoli, 1996).

Kostelanetz, Richard, *A Dictionary of the Avant-Gardes* (New York: Schirmer Books, 2000).

Morris, F. (ed,), *Paris Post-War: Art and Existentialism, 1945–1955* (London: Tate Gallery, 1993).

Osborne, Harold, *The Oxford Companion to Twentieth Century Art* (Oxford: Oxford University Press, 1988).

Pearman, Hugh, *Contemporary World Architecture* (London: Phaidon, 1998).

Terravoli, Valerio (ed.), *1969–1999. Neo-Avant-Guardes. Postmodern and Global Art* (Milan: Skira, 2009).

CHAPTER 31

....

SCIENCE AND TECHNOLOGY IN POSTWAR EUROPE

....

ANDREW JAMISON

INTRODUCTION

....

In the decades that have followed the Second World War, science and technology have come to play ever more central roles in the lives and life worlds of Europeans. Indeed, in the twenty-first century there is very little that goes on in Europe without there being at least some influence from science and technology.[1]

From the never ending stream of research-based technological apparatus that has become so essential for getting us through the day and for keeping us healthy to the political disputes over climate change, genetically modified foods, and environmental pollution, Europe has become a place where scientific 'facts' and technical 'artifacts' permeate our existence. They have infiltrated our languages, altered our behaviour, changed our habits, and, perhaps most fundamentally, imposed their instrumental logic—what philosophers call technological rationality—on our social interaction and the ways in which we communicate with one another.[2]

---

[1] For an intriguing collection of articles and illustrative material on science and technology in contemporary Europe, see Bruno Latour and Peter Weibel (eds), *Making Things Public* (Cambridge, MA: MIT Press, 2005).

[2] Technological rationality is a term that came into use with the so-called Frankfurt School of critical social theorists in the 1930s (Max Horkheimer, Theodor Adorno, Walter Benjamin, Herbert Marcuse, and others). The term has since been widely used to characterize the domination that science and technology exert on the mental disposition of modern societies. A readable history of the early Frankfurt School is Martin Jay, *The Dialectical Imagination* (Boston, MA: Little Brown, 1973). The classic statement of the Frankfurt School is Max Horkheimer and Theodor W. Adorno, *The Dialectic of Enlightenment*, first published in 1944 (English edition, New York: Herder and Herder, 1972).

During the past seventy years, science and technology have considerably expanded both in size and scale, and as they have grown into much larger activities, they have also had a much wider range of societal impacts and implications than they had before the war. They have had serious effects on environmental conditions, both in terms of the sustainability of the European natural landscape, as well as the life-sustaining capabilities of the planet itself, as has been brought to public light in recent years in the debates about climate change. As with environmental problems in general, science and technology are not the cause of climate change, but the particular way in which they have developed during the past three centuries has certainly played a part.[3]

In addition, they have had consequences for all kinds of social, economic, and cultural activities, primarily because of the widespread diffusion and use of information and communication technologies (ICTs), such as personal computers, mobile telephones, and the internet. The cultural appropriation of these technologies has required the development of new kinds of 'socio-technical' competence on the part of engineers, designers, and all sorts of users, and in order to reap the benefits there have been costs, as well—both in terms of training and education as well as broader processes of social and cultural learning. Developments in postwar science and technology have also had a major impact on knowledge production itself, that is, on the ways in which scientists and engineers actually work to create scientific facts and technological artefacts. With the opening of new realms of reality for researchers to investigate—virtual, molecular, sub-atomic, and nanoscale—the traditional boundaries between nature and society, between humans and non-humans have been significantly blurred. In such fields as cognitive science, informatics, synthetic biology, design engineering, and nanotechnology, science and technology have blended together into an amorphous amalgam of 'technosciences' raising a number of challenges for the theory and practice of knowledge making, as well as for science and engineering education.[4]

The changes in the relations between science, technology, and society (STS) since the Second World War have been shaped by longer-term historical processes that have pertained at least since the mid-nineteenth century. The coming of industrialization led to the formation of a number of new scientific and engineering fields—thermodynamics, biochemistry, public health, electrical engineering, city planning, among others—and new forms of higher education and communication, from the technological and scientific universities that came to supplement the traditional ones, to the scientific journals and academic publishing houses that rapidly proliferated in the late-nineteenth and twentieth centuries. In the famous words of Max Weber, in a lecture for students at the University of

---

[3] For a discussion of the contribution of science and technology—and perceptions of science and technology—to climate change, see Mike Hulme, *Why We Disagree about Climate Change: Understanding Controversy, Inaction and Opportunity* (Cambridge: Cambridge University Press, 2009).

[4] There is a substantial literature about the relations between science, technology, and society in sociology, philosophy and history, as well as science and technology studies, communication studies, and cultural studies. For a recent overview, see Edward J. Hackett, Olga Amsterdamska, Michael Lynch and Judy Wajcman (eds), *The Handbook of Science and Technology Studies*, 3rd edn (Cambridge, MA: MIT Press, 2008).

Berlin on the eve of the First World War, science had become a 'vocation' in the course of the nineteenth century. It was no longer the domain of gentlemen working in their 'free time' to follow their own personal curiosity wherever it might lead. It had become, together with its 'mirror image' twin, technology, an integral part of modernizing, industrial societies.[5]

After the science-based destruction of the First World War, with the use of military aircraft and chemical weapons, the rise of 'scientific socialism' in the Soviet Union directly thereafter, and the Nazi ascension to power in Germany in 1933, it became increasingly apparent that the growing social and not least economic importance of science and technology called for new institutional arrangements. In both the Soviet Union and Nazi Germany science was brought actively under the purview of the state, raising fundamental questions about the 'autonomy' of science and the overall relations between science, technology, and society.

While the rest of Europe and the rest of the world would benefit from the migration of scientists and engineers fleeing from Nazi oppression, the Soviet Union provided a very different sort of challenge, offering a fully fledged alternative to the traditional relations between science, technology, and the state. In the words of Loren Graham, 'No previous government in history was so openly and energetically in favor of science. The revolutionary leaders of the Soviet government saw the natural sciences as the answer to both the spiritual and physical problems of Russia.'[6]

In the 1930s, under the inspiration of the Soviet Union, there emerged a loosely organized movement concerned with the 'social relations of science' in Britain and in other European countries; scientists and engineers began to contrast the positive support given to science in the Soviet Union with the situation in their own countries. In the midst of economic depression with many scientists out of work and many of their achievements not effectively appreciated or utilized in the broader society, it seemed to many that the 'contract' separating academic culture from politics and from the broader society that had been institutionalized in the seventeenth century was in need of radical reform. Particularly influential was the Cambridge X-ray crystallographer, John Desmond Bernal, who published a number of pamphlets and articles in the popular press and in 1939 a book-length manifesto, *The Social Function of Science*, which was an ambitious attempt to discuss the broader societal aspects of science and technology, and argue for improvements in their organization as well as increases in their funding and social status.[7] The following year, the coming of war would set in motion many of the changes that Bernal had called for in his book.

---

[5] Max Weber, 'Science as a Vocation', in H.H. Gerth and C. Wright Mills (eds), *From Max Weber: Essays in Sociology* (New York: Oxford University Press, 1946). For historical background on these matters, see Mikael Hård and Andrew Jamison, *Hubris and Hybrids: A Cultural History of Technology and Science* (New York: Routledge, 2005).

[6] Loren Graham, *The Soviet Academy of Sciences and the Communist Party 1927–1932* (Princeton, NJ: Princeton University Press, 1967). See also Loren Graham, *What Have We Learned about Science and Technology from the Russian Experience?* (Stanford, CA: Stanford University Press, 1998).

[7] John Desmond Bernal, *The Social Function of Science* (London: Routledge and Kegan Paul, 1939). On the social relations of the science movement in Britain, see Gary Werskey, *The Visible College: The Collective Biography of British Scientific Socialists in the 1930s* (London: Allen Lane, 1978).

In quantitative terms, the resources devoted to science and technology—both human and financial—have increased enormously over the past seventy years, beginning with the large-scale mobilization of scientists and engineers for the war effort itself and in the massive scaling up from 'little science to big science' that took place throughout the world in the 1940s and 1950s.[8] On the other hand, in qualitative terms, as the ubiquity of personal computers and other science-based consumer products makes ever more apparent, science and technology have tended to become the very stuff by which the 'quality' of European lives are made. The use of buzzwords about the 'age of information', 'knowledge societies', and perhaps especially the 'innovation economy' among scholars, pundits, and policymakers alike, make clear the crucial importance of science and technology in the broader public discourses of contemporary Europeans, as well as in our everyday lives.

During the past seventy years, the unquestioned European superiority in science and technology that had been more or less taken for granted since the 'scientific revolution' of the seventeenth century has largely disappeared and the so-called academic communities that were once considered so vitally important for human enlightenment have faded into the realm of imagination. In the postwar decades, the world has witnessed the emergence of new leaders, as first the United States and the Soviet Union and, more recently, Japan and China have overtaken Europe as the leading force in many fields of science and technology. 'Europe' is no longer the unquestioned source of scientific and technological achievements but ever more the follower, imitator, and consumer of developments emanating elsewhere. At the same time, scientists and technologists have been forced out of their academic cocoons and inbred professional identities to become fully integrated into the contemporary commercial way of life, as entrepreneurs, expert consultants, and citizens. What was thus once a much smaller and more circumscribed set of activities dominated by Europeans has become much larger in size and more diverse in scope, but also ever more 'global' in its range and impact.[9]

The historiography of these processes is partial and highly fragmented, with historians for the most part divided between those who specialize in one or the other, that is, in science or technology. A further division within both sub-disciplines is between those who attend primarily to 'internal' or technical matters in circumscribed fields of science or technology as opposed to those who concern themselves with 'external' relations and contextual issues. There are no general surveys or overviews of postwar history of

---

[8] The terms 'little science' and 'big science' were contrasted by the American historian, Derek De Solla Price in his book, *Little Science, Big Science* (New York: Columbia University Press, 1965) to indicate that there had been an exponential rise in the money and manpower devoted to science and technology in the 1940s and 1950s. The word had first been used by Alvin Weinberg to refer to the kind of science that was carried out at atomic energy research institutes, such as the one at Oak Ridge, Tennessee, where Weinberg served as director. See Alvin Weinberg, *Reflections on Big Science* (Cambridge, MA: MIT Press, 1967) and Peter Galison and Bruce Hevly (eds), *Big Science: The Growth of Large-Scale Research* (Stanford, CA: Stanford University Press, 1992).

[9] For a provocative 'global' history of technology, see David Edgerton, *The Shock of the Old: Technology and Global History since 1900* (Oxford: Oxford University Press, 2007).

science and technology in Europe as a whole, and most historical writings tend to be highly delimited in regard to both time and focus.[10]

In most areas of science and technology, 'Europe' is not widely used for demarcation purposes, since most scientific and technological activity in the postwar era—despite the ambitions of EU policymakers—has continued to be conditioned by national and local factors and has increasingly taken place in international or global contexts. It is therefore perhaps more difficult than in the other chapters in the handbook to present a meaningful account which covers both science and technology in all their ramifications. I have thus chosen to focus primarily on those areas in which I am most knowledgeable, namely at the 'interface' of STS with only passing reference to the more internal aspects of scientific and technological history, and only as they relate to broader societal concerns.

From the 1940s to the 1960s: An Era of Rebuilding and Reconstruction

The wartime mobilization of science and technology among both the allied and Axis countries changed fundamentally the relations between science, technology, and society. Throughout Europe, as in the United States and the Soviet Union, scientists and engineers were asked to play an active part in the war effort, by developing new weapons, as well as in providing strategic advice and 'intelligence'. Natural and physical scientists, as well as social and human scientists, and engineers of all sorts were recruited by the belligerent governments (as well as in the handful of countries, such as Sweden, that remained neutral). As a result, science and technology were transformed in ways that have marked them ever since.

In large-scale, multidisciplinary, and government-funded projects, ranging from operations research, radar, electronics, chemical warfare to atomic energy, many scientists and engineers learned to work according to other sets of rules and organizational procedures than they were accustomed to. At the same time, the wartime experience opened a range of new opportunities for scientists and engineers after the war as attempts were made throughout Europe to make use of science and technology for purposes of postwar reconstruction.

In Europe as elsewhere, governments sought to transform the scientific and technological knowledge embodied in the weapons that had been so important in waging the war into 'peaceful' harbingers of postwar prosperity. They invested heavily in scientific research, especially in relation to atomic energy in the belief that instruments of death could rather easily become techniques for the enhancement of life. In Europe this era of

---

[10] A good short survey of internal developments in science and technology in the twentieth century is John Maddox, 'The Expansion of Knowledge', in Michael Howard and Wm Roger Louis (eds), *The Oxford History of the Twentieth Century* (Oxford: Oxford University Press, 1998).

big science took place within the context of the Cold War, as both the Soviet Union and the United States used the support they offered for science and technology as central components in their hegemonic attempts to rebuild their respective spheres of influence.[11]

The immediate postwar period marked the acceptance throughout the world of an active state involvement in scientific research and technological development (R&D). Research councils, scientific advisory boards, expert commissions, and specialized agencies in particular ministries were created in most countries, and new state-supported R&D institutes in such areas as health, agriculture, and especially atomic energy were added to those that had previously been established in some of the larger industrial corporations and in the military. Because of the major role they had played in the war effort, science and technology were widely seen as key ingredients in the reconstruction of both sides of what would become the 'iron curtain' separating Eastern and Western Europe.

With the Marshall Plan and the efforts to create atomic energy institutes in specific countries—and eventually also at the European level, at CERN in Switzerland—American support for science and technology in Europe became a way of conducting politics and diplomacy by other means. The creation of NATO and the development of research and academic exchanges under NATO auspices helped give science and technology in many European countries in the immediate postwar period a military orientation. Even in countries such as Sweden that stood outside of NATO, a large proportion of the resources devoted to science and technology went into the military, even though a great deal of the military research, in Sweden as well as elsewhere, would later lead to civilian 'spin-offs' ranging from computers and synthetic chemicals to jet aircraft and the internet.

Atomic energy was the major area of scientific and technological development. Developing atomic energy provided a way to turn a weapon of mass destruction into something that could not only serve as the fuel for a new wave of economic growth but also symbolize a new kind of science-based technological progress and provide sources of national pride; as President Vincent Auriol put it when he visited the first French experimental nuclear reactor after scientists had isolated the first milligrams of plutonium, 'This achievement will add to the radiance of France.'[12]

The era of rebuilding and reconstruction was a time of Cold War and in the late 1950s it seemed to many that the Soviets were winning, especially after the launching in 1957 of Sputnik, the first space satellite. One immediate effect was to begin a process that has continued ever since, namely to try to bring 'basic' scientific research into closer contact with technological development. This was done both within the academic world, where new approaches to studying, analysing, and fostering economic innovations started to

---

[11] See John Krige, *American Hegemony and the Postwar Reconstruction of Science in Europe* (Cambridge, MA: MIT Press, 2006).

[12] Gabrielle Hecht, *The Radiance of France: Nuclear Power and National Identity after World War II* (Cambridge, MA: MIT Press, 1998), 2.

develop in business schools and management departments, but also in the wider worlds of business and government. The ambition was to systematize and coordinate the whole process of scientific and technological development—or economic innovation, as it started to be called—so that scientific ideas and technical inventions could become commercially profitable and thus contribute to the competitiveness of European companies in international trade.

As European economies revived, it became apparent that pumping money into atomic energy and other big, prestigious projects was not the most effective way to foster economic growth and more generally provide for the good life. 'Big science' was simply too big and too costly—and, in many respects, too American—to justify the benefits it produced.[13] Especially after Sputnik, it was obvious that science and technology needed to be managed and organized much differently from how they had been in the immediate postwar era. And there would be significant differences within Western Europe as to how science and technology was governed. What Tony Judt, in his book *Postwar,* calls a 'tale of two economies', with the Federal Republic of Germany developing a much more innovation-oriented economy while Britain increasing fell behind in one industrial branch after another, is also, to a large extent the 'story-line' of postwar scientific and technological development.[14]

In the late 1950s, efforts began to strengthen European cooperation in technological development with the establishment of the European Economic Community (EEC) and the European Atomic Energy Association in 1958, and the subsequent establishment of the Organisation for Economic Cooperation and Development (OECD), which included the United States, Canada, and Japan as well as most of the countries of Western Europe. All would be key sites for developing policies for science and technology, with the science policy division at OECD playing a particularly important role in articulating policy doctrines and making proposals for institutional reforms.

From the 1960s to the 1980s: A Period of Debate and Reform

The 1960s would be marked in both Eastern and Western Europe by a widespread questioning of the policies and priorities that had predominated in the era of rebuilding and reconstruction. The questioning had started early, particularly in regard to the

---

[13] In Europe the continuous concern with the 'American challenge' throughout the postwar period has focused to a large extent on American dominance in science and technology, from atomic weapons and basic scientific research to the management and organization of innovation more generally. See for example Jean-Jacques Servan-Schreiber, *The American Challenge* (New York: Atheneum, 1968).

[14] Tony Judt, *Postwar. A History of Europe since 1945* (New York: Penguin, 2005), 354–9. Judt refers specifically to the automobile industry, but the difference between Germany and Britain is relevant in relation to many other fields of science and engineering, and has deep historical roots. See for example Thorstein Veblen, *Imperial Germany and the Industrial Revolution* (New York: Macmillan, 1915).

continuing expansion of the nuclear arms race that took on a frightening new dimension with the detonation of the first hydrogen bomb in 1954. Public demonstrations to 'ban the bomb' arranged by organizations for nuclear disarmament began to be held in the late 1950s, especially in Britain with the philosopher Bertrand Russell and several active atomic scientists among the leading figures.

In the course of the 1960s, the questioning would come to encompass much more than nuclear weapons as the broader challenges that had come with what the French philosopher Jacques Ellul termed 'the technological society' in an influential book that characterized technology as the 'bet of the century'.[15] It would be especially students, but also a good many scientists and engineers themselves, in both Eastern and Western Europe during the second half of the 1960s, who would take part in a wide-ranging public education activity about the ways in which science and technology had been developing.[16]

In Eastern Europe, the Hungarian revolt in 1956 had already made it clear that the imposition of Soviet rule had not been to everyone's liking; and in Hungary, Poland, Yugoslavia, and Czechoslovakia in the 1960s there was a good deal of discussion about the pros and cons of communist society, which included the relations between science, technology, and (socialist) society. In Czechoslovakia, the Academy of Sciences conducted a large, multidisciplinary study on the social implications of the 'scientific and technological revolution'. In the Eastern European countries this was a term that was commonly used to refer to the changes that had taken place in science and technology in the twentieth century, and in particular the increasing use of automation technologies in economic production. When the report of the study was published in 1968, with a range of proposals for the reform of science, technology, and higher education, it entered into the more general spirit of reform that came to be known as Prague Spring. As elsewhere in Eastern Europe, *Civilization at the Crossroads*, as the report was called, was an attempt to foster 'socialism with a human face' but, as the Soviet tanks rolled into Prague in the summer, it was clear that the Soviet leaders were not interested in debate. Many of the participants in the study left Czechoslovakia afterwards, as was the case with dissident scientists from other Eastern European countries.[17]

In the West, the increasingly visible and horrific uses of science and technology in the war in Vietnam as well as a general dissatisfaction with the ways that students were being educated brought on a wave of student revolts in the second half of the 1960s. As science

---

[15] Jacques Ellul, *The Technological Society (La technique ou l' enjeu du siècle)* (New York: Knopf, 1964). Originally published in 1954.

[16] Examples of this public education activity are John Ziman, *Public Knowledge: The Social Dimension of Science* (Cambridge: Cambridge University Press, 1968) and Hilary Rose and Steven Rose, *Science and Society* (Harmondsworth: Penguin, 1969).

[17] Radovan Richta, in collaboration with an interdisciplinary research team, *Civilization at the Crossroads: Social and Human Implications of the Scientific and Technological Revolution* (Prague: Academy of Sciences, 1967). One such participant, Mikuláš Teich, presented the study at a seminar at Harvard in 1968 (which is where I found out about it), and later became professor of history at Cambridge.

and technology had become ever more integrated into the economy and the state—and come to serve as a kind of overarching political 'ideology', as Jürgen Habermas characterized it in an influential essay in 1968[18]—a gap had opened up, not least in education, between what the British chemist-turned-novelist C.P. Snow termed the 'two cultures' in a famous speech in 1959. Snow's argument, which was echoed by many others throughout the world in the course of the 1960s was that both in education as well as in the broader culture, scientists and engineers on the one side, and humanists and writers on the other, had come to form separate cultural identities in the postwar era. Education and communication both in the professional and popular media had become polarized and overly specialized and there was a need for both sides to know more about what the other was doing.[19]

As a 'new left' emerged in Europe as part of the student revolts, alternative ideas about STS were promulgated both among scientists and engineers, as well as among concerned citizens and even policymakers. In several countries, societies for social responsibility in science were established, and in many national governments, as well as the EEC and OECD, new kinds of socially oriented science and technology policies began to be formulated.[20]

As the 1960s developed, a central focus of the questioning concerned the impact that scientific and technological development was having on nature, or what came to be referred to as the natural environment. As in the United States, the environmental debate began in 1962 with the publication of the book, *Silent Spring*, written by the biologist-turned-science writer, Rachel Carson.[21] But it would not be until the end of the 1960s, under the influence of the student and anti-war protests that an environmental 'movement' would develop, particularly in the countries of north-western Europe; Germany, Scandinavia, Britain, and the Netherlands.

While conservationists and other 'nature-lovers' had been discussing the consequences that science-based economic development was having on plants and animals throughout the postwar era, it would be Carson's book, with its detailed exposé of the health and environmental costs of one particular, widely used chemical in agriculture, the insecticide DDT that would bring the environmental cause to the attention of the European public. As in the United States, it would also stimulate a more activist or radical approach to environmental politics than had been characteristic of the older conservation societies which had been established in the late nineteenth and early

---

[18] Jürgen Habermas, 'Science and Technology as Ideology', in *Toward a Rational Society* (London: Heinemann, 1971).

[19] C.P. Snow, *The Two Cultures and the Scientific Revolution* (Cambridge: Cambridge University Press, 1959).

[20] The longtime director of the science policy division at OECD was Jean-Jacques Salomon who also helped establish an International Society for Science Policy Studies. See Jean-Jacques Salomon, *Science and Politics* (Cambridge, MA: MIT Press, 1973).

[21] Rachel Carson, *Silent Spring* (Boston, MA: Little, Brown and Co, 1962). For an early European contribution to the environmental debate, see Max Nicholson, *The Environmental Revolution: A Guide for the New Masters of the World* (Harmondsworth: Penguin, 1970). See also E.S. Mishan, *The Costs of Economic Growth* (Harmondsworth: Penguin, 1969).

twentieth centuries and tended to be located on the conservative side of the political spectrum.

What Carson and other more home-grown European environmentalists argued as the 1960s progressed was that a fully fledged crisis was in the offing if science and technology were not to be changed into more environmentally friendly, or ecological directions. Many of the new kinds of science-based products that had been produced in the postwar era, especially the chemical fertilizers, insecticides, and additives that were used in agriculture and food production, could not be broken down and reused by other species as could the products they replaced, and thus served to destroy the natural environment. Particularly in north-western Europe, new environmental organizations sprang up in the late 1960s and early 1970s to call for and begin to practise 'greener' approaches to science and technology, and environmental science and engineering soon became important new fields of research and higher education.[22]

In 1971 an OECD committee, headed by Harvard engineering professor Harvey Brooks, produced the report, *Science, Growth and Society*, which was one of the most explicit attempts to respond to the questioning and debate of the 1960s. Rather than defining the task of the government primarily in terms of national security and military defence, the report contended that the state should take on a much broader role if society were to benefit from science and technology. In the following years, many European countries would create new agencies to support research in socially relevant fields of science and technology, and there would be a widening of focus in governmental activity so that more policy sectors were given the capability to support and use scientific research and technological development.[23]

One of the most immediate results was the emergence of teaching and research programmes in STS at universities throughout Europe, to try to bridge the 'two cultures' gap. The idea was to offer instruction about the social and cultural contexts of science and technology, but also to provide places where natural scientists, engineers, social scientists, and humanists could meet for discussion seminars and workshops, and eventually carry out research projects together. The field of STS, at least at the beginning, was part of a more general interest within universities to foster interdisciplinary studies in a number of new fields.[24]

In the course of the 1970s, courses and entire departments in gender studies, peace studies, development studies, and environmental studies, as well as STS, would be established throughout Europe, significantly altering the landscape at many universities. A number of new universities were also created, often based on 'student-centered'

---

[22] See Andrew Jamison, Ron Eyerman, Jacqueline Cramer and Jeppe Læssøe, *The Making of the New Environmental Consciousness* (Edinburgh: Edinburgh University Press, 1990).

[23] Organisation for Economic Cooperation and Development, *Science, Growth and Society: A New Perspective* (Paris: OECD, 1971).

[24] For an early collection of STS articles, see Ina Spiegel-Rösing and Derek De Solla Price (eds), *Science, Technology and Society: A Cross-Disciplinary Perspective* (London: Sage, 1977). See also Leslie Sklair, *Organized Knowledge: A Sociological View of Science and Technology* (St Albans: Paladin, 1973); Jerome Ravetz, *Scientific Knowledge and its Social Problems* (London: Open University Press, 1971).

approaches to education that tried to transform the critical energy of the social movements of the times into more constructive directions. When applied to natural science and engineering, problem-based learning proved to be particularly effective as a way to connect academic scientists, engineers, and their students more closely to the broader society and to help identify the sorts of communicative, managerial, and design skills that scientists and engineers would increasingly need in the emerging 'innovation economy' or 'knowledge society', as they would be called in ensuing decades.[25]

There were also a number of centres set up outside the universities for appropriate, alternative, small-scale, and/or intermediate technologies, putting into practice the ideas that were propagated in such books as *Small is Beautiful*, by E.F. Schumacher, an economist who had worked on development projects in India as well as for the British Coal Board.[26] A kind of 'grass-roots' engineering emerged in several European countries, most significantly perhaps in Denmark, where an organization for renewable energy helped people throughout the country to learn how to build their own wind energy plants and solar panels. By the late 1970s, the movement had spawned a number of companies, one of which, VESTAS, is now the leading wind turbine producer in the world and one of Denmark's largest companies.

In the second half of the 1970s environmental movements and movements for women's liberation—what came to be called 'new social movements' by social scientists—provided sites for experimentation with alternative approaches to science and engineering. In collecting and distributing information about air and water pollution and the risks involved with atomic energy, and in developing knowledge about women's health care and gender issues in general, participants in these movements could become 'citizen scientists', challenging the ways in which science and technology were practised and organized, in addition to providing substantive critiques of specific types of science and technology. In the Netherlands, students in Amsterdam set up a 'science shop' at the university for facilitating collaboration with the surrounding society, and their idea spread to other universities in the country, as well as to other European countries.[27]

Around the same time, internal developments in science and technology, especially in molecular biology and genetics, were bringing the worlds of scientific theory into more intimate contact with engineering and the more commercial sites of technological development. Genetic engineering and the other so-called biotechnologies that came into Europe in the 1970s from the United States, as did so much science and technology

---

[25] See Erik De Graaff and Anette Kolmos (eds), *Management of Change: Implementation of Problem-based and Project-based Learning in Engineering* (Rotterdam: Sense Publishers, 2007). It is something of a paradox that many of the universities that were created in the 1970s (my own, for example) have become among the leading 'entrepreneurial universities' in Europe.

[26] E.F. Schumacher, *Small is Beautiful: Economics as if People Mattered* (London: Blond and Briggs, 1973). See also David Dickson, *Alternative Technology and the Politics of Technical Change* (Glasgow: Fontana, 1974).

[27] Alan Irwin, *Citizen Science* (London: Routledge, 1995). See also Alan Irwin and Brian Wynne (eds), *Misunderstanding Science? The Public Reconstruction of Science and Technology* (Cambridge: Cambridge University Press, 1996).

after World War II, were among the first 'technosciences' that would raise a more internal set of challenges which would become increasingly significant in the ensuing decades. These are fields in which the traditional boundaries are blurred between theoretical, or basic scientific knowledge and technological, or more instrumental knowledge. By mixing previously separated fields of knowledge into new combinations, these fields challenged not only the traditional identities of scientists and engineers, but also the traditional ways in which they were educated.

FROM THE 1980S TO THE NEW MILLENNIUM: THE AGE OF COMMERCIALIZATION

Genetic engineering and information technology, and, more recently, nanotechnology and synthetic biology require expertise and skills from a number of scientific fields, as well as an engineering competence, put together in what might be termed a commercializable cocktail. While certainly not all science and technology has come to be integrated into processes of commercial innovation, there can be no denying that the rise of information technology and biotechnology industries—and with them a new 'mode' of knowledge production—has exerted a major influence on scientific research and technological development as a whole, for these are fields that differ from the traditional fields of science and technology in a number of ways.[28]

On the one hand, they are instrument-driven fields, which means that they require major expenditures on expensive scientific instruments for their eventual development and commercialization. And unlike the science-based industries of the early twentieth century, which were, for the most part, applications of a scientific understanding of a particular aspect of nature (microbes, molecules, organisms, etc.), the technosciences are based on what Herbert Simon once called the sciences of the artificial. Information technology is based on scientific understanding of man-made computing machines, and biotechnology is based on scientific understanding of humanly modified organisms. Nanotechnology is the most recent example of a field that is based on the development of scientific instruments to make a previously unreachable realm of reality available for commercial product development.[29]

Second, these are fields that are generic in scope, which means that they have a wide range of potential applications in a number of different economic areas, social sectors, and cultural life worlds. As opposed to earlier generic technologies, or radical innovations—the steam engine, electricity, and atomic energy, for example, which were primarily attempts to find solutions to identified problems—these new fields tend to be

[28] See Michael Gibbons, Camille Limoges, Helga Nowotny, Simon Schwartzman, Peter Scottand Martin Trow, *The New Production of Knowledge: The Dynamics of Science and Research in Contemporary Societies* (London: Sage, 1994).

[29] Herbert Simon, *Sciences of the Artificial* (Cambridge, MA: MIT Press, 1969).

solutions in search of problems. In this respect, information technologies, biotechnologies, and nanotechnologies are idea-based, rather than need-based, which means that, in relation to their societal uses, they are supply-driven, rather then demand-driven. That is one of the reasons why they require such large amounts of marketing and market research for their effective commercialization, and indeed for their development.

Finally, these advanced, or 'high' technology fields are trans-disciplinary in what might be called their underlying knowledge base; that is, their successful transformation into marketable commodities requires knowledge and skills from a variety of different specialist fields of science and engineering. In earlier periods of scientific and technological development, there were clearer lines of demarcation between the specific types of competence and knowledge that were relevant; indeed the classical categories of science and engineering are based on the particular types of scientific and technological theories that were utilized (physical, biological, chemical, mechanical, combustion, aerodynamic, etc.). The genetic engineer and the nanotechnologist certainly must know physics and chemistry and biology, but they do not know and learn these subjects in the same way as physicists, chemists, and biologists. Rather they are taught to know what they need to know, in order to provide the society with new sorts of products. As such, the new fields represent a qualitatively new 'mode' of knowledge production.

From the 1980s onward as the Soviet empire decomposed and other 'new industrial countries' in Asia—South Korea, Singapore, and Taiwan, in particular—joined Japan in the competition for global market shares, especially in information and communications technologies, it became ever more apparent that the individual European countries could not meet the challenges by themselves. This realization has led to a much more selective approach to governing and funding science and technology during the past three decades, with an ever closer eye to the machinations of the commercial marketplace. It has also led to a continual expansion of European-wide programmes and policies in science, technology, and higher education within the European Union and other intergovernmental bodies.

In the late 1970s, the political climate turned to the right in several European countries, as was the case also in the United States. At the same time, the debates about nuclear energy that had been the main focus of public debate in the period of questioning were resolved in parliamentary decisions and negotiated settlements of one kind or another. In response to both processes, many of those who had been active in the critical discussions and movements of the 1970s became more business-minded in their activities, as a kind of institutionalization and professionalization set in within the environmental and renewable energy movements. Green parties and environmental research institutes, as well as a range of new environmental and energy companies, came to replace the more activist groups; there was also a professionalization of activism itself with the coming to many European countries of Greenpeace, with its media savvy and well organized protests, and the environmental 'think tanks', such as the Wuppertal Institute in Germany, that were closely associated with the green parties.

A significant outcome of the professionalization of the environmental debate was the articulation of a new policy doctrine—and eventually of an overarching political discourse—of sustainable development. It was first coined in the 'World Conservation Strategy' of 1980, which was written by three conservation organizations, and was later more widely promulgated in an influential report, *Our Common Future*, published in 1987 by the World Commission for Environment and Development headed by the former Norwegian prime minister, Gro Harlem Brundtland.[30]

Sustainable development was an attempt to redefine the aims of scientific, technological, and socio-economic development to take the needs of future generations into account, specifically in regard to the availability of natural resources and environmental quality. By bringing together representatives of business, government, and civil society, including environmental organizations, the Brundtland Commission tried to formulate an ambitious new global agenda, and in 1992, at the so-called Earth Summit in Brazil, many of the world's nations, and all of the European countries, agreed on a document that specified how sustainable development could be implemented: the so-called Agenda 21.

In the 1990s, many European cities and governments developed local and national agenda 21 activities, as well as scientific research and technological development programmes in sustainable development. Many of these activities sought to foster partnerships between business and government, by emphasizing environmental management systems and eco-efficient, or 'clean' technologies in addition to renewable energy and ecological, or organic, agriculture.[31]

There were some significant differences between the various European countries in regard to the quest for sustainable development, with the Eastern European countries generally much less active than the Western European countries. Within Western Europe, the level of activity has depended a good deal on the political situation; in those countries where social-democratic governments have been in power, often with the support of green parties, R&D programmes in sustainable development have been much more prevalent. And when social-democratic parties have lost power, as has been the case in Germany, Denmark, Sweden, the Netherlands, and Great Britain during the past ten years, the interest in sustainable development has tended to diminish.

In many areas of environmental or green science and technology, particularly in regard to renewable energy, organic agriculture, and eco-design, European companies have been among the world leaders. Many European cities have also been in the forefront in regard to sustainable urban development, and European green business is

[30] *World Conservation Strategy. Living Resource Conservation for Sustainable Development. Prepared by the International Union for Conservation of Nature and Natural Resources* (Gland, Switzerland: IUCN, 1980); The World Commission on Environment and Development, *Our Common Future* (Oxford: Oxford University Press, 1987).

[31] There is by now a huge literature on the politics of sustainable development. For a comparative history of policy trajectories in Britain and the Netherlands, see Maarten Hajer, *The Politics of Environmental Discourse* (Oxford: Oxford University Press, 1995). On Agenda 21, see William Lafferty (ed.), *Implementing LA21 in Europe: New Initiatives for Sustainable Development* (Oslo: ProSus, 1999). See also Andrew Jamison, *The Making of Green Knowledge: Environmental Politics and Cultural Transformation* (Cambridge: Cambridge University Press, 2001).

rapidly finding markets in China and the other emerging economies of Asia. In becoming mainstream, however, and in following the general trend toward commercialization, the question can be raised as to whether certain kinds of environmental challenges—and especially the climate challenge—are amenable to this kind of response strategy, with its overarching belief in technical fixing: that all problems can be solved with more technology. There are those who say that the only way to deal with climate change is to cut down on consumption and develop more sustainable communities, but up until now, these more social or cultural approaches to sustainability have been much weaker than the technical and commercial.[32]

A similar kind of historical trajectory can be seen in relation to the social aspects of science and technology that had been subject to debate in the 1960s and 1970s, both gender issues, as well as issues of access, accountability, and assessment. In many European countries, as well as the European Commission, new units and programmes in technology assessment were brought into the science and technology policy landscape.

The idea had emerged in the United States, and an Office for Technology Assessment had been set up in the American Congress in 1974 to study the social implications of particular areas of scientific and technological development. As the energy debates and movements intensified in the 1970s in Europe, several governments made funding available for similar kinds of studies in relation to energy technologies, and in the 1980s agencies and research programmes were created to provide opportunities for studying the social aspects of other technologies, especially information technologies and biotechnologies.

In Europe, some of these activities took on a more 'participatory' form than in the United States, with the involvement of citizens and municipal authorities in what came to be known as interactive technology assessment.[33] In Denmark, the government board for technology developed what came to be known as consensus conferences, arranging dialogues between lay people and experts that were written up in reports that then entered into the policymaking process. After one such consensus conference in the 1980s, for example, the Danish parliament passed a law banning field experiments with genetically modified food.[34]

In addition to technology assessment, which was primarily a governmental activity, in the course of the 1980s a more academic approach to the social challenges developed in the field of science and technology studies. Centres and institutes were established at

[32] For a brief history of the contending positions in the climate change debate, see Andrew Jamison, 'Climate Change Knowledge and Social Movement Theory', *Wiley Interdisciplinary Reviews: Climate Change* 1:6 November (2010), 811–23. See also Anthony Giddens, *The Politics of Climate Change* (Cambridge: Polity, 2009).

[33] Simon Joss and Sergio Belucci (eds), *Participatory Technology Assessment: European Perspectives* (London: Centre for the Study of Democracy, 2002).

[34] Jesper Lassen, 'Changing Modes of Biotechnology Assessment in Denmark', in Reijo Miettinen (ed.), *Biotechnology and Public Understanding of Science* (Helsinki: Academy of Finland, 1998). See also Simon Joss and John Durant (eds), *Public Participation in Science: The Role of Consensus Conferences in Europe* (London: Science Museum, 1995).

many universities where scientists, engineers, and social scientists could work together on research projects about the social and ethical aspects of science and technology, especially in relation to the newer fields of technoscience, as they started to be called in the 1980s. Science and technology studies represented a kind of institutionalization of the programmes in STS that had grown up in the 1970s, and as the new, more academic and professional style of STS grew in status and significance in the 1990s, both at universities as well as within the government research funding systems, the older programmes that had sought to bridge the 'two cultures' gap tended to diminish. As a result, while new kinds of experts in the social aspects of science and technology were trained and educated, their expertise tended not to be effectively integrated into the education of scientists and engineers.[35]

In relation to the more internal developments in science and technology, the 1980s can be seen as the beginning of a new 'long wave' of growth and expansion based on the cluster of innovations that had come in the 1970s in information technology and biotechnology. In the 1930s, the Austrian Joseph Schumpeter had developed an influential theory of economic history, based on the notion of 'creative destruction' by which he characterized the process of industrialization since the late eighteenth century.[36] He had identified three waves of industrial development that had been instigated by clusters of what he termed radical innovations, both technical and institutional, which had led to far-reaching repercussions throughout the industrial economies: textile machines and the factory system in the first wave; steam-powered transport, machine tools, and joint stock companies in the second; and steel, electrification, and professional management systems in the third. From this perspective, neo-Schumpeterian students of innovation came to identify a fourth wave in the mid-twentieth century, based on petrochemical products, automobiles, and mass production that had begun its decline in the 1970s and was now on the verge of being 'creatively destroyed' by a new wave based on innovations in information technologies, such as personal computers, video recorders, and software systems and biotechnologies, especially genetic modification.[37]

As departments or centres for innovation studies were established at business schools and technological universities, the institutions of science and technology started to be reconfigured, so that the new technologies could be more effectively commercialized. The institutional innovations that were called for involved the establishment of networks

---

[35] It is symptomatic that the acronym STS has come to stand for 'science and technology studies' during the past 20 years, and in the process has become more of an academic field of its own than a space, or interface, for the interaction between 'science, technology and society'. For a presentation of the field in the 1990s in the midst of this transition, Sheila Jasanoff, Gerald Markle, James Petersen and Trevor Pinch (eds), *Handbook of Science and Technology Studies* (London: Sage, 1995).

[36] Joseph Schumpeter, *Business Cycles: A Theoretical, Historical and Statistical Analysis of the Capitalist Process* (New York: McGraw-Hill, 1939). See also Joseph Schumpeter, *Capitalism, Socialism and Democracy* (New York: Harper and Brothers, 1942).

[37] See Chris Freeman and Francisco Louçã, *As Time Goes by: From the Industrial Revolution to the Information Revolution* (Oxford: Oxford University Press, 2001).

or systems of innovation, as they started to be called.[38] In Japan, university scientists and engineers had been brought in by the governmental authorities to identify those areas of science and technology that were especially promising from a commercial point of view. The government also sponsored programmes of cooperative, 'pre-commercial' research in some of the areas that had been identified.[39] Japan, with its top-down approach to innovation policy, could be seen as a contrast to the experience in the United States, where university scientists, particularly in information technology and biotechnology, had established companies based on their research near the universities where they worked (the so-called Silicon Valley near Stanford in California was the prime example). Both the Japanese and the Americans had developed approaches to science and technology that were directly commercial. And in the 1980s, as European countries felt ever more intense competition from both the Japanese and the Americans in relation to developing the new technologies, many governments both individually and together at the EU level established programmes and policies that adopted many of the approaches that had emerged in the US and Japan.

In the course of the 1990s, the European Commission took on more and more responsibility for science and technology funding and coordination. Increasingly, the Commission has tried to create opportunities for all kinds of scientists and engineers to be involved in European cooperative ventures, both in research, development, and education. There are continual efforts to establish student and teacher exchanges, networks of excellence in particular fields, workshops and conferences to initiate new research projects, and a wide range of opportunities for European research projects, both funded by the Commission itself as well as by the European Science Foundation. The Commission has also tried to coordinate national policies in such areas as higher education and environmental protection. Over the past thirty years, Europe has taken some rather large strides forward in creating new forms of scientific and technological practice that transcend national boundaries.[40]

Perhaps nowhere has the new wave of scientific and technological development had a stronger impact on the national economy than in Finland, where one company creatively destroyed and then reconstructed itself to become, in the course of the 1990s, the largest company in the country and the world's largest producer of mobile telephones. Nokia's story—of how a traditional industrial rubber company, which had unsuccessfully tried to diversify into other areas to keep itself afloat transformed itself into a global

---

[38] See Bengt-Åke Lundvall (ed.), *National Systems of Innovation: Towards a Theory of Innovation and Interactive Learning* (London: Pinter, 1992); Charles Edquist (ed.), *Systems of Innovation: Technologies, Institutions and Organizations* (London: Pinter, 1997); Franco Malerba, *Sectoral Systems of Innovation: Concepts, Issues and Analyses of Six Major Sectors in Europe* (Cambridge: Cambridge University Press, 2004).

[39] Christopher Freeman, *Technology Policy and Economic Performance: Lessons from Japan* (London: Pinter, 1987).

[40] See Susanna Borrás, *The Innovation Policy of the European Union: From Government to Governance* (Cheltenham: Edward Elgar, 2004); and, for the broader picture, see Desmond Dinan, *Europe Recast: A History of European Union* (Basingstoke: Palgrave Macmillan, 2004).

powerhouse by focusing on innovation, design, and marketing of a typical technoscientific product—encapsulates both the good and the bad news of postwar European scientific and technological development. On the one hand, it is a classic case of Schumpeterian creative destruction, but on the other hand, by going global, the incredible and rapid growth of the company did not bring about an expansion in employment opportunities in Europe to the same extent that had occurred in previous waves. Instead, Nokia, like all of the other successful, high-tech companies of the past three decades, provides jobs where the labour force is cheaper and where the corporate taxes are lower. The tragic paradox of science and technology in postwar Europe is that while innovation runs rampant with the generous support of the EU and national governments, the economic, social, and, for that matter, cultural benefits of this innovative activity are not really felt by the large proportion of the European population. The global support systems and logistical infrastructures, not least in relation to financing and transport that have been so important for Nokia and other high-tech companies are also problematic, both in terms of regulatory control and political accountability, as well as in relation to the natural environment.

CONCLUSIONS

At the close of the first decade of a new millennium, science and technology in Europe find themselves at a critical juncture. In a time of economic recession with many European governments heavily in debt and levels of unemployment the highest in many years, there is once again, as in the 1960s, a need for questioning the assumptions that have guided policymaking, as well as scientific and technological knowledge making, over the past few decades. In particular, it seems important to question the dominant discourse of commercialization, with its overarching emphasis on linking scientists and engineers ever more intimately with the business world. This has involved both an institutional restructuring of universities, as well as a reshaping of many scientific and engineering fields so that they are more amenable to the needs and values of the commercial marketplace. The widespread fostering of entrepreneurship among scientists and engineers has certainly led to an effusion of new gadgets and high-tech wizardry, but it can be questioned whether this orientation has gone too far.

The typical reaction to commercialization on the part of many scientists and engineers has been to try to return to how it was, or is imagined to have been, in pre-war days, when science was 'autonomous' and the role of science-based technology in society and in the economy was much more limited. The appeal of traditional ways of practising science and technology has become quite strong in certain circles in Europe, as elsewhere, but as in previous periods of change, it seems counterproductive to think that the future can be met by returning to the past.

Instead, as in the 1960s, there is a need for fundamentally rethinking the relations between science, technology, and society, in Europe as well as internationally. In particular, there needs to be much more coordination between policies for science and technology and all the other policies that national governments, as well as local authorities and intergovernmental bodies pursue. In order to meet the challenge of climate change and sustainable development, science and technology will need to be reconfigured so that the 'solutions' they provide can be relevant for the problems that humanity faces. And in order to provide appropriate solutions, scientists and engineers will need to be better educated about the problems that need to be solved.

FURTHER READING

Borrás, Susanna, *The Innovation Policy of the European Union: From Government to Governance* (Cheltenham: Edward Elgar, 2004).

Edgerton, David, *The Shock of the Old: Technology and Global History since 1900* (Oxford: Oxford University Press, 2007).

Gibbons, Michael, Camille Limoges, Helga Nowotny, Simon Schwartzman, Peter Scott and Martin Trow, *The New Production of Knowledge: The Dynamics of Science and Research in Contemporary Societies* (London: Sage, 1994).

Giddens, Anthony, *The Politics of Climate Change* (Cambridge: Polity, 2009).

Hackett, Edward J, Olga Amsterdamska, Michael Lynch and Judy Wajcman (eds), *The Handbook of Science and Technology Studies*, 3rd edn (Cambridge, MA: MIT Press, 2008).

Hajer, Maarten, *The Politics of Environmental Discourse* (Oxford: Oxford University Press, 1995).

Hecht, Gabrielle, *The Radiance of France: Nuclear Power and National Identity after World War II* (Cambridge, MA: MIT Press, 1998).

Krige, John, *American Hegemony and the Postwar Reconstruction of Science in Europe* (Cambridge, MA: MIT Press, 2006).

Latour, Bruno and Peter Weibel (eds), *Making Things Public* (Cambridge, MA: MIT Press, 2005).

Rose, Hilary and Steven Rose, *Science and Society* (Harmondsworth: Penguin, 1969).

CHAPTER 32

···

IMAGES OF EUROPE, EUROPEAN IMAGES: POSTWAR EUROPEAN CINEMA AND TELEVISION CULTURE

···

IB BONDEBJERG

IN 2004 the Danish film production company Zentropa, the German TV station ZDF, the French-German TV channel Arte, and the Danish Film Institute created the short film anthology *Visions of Europe*; twenty-five films from twenty-five European countries by twenty-five different European directors. The films were produced to salute the diversity of culture in Europe after the Copenhagen summit in 2003 and the enlargement of Europe to Europe 25. In many ways this film project is a unique example of the new, more integrated, and unified Europe.

The audio-visual culture of Europe right after 1945 was a culture in ashes in a Europe soon to be divided into east and west under the Cold War. It was a Europe where nation states had to reconstruct and revitalize a cinema culture damaged by war and where television did not emerge until the 1950s, or in some countries even later. The European Community created by the 1957 Treaty of Rome did not have a strong focus on culture, although the treaty talks about: 'the establishment and development of trans-European networks...contribution to education and training of quality and to the flowering of cultures of the member states'.[1] But already during the 1980s a cultural policy and a policy for film and media was starting to develop and both the MEDIA programmes (from 1987),[2]

---

[1] Treaty of Rome, online at: http://europa.eu/legislation_summaries/institutional_affairs/treaties/treaties_eec_en.htm, accessed April 2010.

[2] See Richard Collins, *Broadcasting and Audio-Visual Policy in the European Single Market* (London: John Libbey, 1994).

and the EURIMAGE programme (from 1988) represented the institutionalization of support for the diversity of film and media culture in Europe as a whole. With the Maastricht Treaty (1993), cultural and media policy became an integrated part of the EU with the new article 128 on culture.[3]

Visions of Europe is a tribute to the new Europe, but the film also illustrates the problems of a European film and TV culture: there is no vision of Europe, no single European cultural identity, and in relation to the official EU motto for culture, 'unity in diversity',[4] there is much more diversity than unity. The films also clearly reflect scepticism towards the European Union among citizens in Europe. Jan Troell's film *The Yellow Tag* is a grotesque, satirical film about EU bureaucracy, with EU bureaucrats in dark suits and bowler hats falling from the sky in Brussels as in Magritte's famous painting *Golconda* (1953). In the Danish director Christoffer Boe's *Europe*, a minister cannot even pronounce the word Europe and is clearly distracted when his female secretary in a very sensual way tries to teach him to pronounce it. In Peter Greenaway's *The European Showerbath*, a group of naked people take a shower with national flags painted on their bodies and with more and more people joining in; but as the last group wants to join, the water stops. Rather than celebrating one European vision, these films point to the problems with establishing a European culture and society and refer to a Europe with both great internal differences and problems in a global context.

A EUROPE OF NATIONAL CULTURES

Anthony D. Smith talks about European culture as a 'family of cultures' rather than one common culture.[5] Looking at European culture and history there is no doubt that we do share historical memories and myths. But although we have a certain, common cultural heritage and although since 1957 the EU has developed many integrating policies, Europeans are primarily national citizens. But at the same time Europeans are influenced by globalization, both in everyday life and cultural consumption. Media and communication are pervasive forces of globalization and instruments of mediation and dialogue between national cultures. Arjun Appadurai defines the role of modern media in a global world as 'building blocks of... imagined worlds'.[6] In a modern, globalized world culture, film, news, entertainment, and concepts flow in a very intense way between national cultures. But even though Europeans live in a complex world and possess multiple identities linked to local, national, European, and global cultural elements,

---

[3] http://eur-lex.europa.eu/en/treaties/dat/11992M/htm/11992M.html#0001000001, accessed April 2010.

[4] Constitution for Europe, article 1–8, 2004, online at: http://europa.eu/scadplus/constitution/objectives_en.htm, accessed April 2010.

[5] Anthony D. Smith, 'National Identity and the Idea of European Identity', *International Affairs* 68:1 (1992), 55–76.

[6] Arjun Appadurai, *Modernity at Large: Cultural Dimensions of Globalization* (Minneapolis, MN: University of Minnesota Press, 1996), 33.

data on film and TV consumption show that the primary local/national culture is still the culture people explicitly identify with. But at the same time American films occupy the centre stage as the most popular in all European countries.

EUROPE AND THE BIG AMERICAN OTHER

After the Second World War the US War Department invited representatives of the big Hollywood studios on a tour of Europe. When they returned they issued a joint statement on the importance of American movies abroad. Movies could help 'cleanse the minds, change the attitudes', and they could provide Americans abroad with 'psychological warfare' and make them 'well armed intellectually for a war of ideas'.[7] This confirms the fear of the European elite about American cultural imperialism. But the story of the big American other is a much more complex story of conflict, collaboration, and mutual cultural inspirations.

The American dominance of Europe immediately after 1945 took different forms and national cultural policies did resist and fight back. In France the Blum-Byrnes agreement signed in May 1946 aimed at helping the French economy recover was a disaster for French film culture. American films flooded the cinemas and French film production was drastically reduced. In October 1946 the French created the Centre National de la Cinématographie (CNC) financed by a tax on cinema tickets and using this tax to support French film production. The American postwar 'invasion' thus resulted in the creation of very strong state intervention and regulation of the French film culture and television that are still today among the most prolific in Europe.[8]

In the UK, strong American dominance immediately after 1945 resulted in the creation of the National Film Finance Corporation in 1949 and in 1950 the Eady Levy tax on cinema tickets providing money for the British Film Production Fund. The UK did not develop a protectionist cinema culture with quotas, but they did create incentives to strengthen the production of national films or films co-financed with the Americans but made in the UK.[9] The French and the UK models represent two different poles in a European continuum of different forms of cinema culture also extended to the later television culture.

There are very early historical examples of European global dominance and transnational collaboration in Europe.[10] But since the end of the First World War the Americans have dominated the global market, benefitting from a huge, unified, one language home market and efficient global distribution and marketing. Whereas the American market was dominated from the early days by major production and distribution companies,

---

[7] David Puttnam, *The Undeclared War* (London: Harper Collins, 1997), 204.
[8] Susan Hayward, *French National Cinema* (London: Routledge, 2005), 17 f.
[9] Sarah Street, *British National Cinema* (London: Routledge, 1997), 14.
[10] Anne Jäckel, *European Film Industries* (London: BFI, 2003), 4.

Europe has always been characterized by hundreds of smaller national production and distribution companies. The lack of a common European market and efficient and stable co-production and co-distribution systems together with many languages has historically been the major weakness of the system.

Regional European collaboration in cinema and TV before and after 1945 indicates tendencies in Europe to develop a pan-European audio-visual space and to compete with the dominant American audio-visual culture. The later EU film and media policy follows the same main goals. But the statistics on film consumption in the European market are pretty clear even today: of all the films released in the EU-27 countries between 2000 and 2008, the top fifty are almost completely dominated by films with either only a US production background, US/UK co-production background, or US plus more than one European production background.[11] If we focus on the top ten, the picture is even less diverse (see Table 32.1).

The dominance is really British–American dominance, and it points furthermore to the dominance of a few film genres that seem to travel extremely well, not just in Europe but also in the rest of the world: fantasy, thrillers, and action movies with a few family cartoon films, comedies, and musicals as runners up. No European national productions or European co-productions can compete with the British–American films when it comes to popularity and box office. But a number of European co-productions or even national films have had a certain success in both Europe and the

Table 32.1 Top 10 films EU-27 2000–08

Film	Producing countries	Year	Audience (million)
1. Lord of the Rings: Fellowship of the Ring	US/NZ	2001	58.1
2. Harry Potter and the Philosopher's Stone	GB/US	2001	57.3
3. Lord of the Rings: Two Towers	US/NZ	2002	52.8
4. Harry Potter and the Chamber of Secrets	GB/US	2002	50.1
5. Pirates of the Carribean	US	2006	42.5
6. Harry Potter and the Goblets of Fire	GB/US	2005	42.2
7. Harry Potter and the Prisoner of Azkeban	GB/US	2004	38.8
8. Ice Age: The Meltdown	US	2006	37.8
9. Harry Potter and the Order of the Phoenix	GB/US	2007	36.8
10. The Da Vinci Code	US/GB	2006	34.1

Source: Lumiere database, 2009

[11] Lumiere database, 2009, online at: http://lumiere.obs.coe.int/web/search/, accessed April 2010.

US, and many European directors have since 1945 tried their luck in Hollywood. Roman Polanski's *The Pianist* (2002) had a European cinema audience of 8.7 million and was at the same time seen by 5.2 million Americans. It is a story with universal attraction giving a novel perspective on the Holocaust and European history during the Second World War with appeal for both a European and an American audience. The film was a co-production between several European countries; US–EU collaboration is also quite common.

OVERCOMING FASCISM: NEW WAVES IN SOUTHERN EUROPE

Both in Germany and Italy the fascists made film part of their authoritarian project, and after 1945 film-makers were eager to create a new cinema that could take part in the forming of a new society. When the Cold War began to settle over Europe in the 1950s, Eastern Europe as a whole moved back to totalitarian dominance, despite short periods of cultural thaw in the 1960s. A number of European film festivals were born in the first years after 1945, indicating the wish to re-open the world of culture and create connections both within Europe and with other parts of the world: Cannes, Karlovy Vary and Locarno (1946), Edinburgh (1947), Berlin (1951), and London (1957). At the same time new institutional strongholds were formed in many nations to secure development of the national cinema, and last but not least directors worked together to define a new cinema with a new commitment to reality.

This was maybe most noticeable in Italy, emerging from fascism and the discrediting this had meant for Italian culture. A group of directors, among them Luigi Visconti, Victoria De Sica, and Roberto Rossellini left the studios to film on location in order to catch the reality of everyday life.[12] The movement was called neo-realism and the films they made clearly had a social and political agenda: Rossellini's *Rome Open City* (1945) celebrated the resistance movement; De Sica's *Bicycle Thieves* (1948) and *Umberto D* (1952) told stories of completely ordinary Italians; and Visconti's *La terra trema* (1948) shot on Sicily among local fishermen was the first part of a trilogy aiming at giving regional working-class cultures a place in Italian cinema. But although many of these films won critical and international acclaim they did not do well at the national box office.

The rise of neo-realism was a sign of a new vitality in Italian and European cinema after the war, but it partly rested on the absence of both popular Italian cinema and American cinema in the immediate aftermath of the Second World War. Already around 1950 things had started to return to normal, and popular Italian genre films took over the market together with the return of extremely popular American genre films. But

---

[12] Pierre Sorlin, *Italian National Cinema* (London: Routledge, 1996), 89.

Italian directors from neo-realism and new directors such as Michelangelo Antonioni, Federico Fellini, Bernardo Bertolucci, Ettora Scola, and Paolo Pasolini continued to contribute to the modern, European Art cinema tradition and also to move into the more international circuit of modern European directors. Antonioni for instance made two English language films in the 1960s, *Blow Up* (1967), distributed as an English film, and *Zabriskie Point* (1969), distributed as an American film.

Fellini created a very personal, imaginary world balancing between reality, memoirs, and phantasy in films like *La Strada* (1954) or *La dolce vita* (1960) and *8½* (1963), both with existential art themes, or the poetic historical memory film *Amarcord* (1973). The fact that Fellini in 1996 was given an Oscar for his lifetime achievement indicates the international prestige of European art cinema. Bernardo Bertolucci started with political films like *Il conformista* (1970) about the roots of fascism, but with the daring erotic film *Last Tango in Paris* (1972), starring Marlon Brando, he moved closer to international cinema. His historical masterpiece is *Novecento/1900* (1976), a historical drama about Italian history and the birth of a new century. Bertolucci's later films have moved closer to Hollywood mainstream cinema.

In other European countries such as Spain, Portugal, and Greece, where fascism survived or dictatorships later took power, strong restrictions on film production were common. But also in Spain there was a new wave in the 1960s with directors like Carlos Saura and Marco Ferreri; and after the death of Franco in 1975 a strong wave of experiments, social criticism, and more daring themes became part of a new Spanish film culture that became popular both in Spain and internationally. Clearly the most internationally renowned director is Pedro Almodóvar, who came out of the Madrid subculture in the 1970s but had his major international breakthrough with the strong erotic melodrama *Women on the Verge of a Nervous Breakdown* (1988), and the following international prize winners *All about My Mother* (1999) and *Talk to Her* (2002). Almodóvar is a modern art cinema director capable of combining melodrama, comedy, and other popular genres with an original, aesthetic expression and a deep insight into Spanish everyday life and universal erotic and psychological themes. In Portugal and Greece new cinema since 1945 and 1960 has had much less international success, and a well known Greek art cinema director like Theodor Angelopoulos is one of the few directors that has made important contributions to the European art cinema, for instance with *Eternity and a Day* (1998), which won the Palme d'Or in Cannes.

MODERN EUROPEAN FILM CULTURE
AND THE NEW POSTWAR SOCIETY

Of the European art cinema movements after 1945 the most influential is no doubt the new wave in the 1960s that became a transnational European cinema. The new wave was not an isolated cinematic break with tradition but a sign of more profound changes in European societies, indicating changing norms and cultural traditions of new generations. In Tony Judt's *Postwar: A History of Europe since 1945* (2007), the period after 1960 is simply called 'the age of affluence'. He points to both the enormous economic growth, the rise of a modern consumer culture, the increase of knowledge and education among the younger generations, and also to new forms of communication and culture. The youth culture and rebellion against the old systems symbolized by 1968 was first seen in the British Free Cinema movement of directors like Lindsay Anderson, Karel Reisz, and Tony Richardson,[13] and they were very soon joined by the rock 'n' roll culture of the Rolling Stones and the Beatles. The demographics of European cultures were changing: a decline in agriculture; a more traditional, patriarchal society; and a strong urbanization followed by new norms and lifestyles. Beneath these European developments in different national forms there was also a steadily growing globalization of society, culture, and communication that would have a huge impact on the social and cultural agenda later in the century and after 2000.

The new wave cinema of the 1960s was a cinema trying to find a new and contemporary language for itself in a new and mostly urban culture. But the new wave generation also admired Hollywood and in this sense also became part of a new global culture. A film such as Jean-Luc Godard's *Breathless* (1960) is an emblematic film of the new wave. With its homage to the American gangster movie and its completely new realistic look on urban life in Paris, the moving camera, on-location shots, and its tragic love story, the film clearly signals a new, young culture. François Truffaut's films *The 400 Blows* (1959) and *Jules &Jim* (1962) signal the same kind of new realism and a different look at love and everyday life through the eyes of a new generation.

British cinema after 1960 also made important contributions to both social realism and modernism. A new realism was visible in films like Lindsay Anderson's *Saturday Night and Sunday Morning* (1963) and *If* (1968), or Jack Clayton's *Room at the Top* (1959) with a strong, critical, social edge. But films celebrating a new youth culture, like Tony Richardson's *A Taste of Honey*, also signalled a new momentum in British cinema. A direct line runs from this tradition to Ken Loach and Mike Leigh, who both represent strong social realism in contemporary British cinema with broad international recognition. Ken Loach has had a long television career, for instance with the historical miniseries *Days of Hope* (1975); and has won prizes for several of his films on British everyday life and historical conflicts such as *Raining Stones* (1993) and *The Wind that Shakes the Barley* (2006). Mike Leigh's strength is to catch the deep space of everyday life in films like *Secrets and Lies* (1996). But the new wave also introduced a more experimental cinema represented by, for instance Peter Greenaway with colourful, non-narrative films like *The Cook, the Thief, His Wife and Her Lover* (1989).

---

[13] Sarah Street, *British National Cinema* (London: Routledge, 1997), 78 ff.

SCANDINAVIAN NEW WAVE AND THE RISE
OF A MODERN WELFARE CULTURE

The new wave cinema of the 1960s and the rise of television are also results of intensified national policies for culture, where cultural policy became part of modern welfare policy. The European model for television with either a public service monopoly or a dual system of both public service and commercial channels is part of this cultural offensive. States wanted to secure cultural diversity and believed that a national production of both fictional and factual programmes could resist the pressure from global competition. In much the same way, many European nations increased support for national films that might otherwise be threatened, especially in small nations.

Denmark is a typical example of such a small nation policy.[14] In 1964 the first law for cinema culture was passed and money was allocated to support both art film and documentary film. In 1972 the Danish Film Institute was created, and support mechanisms were established to make sure that the struggling national film industry could survive. The aim of this law was primarily to secure a place for film art, for documentary films, and for films for children that would supplement mainstream cinema and thus create cultural diversity; but in the period 1972–90 it became clear that support even for mainstream cinema was necessary. Starting with the Oscar and Cannes success of Gabriel Axel's *Babette's Feast* (1987), Bille August's *Pelle the Conquerer* (1988) and *The Best Intentions* (1992), Danish cinema had an international breakthrough. In 1997 the new and financially much stronger Danish Film Institute was formed and today Danish film has the highest national audience share (25–30 per cent) in Europe after France.

The situation in Sweden, Norway, and Finland was much the same with minor, national differences, but it was Sweden that first and most strongly put Scandinavian cinema on the global agenda. Just as Denmark had the world famous Carl Theodor Dreyer, celebrated by the French new wave generation for films like *The Word* (1954) and *Gertrud* (1964), Sweden had Ingmar Bergman who stands out as the most internationally recognized Scandinavian director since 1945. In the 1950s he made films such as *Summer with Monika* (1953) and *Wild Strawberries* (1957) that introduced modern art cinema, and with his films from the 1960s onwards he became almost synonymous with Scandinavian new wave, with strong psychological dramas like *The Silence* (1963), *Persona* (1966), and *Cries and Whispers* (1973). Another strong representative of the Scandinavian new wave was Bo Widerberg with much more socially realistic films like *Raven's End* (1963) or *Ådalen 1931* (1969) about a social uprising, but also the poetic romantic drama *Elvira Madigan* (1967), which gave him broad European and international success.

---

[14] See Ib Bondebjerg, 'The Danish Way: Danish Film Culture in a European and Global Perspective', in Andrew Nestingen and Trevor Elkington (eds), *Transnational Cinema in a Global North: Nordic Cinema in Transition* (Detroit, MI: Wayne State University Press, 2005), 111–41.

Neither Norway, Finland, nor Denmark could match the Swedish successes of the 1960s and 1970s and until recently only a director like the Finnish Aki Kaurismäki has reached international fame with absurd, social comedies like *I Hired a Contract Killer* (1990) or *The Man without a Past* (2002). In Denmark only Henning Carlsen made a European entry with the Hamsun film *Hunger* (1966), but the Danish Dogme 95 movement started by Lars von Trier and the so-called Vow of Chastity manifesto, also signed by Thomas Vinterberg,[15] in many ways repeat positions taken by 1960s new wave cinema. The ten rules set out in the manifesto clearly have to do with getting rid of mainstream genre film productions and creating intense realism in themes and form.

The Danish Dogma films received much intellectual attention and some of the films also had limited transnational success. Thomas Vinterberg's *Festen (The Celebration)* (1998) has been seen worldwide in cinema by 3 million people, whereas Lars von Trier's much more radical *The Idiots* (1997) was only seen by 840,000. But the most impressive result of the Dogma manifesto was the fact that more than sixty films internationally were made in accordance with the manifesto rules, a fact that makes the movement just as big internationally as the French new wave.

Lars von Trier is a clear example of the new type of European art cinema director. Although based in Denmark, most of his films are made as huge European co-productions, and the new European system of distribution and promotion together with the festival system has made his work widely known and influential. His religious melodrama *Breaking the Waves* (1996, co-produced by Denmark, France, Germany, and Sweden) was seen by 4 million people worldwide and his very experimental musical *Dancer in the Dark* (2000, co-produced by Denmark, France, Sweden, Germany, Norway, the Netherlands, and Iceland) was seen by almost 5 million. Even the Brecht inspired film *Dogville* (2003, co-produced by Denmark, France, Sweden, Germany, Norway, the Netherlands, and Great Britain) with its very low-key stage settings managed to attract 2.5 million.

EUROPEAN MEDIA CULTURE AND THE COMMUNIST 'ICE AGE'

European media culture after 1945 was not just divided nationally, but also influenced by the long period of Cold War between East and West. Perhaps this was nowhere felt in a more direct way than in Berlin, where a creative centre for film production was divided and where, after 1961, a wall divided Germany into two states. In the German Democratic Republic (GDR) film and television was under strong control from the communist party and the official doctrine was socialist realism.

---

[15] Mette Hjort and Ib Bondebjerg (eds), *The Danish Directors: Dialogues on a Contemporary National Cinema* (Bristol: Intellect Books, 2001), 9.

In the period up until the fall of the Berlin Wall in 1989, the GDR produced more than 700 films; together with a large TV production of documentaries, TV-series, children's programmes, and more, the GDR tried, with imports from other communist nations, to create a communist audio-visual space secluded from the rest of Europe and the world. But figures for film consumption after 1970[16] in the GDR indicate that although 75 per cent of all films shown in cinemas and television were national or from other communist countries, it was the last 25 per cent from the US and Western Europe that had by far the largest audience.

Still, many of the films and TV programmes produced in Eastern Europe belong to the classics of European culture. When German film critics in 1995 were asked to nominate the one hundred best German films of all time, fourteen GDR films (out of the total GDR production of 750 films) were nominated, among them films by Wolfgang Staudte, Konrad Wolf, Frank Beyer, Gerhard Klein, and Heiner Carow.[17] The list of nominated directors and films show that the genres and traditions mostly valued by the critics belonged to the anti-fascist historical drama and the broader realist tradition, with some of the heritage films based on literary classics also nominated.

In Poland, Hungary, and Czechoslovakia films were also made that are part of the new wave cinema, despite control and censorship. In Poland directors such as Andrzej Wajda, Jerzy Skolimowski, Roman Polanski, and not least Krzysztof Kieślowski represented a broader group of film directors, who did not comply with the official party line, but whose films were seen both in Poland and abroad. This limited freedom for film can partly be explained by the rise and popularity of the Solidarity movement in the 1970s. Films by Andrzej Wajda such as *Ashes and Diamonds* (1958) introduced a special Polish tone of symbolic realism, and with *Man of Marble* (1976) and *Man of Iron* (1981) Wajda became the critical realist expressing the mood of the Solidarity movement period.

Kieślowski's films show the complexities of the pre-1989 communist film culture. His documentary films clearly record the bleakness of life in a communist state without directly raising a critical voice. He also made the amazing, nationally and internationally acclaimed TV-series *Decalogue* (10 parts, 1988–89) with freezing images of existential problems and dilemmas of everyday life in a Polish nation on its way out of communism. After 1989, Kieślowski continued as one of the most important European directors, especially with his *Three Colours Trilogy* (1993–94), three films illustrating the modern meaning of the European values of freedom, equality, and brotherhood, through stories with a clear transnational, European theme and plot line.

Kieślowski became a truly European director as a direct result of the fall of communism and the opening of a free European market, but also based on his merits as a filmmaker already established during communism. Another important international director with roots in the Eastern European art cinema is the Czech director Milos Forman, who was already Oscar nominated for his early social comedies such as *Loves of a Blonde* (1965) and *The Firemen's Ball* (1967). He soon moved to America and became

---

[16] Sabine Hake, *German National Cinema* (London: Routledge, 2008).

[17] Daniela Berghahn, 'East German Cinema after Unification', in David Clarke (ed.), *German Cinema since Unification* (London: Continuum, 2006), 79–80.

an important American international director. Films such as *One Flew over the Cuckoo's Nest* (1975) winning five Oscars and *Amadeus* (1984) winning eight, are good examples of the ways in which American cinema has been influenced by European art cinema.

But the fall of communism and the taking over of national and transnational market forces in the former communist region was of course not without problems. In Yugoslavia the fall of communism led to the rise of strong nationalism and ethnic conflicts and a terrible civil war. As a result we now have new nations like Bosnia, Slovenia, Croatia, and Serbia on their way to developing their different national film cultures. We also find some important directors becoming more internationally known after 1989, such as the Bosnian director Emir Kusturica, who already in 1985 had won international acclaim with films like *Father Was Away on Business* (1985, Palme d'Or in Cannes) about post-Second World War Bosnia seen through the eyes of a boy; and *Underground* (1989, Palme d'Or in Cannes), perhaps his best film to date, a grand history of Yugoslavia from the Second World War to the civil wars, told with grotesque humour and surrealism.

The fall of communism created profound changes in all of Eastern Europe. The complete collapse overnight of one state system and the integration into a new, very different system meant that a lot of people lost their jobs in the cultural, as in every other, sector. The transition and the relationship between past and present became central themes for German TV and film.[18] A former East German director such as Andreas Dresen became a central figure in the new Berlin cinema, with films like *Nachtgestalten* (1998), a multi-plot story about three main characters in Berlin during 24 dramatic hours; or the comedy about life in the eastern provinces, *Halbe Treppe* (2002), which won the prize for best German film that year. In Wolfgang Becker's *Goodbye, Lenin!* (2003) the use of satire and humour in the portrait of the former GDR put the past and present on the agenda in a new way. In Florian Henckel von Donnersmarck's *The Lives of Others* (2006), an intense, psychological drama, life behind the wall was suddenly visible in its tragic and human dimensions, and the historical distance also made it possible to give even a Stasi character a human face and dimension. The two films illustrate how much media can contribute to the healing of historical divides and wounds, and how the wall has become a common European symbol and reference point.

EUROPEAN TELEVISION CULTURES: CONSTRUCTING THE NATION AND GLOBALIZING THE HOME

If the historical art cinema tradition is the most important European contribution to world cinema, public service television culture is the European contribution to world television.

---

[18] Ib Bondebjerg, 'Coming to Terms with the Past: Post-1989 Strategies in German Film Culture', *Studies in East European Cinema* 1:1 (2010), 29–42.

A significant change in the audio-visual culture of Europe (and the US) around 1960 was caused by the rise of television and this medium's way of bringing politics, world affairs, and all forms of entertainment directly into European households. The real revolution of television was its breaking down of social and cultural hierarchies and the creation of a mass culture that covered news, factual programming, art and entertainment. Television changed the relationship between the political and cultural elite and the general population, and it changed the borders between the public and the private domain in all forms of communication in the public sphere.

In America television was a purely commercial and market driven phenomenon, whereas the British BBC saw television as part of an educational, cultural, and democratic project supported by the state. Most European countries after 1945 took the public service road and created autonomous, public TV institutions financed by either viewer fees or taxes and guided by demand for diversity in programming. Not all countries followed the BBC model, and public service in Europe after the war developed into different models, just as dual systems of both public service and commercial broadcasting were developed quite early, in the UK as early as 1955 with ITV. In most other European countries we see the same development, but in some countries it was much later.

Different models in Europe clearly reflect national differences and ideological division in Europe. In West Germany, a federal republic founded in 1949, TV from 1954 followed the strong decentralized model of regional states with political autonomy. But these local broadcasters cooperated through the ARD, and responsibility for programme production was distributed according to the size of the broadcaster and regional state, with only some of the programming centrally made.[19] This regional collaboration was further developed in 1963 with ZDF and the further regionalization of ARD the same year with different ARD 3 channels, for instance NDR3.

A very special national construction pertains in the Netherlands, a small country known for its 'pillarized' structure and a 'segmented pluralism'.[20] This basically means that the whole social, political, and cultural system and also media systems have traditionally been organized in four 'pillars'—Calvinist, Catholic, socialist, and liberal—in an attempt to let all voices, opinions, and cultures be heard and represented in the public sphere. But despite this pillarized structure of programming, the Dutch system until 1988 was completely dominated by national public service channels (Netherlands 1 (1951), Netherlands 2 (1964) and Netherlands 3 (1988)) and a structure of regional channels also publicly supported, with different production companies representing the 'pillars' producing for these channels.

The British, Dutch, and German models represent different TV cultures in the Western, democratic part of Europe. But it is important to remember that large parts of

---

[19] Hans Kleinsteuber, 'Germany', in Mary Kelly, Gianpietro Mazzoleni and Denis Mcquail (eds), *The Media in Europe* (London: Sage, 2004), 81.

[20] Kees Brandt, 'The Netherlands', in Kelly, Mazzoleni and Mcquail (eds), *The Media in Europe*, 145.

Europe until 1989 were under authoritarian rule and the media and culture as a whole were carefully controlled, both in the communist, Eastern part of Europe and in Spain and Portugal under postwar fascist regimes. In Spain during the Franco regime (1939–75) the central Television Espanola (TVE, established 1956) was a monolithic propaganda tool for the regime in many programming categories, and even the regional channels established during the 1960s were to a large degree centrally controlled. The same situation could be found in Portugal during the Salazar dictatorship (1930–74) and the shaping of Portuguese Television (RTP) in 1955.

In communist Eastern Europe the media system as a whole up until 1989 was also dominated by heavy state control, with journalism and fiction both subject to censorship. In Poland, a country with a strong film tradition despite communist control, television started in 1951 with one national channel, TVP, a channel still existing today but now split into three (TVP1, TVP2, and TVP3). State control of the channel before 1989 was replaced by a more traditional public service model, and after a chaotic transition period with foreign, private takeovers in many sectors, including the media, a balance between public and private channels was established in Poland.

EUROPEAN ART TELEVISION AND NATIONAL FICTION SERIES

Although American products dominated the small screens of postwar Europe, especially in fiction and entertainment formats, TV has also been a strong factor in constructing a community for the nations of Europe. European television is a story of channels established to serve a nation, to construct an imaginary cultural community of this nation and an inclusive democratic public sphere. In all European countries the national news, national fictional series, and national documentary formats play a crucial role for a national reference to reality and a national sense of belonging. In all European nations it is possible for instance to point to historical drama series that have become cornerstones for a national mass audience. In Denmark the series *Matador* (24 parts, 1978–81) about life in a small Danish provincial town from 1929–47 has been broadcast about six times and has sold out first on video and then on DVD. Its successor, *The Chronicle* (2004–07, 22 parts), following the life of very different families between 1947 and 1972 was just as popular.

In Germany one could mention the tremendous success of Edgar Reitz's *Heimat* (1984, 11 parts) following German everyday life between 1919 and 1982, centred around a small German village and the debate and emotional impact it created in a nation still partly traumatized by Second World War guilt and experiences. Reitz's series was made as a response to the global and German success of the American series *Holocaust* (1978) and its extremely emotional and dramatic reconstruction of a Jewish family during the Holocaust. Reitz wanted to create a national alternative to the American way of interpreting German history.[21] Reitz managed to change the agenda and put a deeper perspective on structures and changes in German everyday life into the public debate.

One of the first European art cinema directors to use the small screen in an artistic way was Swedish Ingmar Bergman with the intense, psychological drama series *Scenes from a Marriage* (1–6, 1973), one of the first TV series to expose private, sexual, and psychological power struggles in a modern family so directly and openly. It was followed by the just as intense family drama series *Fanny and Alexander* (1982), based on Bergman's own family story. This Scandinavian quality tradition is also represented by Jan Troell's internationally acclaimed historical immigrant saga *The Immigrants* (1971) and *The Settlers* (1972).

A national art television tradition can be found in all European countries and often these television series are historical dramas capturing the imagination of the national audience and at the same developing new aesthetic forms. This is the case with the historical series made by Rainer Werner Fassbinder, *Berlin Alexanderplatz* (1–14, 1980), an expressionistic and aesthetically challenging series about culture and society in the Weimar Republic. Just as innovative and experimental was the British television series by Dennis Potter, who took television fiction to new aesthetic levels in series like *Pennies from Heaven* (1–6, 1978) and *The Singing Detective* (1–6, 1986), in which he combines popular culture genres and characters with British social and cultural history and memoirs.[22]

The UK has a huge and internationally very popular production of television fiction based on literary classics or, in some cases, long-running, historical series. Examples of the last category are *A Family at War* (1970–72), dealing with the life of an ordinary middle-class English family during the Second World War; *Upstairs Downstairs* (1971–74), telling a modern story of changes in class distinctions in Edwardian England; or *When the Boat Comes in* (1976–81), about life in a north of England town in the 1920s and 1930s. Literary adaptations include the hugely popular *Brideshead Revisited* (1981), based on Evelyn Waugh's novel about the decaying aristocracy; *The Jewel in the Crown* (1984), about the loss of India and the British Empire during the Second World War and based on Paul Scott's novels; or *Pride and Prejudice* (1995), based on Jane Austin's 1813 novel, and adding to the strong British heritage tradition in both film and television.[23]

This British tradition has to a large degree influenced European television drama and has been broadcast on most European channels. But in France too there is a strong national tradition for national historical series and adaptations. One of the most popular in recent years was the miniseries *Napoleon* (2002). Though very French in theme

[21] Ib Bondebjerg, 'European Art Television and the American Challenge', *Northern Lights* 4 (2005), 206–7.

[22] Ib Bondebjerg, 'Intertextuality and Metafiction: Genre and Naration in the Television Fiction of Dennis Potter', in Michael Skovmand and Kim Schröder (eds), *Media Cultures: Reappraising Transnational Media* (London: Routledge, 1992), 161–80.

[23] Andrew Higson, *English Heritage, English Cinema: Costume Drama since 1980* (Oxford: Oxford University Press, 2003).

and genre this was a co-production with the UK, US, and Canada and thus broadcast both inside and outside Europe. A very special version of French heritage drama based on classical literature is the 2003 miniseries *Dangerous Liaisons,* where Laclos's classical eighteenth-century novel around decadent aristocrats is remade among the 1960s Parisian upper class.

THE TRANSNATIONAL POWER OF TELEVISION

But the power of television to construct a national identity is only one aspect of the medium. The other side is television as part of globalization and to some degree also Europeanization. Already in the early phases of European television, institutional attempts had been made to create pan-European cooperation. The European Broadcasting Union (EBU) was created in 1950 and developed the Eurovision programme production and exchange system of news, entertainment, and sport. The coronation of Queen Elizabeth II in 1953 was a major European media event in early television culture, as were later institutionalized media events such as the Eurovision Song Contest. But the exchange of football events and drama productions also points to the establishment of a European audio-visual space.

After deregulation, commercialization, and globalization of European TV in the 1980s, the growth in the number of channels and hours of transmission have led to an even stronger globalization of TV. The EU's media policy during the 1980s attempted to stimulate the creation of a stronger pan-European television industry by encouraging pan-European investment in the television sector, establishing pan-European generic channels (like Eurosport and Euronews), and by providing better frameworks for investment in programme production and the transnational export of programme formats. A successful company such as the Dutch based Endemol, which created *Big Brother,* one of the largest global successes for a European TV-format ever, is one of the results of this policy.

But the audio-visual area is of course not just a place for pan-European players entering national television culture; it is a global business for huge multimedia conglomerates. Global media events such as the assassination of Kennedy in 1963, the moon landing in 1969, and the first global live satellite transmission of Elvis's *Aloha from Hawaii* concert mark different aspects of the global synchronization of time and space through television. As a consequence of this we see the rise of global channels in Europe during the 1980s and 1990s with, for instance, CNN, BBC World and MTV. An interesting development for many of these channels is regionalization: CNN is now divided into a European and an Asian version and MTV has gone even further and is now divided into five territories in Europe alone (British, Central, Central Europe, Northern and Southern Europe). The idea of a homogenous global audience for a centralized broadcaster is thus replaced by a much more complex strategy for global media speaking to regional cultures and audiences.

Narratives of Reality: The
Documentary Tradition

Documentary film and television is a strong part of European culture and had already since the 1930s become part of public communication and cultural policy. In the UK an influential documentary movement was formed under the leadership of John Grierson.[24] His idea of documentary as 'creative treatment of actuality', and as part of a new vision for steering social and public opinion and a broader democracy, deeply influenced developments in other European countries. Directors like Basil Wright, Harry Watt, and Humphrey Jennings during the 1930s and 1940s managed to put drama, poetry, and vision into films about the modern world of work and everyday life even though they were working under private corporations or public institutions with their own agendas. Humphrey Jennings's existential and poetic documentary *A Diary for Timothy* (1945), looking ahead to postwar developments, marks the beginning of a modern documentary movement.

In many European countries, development after the war gave a new boost to independent documentary films, even though television took over many of the previous roles of documentary films and cinema. In the UK, Free Cinema directors like Lindsay Anderson and Karel Reisz developed a more observational style of documentary with images of modern life and a poetic, symbolic dimension as in for instance Reisz's *We are the Lambeth Boys* (1959) about a group of teenagers in a south London working-class area. In France, Jean Rouch termed the new film form *cinéma verité* and in *Chronicle of a Summer* (1961) he mixed observations, interviews, and a reflexive dimension in a film about how people in Paris experience life. Another French director, Chris Marker, followed this trend in his *La joli mai* (1968) about the student revolts in 1968. In Scandinavia, directors like Stefan Jarl and Arne Sucksdorf from Sweden portrayed modern welfare societies. Arne Sucksdorff, belonging to the older generation, created the poetic city portrait *Människor i stad* (1947), while Stefan Jarl looked at the bleaker sides of life in his trilogy *They Call Us Misfits* (1968), *A Decent Life* (1979), and *Misfits to Yuppies* (1992), following a group of people on the margins of society.

But observational form was not the only form of documentary film after 1945; a strong social and critical tradition and a multifaceted poetic and dramatized documentary tradition runs through postwar Europe. The atrocities of the Holocaust dominate in a number of films where documentary films become important voices and witnesses of history. Alain Resnais's *Night and Fog* (1955) introduced a whole new way of combining present and past voices and pictures, and the impressive documentation of the Holocaust is continued in Claude Lanzman's much later, nine-hour long film *Shoah* (1985) with

---

[24] See for instance Jack C. Ellis and Betsy A. Mclane, *A New History of Documentary Film* (New York: Contiuum, 2005), 57 ff.; Ian Aitken, *Film and Reform: John Grierson and the Documentary Movement* (London: Routledge, 1990).

shocking testimonies from a huge number of people involved, both as victims and culprits.

Another strong, critical documentary voice belongs to the English director Peter Watkins who has specialized in dramatized documentaries on often very controversial historical or contemporary subjects. In *Culloden* (1963), he recreates the crucial battle between the English and the Scots in 1745 in the form of news reportage; in *The War Game* (1965), he illustrates the devastating consequences of a nuclear attack on London and the serious naivety in public efforts to prevent these consequences. The film was so controversial that it was not shown on BBC TV until much later, but only in cinemas around the world.

In other parts of Europe critical voices also developed, taking up new themes. Louis Malle's impressive *Calcutta* (1969) had already opened the door to the global postwar world, but films like *Darwin's Nightmare* (2004, a French, Belgian, Austrian co-production, directed by Hupert Sauper) demonstrate serious environmental problems in Africa, The problem of authoritarian regimes is also taken up in Werner Herzog's *Echoes From a Somber Empire* (1990). The effects of globalization on Europe and the world as such is clearly a major theme in contemporary European documentary cinema. An interesting project trying to deal with the question of transnational democracy and a global civil society is *Why Democracy?*, initiated by the Danish TV station DR2 in collaboration with the BBC, Arte, ZDF, and YLE.[25] The films were partly inspired by the global conflict on the Danish cartoon case and resulted in ten very different documentary films on democracy from all over the world. Also, a film like the Danish *Enemies of Our Happiness* (2006, Eva Mulvad), about the first democratically elected Afghan woman and her difficult and dangerous life, is part of the global documentary dialogue between cultures.

It becomes more and more difficult to draw the dividing line between independent documentary film-making and television documentary in postwar Europe. In the UK, one of the key figures behind the early documentary film movement, Paul Rotha, became head of the BBC's Documentary Department in 1953. He initiated a lengthy development of television documentaries both of a critical, investigative kind and of a more observational, ethnographic nature. Series like *Special Inquiry* (1952–57, BBC), *World in Action* (1963–99, Granada), *This Week* (1956–92, ITV), and *Panorama* (1953 to date, BBC) became important, journalistic, documentary institutions with deeper and broader perspectives than the daily news. Both in the US and in other European countries we see similar developments. A strong European tradition is also the nature documentary, for instance BBC's spectacular series *The Blue Planet* (2001), narrated by the legendary David Attenborough; popular interest for nature documentary is also visible on transnational channels such as Animal Planet and the Discovery Channel. We find just as strong an interest in historical documentaries, both on ordinary channels and the History Channel.

[25] Mette Hjort, 'Living with Diversity: What Difference Can Film-making Make?', *Northern Lights* 7 (2009), 9–27. See also the project website: www.whydemocracy.net, accessed April 2010.

However, there is no doubt that television strongly influenced the development of documentary formats from the 1990s onwards with the rise of so-called 'reality tv'. Paul Watson may have been the first to create a reality series with *Family* (1974), but it was the Dutch production company Endemol that created a global surge with *Big Brother* (1999), a reality show made in national versions all over Europe but following the same formula of voyeuristic observation of the life of a carefully selected group representing the nation, and rules and games to make drama and psychological conflicts during the 24-hour cycle. In many nations of Europe, *Big Brother* became a media event and caused major debates on ethics, democracy, and the decline of public television.

Digital Futures in a European Perspective

In most European countries the period around 2000 meant a switch to digital technology in both the production and distribution of film and TV. With the development of digital cinema and with the possibility of multi-platform use of film and TV material, a new multimedia culture is beginning to take form. Digital technology has cut production costs, but the explosion in channels and platforms for audio-visual material has also dramatically increased the demand for content. The development has also opened up an even more segmented form of programming on special channels to different audiences.

Contrary to many hopes and expectations for greater diversity and choice in production, channels, and programmes in Europe as a whole, the competition following the digital switch shows signs of concentration in ownership and a focus on very few commercial formats like sports and entertainment. Some aspects of the cultural dimensions of the digital revolution are clearly overrated, and in many ways the new digital media culture has turned out to be just a digital version of already existing patterns of communication and cultural consumption. However, the convergence between media and platforms following the digital revolution is a real and fundamental revolution. Citizens of Europe can watch films and television whenever they want and select their own schedule from live or archive material. Visions for a new transnational global sphere also include enhanced possibilities for user driven information and media production, for people sharing cultural products or information on websites and in social networks, as we see for instance on Facebook, YouTube, or MySpace.

The digital revolution has created a whole new framework for the production and distribution of film and television, and many of the technological barriers for a transnational media culture in Europe no longer exist. But technology isn't everything, and the digital revolution cannot in itself create a social, political, and cultural revolution. The vision of a more unified European media culture is still far from reality in Europe. Behind the contours of a new, digital, transnational media culture in Europe lie very old and well established differences, and the stories and images we watch on our now multiple screens are still not European images and stories, but images and stories with a national or an American background.

FURTHER READING

Bignell, Jonathan and Andreas Fickers (eds), *A European Television History* (London: Wiley-Blackwell, 2008).

Bondebjerg, Ib (ed.), *Television in Scandinavia: History, Politics and Aesthetics* (Luton: Acamedia/Luton Press, 1996).

Bondebjerg, Ib and Peter Madsen (eds), *Media, Democracy and European Culture* (Bristol: Intellect Press, 2008).

Collins, Richard, *Media and Identity in Contemporary Europe* (Bristol: Intellect Press, 2002).

Ellis, Jack C. and Betsy A. McLane, *A New History of Documentary Film* (New York: Continuum, 2005).

Elsaesser, Thomas, *European Cinema Face to Face with Hollywood* (Amsterdam: Amsterdam University Press, 2005).

Fowler, Catherine (ed.), *The European Cinema Reader* (London: Routledge, 2002).

Hjort, Mette and Duncan Petrie (eds), *The Cinema of Small Nations* (Edinburgh: Edinburgh University Press, 2007).

Iosifides, Petros, Jeannette Steemers and Mark Wheeler, *European Television Industries* (London: BFI, 2005).

Jäckel, Anne, *European Film Industries* (London: BFI, 2004).

Kovacs, Andresz, *Screening Modernism: European Art Cinema 1950–1980* (Chicago, IL: Chicago University Press, 2007).

Sorlin, Pierre, *European Cinemas, European Societies 1939–1990* (London: Routledge, 1991).

Wood, Mary, *Contemporary European Cinema* (London: Hodder Arnold, 2007).

PART VII

....

COMING TO TERMS WITH THE WAR

....

CHAPTER 33

INTELLECTUALS
AND NAZISM

SAMUEL MOYN

INTRODUCTION

THOUGH Nazism was destroyed totally and decisively at the end of World War II, the relationship of intellectuals to it as the years passed thereafter never proved simple.[1] Its formation and evolution depended above all on two factors. First, intellectuals drew on traditions of conceptualizing the nature of the Nazi ideology and Adolf Hitler's regime forged before the war: anti-fascism and anti-totalitarianism. After the conflict's end, these theories influenced how intellectuals identified what was worst about what had occurred, notably the essence of Nazism's crimes. Second, an evolving politics of recognition of the particularities of Adolf Hitler's agenda, and especially his unique animus towards the Jewish people, proved crucial. In a word, the Holocaust became ever more central to how Nazism's essence and repertory of projects were conceived. Further, if in some places the extent and zeal of implication in Nazi plans were obvious from the start, in others it had to be learned as Holocaust memory crystallized, with the consequence that what originally seemed easily targeted as a purely external evil came to seem much more ambiguous and 'internal'.

The first factor—the persistence of the earliest traditions of interpreting and denouncing Nazism—has been drastically understated in conventional narratives of postwar European history. Without it, a simpler approach has dominated, in which the paradigm shift of Holocaust memory completely supplanted the 'blindness' that reigned before. In Tony Judt's *Postwar*, for example the history of public memory of the Holocaust is not one topic among others. It is extruded from the various narratives of the mammoth book to provide their unifying epilogue, in an almost idealist gesture: the story of the

[1] I am grateful to Abigail Walworth for research assistance, and to Paul A. Hanebrink and Dan Stone for their advice about how to finalize this chapter.

long transit of postwar Europeans from brutality to civility and from ethno-national destruction to cosmopolitan inclusion—the main concern of Judt's book—is not really complete until and unless a parallel history is narrated explaining how Europeans fitfully gained consciousness of that very transformation. In this approach, the relationship of intellectuals to Nazism is one of *Vergangenheitbewältigung*: the belated acknowledgement and acceptance of a past previously evaded.[2]

Yet the same history shows that, from another angle, the need to make sense of the postwar era as an aftermath to Nazism is not really a matter of delayed recognition and slow learning at all. Theories of what had gone wrong predated the war, and were updated immediately after. Similarly, calls to learn from the past and respond accordingly were practically coeval with the aftermath itself, but they depended on what theory of Nazism intellectuals adopted: anti-fascism or anti-totalitarianism. Across the era, intellectuals certainly did change their minds about what evils the past war was thought to involve. But if developing and changing interpretations of Nazism ultimately proved inseparable from the rise of Holocaust memory and thus new understandings of the wartime conduct of nations and intellectuals, the original theories have proved surprisingly long lasting. Instead of being supplanted by Holocaust memory, it may be that each simply made room for it.

THE POSTWAR SCENE

In fact, theories contended from the beginning about the nature of Nazism, and vied with one another, as early perceptions were linked to extraordinary and open-ended contention in the political and cultural realm in the fluid situation of a postwar era that had not yet crystallized in a Cold War of global dimensions. And at the threshold, the crucial fact—however obvious—was that Nazism had been anatomized throughout its life, with its death allowing for many strands of continuity with earlier analyses and reactions. In a landmark study of World War I's legacy, Jay Winter has argued against the common view that that 'great' war introduced a blank caesura in European cultural history, which—he suggests—was reserved for the aftermath of the next great conflict, with its Holocaust and other violence.[3] Yet there may never have been any caesura, in part

---

[2] Tony Judt's writings in this vein continue to set the standard for pan-European accounts. His first venture was 'The Past Is Another Country: Myth and Memory in Postwar Europe', *Daedalus* 121:4 (1992), 83–118, rpt. in István Deák, Jan T. Gross and Tony Judt (eds), *The Politics of Retribution in Europe: World War II and Its Aftermath* (Princeton, NJ: Princeton University Press, 2000), epilogue; and in Jan-Werner Müller (ed.), *Memory and Power in Post-War Europe: Studies in the Presence of the Past* (Cambridge: Cambridge University Press, 2002), 157–83; more recently, see 'From the House of the Dead: On Modern European Memory', *New York Review* (6 October 2005), rpt. as Judt, *Postwar: A History of Europe since 1945* (London: William Heinemann, 2005), epilogue.

[3] J. M. Winter, *Sites of Memory, Sites of Mourning: The Great War in European Cultural History* (Cambridge: Cambridge University Press, 1995).

because the Holocaust was not widely perceived in the postwar moment, but above all because inherited approaches were so powerful.

In 1945, after all, Nazism had long since been viewed as a criminal regime. With the disappearance of its sympathizers and given the tragedy it caused—with tens of millions of soldiers gone, and over 10 million civilians and prisoners of war murdered—its image of criminality became even more lurid. Thus, the evil of what had transpired was the premise for all available positions that would survive World War II, including the clearly dominant ones of anti-facism and anti-totalitarianism. Though few may have realized self-consciously that, as Hannah Arendt famously put it, 'the problem of evil will become the fundamental question of postwar political life in Europe', perhaps the main problem was not that anyone would have disagreed. It was that they then diverged over *what sort* of evil had been involved, and what sort of 'good' should rise in response.[4]

The 'shock of the camps' did occur, but many other things were shocking, too. The Nazis had visited terrible depredations across the English Channel, notably during the fierce aerial bombardments with which the Luftwaffe pounded cities when Britain fought Germany almost alone in 1940. The Soviet Union had perhaps endured most, in terms of soldier and civilian deaths, including specific hecatombs like the three-year siege of Leningrad, which gave way to a culture of remembrance for decades. In every corner of Europe, there was a nearby Nazi outrage to mourn, including 'martyred villages' such as Lidice in Czechoslovakia or Oradour-sur-Glâne in France.[5] Across liberated Europe, intellectuals typically joined their nations in the construction of 'patriotic memory', in which locally felt death and destruction mattered most, and the Nazi regime deserved most opprobrium for causing it. Given the strong basis for such interpretations, it is surprising that other approaches to the Nazi past were ever possible.[6]

As to the camps, the shock occurred based on very partial understanding, and worked through ignorance of what later generations would consider most appalling about Nazi crime. American GIs liberated Buchenwald in April 1945, just as British soldiers were marching into Bergen-Belsen. But the German concentration camp network had been well known as the subject of propaganda and analysis since its inception, with Dachau, in 1933. The Jews, however, had largely died in the eastern precincts conquered by the Soviet Union, and the Nazis had in any event razed the most infernal sites, killing centres like Treblinka that left almost no survivors. The Red Army discovered Majdanek in 1944, it is true, but as at Auschwitz, which it liberated in January 1945, it found not a

[4] Cf. Judt, 'The "Problem of Evil" in Postwar Europe', *New York Review* (14 February 2008), citing H. Arendt, 'Nightmare and Flight', in *Essays in Understanding 1930–1954* (New York: Harcourt Brace, 1994), 134.

[5] See variously Malcolm Smith, *Britain and 1940: History, Myth, and Popular Memory* (New York: Routledge, 2000); Lisa Kirschenbaum, *The Legacy of the Siege of Leningrad, 1941–1995: Myth, Memories, and Monuments* (Cambridge: Cambridge University Press, 2006); Sarah Farmer, *Martyred Village: Commemorating the 1944 Massacre at Oradour-sur-Glâne* (Berkeley, CA: University of California Press, 1999).

[6] The best overall work is Pieter Lagrou, *The Legacy of Nazi Occupation: Patriotic Memory and National Recovery in Western Europe, 1945–1965* (Cambridge: Cambridge University Press, 2000).

'pure' killing centre, but a hybrid institution whose survivors were witnesses to a reality easily assimilable to pre-existing notions of a concentration camp. And while some Soviets were in possession of a more nuanced view of Nazi criminality—like some Soviet Jewish photographers, or like the Jewish writer Vasily Grossman, who visited the Treblinka site and tried to reconstruct what happened on this hastily planted new farmland—the victorious powers concurred on visions of universal victimhood which were useful for many postwar ideologies. The Nuremberg trials, for example, presented even Auschwitz this way: a place where all men had suffered.

Among intellectuals, visions of the concentration camp (not the killing centre) as the nether pole of Nazi crime ruled in touchstone works like German Eugen Kogon's *Der SS-Staat: Das System der deutschen Konzentrationslager* (1946) and Frenchman David Rousset's *L'univers concentrationnaire* (1945). As for the war itself, the reigning understanding of the camps was thus compatible with an inclusive theory of Nazi evil. Patriotic visions of suffering were sometimes purely local, but more often provided inflections to anti-fascism and anti-totalitarianism, which were by any measure the dominant rubrics transnationally for grasping what had gone wrong and forging a response.[7]

THE ANTI-FASCIST LEGACY

Consider anti-fascism first. It had crystallized in the interwar period; and World War II had been fought in some sense as an anti-fascist war, transforming ideological forces that had been felt to be strange bedfellows into commonsense and eventually victorious allies. Originating as a transnational ideology through the Comintern organization in the years immediately following Hitler's seizure of power in 1933, and crystallizing in the era of the Popular Front as the rationale for unity with 'bourgeois' forces, anti-fascism survived the confusing years of 1939–41 when Josef Stalin reached his famous accommodation with Hitler. Many intellectuals, notably literary and visual artists, had been swept up in the mid-1930s formation of transnational anti-fascism, which then provided the central ideology for engagement in the Spanish Civil War and later for what resistance and partisanship there was in occupied and collaborationist lands during World War II, as well as for many exiles abroad.[8]

---

[7] David Shneer, *Through Soviet Jewish Eyes: Photography, War, and the Holocaust* (New Brunswick, NJ: Rutgers University Press, 2010); Vasily Grossman, 'Treblinka', in *The Road* (New York: New York Review of Books, 2011); Samuel Moyn, 'In the Aftermath of Camps', in Frank Biess and Robert Moeller (eds), *Histories of the Aftermath: The Legacies of the Second World War in Europe* (New York: Berghahn Books, 2010), 49–64. On Nuremberg, see Donald Bloxham, *Genocide on Trial: War Crimes Trials and the Formation of Holocaust History and Memory* (Oxford: Oxford University Press, 2001).

[8] See e.g. Leonid Luks, *Entstehung der kommunistischen Faschismustheorie: die Auseinandersetzung der Komintern mit Faschismus und Nationalsozialismus, 1921–1935* (Stuttgart: Deutsche Verlags-Anstalt, 1984) and Anson Rabinbach, 'Paris, Capital of Anti-Fascism', in Warren Breckman et al. (eds), *The Modernist Imagination: Intellectual History and Critical Theory* (New York: Berghahn Books, 2009), 183–209.

According to official anti-fascist theory (not held in every particular by everyone, of course), Nazism counted as a version of fascism—sometimes called 'Hitler-fascism'—which in turn reflected the stage of monopoly capitalism in economic relationships. Political liberalism never had more than a temporary connection to capitalist economics, anti-fascism suggested, and the former simply proved dispensable when the preservation of the latter seemed at risk. While communism's attack on interwar liberal democracy had been in the service of a progressive history, the spectre of socialism it encouraged inevitably led to a dictatorial and terroristic backlash. Nazism, after the conspiracy that led to the Reichstag arson, was its worst form. Anti-fascism located the essence of the regimes it targeted in economic interests, a commitment that prompted less attention to ideological factors such as Hitler's feints in the direction of socialism or his constant Jew baiting.

In the new German Democratic Republic that arose under Walter Ulbricht after World War II, anti-fascism became the ideology of the new state, whose ideological credentials (unlike in the Soviet Union) depended completely on having supplanted Nazi rule; its intellectuals were trained to work within the ambit of anti-fascism to the end.[9] In the eastern lands that the Soviets had conquered (in some cases, reconquered) after years of either Nazi occupation or collaboration, and were soon to become Soviet satellites, versions of anti-fascism also ruled, and provided the template for postwar reckonings with the past.[10] Georgi Dimitrov, who had led the interwar Comintern that had developed classical anti-fascism, became premier of communist Bulgaria, for example.

In the critical years between the end of the war and the communist takeover of Czechoslovakia in February 1948, intellectuals of every stripe were caught up in the anti-fascist narrative of what had transpired in their lands, with Nazi rule following from a bourgeois despotism and national suffering whose justifiable sequel was communism.[11] In spite of a small modicum of attention to the paroxysm of death that had been visited on Hungarian Jewry in 1944, in the years after, the communist regime and its intellectuals made a generalized fascism (or specific 'Horthy-fascism', named after Admiral Miklós Horthy, regent of the country during most of the war), the crime that had been such a dangerous lure in the past.[12] The entire point of anti-fascism in its glory days had been pluralistic unity against a common enemy, and some flexibility remained essential to anti-fascism through the postwar period, in spite of recent allegations by François

---

[9] See Antonia Grunenberg, *Der Antifaschismus: ein deutsches Mythos* (Reinbek bei Hamburg: Rowohlt, 1993).

[10] See Déak et al. (eds), *The Politics of Retribution*, or Benjamin Frommer, *National Cleansing: Retribution against Collaborators in Postwar Czechoslovakia* (Cambridge: Cambridge University Press, 2005).

[11] Bradley F. Abrams, *The Struggle for the Soul of a Nation: Czech Culture and the Rise of Communism* (Lanham, MD: Rowman and Littlefield, 2004), esp. ch. 5.

[12] See Béla Zsolt, *Nine Suitcases: A Memoir* (London: Jonathan Cape, 2004), which originally appeared in a Hungarian newspaper in 1946–47.

Furet and others that its primary outcome was to dupe intellectuals into serving the cause of world communism.[13]

In the interregnum years between war's end and the Cold War's beginning, which was when anti-fascism reached its zenith in continental politics and perceptions of Nazi evil, considerable fluidity still reigned. In Poland, in spite of serious episodes of anti-Jewish violence, there were promising initiatives in integrating Holocaust memory in official memory, such as the state sponsorship of the crucial Centralna Żydowska Komisja Historyczna (Central Jewish Historical Commission).[14] Ilya Ehrenburg, a Soviet Jewish intellectual active in interwar anti-fascism, collaborated with Grossman on a now famous *Black Book*, whose different sections were meant to testify to 'the ruthless murder of Jews by German-Fascist invaders throughout the temporarily occupied regions of the Soviet Union and in the death camps of Poland during the war of 1941–45'. Their version of anti-fascism accommodated a vision of Nazism's worst crimes. Indeed, it is anachronistic to suppose that anti-fascist communists were less likely to acknowledge Nazism's special hatred for Jews than their one-time liberal democratic allies. Even though anti-fascism did not especially favour insight into Jewish victimhood, many—including many Jews—were drawn to communism in hopes it would provide the best antidote to Hitlerian anti-Semitism. As Jeffrey Herf has shown, an important exile community in Mexico City—the second capital for communist exiles from Germany after Moscow itself—promoted a version of anti-fascism that acknowledged the realities of Jewish victimhood.[15]

But such anti-fascist alternatives lost out in an era of Stalinist anti-Semitism, whether centrally imposed on the Eastern bloc or locally imitated.[16] The Soviets destroyed the plates of the *Black Book* on the brink of its publication, as the regime initiated its postwar anti-Semitism. East Germany promoted a version of heroic anti-fascism in which 'cosmopolitanism' was actively targeted for opprobrium, after Nazism's past destruction. When he spoke at the dedication of the memorial at the Sachsenhausen camp in 1961, Ulbricht remembered 'ten thousand martyrs from many countries, and of many different worldviews', but even this minor concession to pluralism did not disturb his conclusion that the main reason for and outcome of remembering Nazism was a communist future.[17] In the West, the struggle of canonical analysts of the brutality of the Nazis in concentration camps—including Kogon in Germany and Rousset in France—to rouse

---

[13] See François Furet, *The Passing of an Illusion: The Idea of Communism in the Twentieth Century* (Chicago, IL: University of Chicago Press, 1999).

[14] Compare Michael C. Steinlauf, *Bondage to the Dead: Poland and the Memory of the Holocaust* (Syracuse: Syracuse University Press, 1997), ch. 3 and Jan T. Gross, *Fear: Anti-Semitism in Poland after Auschwitz* (Princeton, NJ: Princeton University Press, 2006).

[15] Jeffrey Herf, *Divided Memory: The Nazi Past in the Two Germanys* (Cambridge, MA: Harvard University Press, 1997), ch. 2.

[16] Compare Amir Weiner, 'When Memory Counts: War, Genocide, and Postwar Soviet Jewry', in Weiner, ed., *Landscaping the Human Garden: Twentieth-Century Population Management in a Comparative Framework* (Stanford, CA: Stanford University Press, 2003), 167–88.

[17] Ilya Ehrenburg and Vasily Grossman (eds), *The Black Book: The Ruthless Murder of Jews by German-Fascist Invaders...* (New York: Holocaust Library, 1981); Herf, *Divided Memory*, 177.

consciousness among fellow anti-fascists about new camps under Soviet rule led to their stigmatization and denunciation, as communism or fellow-travelling anti-fascism triumphed. (Rousset founded a *Commission Internationale contre le régime concentrationnaire* uniting one-time internees, but even independent leftists like Rousset's one-time ally Jean-Paul Sartre rejected his activities.)

In spite of the extraordinary lift communism—and therefore anti-fascism—gained in the immediate aftermath of World War II in Western Europe, the Cold War soon supervened; and while communism remained strong and even culturally hegemonic at least in France and Italy, it was defanged politically. Italians, of course, had their own specificity, since they had had a self-denominated 'fascist' regime far longer than Germany, and one with considerable autonomy until the later 1930s. Especially after 1949, postwar Italian political culture, one might say, needed to be anti-Fascist more than anti-fascist. This Italian development—shared by communists with the Christian Democrats who ruled the country for decades—ironically meant the comparative marginalization of the National Socialist component of anti-fascism dominant elsewhere; and Italian intellectuals shaped a much less integral sense of themselves as post-Nazi society than Germans or even the French (including among communists in each case). Even as they perpetually faced leftist indictments of their failure to break sufficiently with the Fascist past, the Christian Democrats treated Benito Mussolini's reign as a 'lesser evil' compared to Nazi racism but also the communism that now threatened locally. Yet until a very recent *crisi dell'antifascismo*, the Christian Democrats have been anti-Fascist too.[18] Elsewhere, the transnational implications of anti-fascism stood out far more strongly. In Greece, a bloody civil war in the 1940s turned on whether anti-fascism or anti-totalitarianism should provide the true framework for replacing Nazi occupation. As the Cold War crystallized there and everywhere else, the hegemony of anti-fascism in the East was not shared in the West, which left an opening for the construction of an important anti-totalitarian tendency.

THE ANTI-TOTALITARIAN ALTERNATIVE

Compared to anti-fascism, anti-totalitarianism has proved much more durable as a vision, not least in recent admiration for those intellectuals who resisted or at least later stigmatized Nazism while sparing no criticism of the new Soviet foe. However, far from forming a coherent tradition, anti-totalitarian interpretations of Nazism were quite diverse, and it was not obvious in the beginning whether or how it could take account of the disproportionate victimhood of Jews under Nazi rule. In its original versions,

---

[18] Ruth Ben-Ghiat, 'A Lesser Evil? Italian Fascism in/and the Totalitarian Equation', in Helmut Dubiel and Gabriel Motzkin (eds), *The Lesser Evil: Moral Approaches to Genocide Practices* (New York: Routledge, 2004), 137–53; Sergio Luzzatto, *La crisi dell'antifascismo* (Turin: Einaudi, 2004).

indeed, anti-totalitarianism did not focus on this inconvenient fact, any more than had anti-fascism.

As with anti-fascism, the background of anti-totalitarianism mattered. It had been invented first by Catholic intellectuals, who eventually had their own emigration that would spread it widely. Benito Mussolini's house philosopher Giovanni Gentile had once restored 'totalitarian' as an honorific label for the Italian regime from socialists; but 'mature' totalitarianism theory evolved when European Catholics tried to make it again a critical term after Carl Schmitt praised the breakthrough to the 'total state'. In fact, anti-totalitarianism as a theory, grouping Bolshevism and Nazism under the same rubric, surged in the mid-1930s in direct response to the crystallization of the Popular Front under anti-fascist auspices. By the postwar epoch, 'totalitarianism' functioned, thanks at first to these Catholics, to stigmatize Nazi Germany as a disaster much more similar to the Soviet Union than was the original Italian avatar of the syndrome.[19]

In the first version of the theory, that Nazism and Stalinism were equally 'statist' results of a disastrous modern turn can be traced to various sources, but especially to secularism. Nazism was not a 'stage' in modernity, inevitable as monopoly capitalism reached crisis, and promising some brighter future, but the inevitable outcome of modern delusions about human self-sufficiency. Such theories indeed sometimes insisted that by deifying race or state, totalitarianism's atheism or paganism masked its true status as heresies: they were political or 'secular' religions. In the beginning, in the hands of ideological pioneers like Waldemar Gurian (Schmitt's ex-disciple) and Jacques Maritain, liberal democracy was by no means either the necessary basis or the necessary outcome of the anti-totalitarian perspective. In fact, liberalism with its atomistic individualism and democracy with it slavery-prone masses were part of the syndrome that had led to totalitarianism. But if the original, typically Catholic anti-totalitarians were most likely to recommend corporatist solutions against the Nazi state (including 'Austro-fascism'), or pine for some personalist-cum-communitarian utopia, World War II left the theorization of Nazism as part of a totalitarian syndrome open for appropriation by a wider range of analysts.

If anti-fascists confused by the Hitler–Stalin pact faced the problem of explaining it away ever after, anti-totalitarians who had treated that event as a welcome vindication of their theory of Nazism were then forced to downplay the brute fact of the wartime alliance. After all, one 'totalitarian' power had now proved most crucial for putting down the other. The Cold War—which anti-totalitarians earnestly promoted as an alternative to nerve-wracking anti-fascist compromises during the war—saved them. Its Christian antecedents helped make anti-tolitarianism the ideological backbone not least for transatlantic Christianity and the usually Catholic-led Christian Democracy in Western European countries, as well as the first versions of so-called federalist thought

---

[19] I follow here James Chappel's forthcoming Columbia University dissertation; compare, for the thesis of left-wing sources of totalitarianism theory, Rabinbach, 'Moments of Totalitarianism', *History and Theory* 45 (2006), 72–100; or Enzo Traverso, *Le Totalitarisme: Le XXème siècle en débat* (Paris: Seuil, 2001).

regionally—all three of which had many intellectual defenders. But anti-totalitarianism also beckoned the unclassifiable and now American thinker Arendt (Gurian's friend) and a huge set of Cold War liberals in Western Europe such as Raymond Aron, Isaiah Berlin, Friedrich Hayek, or Karl Popper.[20] All the same, and much as with anti-fascism, a variety of different positions were available within a generally anti-totalitarian world view, even if in the long run Cold War liberalism as the sole alternative to totalitarianism proved to be theoretically the most prestigious among them.

Even the secular-minded among postwar anti-totalitarians inherited a worry that Nazism might have followed from 'modernity' run amok. Decades before modernity was blamed for the Holocaust, it was regularly made the ultimate culprit for Nazism's rise. Roughly, where anti-fascism as an alternative to Nazism had a strong democratic, emancipatory, and even populist streak—one historian has even claimed that the creation of British social democracy under the Labour Party in the postwar age occurred in something similar to an anti-fascist spirit—anti-totalitarians concurred in ranking the hypertrophic modern state first among all evils, especially when it promised collective emancipation and social protection. Democracy itself seemed the source of totalitarianism, unless hemmed in by liberalism. Jacob Talmon, a Central European who ended in Israel, developed these views during a sojourn in Britain, whose 'indigenous' liberalism now owes an astonishing part of its theoretical renown as the charm to use to stave off Nazism and other forms of totalitarianism to one-time émigrés.[21]

For obvious reasons, anti-totalitarian intellectuals tended to be much more pro-American than were anti-fascists, with the United States—sometimes explicitly viewed as Britain's heir in mastering democracy through liberalism—providing the true or at least necessary historical alternative to Nazi barbarity. Such anti-totalitarians founded and promoted the agenda of the American sponsored cultural Cold War, notably the Congress for Cultural Freedom.[22] Nevertheless, anti-totalitarianism accommodated left-wing and dissident visions—its pantheon now most frequently includes Albert Camus, Arthur Koestler, Czeslaw Milosz, and George Orwell along with the later Grossman and Rousset—whose common rejection of Nazism and communism did not always take the limitation on the state at the core of anti-totalitarianism all the way to classical liberalism, either political or economic. Camus's later novels and essays unforgettably staged the anti-totalitarian fear that the threat of despotism—especially when driven by rebellious tendencies of the modern age—remained ever present.

[20] See Müller, 'Fear and Freedom: On "Cold War Liberalism"', *European Journal of Political Theory* 7:1 (2008), 45–64.

[21] Geoff Eley, 'Legacies of Antifascism: Forging Democracy in Postwar Europe', *New German Critique* 67 (1996), 73–100. For the much broader interwar debate about fascism in Britain, prior to the crystallization of Cold War liberalism, see Nigel Copsey and Andrzej Olechnowicz (eds), *Varieties of Anti-Fascism: Britain in the Interwar Period* (New York: Palgrave Macmillan, 2010).

[22] See e.g. Pierre Grémion, *Intelligence de l'anticommunisme: Le Congrès pour la liberté de la culture à Paris (1950–1975)* (Paris: Fayard, 1995); or Giles Scott-Smith, *The Politics of Apolitical Culture: The Congress for Cultural Freedom, the CIA, and Postwar American Hegemony* (New York: Routledge, 2002).

THE WEST GERMAN CONFLICT

In the zones of Germany unoccupied by the Soviets, and in the Federal Republic begin-ning in 1949, there was no denying the past from the beginning, even if it was national aggression, not Jew killing, that initially seemed worst about Nazi designs. There was a 'great debate' about what had occurred, with theories of Nazi evil in contention.[23] Among the ruins, and in spite of considerable self-pity given the fierce bombings at the end of the war and violent expulsion of ethnic Germans from the East immediately after it, Karl Jaspers examined the difficulties of collective guilt; and conservative historian and con-fused nationalist Friedrich Meinecke proposed to found cultural institutes recalling the good parts of German history to counteract international memories of the recent past.[24] In the early years especially, some proposed anti-fascist interpretations of Nazism and radical cures to the malady—including Christians on the left, such as Walter Dirks. But if the 'stigma' of Nazism was, in this early stage, obvious and inexpiable, it is clear that conservative anti-totalitarianism quickly got the upper hand as a ritually organized response to it.[25]

It may have been surprising that Christianity, even Christian anti-totalitarianism, could enjoy a massive renaissance in the immediate postwar years, given the active and tacit support that many Christians had lent Nazism in Germany and across the conti-nent.[26] And given the congenital allergy of anti-totalitarianism to democracy, it might have seemed an uncertain basis for republicanization. But in its insistence that correc-tion against the far right had to be done without incurring a disaster of the far left, the German centre-right won, participating in a decades-long Christian Democratic hegemony that strongly marked Western Europe as a whole. In a version of patriotic memory, Christians constructed a cult of resistance, one that turned around the churches in general, or heroic individuals. These included hagiographies in which national and confessional memory could intersect, as the enormous postwar interest in Dietrich Bonhoeffer or Martin Niemöller in Germany illustrates.

Where anti-fascists tended to stigmatize bankrupt German traditions such as Prussianism and militarism, anti-totalitarians were the ones who worried that such

---

[23] Jean Solchany, *Comprendre le nazisme dans l' Allemagne des années zéro (1945–1949)* (Paris: Presses Universitaires de France, 1997), part 1, ch. 2.

[24] Karl Jaspers, *The Question of German Guilt* (New York: Dial Press, 1948); Friedrich Meinecke, *The German Catastrophe: Reflections and Recollections* (Cambridge, MA: Harvard University Press, 1950).

[25] A. Dirk Moses, 'Sacrifice and Stigma in the Federal Republic of Germany', *History & Memory* 19:2 (2007), 139–80. See also Robert Moeller, *War Stories: The Search for the Usable Past in the Federal Republic of Germany* (Berkeley, CA: University of California Press, 2001).

[26] See Damian von Melis, '"Strengthened and Purified through Ordeal by Fire": Ecclesiastical Triumphalism in the Ruins', in Richard Bessel and Dirk Schumann (eds), *Life after Death: Approaches to a Cultural and Social History of Europe in the 1940s and 1950s* (Cambridge: Cambridge University Press, 2003), 231–41.

callow scapegoating ignored the fact that Nazism arose from modern pathology.[27] Even for many German intellectuals who had long since turned their backs on Christianity, modern godlessness now seemed the source of error. 'After the war', Jerry Z. Muller writes,

> when the terms *conservative* and *national* were discredited by virtue of their association with National Socialism, *Christian* provided a banner under which a broad portion of the centre-right could organize politically... And at a time when the rest of Europe held all things German in disrepute, Christianity served as a cultural bridge to Western Europe.[28]

The roots of Nazism in a perceived crisis of secularism stimulated an orientalist anti-totaliarianism in which the Christianity of 'the West' (*Abendland*) proved the last best hope against a democratic wildfire that had sparked the raging inferno of Nazism and now world communism.[29]

To be sure, there were some whose earlier Nazi temptations—most prominently Martin Heidegger and Carl Schmitt—left them, even when their affiliations had been brief, less than eager to moralize about their mistakes and thus about Nazism's evil. Infamously, Heidegger in the postwar era opined that Nazism had gone wrong but its 'inner truth and greatness' made it somehow still pertinent, at least in its basic riposte to a technology continuing to run wild.[30] Similarly, conservative circles around Heidegger and Schmitt—and Ernst Jünger, who, like many others in a late-breaking German resistance, had given up on National Socialism in favour of conservative-aristocratic visions—kept their distance from the new Federal Republic, even or especially when they were willing to acknowledge the disaster of the Nazi past.[31]

Surely not standard anti-fascists—any more than, in his anxiety about modernity, Heidegger ever came around to anti-totalitarianism—the members of the so-called Frankfurt school verged on worrying about modernity and Nazism's sources in it that was not familiar in leftist traditions up until then. Its original, interwar schemas were a highly complex version of anti-fascism, best known in Franz Neumann's classic work *Behemoth: The Structure and Practice of National-Socialism* (1942).[32] Theodor W. Adorno and Max Horkheimer—long the school's leading members, both of whom returned to

---

[27] Solchany, 'Vom Antimodernismus zum Antitotalitarismus: Konservative Interpretationen des Nationalsozialismus in Deutschland 1945–1949', *Vierteljahrshefte für Zeitgeschichte* 44:3 (1996), 373–94.

[28] Jerry Z. Muller, *The Other God that Failed: Hans Freyer and the Deradicalization of German Conservatism* (Princeton, NJ: Princeton University Press, 1987), 336.

[29] Axel Schildt, *Zwischen Abendland und Amerika: Studien zur westdeutschen Ideenlandschaft der 50er Jahre* (Munich: R. Oldenbourg, 1999).

[30] Martin Heidegger, *Introduction to Metaphysics* (New Haven, CT: Yale University Press, 2000), 213.

[31] See Daniel Morat, *Von der Tat zur Gelassenheit: Konservatives Denken bei Martin Heidegger, Ernst Jünger und Friedrich Georg Jünger 1920–1960* (Göttingen: Wallstein, 2007). On Schmitt's circles, see e.g. Jan-Werner Müller, *A Dangerous Mind: Carl Schmitt and Post-War European Thought* (New Haven, CT: Yale University Press, 2003).

[32] Cf. Michael Wilson, *Der Institut für Sozialforschung und seine Fascismusanalysen* (Frankfurt/M: Campus, 1982).

Germany to teach after the war—offered a version of 'Western Marxism' that surely avoided the simplicities of a vulgar anti-fascism, tracing Nazism to the continuing economic superintendence of the bourgeoisie, now frighteningly restored in an insufficiently democratized West German state. But if they were eventually better than other anti-fascists at acknowledging the Jewish victimhood at Nazi hands that 'Holocaust memory' would make so salient, Adorno, especially, did so only in connection with a depressing picture of the Enlightenment's dialectic that traced Nazi barbarism to reason's work, with no clear dialectical reversal into emancipation in the offing.[33]

All the same, some memory of the anti-fascist claim that the advent of Nazism followed from insufficient modernization, and proved the need for more, remains in Adorno's critique of the postwar conservative restoration in his country. 'National Socialism lives on', he wrote in 1959. 'I consider the continued existence of National Socialism *within* democracy potentially more threatening than the continued existence of fascist tendencies *against* democracy.'[34] And whether in the forms offered by the student intellectuals who rediscovered the Frankfurt school, or in its scion Jürgen Habermas's more guarded versions, in the 1960s and 1970s such charges became very familiar.[35] In the 1960s and 1970s, anti-fascism in many creative new versions seized the foreground in West German culture as lenses through which to interpret Nazism; in an idiosyncratic revival of the Frankfurt School's own interwar integration of psychoanalysis as a tool for understanding domination, for example, Klaus Theweleit offered a brilliant interpretation of the 'male fantasies' on which fascism intrapsychically depended.[36]

After a brief dominance of anti-totalitarianism, anti-fascism also had a revival in the scholarly circles of professional historians, where the roots and nature of National Socialism were never new topics in the postwar age. Figures like Gerhard Ritter, charged with refounding the often superb prior traditions of historical scholarship after their Nazi pollution, willingly signed on in the immediate postwar years to Christian anti-totalitarianism. A member of the religious and conservative resistance towards the end of the regime, Ritter hated democracy and indeed blamed Hitler for it, and thus was desperate for the sequel to it to be some sort of conservative moral reintegration that would wholly reject Nazism as one form of menacing totalitarianism.

---

[33] Consider T.W. Adorno and Max Horkheimer, *Dialectic of Enlightenment* (Stanford, CA: Stanford University Press, 2002); Martin Jay, 'The Jews and the Frankfurt School: Critical Theory's Analysis of Antisemitism', in *Permanent Exiles: Essays on the Intellectual Migration from Germany to America* (New York: Columbia University Press, 1986), 90–100.

[34] Adorno, 'What Does Coming to Terms with the Past Mean?', in Geoffrey Hartman (ed.), *Bitburg in Moral and Political Perspective* (Bloomington, IN: Indiana University Press, 1986), 115.

[35] See A. Dirk Moses, *German Intellectuals and the Nazi Past* (Cambridge: Cambridge University Press, 2007) which concentrates on this era; compare Belinda Davis, 'New Leftists and West Germany: Fascism, Violence, and the Public Sphere, 1967–1974', in Philipp Gassert and Alan Steinweis (eds), *Coping with the Nazi Past: West German Debates on Nazism and Generational Conflict, 1955–1975* (New York: Berghahn Books, 2006), 210–37.

[36] See Klaus Theweleit, *Male Fantasies*, 2 vols (Minneapolis, MN: University of Minnesota Press, 1987–89).

As such, Nazism had in fact been a deviation from German national traditions, he insisted; but unlike many other votaries of the 'Christian West' in German lands, Ritter lionized the moral community of the trans-Atlantic Christian tradition, with its emphases on dignity and rights, as the most plausible alternative to the recrudescence of another totalitarian state in the future—especially given the one across the new East German border. Though part Jewish, and a forced exile at the University of Chicago during the war, Hans Rothfels returned and offered his own revival of conservative nationalism as a better version of German traditions, which Nazism betrayed. The original historiographical response to Nazism was thus a nationalist one, albeit open in new ways to the alliances suggested by transnational Cold War politics (and, often, transnational religion).[37]

Only the appearance of Ernst Nolte's *Three Faces of Fascism* (*Der Faschismus in seiner Epoche*, 1963), which offered an anti-fascist reading of Nazism by grouping it with the Action Française and Italian Fascism, and including much emphasis on its anti-Semitism, broke the academic hegemony of anti-totalitarianism. True, Fritz Fischer, a former Nazi himself, had already suggested two years earlier in his famous *Germany's Aims in the First World War* (*Griff nach der Weltmacht*, 1961) that the nationalist reclamation of German traditions, with the Nazi disaster presented as a recent, exiguous deviation from them, could not work. But unlike Nolte, Fischer concentrated on World War I, so interfered only indirectly with the anti-totalitarian historiographical consensus about Hitler's regime itself. But he did leave its apologetic interpretations of the Nazi era as mere *Betriebsunfall* (accident in the factory) difficult to sustain.[38]

In the wake of Nolte's powerful but idiosyncratic reading, older and explicitly left-wing versions of anti-fascism could be revived in the West German academy as a *Sonderweg* account of Nazism triumphed. In this view, Nazism was not 'modern' except insofar as it proved the outrageous symptom of a false modernization. This approach suggested that it had been the failure to develop a historical basis for democracy that led to fascism in Germany—where, unlike in Western polities, bourgeois elites were insufficiently formed before the advent of mass politics. Scholars close to Habermas, such as Hans-Ulrich Wehler who founded the pre-eminent 'Bielefeld' school of historians, developed this approach in very potent ways.[39] In the brief but broad revival of *Fascismustheorie* in the years of student rebellion and thereafter, it became hard to sustain the anti-totalitarian principle on which the Federal Republic had grown up and which many of its intellectuals had supported. Further, given the rise of Holocaust

---

[37] On Ritter, see S. Moyn, 'The First Historian of Human Rights', *American Historical Review* 116:1 (2011), 58–79; Jan Eckel, 'Hans Rothfels: An Intellectual Biography in the Age of Extremes', *Journal of Contemporary History* 42:3 (2007), 421–46. More generally, see such works as Winfried Schulze, *Deutsche Geschichtswissenschaft nach 1945* (Munich: Deutscher Taschenbuch Verlag, 1989).

[38] John A. Moses, *The Politics of Illusion: The Fischer Controversy in German Historiography* (London: Prior, 1975).

[39] See e.g. Hans-Ulrich Wehler, *Modernisierungstheorie und Geschichte* (Göttingen: Vandenhoeck und Ruprecht, 1975).

scholarship in the same years, it became clear that a modified anti-fascist approach could husband attention to the plight of the Jews in European history as a whole, and in the dark years of the Holocaust itself—something the original versions of anti-fascism and anti-totalitarianism alike had by and large neglected.

FRENCH INTELLECTUALS BETWEEN RESISTANCE AND HOLOCAUST MEMORY

If, for the Germans, there was no way to deny national implication in the Nazi past, however inadequate their reckoning with it now seems, the French scene provides a convenient proxy to examine intellectuals for whom an initial myth of 'resistance' took pride of place. Yet this substantial difference did not substantially alter the choice between anti-fascism and anti-totalitarianism.

Among the French, a myth of resistance quickly crystallized. Those who could or would not find some way to affiliate with it were quickly purged or were blackballed. Sartre set the tone for anti-fascism, which—though he had largely missed out on it during its interwar glory days—he updated and incorporated into the emerging politics of existentialism in the postwar moment. Sartre's notion of intellectual *engagement* reposed essentially on an anti-fascist theory of the writer as the beacon of solidaristic humanity united against barbarism and for the sake of progress. The intellectual, to be sure, could neither vigorously advance nor—as Julien Benda's interwar pamphlet had worried—treasonously betray eternal values, since there were no such things. But he was called upon to affiliate with specific campaigns for freedom, with the Resistance of the immediate past now giving way to new tasks. As Stefan Collini has pointed out, the *engagement* of the French intellectual tradition had no parallel elsewhere; it would certainly be hard to organize an account of British 'intellectuals' (if indeed there have been any) in which the Resistance experience had a comparable pride of place. Yet however existentialized and localized, Sartre's basic attitudes towards the Nazi past were anti-fascist. Similarly, in the first issue of *Les temps modernes*, the classic journal he co-founded with Sartre, fellow existentialist Maurice Merleau-Ponty entitled his contribution: 'The War Took Place'. He meant that Nazism instructed French intellectuals that there was no alternative to the solidaristic engagement against continuing violations.[40]

---

[40] See e.g. Alice Kaplan, *The Collaborator: The Trial and Execution of Robert Brasillach* (Chicago, IL: University of Chicago Press, 2000); cf. Philip Watts, *Allegories of the Purge: How Postwar Literature Responded to the Postwar Trials of Writers and Intellectuals in France* (Stanford, CA: Stanford University Press, 1998); Stefan Collini, *Absent Minds: Intellectuals in Britain* (Oxford: Oxford University Press, 2006); Maurice Merleau-Ponty, 'The War took Place', in *Sense and Nonsense* (Evanston, IL: Northwestern University Press, 1964), 144.

The French case shows that—as elsewhere in the interregnum years between World and Cold War—there was no inevitability to the anti-fascist expulsion of Jewish victim-hood from perception and memory. There may be an argument that Sartre's anti-fascism paid heed to the Jewish question early and relatively often, at least compared to the often pitiless current accounts of how problematic his attempts to be 'philosemitic' were. Sartre's interwar story 'The Childhood of a Leader' targeted rightist personality cults, with rare attention to the special attraction to and repulsion from Jews in fascist politics; while his classic *Antisemite and Jew*, largely drafted in late 1944 when only Majdanek was known, denounced it as a Jewish (and Polish) killing site. In his article, Merleau-Ponty could even write as follows:

> German anti-semitism makes us face a truth we did not know in 1939. We did not think there were Jews or Germans but only men, or even consciousnesses...[I]f men are one day to be human to one another and the relations between conscious-nesses are to become transparent...this will be in a society in which past traumas have been wiped out and the conditions of an effective liberty have from the first been realized.

It is thus certainly true that for both anti-fascist existentialists, if what the Jews had suf-fered was unique, the outcome was to be a reconstructed society beyond particular identities.[41]

Yet even so, it is worth recording that neither the anti-totalitarianism of Aron nor that of Camus paid comparable attention to the Jewish question, even in ways that might now seem problematic. Even before the onset of the Cold War, and certainly after, the former's politics made the Soviet Union (and domestic avatars) the premier enemy. The latter's sometimes melodramatic attempts to square a vestigial leftism with a crystallizing anti-totalitarian morality led him, before his untimely death in 1960, to excuse French crimes in Algeria even as other notable intellectuals like Pierre Vidal-Naquet likened them to Gestapo tactics (only a tiny and unrepresentative few agreed with Aimé Césaire in viewing concern for the hostility of Nazism and its Holocaust as an integral part of anti-colonialism).[42] Indeed, Nazism remained ever less central to French anti-totalitarians as time passed. The thought of Emmanuel Levinas, a Lithuanian Jew who emigrated to France between the wars, had its origins in the new phenomen-ology and in his response to his teacher Heidegger's shocking Nazi affiliation. It may be true that Levinas updated phenomenology to its now famous version as an anti-totalitarian morality in response to the Holocaust. But it is also true that for decades no one cared. At first, then, anti-totalitarianism seemed no better (and perhaps worse)

[41] Merleau-Ponty, 'The War took Place', 144. For a less forgiving account of Sartre, see Jonathan Judaken, *Jean-Paul Sartre and the Jewish Question: Anti-antisemitism and the Politics of the French Intellectual* (Lincoln, NE: University of Nebraska Press, 2006).

[42] See e.g. David Carroll, *Albert Camus the Algerian: Colonialism, Terrorism, Justice* (New York: Columbia University Press, 2007) and Michael Rothberg, *Multidirectional Memory: Remembering the Holocaust in the Age of Decolonization* (Stanford, CA: Stanford University Press, 2009).

positioned at the start to organize opposition to Nazism around what now seem its worst crimes. [43]

In spite of this initial picture, however, in the long view anti-fascism expelled the possibility of Holocaust memory. Just as in the East, Stalin made it deeply anti-Semitic, in the West Holocaust memory emerged over anti-fascist opposition. It may have been on the right, not the left, and as part of an anti-totalitarian view, that the pioneering acceptance of the singularity of Nazi purposes in exterminating Jews occurred. The Catholic novelist and Gaullist François Mauriac increased his explicit condemnation of Nazi Jew-killing in the 1960s, while continuing to view the 'Christian West' as bystander to the crime and the only true alternative to it. Simone de Beauvoir, Sartre's consort, wrote an anti-fascist preface to journalist Jean-François Steiner's *Treblinka* in 1966—the best-selling potboiler put the proper name in his title in circulation across the Western world—but Rousset decried the perversion to anti-fascism of singling out disproportionate Jewish victimhood, even as Mauriac and other anti-totalitarian conservatives rallied around Steiner for recalling the 'Judeo-Christian' truths that alone could stave off barbarism past, present, and future.[44]

Telling this still too unfamiliar story about conservatism and Holocaust memory in the future will depend on the essential point that there was no necessary connection between changes in the understanding of Nazi criminality in France (or anywhere else) and the rise of new insights into local collaboration; at least, conflating the two phenomena risks confusion. But the more familiar story did eventually become the main one. What historian Henry Rousso dubbed the 'Vichy syndrome', in which awareness of French collusion with Nazi designs rose (spectacularly with the publication of Robert O. Paxton's *Vichy France* in 1972), helped set a pattern for all countries. It turned out that many elites—including intellectual elites—had established the myth of heroic resistance as an alternative to reckoning with the past. As a result, bitter disputes swirled around a huge number of figures. For instance Emmanuel Mounier, having been the 'personalist' theoretician viewed as the standard bearer of left Catholic *Esprit* in the postwar years, found his memory besieged by publicists like Bernard-Henry Lévy and Zeev Sternhell who spread allegations of fascistic attitudes and Vichy-era entanglements without limits. In this context, what it meant to be against Nazism had to be rethought: it turned out that few had been so when it mattered. Accordingly, earlier myths of the clarity of opposition gave way to a widespread sense of degrees of implication in the horror, from which no clean escape was possible.[45]

---

[43] See Samuel Moyn, *Origins of the Other: Emmanuel Levinas between Revelation and Ethics* (Ithaca, NY: Cornell University Press, 2005), ch. 5. For Levinas's admiration for Grossman on anti-totalitarian grounds, see Michael L. Morgan, *Discovering Levinas* (Cambridge: Cambridge University Press, 2008), ch. 1.

[44] See Nathan Bracher, *Though the Past Darkly: History and Memory in François Mauriac's 'Bloc-Notes'* (Washington, DC: Catholic University of America Press, 2004); and Samuel Moyn, *A Holocaust Controversy: The Treblinka Affair in Postwar France* (Waltham, MA: Brandeis University Press, 2005).

[45] Henry Rousso, *The Vichy Syndrome: History and Memory in France since 1944* (Cambridge, MA: Harvard University Press, 1991).

Holocaust Memory and the Legacy
of the Frameworks

The rise of Holocaust consciousness put considerable pressure on inherited frameworks; local collaboration especially came to the fore in national memory culture and in intellectual networks.[46] Just as Holocaust memory made the prescriptive high ground harder to mount, given glaring evidence of pervasive collusion with the Nazi new order, it also put pressure on the descriptive premises of anti-fascism and anti-totalitarianism alike. The newly recalled extremity of the Nazi project meant it was less easy to move from opposition to it to opposition to broader syndromes, whether 'fascistic' or 'totalitarian'. Nevertheless, in the long run both founding views of interpreting Nazism were to survive, though perhaps at the price of reinvention. The 'unique' status of the Holocaust never went far enough to pre-empt comparative inquiry into the Nazis or presentist interpretations in which their evil survived in new forms to be combated.

This is not the place to explore the rise of Holocaust consciousness, of course. In time, Holocaust memory will probably need to be seen as an event related to anti-totalitarianism rather than a departure from it; or at least, that its original sites were in Cold War Western Europe, along with the United States in the same era. After the complications of the 1940s and the consolidation of a universalizing anti-fascism, memory of the particular fate of the Jews remained impossible to express publicly in communist lands—until the fall of the Soviet Union forced its rapid incorporation when Western memorial cultures triumphed, just as did its political and economic models. There, several of the formerly communist states had been the killing fields, notably Poland and Ukraine, while in Hungary the events of 1944 cried out for reintegration in national memory.

In the former Soviet bloc, the rude awakening that Holocaust memory involved after the collapse of anti-fascist officialdom meant the painful discovery of considerable local malfeasance, as debates around the Polish translation of Jan Gross's *Neighbors*—which documented an extraordinary episode of Jew-killing by Poles after the Nazi invasion had given them the opportunity—show.[47] There was no less evasion of hard truths in the East than there had been in the West when Holocaust memory was forged, and intellectuals continued to be tempted by a patriotic version of memory, stressing the Nazi savagery towards their nation rather than the Jews within it. All the same, the legitimacy

---

[46] Some valuable general works on European Holocaust memory not hitherto cited include Jeffrey Alexander et al., *Remembering the Holocaust: A Debate* (New York: Oxford University Press, 2009), Annette Wieviorka, *The Era of the Witness* (Ithaca, NY: Cornell University Press, 2006), and Winter, 'Notes on the Memory Boom: War, Remembrance, and the Uses of the Past', in Duncan Bell, ed., *Memory, Trauma and World Politics: Reflections on the Relationship Between Past and Present* (New York: Palgrave Macmillan, 2006), 54–73.

[47] See e.g. Antony Polonsky and Joanna B. Michlic (eds), *The Neighbors Respond: The Controversy over the Jedwabne Massacre in Poland* (Princeton, NJ: Princeton University Press, 2003).

and even hegemony of Holocaust memory was rapidly established. In 2001, Italy set its Holocaust Remembrance Day on the Europe-wide commemoration date of 27 January, when the Soviets had liberated faraway Auschwitz, and drew criticism for thereby evading Italian collusion in the final solution. Meanwhile, Hungary began a similar practice in the same year, but chose 16 April to remember the past, the date when the local ghettoization of Hungary's Jews had begun.[48]

With the disintegration of the communist regimes that had made it state-sanctioned, along with the decline of utopian energies associated with the student movements, anti-fascism suffered the final indignity of the hollowing out of social democracy, which might otherwise have provided a refuge. Correspondingly, together with the backlash against the anti-fascist renaissance of the 1960s and 1970s, the victory of liberal democracy in the Cold War gave anti-totalitarianism an extraordinary new lease on life; it remains dominant albeit in altered form to the present day, to the point of defining not only European memory, but the most prominent interpretations of it.

The historiography of the relationship of intellectuals to Nazism in its own time typically takes the form of indictment of 'reckless minds' who are 'seduced by unreason' into scandalous collusion with barbarism. Meanwhile, the historiography of the relationship of intellectuals to Nazism after the fact usually targets a series of irresponsible denials of the past that finally gave way to Holocaust memory, stressing the need for moral vigilance against totalitarian monsters who perpetually haunt the frontiers of the liberal order. Tony Judt's writings about European memory, or those of the so-called 'new philosophers' in France, have epitomized such a position. Evidently, such interpretations have a kernel of truth, but they disguise how integral anti-totalitarianism has always been to postwar European memory—and understate how much anti-totalitarianism itself had to change to incorporate Holocaust themes.[49]

To be sure, anti-fascism was too powerful, and had too many versions, to disappear entirely. Yet with the disappearance of its social constituencies, it often finds itself exiled to far left circles, and transformed by other currents. A prominent example of an intellectual who has inherited a dose of anti-fascism, but preserved it in association with other impulses, is Italian theorist Giorgio Agamben. In his much discussed *Remnants of Auschwitz*, Agamben interprets (or more accurately, interprets fellow Italian Primo Levi's interpreting) the 'gray zone' of Nazi camp life. In fact, however, Agamben's position incorporates anti-fascist elements both descriptively and morally.

Descriptively, Agamben reverts to Rousset's anti-fascist vision of a *univers concentrationnaire*, in which Auschwitz is a forum for concentration camp life, rather than one of Jewish death as such or directly. Agamben uses Levi to focus on the figure from survivor

[48]   Compare Robert S. C. Gordon, 'The Holocaust in Italian Collective Memory: Il giorno della memoria, 27 January 2001', *Modern Italy* 11:2 (2006), 167–88 and Paul A. Hanebrink, 'The Politics of Holocaust Memory in Hungary', in John-Paul Himka and Joanna Michlic (eds), *Bringing the Dark Past to Light: The Reception of the Holocaust in Post-communist Europe* (forthcoming).

[49]   Mark Lilla, *The Reckless Mind: Intellectuals and Politics* (New York: New York Review of Books, 2001); Richard Wolin, *The Seduction of Unreason: The Intellectual Romance with Fascism from Nietzsche to Postmodernism* (Princeton, NJ: Princeton University Press, 2006).

accounts of the *Muselmann*—the 'Muslim' figure, chosen no doubt by Agamben for emphasis for contemporary political reasons. This figure, whose life could no longer be distinguished from death, was driven for many camp witnesses beyond the boundaries of humanity. Absent from Agamben's vision of 'the camps' is any notion of killing centres where Jews were not even able to spend the night before they were immediately put to death. For Agamben, instead, the *Muselmann* is the central figure, and he goes so far as to say that 'the Jews knew that they would not die at Auschwitz as Jews', but rather as 'Muslims', figures to whom in principle all people could find themselves reduced. (In actual fact, Jews had no monopoly on this sort of victimhood.) As with Rousset and even Hannah Arendt, the effect of Agamben's comparatively homogenizing interpretation of Nazi criminality is to displace analysis from the immediate death that most Jews suffered upon entry into death camps, to the terrible but real survival that those allowed to live in concentration camps were granted—even if such survival was no more real or lasting than the pathetic *Muselmann* could claim.[50]

In his moral call for solidarity against camps, Agamben also inherits a dose of anti-fascism. Agamben's sources are various, to be sure. It is more in the spirit of anti-totalitarianism—and his master Heidegger—that Agamben is tempted to see Auschwitz as the symbol of modernity in crisis. Further, Agamben's favoured inspirations include so-called postmodern ones in which post-humanist figures in the French philosophical tradition often elevated Jews suffering under the Nazis to figures of general significance, while reaching neither the universalism of leftist anti-fascism nor that of liberal anti-totalitarianism. All the same, it is more in the spirit of historic anti-fascism that camps past and present remain a warning in Agamben's view, preparing some sequel that must bring justice to all as compensation for past wrongs. This is so even if the current (indeed all-pervasive) horror of 'the camps' leaves Agamben as vague about what sort of solidaristic opposition could ever overcome it as he is insistent about the need for hope.[51]

That Agamben pays homage to Holocaust memory in framing his project, even in concluding that it is Palestinians who deserve to be the principal beneficiaries of solidaristic concern, also suggests that anti-fascism has had to be transformed to survive. But the same thing has occurred in anti-totalitarian thought, from which the Jewish fate under Nazi rule was long absent. In this vein, Tzvetan Todorov provides a useful example of contemporary anti-totalitarianism in its survival through transformation. Born in Bulgaria, and an émigré to Paris in his early twenties in 1963, Todorov has advanced an anti-totalitarian interpretation of Nazism in many places, but most notably in his *Hope and Memory: Lessons from the Twentieth Century*. Repeating standard tropes from the anti-totalitarian tradition, Todorov insists on the viability of comparing Nazism and

---

[50] Giorgio Agamben, *Remnants of Auschwitz: The Witness and the Archive* (New York: Zone Books, 2002), 52, 45.

[51] For more details, see Moyn, 'In the Aftermath', as well as Mark Mazower, 'Foucault, Agamben: Theory and the Nazis', *boundary 2* 35:1 (2008), 23–34. On French figures, see Sarah Hammerschlag, *The Figural Jew: Politics and Identity in Postwar French Thought* (Chicago, IL: University of Chicago Press, 2010).

communism with 'democracy', the alternative to both. Showing just how far such icons can serve diverse positions, Todorov, like Agamben, invokes Levi, whom he considers an anti-totalitarian, while Rousset earns all his admiration for opposing the camps even when it became known that Soviets also constructed them (omitting Rousset's seemingly inconvenient refusal to acknowledge that Jews suffered most in those made by the Nazis).

Of course, the world has changed for the anti-totalitarian intellectual, even as classic features of the position—like the theory of totalitarianism as a political religion—have gained a new look. Reflecting the power of Holocaust memory, Todorov is clear that one reason to memorialize victims of Nazism is the special fate it visited on European Jews above all others: 'There was never a Treblinka in the Soviet Union.' At the same time, the new element in anti-totalitarianism has not consumed its host, for Todorov also takes up the mission of saving anti-totalitarianism from a Jewish 'cult of memory' that risks sacrificing the breadth of a vision that ranges the various kinds of illiberal evil under the same rubric. Given his biography, and the intensity of a living communist politics for much of his French life, it is understandable that Todorov has participated fully in Parisian debates about how bad communism really was. In a sequel of sorts to Ehrenburg and Grossman, French intellectuals published in 2001 a famous *Black Book* of their own, which indicted the murderous crimes of international communism. Todorov agrees with some of its authors that, in some respects, communism was worse than Nazism, such that the memory of both should inspire anti-totalitarian vigilance.[52]

The persistence of anti-fascism and anti-totalitarianism do not suggest there is nothing new under the sun. Holocaust memory did offer intellectuals a challenge, but it seems to be one that they have faced mainly by adapting old frameworks. Whether their strategy is viable, and whether they choose anti-fascism or anti-totalitarianism to bring up to date, the continuity of the responses to Nazism in postwar European history so far has been seriously underrated. Paradigms of interpretations were there from the start. And if it was never obvious what among intellectuals or in general it meant to be against Nazism, the same remains true today, even after the epoch-making acquisition of Holocaust memory. In some respects, therefore, the standoff of anti-fascism and anti-totalitarianism—the starting position of postwar memory of Nazism and its crimes—remains to this day a constituent part of intellectual life.

Further Reading

Bessel, Richard and Dirk Schumann (eds), *Life after Death: Approaches to a Cultural and Social History of Europe in the 1940s and 1950s* (Cambridge: Cambridge University Press, 2003).

[52] Tzvetan Todorov, *Hope and Memory: Lessons from the Twentieth Century* (Princeton, NJ: Princeton University Press, 2003), 88; cf. S. Moyn's 'The Ghosts of Totalitarianism', *Ethics and International Affairs* 8:2 (2004), 99–104 and esp. Carolyn J. Dean, 'Recent French Discourses on Stalinism, Nazism and "Exorbitant" Jewish Memory', *History & Memory* 18:1 (2006), 43–85. On 'political religion', see e.g. Richard Steigmann-Gall, 'Nazism and the Revival of Political Religion Theory', *Totalitarian Movements and Political Religions* 5:3 (2004), 376–96.

Biess, Frank, and Robert Moeller (eds), *Histories of the Aftermath: The Legacies of the Second World War in Europe* (New York: Berghahn Books, 2010).

Herf, Jeffrey, *Divided Memory: The Nazi Past in the Two Germanys* (Cambridge, MA: Harvard University Press, 1997).

Judt, Tony, 'The "Problem of Evil" in Postwar Europe', *New York Review of Books*, 14, February 2008.

Lagrou, Pieter, *The Legacy of Nazi Occupation: Patriotic Memory and National Recovery in Western Europe, 1945–1965* (Cambridge: Cambridge University Press, 2000).

Moses, A. Dirk, *German Intellectuals and the Nazi Past* (Cambridge: Cambridge University Press, 2008).

Moyn, Samuel, *A Holocaust Controversy: The Treblinka Affair in Postwar France* (Waltham, MA: Brandeis University Press, 2005).

Rothberg, Michael, *Multidirectional Memory: Remembering the Holocaust in the Age of Decolonization* (Stanford, CA: Stanford University Press, 2009).

Shneer, David, *Through Soviet Jewish Eyes: Photography, War, and the Holocaust* (New Brunswick, NJ: Rutgers University Press, 2010).

Solchany, Jean, *Comprendre le nazisme dans l'Allemagne des années zéro 1945–1949* (Paris: Presses Universitaires de France, 1997).

Steinlauf, Michael C., *Bondage to the Dead: Poland and the Memory of the Holocaust* (Syracuse: Syracuse University Press, 1997).

Todorov, Tzvetan, *Hope and Memory: Lessons from the Twentieth Century* (Princeton, NJ: Princeton University Press, 2003).

Wieviorka, Annette, *The Era of the Witness* (Ithaca, NY: Cornell University Press, 2006).

CHAPTER 34

....

THE GREAT PATRIOTIC
WAR IN SOVIET AND
POST-SOVIET
COLLECTIVE MEMORY

....

ROGER MARKWICK

'There is only one religion—FRIENDSHIP
There is only one temple—the FRONT.'
Yuliya Drunina[1]

THE Second World War has never ended for the citizens of the former Soviet Union. Nearly 27 million Soviet citizens died in the course of what Stalin declared to be the Great Patriotic War, half of the total 55 million victims of the world war. Virtually no Soviet family was left unscathed by the 'war of annihilation' that Hitler unleashed on 22 June 1941. Yet the enduring personal trauma and grief that engulfed those who survived, despite the Red Army's victory over fascism, was not matched by Stalin's state of mind, which preferred to forget the war. Not until the ousting of Khrushchev in October 1964 by Brezhnev was official memory of the war really resurrected, assuming particular intensity with the onset of the so-called 'period of stagnation' in the 1970s, when a veritable 'cult' of the Patriotic War erupted, eclipsing even the 1917 Great October Socialist Revolution as the foundational myth of the Soviet Union.[2] The state-sanctified depiction of the war, embodied in massive historical works and numerous, even more massive memorials, prohibited any challenge to the hegemonic, heroic–patriotic, master

---

[1] Cited in Yu. E. Bogacheva, *The Roads We Choose . . . Memoirs and Reflections of a Military Nurse* (Voronezh: IVGU, 2005), 72.

[2] Nina Tumarkin, *The Living and the Dead: The Rise and Fall of the Cult of World War II in Russia* (New York: Basic Books, 1994), 132.

narrative of the war. But the intensely patriotic conservatism associated with the war was not only orchestrated from above by the Brezhnevite party state; it was embraced and encouraged from below by war veterans and the Soviet populace at large. It is testimony to one of the sources of the enduring power of the Great Patriotic War myth, beyond the posturing of monumental state propaganda and despite challenges in East-Central Europe and the Baltic states, that it continues to strike a real resonance with the individual life and death experiences and memories of millions of former Soviet citizens, even after the fall of the Soviet Union. Ironically, the authoritarian Russian post-Soviet state, seeking to construct a credible national narrative, has sought to legitimize itself by mythologizing more than ever the Great Patriotic War, even selectively associating itself with its Soviet past.

In elaborating this thesis about the place of the Second World War in Soviet and post-Soviet collective memory, this chapter sets out to illuminate the sources of the mythology of the Great Patriotic War and the mechanisms by which it has been sustained and even amplified. In this chapter it is assumed that the modern state deliberately constructs a hegemonic national narrative as a means of legitimation that masks and reinforces the coercive power of the state. In this approach, 'collective memory' is more than the sum of individual memories, although it certainly taps into them; it is the constructing, manipulating, and mobilizing of a 'usable past' from the reality of individual memories of lived history in order to forge or 'invent' an unassailable national tradition.[3] Symbolic, cultural power, secured through written histories, rituals, films, commemorations, monuments, museums, and other '*lieux de memoire*', becomes a powerful instrument for shaping the past in order to secure the present and the future.[4]

History is at the core of collective memory, not 'as it really was' but as an idealized history that creates an 'imagined', mythologized, national history, seemingly rising above class or other sectional interests. If an imagined, national history is at the core of collective memory, then war, especially victorious war, is its most powerful symbolic weapon. Death, blood sacrifice, and nation are the holy trinity of an unassailable, sacralized, collective memory; to challenge it is to blaspheme. Nowhere has this been truer than in the former Soviet Union and its Russian successor state.

---

[3] In his classic study, Maurice Halbwachs, *The Collective Memory* (New York: Harper & Row, 1980), esp. ch. 2, pursued a 'social-constructivist' approach to memory, which was by definition 'collective'; Arja Rosenholm and Withold Bonner, 'Introduction', in Rosenholm and Bonner (eds), *Recalling the Past—(Re)constructing the Past. Collective and Individual Memory of World War II in Russia and Germany* (Helsinki: Aleksanteri Institute, 2008), 7–18. Similarly, Alon Confino, 'Collective Memory and Cultural History: Problems of Method', *American Historical Review* 102:5 (1997), 1393–9, maintains that memory, 'fundamentally a concept of culture', cannot simply be reduced to political representation 'constructed by the powerful' nor neglect its social context. Rather, he argues for the 'multiplicity of memory', when elite representation engages with private, invisible, 'popular memories'.

[4] Pierre Nora, 'Between Memory and History: Les Lieux de Mémoire', *Representations* 26 (1989), 7–24; Kathleen E. Smith, *Mythmaking in the New Russia. Politics and Memory during the Yeltsin Era* (Ithaca, NY: Cornell University Press, 2002), 6–7.

A 'SACRED WAR'

From the moment Hitler unleashed his genocidal 'war of annihilation' on the Soviet Union at three o'clock in the morning of 22 June 1941, the Soviets fought a 'sacred', 'patriotic', 'people's war', in defence of the 'Motherland' [*Rodina*] against German fascism. In his radio address to the Soviet people, nine hours after the attack, Foreign Minister Vyacheslav Molotov invoked the victorious 'people's war' against Napoleon in 1812 as guarantee that 'Victory will be ours' in a 'just', defensive war.

Symptomatic of the quasi-religious discourse of a just, defensive war, the very day of the invasion the Russian Orthodox Metropolitan of Moscow celebrated the historic 'holy leaders of the Russian people' who had fulfilled their 'sacred duty before the motherland'; sentiments echoed in the title and refrain of the Soviet battle hymn: 'Sacred War'. Similar quasi-religious, patriotic sentiments permeated Stalin's address after he finally broke his silence, eleven days after the invasion. They did so again in his speech on 7 November 1941, the twenty-fourth anniversary of the Revolution, when, with the *Wehrmacht* at Moscow's gates, he hailed Aleksander Nevsky and Field Marshal Kutuzov, Russian military heroes who had defended the 'glorious Motherland' against the Teutonic knights and Napoleon's Grand Armée.[5] Stalin said not a word about world socialism, class struggle, or Marxism.[6] Stalin's highly gendered, populist, patriotic, religious discourse, intended to appeal to the overwhelming majority of a largely peasant populace at home, and to potential allies abroad, notably the leaders of the USA and Britain, Roosevelt and Churchill, would henceforth shape Soviet and post-Soviet depiction and remembrance of the war, by state and populace alike. For Patriotic War veterans, a half century later, the war was still a 'sacred duty', connoting a religious commitment sealed in blood.[7]

The trauma of this war left nobody unscathed. But with the first defeat of the *Wehrmacht* outside Moscow in December 1941, the Soviet state moved quickly to record popular experiences of the war, following the peculiarly Bolshevik belief in the 'self-educative' efficacy of life stories imbuing ordinary people with communist conviction. A commission was established on the initiative of Aleksandr Shcherbakov, head of the Red Army political department, to record popular experiences of the war, from the fighting to the home and factory fronts; but the Commission for the History of the Great Patriotic War, led by the historian Isaac

---

[5] M.M. Gorinov et al. (eds), *Moskva voennaya: Memuary i arkhivnye dokumenty* (Moscow: Mosgorarkhiv, 1995), 33, 39–41, 44–6, 138–42; Tumarkin, *The Living and the Dead*, 61–3.

[6] Bernd Bonwetsch, 'Der "Grosse Vaterländischen Krieg". Vom öffentliche Schweigen unter Stalin zum Heldenkult unter Breschnew', in Babette Quinckert (ed.), *'Wir sind die Herren dieses Landes'. Ursachen, Verlauf und Folgen des deutschen Überfalls auf die Sowjetunion* (Hamburg: VSA-Verlag, 2002), 166–7.

[7] Roger D. Markwick, '"A Sacred Duty": Red Army Women Veterans Remembering the Great Fatherland War, 1941–45', *Australian Journal of Politics and History* 54:3 (2008), 403–4.

Mints, was dissolved in 1945 and its invaluable records consigned to the archives of the Academy of Sciences' Institute of History, where they remain today, off limits to foreign researchers. In true Stalinist style, only state-sanctioned narratives of the war were permissible.[8]

THE 'GENIUS' GENERALISSIMO

Although Stalin ensured that victory on 9 May 1945 ultimately came to be synonymous with his leadership as marshal and generalissimo of the Red Army, in the course of the war it was popular identification with the motherland, rather than Stalin himself, that rallied the bulk of the populace to fight. 'For the Motherland! For Stalin!' may have been an official battle cry, but it was the former rather than the latter that was most often on Soviet soldiers' lips. And in an attempt to rally popular support, Stalin gave the intelligentsia just enough free rein, after the nightmare of the 1937–38 Terror, to harness them to the patriotic cause. Seeking to distance himself from the catastrophic routs of 1941–42, Stalin temporarily accepted a lower public profile, allowing the fighting Red Army marshals to turn the military tide, especially after the battles of Stalingrad and Kursk in 1943. It was Marshal Georgyi Zhukov, astride a white charger, who took the salute on Red Square, as the victorious Red Army threw down the banners of the defeated Nazi war machine at the foot of the Lenin Mausoleum on the first 'Victory Day' [*Den pobedy*], 24 June 1945. Stalin went on to pay homage to the Red Army, its marshals, the people, especially the Russians whom a month earlier he had elevated to the 'leading people of the Soviet Union', and lastly the Communist Party, as the driving forces of victory.[9] But Stalin was certainly not going to be eclipsed by them.

In the decade following the war, Soviet victory over Nazism became synonymous with Stalin's 'genius'. Faced with hostile western propaganda and historiography attributing the outbreak of war to Molotov's August 1939 non-aggression pact with Nazi Germany, Soviet historians, ever obedient scribes of the state, retold the triumphant version of events sanctioned by Stalin. Official clichés about the Soviet Union's 'peace-loving' foreign policy, especially the non-aggression pact, and Stalin's allegedly 'wise' pursuit of 'active defence and counter-offensive' in 1941–42, a postwar formula devised by Stalin himself to rationalize rout,[10] were uncritically recapitulated by the historians. Dependent as they were on published sources and denied access to archives or diplomatic documents, historians were ignorant about the pact's secret protocols, inter alia,

---

[8] Carmen Scheide, 'Kollektivnye i indivudualnye modeli pamyati o "Velikoi Otechestvennoi voine" (1941–45)', *Ab Imperio* 3 (2004), 216–17.

[9] Elena Zubkova, *Russia after the War: Hopes, Illusions and Disappointments, 1945–1957* (New York: M.E. Sharpe, 1998), 29.

[10] O.V. Druzhba, *Velikaya Otechestvennaya voina v soznanni sovetskogo i postsovetskogo obshchestva: dinamika predstavlenii ob istoricheskom proshlom* (Rostov on Don: DGTU, 2000), 41, 44.

incorporating the Baltics into the Soviet Union, and they were necessarily silent about Stalin's responsibility for the catastrophic defeats of 1941–42.[11]

FORGETTING THE UNFORGETTABLE

Despite the extraordinary cost of the Red Army's victory over fascism—11.2 million dead and 18.3 million wounded[12]—other than mass, 'brotherly graves' and small community and family monuments, only a few official memorials were erected on Soviet soil itself in these years. The most important Soviet war memorial complex was actually located outside the Soviet Union, in Berlin's Treptow Park. Constructed in 1946–49 on the site of a cemetery for 7000 soldiers killed in the battle for Berlin, it depicted a Red Army soldier astride a broken swastika, holding a German girl in one arm.[13] Located as it was on the new, far-flung, Cold War front line, it was more of a statement to Stalin's Cold War opponents than a site where Soviet citizens could grieve. At the same time, the state's monopoly of the media meant that only the heroic depiction of the war, divorced from private memory, reached the public domain. The shocking routs and surrenders, the mass deaths of soldiers and prisoners, the trauma of the wounded, the starvation of the besieged in Leningrad, the deprivation on the home front, the terror of occupation, the shame and discrimination against those suspected of collaboration, and the fate of the invalids; all these experiences were 'expunged' from the public record for decades.[14] Stalin minimized the extraordinary human cost of the war, claiming in March 1946 that only 7 million Soviet citizens had died; 13 million fewer than Khrushchev claimed in 1956 while debunking Stalin's reputation as a wartime leader; and 20 million fewer than the actual total figure. Not until the forty-fifth anniversary of the victory, in the dying days of the Soviet Union, did the Communist Party leadership, under Mikhail Gorbachev, acknowledge the price that had been paid for the victory: 27 million dead.[15]

Mass death was not the only price. With the onset of the Cold War, fearful of popular expectations of liberalization and of 'neo-Decembrist' sentiment infecting millions of demobilized soldiers and prisoners of war (POWs) exposed to prosperous foreign lands, the Stalinist state reprised repression and drew up the drawbridge on the allegedly

[11]   Roger D. Markwick, 'Thaws and Freezes in Soviet Historiography', in Polly Jones (ed.), *The Dilemmas of De-Stalinization: Negotiating Cultural and Social Change in the Khrushchev Era* (London: Routledge, 2006), 181; V. Kulish, 'Sovetskaya istoriografiya Velikoi Otechestvennoi voiny', in Iu. Afanas'ev (ed.), *Sovetskaya istoriografiya* (Moscow: RGGU, 1996), 274–81.

[12]   G.F. Krivosheev et al. (eds), *Rossiya i SSR v voinakh XX veka. Kniga poter* (Moscow: Veche, 2010), 219, 236, tablitsa 139.

[13]   Peter Jahn, 'Opora pamyati – bremya pamyati', in Jahn (ed.), *Triumph und Trauma. Sowjetische und postsowetische Erinnerung an den Krieg 1941–1945/Triumph i bol'. Sovetskaya i postsovetskaya pamyat o voine 1941–45* (Berlin: Ch. Links Verlag, 2005), 14; Scheide, 'Kollektivnye i individual'nye modeli pamyati', 217–18.

[14]   Bonwetsch, 'Der "Grosse Vaterländischen Krieg"', 168.

[15]   Tumarkin, *The Living and The Dead*, 197.

'besieged fortress'.[16] Behind a wall of Russian chauvinism, an anti-Semitic, anti-intellectual, xenophobic, 'anti-cosmopolitan campaign' erupted, which saw the banning in 1946 of *The Complete Black Book of Russian Jewry* and the erasure of the Jewish Holocaust from the patriotic narrative of suffering, resistance, and victory.[17] In the course of the war, the intelligentsia, temporarily off leash from the Agitprop *apparat*, became the vehicle for recording and reporting the war. Towards the end of the war it fell to writers to become the 'healers of wounded souls', in circumstances in which the state and its medical practitioners proved incapable of recognizing, let alone attending to, the psychological needs of those traumatized by war.[18] But in a shattered economy and society, the political noose was once again tightened around the intelligentsia, in the guise of the *Zhadonovshchina*, named after the Communist Party Secretary for Culture and Ideology. From 1946 onwards, literature reverted quickly to the one-dimensional heroic 'Socialist realist' style, and even wartime works that had been awarded the Stalin prize were severely criticized and had to be rewritten; among them was Aleksandr Fadeev's *Young Guard*, the embellished tale of a group of young resistance fighters murdered in 1942.[19] In 1952 Fadeev, Secretary of the Writers' Union, demanded Vasily Grossman rewrite his novel *For a Just Cause* for its failure to depict the war 'in the light of Stalin's words'.[20]

The country was faced with rebuilding a devastated society; military heroes were no longer needed. Heroism on the labour front was the order of the day.[21] Symptomatic of Stalin's determination to erase public commemoration of the war, and with it military heroes such as Marshal Zhukov, was the abolition in 1947 of Victory Day, 9 May, as a holiday, only two years after it was first celebrated; it was not to be reinstated until 1965 under Brezhnev.[22] The downgrading of Victory Day was soon accompanied by Zhukov's own fall from grace and that of other marshals, some of whom found themselves in the Gulag. Military memoirs were virtually banned; a forthcoming anthology, *Storm over Berlin*, was withdrawn from the press. But millions of copies of Stalin's collected speeches on the war were published in 1945, crowned two years later by his *Short Biography*, which gave the impression that 'Stalin's genius' had single-handedly won the war. Ironically, films about the war were few and far between; only four of the 124 films produced between 1946 and Stalin's death in 1953 dealt with the war, among them *The Fall of Berlin* and *Battle for Stalingrad*, which served only to glorify Stalin as a military leader.[23]

[16] Zubkova, *Russia after the War*, 25; Scheide, 'Kollektivnye i indivudual'nye modeli pamyati', 218; Druzhba, *Velikaya Otechestvennaya voina*, 39.

[17] Ilya Ehrenburg and Vasily Grossman, *The Complete Black Book of Russian Jewry* (New Brunswick, NJ: Transaction Publishers, 2002), ix, xiii–xiv.

[18] Anna Krylova, ' "Healers of Wounded Souls": The Crisis of Private Life in Soviet Literature, 1944–1946', *Journal of Modern History* 73 (2001), 307–31.

[19] Bonwetsch, 'Der "Grosse Vaterländischen Krieg" ', 170.

[20] Druzhba, *Velikaya Otechestvennaya voina*, 47.

[21] Jahn, 'Opora pamyati', 12.

[22] Tumarkin, *The Living and the Dead*, 104.

[23] Bonwetsch, 'Der "Grosse Vaterländischen Krieg" ', 171–2; Druzhba, *Velikaya Otechestvennaya voina*, 44–5.

But the net result of an idealized propaganda image of the Soviet Union and its people deciding the 'fate of humanity' meant that 'people saw any criticism as an insult to the dead'.[24]

The 'Thaw'

It took the death of Stalin and the ensuing the political 'thaw' under Khrushchev to clear the way for public remembrance of the war, ten years after war's end. A powerful impetus for the victory over Nazism to assume the pivotal place in Soviet official memory came in 1954–55 with West German 'remilitarization' and its incorporation into NATO; the Soviet state thereby assured a war-fearful populace that in any confrontation with western imperialism it would be victorious.[25] But even before Khrushchev audaciously denounced Stalin's 'cult of the personality', in his so-called 'secret speech' to the Twentieth Communist Party Congress in March 1956, behind the scenes some leading historians and military figures were chipping away at the myth of Stalin and agitating for real historical research and renewed remembrance of the war. The tenth anniversary of the victory saw historians calling for 'profound analysis' and an end to 'citations' of 'dogma'.[26] Meanwhile, Marshal Zhukov, in particular, was urging rehabilitation of Red Army leaders purged in the 1930s; amnesties for ex-Soviet prisoners of war, who were regarded as traitors; the creation of more 'Hero-cities'; and the erection of monuments in keeping with the scale of the Soviet war effort, which already existed in liberated Eastern Europe and Germany but not on Soviet soil.[27]

In his 'secret speech', Khrushchev blamed Stalin's 'incompetent' leadership for the Red Army's catastrophic, initial defeats, particularly his failure to heed dire warnings of the impending attack, and his 'nervousness and hysteria' for subsequent disasters. Khrushchev mocked Stalin's so-called 'active defence' and blamed his paranoia for the 'mass repression' which had decapitated the military in 1937–41. Khrushchev falsely accused Stalin of panic, but in de-mythologizing Stalin's wartime role, Khrushchev's priority was not so much the war's 'historical significance' as its 'political educative and practical significance'.[28] Khrushchev's objective was to recast the political narrative of the war as a triumph of the Soviet people under the collective leadership of the Communist Party, sans Stalin. In Soviet historical practice, '*aktualnost*', the contemporary political relevance of history, was more important than illuminating the past.[29]

[24] Druzhba, *Velikaya Otechestvennaya voina*, 49.

[25] Jahn, 'Opora pamyati', 13.

[26] Druzhba, *Velikaya Otechestvennaya voina*, 56.

[27] Bonwetsch, 'Der "Grosse Vaterländischen Krieg"', 172.

[28] Markwick, 'Thaws and Freezes', 181; Kulish, 'Sovetskaya istoriografiya', 284–5.

[29] Roger D. Markwick, *Rewriting History in Soviet Russia: The Politics of Revisionist Historiography, 1956–1974* (Basingstoke: Palgrave Macmillan, 2001), 159, 247.

The twentieth party congress unleashed a wave of historical revisionism, which the party itself quickly set out to contain, fearful, as Khrushchev himself later confessed, of being 'overwhelmed by a flood'. But history was too important and controversial to be left to the historians. This was particularly true of the war, into which there was considerable research effort, but under the Argus eyes of party and military authorities. In addition to the new *Military-Historical Journal*, several major military history centres were established, overseen by a variety of authorities including the Institute of Marxism–Leninism, the General Staff and the Soviet Academy of Sciences. The result was the publication of a vast amount of material about the war, including new documentary collections. In September 1957, the Party Central Committee sanctioned a collective of party and military functionaries, historians, and archivists to publish an official six volume *History of the Great Patriotic War*, which appeared in 1960–65. Under the imprint of the Academy of Sciences' press 'Nauka', headed by the liberal academician Aleksandr Samsonov, a stream of books and military memoirs was published. Despite this plethora of publications, its overall impact on the historiography of the war was limited, constrained not only by a dearth of archival research but even more so by the shallow 'cult of the personality' analytical framework expounded in party resolutions. Whereas prior to the twentieth party congress historians attributed Soviet military successes to Stalin's 'genius', afterwards he was blamed for all the defeats; the Communist Party was now proclaimed the architect of true victory.[30]

At the height of the Thaw, in the early 1960s, the historical representation of the war became central to the Communist Party's objective of 'educating the entire population in the spirit of scientific communism', which Khrushchev boasted was now in reach of Soviet society. For political and military leaders, such as Zhukov, the war provided ideal norms of Soviet citizenship, 'above all among the young': 'courage', 'heroism', 'Soviet patriotism, love of their armed forces and readiness to do battle with any enemy'. Victory in the war was seen as proof of the inevitable triumph of Soviet socialism over capitalism.[31]

In this spirit, the 1960s finally witnessed a flood of war memoirs, albeit heavily censored. Between 1957 and 1967 more than 150 book-length memoirs and hundreds of articles were published.[32] That decade also saw the publication of fiction, the 'tuning fork' of Soviet public opinion, such as *The Living and the Dead* and *Soldiers are not Born* by the famous war correspondent Konstantin Simonov, and *Goodbye Schoolboy* by the avant-garde bard Bulat Okudzhava, as well as war stories by ordinary soldiers: 'lieutenants' prose'.[33] Despite the censorship, these writings captured the lived reality of the war far more effectively and critically than the tedious, pseudo-scientific tomes produced by teams of bureaucratic historians. At the height of the Thaw, more nuanced, somewhat

[30] Markwick, 'Thaws and Freezes', 181.
[31] Druzhba, *Velikaya Otechestvennaya voina*, 51.
[32] Hiroaki Kuromiya, 'Soviet Memoirs as a Historical Source', in Sheila Fitzpatrick and Lynne Viola (eds), *A Researcher's Guide to Sources on Soviet Social History in the 1930s* (New York: M.E. Sharpe, 1992), 235.
[33] Druzhba, *Velikaya Otechestvennaya voina*, 54, 62–3.

critical, even pacifistic, literary, artistic, and cinematic depictions of the war, such as Mikhail Kalatozov's film *The Cranes are Flying* (1957) and Sergei Bondarchuk's film *The Fate of a Man* (1959), 'moved to the centre of artistic and intellectual production'. It was time when even the writings of the German 'bourgeois pacifist' Eric Maria Remarque, author of *All Quiet on the Western Front* (1929), were extremely popular.[34] With the demise of Khrushchev's liberalization such writings fell out favour; criticized for their 'de-heroisation' and depicting the 'truth of the trenches', they were not republished or even banned on the grounds of 'pacifism', as was Okudzhava's novel.[35]

Tepid as Khrushchev's de-Stalinization was, it nevertheless opened the way for public memorializing of the war, ultimately on a grand scale. Plans were laid in 1958 for the Mamayev Hill memorial complex at Stalingrad, hitherto occupied by a monument to Stalin, which was completed in October 1967, crowned by the towering, sword-wielding goddess of victory. Planning also began in 1958 for the ambitious 'Poklonnaya Gora' [*The Hill of Prostrations*] memorial complex in Moscow, although it would not be completed until the fiftieth anniversary of the victory, almost five years after the demise of the Soviet Union. Such public memorializing of the war became an integral part of the reinvigorated anti-Stalin campaign unleashed by the 1961 twenty-second party congress.[36] But well before such grandiose state proposals for commemoration were launched, millions of ordinary citizens privately grieved, incorporating Victory Day into their own everyday 'ethnic cultural traditions'; elderly women villagers baking 'pancakes, pies and buns' in a 'widows' requiem' for husbands and sons who had never returned. Such private customs provided solid socio-psychological soil for the resurrection of official, collective, remembrance of the war.[37]

THE 'CULT' OF THE WAR

The social 'mood' too in the mid-1960s proved receptive to renewed emphasis on the war; after a decade of Khrushchev's erratic economic and political reforms, there was a popular yearning for stability that the conservative, bureaucratic wing of the party, led by Leonid Brezhnev, could tap into. Soviet triumph in the war would legitimate the overall, steady course of the Communist Party towards socialism, notwithstanding a few 'mistakes' under Stalin and Khrushchev.[38] While Brezhnev's ousting of Khrushchev as party first secretary in October 1964 brought a halt to the debunking of Stalin, a cult of the Great Patriotic War was soon unleashed that would rival Stalin's discredited 'cult of

[34] Mark Edele, *Soviet Veterans of the Second World War: A Popular Movement in an Authoritarian Society 1941–1991* (Oxford, New York: Oxford University Press, 2008), 8; Denise J. Youngblood, *Russian War Films: On the Cinema Front, 1914–2005* (Lawrence, KS: University of Kansas Press, 2007), 117–23.

[35] Bonwetsch, 'Der "Grosse Vaterländischen Krieg"', 174.

[36] Ibid., 173.

[37] Druzhba, *Velikaya Otechestvennaya voina*, 52, 95.

[38] Ibid., 88–9.

the personality' and eclipse the October Revolution as the foundational myth of the Soviet state.

The twentieth anniversary of the defeat of Nazi Germany, 9 May 1965, unleashed the 'cult of the Great Patriotic War' in earnest. Victory Day was re-established as a national holiday; an occasion for military parades and solemn speeches, first and foremost before party and military chiefs arrayed above Lenin's marble tomb on Red Square. Henceforth Victory Day was bestowed with a sacred significance embracing both state and society.[39] Public radio and television instituted observance of a memorial 'Minute of silence' and the week leading up to Victory Day became a 'Watch of memory'—soirées, meetings, exhibitions—to acculturate young people into the mythology of the war.[40] In his 1965 Victory Day speech, Brezhnev not only insinuated Stalin back into the heroic victory narrative, he also tapped into the Thaw literary and artistic emphasis on the role and experiences of ordinary people in the war, shorn of any 'Remarquist', pacifist sentiments, by referring to 'the millions of unknown "participants of the Great Patriotic War"'.[41]

Brezhnev's populist overture was well received, judged by the positive response it received among the populace, according to KGB reports, particularly among war veterans. Veterans and their associations, hitherto an appallingly neglected constituency, especially invalids, at last received some recognition and long-denied, if still menial, social security benefits. Over the next two decades Victory Day became a rallying point for bemedalled, predominantly male, veterans and their associations, who saw themselves an 'entitlement group' which increasingly and successfully lobbied for social benefits (better access to pensions, housing, medical care, and transport) befitting those who had defended the Motherland. By 1988, at the height of *perestroika*, 'Veterans had become an officially recognized pillar of Soviet society', more than half a century after war's end.[42]

The Brezhnev ascendancy was accompanied by a drive to quash the last remnants of the liberalizing Thaw and salvage Stalin's reputation, not least in relation to the war. In October 1965 the new party leadership initiated condemnation of the revisionist history *22 June 1941*, by Aleksander Nekrich. Nekrich's basic thesis was that Stalin's 'mistakes' were directly responsible for the disastrous routs inflicted by Germany following its undeclared attack on the USSR in June 1941. Having signed a non-aggression pact in 1939 to the disadvantage of the USSR, Stalin had ignored all the warnings he had been given of an impending German attack, dismissing them as an attempt by Britain to provoke a war between the Soviet Union and Nazi Germany. The 'Nekrich affair', which went on for two years and saw Nekrich expelled from the party and eventually depart the Soviet Union, was clearly a neo-Stalinist campaign to reassert party orthodoxy about the Great Patriotic War as an unmitigated triumph of Soviet arms and diplomacy and intimidate those historians and the intelligentsia as a whole who might dare to suggest otherwise.[43]

---

[39] Tumarkin, *The Living and the Dead*, 132–6.
[40] Druzhba, *Velikaya Otechestvennaya voina*, 94.
[41] Edele, *Soviet Veterans*, 9–10.
[42] Ibid., 185, 207.
[43] Markwick, *Rewriting History*, 209–12.

The 'Nekrich affair' was the elite, academic dimension of an overarching Brezhnevite campaign to elevate the Great Patriotic War to the pivotal legitimating mythology of the Soviet state, eclipsing both the Great October Socialist Revolution and even 'The great Lenin' himself. As economic growth slowed towards the end of the 1960s and consumer shortages grew, Brezhnev's party-state retreated from Khrushchev's brash aspirations for a classless communist future which would outstrip western capitalism, resorting instead to an increasing celebration of the victorious war to bolster the sagging legitimacy of party and state.[44]

The Brezhnev period saw mass production of publications about the war, intended to affirm that the 'great victory' was testimony to the superiority of Soviet socialism under the leadership of its 'Leninist party'.[45] An army of state historians was mobilized to produce massive, multi-volume, official histories. The twentieth anniversary of the victory saw the publication of a six-volume history of the Great Patriotic War, eclipsed only by a 'bulky, but vacuous', twelve-volume history of the entire Second World War, published over the decade 1973–82. This magnum opus was accompanied by an avalanche of celebratory books on the war; between 1965 and 1988, 20,000 books, totalling one million volumes, were published, particularly to mark the jubilees of the victory.[46] But such publications were carefully vetted. Censorship was the order of the day; a special unit was set up in the political department of the defence ministry to check military memoirs.[47]

Even the most illustrious authors were not immune: Marshal Zhukov's *Recollections and Reflections* only finally appeared in 1969, after passages had been deleted and others, not written by Zhukov, were inserted into the original manuscript, and the memoirs had personally been cleared by Brezhnev himself. Likewise, criticisms of the disastrous Soviet defeats in the first phase of the war were struck from the memoirs of Marshal Rokossovsky, as were his arrest and torture during Stalin's pre-war purges of the Red Army officer corps, one of the deafening 'silences' in Brezhnevite historiography and memoirs that killed their readership in the 1970s and early 1980s.[48] Film too was subject to strict censorship. In the 1970s large-scale, triumphalist films for screen and television focusing on the exploits of the Red Army after 1943 but not the routs of 1941–42, notably the five-part blockbuster *Liberation* [*Osvobozhdenie*] released for the twenty-fifth victory anniversary (1970–72), became important media for the 'militarization of mass consciousness' and the fanning of patriotic sentiment at the expense of flagging socialist ideals.[49]

[44] Jahn, 'Opora pamyati', 13–14.

[45] Druzhba, *Velikaya Otechestvennaya voina*, 92.

[46] Bonwetsch, 'Der "Grosse Vaterländischen Krieg"', 176.

[47] Tumarkin, *The Living and the Dead*, 134–5; Lazar Lazarev, 'Russian Literature on the War and Historical Truth', in John Garrard and Carol Garrard (eds), *World War 2 and the Soviet People* (Basingstoke: St Martin's Press, 1993), 34–5.

[48] Bonwetsch, 'Der "Grosse Vaterländischen Krieg"', 177; Druzhba, *Velikaya Otechestvennaya voina*, 104–5, 110.

[49] Druzhba, *Velikaya Otechestvennaya voina*, 125–6, 130; Youngblood, *Russian War Films*, 158–60.

Given the particularly close scrutiny and censorship of war films, histories, and memoirs in these decades of intellectual stagnation, only fiction, together with some art films such as the anti-heroic *They Fought for the Motherland* (1975), provided any genuine insight into the realities of the war.[50] Only in the fiction of such authors as Vladimir Tendryakov, Konstantin Simonov, Vasil Bykov, Anatoly Kuznetsov, Viktor Nekrasov, Vyacheslav Kondratyev, or Anatoly Rybakov, although not immune from censorship, could readers find out about the less glorious aspects of the war: fear, cowardice, panic (including the Moscow panic of October 1941), punishment battalions, soldiers released from the Gulag, soldiers sacrificed as cannon fodder, the forgotten war invalids, the stigma of collaboration of having survived under occupation, or the Jews as a particular target of Nazi genocide, although not about the Holocaust as whole, which was subsumed within the overall story of Soviet suffering.[51]

The so-called 'period of stagnation' under Brezhnev saw the flourishing of the hero cult around the war, intended to infuse a spirit of 'official optimism' into 'every sphere of life'.[52] 'The immortal feat of the Soviet people and their Armed Forces in achieving their historic victory in the Great Patriotic War' was incorporated into the preamble to Brezhnev's new 1977 Soviet constitution.[53] It also became integral to the high-school history curriculum, where it was treated on a par with the October 1917 Revolution. Not just soldiers but entire cities were declared 'Heroes', accompanied by the awarding of special medals and military orders. By Victory Day 1985 there were twelve Hero Cities.[54]

Mass death generated mass memorialization; by 1980 70,000 monuments dotted the landscape.[55] In addition, vast memorial complexes proliferated in the Brezhnev years; whereas only eleven had been erected in the first decade and a half after the war, fifty-nine were erected in the 1960s, among them the Khatyn memorial in Belarus commemorating the incineration of an entire village and its inhabitants by the Nazis in 1943, followed by a further sixty-seven in the 1970s. Towering above them all was the vast Mamaev Hill memorial at Volgograd, which opened in 1967. Crowned by the 85 metre, sword-wielding 'Motherland' commemorating the battle of the former Stalingrad, Mamaev Hill became the archetypal monument; a massive memorial in which sublime 'heroism and triumph' were elevated over 'suffering and the pain of loss'.[56] The devastated Brest fortress on the Soviet–Polish border, the garrison of which had held out for more than a month against the initial invasion without surrendering, was accorded the special title of 'Hero Fortress' by the Supreme Soviet, as a 'symbol of

[50] Youngblood, *Russian War Films*, 168–70.

[51] Bonwetsch, 'Der "Grosse Vaterländischen Krieg"', 181–2.

[52] Druzhba, *Velikaya Otechestvennaya voina*, 93.

[53] 'Constitution (Fundamental Law) of the Union of Soviet Socialist Republics', 7 October 1977, online at: http://www.departments.bucknell.edu/russian/const/77cons01.html#preamble, accessed April 2010.

[54] Bonwetsch, 'Der "Grosse Vaterländischen Krieg"', 178, 180. Tumarkin, *The Living and The Dead*, 42.

[55] Nurit Schleifman, 'Moscow's Victory Park: A Monumental Change', *History & Memory*, 13:2 (2001), 8.

[56] Jahn, 'Opora pamyati', 14.

the unparalleled determination of the Soviet people'. The ruins of the fortress were subsequently incorporated into the vast 'Brest Fortress-Hero Memorial Ensemble', opened in 1971, which, with its towering titanium coated obelisk, massive sculptures, eternal flame, rows of gravestones, recorded renditions of the battle hymn 'Sacred War', and the original radio announcement of the declaration of war, masked military disaster with mass martyrdom.[57]

Ritualized remembrance became a fine art under Brezhnev. Nothing exemplifies this more than the elaborate rituals that led up to the lighting on 8 May 1967 of the 'Fire of Glory' on Moscow's Tomb of the Unknown Soldier, the remains of whom had been reburied with full military honours in the Alexander Garden beside the Kremlin wall, having been taken from a mass grave outside Moscow in December 1966, the twenty-fifth anniversary of the Red Army's first successful counteroffensive. A torch lit from the flame at Leningrad's Field of Mars, the memorial to the martyrs of the October 1917 revolution, together with soil from Leningrad's vast Piskarevskoe siege cemetery, had been carefully conveyed by armoured car all the way to the Kremlin wall, where the General Secretary of the Communist Party, Brezhnev, received it to ignite the eternal flame. It was a moment that fused the 1917 revolution with the Great Patriotic War, simultaneously re-enshrining the authority of the Communist Party and its Leninist roots, if not Stalin's status. In the lofty rhetoric of Moscow Communist Party Chief, Nikolai Yegorichev: 'The soldiers of the revolution and the soldiers of the Great Patriotic War have closed ranks into one immortal rank, illuminated by the Eternal flame of glory, lit by the living in honour of the fallen who will always live.'[58]

The Brezhnev period witnessed the construction of some twenty massive 'cathedrals' of remembrance, together with memorials, monuments, and museums, hailing the victory and honouring the dead.[59] Lesser monuments, honour rolls, 'Military Glory Rooms' and 'Corners', saturated with war memorabilia, proliferated in enterprises, educational institutions, and public buildings across the Union, while commemorative stamps, matchboxes and miniature posters made remembrance part of everyday life. Newly married couples took to laying flowers at war memorials, a ritual that may have derived from a Russian tradition of laying food on graves.[60] Wartime songs, at least those sanctioned by the state, provided an extremely personal means for both the wartime and younger generations to connect with the war and each other.[61] Mass participation in remembrance ceremonies by bemedalled veterans, with their newly conceded privileges, by uniformed members of party youth organizations, or by those seeking news of friends or relatives who never came back, forged popular, cross-generational, identification with state driven remembrance.

---

[57] Tumarkin, *The Living and the Dead*, 145–6; www.brest.by/ct/indexe.html, accessed April 2010.
[58] Tumarkin, *The Living and the Dead*, 127–8.
[59] Tumarkin, *The Living and the Dead*, 47.
[60] Jahn (ed.), *Triumph und Trauma*, 164, 168–70.
[61] Suzanne Ament, 'Lyric and Legacy, Melody and Memory: World War II Songs and the Shaping of Memory and Identity', in Rosenholm and Bonner (eds), *Recalling the Past*, 191–3.

The cult of the Great Patriotic War thereby effectively re-established the wartime unity between party, state, and society, cementing the 'tacit accord', as Bernd Bonwetsch has called it, between state and society that was the hallmark of the Brezhnev decades, 1964 to 1982. Hence the cultivation of a veritable 'cult without personality' around the arch-bureaucrat Brezhnev, head of party and state, who, in 1976, elevated himself to the pantheon of war heroes as a Red Army Marshal awash with the highest military decorations, although as a political officer during the war he had never held a military command.[62] In this period of growing disillusion with Soviet ideals, the Brezhnev state attempted to stabilize itself by tapping into remembrance of the war which for the wartime generation was a defining, 'moral', moment; a moment which was fast fading among the young. But the carefully crafted, dehumanized, heroic narrative of the war and the glorification of Brezhnev only sowed cynicism, especially among the intelligentsia and the postwar generation, fuelling a 'socio-cultural crisis' in the Soviet system.[63]

PERESTROIKA: 'AN ENTIRELY DIFFERENT WAR'

Perestroika began with high hopes for the renewal and reinvigoration of the Soviet system, in good part by lifting the lid on the Soviet past; it ended with its downfall. A crucial ingredient in its fall was the tarnishing of the 'bronzed saga' of the Great Patriotic War.[64] The fortieth anniversary of the victory, May 1985, was the high point of the Soviet celebration of victory in the Great Patriotic War; newly appointed General Secretary, Mikhail Gorbachev, soon to be the apostle of *perestroika* and *glasnost*, hailed it the 'Hero war'. But in the course of *perestroika*, the Great Patriotic War became one of the most contentious elements of the debates that erupted in 1987 about the notorious 'blank spots' in and outright 'falsification' of Soviet history, principally the crimes of Stalin: forced collectivization of agriculture, mass famine in the 1930s, and the terror; debates that began in the public arena but soon embraced the predominantly conservative historical profession.

The history of the war, which still haunted the living memories of millions of Soviet citizens, ultimately went to the heart of the Soviet past and therefore present. Public argument about the war, specifically whether Soviet POWs and those 'missing without a trace' should be treated as heroes or stigmatized as traitors, peaked in *Izvestiya* and *Pravda* in mid-1987, eliciting an avalanche of letters from veterans. The divorce between personal experiences of the war and authorized depictions of it such as the twelve-volume official history was captured in the blistering outburst, in April 1988, by the Russian nationalist writer Viktor Astafev that 'I was in an entirely different war...A

---

[62] Bonwetsch, 'Der "Grosse Vaterländischen Krieg"', 180–1.
[63] Druzhba, *Velikaya Otechestvennaya voina*, 131, 134–5, 137–45.
[64] Tumarkin, *The Living and the Dead*, 188, 190, 193.

more falsified, concocted publication...I never knew'.[65] Already, in November 1987, the Politburo had authorized a new ten-volume history of the Great Patriotic War intended for publication on the silver jubilee of the victory; it would never be completed.[66]

The 'niches of freedom' opened up by *glasnost* saw the publication of hitherto censored speeches and interviews by Zhukov, Rokossovsky, and Simonov. *Life and Fate*, the epic Stalingrad novel by the deceased war correspondent Vasily Grossman, seized by the KGB in 1961 at the height of the Thaw, finally saw the light of day in 1988.[67] Questions formerly taboo about the war suddenly erupted in popular publications, puncturing the master narrative of unalloyed heroism retold by professional historians: Stalin's responsibility for the military catastrophes of 1941–42; Stalin's ruthless, secret, 'Not a step backwards' Order No 227, issued 28 July 1942 but only published in February 1988; the vast number of casualties; widespread collaboration with the Nazi occupiers; mass deportation of allegedly collaborationist minorities, such as Chechens and Crimean Tartars; and the fate of forced labourers and POWs, who for decades had been treated like traitors, an issue raised by the anti-Stalin human rights organization 'Memorial' formed in mid-1988.[68]

Such revelations about the dark side of the victory, coupled with the mounting publicist campaigns against the icons of Soviet history—initially Stalin, subsequently Lenin himself—took their toll on popular support for the Soviet idea and engulfed the Communist Party itself. At the mid-1988 nineteenth party conference, the war was part of the fierce polemics around hostile depictions of Stalinism in the popular press. Symptomatic of the time was a headline 'The Time for Pompous Monuments has Past' in the *Literary Newspaper* [*Literaturnaya gazeta*], which welcomed the abandonment of a design competition for a war memorial in Moscow, just as the Memorial society's campaign for a memorial to the 'Victims of the Repressions' was taking off.[69]

The intense 'politicization of history' meant that arguments about the Soviet past became weapons in the hands of contending political forces.[70] By mid-1989, Soviet state and party, wracked by the centrifugal forces of economic crisis, social turbulence, and nationalist aspirations, were undergoing a 'desacralization', in the words of a leading Russian revisionist historian, Mikhail Gefter.[71] Revelations about the 'underbelly' of the war were 'painful', even for those who simply wanted to know the truth about the war, such as the poet Evgenii Evtushenko. For the young, it intensified their cynicism about the Soviet system and even resentment against the 'privileges' of veterans, deepening the generational divide. For nationalistic military conservatives, 'pluralism' was

[65] Druzhba, *Velikaya Otechestvennaya voina*, 148; R.W. Davies, *Soviet History in the Gorbachev Revolution* (Basingstoke: Macmillan Press, 1989), 100–11.

[66] Bonwetsch, 'Der "Grosse Vaterländischen Krieg"', 169, n. 9; 181.

[67] Druzhba, *Velikaya Otechestvennaya voina*, 154–5; Robert Chandler, 'Translator's Introduction', in Vasily Grossman, *Life and Fate* (London: Harvill Press, 1995), 9–10.

[68] Jahn, 'Opora pamyati', 16.

[69] Davies, *Soviet History*, 157–8.

[70] Druzhba, *Velikaya Otechestvennaya voina*, 163.

[71] Tumarkin, *The Living and the Dead*, 187.

'being used for a purely provocative aim—"spitting on", disparaging and distorting eve-rything Soviet.'[72] The unravelling of the cult of the war, along with that around Lenin, was the harbinger of Soviet collapse. That collapse began in the periphery, rather than the centre: to be precise—in the Baltic states, whose forced incorporation into the Soviet Union under a secret protocol of the Molotov–Ribbentrop pact, cemented by Red Army occupation in 1944, had been vociferously denied in Moscow. Publication of the protocol, after prolonged internal discussion within the Communist Party Central Committee, triggered a 650 km human chain protest across the Baltic States, to mark its fiftieth anniversary, 23 August 1989. A further body blow to the 'sacred' status of the Great Patriotic War came with Gorbachev's admission on 13 April 1990 that 15,000 Polish officers had been murdered by NKVD at Katyn Forest in the spring of 1940, not by Nazi forces in 1941, as successive Soviet governments since Stalin had claimed. Such about-turns on crucial elements of Soviet eve of war policy struck at the heart of the Great Patriotic War mythology, at home and abroad.[73] Nevertheless, the war would become central to nationalist politics in the newly independent Russian Federation led by the renegade ex-communist Boris Yeltsin, who scuttled Gorbachev's Soviet Union in December 1991.

PATRIOTISM WITHOUT COMMUNISM

The demise of the Soviet Union and its Communist Party left a vacuum of social identity and political purpose, particularly in 1990s Russia as it endured the travail of its trans-formation into a despotic, criminalized capitalism;[74] resurrection of the cult of the Great Patriotic War, together with Russian Orthodoxy, proved an ideal way to fill it. Ironically, in post-Soviet Russia the myth of the war assumed even greater significance than it had in the Soviet Union. The titanic victory over Nazism stood out as the one bright spot in the otherwise seemingly bleak historical landscape of twentieth-century Russian his-tory under Stalinist repression.[75] A survey of Russian citizens in 1993 found that 98 per cent of respondents viewed victory in the Great Patriotic War as one of the most important events in twentieth century Russian history.[76] In Russia, where the war had increasingly been represented as a nationalist rather than a communist party achieve-ment, the challenge was to remove the alleged 'taint of Communism from wartime

---

[72] Druzhba, *Velikaya Otechestvennaya voina*, 158–9, 162.

[73] Tumarkin, *The Living and the Dead*, 175–81; Lisa A. Kirschenbaum and Nancy M. Wingfield, 'Gender and the Construction of Wartime Heroism in Czechoslovakia and the Soviet Union', *European History Quarterly* 39:3 (2009), 481.

[74] Graeme Gill and Roger D. Markwick, *Russia's Stillborn Democracy? From Gorbachev to Yeltsin* (Oxford: Oxford University Press, 2000), 212–13, 256–8.

[75] Jahn, 'Opora pamyati', 17.

[76] Druzhba, *Velikaya Otechestvennaya voina*, 168.

martyrs, heroes, and heroines and to transform them into emblems of national pride and identity'.[77]

ZOYA

Nothing was more emblematic of the struggle around the legacy of the Great Patriotic War mythology than the furore about the fate of the wartime Young Communist heroine, Zoya Kosmodemyanskaya, that erupted in the popular press on the eve of the demise of the Soviet Union and lingered for nearly a decade after. 'Zoya', as she was popularly known, was an 18-year-old partisan who had been tortured and hung by the Germans in November 1941, allegedly crying out, inter alia, 'Stalin is with us! Stalin will come!' The first woman during the war to be awarded the ultimate accolade of 'Hero of the Soviet Union', a carefully constructed media campaign utilizing photographs of her execution and ravaged, frozen, naked corpse ensured that she became the 'Soviet Joan of Arc', epitomizing the ultimate sacrifice for the Motherland and gendering the war effort as feminine.

Memorialized in song and verse, on stage and film, and in numerous museums, monuments, and ceremonies, the myth of Zoya was seemingly unassailable. But at the beginning of the 1990s questions were raised in the popular press about the veracity of the Zoya story.[78] Ultimately, the facts surrounding her execution, with the notable exception of her alleged cries about Stalin, were substantiated.[79] But truth was never the real issue: the mythology of Zoya was much larger than her death. She had died for her Russian *rodina* [Motherland], not for Stalin; accordingly, Zoya could live on beyond the demise of the Soviet system, the fraught Yeltsin years and even flourish in Putin's increasingly patriotic twenty-first century Russia.[80]

The dissolution of the Soviet Union and suppression of its Communist Party after August 1991 saw a hard fought contest—between the so-called 'democrats' led by Russian President Boris Yeltsin and their communist opponents—over the Great Patriotic War and who were the real standard bearers of its legacy. On the eve of the Union's demise, critics of Stalin and the ruling Communist Party were calling for a re-evaluation of the myths surrounding the war, with its terrible toll and disastrous leadership, as a way 'out of a terrible past to...a difficult but normal future'. For the Communist Party and veterans associations, such heretical views struck at the heart of Russian patriotism; seeking to overturn its outlawing after the failed putsch of August 1991, the Communist Party sought to demonstrate in court that its legitimacy derived from its leading role in the Soviet victory.

---

[77] Kirschenbaum and Wingfield, 'Gender and the Construction of Wartime Heroism', 467–8.

[78] Rosalinde Sartori, 'On the Making of Heroes, Heroines, and Saints', in Richard Stites (ed.), *Culture and Entertainment in Wartime Russia* (Bloomington, IN: Indiana University Press, 1995), 182–91.

[79] M.M. Gorinov, 'Zoya Kosmodemyanskaya', *Otechestvennaya istoriya* 1 (2003), 77–91.

[80] Kirschenbaum and Wingfield, 'Gender and the Construction of Wartime Heroism', 482–3.

THE BATTLE FOR VICTORY DAY

In the very first year of independent Russia, Yeltsin sought to give a pacifist twist to Victory Day by substituting a 'peace parade' for the traditional military parade on Red Square, laying a wreath at the tomb of the unknown soldier behind the Kremlin and joining war veterans in Gorky Park, a seeming tribute to the role of ordinary soldiers, at the expense of the Communist Party, which saw the low key observances as a repudiation of Russian patriotism. This contest over Victory Day was exacerbated by the political turbulence in the following two years as Yeltsin and his opponents in the parliament clashed over free market 'shock therapy' and whether president or parliament had the decisive say in affairs of state. Despite Yeltsin's bloody victory over his opponents in October 1993, when he shelled the parliament into submission, by Victory Day 1995, the fiftieth anniversary of the Soviet triumph had been officially resurrected as a patriotic celebration.

Anxious to heal the wounds of a nation divided by his presidential coup and an unpopular war in Chechnya unleashed in December 1994,[81] Yeltsin sought to re-appropriate the patriotic space occupied by his communist and nationalist opponents. The result was competing celebrations; a presidential ceremony at Poklonnaya Gora versus a parliamentary, communist, and nationalist rally in the centre of Moscow. Yeltsin re-established the pomp and ceremony of the Red Square military parade and symbols, such as the Soviet red banner of victory that flew alongside the new Russian tricolor, so revered by veterans. To a journalist with the liberal newspaper *Nezavisimaya gazeta*, Yeltsin's ceremony was a failed attempt to synthesize Russia's 'great power status [*derzhavinstva*] and democracy', overshadowed by Soviet Victory Day rituals: hammers and sickles on red banners 'supplanted the tricolour' as 'Soviet marches and songs' eclipsed 'the Russian hymn'.

A year later the sovietization of Victory Day was even more intense, symbolized by the flying of the red flag that had flown over the Reichstag, as Yeltsin hailed the 'continuity of times contained in our symbols [and] the proud spirit of the motherland in the unity of generations, in each of us.' The 'continuity of the times' included Marshal Zhukov, immortalized by an imposing equestrian statue just off Red Square and erected for the fiftieth anniversary, but still excluded Stalin and the Communist Party; victory had been achieved despite rather than because of them.[82]

TROPHY ART

Parallel with the battle for Victory Day, during 1994–97 a debate raged between Yeltsin and his 'red-brown' opponents about the return or otherwise of 'trophy' art, captured from the defeated Germans. It went to the heart of the place of the Great Patriotic War in

[81] R.W. Davies, *Soviet History in the Yeltsin Era* (Basingstoke: Macmillan Press, 1997), 73.
[82] Smith, *Mythmaking*, 85–90, 99, 178.

post-Soviet collective memory and politics. The willingness of the Yeltsin administration to make good a promise to Germany by Gorbachev in the dying days of the Soviet Union—to return captured cultural treasures—triggered a storm of patriotic opposition, led by a resurgent Communist Party which saw it as an affront to Russia and its war veterans. The terms in which the vitriolic debate was conducted about the restitution of secretly held trophy art, sensational revelations that only came to light in 1991, came straight from the contested landmarks of the Great Patriotic War. Pro-Western, anti-Communist Party journalists depicted the Soviet treasure trove as a 'Cultural Katyn'. Patriotic politicians, who in 1997 successfully opposed the return of what they regarded as legitimate material compensation for Soviet war losses, just as NATO was negotiating membership with the erstwhile Warsaw Pact members Poland, Hungary, and the Czech Republic, saw it as a 'spiritual Stalingrad'.[83]

The Hill of Prostrations

The incorporation of the Great Patriotic War as a core patriotic myth for independent Russia, shorn of Communist Party associations, was grandiosely symbolized by the decision to finally erect in Moscow's Victory Park the long-promised memorial complex at The Hill of Prostrations [*Poklonnaya gora*] to mark the fiftieth anniversary of the Victory. From its inception, the configuration and fate of this hugely expensive project had been determined by the interests of state. In the Brezhnev period, a fountain flanked avenue, with 1418 water jets symbolizing each day of the war, had been proposed, which would lead to a massive museum, crowned by a triumphalist, 70m high red 'Victorious Lenin Banner' with a bas relief of Lenin, surrounded by granite statues of 'The Victorious People', an ensemble that elevated the Communist Party over the *narod* [people]. On the eve of the 1980 Moscow Olympics it was abandoned as too costly. *Perestroika* witnessed two public competitions for a new monumental design, in which Russian Orthodox iconography, centred on grieving mothers, jostled with political triumphalism; neither of the proposed monuments were accepted.

In post-Soviet Russia, heated argument occurred over the most appropriate monument amid a bitter contest between Yeltsin's democrats and a communist party-veterans' alliance for ownership of the 'Victory'. In the end, a triumphalist, eclectic ensemble, featuring classical Greek and Christian motifs, was erected, which excluded Soviet symbolism: a bayonet-like obelisk crowned by the Greek goddess of victory, Nike, at the foot of which was a mounted St George, the patron Saint of Moscow, slaying the Nazi dragon; in the Hall of Memory and Sorrow a Pietà-like Motherland nursed the body of a slain warrior.[84] Designed by architect Zurab Tsereteli, it was a monument that captured Russian,

---

[83] Ibid., ch. 4, esp. 63, 71.
[84] Schleifman, 'Moscow's Victory Park', 13, 25–8.

religious memory of the war, not Soviet, political memory. It also elevated official triumphalism over human suffering. One of Tsereteli's sculptures, *The Tragedy of the Peoples*, featuring gaunt, toppling figures, was consigned to the rear of the museum, after public criticism that its mournful commemoration was more appropriate for Israel.

Nevertheless, concessions to the popular, religious dimensions of the war and its suffering were reflected in the inclusion not only of a Russian Orthodox church, a traditional Russian symbol of military victories which foregrounded the Victory Park museum complex, but subsequently also a synagogue, a mosque, and a separate Jewish memorial; they went ahead, over the opposition of a parliamentary resolution which warned 'a hearth for national and religious conflicts...is completely unacceptable in view of its extreme social danger'.[85] Yeltsin's version of Victory was also unacceptable to many veterans, for whom it represented the theft of their Soviet 'Victory'.[86] The struggle over the Hill of Prostrations monument was clearly a struggle between two competing patriotic narratives—Russian and Soviet—over a *lieu de memoire* of the Great Patriotic War as the defining national moment.[87] The Russian narrative prevailed, but Yeltsin's hand-picked presidential successor, Vladimir Putin, a former member of the KGB, a core institution of the former Soviet state, was more inclined to reincorporate Soviet symbolism into a Russian patriotic narrative.

SOVIETISM SANS SOCIALISM

On the very eve of Putin's accession to the Russian presidency in 2000 he had declared that 'patriotism' would be injected into post-Soviet Russia's 'ideological vacuum' to bolster Russian 'statehood' [*gosudarstvennichestvo*]. The Great Patriotic War would be a central patriotic pillar of the 'Russian idea'. Where Yeltsin had adopted the Tsarist double-headed eagle and a wordless national anthem as symbols of state that would celebrate Russia but not the Soviet Union, Putin moved quickly to resurrect the wartime national anthem, albeit with new words, and the red flag for the military, shorn of hammer and sickle iconography. He also moved quickly to reinvigorate Russian state authority and authoritarianism, starting with a cruel, relentless war in Chechnya and bringing to heel the oligarchs by gaoling one of its more rogue representatives, petroleum magnate Mikhail Khodorkovsky. In the interests of a validating Russian history, scrutiny of the Soviet period has also been curtailed, through more restricted access to key archives and the intimidation of recalcitrant historians; inevitably, there has been a gradual re-valorization of Stalin himself. Although Putin allowed the Presidential Commission

[85] Smith, *Mythmaking*, 106–13; Davies, *Soviet History in the Yeltsin Era*, 74.

[86] Anna Krylova, 'Dancing on the Graves of the Dead: Building a World War II Memorial in Post-Soviet Russia', in Daniel J. Walkowitz and Lisa Mayer Knauer (eds), *Memory and the Impact of Political Transformation in Public Space* (Durham, NC: Duke University Press, 2004), 97.

[87] Schleifman, 'Moscow's Victory Park', 29.

on Rehabilitation of the victims of Stalin to continue, his administration abstained from passing judgement on Stalin or Russia taking responsibility for Soviet era crimes. Although Putin declined to support renaming Volgograd 'Stalingrad' on the sixtieth anniversary of the battle in 2003, like the veterans who advocated the renaming he revelled in Soviet achievements, above all the victory over German fascism.[88]

Celebration of the sixtieth jubilee of the 'Victory' in 2005, widely regarded as the last in which original veterans would participate *en masse*, was central to Putin's drive to reinvigorate Russian patriotism. By presidential decree in August 2000, in accordance with 'proposals by veterans' organizations', his administration took immediate responsibility for the forthcoming celebrations to 'immortalise memory of the fallen' and 'The Victory of the Soviet people in the Great Patriotic War'.[89] Russia's extravagant Victory Day celebrations, festooned with Soviet banners and Red Army veterans, paraded before fifty foreign dignitaries, were intended to reassert the central role Soviet Russia played in the defeat of Nazism, and to repudiate NATO expansion eastwards. For many Soviet successor and allied states, such as Estonia, Lithuania, Poland, and Ukraine, the sixtieth anniversary was another occasion on which to demand an apology for Stalinist repression, which they saw as equivalent to Nazism. Speaking at Auschwitz in January 2005, Putin had vigorously rejected any attempt to equate Stalinist repression with Hitler's Holocaust.[90] In his speech on 9 May, Putin affirmed Victory Day as the most 'sacred', 'inclusive', and 'festive' day for Russia. Far from the 'fall' of the cult of the war with the demise of the Soviet Union, under Putin it had become the decisive unifying element in state ideology and popular consciousness.

Undoubtedly, the Russian state has actively contributed to collective memory of Stalin's triumphal war at the expense of collective memory of Stalinist repression. And yet the state has also abetted the latter, seemingly without cost. In late 2004, on the eve of the sixtieth anniversary of the victory, state television broadcast an 11-part series, *Shtrafbat* [Punishment Battalion], which depicted for the first time the fate of hundreds of thousands of disgraced Red Army officers in NKVD punishment battalions, ordered into suicidal offensives. Notwithstanding the reinvigorated heroic celebration of the victory, *Shtrafbat* captured the public imagination.[91] But such revelations have hardly dented popular identification with the Great Patriotic War, which only intensified under Putin as the wartime generation faded. In 2003, 87 per cent of respondents to the question 'What personally makes you most proud in our history?' referred to the Great Patriotic War; it was also Russia's only 'just war' in the twentieth century. Concomitantly, Stalin has once more become a popular figure. Ironically, such trends point to the

---

[88]   Nancy Adler, 'The Future of the Stalinist Past Remains Unpredictable: The Resurrection of Stalinist Symbols amidst the Exhumation of Mass Graves', *Europe-Asia Studies* 57:8 (2005), 1099–100; Richard Sakwa, *Putin. Russia's Choice*, 2nd edn (London: Routledge, 2008), 216, 218–22, 322–5.

[89]   'Ukaz Prezidenta Rossiisskoi Federatsii 5 avgusta 2000 No. 1441'. www.pobeda-60.ru/main. php?trid=40, accessed April 2010.

[90]   Adler, 'The Future of the Stalinist Past', 1111.

[91]   Jahn, 'Opora pamyati', 18, 207.

resurgence of a Sovietized, sacralized, celebratory, collective memory of the war, fuelled by a multitude of state, social, and media institutions, which denies any private memories, misgivings, or suffering, and legitimates a neo-authoritarian, capitalist state, arisen from the ashes of Stalinist state socialism.[92]

Further Reading

Davies, R.W., *Soviet History in the Gorbachev Revolution* (Basingstoke: Macmillan Press, 1989).

Davies, R.W., *Soviet History in the Yeltsin Era* (Basingstoke: Macmillan Press, 1997).

Grant, Bruce, 'New Moscow Monuments, or, States of Innocence', *American Ethnologist* 28:2 (2001), 332–62.

Harasymiw, Bohdan, 'Memories of the Second World War in Recent Ukrainian Election Campaigns', *Journal of Ukrainian Studies* 32:1 (2007), 97–108.

Ignatieff, Michael, 'Soviet War Memorials', *History Workshop* 17 (1984), 157–63.

Kirschenbaum, L.A., *The Legacy of the Siege of Leningrad, 1941–1995: Myth, Memories, and Monuments* (Cambridge: Cambridge University Press, 2006).

Merridale, Catherine, *Night of Stone: Death and Memory in Twentieth-Century Russia* (New York: Viking, 2001).

Rosenholm, Arja and Withold Bonner (eds), *Recalling the Past – (Re)constructing the Past. Collective and Individual Memory of World War II in Russia and Germany* (Helsinki: Aleksanteri Institute, 2008).

Serbyn, Roman, 'Historical Memory and State Building: The Myth of the Great Patriotic War in Independent Ukraine', *Ukrainian Quarterly* 59:1–2 (2003), 52–79.

Smith, Kathleen E., *Mythmaking in the New Russia: Politics and Memory during the Yeltsin Era* (Ithaca, NY: Cornell University Press, 2002).

Tumarkin, Nina, *The Living and the Dead: The Rise and Fall of the Cult of World War II in Russia* (New York: Basic Books, 1994).

Uldricks, Teddy J., 'War, Politics and Memory. Russian Historians Reevalutae the Origins of World War II', *History and Memory* 21:2 (2009), 60–82.

[92] Lev Gudkov, 'The Fetters of Victory: How the war provides Russia with its identity', 4, 7, 12.. www.eurozine.com/articles/2005-05-03-gudkov-en.html, accessed April 2010.

CHAPTER 35

MEMORY WARS IN THE 'NEW EUROPE'

DAN STONE

'An acceleration of history, like the one we are living through at the present, is not just a very quick passage from yesterday to tomorrow; it is also the abrupt reappearance in the present of the day before yesterday.'

Régis Debray[1]

INTRODUCTION

SEVENTY years since the start of World War II, revisionists across Europe are arguing that Stalin was as much to blame for starting the war as was Hitler. No historical fact, it seems, not even the one that every school pupil knows, that Hitler was responsible for the war, is any longer secure. At the same time, the British Conservative Party, the party of Churchill, has aligned itself in the European Parliament with a far-right grouping, the ECR (European Conservatives and Reformists Group), which includes the Latvian For Fatherland and Freedom Party and the Polish Law and Justice Party. The latter's former spokesman, Michał Kaminski, appealing to the old canard of Judeo–Bolshevism (*Żydokomuna*), explains the murder of Jews in Jedwabne in 1941 with reference to the 'crimes' supposedly committed by Jews during the period of Bolshevik rule in eastern Poland. As Adam Krzeminski rightly says, the Second World War is still being fought.[2]

---

[1] Régis Debray, *Charles de Gaulle: Futurist of the Nation* (London: Verso, 1994), 92. My thanks to Luiza Bialasiewicz, Robert Bideleux, Cathie Carmichael, Martin Evans, Helen Graham, Becky Jinks, Roger Markwick, Dirk Moses, Gavin Schaffer, and the commentators at the CEMES conference, Copenhagen, 24 August 2010 for their comments on earlier drafts of this chapter.

[2] Adam Krzeminski, 'As Many Wars as Nations: The Myths and Truths of World War II', *Sign and Sight*, 6 April 2005, www.signandsight.com/features/96.html, accessed March 2010 (original in *Polityka*, 23 March 2005). Jan T. Gross, *Neighbors: The Destruction of the Jewish Community in Jedwabne, Poland* (Princeton, NJ: Princeton University Press, 2001). Kaminski stood down from the Law and Justice Party in November 2010, saying it was becoming too right-wing.

And, we might add, more intensively today than at any point in the last seven decades.

Today the study of memory has become so all-pervasive that it is hard even to keep up with the review articles on the subject.[3] Yet, as the above example shows—and there are more every day—the study of memory is no idle academic pursuit but goes to the heart of contemporary understandings of the past, and thus of attitudes towards the present and future. 'Forgetting' is as important here as 'remembering'; in the case of communism and Nazism, for example, some participants in recent 'memory politics' debates seem to have forgotten (or want to forget) that, if liberal democracy 'defeated' communism in 1989, that defeat was only possible because communism had defeated Nazism in World War II.[4] There is certainly a tendency, in Russia and elsewhere, to whitewash Stalin's crimes, but correcting that pernicious line need not come at the expense of the victims of fascism and Nazism. Indeed, the Russian 'defence' of Stalin indicates that scholars who insist on the long-term and rather ironic resonance of communist structures of thought on post-communist Russian nationalism are right, for 'a decade of post-Communist history in Eastern Europe suggests that Communist regimes did successfully indoctrinate several generations of their citizens with respect to certain key events—most notably, World War II and the Holocaust.'[5]

In this chapter, I do not present a methodological explication of 'memory studies'; rather, I take a broad definition of 'collective memory', seeing it, with Alon Confino, as a

> set of representations of the past that are constructed by a given social group (be it a nation, a family, a religious community, or other) through a process of invention, appropriation, and selection, and that have bearings on relationships of power within society.[6]

This is a capacious definition, but it is useful to us here because the topic deals with more than just visual or material *lieux de mémoire*. It also explores contemporary power struggles over these representations, and thus emphasizes the element of selection. What is important is not just what is 'remembered', but what is omitted, distorted, falsified, or

---

[3] For example Douglas C. Peifer, 'New Books on Memory, History and the Second World War', *Contemporary European History* 18:2 (2009), 235–44; Christof Dejung, 'A Past That Refuses to Pass: The Commemoration of the Second World War and the Holocaust', *Journal of Contemporary History* 43:4 (2008), 701–10.

[4] Martin Evans, 'Memories, Monuments, Histories: The Re-Thinking of the Second World War since 1989', *National Identities* 8:4 (2006), 335.

[5] Richard Ned Lebow, 'The Memory of Politics in Postwar Europe', in Richard Ned Lebow, Wulf Kansteiner and Claudio Fogu (eds), *The Politics of Memory in Postwar Europe* (Durham, NC: Duke University Press, 2006), 14.

[6] Alon Confino, 'Remembering the Second World War, 1945–1965: Narratives of Victimhood and Genocide', *Cultural Analysis* 4 (2005), 48. See Dan Stone, 'Beyond the Mnemosyne Institute: The Future of Memory after the Age of Commemoration', in Rick Crownshaw, Jane Kilby and Antony Rowland (eds), *The Future of Memory* (Oxford: Berghahn, 2010), 17–36; Stone, 'Genocide and Memory', in Donald Bloxham and A. Dirk Moses (eds), *The Oxford Handbook of Genocide Studies* (Oxford: Oxford University Press, 2010), 102–19.

'forgotten' in the service of the present, and the process by which certain narratives of the past (or the 'past') come to prominence over others. Thus, 'memory' here refers not only to the academic study of memory—although the chapter is anchored in this literature—but primarily to the various manifestations of 'memory politics' that have characterized Europe since the end of the Cold War, that is, the contested accounts of the past that have given rise to controversies and debates in the public sphere. Far from signalling the 'end of history', the end of the Cold War gave rise to a 'new world disorder'.[7] This chapter will show that struggles over memory, in particular over the memory of World War II, lay, as they still lie, at the forefront of this process. In fact, rather than 1989 signalling the end of the 'long Second World War',[8] the further from the postwar years we get, the more vigorously the memory of the war is being fought over.

The significance of memory, both individual and collective, is that it mediates between past and future. Memory, as Hannah Arendt explained, resides between the 'no more' and the 'not yet' in the 'space' of the 'timeless present'. She writes that it is 'the function of memory to "present" (make present) the past and deprive the past of its definitely bygone character. Memory undoes the past.' The result is that 'memory transforms the past into a future possibility',[9] Control of the future demands control over the past, and leads to greater contestation over which version of the past should prevail. The widespread sense that the collapse of communism had invalidated all future-oriented political projects proved a powerful impetus for turning to the past. And given that the past concerned involved war, genocide, and many other forms of oppression, violence, and trauma, acts which radically divided the original participants and which now divide their descendants, the contest over the past was and continues to be especially marked.[10]

OUT OF THE COLD WAR FREEZER

According to the senior Romanian communist and, after 1989, TV-show host Silviu Brucan:

> Old grudges and conflicts from as far back as the Hapsburg and tsarist empires, marvellously preserved in the communist freezer, are floating to surface with the

[7] Ken Jowitt, *New World Disorder: The Leninist Extinction* (Berkeley, CA: University of California Press, 1992).

[8] As R. J. B. Bosworth argues in *Explaining Auschwitz and Hiroshima: History Writing and the Second World War 1945–1990* (London: Routledge, 1993), 3.

[9] Hannah Arendt, 'No Longer and Not Yet', in Jerome Kohn (ed.), *Essays in Understanding, 1930–1954* (New York: Harcourt Brace, 1994), 158–62; Arendt, *Love and Saint Augustine*, ed. Joanna Vecchiarelli Scott and Judith Chelius Stark (Chicago, IL: University of Chicago Press, 1996), 48. See also Joanna Vecchiarelli Scott, 'Hannah Arendt Twenty Years Later: A German Jewess in the Age of Totalitarianism', *New German Critique* 86 (2002), 30.

[10] Gavriel D. Rosenfeld, 'A Looming Crash or a Soft Landing? Forecasting the Future of the Memory "Industry"', *Journal of Modern History* 81:1 (2009), 127, 135.

thawing of the Cold War and the lifting of the Stalinist coercion and repression. Territorial, religious, and ethnic claims long suppressed are striking back with a vengeance, while national liberation, secessions, and declarations of independence are coming first on the political agenda.[11]

In this view, the years since 1989 are the 'real' postwar years, for only with the demise of the Cold War could a true debate over the meaning of World War II, in which all sides could be heard, take place. What has happened since the 'post-war parenthesis' ended can be regarded both as a liberation from tyranny (in the East) and a chance to debunk longstanding myths, but also, more darkly, a freedom to express views that were long regarded as dead or, at best, marginal (in East and West). The years 1945–89 now appear as 'an extended epilogue to the European civil war that had begun in 1914, a forty-year interregnum between the defeat of Adolf Hitler and the final resolution of the unfinished business left behind by his war.'[12] Perhaps, as Geoff Eley suggests, the Cold War years, which brought social democracy and class cooperation to Western Europe, and welfare states of one variety or another to all of Europe, were an aberration in European history.[13] Is Europe now reverting to type?

Of course, it is not the case that there was no discussion of the past before 1989. In Yugoslavia, for example, a certain rendering of wartime atrocity was central to the Titoist slogan of 'brotherhood and unity' (*bratstvo i jedinstvo*). The point is that what had gone before was distorted to fit new ideological realities, in this instance the deaths of some 300,000 Bosnians at the hands of Croatian fascist Ustashe and Serbian royalist Chetniks, which were subsumed into a narrative of the partisan, anti-fascist struggle.[14] Similarly, indigenous fascism and support for Hitler's New Order were brushed under the carpet in Eastern Europe, as the Soviet narrative of working-class anti-fascism was imposed from above, a process which facilitated the Soviets' carrying out massive social restructuring through land 'redistribution'.

In the West, the suffering caused by the liberation process—through bombing, looting, and sexual violence—was brushed aside by the Allies in favour of 'triumphalist narratives' that could compete with the Soviets'. Widespread collaboration with Nazism or the weakness of resistance movements were topics too uncomfortable to mention in liberated countries. Instead, mythic narratives of resistance, Allied solidarity, and democratic renewal quickly took hold, in the interests of relatively frictionless reconstruction.[15]

[11] Silviu Brucan, *The Wasted Generation: Memoirs of the Romanian Journey from Capitalism to Socialism and Back* (Boulder, CO: Westview Press, 1993), x.

[12] Tony Judt, *Postwar: A History of Europe since 1945* (London: William Heinemann, 2005), 749.

[13] Geoff Eley, 'Historicizing the Global, Politicizing Capital: Giving the Present a Name', *History Workshop Journal* 63:1 (2007), 154–88. Cf. Carl Tighe, 'Pax Germanica', in *Pax Variations* (Manchester: IMPress, 2000), 89–141.

[14] Tomislav Dulić, *Utopias of Nation: Local Mass Killing in Bosnia and Herzegovina, 1941–42* (Uppsala: Uppsala University Press, 2005); Dubravka Ugrešić, 'The Confiscation of Memory', in *The Culture of Lies: Antipolitical Essays* (London: Phoenix, 1998), 217–35.

[15] William I. Hitchcock, *Liberation: The Bitter Road to Freedom, Europe 1944–1945* (London: Faber and Faber, 2009), 369; Pieter Lagrou, 'Victims of Genocide and National Memory: Belgium, France and the Netherlands 1945–1965', *Past and Present* 154 (1997), 181–222.

And in Germany an 'exculpatory identity of victimhood', based on an unwillingness 'to accept the relationship between cause and effect', coupled in the western zones with a useful anti-communist stance, swiftly did away with the rare statements of guilt or remorse that had appeared in 1945–46.[16] There were many commemorations of the war in the Cold War years, but they did not encompass all Europeans' opinions. Those whose views did not conform to the anti-fascist consensus expressed them in private or not at all in the East or in more or less fringe venues in the West.

The end of the Cold War permitted the articulation of sentiments that had been hitherto suppressed. Something, Richard Ned Lebow writes, 'resembling a tacit conspiracy to tiptoe quietly around the past developed between major forces on the right and left' in the postwar years.[17] It is true that 'revisions of World War II collective memory in Eastern Europe started in the mid-1980s, well before the fall of the Berlin Wall', but such revisions could only be freely voiced on a large scale after 1989.[18] On the one hand, postwar myths that contributed to smoothing the path of social reconstruction were dismantled even faster than was already the case; for example, the notion of widespread involvement in and support for the French resistance was something that scholars and filmmakers had been taking apart since the late 1960s, the most famous example being *The Sorrow and the Pity*, Marcel Ophüls's dissection of Clermont-Ferrand during the war. On the other hand, the loosening grip of such myths also enabled the return of arguments that characterized the 'other side' of the consensus. Fascist, ultra-nationalist, anti-semitic, and xenophobic positions that it had been impossible (in the East) or difficult (in the West) openly to articulate gained strength and confidence as the demise of communism signalled, for some, the death of all liberal–leftist ideologies stemming from Enlightenment thought.

Particularly in the eastern half of the continent, what Vladimir Tismaneanu names 'fantasies of salvation' appeared rapidly on the scene—often directly reprising local interwar and wartime fascist movements—as the collapse of communism encouraged the search for a national heritage untainted by association with communism.[19] Unfortunately, in a region in which few countries had a tradition of liberalism, anti-communism before and during World War II often meant ultra-nationalism or fascism, and not a few war criminals, such as Ion Antonescu, Jozef Tiso, or Ferenc Szálasi were rehabilitated as national heroes in the immediate post-Cold War years. Romania's Memorial of the Victims of Communism and Anticommunist Resistance in Sighet

---

[16] Hitchcock, *Liberation*, 370–1; Jeffrey Herf, *Divided Memory: The Nazi Past in the Two Germanys* (Cambridge, MA: Harvard University Press, 1997); Robert G. Moeller, *War Stories: The Search for a Usable Past in the Federal Republic of Germany* (Berkeley, CA: University of California Press, 2001).

[17] Lebow, 'The Memory of Politics in Postwar Europe', 19.

[18] Claudio Fogu and Wulf Kansteiner, 'The Politics of Memory and the Poetics of History', in Lebow, Kansteiner, and Fogu (eds), *The Politics of Memory in Postwar Europe*, 295.

[19] Vladimir Tismaneanu, *Fantasies of Salvation: Democracy, Nationalism, and Myth in Post-Communist Europe* (Princeton, NJ: Princeton University Press, 1998).

exemplifies the phenomenon.[20] As Tismaneanu writes, although 'historical memory is incessantly invoked in public debates, narratives of self-pity and self-glorification prevail over lucid scrutiny of the past'.[21]

With the exception of Yugoslavia in the 1990s, when World War II memory was mobilized to fuel ethno-nationalist war on a scale not seen on the continent since 1945,[22] the direst predictions of a return to local traditions of fascism, nationalism, or peasantism have not materialized, thanks partly to the incorporation of East-Central Europe into the EU and partly to the widespread acceptance of liberal democracy, whether espoused by centre-right or revamped communist parties. But such political traditions—which are also by no means unknown in the EU's longer-standing members—remain potent as possible sources of alternative ideologies, and populist politicians are now in or close to government.[23] Indeed, although stability is the most noteworthy fact about the post-communist years, some commentators argue that the region is backsliding, with populism now 'the new condition of the political in Europe', especially in countries where 'long-maintained forms of amnesia' concerning fascist and communist crimes are 'bound to fuel discontent, outrage, and frustration and to encourage the rise of demagogues'.[24] In Western Europe, the demise of the anti-fascist consensus that dominated postwar politics after 1945, whether Social or Christian Democrats were in power, started to crack, as confusion over the meaning of 'left' and 'right' took hold. The ensuing vacuum in political theory was exacerbated by such phenomena as globalization and the rise of the unregulated global market and, after 11 September 2001, the 'war on terror'.

In contemporary Europe, far-right politicians clearly share a heritage with 'classic fascism', but advance their populist agenda on the basis of more topical fears: of Muslims, financial crisis, immigration, and the threat posed to local, 'indigenous' populations by

[20] Gabriela Cristea and Simina Radu-Bucurenci, 'Raising the Cross: Exorcising Romania's Communist Past in Museums, Memorials and Monuments', in Oksana Sarkisova and Péter Apor (eds), *Past for the Eyes: East European Representations of Communism in Cinema and Museums after 1989* (Budapest: Central European University Press, 2008), 275–305, esp. 297–303.

[21] Vladimir Tismaneanu, 'Civil Society, Pluralism, and the Future of East and Central Europe', *Social Research* 68:4 (2001), 989.

[22] Robert M. Hayden, 'Mass Killings and Images of Genocide in Bosnia, 1941–5 and 1992–5', in Dan Stone (ed.), *The Historiography of Genocide* (Basingstoke: Palgrave Macmillan, 2008), 487–516.

[23] Marc Morjé Howard, 'The Leninist Legacy Revisited', in Vladimir Tismaneanu, Marc Morjé Howard and Rudra Sil (eds), *World Disorder after Leninism: Essays in Honor of Ken Jowitt* (Seattle, WA: University of Washington Press, 2006), 34–46; Jeffrey Kopstein, '1989 as a Lens for the Communist Past and Post-communist Future', *Contemporary European History* 18:3 (2009), 289–302. On the role of the EU, see Milada Anna Vachudova, *Europe Undivided: Democracy, Leverage, and Integration after Communism* (Oxford: Oxford University Press, 2005).

[24] Ivan Krastev, 'The Strange Death of the Liberal Consensus', *Journal of Democracy* 18:4 (2007), 63; Vladimir Tismaneanu, 'Leninist Legacies, Pluralist Dilemmas', *Journal of Democracy* 18:4 (2007), 38; cf. Charles S. Maier, 'What Have We Learned since 1989?', *Contemporary European History* 18:3 (2009), 253–69; Michael Shafir, 'From Historical to "Dialectical" Populism: The Case of Post-Communist Romania', *Canadian Slavonic Papers* 50:3–4 (2008), 425–70.

these ideological, economic, and population movements.[25] While racism in the sense of biological determinism still exists, it has been largely replaced by an older form of race understood through culture, in which somatic characteristics are understood as markers of cultural and religious difference rather than of 'a biological heredity'.[26]

Other chapters in this book deal specifically with memory in the Soviet Union, Germany, Yugoslavia, and Spain. Historians have provided richly detailed accounts of the construction of memory regimes in Western and Eastern Europe after 1945.[27] In particular, they have rigorously scrutinized the gradual development of 'Holocaust consciousness'.[28] In what follows, I will focus on how the memory boom since the end of the Cold War, and especially in the new millennium, reflects and brings about new challenges to European identity and politics. The common theme is the demise of the postwar consensus and the revival of previously marginalized ways of thinking, which means that an unprecedented assault on the values of the postwar period has taken place on the one hand and that an exaggerated version of them has survived on the other.

Nothing illustrates the first effect—the collapse of the postwar consensus—better than the creation of the so-called 'second republic' in Italy after 1994.[29] After 1944, postwar Italy, following the general trend in Western Europe, was stabilized with the aid of the founding myth of the country as a nation of anti-fascists. The result, according to Renzo De Felice, was 'to obscure the actual history of fascism and the war, and to allow many decidedly undemocratic political elements (Fascists and Communists) to hide behind the mask of Italy's so-called antifascist republic.'[30] Although historians had debated the role played by fascism and anti-fascism before the end of the Cold War, the collapse of communism and the birth of the 'second republic' sundered Italy's postwar

[25]   Dieter Prowe, '"Classic" Fascism and the New Radical Right in Western Europe: Comparisons and Contrasts', *Contemporary European History* 3:3 (1994), 289–314; Richard Golsan (ed.), *Fascism's Return: Scandal, Revision, and Ideology since 1980* (Lincoln, NE: University of Nebraska Press, 1998); Tamir Bar-On, 'Fascism to the Nouvelle Droite: The Dream of Pan-European Empire', *Journal of Contemporary European Studies* 16:3 (2008), 327–45.

[26]   Etienne Balibar, 'Is There a "Neo-Racism"?', in Balibar and Immanuel Wallerstein, *Race, Nation, Class: Ambiguous Identities* (London: Verso, 1991), 17–28; Lisa Lampert, 'Race, Periodicity, and the (Neo-) Middle Ages', *Modern Language Quarterly* 65:3 (2004), 391–421.

[27]   For example: Jan-Werner Müller (ed.), *Memory and Power in Post-War Europe: Studies in the Presence of the Past* (Cambridge: Cambridge University Press, 2002); Małgorzata Pakier and Bo Stråth (eds), *A European Memory? Contested Histories and Politics of Remembrance* (New York: Berghahn, 2010).

[28]   For example Harold Marcuse, 'The Revival of Holocaust Awareness in West Germany, Israel, and the United States', in Carole Fink, Philipp Gassert and Detlef Junker (eds), *1968: A Year Transformed* (Cambridge: Cambridge University Press, 1998), 421–38; Susan Rubin Suleiman, *Crises of Memory and the Second World War* (Cambridge, MA: Harvard University Press, 2006); Andy Pearce, 'The Development of Holocaust Consciousness in Contemporary Britain, 1979–2001', *Holocaust Studies* 14:2 (2008), 71–94; Hasia R. Diner, *We Remember with Reverence and Love: American Jews and the Myth of Silence after the Holocaust, 1945–1962* (New York: New York University Press, 2009).

[29]   Claudio Fogu, '*Italiani brava gente*: The Legacy of Fascist Historical Culture on Italian Politics of Memory', in Lebow, Kansteiner and Fogu (eds), *The Politics of Memory in Postwar Europe*, 161–5.

[30]   Robert A. Ventresca, 'Mussolini's Ghost: Italy's *Duce* in History and Memory', *History & Memory* 18:1 (2006), 96–7.

mythic narrative and opened up an uneasy space for multiple, competing versions of the past. Within a very short space of time, 'neo-fascists', led by Gianfranco Fini, found their way into Berlusconi's government.

Although the party changed its name from the fascist-connoted Movimento Sociale Italiano to the Alleanza Nazionale, its message was the revisionist one, that all sides had been victims in the war, that Italy had overcome the divisions of the past, and that the Italian people were all 'post-fascists' now.[31] In one of the most striking examples, the Risiera di San Sabba in Trieste—Italy's most notorious concentration camp during World War II—has become the focus of a vigorous struggle over wartime memory, which has seen the *foibe* (the murder by Yugoslav partisans of Italian soldiers and civilians in 1943 and 1945) set alongside the Holocaust, thus driving revisionist claims by instrumentalizing Holocaust victims' experiences.[32] In fact, this drive to moral equivalence actually perpetuates, as Ruth Ben-Ghiat notes, 'black holes' in memory, with very little discussion taking place about Italian atrocities in the Balkans or colonial territories, Italian concentration camps, or Jewish forced labour in Italian cities and countryside.[33]

The same phenomenon is observable in states which were victims of Nazi aggression but in which collaboration played a significant role. In the Netherlands, the 1940s and 1950s saw a kind of 'truce'—Ido de Haan calls it 'a shifting political compromise between silence and speaking out'—over the question of who had suffered more, those deported to Germany as forced labourers, Jews deported to concentration and death camps, and those who had endured the 'Hunger Winter' of 1944–45.[34] Although Jewish victims made up about half of all Dutch wartime deaths,[35] their experiences were subsumed into

[31]   Ventresca, 'Mussolini's Ghost', 102–4. See also Ventresca, 'Debating the Meaning of Fascism in Contemporary Italy', *Modern Italy* 11:2 (2006), 189–209; Andrea Mammone, 'A Daily Revision of the Past: Fascism, Anti-Fascism, and Memory in Contemporary Italy', *Modern Italy* 11:2 (2006), 211–26; Joshua Arthurs, 'Fascism as "Heritage" in Contemporary Italy', in Andrea Mammone and Giuseppe A. Veltri (eds), *Italy Today: The Sick Man of Europe* (London: Routledge, 2010), 114–27.

[32]   Pamela Ballinger, 'Who Defines and Remembers Genocide after the Cold War? Contested Memories of Partisan Massacre in Venezia Giulia in 1943–1945', *Journal of Genocide Research* 2:1 (2000), 11–30; Gaia Baracetti, '*Foibe*: Nationalism, Revenge and Ideology in Venezia Giulia and Istria, 1943–5', *Journal of Contemporary History* 44:4 (2009), 657–74; Martin Purvis and David Atkinson, 'Performing Wartime Memories: Ceremony as Contest at the Risiera di San Sabba Death Camp, Trieste', *Social and Cultural Geography* 10:3 (2009), 337–56.

[33]   Ruth Ben-Ghiat, 'A Lesser Evil? Italian Fascism in/and the Totalitarian Equation', in Helmut Dubiel and Gabriel Motzkin (eds), *The Lesser Evil: Moral Approaches to Genocide Practices* (London: Routledge, 2004), 147; cf. James Walston, 'History and Memory of the Italian Concentration Camps', *The Historical Journal* 40:1 (1997), 169–83; Robert S. C. Gordon, 'The Holocaust in Italian Collective Memory: *Il giorno della memoria*, 27 January 2001', *Modern Italy* 11:2 (2006), 167–88.

[34]   Ido De Haan, 'Paths of Normalization after the Persecution of the Jews: The Netherlands, France, and West Germany', in Richard Bessel and Dirk Schumann (eds), *Life after Death: Approaches to a Cultural and Social History of Europe during the 1940s and 1950s* (Cambridge: Cambridge University Press, 2003), 69.

[35]   Ido De Haan, 'Routines and Traditions: The Reactions of Non-Jews and Jews in the Netherlands to War and Persecution', in David Bankier and Israel Gutman (eds), *Nazi Europe and the Final Solution* (Jerusalem: Yad Vashem, 2003), 437.

a narrative of national heroism that animated the postwar reconstruction. That narrative began to break down long before 1989, but since the end of the Cold War, greater openness about Dutch–German collaboration and the role of the Dutch police and state bureaucracy in deporting Jews to the death camps has been accompanied by a revival of right-wing populism, most often manifest as a 'defence' of Dutch liberty from 'radical Islam'. In France, the combination of the memory of Vichy and the recent reawakening of interest in the Algerian War (1954–62) has been a potent brew for memory wars, which have seen laws passed and retracted on the teaching of colonialism's 'positive' side, and unseemly debates, sparked by the publication of *The Black Book of Communism* (1997) about whether communism was 'worse' than Nazism.[36]

A particularly interesting case is Spain, where Franco's regime survived the war by playing up its alleged neutrality, talking the language of anti-communism, and providing a useful base for the US air force. The literal exhumation of the past in the form of mass graves of victims of Francoist repression, combined with an assault on the dictatorship's 'repressive distortion of memory' (removing monuments of Franco, for example) has engendered a substantial public movement towards recovering 'lost' memories and investigating the extent of what really happened after the civil war.[37]

The transition to democracy after 1975 was negotiated by reformist Francoists and the democratic opposition on the basis of a consensus that the civil war was a 'tragedy' over which a veil of silence should be drawn, a strategy aided by the 1977 Amnesty Law.[38] This consensus broke down in the 1990s 'history wars', when groups representing victims of Franco began to demand not just accurate historical facts but official condemnation of the dictatorship, because, they argued, the 'model transition' had allowed perpetrators to evade justice and had created a democratic deficit. A strong government-backed expression of support for the victims of Francoist violence came in 2007, with the passing of the Law of Historical Memory. 'The revision of official memory to include the individual memories of those previously silenced', Carolyn Boyd writes, 'was understood to be a necessary first step toward reconciliation and democratic consolidation.'[39] Whether it was

---

[36] William B. Cohen, 'The Algerian War and French Memory', *Contemporary European History* 9:3 (2000), 489–500; Vladimir Tismaneanu, 'Communism and the Human Condition: Reflections on *The Black Book of Communism*', *Human Rights Review* 2:2 (2001), 125–34.

[37] Michael Richards, 'Between Memory and History: Social Relationships and Ways of Remembering the Spanish Civil War', *International Journal of Iberian Studies* 19:1 (2006), 86; Francisco Ferrándiz, 'Cries and Whispers: Exhuming and Narrating Defeat in Spain Today', *Journal of Spanish Cultural Studies* 9:2 (2008), 177–92.

[38] I am grateful to Helen Graham for the wording of this sentence.

[39] Carolyn P. Boyd, 'The Politics of History and Memory in Democratic Spain', *Annals of the American Academy of Political and Social Science* 617 (2008), 142–3. See also Carsten Jacob Humlebæk, 'Political Uses of the Recent Past in the Spanish Post-Authoritarian Democracy', in Max Paul Friedman and Padraic Kenney (eds), *Partisan Histories: The Past in Contemporary Global Politics* (New York: Palgrave Macmillan, 2005), 75–88; Paloma Aguilar and Carsten Humlebæk, 'Collective Memory and National Identity in the Spanish Democracy', *History & Memory* 14:1/2 (2002), 121–64. For a moving example, see Ramón Sender Barayón, *A Death in Zamora* (Albuquerque, NM: University of New Mexico Press, 1989).

appropriate to use legislation to mandate the control of memory (for example banning Francoist events at the Valley of the Fallen) is hotly contested, but Spain's example is perhaps no different from laws banning Nazi symbols in Germany or Holocaust denial in France. Indeed, it is striking that the 2007 law was passed at the same time as there was a rapid development of 'Holocaust consciousness' in Spain—with Holocaust-related plays, monuments, and novels all appearing at a rapid rate since 2000—and while Holocaust commemoration was becoming a defining aspect of European identity. Condemning the Franco dictatorship, even if Spaniards still do not know how to exhibit its legacy,[40] can thus be seen as an integral part of a pan-European memory phenomenon.

This breaking down of the postwar consensus can also be seen at work in the rhetoric of the 'double genocide' that informs a wave of new museums in post-communist Eastern Europe. In Budapest's Terror House, in Tallinn's and Riga's Occupation Museums, and in Vilnius's Museum of the Victims of Genocide, the memories of Nazism and communism are placed in competition with each other, and anti-fascism is only employed insofar as it does not impinge on the anti-communist narrative. In Budapest, the museum sets great store by the fact that the communist regime lasted decades as opposed to the mere months of the Nazi occupation, forgetting, as István Rév notes, that 'there was a sort of connection between the coming in of the Soviets and the end of the Arrow-Cross rule'. Indeed, Rév goes so far as to argue that the Terror House, with its overwhelming focus on the communist period, is not meant as a space of memory at all, but is 'a total propaganda space, where death and victims are used as rhetorical devices'.[41]

In Tallinn, images of local support for the Nazi invasion are willingly shown, since they imply the horror of the first Soviet occupation (June 1940–June 1941) and thus 'confirm the anti-communist script'.[42] The exaggerated nature of this 'equality of suffering' argument, with its suggestion that the Nazi invasion constituted a 'national liberation' from Soviet terror, and with its antisemitic subtext which 'justifies' Jewish persecution in terms of Jews' alleged support for communism, is explicable as an over-compensation for or a counter-memory to the rejection of communism after 1989 (1991 in the case of the Baltic States), in an attempt to remind Western Europeans of Eastern Europe's continued suffering after the end of World War II.[43] It reveals too how what is aptly called

---

[40] Antonio Monegal, 'Exhibiting Objects of Memory', *Journal of Spanish Cultural Studies* 9:2 (2008), 239–51.

[41] István Rév, *Retroactive Justice: Prehistory of Post-Communism* (Stanford, CA: Stanford University Press, 2005), 282, 296. See also Mark Pittaway, 'The "House of Terror" and Hungary's Politics of Memory', *Austrian Studies Newsletter* 15:1 (2003), 16–17; Judt, *Postwar*, 827–8.

[42] Evans, 'Memorials, Monuments, Histories', 319–21; James Mark, 'Containing Fascism: History in Post-Communist Baltic Occupation and Genocide Museums', in Sarkisova and Apor (eds), *Past for the Eyes*, 352.

[43] William Outhwaite and Larry Ray, *Social Theory and Postcommunism* (Oxford: Blackwell, 2005), 184–6. See also Richard Shorten, 'Hannah Arendt on Totalitarianism: Moral Equivalence and Degrees of Evil in Modern Political Violence', in Richard H. King and Dan Stone (eds), *Hannah Arendt and the Uses of History: Imperialism, Nation, Race, and Genocide* (New York: Berghahn, 2007), 173–90; Michael Geyer and Sheila Fitzpatrick (eds.), *Beyond Totalitarianism: Stalinism and Nazism Compared* (Cambridge: Cambridge University Press, 2009).

'geopolitical vertigo'[44] informs the ambivalent relationship of Eastern European states with Western European narratives of the 'good war': the memory of World War II is employed both to challenge 'smug' Western European accounts and to assure 'core Europe' of Eastern European commitment to a shared definition of 'Europe'.[45]

Apart from the breakdown of the anti-fascist consensus, the second process—the caricatured afterlife of postwar values—is best shown by analysing the role played by the Great Patriotic War in Russia. Since the Russian master narrative of the war has been subjected to tendentious revisionism in the Baltic States and other former parts of the Soviet Union, it should come as no surprise that in Russia itself under Putin and his successors, the cult of the Great Patriotic War has been revived. Indeed, as Martin Evans writes, 'the more Russia's loss of superpower status became apparent, the more the defeat of fascism has been held up as a source of national pride that transcends the end of the USSR'.[46]

It is noteworthy that the Central Museum of the Great Patriotic War in Moscow's Victory Park was not opened until after the collapse of the Soviet Union, in 1995, even though the decision to build a museum on the site had been taken as early as 1942,[47] and that a museum to commemorate the siege of Leningrad was built in 1989 on the same site as the original museum, constructed during the siege itself (and which closed in 1953).[48] Post-communist Russian governments want to bask in the glow that the memory of the war emits, for it is one of the few sources of continuity and popular legitimacy in a country that had always been synonymous with its empire and is therefore still grappling with its national identity. Thus, dissenters such as the Belorussian writer Ales Adamovich believe that the overburdened term 'Great Patriotic War' should be dropped in favour of 'the war with Hitler'; and Viktor Suvorov scurrilously though understandably in the context of the break-up of the USSR argued that Stalin had supported Nazi Germany from the outset because he believed that Hitler would unleash a destructive

[44] Stuart Elden and Luiza Bialasiewicz, 'The New Geopolitics of Division and the Problem of a Kantian Europe', *Review of International Studies* 32:4 (2006), 627.

[45] Maria Mälksoo, 'The Memory Politics of Becoming European: The East European Subalterns and the Collective Memory of Europe', *European Journal of International Relations* 15:4 (2009), 653–80. See also Claus Leggewie, 'A Tour of the Battleground: The Seven Circles of Pan-European Memory', *Social Research* 75:1 (2008), 217–34; Robert Bideleux, 'Rethinking the Eastward Extension of the EU Civil Order and the Nature of Europe's New East-West Divide', *Perspectives on European Politics and Society* 10:1 (2009), 118–36; Jörg Hackmann, 'From National Victims to Transnational Bystanders? The Changing Commemoration of World War II in Central and Eastern Europe', *Constellations* 16:1 (2009), 167–81.

[46] Evans, 'Memorials, Monuments, Histories', 333. See also Maria Todorova and Zsuzsa Gille (eds), *Post-Communist Nostalgia* (New York: Berghahn, 2010); Gregory Carleton, 'Victory in Death: Annihilation Narratives in Russia Today', *History & Memory* 22:1 (2010), 135–68; Roger Markwick's chapter in this volume.

[47] Nurit Schleifman, 'Moscow's Victory Park: A Monumental Change', *History & Memory* 13:2 (2001), 5–34.

[48] Lisa A. Kirschenbaum, 'Commemorations of the Siege of Leningrad: A Catastrophe in Memory and Myth', in Peter Gray and Kendrick Oliver (eds), *The Memory of Catastrophe* (Manchester: Manchester University Press, 2004), 111.

war that would act as the 'icebreaker' for revolution in Europe.[49] If it is something of an exaggeration to argue, as some do, that debates about the past contributed to the collapse of the Soviet Union,[50] Ilya Prizel is nevertheless correct to state that: 'Contemporary Russia has not yet arrived at a consensus about its past, and thus is forced to contend with conflicting and contradictory visions of its future.'[51] Prizel's point is apparent, for example, in continued denials of the existence of the secret clauses in the Molotov-Ribbentrop Pact.[52]

These specific examples could easily be multiplied. What is striking is that the Holocaust, which, in Judt's felicitous phrase, has been made the 'entry ticket' to contemporary Europe, has been the subject of historical commissions across Europe and, since the Stockholm Forum of 2000, has been enshrined in official European collective memory.[53] Questions of compensation for slave labour and the restitution of stolen property and land—topics which were impossible to discuss under communism—have become burning issues.[54] At the same time, most Eastern European countries have conducted commissions into the experience of communism. These two sets of commissions have been conducted with remarkably scholarly dispassion and expertise, and even in the most difficult cases, such as Romania, with its history of ethno-nationalism and a communist regime akin to a form of 'totalitarianism-cum-Sultanism',[55] they have provided

[49] Adamovich and Suvorov cited in Nina Tumarkin, *The Living and the Dead: The Rise and Fall of the Cult of World War II in Russia* (New York: Basic Books, 1994), 207, 211–12.

[50] Benjamin Forest, Juliet Johnson and Karen Till, 'Post-totalitarian National Identity: Public Memory in Germany and Russia', *Social and Cultural Geography* 5:3 (2004), 368.

[51] Ilya Prizel, 'Nationalism in Postcommunist Russia: From Resignation to Anger', in Sorin Antohi and Vladimir Tismaneanu (eds), *Between Past and Future: The Revolutions of 1989 and Their Aftermath* (Budapest: Central European University Press, 2000), 337. See also Alexander Etkind, 'Hard and Soft in Cultural Memory: Political Mourning in Russia and Germany', *Grey Room* 16 (2004), 36–59; Thomas C. Wolfe, 'Past as Present, Myth, or History? Discourses of Time and the Great Fatherland War', in Lebow, Kansteiner and Fogu (eds), *The Politics of Memory in Postwar Europe*, 249–83; David Reynolds, 'World War II and Modern Meanings', *Diplomatic History* 25:3 (2001), 457–72, esp. 464–6.

[52] James V. Wertsch, 'Blank Spots in History and Deep Memory: Revising the Official Narrative of the Molotov-Ribbentrop Pact', in Ene Kõresaar, Epp Lauk and Kristin Kuutma (eds), *The Burden of Remembering: Recollections and Representations of the 20th Century* (Helsinki: Finnish Literature Society, 2009), 37–56.

[53] Judt, *Postwar*, 803. Jens Kroh, 'Erinnerungskultureller Akteur und geschichtspolitisches Netzwerk: Die "Task Force for International Cooperation on Holocaust Education, Remembrance and Research"', and Harald Schmid, 'Europäisierung des Auschwitzgedenkens? Zum Aufstieg des 27. Januar 1945 als "Holocaustgedenktag" in Europa', both in Jan Eckel and Claudia Moisel (eds), *Universalisierung des Holocaust? Erinnerungskultur und Geschichtspolitik in internationaler Perspektive* (Göttingen: Wallstein, 2008), 156–73 and 174–202; Lothar Probst, 'Founding Myths in Europe and the Role of the Holocaust', *New German Critique* 90 (2003), 45–58.

[54] Avi Beker (ed.), *The Plunder of Jewish Property during the Holocaust: Confronting European History* (New York: New York University Press, 2001); Martin Dean, Constantin Goschler, and Philipp Ther (eds), *Robbery and Restitution: The Conflict over Jewish Property in Europe* (New York: Berghahn, 2007); Martin Dean, *Robbing the Jews: The Confiscation of Jewish Property in the Holocaust, 1933–1945* (Cambridge: Cambridge University Press, 2008).

[55] Juan J. Linz and Alfred Stepan, *Problems of Democratic Transition and Consolidation: Southern Europe, South America, and Post-Communist Europe* (Baltimore, MD: Johns Hopkins University Press, 1996), 344–65.

judicious and impartial models for examining difficult pasts.[56] Yet these 'EU-friendly' measures are simultaneously being challenged (in all parts of the continent) both at the official level, by government-sponsored revisionist museums, or populist state-controlled media, for example; and at the grassroots, by the resurgence of populism, which breeds on resentment towards Eurocrats and anger at 'exorbitant' Holocaust memory, itself a recapitulation of resentment towards minority treaties.[57] The balance of the commissions needs to be brought into mainstream discussions, where many have yet to discover that a recovery of Holocaust memory need not come at the expense of the memory of communism: between transnational commemoration of the Holocaust and recognition of specific national and regional suffering under communism there can be coexistence. Memory need not be a zero-sum game.

The International Context

Although the focus of this book is Europe, it is worth briefly situating these European memory wars into a broader context, since they occur worldwide, especially in societies scarred by civil war, genocide, and authoritarianism, such as post-apartheid South Africa, Rwanda, Guatemala, and Argentina. Besides, many of the European memory wars have a far wider resonance than their national or intra-European contexts might suggest; after all, many of the debates over memory concern colonial legacies, and therefore debates over Belgium's role in the Congo, or France's in Algeria or Indochina, for example, are obviously not merely European issues.[58] However, the impact of these memories varies considerably depending on local context. The recent revelations of British atrocities in Kenya during the Mau Mau emergency revealed that there is more appetite for revising histories of colonialism in some countries than others: in the UK, there is no need to pass laws teaching the benefits of imperial rule, not because Britain's imperial past constitutes an unblemished record, but because for most people it has vanished without trace.[59] Memories of Britain 'standing alone' in 1940 have facilitated 'a fifty

[56] Vladimir Tismaneanu, 'Democracy and Memory: Romania Confronts Its Communist Past', *Annals of the American Academy of Political and Social Science* 617 (2008), 166–80; Ruxandra Cesereanu, 'The Final Report on the Holocaust and the Final Report on the Communist Dictatorship in Romania', *East European Politics and Societies* 22:2 (2008), 270–81. See also the United States Holocaust Memorial Museum's 'List of Government-Appointed Historical Commissions Concerning the Holocaust', online at: www.holocausttaskforce.org/teachers/index.php?content=commission, accessed March 2010.

[57] Carolyn J. Dean, 'Recent French Discourses on Stalinism, Nazism and "Exorbitant" Jewish Memory', *History & Memory* 18:1 (2006), 43–85.

[58] Adam Hochschild, 'In the Heart of Darkness', *New York Review of Books* (6 October 2005), 39–42; Ludo De Witte, *The Assassination of Lumumba* (London: Verso, 2002); Martin Ewans, *European Atrocity, African Catastrophe: Leopold II, the Congo Free State and its Aftermath* (London: Routledge, 2002).

[59] Caroline Elkins, *Britain's Gulag: The Brutal End of Empire in Kenya* (London: Jonathan Cape, 2004); David Anderson, *Histories of the Hanged: Britain's Dirty War in Kenya and the End of Empire* (London: Weidenfeld and Nicolson, 2004).

year inflation of the national ego' and still inform British attitudes towards the EU, with a popular suspicion that it constitutes 'simply a peaceful form of German domination'.[60] Perhaps the different emphases that colonial histories have had in French and Belgian memory debates in comparison with Britain have something to do with the former countries' experience of World War II, and the rise of English as a world language—certainly as the language of European diplomacy—and is not solely a reflection of the violence that characterized their decolonization processes?[61]

Once again, it is obvious that World War II is central to these debates. Since it really was a *world* war (in a way that even World War I was not), its effects are being debated more than ever across the world, now that the Cold War lenses have been removed.[62] Issues of race, for example, or American awareness of the Soviet war effort, have recently come to the fore.[63] However, memory wars taking place outside of the European public sphere have tended to be focused less on World War II than on postwar phenomena, such as Apartheid, the putting down of anti-colonial resistance movements, and national traumas such as the 'disappeared' in Argentina or the 'stolen children' in Australia. 'Truth and reconciliation committees' have been a notable characteristic of the post-Cold War years, as have related phenomena such as states apologizing for former crimes or the search for forms of justice other than retribution.[64] Richard King notes that, like memory, restitution and compensation processes need not be zero-sum games: compensating one formerly abused group can be in the best interests of society as a whole.[65] The reality, however, is that such bodies as Guatemala's Commission for Historical Clarification or Rwanda's *gacaca* system of local trials for relatively minor *génocidaires* create new divisions even as they help to heal old wounds.[66]

Just as important as these phenomena has been the rise to prominence of a human rights agenda, since 1945 (and inspired by it—most obviously in the 1948 United Nations

[60] Kenneth O. Morgan, 'The Second World War and British Culture', in Brian Brivati and Harriet Jones (eds), *From Reconstruction to Integration: Britain and Europe since 1945* (Leicester: Leicester University Press, 1993), 45 (national ego); Reynolds, 'World War II and Modern Meanings', 470(German domination); cf. Wendy Webster, '"Europe against the Germans": The British Resistance Narrative, 1940–1950', *Journal of British Studies* 48 (2009), 958–82.

[61] Caroline Elkins, 'Race, Citizenship, and Governance: Settler Tyranny and the End of Empire', in Elkins and Susan Pedersen (eds), *Settler Colonialism in the Twentieth Century: Projects, Practices, Legacies* (New York: Routledge, 2005), 203–22.

[62] Matthew Connelly, 'Taking Off the Cold War Lens: Visions of North-South Conflict During the Algerian War for Independence', *American Historical Review* 105:3 (2000), 739–69.

[63] Edward T. Linenthal and Tom Engelhardt, *History Wars: The Enola Gay and Other Battles for the American Past* (New York: Henry Holt & Co, 1996); Phillips P. O'Brien, 'East versus West in the Defeat of Nazi Germany', *Strategic Studies* 23:2 (2000), 89–113; Mark A. Stoler, 'The Second World War in US History and Memory', *Diplomatic History* 25:3 (2001), 383–92.

[64] John Torpey, '"Making Whole What Has Been Smashed": Reflections on Reparations', *Journal of Modern History* 73:2 (2001), 333–58; Elazar Barkan, *The Guilt of Nations: Restitution and Negotiating Historical Injustices* (Baltimore, MD: Johns Hopkins University Press, 2000).

[65] Richard H. King, '"What Kind of People Are We?" The United States and the Truth and Reconciliation Idea', in Wilfred M. Mcclay (ed.), *Figures in the Carpet: Finding the Human Person in the American Past* (Grand Rapids, MI: Eerdmans, 2007), 496.

[66] Christopher J. Le Mon, 'Rwanda's Troubled Gacaca Courts', *Human Rights Brief* 14:2 (2007), 16–20.

Genocide Convention and Universal Declaration of Human Rights and 1951 Refugees Convention), but especially since 1989. The development of a human rights culture has gone hand in hand with the globalization of Holocaust memory, although the precise relationship between the two is unclear.[67] After World War II, the League of Nations' dedication to group rights, which had failed miserably, was partially replaced with the weaker but politically expedient United Nations' commitment to individual rights.[68] The emphasis in twentieth-century diplomacy on 'state sovereignty rooted in national homogeneity' meant that humanitarian intentions went hand in hand with forced deportations and territorial partition along ethnic lines.[69]

Although the history of human rights predates World War II, its advocates employ the memory of the war to justify the concept and to provide a linear, progressive history of its unfolding towards global prominence. This history is both complicated/disrupted and reinvigorated by recent catastrophes, such as the wars in the former Yugoslavia and genocide in Rwanda or Darfur. Competing versions of the origins and necessity to protect human rights are bound up with debates over humanitarian intervention, preemptive wars, and the rights and wrongs of 'regime change', and are thus prime examples of how memory informs contemporary international relations and political action. Indeed, following Jens Bartelson, we might argue that human rights discourse has been *remembered* into existence as a constituent part of an argument that justifies action on behalf of human rights.[70]

Conclusion

It has been suggested recently that the 'memory boom' of the last decades cannot be sustained. The relatively stable and apparently 'post-ideological' years of the 1990s have given way in the new millennium to a new 'war' on a global scale; demands for national unity and the rejection of 'postmodern relativism' are turning the tide against the focus

---

[67] Jeffrey C. Alexander, 'On the Social Construction of Moral Universals: The "Holocaust" from War Crime to Trauma Drama', *European Journal of Social Theory* 5:1 (2002), 5–85; Daniel Levy and Natan Sznaider, 'Memories of Europe: Cosmopolitanism and Its Others', in Chris Rumford (ed.), *Cosmopolitanism and Europe* (Liverpool: Liverpool University Press, 2007), 158–77; Gerard Delanty, 'The Idea of a Cosmopolitan Europe: On the Cultural Significance of Europeanization', *International Review of Sociology* 15:3 (2005), 405–21.

[68] Mark Mazower, 'The Strange Triumph of Human Rights, 1933–1950', *The Historical Journal* 47:2 (2004), 379–98.

[69] Eric D. Weitz, 'From the Vienna to the Paris System: International Politics and the Entangled Histories of Human Rights, Forced Deportations, and Civilizing Missions', *American Historical Review* 113:5 (2008), 1313–43.

[70] Jens Bartelson, 'We Could Remember it for You Wholesale: Myths, Monuments and the Constitution of National Memories', in Duncan Bell (ed.), *Memory, Trauma and World Politics: Reflections on the Relationship Between Past and Present* (Basingstoke: Palgrave Macmillan, 2006), 51.

on the past that characterized the first post-Cold War decade.[71] Irrespective of the fact that the condemnation of 'relativism' seems terribly misplaced in an age in which the most dangerous threats come from those with firm beliefs (including the attack on science and reason that characterizes the new age of superstition which appears to be upon us), it is no doubt the case, if only because of the cycles of fashion, that the 'memory boom' has reached its zenith. The scholarly assault on 'trauma studies' means that more care needs to be taken when deploying this medical term in the context of social experience of atrocity,[72] and the remarkably popular phenomena of confessional literature and celebrity culture seem to be waning somewhat, indicating that the appetite for testimony as a genre will become less fashionable and that testimony will turn into just another tool in the scholarly kit—as Saul Friedländer's *The Years of Extermination* indicates.[73] Furthermore, as Tony Judt suggests, when it comes to Holocaust commemoration the greatest challenge to meaningful (i.e. critically-engaged) memory may not be ignorance or hostility but the 'banality of overuse', that is, 'the flattening, desensitizing effect of seeing or saying or thinking the same thing too many times until we have numbed our audience and rendered them immune to the evil we are describing'.[74]

Yet memory, as Michael Rothberg stresses, is 'multidirectional'. That is to say, sometimes a process takes place 'in which transfers occur between events that have come to seem separate from each other'.[75] He gives the examples of the Holocaust and decolonization, but there are others, such as slavery, the use of the atom bomb, and genocides of indigenous peoples. One cannot easily predict how the contested memories of one event will help or hinder the 'discovery' of memories of other events, which may then become equally contentious. Besides, as recent arguments about World War II show, one can hardly suggest that memory animates public and academic concerns less now than it did twenty years ago.

Germany may present an exemplary face of a nation that has confronted its dark past (if one brackets off for the moment the critical voices which regard this self-satisfaction as a kind of *Sündenstolz*, or pride in one's own sins); but Russia has yet to do so, and most of the countries of the former eastern bloc have barely begun the process (not to mention other areas of the world in Latin America or Africa where such processes are also relevant). Spain is another major European example where memory politics are

[71] Rosenfeld, 'A Looming Crash'.

[72] Ido De Haan, 'The Construction of a National Trauma: The Memory of the Persecution of the Jews in the Netherlands', *Netherlands Journal of Social Sciences* 34:2 (1998), 196–217.

[73] Wulf Kansteiner, 'Genealogy of a Category Mistake: A Critical Intellectual History of the Cultural Trauma Metaphor', *Rethinking History* 8:2 (2004), 193–221; Kansteiner, 'Testing the Limits of Trauma: The Long-Term Psychological Effects of the Holocaust on Individuals and Collectives', *History of the Human Sciences* 17:2–3 (2004), 97–123. On Friedländer's use of testimony, see Amos Goldberg, 'The Victim's Voice and Melodramatic Aesthetics in History', *History and Theory* 48 (2009), 220–37.

[74] Tony Judt, 'The "Problem of Evil" in Postwar Europe', *New York Review of Books* (14 February 2008).

[75] Michael Rothberg, 'The Work of Testimony in the Age of Decolonization: Chronicle of a Summer, Cinema Verité, and the Emergence of the Holocaust Survivor', *PMLA* 119:5 (2004), 1243.

fundamental to contemporary life. One cannot look to Germany and argue that because the job has been done there, the trajectory to be followed by other states is mapped out and thus, for scholars, predictable and boring. Indeed, the reverse seems to be the case: the more that the myth of the Holocaust as an act committed by an impersonal evil force called Nazism that has nothing to do with 'us' is challenged, the more resistance in European countries to official commemoration seems to grow. In other words, the more uncertain the present and the future look, the more memory—precisely because it is future-oriented—will continue to be an arena of contestation, giving rise in some cases to conflict, in others to reconciliation.[76] In case of the former, it might turn out that the 'negation of nationalism as the central force in politics was a short interlude that lasted less than an intellectual generation'.[77] In case of the latter, we might argue that with the extension of the EU, the upsurge of populism will be contained within democratic structures and thus that Europe 'has not had such a good opportunity to establish lasting peace since the Congress of Vienna'.[78] Postwar Europe, especially post-Cold War Europe, has been a period of intense memory scrutiny, primarily of World War II. Now that postwar Europe is itself fast on the road to becoming history, its very past-ness means it too is ripe for inclusion in ongoing struggles to control memory and thus to shape the 'new Europe'.

FURTHER READING

Crownshaw, Richard, Jane Kilby and Antony Rowland (eds), *The Future of Memory* (Oxford: Berghahn Books, 2010).

Eley, Geoff, 'Historicizing the Global, Politicizing Capital: Giving the Present a Name', *History Workshop Journal* 63:1 (2007), 154–88.

Lebow, Richard Ned, Wulf Kansteiner and Claudio Fogu (eds), *The Politics of Memory in Postwar Europe* (Durham, NC: Duke University Press, 2006).

Mälksoo, Maria, 'The Memory Politics of Becoming European: The East European Subalterns and the Collective Memory of Europe', *European Journal of International Relations* 15:4 (2009), 653–80.

Sarkisova, Oksana and Péter Apor (eds), *Past for the Eyes: East European Representations of Communism in Cinema and Museums after 1989* (Budapest: Central European University Press, 2008).

[76] Richard Ned Lebow, 'The Future of Memory', *Annals of the American Academy of Political and Social Science* 617 (2008), 25–41.

[77] Prizel, 'Nationalism in Postcommunist Russia', 334.

[78] Georges-Henri Soutou, 'Was There a European Order in the Twentieth Century? From the Concert of Europe to the End of the Cold War', *Contemporary European History* 9:3 (2000), 330. See, for examples: Jeffrey S. Kopstein, 'The Politics of National Reconciliation: Memory and Institutions in German-Czech Relations since 1989', *Nationalism and Ethnic Politics* 3:2 (1997), 57–78; Jan C. Behrends, 'Jan Józef Lipskis europäischer Traum: Zur Geschichtskultur in Polen, Russland und Deutschland nach 1989', *Themenportal Europäische Geschichte* (2007), online at: www.europa.clio-online.de/2007/ Article=246, accessed March 2010; and the forum ed. Elazar Barkan, *American Historical Review* 114:4 (2009).

Stone, Dan, *Histories of the Holocaust* (Oxford: Oxford University Press, 2010).

Suleiman, Susan Rubin, *Crises of Memory and the Second World War* (Cambridge, MA: Harvard University Press, 2006).

Tismaneanu, Vladimir, Marc Morjé Howard and Rudra Sil (eds), *World Disorder after Leninism: Essays in Honor of Ken Jowitt* (Seattle, WA: University of Washington Press, 2006).

Todorova, Maria, and Zsuzsa Gille (eds), *Post-Communist Nostalgia* (New York: Berghahn Books, 2010).

Index

Bold page numbers refer to a quotation made by the person concerned

The manufacturer's authorised representative in the EU for product
safety is Oxford University Press España S.A. of El Parque Empresarial
San Fernando de Henares, Avenida de Castilla, 2 - 28830 Madrid
(www.oup.es/en or product.safety@oup.com). OUP España S.A. also acts
as importer into Spain of products made by the manufacturer.
Printed and bound by CPI Group (UK) Ltd, Croydon, CR0 4YY

31/10/2025
01988715-0001